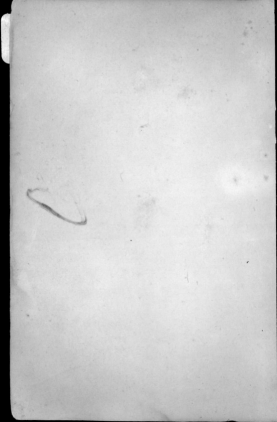

SPANISH·ENGLISH
ENGLISH·SPANISH
ESPAÑOL·INGLÉS
INGLÉS·ESPAÑOL

COLLINS
GEM
DICTIONARY

SPANISH · ENGLISH
ENGLISH · SPANISH

ESPAÑOL · INGLÉS
INGLÉS · ESPAÑOL

Mike Gonzalez

completely new edition
edición totalmente revisada

Collins
London and Glasgow
Grijalbo
Barcelona

first published in this edition 1982
latest reprint/última reimpresión 1986

ISBN 0 00 458647 6

© William Collins Sons & Co. Ltd. 1982

contributors/con la colaboración de
Margaret Tejerizo, John Forry,
Carmen Billinghurst, Liam Kane,
Pat Feehan

editorial staff/redacción
Irene Lakhani

Printed in Great Britain
Collins Clear-Type Press

INTRODUCCIÓN

Quien desee leer y entender el inglés encontrará en este diccionario un extenso léxico moderno que abarca una amplia gama de locuciones de uso corriente. Igualmente encontrará, en su debido orden alfabético, las abreviaturas, las siglas, los nombres geográficos más conocidos y, además, las principales formas de verbo irregulares, donde se le referirá a las respectivas formas de base, hallándose allí la traducción.

Quien aspire comunicarse y expresarse en lengua extranjera, hallará aquí una clara y detallada explicación de las palabras básicas, empleándose un sistema de indicadores que le remitirán a la traducción más apta y le señalarán su correcto uso.

INTRODUCTION

The user whose aim is to read and understand Spanish will find a comprehensive and up-to-date wordlist including numerous phrases in current use. He will also find listed alphabetically the main irregular forms with a cross-reference to the basic form where a translation is given, as well as some of the most common abbreviations, acronyms and geographical names.

The user who wishes to communicate and to express himself in the foreign language will find clear and detailed treatment of all the basic words, with numerous indicators pointing to the appropriate translation, and helping him to use it correctly.

adjetivo, locución adjetivo	**a**	adjective, adjectival phrase
abreviatura	**ab(b)r**	abbreviation
adverbio, locución adverbial	**ad**	adverb, adverbial phrase
administración, lengua administrativa	**ADMIN**	administration
agricultura	**AGR**	agriculture
América Latina	**AM**	Latin America
anatomía	**ANAT**	anatomy
arquitectura	**ARQ, ARCH**	architecture
astrología, astronomía	**ASTRO**	astrology, astronomy
el automóvil	**AUT(O)**	the motor car and motoring
aviación, viajes aéreos	**AVIAT**	flying, air travel
biología	**BIO(L)**	biology
botánica, flores	**BOT**	botany
inglés británico	**Brit**	British English
química	**CHEM**	chemistry
conjunción	**conj**	conjunction
lengua familiar	**col**	colloquial usage
comercio, finanzas, banca	**COM(M)**	commerce, finance, banking
construcción	**CONSTR**	building
compuesto	**cpd**	compound element
cocina	**CULIN**	cookery
determinante, artículo	**det**	determiner, article
economía	**ECON**	economics
electricidad, electrónica	**ELEC**	electricity, electronics
enseñanza, sistema escolar y universitario	**ESCOL**	schooling, schools and universities
especialmente	**esp**	especially
exclamación, interjección	**excl**	exclamation, interjection
femenino	**f**	feminine
lengua familiar	**fam**	colloquial usage
ferrocarril	**FERRO**	railways
uso figurado	**fig**	figurative use
fotografía	**FOTO**	photography
(verbo inglés) del cual la partícula es inseparable	**fus**	(phrasal verb) where the particle is inseparable
generalmente	**gen**	generally
geografía, geología	**GEO**	geography, geology
geometría	**GEOM**	geometry
invariable	**inv**	invariable
irregular	**irg**	irregular
lo jurídico	**JUR**	law
gramática, lingüística	**LING**	grammar, linguistics

masculino	m	masculine
matemáticas	MAT(H)	mathematics
medicina	MED	medical term, medicine
masculino/femenino	m/f	masculine/feminine
o militar, ejército	MIL	military matters
música	MUS	music
sustantivo, nombre	n	noun
navegación, náutica	NAUT	sailing, navigation
sustantivo numérico	num	numeral noun
complemento	obj	(grammatical) object
	o.s.	oneself
peyorativo	pey, pej	derogatory, pejorative
fotografía	PHOT	photography
fisiología	PHYSIOL	physiology
plural	pl	plural
política	POL	politics
participio de pasado	pp	past participle
prefijo	pref	prefix
preposición	prep	preposition
pronombre	pron	pronoun
psicología, psiquiatría	PSICO, PSYCH	psychology, psychiatry
tiempo pasado	pt	past tense
sustantivo no empleado en el plural	q	collective (uncountable) noun, not used in plural
ferrocarril	RAIL	railways
religión, lo eclesiástico	REL	religion, church service
	sb	somebody
escolar, universitario	SCOL	schools, universities
singular	sg	singular
	sth	something
sujeto	su(b)j	(grammatical) subject
sufijo	suff	suffix
tauromaquia	TAUR	bullfighting
técnica, tecnología	TEC(H)	technical term, technology
telecomunicaciones	TELEC, TEL	telecommunications
televisión	TV	television
imprenta, tipografía	TYP	typography, printing
inglés norteamericano	US	American English
verbo	vb	verb
verbo intransitivo	vi	intransitive verb
verbo pronominal	vr	reflexive verb
verbo transitivo	vt	transitive verb
zoología, animales	ZOOL	zoology
marca registrada	®	registered trademark
indica un equivalente cultural	≈	introduces a cultural equivalent

SPANISH PRONUNCIATION

Consonants

c	[k]	caja	c before a, o or u is pronounced as i cat
ce, ci	[θe, θi]	cero cielo	c before e or i is pronounced as i thin
ch	[tʃ]	chiste	ch is pronounced as ch in chair
d	[d, ð]	danés ciudad	at the beginning of a phrase or after or n, d is pronounced as in English In any other position it is pronounce like th in the
g	[g, ɣ]	gafas paga	g before a, o or u is pronounced as i gap, if at the beginning of a phrase (after n. In other positions the soun is softened
ge, gi	[xe, xi]	gente girar	g before e or i is pronounced simila to ch in Scottish loch
h		haber	h is always silent in Spanish
j	[x]	jugar	j is pronounced similar to ch i Scottish loch
ll	[ʎ]	talle	ll is pronounced like the lli in millio
ñ	[ɲ]	niño	ñ is pronounced like the ni in onio
q	[k]	que	q is pronounced as k in king
r, rr	[r, rr]	quitar garra	r is always pronounced in Spanish unlike the silent r in dancer. rr i trilled, like a Scottish r
s	[s]	quizás isla	s is usually pronounced as in pass but before b, d, g, l, m or n it i pronounced as in rose
v	[b, ß]	vía dividir	v is pronounced something like b. A the beginning of a phrase or after n or n it is pronounced as b in boy. I any other position the sound i softened
z	[θ]	tenaz	z is pronounced as th in thin

b, f, k, l, m, n, p, t and x are pronounced as in English.

Vowels

[a]	pata	not as long as *a* in far. When followed by a consonant in the same syllable (i.e. in a closed syllable), as in amante, the *a* is short, as in bat
[e]	me	like *e* in they. In a closed syllable, as in gente, the *e* is short as in pet
[i:]	pino	as in mean or machine
[o]	lo	as in local. In a closed syllable, as in control, the *o* is short as in cot
[u:]	lunes	as in rule. It is silent after *q*, and in *gue*, *gui*, unless marked *güe*, *güi* e.g. antigüedad

Diphthongs

ai, ay	baile	as *i* in ride
au	auto	as *ou* in shout
ei, ey	buey	as *ey* in grey
eu	deuda	both elements pronounced independently [e]+[u:]
oi, oy	hoy	as *oy* in toy

Stress

The rules of stress in Spanish are as follows:

(a) when a word ends in a vowel or in *n* or *s*, the second last syllable is stressed: patata, patatas, come, comen

(b) when a word ends in a consonant other than *n* or *s*, the stress falls on the last syllable: pared, hablar

(c) when the rules set out in a and b are not applied, an acute accent appears over the stressed vowel: común, geografía, inglés

In the phonetic transcription, the symbol ['] precedes the syllable on which the stress falls.

PRONUNCIACIÓN INGLESA

Vocales y diptongos

	Ejemplo inglés	Ejemplo español/explicación
a:	father	Entre a de padre y o de noche
ʌ	but, come	a muy breve
æ	man, cat	Se mantienen los labios en la posició de e en pena y luego se pronuncia e sonido a
ə	father, ago	Sonido indistinto parecido a una e u casi mudas
ə:	bird, heard	Entre e abierta, y o cerrada, sonid alargado
ɛ	get, bed	como en perro
ɪ	it, big	Más breve que en si
i:	tea, see	Como en fíno
ɔ	hot, wash	Como en torre
ɔ:	saw, all	Como en por
u	put, book	Sonido breve, más cerrado que burr
u:	too, you	Sonido largo, como en uno
aɪ	fly, high	Como en fraile
au	how, house	Como en pausa
ɛə	there, bear	Casi como en vea, pero el sonido a s mezcla con el indistinto [ə]
eɪ	day, obey	e cerrada seguida por una i débil
ɪə	here, hear	Como en manía, mezclándose e sonido a con el indistinto [ɔ]
əu	go, note	[ɔ] seguido por una breve u
ɔɪ	boy, oil	Como en voy
uə	poor, sure	u bastante larga más el sonid indistinto [ə]

x

Consonantes

	Ejemplo inglés	Ejemplo español/explicación
d	men*d*ed	Como en con*d*e, an*d*ar
g	*g*o, *g*et, bi*g*	Como en *g*rande, *g*ol
dʒ	*g*in, *j*udge	Como en la *ll* andaluza y en Generalitat (catalán)
ŋ	si*ng*	Como en ví*n*culo
h	*h*ouse, *h*e	Como la *j*ota hispanoamericana
j	*y*oung, *y*es	Como en *y*a
k	*c*ome, mo*ck*	Como en *c*aña, Es*c*ocia
r	*r*ed, t*r*ead	Se pronuncia con la punta de la lengua hacia atrás y sin hacerla vibrar
s	*s*and, ye*s*	Como en ca*s*a, *s*esión
z	ro*s*e, *z*ebra	Como en de*s*de, mi*s*mo
ʃ	*sh*e, ma*ch*ine	Como en *ch*ambre (francés), ro*x*o (portugués)
tʃ	*ch*in, ri*ch*	Como en *ch*ocolate
v	*v*alley	Como en f, pero se retiran los dientes superiores vibrándolos contra el labio inferior
w	*w*ater, *wh*ich	Como en la *u* de *hu*evo, p*u*ede
ʒ	vi*s*ion	Como en *j*ournal (francés)
θ	*th*ink, my*th*	Como en re*c*eta, *z*apato
ð	*th*is, *th*e	Como en la *d* de hablado, ver*d*ad

b, p, f, m, n, l, t iguales que en español

El signo * indica que la r final escrita apenas se pronuncia en inglés británico cuando le palabra siguiente empieza con vocal. El signo ['] indica la sílaba acentuada.

xi

ESPAÑOL - INGLÉS
SPANISH - ENGLISH

A

a [a] *prep* (a + el = al) *(lugar)* at, in, on; *(dirección)* to; *(destino)* to; towards; *(tiempo)* at; ~ **la derecha/izquierda** on the right/left; **al lado de** beside, at the side of; **subir** ~ **un avión/tren** to get on *or* board a plane/train; **hablar** ~ **larga distancia** to speak long distance; ~ **las cuatro** at four o'clock; ¿~ **qué hora?** at what time?; ~ **los 30 años** at 30 years of age; **al día siguiente** the next day; ~ **eso de las cuatro** at about four o'clock; **al poco tiempo** a short time later; **al verlo yo** when I saw it; *(manera)*: **hacerlo** ~ **la fuerza** to do it by force; **ir** ~ **caballo/pie** to go on horse-back/foot; *(evaluación)*: **poco** ~ **poco** little by little; **de dos** ~ **tres** from two to three; **ocho horas al día** eight hours a day *or* per day; ~ **30 pias el kilo** 50 pesetas a kilo; *(con verbo)*: **empezó** ~ **llover** it started raining; **enseñar** ~ **leer** to teach to read; **voy** ~ **llevarlo** I am going to carry it; *(complemento de objeto)*: **quiero** ~ **mis padres** (not translated) I love my parents; *(complemento circunstancial)*: **cercano/near (to)**; **por miedo** ~ **out of fear of;** *(frases elípticas)*: **a comer!** let's eat; ¿~ **qué viene eso?** what's the meaning of this?; ~ **ver** let's see.

abacero, a [aßa'θero, a] *nm/f* grocer.

abad, esa [a'ßað, 'ßesa] *nm/f* abbot/abbess; ~**ía** *nf* abbey.

abajo [a'ßaxo] *ad (situación)* down, below, underneath; *(en casa)* downstairs, *(dirección)* down, downwards; ~ **de** *prep* below, under; **el piso de** ~ the downstairs flat; **la parte de** ~ the lower part; **¡~ el gobierno!** down with the government!; **cuesta/río** ~ downhill/downstream; **de arriba** ~ from top to bottom; **el** ~ **firmante** the undersigned; **más** ~ lower *or* further down; **echar** ~ to bring down.

abalanzar [aßalan'θar] *vt* to weigh; *(equilibrar)* to balance; *(arrojar)* to hurl; ~**se** *vr*: ~**se sobre** *o* **contra** to throw o.s. at.

abandonado, a [aßando'naðo, a] *a* derelict; *(desatendido)* abandoned; *(desierto)* deserted; *(descuidado)* neglected.

abandonar [aßando'nar] *vt (dejar)* to leave, abandon, desert; *(descuidar)* to neglect; *(ceder, dejar de)* to give up; ~**se** *vr*: ~**se a** to abandon o.s. to.

abandono [aßan'dono] *nm (acto)* desertion, abandonment; *(estado)* abandon, neglect; *(renuncia)* withdrawal, retirement; **perdió por** ~ he lost by default.

abanicar [aßani'kar] *vt* to fan; **abanico** *nm* fan; *(NAUT)* derrick.

abaratar [aßara'tar] *vt* to lower (the price of) // *vi*, ~**se** *vr* to go *or* come down in price.

abarcar [aßar'kar] *vt* to include, embrace, take in; *(AM)* to monopolize.

abarrotar [aßarro'tar] *vt* to bar; *(NAUT)* to stow; *(fig)* to overstock.

abarrote [aßa'rrote] *nm* packing; ~**s** *nmpl (AM)* groceries, provisions; ~**ro** *nm (AM)* grocer.

abastecer [aßaste'θer] *vt* to supply; **abastecimiento** *nm* supply; *(suministrar)* supplying.

abasto [a'ßasto] *nm* supply; *(abundancia)* abundance; **dar** ~ **con** to manage to finish.

abatido, a [aßa'tiðo, a] *a* dejected, downcast.

abatimiento [aβati'mjento] nm
(acto) demolition; (moral)
dejection, depression.

abatir [aβa'tir] vt (muro) to
demolish; (pájaro) to shoot, bring
down; (fig) to depress; (humillar) to
humiliate // vi to go off course; ~se
vr to be depressed; ~se sobre to
swoop or pounce on.

abdicación [aβðika'θjon] nf
abdication; **abdicar** vi to abdicate.

abdomen [aβ'ðomen] nm abdomen.

abecedario [aβeθe'ðarjo] nm
alphabet; (libro) spelling book.

abedul [aβe'ðul] nm birch.

abeja [a'βexa] nf bee.

aberración [aβerra'θjon] nf
aberration.

abertura [aβer'tura] nf opening,
gap; (fig) openness.

abeto [a'βeto] nm fir.

abierto, a [a'βjerto, a] pp de **abrir**
// a open; (AM) generous.

abigarrado, a [aβiɣa'rraðo, a] a
multi-coloured.

abismar [aβis'mar] vt to humble,
cast down; ~se vr to sink; ~se en
(fig) to be plunged into.

abismo [a'βismo] nm abyss.

abjurar [aβxu'rar] vt, vi to abjure,
forswear.

ablandar [aβlan'dar] vt to soften
up; (AUTO) to run in // vi, ~se vr to
grow softer.

ablución [aβlu'θjon] nf ablution.

abnegación [aβneɣa'θjon] nf self-
denial; **abnegarse** vr to act
unselfishly.

abobado, a [aβo'βaðo, a] a silly.

abobar [aβo'βar] vt to daze.

abocar [aβo'kar] vt to seize in one's
mouth; ~se vr to approach.

abochornar [aβotʃor'nar] vt to
embarrass; ~se vr to get flustered;
(BOT) to wilt.

abofetear [aβofete'ar] vt to slap
(in the face).

abogacía [aβoɣa'θia] nf legal
profession; (ejercicio) practice of

the law; **abogado** nm lawyer.

abogar [aβo'ɣar] vi: ~ **por** to plead
for; (fig) to advocate.

abolengo [aβo'lengo] nm ancestry
lineage.

abolición [aβoli'θjon] nf abolition.

abolir [aβo'lir] vt to abolish;
(cancelar) to cancel.

abolladura [aβoʎa'ðura] nf dent;
(chichón, choque) bump; **abollar** vt
to dent; to raise a bump on.

abominación [aβomina'θjon] nf
abomination.

abonado, a [aβo'naðo, a] a (deuda)
paid // nm/f subscriber.

abonar [aβo'nar] vt (deuda) to
settle; (terreno) to fertilize; (idea) to
endorse; ~se vr to subscribe; **abono**
nm payment; fertilizer; subscription.

abordar [aβor'ðar] vt to board;
(fig) to broach.

aborigen [aβo'rixen] nm aborigine.

aborrecer [aβorre'θer] vt to hate,
loathe; **aborrecible** a hateful,
loathsome.

abortar [aβor'tar] vi (malparir) to
have a miscarriage; (deliberada-
mente) to have an abortion;
hacerse ~ to have an abortion;
aborto nm miscarriage; abortion.

abotonar [aβoto'nar] vt to button
(up), do up // vi to bud.

abovedado, a [aβoβe'ðaðo, a] a
vaulted, domed.

abrasar [aβra'sar] vt to burn (up);
(AGR) to dry up, parch.

abrazar [aβra'θar] vt to embrace.

abrazo [a'βraθo] nm embrace, hug;
un ~ (en carta) with best wishes.

abrelatas [aβre'latas] nm inv tin
opener.

abreviar [aβre'βjar] vt to
abbreviate; (texto) to abridge;
(plazo) to reduce; **abreviatura** nf
abbreviation.

abrigar [aβri'ɣar] vt (proteger) to
shelter; (suj: ropa) to keep warm;
(fig) to cherish; **abrigo** nm shelter;
(apoyo) support; (prenda) coat,
overcoat.

abril [a'βril] *nm* April.

abrir [a'βrir] *vt* to open (up) // *vi* to open; ~**se** *vr* to open (up); (*extenderse*) to open out; (*cielo*) to clear; ~**se paso** to find or force a way through.

abrochar [aβro'tʃar] *vt* (*vestido*) to button (up); (*AM*) to staple; (*zapato*) to buckle; (*atar*) to lace up.

abrumar [aβru'mar] *vt* to overwhelm; (*sobrecargar*) to weigh down; (*agotar*) to wear out; ~**se** *vr* to become foggy.

abrupto, a [a'βrupto, a] *a* abrupt; (*empinado*) steep.

absceso [aβs'θeso] *nm* abscess.

absolución [aβsolu'θjon] *nf* (*REL*) absolution; (*JUR*) pardon; (: *de acusado*) acquittal.

absoluto, a [aβso'luto, a] *a* absolute; **en ~** *ad* in no way, not at all.

absolver [aβsol'βer] *vt* to absolve; (*JUR*) to pardon; (: *acusado*) to acquit.

absorber [aβsor'βer] *vt* to absorb; (*embeber*) to soak up.

absorción [aβsor'θjon] *nf* absorption.

absorto, a [aβ'sorto, a] *pp de* **absorber** // *a* absorbed, engrossed.

abstemio, a [aβs'temjo, a] *a* teetotal.

abstención [aβsten'θjon] *nf* abstention; **abstenerse** *vr* to abstain or refrain from.

abstinencia [aβsti'nenθja] *nf* abstinence; (*ayuno*) fasting.

abstracción [aβstrak'θjon] *nf* abstraction; (*despiste*) absentmindedness; ~ **hecha de** leaving aside.

abstraer [aβstra'er] *vt* to abstract // *vi* ... to leave aside; ~**se** *vr* to be/become distracted.

abstraído, a [aβstra'iðo, a] *a* preoccupied; (*despistado*) absentminded.

absuelto [aβ'swelto] *pp de* **absolver**.

absurdo, a [aβ'surðo, a] *a* absurd.

abuelo, a [a'βwelo, a] *nm/f* grandfather/mother.

abulia [a'βulja] *nf* spinelessness, weakness.

abultado, a [aβul'taðo, a] *a* bulky.

abultar [aβul'tar] *vt* to enlarge; (*aumentar*) to increase; (*fig*) to exaggerate // *vi* to be bulky.

abundancia [aβun'danθja] *nf* abundance, plenty; **abundante** *a* abundant, plentiful; **abundar** *vi* to abound, be plentiful.

aburrido, a [aβu'rriðo, a] *a* (*hastiado*) bored; (*que aburre*) boring; **aburrimiento** *nm* boredom, tedium; **aburrir** *vt* to bore; **aburrirse** *vr* to be bored, get bored.

abusar [aβu'sar] *vi* to go too far; ~ **de** to abuse; **abuso** *nm* imposition; abuse.

abyecto, a [aβ'jekto, a] *a* wretched, abject.

A.C. *abr de* **Año de Cristo** A.D. (Anno Domini)

a/c *abr de* **al cuidado de** c/o (care of).

acá [a'ka] *ad* (*lugar*) here; (*tiempo*) now.

acabado, a [aka'βaðo, a] *a* finished, complete; (*perfecto*) perfect; (*agotado*) worn out; (*fig*) masterly // *nm* finish.

acabar [aka'βar] *vt* (*llevar a su fin*) to finish, complete; (*llegar al final de*) to finish, conclude; (*perfeccionar*) to complete; (*consumir*) to use up; (*rematar*) to finish off // *vi* to finish, end, come to an end; ~ **con** to put an end to; ~ **de llegar** to have just arrived; ~ **por** to end (up) by; ~**se** *vr* to finish, stop; (*terminarse*) to be over; (*agotarse*) to run out; **¡se acabó!** that's enough!, it's all over!

academia [aka'ðemja] *nf* academy; **académico, a** *a* academic.

acaecer [akae'θer] *vi* to happen, occur; **acaecimiento** *nm* occurrence, happening.

acalorar [akalo'rar] *vt* to heat; (*fig*) to inflame; ~se *vr* (*fig*) to get heated.

acampar [akam'par] *vi* to camp.

acanalar [akana'lar] *vt* to groove; (*ondular*) to corrugate.

acantilado, a [akanti'laðo, a] *a* steep, sheer // *nm* cliff.

acaparar [akapa'rar] *vt* to monopolize; (*acumular*) to hoard.

acariciar [akari'θjar] *vt* to caress; (*fig*) to cherish.

acarrear [akarre'ar] *vt* to transport; (*fig*) to cause, result in; **acarreo** *nm* transport, haulage; (*precio*) carriage.

acaso [a'kaso] *ad* perhaps, maybe // *nm* chance; **por si** ~ just in case; **si** ~ in case; **al** ~ at random.

acatamiento [akata'mjento] *nm* respect; (*reverencia*) reverence; (*deferencia*) deference; **acatar** *vt* to respect; to revere; (*obedecer*) to obey.

acatarrarse [akata'rrarse] *vr* to catch a cold.

acaudalado, a [akauða'laðo, a] *a* well-off; **acaudalar** *vt* to accumulate.

acaudillar [akauði'ʎar] *vt* to lead, command.

acceder [akθe'ðer] *vi* to accede, agree.

accesible [akθe'siβle] *a* accessible.

acceso [ak'θeso] *nm* access, entry; (*camino*) access road; (*MED*) attack, fit.

accesorio, a [akθe'sorjo, a] *a, nm* accessory.

accidentado, a [akθiðen'taðo, a] *a* uneven; (*áspero*) rough; (*montañoso*) hilly; (*azaroso*) eventful // *nm*/*f* injured person.

accidental [akθiðen'tal] *a* accidental; **accidentarse** *vr* to have an accident.

accidente [akθi'ðente] *nm* accident; (*MED*) faint; ~s *nmpl* unevenness *sg*, roughness *sg*.

acción [ak'θjon] *nf* action; (*acto*)

action, act, deed; (*COM*) share; (*JUR*) action, lawsuit; ~ **ordinaria** ordinary/preference referente share; **accionar** *vt* to work, operat // *vi* to gesticulate.

accionista [akθjo'nista] *nm*/ shareholder.

acebo [a'θeβo] *nm* holly; (*árbol* holly tree.

acechanza [aθe't'ʃanθa] *nf* = **acecho.**

acechar [aθe't'ʃar] *vt* to spy on (*aguardar*) to lie in wait for; **aceche** *nm* spying, watching; (*fig*) snoop.

acedía [aθe'ðia] *nf* acidity; (*MED* heartburn; (*fig*) sourness.

aceitar [aθei'tar] *vt* to oil, lubricate **aceite** *nm* oil; (*de oliva*) olive oil **aceitera** *nf* oilcan; **aceitoso, a** *a* oily

aceituna [aθei'tuna] *nf* olive.

acelerar [aθele'rar] *vt* t accelerate.

acento [a'θento] *nm* accent; (*acer tuación*) stress; **acentuar** *vt* t accent; to stress; (*fig*) to accentuate

acepción [aθep'θjon] *nf* meaning (*preferencia*) preference.

acepillar [aθepi'ʎar] *vt* to brush (*alisar*) to plane.

aceptación [aθepta'θjon] *n* acceptance; (*aprobación*) approval **aceptar** *vt* to accept; to approve.

acequia [a'θekja] *nf* irrigation ditch.

acera [a'θera] *nf* pavement.

acerado, a [aθe'raðo, a] *a* steel (*afilado*) sharp; (*fig: duro*) steely; (* mordaz*) biting.

acerbo, a [a'θerβo, a] *a* bitter; (*fig* harsh.

acerca [a'θerka]: ~ **de** *ad* about concerning.

acercar [aθer'kar] *vt* to bring o move nearer; ~se *vr* to approach come near.

acero [a'θero] *nm* steel.

acérrimo, a [a'θerrimo, a] *a* out and-out, staunch.

acertado, a [aθer'taðo, a] *a*

correct; (apropiado) apt; (sensato) sensible.

acertar [aθer'tar] vt (dar en: el blanco) to hit; (llegar a encontrar) to get right; (adivinar) to guess; (alcanzar) to achieve // vi to get it right, be right; ~ a to manage to; ~ con to happen on.

acertijo [aθer'tixo] nm riddle, puzzle.

acervo [a'θerβo] nm heap; ~ común undivided estate.

acicalar [aθika'lar] vt to polish; (adornar) to bedeck, ~se vr to smarten o.s. up.

acicate [aθi'kate] nm spur.

acidez [aθi'δeθ] nf acidity.

ácido, a ['aθiδo, a] a sour, acid // nm acid.

acierto [a'θjerto] nm success; (buen paso) wise move; (solución) solution; (habilidad) skill, ability.

aclamación [oklama'θjon] nf acclamation; (aplausos) applause; **aclamar** vt to acclaim; to applaud.

aclaración [aklara'θjon] nf rinsing, rinse; (clasificación) classification.

aclarar [akla'rar] vt to clarify, explain; (ropa) to rinse // vi to clear up; ~se vr: ~se la garganta to clear one's throat.

aclimatación [aklimataθjon] nf acclimatization; **aclimatar** vt to acclimatize; **aclimatarse** vr to become acclimatized.

acobardar [akoβar'δar] vt to daunt, intimidate.

acodarse [ako'δarse] vr: ~ en to lean on.

acogedor, a [akoxe'δor, a] a welcoming; (hospitalario) hospitable; **acoger** vt to welcome; (abrigar) to shelter; **acogerse** vr to take refuge; **acogida** nf reception; refuge.

acolchar [akol'tʃar] vt to pad; (tapizar) to upholster; (fig) to cushion.

acometer [akome'ter] vt to attack; (emprender) to undertake; **acometida** nf attack, assault.

acomodadizo, a [akomoδa'δiθo, a] a obliging, acquiescent.

acomodado, a [akomo'δaδo, a] a suitable; (precio) moderate; (persona) well-to-do.

acomodador, a [akomoδa'δor, a] nm/f usher/ette.

acomodar [akomo'δar] vt to adjust; (alojar) to accommodate; (convenir) to suit; (reparar) to repair; (reconciliar) to reconcile // vi to be suitable; ~se vr to conform; (instalarse) to install o.s.; (adaptarse) to adapt o.s.

acomodo [ako'moδo] nm arrangement; (puesto) post.

acompañar [akompa'nar] vt to accompany; (documentos) to enclose.

acondicionar [akondiθjo'nar] vt to arrange, prepare; (determinar) to condition.

acongojar [akongo'xar] vt to distress, grieve.

aconsejar [akonse'xar] vt to advise, counsel; ~se vr: ~se con to consult.

acontecer [akonte'θer] vi to happen, occur; **acontecimiento** nm event.

acopio [a'kopjo] nm store, stock; (asamblea) gathering.

acoplamiento [akopla'mjento] nm coupling, joint; **acoplar** vt to fit, couple; (unir) to connect.

acorazado, a [akora'θaδo, a] a armour-plated, armoured // nm battleship.

acordar [akor'δar] vt (resolver) to agree, resolve; (recordar) to remind; (MUS) to tune; ~se vr to agree; ~se (de) to remember; **acorde** a in agreement; (MUS) harmonious // nm chord.

acordeón [akorδe'on] nm accordion.

acordonado, a [akorδo'naδo, a] a corded, ribbed.

acorralar [akorra'lar] vt to round up, corral.

acortar [akor'tar] *vt* to shorten; *(duración)* to cut short; *(cantidad)* to reduce; ~**se** *vr* to become shorter.

acosar [ako'sar] *vt* to pursue relentlessly; *(fig)* to hound, pester.

acostar [akos'tar] *vt* *(en cama)* to put to bed; *(en suelo)* to lay down; *(barco)* to bring alongside; ~**se** *vr* to go to bed; to lie down.

acostumbrar [akostum'brar] *vt*: ~ **a uno a** to accustom sb to // *vi*: ~ **a** to be used to; ~**se** *vr*: ~**se a** to get used to.

acotación [akota'θjon] *nf* marginal note; *(GEO)* elevation mark; *(de límite)* boundary mark; *(TEATRO)* stage direction.

acre ['akre] *a* sharp, bitter; *(fig)* biting // *nm* acre.

acrecentar [akreθen'tar] *vt* to increase, augment.

acreditar [akreδi'tar] *vt* *(garantizar)* to vouch for, guarantee; *(autorizar)* to authorize; *(dar prueba de)* to prove; *(COM: abonar)* to credit; *(embajador)* to accredit; ~**se** *vr* to become famous.

acreedor, a [akree'δor, a] *a*: ~ **a** worthy of // *nm/f* creditor.

acribillar [akriβi'λar] *vt*: ~ **a balazos** to riddle with bullets.

acrimonia [akri'monja], **acritud** [akri'tuδ] *nf* acrimony.

acta ['akta] *nf* certificate; *(de comisión)* minutes *pl*, record; ~ **de nacimiento/matrimonial** birth/marriage certificate; ~ **notarial** affidavit.

actitud [akti'tuδ] *nf* attitude; *(postura)* posture.

activar [akti'βar] *vt* to activate; *(acelerar)* to expedite.

actividad [aktiβi'δað] *nf* activity.

activo, a [ak'tiβo, a] *a* active; *(vivo)* lively // *nm* assets *pl*.

acto ['akto] *nm* act, action; *(ceremonia)* ceremony; *(TEATRO)* act; **en el ~** immediately.

actor [ak'tor] *nm* actor; *(JUR)* plaintiff.

actora [ak'tora] *a*: **parte ~** prosecution; *(demandante)* plaintiff.

actriz [ak'triθ] *nf* actress.

actuación [aktwa'θjon] *nf* action; *(comportamiento)* conduct, behaviour; *(JUR)* proceedings *pl*; *(desempeño)* performance.

actual [ak'twal] *a* present(-day), current; ~**idad** *nf* present, present time; ~**idades** *nfpl* news *sg*; *(película, nodo)* newsreel *sg*; **en la ~idad** nowadays, at the present time.

actualizar [aktwali'θar] *vt* to update, modernize.

actualmente [aktwal'mente] *ad* now, nowadays, at present.

actuar [ak'twar] *vi (obrar)* to work, operate; *(actor)* to act, perform // *vt* to work, operate; ~ **de** to act as.

actuario [ak'twarjo] *nm* clerk; *(COM)* actuary.

acuarela [akwa'rela] *nf* watercolour.

acuario [a'kwarjo] *nm* aquarium; **A~** *(ASTRO)* Aquarius.

acuático, a [a'kwatiko, a] *a* aquatic.

acuciar [aku'θjar] *vt* to urge on.

acuclillarse [akukli'λarse] *vr* to crouch down.

acudir [aku'δir] *vi* to come along, turn up; ~ **a** to turn to; ~ **en ayuda de** to go to the aid of.

acuerdo *etc vb ver* **acordar** // [a'kwerðo] *nm* agreement; ¡**de ~!** agreed!; **de ~ con** *(persona)* in agreement with; *(acción, documento)* in accordance with.

acumulador [akumula'δor] *nm* storage battery; **acumular** *vt* to accumulate, collect.

acuñar [aku'nar] *vt (moneda)* to coin, mint; *(poner cuñas)* to wedge.

acuoso, a [a'kwoso, a] *a* watery.

acurrucarse [akurru'karse] *vr* to crouch; *(ovillarse)* to curl up.

acusación [akusa'θjon] *nf* accusation; **acusar** *vt* to accuse;

(revelar) to reveal; *(denunciar)* to denounce.

acuse [a'kuse] *nm*: ~ **de recibo** acknowledgement of receipt.

acústico, a [a'kustiko, a] a acoustic // *nm* hearing aid

achacar [atʃa'kar] *vt* to attribute.

achacoso, a [atʃa'koso, a] a sickly.

achaque [a'tʃake] *nm* ailment.

achicar [atʃi'kar] *vt* to reduce; *(humillar)* to humiliate; *(NAUT)* to bale out.

achicoria [atʃi'korja] *nf* chicory.

achicharrar [atʃitʃa'rrar] *vt* to scorch, burn.

adagio [a'ðaxjo] *nm* adage; *(MUS)* adagio.

adaptación [aðapta'θjon] *nf* adaptation; **adaptar** *vt* to adapt; *(acomodar)* to fit.

a de C *abr* = **a. de J.C.**

A. de C *abr* = **A.C.**

adecuado, a [aðe'kwaðo, a] a adequate; *(apto)* suitable; *(oportuno)* appropriate; **adecuar** *vt* to adapt; to make suitable.

a. de J.C. *abr de* **antes de Jesucristo** B.C. (before Christ).

adelantado, a [aðelan'taðo, a] a advanced; *(reloj)* fast; **pagar por** ~ to pay in advance; **adelantamiento** *nm* advance, advancement; *(AUTO)* overtaking; *(progreso)* progress.

adelantar [aðelan'tar] *vt* to move forward; *(avanzar)* to advance; *(acelerar)* to speed up // *vi*, ~**se** *vr* to go forward, advance; *(AUTO)* to overtake.

adelante [aðe'lante] ad forward(s), onward(s), ahead // *excl* come in!; **de hoy en** ~ from now on; **más** ~ *later on*; *(más allá)* further on.

adelanto [aðe'lanto] *nm* advance; *(mejora)* improvement; *(progreso)* progress.

adelgazar [aðelxa'θar] *vt* to thin (down); *(afilar)* to taper // *vi*, ~**se** *vr* to grow thin.

ademán [aðe'man] *nm* gesture;

ademanes *nmpl* manners; **en** ~ **de** as if to.

además [aðe'mas] *ad* besides; *(por otra parte)* moreover; *(también)* also; ~ **de** besides, in addition to.

adentro [a'ðentro] *ad* inside, in; **mar** ~ out at sea; **tierra** ~ inland.

adepto, a [a'ðepto, a] *nm/f* supporter.

aderezar [aðere'θar] *vt* to prepare; *(persona, ensalada)* to dress; *(comida)* to season; ~**se** *vr* to dress up; **aderezo** *nm* preparation; dressing; seasoning.

adeudar [aðeu'ðar] *vt* to owe // *vi* to become related by marriage; ~**se** *vr* to run into debt.

adherirse [aðe'rirse] *vr*: ~ **a** to adhere to.

adhesión [aðe'sjon] *nf* adhesion; *(fig)* adherence.

adición [aði'θjon] *nf* addition.

adicionar [aðiθjo'nar] *vt* to add.

adicto, a [a'ðikto, a] a: ~ **a** adhere to; *(dedicado)* devoted to // *nm/f* supporter, follower.

adiestrar [aðjes'trar] *vt* to train, teach; *(conducir)* to guide, lead; ~**se** *vr* to practise; *(enseñarse)* to train o.s.

adinerado, a [aðine'raðo a] a wealthy.

adiós [a'ðjos] *excl (para despedirse)* goodbye!, cheerio!; *(para saludar)* hello!

aditivo [aði'tiβo] *nm* additive.

adivinanza [aðiβi'nanθa] *nf* riddle; **adivinar** *vt* to prophesy; *(conjeturar)* to guess, **adivino, a** *nm/f* fortune-teller.

adj *a abr de* **adjunto** *encl.* (enclosed).

adjetivo [aðxe'tiβo] *nm* adjective.

adjudicación [aðxuðika'θjon] *nf* award; **adjudicar** *vt* to award; **adjudicarse** *vr*: **adjudicarse algo** to appropriate sth.

adjuntar [aðxun'tar] *vt* to attach, enclose; **adjunto, a** a attached, enclosed // *nm/f* assistant.

administración [aðminitra'θjon] nf administration; (dirección) management; **administrador, a** nm/f administrator; manager/ess.

administrar [aðminis'trar] vt to administer; **administrativo, a** a administrative.

admirable [aðmi'raßle] a admirable; **admiración** nf admiration; (asombro) wonder; (LING) exclamation mark; **admirar** vt to admire; (extrañar) to surprise; **admirarse** vr to be surprised.

admisible [aðmi'sißle] a admissible.

admitir [aðmi'tir] vt to admit; (aceptar) to accept.

admonición [aðmoni'θjon] nf warning.

adobe [a'ðoße] nm adobe, sun-dried brick.

adolecer [aðole'θer] vi to be ill, fall ill; ~ **de** to suffer from.

adolescente [aðoles'θente] nm/f adolescent.

adonde [a'ðonðe] conj (to) where.

adónde [a'ðonðe] ad = **dónde.**

adopción [aðop'θjon] nf adoption.

adoptar [aðop'tar] vt to adopt.

adoquín [aðo'kin] nm paving stone.

adorar [aðo'rar] vt to adore.

adormecer [aðorme'θer] vt to put to sleep; ~**se** vr to become sleepy, fall asleep.

adornar [aðor'nar] vt to adorn.

adorno [a'ðorno] nm adornment; (decoración) decoration.

adquiero etc vb ver **adquirir.**

adquirir [aðki'rir] vt to acquire, obtain.

adquisición [aðkisi'θjon] nf acquisition.

adrede [a'ðreðe] ad on purpose.

adscribir [aðskri'ßir] vt to appoint.

aduana [a'ðwana] nf customs pl.

aduanero, a [aðwa'nero, a] a customs cpd // nm/f customs officer.

aducir [aðu'θir] vt to adduce; (dar como prueba) to offer as proof.

adueñarse [aðwe'ɲarse] vr: ~ **de** to take possession of.

adulación [aðula'θjon] nf flattery.

adular [aðu'lar] vt to flatter.

adulterar [aðulte'rar] vt to adulterate // vi to commit adultery.

adulterio [aðul'terjo] nm adultery.

adulto, a [a'ðulto, a] a, nm/f adult.

adusto, a [a'ðusto, a] a stern; (austero) austere.

advenedizo, a [aðßene'ðiθo, a, nm/f upstart.

advenimiento [aðßeni'mjento] nm arrival; (al trono) accession.

adverbio [að'ßerßjo] nm adverb.

adversario, a [aðßer'sarjo, a] nm/f adversary.

adversidad [aðßersi'ðað] nf adversity; (contratiempo) setback.

adverso, a [að'ßerso, a] a adverse, (opuesto) opposite.

advertencia [aðßer'tenθja] n. warning; (prefacio) preface, foreword.

advertir [aðßer'tir] vt to notice (avisar) to warn // vi: ~ **en** to notice.

Adviento [að'ßjento] nm Advent.

adyacente [aðja'θente] a adjacent.

aéreo, a [a'ereo, a] a aerial.

aerodeslizador [aeroðesli'θa'ðor] **aerodeslizante** [aeroðesli'ßante] nm hovercraft.

aeronáutica [aero'nautika] n aeronautics sg.

aeropuerto [aero'pwerto] nm airport.

afabilidad [afaßili'ðað] nf friendliness; **afable** a affable.

afán [a'fan] nm hard work; (deseo) desire.

afanar [afa'nar] vt to harass; ~**se** vr: ~**se por** to strive for; **afanoso, a** a hard; (trabajador) industrious.

afear [afe'ar] vt to make ugly; (mutilar) to deface.

afección [afek'θjon] nf affection; (MED) disease.

afectación [afekta'θjon] nf affectation; **afectado, a** a affected; **afectar** vt to affect.

afectísimo, a [afek'tisimo, a] a affectionate; ~ **suyo** yours truly.

afecto, a [a'fekto, a] a affectionate // nm affection; ~ **a** fond of.

afectuoso, a [afek'twoso, a] a affectionate.

afeitar [afei'tar] vt to shave; ~**se** vr to shave.

afeminado, a [afemi'naðo, a] a effeminate.

aferrado, a [afe'rraðo, a] a stubborn.

aferrar [afe'rrar] vt to moor; (fig) to grasp // vi to moor.

afianzamiento [afjanθa'mjento] nm strengthening; (garantía) guarantee; (COM) security; **afianzar** vt to strengthen; to guarantee; to secure; **afianzarse** vr to become established.

afición [afi'θjon] nf fondness; liking; **la ~** the fans pl; **pinto por ~** I paint as a hobby; **aficionado, a** a keen, enthusiastic; amateur // nm/f enthusiast; fan; amateur.

aficionar [afiθjo'nar] vt: ~ **a uno a algo** to make sb like sth; ~**se** vr: ~**se a algo** to grow fond of sth.

afilado, a [afi'laðo, a] a sharp.

afilar [afi'lar] vt to sharpen.

afiliarse [afi'ljarse] vr to become affiliated to.

afín [a'fin] a bordering, adjacent; (parecido) similar; (conexo) related.

afinar [afi'nar] vt (TEC) to refine; (MUS) to tune // vi to play/sing in tune.

afinidad [afini'ðað] nf affinity; (parentesco) relationship; **por** ~ by marriage.

afirmación [afirma'θjon] nf affirmation; **afirmar** vt to affirm, state; (sostener) to strengthen; **afirmativo, a** a affirmative.

aflicción [aflik'θjon] nf affliction; (dolor) grief.

afligir [afli'xir] vt to afflict,

(apenar) to distress; ~**se** vr to grieve.

aflojar [aflo'xar] vt to slacken; (desatar) to loosen, undo; (relajar) to relax // vi to drop; (bajar) to go down; ~**se** vr to relax.

afluente [aflu'ente] a flowing; (elocuente) eloquent // nm tributary.

afluir [aflu'ir] vi to flow.

afmo, a abr de **afectísimo(a) suyo(a)**.

afónico, a [a'foniko, a] a (ronco) hoarse; (sin voz) voiceless.

afortunado, a [afortu'naðo, a] a fortunate, lucky.

afrancesado, a [afranθe'saðo, a] a francophile; (pey) frenchified.

afrenta [a'frenta] nf affront, insult; (deshonra) dishonour, shame; **afrentar** vt to affront; to dishonour; **afrentarse** vr to be ashamed; **afrentoso, a** a insulting.

África [a'frika] nf África; ~ **del Sur** South Africa; **africano, a** a, nm/f African.

afrontar [afron'tar] vt to confront; (poner cara a cara) to bring face to face.

afuera [a'fwera] ad out, outside; ~**s** nfpl outskirts, suburbs.

agachar [aɣa'tʃar] vt to bend, bow; ~**se** vr to stoop, bend.

agalla [a'ɣaʎa] nf (ZOOL) gill; ~**s** nfpl (MED) tonsillitis sg; (ANAT) tonsils.

agarradera [aɣarra'ðera] nf (AM), **agarradero** [aɣarra'ðero] nm handle; ~**s** nfpl pull sg, influence sg

agarrado, a [aɣa'rraðo, a] a mean, stingy.

agarrar [aɣa'rrar] vt to grasp, grab; (AM) to take, catch // vi (planta) to take root; ~**se** vr to hold on (tightly).

agarrotar [aɣarro'tar] vt (lío) to tie tightly; (persona) to squeeze tightly; (reo) to garrotte; ~**se** vr (motor) to seize up; (MED) to stiffen.

agasajar [aɣasa'xar] vt to flatter

well, fête; **agasajo** *nm* lavish hospitality.

agencia [a'xenθja] *nf* agency; ~ **de viajes/inmobiliaria** travel/estate agency.

agenda [a'xenda] *nf* diary.

agente [a'xente] *nm* agent; (*de policía*) policeman; ~ **femenino** policewoman.

ágil ['axil] *a* agile, nimble; **agilidad** *nf* agility, nimbleness.

agio ['axjo] *nm* speculation.

agiotista [axjo'tista] *nm* (*stock*)jobber; (*especulador*) speculator.

agitación [axita'θjon] *nf* shaking, waving, stirring; (*del mar*) roughness; (*fig*) agitation.

agitar [axi'tar] *vt* to wave, shake, stir; (*fig*) to stir up, excite; ~**se** *vr* to get excited.

aglomerar [axlome'rar] *vt*, ~**se** *vr* to agglomerate, crowd together.

agnóstico, a [ax'nostiko, a] *a*, *nm/f* agnostic.

agobiar [axo'βjar] *vt* to weigh down; (*oprimir*) to oppress; (*cargar*) to burden.

agolparse [axol'parse] *vr* to crowd together.

agonía [axo'nia] *nf* agony, anguish.

agonizante [axoni'θante] *a* dying.

agonizar [axoni'θar] *vi* (*también* **estar agonizando**) to be dying.

agosto [a'xosto] *nm* August.

agotado, a [axo'taðo, a] *a* exhausted; (*libros*) out of print; (*acabado*) finished; (*mercancías*) sold out; **agotamiento** *nm* exhaustion.

agotar [axo'tar] *vt* to exhaust; (*consumir*) to drain; (*recursos*) to use up, deplete; ~**se** *vr* to be exhausted; (*acabarse*) to run out; (*libro*) to go out of print.

agraciar [axra'θjar] *vt* (*JUR*) to pardon; (*con premio*) to reward.

agradable [axra'ðaβle] *a* pleasing, pleasant, nice.

agradar [axra'ðar] *vt*, *vi* to please.

agradecer [axraðe'θer] *vt* to thank (*favor etc*) to be grateful for **agradecimiento** *nm* thanks *pl* gratitude.

agrado [a'xraðo] *nm* affability (*gusto*) liking.

agrandar [axran'dar] *vt* to enlarge (*fig*) to exaggerate; ~**se** *vr* to ge bigger.

agrario, a [a'xrarjo, a] *a* agrarian.

agravar [axra'βar] *vt* to make heavier; (*irritar*) to aggravate (*oprimir*) to oppress; ~**se** *vr* to worsen, get worse.

agraviar [axra'βjar] *vt* to offend (*ser injusto con*) to wrong; ~**se** *vr* to take offence; **agravio** *nm* offence wrong; (*ofensa*) grievance.

agregado [axre'xaðo] *nm* aggregate; (*persona*) attaché.

agregar [axre'xar] *vt* to gather (*añadir*) to add; (*persona*) to appoint.

agresión [axre'sjon] *nf* aggression; **agresivo, a** *a* aggressive.

agriar [a'xrjar] *vt* to (turn) sour ~**se** *vr* to turn sour.

agricultor, a [axrikul'tor, a] *nm/i* farmer; **agricultura** *nf* agriculture farming.

agridulce [axri'ðulθe] *a* bitter-sweet.

agrietarse [axrje'tarse] *vr* to crack; (*la piel*) to chap.

agrio, a ['axrjo, a] *a* bitter.

agronomía [axrono'mia] *nf* agronomy, agriculture.

agrupación [axrupa'θjon] *nf* group; (*acto*) grouping.

agrupar [axru'par] *vt* to group.

agua ['axwa] *nf* water; (*lluvia*) rain; (*NAUT*) wake; (*ARQ*) slope of a roof; ~**s** *nfpl* (*de piedra*) water *sg*, sparkle *sg*; (*MED*) water *sg*, urine *sg*; (*NAUT*) waters; ~**s abajo/arriba** downstream/upstream; ~ **bendita/destilada/potable** holy/dis-tilled/drinking water; ~ **corriente** running water; ~ **de colonia** eau de cologne; ~**s jurisdiccionales**

territorial waters; ~s mayores excrement sg.

aguacate [axwa'kate] nm avocado pear.

aguacero [axwa'θero] nm (heavy) shower.

aguado, a [a'xwaðo, a] a watery, watered down // nf (AGR) watering place; (NAUT) water supply; (ARTE) water-colour.

aguafiestas [axwa'fjestas] nm/f inv spoilsport.

aguafuerte [axwa'fwerte] nf etching.

aguamar [axwa'mar] nm jellyfish.

aguantable [axwan'taßle] a bearable; aguantar vt to bear, put up with; (contener) to hold; (sostener) to hold up // vi to last; aguantarse vr to restrain o.s.

aguante [a'xwante] nm (paciencia) patience; (resistencia) endurance.

aguar [a'xwar] vt to water down.

aguardar [axwar'ðar] vt to wait for.

aguardiente [axwar'ðjente] nm brandy.

aguarrás [axwa'rras] nm turpentine.

agudeza [axu'ðeθa] nf sharpness; (ingenio) wit; agudo, a a sharp; (voz) high-pitched, piercing; (dolor, enfermedad) acute.

agüero [a'xwero] nm omen; (pronóstico) prediction.

aguijar [axi'xar] vt to goad; (incitar) to urge on // vi to hurry along.

aguijón [axi'xon] nm sting; (BOT) spine (estímulo, fig) spur; aguijonear vt = aguijar.

águila ['axila] nf eagle; (fig) genius.

aguileño, a [axi'leɲo, a] a aquiline; (facciones) sharp-featured.

aguinaldo [axi'naldo] nm Christmas box.

aguja [a'xuxa] nf needle; (de reloj) hand; (ARQ) spire; (TEC) firing-pin; ~s nfpl (ZOOL) ribs; (FERRO) points.

agujerear [axuxere'ar] vt to make holes in; agujero nm hole.

agujetas [axu'xetas] nfpl stitch sg; (rigidez) stiffness sg.

aguzar [axu'θar] vt to sharpen; (fig) to incite.

ahí [a'i] ad there; de ~ que so that, with the result that; ~ llega here he comes; por ~ that way; (allá) over there.

ahijado, a [ai'xaðo, a] nm/f godson/daughter.

ahínco [a'inko] nm earnestness.

ahitar [ai'tar] vt to surfeit; ~se vr to stuff o.s.

ahíto, a [a'ito, a] a: estoy ~ I have indigestion // nm indigestion.

ahogar [ao'xar] vt to drown; (asfixiar) to suffocate, smother; (fuego) to put out; ~se vr (en el agua) to drown; (suicidio) to drown o.s.; (por asfixia) to suffocate.

ahogo [a'oxo] nm shortness of breath; (fig) financial difficulty.

ahondar [aon'dar] vt to deepen, make deeper; (fig) to go deeply into // vi: ~ en to go deeply into.

ahora [a'ora] ad now; (poco tiempo ha) a moment ago, just now; (dentro de poco) in a moment // conj now; ~ voy I'm coming; ~ mismo right now; ~ bien now then; por ~ for the present.

ahorcar [aor'kar] vt to hang; ~se vr to hang o.s.

ahorita [ao'rita] ad (fam) right now.

ahorrar [ao'rrar] vt (dinero) to save; (esfuerzos) to save, avoid; ahorro nm economy, saving; (frugalidad) thrift; ahorros nmpl savings.

ahuecar [awe'kar] vt to hollow (out); (voz) to deepen; ~se vr to give o.s. airs.

ahumar [au'mar] vt to smoke, cure; (llenar de humo) to fill with smoke // vi to smoke; ~se vr to fill with smoke.

ahuyentar [aujen'tar] vt to drive off, frighten off; (fig) to dispel; ~se vr to run away.

airado, a [ai'raðo, a] *a* angry; **airar** *vt* to anger; **airarse** *vr* to get angry.

aire ['aire] *nm* air; (*viento*) wind; (*corriente*) draught; (*MUS*) tune; ~**s** *nmpl:* **darse** ~**s** to give o.s. airs; **al** ~ **libre** in the open air; ~ **acondicionado** air conditioning; **airoso, a** *a* windy; draughty; (*fig*) graceful.

aislador [aisla'ðor] *nm* insulator; **aislar** *vt* to isolate; (*ELEC*) to insulate.

ajar [a'xar] *vt* to spoil; (*fig*) to abuse.

ajedrez [axe'ðreθ] *nm* chess.

ajeno, a [a'xeno, a] *a* (*que pertenece a otro*) somebody else's; (*impropio*) inappropriate; (*extraño*) alien, foreign; ~ **a** foreign to; ~ **de** free from, devoid of.

ajetreo [axe'treo] *nm* bustle.

ají [a'xi] *nm* chili, red pepper; (*salsa*) chili sauce.

ajo ['axo] *nm* garlic; ~ **porro** *o* **puerro** leek.

ajorca [a'xorka] *nf* bracelet.

ajuar [a'xwar] *nm* household furnishings *pl*; (*de novia*) trousseau; (*de niño*) layette.

ajustado, a [axus'taðo, a] *a* (*tornillo*) tight; (*cálculo*) right; (*ropa*) tight-fitting; (*DEPORTE: resultado*) close.

ajustar [axus'tar] *vt* (*adaptar*) to adjust; (*encajar*) to fit; (*TEC*) to engage; (*contratar*) to hire; (*IMPRENTA*) to make up; (*apretar*) to tighten; (*concertar*) to agree (on); (*reconciliar*) to reconcile; (*cuenta*) to settle // *vi* to fit; ~**se** *vr* to come to an agreement.

ajuste [a'xuste] *nm* adjustment; (*TEC, costura*) fitting; (*acuerdo*) compromise; (*de cuenta*) settlement.

al [al] = **a + el**, *ver* **a**.

ala ['ala] *nf* wing; (*de sombrero*) brim; (*futbolista*) winger.

alabanza [ala'ßanθa] *nf* praise.

alabar [ala'ßar] *vt* to praise; ~**se** *vr:* ~**se de** to boast of (being).

alabear [alaße'ar] *vt*, ~**se** *vr* to warp.

alacena [ala'θena] *nf* cupboard.

alacrán [ala'kran] *nm* scorpion.

alambicado, a [alambi'kaðo, a] *a* distilled; (*fig*) affected.

alambicar [alambi'kar] *vt* to distil.

alambique [alam'bike] *nm* still.

alambrado [alam'braðo] *nm* wire fence; (*red*) wire netting; **alambre** *nm* wire; **alambre de púas** barbed wire; **alambrista** *nm/f* tightrope walker.

alameda [ala'meða] *nf* (*plantío*) poplar grove; (*lugar de paseo*) avenue, tree-lined walk.

álamo ['alamo] *nm* poplar; ~ **temblón** aspen.

alano [a'lano] *nm* mastiff.

alar [a'lar] *nm* eaves *pl.*

alarde [a'larðe] *nm* (*MIL*) review; (*ostentación*) show, display; **hacer** ~ **de** to boast of.

alargar [alar'xar] *vt* to lengthen, extend; (*paso*) to hasten; (*brazo*) to stretch out; (*cuerda*) to pay out; (*conversación*) to spin out; ~**se** *vr* to get longer; ~**se en** to enlarge upon; (*pey*) to drag out.

alarido [ala'riðo] *nm* shriek.

alarma [a'larma] *nf* alarm.

alazán [ala'θan] *nm* sorrel.

alba ['alßa] *nf* dawn.

albacea [alßa'θea] *nm/f* executor/trix.

Albania [al'ßanja] *nf* Albania.

albañal [alßa'nal] *nm* drain, sewer.

albañil [alßa'nil] *nm* bricklayer; (*cantero*) mason.

albaricoque [alßari'koke] *nm* apricot.

albedrío [alße'ðrio] *nm:* **libre** ~ free will.

alberca [al'ßerka] *nf* reservoir.

albergar [alßer'xar] *vt*, ~**se** *vr* to shelter.

albergue [al'ßerxe] *nm* shelter, refuge; ~ **de juventud** youth hostel.

albóndiga [al'ßondixa] *nf* meatball.

albor [al'βor] nm whiteness; (amanecer) dawn; ~ada nf dawn; (diana) reveille; ~ear vi to dawn.

albornoz [alβor'noθ] nm (de los árabes) burnous; (para el baño) bathrobe.

alborotar [alβoro'tar] vi to make a row // vt to agitate, stir up; ~se vr to get excited; (mar) to get rough; **alboroto** nm row, uproar.

alborozar [alβoro'θar] vt to gladden; ~se vr to rejoice.

alborozo [alβo'roθo] nm joy.

albricias [al'βriθjas] nfpl reward sg // excl good news!

álbum ['alβum] nm album.

albumen [al'βumen] nm egg white.

alcachofa [alka'tʃofa] nf artichoke.

alcalde [al'kalde] nm mayor.

alcaldía [alkal'dia] nf mayoralty; (lugar) mayor's office.

alcance [al'kanθe] nm reach; (COM) adverse balance; (de periódico) stop-press (news), de pocos ~s not very clever; ~ de última hora late postal collection.

alcancía [alkan'θia] nf money box.

alcantarilla [alkanta'riʎa] nf (de aguas cloacales) sewer; (en la calle) gutter.

alcanzar [alkan'θar] vt (algo: con la mano, el pie) to reach; (alguien en el camino) to catch up with; (autobús) to catch; (suj: bala) to hit, strike // vi: ~ a hacer to manage to do.

alcatraz [alka'traθ] nm gannet.

alcázar [al'kaθar] nm fortress; (palacio) royal palace; (NAUT) quarter-deck.

alcoba [al'koβa] nf bedroom.

alcohol [al'kol] nm alcohol; **alcohólico, a** a alcoholic; ~ismo nm alcoholism.

alcornoque [alkor'noke] nm cork tree.

aldaba [al'daβa] nf (door) knocker.

aldea [al'dea] nf village; ~no, a a village cpd // nm/f villager.

aleación [alea'θjon] nf alloy.

aleccionar [alekθjo'nar] vt to instruct; (adiestrar) to train.

alegación [alexa'θjon] nf allegation; **alegar** vt to allege; (JUR) to plead; (AM) to dispute, argue.

alegato [ale'xato] nm (JUR) allegation; (AM) argument.

alegoría [alexo'ria] nf allegory.

alegrar [ale'xrar] vt (causar alegría) to cheer (up); (fuego) to poke; (fiesta) to liven up; ~se vr to get merry or tight; ~se de to be glad about.

alegre [a'lexre] a happy, cheerful; (fam) merry, tight; (licencioso) risqué, blue; **alegría** nf happiness, merriment.

alejamiento [alexa'mjento] nm removal; (distancia) remoteness.

alejar [ale'xar] vt to remove; (fig) to estrange; ~se vr to move away.

aleluya [ale'luja] nm (canto) hallelujah; (Pascuas) Easter time // nf Easter print.

alemán, ana [ale'man, ana] a, nm/f German // nm (lengua) German.

Alemania [ale'manja] nf: ~ Federal/Oriental West/East Germany.

alentado, a [alen'tado, a] pp de **alentar** // a brave; (orgulloso) proud; (fuerte) strong.

alentador, a [alenta'ðor, a] a encouraging.

alentar [alen'tar] vt to encourage; ~se vr to cheer up.

alerce [a'lerθe] nm larch.

alergia [a'lerxja] nf allergy.

alero [a'lero] nm (de tejado) eaves pl; (de carruaje) mudguard.

alerta [a'lerta] a, nm alert.

aleta [a'leta] nf (de pez) fin; (de ave) wing; (de coche) mudguard.

aletargar [aletar'xar] vt to make drowsy; (entumecer) to make numb; ~se vr to grow drowsy; to become numb.

aletazo [ale'taθo] nm wingbeat, flap of the wing.

aletear [alete'ar] *vi* to flutter.

aleve [a'leβe] *a* treacherous.

alevosía [aleβo'sia] *nf* treachery.

alfabeto [alfa'βeto] *nm* alphabet.

alfarería [alfare'ria] *nf* pottery; (*tienda*) pottery shop; **alfarero** *nm* potter.

alférez [al'fereθ] *nm* (MIL) second lieutenant; (NAUT) ensign.

alfiler [alfi'ler] *nm* pin; (*broche*) clip; ~ **de seguridad** safety pin.

alfombra [al'fombra] *nf* carpet; (*más pequeña*) rug; **alfombrar** *vt* to carpet; **alfombrilla** *nf* rug, mat; (MED) German measles.

alforja [al'forxa] *nf* saddlebag.

alforza [al'forθa] *nf* pleat.

alga ['alɣa] *nf* seaweed, alga.

algarabía [alɣara'βia] *nf* (*fam*) gibberish; (BOT) cornflower.

algarrobo [alɣa'rroβo] *nm* carob tree.

algazara [alɣa'θara] *nf* din, uproar.

álgebra ['alxeβra] *nf* algebra.

algo ['alɣo] *pron* something; anything // *ad* somewhat, rather; **por ~ será** there must be some reason for it.

algodón [alɣo'ðon] *nm* cotton; (*planta*) cotton plant; (*dulce*) candy floss; ~ **hidrófilo** cotton wool.

algodonero, a [alɣoðo'nero, a] *a* cotton *cpd* // *nm/f* cotton grower // *nm* cotton plant.

alguacil [alɣwa'θil] *nm* bailiff; (TAUR) mounted official.

alguien ['alxjen] *pron* someone, somebody, anybody.

alguno, a [al'ɣuno, a], **algún** [al'xun] *a* some, any // *pron* some; one; someone, somebody; ~ **que otro libro** some book or other; **algún día iré** I'll go one *or* some day; **sin interés** ~ without the slightest interest; ~ **que otro** an occasional one; ~**s piensan** some (people) think.

alhaja [a'laxa] *nf* jewel; (*tesoro*) precious object, treasure; (*pey*) rogue.

aliado, a [a'ljaðo, a] *a* allied.

alianza [a'ljanθa] *nf* alliance.

aliar [a'ljar] *vt* to ally; ~**se** *vr* to form an alliance.

alias ['aljas] *ad* alias.

alicantino, a [alikan'tino, a] *a* of *or* from Alicante.

alicates [ali'kates] *nmpl*: ~ **de uñas** nail clippers.

aliciente [ali'θjente] *nm* incentive; (*atracción*) attraction.

alienación [aljena'θjon] *nf* alienation.

aliento [a'ljento] *nm* breath; (*respiración*) breathing; **sin** ~ breathless.

aligerar [alixe'rar] *vt* to lighten; (*reducir*) to shorten; (*aliviar*) to alleviate; (*mitigar*) to ease.

alimaña [ali'maɲa] *nf* pest.

alimentación [alimenta'θjon] *nf* (*comida*) food; (*acción*) feeding; (*tienda*) grocer's (shop); **alimentar** *vt* to feed; (*nutrir*) to nourish; **alimentarse** *vr* to feed.

alimenticio, a [alimen'tiθjo, a] *a* nourishing.

alimento [ali'mento] *nm* food; (*nutritivo*) nourishment; ~**s** *nmpl* (JUR) alimony *sg*.

alinear [aline'ar] *vt* to align; ~**se** *vr*: ~**se en** to fall in with.

aliñar [ali'ɲar] *vt* to adorn; (*preparar*) to prepare; (CULIN) to season; **aliño** *nm* decoration; (*esmero*) neatness; (CULIN) dressing.

alisar [ali'sar] *vt* to smooth; (*pulir*) to polish.

aliso [a'liso] *nm* alder.

alistamiento [alista'mjento] *nm* recruitment; **alistar** *vt* to recruit; (*inscribir*) to enrol; **alistarse** *vr* to enlist; to enrol.

aliviar [ali'βjar] *vt* (*carga*) to lighten; (*persona*) to relieve; (*dolor*) to alleviate; ~**se** *vr*: ~**se de** to unburden o.s. of.

alivio [a'liβjo] *nm* alleviation, relief.

aljibe [al'xiβe] *nm* cistern; (AUTO) oil tanker.

aljofaina [alxo'faina] *nf* = **jofaina.**

alma ['alma] *nf* soul; (*persona*) person; (*que anima*) life and soul; (*TEC*) core.

almacén [alma'θen] *nm* (*depósito*) warehouse, store; (*MIL*) magazine; (*AM*) shop; **almacenes** *nmpl* department store *sg*; **almacenaje** *nm* storage.

almacenar [almaθe'nar] *vt* to store, put in storage; (*proveerse*) to stock up (with); **almacenero** *nm* warehouse-man.

almanaque [alma'nake] *nm* almanac.

almeja [al'mexa] *nf* shellfish, clam.

almendra [al'mendra] *nf* almond; **almendro** *nm* almond tree.

almiar [al'mjar] *nm* hayrick.

almíbar [al'mißar] *nm* syrup; **almibarado, a** *a* syrupy.

almidón [almi'ðon] *nm* starch; **almidonar** *vt* to starch.

almirantazgo [almiran'taðxo] *nm* admiralty; **almirante** *nm* admiral.

almohada [almo'aða] *nf* pillow; (*funda*) pillowcase; **almohadilla** *nf* cushion; (*TEC*) pad; (*AM*) pincushion.

almoneda [almo'neða] *nf* auction; (*liquidación*) clearance sale.

almorranas [almo'rranas] *nfpl* piles, haemorrhoids.

almorzar [almor'θar] *vt*: ~ **una tortilla** to have an omelette for lunch // *vi* to (have) lunch.

almuerzo [al'mwerθo] *nm* lunch.

alnado, a [al'naðo, a] *nm/f* stepson/daughter.

alocado, a [alo'kaðo, a] *a* crazy.

alojamiento [aloxa'mjento] *nm* lodging(s) (*pl*); (*viviendas*) housing.

alojar [alo'xar] *vt* to lodge; ~**se** *vr* to lodge, stay.

alondra [a'londra] *nf* lark, skylark.

alpargata [alpar'xata] *nf* rope soled sandal; (*de lona*) canvas shoe.

Alpes ['alpes] *nmpl*. **los** ~ the Alps.

alpinismo [alpi'nismo] *nm* mountaineering, climbing; **alpinista** *nm/f* mountaineer, climber.

alquería [alke'ria] *nf* farmhouse.

alquilar [alki'lar] *vt* to rent (out), let, hire (out); (*de inquilino*) to rent, hire; **se alquilan casas** houses to let.

alquiler [alki'ler] *nm* renting, letting, hiring; (*arriendo*) rent, hire charge; **de** ~ for hire.

alquimia [al'kimja] *nf* alchemy.

alquitrán [alki'tran] *nm* tar.

alrededor [alreðe'ðor] *ad* around, about; ~**es** *nmpl* surroundings; **de pre** around, about; **mirar a su** ~ to look (round) about one.

alta ['alta] *nf* ver **alto.**

altanería [altane'ria] *nf* haughtiness, arrogance; **altanero, a** *a* arrogant, haughty.

altar [al'tar] *nm* altar.

altavoz [alta'βoθ] *nm* loudspeaker; (*amplificador*) amplifier.

alteración [altera'θjon] *nf* alteration; (*alboroto*) disturbance; (*discusión*) quarrel; **alterar** *vt* to alter; to disturb; **alterarse** *vr* (*alimento etc*) to go bad or off; (*voz*) to falter; (*persona*) to get upset.

altercado [alter'kaðo] *nm* argument.

alternar [alter'nar] *vt* to alternate // *vi*, ~**se** *vr* to alternate; (*turnar*) to take turns; ~ **con** to mix with; **alternativo, a** *a* alternative; (*alterno*) alternating // *nf* alternative; (*elección*) choice; **alternativas** *nfpl* ups and downs.

alteza [al'teθa] *nf* (*tratamiento*) highness; (*altura*) height.

altibajos [alti'βaxos] *nmpl* ups and downs.

altiplanicie [altipla'niθje] *nf*, **altiplano** [alti'plano] *nm* high plateau.

altisonante [altiso'nante] *a* high-flown.

altitud [alti'tuð] *nf* altitude.

altivez [alti'βeθ] *nf* haughtiness, arrogance; **altivo, a** *a* haughty, arrogant.

alto, a ['alto, a] a high; (de tamaño) tall; (precio, importante) high; (sonido) high, sharp; (noble) high, lofty // nm halt; (MUS) alto; (GEO) hill; (AM) pile // ad (de sitio) high; (de sonido) loud, loudly // nf (certificate of) discharge // excl halt!; **tiene 2 metros de** ~ he is 2 metres tall; **en** ~**a mar** on the high seas; **en voz** ~**a** in a loud voice; **las** ~**as horas de la noche** the small hours; **en lo** ~ **de** at the top of; **pasar por** ~ to overlook; **dar de** ~**a** to discharge.

altoparlante [altopar'lante] nm (AM) loudspeaker.

altura [al'tura] nf height; (NAUT) depth; (GEO) latitude; **tiene 1.80 de** ~ he is 1 metre 80cm tall; **a esta** ~ **del año** at this time of the year.

alubia [a'luβja] nf French bean, kidney bean.

alucinación [aluθina'θjon] nf hallucination; **alucinar** vi to hallucinate // vt to deceive; (fascinar) to fascinate.

alud [a'luð] nm avalanche.

aludir [alu'ðir] vi: ~ **a** to allude to; **darse por** ~ to take the hint.

alumbrado [alum'braðo] nm lighting; **alumbramiento** nm lighting; (MED) childbirth, delivery.

alumbrar [alum'brar] vt to light (up); (ciego) to restore the sight of // vi to give birth.

aluminio [alu'minjo] nm aluminium.

alumno, a [a'lumno, a] nm/f pupil, student.

alunizar [aluni'θar] vi to land on the moon.

alusión [alu'sjon] nf allusion.

alusivo, a [alu'siβo, a] a allusive.

aluvión [alu'βjon] nm alluvium; (fig) flood.

alza ['alθa] nf rise; ~**s** nfpl sights.

alzada [al'θaða] nf (de caballos) height; (JUR) appeal.

alzamiento [alθa'mjento] nm (aumento) rise, increase; (acción)

lifting, raising; (mejor postura) higher bid; (rebelión) rising; (COM) fraudulent bankruptcy.

alzar [al'θar] vt to lift (up); (precio, muro) to raise; (cuello de abrigo) to turn up; (AGR) to gather in; (IMPRENTA) to gather; ~**se** vr to get up, rise; (rebelarse) to revolt; (COM) to go fraudulently bankrupt; (JUR) to appeal.

allá [a'ʎa] ad (lugar) there; (por ahí) over there; (tiempo) then; ~ **abajo** down there; **más** ~ further on; **más** ~ **de** beyond; ¡~ **tu!** that's your problem!

allanar [aʎa'nar] vt to flatten, level (out); (igualar) to smooth (out); (fig) to subdue; (JUR) to burgle, break into; ~**se** vr to fall down; ~**se a** to submit to, accept.

allegado, a [aʎe'xaðo, a] a near, close // nm/f relation.

allegar [aʎe'xar] vt to gather (together); (añadir) to add; ~**se** vr to approach.

allí [a'ʎi] ad there; ~ **mismo** right there; **por** ~ over there; (por ese camino) that way.

ama ['ama] nf lady of the house; (dueña) owner; (institutriz) governess; (madre adoptiva) foster mother; ~ **de cría** o **de leche** wet-nurse; ~ **de llaves** housekeeper.

amabilidad [amaβili'ðað] nf kindness; (simpatía) niceness; **amable** a kind; nice.

amado, a [a'maðo, a] nm/f beloved, sweetheart.

amaestrar [amaes'trar] vt to train; (preparar) to coach.

amagar [ama'xar] vt, vi to threaten; **amago** nm threat; (gesto) threatening gesture; (MED) symptom.

amalgama [amal'xama] nf amalgam; **amalgamar** vt to amalgamate; (combinar) to combine, mix.

amamantar [amaman'tar] vt to suckle, nurse.

amanecer [amane'θer] vi to dawn // nm dawn; **el niño amaneció afiebrado** the child woke up with a fever.

amanerado, a [amane'raðo, a] a affected.

amansar [aman'sar] vt to tame; (templar) to subdue.

amante [a'mante] a: ~ **de** fond of // nm/f lover.

amapola [ama'pola] nf poppy.

amar [a'mar] vt to love.

amargado, a [amar'xaðo, a] a bitter; **amargar** vt to make bitter; (fig) to embitter; **amargarse** vr to get bitter.

amargo, a [a'marvo, a] a bitter; **amargura** nf bitterness.

amarillento, a [amari'λento, a] a yellowish; (tez) sallow; **amarillo, a** a, nm yellow.

amarrar [ama'rrar] vt to moor; (sujetar) to tie up.

amartelar [amarte'lar] vt to make jealous, (enamorar) to win the heart of, ~ se vr: ~se de to fall in love with.

amartillar [amarti'λar] vt → **martillar**.

amasar [ama'sar] vt to knead; (mezclar) to mix, prepare; (MED) to massage; (confeccionar) to concoct; **amasijo** nm kneading; mixing; (masa) dough; (pasta) paste; (fig) hotchpotch.

amateur ['amatur] nm/f amateur.

amatista [ama'tista] nf amethyst.

amazona [ama'θona] nf horsewoman; **A~s** nm: **el A~s** the Amazon.

ambages [am'baxes] nmpl. **sin** ~ in plain language.

ámbar ['ambar] nm amber.

ambición [ambi'θjon] nf ambition; **ambicionar** vt to aspire to; **ambicioso, a** a ambitious.

ambidextro, a [ambi'dekstro, a] a ambidextrous.

ambiente [am'bjente] nm atmosphere; (medio) environment.

ambigüedad [ambixwe'ðað] nf ambiguity; **ambiguo, a** a ambiguous.

ámbito ['ambito] nm compass; (campo) field; (límite) boundary; (fig) scope.

ambos, as ['ambos, as] apl, pron pl both.

ambulancia [ambu'lanθja] nf ambulance.

ambulante [ambu'lante] a walking cpd, itinerant.

ambulatorio [ambula'torjo] nm national health clinic.

amedrentar [ameðren'tar] vt to scare.

amén [a'men] excl amen; ~ **de** except for.

amenaza [ame'naθa] nf threat; **amenazar** vt, vi to threaten.

amenguar [amen'gwar] vt to diminish; (fig) to dishonour.

amenidad [ameni'ðað] nf pleasantness.

ameno, a [a'meno, a] a pleasant.

América [a'merika] nf America; ~ **del Norte/del Sur** North/South America; ~ **Central/Latina** Central/Latin America; **americano, a** a, nm/f American // (cod) jacket.

ametralladora [ametraλa'ðora] nf machine gun.

amigable [ami'xaβle] a friendly.

amígdala [a'mixðala] nf tonsil; **amigdalitis** nf tonsillitis.

amigo, a [a'mixo, a] a friendly // nm/f friend.

amilanar [amila'nar] vt to scare.

aminorar [amino'rar] vt to diminish; (reducir) to reduce.

amistad [amis'tað] nf friendship; ~**es** nfpl friends; **amistoso, a** a friendly.

amnesia [am'nesja] nf amnesia.

amnistía [amnis'tia] nf amnesty.

amo ['amo] nm owner; (dueño) boss; ~ **de casa** householder.

amodorrarse [amoðo'rrarse] vr to get sleepy.

amolar [amo'lar] vt to sharpen; (fig) to bore.

amoldar [amol'dar] *vt* to mould; (*adaptar*) to adapt.

amonestación [amonesta'θjon] *nf* warning; **amonestaciones** *nfpl* marriage banns; **amonestar** *vt* to warn; to publish the banns of.

amontonar [amonto'nar] *vt* to collect, pile up; ~**se** *vr* to crowd together; (*acumularse*) to pile up.

amor [a'mor] *nm* love; (*amante*) lover; **hacer el** ~ to make love; (*cortejar*) to court.

amoratado, a [amora'taðo, a] *a* a purple, blue with cold.

amordazar [amorða'θar] *vt* to muzzle; (*fig*) to gag.

amorío [amo'rio] *nm* (*fam*) love affair.

amoroso, a [amo'roso, a] *a* affectionate, loving.

amortajar [amorta'xar] *vt* to shroud.

amortiguador [amortigwa'ðor] *nm* shock absorber; (*parachoques*) bumper; (*silenciador*) silencer; **amortiguar** *vt* to deaden; (*ruido*) to muffle; (*color*) to soften.

amortización [amortiθa'θjon] *nf* redemption, repayment.

amotinar [amoti'nar] *vt* to stir up, incite (to riot); ~**se** *vr* to mutiny.

amparar [ampa'rar] *vt* to protect; ~**se** *vr* to seek protection; (*abrigar*) to shelter; **amparo** *nm* help, protection.

ampliación [amplja'θjon] *nf* enlargement; (*extensión*) extension; **ampliar** *vt* to enlarge; to extend.

amplificación [amplifika'θjon] *nf* enlargement; **amplificador** *nm* amplifier; **amplificar** *vt* to amplify.

amplio, a [am'pljo, a] *a* spacious; (*de falda etc*) full; (*extenso*) extensive; (*ancho*) wide; **amplitud** *nf* spaciousness; extent; (*fig*) amplitude.

ampolla [am'poʎa] *nf* blister; (*MED*) ampoule.

amputar [ampu'tar] *vt* to cut off, amputate.

amueblar [amwe'βlar] *vt* to furnish.

amurallar [amura'ʎar] *vt* to wall up/in.

anacronismo [anakro'nismo] *nm* anachronism.

ánade ['anaðe] *nm* duck.

anadear [anaðe'ar] *vi* to waddle.

anales [a'nales] *nmpl* annals.

analfabetismo [analfaβe'tismo] *nm* illiteracy; **analfabeto, a** *a* illiterate.

análisis [a'nalisis] *nm* analysis.

analizar [anali'θar] *vt* to analyse.

analogía [analo'xia] *nf* analogy.

analógico, a [analo'xiko, a] *a*

ananá(s) [ana'na(s)] *nm* pineapple.

anaquel [ana'kel] *nm* shelf.

anarquía [anar'kia] *nf* anarchy; **anarquismo** *nm* anarchism; **anarquista** *nm/f* anarchist.

anatomía [anato'mia] *nf* anatomy.

anciano, a [an'θjano, a] *a* old, aged // *nm/f* old man/woman // *nm* elder.

ancla ['ankla] *nf* anchor; ~**dero** *nm* anchorage; **anclar** *vi* to (drop) anchor.

ancho, a ['antʃo, a] *a* wide; (*falda*) full; (*fig*) liberal // *nm* width; (*FERRO*) gauge; **ponerse** ~ to get conceited; **estar a sus** ~ as to be at one's ease.

anchoa [an'tʃoa] *nf* anchovy.

anchura [an'tʃura] *nf* width; (*extensión*) wideness; (*fig*) freedom.

andaderas [anda'ðeras] *nfpl* baby walker *sg*.

andadura [anda'ðura] *nf* gait, pace.

Andalucía [andalu'θia] *nf* Andalusia; **andaluz, a** *a, nm/f* Andalusian.

andamio [an'damjo], **andamiaje** [anda'mjaxe] *nm* scaffold.

andar [an'dar] *vt* to go, cover, travel // *vi* to go, walk, travel; (*funcionar*) to go, work; (*estar*) to be // *nm* walk, gait, pace; ~**se** *vr* to go away; ~ **a pie/a caballo/en bicicleta** to go on foot/on horseback/by bicycle; **¡anda!**

¡andando! go on!; (vamos) come on!; (bien) well!; **anda en los 40** he's about 40.

andariego, a [anda'rjexo, a] a fond of travelling.

andén [an'den] nm (FERRO) platform; (NAUT) quayside; (AUTO) hard shoulder.

Andes ['andes] nmpl: **los ~** the Andes.

Andorra [an'dorra] nf Andorra.

andrajo [an'draxo] nm rag; **~so, a** a ragged.

andurriales [andur'rjales] nmpl out-of-the-way place sg.

anduve etc vb ver **andar**.

anécdota [a'neƙðota] nf anecdote, story.

anegar [ane'xar] vt to flood; (ahogar) to drown; **~se** vr to drown; (hundirse) to sink.

anemia [a'nemja] nf anaemia.

anestésico [anes'tesiko] nm anaesthetic.

anexar [anek'sar] vt to annex; (documento) to attach; **anexo, a** a attached // nm annexe.

anfibio, a [an'fiβjo, a] a amphibious // nm amphibian.

anfiteatro [anfite'atro] nm amphitheatre; (TEATRO) dress circle.

anfitrión, ona [anfi'trjon, ona] nm/f host.

ángel ['anxel] nm angel; **angélico, a**, **angelical** a angelic(al).

angina [an'xina] nf (MED) inflammation of the throat; **~ de pecho** angina (pectoris).

anglicano, a [angli'kano, a] a, nm/f Anglican.

angosto, a [an'gosto, a] a narrow.

angostura [angos'tura] nf narrowness; (paso) narrow passage.

anguila [an'gila] nf eel; **~s** nfpl slipway sg.

ángulo ['angulo] nm angle; (esquina) corner; (curva) bend.

angustia [an'gustja] nf anguish; **angustiar** vt to distress, grieve.

anhelante [ane'lante] a eager; (deseoso) longing; **anhelar** vt to be eager for; to long for, desire // vi to pant, gasp; **anhelo** nm eagerness; desire.

anidar [ani'ðar] vi to nest.

anillo [a'niƙo] nm ring; **~ de boda** wedding ring.

ánima ['anima] nf soul; **las ~s** the Angelus (bell) sg.

animación [anima'θjon] nf liveliness; (vitalidad) life; (actividad) bustle; **animado, a** a lively; (vivaz) animated.

animadversión [animaðβer'sjon] nf ill-will, antagonism.

animal [ani'mal] a animal; (fig) stupid // nm animal; (fig) fool; (bestia) brute.

animar [ani'mar] vt (BIO) to animate, give life to; (fig) to liven up, brighten up, cheer up; (estimular) to stimulate; **~se** vr to cheer up, feel encouraged; (decidirse) to make up one's mind.

ánimo ['animo] nm soul, mind; (valentía) courage // excl cheer up!

animosidad [animosi'ðað] nf animosity.

animoso, a [ani'moso, a] a brave; (vivo) lively.

aniquilar [aniki'lar] vt to annihilate, destroy; **~se** vr to be wiped out, disappear; (emporcarse) to deteriorate.

anís [a'nis] nm aniseed.

aniversario [aniβer'sarjo] nm anniversary.

anoche [a'notʃe] ad last night; **antes de ~** the night before last.

anochecer [anotʃe'θer] vi to get dark // nm nightfall, dusk.

anomalía [anoma'lia] nf anomaly.

anonadamiento [anonaða'mjento] nm annihilation; (desaliento) discouragement; **anonadar** vt to annihilate; to discourage; **anonadarse** vr to get discouraged.

anónimo, a [a'nonimo, a] a

anonymous; (COM) limited // nm anonymity.

anormal [anor'mal] a abnormal.

anotación [anota'θjon] nf note.

anotar [ano'tar] vt to note down; (comentar) to annotate.

ansia ['ansja] nf anxiety; (añoranza) yearning; **ansiar** vt to long for.

ansiedad [ansje'ðað] nf anxiety.

ansioso, a [an'sjoso, a] a anxious; (anhelante) eager.

antagónico, a [anta'xoniko, a] a antagonistic; (opuesto) contrasting; **antagonista** nm/f antagonist.

antaño [an'taɲo] ad long ago.

Antártico [an'tartiko] nm: **el ~** the Antarctic.

ante ['ante] prep before, in the presence of; (encarado con) faced with // nm suede, buckskin; **~ todo** above all.

anteanoche [antea'notʃe] ad the night before last.

anteayer [antea'jer] ad the day before yesterday.

antebrazo [ante'ßraθo] nm forearm.

antecedente [anteθe'ðente] a previous // nm antecedent; **~s** nmpl record sg, background sg.

anteceder [anteθe'ðer] vt to precede, go before.

antecesor, a [anteθe'sor, a] nm/f predecessor; (antepasado) ancestor.

antedicho, a [ante'ðitʃo, a] a aforementioned.

antelación [antela'θjon] nf: **con ~** in advance.

antemano [ante'mano]: **de ~** ad beforehand, in advance.

antena [an'tena] nf antenna; (de televisión etc) aerial.

anteojo [ante'oxo] nm eyeglass; **~s** nmpl spectacles, glasses.

antepasados [antepa'saðos] nmpl ancestors.

antepecho [ante'petʃo] nm guardrail, parapet; (repisa) ledge, sill.

anteponer [antepo'ner] vt to place

in front; (fig) to prefer; **~se** vr: **~se a** to overcome.

anteproyecto [antepro'jekto] nm preliminary sketch; (fig) blueprint.

anterior [ante'rjor] a preceding, previous; **~idad** nf: **con ~idad a** prior to, before.

antes ['antes] ad sooner; (primero) first; (con prioridad) before; (hace tiempo) previously, once; (más bien) rather // prep: **~ de** before // conj: **~ (de) que** before; **~ bien** (but) rather; **dos días ~** two days before or previously; **~ muerto que esclavo** better dead than enslaved; **tomo el avión ~ que el barco** I take the plane rather than the boat; **cuanto ~, lo ~ posible** as soon as possible.

antesala [ante'sala] nf anteroom.

antibiótico [anti'ßjotiko] nm antibiotic.

anticipación [antiθipa'θjon] nf anticipation; (COM) advance; **con 10 minutos de ~** 10 minutes early; **anticipado, a** a (in) advance.

anticipar [antiθi'par] vt to anticipate; (adelantar) to bring forward; (COM) to advance; **~se** vr: **~se a su época** to be ahead of one's time.

anticipo [anti'θipo] nm = **anticipación**.

anticonceptivo, a [antikonθep'tißo, a] a, nm contraceptive.

anticongelante [antikonxe'lante] nm antifreeze.

anticuado, a [anti'kwaðo, a] a out-of-date, old-fashioned; (desusado) obsolete.

anticuario [anti'kwarjo] nm antique dealer.

antídoto [an'tiðoto] nm antidote.

antifaz [anti'faθ] nm mask; (velo) veil.

antigualla [anti'ɣwaʎa] nf antique; (reliquia) relic.

antiguamente [antiɣwa'mente] ad formerly; (hace mucho tiempo) long ago.

antigüedad [antixweˈðað] nf antiquity; (artículo) antique; (rango) seniority; **antiguo, a** old, ancient; (que fue) former.

antílope [anˈtilope] nm antelope.

antillano, a [antiˈʎano, a] a, nm/f West Indian.

Antillas [anˈtiʎas] nfpl: **las ~** the West Indies.

antipara [antiˈpara] nf screen.

antipatía [antipaˈtia] nf antipathy, dislike; **antipático, a** disagreeable, unpleasant.

antisemita [antiseˈmita] nm/f antisemite.

antítesis [anˈtitesis] nf antithesis.

antojadizo, a [antoxaˈðiθo, a] a capricious.

antojarse [antoˈxarse] vr (desear): **se me antoja comprarlo** I have a mind to buy it; (pensar): **se me antoja que** I have a feeling that.

antojo [anˈtoxo] nm caprice, whim; (rosa) birthmark; (lunar) mole.

antología [antoloˈxia] nf anthology.

antorcha [anˈtortʃa] nf torch.

antro [ˈantro] nm cavern.

antropófago, a [antroˈpofaxo, a] a, nm/f cannibal.

antropología [antropoloˈxia] nf anthropology.

anual [aˈnwal] a annual.

anualidad [anwaliˈðað] nf annuity.

anuario [aˈnwarjo] nm yearbook.

anublar [anuˈβlar] vt to cloud; (oscurecer) to darken; **~se** vr to become cloudy, cloud over; (BOT) to wither.

anudar [anuˈðar] vt to knot, tie (unir) to join; **~se** vr to get tied up.

anulación [anulaˈθjon] nf annulment; (cancelación) cancellation; **anular** vt to annul, to cancel; (revocar) to revoke, repeal // nm ring finger.

anunciación [anunθjaˈθjon] nf announcement; **anunciar** vt to announce; (proclamar) to proclaim; (COM) to advertise.

anuncio [aˈnunθjo] nm announce-

ment; (señal) sign; (COM) advertisement; (cartel) poster.

anzuelo [anˈθwelo] nm hook; (para pescar) fish hook.

añadidura [aɲaðiˈðura] nf addition, extra; **por ~** besides, in addition.

añadir [aɲaˈðir] vt to add.

añejo, a [aˈɲexo, a] a old.

añicos [aˈɲikos] nmpl: **hacer ~** to smash, shatter.

año [ˈaɲo] nm year; **¡Feliz A~ Nuevo!** Happy New Year!; **tener 15 ~s** to be 15 (years old); **los ~s 60** the sixties; **~ bisiesto/escolar** leap/school year.

añoranza [aɲoˈranθa] nf nostalgia; (anhelo) longing.

apacentar [apaθenˈtar] vt to pasture, graze.

apacible [apaˈθiβle] a gentle, mild.

apaciguar [apaθiˈɣwar] vt to pacify, calm (down).

apadrinar [apaðriˈnar] vt to sponsor, support; (REL) to act as godfather to.

apagado, a [apaˈɣaðo, a] a out; (volcán) extinct; (cal) slaked; (color) dull; (voz) quiet, timid; (sonido) muted, muffled; (apático) listless.

apagar [apaˈɣar] vt to put out, (sonido) to silence, muffle; (sed) to quench; (fig) to kill.

apagón [apaˈɣon] nm blackout, power cut.

apalabrar [apalaˈβrar] vt to agree to; (obrero) to engage.

apalear [apaleˈar] vt to beat, thrash, (AGR) to winnow.

apañar [apaˈɲar] vt to pick up; (asir) to take hold of, grasp; (vestir) to dress up; (reparar) to mend, patch up; **~se** vr to manage, get along.

aparador [apaɾaˈðoɾ] nm sideboard, (establecer) shop window.

aparato [apaˈrato] nm apparatus; (máquina) machine; (doméstico) appliance; (boato) ostentation; **~so, a** a showy, ostentatious.

aparcamiento [aparka'mjento] *nm* car park.

aparcar [apar'kar] *vt, vi* to park.

aparecer [apare'θer] *vi*, ~**se** *vr* to appear.

aparejado, a [apare'xaðo, a] *a* fit, suitable.

aparejar [apare'xar] *vt* to prepare; (*caballo*) to saddle, harness; (*NAUT*) to fit out, rig out; **aparejo** *nm* preparation; harness; rigging; (*de poleas*) block and tackle.

aparentar [aparen'tar] *vt* to feign; (*parecer*) to look, seem (to be).

aparente [apa'rente] *a* apparent; (*adecuado*) suitable.

aparición [apari'θjon] *nf* appearance; (*de libro*) publication.

apariencia [apa'rjenθja] *nf* (*outward*) appearance; **en** ~ outwardly, seemingly.

apartado, a [apar'taðo, a] *a* separate; (*lejano*) remote // *nm* post office box; (*tipográfico*) paragraph.

apartamento [aparta'mento] *nm* apartment, flat.

apartamiento [aparta'mjento] *nm* separation; (*aislamiento*) remoteness; (*AM*) apartment, flat.

apartar [apar'tar] *vt* to separate; (*quitar*) to remove; (*MINEROLOGÍA*) to extract; ~**se** *vr* to separate, part; (*irse*) to move away, keep away; **aparte** *ad* (*separadamente*) separately; (*además*) besides // *nm* aside; (*tipográfico*) new paragraph.

apasionado, a [apasjo'naðo, a] *a* passionate; biassed, prejudiced.

apasionar [apasjo'nar] *vt* to arouse passion in; ~**se** *vr* to get excited.

apatía [apa'tia] *nf* apathy.

apático, a [a'patiko, a] *a* apathetic.

apdo *nm abr de* **apartado** (*de correos*).

apeadero [apea'ðero] *nm* halt, wayside station.

apearse [ape'arse] *vr* to dismount; (*bajarse*) to get down/out.

apedrear [apeðre'ar] *vt* to stone.

apegarse [ape'xarse] *vr*: ~**se a** to become attached to; **apego** *nm* attachment, fondness.

apelación [apela'θjon] *nf* appeal.

apelante [ape'lante] *nm/f* appellant.

apelar [ape'lar] *vi* to appeal; ~ **a** to resort to.

apellidar [apeʎi'ðar] *vt* to call name; ~**se** *vr* to be called; **apellido** *nm* surname, name.

apenar [ape'nar] *vt* to grieve trouble; ~**se** *vr* to grieve.

apenas [a'penas] *ad* scarcely hardly // *conj* as soon as, no sooner.

apéndice [a'pendiθe] *nm* appendix **apendicitis** *nf* appendicitis.

apercibir [aperθi'βir] *vt* prepare; (*avisar*) to warn; (*JUR*) to summon; (*AM*) to notice, see; ~**se** to get ready.

aperitivo [aperi'tiβo] *nm* aperitif.

apertura [aper'tura] *nf* opening.

apesadumbrar [apesaðum'brar *vt* to grieve, sadden; ~**se** *vr* to distress o.s.

apestar [apes'tar] *vt* to infect // *v* to stink.

apetecer [apete'θer] *vt*: ¿**te apetece una tortilla?** do you fancy an omelette?; **apetecible** *a* desirable; (*llamativo*) attractive.

apetito [ape'tito] *nm* appetite; ~**so a** *a* appetizing; (*fig*) tempting.

apiadarse [apja'ðarse] *vr*: ~ **de** to take pity on.

ápice ['apiθe] *nm* apex; (*fig*) whit iota.

apio ['apjo] *nm* celery.

aplacar [apla'kar] *vt* to placate ~**se** *vr* to calm down.

aplanamiento [aplana'mjento *nm* smoothing, levelling.

aplanar [apla'nar] *vt* to smooth level; (*allanar*) to roll flat, flatten.

aplastar [aplas'tar] *vt* to squash (flat); (*fig*) to crush.

aplaudir [aplau'ðir] *vt* to applaud.

aplauso [a'plauso] *nm* applause (*fig*) approval, acclaim.

aplazamiento [aplaθa'mjento] nm postponement, adjournment; **aplazar** vt to postpone, defer.

aplicación [aplika'θjon] nf application; (esfuerzo) effort.

aplicado, a [apli'kaðo, a] a diligent, hard-working.

aplicar [apli'kar] vt (ejecutar) to apply; ~se vr to apply o.s.

aplomo [a'plomo] nm aplomb, self-assurance.

apocado, a [apo'kaðo, a] a timid.

apocamiento [apoka'mjento] nm timidity, (depresión) depression.

apocar [apo'kar] vt to reduce; ~se vr to feel small, feel humiliated.

apodar [apo'ðar] vt to nickname.

apoderado [apoðe'raðo] nm agent, representative; **apoderar** vt to authorize, empower; (JUR) to grant (a) power of attorney to; **apoderarse** vr: **apoderarse de** to take possession of.

apodo [a'poðo] nm nickname.

apogeo [apo'xeo] nm peak, summit.

apología [apolo'xia] nf eulogy; (defensa) defence.

apoplejía [aple'xia] nf apoplexy, stroke.

aporrear [aporre'ar] vt to beat (up); **aporreo** nm beating.

aportar [apor'tar] vt to contribute // vi to reach port; ~se vr (AM) to arrive, come.

aposentar [aposen'tar] vt to lodge, put up; **aposento** nm lodging; (habitación) room.

apostar [apos'tar] vt to bet, stake; (destinar) to station, post // vi to bet.

apostilla [apos'tiʎa] nf note, comment.

apóstol [a'postol] nm apostle.

apóstrofe [a'postrofe] nm insult; (reprimenda) reprimand.

apóstrofo [a'postrofo] nm apostrophe.

apostura [apos'tura] nf neatness, elegance.

apoyar [apo'jar] vt to lean, rest;

(fig) to support, back; ~se vr: ~se en to lean on; **apoyo** nm support, backing; (sostén) prop.

apreciable [apre'θjaßle] a considerable; (fig) esteemed.

apreciación [apreθja'θjon] nf (COM) valuation; **apreciar** vt to evaluate, assess; (COM) to appreciate, value.

aprecio [a'preθjo] nm valuation, estimate; (fig) appreciation.

aprehender [apreen'der] vt to apprehend, seize; **aprehensión** nf detention, capture.

apremiante [apre'mjante] a urgent, pressing; **apremiar** vt to compel, force // vi to be urgent, press; **apremio** nm compulsion; urgency.

aprender [apren'der] vt, vi to learn.

aprendiz, a [apren'diθ, a] nm/f apprentice; (principiante) learner; ~aje nm apprenticeship.

aprensión [apren'sjon] nm apprehension, fear; (delicadeza) squeamishness; **aprensivo, a** a apprehensive; (nervioso) nervous, timid.

apresar [apre'sar] vt to seize; (capturar) to capture.

aprestar [apres'tar] vt to prepare, get ready; (TEC) to prime, size; ~se vr to get ready.

apresurado, a [apresu'raðo, a] a hurried, hasty; **apresuramiento** nm hurry, haste.

apresurar [apresu'rar] vt to hurry, accelerate; ~se vr to hurry, make haste.

apretado, a [apre'taðo, a] a tight; (escritura) cramped; (difícil) difficult; (fam) stingy.

apretar [apre'tar] vt to squeeze, press; (TEC) to tighten; (presionar) to press together, pack // vi to be too tight; (insistir) to insist.

apretón nm squeeze; (abrazo) hug; (aglomeración) crush; (dificultad) difficulty, jam; (carrera) dash, sprint; ~ **de manos**

handshake; **apretura** nf squeeze; hug; crush; difficulty, jam; (escasez) scarcity.

aprieto [a'prjeto] nm squeeze, press; (dificultad) difficulty, jam.

aprisionar [aprisjo'nar] vt to imprison.

aprobación [aproβa'θjon] nf approval; (de examen) pass; (nota) pass mark; **aprobar** vt to approve (of); to pass // vi to pass.

apropiación [apropja'θjon] nf appropriation.

apropiado, a [apro'pjaðo, a] a appropriate.

apropiar [apro'pjar] vt to adapt, make fit; ~**se** vr: ~**se de** to appropriate.

aprovechado, a [aproβe'tʃaðo, a] a diligent, hardworking; (económico) thrifty; (pey) unscrupulous, grasping; **aprovechamiento** nm use, exploitation.

aprovechar [aproβe'tʃar] vt to use, exploit, profit from; (sacar partido de) to take advantage of // vi to progress, improve; ~**se** vr: ~**se de** to make use of, take advantage of; **¡que aproveche!** enjoy your meal!

aproximación [aproksima'θjon] nf approximation; (cercanía) nearness; (de lotería) consolation prize; **aproximado, a** a approximate; **aproximar** vt to bring nearer; **aproximarse** vr to come near, approach.

aptitud [apti'tuð] nf aptitude; (idoneidad) suitability.

apto, a ['apto, a] a suitable.

apuesto [a'pwesto, a] a neat, elegant // nf bet, wager.

apuntador [apunta'ðor] nm prompter.

apuntalar [apunta'lar] vt to prop up.

apuntar [apun'tar] vt (con arma) to aim at; (con dedo) to point at or to; (anotar) to note (down); (TEATRO) to prompt; (dinero) to stake; ~**se** vr to score a point.

apunte [a'punte] nm note.

apuñalar [apuɲa'lar] vt to stab.

apurado, a [apu'raðo, a] a needy; (difícil) difficult, dangerous; (agotado) exhausted; (AM) hurried, rushed.

apurar [apu'rar] vt (purificar) to purify; (agotar) to drain; (recursos) to use up; (molestar) to annoy; ~**se** vr to worry; (AM) to hurry.

apuro [a'puro] nm (aprieto) fix, jam; (escasez) want, hardship; (aflicción) distress; (AM) haste, urgency.

aquejar [ake'xar] vt to distress, grieve; (MED) to afflict.

aquel, aquella, aquellos, a [a'kel, a'keʎa, a'keʎos, as] det that; (pl) those.

aquél, aquélla, aquéllos, a [a'kel, a'keʎa, a'keʎos, as] pron that (one); (pl) those (ones).

aquello [a'keʎo] pron that, that business.

aquí [a'ki] ad (lugar) here; (tiempo) now; ~ **arriba** up here; ~ **mismo** right here; ~ **yace** here lies; **de** ~ **siete días** a week from now.

aquietar [akje'tar] vt to quieten (down), calm (down).

árabe ['araβe] a Arab, Arabian, Arabic // nm/f Arab // nm (lengua) Arabic.

Arabia Saudita [a'raβjasau'ðita] nf Saudi Arabia.

arado [a'raðo] nm plough.

aragonés, esa [araxo'nes, esa] a nm/f Aragonese.

arancel [aran'θel] nm tariff, duty; ~ **de aduanas** customs duty.

araña [a'raɲa] nf (ZOOL) spider; (de luces) chandelier.

arañar [ara'ɲar] vt to scratch.

arañazo [ara'ɲaθo] nm scratch.

arar [a'rar] vt to plough, till.

arbitrador, a [arβitra'ðor, a] nm/f arbiter.

arbitraje [arβi'traxe] nm arbitration.

arbitrar [arβi'trar] vt to arbitrate

in; (DEPORTE) to referee // vi to arbitrate.

arbitrariedad [arβitrarje'ðað] nf arbitrariness; (acto) arbitrary act.

arbitrario, a a arbitrary.

arbitrio [ar'βitrjo] nm free will; (JUR) adjudication, decision.

árbitro ['arβitro] nm arbitrator; (DEPORTE) referee; (TENIS) umpire.

árbol [ar'βol] nm (BOT) tree; (NAUT) mast; (TEC) axle, shaft; **arbolado, a** a a wooded, tree-lined // nm woodland.

arboladura [arβola'ðura] nf rigging; **arbolar** vt to hoist, raise; **arbolarse** vr to rear up.

arboleda [arβo'leða] nf grove, plantation.

arbusto [ar'βusto] nm bush, shrub.

arca ['arka] nf chest, box; (caja fuerte) strongbox.

arcada [ar'kaða] nf arcade; (de puente) arch, span; ~s nfpl retching sg.

arcaduz [arka'ðuθ] nm pipe, conduit.

arcaico, a [ar'kaiko, a] a archaic.

arce ['arθe] nm maple tree.

arcediano [arθe'ðjano] nm archdeacon.

arcilla [ar'θiλa] nf clay.

arco ['arko] nm arc; (MAT) arc; (MIL, MUS) bow; ~ **iris** rainbow.

archipiélago [artʃi'pjelaɣo] nm archipelago.

archivar [artʃi'βar] vt to file (away); **archivo** nm archive(s) (pl).

arder [ar'ðer] vi, vt to burn.

ardid [ar'ðið] nm ruse.

ardiente [ar'ðjente] a burning, (apasionado) ardent.

ardilla [ar'ðiλa] nf squirrel.

ardor [ar'ðor] nm (calor) heat, warmth; (fig) ardour; ~ **de estómago** heartburn; ~**oso, a** a = **ardiente**.

arduo, a ['arðwo, a] a arduous.

área ['area] nf area; (DEPORTE) penalty area.

arena [a'rena] nf sand; (de una lucha) arena; (MED) stone.

arenal [are'nal] nm sandy ground; (arena movediza) quicksand.

arengar [aren'gar] vt to harangue.

arenisco, a [are'nisko, a] a sandy // nf sandstone; (cascajo) grit.

arenoso, a [are'noso, a] a sandy.

arenque [a'renke] nm herring.

arete [a'rete] nm earring.

argamasa [arɣa'masa] nf mortar, plaster; **argamasar** vt to mortar, plaster.

Argel [ar'xel] n Algiers; ~**ia** nf Algeria; **argelino, a** a, nm/f Algerian.

argentino, a [arxen'tino, a] a Argentinian; (de plata) silvery // nm/f Argentinian // nf: A~a Argentina.

argolla [ar'xoλa] nf (large) ring; (juego) croquet.

argot [ar'xo] nm slang.

argucia [ar'xuθja] nf subtlety, sophistry.

argüir [ar'xwir] vt to deduce; (discutir) to argue; (indicar) to indicate, imply; (censurar) to reproach // vi to argue.

argumentación [arxumenta'θjon] nf (line of) argument; **argumentar** vt, vi to argue.

argumento [arxu'mento] nm argument; (de obra) plot.

aria ['arja] nf aria.

aridez [ari'ðeθ] nf aridity, dryness.

árido, a ['ariðo, a] a arid, dry; ~s nmpl dry goods.

Aries ['arjes] nm Aries.

ariete [a'rjete] nm battering ram.

ario, a ['arjo, a] a Aryan.

arisco, a [a'risko, a] a surly; (insociable) unsociable.

aristócrata [aris'tokrata] nm/f aristocrat.

aritmética [arit'metika] nf arithmetic.

arma ['arma] nf arm; ~s nfpl arms; ~ **blanca** blade, knife; (espada) sword; ~ **de fuego** firearm; ~**s cortas** small arms.

armadillo [arma'ðiʎo] *nm* armadillo.

armado, a [ar'maðo, a] *a* armed; (TEC) reinforced // *a* armada; (flota) fleet.

armadura [arma'ðura] *nf* (MIL) armour; (TEC) framework; (ZOOL) skeleton; (FÍSICA) armature.

armamento [arma'mento] *nm* armament; (buque) fitting-out.

armar [ar'mar] *vt* (soldado) to arm; (máquina) to assemble; (navío) to fit out; ~ **la, ~ un lío** to start a row.

armario [ar'marjo] *nm* wardrobe.

armatoste [arma'toste] *nm* large useless object, contraption.

armazón [arma'θon] *nf* body, chassis; (de mueble etc) frame; (ARQ) skeleton.

armería [arme'ria] *nf* (museo) military museum; (tienda) gunsmith's.

armiño [ar'miɲo] *nm* stoat; (piel) ermine.

armisticio [armis'tiθjo] *nm* armistice.

armonía [armo'nia] *nf* harmony.

armónica [ar'monika] *nf* harmonica.

armonioso, a [armo'njoso, a] *a* harmonious.

arnés [ar'nes] *nm* armour; **arneses** *nmpl* harness sg.

aro ['aro] *nm* ring; (tejo) quoit; (pendiente) earring.

aroma [a'roma] *nm* aroma.

aromático, a [aro'matiko, a] *a* aromatic.

arpa ['arpa] *nf* harp.

arpía [ar'pia] *nf* shrew.

arpista [ar'pista] *nm/f* harpist.

arpón [ar'pon] *nm* harpoon.

arquear [arke'ar] *vt* to arch, bend; ~**se** *vr* to arch, bend; **arqueo** *nm* (gen) arching, curve; (de navío) tonnage.

arqueología [arkeolo'xia] *nf* archaeology; **arqueólogo, a** *nm/f* archaeologist.

arquero [ar'kero] *nm* archer bowman.

arquetipo [arke'tipo] *nm* a chetype.

arquitecto [arki'tekto] *nf* architect; **arquitectura** *nf* arch tecture.

arrabal [arra'βal] *nm* suburb; (AM slum.

arraigado, a [arrai'xaðo, a deep-rooted; (fig) established.

arraigar [arrai'xar] *vt* to establis // *vi*, ~**se** *vr* to take root.

arrancar [arran'kar] *vt* (sacar) t pull up, extract, pull out; (separar to snatch (away), wrest; (fig) t extract // *vi* to start, pull out.

arranque [a'rranke] *nm* sudde start; (AUTO) start; (fig) fit, outburst

arras ['arras] *nfpl* pledge s security sg.

arrasar [arra'sar] *vt* (aplanar) t level, flatten; (destruir) to demolish (llenar) to fill up // *vi* to clear.

arrastrado, a [arras'traðo, a poor, wretched; (AM) servile.

arrastrar [arras'trar] *vt* to dra (along); (fig) to drag down, degrade (suj: agua, viento) to carry away / *vi* to drag, trail on the ground; ~**s** *vr* to crawl; (fig) to grovel; lleva algo arrastrado to drag sth along.

arrastre [a'rrastre] *nm* dra dragging; (DEPORTE) crawl.

arrayán [arra'jan] *nm* myrtle.

arrear [arre'ar] *vt* to drive, urg on; (enganchar) to harness // *vi* t hurry along; **¡arre(a)!** get up!, ge up!

arrebatado, a [arreβa'taðo, a rash, impetuous; (repentino) sudde hasty.

arrebatar [arreβa'tar] *vt* to snatc (away), seize; (fig) to captivate ~**se** *vr* to get carried away, ge excited.

arrebato [arre'βato] *nm* fit of rag fury; (éxtasis) rapture.

arreglado, a [arre'xlaðo, a (ordenado) neat, orderly; (mode *rado)* moderate, reasonable.

rreglar [arre'slar] *vt (poner orden)* to tidy up; *(algo roto)* to fix, repair; *(problema)* to solve; *(MUS)* to arrange; ~**se** *vr* to reach an understanding; **arreglárselas** *(fam)* to get by, manage.

rreglo [a'rreglo] *nm* settlement; *(orden)* order; *(acuerdo)* agreement; *(MUS)* arrangement, setting.

rremangar [arreman'gar] *vt* to roll up, turn up; ~**se** *vr* to roll up one's sleeves.

rremeter [arreme'ter] *vi* to attack, assault.

rrendador, a [arrenda'ðor, a] *nm/f* landlord/lady; *(inquilino)* tenant.

rrendamiento [arrenda'mjento] *nm* letting; *(alquilar)* hiring; *(contrato)* lease, *(alquiler)* rent; **arrendar** *vt* to let, lease; to rent; **arrendatario, a** *nm/f* tenant.

rrepentimiento [arrepenti'mjento] *nm* regret, repentance.

rrepentirse [arrepen'tirse] *vr:* ~ **de** to regret, repent of.

rrestar [arres'tar] *vt* to arrest; *(encarcelar)* to imprison; **arresto** *nm* arrest; *(MIL)* detention; *(audacia)* boldness, daring; **arresto domiciliario** house arrest.

rriar [a'rrjar] *vt (velas, bandera)* to lower, strike; *(un cable)* to pay out; ~**se** *vr* to flood.

rriba [a'rrißa] *ad (posición)* above, overhead, on top; *(en casa)* upstairs; *(dirección)* up, upwards; ~ **de** above, higher (up) than; **de abajo** the flat upstairs; **de ~ abajo** from top to bottom; **calle** ~ up the street; **lo ~ mencionado** the aforementioned; ~ **de 20 pesetas** more than 20 pesetas; **¡~ las manos!** hands up!

rribar [arri'ßar] *vi* to put into port; *(llegar)* to arrive.

arribista [arri'ßista] *nm/f* parvenu/e, upstart.

arriendo [a'rrjendo] *nm* = **arrendamiento**.

arriero [a'rrjero] *nm* muleteer.

arriesgado, a [arrjes'xaðo, a] *a (peligroso)* risky; *(audaz)* bold, daring; **arriesgar** *vt* to risk; *(poner en peligro)* to endanger; **arriesgarse** *vr* to take a risk.

arrimar [arri'mar] *vt (acercar)* to bring close; *(poner de lado)* to set aside; ~**se** *vr* to come close *or* closer; ~**se a** to lean on; **arrimo** *nm* approach, *(fig)* support.

arrinconado, a [arrinko'naðo, a] *a* forgotten, neglected; **arrinconar** *vt* to put in a corner; *(fig)* to put on one side; *(abandonar)* to push aside; **arrinconarse** *vr* to withdraw from the world.

arrodillarse [arroði'Aarse] *vr* to kneel, kneel down.

arrogancia [arro'xanθja] *nf* arrogance; **arrogante** *a* arrogant.

arrojar [arro'xar] *vt* to throw, hurl; *(humo)* to emit, give out; *(COM)* to yield, produce; ~**se** *vr* to throw *or* hurl o.s.

arrojo [a'rroxo] *nm* daring.

arrollador, a [arroAa'ðor, a] *a* crushing, overwhelming.

arropar [arro'par] *vt* to cover, wrap up; ~**se** *vr* to wrap o.s. up.

arrope [a'rrope] *nm* syrup.

arrostrar [arros'trar] *vt* to face (up to); ~**se** *vr* to rush into the fight.

arroyo [a'rrojo] *nm* stream; *(de la calle)* gutter.

arroz [a'rroθ] *nm* rice; ~ **con leche** rice pudding.

arruga [a'rruxa] *nf* fold; *(de cara)* wrinkle; *(de vestido)* crease; **arrugar** *vt* to fold; to wrinkle; to crease; **arrugarse** *vr* to get creased.

arruinar [arrwi'nar] *vt* to ruin, wreck; ~**se** *vr* to be ruined.

arrullar [arru'Aar] *vt* to coo // *vt* to lull to sleep.

arsenal [arse'nal] *nm* naval

dockyard; (MIL) arsenal.
arsénico [ar'seniko] nm arsenic.
arte ['arte] nm (gen m en sg y siempre f en pl) art; (maña) skill, guile; ~s nfpl arts.
artefacto [arte'fakto] nm appliance; (ARQUEOLOGÍA) artefact.
artejo [ar'texo] nm knuckle.
arteria [ar'terja] nf artery.
artesanía [artesa'nia] nf craftsmanship; (artículos) handicrafts pl; **artesano** nm artisan, craftsman.
ártico, a [ar'tiko, a] a Arctic // nm: el A~ the Arctic.
articulación [artikula'θjon] nf articulation; (MED, TEC) joint; **articulado, a** a articulated; jointed; **articular** vt to articulate; to join together.
artículo [ar'tikulo] nm article; (cosa) thing, article; ~s nmpl goods.
artífice [ar'tifiθe] nm artist, craftsman; (fig) architect.
artificial [artifi'θjal] a artificial.
artificio [arti'fiθjo] nm art, skill; (artesanía) craftsmanship; (astucia) cunning; ~so, a a skilful, clever; cunning.
artillería [artiʎe'ria] nf artillery.
artillero [arti'ʎero] nm artilleryman, gunner.
artimaña [arti'maɲa] nf trap, snare; (astucia) cunning.
artista [ar'tista] nm/f (pintor) artist, painter; (TEATRO) artist, artiste; **artístico, a** a artistic.
artritis [ar'tritis] nf arthritis.
arzobispo [arθo'βispo] nm archbishop.
as [as] nm ace.
asa ['asa] nf handle; (fig) lever.
asado [a'saðo] nm roast (meat).
asador [asa'ðor] nm spit.
asalariado, a [asala'rjaðo; a] a paid, wage-earning // nm/f wage earner.
asaltabancos [asalta'bankos] nm inv bank robber.
asaltador, a [asalta'ðor, a],

asaltante [asal'tante] nm assailant; **asaltar** vt to attac assault; (fig) to assail; **asalto** n attack, assault; (DEPORTE) round.
asamblea [asam'blea] nf assembl (reunión) meeting.
asar [a'sar] vt to roast.
asbesto [as'βesto] nm asbestos.
ascendencia [asθen'denθja] n ancestry; (AM) ascendancy.
ascender [asθen'der] vi (subir) ascend, rise; (ser promovido) to ga promotion // vt to promote; ~ a amount to; **ascendiente** nm ascendency, influence // nm ancestor.
ascensión [asθen'sjon] nf ascent; A~ the Ascension.
ascensionista [asθensjo'nist nm/f balloonist.
ascenso [as'θenso] nm ascen (promoción) promotion.
ascensor [asθen'sor] nm li elevator.
ascético, a [as'θetiko, a] a ascetic.
asco ['asko] nm loathing, disgus (cosa) loathsome thing; **el ajo me d** ~ I hate o loathe garlic.
ascua ['askwa] nf ember.
aseado, a [ase'aðo, a] a clea (arreglado) tidy; (pulcro) smar **asear** vt to clean, wash; to tidy (up (adornar) to adorn.
asediar [ase'ðjar] vt to besiege, la siege to; (fig) to chase, peste **asedio** nm siege; (COM) run.
asegurado, a [asexu'raðo, a] insured; **asegurador, a** nm/f insure underwriter.
asegurar [asexu'rar] vt (co solidar) to secure, fasten; (da garantía de) to guarantee; (prese var) to safeguard; (afirmar, dar po cierto) to assure, affirm; (tranqui zar) to reassure; (tomar un seguro to insure; ~se vr to assure o.s make sure.
asemejarse [aseme'xarse] vr be alike; ~ a to be like, resemble.

asentado, a [asen'taðo, a] a established, settled.

asentar [asen'tar] vt (sentar) to seat, sit down; (poner) to place, establish; (alisar) to level, smooth down or out; (anotar) to note down; (afirmar) to affirm, assert; (afinar) to sharpen, hone // vi to be suitable, suit.

asentir [asen'tir] vi to assent, agree.

asco [a'seo] nm cleanliness; ~s nmpl toilet sg, cloakroom sg.

asequible [ase'kiβle] a attainable, available.

aserradero [aserra'ðero] nm sawmill; aserrar vt to saw.

aserrín [ase'rrin] nm sawdust.

asesinar [asesi'nar] vt to murder; (POL) to assassinate; (fig) to pester; asesinato nm murder; assassination.

asesino, a [ase'sino, a] nm/f murderer, killer; (POL) assassin.

asesor, a [ase'sor, a] nm/f adviser, consultant.

asfalto [as'falto] nm asphalt.

asfixia [as'fiksja] nf suffocation.

asfixiar [asfik'sjar] vt, ~se vr to asphyxiate, suffocate.

asgo etc vb ver asir.

así [a'si] ad (de esta manera) so, in this way, like this; thus; (aunque) although; (tan luego como) as soon as; ~ que so, therefore; ~ como as well as; ~ y todo even so, ¿no es ~? isn't it?, didn't you?

Asia [asja] nf Asia; asiático, a a Asiatic, Asian.

asidero [asi'ðero] nm handle.

asiduidad [asiðwi'ðað] nf assiduousness; asiduo, a a assiduous; (frecuente) frequent // nm/f regular (customer).

asiento [a'sjento] nm (mueble) seat, chair; (de coche, en tribunal etc) seat; (localidad) seat; (fundamento) base, bottom; (establecimiento) (deposito) sediment; (cordura) good sense; ~ delan-

tero/trasero front/back seat.

asignación [asixna'θjon] nf (atribución) assignment; (reparto) allocation; (cita) appointment; (sueldo) salary; asignar vt to assign, allocate.

asignatura [asixna'tura] nf subject.

asilo [a'silo] nm (refugio) asylum, refuge; (establecimiento) home, institution.

asimilación [asimila'θjon] nf assimilation.

asimilar [asimi'lar] vt to assimilate; ~se vr: ~se a to resemble; (incorporarse) to become assimilated to.

asimismo [asi'mismo] ad in the same way, likewise.

asir [a'sir] vt to seize, grasp.

asistencia [asis'tenθja] nf audience; (MED) attendance; (ayuda) assistance; asistir vt to assist // vi to attend, be present.

asma [asma] nf asthma.

asno ['asno] nm donkey; (fig) ass.

asociación [asoθja'θjon] nf association; (COM) partnership; ~ aduanera customs union; asociado, a a associate // nm/f associate, partner.

asociar [aso'θjar] vt to combine.

asolear [asole'ar] vt to put in the sun; ~se vr to sunbathe.

asomar [aso'mar] vt to show, stick out // vi to appear, ~se vr to appear, show up; ~ la cabeza por la ventana to put one's head out of the window.

asombrar [asom'brar] vt (causar admiración, sorpresa) to amaze, astonish; (asustar) to frighten; (dar sombra a) to shade; ~se vr (sorprenderse) to be amazed; to be frightened; asombro nm amazement, astonishment; fright, asombroso, a a amazing.

asomo [aso'mo] nm (apar-

aspa ['aspa] nf (cruz) cross; (de molino) sail.

aspar [as'par] vt to reel, wind; (fig) to vex, annoy.

aspaviento [aspa'βjento] nm exaggerated display of feeling; (fam) fuss.

aspecto [as'pekto] nm (apariencia) look, appearance; (fig) aspect.

aspereza [aspe'reθa] nf roughness; (agrura) sourness; (severidad) harshness, surliness; **áspero, a** a rough; bitter, sour; harsh.

aspersión [asper'sjon] nf sprinkling.

áspid [as'piδ] nm asp.

aspiración [aspira'θjon] nf breath, inhalation; (MUS) short pause; **aspiraciones** nfpl (AM) aspirations.

aspiradora [aspira'δora] nf vacuum cleaner.

aspirar [aspi'rar] vt to breathe in // vi: ~ a to aspire to.

aspirina [aspi'rina] nf aspirin.

asquear [aske'ar] vt to sicken // vi to be sickening; ~se vr to feel disgusted; **asqueroso, a** a disgusting, sickening.

asta ['asta] nf lance; (arpón) spear; (mango) shaft, handle; (ZOOL) horn; **a media** ~ at half mast.

astilla [as'tiʎa] nf splinter; (pedacito) chip; ~s nfpl firewood sg.

astillero [asti'ʎero] nm shipyard.

astringente [astrin'xente] a, nm astringent.

astringir [astrin'xir] vt to bind.

astro ['astro] nm star.

astrología [astrolo'xia] nf astrology; **astrólogo, a** nm/f astrologer.

astronauta [astro'nauta] nm/f astronaut.

astronomía [astrono'mia] nf astronomy; **astrónomo** nm astronomer.

astucia [as'tuθja] nf astuteness; (destreza) clever trick; **astuto, a** a astute, cunning.

asueto [a'sweto] nm holiday; (tiempo libre) time off q.

asumir [asu'mir] vt to assume.

asunción [asun'θjon] nf assumption.

asunto [a'sunto] nm (tema) matter, subject; (negocio) business.

asustar [asus'tar] vt to frighten; ~se vr to be/become frightened.

atacar [ata'kar] vt to attack.

atadura [ata'δura] nf bond, tie.

atajo [a'taxo] nm short cut; (DEPORTE) tackle.

ataque [a'take] nm attack; ~ **cardíaco** heart attack.

atar [a'tar] vt to tie, tie up; ~se (fig) to be or get embarrassed.

atardecer [ataρδe'θer] vi to get dark // nm evening; (crepúsculo) dusk.

atareado, a [atare'aδo, a] a busy.

atarear [atare'ar] vt to give a job to; ~se vr to be busy, keep busy.

atascamiento [ataska'mjento] nm = **atasco**.

atascar [atas'kar] vt to clog up; (obstruir) to jam; (fig) to hinder; ~se vr to stall; (cañería) to get clogged up; **atasco** nm obstruction; (AUTO) traffic jam.

ataúd [ata'uδ] nm coffin.

ataviar [ata'βjar] vt to deck, array; ~se vr to dress up.

atavío [ata'βio] nm attire, dress; ~ nmpl finery sg.

atemorizar [atemori'θar] vt to frighten, scare; ~se vr to get scared.

Atenas [a'tenas] n Athens.

atención [aten'θjon] nf attention; (bondad) kindness; (cortesía) civility // excl (be) careful!, look out!

atender [aten'der] vt to attend to, look after // vi to pay attention.

atenerse [ate'nerse] vr: ~ a to abide by, adhere to.

atentado [aten'taδo] nm crime, illegal act; (asalto) assault; (contra la vida de uno) attempt on sb's life.

atentar [aten'tar] vi: ~ a o contra to commit an outrage against.

atento, a [a'tento, a] a attentive, observant; (cortés) polite, thoughtful.

atenuación [atenwa'θjon] nf attenuation, lessening; **atenuante** a attenuating, extenuating; **atenuar** vt to attenuate; (disminuir) to lessen, minimize.

ateo, a [a'teo, a] a atheistic // nm/f atheist.

aterrador, a [aterra'ðor, a] a frightening.

aterrar [ate'rrar] vt to pull down, demolish; (AGR) to cover with earth; (espantar) to frighten; ~se vr to be frightened.

aterrizar [aterri'θar] vi to land.

aterrorizar [aterrori'θar] vt to terrify; (MIL, POL) to terrorize.

atesorar [ateso'rar] vt to hoard, store up.

atestar [ates'tar] vt to pack, stuff; (JUR) to attest, testify to.

atestiguar [atesti'wwar] vt to testify to, bear witness to.

atiborrar [atiβo'rrar] vt to fill, stuff; ~se vr to stuff o.s.

ático ['atiko] nm attic.

atildar [atil'dar] vt to criticize; ~se vr to spruce o.s. up.

atisbar [atis'βar] vt to spy on; (echar ojeada) to peep at.

atizar [ati'θar] vt to poke; (horno etc) to stoke; (fig) to stir up, rouse.

atlántico, a [at'lantiko, a] a Atlantic // nm: el (océano) A~ the Atlantic (Ocean).

atlas ['atlas] nm atlas.

atleta [at'leta] nm athlete; **atlético, a** a athletic; **atletismo** nm athletics sg.

atmósfera [at'mosfera] nf atmosphere.

atolondramiento [atolondra'mjento] nm bewilderment; (insensatez) silliness.

atollar [ato'Kar] vi: ~se vr to get stuck; (fig) to get into a jam.

atómico, a [a'tomiko, a] a atomic.

atomizador [atomiθa'ðor] nm atomizer.

átomo ['atomo] nm atom.

atónito, a [a'tonito, a] a astonished, amazed.

atontado, a [aton'taðo, a] a stunned; (bobo) silly, daft.

atontar [aton'tar] vt to stun; ~se vr to become bewildered.

atormentar [atormen'tar] vt to torture; (molestar) to torment; (acosar) to plague, harass.

atornillar [atorni'Kar] vt to screw in or down.

atracar [atra'kar] vt (NAUT) to moor; (robar) to hold up, rob; (fam) to stuff (with food) // vi to moor.

atracción [atrak'θjon] nf attraction.

atraco [a'trako] nm holdup, robbery.

atractivo, a [atrak'tiβo, a] a attractive // nm attraction; (belleza) attractiveness.

atraer [atra'er] vt to attract.

atrancar [atran'kar] vi (con tranca, barra) to bar, bolt.

atrapar [atra'par] vt to trap (fig) to take in, deceive.

atrás [a'tras] ad (movimiento) back, backwards; (lugar) behind; (tiempo) previously; **ir hacia** ~ to go back or backwards; to go to the rear; **estar** ~ to be behind or at the back.

atrasado, a [atra'saðo, a] a slow; (pago) overdue, late; (país) backward.

atrasar [atra'sar] vi to be slow; ~se vr to remain behind; (llegar tarde) to arrive late; **atraso** nm slowness; lateness, delay; (de país) backwardness; **atrasos** nmpl arrears.

atravesar [atraβe'sar] vt (cruzar) to cross (over); (traspasar) to pierce, go through; (poner al través) to lay or put across; ~se vr to come in between; (intervenir) to interfere.

atrayente [atra'jente] a attra

atreverse [atre'ßerse] *vr* to dare; (*insolentarse*) to be insolent; **atrevido, a** *a* daring; insolent; **atrevimiento** *nm* daring; insolence.

atribuir [atrißu'ir] *vt* to attribute; (*funciones*) to confer.

atribular [atrißu'lar] *vt* to afflict, distress; **~se** *vr* to grieve, be distressed.

atributo [atri'ßuto] *nm* attribute.

atrocidad [atroθi'ðað] *nf* atrocity, outrage.

atropellar [atrope'ʎar] *vt* (*derribar*) to knock over, knock down; (*empujar*) to push (aside); (*pasar por encima de*) to run over, run down; (*agraviar*) to insult; **~se** *vr* to act hastily; **atropello** *nm* accident; push; insult; (*agravio*) wrong; (*atrocidad*) outrage.

atroz [a'troθ] *a* atrocious, awful.

atto. a *abr de* **atento**.

atuendo [a'twendo] *nm* dress.

atún [a'tun] *nm* tuna, tunny.

aturdir [atur'ðir] *vt* to stun; (*de ruido*) to deafen; (*fig*) to dumbfound, bewilder.

audacia [au'ðaθja] *nf* boldness, audacity; **audaz** *a* bold, audacious; (*descarado*) cheeky, impudent.

audible [au'ðißle] *a* audible.

audición [auði'θjon] *nf* hearing; (*TEATRO*) audition.

audiencia [au'ðjenθja] *nf* audience; (*JUR*) high court.

auditor [auði'tor] *nm* (*JUR*) judge-advocate; (*COM*) auditor.

auditorio [auði'torjo] *nm* audience; (*sala*) auditorium.

auge ['auxe] *nm* boom; (*clímax*) climax.

augurar [auxu'rar] *vt* to predict; (*presagiar*) to portend; **augurio** *nm* omen; **augurios** *nmpl* good wishes.

aula ['aula] *nf* classroom.

aullar [au'ʎar] *vi* to howl, yell.

aullido [au'ʎiðo] *nm* howl, yell.

aumentar [aumen'tar] *vt* (*precios, sueldo*) to raise; (*producción*) to increase; (*con microscopio,*

anteojos) to magnify // *vi*, **~se** *vr* to increase; (*subirse*) to rise; (*multiplicarse*) to multiply; **aumento** *nm* increase; rise.

aun [a'un] *ad* even.

aún [a'un] *ad* still, yet.

aunque [a'unke] *conj* though although, even though, even if.

aura ['aura] *nf* gentle breeze; (*fig* popularity.

aureola [aure'ola] *nf* halo.

auricular [auriku'lar] *nm* (*dedo* little finger; (*del teléfono*) earpiece receiver; **~es** *nmpl* headphones.

ausencia [au'senθja] *nf* absence.

ausentarse [ausen'tarse] *vr* t go/stay away, absent o.s.

ausente [au'sente] *a* absent.

auspicios [aus'piθjos] *nmpl* aus pices; (*protección*) protection *sg*.

austeridad [austeri'ðað] *nf* aus terity; **austero, a** *a* austere.

austral [aus'tral] *a* southern.

Australia [aus'tralja] *nf* Australia **australiano, a** *a, nm/f* Australian.

Austria ['austrja] *nf* Austria **austríaco, a** *a, nm/f* Austrian.

autenticar [autenti'kar] *vt* t authenticate; **auténtico, a** *a* authentic.

auto ['auto] *nm* (*JUR*) edict, decree (: *orden*) writ; (*fam*) car; **~s** *nmp* (*JUR*) proceedings; (: *acta*) cour record *sg*.

autobiografía [autoßjoxra'fia] *nf* autobiography.

autobús [auto'ßus] *nm* bus.

autocar [auto'kar] *nm* coach.

autócrata [au'tokrata] *nm* autocrat.

autóctono, a [au'toktono, a] *a* native, indigenous.

autodefensa [autoðe'fensa] *nf* sel defence.

autodeterminación [autoðete mina'θjon] *nf* self-determination.

autoescuela [autoes'kwela] driving school.

autógrafo [au'toxrafo] *nm* aut graph.

autómata [au'tomata] nm automaton.

automático, a [auto'matiko, a] a automatic.

automotor, triz [automo'tor, 'triz] a self-propelled // nm Diesel train.

automóvil [auto'moβil] nm (motor) car, automobile; **automovilístico, a** a driving cpd, motoring cpd.

autonomía [autono'mia] nf autonomy; **autónomo, a** a autonomous.

autopista [auto'pista] nf motorway.

autopsia [au'topsja] nf autopsy.

autor, a [au'tor, a] nm/f author.

autoridad [autori'ðað] nf authority; **autoritario, a** a authoritarian.

autorización [autoriθa'θjon] nf authorization; **autorizado, a** a authorized; (aprobado) approved; **autorizar** vt to authorize; to approve.

autorretrato [autorre'trato] nm self-portrait.

autoservicio [autoser'βiθjo] nm self-service restaurant.

autostop [auto'stop] nm hitch-hiking; **hacer el ~** to hitch-hike; **~ista** nm/f hitch-hiker.

autosuficiencia [autosufi'θjenθja] nf self-sufficiency.

auxiliar [auksi'ljar] vt to help // nm/f assistant; **auxilio** nm assistance, help; **primeros auxilios** first aid sg.

Av abr de **Avenida**.

aval [a'βal] nm guarantee; (persona) guarantor.

avalancha [aβa'lantʃa] nf avalanche.

avaluar [aβalu'ar] vt to value, appraise.

avance [a'βanθe] nm advance; (pago) advance payment.

avanzar [aβan'θar] vt, ~se vr to advance.

avaricia [aβa'riθja] nf avarice, greed, **avariento, a** a avaricious, greedy.

avaro, a [a'βaro, a] a miserly, mean // nm/f miser.

avasallar [aβasa'ʎar] vt to subdue, subjugate; ~se vr to submit.

Avda abr de **Avenida**.

ave ['aβe] nf bird; ~ **de rapiña** bird of prey.

avellana [aβe'ʎana] nf hazelnut; **avellano** nm hazel tree.

avemaría [aβema'ria] nf Hail Mary, Ave Maria.

avena [a'βena] nf oats pl.

avenencia [aβe'nenθja] nf agreement; (COM) bargain.

avenida [aβe'niða] nf (calle) avenue; (de río) flood, spate.

avenir [aβe'nir] vt to reconcile; ~se vr to come to an agreement, reach a compromise.

aventajado, a [aβenta'xaðo, a] a outstanding; **aventajar** vt (sobrepasar) to surpass, outstrip; (preferir) to prefer; **aventajarse** vr to surpass or excel o.s.

aventar [aβen'tar] vt to fan, blow; (esparcir) to scatter; (grano) to winnow; ~se vr to fill with air.

aventura [aβen'tura] nf adventure; (casualidad) chance; **aventurado, a** a risky; **aventurero, a** a adventurous.

avergonzar [aβerxon'θar] vt to shame; (desconcertar) to embarrass; ~se vr to be ashamed; to be embarrassed.

avería [aβe'ria] nf damage; (TEC) breakdown, fault.

averiguación [aβerixwa'θjon] nf investigation; (determinación) ascertainment, **averiguar** vt to investigate, to find out, ascertain.

aversión [aβer'sjon] nf aversion, dislike.

avestruz [aβes'truθ] nm ostrich.

avezarse [aβe'θarse] vr; ~se a algo to get used to sth.

aviación [aβja'θjon] nf aviation; (fuerzas aéreas) air force.

aviador, a [aβja'ðor, a] nm/f aviator, airman/woman.

avicultura [aβikul'tura] *nf* poultry farming.

avidez [aβi'ðeθ] *nf* avidity, eagerness; **ávido, a** *a* avid, eager.

avinagrado, a [aβina'xraðo, a] *a* sour, acid; **avinagrarse** *vr* to turn sour.

avío [a'βio] *nm* preparation; ~ *nmpl* gear *sg*, kit *sg*.

avión [a'βjon] *nm* aeroplane; (*ave*) martin; ~ **de reacción** jet plane.

avisar [aβi'sar] *vt* (*advertir*) to warn, notify; (*informar*) to tell; (*aconsejar*) to advise, counsel; **aviso** *nm* warning; (*noticia*) notice; (*prudencia*) caution, discretion.

avispa [a'βispa] *nf* wasp.

avispado, a [aβis'paðo, a] *a* sharp, clever.

avispar [aβis'par] *vt* to spur (on); ~**se** *vr* to fret, worry.

avispero [aβis'pero] *nm* wasp's nest.

avispón [aβis'pon] *nm* hornet.

avistar [aβis'tar] *vt* to sight, spot; ~**se** *vr* to have an interview.

avituallar [aβitwa'ʎar] *vt* to supply with food.

avivar [aβi'βar] *vt* to strengthen, intensify; ~**se** *vr* to revive, acquire new life.

avizorar [aβiθo'rar] *vt* to spy on.

axila [ak'sila] *nf* armpit.

axioma [ak'sjoma] *nm* axiom.

ay [ai] *excl* (*dolor*) ow!, ouch!; (*aflicción*) oh!, oh dear!; ¡~ **de mí!** poor me!; ¡~ **del que!** pity help or woe betide whoever!

aya ['aja] *nf* governess; (*niñera*) children's nurse.

ayer [a'jer] *ad, nm* yesterday; **antes de** ~ the day before yesterday.

ayo ['ajo] *nm* tutor.

ayuda [a'juða] *nf* help, assistance; (*MED*) enema; (*AM*) laxative // *nm* page; **ayudante, a** *nm/f* assistant, helper; (*ESCOL*) assistant; (*MIL*) adjutant; **ayudar** *vt* to help, assist.

ayunar [aju'nar] *vi* to fast; **ayunas** *nfpl*: **estar en ayunas** (*no haber*

comido) to be fasting; (*ignorante*) be in the dark; **ayuno** *nm* fasting, ignorance.

ayuntamiento [ajunta'mjent... *nm* (*consejo*) council; (*edificio* town hall; (*cópula*) sexual inte... course.

azabache [aθa'βatʃe] *nm* jet.

azada [a'θaða] *nf* hoe.

azafata [aθa'fata] *nf* air hostess.

azafrán [aθa'fran] *nm* saffron.

azahar [aθa'ar] *nm* orange/lemo... blossom.

azar [a'θar] *nm* (*casualidad*) chance fate; (*desgracia*) misfortun... accident; **por** ~ by chance; **al** ~ ... random.

azarearse [aθare'arse] *vr* ... **azorarse.**

azogue [a'θoxe] *nm* mercury.

azoramiento [aθora'mjento] *n... alarm; (*confusión*) confusion.

azorar [aθo'rar] *vt* to alarm; ~**se** to get alarmed.

Azores [a'θores] *nmpl*: **los** ~ th... Azores.

azotar [aθo'tar] *vt* to whip, bea... (*pegar*) to spank; **azote** *nm* (*látig*... whip; (*latigazo*) lash, stroke; (*en la... nalgas*) spank; (*calamidad*) ca... lamity.

azotea [aθo'tea] *nf* terrace roof.

azteca [aθ'teka] *a, nm/f* Aztec.

azúcar [a'θukar] *nm* suga... **azucarado, a** *a* sugary, sweet.

azucarero, a [aθuka'rero, a] ... sugar *cpd* // *nm* sugar bowl.

azucena [aθu'θena] *nf* white lily.

azufre [a'θufre] *nm* sulphur.

azul [a'θul] *a, nm* blue.

azulejo [aθu'lexo] *nm* glazed tile.

azuzar [aθu'θar] *vt* to incite, egg ...

B

A. abr de **Buenos Aires.**

.ba ['baβa] nf spittle, saliva;

abear vi to drool, slaver.

abel [ba'βel] nm o f bedlam.

abero [ba'βero] nm bib.

abor [ba'βor] nm port (side).

abucha [ba'βutʃa] nf whistle.

acalao [baka'lao] nm cod(fish).

acía [ba'θia] nf basin.

acín [ba'θin] nm chamber pot.

acteria [bak'terja] nf bacterium, -erm.

.culo ['bákulo] nm stick, staff.

ache ['batʃe] nm pothole, rut; (fig) ad patch.

achillerato [batʃiʎe'rato] nm (ESCOL) school-leaving examination.

.gaje [ba'saxe] nm baggage.

.gatela [basa'tela] nf trinket, ifle.

ahía [ba'ia] nf bay.

ailar [bai'lar] vt, vi to dance; ~ín, ...a nm/f (ballet) dancer; **baile** nm ance; (formal) ball.

aja ['baxa] nf ver **bajo.**

ajada [ba'xaða] nf descent; camino) slope; (de aguas) ebb.

ajamar [baxa'mar] nf low tide.

ajar [ba'xar] vi to go/come down; temperatura, precios) to drop; (de coche) to get out; (de autobús) o get off // vt (cabeza) to bow, end; (escalera) to go/come down, brecto, voz) to lower; (llevar abajo) o take down; ~se vr to bend down; o get out of, to get off; (fig) to umble o.s.

ajeza [ba'xeθa] nf baseness q; (una ~) vile deed.

ajío [ba'xio] nm shoal, sandbank; AM) lowlands pl.

ajo, a ['baxo, a] a (terreno) ow-(lying); (mueble, número, pre- io) low; (piso) ground; (de ultu-a) small, short; (color) pale; (sonido) faint, soft, low; (voz: en ...) deep; (metal) base; (humilde)

low, humble // ad (hablar) low, quietly; (volar) low // prep under, below, underneath // nm (MUS) bass // nf drop, fall; (MIL) casualty; ~ la lluvia in the rain; **dar de** ~**a** (soldado) to discharge; (empleado) to dismiss, sack.

bajón [ba'xon] nm (MUS) bassoon; (baja) decline, fall, drop.

bajorrelieve [baxorre'ljeβe] nm bas-relief.

bala ['bala] nf bullet.

baladí [bala'ði] a trivial.

baladrón, ona [bala'ðron, ona] a boastful.

bálago ['balaxo] nm thatch.

balance [ba'lanθe] nm (balanceo) oscillation, rocking; (NAUT) roll; (COM) balance; (: libro) balance sheet; (: cuenta general) stock-taking; ~**ar** vt to balance // vi, ~**se** vr to swing (to and fro); (vacilar) to hesitate; **balanceo** nm swinging.

balanza [ba'lanθa] nf balance, scales pl; ~ **comercial** balance of trade; ~ **de pagos** balance of payments; (ASTRO) **B~** = **Libra.**

balar [ba'lar] vi to bleat.

balazo [ba'laθo] nm (golpe) shot; (herida) bullet wound.

balbucear [balβuθe'ar] vi, vt to stammer, stutter; **balbuceo** nm stammering, stuttering.

balbucir [balβu'θir] vi, vt to stammer, stutter.

balcón [bal'kon] nm balcony.

baldaquín [balda'kin], **baldaquino** [balda'kino] nm canopy.

baldar [bal'dar] vt to cripple.

balde ['balde] nm bucket, pail; de ~ ad (for) free, for nothing; **en** ~ ad in vain.

baldío, a [bal'dio, a] a uncultivated // nm waste land.

baldón [bal'don] nm (afrenta) insult, (deshonra) disgrace.

baldosa [bal'dosa] nf paving stone.

Baleares [bale'ares] nfpl: las (Islas) ~ the Balearic Islands.

balido [ba'liðo] nm bleat, bleating.

balística [ba'listika] nf ballistics pl.

baliza [ba'liθa] nf (AVIAT) beacon; (NAUT) buoy.

balneario, a [balne'arjo, a] a: **estación** ~a a bathing resort // nm spa, health resort.

balón [ba'lon] nm ball.

baloncesto [balon'θesto] nm basketball.

balsa ['balsa] nf raft; (BOT) balsa wood.

bálsamo ['balsamo] nm balsam, balm.

baluarte [ba'lwarte] nm bastion, bulwark.

ballena [ba'ʎena] nf whale.

ballesta [ba'ʎesta] nf crossbow; (AUTO) spring.

ballet [ba'le] nm ballet.

bambolear [bambole'ar] vi, ~se vr to swing, sway; (silla) to wobble; **bamboleo** nm swinging, swaying; wobbling.

bambú [bam'bu] nm bamboo.

banca ['banka] nf (asiento) bench; (COM) banking; ~da nf (banco) stone bench; (TEC) bench.

bancario, a [ban'karjo, a] a banking cpd, bank cpd.

bancarrota [banka'rrota] nf (esp fraudulent) bankruptcy.

banco ['banko] nm bench, seat; (ESCOL) desk; (COM) bank; (GEO) stratum; ~ **de crédito/de ahorros** credit/savings bank; ~ **de arena** sandbank; ~ **de hielo** iceberg.

banda ['banda] nf band; (pandilla) gang; (NAUT) side, edge; **la B~ Oriental** Uruguay; ~ **sonora** soundtrack.

bandada [ban'daða] nf (de pájaros) flock; (de peces) shoal.

bandeja [ban'dexa] nf tray.

bandera [ban'dera] nf (de tela) flag; (estandarte) banner.

banderilla [bande'riʎa] nf banderilla.

banderola [bande'rola] nf banderole, pennant.

bandido [bandi'ðaxe] nm ban

ditry; **bandido** nm bandit.

bando ['bando] nm (edicto) ed proclamation; (facción) faction; ~s the banns.

bandolero [bando'lero] nm ban brigand.

banquero [ban'kero] nm banker

banqueta [ban'keta] nf (asien bench; (escabel) stool.

banquete [ban'kete] nm banqu (para convidados) formal dinner.

banquillo [ban'kiʎo] nm (J dock, prisoner's bench; (ban bench; (para los pies) footstool.

bañador [baɲa'ðor] nm swimm costume.

bañar [ba'ɲar] vt (niño) to ba bathe; (objeto) to dip; (de barniz coat; ~**se** vr (en el mar) to bat swim; (en la bañera) to bath, hav bath.

bañera [ba'ɲera] nf bath(tub).

bañero [ba'ɲero] nm lifeguard.

bañista [ba'ɲista] nm/f bather.

baño ['baɲo] nm (en bañera) ba (en río) dip, swim; (cuarto) ba room; (bañera) bath(tub); (ca coating.

baptista [bap'tista] nm/f baptist.

baqueta [ba'keta] nf (M drumstick.

bar [bar] nm bar.

barahúnda [bara'unda] nf upro hubbub.

baraja [ba'raxa] nf pack (of car **barajar** vt (naipes) to shuffle; (to jumble up.

baranda [ba'randa] nf rail, railin

barandilla [baran'diʎa] nf r railing.

baratija [bara'tixa] nf trinket.

baratillo [bara'tiʎo] nm (tien junkshop; (subasta) bargain s (conjunto de cosas) secondha goods pl.

barato, a [ba'rato, a] a cheap nm bargain sale // ad che cheaply; **baratura** nf cheapness.

baraúnda [bara'unda] nf = **barahúnda.**

barba [ˈbarβa] nf (ANAT) chin; (pelo) beard, whiskers pl.

barbacoa [barβaˈkoa] nf (parrilla) barbecue; (carne) barbecued meat.

barbado, a [barˈβaðo, a] a bearded // nm seedling.

barbaridad [barβariˈðað] nf barbarity; (acto) barbarism; (atrocidad) outrage; **una ~** (fam) a huge amount; ¡qué ~! (fam) how awful!

barbarie [barˈβarje] nf, **barbarismo** [barβaˈrismo] nm barbarism; (crueldad) barbarity.

bárbaro, a [ˈbarβaro, a] a barbarous, cruel; (grosero) rough, uncouth // nm/f barbarian // a: **lo pasamos ~** (fam) we had a tremendous time; ¡qué ~! (fam) how marvellous!; **un éxito ~** (fam) a terrific success; **es un tipo ~** (fam) he's a splendid chap.

barbear [barβeˈar] vt (AM) to shave.

barbecho [barˈβetʃo] nm fallow land.

barbero [barˈβero] nm barber, hairdresser.

barbilampiño [barβilamˈpiɲo] a smooth-faced; (fig) inexperienced.

barbilla [barˈβiʎa] nf chin, tip of the chin.

barbotar [barβoˈtar], **barbotear** [barβoteˈar] vt, vi to mutter, mumble.

barbudo, a [barˈβuðo, a] a bearded.

barca [ˈbarka] nf (small) boat; **~ de pesca** fishing boat, **~ de pasaje** ferry; **~ of barge**; **~ de desembarco** landing craft.

barcelonés, esa [barθeloˈnes, esa] a nf or from Barcelona.

barco [ˈbarko] nm boat; (buque) ship; **~ de carga** cargo boat.

bardar [barˈdar] vt to thatch.

barítono [baˈritono] nm baritone.

barman [ˈbarman] nm barman.

Barna abr de Barcelona.

barniz [barˈniθ] nm varnish; (en la loza) glaze; (fig) veneer; **~ para las**

uñas nail varnish; **~ar** vt to varnish; (loza) to glaze.

barómetro [baˈrometro] nm barometer.

barquero [barˈkero] nm boatman.

barquillo [barˈkiʎo] nm cone, cornet.

barra [ˈbarra] nf bar, rod; (de un bar, café) bar; (de pan) small loaf; (palanca) lever; **~ de carmín o de labios** lipstick.

barraca [baˈrraka] nf hut, cabin.

barranca [baˈrranka] nf ravine, gully; **barranco** nm ravine; (fig) difficulty.

barrena [baˈrrena] nf drill; **barrenar** vt to drill (through), bore; **barreno** nm large drill, borer.

barrer [baˈrrer] vt to sweep; (quitar) to sweep away.

barrera [baˈrrera] nf barrier.

barriada [baˈrrjaða] nf quarter, district.

barricada [barriˈkaða] nf barricade.

barrido [baˈrriðo] nm, **barrida** [baˈrriða] nf sweep, sweeping.

barriga [baˈrriɣa] nf belly; (panza) paunch; **barrigón, ona, barrigudo, a** a fat, potbellied.

barril [baˈrril] nm barrel, cask.

barrio [ˈbarrjo] nm (en el pueblo) district, quarter; (fuera del pueblo) suburb.

barro [ˈbarro] nm (lodo) mud; (objetos) earthenware; (MED) pimple.

barroco, a [baˈrroko, a] a, nm baroque.

barroso, a [baˈrroso, a] a (lodoso) muddy; (MED) pimply.

barruntar [barrunˈtar] vt (conjeturar) to guess; (presentir) to suspect; **barrunto** nm (presentir) suspicion.

bartola [barˈtola]: **a la ~** ad: **tirarse a la ~** to take it easy, do nothing.

bártulos [ˈbartulos] nmpl things, belongings.

barullo [baˈruʎo] nm row, uproar.

basa ['basa] *nf* base; *(fig)* basis; ~**mento** *nm* base, plinth.

basar [ba'sar] *vt* to base; ~**se** *vr*: ~**se en** to be based on.

basca ['baska] *nf* nausea.

báscula ['baskula] *nf* (platform) scales *pl*.

base ['base] *nf* base; **a** ~ **de** on the basis of.

básico, a ['basiko, a] *a* basic.

basílica [ba'silika] *nf* basilica.

bastante [bas'tante] *a (suficiente)* enough, sufficient; *(no poco(s))* quite a lot of // *ad (suficientemente)* enough, sufficiently; *(muy)* quite, rather.

bastar [bas'tar] *vi* to be enough *or* sufficient; ~**se** *vr* to be self-sufficient; ~ **para** to be enough to; ¡**basta**! (that's) enough!

bastardilla [bastar'ðiλa] *nf* italics *pl*.

bastardo, a [bas'tarðo, a] *a, nm/f* bastard.

bastidor [basti'ðor] *nm* frame; *(de coche)* chassis.

basto, a ['basto, a] *a* coarse, rough; ~**s** *nmpl (NAIPES)* clubs.

bastón [bas'ton] *nm (gen)* stick, staff; *(para el paseo)* walking stick.

basura [ba'sura] *nf* rubbish, refuse.

basurero [basu'rero] *nm (hombre)* dustman; *(lugar)* rubbish dump; *(cubo)* (rubbish) bin.

bata ['bata] *nf (salto de cama)* dressing gown, housecoat; *(de alumno etc)* smock, overall.

batalla [ba'taλa] *nf* battle; **de** ~ everyday, for everyday use.

batallar [bata'λar] *vi* to fight.

batallón [bata'λon] *nm* battalion.

bate ['bate] *nm* bat; ~**ador** *nm* batter, batsman.

batería [bate'ria] *nf* battery; *(MUS)* drums *pl*; ~ **de cocina** kitchen utensils *pl*.

batido, a [ba'tiðo, a] *a (camino)* beaten, well-trodden // *nm (CULIN)* batter; ~ **de leche** milk shake.

batidora [bati'ðora] *nf* beater, mixer.

batir [ba'tir] *vt* to beat, strike; *(vencer)* to beat, defeat; *(revolver)* to beat, mix; *(acuñar)* to strike, mint; *(pelo)* to comb; ~**se** *vr* to fight; ~ **palmas** to clap, applaud.

batuta [ba'tuta] *nf* baton.

baúl [ba'ul] *nm* trunk; *(AUTO)* boot.

bautismo [bau'tismo] *nm* baptism, christening.

bautizar [bauti'θar] *vt* to baptize, christen; *(fam)* to water down; **bautizo** *nm* baptism, christening.

bayo, a ['bajo, a] *a* bay // *nf* berry.

bayoneta [bajo'neta] *nf* bayonet.

baza ['baθa] *nf* trick.

bazar [ba'θar] *nm* bazaar.

bazofia [ba'θofja] *nf* left-overs *pl*.

beato, a [be'ato, a] *a* blessed; *(piadoso)* pious // *nm/f* lay brother/sister.

bebé [be'ße] *nm* baby.

bebedero, a [beße'ðero, a] *a* drinkable // *nm (para animales)* drinking trough; *(de vasija)* spout.

bebedizo, a [beße'ðiθo, a] *a* drinkable // *nm* potion.

bebedor, a [beße'ðor, a] *a* hard-drinking.

beber [be'ßer] *vt, vi* to drink.

bebida [be'ßiða] *nf* drink.

beca ['beka] *nf* grant, scholarship.

befa ['befa] *nf ver* **befo.**

befar [be'far] *vt* to scoff at.

befo, a ['befo, a] *a* thick-lipped // *nm* lip // *nf*: **hacer** ~**a de** to jeer, mock.

beldad [bel'dað] *nf* beauty.

belfo, a ['belfo, a] *a* = **befo.**

belga ['belɣa] *a, nm/f* Belgian.

Bélgica ['belxika] *nf* Belgium.

bélico, a ['beliko, a] *a* warlike, martial; **belicoso, a** *a (guerrero)* warlike; *(agresivo)* aggressive, bellicose.

beligerante [belixe'rante] *a* belligerent.

bellaco, a [be'λako, a] *a* sly, cunning // *nm* villain, rogue;

bellaquería *nf* (*acción*) dirty trick; (*calidad*) wickedness.

belleza [be'λeθa] *nf* beauty.

bello, a [a 'beλo, a] *a* beautiful, lovely; ~**as artes** fine arts.

bellota [be'λota] *nf* acorn.

bemol [be'mol] *nm* (*MUS*) flat; **esto tiene** ~**es** (*fam*) this is a real problem.

bendecir [bende'θir] *vt* to bless.

bendición [bendi'θjon] *nf* blessing.

bendito, a [ben'dito, a] *pp de* **bendecir // a** *a* holy; (*afortunado*) lucky; (*feliz*) happy; (*sencillo*) simple // *nm/f* simple soul.

benedictino, a [beneðik'tino, a] *a, nm* Benedictine.

beneficencia [benefi'θenθja] *nf* charity.

beneficiar [benefi'θjar] *vt* (*hacer bien a*) to benefit, be of benefit to; (*tierra*) to cultivate; (*mina*) to exploit; (*mineral*) to process, treat; ~**se** *vr* to benefit, profit; ~**io, a** *nm/f* beneficiary.

beneficio [bene'fiθjo] *nm* (*bien*) benefit, advantage; (*ganancia*) profit, gain; (*AGR*) cultivation; ~**so, a** *a* beneficial.

benéfico, a [be'nefiko, a] *a* beneficent, charitable.

beneplácito [bene'plaθito] *nm* approval, consent.

benevolencia [beneßo'lenθja] *nf* benevolence, kindness; **benévolo, a** *a* benevolent, kind.

benignidad [beniɣni'ðað] *nf* (*afabilidad*) kindness; (*suavidad*) mildness; **benigno, a** *a* kind, mild; mild.

beodo, a [be'oðo, a] *a* drunk.

berenjena [beren'xena] *nf* aubergine, eggplant.

Berlín [ber'lin] *nm* Berlin; **berlinés, esa** *a* of or from Berlin // *nm/f* Berliner.

bermejo, a [ber'mexo, a] *a* red.

Berna ['berna] *n* Berne.

berrear [berre'ar] *vi* to bellow, low.

berrido [be'rriðo] *nm* bellow, bellowing.

berrinche [be'rrintʃe] *nm* (*fam*) temper, tantrum.

berro ['berro] *nm* watercress.

berza ['berθa] *nf* cabbage.

besar [be'sar] *vt* to kiss; (*fig*) to graze; ~**se** *vr* to kiss (one another); **beso** *nm* kiss.

bestia ['bestja] *nf* beast, animal; (*fig*) idiot; ~ **de carga** beast of burden.

bestial [bes'tjal] *a* bestial; (*fam*) terrific; ~**idad** *nf* bestiality; (*fam*) stupidity.

besuquear [besuke'ar] *vt* to cover with kisses; ~**se** *vr* to kiss and cuddle.

betún [be'tun] *nm* bitumen, asphalt; (*para calzado*) shoe polish.

biberón [biße'ron] *nm* feeding bottle.

Biblia ['bißlja] *nf* Bible.

bíblico, a ['bißliko, a] *a* biblical.

bibliografía [bißljoɣra'fia] *nf* bibliography.

biblioteca [bißljo'teka] *nf* library; (*mueble*) bookshelves *pl*; ~ **de consulta** reference library; ~**rio, a** *nm/f* librarian.

B.I.C. *nf abr de* **Brigada de Investigación Criminal** CID (Criminal Investigation Department); FBI (Federal Bureau of Investigation) (*US*).

bicarbonato [bikarßo'nato] *nm* bicarbonate.

bicicleta [biθi'kleta] *nf* bicycle, bike.

bicho ['bitʃo] *nm* (*animal*) small animal; (*sabandija*) bug, insect; (*TAUR*) bull.

bidé [bi'ðe] *nm* bidet.

bien [bjen] *nm* good; (*interés*) advantage, benefit // *ad* well; (*correctamente*) properly, right; (*oler*) nice; (*muy*) very; **más rather** // *a* (*muy*) ~**! well done!** // *conj*: **no** ~ **llovió, bajó la temperatura** no sooner had it rained than the temperature dropped; ~ **que** although; ~**es**

inmuebles/muebles real estate *sg*/personal property *sg*; **~es de consumo** consumer goods; **~es raíces** real estate *sg*.

bienal [bje'nal] *a* biennial.

bienandanza [bjenan'danθa] *nf* happiness.

bienaventurado, a [bjenaβentu'raðo, a] *a* (*feliz*) happy, fortunate; (*sencillo*) simple, naïve.

bienestar [bjenes'tar] *nm* well-being.

bienhechor, a [bjene'tʃor, a] *a* beneficent.

bienvenida [bjenβe'niða] *nf* welcome; **bienvenido** *excl* welcome!

biftec [bif'tek] *nm* (beef)steak.

bifurcación [bifurka'θjon] *nf* fork.

bigamia [bi'xamja] *nf* bigamy; **bígamo, a** *a* bigamous // *nm/f* bigamist.

bigote [bi'xote] *nm* moustache; **bigotudo, a** *a* moustached.

bilbaíno, a [bilβa'ino, a] *a* of or from Bilbao.

bilingüe [bi'lingwe] *a* bilingual.

billar [bi'ʎar] *nm* billiards *sg*; (*lugar*) billiard hall.

billete [bi'ʎete] *nm* ticket; (*de banco*) banknote; (*carta*) note; **~ simple** single (ticket); **~ de ida y vuelta** return (ticket); **~ kilométrico** runabout ticket.

billetera [biʎe'tera] *nf*, **billetero** [biʎe'tero] *nm* wallet.

billón [bi'ʎon] *nm* billion.

bimensual [bimen'swal] *a* twice monthly.

bimotor [bimo'tor] *a* twin-engined // *nm* twin-engined plane.

binóculo [bi'nokulo] *nm* pince-nez.

biografía [bjoxra'fia] *nf* biography; **biógrafo, a** *nm/f* biographer.

biología [bjolo'xia] *nf* biology; **biológico, a** *a* biological; **biólogo, a** *nm/f* biologist.

biombo [bjombo] *nm* (folding) screen.

biopsia [bi'opsja] *nf* biopsy.

biplano [bi'plano] *nm* biplane.

birlar [bir'lar] *vt* (*derribar*) t knock down; (*matar*) to kill; (*fam* to pinch.

bis [bis] *excl* encore! // *ad*: **viven e el 27 ~** they live at 27a.

bisabuelo, a [bisa'βwelo, a] *nm* great-grandfather/mother.

bisagra [bi'saxra] *nf* hinge.

bisbisar [bisβi'sar], **bisbisea** [bisβise'ar] *vt* to mutter, mumble.

bisexual [bisek'swal] *a* bisexual.

bisiesto [bi'sjesto] *a*: **año ~** lea year.

bisnieto, a [bis'njeto, a] *nm* great-grandson/daughter.

bisonte [bi'sonte] *nm* bison.

bisoño, a [bi'soɲo, a] *a* green inexperienced.

bistec [bis'tek], **bisté** [bis'te] *nm* steak.

bisturí [bistu'ri] *nm* scalpel.

bisutería [bisute'ria] *nf* imitatio or costume jewellery.

bizarría [biθa'rria] *nf* (*valor* bravery; (*generosidad*) generosity **bizarro, a** *a* brave; generous.

bizcar [biθ'kar] *vi* to squint; **bizco, a** a cross-eyed.

bizcocho [biθ'kotʃo] *nm* (CULIN sponge cake.

bizquear [biθke'ar] *vi* to squint.

blanco, a ['blanko, a] *a* white // *nm/f* white man/woman, white // *nm* (*color*) white; (*intervalo*) space interval; (*en texto*) blank; (MIL, *fig*) target // *nf* (MUS) minim; **en ~** blank; **noche en ~** sleepless night; **estar sin ~** to be broke.

blancura [blan'kura] *nf* whiteness.

blandir [blan'dir] *vt* to brandish.

blando, a ['blando, a] *a* soft (*tierno*) tender, gentle; (*carácter*) mild; (*fam*) cowardly; **blandura** *n* softness; tenderness; mildness.

blanquear [blanke'ar] *vt* to whiten; (*fachada*) to whiten; (*paño*) to bleach // *vi* to turn white; **blanquecino, a** *a* whitish; **blanqueo** *nm* whitewashing; bleaching.

blanquillo, a [blaŋˈkiʎo, a] *a* white.

blasfemar [blasfeˈmar] *vi* to blaspheme, curse; **blasfemia** *nf* blasphemy.

blasón [blaˈson] *nm* coat of arms; *(fig)* honour; **blasonar** *vt* to emblazon // *vi* to boast, brag.

bledo [ˈbleðo] *nm*: **(no) me importa un ~** I don't care two hoots.

blindaje [blinˈdaxe] *nm* armour, armour-plating; **blindar** *vt* to armour, armour-plate.

bloc [blok] *nm* writing pad.

bloque [ˈbloke] *nm* block; *(POL)* bloc; **~ de cilindros** cylinder block.

bloquear [blokeˈar] *vt* to blockade; **bloqueo** *nm* blockade; *(COM)* freezing, blocking.

bluejean [bludˈʒin] *nm* inv jeans *pl*.

blusa [ˈblusa] *nf (de alumno)* smock; *(de mujer)* blouse.

boardilla [boarˈðiʎa] *nf* = **buhardilla**.

boato [boˈato] *nm* show, ostentation.

bobada [boˈβaða], **bobería** [boβeˈria] *nf* foolish action/statement.

bobina [boˈβina] *nf (TEC)* bobbin; *(FOTO)* spool; *(ELEC)* coil; **bobinar** *vt* to wind.

bobo, a [ˈboβo, a] *a (tonto)* daft, silly; *(cándido)* naive // *nm (TEATRO)* clown, funny man, fool.

boca [ˈboka] *nf* mouth; *(de crustáceo)* pincer; *(de cañón)* muzzle; *(de vino)* flavour, taste; *(entrada)* mouth, entrance; **~s** *nfpl (de río)* mouth *sg*; **~ abajo/arriba** face down/up; **a ~ de jarro** point-blank; **se me hace la ~ agua** my mouth is watering.

bocacalle [bokaˈkaʎe] *nf* entrance to a street.

bocadillo [bokaˈðiʎo] *nm (emparedado)* sandwich; *(comida ligera)* snack.

bocado [boˈkaðo] *nm* mouthful, bite; *(de caballo)* bridle; **~ de Adán** Adam's apple.

bocanada [bokaˈnaða] *nf (de vino)* mouthful, swallow; *(de aire)* gust, puff.

boceto [boˈθeto] *nm* sketch, outline.

bocina [boˈθina] *nf (MUS)* trumpet; *(AUTO)* horn; *(para hablar)* megaphone; *(para sordos)* ear trumpet.

bocha [ˈbotʃa] *nf* bowl; **~s** *nfpl* bowls.

bochinche [boˈtʃintʃe] *nm (fam)* uproar.

bochorno [boˈtʃorno] *nm (calor)* sultry weather; *(vergüenza)* embarrassment; **~so, a** *a* sultry; embarrassing; *(sofocante)* stuffy.

boda [ˈboða] *nf (también* **~s** *nfpl)* wedding, marriage; *(fiesta)* wedding reception; **~s de plata/de oro** silver/golden wedding.

bodega [boˈðexa] *nf (de vino)* (wine) cellar; *(depósito)* storeroom; *(de barco)* hold.

bodegón [boðeˈxon] *nm* cheap restaurant; *(ARTE)* still life.

bofe [ˈbofe] *nm (también* **~s** *nmpl)* lung.

bofetada [bofeˈtaða] *nf* slap (in the face).

bofetón [bofeˈton] *nm* punch (in the face).

boga [ˈboxa] *nf (NAUT)* rowing; *(fig)* vogue, fashion // *nm/f* rower; **en ~** in vogue; **bogar** *vi (remar)* to row; *(navegar)* to sail.

Bogotá [boxoˈta] *n* Bogota; **bogotano, a** *a* of or from Bogota.

bohardilla [boarˈðiʎa] *nf* = **buhardilla**.

bohemio, a [boˈemjo, a] *a, nm/f* Bohemian.

boicot [boiˈkot] *nm* boycott; **~ear** *vt* to boycott; **~eo** *nm* boycott.

boina [ˈboina] *nf* beret.

bola [ˈbola] *nf (en gen)* ball; *(canica)* marble; *(NAIPES)* slam; *(betún)* shoe polish; **~ de billar** billiard ball; **~ de nieve** snowball.

bolchevique [boltʃeˈβike] *nm/f* Bolshevik.

boleadoras [boleaˈðoras] *nfpl* (AM)
bolas.

bolera [boˈlera] *nf* skittle alley.

boleta [boˈleta] *nf* (*billete*) ticket;
(*permiso*) pass, permit.

boletín [boleˈtin] *nm* bulletin;
(*periódico*) journal, review; (*billete*)
ticket; ~ **escolar** school report; ~
de noticias news bulletin; ~ **de
pedido** application form; ~ **de
precios** price list; ~ **de prensa**
press release.

boleto [boˈleto] *nm* ticket.

boliche [boˈlitʃe] *nm* (*bola*) jack;
(*juego*) bowls *sg*; (*lugar*) bowling
alley.

bolígrafo [boˈliɣrafo] *nm* ball-point
pen.

bolívar [boˈliβar] *nm* monetary unit
of Venezuela.

Bolivia [boˈliβja] *nf* Bolivia; **boli-
viano, a** *a, nm/f* Bolivian.

bolo [ˈbolo] *nm* skittle; (*píldora*)
(large) pill; (*juego de*) ~**s** skittles
sg.

bolsa [ˈbolsa] *nf* (*cartera*) purse;
(*saco*) bag; (ANAT) cavity, sac; (COM)
stock exchange; (MINERÍA) pocket;
~ **de agua caliente** hot water
bottle; ~ **de aire** air pocket; ~ **de
papel** paper bag.

bolsillo [bolˈsiʎo] *nm* pocket;
(*cartera*) purse; de ~ pocket(-size).

bolsista [bolˈsista] *nm/f* stockbroker.

bolso [ˈbolso] *nm* (*bolsa*) bag; (*de
mujer*) handbag.

bollo [ˈboʎo] *nm* (*pan*) roll; (*bulto*)
bump, lump; (*abolladura*) dent.

bomba [ˈbomba] *nf* (MIL) bomb;
(TEC) pump // a (*fam*): **noticia** ~
shattering piece of news // *ad*
(*fam*): **pasarlo** ~ to have a great
time; ~ **atómica/de humo/de
retardo** atomic/smoke/ time bomb;
~ **de gasolina** petrol pump; ~ **de
mano** grenade; ~ **lacrimógena** tear
gas bomb.

bombardear [bombarðeˈar] *vt* to
bombard; (MIL) to bomb;

bombardeo *nm* bombardment/
bombing.

bombardero [bombarˈðero] *nm*
bomber.

bombear [bombeˈar] *vt* (*agua*) to
pump (out *or* up); (MIL) to bomb;
~**se** *vr* to warp.

bombero [bomˈbero] *nm* fireman.

bombilla [bomˈbiʎa] *nf* bulb.

bombín [bomˈbin] *nm* bowler hat.

bombo [ˈbombo] *nm* (MUS) bass
drum; (TEC) drum.

bombón [bomˈbon] *nm* chocolate.

bonachón, ona [bonaˈtʃon, ona] *a*
good-natured, easy-going.

bonaerense [bonaeˈrense] *a* of *or*
from Buenos Aires.

bonancible [bonanˈθiβle] *a*
(*tiempo*) fair, calm.

bonanza [boˈnanθa] *nf* (NAUT) fair
weather; (*fig*) bonanza; (MINERÍA)
rich pocket *or* vein.

bondad [bonˈdað] *nf* goodness,
kindness; **tenga la** ~ **de** (please) be
good enough to; ~**oso, a** *a* good,
kind.

bonito, a [boˈnito, a] *a* (*lindo*)
pretty; (*agradable*) nice.

bono [ˈbono] *nm* voucher; (FIN)
bond.

boquear [bokeˈar] *vi* to gasp.

boquerón [bokeˈron] *nm* (*anchoa*)
anchovy; (*agujero*) large hole.

boquete [boˈkete] *nm* gap, hole.

boquiabierto, a [bokiaˈβjerto, a] *a*
open-mouthed (in astonishment).

boquilla [boˈkiʎa] *nf* (*para riego*)
nozzle; (*para cigarro*) cigarette
holder; (MUS) mouthpiece.

borbollar [borβoˈʎar], **borbo-
llear** [borβoʎeˈar], **borbotar**
[borβoˈtar] *vi* to bubble.

borbotón [borβoˈton] *nm* bubbling.

bordado [borˈðaðo] *nm* embroidery.

bordar [borˈðar] *vt* to embroider.

borde [ˈborðe] *nm* edge, border; (*de
camino etc*) side; (*en la costura*)
hem; **al** ~ **de** (*fig*) on the verge *or*
brink of; ~**ar** *vt* to border.

bordo ['borðo] nm (NAUT) side; **a ~** on board.

Borinquén [borin'ken] nm Puerto Rico; **borinqueño, a** a, nm/f Puerto Rican.

borra ['borra] nf (pelusa) fluff; (sedimento) sediment.

borrachera [borra'tʃera] nf (ebriedad) drunkenness; (orgía) sprec, binge.

borracho, a [bo'rratʃo, a] a drunk // nm/f (que bebe mucho) drunkard, drunk; (temporalmente) drunk, drunk man/woman.

borrador [borra'ðor] nm (escritura) first draft, rough sketch; (cuaderno) scribbling pad; (goma) rubber, eraser.

borrajear [borraxe'ar] vt, vi to scribble.

borrar [bo'rrar] vt to erase, rub out.

borrascoso, a [borras'koso, a] a stormy.

borrica [bo'rrika] nf she-donkey; (fig) stupid woman; **~da** nf foolish action/statement.

borrico [bo'rriko] nm donkey; (fig) stupid man.

borrón [bo'rron] nm (mancha) stain; (proyecto) rough draft; (de cuadro) sketch.

borroso, a [bo'rroso, a] a vague, unclear; (escritura) illegible.

bosque ['boske] nm wood, forest.

bosquejar [boske'xar] vt to sketch; **bosquejo** nm sketch.

bosta ['bosta] nf dung, manure.

bostezar [boste'θar] vi to yawn; **bostezo** nm yawn.

bota ['bota] nf (saco) leather wine bottle; (calzado) boot.

botadura [bota'ðura] nf launching.

botánico, a [bo'taniko, a] a nm/f botanist // nf botany.

botar [bo'tar] vt to throw, hurl; (NAUT) to launch; (fam) to throw out // vi to bounce.

bote ['bote] nm (salto) bounce; (golpe) thrust; (vasija) tin, can; (embarcación) boat; **de ~ en ~**

packed, jammed full; **~ salvavidas** lifeboat.

botella [bo'teʎa] nf bottle.

botica [bo'tika] nf chemist's (shop), pharmacy; **~rio, a** nm/f chemist, pharmacist.

botija [bo'tixa] nf (earthenware) jug; **botijo** nm (earthenware) jug; (tren) excursion train.

botín [bo'tin] nm (calzado) half boot; (polaina) spat; (MIL) booty.

botiquín [boti'kin] nm (armario) medicine cabinet; (portátil) first-aid kit.

botón [bo'ton] nm button; (BOT) bud; (de florete) tip; **~ de oro** buttercup.

botones [bo'tones] nm buttons sg, bellboy.

bóveda ['boβeða] nf (ARQ) vault.

boxeador [boksea'ðor] nm boxer.

boxeo [bok'seo] nm boxing.

boya ['boja] nf (NAUT) buoy; (flotador) float.

bozal [bo'θal] a (novato) raw, green; (tonto) stupid; (salvaje) wild // nm (de caballo) halter; (de perro) muzzle.

bracear [braθe'ar] vi (agitar los brazos) to wave one's arms; (nadar) to swim (the crawl).

bracero [bra'θero] nm labourer; (en el campo) farmhand.

bracete [bra'θete]: **de ~** ad arm in arm.

braga ['braɣa] nf (cuerda) sling, rope; (de bebé) nappy; **~s** nfpl (de mujer) panties.

bragueta [bra'xeta] nf fly, flies nf braille [bra'il] nm braille.

bramar [bra'mar] vi to bellow, roar; **bramido** nm bellow, roar.

brasa ['brasa] nf live coal.

brasero [bra'sero] nm brazier.

Brasil [bra'sil] nm: **el ~** Brazil; **brasileño, a** a, nm/f Brazilian.

bravata [bra'βata] nf boast.

braveza [bra'βeθa] nf (valor) bravery; (ferocidad) ferocity.

bravío, a [bra'βio, a] a wild; (feroz) fierce.

bravo, a ['braβo, a] a (*valiente*) brave; (*bueno*) fine, splendid; (*feroz*) ferocious; (*salvaje*) wild // *excl* bravo!; **bravura** nf bravery; ferocity; (*pey*) boast.

braza ['braθa] nf fathom; **nadar a la ~** to swim the breast-stroke.

brazada [bra'θaða] nf stroke.

brazado [bra'θaðo] nm armful.

brazalete [braθa'lete] nm (*pulsera*) bracelet; (*banda*) armband.

brazo ['braβo] nm arm; (*ZOOL*) foreleg; (*BOT*) limb, branch; **a ~ partido** hand-to-hand; **del ~** arm in arm.

brea ['brea] nf pitch, tar.

brebaje [bre'βaxe] nm potion.

brecha ['bretʃa] nf breach, gap, opening.

brega ['breγa] nf (*lucha*) struggle; (*trabajo*) hard work.

breve ['breβe] a short, brief // nf breve; **~dad** nf brevity, shortness.

brezal [bre'θal] nm moor(land), heath; **brezo** nm heather.

bribón, ona [bri'βon, ona] a idle, lazy // nm/f (*vagabundo*) vagabond; (*pícaro*) rascal, rogue.

bricolaje [briko'laxe] nm do-it-yourself, DIY.

brida ['briða] nf bridle, rein; (*TEC*) clamp; **a toda ~** at top speed.

bridge [britʃ] nm bridge.

brigada [bri'γaða] nf (*unidad*) brigade; (*trabajadores*) squad, gang // nm ≈ staff-sergeant, sergeant-major.

brillante [bri'ʎante] a brilliant // nm diamond; **brillar** vi to shine.

brillo ['briʎo] nm shine; (*brillantez*) brilliance; (*fig*) splendour; **sacar ~** to polish.

brincar [brin'kar] vi to skip about, hop about, jump about; **está que brinca** he's hopping mad.

brinco ['brinko] nm hop, skip, jump.

brindar [brin'dar] vi: **~ a o por** to drink (a toast) to // vt to offer, present.

brindis ['brindis] nm toast; (*TAUR*)

(ceremony of) dedicating the bull.

brío ['brio] nm spirit, dash; **brioso, a** a spirited, dashing.

brisa ['brisa] nf breeze.

británico, a [bri'taniko, a] a British // nm/f Briton, British person.

brocal [bro'kal] nm rim.

brocha ['brotʃa] nf brush.

broche ['brotʃe] nm brooch; **~ para papeles** (*AM*) paper clip.

broma ['broma] nf (*bulla*) fun; (*chanza*) joke; **en ~** in fun, as a joke; **bromear** vi to joke.

bromista [bro'mista] a fond of joking // nm/f joker, wag.

bronca ['bronka] nf row.

bronce ['bronθe] nm bronze; **~ado, a** a bronze; (*por el sol*) tanned // nm (*sun*)tan; (*TEC*) bronzing.

broncearse [bronθe'arse] vr to get a suntan.

bronco, a ['bronko, a] a (*superficie*) rough; (*manera*) rude, surly; (*voz*) harsh.

bronquitis [bron'kitis] nf bronchitis.

brotar [bro'tar] vi (*BOT*) to sprout; (*aguas*) to gush (forth), flow; (*MED*) to break out; **brote** nm (*BOT*) shoot; (*MED, fig*) outbreak.

bruces ['bruθes]: **de ~ ad: caer o dar de ~** to fall headlong, fall flat; **estar de ~** to lie face downwards.

bruja ['bruxa] nf witch; (*lechuza*) owl; **brujería** nf witchcraft.

brujo ['bruxo] nm wizard, magician.

brújula ['bruxula] nf compass.

bruma ['bruma] nf mist; **brumoso, a** a misty.

bruñido [bru'niðo] nm polish; **bruñir** vt to polish.

brusco, a ['brusko, a] a (*súbito*) sudden; (*áspero*) brusque.

Bruselas [bru'selas] n Brussels.

brutal [bru'tal] a brutal; (*fig*) sudden; **~idad** nf brutality.

bruto, a ['bruto, a] a (*idiota*) stupid; (*bestial*) brutish; (*peso*) gross;

(diamante etc) raw, uncut; **en ~** raw, unworked.

Bs.As. *abr de* **Buenos Aires.**

buba ['buβa] *nf* tumour.

bucal [bu'kal] *a:* **por vía ~** by or through the mouth, orally.

bucear [buθe'ar] *vi* to dive // *vt* to explore; **buceo** *nm* diving; *(fig)* investigation.

bucle ['bukle] *nm* curl.

budismo [bu'ðismo] *nm* Buddhism.

buenamente [bwena'mente] *ad* *(fácilmente)* easily; *(voluntariamente)* willingly.

buenaventura [bwenaßen'tura] *nf (suerte)* good luck; *(adivinación)* fortune.

bueno, a ['bweno, a], **buen** [bwen] *a (amable)* kind; *(MED)* well; *(guapo)* attractive; **¡~as!** hello!; **buen día, ~os días** good morning!; good afternoon!; hello!; **~as tardes** good afternoon!; good evening!; **~as noches** good night!; **buen sinvergüenza resultó** a fine rascal he turned out to be // *excl* right!, all right!; **~, ¿y qué?** well, so what?

buey [bwei] *nm* ox.

búfalo ['bufalo] *nm* buffalo.

bufanda [bu'fanda] *nf* scarf, muffler.

bufar [bu'far] *vi* to snort.

bufete [bu'fete] *nm (mesa)* desk; *(de abogado)* lawyer's office.

bufo, a ['bufo, a] *a* comic.

bufón, ona [bu'fon, ona] *a* funny // *nm* clown.

buhardilla [buar'ðiʎa] *nf (ventana)* skylight; *(desván)* attic.

búho ['buo] *nm* owl; *(fig)* hermit, recluse.

buhonero [buo'nero] *nm* pedlar.

buitre ['bwitre] *nm* vulture.

bujía [bu'xia] *nf (vela)* candle; *(ELEC)* candle (power); *(AUTO)* spark plug.

bula ['bula] *nf (papal)* bull.

bulbo ['bulßo] *nm* bulb.

búlgaro, a ['bulxaro, a] *a, nm/f* Bulgarian.

bulto ['bulto] *nm (paquete)* package; *(fardo)* bundle; *(tamaño)* size, bulkiness; *(MED)* swelling, lump; *(silueta)* vague shape; *(estatua)* bust, statue; **de mucho/poco ~** important/unimportant.

bulla ['buʎa] *nf (ruido)* uproar; *(de gente)* crowd.

bullicio [bu'ʎiθjo] *nm (ruido)* uproar; *(movimiento)* bustle.

bullir [bu'ʎir] *vi (hervir)* to boil; *(burbujear)* to bubble; *(mover)* to move, stir.

buñuelo [bu'ɲwelo] *nm* fritter.

buque ['buke] *nm* ship, vessel.

burbuja [bur'βuxa] *nf* bubble; **burbujear** *vi* to bubble.

burdel [bur'ðel] *nm* brothel.

burdo, a ['burðo, a] *a* coarse, rough.

burgués, esa [bur'xes, esa] *a* middle-class, bourgeois; **burguesía** *nf* middle class, bourgeoisie.

burla ['burla] *nf (mofa)* gibe; *(broma)* joke; *(engaño)* trick.

burladero [burla'ðero] *nm* (bullfighter's) refuge.

burlador, a [burla'ðor, a] *a* mocking // *nm (bromista)* joker; *(libertino)* seducer.

burlar [bur'lar] *vt (engañar)* to deceive, *(seducir)* to seduce // *vi*, **~se vr** to joke; **~se de** to make fun of.

burlesco, a [bur'lesko, a] *a* burlesque.

burlón, ona [bur'lon, ona] *a* mocking.

burocracia [buro'kraθja] *nf* civil service; *(pey)* bureaucracy.

burócrata [bu'rokrata] *nm/f* civil servant; *(pey)* bureaucrat.

burra ['burra] *nf* (she-)donkey; *(fig)* stupid woman.

burro ['burro] *nm* donkey; *(fig)* ass, idiot.

bursátil [bur'satil] *a* stock-exchange *cpd*.

busca ['buska] *nf* search, hunt; **en ~ de** in search of.

buscapleitos [buska'pleitos] *nm/f inv* troublemaker.

buscar [bus'kar] *vt* to look for, search for, seek // *vi* to look, search, seek; **se busca empleado** employee wanted.

buscón, ona [bus'kon, ona] *a* a thieving // *nm* petty thief // *nf* whore.

busilis [bu'silis] *nm* (*fam*) snag.

busque *etc vb ver* **buscar.**

búsqueda ['buskeða] *nf* = **busca.**

busto ['busto] *nm* bust.

butaca [bu'taka] *nf* armchair; (*de cine, teatro*) stall, seat.

butano [bu'tano] *nm* butane.

buzo ['buðo] *nm* diver.

buzón [bu'θon] *nm* letter box; (*en la calle*) pillar box.

C

c. *abr de* **capítulo.**

C. *abr de* **centígrado; compañía.**

C/ *abr de* **calle.**

c.a. *abr de* **corriente alterna.**

cabal [ka'βal] *a* (*exacto*) exact; (*correcto*) right, proper; (*acabado*) finished, complete; **~es** *nmpl*: **estar en sus ~es** to be in one's right mind.

cabalgadura [kaβalxa'ðura] *nf* mount, horse.

cabalgar [kaβal'xar] *vt, vi* to ride.

caballa [ka'βaʎa] *nf* mackerel.

caballeresco, a [kaβaʎe're̞sko, a] *a* noble, chivalrous.

caballería [kaβaʎe'ria] *nf* mount; (*MIL*) cavalry.

caballeriza [kaβaʎe'riθa] *nf* stable; **caballerizo** *nm* groom, stableman.

caballero [kaβa'ʎero] *nm* rider, horseman; (*hombre galante*) gentleman; (*de la orden de caballería*) knight; (*hidalgo*) noble(man);

(*señor, término de cortesía*) sir.

caballerosidad [kaβaʎerosi'ðað] *nf* chivalry.

caballo [ka'βaʎo] *nm* horse (*AJEDREZ*) knight; (*NAIPES*) queen; ~ **de vapor** *o* **de fuerza** horsepower.

cabaña [ka'βaɲa] *nf* (*casita*) hut, cabin; (*rebaño*) flock.

cabaré, cabaret (*pl* **cabarets** [kaßa're] *nm* cabaret.

cabás [ka'βas] *nm* satchel.

cabecear [kaβeθe'ar] *vt* to head // *vi* to nod; (*negar*) to shake one's head.

cabecera [kaβe'θera] *nf* (*gen*) head; (*de distrito*) chief town; (*IMPRENTA*) headline.

cabecilla [kaβe'θiʎa] *nm/f* ringleader; (*fig: fam*) hothead.

cabellera [kaβe'ʎera] *nf* hair; (*de cometa*) tail.

cabello [ka'βeʎo] *nm* (*también* ~s *nmpl*) hair *sg*; **cabelludo, a** a a hairy.

caber [ka'βer] *vi* (*entrar*) to fit, go; (*tener lugar*) to have enough room; **caben 3 más** there's room for 3 more.

cabestrillo [kaβes'triʎo] *nm* sling.

cabestro [ka'βestro] *nm* halter.

cabeza [ka'βeθa] *nf* head; (*POL*) chief, leader; ~**da** *nf* (*golpe*) butt; (*al dormirse*) nod.

cabezudo, a [kaβe'θuðo, a] a bigheaded; (*fig*) pigheaded.

cabida [ka'βiða] *nf* space.

cabildo [ka'βildo] *nm* (*de iglesia*) chapter; (*POL*) town council.

cabina [ka'βina] *nf* booth; (*de camión*) cabin.

cabizbajo, a [kaβiθ'βaxo, a] a crestfallen, dejected.

cable [ka'βle] *nm* cable; ~ **grama** *nm* cablegram.

cabo ['kaβo] *nm* (*de objeto*) end, extremity; (*de tiempo, proceso*) end; (*persona*) head, chief; (*MIL*) corporal; (*NAUT*) rope, cable; (*GEO*) cape; **al ~ de 3 días** after 3 days; **al fin y al ~** in the end.

cabra ['kaβra] *nf* (she-)goat, nanny goat.

cabré *etc vb ver* **caber.**

cabria ['kaβrja] *nf* hoist, derrick.

cabrío, a [ka'βrio, a] *a* goatish; **macho ~** (he-)goat, billy goat.

cabriola [ka'βrjola] *nf* caper.

cabritilla [kaβri'tiʎa] *nf* kid, kidskin.

cabrito [ka'βrito] *nm* kid.

cabrón [ka'βron] *nm* cuckold; (*fig: fam*) bastard (*fam!*).

cacahuete [kaka'wete] *nm* peanut, monkey nut.

cacao [ka'kao] *nm* cocoa; (*BOT*) cacao.

cacarear [kakare'ar] *vi* (*persona*) to boast; (*gallo*) to cackle.

cacería [kaθe'ria] *nf* hunting, shooting.

cacerola [kaθe'rola] *nf* pan, saucepan.

cacique [ka'θike] *nm* chief, local ruler; (*POL*) local boss; **caciquismo** *nm* (system of) dominance by the local boss.

caco ['kako] *nm* pickpocket.

cacto ['kakto], **cactus** ['kaktus] *nm* cactus.

cacumen [ka'kumen] *nm* (*fig: fam*) acumen.

cachar [ka'tʃar] *vt* to smash, break.

cacharro [ka'tʃarro] *nm* earthenware pot.

cachear [katʃe'ar] *vt* to search, frisk.

cachemira [katʃe'mira] *nf* cashmere.

cacheo [ka'tʃeo] *nm* searching, frisking.

cachimba [ka'tʃimba] *nf*, **cachimbo** [ka'tʃimbo] *nm* pipe.

cachiporra [katʃi'porra] *nf* truncheon.

cachivache [katʃi'βatʃe] *nm* pot; (*utensilio*) utensil; (*persona*) good-for-nothing.

cacho, a ['katʃo, a] *a* bent, crooked // *nm* (small) bit.

cachondeo [katʃon'deo] *nm* (*fam*) farce, joke.

cachondo, a [ka'tʃondo, a] *a* (*ZOOL*) on heat; (*vulg*) randy, sexy; (*gracioso*) funny.

cachorro, a [ka'tʃorro, a] *nm/f* (*perro*) pup, puppy; (*león*) cub.

cada ['kaða] *a inv* each; (*antes de número*) every; **~ día** each day, every day; **~ uno/a** each one, every one; **~ vez más** more and more; **uno de ~ diez** one out of every ten.

cadalso [ka'ðalso] *nm* scaffold.

cadáver [ka'ðaβer] *nm* (dead) body, corpse.

cadena [ka'ðena] *nf* chain; (*TV*) channel; **trabajo en ~** assembly line work.

cadencia [ka'ðenθja] *nf* cadence, rhythm.

cadera [ka'ðera] *nf* hip.

cadete [ka'ðete] *nm* cadet.

caducar [kaðu'kar] *vi* (*permiso, ley*) to lapse, expire; (*persona*) to become senile; **caduco, a** *a* expired; (*persona*) very old.

C.A.F. *abr de* **cóbrese al entregar** COD (cash on delivery).

caer [ka'er] *vi, ~se vr* to fall (down); **~ bien/mal** to make a good/bad impression; **el pago se mañana** the payment is due tomorrow; **~ en la cuenta** to cotton on.

café [ka'fe] (*pl ~s*) *nm* (*bebida, planta*) coffee; (*lugar*) café // (*color*) brown; **cafetal** *nm* coffee plantation.

cafetera, a [kafe'tero, a] *a* coffee *cpd* // *nf* coffee pot.

cáfila ['kafila] *nf* (*de personas*) group; (*de ovejas*) flock.

caída [ka'iða] *nf* (*gen*) fall; (*declive*) slope; (*disminución*) fall, drop.

caigo *etc vb ver* **caer.**

caimán [kai'man] *nm* alligator.

caimiento [kai'mjento] *nm* fall, falling.

caja ['kaxa] *nf* box; (*para reloj*) case; (*de ascensor*) shaft; (*COM*) cashbox; (donde se hacen los pagos) cashdesk; ~ **de ahorros** savings bank; ~ **de cambios** gearbox; ~ **fuerte**, ~ **de caudales** safe, strongbox.

cajero, a [ka'xero, a] nm/f cashier.

cajetilla [kaxe'tiʎa] nf small box; (de cigarrillos) packet.

cajón [ka'xon] nm big box; (de mueble) drawer.

cal [kal] nf lime.

cala ['kala] nf (GEO) cove, inlet; (de barco) hold; (MED) suppository.

calabaza [kala'βaθa] nf (BOT) pumpkin.

calabozo [kala'βoθo] nm prison (cell).

calamar [kala'mar] nm squid.

calambre [ka'lambre] nm cramp.

calamidad [kalami'ðað] nf calamity, disaster.

calamina [kala'mina] nf calamine.

calaña [ka'laɲa] nf model, pattern.

calar [ka'lar] vt to soak, drench; (penetrar) to pierce, penetrate; (comprender) to see through; (vela, red) to lower; ~**se las gafas** to stick one's glasses on.

calavera [kala'βera] nf skull.

calcañar [kalka'ɲar], **calcañal** [kalka'ɲal], **calcaño** [kal'kaɲo] nm heel.

calcar [kal'kar] vt (reproducir) to trace; (imitar) to copy.

calceta [kal'θeta] nf (knee-length) stocking; **hacer** ~ to knit; **calcetín** nm sock.

calcina [kal'θina] nf concrete.

calcinar [kalθi'nar] vt to burn, blacken.

calcio ['kalθjo] nm calcium.

calco ['kalko] nm tracing.

calcomanía [kalkoma'nia] nm transfer.

calculadora [kalkula'ðora] nf calculator; ~ **de bolsillo** pocket calculator.

calcular [kalku'lar] vt (MAT) to calculate, compute; (suponer, creer)

to reckon, expect; **cálculo** nm calculation; reckoning.

caldear [kalde'ar] vt to warm (up), heat (up); (los metales) to weld.

caldera [kal'dera] nf boiler.

calderilla [kalde'riʎa] nf (REL) vessel for holy water; (moneda) small change.

caldero [kal'dero] nm small boiler.

calderón [kalde'ron] nm cauldron.

caldo ['kaldo] nm stock; (consomé) consommé; (para la ensalada) dressing.

calefacción [kalefak'θjon] nf heating.

calendario [kalen'darjo] nm calendar.

calentador [kalenta'ðor] nm heater.

calentar [kalen'tar] vt to heat (up); ~**se** vr to heat up, warm up; (fig) to get heated.

calentura [kalen'tura] nf (MED) fever, (high) temperature; **calenturiento, a** a feverish.

calero, a [ka'lero, a] a lime cpd.

calibrar [kali'βrar] vt to gauge, measure; **calibre** nm (de cañón) calibre, bore; (diámetro) diameter; (fig) calibre.

calidad [kali'ðað] nf quality; **en ~ de** in the capacity of.

cálido, a ['kaliðo, a] a hot; (fig) warm.

caliente [ka'ljente] a hot; (sin exceso) warm; (fig) fiery; (disputa) heated.

calificación [kalifika'θjon] nf qualification; (de alumno) grade, mark.

calificado, a [kalifi'kaðo, a] a qualified, competent; (trabajador) skilled.

calificar [kalifi'kar] vt (enaltecer) to distinguish; (alumno) to grade, mark; (determinar) to describe.

calma ['kalma] nf calm; (pachorra) slowness.

calmante [kal'mante] *nm* sedative, tranquillizer.

calmar [kal'mar] *vt* to calm, calm down // *vi* (*tempestad*) to abate; (*mente etc*) to become calm.

calmoso, a [kal'moso, a], **calmudo, a** [kal'muðo, a] *a* calm, quiet.

calofrío [kalo'frio] *nm* = **escalofrío**.

calor [ka'lor] *nm* heat; (~ *agradable*) warmth.

caloría [kalo'ria] *nf* calorie.

calorífero, a [kalo'rifero, a] *a* heat-producing, heat-giving // *nm* heating system.

calumnia [ka'lumnja] *nf* calumny, slander; **calumnioso, a** *a* slanderous.

caluroso, a [kalu'roso, a] *a* hot; (*sin exceso*) warm; (*fig*) enthusiastic.

calva ['kalβa] *nf* bald patch; (*en bosque*) clearing.

calvario [kal'βarjo] *nm* stations *pl* of the cross.

calvicie [kal'βiθje] *nf* baldness.

calvo, a ['kalβo, a] *a* bald; (*terreno*) bare, barren; (*tejido*) threadbare.

calza ['kalθa] *nf* wedge, chock.

calzado, a [kal'θaðo, a] *a* shod // *nm* footwear // *nf* roadway, highway.

calzador [kalθa'ðor] *nm* shoehorn.

calzar [kal'θar] *vt* to put on; (*un mueble*) to put a wedge under; ~se *vr:* ~se los zapatos to put on one's shoes; ¿qué (número) calza? what size do you wear or take?

calzón [kal'θon] *nm* (*también* calzones *nmpl*) shorts *pl*.

calzoncillos [kalθon'θiʎos] *nmpl* underpants.

callado, a [ka'ʎaðo, a] *a* quiet.

callar [ka'ʎar] *vt* to keep quiet about, say nothing about // *vi*, ~se *vr* to keep quiet, be silent.

calle [ka'ʎe] *nf* street; (*DEPORTE*) lane; ~ arriba/abajo up/down the street; ~ de un solo sentido one-way street.

calleja [ka'ʎexa] *nf* alley, narrow street; **callejear** *vi* to wander about the streets; **callejero, a** *a* street *cpd*.

callejón [kaʎe'xon] *nm* alley, passage; ~ sin salida one-way street.

callejuela [kaʎe'xwela] *nf* side-street, alley.

callista [ka'ʎista] *nm/f* chiropodist.

callo ['kaʎo] *nm* callus; (*en el pie*) corn; ~s *nmpl* tripe *sg*; ~so, a *a* horny, rough.

cama ['kama] *nf* bed; (*GEO*) stratum; ~ de matrimonio double bed.

camada [ka'maða] *nf* litter; (*de personas*) gang, band.

camafeo [kama'feo] *nm* cameo.

camandulear [kamandule'ar] *vi* to be a hypocrite.

cámara ['kamara] *nf* (*gen*) chamber; (*habitación*) room; (*sala*) hall; (*CINE*) cine camera; (*fotográfica*) camera; ~ de aire inner tube.

camarada [kama'raða] *nm* comrade, companion.

camarera [kama'rera] *nf* (*en restaurante*) waitress; (*en casa, hotel*) maid.

camarero [kama'rero] *nm* waiter.

camarilla [kama'riʎa] *nf* (*clan*) clique; (*POL*) lobby.

camarín [kama'rin] *nm* dressing room.

camarón [kama'ron] *nm* shrimp.

camarote [kama'rote] *nm* cabin.

cambiable [kam'bjaβle] *a* (*variable*) changeable, variable; (*intercambiable*) interchangeable.

cambiante [kam'bjante] *a* variable // *nm* moneychanger.

cambiar [kam'bjar] *vt* (*gen*) to change; (*de moneda*) to change; (*dinero*) to exchange // *vi* (*gen*) to change; ~se *vr* (*mudarse*) to move, (*de ropa*) to change; ~(se) de... to change one's ...

cambio ['kambjo] *nm* change; (*trueque*) exchange; (*COM*) rate of exchange; (*oficina*) (foreign) ex change office; (*dinero menudo*) small change; **en** ~ on the other hand; (*en lugar de eso*) instead; ~ **de velocidades** gear lever; ~ **de vía** points *pl*.

cambista [kam'bista] *nm* (COM) exchange broker; (FERRO) switch-man.

camelar [kame'lar] *vt* (*galantear*) to flirt with; (*engañar*) to cajole.

camello [ka'meʎo] *nm* camel.

camilla [ka'miʎa] *nf* (*cama*) cot; (MED) stretcher.

caminante [kami'nante] *nm/f* traveller.

caminar [kami'nar] *vi* (*marchar*) to walk, go; (*viajar*) to travel, journey // *vt* (*recorrer*) to cover, travel.

caminata [kami'nata] *nf* long walk.

camino [ka'mino] *nm* (*gen*) way, road; (*senda*) track; **a medio** ~ halfway (there); **en el** ~ on the way, en route.

camión [ka'mjon] *nm* lorry, truck.

camisa [ka'misa] *nf* shirt; (BOT) skin; ~ **de dormir** nightdress; ~ **de fuerza** straitjacket; **camisería** *nf* outfitter's (shop).

camiseta [kami'seta] *nf* (*prenda*) vest; (*de deportista*) singlet.

camisón [kami'son] *nm* nightdress, nightgown.

campamento [kampa'mento] *nm* camp.

campana [kam'pana] *nf* bell; ~**da** *nf* peal; ~**rio** *nm* belfry.

campanilla [kampa'niʎa] *nf* (*campana*) small bell; (*burbuja*) bubble.

campaña [kam'paɲa] *nf* (MIL, POL) campaign; (*campo*) countryside.

campar [kam'par] *vi* to camp; (*sobresalir*) to excel, stand out.

campeón, ona [kampe'on, ona] *nm/f* champion; **campeonato** *nm* championship.

campesino, a [kampe'sino, a] *a* country *cpd*, rural // *nm/f*

countryman/woman; (*agricultor*) farmer.

campestre [kam'pestre] *a* country *cpd*, rural.

camping ['kampin] *nm* camping (*lugar*) campsite; **hacer** ~ to go camping.

campiña [kam'piɲa] *nf* country side.

campo ['kampo] *nm* (*fuera de la ciudad*) country, countryside; (AGR, ELEC) field; (*de fútbol*) ground, pitch; (*de golf*) course; (*de tenis*) court (MIL) camp.

camposanto [kampo'santo] *nm* cemetery.

camuflaje [kamu'flaxe] *nm* camouflage.

Canadá [kana'ða] *nm* Canada **canadiense** *a, nm/f* Canadian // fur-lined jacket.

canal [ka'nal] *nm* canal; (GEO) channel, strait; (*de televisión*) channel; (*de tejado*) gutter; ~**izar** *v* to channel.

canalón [kana'lon] *nm* (*conducto vertical*) drainpipe; (*del tejado*) gutter.

canalla [ka'naʎa] *nf* rabble, mob // *nm* swine, rotter.

canapé [kana'pe] (*pl* ~**s**) *nm* sofa settee; (CULIN) canapé.

canario, a [ka'narjo, a] *a, nm/f* (native) of the Canary Isles // *nm* canary.

canasta [ka'nasta] *nf* (*round*) basket; **canasto** *nm* large basket.

cancelación [kanθela'θjon] *nf* cancellation.

cancelar [kanθe'lar] *vt* to cancel; (*una deuda*) to write off.

cáncer ['kanθer] *nm* (MED) cancer; **C**~ (ASTRO) Cancer.

canciller [kanθi'ʎer] *nm* chancellor.

canción [kan'θjon] *nf* song; ~ **de cuna** lullaby; **cancionero** *nm* song book.

candado [kan'daðo] *nm* padlock.

candela [kan'dela] *nf* candle.

candelero [kande'lero] *nm* (*para vela*) candlestick; (*de aceite*) oil lamp.

candente [kan'dente] *a* red-hot; (*fig*) burning.

candidato [kandi'ðato] *nm/f* candidate.

candidez [kandi'ðeθ] *nf* (*sencillez*) simplicity; (*simpleza*) naiveté; **cándido, a** *a* simple; naive.

candil [kan'dil] *nm* oil lamp; **~eja** *nf* small oil lamp.

candor [kan'dor] *nm* (*sinceridad*) frankness; (*inocencia*) innocence.

canela [ka'nela] *nf* cinnamon.

canelón [kane'lon] *nm* (*canal*) drainpipe; (*carámbano*) icicle.

cangrejo [kan'grexo] *nm* crab.

canguro [kan'guro] *nm* kangaroo.

caníbal [ka'niβal] *a, nm/f* cannibal.

canica [ka'nika] *nf* marble.

canijo, a [ka'nixo, a] *a* frail, sickly.

canino, a [ka'nino, a] *a* canine // *nm* canine (tooth).

canjear [kanxe'ar] *vt* to exchange.

cano, a [kano, a] *a* grey-haired, white-haired.

canoa [ka'noa] *nf* canoe.

canon ['kanon] *nm* canon; (*pensión*) rent; (*com*) tax.

canónigo [ka'noniɣo] *nm* canon.

canonizar [kanoni'θar] *vt* to canonize.

canoro, a [ka'noro, a] *a* melodious.

cansado, a [kan'saðo, a] *a* tired, weary; (*tedioso*) tedious, boring.

cansancio [kan'sanθjo] *nm* tiredness, fatigue.

cansar [kan'sar] *vt* (*fatigar*) to tire, tire out, weary; (*aburrir*) to bore; (*fastidiar*) to bother; **se** *vr* to tire, get tired; (*aburrirse*) to get bored.

cantante [kan'tante] *a* singing // *nm/f* singer.

cantar [kan'tar] *vt* to sing // *vi* (*gen*) to sing; (*insecto*) to chirp; (*rechinar*) to squeak // *nm* (*acción*) singing; (*canción*) song; (*poema*) poem.

cántara ['kantara] *nf* large pitcher.

cántaro ['kantaro] *nm* pitcher, jug.

cantatriz [kanta'triθ] *nf* singer.

cante ['kante] *nm*: **~ jondo** flamenco singing.

cantera [kan'tera] *nf* quarry.

cantidad [kanti'ðað] *nf* quantity, amount.

cantilena [kanti'lena] *nf* = **cantinela**.

cantimplora [kantim'plora] *nf* (*frasco*) water bottle, canteen; (*sifón*) syphon.

cantina [kan'tina] *nf* canteen; (*de estación*) buffet; (*sótano*) wine cellar.

cantinela [kanti'nela] *nf* ballad, song.

canto ['kanto] *nm* (*gen*) singing; (*canción*) song; (*borde*) edge, rim; (*de un cuchillo*) back; **~ rodado** boulder.

cantor, a [kan'tor, a] *nm/f* singer.

canturrear [kanturre'ar], **canturriar** [kanturrjar] *vi* to sing softly.

caña ['kaɲa] *nf* (*bot: tallo*) stem, stalk; (*carrizo*) reed; (*de cerveza*) glass; (*anat: del brazo*) long bone; (: *de la pierna*) shinbone; (*minería*) gallery; **~ de azúcar** sugar cane.

cañada [ka'ɲaða] *nf* (*entre dos montañas*) gully, ravine; (*camino*) cattle track.

caño ['kaɲo] *nm* (*tubo*) tube, pipe; (*de aguas servidas*) sewer; (*mus*) pipe; (*naut*) navigation channel; (*de fuente*) jet.

cañón [ka'ɲon] *nm* tube, pipe; (*mil*) cannon; (*de fusil*) barrel; (*geo*) canyon, gorge.

cañonero [kaɲo'nero] *nm* gunboat.

caoba [ka'oβa] *nf* mahogany.

caos ['kaos] *nm* chaos.

cap. *abr de* **capítulo**.

capa ['kapa] *nf* cloak, cape; (*geo*) layer, stratum; (*pretexto*) pretence.

capacidad [kapaθi'ðað] *nf* (*medida*) capacity; (*aptitud*) capacity, ability.

capacitación [kapaθita'θjon] *nf* training.

capar [ka'par] *vt* to castrate, geld.

caparazón [kapara'θon] *nm* shell.

capataz [kapa'taθ] *nm* foreman.

capaz [ka'paθ] *a* able, capable; *(amplio)* capacious, roomy.

capcioso, a [kap'θjoso, a] *a* wily, deceitful.

capellán [kape'ʎan] *nm* chaplain; *(sacerdote)* priest.

caperuza [kape'ruθa] *nf* hood; **caperucita** *nf*: **Caperucita Roja** Little Red Riding Hood.

capilla [ka'piʎa] *nf* chapel; *(capucha)* hood, cowl.

capital [kapi'tal] *a* capital // *nm (COM)* capital // *nf* capital; **~ social** share capital.

capitalismo [kapita'lismo] *nm* capitalism; **capitalista** *a, nm/f* capitalist.

capitalizar [kapitali'θar] *vt* to capitalize.

capitán [kapi'tan] *nm* captain.

capitana [kapi'tana] *nf* flagship.

capitanear [kapitane'ar] *vt* to captain.

capitolio [kapi'toljo] *nm* capitol.

capitoné [kapito'ne] *nm* removal van.

capitulación [kapitula'θjon] *nf (rendición)* capitulation, surrender; *(acuerdo)* agreement, pact.

capitular [kapitu'lar] *vi* to come to terms, make an agreement // a chapter *cpd*.

capítulo [ka'pitulo] *nm* chapter; **~s** *nmpl*: **~s matrimoniales** marriage contract *sg*.

capó [ka'po] *nm* bonnet.

caporal [kapo'ral] *nm* chief, leader.

capota [ka'pota] *nf (de mujer)* bonnet; *(de coche)* hood, roof.

capote [ka'pote] *nm (abrigo: de militar)* greatcoat; *(de torero)* cloak; *(NAIPES)* slam.

Capricornio [kapri'kornjo] *nm* Capricorn.

capricho [ka'pritʃo] *nm* whim,

caprice; **~so, a** *a* capricious.

cápsula ['kapsula] *nf* capsule; *(de botella)* cap.

captar [kap'tar] *vt* to win (over).

captura [kap'tura] *nf* capture; *(JUR)* arrest; **capturar** *vt* to capture; to arrest.

capucha [ka'putʃa] *nf* hood, cowl.

cara ['kara] *nf (ANAT)* face; *(aspecto)* appearance; *(de moneda)* face; *(de disco)* side; *(fig)* boldness; **~ a** *ad* facing; **de ~** opposite, facing; **dar la ~** to face the consequences; **¿~ o cruz?** heads or tails?

carabina [kara'βina] *nf* carbine, rifle.

caracol [kara'kol] *nm (ZOOL)* snail; *(concha)* shell.

caracolear [karakole'ar] *vi* to prance about.

carácter [ka'rakter] *(pl caracteres) nm* character.

característico, a [karakte'ristiko, a] *a* characteristic // *nf* characteristic.

caracterizar [karakteri'θar] *vt (distinguir)* to characterize, typify; *(honrar)* to confer (a) distinction on.

caramba [ka'ramba] *excl* well!, good gracious!

carámbano [ka'rambano] *nm* icicle.

caramelo [kara'melo] *nm (dulce)* sweet; *(dulce de ~)* toffee; *(azúcar fundida)* caramel.

caramillo [kara'miʎo] *nm (flauta)* recorder; *(montón)* untidy heap; *(chisme, enredo)* bit of gossip.

carapacho [kara'patʃo] *nm* shell, carapace.

caraqueño, a [kara'keɲo, a] *a, nm/f* (native) of Caracas.

carátula [ka'ratula] *nf (careta, máscara)* mask; *(TEATRO)*: **la ~** the stage.

caravana [kara'βana] *nf* caravan; *(fig)* group; *(sucesión de autos)* stream; *(embotellamiento)* traffic jam.

carbón [kar'βon] nm coal; **papel ~** carbon paper; **carbonero** nm/f coal merchant; **carbonilla** nf coal dust.

carbonizar [karβoni'θar] vt to carbonize; (quemar) to char.

carbono [kar'βono] nm carbon.

carburador [karβura'ðor] nm carburettor.

carcajada [karka'xaða] nf (loud) laugh, guffaw.

cárcel [kar'θel] nf prison, jail; (TEC) clamp; **carcelero, a** a prison cpd // nm/f warder.

carcomer [karko'mer] vt to bore into, eat into; (fig) to undermine; **~se** vr to become worm-eaten, (fig) to decay.

carcomido, a [karko'miðo, a] a worm-eaten; (fig) rotten.

cardenal [karðe'nal] nm (REL) cardinal; (equimosis) bruise.

cárdeno, a ['karðeno, a] a purple; (lívido) livid.

cardíaco, a [kar'ðiako, a] a cardiac, heart cpd.

cardinal [karði'nal] a cardinal.

cardo ['karðo] nm thistle.

cardumen [kar'ðumen] nm shoal.

carear [kare'ar] vt to bring face to face; (comparar) to compare; **~se** vr to come face to face, meet.

carecer [kare'θer] vi: **~ de** to lack, be in need of.

carencia [ka'renθja] nf lack; (escasez) shortage; (MED) deficiency

carente [ka'rente] a: **~ de** lacking, devoid of.

carestía [kares'tia] nf (escasez) scarcity, shortage; (COM) high cost.

careta [ka'reta] nf mask.

carga ['karɣa] nf (peso, ELEC) load; (de barco) cargo, freight; (MIL) charge; (obligación, responsabilidad) duty, obligation

cargadero [karɣa'ðero] nm goods platform, loading bay.

cargado, a [kar'ɣaðo, a] a loaded; (ELEC) live; (café, te) strong; (el cielo) overcast.

cargamento [karɣa'mento] nm (acción) loading; (mercancías) load, cargo.

cargar [kar'xar] vt (barco, arma) to load; (ELEC) to charge; (COM: algo en cuenta) to charge, debit; (MIL: enemigo) to charge // vi to load (up); (inclinarse) to lean; **~ con** to pick up, carry away.

cargo ['karɣo] nm (puesto) post, office; (responsabilidad) duty, obligation; (fig) weight, burden; (JUR) charge; **hacerse ~ del gobierno** to take charge of the government.

carguero [kar'ɣero] nm freighter, cargo boat; (avión) freight plane.

caribe [ka'riβe] a, nm/f (native) of the Caribbean.

Caribe [ka'riβe] nm: **el ~ the** Caribbean.

caricatura [karika'tura] nf caricature.

caricia [ka'riθja] nf caress.

caridad [kari'ðað] nf charity.

cariño [ka'riɲo] nm affection, love; (caricia) caress; (en carta) love...; **~so, a** a affectionate.

caritativo, a [karita'tiβo, a] a charitable.

carmesí [karme'si] a, nm crimson.

carnal [kar'nal] a carnal; **primo ~** first cousin.

carnaval [karna'βal] nm carnival.

carne ['karne] nf flesh; (CULIN) meat; **echar ~s** to put on weight.

carnero [kar'nero] nm sheep, ram; (carne) mutton.

carnet [kar'ne] nm: **~ de conducir** driving licence.

carnicería [karniθe'ria] nf butcher's (shop); (mercado) meat market.

carnicero, a [karni'θero, a] a carnivorous // nm/f butcher // nm carnivore.

carnívoro, a [kar'niβoro, a] a carnivorous.

carnoso, a [kar'noso, a] a beefy, fat.

caro, a ['karo, a] a dear; (*COM*) dear, expensive // ad dear, dearly.

carpeta [kar'peta] nf table cover; (*para documentos*) folder, file.

carpintería [karpinte'ria] nf carpentry, joinery; **carpintero** nm carpenter.

carraspera [karras'pera] nf hoarseness.

carrera [ka'rrera] nf (*DEPORTE*) running; (*espacio recorrido*) run; (*certamen*) race; (*trayecto*) course; (*profesión*) career; (*ESCOL*) course.

carreta [ka'rreta] nf wagon, cart.

carrete [ka'rrete] nm reel, spool; (*TEC*) coil.

carretel [karre'tel] nm reel, spool.

carretera [karre'tera] nf (*main*) road, highway.

carretilla [karre'tiʎa] nf trolley; (*AGR*) (wheel)barrow.

carril [ka'rril] nm furrow; (*de autopista*) lane; (*FERRO*) rail.

carrillo [ka'rriʎo] nm (*ANAT*) cheek; (*TEC*) pulley.

carrizo [ka'rriθo] nm reed.

carro ['karro] nm cart, wagon; (*MIL*) tank; (*AM: coche*) car.

carrocería [karroθe'ria] nf bodywork, coachwork.

carta ['karta] nf letter; (*CULIN*) menu; (*naipe*) card; (*mapa*) map; (*JUR*) document; **~ de crédito** credit card; **~ certificada** registered letter.

cartel [kar'tel] nm (*anuncio*) poster, placard; (*alfabeto*) wall chart; (*COM*) cartel.

cartera [kar'tera] nf (*de bolsillo*) wallet; (*de colegial, cobrador*) satchel; (*de señora*) handbag; (*para documentos*) briefcase; (*COM, POL*) portfolio.

cartero [kar'tero] nm postman.

cartón [kar'ton] nm cardboard; (*ARTE*) cartoon.

cartucho [kar'tutʃo] nm (*MIL*) cartridge.

casa ['kasa] nf house; (*hogar*) home; (*edificio*) building; (*COM*) firm,

company; (*de tablero de ajedrez*) square; **~ consistorial** town hall; **~ de huéspedes** boarding house; **~ de socorro** first aid post; **~ editorial** publishing house.

casamiento [kasa'mjento] nm marriage, wedding.

casar [ka'sar] vt to marry; (*JUR*) to quash, annul // nm hamlet; **~se** vr to marry, get married.

cascada [kas'kaða] nf waterfall.

cascar [kas'kar] vt, **~se** vr to crack, split, break (open).

cáscara ['kaskara] nf (*de huevo, fruta seca*) shell; (*de fruta*) skin; (*de limón*) peel.

casco ['kasko] nm (*de bombero, soldado*) helmet; (*cráneo*) skull; (*de botella, obús*) fragment; (*BOT: de cebolla*) skin; (*tonel*) cask, barrel; (*NAUT: de barco*) hull; (*ZOOL: de caballo*) hoof; (*botella*) empty bottle.

caserío [kase'rio] nm hamlet; (*casa*) country house.

casero, a [ka'sero, a] a domestic, household cpd // nm/f (*propietario*) landlord/lady; (*portero*) caretaker; (*COM*) house agent.

caseta [ka'seta] nf hut; (*para bañista*) cubicle; (*de feriantes*) stall.

casi ['kasi] ad almost; **~ te caes** you almost fell.

casilla [ka'siʎa] nf (*casita*) hut, cabin; (*TEATRO*) box office; (*de ajedrez*) square.

casino [ka'sino] nm club.

caso ['kaso] nm case; **en ~ de...** in case of...; **el ~ es que** the fact is that; **hacer ~ a** to pay attention to; **hacer o venir al ~** to be relevant.

caspa ['kaspa] nf dandruff.

cassette [ka'set] nf cassette.

casta ['kasta] nf caste; (*raza*) breed; (*linaje*) lineage.

castaña [kas'taɲa] nf chestnut.

castaño, a [kas'taɲo, a] a chestnut-brown // nm chestnut tree.

castañuela [kasta'ɲwela] nf castanet.

castellano, a [kaste'ʎano, a] a

Castilian // nm (lengua) Castilian, Spanish.

castidad [kasti'ðað] nf chastity, purity.

castigar [kasti'ɣar] vt to punish; (DEPORTE) to penalize; (afligir) to afflict; **castigo** nm punishment; (DEPORTE) penalty.

castillo [kas'tiʎo] nm castle.

castizo, a [kas'tiθo, a] a (LING) pure; (de buena casta) purebred, pedigree.

casto, a ['kasto, a] a chaste, pure.

castor [kas'tor] nm beaver.

castrar [kas'trar] vt to castrate.

casual [ka'swal] a fortuitous, accidental; (DEPORTE) nf chance, accident; (combinación de circunstancias) coincidence.

cataclismo [kata'klismo] nm cataclysm.

catalán, ana [kata'lan, ana] a, nm/f Catalan, Catalonian.

catalizador [kataliθa'ðor] nm catalyst.

catálogo [ka'taloɣo] nm catalogue.

Cataluña [kata'luɲa] nf Catalonia.

cataplasma [kata'plasma] nf poultice.

catar [ka'tar] vt to taste, sample.

catarata [kata'rata] nf (GEO) waterfall, falls pl; (MED) cataract.

catarro [ka'tarro] nm catarrh, (constipado) cold.

catástrofe [ka'tastrofe] nf catastrophe.

catedral [kate'ðral] nf cathedral.

catedrático, a [kate'ðratiko, a] a nm/f professor.

categoría [kateɣo'ria] nf category; (rango) rank, standing; (calidad) quality.

categórico, a [kate'ɣoriko, a] a categorical.

catolicismo [katoli'θismo] nm Catholicism.

católico, a [ka'toliko, a] a, nm/f Catholic.

catorce [ka'torθe] num fourteen.

caución [kau'θjon] nf bail,

caucionar vt to prevent, guard against; (JUR) to bail, go bail for.

caucho ['kautʃo] nm rubber.

caudal [kau'ðal] nm (de río) volume, flow; (fortuna) wealth; (abundancia) abundance; **~oso, a** a (río) large; (aguas) copious; (persona) wealthy, rich.

caudillo [kau'ðiʎo] nm leader, chief.

causa ['kausa] nf cause; (razón) reason; (JUR) lawsuit, case; **causar** vt to cause.

cáustico, a ['kaustiko, a] a caustic.

cautela [kau'tela] nf caution, cautiousness; **cauteloso, a** a cautious, wary, careful.

cautivar [kauti'ßar] vt to capture; (fig) to captivate.

cautiverio [kauti'ßerjo] nm, **cautividad** [kautißi'ðað] nf captivity.

cautivo, a [kau'tißo, a] a, nm/f captive.

cauto, a ['kauto, a] a cautious, careful.

cavar [ka'ßar] vt to dig.

caverna [ka'ßerna] nf cave, cavern.

cavidad [kaßi'ðað] nf cavity.

cavilar [kaßi'lar] vt to ponder.

cayado [ka'jaðo] nm (de pastor) staff, crook; (de obispo) crozier.

cayó etc vb ver **caer.**

caza ['kaθa] nf (gén) hunting, shooting; (una ~) hunt, chase; (animales) game // nm (AVIAT) fighter.

cazador, a [kaθa'ðor] nm/f hunter.

cazar [ka'θar] vt to hunt; (perseguir) to chase; (coger) to catch.

cazo ['kaθo] nm saucepan.

cazuela [ka'θwela] nf pan; (guisado) casserole.

cebada [θe'ßaða] nf barley.

cebar [θe'ßar] vt (animal) to fatten (up); (anzuelo) to bait; (MIL, TEC) to prime; (pasión) to nourish; (ira) to inflame.

cebo ['θeßo] nm (para animales)

feed, food; *(para peces, fig)* bait; *(de arma)* charge.

cebolla [θe'βoʎa] *nf* onion.

cebra [θeβra] *nf* zebra.

cecear [θeθe'ar] *vi* to lisp; **ceceo** *nm* lisp.

cedazo [θe'δaθo] *nm* sieve.

ceder [θe'δer] *vt* to hand over, give up, part with // *vi (renunciar)* to give in, yield; *(disminuir)* to diminish, decline; *(romperse)* to give way.

cedro ['θeδro] *nm* cedar.

cédula [θe'δula] *nf* certificate, document; ~ **de aduana** customs permit.

C.E.E. *nf abr de* **Comunidad Económica Europea** E.E.C. (European Economic Community).

cegar [θe'xar] *vt* to blind; *(fig: pozo)* to block up, fill up // *vi* to go blind; ~**se** *vr* to be blinded *(de by)*.

ceguedad [θexe'δaδ], **ceguera** [θe'βera] *nf* blindness.

ceja ['θexa] *nf* eyebrow.

cejar [θe'xar] *vi* to move back, go back; *(fig)* to back down.

cejijunto, a [θexi'xunto, a] *a* with bushy eyebrows; *(fig)* scowling.

celada [θe'laδa] *nf* ambush, trap.

celador, a [θela'δor, a] *nm/f (de edificio)* watchman; *(de museo etc)* attendant.

celar [θe'lar] *vt (vigilar)* to watch over; *(encubrir)* to conceal, hide.

celda ['θelda] *nf* cell.

celebración [θeleβra'θjon] *nf* celebration.

celebrar [θele'βrar] *vt* to celebrate; *(alabar)* to praise // *vi* to be glad; ~**se** *vr* to occur, take place.

célebre ['θelebre] *a* famous; *(chistoso)* witty, funny.

celebridad [θeleβri'δaδ] *nf (gen)* fame; *(persona)* celebrity; *(festividad)* celebration(s) *(pl)*.

celeste [θe'leste] *a* celestial, heavenly.

celestial [θeles'tjal] *a* celestial, heavenly.

celibato [θeli'βato] *nm* celibacy.

célibe [θe'liβe] *a* celibate // *nm* unmarried person.

celo ['θelo] *nm* zeal; *(REL)* fervour; *(pey)* envy; *(de animales)* rut, heat; ~**s** *nmpl* jealousy *sg*.

celofán [θelo'fan] *nm* cellophane.

celoso, a [θe'loso, a] *a (envidioso)* jealous; *(trabajo)* zealous; *(desconfiado)* suspicious.

celta ['θelta] *nm/f* Celt.

célula ['θelula] *nf* cell.

cementar [θemen'tar] *vt* to cement.

cementerio [θemen'terjo] *nm* cemetery, graveyard.

cemento [θe'mento] *nm* cement; *(hormigón)* concrete.

cena ['θena] *nf* evening meal.

cenagal [θena'xal] *nm* bog, quagmire.

cenar [θe'nar] *vt* to have for supper // *vi* to dine.

cenicero [θeni'θero] *nm* ashtray.

cenit [θe'nit] *nm* zenith.

ceniza [θe'niθa] *nf* ash, ashes *pl*.

censo ['θenso] *nm (empadronamiento)* census; *(JUR)* tax; *(renta)* rent; *(carga sobre una casa)* mortgage.

censor [θen'sor] *nm* censor.

censura [θen'sura] *nf (POL)* censorship; *(moral)* censure, criticism.

censurar [θensu'rar] *vt (idea)* to censure; *(cortar: película)* to censor.

centella [θen'teʎa] *nf* spark.

centellar [θenteʎe'ar], **centellear** [θenteʎe'ar] *vi (metal)* to gleam; *(estrella)* to twinkle; *(fig)* to sparkle; **centelleo** *nm* gleam(ing); twinkling; sparkling.

centenar [θente'nar] *nm* hundred.

centenario, a [θente'narjo, a] *a* centenary.

centésimo, a [θen'tesimo, a] *a* hundredth.

centígrado, a [θen'tixraδo, a] *a* centigrade.

centímetro [θen'timetro] *nm* centimetre.

céntimo, a ['θentimo, a] *a* a hundredth // *nm* cent.

centinela [θenti'nela] *nm* sentry, guard.

central [θen'tral] *a* central // *nf* head office; (TEC) plant; (TELEC) exchange.

centralización [θentraliθa'θjon] *nf* centralization.

centralizar [θentrali'θar] *vt* to centralize.

centrar [θen'trar] *vt* to centre.

céntrico, a ['θentriko, a] *a* centre.

centro [θentro] *nm* centre.

centroamericano, a [θentroameri'kano, a] *a, nm/f* Central American.

ceñidor [θeni'ðor] *nm* sash.

ceñir [θe'nir] *vt* (rodear) to encircle, surround; (ajustar) to fit (tightly); (apretar) to tighten.

ceño [θeno] *nm* frown, scowl; **fruncir el ~** to frown, knit one's brow.

cepillar [θepi'λar] *vt* to brush; (madera) to plane (down); **cepillo** *nm* (gen) brush; (TEC) plane.

cera [θera] *nf* wax.

cerámico, a [θe'ramiko, a] *a* ceramic // *nf* ceramics *sg*.

cerca [θerka] *nf* fence // *ad* near, nearby, close; **~s** *nmpl* foreground *sg*, **~ de** *prep* near, close to.

cercanía [θerka'nia] *nf* nearness, closeness; **~s** *nfpl* outskirts.

cercano, a [θer'kano, a] *a* close, near.

cercar [θer'kar] *vt* to fence in; (rodear) to surround.

cerciorar [θerθjo'rar] *vt* (informar) to inform; (asegurar) to assure; **~se** *vr* (descubrir) to find out; (asegurarse) to make sure.

cerco ['θerko] *nm* (AGR) enclosure; (AM) fence; (MIL) siege.

cerdo [θerðo] *nm* pig.

cereal [θere'al] *nm* cereal.

cerebro [θe'reβro] *nm* brain; (fig) brains *pl*.

ceremonia [θere'monja] *nf* ceremony; **ceremonial** *a, nm* ceremonial; **ceremonioso, a** *a* ceremonious; (cumplido) formal.

cereza [θe'reθa] *nf* cherry.

cerilla [θe'riλa] *nf* (fósforo) match.

cerner [θer'ner] *vt* to sift, sieve, (fig) to scan, watch // *vi* to blossom; (lloviznar) to drizzle; **~se** *vr* to hover.

cernidor [θerni'ðor] *nm* sieve.

cero ['θero] *nm* nothing, zero.

cerrado, a [θe'rraðo, a] *a* closed, shut; (con llave) locked; (tiempo) cloudy, overcast; (curva) sharp; (acento) thick, broad.

cerradura [θerra'ðura] *nf* (acción) closing; (mecanismo) lock.

cerraja [θe'rraxa] *nf* lock.

cerrar [θe'rrar] *vt* to close, shut; (paso, carretera) to close; (grifo) to turn off; (trato, cuenta, negocio) to close; **con llave to lock // vi to** close, shut; (la noche) to come down; **~se** *vr* to close, shut.

cerro [θerro] *nm* hill.

cerrojo [θe'rroxo] *nm* (herramienta) bolt; (de puerta) latch.

certamen [θer'tamen] *nm* competition, contest.

certero, a [θer'tero, a] *a* accurate; (cierto) sure, certain.

certeza [θer'teθa], **certidumbre** [θerti'ðumbre] *nf* certainty.

certificado [θertifi'kaðo] *nm* certificate.

certificar [θertifi'kar] *vt* (asegurar, atestar) to certify; (carta) to register.

cervato [θer'βato] *nm* fawn.

cervecería [θerβeθe'ria] *nf* (fábrica) brewery; (tienda) public house.

cerveza [θer'βeθa] *nf* beer.

cesación [θesa'θjon] *nf* cessation; (suspensión) suspension.

cesante [θe'sante] *a* out of a job.

cesar [θe'sar] *vi* to cease, stop.

cese [ˈθese] *nm* (*de trabajo*) dismissal; (*de pago*) suspension.

césped [ˈθespeð] *nm* grass, lawn.

cesta [ˈθesta] *nf* basket; **cesto** *nm* (large) basket, hamper.

ch... *ver bajo la letra* CH, *después de* C.

Cía *abr de* **compañía.**

cianuro [θjaˈnuro] *nm* cyanide.

ciar [θjar] *vi* to go backwards.

cicatriz [θikaˈtriθ] *nf* scar.

ciclismo [θiˈklismo] *nm* cycling.

ciclo [ˈθiklo] *nm* cycle.

ciclón [θiˈklon] *nm* cyclone.

ciego, a [ˈθjeɣo, a] *a* blind // *nm/f* blind man/woman.

cielo [ˈθjelo] *nm* sky; (REL) heaven; **¡~s!** good heavens!

ciempiés [θjemˈpjes] *nm* centipede.

cien [θjen] *num ver* **ciento.**

ciénaga [ˈθjenaɣa] *nf* marsh, swamp.

ciencia [ˈθjenθja] *nf* science; **~-ficción** *nf* science fiction.

cieno [ˈθjeno] *nm* mud, mire.

científico, a [θjenˈtifiko, a] *a* scientific // *nm/f* scientist.

ciento [ˈθjento], **cien** *num* hundred; **pagar al 10 por ~** to pay at 10 per cent.

cierne [ˈθjerne] *nm:* **en ~** in blossom.

cierre [ˈθjerre] *nm* closing, shutting; (*con llave*) locking; **~ a cremallera** zip fastener.

cierro *etc vb ver* **cerrar.**

cierto, a [ˈθjerto, a] *a* sure, certain; (*un tal*) a certain; (*correcto*) right, correct; **~ hombre** a certain man; **sí, es ~** yes, that's correct.

ciervo [ˈθjerβo] *nm* (*especie*) deer; (*macho*) stag.

cierzo [ˈθjerθo] *nm* north wind.

cifra [ˈθifra] *nf* number, numeral; (*cantidad*) number, quantity; (*secreta*) code; (*siglas*) abbreviation.

cifrar [θiˈfrar] *vt* to code, write in code; (*resumir*) to abridge.

cigarra [θiˈɣarra] *nf* cicada.

cigarrera [θiɣaˈrrera] *nf* cigar case.

cigarrillo [θiɣaˈrriʎo] *nm* cigarette.

cigarro [θiˈɣarro] *nm* cigarette; (*puro*) cigar.

cigüeña [θiˈɣweɲa] *nf* stork.

cilíndrico, a [θiˈlindriko, a] *a* cylindrical.

cilindro [θiˈlindro] *nm* cylinder; (*rodillo*) roller.

cima [ˈθima] *nf* (*de montaña*) top, peak; (*de árbol*) top; (*fig*) summit, height.

címbalo [ˈθimbalo] *nm* cymbal.

cimbrar [θimˈbrar], **cimbrear** [θimbreˈar] *vt* to brandish; **~se** *vr* (*al viento*) to sway.

cimentar [θimenˈtar] *vt* to lay the foundations of.

cimiento [θiˈmjento] *nm* foundation.

cinc [θink] *nm* zinc.

cincel [θinˈθel] *nm* chisel; **~ar** *vt* to chisel.

cinco [ˈθinko] *num* five.

cincuenta [θinˈkwenta] *num* fifty.

cincho [ˈθintʃo] *nm* sash, belt.

cine [ˈθine] *nm* cinema.

cinematográfico, a [θinemaˈtoˈɣrafiko, a] *a* cine-, film *cpd.*

cínico, a [ˈθiniko, a] *a* cynical // *nm/f* cynic.

cinismo [θiˈnismo] *nm* cynicism.

cinta [ˈθinta] *nf* band, strip; (*de seda, lana, algodón*) ribbon, tape; (*película*) reel; (*de máquina de escribir*) ribbon; (*métrica*) tape measure; (*magnetofónica*) tape; (*adhesiva*) adhesive tape.

cinto [ˈθinto] *nm* belt, girdle.

cintura [θinˈtura] *nf* waist.

cinturón [θintuˈron] *nm* belt; **~ de seguridad** safety belt.

ciprés [θiˈpres] *nm* cypress (tree).

circo [ˈθirko] *nm* circus.

circuito [θirˈkwito] *nm* circuit.

circulación [θirkulaˈθjon] *nf* circulation; (AUTO) traffic.

circular [θirku'lar] *a*, *nf* circular // *vi*, *vt* to circulate.

círculo [θirkulo] *nm* circle.

circuncidar [θirkunθi'dar] *vt* to circumcise; **circuncisión** *nf* circumcision; **circunciso, a** *pp* de **circuncidar** // *a* circumcised.

circundar [θirkun'dar] *vt* to surround.

circunferencia [θirkunfe'renθja] *nf* circumference.

circunlocución [θirkunloku'θjon] *nf*, **circunloquio** [θirkun'lokjo] *nm* circumlocution.

circunscribir [θirkunskri'βir] *vt* to circumscribe; **~se** *vr* to be limited.

circunscripción [θirkunskrip'θjon] *nf* division; (*POL*) constituency.

circunspección [θirkunspek'θjon] *nf* circumspection.

circunspecto, a [θirkuns'pekto, a] *a* circumspect, cautious.

circunstancia [θirkuns'tanθja] *nf* circumstance.

circunstante [θirkuns'tante] *nm/f* onlooker, bystander.

cirio [θirjo] *nm* (wax) candle.

ciruela [θi'rwela] *nf* plum; **~ pasa** prune.

cirugía [θiru'xia] *nf* surgery; **~ estética** plastic surgery.

cirujano [θiru'xano] *nm* surgeon.

cisne [θisne] *nm* swan.

cisterna [θis'terna] *nf* cistern.

cita [θita] *nf* appointment, engagement; (*de novios*) date; (*referencia*) quotation.

citación [θita'θjon] *nf* (*JUR*) summons *sg*; (*referencia*) quotation.

citar [θi'tar] *vt* (*gen*) to make an appointment with; (*JUR*) to summons; (*un autor, texto*) to quote.

citrón [θi'tron] *nm* lemon.

ciudad [θju'ðað] *nf* town; (*capital de país etc*) city; **~anía** *nf* citizenship; **~ano/a** *nm/f* citizen; **~ela** *nf* citadel, fortress.

cívico, a [θiβiko, a] *a* civic.

civil [θi'βil] *a* civil // *nm* (*guardia*)

policeman; **~idad** *nf* civility, courtesy.

civilización [θiβiliθa'θjon] *nf* civilization.

civilizar [θiβili'θar] *vt* to civilize.

civismo [θi'βismo] *nm* public spirit.

cizaña [θi'θaɲa] *nf* discord.

clamar [kla'mar] *vt* to clamour for // *vi* to cry out, clamour.

clamor [kla'mor] *nm* (*grito*) cry, shout; (*gemido*) whine; (*de campana*) knell; (*fig*) clamour, protest.

clamorear [klamore'ar] *vt* to clamour for // *vi* (*campana*) to toll, **clamoreo** [klamo'reo] *nm* clamour(ing).

clandestino, a [klandes'tino, a] *a* clandestine; (*POL*) underground.

clara [klara] *nf* (*de huevo*) white of an egg; (*del día*) bright interval.

claraboya [klara'βoja] *nf* skylight.

clarear [klare'ar] *vi* (*el día*) to dawn; (*el cielo*) to clear up, brighten up; **~se** *vr* to be transparent.

claridad [klari'ðað] *nf* (*del día*) brightness; (*de estilo*) clarity.

clarificar [klarifi'kar] *vt* to clarify.

clarín [kla'rin] *nm* bugle.

clarinete [klari'nete] *nm* clarinet.

clarividencia [klariβi'ðenθja] *nf* clairvoyance; (*fig*) far-sightedness.

claro, a [klaro, a] *a* (*gen*) clear; (*luminoso*) bright; (*poco subido*) light; (*evidente*) clear, evident; (*ralo*) sparse; (*poco espeso*) thin // *nm* (*en escritura*) space; (*en bosque*) clearing // *ad* clearly // *excl* of course!

clase [klase] *nf* class, **alta/media/obrera** upper/middle/working class.

clásico, a [klasiko, a] *a* classical; (*fig*) classic.

clasificación [klasifika'θjon] *nf* classification; (*DEPORTE*) league.

clasificar [klasifi'kar] *vt* to classify.

claudicar [klauði'kar] *vi* to limp; (*fig*) to back down.

claustro [klaustro] *nm* cloister.

cláusula [ˈklausula] nf clause.

clausura [klauˈsura] nf closing, closure.

clavar [klaˈβar] vt (clavo) to knock in, drive in; (cuchillo, tenedor) to stick, thrust; (mirada) to fix.

clave [ˈklaβe] nf key; (MUS) clef.

clavel [klaˈβel] nm carnation.

clavícula [klaˈβikula] nf collar bone.

clavija [klaˈβixa] nf peg, dowel, pin; (ELEC) plug.

clavo [ˈklaβo] nm (de metal) nail; (BOT) clove; (callo) corn.

claxon [ˈklakson] nm horn.

clemencia [kleˈmenθja] nf mercy, clemency; **clemente** a merciful, clement.

cleptómano, a [klepˈtomano, a] nm/f kleptomaniac.

clerical [kleriˈkal] a clerical // nm clergyman.

clérigo [ˈkleriɣo] nm clergyman.

clero [ˈklero] nm clergy.

cliente [ˈkljente] nm/f client, customer.

clientela [kljenˈtela] nf clientele, customers pl.

clima [ˈklima] nm climate.

clínica [ˈklinika] nf clinic; (particular) private hospital.

clip [klip] nm paper clip.

clorhídrico, a [kloˈridriko, a] a hydrochloric.

cloroformo [kloroˈformo] nm chloroform.

club [klub] (pl ~s o ~es) nm club.

C.N.T. abr de **Confederación Nacional de Trabajo**.

coacción [koakˈθjon] nf coercion, compulsion.

coalición [koaliˈθjon] nf coalition.

coartar [koarˈtar] vt to limit, restrict.

cobarde [koˈβarðe] a cowardly // nm coward; **cobardía** nf cowardice.

cobertizo [koβerˈtiθo] nm shelter.

cobertor [koβerˈtor] nm bedspread.

cobertura [koβerˈtura] nf cover.

cobija [koˈβixa] nf roof; **cobijar** vt (cubrir) to cover; (abrigar) to shelter.

cobra [ˈkoβra] nf cobra.

cobrador [koβraˈðor] nm (de autobús) conductor; (de impuestos, gas) collector.

cobrar [koˈβrar] vt (cheque) to cash; (sueldo) to collect, draw; (objeto) to recover; (precio) to charge; (deuda) to collect // vi to draw one's pay; ~se vr to recover, get well; **cóbrese al entregar** cash on delivery (COD).

cobre [ˈkoβre] nm copper; ~s nmpl brass instruments.

cobro [ˈkoβro] nm recovery; (paga) payment.

cocaína [kokaˈina] nf cocaine.

cocción [kokˈθjon] nf cooking.

cocear [koθeˈar] vi to kick.

cocer [koˈθer] vt, vi to cook; (en agua) to boil; (en horno) to bake; ~se vr to suffer intensely.

cocido [koˈθiðo] nm stew.

cocina [koˈθina] nf kitchen; (aparato) cooker, stove; (acto) cookery; **cocinar** vt, vi to cook.

cocinero, a [koθiˈnero, a] nm/f cook.

coco [ˈkoko] nm (árbol) coconut palm; (fruto) coconut.

cocodrilo [kokoˈðrilo] nm crocodile.

coche [ˈkotʃe] nm car, motorcar; (de tren, de caballos) coach, carriage; (fúnebre) hearse; (para niños) pram; ~ **celular** Black Maria, prison van.

coche-cama [ˈkotʃekama] (pl **coches-camas**) nm sleeping car, sleeper.

cochera [koˈtʃera] nf garage.

cochero [koˈtʃero] nm coachman.

cochino, a [koˈtʃino, a] a filthy, dirty // nm pig.

codazo [koˈðaθo] nm jab, poke (with the elbow).

codear [koðeˈar] vi to elbow, jostle;

~se *vr*: ~se con to rub shoulders with.

códice [ˈkoðiθe] *nm* manuscript, codex.

codicia [koˈðiθja] *nf* greed; (*fig*) lust; **codiciar** *vt* to covet; **codicioso, a** *a* covetous.

código [ˈkoðixo] *nm* code; ~ **civil** common law.

codillo [koˈðiʎo] *nm* (*zool*) knee; (*tec*) elbow (joint).

codo [ˈkoðo] *nm* (*anat, de tubo*) elbow; (*zool*) knee.

codorniz [koðorˈniθ] *nf* quail.

coerción [koerˈθjon] *nf* coercion.

coetáneo, a [koeˈtaneo, a] *a* contemporary.

coexistencia [koeksisˈtenθja] *nf* coexistence; **coexistir** *vi* to coexist.

cofradía [kofraˈðia] *nf* brotherhood, fraternity.

cofre [ˈkofre] *nm* chest.

coger [koˈxer] *vt* (*gen*) to take (hold of); (*objeto caído*) to pick up; (*frutas*) to pick, harvest; (*resfriado, ladrón, pelota*) to catch // *vi*: ~ **por el buen camino** to take the right road; ~se *vr* to catch; (*robar*) to steal.

cogida [koˈxiða] *nf* gathering, harvesting; (*de peces*) catch.

cogote [koˈxote] *nm* back or nape of the neck.

cohabitar [koaβiˈtar] *vi* to live together, cohabit.

cohechar [koeˈtʃar] *vt* to bribe; **cohecho** *nm* (*acción*) bribery; (*soborno*) bribe.

coherente [koeˈrente] *a* coherent.

cohesión [koeˈsjon] *nf* cohesion.

cohete [koˈete] *nm* rocket.

cohibición [koiβiˈθjon] *nf* restraint, restriction.

cohibir [koiˈβir] *vt* to restrain, restrict.

coincidencia [koinθiˈðenθja] *nf* coincidence; (*acuerdo*) agreement.

coincidir [koinθiˈðir] *vi* (*en idea*) to coincide, agree; (*en lugar*) to coincide.

coito [ˈkoito] *nm* intercourse, coitus.

cojear [koxeˈar] *vi* (*persona*) to limp, hobble; (*mueble*) to wobble, rock.

cojera [koˈxera] *nf* lameness; (*andar cojo*) limp.

cojín [koˈxin] *nm* cushion; **cojinete** *nm* small cushion, pad; (*tec*) ball bearing.

cojo, a [ˈkoxo, a] *a* (*que no puede andar*) lame; (*manco*) crippled; (*mueble*) shaky // *nm/f* lame person; cripple.

col [kol] *nf* cabbage; ~ **de Bruselas** Brussels sprouts.

cola [ˈkola] *nf* (*gen*) tail; (*de gente*) queue; (*lugar*) end, last place; (*para pegar*) glue, gum; **hacer la** ~ to queue (up).

colaborador, a [kolaβoraˈðor, a] *nm/f* collaborator.

colaborar [kolaβoˈrar] *vi* to collaborate.

coladera [kolaˈðera] *nf* strainer.

coladura [kolaˈðura] *nf* (*filtración*) straining; (*residuo*) grounds *pl*, dregs *pl*.

colapso [koˈlapso] *nm* collapse; ~ **nervioso** nervous breakdown.

colar [koˈlar] *vt* (*líquido*) to strain off; (*ropa*) to bleach; (*metal*) to cast // *vi* to ooze, seep (through); ~se *vr* to slip in *or* past.

colateral [kolateˈral] *nm* collateral.

colcha [ˈkoltʃa] *nf* bedspread.

colchón [kolˈtʃon] *nm* mattress.

colear [koleˈar] *vi* to wag its tail.

colección [kolekˈθjon] *nf* collection; **coleccionista** *nm/f* collector.

colecta [koˈlekta] *nf* collection.

colectar [kolekˈtar] *vt* to collect.

colectivo, a [kolekˈtiβo, a] *a* collective joint.

colector [kolekˈtor] *nm* collector; (*sumidero*) sewer.

colega [koˈlexa] *nm/f* colleague.

colegio [koˈlexjo] *nm* (*gen*) college; (*escuela*) (private) school; (*de* *abogados etc*) association.

colegir [kole'xir] *vt* (*juntar, reunir*) to collect, gather; (*deducir*) to infer, conclude.

cólera ['kolera] *nf* (*ira*) anger; (*MED*) cholera.

colérico, a [ko'leriko, a] *a* angry, furious.

coleta [ko'leta] *nf* pigtail.

colgadero [kolxa'ðero] *nm* (*gancho*) hook; (*percha*) hanger.

colgadura [kolxa'ðura] *nf* hangings *pl*, drapery.

colgante [kol'ɣante] *a* hanging // *nm* drop earring.

colgar [kol'ɣar] *vt* to hang (up); (*ropa*) to hang (out); (*teléfono*) to hang up // *vi* to hang.

coliflor [koli'flor] *nf* cauliflower.

colilla [ko'liʎa] *nf* fag end, butt.

colina [ko'lina] *nf* hill.

colindante [kolin'dante] *a* adjacent, neighbouring.

colindar [kolin'dar] *vi* to adjoin, be adjacent.

colisión [koli'sjon] *nf* collision; (*choque*) crash.

colmado, a [kol'maðo, a] *a* abundant, copious; (*cuchara etc*) heaped.

colmar [kol'mar] *vt* to fill to the brim; (*fig*) to fulfil, realize.

colmena [kol'mena] *nf* beehive.

colmillo [kol'miʎo] *nm* (*diente*) eye tooth; (*de elefante*) tusk; (*de perro*) fang.

colmo ['kolmo] *nm* height, summit.

colocación [koloka'θjon] *nf* placing; (*empleo*) job, position; (*de mueble*) place, position.

colocar [kolo'kar] *vt* to place, put, position; (*poner en empleo*) to find a job for.

Colombia [ko'lombja] *nf* Colombia; **colombiano, a** *a, nm/f* Colombian.

colon ['kolon] *nm* colon.

colonia [ko'lonja] *nf* colony; (*de casas*) housing estate; (*agua de ~*) cologne.

colonización [koloniθa'θjon] *nf* colonization.

colonizador, a [koloniθa'ðor, a] *a* colonizing // *nm/f* colonist, settler.

colonizar [koloni'θar] *vt* to colonize.

coloquio [ko'lokjo] *nm* conversation; (*congreso*) conference.

color [ko'lor] *nm* colour.

colorado, a [kolo'raðo, a] *a* (*que tiene color*) coloured; (*rojo*) red.

colorar [kolo'rar] *vt* to colour; (*teñir*) to dye.

colorear [kolore'ar] *vt* to colour // *vi* to redden.

colorido [kolo'riðo] *nm* colouring.

colosal [kolo'sal] *a* colossal.

columbrar [kolum'brar] *vt* to glimpse, spy.

columna [ko'lumna] *nf* column; (*pilar*) pillar; (*apoyo*) support.

columpiar [kolum'pjar] *vt*, ~**se** *vr* to swing; **columpio** *nm* swing.

collar [ko'ʎar] *nm* necklace; (*de perro*) collar.

coma ['koma] *nf* comma // *nm* coma.

comadre [ko'maðre] *nf* (*partera*) midwife; (*madrina*) godmother; (*vecina*) neighbour; ~**ar** *vi* to gossip.

comandancia [koman'danθja] *nf* command.

comandante [koman'dante] *nm* commandant.

comandar [koman'dar] *vt* to command.

comarca [ko'marka] *nf* region.

comarcar [komar'kar] *vi*: ~ **con** to border on, be adjacent to.

combar [kom'bar] *vt* to bend, curve.

combate [kom'bate] *nm* fight; (*fig*) battle; **combatiente** *nm* combatant.

combatir [komba'tir] *vt* to fight, combat.

combinación [kombina'θjon] *nf* combination; (*QUÍMICA*) compound; (*bebida*) cocktail; (*plan*) scheme, setup.

combinar [kombi'nar] vt to combine.

combustible [kombus'tiβle] nm fuel.

combustión [kombus'tjon] nf combustion.

comedia [ko'meðja] nf comedy; (TEATRO) play, drama.

comediante [kome'ðjante] nm/f (comic) actor/actress.

comedido, a [kome'ðiðo, a] a moderate; (cortés) courteous.

comedirse [kome'ðirse] vr to behave moderately; (ser cortés) to be courteous.

comedor, a [kome'ðor, a] nm/f (persona) glutton // nm (habitación) dining room; (restaurante) restaurant; (cantina) canteen.

comentador, a [komenta'ðor, a] nm/f = **comentarista**.

comentar [komen'tar] vt to comment on; (fam) to discuss.

comentario [komen'tarjo] nm comment, remark; (literario) commentary; ~s nmpl gossip sg.

comentarista [komenta'rista] nm/f commentator.

comento [ko'mento] nm = **comentario**.

comenzar [komen'θar] vt, vi to begin, start, commence.

comer [ko'mer] vt (gen) to eat; (DAMAS, AJEDREZ) to take, capture // vi to eat; (almorzar) to have lunch; ~se vr to eat up.

comercial [komer'θjal] a commercial; (relativo al negocio) business cpd.

comerciante [komer'θjante] nm/f trader, merchant.

comerciar [komer'θjar] vi to trade, do business.

comercio [ko'merθjo] nm commerce; (tráfico) trade; (negocio) business; (fig) dealings pl.

comestible [komes'tiβle] a eatable, edible // nm foodstuff.

cometa [ko'meta] nm comet // nf kite.

cometer [kome'ter] vt to commit.

cometido [kome'tiðo] nm (misión) task, assignment; (deber) commitment.

comezón [kome'θon] nf itch, itching.

cómico, a ['komiko, a] a comic(al) // nm/f comedian; (de teatro) (comic) actor/actress.

comida [ko'miða] nf (alimento) food; (almuerzo, cena) meal; (de mediodía) lunch.

comienzo [ko'mjenθo] nm beginning, start.

comillas [ko'miʎas] nfpl inverted commas.

comisario [komi'sarjo] nm commissary; (POL) commissar.

comisión [komi'sjon] nf commission.

comité [komi'te] nm committee.

como ['komo] ad as; (tal ~) like; (aproximadamente) about, approximately // conj (ya que, puesto que) as, since; (en seguida que) as soon as; ¡~ no! of course!; ~ no lo haga hoy unless he does it today; ~ si as if; es tan alto ~ ancho it is as high as it is wide.

cómo ['komo] ad how?, why? // excl what?, I beg your pardon? // nm: el ~ y el porqué the whys and wherefores.

comodidad [komoði'ðað] nf comfort; venga a su ~ come at your convenience.

comodín [komo'ðin] nm joker.

cómodo, a ['komoðo, a] a comfortable; (práctico, de fácil uso) convenient.

compacto, a [kom'pakto, a] a compact.

compadecer [kompaðe'θer] vt to pity, be sorry for; ~se vr: ~se de to pity, be sorry for.

compadre [kom'paðre] nm (padrino) godfather; (amigo) friend, pal.

compañero, a [kompa'ɲero, a] *nm/f* companion; ~ **de clase** classmate.

compañía [kompa'ɲia] *nf* company.

comparación [kompara'θjon] *nf* comparison; **en ~ con** in comparison with.

comparar [kompa'rar] *vt* to compare.

comparativo, a [kompara'tiβo, a] *a* comparative.

comparecer [kompare'θer] *vi* to appear (in court).

compartimiento [komparti-'mjento] *nm* division; (*distribución*) distribution; (*FERRO*) compartment.

compartir [kompar'tir] *vt* to divide (up), share (out).

compás [kom'pas] *nm* (*MUS*) beat, rhythm; (*MAT*) compasses *pl*; (*NAUT*) compass.

compasión [kompa'sjon] *nf* compassion, pity.

compasivo, a [kompa'siβo, a] *a* compassionate.

compatibilidad [kompatiβili'ðað] *nf* compatibility.

compatible [kompa'tiβle] *a* compatible.

compatriota [kompa'trjota] *nm/f* compatriot.

compeler [kompe'ler] *vt* to compel.

compendiar [kompen'djar] *vt* to summarize; (*libro*) to abridge; **compendio** *nm* summary; abridgement.

compensación [kompensa'θjon] *nf* compensation.

compensar [kompen'sar] *vt* to compensate.

competencia [kompe'tenθja] *nf* (*incumbencia*) domain, field; (*aptitud, idoneidad*) competence; (*rivalidad*) competition.

competente [kompe'tente] *a* (*persona, jurado, tribunal*) competent; (*conveniente*) fit, suitable.

competición [kompeti'θjon] *nf* competition.

competir [kompe'tir] *vi* to compete.

compilar [kompi'lar] *vt* to compile.

complacencia [kompla'θenθja] *nf* (*placer*) pleasure; (*satisfacción*) satisfaction; (*buena voluntad*) willingness.

complacer [kompla'θer] *vt* to please; ~**se** *vr* to be pleased.

complaciente [kompla'θjente] *a* kind, obliging, helpful.

complejo, a [kom'plexo, a] *a, nm* complex.

complementario, a [komplemen'tarjo, a] *a* complementary.

completar [komple'tar] *vt* to complete.

completo, a [kom'pleto, a] *a* complete; (*perfecto*) perfect; (*lleno*) full // *nm* full complement.

complicar [kompli'kar] *vt* to complicate.

cómplice ['kompliθe] *nm/f* accomplice.

complot [kom'plot] *nm* plot; (*conspiración*) conspiracy.

componenda [kompo'nenda] *nf* compromise; (*pey*) shady deal.

componer [kompo'ner] *vt* to make up, put together; (*MUS, LITERATURA, IMPRENTA*) to compose; (*algo roto*) to mend, repair; (*adornar*) to adorn; (*arreglar*) to arrange; (*reconciliar*) to reconcile; ~**se** *vr*: ~**se de** to consist of.

comportamiento [komporta-'mjento] *nm* behaviour, conduct.

comportarse [kompor'tarse] *vr* to behave.

composición [komposi'θjon] *nf* composition.

compositor, a [komposi'tor, a] *nm/f* composer.

compostura [kompos'tura] *nf* (*reparación*) mending, repair; (*arreglo*) arrangement; (*acuerdo*) agreement; (*actitud*) composure.

compra ['kompra] *nf* purchase; ~**s** *nfpl* purchases, shopping *sg*.

comprador, a [kompra'ðor, a] *nm/f* buyer, purchaser.

comprar [kom'prar] *vt* to buy, purchase.

comprender [kompren'der] *vt* to understand; (*incluir*) to comprise, include.

comprensión [kompren'sjon] *nf* understanding; (*totalidad*) comprehensiveness.

comprensivo, a [kompren'siβo, a] *a* comprehensive; (*actitud*) understanding.

compresión [kompre'sjon] *nf* compression.

comprimir [kompri'mir] *vt* to compress; (*fig*) to control.

comprobante [kompro'βante] *a* verifying, supporting // *nm* receipt.

comprobar [kompro'βar] *vt* to check, (*probar*) to prove; (*TEC*) to check, test.

comprometer [komprome'ter] *vt* to compromise; (*exponer*) to endanger; ~se *vr* to compromise o.s.; (*involucrarse*) to get involved.

compromiso [kompro'miso] *nm* (*obligación*) obligation; (*cometido*) commitment; (*convenio*) agreement; (*dificultad*) awkward situation.

compuesto, a [kom'pwesto, a] *a:* ~ **de** composed of, made up of // *nm* compound.

compulsión [kompul'sjon] *nf* compulsion.

compunción [kompun'θjon] *nf* compunction, regret.

computador [komputa'ðor] *nm*, **computadora** [komputa'ðora] *nf* computer.

comulgar [komul'xar] *vi* to receive communion.

común [ko'mun] *a* common // *nm:* **el** ~ the community.

comunicación [komunika'θjon] *nf* communication; (*ponencia*) report.

comunicar [komuni'kar] *vt, vi,* ~se *vr* to communicate; **comunicativo, a** *a* communicative.

comunidad [komuni'ðað] *nf* community.

comunión [komu'njon] *nf* communion.

comunismo [komu'nismo] *nm* communism; **comunista** *a, nm/f* communist.

con [kon] *prep* with; (*a pesar de*) in spite of; **- que** so, and so, ~ **apretar el botón** by pressing the button.

concebir [konθe'βir] *vt, vi* to conceive.

conceder [konθe'ðer] *vt* to concede.

concejo [kon'θexo] *nm* council.

concentración [konθentra'θjon] *nf* concentration.

concentrar [konθen'trar] *vt,* ~se *vr* to concentrate.

concepción [konθep'θjon] *nf* conception.

concepto [kon'θepto] *nm* concept.

concertar [konθer'tar] *vt* (*MUS*) to harmonize; (*acordar*: precio) to agree, (. *tratado*) to conclude; (*trato*) to arrange, fix up; (*combinar*: esfuerzos) to coordinate; (*reconciliar*: personas) to reconcile // *vi* to harmonize, be in tune.

concesión [konθe'sjon] *nf* concession.

conciencia [kon'θjenθja] *nf* conscience.

concienzudo, a [konθjen'θuðo, a] *a* conscientious.

concierto [kon'θjerto] *nm* concert; (*obra*) concerto.

conciliar [konθi'ljar] *vt* to reconcile.

concilio [kon'θiljo] *nm* council.

conciso, a [kon'θiso, a] *a* concise.

concluir [konklu'ir] *vt, vi,* ~se *vr* to conclude.

conclusión [konklu'sjon] *nf* conclusion.

concordar [konkor'ðar] *vt* to reconcile // *vi* to agree, tally; **concordia** *nf* concord, harmony.

concretar [konkre'tar] *vt* to make

concrete, make more specific; ~**se** *vr* to become more definite.

concreto, a [kon'kreto, a] *a, nm* (*AM*) concrete; **en ~** (*en resumen*) to sum up; (*especificamente*) specifically; **no hay nada en ~** there's nothing definite.

concurrir [konku'rrir] *vi* (*juntarse: ríos*) to meet, come together; (: *personas*) to gather, meet; (*ponerse de acuerdo, coincidir*) to concur; (*competir*) to compete; (*contribuir*) to contribute.

concurso [kon'kurso] *nm* (*de público*) crowd; (*ESCOL, DEPORTE, competencia*) competition; (*coincidencia*) coincidence; (*ayuda*) help, cooperation.

concusión [konku'sjon] *nf* concussion.

concha ['kontʃa] *nf* shell.

conde ['konde] *nm* count.

condecorar [kondeko'rar] *vt* to decorate.

condena [kon'dena] *nf* sentence.

condenación [kondena'θjon] *nf* (*gen*) condemnation; (*condena*) sentence; (*REL*) damnation.

condenar [konde'nar] *vt* to condemn; (*JUR*) to convict; ~**se** *vr* (*JUR*) to confess (one's guilt); (*REL*) to be damned.

condensar [konden'sar] *vt* to condense.

condescender [kondesθen'der] *vi* to acquiesce, comply.

condición [kondi'θjon] *nf* condition; **condicionado, a** *a* conditioned.

condicional [kondiθjo'nal] *a* conditional.

condimento [kondi'mento] *nm* seasoning.

condolerse [kondo'lerse] *vr* to sympathize.

conducir [kondu'θir] *vt* to take, convey; (*AUTO*) to drive // *vi* to drive; (*fig*) to lead; ~**se** *vr* to behave.

conducta [kon'dukta] *nf* conduct, behaviour.

conducto [kon'dukto] *nm* pipe, tube; (*fig*) channel.

conductor, a [konduk'tor, a] *a* leading, guiding // *nm* (*FÍSICA*) conductor; (*de vehículo*) driver.

conduje *etc vb ver* **conducir.**

conduzco *etc vb ver* **conducir.**

conectar [konek'tar] *vt* to connect (up), plug in.

conejo [ko'nexo] *nm* rabbit.

conexión [konek'sjon] *nf* connection.

confeccionar [konfekθjo'nar] *vt* to make (up).

confederación [konfeðera'θjon] *nf* confederation.

conferencia [konfe'renθja] *nf* conference; (*lección*) lecture; (*TELEC*) call.

conferir [konfe'rir] *vt* to award.

confesar [konfe'sar] *vt* to confess, admit.

confesión [konfe'sjon] *nf* confession.

confesionario [konfesjo'narjo] *nm* confessional.

confiado, a [kon'fjaðo, a] *a* (*crédulo*) trusting; (*presumido*) confident; (*pey*) conceited, vain.

confianza [kon'fjanθa] *nf* trust; (*aliento, confidencia*) confidence; (*familiaridad*) intimacy, familiarity; (*pey*) vanity, conceit.

confiar [kon'fjar] *vt* to entrust // *vi* to trust.

confidencia [konfi'ðenθja] *nf* confidence.

confidencial [konfiðen'θjal] *a* confidential.

confidente [konfi'ðente] *nm/f* confidant/e; (*policial*) informer.

configurar [konfixu'rar] *vt* to shape, form.

confín [kon'fin] *nm* limit; ~**es** *nmpl* edges.

confinar [konfi'nar] *vi* to confine; (*desterrar*) to banish.

confirmar [konfir'mar] *vt* to confirm.

confiscar [konfis'kar] vt to confiscate.

confitería [konfite'ria] nf confectionery; (*tienda*) confectioner's (shop).

confitura [konfi'tura] nf jam.

conflicto [kon'flikto] nm conflict; (*fig*) clash.

conformar [konfor'mar] vt to shape, fashion // vi to agree; ~se con to conform; (*resignarse*) to resign o.s.

conforme [kon'forme] a (*gen*) alike, similar; (*de acuerdo*) agreed, in agreement; (*resignado*) resigned // ad as // excl agreed! // nm agreement // prep: ~ a in accordance with.

conformidad [konformi'ðað] nf (*semejanza*) similarity; (*acuerdo*) agreement; (*resignación*) resignation.

confortable [konfor'taßle] a comfortable.

confortar [konfor'tar] vt to comfort.

confrontar [konfron'tar] vt to confront; (*dos personas*) to bring face to face with; (*cotejar*) to compare // vi to border.

confundir [konfun'dir] vt to blur; (*equivocar*) to mistake, confuse; (*mezclar*) to mix; (*turbar*) to confuse; ~se vr to become blurred; (*turbarse*) to get confused; (*equivocarse*) to make a mistake; (*mezclarse*) to mix.

confusión [konfu'sjon] nf confusion.

confuso, a [kon'fuso, a] a confused.

congelar [konxe'lar] vt to freeze; ~se vr (*sangre, grasa*) to congeal.

congeniar [konxe'njar] vi to get on (well).

conglomeración [konglomera-

congoja [kon'goxa] nf distress, grief.

congratular [kongratu'lar] vt to congratulate.

congregación [kongreɣa'θjon] nf congregation.

congresista [kongre'sista] nm/f delegate, congressman/woman.

congreso [kon'greso] nm congress.

conjetura [konxe'tura] nf guess; **conjeturar** vt to guess.

conjugar [konxu'xar] vt to combine, fit together; (*un verbo*) to conjugate.

conjunción [konxun'θjon] nf conjunction.

conjunto, a [kon'xunto, a] a joint, united // nm whole; (*MUS*) group; **en** ~ as a whole.

conmemoración [konmemora-'θjon] nf commemoration.

conmemorar [konmemo'rar] vt to commemorate.

conmigo [kon'mixo] pron with me; with myself.

conminar [konmi'nar] vt to threaten.

conmiseración [konmisera'θjon] nf pity, commiseration.

conmoción [konmo'θjon] nf shock; (*MED*) concussion; (*fig*) upheaval.

conmovedor, a [konmoße'ðor, a] a touching, moving; (*impresionante*) exciting.

conmover [konmo'ßer] vt to shake, disturb; (*fig*) to move.

conmutador [konmuta'ðor] nm switch.

conocedor, a [konoθe'ðor, a] a expert, knowledgeable // nm/f expert.

conocer [kono'θer] vt (*gen*) to know; (*por primera vez*) to meet; **~ se** to get to know; (*entender*) to know about; (*reconocer*) to know, recognize; ~se vr (*una persona*) to know o.s.; (*dos personas*) to (get to) know each other.

conocido, a [kono'θiðo, a] a (well)-known // nm/f acquaintance.

conocimiento [konoθi'mjento] nm knowledge; (*MED*) consciousness; ~s nmpl (*personas*) acquaintances; (*ciencia*) knowledge sg.

conozco etc vb ver **conocer.**

conque ['konke] conj and so, so then.

conquista [kon'kista] nf conquest.

conquistador, a [konkista'ðor, a] a conquering // nm conqueror.

conquistar [konkis'tar] vt to conquer.

consagrar [konsa'xrar] vt (REL) to consecrate; (fig) to devote.

consciente [kons'θjente] a conscious.

consecución [konseku'θjon] nf acquisition; (de fin) attainment.

consecuencia [konse'kwenθja] nf consequence, outcome; (firmeza) consistency.

consecuente [konse'kwente] a consistent.

consecutivo, a [konseku'tiβo, a] a consecutive.

conseguir [konse'xir] vt to get, obtain; (sus fines) to attain.

consejero, a [konse'xero, a] nm/f adviser, consultant; (POL) councillor.

consejo [kon'sexo] nm advice; (POL) council.

consenso [kon'senso] nm consensus.

consentimiento [konsenti-'mjento] nm consent.

consentir [konsen'tir] vt (permitir, tolerar) to consent to; (mimar) to pamper, spoil; (admitir) to admit // vi to agree, consent.

conserje [kon'serxe] nm caretaker; (portero) porter.

conserva [kon'serβa] nf (acción) preserving; (alimento) preserved food.

conservación [konserβa'θjon] nf conservation; (de alimentos, vida) preservation.

conservador, a [konserβa'ðor, a] a preservative; (POL) conservative // nm/f conservative; (de museo) keeper.

conservar [konser'βar] vt to conserve, keep; (alimentos, vida) to preserve; ~**se** vr to survive.

considerable [konsiðe'raβle] a considerable.

consideración [konsiðera'θjon] nf consideration; (estimación) respect.

considerado, a [konsiðe'raðo, a] a (prudente, respetado) considerate; (respetado) respected.

considerar [konsiðe'rar] vt to consider.

consigna [kon'sixna] nf (orden) consign, instruction; (para equipajes) left-luggage office.

consigo [kon'sixo] pron (m) with him; (f) with her; (Vd.) with you; (reflexivo) with o.s.

consiguiente [konsi'xjente] a consequent; **por** ~ and so, therefore, consequently.

consistente [konsis'tente] a consistent; (sólido) solid, firm; (válido) sound.

consistir [konsis'tir] vi: ~ **en** (componerse de) to consist of; (ser resultado de) to be due to.

consolación [konsola'θjon] nf consolation.

consolar [konso'lar] vt to console.

consolidar [konsoli'ðar] vt to consolidate.

consomé [konso'me] nm consommé, clear soup.

consonante [konso'nante] a consonant, harmonious // nf consonant.

conspicuo, a [kons'pikwo, a] a conspicuous.

conspiración [konspira'θjon] nf conspiracy.

conspirador, a [konspira'ðor, a] nm/f conspirator.

conspirar [konspi'rar] vi to conspire.

constante [kons'tante] a constant.

constar [kons'tar] vi (evidenciarse) to be clear or evident; ~ **de** to consist of.

consternación [konsterna'θjon] nf consternation.

constipación [konstipa'θjon] nf = **constipado.**

constipado, a [konsti'paðo, a] a: **estar ~** to have a cold // nm cold.

constitución [konstitu'θjon] nf constitution; **constitucional** a constitutional.

constituir [konstitu'ir] vt (formar, componer) to constitute, make up; (fundar, erigir, ordenar) to constitute, establish.

constitutivo, a [konstitu'tiβo, a] a constitutive, constituent.

constituyente [konstitu'jente] a constituent.

constreñir [konstre'pir] vt (obligar) to compel, oblige; (restringir) to restrict.

construcción [konstruk'θjon] nf construction, building.

constructor, a [konstruk'tor, a] nm/f builder.

construir [konstru'ir] vt to build, construct.

consuelo [kon'swelo] nm consolation, solace.

cónsul ['konsul] nm consul; **consulado** nm consulate.

consulta [kon'sulta] nf consultation.

consultar [konsul'tar] vt to consult.

consultorio [konsul'torjo] nm information bureau; (MED) surgery.

consumar [konsu'mar] vt to complete, carry out; (crimen) to commit; (matrimonio) to consummate.

consumición [konsumi'θjon] nf consumption; (bebida) drink; (en restaurante) meal.

consumidor, a [konsumi'ðor, a] nm/f consumer.

consumir [konsu'mir] vt to consume; ~**se** vr to be consumed; (persona) to waste away.

consumo [kon'sumo] nm, **consunción** [konsun'θjon] nf consumption.

contabilidad [kontaβili'ðað] nf accounting, book-keeping; (profesión) accountancy.

contacto [kon'takto] nm contact.

contado, a [kon'taðo, a] a: ~**s** (escasos) numbered, scarce, few // nm: **al ~** for cash.

contador [konta'ðor] nm (aparato) meter; (COM) accountant; (de café) counter.

contagiar [konta'xjar] vt (enfermedad) to pass on, transmit; (persona) to infect; ~**se** vr to become infected.

contagio [kon'taxjo] nm infection.

contagioso, a [konta'xjoso, a] a infectious; (fig) catching.

contaminación [kontamina'θjon] nf contamination.

contaminar [kontami'nar] vt to contaminate.

contar [kon'tar] vt (páginas, dinero) to count; (anécdota) to tell // vi to count; ~ **con** to rely on, count on.

contemplación [kontempla'θjon] nf contemplation.

contemplar [kontem'plar] vt to contemplate; (mirar) to look at.

contemporáneo, a [kontempo'raneo, a] a, nm/f contemporary.

contender [konten'der] vi (gen) to contend; (en un concurso) to compete.

contener [konte'ner] vt to contain, hold; (retener) to hold back, contain.

contenido, a [konte'niðo, a] a (moderado) restrained; (reprimido) suppressed // nm contents pl, content.

contentar [konten'tar] vt (satisfacer) to satisfy; (complacer) to please; ~**se** vr to be satisfied.

contento, a [kon'tento, a] a (contented, content; (alegre) pleased; (feliz) happy // nm contentment; (felicidad) happiness.

contestación [kontesta'θjon] nf answer, reply.

contestar [kontes'tar] vt to answer, reply; (JUR) to corroborate, confirm.

contigo [kon'tixo] pron with you.

contiguo, a [kon'tixwo, a] a (de al

lado) next; (*vecino*) adjacent, adjoining.

continental [kontinen'tal] *a* continental.

continente [konti'nente] *a, nm* continent.

contingencia [kontin'xenθja] *nf* contingency; (*riesgo*) risk; **contingente** *a, nm* contingent.

continuación [kontinwa'θjon] *nf* continuation; **a ~** then, next.

continuar [konti'nwar] *vt* to continue, go on with // *vi* to continue, go on.

continuidad [kontinwi'ðað] *nf* continuity.

continuo, a [kon'tinwo, a] *a* (*sin interrupción*) continuous; (*acción perseverante*) continual.

contorno [kon'torno] *nm* outline; (*GEO*) contour; **~s** *nmpl* neighbourhood *sg*, environs.

contorsión [kontor'sjon] *nf* contortion.

contra ['kontra] *prep, ad* against // *nm* con.

contraataque [kontraa'take] *nm* counter-attack.

contrabajo [kontra'βaxo] *nm* double bass.

contrabandista [kontraβan'dista] *nm/f* smuggler.

contrabando [kontra'βando] *nm* (*acción*) smuggling; (*mercancías*) contraband.

contracción [kontrak'θjon] *nf* contraction; (*encogimiento*) shrinkage.

contracepción [kontraθep'θjon] *nf* contraception.

contraceptivo [kontraθep'tiβo] *nm* contraceptive.

contradecir [kontraðe'θir] *vt* to contradict.

contradicción [kontraðik'θjon] *nf* contradiction.

contradictorio, a [kontraðik'torjo, a] *a* contradictory.

contraer [kontra'er] *vt* to contract; (*encoger*) to shrink; (*limitar*) to

restrict; **~se** *vr* to contract; to shrink; (*limitarse*) to limit o.s.

contragolpe [kontra'xolpe] *nm* backlash.

contrahacer [kontraa'θer] *vt* to copy, imitate; (*falsificar*) to forge.

contramaestre [kontrama'estre] *nm* foreman.

contrapelo [kontra'pelo]: **a ~** *ad* the wrong way.

contrapesar [kontrape'sar] *vt* to counterbalance; (*fig*) to offset.

contrariar [kontra'rjar] *vt* (*oponerse*) to oppose; (*poner obstáculo*) to impede; (*enfadar*) to vex.

contrariedad [kontrarje'ðað] *nf* (*oposición*) opposition; (*obstáculo*) obstacle, setback; (*disgusto*) vexation, annoyance.

contrario, a [kon'trarjo, a] *a* contrary; (*de persona*) opposed; (*sentido, lado*) opposite // *nm/f* enemy, adversary; (*DEPORTE*) opponent; **de lo ~** otherwise.

contrarrestar [kontrarres'tar] *vt* to counteract; (*pelota*) to return.

contrastar [kontras'tar] *vt* to resist // *vi* to contrast.

contraste [kon'traste] *nm* contrast.

contratante [kontra'tante] *nm/f* contractor.

contratar [kontra'tar] *vt* (*firmar un acuerdo para*) to contract for; (*empleados, obreros*) to hire, engage; **~se** *vr* to sign on.

contratiempo [kontra'tjempo] *nm* setback.

contratista [kontra'tista] *nm/f* contractor.

contrato [kon'trato] *nm* contract.

contravención [kontraβen'θjon] *nf* contravention, violation.

contravenir [kontraβe'nir] *vi*: **~ a** to contravene, violate.

contraventana [kontraβen'tana] *nf* shutter.

contribución [kontriβu'θjon] *nf* (*municipal etc*) tax; (*ayuda*) contribution.

contribuir [kontriβu'ir] *vt, vi* to

contribute; (COM) to pay (in taxes).

contribuyente [kontriβu'jente] nm/f (COM) taxpayer; (que ayuda) contributor.

control [kon'trol] nm control; (inspección) inspection, check; ~ar vt to control; to inspect, check.

controversia [kontro'βersja] nf controversy.

convalecencia [konβale'θenθja] nf convalescence.

convalecer [konβale'θer] vi to convalesce, get better.

convaleciente [konβale'θjente] a, nm/f convalescent.

convencer [konβen'θer] vt to convince; (persuadir) to persuade.

convencimiento [konβenθi-'mjento] nm convincing; (persuasión) persuasion; (certidumbre) conviction.

convención [konβen'θjon] nf convention.

convencional [konβenθjo'nal] a conventional.

convenido, a [konβe'niðo, a] a agreed.

conveniencia [konβe'njenθja] nf suitability; (conformidad) agreement; (utilidad, provecho) usefulness; ~s nfpl conventions; (COM) property sg.

conveniente [konβe'njente] a suitable; (útil) useful.

convenio [kon'βenjo] nm agreement, treaty.

convenir [konβe'nir] vi (estar de acuerdo) to agree, (ser conveniente) to suit, be suitable; ~se vr to agree.

convento [kon'βento] nm monastery; (de monjas) convent.

converger [konβer'xer], **convergir** [konβer'xir] vi to converge.

conversación [konβersa'θjon] nf conversation.

conversar [konβer'sar] vi to talk, converse.

conversión [konβer'sjon] nf conversion.

convertir [konβer'tir] vt to convert.

convicción [konβik'θjon] nf conviction.

convicto, a [kon'βikto, a] a convicted, found guilty; (condenado) condemned.

convidado, a [konβi'ðaðo, a] nm/f guest.

convidar [konβi'ðar] vt to invite.

convincente [konβin'θente] a convincing.

convite [kon'βite] nm invitation; (banquete) banquet.

convivencia [konβi'βenθja] nf coexistence, living together.

convocar [konβo'kar] vt to summon, call (together).

convulsión [konβul'sjon] nf convulsion.

conyugal [konju'sal] a conjugal.

coñac [ko'nak] nm cognac, brandy.

cooperación [koopera'θjon] nf cooperation.

cooperar [koope'rar] vi to cooperate.

cooperativo, a [koopera'tiβo, a] a cooperative // nf cooperative.

coordinación [koorðina'θjon] nf coordination.

coordinar [koorði'nar] vt to coordinate.

copa [kopa] nf cup; (vaso) glass; (de árbol) top; (de sombrero) crown; ~s nfpl (NAIPES) ~ hearts.

copia [kopja] nf copy; **copiar** vt to copy.

copioso, a [ko'pjoso, a] a copious, plentiful.

copita [ko'pita] nf (small) glass; (GOLF) tee.

copla ['kopla] nf verse; (canción) (popular) song.

coqueta [ko'keta] a flirtatious, coquettish; **coquetear** vi to flirt.

coraje [ko'raxe] nm courage; (ánimo) spirit; (ira) anger.

coral [ko'ral] a choral // nf choir.

corazón [kora'θon] nm heart.

corazonada [koraθo'naða] nf

impulse; (*presentimiento*) presentiment, hunch.

corbata [kor'βata] *nf* tie.

corcovado, a [korko'βaðo, a] *a* hunchbacked.

corchete [kor'tʃete] *nm* catch, clasp.

corcho ['kortʃo] *nm* cork; (*PESCA*) float.

cordel [kor'ðel] *nm* cord, line.

cordero [kor'ðero] *nm* lamb.

cordial [kor'ðjal] *a* cordial; **~idad** *nf* warmth, cordiality.

cordillera [korði'ʎera] *nf* range, chain (of mountains).

Córdoba ['korðoβa] *n* Cordoba; **cordobés, esa** *a* *of* or *from* Cordoba.

cordón [kor'ðon] *nm* (*cuerda*) cord, string; (*de zapatos*) lace; (*policía*) cordon.

corneta [kor'neta] *nf* bugle.

coro ['koro] *nm* chorus; (*conjunto de cantores*) choir.

corolario [koro'larjo] *nm* corollary.

corona [ko'rona] *nf* crown; (*de flores*) garland; **~ción** *nf* coronation; **coronar** *vt* to crown.

coronel [koro'nel] *nm* colonel.

coronilla [koro'niʎa] *nf* crown (of the head).

corporación [korpora'θjon] *nf* corporation.

corporal [korpo'ral] *a* corporal.

corpulento, a [korpu'lento] *a* (*árbol*) stout; (*persona*) well-built.

corral [ko'rral] *nm* farmyard; **~illo** *nm* playpen.

correa [ko'rrea] *nf* strap; (*cinturón*) belt.

corrección [korrek'θjon] *nf* correction; (*reprensión*) rebuke; **correccional** *nm* reformatory.

correcto, a [ko'rrekto, a] *a* correct; (*persona*) well-mannered.

corredor, a [korre'ðor, a] *a* running; (*rápido*) fast // *nm* (*COM*) agent, broker; (*pasillo*) corridor, passage; (*DEPORTE*) runner.

corregir [korre'xir] *vt* (*error*) to

correct; (*amonestar, reprender*) to rebuke, reprimand; **~se** *vr* to reform.

correo [ko'rreo] *nm* post, mail; (*persona*) courier; (*cartero*) postman; **C~** Post Office; **~ aéreo** airmail.

correr [ko'rrer] *vt* to run; (*viajar*) to cover, travel; (*cortinas*) to draw; (*cerrojo*) to shoot // *vi* to run; (*líquido*) to run, flow; (*moneda*) to pass, be valid; **~se** *vr* to slide, move; (*colores*) to run.

correspondencia [korrespon'denθja] *nf* correspondence; (*FERRO*) connection.

corresponder [korrespon'der] *vi* to correspond; (*convenir*) to be suitable; (*pertenecer*) to belong; (*tocar*) to concern; **~se** *vr* (*por escrito*) to correspond; (*amarse*) to have mutual affection.

correspondiente [korrespon'djente] *a* corresponding // *nm* correspondent.

corrido, a [ko'rriðo, a] *a* (*avergonzado*) abashed; (*fluido*) fluent // *nf* run, dash; (*de toros*) bullfight; **3 noches ~as** 3 nights running; **un kilo ~** a good kilo.

corriente [ko'rrjente] *a* (*agua*) running; (*fig*) flowing; (*dinero etc*) current; (*común*) ordinary, normal // *nf* current // *nm* current month.

corrillo [ko'rriʎo] *nm* huddle, clique.

corro ['korro] *nm* ring, circle (of people).

corroborar [korroβo'rar] *vt* to corroborate.

corroer [korro'er] *vt* to corrode; (*GEO*) to erode.

corromper [korrom'per] *vt* (*madera*) to rot; (*alimento*) to turn bad; (*fig*) to corrupt.

corrosivo, a [korro'siβo, a] *a* corrosive.

corrupción [korrup'θjon] *nf* rot, decay; (*fig*) corruption.

corsé [kor'se] *nm* corset.

cortado, a [kor'taðo, a] *a* (*con cuchillo*) cut; (*leche*) sour; (*confuso*) confused; (*desconcertado*) embarrassed; (*estilo*) abrupt // *nm* white coffee (with just a little milk).

cortador, a [korta'ðor, a] *a* cutting // *nf* cutter, slicer.

cortadura [korta'ðura] *nf* cut.

cortar [kor'tar] *vt* to cut; (*el agua*) to cut off; (*un pasaje*) to cut out // *vi* to cut; ~**se** *vr* (*turbarse*) to become embarrassed; (*leche*) to turn, curdle; ~**se el pelo** to have one's hair cut.

corte ['korte] *nm* cut, cutting; (*filo*) edge; (*de tela*) piece, length; **las C~s** the Spanish Parliament.

cortedad [korte'ðað] *nf* shortness; (*fig*) bashfulness, timidity.

cortejar [korte'xar] *vt* to court.

cortejo [kor'texo] *nm* entourage; ~ **fúnebre** funeral procession.

cortés [kor'tes] *a* courteous, polite.

cortesía [korte'sia] *nf* courtesy.

corteza [kor'teθa] *nf* (*de árbol*) bark, (*de pan*) crust.

cortina [kor'tina] *nf* curtain.

corto, a ['korto, a] *a* (*breve*) short; (*tímido*) bashful; (*poco inteligente*) not very clever; (*de vista*) short-sighted; **estar ~ de fondos** to be short of funds.

corvo, a ['korβo, a] *a* curved.

cosa ['kosa] *nf* thing; (*asunto*) affair; ~ **de** about; **eso es ~ mía** that's my affair.

cosecha [ko'setʃa] *nf* (*AGR*) harvest; (*de vino*) vintage.

cosechar [kose'tʃar] *vt* to harvest, gather (in).

coser [ko'ser] *vt* to sew.

cosmético, a [kos'metiko, a] *a, nm* cosmetic.

cosquillas [kos'kiʎas] *nfpl*: **hacer ~** to tickle; **tener ~** to be ticklish.

cosquilloso, a [koski'ʎoso, a] *a* ticklish; (*fig*) touchy.

costa ['kosta] *nf* (*gasto*) cost; (*GEO*) coast.

costado [kos'taðo] *nm* side.

costal [kos'tal] *nm* sack.

costar [kos'tar] *vt* (*valer*) to cost; (*necesitar*) to require, need; **me cuesta hacer** I find it hard to do.

Costa Rica [kosta'rika] *nf* Costa Rica; **costarricense, costarriqueño, a** *a, nm/f* Costa Rican.

coste ['koste] *nm* = **costo**.

costilla [kos'tiʎa] *nf* rib; (*CULIN*) chop.

costo ['kosto] *nm* cost, price; ~ **de la vida** cost of living; ~**so, a** *a* costly, expensive.

costra ['kostra] *nf* crust; (*MED*) scab.

costumbre [kos'tumbre] *nf* custom, habit.

costura [kos'tura] *nf* sewing, needlework; (*de medias*) seam.

costurera [kostu'rera] *nf* dressmaker.

costurero [kostu'rero] *nm* sewing box or case.

cotejar [kote'xar] *vt* to compare.

cotejo [ko'texo] *nm* comparison.

cotidiano, a [koti'ðjano, a] *a* daily, day to day.

cotización [kotiθa'θjon] *nf* (*COM*) quotation, price; (*cuota*) dues *pl*.

cotizar [koti'θar] *vt* (*COM*) to quote, price; ~**se** *vr*: ~**se a** to sell at, fetch.

coto ['koto] *nm* (*terreno cercado*) enclosure; (*de caza*) reserve.

coyote [ko'jote] *nm* coyote, prairie wolf.

coyuntura [kojun'tura] *nf* (*ANAT*) joint; (*oportunidad*) opportunity.

cráneo ['kraneo] *nm* skull, cranium.

cráter ['krater] *nm* crater.

creación [krea'θjon] *nf* creation.

creador, a [krea'ðor, a] *a* creative // *nm/f* creator.

crear [kre'ar] *vt* to create, make.

crecer [kre'θer] *vi* (*niño*) to grow; (*precios*) to rise; (*días*) to lengthen; (*mar*) to swell.

crecido, a [kre'θiðo, a] *a* (*persona, planta*) full-grown; (*cantidad*) large; (*fig*) conceited.

creciente [kre'θjente] a *(persona)* growing; *(cantidad)* increasing; *(luna)* crescent // *nm* crescent // *nf* flood.

crecimiento [kreθi'mjento] *nm* growth; *(aumento)* increase.

credenciales [kreðen'θjales] *nfpl* credentials.

crédito ['kreðito] *nm* credit.

credo ['kreðo] *nm* creed.

crédulo, a ['kreðulo, a] a credulous.

creencia [kre'enθja] *nf* belief.

creer [kre'er] *vt, vi* to think, believe; ~**se** *vr* to believe o.s. (to be); ¡ya lo creo! I should think so!

creíble [kre'iβle] a credible, believable.

crema ['krema] *nf* cream; *(de huevo)* custard.

cremallera [krema'ʎera] *nf* zip (fastener).

crepúsculo [kre'puskulo] *nm* twilight, dusk.

crespón [kres'pon] *nm* crêpe.

creta ['kreta] *nf* chalk.

creyente [kre'jente] *nm/f* believer.

creyó *etc vb ver* **creer**.

cría ['kria] *nf (de animales)* rearing, breeding; *(animal)* baby animal; *(niño)* child.

criadero [kria'ðero] *nm* nursery; *(ZOOL)* breeding place.

criado, a [kri'aðo, a] a bred, reared // *nm* servant // *nf* servant, maid; **mal/bien** ~ badly/well brought up.

criador [kria'ðor] *nm* breeder.

crianza [kri'anθa] *nf* rearing, breeding; *(fig)* breeding.

criar [kri'ar] *vt* to suckle, feed; *(educar)* to bring up; *(producir)* to grow, produce; *(animales)* to breed.

criatura [kria'tura] *nf* creature; *(niño)* baby, (small) child.

criba ['kriβa] *nf* sieve; **cribar** *vt* to sieve.

crimen ['krimen] *nm* crime.

criminal [krimi'nal] a, *nm/f* criminal.

crin [krin] *nf (también* ~**es** *nfpl)* mane.

crisis ['krisis] *nf inv* crisis.

crispar [kris'par] *vt (músculo)* to make contract; *(nervios)* to set on edge.

cristal [kris'tal] *nm* crystal; *(de ventana)* glass, pane; *(lente)* lens; ~**ino, a** a crystalline; *(fig)* clear // *nm* lens of the eye; ~**izar** *vt, vi* to crystallize.

cristiandad [kristjan'daθ] *nf* Christianity.

cristianismo [kristja'nismo] *nm* Christianity.

cristiano, a [kris'tjano, a] a, *nm/f* Christian.

Cristo ['kristo] *nm (dios)* Christ; *(crucifijo)* crucifix.

criterio [kri'terjo] *nm* criterion; *(juicio)* judgement.

criticar [kriti'kar] *vt* to criticize.

crítico, a ['kritiko, a] a critical // *nm* critic // *nf* criticism.

cromo ['kromo] *nm* chrome.

crónico, a ['kroniko, a] a chronic // *nf* chronicle, account.

cronista [kro'nista] *nm/f* chronicler.

cruce ['kruθe] *nm* crossing; *(de carreteras)* crossroads.

crucificar [kruθifi'kar] *vt* to crucify.

crucifijo [kruθi'fixo] *nm* crucifix.

crucigrama [kruθi'xrama] *nm* crossword (puzzle).

crudo, a [kruðo, a] a raw; *(no maduro)* unripe; *(petróleo)* crude; *(rudo, cruel)* cruel.

cruel [krwel] a cruel.

crueldad [krwel'daθ] *nf* cruelty.

crujido [kru'xiðo] *nm* creak.

crujir [kru'xir] *vi (madera)* to creak; *(dedos)* to crack; *(dientes)* to grind; *(nieve, arena)* to crunch.

cruz [kruθ] *nf* cross; *(de moneda)* tails *sg.*

cruzado, a [kru'θaðo, a] a crossed // *nm* crusader // *nf* crusade.

cruzar [kru'θar] *vt* to cross; ~**se** *vr*

to cross; (*personas*) to pass each other.

cuaderno [kwa'ðerno] *nm* notebook; (*de escuela*) exercise book; (*NAUT*) logbook.

cuadra ['kwaðra] *nf* (*caballeriza*) stable; (*gran sala*) hall.

cuadrado, a [kwa'ðraðo, a] *a* square // *nm* (*MAT*) square; (*regla*) ruler.

cuadrar [kwa'ðrar] *vt* to square // *vi*: ~ **con** to square with, tally with; ~**se** *vr* (*soldado*) to stand to attention.

cuadrilla [kwa'ðriʎa] *nf* party, group.

cuadro ['kwaðro] *nm* square; (*de vidrio*) frame; (*PINTURA*) painting; (*TEATRO*) scene.

cuádruplo, a ['kwaðruplo, a], **cuádruple** ['kwaðruple] *a* quadruple.

cuajar [kwa'xar] *vt* to thicken; (*leche*) to curdle; (*sangre*) to congeal; (*adornar*) to adorn, ~**se** *vr* to curdle; to congeal; (*llenarse*) to fill up.

cual [kwal] *ad* like, as // *pron*: **el** ~ *etc* which; (*persona: sujeto*) who; (: *objeto*) whom // *a* such as; **cada** ~ each one; ~ **más**, ~ **menos** some more, some less, tal ~ just as it is.

cuál [kwal] *pron interr* which (one).

cualesquier(a) [kwales'kjer(a)] *pl de* cualquier(a).

cualidad [kwali'ðað] *nf* quality.

cualquiera [kwal'kjera], **cualquier** [kwal'kjer] *a any // pron* anybody, anyone; (*quienquiera*) whoever; **en cualquier parte** anywhere; ~ **que sea** whichever it is; (*persona*) whoever it is.

cuando ['kwando] *ad* when; (*aún si*) if, even if; *conj* (*puesto que*) since // *prep*: ~, when I'm a child...; ~ **no sea** even if it is not so; ~ **más** the more; ~ **menos** the less; ~ **no** if not, otherwise; **de** ~ **en** ~ from time to time.

cuándo ['kwando] *ad* when; ¿desde

~ ?, ¿de ~ acá? since when?

cuanto, a ['kwanto, a] *a* all that, as much as // *pron* all that (which), as much as; **llévate todo** ~ **quieras** take as much as you like; **en** ~ (*en seguida que*) as soon as; (*ya que*) since, inasmuch as; **en** ~ **profesor** as a teacher; **en** ~ **a** as for; ~ **más difícil sea** the more difficult it is; ~ **más hace** (**tanto**) **menos avanza** the more he does, the less he progresses; ~ **antes** as soon as possible; **unos** ~**s libros** a few books.

cuánto, a ['kwanto, a] *a what a lot of*; (*interr: sg*) how much?; (: *pl*) how many? // *pron, ad* how; (*interr: sg*) how much?; (: *pl*) how many?; ¡~**a gente!** what a lot of people!; ¿~ **cuesta?** how much does it cost?; ¿**a** ~ **s estamos?** what's the date?; **Señor no sé** ~**s** Mr. So-and-So.

cuarenta [kwa'renta] *num* forty.

cuarentena [kwaren'tena] *nf* quarantine.

cuartear [kwarte'ar] *vt* to quarter; (*dividir*) to divide up; ~**se** *vr* to crack, split.

cuartel [kwar'tel] *nm* (*de ciudad*) quarter, district; (*MIL*) barracks *pl*; ~ **general** headquarters *pl*.

cuarteto [kwar'teto] *nm* quartet.

cuarto, a ['kwarto, a] *a* a fourth // *nm* (*MAT*) quarter, fourth; (*habitación*) room // *nf* (*MAT*) quarter, fourth; (*palmo*) span; ~ **de baño** bathroom; ~ **de hora** quarter (of an) hour.

cuatro ['kwatro] *num* four.

cuba ['kuβa] *nf* cask, barrel; (*fig*) drunkard.

Cuba ['kuβa] *nf* Cuba; **cubano, a** *a*, *nm/f* Cuban.

cúbico, a ['kuβiko, a] *a* cubic.

cubierto, a [ku'βjerto, a] *pp de* **cubrir** // *a* covered, (*ARQ*) covered (*en la mesa*) place; ~**s** *nmpl* cutlery *sg* // *nf* cover, covering; (*neumático*) tyre; (*NAUT*) deck; **a** ~ **de** covered with or in.

cubo ['kuβo] *nm* cube; *(de madera)* bucket, tub; *(TEC)* drum.

cubrir [ku'βrir] *vt* to cover; **~se** *vr (cielo)* to become overcast.

cucaracha [kuka'ratʃa] *nf* cockroach.

cuchara [ku'tʃara] *nf* spoon; *(TEC)* scoop; **~da** *nf* spoonful; **~dita** *nf* teaspoonful.

cucharita [kutʃa'rita] *nf* teaspoon.

cucharón [kutʃa'ron] *nm* ladle.

cuchichear [kutʃitʃe'ar] *vi* to whisper.

cuchilla [ku'tʃiʎa] *nf* (large) knife; *(de arma blanca)* blade.

cuchillo [ku'tʃiʎo] *nm* knife.

cuello ['kweʎo] *nm (ANAT)* neck; *(de vestido, camisa)* collar.

cuenca ['kweŋka] *nf (escudilla)* hollow; *(ANAT)* eye socket; *(GEO)* bowl, deep valley.

cuenta *etc vb ver* **contar** // ['kwenta] *nf (cálculo)* count, counting; *(en café, restaurante)* bill; *(COM)* account; *(de collar)* bead; *(fig)* account; **a fin de ~s** in the end; **caer en la ~** to catch on; **darse ~ de** to realize; **tener en ~** to bear in mind; **echar ~s** to take stock; **~ corriente/de ahorros** current/savings account.

cuento *etc vb ver* **contar** // ['kwento] *nm* story.

cuerdo, a ['kwerðo, a] *a* sane; *(prudente)* wise, sensible // *nf* rope; *(hilo)* string; *(de reloj)* spring; **dar ~a a un reloj** to wind up a clock.

cuerno ['kwerno] *nm* horn.

cuero ['kwero] *nm (ZOOL)* skin, hide; *(TEC)* leather; **en ~s** stark naked; **~ cabelludo** scalp.

cuerpo ['kwerpo] *nm* body.

cuesta ['kwesta] *nf* slope; *(en camino etc)* hill; **~ arriba/abajo** uphill/downhill; **a ~s** on one's back.

cuestión [kwes'tjon] *nf* matter, question, issue; *(riña)* quarrel, dispute.

cuesto *etc vb ver* **costar.**

cueva ['kweβa] *nf* cave; *(bodega)* cellar.

cuidado [kwi'ðaðo] *nm* care, carefulness; *(preocupación)* care, worry; *excl* careful!, look out!

cuidadoso, a [kwiða'ðoso, a] *a* careful; *(preocupado)* anxious.

cuidar [kwi'ðar] *vt (MED)* to care for; *(ocuparse de)* to take care of, look after // *vi:* **~ de** to take care of, look after; **~se** *vr* to look after o.s.; **~se de hacer algo** to take care not to do something.

culebra [ku'leβra] *nf* snake.

culebrear [kuleβre'ar] *vi* to wriggle along; *(río)* to meander.

culinario, a [kuli'narjo, a] *a* culinary, cooking *cpd.*

culminación [kulmina'θjon] *nf* culmination.

culminar [kulmi'nar] *vi* to culminate.

culo ['kulo] *nm* bottom, backside.

culpa ['kulpa] *nf* fault; *(JUR)* guilt; **tener la ~ (de)** to be to blame (for); **culpabilidad** [kulpaβili'ðað] *nf* guilt.

culpable [kul'paβle] *a* guilty // *nm/f* culprit.

culpar [kul'par] *vt* to blame; *(acusar)* to accuse.

cultivador, a [kultiβa'ðor, a] *nm/f* farmer // *nf* cultivator.

cultivar [kulti'βar] *vt* to cultivate.

cultivo [kul'tiβo] *nm* cultivation; *(plantas)* crop.

culto, a ['kulto, a] *a (cultivado)* cultivated; *(que tiene cultura)* cultured // *nm (homenaje)* worship; *(religión)* cult.

cultura [kul'tura] *nf* culture.

cumbre ['kumbre] *nf* summit, top.

cumpleaños [kumple'aɲos] *nm* birthday.

cumplido, a [kum'pliðo, a] *a* complete, perfect; *(abundante)* plentiful; *(cortés)* courteous // *nm* compliment; *(cortesía)* courtesy.

cumplimentar [kumplimen'tar] *vt* to congratulate.

cumplimiento [kumpli'mjento] *nm (de un deber)* fulfilment; *(acabamiento)* completion; *(cumplido)* compliment.

cumplir [kum'plir] vt (orden) to carry out, carry out, fulfil; (condena) to serve; (años) to reach, attain // vi: ~ **con** (deberes) to carry out, fulfil; ~**se** vr (plazo) to expire.

cuna ['kuna] nf cradle, cot.

cuñado, a [ku'naðo, a] nm/f brother/sister-in-law.

cuota ['kwota] nf (parte proporcional) share; (cotización) fee, dues pl.

cupe etc vb ver **caber**.

cura ['kura] nf (curación) cure; (método curativo) treatment // nm priest.

curación [kura'θjon] nf cure; (acción) curing.

curar [ku'rar] vt (herida) to treat, dress; (enfermo) to cure; (carne, pescado) to cure, salt; (cuero) to tan // vi, ~**se** vr to get well, recover.

curiosear [kurjose'ar] vt to glance at, look over // vi to look round, wander about.

curiosidad [kurjosi'ðað] nf curiosity.

curioso, a [ku'rjoso, a] a curious // nm/f bystander, onlooker.

cursi ['kursi] a (fam) in bad taste, vulgar.

cursivo, a [kur'siβo, a] a italic // nf italics pl.

curso ['kurso] nm course; **en** ~ (año) current; (proceso) going on, under way.

curvo, a ['kurβo, a] a (gen) curved; (torcido) bent // nf (gen) curve, bend.

custodia [kus'toðja] nf care, safekeeping, custody.

custodiar [kusto'ðjar] vt (guardar) to keep, take care of; (vigilar) to guard, watch over.

custodio [kus'toðjo] nm guardian, keeper.

cutis ['kutis] nm skin, complexion.

cuyo, a ['kujo, a] pron (de quien) whose, of whom; (de que) of which.

CH

chabacano, a [tʃaβa'kano, a] a vulgar, coarse.

chacal [tʃa'kal] nm jackal.

chacota [tʃa'kota] nf fun (and games).

chal [tʃal] nm shawl.

chalán [tʃa'lan] nm (pey) shady dealer.

chaleco [tʃa'leko] nm waistcoat, vest (us); ~ **salvavidas** life jacket.

chalupa [tʃa'lupa] nf launch, boat.

champán [tʃam'pan] nm, **champaña** [tʃam'paɲa] nm champagne.

champiñón [tʃampi'ɲon] nm mushroom.

champú [tʃam'pu] nm shampoo.

chamuscar [tʃamus'kar] vt to scorch, sear, singe.

chantaje [tʃan'taxe] nm blackmail.

chapa ['tʃapa] nf (de metal) plate, sheet; (de madera) board, panel.

chaparrón [tʃapa'rron] nm downpour, cloudburst.

chapotear [tʃapote'ar] vt to sponge down // vi (fam) to splash about.

chapucero, a [tʃapu'θero, a] a rough, crude // nm/f bungler.

chapurrar [tʃapu'rrar], **chapurrear** [tʃapurre'ar] vt (idioma) to speak badly; (bebidas) to mix.

chapuzar [tʃapu'θar] vi to duck.

chaqueta [tʃa'keta] nf jacket.

charca ['tʃarka] nf pond, pool.

charco ['tʃarko] nm pool, puddle.

charla ['tʃarla] nf talk, chat; (conferencia) lecture.

charlar [tʃar'lar] vi to talk, chat.

charlatán, ana [tʃarla'tan, ana] nm/f chatterbox; (embaidor) trickster; (curandero) charlatan.

charol [tʃa'rol] nm varnish; (cuero) patent leather.

chascarrillo [tʃaskarri'(l)o] nm (fam) funny story.

chasco ['tʃasko] nm (broma) trick, joke; (desengaño) disappointment.

chasquear [tʃaske'ar] vt (engañar)

to disappoint; (*bromear*) to play a trick on; (*látigo*) to crack; (*lengua*) to click.

chasquido [tʃas'kiðo] *nm* (*de lengua*) click; (*de látigo*) crack.

chato, a [tʃato, a] *a* flat // *excl* hey handsome/beautiful!

chaval, a [tʃa'βal, a] *nm/f* lad/girl.

checo(e)slovaco, a [tʃeko(e)slo-'βako, a] *a*, *nm/f* Czech, Czecho-slovak.

Checo(e)slovaquia [tʃeko(e)slo-'βakja] *nf* Czechoslovakia.

cheque [tʃeke] *nm* cheque.

chequeo [tʃe'keo] *nm* (*MED*) check-up; (*AUTO*) service.

chequera [tʃe'kera] *nf* cheque-book.

chico, a [tʃiko, a] *a* small, little // *nm/f* (*niño, niña*) child; (*muchacho, muchacha*) boy/girl.

chicharrón [tʃitʃa'rron] *nm* crackling.

chichón [tʃi'tʃon] *nm* bump, hump.

chiflado, a [tʃi'flaðo, a] *a* daft, barmy.

chiflar [tʃi'flar] *vt* to hiss, boo; ~**se** *vr*: ~**se por** to be/go crazy about.

chile [tʃile] *nm* chilli, red pepper.

Chile [tʃile] *nm* Chile; **chileno, a** *a*, *nm/f* Chilean.

chillar [tʃi'ʎar] *vi* (*persona*) to yell, scream; (*animal salvaje*) to howl; (*cerdo*) to squeal; (*puerta*) to creak.

chillido [tʃi'ʎiðo] *nm* (*de persona*) yell, scream; (*de animal*) howl; (*de frenos*) screech(ing).

chillón, ona [tʃi'ʎon, ona] *a* (*niño*) noisy; (*color*) loud, gaudy.

chimenea [tʃime'nea] *nf* chimney; (*hogar*) fireplace.

China [tʃina] *nf*: **la ~** China.

chinche [tʃintʃe] *nf* bug; (*TEC*) drawing pin // *nm/f* nuisance, pest.

chino, a [tʃino, a] *a*, *nm/f* Chinese // *nm* (*lengua*) Chinese.

Chipre [tʃipre] *nm* Cyprus; **chi-priota, chipriote** *a*, *nm/f* Cypriot.

chiquito, a [tʃi'kito, a] *a* very small, tiny // *nm/f* kid.

chirle [tʃirle] *a* watery, wishy-washy.

chirriar [tʃi'rrjar] *vi* (*goznes*) to creak, squeak; (*pájaros*) to chirp, sing.

chirrido [tʃi'rriðo] *nm* creak(ing), squeak(ing); (*de pájaro*) chirp(ing).

chis [tʃis] *excl* sh!

chisme [tʃisme] *nm* (*habladurías*) piece of gossip; (*fam: objeto*) thing, thingummyjig.

chismoso, a [tʃis'moso, a] *a* gossiping // *nm/f* gossip.

chispa [tʃispa] *nf* spark; (*fig*) sparkle; (*ingenio*) wit; (*fam*) drunkenness.

chispeante [tʃispe'ante] *a* spar-kling, scintillating.

chispear [tʃispe'ar] *vi* to spark; (*lloviznar*) to drizzle.

chisporrotear [tʃisporrote'ar] *vi* (*fuego*) to throw out sparks; (*leña*) to crackle; (*aceite*) to hiss, splutter.

chiste [tʃiste] *nm* joke, funny story.

chistoso, a [tʃis'toso, a] *a* (*gracioso*) funny, amusing; (*bro-mista*) witty.

chivo, a [tʃiβo, a] *nm/f* (billy/nanny-)goat.

chocante [tʃo'kante] *a* a startling; (*extraño*) odd; (*ofensivo*) shocking; (*antipático*) annoying.

chocar [tʃo'kar] *vi* (*coches, trenes*) to collide, crash // *vt* to shock; (*sorprender*) to startle; ~ **con** to collide with; (*fig*) to run into or up against; ¡**chócala!** put it there!

chocolate [tʃoko'late] *a*, *nm* chocolate.

chochear [tʃotʃe'ar] *vi* to dodder, be senile.

chocho, a [tʃotʃo, a] *a* doddering, senile; (*fig*) soft, doting.

chollo [tʃoʎo] *nm* (*fam*) bargain, snip.

choque [tʃoke] *nm* (*impacto*) impact; (*golpe*) jolt; (*AUTO*) crash; (*ELEC, MED*) shock; (*MIL*) clash; (*fig*) conflict.

chorizo [tʃo'riθo] *nm* hard pork sausage, salami.

chorrear [tʃorre'ar] *vi* to gush, spout (out); (*gotear*) to drip, trickle.

chorro ['tʃorro] *nm* jet; (*fig*) stream.

choza ['tʃoθa] *nf* hut, shack.

chuleta [tʃu'leta] *nf* chop, cutlet.

chulo ['tʃulo] *nm* (*pícaro*) rascal; (*fam: joven lindo*) dandy.

chupado, a [tʃu'paðo, a] *a* (*delgado*) skinny, gaunt; (*ajustado*) tight.

chupar [tʃu'par] *vt* to suck; (*absorber*) to absorb; ~**se** *vr* to grow thin.

churro, a ['tʃurro, a] *a* coarse // *nm* fritter.

chuscada [tʃus'kaða] *nf* funny remark, joke.

chusco, a ['tʃusko, a] *a* funny; (*persona*) coarse but amusing.

chusma ['tʃusma] *nf* rabble, mob.

D

D. *abr de* **Don**.

Da. *abr de* **Doña.**

dactilógrafo, a [dakti'loɣrafo, a] *nm/f* typist.

dádiva ['daðiβa] *nf* (*donación*) donation; (*regalo*) gift.

dado, a ['daðo, a] *pp de* **dar** // *nm* die; ~**s** *nmpl* dice; ~ **que** *conj* given that.

dador, a [da'ðor, a] *nm/f* (*gen*) giver

dama ['dama] *nf* (*gen*) lady, (*AJEDREZ*) queen; ~**s** *nfpl* draughts.

damasco [da'masko] *nm* (*tela*) damask.

damnificar [damnifi'kar] *vt* (*cosa*) to damage; (*persona*) to injure.

danés, esa [da'nes, esa] *a* Danish // *nm/f* Dane.

danzar [dan'θar] *vt, vi* to dance.

dañar [da'ɲar] *vt* (*objeto*) to

damage; (*persona*) to hurt; ~**se** *vr* to get hurt.

dañino, a [da'ɲino, a] *a* harmful.

daño ['daɲo] *nm* (*a un objeto*) damage; (*a una persona*) harm, injury; ~**s y perjuicios** (*JUR*) damages; **hacer** ~ **a** to damage; to harm, injure.

dar [dar] *vt* (*gen*) to give; (*TEATRO*) to perform, put on; (*película*) to show; (*intereses*) to yield; (*naipes*) to deal; (*la hora*): **las 3** to strike 3 // *vi*: ~ **a** to look out on(to), overlook; ~ **con** (*persona etc*) to meet, run into; (*idea*) to hit on, ~ **contra** to knock against, bang into; ~ **de cabeza** to fall on one's head; ~ **en** (*objeto*) to strike, hit; (*broma*) to catch on to; ~ **de sí** to give, stretch; ~**se** *vr* (*pasar*) to happen; (*presentarse*) to occur; ~**se a** to be given to; ~**se por** to consider o.s.; **dárselas de** to pose as; ~ **de comer/beber a uno** to give sth/sb in eat/drink; **da lo mismo** *o* **qué más da** it's all the same; ~ **en el blanco** to hit the mark; **me da pena it** saddens me; ~**se prisa** to hurry (up).

dardo ['darðo] *nm* dart.

dársena ['darsena] *nf* dock.

datar [da'tar] *vi*: ~ **de** to date from.

dátil ['datil] *nm* date.

dato ['dato] *nm* fact, piece of information.

d. de J. C. *abr de* **después de Jesucristo** A.D. (*Anno Domini*)

de [de] *prep* of; from; **libro** ~ **cocina** cookery book; **el hombre** ~ **largos cabellos** the man with long hair; **guantes** ~ **cuero** leather gloves; **fue a Londres** ~ **profesor** he went to London as a teacher; **uno** ~ **dos** one or the other; ~ **mañana in** the morning; **vestido** ~ **negro** dressed in black; ~**las/menos** ~ **un mes/less than;** ~ **cabeza** un **one's head;** ~ **cara a** facing.

deambular [deambu'lar] *vi* to stroll, wander.

debajo [de'βaxo] ad underneath; ~ **de** below, under; **por** ~ **de** beneath.

debate [de'βate] nm debate; **debatir** vt to debate.

deber [de'βer] nm duty // vt to owe // vi: **debe (de)** it must, it should; **debo hacerlo** I must do it; **debe de ir** he should go; ~**se** vr: ~**se a** to be owing o due to.

debido, a [de'βiðo, a] a proper, just; ~ **a** due to, because of.

débil ['deβil] a (persona, carácter) weak; (luz) dim; **debilidad** nf weakness; dimness; **debilidad senil** senility.

debilitar [deβili'tar] vt to weaken; ~**se** vr to grow weak.

débito [de'βito] nm debit.

década ['dekaða] nf decade.

decadencia [deka'ðenθja] nf decadence.

decaer [deka'er] vi (declinar) to decline; (debilitarse) to weaken.

decaimiento [dekai'mjento] nm (declinación) decline; (desaliento) discouragement; (MED: empeoramiento) weakening; (: estado débil) weakness.

decano [de'kano] a, nm/f dean.

decapitar [dekapi'tar] vt to behead.

decena [de'θena] nf: **una** ~ ten (or so).

decencia [de'θenθja] nf (modestia) modesty; (honestidad) respectability.

decente [de'θente] a (correcto) seemly, proper; (honesto) respectable.

decepción [deθep'θjon] nf disappointment; **decepcionar** vt to disappoint.

decidir [deθi'ðir] vt (persuadir) to convince, persuade; (resolver) to decide // vi to decide; ~**se** vr: ~**se a** to make up one's mind to.

décimo, a ['deθimo, a] a tenth // nm tenth.

decir [de'θir] vt (expresar) to say; (contar) to tell; (hablar) to speak //

nm saying; ~**se** vr: **se dice que** it is said that; ~ **para/entre sí** to say to o.s.; **querer** ~ to mean.

decisión [deθi'sjon] nf (resolución) decision; (firmeza) decisiveness.

decisivo, a [deθi'siβo, a] a decisive.

declamar [dekla'mar] vt, vi to declaim.

declaración [deklara'θjon] nf (manifestación) statement; (explicación) explanation; **declarar** vt to declare, state; to explain // vi to declare; (JUR) to testify; **declararse** vr to propose.

declinar [dekli'nar] vt (gen) to decline; (JUR) to reject // vi (el día) to draw to a close; (salud) to deteriorate.

declive [de'kliβe] nm (cuesta) slope; (inclinación) incline.

decolorarse [dekolo'rarse] vr to become discoloured.

decoración [dekora'θjon] nf decoration.

decorado [deko'raðo] nm scenery, set.

decorar [deko'rar] vt to decorate; **decorativo, a** a ornamental, decorative.

decoro [de'koro] nm (respeto) respect; (dignidad) decency; (recato) decorum, propriety; ~**so, a** a (decente) decent; (modesto) modest; (digno) proper.

decrecer [dekre'θer] vi to decrease, diminish.

decrépito, a [de'krepito, a] a decrepit.

decretar [dekre'tar] vt to decree; **decreto** nm decree.

dedal [de'ðal] nm thimble.

dedicación [deðika'θjon] nf dedication; **dedicar** vt (libro) to dedicate; (tiempo, dinero) to devote; (palabras: decir, consagrar) to dedicate, devote; **dedicatoria** nf (de libro) dedication.

dedo ['deðo] nm finger; ~ **(del pie)** toe; ~ **pulgar** thumb; ~ **índice** index finger; ~ **mayor** o **cordial**

middle finger; ~ **anular** ring finger; ~ **meñique** little finger.

deducción [deðuk'θjon] nf deduction.

deducir [deðu'θir] vt (concluir) to deduce, infer; (COM) to deduct.

defecto [de'fekto] nm defect, flaw; (ELEC) fault, **defectuoso, a** a defective, faulty.

defender [defen'der] vt to defend.

defensa [de'fensa] nf defence; (DEPORTE) back; **defensivo, a** a defensive // nf: **a la defensiva** on the defensive.

defensor, a [defen'sor, a] a defending // nm/f (abogado) defending counsel; (protector) protector.

deficiencia [defi'θjenθja] nf deficiency; **deficiente** a (defectuoso) defective; (imperfecto) deficient, wanting.

déficit ['defiθit] nm deficit.

definición [defini'θjon] nf definition.

definir [defi'nir] vt (determinar) to determine, establish; (decidir) to define; (aclarar) to clarify; **definitivo, a** a definitive; **en definitiva** definitively.

deformación [deforma'θjon] nf (alteración) deformation; (distorsión) distortion.

deformar [defor'mar] vt (gen) to deform; ~**se** vr to become deformed; **deforme** a (informe) deformed; (feo) ugly; (mal hecho) misshapen.

defraudar [defrau'ðar] vt (decepcionar) to disappoint; (estafar) to cheat, defraud; (engañar) to deceive.

defunción [defun'θjon] nf decease, demise.

degeneración [dexenera'θjon] nf (de las células) degeneration; (moral) degeneracy; **degenerar** vi to degenerate.

degollar [deɣo'ʎar] vt (animal) to

slaughter; (decapitar) to behead, decapitate.

degradar [deɣra'ðar] vt to debase, degrade; ~**se** vr to demean o.s.

degüello [de'ɣweʎo] nm: **entrar a** ~ to slaughter, put to the sword.

degustación [deɣusta'θjon] nf sampling, tasting.

deidad [dei'ðað] nf deity, divinity.

deificar [deifi'kar] vt (persona) to deify.

dejación [dexa'θjon] nf (abandono) abandonment.

dejadez [dexa'ðeθ] nf (negligencia) neglect; (descuido) untidiness, carelessness; **dejado, a** a (negligente) careless; (indolente) lazy.

dejar [de'xar] vt (gen) to leave; (permitir) to allow, let; (abandonar) to abandon, forsake; (beneficios) to produce, yield // vi: ~ **de** (parar) to stop; (no hacer) to fail to; ~ **a un lado** to leave o put aside.

dejo ['dexo] nm (LING) accent; (sabor fuerte) tang; (sabor que queda) aftertaste.

del [del] = **de + el**, ver **de**.

delantal [delan'tal] nm apron.

delante [de'lante] ad in front; (enfrente) opposite; (adelante) ahead; ~ **de** in front of, before.

delantero, a [delan'tero, a] a front // nm (DEPORTE) forward // nf (de vestido, casa) front part; (DEPORTE) forward line; **llevar la ~ a** a uno to be ahead of sb.

delatar [dela'tar] vt to inform on o against, betray, **delator, a** nm/f informer.

delegación [delexa'θjon] nf delegation; (COM) office, branch; ~ **de policía** police station; ~ **municipal** local government office; **delegado, a** nm/f delegate; (COM) agent; **delegar** vt to delegate.

deleitar [delei'tar] vt to delight; ~ **se** vr: ~**se con o en** to delight in, take pleasure in; **deleite** nm delight, pleasure.

deletrear [deletre'ar] vi to spell

(out); (*fig*) to interpret, decipher;
deletreo nm spelling; interpretation,
decipherment.

deleznable [deleθ'naβle] *a inv*
(*frágil*) fragile; (*resbaloso*) slippery;
(*fugaz*) fleeting.

delfín [del'fin] nm dolphin.

delgadez [delxa'ðeθ] nf thinness,
slimness; **delgado, a** *a* (*gen*) thin;
(*persona*) slim, thin; (*tierra*) poor;
(*tela etc*) light, delicate.

deliberación [deliβera'θjon] nf
deliberation; **deliberar** vt to debate,
discuss.

delicadeza [delika'ðeθa] nf (*gen*)
delicacy; (*refinamiento, sutileza*)
refinement.

delicado, a [deli'kaðo, a] *a* (*gen*)
delicate; (*sensible*) sensitive; (*quisquilloso*) touchy.

delicia [de'liθja] nf delight.

delicioso, a [deli'θjoso, a] *a*
(*gracioso*) delightful, agreeable;
(*placentero*) pleasant; (*exquisito*)
delicious.

delincuencia [delin'kwenθja] nf
delinquency; **delincuente** nm/f
delinquent, criminal.

delinquir [delin'kir] vi to commit
an offence.

delirante [deli'rante] *a* delirious;
delirar vi to be delirious, rave.

delirio [de'lirjo] nm (*MED*) delirium;
(*palabras insensatas*) wanderings pl,
ravings pl.

delito [de'lito] nm (*infracción*)
offence; (*crimen*) crime; ~
político/común political/common
crime.

demagogo [dema'xoxo] nm dema-
gogue.

demanda [de'manda] nf (*pedido,
COM*) demand; (*petición*) request;
(*JUR*) action, lawsuit; **demandante**
nm/f claimant.

demandar [deman'dar] vt (*gen*) to
demand; (*JUR*) to sue.

demarcación [demarka'θjon] nf
(*de terreno*) demarcation; **demar-
car** vt to demarcate.

demás [de'mas] *a*: **los ~ niños** the
other children, the remaining
children // *pron*: **los/las ~** the
others, the rest (of them); **lo ~** the
rest (of it) // *ad* besides.

demasía [dema'sia] nf (*exceso*)
excess, surplus; (*atrevimiento*)
boldness; (*insolencia*) outrage;
comer en ~ to eat to excess.

demasiado, a [dema'sjaðo, a] *a*
too, too much; ~**s** too many // *ad*
too, too much; **¡es ~!** it's too much!

demencia [de'menθja] nf (*locura*)
madness; **demente** nm/f lunatic // *a*
mad, insane.

democracia [demo'kraθja] nf
democracy.

demócrata [de'mokrata] nm/f
democrat; **democrático, a** *a*
democratic.

demoler [demo'ler] vt to demolish;
demolición nf demolition.

demonio [de'monjo] nm devil,
demon; **¡~s!** hell!, confound it!;
¿cómo ~s? how the hell?

demora [de'mora] nf delay;
demorar vt (*retardar*) to delay, hold
back; (*dilatar*) to hold up // vi to
linger, stay on.

demostración [demostra'θjon] nf
(*de teorema*) demonstration; (*de
afecto*) show, display.

demostrar [demos'trar] vt
(*probar*) to prove; (*mostrar*) to
show; (*manifestar*) to demonstrate;
demostrativo, a *a* demonstrative.

denegar [dene'xar] vt (*rechazar*) to
refuse; (*JUR*) to reject.

denigrar [deni'xrar] vt (*desacreditar, infamar*) to denigrate;
(*injuriar*) to insult.

denominación [denomina'θjon] nf
(*nombramiento*) designation;
(*clase*) denomination.

denotar [deno'tar] vt (*indicar*) to
indicate; (*significar*) to denote.

densidad [densi'ðað] nf (*FÍSICA*)
density; (*fig*) thickness.

denso, a ['denso, a] *a* (*apretado*)

dentadura   83   derrame

solid; (espeso, pastoso) thick; (fig) heavy.

dentadura [denta'ðura] nf (set of) teeth pl; ~ **postiza** false teeth pl.

dentera [den'tera] nf (sensación desagradable) the shivers pl, the shudders pl; (envidia) envy, jealousy; (deseo) desire.

dentista [den'tista] nm/f dentist.

dentro ['dentro] ad inside // prep: ~ **de** in, inside, within; **vayamos a** ~ let's go inside; **mirar por** ~ to look inside; ~ **de tres meses** within three months.

denuedo [de'nweðo] nm boldness, daring.

denuncia [de'nunθja] nf (delación) denunciation; (acusación) accusation; (de accidente) report; **denunciar** vt to report, (delatar) to inform on or against.

departamento [departa'mento] nm (sección administrativa) department, section; (de caja, tren) compartment; (AM: piso) apartment, flat.

dependencia [depen'denθja] nf dependence; (POL) dependency; (COM) office, section.

depender [depen'der] vi: ~ **de** to depend on.

dependienta [depen'djenta] nf saleswoman, shop assistant; **dependiente** a dependent // nm salesman.

deplorable [deplo'raβle] a deplorable; **deplorar** vt to deplore.

deponer [depo'ner] vt to lay down // vi (JUR) to give evidence; (declarar) to testify.

deportar [depor'tar] vt to deport.

deporte [de'porte] nm sport; **deportista** a sports cpd // nm/f sportsman/woman.

depositante [deposi'tante], **depositador, a** [deposita'ðor, a] nm/f depositor.

depositar [deposi'tar] vt (dinero) to deposit; (mercaderías) to put away, store; (AM: persona) to confide; ~**se** vr to settle; ~**io, a** nm/f trustee.

depósito [de'posito] nm (gen) deposit; (de mercaderías) warehouse, store; (de agua, gasolina etc) tank; ~ **de equipajes** cloakroom.

depravar [depra'βar] vt to deprave; ~**se** vr to become depraved.

depreciar [depre'θjar] vt to depreciate, reduce the value of; ~**se** vr to depreciate, lose value.

depredación [depreða'θjon] nf (saqueo, pillaje) pillage; (malversación) depredation.

depresión [depre'sjon] nf depression.

deprimido, a [depri'miðo, a] a depressed.

deprimir [depri'mir] vt to depress; ~**se** vr (persona) to become depressed.

depuración [depura'θjon] nf purification; (POL) purge; **depurar** vt to purify, (purgar) to purge.

derecha [de'retʃa] nf right(-hand) side; (POL) right.

derechamente [deretʃa'mente] ad (dirección) straight.

derecho, a [de'retʃo, a] a right, right-hand // nm (privilegio) right; (lado) right(-hand) side; (leyes) law // ad straight, directly; ~ nmpl (de aduana) duty sg; (de autor) royalties; **tener** ~ **a** to have a right to.

deriva [de'riβa] nf: **ir** o **estar a la** ~ to drift, be adrift.

derivación [deriβa'θjon] nf derivation.

derivar [deri'βar] vt (gen) to derive; (desviar) to drift; ~**se** vr to derive, be derived; to drift.

derramamiento [derrama'mjento] nm (de sangre) shedding; (dispersión) spilling.

derramar [derra'mar] vt to spill; (verter) to pour out; (esparcir) to scatter; ~**se** vr to pour out; ~ **lágrimas** to weep.

derrame [de'rrame] nm (de líquido) spilling; (de sangre) shedding; (de tubo etc) overflow; (perdida) loss, leakage; (MED) discharge; (declive) slope.

derredor [derreˈðor] ad: **al** o **en ~ de** around, about.

derretido, a [derreˈtiðo, a] a melted, molten.

derretir [derreˈtir] vt (gen) to melt; (nieve) to thaw; (fig) to squander; **~se** vr to melt.

derribar [derriˈβar] vt to knock down; (construcción) to demolish; (persona, gobierno, político) to bring down; **~se** vr to fall down.

derrocar [derroˈkar] vt (despeñar) to demolish, knock down; (gobierno) to bring down, overthrow.

derrochar [derroˈtʃar] vt to squander; **derroche** nm (despilfarro) waste, squandering.

derrota [deˈrrota] nf (camino, vereda) road, route; (NAUT) course; (MIL) defeat, rout; (fig) disaster; **derrotar** vt (gen) to defeat; (destruir) to ruin; **derrotero** nm (rumbo) course.

derrumbar [derrumˈbar] vt to throw down; **~se** vr (despeñarse) to collapse; (precipitarse) to throw o.s. down.

desabotonar [desaβotoˈnar] vt to unbutton, undo // vi to open out; **~se** vr to come undone.

desabrido, a [desaˈβriðo, a] a (insípido, soso) insipid, tasteless; (persona) rude, surly; (respuesta) sharp.

desabrochar [desaβroˈtʃar] vt (botones, broches) to undo, unfasten; (fig) to expose; **~se** vr to confide, unburden o.s.

desacato [desaˈkato] nm (falta de respeto) disrespect; (irreverencia) insulting behaviour; (JUR) contempt.

desacertado, a [desaθerˈtaðo, a] a (equivocado) mistaken; (inoportuno) unwise.

desacertar [desaθerˈtar] vi (errar) to be mistaken; (destinar) to act unwisely.

desacierto [desaˈθjerto] nm mistake, error.

desacomodar [desakomoˈðar] vt (molestar) to put out, inconvenience; **desacomodo** nm (incomodidad) inconvenience; (molestia) trouble.

desaconsejado, a [desakonseˈxaðo, a] a ill-advised; **desaconsejar** vt to dissuade, advise against.

desacordarse [desakorˈdarse] vr (MUS) to get out of tune; **desacorde** a inv discordant.

desacreditar [desakreðiˈtar] vt (desprestigiar) to discredit, bring into disrepute; (denigrar) to run down.

desacuerdo [desaˈkwerðo] nm (conflicto) discord, disagreement; (error) error, blunder.

desafecto, a [desaˈfekto, a] a (opuesto) disaffected // (hostilidad) disaffection.

desafiar [desaˈfjar] vt (retar) to challenge; (enfrentarse a) to defy.

desafilar [desafiˈlar] vt to blunt; **~se** vr to become blunt.

desafinado, a [desafiˈnaðo] a: **estar ~** to be out of tune; **desafinarse** vr (MUS) to go out of tune.

desafío [desaˈfio] nm (reto) challenge; (combate) duel; (resistencia) defiance; (competición) competition.

desafortunado, a [desaforturˈnaðo, a] a (desgraciado) unfortunate, unlucky.

desagradable [desaxraˈðaβle] a (fastidioso, enojoso) unpleasant; (irritante) disagreeable.

desagradar [desaxraˈðar] vi (disgustar) to displease; (molestar) to bother; **desagradecido, a** a ungrateful.

desagrado [desaˈxraðo] nm (disgusto) displeasure; (contrariedad) dissatisfaction.

desagraviar [desaxraˈβjar] vt to make amends to; **desagravio** nm (*recompensa*) amends; (: *en efectivo*) compensation.

desaguadero [desaxwa'ðero] *nm* drain.

desagüe [des'axwe] *nm* (*de un líquido*) drainage; (*cañería*) drainpipe.

desaguisado, a [desaɣi'saðo, a] *a* illegal // *nm* outrage.

desahogado, a [desao'xaðo, a] *a* (*descarado*) brazen, impudent; (*holgado*) comfortable; (*espacioso*) roomy.

desahogar [desao'xar] *vt* (*consolar*) to console; (*aliviar*) to ease, relieve; (*ira*) to vent; ~**se** *vr* (*distenderse*) to take it easy; (*desfogarse*) to let off steam.

desahogo [desa'oxo] *nm* (*alivio*) relief; (*comodidad*) comfort, ease; (*descaro*) impudence.

desahuciar [desau'θjar] *vt* (*enfermo*) to give up hope for; (*inquilino*) to evict; **desahucio** *nm* eviction.

desairado, a [desai'raðo, a] *a* (*menospreciado*) disregarded; (*desgarbado*) shabby.

desairar [desai'rar] *vt* (*menospreciar*) to slight, snub; (*ultrajar*) to dishonour.

desaire [des'aire] *nm* (*afrenta*) rebuff; (*menosprecio*) slight; (*falta de garbo*) unattractiveness, lack of charm.

desajustar [desaxus'tar] *vt* (*desarreglar*) to disarrange; (*desconcertar*) to throw off balance; ~**se** *vr* to get out of order; (*cintura*) to loosen.

desajuste [desa'xuste] *nm* (*de máquina*) disorder; (*situación*) imbalance.

desalentador, a [desalenta'ðor, a] *a* disheartening, **desalentar** *vt* (*desanimar*) to discourage; **desalentar a uno** to make sb breathless; **desaliento** [desa'ljento] *nm* discouragement.

desalinear [desaline'ar] *vt* to throw out of the straight; ~**se** *vr* to go off the straight.

desaliño [desa'liɲo] *nm* (*negligencia*) slovenliness.

desalmado, a [desal'maðo, a] *a* (*cruel*) cruel, heartless.

desalojamiento [desaloxa'mjento] *nm* ousting; (*cambio de residencia*) removal; (*. forzado*) eviction.

desalojar [desalo'xar] *vt* (*expulsar, echar*) to eject; (*abandonar*) to abandon, evacuate // *vi* to move out.

desamarrar [desama'rrar] *vt* to untie; (*NAUT*) to cast off.

desamor [desa'mor] *nm* (*frialdad*) indifference; (*odio*) dislike; (*enemistad*) enmity.

desamparado, a [desampa'raðo, a] *a* (*persona*) helpless; (*lugar: expuesto*) exposed; (*desierto*) deserted.

desamparar [desampa'rar] *vt* (*abandonar*) to desert, abandon; (*JUR*) to leave defenceless; (*barco*) to abandon.

desandar [desan'dar] *vt*: ~ **lo andado** *o* **el camino** to retrace one's steps.

desanimado, a [desani'maðo, a] *a* (*persona*) downhearted; (*espectáculo, fiesta*) dull; **desanimar** *vt* (*desalentar*) to discourage; (*deprimir*) to depress.

desapacible [desapa'θiβle] *a* (*gen*) unpleasant; (*carácter*) disagreeable; (*voz*) harsh.

desaparecer [desapare'θer] *vt* (*gen*) to hide // *vi* (*gen*) to disappear; (*el sol, la luz*) to vanish; **desaparición** *nf* disappearance.

desapego [desa'pexo] *nm* (*frialdad*) coolness; (*distancia*) detachment.

desapercibido, a [desaperθi'βiðo, a] *a* (*desprevenido*) unprepared; **pasar** ~ to go unnoticed.

desaplicación [desaplika'θjon] *nf* (*negligencia*) slackness; (*ocio*) laziness; **desaplicado, a** *a* slack; lazy.

desaprensivo, a [desapren'siβo, a] *a* unscrupulous.

desaprobar [desapro'βar] *vt* (*reprobar*) to disapprove of; (*condenar*) to condemn; (*no consentir*) to reject.

desaprovechado, a [desaproβe-'tʃaðo, a] *a* (*improductivo*) unproductive; (*atrasado*) backward; **desaprovechar** *vt* to waste.

desarmar [desar'mar] *vt* (MIL, *fig*) to disarm; (TEC) to take apart, dismantle; **desarme** *nm* disarmament.

desarraigar [desarrai'ɣar] *vt* to uproot; **desarraigo** *nm* uprooting.

desarreglado, a [desarre'xlaðo, a] *a* (TEC) out of order; (*desordenado*) disorderly, untidy.

desarreglar [desarre'xlar] *vt* (*desordenar*) to disarrange; (*mecánica*) to put out of order; (*trastocar*) to upset, disturb. **desarreglo** [desa'rrexlo] *nm* (de *casa*, *persona*) untidiness; (*desorden*) disorder.

desarrollar [desarro'ʎar] *vt* (*gen*) to develop; (*extender*) to unfold; ~**se** *vr* to develop; (*extenderse*) to open (out); (*film*) to develop; **desarrollo** *nm* development.

desarticular [desartiku'lar] *vt* (*hueso*) to put out; (*objeto*) to take apart; (*fig*) to break up.

desaseo [desa'seo] *nm* (*suciedad*) slovenliness; (*desarreglo*) untidiness.

desasir [desa'sir] *vt* to loosen; ~**se** *vr* to extricate o.s.; ~**se de** to let go, give up.

desasosegar [desasose'ɣar] *vt* (*inquietar*) to disturb; (*afligir*) to make uneasy; ~**se** *vr* to become uneasy.

desasosiego [desaso'sjeɣo] *nm* (*intranquilidad*) uneasiness; (*aflicción*) restlessness; (*ansiedad*) anxiety.

desastrado, a [desas'traðo, a] *a* (*desaliñado*) shabby; (*sucio*) dirty; (*desgraciado*, *adverso*) wretched.

desastre [de'sastre] *nm* disaster; **desastroso, a** *a* disastrous.

desatado, a [desa'taðo, a] *a* (*desligado*) untied; (*violento*) violent, wild.

desatar [desa'tar] *vt* (*nudo*) to untie; (*paquete*) to undo; (*separar*) to detach; ~**se** *vr* (*zapatos*) to come untied; (*tormenta*) to break.

desatender [desaten'der] *vt* (*no prestar atención a*) to disregard; (*abandonar*) to neglect; (*invitado*) to slight.

desatento, a [desa'tento, a] *a* (*distraído*) inattentive; (*descortés*) discourteous.

desatinado, a [desati'naðo, a] *a* (*disparatado*) wild, reckless; (*absurdo*) foolish, silly; **desatinar** *vi* (*desvariar*) to behave foolishly; **desatino** *nm* (*idiotez*) foolishness, folly; (*error*) blunder.

desautorizado, a [desautori'θaðo, a] *a* unauthorized; **desautorizar** *vt* (*oficial*) to deprive of authority; (*informe*) to deny.

desavenencia [desaβe'nenθja] *nf* (*desacuerdo*) disagreement; (*discrepancia*) rift, quarrel.

desaventajado, a [desaβenta-'xaðo, a] *a* (*inferior*) inferior; (*poco ventajoso*) disadvantageous.

desayunar [desaju'nar] *vi* to have breakfast // *vt* to have for breakfast; **desayuno** *nm* breakfast.

desazón [desa'θon] *nf* (*insipidez*) tastelessness; (*angustia*) anxiety; (*fig*) annoyance.

desazonar [desaθo'nar] *vt* to make tasteless; (*fig*) to annoy, upset; ~**se** *vr* (*enojarse*) to be annoyed; (*preocuparse*) to worry, be anxious; (MED) to be off colour.

desbandarse [desβan'darse] *vr* (MIL) to disband; (*fig*) to flee in disorder.

desbarajuste [desβaraˈxuste] nm confusion, disorder.

desbaratar [desβaraˈtar] vt (deshacer, destruir) to ruin; (malgastar) to squander; (mecánica) to take apart.

desbordar [desβorˈðar] vt (sobrepasar) to go beyond; (exceder) to exceed // vi, ~se vr (río) to overflow; (entusiasmo) to erupt; (persona) to express one's feelings freely.

descabalgar [deskaβalˈɣar] vi to dismount.

descabellado, a [deskaβeˈʎaðo, a] a (disparatado) wild, crazy; (insensato) ridiculous.

descabellar [deskaβeˈʎar] vt to ruffle; (TAUR: toro) to give the coup de grace to.

descabezar [deskaβeˈθar] vt (persona) to behead; (árbol) to lop; ~se vr (AGR) to shed the grain; (fig) to rack one's brains.

descafeinado [deskafeiˈnaðo] nm decaffeinated coffee.

descalabro [deskaˈlaβro] nm blow; (desgracia) misfortune.

descalzar [deskalˈθar] vt (zapato) to take off; **descalzo, a** barefoot(ed); (fig) destitute.

descaminado, a [deskamiˈnaðo, a] a (equivocado) on the wrong road; (fig) misguided.

descaminar [deskamiˈnar] vt (alguien) to misdirect; (: fig) to lead astray; ~se vr (en la ruta) to go the wrong way; (fig) to go astray.

descansado, a [deskanˈsaðo, a] a (gen) rested; (que tranquiliza) restful; **descansar** vt (gen) to rest // vi to rest, have a rest; (echarse) to lie down

descanso [desˈkanso] nm (reposo) rest, (alivio) relief (pausa) break; (DEPORTE) interval, half time.

descarado, a [deskaˈraðo, a] a (sin vergüenza) shameless; (insolente) cheeky; **descararse** vr to be insolent or cheeky.

descarga [desˈkarɣa] nf (ARQ, ELEC, MIL) discharge; (NAUT) unloading

descargadero [deskarɣaˈðero] nm wharf.

descargar [deskarˈɣar] vt to unload; (golpe) to let fly; ~se vr to unburden o.s.; **descargo** nm unloading; (COM) receipt; (JUR) evidence.

descarnado, a [deskarˈnaðo, a] a scrawny; (fig) bare.

descaro [desˈkaro] nm (atrevimiento) shamelessness, nerve; (insolencia) cheek

descarriar [deskaˈrrjar] vt (descaminar) to misdirect, (fig) to lead astray; ~se vr (perderse) to lose one's way; (separarse) to stray; (pervertirse) to err, go astray.

descarrilamiento [deskarrilaˈmjento] nm (de tren) derailment

descartar [deskarˈtar] vt (rechazar) to reject; (poner a un lado) to set aside; (eliminar) to rule out; ~se vr (NAIPES) to discard; ~se de to shirk; **descartado, a** a rejected; set aside, eliminated.

descendencia [desθenˈdenθja] nf (origen) origin, descent; (hijos) offspring.

descender [desθenˈder] vt (bajar: escalera:) to go down; (: equipajes) to take down // vi to descend; (temperatura, nivel) to fall, drop; ~ de to be descended from.

descendiente [desθenˈdjente] nm/f descendant.

descenso [desˈθenso] nm descent; (de temperatura) drop.

descifrar [desθiˈfrar] vt to decipher.

descolgar [deskolˈɣar] vt (bajar) to take down; (teléfono) to pick up, ~se vr to let o.s. down.

descolorir [deskoloˈrir], **descolorar** [deskoloˈrar] vt = **decolorar**.

descomedido, a [deskomeˈðiðo, a] a (descortés) rude; (excesivo) excessive.

descompaginar [deskompaxi'nar] vt (desordenar) to disarrange, mess up.

descompasado, a [deskompa'saðo, a] a (sin proporción) out of all proportion; (excesivo) excessive.

descomponer [deskompo'ner] vt (desordenar) to disarrange, disturb; (TEC) to put out of order; (dividir) to break down (into parts); (fig) to provoke; ~se vr (corromperse) to rot, decompose; (el tiempo) to change (for the worse); (TEC) to break down; (irritarse) to lose one's temper.

descomposición [deskomposi'θjon] nf (gen) breakdown; (de fruta etc) decomposition.

descompostura [deskompos'tura] nf (TEC) breakdown; (desorganización) disorganization; (desorden) untidiness.

descompuesto, a [deskom'pwesto, a] a (corrompido) decomposed; (roto) broken; (descarado) brazen; (furioso) angry.

desconcertado, a [deskonθer'taðo, a] a disconcerted, bewildered.

desconcertar [deskonθer'tar] vt (confundir) to baffle; (incomodar) to upset, put out; (TEC) to put out of order; ~se vr (turbarse) to be upset.

desconcierto [deskon'θjerto] nm (gen) disorder; (daño) damage; (desorientación) uncertainty; (inquietud) uneasiness.

desconectar [deskonek'tar] vt to disconnect.

desconfianza [deskon'fjanθa] nf distrust; **desconfiar** vi to be distrustful; desconfiar de to distrust, suspect.

desconocer [deskono'θer] vt (alguien) to ignore; (ignorar) not to know, be ignorant of; (no recordar) to fail to remember; (no aceptar) to deny; (repudiar) to disown.

desconocimiento [deskonoθi'mjento] nm (falta de conocimientos)

ignorance; (repudio) disregard; (ingratitud) ingratitude.

desconsiderado, a [deskonsiðe'raðo, a] a (descuidado) inconsiderate; (insensible) thoughtless.

desconsolar [deskonso'lar] vt to distress; ~se vr to despair.

desconsuelo [deskon'swelo] nm (tristeza) distress; (desesperación) despair.

descontar [deskon'tar] vt (deducir) to take away, deduct; (rebajar) to discount; (predecir, dar por cierto) to take for granted.

descontento, a [deskon'tento, a] a dissatisfied // nm dissatisfaction, discontent.

descorazonar [deskoraθo'nar] vt to discourage, dishearten.

descorchar [deskor't∫ar] vt to uncork.

descortés [deskor'tes] a (mal educado) discourteous; (grosero) rude.

descoser [desko'ser] vt to unstitch; ~se vr to come apart (at the seams).

descosido, a [desko'siðo, a] a (costura) unstitched; (indiscreto) indiscreet; (desordenado) disjointed.

descoyuntar [deskojun'tar] vt (ANAT) to dislocate.

descrédito [des'kreðito] nm discredit.

descreído, a [deskre'iðo, a] a (incrédulo) incredulous; (falto de fe) unbelieving.

describir [deskri'βir] vt to describe.

descripción [deskrip'θjon] nf description.

descrito [des'krito] pp de **describir.**

descuajar [deskwa'xar] vt (disolver) to melt; (planta) to pull out by the roots.

descubierto, a [desku'βjerto, a] pp de descubrir // a uncovered, bare; (persona) bareheaded; al ~ in the open.

descubrimiento [deskuβri'mjento] nm (hallazgo) discovery; (revelación) revelation.

descubrir [desku'βrir] vt to discover, find; (inaugurar) to unveil; (vislumbrar) to detect; (revelar) to reveal, show; (quitar la tapa) to uncover; ~ se vr to reveal o.s.; (quitarse sombrero) to take off one's hat; (confesar) to confess.

descuento etc [des'kwento] nm discount; ~ jubilatorio retirement pension.

descuidado, a [deskwi'ðaðo, a] a (sin cuidado) careless; (desordenado) untidy; (olvidadizo) forgetful; (dejado) neglected; (desprevenido) unprepared.

descuidar [deskwi'ðar] vt (dejar) to neglect; (olvidar) to overlook // vi, ~ se vr (distraerse) to be careless; (estar desaliñado) to let o.s. go; (desprevenirse) to drop one's guard; ¡descuida! don't worry!; **descuido** nm (dejadez) carelessness; (olvido) negligence.

desde ['desðe] ad from; ~ que since; ~ lejos from afar; ~ ahora en adelante from now onwards; ~ hace 3 días from 3 days now; ~ luego of course.

desdecirse [desðe'θirse] vr (de promesa) to go back on one's word.

desdén [des'ðen] nm scorn.

desdeñar [desðe'ɲar] vt (despreciar) to scorn.

desdicha [des'ðitʃa] nf (desgracia) misfortune; (infelicidad) unhappiness; **desdichado, a** a (sin suerte) unlucky; (infeliz) unhappy.

desdoblar [desðo'βlar] vt (extender) to spread out; (desplegar) to unfold; (separar en dos) to split.

desear [dese'ar] vt to want, desire, wish for.

desecar [dese'kar] vt, ~ se vr to dry up.

desechar [dese'tʃar] vt (basura) to throw out or away; (ideas) to reject,

discard; **desechos** nmpl rubbish sg, waste sg.

desembalar [desemba'lar] vt to unpack.

desembarazado, a [desembara'θaðo, a] a (libre) clear, free; (desenvuelto) free and easy.

desembarazar [desembara'θar] vt (desocupar) to clear; (desenredar) to free; ~ se vr: ~ se de to free o.s. of, get rid of.

desembarcar [desembar'kar] vt, vi, ~ se vr to land.

desembocadura [desemboka'ðura] nf (de río) mouth; (de calle) opening.

desembocar [desembo'kar] vi to flow into; (fig) to result in.

desembolso [desem'bolso] nm payment; ~ s nmpl expenses; ~ inicial deposit, down payment.

desemejante [deseme'xante] a dissimilar, unlike; **desemejanza** nf dissimilarity.

desempeñar [desempe'ɲar] vt (cargo) to hold; (papel) to perform; (lo empeñado) to redeem; ~ se vr to get out of debt; ~ un papel (fig) to play (a role).

desempeño [desem'peɲo] nm redeeming; (de cargo) occupation; (TEATRO, fig) performance.

desempleado, a [desemple'aðo, a] nm/f unemployed person; **desempleo** nm unemployment.

desencadenar [desenkaðe'nar] vt to unchain; (ira) to unleash; ~ se vr to break loose; (tormenta) to burst.

desencajar [desenka'xar] vt (hueso) to put out of joint; (mandíbula) to dislocate; (mecanismo, pieza) to disconnect, disengage.

desencanto [desen'kanto] nm disillusionment.

desenfadado, a [desenfa'ðaðo, a] a (desenvuelto) uninhibited; (descarado) forward; **desenfado** nm (libertad) freedom; (comportamiento) free and easy manner; (descaro) forwardness.

desenfrenado, a [desenfre'naðo, a] a (descontrolado) uncontrolled; (inmoderado) unbridled; **desenfreno** nm (vicio) wildness; (de las pasiones) lack of self-control.

desengañar [desenga'ɲar] vt to disillusion; ~se vr to become disillusioned; **desengaño** nm disillusionment; (decepción) disappointment.

desenlace [desen'laθe] nm outcome.

desenmarañar [desenmara'ɲar] vt (desenredar) to disentangle; (fig) to unravel.

desenredar [desenre'ðar] vt to resolve; (intriga) to unravel; ~se vr to extricate o.s.

desentenderse [desenten'derse] vr: ~ de to pretend to be ignorant about; (apartarse) to have nothing to do with.

desenterrar [desente'rrar] vt to exhume; (tesoro, fig) to unearth, dig up.

desentrañar [desentra'ɲar] vt to disembowel; (misterio) to unravel.

desentumecer [desentume'θer] vt (pierna etc) to stretch; (DEPORTE) to loosen up.

desenvoltura [desenßol'tura] nf (libertad, gracia) ease; (descaro) free and easy manner; (desvergüenza) forwardness.

desenvolver [desenßol'ßer] vt (paquete) to unwrap; (madeja) to disentangle; (fig) to develop; ~se vr (desarrollarse) to unfold, develop; (arreglárselas) to extricate o.s.

deseo [de'seo] nm desire, wish; ~so, a a: estar ~so de to be anxious to.

desequilibrado, a [desekili-'ßraðo, a] a unbalanced.

desertar [deser'tar] vi to desert.

desesperación [desespera'θjon] nf (impaciencia) desperation, despair; (irritación) fury.

desesperar [desespe'rar] vt to drive to despair; (exasperar) to drive to distraction // vi: ~ de to despair of; ~se vr to despair, lose hope.

desestimar [desesti'mar] vt (menospreciar) to have a low opinion of; (rechazar) to reject.

desfachatez [desfaʧa'teθ] nf (insolencia) impudence; (descaro) cheek.

desfalco [des'falko] nm embezzlement.

desfallecer [desfaʎe'θer] vi (perder las fuerzas) to become weak; (desvanecerse) to faint.

desfavorable [desfaßo'raßle] a unfavourable.

desfigurar [desfiɣu'rar] vt (cara) to disfigure; (cuerpo) to deform.

desfilar [desfi'lar] vt to parade; **desfile** nm procession.

desgaire [des'xaire] nm (desaliño, desgano) slovenliness; (menosprecio) disdain.

desgajar [desxa'xar] vt (arrancar) to tear off; (romper) to break off; ~se vr to come off.

desgana [des'xana] nf (falta de apetito) loss of appetite; (renuncia) unwillingness; **desganarse** vr to lose one's appetite; (cansarse) to become bored.

desgarrar [desxa'rrar] vt to tear (up); (fig) to shatter; **desgarro** nm (muscular) tear; (aflicción) grief; (descaro) impudence.

desgastar [desxas'tar] vt (deteriorar) to wear away or down; (estropear) to spoil; ~se vr to get worn out; **desgaste** nm wear and tear; (MED) weakening, decline.

desgracia [des'xraθja] nf misfortune; (accidente) accident; (vergüenza) disgrace; (contratiempo) setback; **por** ~ unfortunately.

desgraciado, a [desxra'θjaðo, a] a (infortunado) unlucky, unfortunate; (miserable) wretched; (infeliz) miserable; (*feo*) ugly; (*desagradable*) unpleasant.

desgreñado, a [desxre'naðo, a] *a* dishevelled.

deshacer [desa'θer] *vt* (*casa*) to break up; (*dañar*) to damage; (*TEC*) to take apart; (*enemigo*) to defeat; (*diluir*) to melt; (*contrato*) to break; (*intriga*) to solve; ~**se** *vr* (*disolverse*) to melt; (*despedazarse*) to come apart or undone; ~**se de** to get rid of; ~**se en lágrimas** to burst into tears.

deshecho, a [des'etʃo, a] *a* undone.

deshelar [dese'lar] *vt* (*cañería*) to thaw; (*heladera*) to defrost.

desheredar [desere'ðar] *vt* to disinherit.

deshielo [des'jelo] *nm* (*de cañería*) thaw; (*de heladera*) defrosting.

deshilar [desi'lar] *vt* (*tela*) to unravel.

deshonesto, a [deso'nesto, a] *a* indecent.

deshonra [des'onra] *nf* (*deshonor*) dishonour; (*vergüenza*) shame; **deshonrar** *vt* to dishonour; (*insultar*) to insult.

deshora [des'ora]: **a ~** *ad* at the wrong time.

designar [desix'nar] *vt* (*nombrar*) to designate; (*indicar*) to fix.

designio [de'sixnjo] *nm* (*proyecto*) plan; (*destino*) fate.

desigual [desi'ɣwal] *a* (*terreno*) uneven; (*lucha etc*) unequal.

desilusión [desilu'sjon] *nf* disappointment, disillusionment; **desilusionar** *vt* to disappoint; **desilusionarse** *vr* to become disillusioned.

desinfectar [desinfek'tar] *vt* to disinfect.

desinflar [desin'flar] *vt* to deflate.

desintegración [desinteɣra'θjon] *nf* disintegration.

desinterés [desinte'res] *nm*

(*objetividad*) disinterestedness; (*altruismo*) unselfishness.

desistir [desis'tir] *vi* (*renunciar*) to stop, desist.

desleal [desle'al] *a* (*infiel*) disloyal; ~**tad** *nf* disloyalty.

deslenguado, a [deslen'ɣwaðo, a] *a* (*grosero*) foul-mouthed.

desligar [desli'ɣar] *vt* (*desatar*) to untie, undo; (*separar*) to separate; ~**se** *vr* (*dos personas*) to break up, separate; (*de un compromiso*) to extricate o.s.

desliz [des'liθ] *nm* (*de coche*) skid; (*de persona*) slip, slide; (*fig*) lapse; ~**ar** *vt* to slip, slide; ~**arse** *vr* (*escurrirse*: *persona*) to slip, slide; (*coche*) to skid; (*aguas mansas*) to flow gently; (*error*) to slip in.

deslucido, a [deslu'θiðo, a] *a* (*gen*) dull; (*torpe*) awkward, graceless; (*marchitado*) tarnished.

deslumbrar [deslum'brar] *vt* to dazzle.

desmán [des'man] *nm* (*exceso*) outrage; (*abuso de poder*) abuse.

desmandarse [desman'darse] *vr* (*abusarse*) to behave badly; (*excederse*) to get out of hand; (*caballo*) to bolt.

desmantelar [desmante'lar] *vt* (*deshacer*) to dismantle; (*casa*) to strip.

desmayado, a [desma'jaðo, a] *a* (*sin sentido*) unconscious; (*carácter*) dull; (*débil*) faint, weak.

desmayar [desma'jar] *vi* to lose heart; ~**se** *vr* (*MED*) to faint; **desmayo** *nm* (*desvanecimiento*) faint; (*sin conciencia*) unconsciousness; (*depresión*) dejection.

desmedido, a [desme'ðiðo, a] *a* excessive; **desmedirse** *vr* to go too far, forget o.s.

desmejorar [desmexo'rar] *vt* (*dañar*) to impair, spoil; (*MED*) to weaken.

desmembrar [desmem'brar] *vt* (*MED*) to dismember; (*fig*) to separate.

desmentir [desmen'tir] vt (contradecir) to contradict; (refutar) to deny // vi: ~ **de** to refute; ~**se** vr to contradict o.s.

desmenuzar [desmenu'θar] vt (deshacer) to crumble; (examinar) to examine closely.

desmerecer [desmere'θer] vt to be unworthy of // vi (deteriorarse) to deteriorate.

desmesurado, a [desmesu'raðo, a] a disproportionate.

desmontar [desmon'tar] vt (deshacer) to dismantle; (tierra) to level // vi to dismount.

desmoralizar [desmorali'θar] vt to demoralize.

desmoronar [desmoro'nar] vt to wear away, erode; ~**se** vr (edificio, dique) to fall into disrepair; (sociedad) to decay; (economía) to decline.

desnivel [desni'βel] nm (de terreno) unevenness; **paso a** ~ (AUTO) flyover.

desnudar [desnu'ðar] vt (desvestir) to undress; (despojar) to strip; ~**se** vr (desvestirse) to get undressed; **desnudo, a** a naked // nm/f nude; **desnudo de** devoid or bereft of.

desobedecer [desoβeðe'θer] vt, vi to disobey; **desobediencia** nf disobedience.

desocupación [desokupa'θjon] nf (ocio) leisure; (desempleo) unemployment; **desocupado, a** a at leisure; unemployed; (deshabitado) empty, vacant; **desocupar** vt to vacate.

desodorante [desoðo'rante] nm deodorant.

desolación [desola'θjon] nf (lugar) desolation; (fig) grief; **desolar** vt to ruin, lay waste; **desolarse** vr to grieve.

desorden [des'orðen] nm confusion; (político) disorder.

desorganizar [desorvani'θar] vt (desordenar) to disorganize; (deshacer) to disrupt.

desorientar [desorjen'tar] vt (extraviar) to mislead; (confundir, desconcertar) to confuse; ~**se** vr (perderse) to lose one's way.

despabilado, a [despaβi'laðo, a] a (despierto) wide-awake; (fig) alert, sharp.

despabilar [despaβi'lar] vt (vela) to snuff; (el ingenio) to sharpen; (fortuna, negocio) to squander // vi, ~**se** vr to wake up.

despacio [des'paθjo] ad slowly.

despachar [despa'tʃar] vt (negocio) to do, complete; (enviar) to send, dispatch; (vender) to sell, deal in; (billete) to issue; (mandar ir) to send away.

despacho [des'patʃo] nm (oficina) office; (de paquetes) dispatch; (venta) sale; (comunicación) message; (eficacia) efficiency; (rapidez) promptness.

desparramar [desparra'mar] vt (esparcir) to scatter; (noticia) to spread; (dinero, fortuna) to squander; (líquido) to spill.

despavorido, a [despaβo'riðo, a] a terrified.

despectivo, a [despek'tiβo, a] a (despreciativo) derogatory; (LING) pejorative.

despecho [des'petʃo] nm spite; **a** ~ **de** in spite of.

despedazar [despeða'θar] vt to tear to pieces.

despedida [despe'ðiða] nf (adios) farewell; (de obrero) sacking.

despedir [despe'ðir] vt (visita) to see off, show out; (licenciar: empleado) to discharge; (inquilino) to evict; (objeto) to hurl; (flecha) to fire; (olor etc) to give out or off; ~**se** vr: ~**se de** to say goodbye to.

despegar [despe'var] vt to unstick // vi to take off; ~**se** vr to come loose, come unstuck; **despego** nm detachment.

despegue [des'peɣe] nm takeoff.

despeinado, a [despei'naðo, a] a dishevelled, unkempt.

despejado, a [despe'xaðo, a] *a (lugar)* clear, free; *(cielo)* cloudless, clear; *(persona)* wide-awake.

despejar [despe'xar] *vt (gen)* to clear; *(misterio)* to clarify, clear up // *vi (el tiempo)* to clear; ~**se** *vr (tiempo, cielo)* to clear (up); *(misterio)* to become clearer; *(persona)* to relax.

despejo [des'pexo] *nm (de casa, calle etc)* brightness; *(desenvoltura)* self-confidence; *(talento, ingenio)* alertness.

despensa [des'pensa] *nf* larder.

despeñadero [despeɲa'ðero] *nm (GEO)* cliff, precipice.

desperdicio [desper'ðiθjo] *nm (despilfarro)* squandering; *(residuo)* waste.

desperezarse [despere'θarse] *vr* to stretch (o.s.).

desperfecto [desper'fekto] *nm (deterioro)* slight damage; *(defecto)* flaw, imperfection.

despertador [desperta'ðor] *nm* alarm clock.

despertar [desper'tar] *vt (persona)* to wake up; *(vocación)* to awaken; *(recuerdos)* to revive; *(apetito)* to arouse // *vi,* ~**se** *vr* to awaken, wake up // *nm* awakening.

despido [des'piðo] *nm* dismissal, sacking.

despierto *etc vb ver* **despertar.**

despierto, a [des'pjerto, a] *a* awake; *(fig)* sharp, alert.

despilfarro [despil'farro] *nm (derroche)* squandering; *(lujo desmedido)* extravagance.

despistar [despis'tar] *vt* to throw off the track or scent; *(fig)* to mislead, confuse; ~**se** *vr* to take the wrong road; *(fig)* to become confused.

desplazamiento [desplaθa'mjento] *nm* displacement; *(de tierras)* landslip.

desplegar [desple'ɣar] *vt (tela, papel)* to unfold, open out; *(bandera)* to unfurl.

despoblar [despo'βlar] *vt (de gente)* to depopulate.

despojar [despo'xar] *vt (alguien: de sus bienes)* to divest of, deprive of; *(casa)* to strip, leave bare; *(alguien: de su cargo)* to strip of; **despojo** *nm (acto)* plundering; *(objetos)* plunder, loot; **despojos** *nmpl* waste *sg; (rocas, ladrillos)* debris *sg.*

desposado, a [despo'saðo, a] *a, nm/f* newly-wed.

desposeer [despose'er] *vt (despojar)* to dispossess.

déspota ['despota] *nm* despot.

despreciar [despre'θjar] *vt (desdeñar)* to despise, scorn; *(afrentar)* to slight; **desprecio** *nm* scorn, contempt; slight.

desprender [despren'der] *vt (separar)* to separate; *(desatar)* to unfasten; *(olor)* to give off; ~**se** *vr (botón: caerse)* to fall off; *(: abrirse)* to unfasten; *(olor, perfume)* to be given off; ~**se de** to follow from; **se desprende que** it transpires that.

desprendimiento [desprendi'mjento] *nm (gen)* loosening; *(de botón que se cae)* detachment; *(de botón que se abre)* unfastening; *(generosidad)* disinterestedness; *(indiferencia)* detachment; *(de gas)* release; *(de tierra, rocas)* landslide.

despreocupado, a [despreoku'paðo, a] *a (sin preocupación)* unworried, nonchalant; *(desprejuiciado)* impartial; *(negligente)* careless; **despreocuparse** *vr* to be carefree; **despreocuparse de** to have no interest in.

desprevenido, a [despreβe'niðo, a] *a (no preparado)* unprepared, unready.

desproporción [despropor'θjon] *nf* disproportion, lack of proportion.

después [des'pwes] *ad* afterwards, later; *(próximo paso)* next; ~ **de** comer after eating; **un año** ~ a year later; ~ **se debatió** el tema the matter was discussed; ~ **de**

corregido el texto after the text had been corrected; **~ de todo** after all.

desquite [des'kite] nm (satisfacción) satisfaction; (venganza) revenge.

destacar [desta'kar] vt to emphasize, point up; (MIL) to detach, detail // vi, **~se** vr (resaltarse) to stand out; (persona) to be outstanding or exceptional.

destajo [des'taxo] nm: **trabajar a ~** to do piecework.

destapar [desta'par] vt (gen) to open; (cacerola) to take the lid off, uncover; **~se** vr (revelarse) to reveal one's true character.

destartalado, a [destarta'laðo, a] a (desordenado) untidy; (ruinoso) tumbledown.

destello [des'teʎo] nm (de estrella) twinkle; (de faro) signal light.

destemplado, a [destem'plaðo, a] a (MUS) out of tune; (voz) harsh; (MED) out of sorts, indisposed.

desteñir [deste'ɲir] vt to fade // vi, **~se** vr (color) to fade; **esta tela no destiñe** this fabric will not run.

desterrar [deste'rrar] vt (exilar) to exile; (fig) to banish, dismiss.

destierro [des'tjerro] nm exile.

destilación [destila'θjon] nf distillation; **destilar** vt to distil; **destilería** nf distillery.

destinar [desti'nar] vt to destine; (funcionario) to appoint, assign; (fondos) to set aside (a for); **~se** vr to be destined.

destinatario, a [destina'tarjo, a] nm/f addressee.

destino [des'tino] nm (suerte) destiny; (de viajero) destination; (función) use.

destituir [destitu'ir] vt to dismiss.

destornillador [destorniʎa'ðor] nm screwdriver; **destornillar** vt, **destornillarse** vr (tornillo) to unscrew.

destreza [des'treθa] nf (habilidad) skill; (maña) dexterity; (facilidad) handiness.

destrozar [destro'θar] vt (romper) to smash, break (up); (estropear) to ruin; (deshacer) to shatter; (el corazón) to break.

destrozo [des'troθo] nm (acción) destruction; (desastre) smashing; **~s** nmpl (pedazos) pieces; (daños) havoc sg.

destrucción [destruk'θjon] nf destruction.

destruir [destru'ir] vt to destroy.

desunir [desu'nir] vt to separate; (TEC) to disconnect; (fig) to cause a quarrel or rift between.

desusado, a [desu'saðo, a] a (anticuado) obsolete.

desvalido, a [desβa'liðo, a] a (desprotegido) destitute; (POL) underprivileged; (sin fuerzas) helpless.

desván [des'βan] nm attic.

desvanecer [desβane'θer] vt (disipar) to dispel; (borrar) to blur; **~se** vr (humo) to vanish, disappear; (color) to fade; (recuerdo) to fade away.

desvanecimiento [desβaneθi'mjento] nm (desaparición) disappearance; (de colores) fading; (evaporación) evaporation; (MED) fainting fit.

desvariar [desβa'rjar] vi (enfermo) to be delirious; **desvarío** nm delirium.

desvelar [desβe'lar] vt to keep awake; **~se** vr to stay awake; (fig) to be vigilant or watchful; **desvelo** nm lack of sleep; (insomnio) sleeplessness; (fig) vigilance.

desventaja [desβen'taxa] nf disadvantage.

desventura [desβen'tura] nf misfortune.

desvergonzado, a [desβerɣon'θaðo, a] a shameless.

desvergüenza [desβer'ɣwenθa] nf (descaro) shamelessness; (insolencia) impudence; (mala conducta) effrontery.

desviación [desβja'θjon] nf deviation.

desviar [des'βjar] vt to turn aside; (río) to alter the course of; (navío) to divert, re-route; (conversación) to sidetrack; ~se vr (apartarse del camino) to turn aside, deviate; (: barco) to go off course.

desvío [des'βio] nm (desviación) detour, diversion; (fig) indifference.

desvirtuar [desβir'twar] vt, ~se vr to spoil.

desvivirse [desβi'βirse] vr: ~ por to long for, crave for.

detallar [deta'ʎar] vt to detail; (COM) to sell retail.

detalle [de'taʎe] nm detail; (fig) gesture, token; **al** ~ in detail.

detallista [deta'ʎista] nm/f retailer.

detener [dete'ner] vt (tren, persona) to stop; (JUR) to arrest; (objeto) to keep; ~se vr to stop; (demorarse): ~se en to delay over, linger over.

detenido, a [dete'niðo, a] a (preso) arrested, under arrest; (minucioso) detailed; (tímido) timid // nm/f person under arrest, prisoner.

detergente [deter'xente] nm detergent.

deteriorar [deterjo'rar] vt to spoil, damage; ~se vr to deteriorate; (relaciones) to become damaged; **deterioro** nm deterioration.

determinación [determina'θjon] nf (empeño) determination; (decisión) decision; **determinar** vt (plazo) to fix; (precio) to settle; **determinarse** vr to decide.

detestar [detes'tar] vt to detest.

detonar [deto'nar] vi to detonate.

detrás [de'tras] ad behind; (atrás) at the back; ~ **de** behind.

detrimento [detri'mento] nm harm, damage; **en** ~ **de** to the detriment of.

deuda ['deuða] nf (condición) indebtedness, debt; (cantidad) debt.

deudor, a [deu'ðor, a] a: **saldo** ~ debit balance // nm/f debtor.

devaluación [deβalwa'θjon] nf devaluation.

devastar [deβas'tar] vt (destruir) to devastate.

devoción [deβo'θjon] nf devotion.

devolución [deβolu'θjon] nf (reenvío) return, sending back; (reembolso) repayment.

devolver [deβol'βer] vt (gen) to return; (carta al correo) to send back; (COM) to repay, refund; (visita, la palabra) to return.

devorar [deβo'rar] vt to devour.

devoto, a [de'βoto, a] a devout // nm/f admirer.

di vb ver **dar; decir**.

día ['dia] nm day; **¿qué** ~ **es?** what's the date?; **estar/poner al** ~ to be/keep up to date; **el** ~ **de hoy/de mañana** today/tomorrow; **al** ~ **siguiente** on the following day; **vivir al** ~ to live from hand to mouth; **de** ~ by day, in daylight; **en pleno** ~ in full daylight.

diablo ['djaβlo] nm devil; **diablura** nf prank; **diabluras** nfpl mischief sg.

diabólico, a [dja'βoliko, a] a diabolical.

diafragma [dja'fraxma] nm diaphragm.

diagnosis [djax'nosis] nf, **diagnóstico** [djax'nostiko] nm diagnosis.

dialecto [dja'lekto] nm dialect.

diálogo ['djalovo] nm dialogue.

diamante [dja'mante] nm diamond.

diapositiva [djaposi'tiβa] nf (FOTO) slide, transparency.

diario, a ['djarjo, a] a daily // nm newspaper.

diarrea [dja'rrea] nf diarrhoea.

dibujar [diβu'xar] vt to draw, sketch; **dibujo** nm drawing; **dibujos animados** cartoons.

diccionario [dikθjo'narjo] nm dictionary.

dice etc vb ver **decir**.

diciembre [di'θjembre] nm December.

dictado [dik'taðo] nm dictation.

dictador [dikta'ðor] nm dictator; **dictadura** nf dictatorship.

dictamen [dik'tamen] nm (opinión) opinion; (juicio) judgment.

dicho, a ['ditʃo, a] pp de **decir** // a: en ~s países in the aforementioned countries // nm saying // nf happiness.

diente ['djente] nm (ANAT, TEC) tooth; (ZOOL) fang; (: de elefante) tusk; (de ajo) clove; **da ~ con ~** his teeth are chattering; **hablar entre ~s** to mutter, mumble.

dieron vb ver **dar.**

diesel ['disel] a: **motor ~** diesel engine.

dieta ['djeta] nf diet.

diez [djeθ] num ten.

diferencia [dife'renθja] nf difference; **diferenciar** vt to differentiate between // vi to differ; **diferenciarse** vr to differ, be different; (distinguirse) to distinguish o.s.

diferente [dife'rente] a different.

difícil [di'fiθil] a difficult.

dificultad [difikul'taθ] nf difficulty; (problema) trouble.

dificultar [difikul'tar] vt (complicar) to complicate, make difficult; (estorbar) to obstruct.

difundir [difun'dir] vt (esparcir) to spread, diffuse; (divulgar) to divulge; **~se** vr to spread (out).

difunto, a [di'funto, a] a dead, deceased // nm/f deceased (person).

digerir [dixe'rir] vt to digest; (fig) to absorb.

digital [dixi'tal] a digital.

dignarse [dix'narse] vr to deign to.

dignidad [dixni'ðaθ] nf dignity; (honra) honour.

digno, a ['dixno, a] a worthy.

digo etc vb ver **decir.**

dije etc vb ver **decir.**

dilatación [dilata'θjon] nf (expansión) dilation.

dilatado, a [dila'taðo, a] a dilated; (ancho) widened; (largo) long drawn-out; (extenso) extensive.

dilatar [dila'tar] vt (cuerpo) to dilate; (prolongar) to stretch; (en el tiempo) to prolong.

dilema [di'lema] nm dilemma.

diligencia [dili'xenθja] nf diligence; (ocupación) errand, job; ~s nfpl (JUR) formalities; **diligente** a diligent.

diluir [dilu'ir] vt to dilute.

diluvio [di'luβjo] nm deluge, flood.

dimensión [dimen'sjon] nf dimension.

diminuto, a [dimi'nuto, a] a tiny.

dimitir [dimi'tir] vi to resign.

dimos vb ver **dar.**

Dinamarca [dina'marka] nf Denmark; **dinamarqués, esa** a Danish // nm/f Dane.

dinámico, a [di'namiko, a] a dynamic.

dinamita [dina'mita] nf dynamite.

dínamo [di'namo] nf dynamo.

dineral [dine'ral] nm large sum of money, fortune.

dinero [di'nero] nm money; ~ **efectivo** cash, ready cash.

dio vb ver **dar.**

dios [djos] nm god.

diosa [di'josa] nf goddess.

diplomacia [diplo'maθja] nf diplomacy; (fig) tact; **diplomático, a** a diplomatic // nm/f diplomat.

diputado, a [dipu'taðo, a] nm/f delegate; (Cortes) deputy.

diré etc vb ver **decir.**

dirección [direk'θjon] nf direction; (señas) address; (AUTO) steering; (gerencia) management; (POL) leadership; ~ **única** o **obligatoria** o **prohibida** one-way.

directo, a [di'rekto, a] a direct; **transmitir en ~** to broadcast live.

director, a [direk'tor, a] a leading // nm/f director; ~ **de cine/de escena** producer/stage manager.

dirigir [diriˈxir] *vt* to direct; (*carta*) to address; (*obra de teatro, film*) to produce, direct; (*coche, barco*) to steer; (*avión*) to fly; (*MUS*) to conduct; (*comercio*) to manage; ~**se** *vr*: ~**se a** to go towards, make one's way towards; (*fig*) to speak to.

discernir [disθerˈnir] *vt* (*distinguir, discriminar*) to discern.

disciplina [disθiˈplina] *nf* discipline; **disciplinar** *vt* to discipline.

discípulo, a [disˈθipulo, a] *nm/f* disciple.

disco [ˈdisko] *nm* disc; (*DEPORTE*) discus; (*TELEC*) dial; (*AUTO*) signal; (*fam*) boring affair; ~ **de larga duración/de duración extendida** long-playing record (L.P.)/extended play record (E.P.); ~ **de freno** brake disc.

discordia [disˈkorðja] *nf* discord.

discoteca [diskoˈteka] *nf* discotheque.

discreción [diskreˈθjon] *nf* discretion; (*reserva*) prudence; (*secreto*) secrecy; **comer a** ~ **lo** to eat as much as one wishes; **discrecional** *a* (*facultativo*) discretionary.

discrepancia [diskreˈpanθja] *nf* (*diferencia*) discrepancy; (*desacuerdo*) disagreement.

discreto, a [disˈkreto, a] *a* (*diplomático*) discreet; (*sensato*) sensible; (*listo*) shrewd; (*reservado*) quiet; (*sobrio*) sober; (*retraído*) unobtrusive; (*razonable*) reasonable.

discriminación [diskriminaˈθjon] *nf* discrimination.

disculpa [disˈkulpa] *nf* excuse; (*pedir perdón*) apology; **disculpar** *vt* to excuse, pardon; **disculparse** *vr* to excuse o.s.; to apologize.

discurrir [diskuˈrrir] *vt* to invent (*pensar, reflexionar*) to think; **meditate** (*decurrir*) to roam, wander; (*el tiempo*) to pass, flow by.

discurso [disˈkurso] *nm* speech; (*razonamiento*) reasoning power.

discutir [diskuˈtir] *vt* (*debatir*) to

discuss; (*pelear*) to argue about; (*contradecir*) to contradict.

diseminar [disemiˈnar] *vt* to disseminate, spread.

diseño [diˈseɲo] *nm* (*dibujo*) design.

disfraz [disˈfraθ] *nm* (*máscara*) disguise; (*excusa*) pretext; ~**ar** *vt* to disguise; ~**arse** *vr*: ~**arse de** to disguise o.s. as.

disfrutar [disfruˈtar] *vt* to enjoy // *vi* to enjoy o.s.; ~ **de** to enjoy, possess.

disgustar [disɣusˈtar] *vt* (*no gustar*) to displease; (*contrariar, enojar*) to annoy, upset; ~**se** *vr* to be annoyed; (*dos personas*) to fall out.

disgusto [disˈɣusto] *nm* (*repugnancia*) disgust; (*contrariedad*) annoyance; (*tristeza*) grief; (*riña*) quarrel; (*avería*) misfortune.

disidente [disiˈðente] *nm* dissident.

disimular [disimuˈlar] *vt* (*ocultar*) to hide, conceal; (*perdonar*) to excuse // *vi* to dissemble.

disipar [disiˈpar] *vt* to dispel; (*fortuna*) to squander; ~**se** *vr* (*nubes*) to vanish; (*indisciplinarse*) to dissipate.

disminución [disminuˈθjon] *nf* diminution.

disminuir [disminuˈir] *vt* (*acortar*) to decrease; (*achicar*) to diminish; (*estrechar*) to lessen.

disoluto, a [disoˈluto, a] *a* dissolute.

disolver [disolˈβer] *vt* (*gen*) to dissolve; ~**se** *vr* to be dissolved.

disparar [dispaˈrar] *vt, vi* to shoot, fire.

disparate [dispaˈrate] *nm* (*tontería*) foolish remark; (*error*) blunder.

disparo [disˈparo] *nm* shot.

dispensar [dispenˈsar] *vt* to dispense; (*disculpar*) to excuse.

dispersar [disperˈsar] *vt* to disperse; ~**se** *vr* to scatter.

disponer [dispoˈner] *vt* (*arreglar*) to arrange; (*ordenar*) to put in order; (*preparar*) to prepare, get

ready // vi: ~ **de** to have, own; ~**se
vr**: ~**se para** to prepare to, prepare
for.

disponible [dispo'niβle] a available.

disposición [disposi'θjon] nf arrangement, disposition; (aptitud)
aptitude; **a la ~ de** at the disposal
of.

dispuesto, a [dis'pwesto, a] pp de
disponer // a (arreglado) arranged;
(preparado) disposed.

disputar [dispu'tar] vt (discutir) to
dispute, question; (contender) to
contend for // vi to argue.

distanciar [distan'θjar] vt to space
out; ~**se vr** to become estranged.

distante [dis'tante] a distant.

diste, disteis vb ver **dar.**

distinción [distin'θjon] nf (gen)
distinction; (claridad) clarity; (elegancia) elegance; (honor) honour.

distinguir [distin'gir] vt to distinguish; (escoger) to single out;
~**se vr** to be distinguished.

distinto, a [dis'tinto, a] a different;
(claro) clear.

distracción [distrak'θjon] nf
(pasatiempo) hobby, pastime;
(olvido) absent-mindedness, distraction.

distraer [distra'er] vt (entretener)
to entertain; (divertir) to amuse;
(fondos) to embezzle; ~**se vr**
(entretenerse) to amuse o.s.; (perder
la concentración) to allow one's
attention to wander.

distraído, a [distra'iðo, a] a (gen)
absent-minded; (entretenido) amusing.

distribuir [distriβu'ir] vt to
distribute.

distrito [dis'trito] nm (sector,
territorio) region; (barrio) district.

disturbio [dis'turβjo] nm disturbance.

disuadir [diswa'ðir] vt to dissuade.

disuelto [di'swelto] pp de
disolver.

divagar [diβa'xar] vi (desviarse) to

digress; (errar) to wander.

diván [di'βan] nm divan.

divergencia [diβer'xenθja] nf
divergence.

diversidad [diβersi'ðað] nf
diversity, variety.

diversificar [diβersifi'kar] vt to
diversify.

diversión [diβer'sjon] nf (gen)
entertainment; (actividad) hobby,
pastime.

diverso, a [di'βerso, a] a diverse;
~**s** sundry.

divertir [diβer'tir] vt (entretener,
recrear) to amuse, entertain;
(apartar, distraer) to divert; ~**se vr**
(pasarlo bien) to have a good time;
(distraerse) to amuse o.s.

dividir [diβi'ðir] vt (gen) to divide;
(separar) to separate; (distribuir)
to distribute, share out.

divino, a [di'βino, a] a divine.

divisa [di'βisa] nf (emblema,
moneda) emblem, badge; ~**s** nfpl
currency sg.

división [diβi'sjon] nf (gen)
division; (de partido) split; (de país)
partition; (LING) hyphen; (divergencia) divergence.

divorciar [diβor'θjar] vt to divorce;
~**se vr** to get divorced; **divorcio** nm
divorce.

divulgar [diβul'xar] vt (desparramar) to spread; (hacer circular)
to divulge, circulate; ~**se vr** to leak
out.

doblar [do'βlar] vt (gen) to double;
(papel) to fold; (caño) to bend; (la
esquina) to turn, go round; (film) to
dub // vi to turn; (campana) to toll;
~**se vr** (plegarse) to fold (up),
crease; (encorvarse) to bend; ~**se
de risa/dolor** to be doubled up with
laughter/pain.

doble [do'βle] a (gen) double; (de
dos aspectos) dual; (fig) two-faced
// nm double; (campana) toll(ing);
~**s** nmpl (DEPORTE) doubles sg //
nm/f (TEATRO) double, stand-in; **con
~ sentido** with a double meaning.

doblegar [doβle'xar] *vt* to fold, crease; **~se** *vr* to yield.

doce [ˈdoθe] *num* twelve.

docena [doˈθena] *nf* dozen.

dócil [ˈdoθil] *a* (*pasivo*) docile; (*obediente*) obedient.

doctor, a [dokˈtor, a] *nm/f* doctor.

doctrina [dokˈtrina] *nf* doctrine, teaching.

documentación [dokumentaˈθjon] *nf* documentation, papers *pl.*

documento [dokuˈmento] *nm* (*certificado*) document.

dólar [ˈdolar] *nm* dollar.

doler [doˈler] *vt*, *vi* to hurt; (*fig*) to grieve; **~se** *vr* (*de su situación*) to grieve, feel sorry; (*de las desgracias ajenas*) to sympathize; **me duele el brazo** my arm hurts.

dolor [doˈlor] *nm* pain; (*fig*) grief, sorrow.

domar [doˈmar], **domesticar** [domestiˈkar] *vt* to tame.

domicilio [domiˈθiljo] *nm* home; **~ particular** private residence; **~ social** head office.

dominante [domiˈnante] *a* dominant; (*person*) domineering.

dominar [domiˈnar] *vt* (*gen*) to dominate; (*idiomas etc*) to have a command of // *vi* to dominate, prevail; **~se** *vr* to control o.s.

domingo [doˈmiŋgo] *nm* Sunday.

dominio [doˈminjo] *nm* (*tierras*) domain; (*autoridad*) power, authority; (*de las pasiones*) grip, hold; (*de varios idiomas*) command

don [don] *nm* (*talento*) gift; **~ Juan Gómez** Mr Juan Gómez or Juan Gómez Esq.

donaire [doˈnaire] *nm* charm.

doncella [donˈθeʎa] *nf* (*criada*) maid; (*muchacha*) girl.

donde [ˈdonde] *ad* where // *prep*: **el coche está allí ~ el parquímetro** the car is over there by the lamppost or where the lamppost is; **por ~** through which; **en ~** where, in which.

dónde [ˈdonde] *ad interr* where?; ¿a

~ vas? where are you going (to)?; ¿**de ~ vienes?** where have you come from?; ¿**por ~?** where?, whereabouts?

dondequiera [dondeˈkjera] *ad* anywhere; **por ~** everywhere, all over the place // *conj*: **~ que** wherever.

doña [ˈdoɲa] *nf* título de mujer que no se traduce.

dorado, a [doˈraðo, a] *a* (*color*) golden; (*TEC*) gilt.

dormir [dorˈmir] *vt*: **~ la siesta por la tarde** to have an afternoon nap // *vi* to sleep; **~se** *vr* to go to sleep.

dormitar [dormiˈtar] *vi* to doze.

dormitorio [dormiˈtorjo] *nm* bedroom; **~ común** dormitory.

dos [dos] *num* two.

dosis [ˈdosis] *nf inv* dose, dosage.

dotado, a [doˈtaðo, a] *a* gifted; **~ de** endowed with.

dotar [doˈtar] *vt* to endow; **dote** *nf* dowry; **dotes** *nfpl* gifts.

doy *vb* ver **dar.**

drama [ˈdrama] *nm* drama.

dramaturgo [dramaˈturxo] *nm* dramatist, playwright.

droga [ˈdroxa] *nf* drug.

drogadicto, a [droxaˈðikto, a] *nm/f* drug addict.

ducha [ˈdutʃa] *nf* (*baño*) shower; (*MED*) douche; **ducharse** *vr* to take a shower.

duda [ˈduða] *nf* doubt.

dudoso, a [duˈðoso, a] *a* (*incierto*) hesitant; (*sospechoso*) doubtful.

duelo [ˈdwelo] *nm* (*combate*) duel; (*luto*) mourning.

duende [ˈdwende] *nm* imp, goblin.

dueño, a [ˈdweɲo, a] *nm/f* (*propietario*) owner; (*de casa*) landlord/lady; (*empresario*) employer.

duermo *etc vb ver* **dormir.**

dulce [ˈdulθe] *a* sweet // *ad* gently, softly // *nm* sweet.

dulzura [dulˈθura] *nf* sweetness; (*ternura*) gentleness.

duplicar [dupli'kar] *vt* (*hacer el doble de*) to duplicate; **~se** *vr* to double.

duque ['duke] *nm* duke.

duquesa [du'kesa] *nf* duchess.

duración [dura'θjon] *nf* duration.

duradero, a [dura'ðero, a] *a* lasting.

durante [du'rante] *ad* during.

durar [du'rar] *vi* (*permanecer*) to last; (*recuerdo*) to remain.

dureza [du'reθa] *nf* (*calidad*) hardness.

durmí *etc vb ver* **dormir.**

durmiente [dur'mjente] *nm/f* sleeper.

duro, a [''duro, a] *a* (*gen*) hard; (*carácter*) tough // *ad* hard // *nm* (*moneda*) five peseta coin/note.

E

e [e] *conj* and.

E *abr de* **este.**

ebanista [eβa'nista] *nm* cabinetmaker.

ébano ['eβano] *nm* ebony.

ebrio, a [''eβrjo, a] *a* drunk.

ebullición [eβuʎi'θjon] *nf* boiling; (*fig*) ferment.

eclesiástico, a [ekle'sjastiko, a] *a* ecclesiastical.

eclipse [e'klipse] *nm* eclipse.

eco ['eko] *nm* echo; **tener ~** to catch on.

ecología [ekolo'xia] *nf* ecology.

economato [ekono'mato] *nm* cooperative store.

economía [ekono'mia] *nf* (*sistema*) economy; (*cualidad*) thrift.

económico, a [eko'nomiko, a] *a* (*barato*) cheap, economical; (*persona*) thrifty; (*COM: plan*) financial; (*: situación*) economic.

economista [ekono'mista] *nm/f* economist.

ecuador [ekwa'ðor] *nm* equator; **el E~** Ecuador.

ecuánime [e'kwanime] *a* (*carácter*) level-headed; (*estado*) calm.

ecuestre [e'kwestre] *a* equestrian.

echar [e't∫ar] *vt* to throw; (*agua, vino*) to pour (out); (*empleado: despedir*) to fire, sack; (*bigotes*) to grow; (*hojas*) to sprout; (*cartas*) to post; (*humo*) to emit, give out // *vi*: **~ a correr/llorar** to break into a run/burst into tears; **~se** *vr* to lie down; **~ llave a** to lock (up); **~ abajo** (*gobierno*) to overthrow; (*edificio*) to demolish; **~ mano a** to lay hands on.

edad [e'ðað] *nf* age; **¿qué ~ tienes?** how old are you?; **tiene ocho años de ~** he is eight (years old); **de ~ mediana/avanzada** middle-aged/ advanced in years; **la E~ Media** the Middle Ages.

edición [eði'θjon] *nf* (*acto*) publication; (*ejemplar*) edition.

edicto [e'ðikto] *nm* edict, proclamation.

edificio [eði'fiθjo] *nm* building; (*fig*) edifice, structure.

editar [eði'tar] *vt* (*publicar*) to publish; (*preparar textos*) to edit.

editor, a [eði'tor, a] *nm/f* (*que publica*) publisher; (*de periódico etc*) editor // *a*: **casa ~a** publishing house; **~ial** *a* editorial // *nm* leading article, editorial; **casa ~ial** publishing house.

educación [eðuka'θjon] *nf* education; (*crianza*) upbringing; (*modales*) (good) manners *pl*.

educar [eðu'kar] *vt* to educate; (*criar*) to bring up; (*voz*) to train.

EE. UU. *nmpl abr de* **Estados Unidos** USA (United States of America).

efectivo, a [efek'tiβo, a] *a* effective; (*real*) actual, real // *nm*: **pagar en ~** to pay (in) cash; **hacer ~ un cheque** to cash a cheque.

efecto [e'fekto] *nm* effect, result; **~s** *nmpl* goods; (*COM*) assets; **en**

in fact; (*respuesta*) exactly, indeed.

efectuar [efek'twar] *vt* to carry out; (*viaje*) to make.

eficacia [efi'kaθja] *nf* (*de persona*) efficiency; (*de medicamento*) effectiveness.

eficaz [efi'kaθ] *a* (*persona*) efficient; (*acción*) effective.

egipcio, a [e'xipθjo, a] *a, nm/f* Egyptian.

Egipto [e'xipto] *nm* Egypt.

egoísmo [exo'ismo] *nm* egoism.

egoísta [exo'ista] *a* egoistical, selfish // *nm/f* egoist.

egregio, a [e'xrexjo, a] *a* eminent, distinguished.

Eire ['eire] *nm* Eire.

ej. *abr de* **ejemplo.**

eje ['exe] *nm* (GEO, MAT) axis; (*de rueda*) axle; (*de máquina*) shaft, spindle; **la idea ~** the central idea.

ejecución [exeku'θjon] *nf* (*gen*) execution; (*cumplimiento*) fulfilment; (*actuación*) performance; (JUR: *embargo de deudor*) attachment, distraint.

ejecutar [exeku'tar] *vt* (*gen*) to execute, carry out; (*matar*) to execute; (*cumplir*) to fulfil; (MUS) to perform; (JUR: *embargar*) to attach, distrain (on).

ejecutivo, a [exeku'tiβo, a] *a* executive; **el poder ~** the Executive (Power).

ejemplar [exem'plar] *a* exemplary // *nm* example; (ZOOL) specimen; (*de libro*) copy; (*de periódico*) number, issue.

ejemplo [e'xemplo] *nm* example; **por ~** for example.

ejercer [exer'θer] *vt* to exercise; (*influencia*) to exert; (*un oficio*) to practise // *vi* (*practicar*) to practise (*de ...*); (*tener oficio*) to hold office.

ejercicio [exer'θiθjo] *nm* exercise; (*período*) tenure; **~ comercial** financial year.

ejército [e'xerθito] *nm* army; **entrar en el ~** to join the army, join up.

el [el] *det* the.

él [el] *pron* (*persona*) he; (*cosa*) it; (*después de prep: persona*) him; (: *cosa*) it.

elaborar [elaβo'rar] *vt* to elaborate; (*hacer*) to make; (*preparar*) to prepare; (*trabajar*) to work; (*calcular*) to work out.

elasticidad [elastiθi'ðað] *nf* elasticity; **elástico, a** *a* elastic; (*flexible*) flexible // *nm* elastic.

elección [elek'θjon] *nf* election; (*selección*) choice, selection.

electorado [elekto'raðo] *nm* electorate, voters *pl*.

electricidad [elektriθi'ðað] *nf* electricity.

electricista [elektri'θista] *nm/f* electrician.

eléctrico, a [e'lektriko, a] *a* electric // *nm* electric train.

electrizar [elektri'θar] *vt* to electrify.

electro... [elektro] *pref* electro...; **~cardiógrafo** *nm* electrocardiograph; **~cución** *nf* electrocution; **~cutar** *vt* to electrocute; **~chapado, a** *a* electroplated; **electrodo** *nm* electrode; **~domésticos** *nmpl* (electrical) household appliances; **~imán** *nm* electromagnet; **~magnético, a** *a* electromagnetic; **~motor** *nm* electric motor.

electrónico, a [elek'troniko, a] *a* electronic // *nf* electronics *sg*.

electrotecnia [elektro'teknja] *nf* electrical engineering; **electrotécnico, a** *nm/f* electrical engineer.

electrotermo [elektro'termo] *nm* immersion heater.

elefante [ele'fante] *nm* elephant; **~ marino** elephant seal.

elegancia [ele'sanθja] *nf* (*gracia*) elegance, grace; (*estilo*) stylishness; **elegante** *a* elegant, graceful, stylish; (*moda*) fashionable.

elegía [ele'xia] *nf* elegy.

elegir [ele'xir] *vt* (*escoger*) to

choose, select; *(optar)* to opt for; *(presidente)* to elect.

elemental [elemen'tal] *a (claro, obvio)* elementary; *(fundamental)* elemental, fundamental.

elemento [ele'mento] *nm* element; *(fig)* ingredient; ~s *nmpl* elements, rudiments.

elevación [eleβa'θjon] *nf* elevation; *(acto)* raising, lifting; *(de precios)* rise; *(GEO etc)* height, altitude; *(de persona)* loftiness; *(pey)* conceit, pride.

elevar [ele'βar] *vt* to raise, lift (up); *(precio)* to put up; ~se *vr (edificio)* to rise; *(precios)* to go up; *(transportarse, enajenarse)* to get carried away; *(engreírse)* to become conceited.

eliminar [elimi'nar] *vt* to eliminate, remove.

eliminatoria [elimina'torja] *nf* heat, preliminary (round).

elite [e'lite] *nf* elite.

elocuencia [elo'kwenθja] *nf* eloquence.

elogiar [elo'xjar] *vt* to praise, eulogize; **elogio** *nm* praise; *(tributo)* tribute.

eludir [elu'ðir] *vt (evitar)* to avoid, evade; *(escapar)* to escape, elude.

ella ['eʎa] *pron (persona)* she; *(cosa)* it; *(después de prep: persona)* her; *(: cosa)* it.

ellas ['eʎas] *pron (personas y cosas)* they; *(después de prep)* them.

ello ['eʎo] *pron* it.

ellos ['eʎos] *pron* they; *(después de prep)* them.

emanar [ema'nar] *vi:* ~ **de** to emanate from, come from; *(derivar de)* to originate in.

emancipar [emanθi'par] *vt* to emancipate; ~se *vr* to become emancipated, free o.s.

embadurnar [embaður'nar] *vt* to smear.

embajada [emba'xaða] *nf* embassy; *(mensaje)* message, errand.

embajador, a [embaxa'ðor, a]

nm/f ambassador/ambassadress.

embalar [emba'lar] *vt (envolver)* to parcel, wrap (up); *(envasar)* to package // *vi* to sprint.

embarazada [embara'θaða] *a* pregnant // *nf* pregnant woman.

embarazar [embara'θar] *vt* to obstruct, hamper; *(a una mujer)* to make pregnant; ~se *vr (aturdirse)* to become embarrassed; *(confundirse)* to get into a muddle; *(mujer)* to become pregnant.

embarazo [emba'raθo] *nm (de mujer)* pregnancy; *(impedimento)* obstacle, obstruction; *(timidez)* embarrassment.

embarcación [embarka'θjon] *nf (barco)* boat, craft; *(acto)* embarkation.

embarcadero [embarka'ðero] *nm* pier, landing stage.

embarcar [embar'kar] *vt (cargamento)* to ship, stow; *(personas)* to embark, put on board; ~se *vr* to embark, go on board.

embargar [embar'ɣar] *vt (impedir)* to impede, hinder; *(JUR)* to seize, impound.

embarque [em'barke] *nm* shipment, loading.

embaular [embau'lar] *vt* to pack (into a trunk); *(fig)* to stuff o.s. with.

embebecerse [embeβe'θerse] *vr (extasiarse)* to be lost in wonder, be amazed.

embeber [embe'βer] *vt (absorber)* to absorb, soak up; *(empapar)* to saturate // *vi* to shrink; ~se *vr:* ~se **en la lectura** to be engrossed or absorbed in a book.

embellecer [embeʎe'θer] *vt* to embellish, beautify.

embestida [embes'tiða] *nf* attack, onslaught; *(carga)* charge; **embestir** *vt* to attack, assault; *vt* to charge, attack // *vi* to attack.

emblema [em'blema] *nm* emblem.

embobado, a [embo'βaðo, a] *a (atontado)* stunned, bewildered.

embocadura [emboka'ðura] *nf*

narrow entrance; (de río) mouth; (MUS) mouthpiece.

émbolo ['embolo] nm (AUTO) piston.

embolsar [embol'sar] vt to pocket, put in one's pocket.

emborrachar [emborra'tʃar] vt to intoxicate, make drunk; ~se vr to get drunk.

emboscada [embos'kaða] nf (celada) ambush.

embotar [embo'tar] vt to blunt, dull; ~se vr (adormecerse) to go numb.

embotellar [embote'ʎar] vt to bottle; ~se vr (circulación) to get into a jam.

embozar [embo'θar] vt to muffle (up).

embragar [embra'xar] vi to let in the clutch.

embrague [em'braxe] nm (también pedal de ~) clutch.

embravecer [embraβe'θer] vt to enrage, infuriate; ~se vr to become furious, (el mar) to get rough; (tormenta) to rage.

embriagado, a [embrja'xaðo, a] a (emborrachado) intoxicated, drunk.

embriagar [embrja'xar] vt (emborrachar) to intoxicate, make drunk; (alegrar) to delight; ~se vr (emborracharse) to get drunk.

embriaguez [embrja'xeθ] nf (borrachera) drunkenness; (fig) rapture, delight.

embrollar [embro'ʎar] vt (el asunto) to confuse, complicate; (persona) to involve, embroil; ~se vr (confundirse) to get into a muddle or mess; ~se con uno to get into an argument with sb.

embrollo [em'broʎo] nm (enredo) muddle, confusion; (aprieto) fix, jam; (poy: engaño) fraud; (: trampa) trick.

embromar [embro'mar] vt (burlarse de) to tease, make fun of.

embrutecer [embrute'θer] vt (brutalizar) to brutalize; (depravar) to deprave; (atontar) to stupefy;

~se vr to become brutal; to become depraved.

embudo [em'buðo] nm funnel; (fig: engaño) fraud; (: trampa) trick.

embuste [em'buste] nm trick; (impostura) imposture; (mentira) lie; (hum) fib; **~ro, a** a lying, deceitful // nm/f (tramposo) cheat; (impostor) impostor; (mentiroso) liar; (hum) fibber.

embutido [embu'tiðo] nm (CULIN) sausage; (TEC) inlay.

embutir [embu'tir] vt (TEC) to inlay; (llenar) to pack tight, cram, stuff.

emergencia [emer'xenθja] nf emergency; (surgimiento) emergence.

emerger [emer'xer] vi to emerge, appear.

emigración [emixra'θjon] nf (éxodo) migration; (destierro) emigration.

emigrar [emi'xrar] vi (pájaros) to migrate; (personas) to emigrate.

eminencia [emi'nenθja] nf eminence; **eminente** a eminent, distinguished; (GEO) high.

emisario [emi'sarjo] nm emissary.

emisión [emi'sjon] nf (acto) emission; (COM etc) issue; (RADIO, TV: acto) broadcasting; (: programa) broadcast, programme.

emisora [emi'sora] nf (de onda corta) shortwave radio station; (aparato) broadcasting station.

emitir [emi'tir] vt (olor etc) to emit, give off; (moneda etc) to issue; (opinión) to express; (RADIO) to broadcast.

emoción [emo'θjon] nf emotion; (excitación) excitement; (turbación) worry, anxiety.

emocionante [emoθjo'nante] a (emotante) exciting, thrilling; (conmovedor) moving, touching; (impresionante) striking, impressive.

emocionar [emoθjo'nar] vt (excitar) to excite, thrill; (conmover) to move, touch; (*impresionar*) to impress.

empacho [em'patʃo] *nm* (MED) indigestion; (*fig*) embarrassment.

empalagoso, a [empala'xoso, a] *a* cloying; (*fig*) tiresome.

empalmar [empal'mar] *vt* to join, connect // *vi* (*dos caminos*) to meet, join; **empalme** *nm* joint, connection; junction; (*de trenes*) connection.

empanada [empa'naða] *nf* pie, patty.

empantanarse [empanta'narse] *vr* to get swamped; (*fig*) to get bogged down.

empañar [empa'ɲar] *vt* (*niño*) to swaddle, wrap up; **~se** *vr* (*nublarse*) to get misty, steam up.

empapar [empa'par] *vt* (*mojar*) to soak, saturate; (*absorber*) to soak up, absorb; **~se** *vr*: **~se de** to soak up.

empapelar [empape'lar] *vt* (*paredes*) to paper; (*envolver con papel*) to wrap (up) in paper.

empaquetar [empake'tar] *vt* to pack, parcel up.

empastar [empas'tar] *vt* (*embadurnar*) to paste; (*diente*) to fill.

empatar [empa'tar] *vi* to draw, tie; **empate** *nm* draw, tie.

empedernido, a [empeðer'niðo, a] *a* hard, heartless; (*fijado*) hardened, inveterate.

empedernir [empeðer'nir] *vt* to harden.

empedrado, a [empe'ðraðo, a] *a* paved // *nm* paving; **empedrar** *vt* to pave.

empeñado, a [empe'ɲaðo, a] *a* (*objeto*) pawned; (*persona*) determined.

empeñar [empe'ɲar] *vt* (*objeto*) to pawn, pledge; (*persona*) to compel; **~se** *vr* (*obligarse*) to bind o.s., pledge o.s.; (*endeudarse*) to get into debt; **~se en** to be set on, be determined to.

empeño [em'peɲo] *nm* (*cosa prendada*) pledge; (*determinación*,

insistencia) determination, insistence; **banco de ~s** pawnshop.

empeorar [empeo'rar] *vt* to make worse, worsen // *vi* to get worse, deteriorate.

empequeñecer [empekeɲe'θer] *vt* to dwarf; (*fig*) to belittle.

emperador [empera'ðor] *nm* emperor.

emperatriz [empera'triθ] *nf* empress.

empezar [empe'θar] *vt, vi* to begin, start.

empiezo *etc vb ver* **empezar**.

empinar [empi'nar] *vt* to raise (up) // *vi* (*fam*) to drink, booze (*fam*); **~se** *vr* (*persona*) to stand on tiptoe; (*animal*) to rear up; (*camino*) to climb steeply; (*edificio*) to tower.

empírico, a [em'piriko, a] *a* empirical.

emplasto [em'plasto], **emplaste** [em'plaste] *nm* (MED) plaster; (: *cataplasma*) poultice; (*componenda*) compromise.

emplazamiento [emplaθa-'mjento] *nm* site, location; (JUR) summons *sg*.

emplazar [empla'θar] *vt* (*ubicar*) to site, place, locate; (JUR) to summons; (*convocar*) to summon.

empleado, a [emple'aðo, a] *nm/f* (*gen*) employee; (*de banco etc*) clerk.

emplear [emple'ar] *vt* (*usar*) to use, employ; (*dar trabajo a*) to employ; **~se** *vr* (*conseguir trabajo*) to be employed; (*ocuparse*) to occupy o.s.

empleo [em'pleo] *nm* (*puesto*) job; (*puestos: colectivamente*) employment; (*uso*) use, employment.

empobrecer [empoβre'θer] *vt* to impoverish; **~se** *vr* to become poor or impoverished; **empobrecimiento** *nm* impoverishment.

emporio [em'porjo] *nm* emporium, trading centre; (*gran almacén*) department store.

emprender [empren'der] *vt*

(*empezar*) to begin, embark on; (*acometer*) to tackle, take on.

empreñar [empre'ɲar] vt to make pregnant; **~se** vr to become pregnant.

empresa [em'presa] nf enterprise.

empréstito [em'prestito] nm (public) loan.

empujar [empu'xar] vt to push, shove; **empuje** nm thrust; (*presión*) pressure; (*fig*) vigour, drive.

empujón [empu'xon] nm push, shove.

empuñar [empu'ɲar] vt (*asir*) to grasp, take (firm) hold of.

emular [emu'lar] vt to emulate; (*rivalizar*) to rival.

émulo, a ['emulo, a] nm/f rival, competitor.

en [en] prep (*gen*) in; (*sobre*) on, upon; meter ~ el bolsillo to put in or into one's pocket; (*lugar*): vivir ~ Toledo to live in Toledo; ~ casa at home; (*tiempo*): lo terminó ~ 6 días he finished it in 6 days; ~ el mes de enero in the month of January; ~ **aquel momento**/**aquella época** at that moment/that time; ~ **aquel día**/**aquella ocasión** on that day/that occasion; ~ **serio** seriously; ~ **fin** well, well then; ir **de puerta** ~ **puerta** to go from door to door; ~ **tren** by train.

enajenación [enaxena'θjon] nf, **enajenamiento** [enaxena-'mjento] nm alienation; (*fig: distracción*) absent-mindedness; (*: embelesamiento*) rapture, trance; (*extrañamiento*) estrangement.

enajenar [enaxe'nar] vt to alienate; (*fig*) to carry away; **~se** vr (*de un bien*) to deprive o.s.; (*amigos*) to become estranged, fall out.

enamorado, a [enamo'raðo, a] a in love; **enamorar** vt to inspire love; **enamorarse** vr to fall in love.

enano, a [e'nano, a] a tiny // nm/f dwarf.

enardecer [enarðe'θer] vt

(*pasiones*) to fire, inflame; (*persona*) to fill with enthusiasm; (*: llenar de ira*) to fill with anger; **~se** vr to get excited; (*entusiasmarse*) to get enthusiastic (*por* about); (*de cólera*) to blaze.

encabezamiento [enkaβeθa-'mjento] nm (*de carta*) heading; (*de periódico*) headline; (*preámbulo*) foreword, preface; (*registro*) roll, register.

encabezar [enkaβe'θar] vt (*manifestación*) to lead, head; (*lista*) to be at the top of; (*carta*) to put a heading to; (*libro*) to entitle, (*empadronar*) to register.

encadenar [enkaðe'nar] vt to chain (together); (*poner grilletes a*) to shackle.

encajar [enka'xar] vt (*ajustar*) to fit (into); (*golpe*) to give, deal; (*entrometer*) to insert // vi to fit (well); (*fig: corresponder a*) to match; **~se** vr to intrude; **~se en un sillón** to squeeze into a chair.

encaje [en'kaxe] nm (*labor*) lace; (*inserción*) insertion; (*ajuste*) fitting.

encajonar [enkaxo'nar] vt to box (up), put in a box.

encaminar [enkami'nar] vt to direct, send; **~se** vr: **~se a** to set out for.

encandilar [enkandi'lar] vt to dazzle; (*fuego*) to poke.

encantador, a [enkanta'ðor, a] a charming, lovely // nm/f magician, enchanter/tress.

encantar [enkan'tar] vt to charm, delight; (*hechizar*) to bewitch, cast a spell on; **encanto** nm (*magia*) spell, charm; (*fig*) charm, delight.

encarcelar [enkarθe'lar] vt to imprison, jail.

encarecer [enkare'θer] vt to put up the price of; (*pedir*) to recommend, urge // vi, **~se** vr to get dearer.

encarecimiento [enkareθi-'mjento] nm price increase; (*pedido insistente*) urging.

encargado, a [enkar'ɣaðo, a] *a* in charge // *nm/f* agent, representative; (*responsable*) person in charge; ~ **de negocios** chargé d'affaires.

encargar [enkar'ɣar] *vt* to entrust; (*recomendar*) to urge, recommend; ~**se** *vr*: ~**se de** to look after, take charge of.

encargo [en'karɣo] *nm* (*pedido*) assignment, job; (*responsabilidad*) responsibility; (*recomendación*) recommendation; (*COM*) order.

encarnación [enkarna'θjon] *nf* incarnation, embodiment.

encarrilar [enkarri'lar] *vt* to correct, put on the right track; (*tren*) to put back on the rails.

encausar [enkau'sar] *vt* to prosecute, sue.

encauzar [enkau'θar] *vt* to channel.

enceguecer [enθeɣe'θer] *vt* to blind // *vi*, ~**se** *vr* to go blind.

encendedor [enθende'dor] *nm* lighter.

encender [enθen'der] *vt* (*con fuego*) to light; (*incendiar*) to set fire to; (*luz, radio*) to put on, switch on; (*inflarse*) to inflame; ~**se** *vr* to catch fire; (*excitarse*) to get excited; (*de cólera*) to flare up; (*el rostro*) to blush.

encendido [enθen'diðo] *nm* ignition.

encerrar [enθe'rrar] *vt* (*confinar*) to shut in, shut up; (*comprender, incluir*) to include, contain.

encía [en'θia] *nf* gum.

encierro [en'θjerro] *nm* shutting in, shutting up; (*calabozo*) prison.

encima [en'θima] *ad* (*sobre*) above, over; (*además*) besides; ~ **de** (*en*) on, on top of; (*sobre*) above, over; (*además de*) besides, on top of; **por** ~ **de** over; **¿llevas dinero** ~**?** have you any money on you?; **se me vino** ~ it got on top of me.

encinta [en'θinta] *a* pregnant.

enclavar [enkla'ßar] *vt* (*clavar*) to

nail; (*atravesar*) to pierce; (*sitio*) to set; (*fig: fam*) to swindle.

encoger [enko'xer] *vt* (*gen*) to shrink, contract; (*fig: asustar*) to scare; (: *desanimar*) to discourage; ~**se** *vr* to shrink, contract; (*fig*) to cringe; ~**se de hombros** to shrug one's shoulders.

encojar [enko'xar] *vt* to lame; (*tullir*) to cripple; ~**se** *vr* to go lame; to become crippled.

encolar [enko'lar] *vt* (*engomar*) to glue, paste; (*pegar*) to stick down.

encolerizar [enkoleri'θar] *vt* to anger, provoke; ~**se** *vr* to get angry.

encomendar [enkomen'dar] *vt* to entrust, commend; ~**se** *vr*: ~**se a** to put one's trust in.

encomiar [enko'mjar] *vt* to praise, pay tribute to.

encomienda [enko'mjenda] *nf* (*encargo*) charge, commission; (*precio*) price; (*elogio*) tribute; ~ **postal** (*AM*) parcel post.

encomio [en'komjo] *nm* praise, tribute.

enconado, a [enko'naðo, a] *a* (*MED*) inflamed; (: *dolorido*) sore; (*fig*) angry.

enconar [enko'nar] *vt* (*MED*) to inflame; (*fig*) to anger, irritate; ~**se** *vr* (*MED*) to become inflamed; (*fig*) to get angry or irritated.

encono [en'kono] *nm* (*rencor*) rancour, spite; (*odio*) ill-feeling.

encontrado, a [enkon'traðo, a] *a* (*contrario*) contrary, conflicting; (*hostil*) hostile.

encontrar [enkon'trar] *vt* (*hallar*) to find; (*inesperadamente*) to meet, run into; ~**se** *vr* to meet (each other); (*situarse*) to be (situated); (*entrar en conflicto*) to crash, collide; ~**se con** to meet (with); ~**se bien de salud** to feel well.

encorvar [enkor'ßar] *vt* to curve; (*inclinar*) to bend (down); ~**se** *vr* to bend down, bend over, stoop.

encrespar [enkres'par] *vt* (*cabe-*

llos) to curl; (*agua*) to ripple; (*fig*) to anger, irritate; ~**se** *vr* (*el mar*) to get rough; (*fig*) to get annoyed, irritated.

encrucijada [enkruθi'xaða] *nf* crossroads *sg*; (*empalme*) junction.

encuadernación [enkwaðerna-'θjon] *nf* binding.

encuadernador, a [enkwaðerna-na'ðor, a] *nm/f* bookbinder.

encuadrar [enkwa'ðrar] *vt* (*retrato*) to frame, (*ajustar*) to fit, insert; (*encerrar*) to contain.

encubrir [enku'βrir] *vt* (*ocultar*) to hide, conceal; (*criminal*) to harbour, shelter.

encuentro *etc vb ver* **encontrar** // [en'kwentro] *nm* (*de personas*) meeting, (*de tropas*) collision, crash; (DEPORTE) match, game; (MIL) encounter.

encuesta [en'kwesta] *nf* inquiry, investigation; ~ **judicial** post mortem.

encumbrado, a [enkum'braðo, a] *a* (*edificio*) lofty, towering; (*persona*) eminent, distinguished.

encumbrar [enkum'brar] *vt* (*edificio*) to raise; (*elevar*) to elevate; (*persona*) to exalt; ~**se** *vr* to rise, tower; (*fig*) to become conceited.

encharcado, a [entʃar'kaðo, a] *a* still; (*estancado*) stagnant.

enchufar [entʃu'far] *vt* (ELEC) to plug in; (TEC) to connect, fit together; **enchufe** *nm* (ELEC) clavija) plug; (: *toma*) plug, socket; (*de dos tubos*) joint, connection; (*fam*: *influencia*) contact, connection; (: *puesto*) cushy job.

endemoniado, a [endemo'njaðo, a] *a* possessed (of the devil); (*endiablado*) devilish; (*furioso*) furious, wild.

endentar [enden'tar] *vt, vi* to engage, mesh.

enderezar [endere'θar] *vt* (*poner derecho*) to straighten (out); (: *verticalmente*) to set upright; (*carta*) to address; (*fig*) to

straighten *or* sort out; (*dirigir*) to direct; ~**se** *vr* (*persona sentado*) to stand up; (*fig*) to correct one's ways.

endeudarse [endeu'ðarse] *vr* to get into debt.

endiablado, a [endja'βlaðo, a] *a* devilish, diabolical; (*hum*) mischievous; (*fig*) furious, angry.

endomingarse [endomin'garse] *vr* to dress up, put on one's best clothes.

endosar [endo'sar] *vt* (*cheque etc*) to endorse.

endulzar [endul'θar] *vt* to sweeten, (*fig*) to soften.

endurecer [endure'θer] *vt* to harden; (*fig*) to toughen; ~**se** *vr* to harden, grow hard.

endurecido, a [endure'θiðo, a] *a* (*duro*) hard; (*fig*) hardy, tough; **estar** ~ **a algo** to be hardened *or* used to sth.

endurecimiento [endureθi-'mjento] *nm* (*acto*) hardening; (*tenacidad*) toughness; (*crueldad*) cruelty; (*insensibilidad*) callousness.

enemigo, a [ene'miɣo, a] *a* enemy, hostile // *nm/f* enemy // *nf* enmity, hostility.

enemistad [enemis'tað] *nf* enmity.

enemistar [enemis'tar] *vt* to make enemies of, cause a rift between; ~**se** *vr* to become enemies; (*amigos*) to fall out.

energía [ener'xia] *nf* (*vigor*) energy, drive; (TEC, ELEC) energy, power.

enérgico, a [e'nerxiko, a] *a* (*gen*) energetic; (*voz, modales*) forceful.

enero [e'nero] *nm* January.

enfadar [enfa'ðar] *vt* to anger, annoy; ~**se** *vr* to get angry *or* annoyed.

enfado [en'faðo] *nm* (*enojo*) anger, annoyance; (*disgusto*) trouble, bother; ~**so** *a* annoying; (*aburrido*) tedious.

énfasis ['enfasis] *nm* emphasis, stress.

enfático, a [en'fatiko, a] *a* a

emphatic; (*afectado*) pompous.

enfermar [enfer'mar] *vt* to make ill // *vi* to fall ill, be taken ill.

enfermedad [enferme'ðað] *nf* illness; ~ **venérea** venereal disease.

enfermería [enferme'ria] *nf* infirmary; (*de colegio etc*) sick bay.

enfermero, a [enfer'mero, a] *nm // nf* male nurse/nurse.

enfermizo, a [enfer'miθo, a] *a* (*persona*) sickly, unhealthy; (*lugar*) unhealthy.

enfermo, a [en'fermo, a] *a* ill, sick // *nm // nf* invalid, sick person; (*en hospital*) patient.

enflaquecer [enflake'θer] *vt* (*adelgazar*) to make thin; (*debilitar*) to weaken; ~**se** *vr* (*adelgazarse*) to become thin, lose weight; (*debilitarse*) to grow weak; (*fig*) to lose heart.

enfocar [enfo'kar] *vt* (*foto etc*) to focus; (*problema etc*) to approach, look at.

enfoque [en'foke] *nm* focus.

enfrentar [enfren'tar] *vt* (*peligro*) to face (up to), confront; (*oponer, carear*) to put face to face; ~**se** *vr* (*dos personas*) to face or confront each other; (*dos equipos*) to meet; ~**se** *a o con* to face up to, confront.

enfrente [en'frente] *ad* opposite; ~ **de** *prep* opposite, facing; **la casa de** ~ the house opposite, the house across the street.

enfriamiento [enfria'mjento] *nm* chilling, refrigeration; (*MED*) cold, chill.

enfriar [enfri'ar] *vt* (*alimentos*) to cool, chill; (*algo caliente*) to cool down; (*habitación*) to air, freshen; ~**se** *vr* to cool down; (*MED*) to catch a chill; (*amistad*) to cool.

enfurecer [enfure'θer] *vt* to enrage, madden; ~**se** *vr* to become furious, fly into a rage; (*mar*) to get rough.

engalanar [engala'nar] *vt* (*adornar*) to adorn; (*ciudad*) to decorate;

~**se** *vr* to get dressed up.

enganchar [engan't∫ar] *vt* (*gen*) to hook; (*ropa*) to hang up; (*dos vagones*) to hitch up; (*TEC*) to couple, connect; (*MIL*) to recruit; (*fig: fam: persona*) to rope into; ~**se** *vr* (*MIL*) to enlist, join up.

enganche [en'gant∫e] *nm* hook; (*TEC*) coupling, connection; (*acto*) hooking (up); (: *ropa*) hanging up; (*MIL*) recruitment, enlistment.

engañar [enga'nar] *vt* to deceive; (*trampear*) to cheat, swindle; ~**se** *vr* (*equivocarse*) to be wrong; (*disimular la verdad*) to deceive or kid o.s.

engaño [en'gaɲo] *nm* deceit; (*trampa*) trick, swindle; (*error*) mistake, misunderstanding; (*ilusión*) delusion; ~**so, a** *a* (*tramposo*) crooked; (*mentiroso*) dishonest, deceitful; (*aspecto*) deceptive; (*consejo*) misleading, wrong.

engarzar [engar'θar] *vt* (*joya*) to set, mount; (*fig*) to link, connect.

engatusar [engatu'sar] *vt* (*fam*) to coax.

engendrar [enxen'drar] *vt* to breed; (*procrear*) to beget; (*fig*) to cause, produce; **engendro** *nm* (*BIO*) foetus; (*fig*) monstrosity; (*idea*) brainchild.

engolfarse [engol'farse] *vr*: ~ **en** to bury o.s. in, become deeply involved in.

engomar [engo'mar] *vt* to gum, glue, stick.

engordar [engor'ðar] *vt* to fatten // *vi* to get fat, put on weight.

engranaje [engra'naxe] *nm* gear.

engranar [engra'nar] *vt* to put into gear // *vi* to interlock.

engrandecer [engrande'θer] *vt* to enlarge, magnify; (*alabar*) to praise, speak highly of; (*exagerar*) to exaggerate.

engrasar [engra'sar] *vt* (*TEC: poner grasa*) to grease; (: *lubricar*) to lubricate, oil; (*manchar*) to make greasy; (*animal*) to fatten.

engreído, a [eŋgreˈiðo, a] a vain, conceited; **engreírse** vr to become conceited.

engrosar [eŋgroˈsar] vt (ensanchar) to enlarge; (aumentar) to increase; (hinchar) to swell // vi to get fat; ~**se** vr to increase; to swell.

enhebrar [eneˈβrar] vt to thread.

enhorabuena [enoraˈβwena] nf congratulations pl // ad well and good.

enigma [eˈnixma] nm enigma; (problema) puzzle; (misterio) mystery.

enjabonar [enxaβoˈnar] vt to soap; (fam: adular) to soft-soap; (: regañar) to scold.

enjambre [enˈxamβre] nm swarm.

enjaular [enxauˈlar] vt to put in a cage; (fam) to jail, lock up.

enjuagar [enxwaˈɣar] vt (ropa) to rinse (out).

enjugar [enxuˈɣar] vt to wipe (off); (lágrimas) to dry; (déficit) to wipe out.

enjuiciar [enxwiˈθjar] vt (JUR: procesar) to prosecute, try; (fig) to judge.

enjuto, a [enˈxuto, a] a dry, dried up; (fig) lean, skinny.

enlace [enˈlaθe] nm link, connection; (relación) relationship; (casamiento) marriage; (de carretera, trenes) connection; **agente de** ~ broker; ~ **sindical** shop steward.

enlazar [enlaˈθar] vt (atar) to tie; (conectar) to link, connect; (AM) to lasso; ~**se** vr (novios) to get married; (dos familias) to become related by marriage; (conectarse) to link (up), be linked.

enlodar [enloˈðar], **enlodazar** [enloðaˈθar] vt to muddy, cover in mud; (fig: manchar) to stain; (: rebajar) to debase.

enloquecer [enlokeˈθer] vt to drive mad // vi, ~**se** vr to go mad.

enlutar [enluˈtar] vt to dress in mourning; ~**se** vr to go into mourning.

enmarañar [enmaraˈɲar] vt (enredar) to tangle (up), entangle; (complicar) to complicate; (confundir) to confuse; ~**se** vr (enredarse) to become entangled; (confundirse) to get confused; (nublarse) to cloud over.

enmascarar [enmaskaˈrar] vt to mask; ~**se** vr to put on a mask; ~**se** to masquerade as.

enmendar [enmenˈdar] vt to emend, correct; (constitución etc) to amend; (compensar) to make good; (comportamiento) to reform; ~**se** vr to reform, mend one's ways; **enmienda** nf correction; amendment; reform; (compensación) compensation, indemnity.

enmohecerse [enmoeˈθerse] vr (metal) to rust, go rusty; (muro, plantas) to get mouldy.

enmudecer [enmuðeˈθer] vt to silence // vi, ~**se** vr (perder el habla) to go silent; (guardar silencio) to keep quiet.

ennegrecer [ennexreˈθer] vt (poner negro) to blacken; (oscurecer) to darken; ~**se** vr to turn black; (oscurecerse) to get dark.

ennoblecer [ennoβleˈθer] vt to ennoble; (fig) to embellish, adorn.

enojadizo, a [enoxaˈðiθo, a] a irritable, short-tempered.

enojar [enoˈxar] vt (encolerizar) to anger; (disgustar) to annoy, upset; ~**se** vr to get angry; to get annoyed.

enojo [eˈnoxo] nm (cólera) anger; (disgusto) annoyance; ~**s** nmpl trials, problems; ~**so, a** a annoying.

enorgullecerse [enoryuʎeˈθerse] vr to be proud; ~ **de** to pride o.s. on, be proud of.

enorme [eˈnorme] a enormous, huge; (fig) monstrous; **enormidad** nf hugeness, immensity; (despropósito) absurdity; **piece of** nonsense; (perversidad) monstrosity.

enraizar [enraiˈθar] vi to take root.

enredadera [enreðaˈðera] nf (BOT) creeper, climbing plant.

enredar [enre'ðar] vt (ovillo) to tangle (up), entangle; (peces) to net; (situación) to complicate, confuse; (meter cizaña) to sow discord among or between; (implicar) to embroil, implicate; ~se vr to get entangled, get tangled (up); (situación) to get complicated; (persona) to get embroiled (AM: fam) to meddle.

enredo [en'reðo] nm (maraña) tangle; (confusión) mix-up, confusion; (intriga) intrigue.

enrevesada, a [enreße'saðo, a] a unruly, uncontrollable; (enredado) complicated, involved.

enriquecer [enrike'θer] vt to make rich, enrich; ~se vr to get rich.

enrojecer [enroxe'θer] vt to redden // vi, ~se vr (metal) to become red hot; (persona) to blush.

enrollar [enro'λar] vt to roll (up), wind (up).

enroscar [enros'kar] vt (torcer, doblar) to coil (round), wind; (tornillo, rosca) to screw in; ~se vr to coil, wind.

ensalada [ensa'laða] nf salad; **ensaladilla** nf Russian salad.

ensalzar [ensal'θar] vt (alabar) to praise, extol; (exaltar) to exalt.

ensambladura [ensambla'ðura] nf, **ensamblaje** [ensam'blaxe] nm assembly; (TEC) joint; **ensamblar** vt to assemble.

ensanchar [ensan'tʃar] vt (hacer más ancho) to widen; (agrandar) to enlarge, expand; ~se vr to get wider, expand; (pey) to give o.s. airs; **ensanche** nm (de vestido, calle) widening; (de negocio) expansion.

ensangrentar [ensangren'tar] vt to stain with blood; ~se vr (fig) to get angry.

ensañar [ensa'ɲar] vt to enrage; ~se vr: ~se con to delight in tormenting.

ensartar [ensar'tar] vt (gen) to string (together); (aguja) to thread.

ensayar [ensa'jar] vt to test, try (out); (TEATRO) to rehearse.

ensayista [ensa'jista] nm/f essayist.

ensayo [en'sajo] nm test, trial; (QUIMICA) experiment; (TEATRO) rehearsal; (DEPORTE) try; (obra literaria) essay.

ensenada [ense'naða] nf inlet, cove.

enseñanza [ense'ɲanθa] nf (educación) education; (acción) teaching; (doctrina) teaching, doctrine.

enseñar [ense'ɲar] vt (educar) to teach; (instruir) to teach, instruct; (mostrar, señalar) to show.

enseres [en'seres] nmpl goods and chattels, things.

ensimismarse [ensimis'marse] vr (abstraerse) to become lost in thought; (estar absorto) to be lost in thought; (AM) to become conceited.

ensoberbecerse [ensoßerße'θerse] vr to become proud; (hacerse arrogante) to become arrogant; (mar) to get rough.

ensordecer [ensorðe'θer] vt to deafen // vi to go deaf.

ensortijar [ensorti'xar] vt, ~se v (cabellos) to curl.

ensuciar [ensu'θjar] vt (manchar) to dirty, soil; (fig) to defile; ~se vr (mancharse) to get dirty; (fig) to dirty/wet o.s.

ensueño [en'sweɲo] nm (sueño) dream, fantasy; (ilusión) illusion; (soñando despierto) reverie.

entablado [enta'blaðo] nm (piso) floorboards pl; (armazón) boarding.

entablar [enta'blar] vt (recubrir to board (up); (AJEDREZ, DAMAS) to set up; (conversación) to strike up (JUR) to file // vi to draw.

entallar [enta'λar] vt (piedra) to sculpt; (madera) to carve; (grabar) to engrave; (traje) to tailor // vi: el traje entalla bien the suit fits well.

entender [enten'der] vt (comprender) to understand; (darse cuenta to realize; (*creer, pensar*) to think, believe; (*querer decir*) to mean // *vi*: ~ **de** to know all about; ~ **en** to deal with, have to do with; ~**se** *vr* (*comprenderse*) to be understood; (*ponerse de acuerdo*) to understand one another, have an understanding; (*aliarse*) to agree, reach an agreement; (*fam*) to have an affair; **me entiendo con la mecánica** I'm (quite) good at mechanics.

entendido, a [enten'diðo, a] *a* (*comprendido*) understood; (*hábil*) skilled; (*inteligente*) knowledgeable // *nm/f* (*experto*) expert; (*docto*) knowledgeable person // *excl* agreed!; **entendimiento** *nm* (*comprensión*) understanding; (*facultad intelectual*) the mind, intellect; (*juicio*) judgement.

enterado, a [ente'raðo, a] *a* a well-informed; **estar** ~ **de** to know about, be aware of.

enteramente [entera'mente] *ad* entirely, completely.

enterar [ente'rar] *vt* (*informar*) to inform, tell; ~**se** *vr* to find out, get to know.

entereza [ente'reθa] *nf* (*totalidad*) entirety; (*fig: energía*) strength of mind; (*honradez*) integrity; (*severidad*) strictness, severity.

enternecer [enterne'θer] *vt* (*ablandar*) to soften; (*apiadar*) to touch, move; ~**se** *vr* to be touched, be moved.

entero, a [en'tero, a] *a* (*total*) whole, entire; (*fig: recto*) honest; (: *firme*) firm, resolute //: *nm* (*COM: punto*) point; (*AM: pago*) payment.

enterrador [enterra'ðor] *nm* gravedigger.

enterrar [ente'rrar] *vt* to bury.

entibiar [enti'βjar] *vt* to cool; (*fig*) to cool (...)

entidad [enti'ðað] *nf* (*empresa*) firm, company; (*organismo*) body; (*sociedad*) society; (*FILOSOFÍA*) entity.

entiendo etc *vb ver* **entender.**

entierro [en'tjerro] *nm* (*acción*) burial; (*funeral*) funeral.

entomología [entomolo'xia] *nf* entomology.

entonación [entona'θjon] *nf* (*LING*) intonation; (*fig*) conceit.

entonado, a [ento'naðo, a] *a* (*MUS*) in tune; (*fig*) conceited.

entonar [ento'nar] *vt* (*canción*) to intone; (*colores*) to tone; (*MED*) to tone up // *vi* to be in tune; ~**se** *vr* (*engreírse*) to give o.s. airs.

entonces [en'tonθes] *ad* then, at that time; **desde** ~ since then; **en aquel** ~ at that time; (**pues**) ~ and so.

entornar [entor'nar] *vt* (*puerta, ventana*) to half close, leave ajar; (*los ojos*) to screw up.

entorpecer [entorpe'θer] *vt* (*adormecer los sentidos*) to dull, benumb; (*impedir*) to obstruct, hinder; (: *tránsito*) to slow down, delay; **entorpecimiento** *nm* numbness; slowing-down, delay; (*letargia*) lethargy.

entrado, a [en'traðo, a] *a*: ~ **en años** elderly; **una vez** ~ **el verano** in the summer(time), when summer comes // *nf* (*acción*) entry, access; (*sitio*) entrance, way in; (*COM*) receipts *pl*, takings *pl*; (*CULIN*) entree; (*DEPORTE*) innings *sg*; (*TEATRO*) house, audience; (*para el cine etc*) ticket; (*COM*): ~**as y salidas** income and expenditure; (*TEC*): ~**a de aire** air intake or inlet.

entrante [en'trante] *a* next, coming // *nm* inlet; **ser** ~ **en una casa** to have the run of a house.

entraña [en'traɲa] *nf* (*fig: centro*) heart, core; (*raíz*) root; ~**s** *nfpl* (*ANAT*) entrails; **entrañable** a close, intimate.

entrar [en'trar] *vt* (*introducir*) to bring in ... // *vi* (*meterse*) to go/come in, enter; (*comenzar*) ... begin by saying; **no me entra** I can't get the hang of it; **el año que entra** next year.

entre ['entre] *prep* (*dos*) between; (*más de dos*) among(st); **pensaba ~ mí** I thought to myself.

entreabrir [entrea'βrir] *vt* to half-open, open halfway.

entrecejo [entre'θexo] *nm*: **fruncir el ~** to frown.

entredicho [entre'ðitʃo] *nm* prohibition, ban; (*JUR*) injunction.

entrega [en'treɣa] *nf* (*de mercancías*) delivery; (*rendición*) surrender; **novela por ~s** serial, novel in instalments.

entregar [entre'ɣar] *vt* (*dar*) to hand (over), deliver; (*ceder*) to give up; **~se** *vr* (*rendirse*) to surrender, give in, submit; (*dedicarse*) to devote o.s.

entrelazar [entrela'θar] *vt* to entwine.

entremés [entre'mes] *nm* (*CULIN*) side-dish; **entremeses** *nmpl* hors d'œuvres.

entremeter [entreme'ter] *vt* to insert, put in; **~se** *vr* to meddle, interfere; **entremetido, a** *a* meddling, interfering.

entremezclar [entremeθ'klar] *vt*, **~se** *vr* to intermingle.

entrenador [entrena'ðor] *nm* trainer, coach; **entrenarse** *vr* to train.

entreoír [entreo'ir] *vt* to half hear.

entresacar [entresa'kar] *vt* to pick out, select.

entresuelo [entre'swelo] *nm* (*sótano*) basement.

entretanto [entre'tanto] *ad* meanwhile, meantime; **en el ~** in the meantime.

entretejer [entrete'xer] *vt* to interweave.

entretener [entrete'ner] *vt* (*divertir*) to entertain, amuse; (*detener*) to hold up, delay; (*cuidar*) to maintain; **~se** *vr* (*divertirse*) to amuse o.s.; (*retrasarse*) to delay, linger; **entretenido, a** *a* entertaining, amusing; **entretenimiento** *nm* entertainment, amusement; (*cuida-*

do) upkeep, maintenance.

entrever [entre'βer] *vt* to glimpse, catch a glimpse of.

entreverar [entreβe'rar] *vt* to mix (up).

entrevista [entre'βista] *nf* interview; **entrevistar** *vt* to interview; **entrevistarse** *vr* to have an interview.

entristecer [entriste'θer] *vt* to sadden, grieve; **~se** *vr* to grow sad.

entrometer [entrome'ter] *etc* = **entremeter** *etc*.

entroncar [entron'kar] *vi* to be connected *or* related.

entronque [en'tronke] *nm* connection, link.

entuerto [en'twerto] *nm* wrong, injustice.

entumecer [entume'θer] *vt* to numb, benumb; **~se** *vr* (*por el frío*) to go *or* become numb; **entumecido, a** a numb, stiff.

enturbiar [entur'βjar] *vt* (*el agua*) to disturb, make cloudy; (*fig*) to fog, confuse; **~se** *vr* (*oscurecerse*) to become cloudy; (*fig*) to get confused, become obscure.

entusiasmar [entusjas'mar] *vt* to excite, fill with enthusiasm; (*gustar mucho*) to delight; **~se** *vr*: **~se con** *o* **por** to get enthusiastic *or* excited about.

entusiasmo [entu'sjasmo] *nm* enthusiasm; (*deleite*) delight; (*excitación*) excitement.

entusiasta [entu'sjasta] *a* enthusiastic // *nm/f* enthusiast.

enumerar [enume'rar] *vt* to enumerate.

enunciación [enunθja'θjon] *nf*, **enunciado** [enun'θjaðo] *nm* enunciation; (*declaración*) declaration, statement; **enunciar** *vt* to enunciate; to declare, state.

envainar [enßai'nar] *vt* to sheathe.

envalentonar [enßalento'nar] *vt* to give courage to; **~se** *vr* to take courage, become bolder; (*pey: jactarse*) to boast, brag.

envanecer [enßane'θer] vt to make conceited; ~se vr to grow vain or conceited.

envasar [enßa'sar] vt (empaquetar) to pack, wrap; (enfrascar) to bottle; (enlatar) to tin; (embolsar) to pocket // vi (fig: fam: vino) to knock back; **envase** nm packing, wrapping; bottling; tinning, canning; (recipiente) container; (paquete) package; (botella) bottle; (lata) tin, can.

envejecer [enßexe'θer] vt to make old, age // vi, ~se vr (volverse viejo) to grow old; (fig) to become old-fashioned.

envenenar [enßene'nar] vt to poison; (fig) to embitter.

envergadura [enßerɣa'ðura] nf (fig) scope, compass.

envés [en'ßes] nm (de tela) back, wrong side.

enviar [en'ßjar] vt to send.

envidia [en'ßiðja] nf (deseo ferviente) envy; (celos) jealousy; **envidiar** vt (desear) to envy; (tener celos de) to be jealous of.

envilecer [enßile'θer] vt to debase, degrade; ~se vr to lower o.s.

envío [en'ßio] nm (acción) sending; (de mercancías) consignment; (COM) remittance.

enviudar [enßju'ðar] vi to be widowed.

envoltura [enßol'tura] nf (cobertura) cover; (embalaje) wrapper, wrapping; (funda) case.

envolver [enßol'ßer] vt to wrap (up); (cubrir) to cover; (enemigo) to surround; (implicar) to involve, implicate; ~se vr (cubrirse) to wrap o.s. up; (implicarse) to become involved.

envuelto [en'ßwelto] pp de **envolver**.

enzarzar [enθar'θar] vt (fig) to involve (in a dispute).

épico, a ['epiko, a] a epic // nf epic.

epidemia [epi'ðemja] nf epidemic; **epidémico, a** a epidemic.

epifanía [epifa'nia] nf Epiphany.

epilepsia [epi'lepsja] nf epilepsy.

epílogo [e'piloxo] nm epilogue.

episodio [epi'soðjo] nm episode.

epístola [e'pistola] nf epistle; (fam) letter.

epitafio [epi'tafjo] nm epitaph.

época ['epoka] nf period, time; (HISTORIA) age, epoch; **hacer** ~ to be epoch-making.

equidad [eki'ðað] nf equity.

equilibrar [ekili'ßrar] vt to balance; **equilibrio** nm balance, equilibrium; **equilibrista** nm/f (funámbulo) tightrope walker; (acróbata) acrobat.

equipaje [eki'paxe] nm luggage; (equipo) equipment, kit; (NAUT: tripulación) crew; ~ de mano hand luggage.

equipar [eki'par] vt (proveer) to equip.

equipararse [ekipa'rarse] vr: ~ con to be on a level with.

equipo [e'kipo] nm (materiales) equipment; (grupo) team; (: de obreros) shift.

equis ['ekis] nf (the letter) X.

equitación [ekita'θjon] nf (acto) riding; (arte) horsemanship.

equitativo, a [ekita'tißo, a] a equitable, fair.

equivalente [ekißa'lente] a, nm equivalent; **equivaler** vi to be equivalent or equal.

equivocación [ekißoka'θjon] nf mistake, error; **equivocarse** vr to be wrong, make a mistake; **equivocarse de camino** to take the wrong road; **equívoco, a** a (dudoso) suspect; (ambiguo) ambiguous // nm ambiguity; (juego de palabras) play on words.

era vb ver ser // ['era] nf era, age.

eras vb ver ser.

eran vb ver ser.

erario [e'rarjo] nm exchequer, treasury.

eras vb ver ser.

eres *vb ver* **ser.**

erguir [er'ɣir] *vt* to raise, lift; *(poner derecho)* to straighten; ~ **se** *vr* to straighten up; *(fig)* to swell with pride.

erigir [eri'xir] *vt* to erect, build; ~ **se** *vr*: ~ **se en** to set o.s. up as.

erizado, a [eri'θaðo, a] *a* bristly.

erizarse [eri'θarse] *vr* to stand on end.

erizo [e'riθo] *nm* hedgehog; (~ **de mar**) sea-urchin.

ermitaño, a [ermi'taɲo, a] *nm/f* hermit.

erótico, a [e'rotiko, a] *a* erotic; **erotismo** *nm* eroticism.

erradicar [errað̃i'kar] *vt* to eradicate.

errado, a [e'rraðo, a] *a* mistaken, wrong.

errante [e'rrante] *a* wandering, errant.

errar [e'rrar] *vi (vagar)* to wander, roam; *(equivocarse)* to err, make a mistake // *vt*: ~ **el camino** to take the wrong road; ~ **el tiro** to miss.

erróneo, a [e'rroneo, a] *a (equivocado)* wrong, mistaken; *(falso)* false, untrue.

error [e'rror] *nm* error, mistake; ~ **de imprenta** misprint.

eructar [eruk'tar] *vt* to belch.

erudición [eruð̃i'θjon] *nf* erudition, learning.

erudito, a [eru'ð̃ito, a] *a* erudite, learned.

erupción [erup'θjon] *nf* eruption; *(MED)* rash.

es *vb ver* **ser.**

esa, esas *det ver* **ese.**

ésa, ésas *pron ver* **ése.**

esbelto, a [es'ßelto, a] *a* slim, slender.

esbozo [es'ßoßo] *nm* sketch, outline.

escabeche [eska'ßetʃe] *nm* brine; *(de aceitunas etc)* pickle; **pescado en** ~ pickled fish.

escabel [eska'ßel] *nm* (low) stool.

escabroso, a [eska'ßroso, a] *a (accidentado)* rough, uneven; *(fig)*

tough, difficult; *(: atrevido)* risqué.

escabullirse [eskaßu'ʎirse] *vr* to slip away; *(irse)* to clear out.

escala [es'kala] *nf (proporción, MUS)* scale; *(de mano)* ladder; *(AVIAT)* stopover; **hacer** ~ **en** to stop or call in at; ~ **de colores** range of colours.

escalafón [eskala'fon] *nm (escala de salarios)* salary scale, wage scale; *(lista etc)* list; *(registro)* register.

escalar [eska'lar] *vt (montaña etc)* to climb, scale; *(casa)* to burgle, break into.

escalera [eska'lera] *nf* stairs *pl*, staircase; *(escala)* ladder; *(NAIPES)* run; ~ **mecánica** escalator; ~ **de caracol** spiral staircase.

escalinata [eskali'nata] *nf* outside staircase.

escalofrío [eskalo'frio] *nm* chill; ~ **s** *nmpl (fig)* shivers; **escalofriante** *a* chilling.

escalón [eska'lon] *nm* step, stair; *(de escalera)* rung.

escama [es'kama] *nf (de pez, serpiente)* scale; *(de jabón)* flake; *(fig)* resentment.

escamado, a [eska'maðo, a] *a* wary, cautious.

escamotear [eskamote'ar], **escamotar** [eskamote'ar] *vt (quitar)* to lift, swipe *(fam)*; *(hacer desaparecer)* to make disappear.

escampar [eskam'par] *vb impersonal* to stop raining; *(del cielo)* to clear (up).

escandalizar [eskandali'θar] *vt* to scandalize, shock; ~ **se** *vr* to be shocked; *(ofenderse)* to be offended.

escándalo [es'kandalo] *nm* scandal; *(alboroto, tumulto)* row, uproar; **escandaloso, a** *a* scandalous, shocking.

escandinavo, a [eskandi'naßo, a] *a*, *nm/f* Scandinavian.

escaño [es'kaɲo] *nm* bench; *(POL)* seat.

escapar [eska'par] *vi (gen)* to

escape, run away; (DEPORTE) to break away; **~se** vr to escape, get away; (gas) to leak (out).

escaparate [eskapa'rate] nm shop window; (AM) wardrobe.

escape [es'kape] nm (de gas) leak; (de motor) exhaust; (de persona) escape.

escarabajo [eskara'βaxo] nm beetle; **~s** nmpl (fam) scribble sg.

escaramuza [eskara'muθa] nf skirmish; (fig) brush.

escarbar [eskar'βar] vt (gallina) to scratch; (dientes) to pick; (orejas) to clean; (fig) to inquire into, investigate.

escarcha [es'kartʃa] nf frost.

escarlata [eskar'lata] a inv scarlet; **escarlatina** nf scarlet fever.

escarmentar [eskarmen'tar] vt to punish severely // vi to learn one's lesson; **escarmiento** nm (ejemplo) lesson, example; (castigo) punishment.

escarnecer [eskarne'θer] vt to mock, ridicule; **escarnio**, **escarnecimiento** nm mockery; (injuria) insult.

escarpado, a [eskar'paðo, a] a (abrupto) sheer; (inclinado) steep; (accidentado) craggy.

escasear [eskase'ar] vt to skimp (on) // vi to be scarce.

escasez [eska'seθ] nf (falta) shortage, scarcity; (pobreza) poverty; (mezquindad) meanness.

escaso, a [es'kaso, a] a (poco) scarce; (raro) rare; (ralo) thin, sparse; (limitado) limited.

escatimar [eskati'mar] vt (limitar) to skimp (on); (reducir) to curtail, cut down.

escena [es'θena] nf scene.

escenario [esθe'narjo] nm (TEATRO) stage; (CINE) set; (fig) scene.

escepticismo [esθepti'θismo] nm scepticism; **escéptico, a** a sceptical // nm/f sceptic.

esclarecer [esklare'θer] vt (iluminar) to light up, illuminate; (misterio, problema) to shed light on; (ennoblecer) to ennoble.

esclavitud [esklaβi'tuð] nf slavery.

esclavizar [esklaβi'θar] vt to enslave.

esclavo, a [es'klaβo, a] nm/f slave.

escoba [es'koβa] nf broom.

escocer [esko'θer] vt to annoy // vi to burn, sting; **~se** vr to chafe, get chafed.

escocés, esa [esko'θes, esa] a Scottish // nm/f Scotsman/woman, Scot.

Escocia [es'koθja] nf Scotland.

escoger [esko'xer] vt to choose, pick, select; **escogido, a** a chosen, selected; (calidad) choice, select; **escogimiento** nm choice.

escolar [esko'lar] a school cpd // nm/f schoolboy/girl, pupil.

escolta [es'kolta] nf escort; **escoltar** vt to escort.

escombro [es'kombro] nm mackerel; **~s** nmpl (basura) rubbish sg; (restos) debris sg.

esconder [eskon'der] vt to hide, conceal; **~se** vr to hide; **escondite** nm hiding place; (juego) hide-and-seek.

escondrijo [eskon'drixo] nm hiding-place, hideout.

escopeta [esko'peta] nf shotgun.

escoplo [es'koplo] nm chisel.

Escorpio [es'korpjo] nm Scorpio.

escorpión [eskor'pjon] nm scorpion.

escote [es'kote] nm (de vestido) low neck; (parte) share; **pagar a ~** to share the expenses.

escotillón [eskoti'ʎon] nm trapdoor.

escozor [esko'θor] nm (dolor) sting(ing); (fig) grief, heartache.

escribano, a [eskri'βano, a], **escribiente** [eskri'βjente] nm/f clerk.

escribir [eskri'βir] vt, vi to write; **~ a máquina** to type; **¿cómo se escribe?** how do you spell it?

escrito, a [es'krito, a] pp de

escribir // nm (documento) document; (manuscrito) text, manuscript; **por ~** in writing.

escritor, a [eskri'tor, a] nm/f writer.

escritorio [eskri'torjo] nm desk; (oficina) office.

escritura [eskri'tura] nf (acción) writing; (caligrafía) (hand)writing; (JUR: documento) deed.

escrúpulo [es'krupulo] nm scruple; (minuciosidad) scrupulousness; **escrupuloso, a** a scrupulous.

escrutar [eskru'tar] vt to scrutinize, examine; (votos) to count.

escrutinio [eskru'tinjo] nm (examen atento) scrutiny; (recuento de votos) poll; (resultado de elección) voting, ballot.

escuadra [es'kwaðra] nf (MIL etc) squad; (NAUT) squadron; (de coches etc) fleet; **escuadrilla** nf (de aviones) squadron; (AM: de obreros) gang.

escuadrón [eska'ðron] nm squadron.

escuálido, a [es'kwaliðo, a] a (flaco, macilento) pale, wan; (sucio) squalid.

escuchar [esku't∫ar] vt to listen to // vi to listen.

escudilla [esku'ðiʎa] nf bowl, basin.

escudo [es'kuðo] nm shield.

escudriñar [eskuðri'nar] vt (examinar) to investigate, examine closely; (mirar de lejos) to scan.

escuela [es'kwela] nf school.

escueto, a [es'kweto, a] a plain, unadorned.

esculpir [eskul'pir] vt to sculpt; (grabar) to engrave; (tallar) to carve; **escultor, a** nm/f sculptor/tress; **escultura** nf sculpture.

escupidora [eskupi'ðora], **escupidera** [eskupi'ðera] nf spittoon; (orinal) bedpan.

escupir [esku'pir] vt, vi to spit (out).

escurridero [eskurri'ðero] nm draining-board.

escurridizo, a [eskurri'ðiθo, a] a slippery.

escurrir [esku'rrir] vt (ropa) to wring out; (verduras) to strain; (platos) to drain // vi (los líquidos) to drip; (resbalarse) to slip, slide; **~se** vr (gotear) to drip; (secarse) to drain; (resbalarse) to slip, slide; (escaparse) to slip away.

ese, esa, esos, esas ['ese, 'esa, 'esos, 'esas] det (sg) that; (pl) those.

ése, ésa, ésos, ésas ['ese, 'esa, 'esos, 'esas] pron (sg) that (one); (pl) those (ones); **~... éste...** the former...; the latter...; **¡no me vengas con ~s** as don't give me any more of that nonsense.

esencia [e'senθja] nf essence; **esencial** a essential.

esfera [es'fera] nf sphere; (de reloj) face; **esférico, a** a spherical.

esforzado, a [esfor'θaðo, a] a (enérgico) energetic, vigorous; (valiente) brave.

esforzar [esfor'θar] vt (fortalecer) to strengthen; (alentar) to encourage; **~se** vr to exert o.s., make an effort.

esfuerzo [es'fwerθo] nm effort; (TEC) stress; (valor) courage, spirit.

esfumarse [esfu'marse] vr to fade away.

esgrima [es'γrima] nf fencing.

esguince [es'γinθe] nm (MED) sprain; (ademán) swerve, dodge; (ceño) scowl, frown.

eslabón [esla'βon] nm link; **eslabonar** vt to link, connect.

esmaltar [esmal'tar] vt to enamel; (las uñas) to paint, varnish; **esmalte** nm enamel; **esmalte de uñas** nail varnish, nail polish.

esmerado, a [esme'raðo, a] a careful, neat.

esmeralda [esme'ralda] nf emerald.

esmerarse [esme'rarse] vr (aplicarse) to take great pains, exercise great care; (*brillar*) to shine, do well.

esmero [es'mero] *nm* (great) care.

esnob [es'nob] *a inv* (*persona*) snobbish; (*coche etc*) posh // *nm/f* snob; ~**ismo** *nm* snobbery.

eso ['eso] *pron* that, that thing or matter; ~ **dé su coche** all that about his car; ~ **de ir al cine** all that about going to the cinema, the idea of going to the cinema; **a** ~ **de las cinco** at about five o'clock; **en** ~ thereupon, at that point; ~ **sí que es vida!** now this is really living!; **por** ~ **te lo dije** that's why I told you.

esos ['esos] *det ver* **ese**.

ésos ['esos] *pron ver* **ése**.

espabilar [espaßi'lar] *vt* (*vela*) to snuff; ~**se** *vr* (*despertarse*) to wake up; (*animarse*) to liven up, look lively.

espacial [espa'θjal] *a inv* (*del espacio*) space *cpd*.

espaciar [espa'θjar] *vt* to space (out), (*divulgar*) to spread; ~**se** *vr*: ~**se en un tema** to enlarge on a subject.

espacio [es'paθjo] *nm* space; (*MUS*) interval; (*emisión*) (short) programme, *spot*; **el** ~ **space**; ~**so, a** *a* spacious, roomy; (*lento*) slow.

espada [es'paða] *nf* sword; ~**s** *nfpl* (*NAIPES*) spades.

espaguetis [espa'xetis] *nmpl* spaghetti *sg*.

espalda [es'palda] *nf* (*gen*) back; ~**s** *nfpl* (*hombros*) shoulders; **a** ~**s de uno** behind sb's back; **cargado de** ~ round-shouldered; **tenderse de** ~ to lie (down) on one's back; **volver la** ~ **a alguien** to give sb the cold shoulder.

espaldar [espal'dar] *nm* (*de asiento*) back.

espaldilla [espal'ðiʎa] *nf* shoulder blade.

espantadizo, a [espanta'ðiθo, a] *a* timid, easily frightened.

espantajo [espan'taxo] *nm*,

espantapájaros [espanta'paxaros] *nmpl inv* scarecrow *sg*.

espantar [espan'tar] *vt* (*asustar*) to frighten, scare; (*ahuyentar*) to frighten off; (*asombrar*) to horrify, appal; ~**se** *vr* to get frightened or scared; to be appalled.

espanto [es'panto] *nm* (*susto*) fright; (*terror*) terror; (*fantasma*) ghost; (*asombro*) astonishment; ~**so, a** *a* frightening, terrifying; astonishing.

España [es'paɲa] *nf* Spain; **español** a Spanish // *nm/f* Spaniard // *nm* (*lengua*) Spanish.

esparadrapo [espara'ðrapo] *nm* sticking plaster.

esparcido, a [espar'θiðo, a] *a* scattered; (*fig*) jolly, cheerful.

esparcimiento [esparθi'mjento] *nm* (*de líquido*) spilling; (*dispersión*) spreading; (*derramamiento*) scattering; (*fig*) cheerfulness.

esparcir [espar'θir] *vt* to spread; (*derramar*) to scatter; (*líquido*) to spill; ~**se** *vr* to spread (out); to scatter, to spill; (*divertirse*) to enjoy o.s.

espárrago [es'parraxo] *nm* asparagus.

espasmo [es'pasmo] *nm* spasm.

especia [es'peθja] *nf* spice.

especial [espe'θjal] *a* special; ~**idad** *nf* speciality.

especie [es'peθje] *nf* (*BIO*) species; (*clase*) kind, sort; (*asunto*) matter; (*comentario*) remark, comment; **en** ~ in kind.

especificar [espeθifi'kar] *vt* to specify; **específico, a** *a* specific.

espécimen [es'peθimen] (*pl* **especímenes**) *nm* specimen.

especioso, a [espe'θjoso, a] *a* (*perfecto*) perfect; (*fig*) deceitful.

espectáculo [espek'takulo] *nm* (*gen*) spectacle; (*TEATRO etc*) show.

espectador, a [espekta'ðor, a] *nm/f* spectator.

espectro [es'pektro] *nm* ghost; (*fig*) spectre.

especular [espeku'lar] vt, vi to speculate; **especulativo, a** a speculative.

espejismo [espe'xismo] nm mirage.

espejo [es'pexo] nm mirror; (fig) model; ~ **de retrovisión** rear-view mirror.

espeluznante [espelu0'nante] a inv horrifying, hair-raising.

espera [es'pera] nf (pausa, intervalo) wait, period of waiting; (JUR: plazo) respite; **en** ~ **de** waiting for; (con expectativa) expecting.

esperanza [espe'ranθa] nf (confianza) hope; (expectativa) expectation; (perspectiva) prospect; **esperanzar** vt to give hope to.

esperar [espe'rar] vt (aguardar) to wait for; (tener expectativa de) to expect; (desear) to hope for // vi to wait; to expect; to hope.

esperma [es'perma] nf sperm.

espesar [espe'sar] vt to thicken; ~**se** vr to thicken, get thicker.

espeso, a [es'peso, a] a thick; **espesor** nm thickness.

espetar [espe'tar] vt (pollo) to put on a spit or skewer; (pregunta) to pop; (dar: reto, sermón) to give.

espetón [espe'ton] nm (asador) spit, skewer; (aguja) large pin; (empujón) jab, poke.

espía [es'pia] nm/f spy; **espiar** vt (observar) to spy on; (acechar) to watch out for.

espina [es'pina] nf thorn; (de madera, astilla) splinter; (de pez) bone; ~ **dorsal** spine.

espinaca [espi'naka] nf spinach.

espinar [espi'nar] vt (herir) to prick; (fig) to sting, hurt.

espinazo [espi'naθo] nm spine, backbone.

espino [es'pino] nm hawthorn.

espinoso, a [espi'noso, a] a (planta) thorny, prickly; (fig) bony.

espionaje [espjo'naxe] nm spying, espionage.

espiral [espi'ral] a, nf spiral.

espirar [espi'rar] vt to breathe out, exhale.

espiritista [espiri'tista] a, nm/f spiritualist.

espíritu [es'piritu] nm spirit; **espiritual** a spiritual.

espita [es'pita] nf tap; (fig: fam) drunkard.

esplendidez [esplendi'ðeθ] nf (abundancia) lavishness; (magnificencia) splendour.

esplendor [esplen'dor] nm splendour.

espolear [espole'ar] vt to spur on.

espolvorear [espolβore'ar] vt (echar polvos) to dust; (esparcir) to dust, sprinkle.

esponja [es'ponxa] nf sponge; (fig) sponger.

esponjarse [espon'xarse] vr (fam: hincharse) to swell with pride; (de salud) to glow with health.

esponjoso, a [espon'xoso, a] a spongy, porous.

espontaneidad [espontanei'ðað] nf spontaneity; **espontáneo, a** a spontaneous.

esposa [es'posa] nf wife; ~**s** nfpl handcuffs; **esposar** vt to handcuff.

esposo [es'poso] nm husband.

espuela [es'pwela] nf spur.

espuma [es'puma] nf foam; (de cerveza) froth, head; (de jabón) lather; **espumoso, a** a frothy, foamy; (vino) sparkling.

esqueleto [eske'leto] nm skeleton.

esquema [es'kema] nm (diagrama) diagram; (dibujo) plan; (plan) scheme; (FILOSOFÍA) schema.

esquí [es'ki] (pl esquís) nm (objeto) ski; (deporte) skiing.

esquilar [eski'lar] vt to shear.

esquilmar [eskil'mar] vt (cosechar) to harvest; (empobrecer: suelo) to exhaust; (fig) to skin.

esquimal [eski'mal] a, nm/f Eskimo.

esquina [es'kina] nf corner.

esquirol [eski'rol] nm (fam) blackleg.

esquivar [eski'βar] *vt* to avoid; (*evadir*) to dodge, elude; **~se** *vr* to withdraw.

esquivez [eski'βeθ] *nf* (*altanería*) aloofness; (*desdeño*) scorn, disdain; **esquivo, a a** (*altanero*) aloof; (*desdeñoso*) scornful, disdainful.

esta ['esta] *det ver* **este**.

ésta ['esta] *pron ver* **éste**.

está *vb ver* **estar**.

estabilidad [estaβili'ðað] *nf* stability; **estable a** stable.

establecer [estaβle'θer] *vt* to establish; **~se** *vr* to establish o.s.; (*echar raíces*) to settle; **establecimiento** *nm* establishment.

estaca [es'taka] *nf* stake, post; (*para tiendas*) peg.

estacada [esta'kaða] *nf* (*cerca*) fence, fencing; (*palenque*) stockade.

estación [esta'θjon] *nf* station; (*del año*) season; **~ de autobuses** bus station.

estacionamiento [estaθjona'mjento] *nm* (*AUTO*) parking; (*MIL*) stationing; (*colocación*) placing

estacionar [estaθjo'nar] *vt* (*AUTO*) to park; (*MIL*) to station; (*colocar*) to place; **~io, a a** stationary; (*COM. mercado*) slack.

estadio [es'taðjo] *nm* (*fase*) stage, phase; (*DEPORTE*) stadium.

estadista [esta'ðista] *nm* (*POL*) statesman; (*ESTADÍSTICA*) statistician.

estadística [esta'ðistika] *nf* (*una ~*) figure, statistic; (*ciencia*) statistics *pl*.

estado [es'taðo] *nm* (*POL: condición*) state; (*social*) status; **~ de las cuentas** statement of accounts; **~ mayor** staff; **E ~ Unidos** (*EE. UU.*) United States (*USA*).

estafa [es'tafa] *nf* swindle, trick; **estafar** *vt* to swindle, defraud.

estafeta [esta'feta] *nf* (*correo*) post; (*oficina de correos*) post office; **~ diplomática** diplomatic bag.

estallar [esta'ʎar] *vi* to burst; (*explotar*) to explode; (*epidemia,*

rebelión) to break out; **~ en llanto** to burst into tears; **estallido** *nm* explosion; (*fig*) outbreak.

estampa [es'tampa] *nf* (*imagen*) image; (*impresión, imprenta*) print, engraving; (*imagen, figura: de persona*) appearance; (*fig: huella*) footprint.

estampado, a [estam'paðo, a] *a* printed // *nm* (*impresión: acción*) printing; (: *efecto*) print; (*marca*) stamping.

estampar [estam'par] *vt* (*imprimir*) to print; (*marcar*) to stamp; (*metal*) to engrave; (*poner sello en*) to stamp; (*fig*) to stamp, imprint.

estampida [estam'piða] *nf* stampede; (*estampido*) bang, report.

estampido [estam'piðo] *nm* bang, report.

estampilla [estam'piʎa] *nf* stamp.

están *vb ver* **estar**.

estancar [estaŋ'kar] *vt* (*aguas*) to hold up, hold back; (*COM*) to monopolize; (*fig*) to block, hold up; **~se** *vr* to stagnate.

estancia [es'tanθja] *nf* (*permanencia*) stay; (*sala*) living-room; (*AM*) farm, ranch; **estanciero** *nm* farmer, rancher.

estanco, a [es'taŋko, a] *a* watertight // *nm* (*monopolio*) state monopoly; (*tienda*) tobacconist's (*shop*).

estandarizar [estandari'θar] *vt* to standardize.

estandarte [estan'darte] *nm* banner, standard.

estanque [es'taŋke] *nm* (*lago*) pool, pond; (*AGR*) reservoir.

estanquero, a [estaŋ'kero, a], **estanquillero, a** [estaŋki'ʎero, a] *nm/f* tobacconist.

estante [es'tante] *nm* (*armario*) rack, stand; (*biblioteca*) bookcase; (*anaquel*) shelf; (*AM*) prop; **estantería** *nf* shelving, shelves *pl*.

estantigua [estan'tiɣwa] *nf* (*fantasma*) apparition.

estaño [es'tano] *nm* tin.

estar [es'tar] vi (gen) to be; (en casa) to be in; (ubicarse) to be found; (presente) to be present; **estamos a 2 de mayo** it is the 2nd May; ¿**cómo está Ud?** how are you?; ~ **enfermo** to be ill; ~ **viejo/joven** (parecerse) to seem old/young; (seguido de una preposición): ¿**a cuánto estamos de Madrid?** how far are we from Madrid?; ~ **de fiesta** o **vacaciones** to be on holiday; **las uvas están a 5 pesetas** grapes are at 5 pesetas; **María no está** Maria isn't in; ~ **por** o: (moción) to be in favour of; (: persona) to support, back; **está por hacer** it remains to be done; ¿**estamos?** are we agreed?

estas ['estas] det ver **este**.

éstas ['estas] pron ver **éste**.

estás vb ver **estar**.

estatal [esta'tal] a inv state cpd.

estático, a [es'tatiko, a] a static.

estatificar [estatifi'kar] vt to nationalize.

estatua [es'tatwa] nf statue.

estatuir [estatu'ir] vt (establecer) to establish; (determinar) to prove.

estatura [esta'tura] nf stature, height.

estatuto [esta'tuto] nm (JUR) statute; (de ciudad) bye-law; (de comité) rule.

este ['este] nm east.

este, esta, estos, estas ['este, 'esta, 'estos, 'estas] det (sg) this; (pl) these.

éste, ésta, éstos, éstas ['este, 'esta, 'estos, 'estas] pron (sg) this (one); (pl) these (ones); ~ ... **ése**... the latter... the former... .

esté etc vb ver **estar**.

estela [es'tela] nf wake, wash; (fig) trail.

estenografía [estenoɤra'fia] nf shorthand, stenography.

estepa [es'tepa] nf (GEO) steppe.

estera [es'tera] nf mat(ting).

estereo... [estereo] pref stereo...; ~**fónico, a** a stereophonic; ~**tipar**

vt to stereotype; ~**tipo** nm stereotype.

estéril [es'teril] a sterile, barren; (fig) vain, futile.

esterlina [ester'lina] a: **libra** ~ pound sterling.

estético, a [es'tetiko, a] a aesthetic // nf aesthetics sg.

estiércol [es'tjerkol] nm dung, manure.

estigma [es'tiɣma] nm stigma.

estilar [esti'lar] vi, ~**se** vr to be in fashion, be used, be worn.

estilo [es'tilo] nm style; (TEC) stylus; (DEPORTE) stroke; **algo por el** ~ something of the sort.

estima [es'tima] nf esteem, respect.

estimación [estima'θjon] nf (evaluación) estimation; (aprecio, afecto) esteem, regard.

estimar [esti'mar] vt (evaluar) to estimate; (valorar) to value; (apreciar) to esteem, respect; (pensar, considerar) to think, reckon; ¡**se estima!** thanks very much!

estimulante [estimu'lante] a stimulating // nm stimulant; **estimular** vt to stimulate; (excitar) to excite; (animar) to encourage; **estímulo** nm stimulus; (ánimo) encouragement.

estío [es'tio] nm summer.

estipulación [estipula'θjon] nf stipulation, condition; **estipular** vt to stipulate.

estirado, a [esti'rado, a] a (tenso) (stretched o drawn) tight; (fig) stiff, pompous.

estirar [esti'rar] vt to stretch; (conversación, presupuesto) to stretch out; ~**se** vr to stretch.

estirón [esti'ron] nm pull, tug; (crecimiento) spurt, sudden growth; **dar un** ~ to shoot up.

estirpe [es'tirpe] nf stock, lineage.

estival [esti'βal] a summer cpd.

esto ['esto] pron this, this thing o matter; ~ **de la boda** this business about the wedding.

estofa [es'tofa] nf (tela) quilting.

(calidad, clase) quality, class.

estofado, a [esto'faðo, a] *a (CULIN)* stewed; *(bordado)* quilted // *nm* stew.

estofar [esto'far] *vt (bordar)* to quilt; *(CULIN)* to stew.

estoico, a [es'toiko, a] *a (FILOSOFÍA)* stoic(al); *(fig)* cold, indifferent.

estólido, a [es'toliðo, a] *a* stupid.

estómago [es'tomaɣo] *nm* stomach; **tener ~** to be thick-skinned.

estorbar [estor'ßar] *vt* to hinder, obstruct; *(fig)* to bother, disturb // *vi* to be in the way; **estorbo** *nm (molestia)* bother, nuisance; *(obstáculo)* hindrance, obstacle.

estornudar [estornu'ðar] *vi* to sneeze.

ostos ['estos] *det ver* este.

éstos ['estos] *pron ver* éste.

estoy *vb ver* estar.

estrafalario, a [estrafa'larjo, a] *a* odd, eccentric; *(desarreglado)* slovenly, sloppy.

estragar [estra'ɣar] *vt* to deprave, corrupt; *(deteriorar)* to ruin; **estrago** *nm* ruin, destruction; **hacer estragos en** to wreak havoc among.

estragón [estra'ɣon] *nm (CULIN)* tarragon.

estrangul [estran'ɣul] *nm* mouthpiece.

estrangulación [estranɣula'θjon] *nf* strangulation.

estrangulador, a [estranɣula'ðor, a] *nm/f* strangler // *nm (TEC)* throttle; *(AUTO)* choke.

estrangulamiento [estranɣula'mjento] *nm (AUTO)* bottleneck.

estrangular [estranɣu'lar] *vt (persona)* to strangle; *(MED)* to strangulate.

estraperlo [estra'perlo] *nm* black market.

estratagema [estrata'xema] *nf (MIL)* stratagem; *(astucia)* cunning.

estrategia [estra'texja] *nf* strategy; **estratégico, a** *a* strategic.

estratificar [estratifi'kar] *vt* to stratify.

estrato [es'trato] *nm* stratum, layer.

estrechar [estre'tʃar] *vt (reducir)* to narrow; *(vestido)* to take in; *(persona)* to hug, embrace; **~se** *vr (reducirse)* to narrow, grow narrow; *(apretarse)* to embrace; *(reducir los gastos)* to economize; **~ la mano** **a alguien** to shake hands; **~ amistad con** **alguien** to become very friendly with sb.

estrechez [estre'tʃeθ] *nf* narrowness; *(de ropa)* tightness; *(intimidad)* intimacy; *(COM)* want or shortage of money; **estrecheces** *nfpl* financial difficulties; **~ de conciencia** small-mindedness; **~ de miras** narrow-mindedness.

estrecho, a [es'tretʃo, a] *a* narrow; *(apretado)* tight; *(íntimo)* close, intimate; *(miserable)* mean // *nm* strait.

estregar [estre'ɣar] *vt (sobar)* to rub (hard); *(rascar)* to scrape.

estrella [es'treʎa] *nf* star; **~ de** **mar** starfish.

estrellar [estre'ʎar] *vt (hacer añicos)* to smash (to pieces); *(huevos)* to fry; **~se** *vr* to smash; *(chocarse)* to crash; *(fracasar)* to be smashed to pieces.

estremecer [estreme'θer] *vt* to shake; *(hacer temblar)* to tremble; **estremecimiento** *nm (conmoción)* tremor; *(sobresalto)* shock, *(temblor)* trembling, shaking.

estrenar [estre'nar] *vt (vestido)* to wear for the first time; *(casa)* to move into; *(película, obra de teatro)* to present for the first time; **~se** *vr (persona)* to make one's début; **estreno** *nm (primer uso)* first use; *(en un empleo)* début, first appearance; *(CINE, etc)* première.

estreñir [estre'ɲir] *vt* to constipate; **~se** *vr* to become constipated.

estrépito [es'trepito] *nm* noise, racket; *(fig)* fuss; **estrepitoso, a** *a* noisy; (*fiesta*) rowdy, boisterous.

estría [es'tria] *nf* groove.

estribar [estri'βar] *vi*: ~ **en** to rest on, be supported by.

estribo [es'triβo] *nm* (*de jinete*) stirrup; (*de coche, tren*) step; (*de puente*) support; (*fig*) basis, foundation; (*GEO*) spur.

estribor [estri'βor] *nm* starboard.

estricnina [estrik'nina] *nf* strychnine.

estricto, a [es'trikto, a] *a* (*riguroso*) strict; (*severo*) severe.

estro ['estro] *nm* inspiration.

estropajo [estro'paxo] *nm* scourer.

estropear [estrope'ar] *vt* (*arruinar*) to spoil; (*dañar*) to damage; (*lisiar*) to maim; (*tullir*) to cripple; ~**se** *vr* (*objeto*) to get damaged; (*persona*) to be crippled.

estructura [estruk'tura] *nf* structure.

estruendo [es'trwendo] *nm* (*ruido*) racket, din; (*fig: alboroto*) uproar, turmoil; (*pompa*) pomp.

estrujar [estru'xar] *vt* (*apretar*) to squeeze; (*aplastar*) to crush; (*magullar*) to bruise; (*fig*) to drain, bleed.

estuario [es'twarjo] *nm* estuary.

estuche [es'tutʃe] *nm* box, case.

estudiante [estu'ðjante] *nm/f* student; **estudiantil** *a inv* student *cpd*.

estudiantina [estuðjan'tina] *nf* student music group.

estudiar [estu'ðjar] *vt* to study.

estudio [es'tuðjo] *nm* study; (*CINE, ARTE, RADIO*) studio; ~**s** *nmpl* studies; (*erudición*) learning *sg*; ~**so, a** a studious.

estufa [es'tufa] *nf* heater, fire.

estulticia [estul'tiθja] *nf* foolishness.

estupefacto, a [estupe'fakto, a] *a* speechless, thunderstruck.

estupendo, a [estu'pendo, a] *a* wonderful, terrific; (*fam*) great; ¡~! that's great!, fantastic!

estupidez [estupi'ðeθ] *nf* (*torpeza*) stupidity; (*tontería*) piece of nonsense.

estúpido, a [es'tupiðo, a] *a* stupid, silly.

estupor [estu'por] *nm* stupor; (*fig*) astonishment, amazement.

estupro [es'tupro] *nm* rape.

estuve etc *vb ver* **estar**.

etapa [e'tapa] *nf* stage; (*DEPORTE*) leg; (*parada*) stopping place; (*fig*) stage, phase.

eternidad [eterni'ðað] *nf* eternity; **eterno, a** a eternal, everlasting.

ético, a ['etiko, a] *a* ethical // *nf* ethics *pl*.

etíope [e'tiope] a, *nm/f* Ethiopian.

Etiopía [etjo'pia] *nf* Ethiopia.

etiqueta [eti'keta] *nf* (*modales*) etiquette; (*papel*) label, tag.

eucalipto [euka'lipto] *nm* eucalyptus.

Eucaristía [eukaris'tia] *nf* Eucharist.

eufemismo [eufe'mismo] *nm* euphemism.

euforia [eu'forja] *nf* euphoria.

eugenesia [euxe'nesja] *nf*, **eugenismo** [euxe'nismo] *nm* eugenics *sg*.

eunuco [eu'nuko] *nm* eunuch.

Europa [eu'ropa] *nf* Europe; **europeo, a** a, *nm/f* European.

éuscaro, a [e'uskaro, a] a Basque // *nm* (*lengua*) Basque.

Euskadi [eus'kaði] *nm* the Basque Provinces *pl*.

eutanasia [euta'nasja] *nf* euthanasia.

evacuación [eβakwa'θjon] *nf* evacuation; **evacuar** [e-] vt to evacuate.

evadir [eβa'ðir] *vt* to evade, avoid; ~**se** *vr* to escape.

evaluar [eβa'lwar] *vt* to evaluate.

evangélico, a [eβan'xeliko, a] a evangelic(al).

evangelio [eβan'xeljo] *nm* gospel.

evaporación [eβapora'θjon] *nf* evaporation.

evaporar [eβapo'rar] *vt* to evaporate; ~**se** *vr* to vanish.

evasión [eßa'sjon] *nf* escape, flight; (*fig*) evasion.

evasivo, a [eßa'sißo, a] *a* evasive, non-commital.

evento [e'ßento] *nm* unforeseen event; (*eventualidad*) eventuality; **a cualquier ~** in any event.

eventual [eßen'twal] *a* possible, conditional (*upon circumstances*); (*trabajador*) casual, temporary.

evidencia [eßi'ðenθja] *nf* (*certidumbre*) evidence, proof; **evidenciar** *vt* (*hacer patente*) to make evident; (*probar*) to prove, show; **evidenciarse** *vr* to be evident.

evidente [eßi'ðente] *a* obvious, clear, evident.

evitar [eßi'tar] *vt* (*evadir*) to avoid; (*impedir*) to prevent.

evocar [eßo'kar] *vt* to evoke, call forth.

evolución [eßolu'θjon] *nf* (*desarrollo*) evolution, development; (*cambio*) change, (*MIL*) manoeuvre; **evolucionar** *vi* to evolve; (*MIL*, *AVIAT*) to manoeuvre.

ex [eks] *a* ex-; **el ~ ministro** the former minister, the ex-minister.

exacerbar [eksaθer'ßar] *vt* to irritate, annoy; (*agravar*) to aggravate.

exactitud [eksakti'tuð] *nf* exactness, (*precisión*) accuracy; (*puntualidad*) punctuality, **exacto, a** *a* exact; **accurate**; punctual; **¡exacto!** exactly!

exageración [eksaxera'θjon] *nf* exaggeration; **exagerar** *vt, vi* to exaggerate.

exaltado, a [eksal'taðo, a] *a* (*apasionado*) over-excited, worked-up, (*exagerado*) extreme; (*excitado*) elated.

exaltar [eksal'tar] *vt* to exalt, glorify; **~se** *vr* (*excitarse*) to get excited or worked-up; (*arrebatarse*) to get carried away.

examen [ek'samen] *nm* examination.

examinar [eksami'nar] *vt* to examine; **~se** *vr* to be examined, sit an examination.

exangüe [ek'sangwe] *a* (*desangrado*) bloodless; (*sin fuerzas*) weak.

exasperar [eksaspe'rar] *vt* to exasperate; **~se** *vr* to get exasperated, lose patience.

Exca. *abr de* **Excelencia.**

excedente [eksθe'ðente] *a, nm* excess, surplus.

exceder [eksθe'ðer] *vt* to exceed, surpass; **~se** *vr* (*extralimitarse*) to go too far; (*subrepasarse*) to excel o.s.

excelencia [eksθe'lenθja] *nf* excellence; **E~** Excellency; **excelente** *a* excellent.

excelso, a [eks'θelso, a] *a* lofty, sublime.

excentricidad [eksθentriθi'ðað] *nf* eccentricity; **excéntrico, a** *a, nm/f* eccentric.

excepción [eksθep'θjon] *nf* exception; **excepcional** *a* exceptional.

excepto [eks'θepto] *ad* excepting, except (for).

exceptuar [eksθep'twar] *vt* to except, exclude.

excesivo, a [eksθe'sißo, a] *a* excessive.

exceso [eks'θeso] *nm* (*gen*) excess; (*COM*) surplus.

excitación [eksθita'θjon] *nf* (*sensación*) excitement; (*acción*) excitation.

excitado, a [eksθi'taðo, a] *a* excited, (*emociones*) aroused; **excitar** *vt* to excite, (*incitar*) to urge; **excitarse** *vr* to get excited.

exclamación [eksklama'θjon] *nf* exclamation; **exclamar** *vi* to exclaim.

excluir [eksklu'ir] *vt* to exclude; (*dejar fuera*) to shut out; (*descartar*) to reject; **exclusión** *nf* exclusion; (*descarte*) rejection; **con exclusión de** excluding.

exclusiva [eksklu'sißa] *nf*; **exclusividad** [eksklusißi'ðað] *nf* exclusiveness; (PRENSA) exclusive; (COM) sole right or agency.

exclusivo, a [eksklu'siβo, a] a exclusive; (único) sole.

Excmo. abr de **excelentísmo.**

excomulgar [ekskomul'xar] vt (REL) to excommunicate; (excluir) to ban, banish.

excomunión [ekskomu'njon] nf excommunication.

excoriar [eksko'rjar] vt to flay, skin.

excursión [ekskur'sjon] nf excursion, outing; **excursionismo** nm sightseeing.

excusa [eks'kusa] nf excuse; (disculpa) apology.

excusado, a [eksku'saðo, a] a unnecessary; (disculpado) excused, forgiven // nm lavatory, toilet.

excusar [eksku'sar] vt to excuse; (evitar) to avoid; (impedir) to prevent; **~se** vr (rehusarse) to decline a request; (disculparse) to apologize.

execrar [ekse'krar] vt to loathe.

exención [eksen'θjon] nf exemption.

exento, a [ek'sento, a] pp de **eximir** // a exempt; **~ de derechos** tax-free.

exequias [ek'sekjas] nfpl funeral rites, obsequies.

exhalación [eksala'θjon] nf (del aire) exhalation; (vapor) fumes pl, vapour; (rayo) shooting star.

exhalar [eksa'lar] vt to exhale, breathe out; (olor etc) to give off; (suspiro) to breathe, heave.

exhausto, a [ek'sausto, a] a exhausted.

exhibición [eksiβi'θjon] nf exhibition, display, show.

exhibir [eksi'βir] vt to exhibit, display, show.

exhortación [eksorta'θjon] nf exhortation; **exhortar** vt: **exhortar a** to exhort to.

exigencia [eksi'xenθja] nf demand,

requirement; **exigente** a demanding.

exigir [eksi'xir] vt (gen) to demand, require; (pago) to exact.

exilio [ek'siljo] nm exile.

eximio, a [ek'simjo, a] a (excelente) choice, select; (eminente) distinguished, eminent.

eximir [eksi'mir] vt to exempt.

existencia [eksis'tenθja] nf existence; **~s** nfpl stock(s) (pl).

existir [eksis'tir] vi to exist, be.

éxito ['eksito] nm (resultado) result, outcome; (triunfo) success; **tener ~** to be successful.

exonerar [eksone'rar] vt to exonerate; **~ de una obligación** to free from an obligation.

exorcizar [eksorθi'θar] vt to exorcize.

exótico, a [ek'sotiko, a] a exotic.

expandir [ekspan'dir] vt to expand.

expansión [ekspan'sjon] nf expansion.

expatriarse [ekspa'trjarse] vr to emigrate; (POL) to go into exile.

expectativa [ekspekta'tiβa] nf (espera) expectation; (perspectiva) prospect.

expedición [ekspeði'θjon] nf (excursión) expedition; (envío) shipment; (rapidez) speed.

expediente [ekspe'ðjente] nm expedient; (JUR: procedimento) action, proceedings pl; (: papeles) dossier, file, record.

expedir [ekspe'ðir] vt (despachar) to send, forward; (libreta cívica, pasaporte) to issue; (fig) to deal with.

expedito, a [ekspe'ðito, a] a (libre) clear, free; (pronto) prompt, speedy.

expendedor, a [ekspende'ðor, a] nm/f (vendedor) dealer; (aparato) (vending) machine; **~ de cigarrillos** cigarette machine.

expendeduría [ekspendeðu'ria] nf shop; (estanco) tobacconist's shop.

expensas [eks'pensas] nfpl expenses; **a ~ de** at the expense of.

experiencia [ekspe'rjenθja] nf experience; (científica) experiment.

experimentado, a [eksperimen'taðo, a] a experienced.

experimentar [eksperimen'tar] vt (en laboratorio) to experiment with; (probar) to test, try out; (notar, observar) to experience; (sufrir) to suffer; **experimento** nm experiment.

experto, a [eks'perto, a] a (práctico) expert, (diestro) skilled, experienced // nm/f expert.

expiar [ekspi'ar] vt to atone for.

expirar [ekspi'rar] vi to expire.

explayar [ekspla'jar] vt to extend, expand; ~se vr to extend, spread; ~se con uno to confide in sb.

explicación [eksplika'θjon] nf explanation; **explicar** vt to explain; **explicarse** vr to explain (o.s.).

explícito, a [eks'pliθito, a] a explicit.

explorador, a [eksplora'ðor, a] nm/f (pionero) explorer; (MIL) scout // nm (MED) probe; (TEC) (radar) scanner; **los E~s** the Scouts.

explorar [eksplo'rar] vt to explore; (MED) to probe; (radar) to scan.

explosión [eksplo'sjon] nf explosion; **explosivo, a** a explosive.

explotación [eksplota'θjon] nf exploitation; (de planta etc) running, operation; **explotar** vt to exploit; to run, operate // vi to explode.

exponer [ekspo'ner] vt to expose; (cuadro) to display; (vida) to risk; (idea) to explain; ~se vr to expose o.s., leave o.s. open.

exportación [eksporta'θjon] nf (acción) export; (mercancías) exports pl; **exportar** vt to export.

exposición [eksposi'θjon] nf exposure; (de arte) show, exhibition; (petición) petition; (explicación) explanation; (narración) account, statement.

exposímetro [ekspo'simetro] nm (FOTO) exposure meter.

exprés [eks'pres] nm (AM) express (train).

expresar [ekspre'sar] vt to express; **expresión** nf expression; **expresiones** nfpl regards.

expreso, a [eks'preso, a] pp de **exprosar** // a (claro) specific, clear; (rápido) fast // nm: **mandar por ~** to send by express (delivery).

exprimir [ekspri'mir] vt (fruta) to squeeze (out); (ropa) to wring out; (fig) to express emphatically.

expropiar [ekspro'pjar] vt to expropriate.

expuesto, a [eks'pwesto, a] a exposed; (cuadro etc) on show, on display.

expugnar [ekspuɣ'nar] vt to take by storm.

expulsar [ekspul'sar] vt (echar) to eject; (arrojar) to throw out; (expeler) to expel; (desalojar) to drive out; (despedir) to sack, fire; (a un futbolista) to send off; **expulsión** nf expulsion; sending-off.

expurgar [ekspur'sar] vt to expurgate.

exquisito, a [ekski'sito, a] a exquisite; (agradable) delightful.

éxtasis ['ekstasis] nm ecstasy.

extender [eksten'der] vt (gen) to extend; (los brazos) to stretch out, hold out; (mapa) to spread (out), open (out); (mantequilla) to spread; (certificado) to issue; (cheque, recibo) to make out; (documento) to draw up; ~se vr (gen) to extend; (en el suelo) to stretch out; (epidemia) to spread; **extendido, a** a (abierto) spread out, open; (brazos) outstretched; (prevaleciente) widespread; **extensión** nf (de país) expanse, stretch; (de libro) extent; (de tiempo) length, duration; (AM) extensión; **en toda la extensión de la palabra** in every sense of the word; **extenso, a** a extensive; (prevaleciente) widespread.

extenuar [ekste'nwar] vt (agotar) to exhaust; (debilitar) to weaken.

exterior [ekste'rjor] a inv (de fuera) external; (afuera) outside, exterior; (apariencia) outward; (comercio) foreign // nm (gen) exterior, outside; (aspecto) outward appearance; (DEPORTE) wing(er); el ~ foreign parts pl; al ~ outwardly, on the surface.

exterminar [ekstermi'nar] vt to exterminate; **exterminio** nm extermination.

externo, a [eks'terno, a] a (exterior) external, outside; (superficial) outward // nm/f day pupil.

extinguir [ekstin'gir] vt (fuego) to extinguish, put out; (raza, población) to wipe out; **~se** vr (fuego) to go out; (BIO) to die out, become extinct.

extinto, a [eks'tinto, a] a extinct.

extintor [ekstin'tor] nm (fire) extinguisher.

extra ['ekstra] a, nm/f extra // nm extra; (bono) bonus.

extracción [ekstrak'θjon] nf extraction; (en lotería) draw.

extracto [eks'trakto] nm extract.

extraer [ekstra'er] vt to extract, take out.

extralimitarse [ekstralimi'tarse] vr to go too far.

extranjero, a [ekstran'xero, a] a foreign // nm/f foreigner // nm foreign lands pl; **en el ~** abroad.

extrañar [ekstra'ɲar] vt (desterrar) to exile; (sorprender) to find strange or odd; (AM) to miss; **~se** vr (sorprenderse) to be amazed, be surprised; (distanciarse) to become estranged, grow apart.

extrañeza [ekstra'ɲeθa] nf (rareza) strangeness, oddness; (asombro) amazement, surprise.

extraño, a [eks'traɲo, a] a (extranjero) foreign; (raro, sorprendente) strange, odd.

extraordinario, a [ekstraordi'narjo, a] a extraordinary; (edición, número) special // nm (plato) special dish; (de periódico) special edition; **horas ~as** overtime sg.

extravagancia [ekstraβa'xanθja] nf extravagance; **extravagante** a extravagant; (extraño) strange, odd; (excéntrico) eccentric; (estrafalario) outlandish.

extraviado, a [ekstra'βjaðo, a] a lost, missing.

extraviar [ekstra'βjar] vt (desviar) to mislead; (perder) to lose, misplace; **~se** vr to lose one's way, get lost.

extravío [ekstra'βio] nm loss; (fig) deviation.

extremar [ekstre'mar] vt to carry to extremes; **~se** vr to do one's utmost, make every effort.

extremaunción [ekstremaun'θjon] nf extreme unction.

extremeño, a [ekstre'meɲo, a] a, nm/f Extremaduran.

extremidad [ekstremi'ðað] nf (punta) extremity; (fila) edge; **~es** nfpl (ANAT) extremities.

extremo, a [eks'tremo, a] a extreme; (último) last // nm end; (límite, grado sumo) extreme; **en último ~** as a last resort; **~ derecho/izquierdo** outside-right/outside-left.

extrínseco, a [eks'trinseko, a] a extrinsic.

extrovertido, a [ekstroβer'tiðo, a] a, nm/f extrovert.

exuberancia [eksuβe'ranθja] nf exuberance; **exuberante** a exuberant; (fig) luxuriant, lush.

exvoto [eks'βoto] nm votive offering.

eyacular [ejaku'lar] vt, vi to ejaculate.

F

f.a.b. abr de **franco a bordo** f.o.b. (free on board).

fábrica ['faβrika] nf factory; **marca**

de ~ trademark; **precio de ~** factory price.

fabricación [faβrika'θjon] nf (*manufactura*) manufacture; (*producción*) production; **de ~ casera** home-made; **~ en serie** mass production.

fabricante [faβri'kante] nm/f manufacturer.

fabricar [faβri'kar] vt (*hacer*) to manufacture, make; (*construir*) to build; (*elaborar*) to fabricate, devise.

fabril [fa'βril] a: **industria ~** manufacturing industry.

fábula ['faβula] nf (*cuento*) fable; (*chisme*) rumour.

facción [fak'θjon] nf (*POL*) faction; (*del rostro*) feature.

fácil ['faθil] a (*simple*) easy; (*probable*) likely

facilidad [faθili'ðað] nf (*capacidad*) ease; (*sencillez*) simplicity; (*de palabra*) fluency; **~es** nfpl facilities.

facilitar [faθili'tar] vt (*hacer fácil*) to make easy; (*proporcionar*) to provide; (*hacer posible*) to arrange; (*hacer más fácil*) to facilitate.

fácilmente ['faθilmente] ad easily.

factible [fak'tiβle] a feasible.

factor [fak'tor] nm factor.

factura [fak'tura] nf (*cuenta*) bill; (*hechura*) manufacture; **facturar** vt (*COM*) to invoice, charge for.

facultad [fakul'tað] nf (*aptitud*, *ESCOL etc*) faculty; (*poder*) power.

facha ['faʃa] nf (*fam: aspecto*) look; (: *desagradable*) unpleasant look.

fachada [fa'tʃaða] nf (*ARQ*) façade.

faena [fa'ena] nf (*trabajo*) work; (*quehacer*) task; **~ de la casa** housework sg.

fagot [fa'got] nm (*MUS*) bassoon.

faisán [fai'san] nm pheasant.

faja ['faxa] nf (*para la cintura*) sash; (*de mujer*) corset; (*de tierra*) strip; (*venda*) bandage.

falange [fa'lanxe] nf (*POL*) Falange.

falda ['falda] nf (*prenda de vestir*) skirt.

falibilidad [faliβili'ðað] nf fallibility.

fálico, a ['faliko, a] a phallic.

falo ['falo] nm phallus.

falsedad [false'ðað] nf (*hipocresía*) falseness; (*mentira*) falsehood.

falsificar [falsifi'kar] vt (*firma etc*) to forge; (*voto etc*) to rig; (*moneda*) to counterfeit.

falso, a ['falso, a] a (*gen*) false; (*erróneo*) mistaken; (*moneda etc*) fake; **en ~** falsely.

falta ['falta] nf (*defecto*) fault, flaw; (*privación*) lack, want; (*ausencia*) absence; (*carencia*) shortage; (*equivocación*) mistake; (*DEPORTE*) foul; **hacer ~** to be missing or lacking.

faltar [fal'tar] vi (*escasear*) to be lacking, be wanting; (*ausentarse*) to be absent, be missing; (*fallar: mecanismo*) to go wrong, break down; **faltan 2 horas para llegar** there are 2 hours to go till arrival; **~ el respeto a alguien** to be disrespectful to sb; **echar a ~ alguien** to miss sb; **¡no faltaba más!** that's the last straw!

falto, a ['falto, a] a (*desposeído*) deficient, lacking; (*necesitado*) poor, wretched.

fallo ['faʎo] nf (*defecto*) fault, flaw; (*fracaso*) failure.

fallar [fa'ʎar] vt (*JUR*) to pronounce sentence on // vi (*memoria*) to fail; (*motor*) to miss.

fallecer [faʎe'θer] vi to pass away, die; **fallecimiento** nm decease, demise.

fallo ['faʎo] nm (*JUR*) verdict, ruling; (*fracaso*) failure.

fama ['fama] nf (*renombre*) fame; (*reputación*) reputation.

familia [fa'milja] nf family.

familiar [fami'ljar] a (*relativo a la familia*) family *cpl*; (*conocido, informal*) familiar // nm relative; **~idad** nf (*gen*) familiarity;

(*informalidad*) homeliness; ~**izarse**
vr to familiarize o.s. with.

famoso, a [fa'moso, a] *a*
(*renombrado*) famous; (*fam:
fabuloso*) great.

fanático, a [fa'natiko, a] *a*
fanatical // *nm/f* (*gen*) fanatic;
(*CINE etc*) fan; (*de deportes*)
supporter; **fanatismo** *nm*
fanaticism.

fanfarrón, ona [fanfa'rron, ona] *a*
a boastful(-pey) showy.

fango ['faŋgo] *nm* mud; ~**so, a** *a*
muddy.

fantasía [fanta'sia] *nf* fantasy,
imagination; (*fam*) conceit, vanity;
joyas de ~ imitation jewellery *sg*.

fantasma [fan'tasma] *nm* (*espectro*) ghost, apparition.

fantástico, a [fan'tastiko, a] *a* *a*
fantastic.

farmacéutico, a [farma'θeutiko,
a] *a* pharmaceutical // *nm/f*
chemist, pharmacist.

farmacia [far'maθja] *nf* chemist's
(shop), pharmacy; ~ **de turno** all-
night chemist.

faro ['faro] *nm* (*NAUT: torre*)
lighthouse; (*AUTO*) headlamp; ~**s
laterales** sidelights; ~**s traseros**
rear lights.

farol [fa'rol] *nm* (*luz*) lantern, lamp;
(*de calle*) streetlamp.

farsa ['farsa] *nf* (*gen*) farce.

farsante [far'sante] *nm/f* fraud,
fake.

fascinar [fasθi'nar] *vt* (*deslumbrar*) to fascinate.

fascismo [fas'θismo] *nm* fascism;
fascista *a, nm/f* fascist.

fase ['fase] *nf* phase.

fastidiar [fasti'δjar] *vt* (*disgustar*)
to annoy, bother; (*estropear*) to
spoil; (*aburrir*) to bore; ~**se** *vr*
(*dañarse*) to harm o.s.; (*disgustarse*)
to get annoyed or cross.

fastidio [fas'tiδjo] *nm* (*disgusto*)
annoyance; (*tedio*) boredom; ~**so, a**
a (*molesto*) annoying; (*aburrido*)
tedious.

fatal [fa'tal] *a* (*gen*) fatal;
(*inevitable*) unavoidable; (*desgraciado*) ill-fated; (*fam: malo, pésimo*)
awful; (*mala suerte*) fate;
(*mala suerte*) misfortune.

fatiga [fa'tixa] *nf* (*cansancio*)
fatigue, weariness; **fatigar** *vt* to tire,
weary; **fatigarse** *vr* to get tired;
fatigoso, a *a* (*cansador*) tiring;
(*aburrido*) tiresome.

fatuo, a [fa'two, a] *a* (*vano*) fatuous;
(*presuntuoso*) conceited.

fauces [fau'θes] *nfpl* jaws, mouth *sg*.

favor [fa'βor] *nm* favour; **entrada
de** ~ complimentary ticket; **haga el
favor de...** would you be so good as to...,
kindly...; **por** ~ please; ~**able** *a*
favourable.

favorecer [faβore'θer] *vt* (*gen*) to
favour; (*vestido etc*) to become,
flatter; **este peinado le favorece**
this hairstyle suits her.

favorito, a [faβo'rito, a] *a, nm/f*
favourite.

faz [faθ] *nf*: **la** ~ **de la tierra** the
face of the earth.

fe [fe] *nf* (*REL*) faith; (*confianza*)
belief; (*documento*) certificate;
(*lealtad*) fidelity, loyalty; **prestar** ~
a to believe, credit; **actuar con
buena/mala** ~ to act in good/bad
faith; **dar** ~ to bear witness to.

fealdad [feal'daδ] *nf* ugliness.

febrero [fe'βrero] *nm* February.

febril [fe'βril] *a* feverish.

fecundar [fekun'dar] *vt* (*generar*)
to fertilize, make fertile; **fecundo, a**
a (*fértil*) fertile; (*prolífico*) prolific;
(*fructífero*) fruitful; (*abundante*)
abundant; (*productivo*) productive.

fecha ['fetʃa] *nf* date; **en** ~ **próxima**
soon; **hasta la** ~ to date, so far;
poner ~ to date; **con** ~ **adelantada**
post-dated.

federación [federa'θjon] *nf* federation.

federal [feðe'ral] *a* federal; ~**ismo**
nm federalism.

felicidad [feliθi'δaδ] *nf* (*satisfacción, contento*) happiness; (*suerte fe-*

liz) (good) luck; ~**es** nfpl best wishes, congratulations.

felicitación [feliθita'θjon] nf congratulation; **felicitar** vt to congratulate.

feligrés, esa [feli'γres, esa] nm/f parishioner.

feliz [fe'liθ] a (contento) happy; (afortunado) lucky.

felonía [felo'nia] nf felony, crime.

felpudo [fel'puðo] nm doormat.

femenino, a [feme'nino, a] a, nm feminine.

feminista [femi'nista] nf feminist.

fénix ['feniks] nm (ave) phoenix.

fenómeno [fe'nomeno] nm phenomenon; (fig) freak, accident // a inv great // excl smashing!, marvellous!

feo, a ['feo, a] a (gen) ugly; (desagradable) bad, nasty.

féretro ['feretro] nm (ataúd) coffin; (sarcófago) bier.

feria ['ferja] nf (gen) fair; (AM) village market; (día de asueto) holiday, rest day.

fermentar [fermen'tar] vi to ferment.

ferocidad [feroθi'ðað] nf fierceness, ferocity.

feroz [fe'roθ] a (cruel) cruel; (salvaje) fierce.

férreo, a ['ferreo, a] a iron.

ferretería [ferrete'ria] nf (trastes) ironmongery; (tienda) ironmonger's (shop), hardware store.

ferrocarril [ferroka'rril] nm railway; ~ **de cremallera** rack railway.

fértil ['fertil] a (productivo) fertile; (rico) rich; **fertilidad** nf (gen) fertility; (productividad) fruitfulness; **fertilizar** vt to fertilize.

fervor [fer'βor] nm fervour; ~**oso, a** a fervent.

festejar [feste'xar] vt (agasajar) to entertain lavishly; (galantear) to court; (su cumpleaños) to celebrate; **festejo** nm (diversión) entertain-

ment; (galanteo) courtship; (fiesta) celebration.

festividad [festiβi'ðað] nf festivity.

festivo, a [fes'tiβo, a] a (de fiesta) festive; (fig) witty; (CINE, LITERATURA) humorous.

fétido, a ['fetiðo, a] a (hediondo) foul-smelling; (podrido) rotten.

fiado [fi'aðo] nm: **comprar al** ~ to buy on credit.

fiador, a [fia'ðor, a] nm/f (JUR) surety, guarantor; (COM) backer // nm (de arma) safety catch; (cerrojo) tumbler; **salir** ~ **por alguien** to go bail for sb.

fiambre ['fjambre] nm cold meat.

fianza ['fjanθa] nf surety; (JUR): **libertad bajo** ~ release on bail.

fiar [fi'ar] vt (salir garante de) to guarantee; (vender a crédito) to sell on credit // vi to trust; ~**se** vr to trust (in), rely on; ~**se de uno** to rely on sb.

fiasco ['fjasko] nm fiasco.

fibra ['fiβra] nf fibre.

ficción [fik'θjon] nf fiction.

ficticio, a [fik'tiθjo, a] a (imaginario) fictitious; (falso) fabricated.

ficha ['fitʃa] nf (en juegos) token, counter; (tarjeta) (index) card; (ELEC) plug; **fichar** vt (archivar) to file, index; **estar fichado** to have a record; **fichero** nm card index.

fidelidad [fiðeli'ðað] nf (lealtad) fidelity, loyalty; **alta** ~ high fidelity, hi-fi.

fideos [fi'ðeos] nmpl noodles.

fiebre ['fjeβre] nf (MED) fever; (fig) feverish excitement; ~ **amarilla/del heno** yellow/hay fever; ~ **palúdica** malaria; **tener** ~ to have a temperature.

fiel [fjel] a (leal) faithful, loyal; (fiable) reliable; (exacto) accurate; // nm (aguja de balanza) needle, pointer; **los** ~**es** the faithful.

fieltro ['fjeltro] nm felt.

fiereza [fje'reθa] nf (bravura) fierceness; (fealdad) ugliness.

fiero, a ['fjero, a] a (*cruel*) cruel; (*feroz*) fierce; (*duro*) harsh // nf (*animal feroz*) wild animal or beast.

fiesta ['fjesta] nf party; (*de pueblo*) festival; ~**s** nfpl (*caricias*) endearments; (*vacaciones*) holiday sg; (*broma*) jokes; (*juerga*) fun and games; (REL:) ~ **de guardar** day of obligation.

figura [fi'ɣura] nf (*gen*) figure; (*forma, imagen*) shape, form; (*cara*) face; (TEATRO) marionette; (NAIPES) face card.

figurar [fiɣu'rar] vt (*representar*) to represent; (*fingir*) to figure // vi to figure; ~**se** vr (*imaginarse*) to imagine; (*suponer*) to suppose.

fijar [fi'xar] vt (*gen*) to fix; (*estampilla*) to affix, stick (on); (*fig*) to settle (on), decide; ~ **con hilos** to sew on; ~**se** vr: ~**se en** to notice.

fijo, a ['fixo, a] a (*gen*) fixed; (*firme*) firm; (*permanente*) permanent // ad: **mirar** ~ to stare.

fila ['fila] nf row; (*cola, columna*) queue; (*cadena*) line; **ponerse en** ~ to line up, get into line.

filántropo [fi'lantropo] nm philanthropist.

filatelia [fila'telja] nf philately.

filete [fi'lete] nm (*carne*) steak; (*pescado*) fillet.

filial [fi'ljal] a filial // nf subsidiary.

Filipinas [fili'pinas] nfpl: **las** ~ the Philippines.

filmar [fil'mar] vt to film, shoot.

filo ['filo] nm (*gen*) edge; **sacar** ~ **a** to sharpen; **al** ~ **del mediodía** at about midday; **de doble** ~ double-edged.

filosofía [filoso'fia] nf philosophy; **filósofo** nm philosopher.

filtrar [fil'trar] vt, vi to filter, strain; ~**se** vr to filter; (*fig*) to dwindle; **filtro** nm (TEC, *utensilio*) filter; (CULIN) strainer.

fin [fin] nm (*gen*) end; (*objetivo*) aim, purpose; **al** ~ **y al cabo** when all's said and done; **a** ~ **de** in order to; **por** ~ finally; **en** ~ in short; ~

de semana weekend; ~**al** a final // nm end, conclusion // nf final; ~**alista** nm/f finalist; ~**alizar** vt to end, finish // vi, ~**alizarse** vr to end, come to an end.

financiar [finan'θjar] vt to finance; **financiero, a** a financial.

finca ['finka] nf country estate; (*casa*) country house.

fingir [fin'xir] vt (*simular*) to simulate; (*pretextar*) to sham, fake // vi (*aparentar*) to pretend, feign; ~**se** vr to pretend to be.

finlandés, esa [finlan'des, esa] a Finnish // nm/f Finn // nm (*lengua*) Finnish.

Finlandia [fin'landja] nf Finland.

fino, a ['fino, a] a (*gen*) fine; (*delgado*) slender; (*puro*) pure; (*de buenas maneras*) polite, refined; (*inteligente*) shrewd.

firma ['firma] nf signature; (COM) firm, company; **firmar** vt to sign.

firme ['firme] a (*gen*) firm; (*estable*) stable; (*sólido*) solid; (*compacto*) compact; (*constante*) steady; (*decidido*) resolute // nm road (surface); ~**mente** ad firmly; ~**za** nf firmness; (*constancia*) steadiness; (*solidez*) solidity.

fiscal [fis'kal] a fiscal // nm Public Prosecutor.

fisgar [fis'ɣar] vt to pry into; (*pescar*) to spear, harpoon.

físico, a ['fisiko, a] a physical // nm physique // nm/f physicist // nf physics sg.

fiasco, a ['flako, a] a (*muy delgado*) skinny, lean; (*débil*) weak, feeble.

flagrante [fla'ɣrante] a flagrant.

flamante [fla'mante] a brilliant; (*nuevo*) brand-new.

flamenco, a [fla'menko, a] a (*de Flandes*) Flemish; (*agitanado*) gipsy // nm (*canto y baile*) flamenco.

flan [flan] nm creme caramel.

flaqueza [fla'keθa] nf (*delgadez*) leanness; (*fig*) weakness.

flash [flaʃ] nm (FOTO) flash.

flauta ['flauta] nf flute.

fleco ['fleko] nm fringe.

flecha ['fletʃa] nf arrow.

flema ['flema] nm phlegm.

flequillo [fle'kiʎo] nm (pelo) fringe.

flete ['flete] nm (carga) freight; (alquiler) charter; (precio) freightage.

flexible [flek'siβle] a flexible.

flojo, a ['floxo, a] a (gen) loose; (sin fuerzas) limp; (débil) weak.

flor [flor] nf flower; (piropo) compliment; **a ~ de** on the surface of; **~ecer** a (BOT) to flower; (fig) to flourish; **~eciente** a (BOT) in flower, flowering; (fig) thriving.

flota ['flota] nf fleet.

flotar [flo'tar] vi (gen) to float; (colgar) to hang; **flote** nm: **a flote** afloat; **sacar a flote** (fig) to get back on one's feet.

fluctuar [fluk'twar] vi (oscilar) to fluctuate; (vacilar) to waver.

fluidez [flui'ðeθ] nf fluidity; (fig) fluency.

fluido, a ['fluiðo, a] a, nm fluid.

fluir [flu'ir] vi to flow.

flujo ['fluxo] nm flow; **~ y reflujo** ebb and flow; **~ de sangre** (MED) loss of blood.

foca ['foka] nf seal.

foco ['foko] nm focus; (ELEC) floodlight.

fogón [fo'ɣon] nm (de cocina) stove.

fogoso, a [fo'ɣoso, a] a spirited.

follaje [fo'ʎaxe] nm foliage.

folleto [fo'ʎeto] nm pamphlet.

fomentar [fomen'tar] vt (MED) to foment; **fomento** nm (MED) fomentation; (promoción) promotion; **Ministerio de Fomento** ≈ Ministry of Public Works.

fonda ['fonda] nf (= restaurante) buffet.

fondo ['fondo] nm (de mar) bottom; (cuarto) back; (ARTE etc) background; (reserva) fund; **~s** nmpl (COM) funds, resources; **una investigación a ~** a thorough investigation; **en el ~** at bottom, deep down.

fontanería [fontane'ria] nf plumbing; **fontanero** nm plumber.

forastero, a [foras'tero, a] a (extraño) alien, strange // nm/f stranger.

forcejear [forθexe'ar] vi (luchar) to struggle; (esforzarse) to make violent efforts.

forjar [for'xar] vt to forge.

forma ['forma] nf (figura) form, shape; (molde) mould, pattern; (MED) fitness; (método) way, means; **las ~s** the conventions.

formación [forma'θjon] nf (gen) formation; (educación) education.

formal [for'mal] a (gen) formal; (fig: persona) serious; **~idad** nf formality; seriousness.

formar [for'mar] vt (componer) to form, shape; (constituir) to make up, constitute; (ESCOL) to train, educate; **~se** vr (cobrar forma) to form, take form; (hacer línea) to form up; (desarrollarse) to develop.

formidable [formi'ðaβle] a (temible) formidable; (asombroso) tremendous.

formulario [formu'larjo] nm form.

fornido, a [for'niðo, a] a strapping, well-built.

foro ['foro] nm (gen) forum; (JUR) court.

forrar [fo'rrar] vt (abrigo) to line; (libro) to cover, **forro** nm (de cuaderno) cover; (costura) lining; (de sillón) upholstery; **forro de freno** brake lining.

fortalecer [fortale'θer] vt to strengthen.

fortaleza [forta'leθa] nf (gen) strength; (determinación) resolution.

fortuito, a [for'twito, a] a accidental.

fortuna [for'tuna] nf (suerte) fortune, (good) luck; (riqueza, caudal) fortune, wealth.

forzar [for'θar] vt (puerta) to force

(open); (*casa*) to break into; (*compeler*) to compel.

forzoso, a [for'θoso, a] *a* necessary.

fosa ['fosa] *nf* (*sepultura*) grave; (*en tierra*) pit; (*MED*) cavity.

fósforo ['fosforo] *nm* (*metaloide*) phosphorus; (*AM*) match.

foso ['foso] *nm* ditch; (*TEATRO*) pit; (*AUTO*): ~ **de reconocimiento** inspection pit.

foto ['foto] *nf* photo, snap(shot); ~**copia** *nf* photocopy; ~**copiador** *nm* photocopier; ~**copiar** *vt* to photocopy.

fotografía [fotoɤra'fia] *nf* (*gen*) photography; (*una* ~) photograph; **fotografiar** *vt* to photograph.

fotógrafo, a [fo'toɤrafo, a] *nm/f* photographer.

fracaso [fra'kaso] *nm* (*desgracia, revés*) failure; **fracasar** *vi* (*gen*) to fail.

fracción [frak'θjon] *nf* fraction; (*POL*) faction; **fraccionar** *vt* to divide, break up.

fractura [frak'tura] *nf* fracture, break.

fragancia [fra'ɣanθja] *nf* (*olor*) fragrance; (*perfume*) perfume.

frágil ['fraxil] *a* (*débil*) fragile; (*quebradizo*) breakable; **fragilidad** *nf* fragility; (*de persona*) frailty.

fragmento [fraɣ'mento] *nm* (*pedazo*) fragment.

fragor [fra'ɣor] *nm* (*ruido intenso*) din; (*de gente*) uproar.

fragua ['fraɣwa] *nf* forge; **fraguar** *vt* to forge; (*fig*) to concoct // *vi* to harden.

fraile ['fraile] *nm* (*REL*) friar; (: *monje*) monk.

frambuesa [fram'bwesa] *nf* raspberry.

francés, esa [fran'θes, esa] *a* French // *nm/f* Frenchman/ woman // *nm* (*lengua*) French.

Francia ['franθja] *nf* France.

franco, a ['franko, a] *a* (*leal, abierto*) frank, open; (*generoso, liberal*) generous, liberal; (*COM*:

exento) free // *nm* franc.

francotirador, a [frankotira'ðor, a] *nm/f* sniper.

franela [fra'nela] *nf* flannel.

franja ['franxa] *nf* fringe.

franquear [franke'ar] *vt* (*camino*) to clear; (*carta, paquete postal*) to frank, stamp; (*obstáculo*) to overcome; ~**se** *vr* (*ceder*) to give way; (*confiarse a alguien*) to unburden o.s.

franqueo [fran'keo] *nm* postage.

franqueza [fran'keθa] *nf* (*candor*) frankness; (*generosidad*) generosity.

frasco ['frasko] *nm* bottle; (*al vacío*) (*vacuum*) flask.

frase ['frase] *nf* sentence; ~ **hecha** set phrase.

fraude ['frauðe] *nm* (*cualidad*) dishonesty; (*acto*) fraud; **fraudulento, a** *a* fraudulent.

frecuencia [fre'kwenθja] *nf* frequency; **con** ~ frequently, often.

fregadero [freɣa'ðero] *nm* sink.

fregar [fre'ɣar] *vt* (*frotar*) to scrub; (*platos*) to wash (up); (*AM*) to annoy.

freír [fre'ir] *vt* to fry.

frenar [fre'nar] *vt* to brake; (*fig*) to check.

frenesí [frene'si] *nm* frenzy; **frenético, a** *a* frantic.

freno ['freno] *nm* (*TEC, AUTO*) brake; (*de cabalgadura*) bit; (*fig*) check.

frente ['frente] *nm* (*ARQ, POL*) front; (*de objeto*) front part // *nf* forehead, brow; **en** ~ **de** in front of; (*en situación opuesta de*) opposite; **chocar de** ~ to crash head-on; **hacer** ~ **a** to face up to.

fresa ['fresa] *nf* strawberry.

fresco, a ['fresko, a] *a* (*nuevo*) fresh; (*frío*) cool // *nm* (*aire*) fresh air; (*ARTE*) fresco; (*fam*) shameless person; (*persona insolente*) impudent person // *nf* cool part of the day; **tomar el** ~ to get some fresh air; **frescura** *nf* freshness; (*descaro*) cheek, nerve; (*calma*) calmness.

frialdad [frial'daθ] *nf* (*gen*)

coldness; *(indiferencia)* indifference.

fricción [frik'θjon] *nf (gen)* friction; *(acto)* rub(bing); *(MED)* massage.

frigidez [frixi'δeθ] *nf* frigidity.

frigorífico, a [frixo'rifiko] *nm* refrigerator.

fríjol [fri'xol] *nm* kidney bean.

frío, a [ˈfrio, a] *a* cold // *nm* cold(ness).

frito, a [ˈfrito, a] *a* fried; **me trae ~ ese hombre** I'm sick and tired of that man.

frívolo, a [ˈfriβolo, a] *a* frivolous.

frontera [fron'tera] *nf* frontier; **fronterizo, a** *a* frontier *cpd*; *(contiguo)* bordering.

frontón [fron'ton] *nm (DEPORTE)* pelota court.

frotar [fro'tar] *vt* to rub; **~se** *vr*: **~se las manos** to rub one's hands.

fructífero, a [fruk'tifero, a] *a* fruitful.

frugal [fru'xal] *a* frugal.

fruncir [frun'θir] *vt* to pucker; *(costura)* to pleat; **~ el ceño** to knit one's brow.

frustrar [frus'trar] *vt* to frustrate.

fruta [ˈfruta] *nf* fruit; **frutería** *nf* fruit shop.

fue *vb ver* **ser, ir**.

fuego [ˈfweɣo] *nm (gen)* fire; *(MED)* rash; **a ~ lento** on a low flame or gas; **¿tienes ~?** have you a light?

fuente [ˈfwente] *nf (de una plaza)* fountain; *(manantial, fig)* spring; *(origen)* source; *(plato)* large dish.

fuera *etc vb ver* **ser, ir** // [ˈfwera] *ad* out(side); *(en otra parte)* away; *(excepto, salvo)* except, save // *prep*: **~ de** outside; *(fig)* besides; **~ de sí** beside o.s.

fuerte [ˈfwerte] *a (gen)* strong; *(golpe)* hard; *(ruido)* loud; *(comida)* rich; *(lluvia)* heavy; *(dolor)* intense // *ad* strongly; hard; loud(ly).

fuerza [ˈfwerθa] *nf (fortaleza)* strength; *(TEC, ELEC)* power; *(coacción)* force; *(MIL)* forces *pl*; a

~ de by dint of; **cobrar ~s** to recover one's strength; **tener ~s para** to have the strength to; **a la ~,** **por ~** forcibly, by force.

fuga [ˈfuɣa] *nf (huida)* flight, escape; *(de gas)* leak; **fugarse** *vr* to flee, escape; **fugaz** a fleeting; *fugitivo, a,* *nm/f* fugitive.

fui *vb ver* **ser, ir**.

fulano, a [fuˈlano, a] *nm/f* so-and-so, what's-his-name.

fulgor [fulˈɣor] *nm* brilliance.

fumar [fuˈmar] *vt, vi* to smoke; **~se** *vr (disipar)* to squander; **~ en pipa** to smoke a pipe.

funámbulo, a [fuˈnambulo, a] *nm/f* tightrope-walker.

función [funˈθjon] *nf* function; *(de puesto)* duties *pl*; *(espectáculo)* show; **entrar en funciones** to take up one's duties, **funcionar** *vi (gen)* to function; *(máquina)* to work.

funcionario, a [funθjoˈnarjo, a] *nm/f* official; *(público)* civil servant.

funda [ˈfunda] *nf (gen)* cover; *(de almohada)* pillowcase.

fundación [fundaˈθjon] *nf* foundation.

fundamental [fundamenˈtal] *a* fundamental, basic.

fundamentar [fundamenˈtar] *vt (poner base)* to lay the foundations of; *(establecer)* to found; *(fig)* to base; **fundamento** *nm (base)* foundation.

fundar [funˈdar] *vt* to found; *(dotar de fondos)* to endow; **~se** *vr*: **~se en** to be founded on.

fundición [fundiˈθjon] *nf* fusing; *(fábrica)* foundry.

fundir [funˈdir] *vt (gen)* to fuse; *(metal)* to smelt, melt down; *(COM)* to merge; *(estatua)* to cast; **~se** *vr (sólido)* to merge, blend; *(unirse)* to fuse together.

fúnebre [ˈfuneβre] *a* funeral *cpd*, funereal.

funeral [funeˈral] *nm* funeral.

furgón [furˈɣon] *nm* wagon.

furia [ˈfurja] *nf (ira)* fury;

(violencia) violence; **furibundo, a** a furious; **furioso, a** a *(iracundo)* furious; *(violento)* violent; **furor** nm *(cólera)* rage.

furtivo, a [fur'tiβo, a] a furtive.

furúnculo [fu'runkulo] nm *(MED)* boil.

fusible [fu'siβle] nm fuse.

fusil [fu'sil] nm rifle; **~ar** vt to shoot.

fusión [fu'sjon] nf *(gen)* melting; *(unión)* fusion; *(COM)* merger.

fútbol ['futβol] nm football; **futbolín** nm table football; **futbolista** nm footballer.

fútil ['futil] a trifling; **futilidad, futileza** nf triviality.

futuro, a [fu'turo, a] a, nm future.

G

gabacho, a [ga'βatʃo, a] a Pyrenean; *(fam)* frenchified // nm/f Pyrenean villager.

gabán [ga'βan] nm overcoat.

gabardina [gaβar'ðina] nf raincoat, gabardine.

gabinete [gaβi'nete] nm *(POL)* cabinet; *(estudio)* study; *(de abogados etc)* office.

gaceta [ga'θeta] nf gazette; **gacetilla** nf *(en periódico)* news in brief; *(de personalidades)* gossip column.

gacha ['gatʃa] nf mush; **~s** nfpl porridge sg.

gafas ['gafas] nfpl glasses; **~ oscuras** dark glasses.

gaita ['gaita] nf flute; *(~ gallega)* bagpipes pl.

gajes ['gaxes] nmpl *(salario)* pay; **los ~ del oficio** occupational hazards.

gajo ['gaxo] nm *(gen)* bunch; *(de árbol)* bough; *(de naranja)* segment.

gala ['gala] nf full dress; *(fig: lo mejor)* cream, flower; **~s** nfpl

finery sg; **estar de ~** to be in one's best clothes; **hacer ~ de** to display, show off.

galán [ga'lan] nm lover, gallant; *(hombre atractivo)* ladies' man; *(TEATRO)*: **primer ~** leading man.

galano, a [ga'lano, a] a *(elegante)* elegant; *(bien vestido)* smart.

galante [ga'lante] a gallant; **galantear** vt *(hacer la corte a)* to court, woo; **galanteo** nm *(coqueteo)* flirting; *(de pretendiente)* wooing; **galantería** nf *(caballerosidad)* gallantry; *(cumplido)* politeness; *(comentario)* compliment.

galaxia [ga'laksja] nf galaxy.

galera [ga'lera] nf *(nave)* galley; *(carro)* wagon; *(MED)* hospital ward; *(IMPRENTA)* galley.

galería [gale'ria] nf *(gen)* gallery; *(balcón)* veranda(h); *(de casa)* corridor.

Gales ['gales] nm Wales; **galés, esa** a Welsh // nm/f Welshman/woman // nm *(lengua)* Welsh.

galgo, a [ga'lɣo, a] nm/f greyhound.

galimatías [galima'tias] nmpl *(lenguaje)* gibberish sg, nonsense sg.

galón [ga'lon] nm *(MIL)* stripe; *(medida)* gallon.

galopar [galo'par] vi to gallop; **galope** nm gallop.

galvanizar [galβani'θar] vt to galvanize.

gallardía [gaʎar'ðia] nf *(galantería)* dash; *(valor)* bravery; *(elegancia)* elegance.

gallego, a [ga'ʎeɣo, a] a, nm/f Galician.

galleta [ga'ʎeta] nf biscuit.

gallina [ga'ʎina] nf hen // nm *(fam)* coward; **~ ciega** blind man's buff.

gallo [ga'ʎo] nm cock, rooster.

gama ['gama] nf *(MUS)* scale; *(fig)* range.

gamba ['gamba] nf prawn.

gamberro, a [gam'berro, a] nm/f hooligan, lout.

gamuza [ga'muθa] *nf* chamois.

gana ['gana] *nf (deseo)* desire, wish; *(apetito)* appetite; *(voluntad)* will; *(añoranza)* longing; **de buena ~** willingly; **de mala ~** reluctantly; **me da la ~ de** I feel like, I want to; **tener ~s de** to feel like.

ganadería [ganaðe'ria] *nf (ganado)* livestock; *(ganado vacuno)* cattle *pl*, *(cría, comercio)* cattle raising.

ganado [ga'naðo] *nm* livestock; **~ lanar** sheep *pl*, **~ vacuno** cattle *pl*; **~ porcino** pigs *pl*.

ganador, a [gana'ðor, a] *a* winning // *nm/f* winner.

ganancia [ga'nanθja] *nf (lo ganado)* gain; *(aumento)* increase; *(beneficio)* profit; **~s** *nfpl (ingresos)* earnings; *(beneficios)* profit *sg*, winnings.

ganapán [gana'pan] *nm (obrero casual)* odd-job man; *(individuo tosco)* lout.

ganar [ga'nar] *vt (obtener)* to get, obtain; *(sacar ventaja)* to gain; *(COM)* to earn; *(DEPORTE, premio)* to win; *(derrotar a)* to beat; *(alcanzar)* to reach // *vi (DEPORTE)* to win; **~se** *vr*: **~se la vida** to earn one's living.

gancho ['gantʃo] *nm (gen)* hook; *(colgador)* hanger.

gandul, a [gan'dul, a] *a, nm/f* good-for-nothing.

ganga ['ganga] *nf (cosa buena y barata)* bargain; *(buena situación)* cushy job.

gangrena [gan'grena] *nf* gangrene.

gansada [gan'saða] *nf (fam)* stupid thing to do.

ganso, a ['ganso, a] *nm/f (ZOOL)* gander/goose; *(fam)* idiot.

ganzúa [gan'θua] *nf* skeleton key // *nm/f* burglar.

gañán [ga'ɲan] *nm* farmhand, farm labourer.

garabato [gara'ßato] *nm (gancho)* hook; *(garfio)* grappling iron; *(escri-* tura) scrawl, scribble; *(fam)* sex appeal.

garaje [ga'raxe] *nm* garage.

garante [ga'rante] *a* responsible // *nm/f* guarantor.

garantía [garan'tia] *nf* guarantee.

garantizar [garanti'θar], **garantir** [garan'tir] *vt (hacerse responsable de)* to vouch for; *(asegurar)* to guarantee.

garbanzo [gar'ßanθo] *nm* chickpea.

garbo ['garßo] *nm* grace, elegance; **~so, a** a graceful, elegant.

garfa ['garfa] *nf* claw.

garfio ['garfjo] *nm* grappling iron.

garganta [gar'ganta] *nf (interna)* throat; *(externa, de botella)* neck; **gargantilla** *nf* necklace.

gárgara ['gargara] *nf* gargle, gargling.

gárgola ['gargola] *nf* gargoyle.

garita [ga'rita] *nf (cabin, hut; (MIL)* sentry box; *(de camión)* cab.

garra ['garra] *nf (de gato, TEC)* claw; *(de ave)* talon; *(fam)* hand, paw *(fam)*.

garrafa [ga'rrafa] *nf* carafe, decanter.

garrido, a [ga'rriðo, a] *a* handsome.

garrote [ga'rrote] *nm (palo)* stick; *(porra)* cudgel; *(suplicio)* garrote; *(MED)* tourniquet.

garrulería [garrule'ria] *nf* chatter.

gárrulo, a ['garrulo, a] *a (charlatán)* talkative; *(ave)* twittering; *(arroyo)* murmuring.

garzo, a ['garθo, a] *a* blue // *nf* heron.

gas [gas] *nm* gas.

gasa ['gasa] *nf* gauze.

gaseoso, a [gase'oso, a] *a* gassy, fizzy // *nf* lemonade, fizzy drink; *(fam)* pop.

gasolina [gaso'lina] *nf* petrol, gas(oline) *(US)*; **gasolinera** *nf* petrol station.

gasómetro [ga'sometro] *nm* gasometer.

gastado, a [gas'taðo, a] *a* (*rendido*) spent; (*raído*) worn, threadbare; (*usado*: *frase etc*) trite.

gastar [gas'tar] *vt* (*dinero, tiempo*) to spend; (*fuerzas*) to use up; (*desperdiciar*) to waste; (*llevar*) to wear; **~se** *vr* to wear out; (*estropearse*) to waste; **~ bromas** to crack jokes.

gasto ['gasto] *nm* (*desembolso*) expenditure, spending; (*consumo, uso*) use; **~s** *nmpl* (*desembolsos*) expenses; (*cargos*) charges, costs.

gatear [gate'ar] *vi* (*andar a gatas*) to go on all fours; (*trepar*) to climb // *vt* to scratch.

gatillo [ga'tiʎo] *nm* (*de arma de fuego*) trigger; (*de dentista*) forceps.

gato, a ['gato, a] *nm/f* cat // *nm* (*TEC*) jack; **andar a ~as** to go on all fours.

gatuno, a [ga'tuno, a] *a* feline.

gaucho ['gautʃo] *nm* gaucho.

gaveta [ga'ßeta] *nf* drawer.

gavilla [ga'ßiʎa] *nf* sheaf.

gaviota [ga'ßjota] *nf* seagull.

gay [ge] *a* a gay, homosexual.

gayo, a ['gajo, a] *a* gay, merry.

gazapera [gaθa'pera] *nf* (*conejera*) rabbit warren; (*de gente*) den of thieves; **gazapo** *nm* young rabbit; (*fam*) sly fellow.

gazmoño, a [gaθ'moɲo, a], **gazmoñero, a** [gaθmo'ɲero, a] *nm/f* prude; (*pretencioso*) prig; (*hipócrita*) hypocrite.

gazpacho [gaθ'patʃo] *nm* gazpacho, cold vegetable soup.

gelatina [xela'tina] *nf* (*plato*) jelly; (*polvos etc*) gelatine.

gema ['xema] *nf* gem.

gemelo, a [xe'melo, a] *a, nm/f* twin; **~s** *nmpl* (*de camisa*) cufflinks; **G~s** *pl* (*ASTRO*) Gemini *sg*; **~s de campo** field glasses.

gemido [xe'miðo] *nm* (*quejido*) moan, groan; (*aullido*) howl.

gemir [xe'mir] *vi* (*quejarse*) to moan, groan; (*aullar*) to howl.

genealogía [xenealo'xia] *nf* genealogy.

generación [xenera'θjon] *nf* generation.

generador [xenera'ðor] *nm* generator.

general [xene'ral] *a* a general // *nm* general; **por lo o en ~** in general; **~idad** *nf* generality; **G~itat** *nf* Catalan parliament; **~ización** *nf* generalization; **~izar** *vt* to generalize; **~izarse** *vr* to become generalised, spread; **~mente** *ad* generally.

generar [xene'rar] *vt* to generate.

genérico, a [xe'neriko, a] *a* generic.

género ['xenero] *nm* (*clase*) kind, sort; (*tipo*) type; (*BIO*) genus; (*LING*) gender; (*COM*) material; **~ humano** human race.

generosidad [xenerosi'ðað] *nf* generosity; **generoso, a** *a* generous.

genial [xe'njal] *a* (*idea*) inspired; brilliant; (*afable*) genial.

genio ['xenjo] *nm* (*carácter*) nature, disposition; (*humor*) temper; (*facultad creadora*) genius; **de mal ~** bad-tempered.

gente ['xente] *nf* (*personas*) people *pl*; (*raza*) race; (*nación*) nation; (*parientes*) relatives *pl*.

gentil [xen'til] *a* (*elegante*) graceful; (*encantador*) charming; **~eza** *nf* grace; charm; (*cortesía*) courtesy.

gentío [xen'tio] *nm* crowd, throng.

genuflexión [xenuflek'sjon] *nf* genuflexion.

genuino, a [xe'nwino, a] *a* genuine.

geografía [xeoxra'fia] *nf* geography.

geología [xeolo'xia] *nf* geology.

geometría [xeome'tria] *nf* geometry.

gerencia [xe'renθja] *nf* management; **gerente** *nm* (*supervisor*) manager; (*jefe*) director.

germen ['xermen] *nm* germ.

germinar [xermi'nar] vi to germinate.

gesticulación [xestikula'θjon] nf (ademán) gesticulation; (mueca) grimace.

gestión [xes'tjon] nf management; (diligencia, acción) negotiation; (esfuerzo) effort; **gestionar** vt (lograr) to try to arrange; (llevar) to manage; (discutir) to negotiate.

gesto ['xesto] nm (mueca) grimace; (ademán) gesture.

gestoría [xesto'ria] nf estate agent's

Gibraltar [xiβral'tar] nm Gibraltar.

gigante [xi'xante] a, nm/f giant.

gilipollas [xili'poʎas] excl (fam) bastard! (fam).

gimnasia [xim'nasja] nf gymnastics pl; **gimnasio** nm gymnasium; **gimnasta** nm/f gymnast.

gimotear [ximote'ar] vi to whine, whimper.

ginebra [xi'neβra] nf gin.

ginecólogo, a [xine'koloxo, a] nm/f gynecologist.

gira ['xira] nf tour, trip.

girar [xi'rar] vt (dar la vuelta) to turn (around); (: rápidamente) to spin; (COM: cheque) to draw; (comerciar: letra de cambio) to issue // vi to turn (round); (rápido) to spin; (COM) to draw.

girasol [xira'sol] nm sunflower.

giratorio, a [xira'torjo, a] a (gen) revolving; (puente) swing.

giro ['xiro] nm (movimiento) turn, revolution; (LING) expression, (COM) draft; ~ **bancario/postal** money/postal order.

gitano, a [xi'tano, a] a, nm/f gypsy.

glacial [gla'θjal] a icy, freezing.

glándula ['glandula] nf gland.

globo ['gloβo] nm (esfera) globe, sphere; (aerostato, juguete) balloon.

gloria ['glorja] nf glory; **gloriarse** vr to boast.

glorieta [glo'rjeta] nf (de jardín)

bower, arbour; (plazoleta) roundabout.

glorificar [glorifi'kar] vt (enaltecer) to glorify, praise; ~**se** vr: ~**se de** to boast of.

glorioso, a [glo'rjoso, a] a glorious.

glosa ['glosa] nf comment; **glosar** vt (comentar) to comment on; (fig) to criticize.

glosario [glo'sarjo] nm glossary

glotón, ona [glo'ton, ona] a gluttonous, greedy; **glotonería** nf gluttony, greed.

gobernación [goβerna'θjon] nf government, governing; **gobernador, a** a governing // nm governor; **gobernante** a governing.

gobernar [goβer'nar] vt (dirigir) to guide, direct; (regir) to rule, govern // vi to govern; (NAUT) to steer.

gobierno [go'βjerno] nm (pol) government; (dirección) guidance, direction; (NAUT) steering.

goce ['goθe] nm enjoyment.

gol [gol] nm goal.

gola ['gola] nf gullet; (garganta) throat.

golf [golf] nm golf.

golfa ['golfa] nf (fam) tart, whore.

golfo ['golfo] nm (GEO) gulf; (fam: niño) urchin; (gamberro) lout.

golondrina [golon'drina] nf swallow

golosina [golo'sina] nf (gen) titbit; (dulce) sweet, **goloso, a** a sweet-toothed.

golpe ['golpe] nm (gen) blow; (de puño) punch; (de mano) smack; (de cabeza) beat; (de remo) stroke; (fig: choque) clash; **no dar** ~ to be bone idle; **de un** ~ with one blow, **de** ~ suddenly; ~ **de estado** coup d'état; **golpear** vt, vi to strike, knock; (asestar) to beat; (de puño) to punch; (golpetear) to tap.

goma ['goma] nf (caucho) rubber; (elástico) elastic; ~ **espuma** foam rubber; ~ **de pegar** gum, glue.

gomita [go'mita] nf elastic band.

góndola ['gondola] *nf* (*barco*) gondola; (*de tren*) goods wagon.

gordo, a [gorðo, a] *a* (*gen*) fat; (*persona*) plump; (*tela*) coarse; (*fam*) enormous; **el premio ~** (*en lotería*) first prize; **gordura** *nf* fat; (*corpulencia*) fatness, stoutness.

gorgojo [gor'xoxo] *nm* (*insecto*) grub; (*fam*) runt.

gorila [go'rila] *nm* gorilla.

gorjear [gorxe'ar] *vi* to twitter, chirp; **gorjeo** *nm* twittering, chirping.

gorra ['gorra] *nf* (*gen*) cap; (*de niño*) bonnet; (*militar*) bearskin // *nm* scrounger.

gorrión [go'rrjon] *nm* sparrow.

gorro ['gorro] *nm* (*gen*) cap; (*de niño, mujer*) bonnet.

gorrón [go'rron] *nm* pebble.

gota ['gota] *nf* (*gen*) drop; (*de sudor*) bead; (*MED*) gout; **gotear** *vi* to drip; (*lloviznar*) to drizzle; **gotera** *nf* leak.

gótico, a [gotiko, a] *a* Gothic.

gozar [go'θar] *vi* to enjoy o.s.; **~ de** (*disfrutar*) to enjoy; (*poseer*) to possess.

gozne ['goθne] *nm* hinge.

gozo ['goθo] *nm* (*alegría*) joy; (*placer*) pleasure; **~so, a** *a* joyous, joyful.

grabación [graβa'θjon] *nf* recording.

grabado [gra'βaðo] *nm* print, engraving; **grabador** *nm* engraver.

grabadora [graβa'ðora] *nf* tape-recorder.

grabar [gra'βar] *vt* to engrave; (*discos, cintas*) to record.

gracejo [gra'θexo] *nm* (*humor*) wit, humour; (*elegancia*) grace.

gracia ['graθja] *nf* (*encanto*) grace, gracefulness; (*chiste*) joke; (*humor*) humour, wit; **¡~s!** thanks!; **muchas ~s!** thanks very much!; **~s a** thanks to; **tener ~** to be funny; **no me hace ~** I am not keen; **gracioso, a** (*divertido*) funny, amusing;

(*cómico*) comical // *nm* (*TEATRO*) comic character.

grada ['graða] *nf* (*de escalera*) step; (*de anfiteatro*) tier, row.

gradación [graða'θjon] *nf* gradation.

gradería [graðe'ria] *nf* (*gradas*) (flight of) steps *pl*; (*de anfiteatro*) tiers *pl*, rows *pl*; **~ cubierta** covered stand.

grado ['graðo] *nm* degree; (*de aceite, vino*) grade; (*grada*) step; (*MIL*) rank; **de buen ~** willingly.

graduación [graðwa'θjon] *nf* (*del alcohol*) proof, strength; (*ESCOL*) graduation.

gradual [gra'ðwal] *a* gradual.

graduar [gra'ðwar] *vt* (*gen*) to graduate; (*clasificar*) to grade; (*MIL*) to commission; **~se** *vr* to graduate.

gráfico, a [grafiko, a] *a* graphic // *nm* diagram // *nf* graph.

grajo [graxo] *nm* rook.

Gral *abr de* **General.**

gramática [gra'matika] *nf* grammar.

gramo ['gramo] *nm* gramme.

gran [gran] *a ver* **grande.**

grana ['grana] *nf* (*BOT*) seedling; (*ZOOL*) cochineal; (*color, tela*) scarlet.

Granada [gra'naða] *n* Granada.

granada [gra'naða] *nf* pomegranate; (*MIL*) grenade; **granadina** *nf* grenadine.

granadino, a [grana'ðino, a] *a* of Granada // *nm/f* native or inhabitant of Granada.

granado, a [gra'naðo, a] *a* choice, select // *nm* pomegranate tree.

granar [gra'nar] *vi* to seed.

granate [gra'nate] *nm* garnet.

Gran Bretaña [granbre'taɲa] *nf* Great Britain.

grande [grande], **gran** [gran] *a* (*de tamaño*) big, large; (*alto*) tall; (*distinguido*) great; (*impresionante*) grand // *nm* grandee; **grandeza** *nf* greatness.

grandioso, a [gran'djoso, a] a magnificent, grand.

grandor [gran'dor] nm size.

granel [gra'nel]: **a ~** ad in abundance; (COM) in bulk.

granero [gra'nero] nm granary, barn.

granito [gra'nito] nm (AGR) small grain; (roca) granite; (MED) pimple.

granizado [grani'θaðo] nm iced drink; **granizar** vi to hail; **granizo** nm hail.

granja ['granxa] nf (gen) farm; (lechería) dairy, (café) milk bar.

granjear [granxe'ar] vt (cobrar) to earn; (ganar) to win; (avanzar) to gain; **granjería** nf (COM) profit; (AGR) farming.

grano ['grano] nm grain; (semilla) seed; (baya) berry; (MED) pimple; **~s** nmpl cereals.

granoso, a [gra'noso, a] a granulated.

granuja [gra'nuxa] nf grape seed // nm rogue; (golfillo) urchin.

grapa ['grapa] nf staple; (TEC) clamp.

grasa ['grasa] nf (gen) grease; (de cocina) fat, lard; (sebo) suet; (mugre) filth; (escoria) dross; **grasiento, a** a greasy; (de aceite) oily.

gratificación [gratifika'θjon] nf (propina) tip; (bono) bonus; (recompensa) reward; **gratificar** vt to tip, to reward.

gratis ['gratis] ad free.

gratitud [grati'tuð] nf gratitude.

grato, a ['grato, a] a (agradable) pleasant, agreeable; (bienvenido) welcome.

gratuito, a a [gra'twito, a] a (gratis) free; (sin razón) gratuitous.

gravamen [gra'βamen] nm (carga) burden; (impuesto) tax.

gravar [gra'βar] vt to burden.

grave ['graβe] a heavy; (serio) grave, serious; **~dad** nf gravity.

grávido, a ['graβiðo, a] a (preñada) pregnant; (lleno, cargado) full.

gravitación [graβita'θjon] nf gravitation; **gravitar** vi to gravitate; **gravitar sobre** to rest on.

gravoso, a [gra'βoso, a] a (pesado) burdensome; (costoso) costly.

graznar [graθ'nar] vi (cuervo) to squawk; (pato) to quack; (hablar ronco) to croak; **graznido** nm squawk; croak.

Grecia ['greθja] nf Greece.

greguería [greχe'ria] nf hubbub.

gremio ['gremjo] nm (sindicato) trade union; (asociación) professional association.

greña ['greña] nf (cabellos) shock of hair; (maraña) tangle; **greñudo, a** a (persona) dishevelled; (hair) tangled.

gresca ['greska] nf uproar.

grey [grei] nf flock.

griego, a a ['grjeχo, a] a, nm/f Greek.

grieta ['grjeta] nf crack; **grietarse** vr = agrietarse.

grifo ['grifo, a] a curly, kinky // nm tap.

grillo ['griʎo] nm (ZOOL) cricket; (BOT) shoot; **~s** nmpl shackles, irons.

gripe ['gripe] nf flu, influenza.

gris [gris] a (color) grey.

grita ['grita] nf uproar; **gritar** vt to shout, yell; **grito** nm shout, yell; (de horror) scream; **a grito pelado** at the top of one's voice.

grosella [gro'seʎa] nf (red)currant; **~ negra** blackcurrant.

grosería [grose'ria] nf (actitud) rudeness; (comentario) vulgar comment; **grosero, a** a (poco cortés) rude; (ordinario) vulgar, crude.

grosor [gro'sor] nm thickness.

grotesco, a [gro'tesko, a] a grotesque.

grúa ['grua] nf (TEC) crane; (de petróleo) derrick.

grueso, a ['grweso, a] a thick; (voluminoso) stout // nm bulk // nf gross; **el ~ de** the bulk of.

grulla ['gruʎa] nf crane.

gruñido [gruˈɲiðo] *nm* grunt; *(fig)* grumble; **gruñir** *vi* *(animal)* to growl; *(fam)* to grumble.

grupa [ˈgrupa] *nf* (ZOOL) rump.

grupo [ˈgrupo] *nm* group; (TEC) unit, set.

gruta [ˈgruta] *nf* grotto.

guadamecí [gwaðameˈθi], **guadamecil** [gwaðameˈθil] *nm* embossed leather.

guadaña [gwaˈðaɲa] *nf* scythe; **guadañar** *vt* to scythe, mow.

guano [ˈgwano] *nm* (AM) guano.

guante [ˈgwante] *nm* glove.

guapo, a [ˈgwapo, a] *a* good-looking, attractive; *(hombre)* handsome; *(elegante)* smart // *nm* lover, gallant.

guarda [ˈgwarða] *nm* guard, keeper // *nf* guarding; *(custodia)* custody; **~bosque** *nm* gamekeeper; **~costas** *nm inv* coastguard vessel; **~dor, a** *a* protective // *nm/f* guardian, protector; **~espaldas** *nm/f inv* bodyguard; **~polvo** *nm* dust cover; *(de niño)* smock; *(para el trabajo)* overalls *pl*; **guardar** *vt* (gen) to keep; *(vigilar)* to guard, watch over; *(dinero: ahorrar)* to save, put by; **guardarse** *vr* *(preservarse)* to protect o.s.; *(evitar)* to avoid; **guardarropa** *nm* *(armario)* wardrobe; *(en establecimiento público)* cloakroom.

guardería [gwarðeˈria] *nf* (children's) nursery.

guardia [ˈgwarðja] *nf* (MIL) guard; *(cuidado)* care, custody // *nm* guard; *(policía)* policeman; **estar de ~** to be on guard; **montar ~** to mount guard; **G~ Civil** Civil Guard; **G~ Nacional** police; **~ urbano** traffic policeman.

guardián, ana [gwarˈðjan, ana] *nm/f* (gen) guardian, keeper; *(sereno)* watchman.

guardilla [gwarˈðiʎa] *nf* attic.

guarecer [gwareˈθer] *vt* *(proteger)* to protect; *(abrigar)* to shelter; **~se** *vr* to take refuge.

guarida [gwaˈriða] *nf* *(de animal)* den, lair; *(refugio)* refuge.

guarismo [gwaˈrismo] *nm* figure, number.

guarnecer [gwarneˈθer] *vt* *(equipar)* to provide; *(adornar)* to adorn; (TEC) to reinforce; **guarnición** *nf* *(de vestimenta)* trimming; *(de piedra)* mount; *(CULIN)* garnish; *(arneses)* harness; *(MIL)* garrison.

guarro, a [ˈgwarro, a] *nm/f* pig.

guasa [ˈgwasa] *nf* joke; **guasón, ona** *a* witty; *(bromista)* joking // *nm/f* wit; joker.

Guatemala [gwateˈmala] *nf* Guatemala.

gubernativo, a [guβernaˈtiβo, a] *a* governmental.

guedeja [geˈðexa] *nf* long hair; *(de león)* mane.

guerra [ˈgerra] *nf* war; *(pelea)* struggle; **~ fría** cold war; **dar ~** to annoy; **guerrear** *vi* to wage war; **guerrero, a** *a* fighting; *(carácter)* warlike // *nm/f* warrior.

guerrilla [geˈrriʎa] *nf* guerrilla warfare; *(tropas)* guerrilla band or group.

guía [ˈgia] *nm/f* guide // *nf* *(libro)* guidebook; **~ de ferrocarriles** railway timetable; **~ de teléfonos** telephone directory; **guiar** *vt* to guide, direct; *(AUT)* to steer; **guiarse** *vr*: **guiarse por** to be guided by.

guija [ˈgixa] *nf*, **guijarro** [giˈxarro] *nm* pebble; *(camino)* cobblestone.

guijo [ˈgixo] *nm* gravel; *(de playa)* shingle.

guillotina [giʎoˈtina] *nf* guillotine.

guinda [ˈginda] *nf* morello cherry.

guindar [ginˈdar] *vt* to hoist.

guindilla [ginˈdiʎa] *nf* Guinea pepper.

guiñapo [giˈɲapo] *nm* *(harapo)* rag; *(persona)* reprobate, rogue.

guiñar [giˈɲar] *vi* to wink; *(parpadear)* to blink.

guión [giˈon] *nm* *(conductor)* leader; (LING) hyphen, dash; *(CINE)* script; **guionista** *nm/f* scriptwriter.

guirnalda [gir'nalda] *nf* garland.

guisa ['gisa] *nf*: a ~ de as, like, in the way of.

guisado [gi'saðo] *nm* stew.

guisante [gi'sante] *nm* pea; ~ de olor sweet pea.

guisar [gi'sar] *vt, vi* to cook; **guiso** *nm* cooked dish.

guita ['gita] *nf* twine.

guitarra [gi'tarra] *nf* guitar.

gula ['gula] *nf* gluttony, greed.

gusano [gu'sano] *nm* maggot; (*lombriz*) earthworm; ~ de luz glowworm; ~ de seda silk-worm.

gustar [gus'tar] *vt* to taste, sample // *vi* to please, be pleasing; ~ de algo to like or enjoy sth; me gustan las uvas I like grapes.

gusto ['gusto] *nm* (*sentido, sabor*) taste, (*placer*) pleasure; tiene ~ a menta it tastes of mint; tener buen ~ to have good taste; sentirse a ~ to feel at ease; mucho ~ en conocerle pleased to meet you, el ~ es mío the pleasure is mine; con ~ willingly, gladly; ~so, a (*sabroso*) tasty; (*agradable*) pleasant.

gutural [gutu'ral] *a* guttural.

H

ha *vb ver* **haber.**

haba ['aβa] *nf* bean.

Habana [a'βana] *nf*: la ~ Havana.

habano [a'βano] *nm* Havana cigar

haber [a'βer] *vb auxiliar* to have; de ~ lo sabido if I had known (it); ~ de to have to // *vb impersonal*: hay there is/are; hay que it is necessary to, one must; ¿qué hay? how's it going?; no hay de qué don't mention it // *nm* (*ingreso*) income; (*com crédito*) credit; ~es *nmpl* assets.

habichuela [aβi't∫wela] *nf* kidney bean.

hábil ['aβil] *a* (*listo*) clever, smart;

(*capaz*) fit, capable; (*experto*) expert; **día** ~ working day; **habilidad** *nf* (*gen*) skill, ability; (*inteligencia*) cleverness.

habilitación [aβilita'θjon] *nf* qualification; (*colocación de muebles*) fitting out; (*financiamiento*) financing.

habilitar [aβili'tar] *vt* (*capacitar*) to enable; (*dar instrumentos*) to equip; (*financiar*) to finance.

hábilmente [aβil'mente] *ad* skilfully, expertly.

habitación [aβita'θjon] *nf* (*cuarto*) room; (*casa*) dwelling, abode; (*biol, morada*) habitat; ~ sencilla o particular single room; ~ doble o matrimonial double room.

habitante [aβi'tante] *nm/f* inhabitant.

habitar [aβi'tar] *vt* (*residir en*) to inhabit; (*ocupar*) to occupy // *vi* to live.

hábito ['aβito] *nm* habit; **habitual** *a* habitual.

habituar [aβi'twar] *vt* to accustom; ~se *vr*: ~se a to get used to.

habla ['aβla] *nf* (*capacidad de hablar*) speech; (*idioma*) language; (*dialecto*) dialect; perder el ~ to become speechless; de ~ francesa French-speaking; estar al ~ to be in contact; ¡González al ~! González speaking!

hablador, a [aβla'ðor, a] *a* talkative // *nm/f* chatterbox.

habladuría [aβlaðu'ria] *nf* rumour; (*sarcasmo*) sarcastic comment; ~s *nfpl* gossip *sg*.

hablar [a'βlar] *vt* to speak, talk // *vi* to speak; ~se *vr* to speak to each other; ~ con to speak to; ~ de to speak of or about; 'se habla inglés' 'English spoken here'.

hablilla [a'βliʎa] *nf* story, rumour.

habré *etc vb ver* **haber.**

hacedero, a [aθe'ðero, a] *a* feasible.

hacedor, a [aθe'ðor, a] *nm/f* maker.

hacendoso, a [aθen'doso, a] *a* industrious.

hacer [a'θer] *vt* (*gen*) to make; (*crear*) to create; (*TEC*) to manufacture; (*preparar*) to prepare; (*ejecutar*) to do, execute; (*obligar*) to force, compel // (*comportarse*) to act, behave; (*disimular*) to pretend; (*importar*) to be important, matter; (*convenir, ser apto*) to be suitable; ~**se** *vr* (*fabricarse*) to be made, be done; (*volverse*) to become; (*acostumbrarse a*) to get used to; ~ **la maleta** to pack; ~ **una pregunta** to ask a question; ~ **una visita** to visit; ~ **bien/mal** to act rightly/wrongly; **hace frío/calor** it's cold/hot; **hace dos años** two years ago; **hace poco** a little while ago; ~ **el malo** (*TEATRO*) to play (the part of) the villain; ¿**qué** ~? what is to be done?; ~ **como que o como si** to act as though or as if; ~ **de** to act as; **me hice un traje** I had a suit made; ~**se el sordo** to turn a deaf ear; ~**se viejo** to grow old; ~**se con algo** to get hold of sth; ~**se a un lado** to stand aside.

hacia ['aθja] *prep* (*en dirección de*) towards; (*cerca de*) near; ~ **arriba/abajo** up(wards)/down(wards); ~ **mediodía** about noon.

hacienda [a'θjenda] *nf* (*propiedad*) property; (*estancia*) farm, ranch; (*AM*) plantation; ~ **pública** public finance; (**Ministerio de**) **H~** Treasury, Exchequer.

hacina [a'θina] *nf* pile, stack.

hacha ['atʃa] *nf* axe; (*antorcha*) torch.

hache ['atʃe] *nf* (the letter) H.

hada ['aða] *nf* fairy.

hago *etc vb ver* **hacer**.

Haití [ai'ti] *nm* Haiti.

halagar [ala'ɣar] *vt* (*mostrar afecto*) to show affection to; (*lisonjear*) to flatter.

halago [a'laxo] *nm* pleasure, delight; (*atractivo*) attraction; (*adulación*) flattery; **halagüeño, a** *a*

pleasing; attractive; flattering.

halcón [al'kon] *nm* falcon, hawk.

hálito ['alito] *nm* breath.

hallar [a'ʎar] *vt* (*gen*) to find; (*descubrir*) to discover; (*toparse con*) to run up against; ~**se** *vr* to be (situated); **hallazgo** *nm* discovery; (*cosa*) find.

hamaca [a'maka] *nf* hammock; ~ **plegable** deckchair.

hambre ['ambre] *nf* hunger; (*carencia*) famine; (*fig*) longing; **tener** ~ to be hungry; ~**ar** *vi, vt* to starve; **hambriento, a** *a* hungry, starving.

hamburguesa [ambur'xesa] *nf* hamburger.

hampa ['ampa] *nf* underworld; **hampón** *nm* tough.

han *vb ver* **haber**.

haragán, ana [ara'xan, ana] *a, nm/f* good-for-nothing; **haraganear** *vi* to idle, loaf about.

harapiento, a [ara'pjento, a] *a* tattered, in rags; **harapo** *nm* rag.

haré *etc vb ver* **hacer**.

harina [a'rina] *nf* flour; (*polvo*) powder; **harinero, a** *nm/f* flour merchant; **harinoso, a** *a* floury.

hartar [ar'tar] *vt* to satiate, glut; (*fig*) to tire, sicken; ~**se** *vr* (*de comida*) to fill o.s., gorge o.s.; (*cansarse*) to get fed up (*de* with); **hartazgo** *nm* surfeit, glut; **harto, a** *a* (*lleno*) full; (*cansado*) fed up // *ad* (*bastante*) enough; (*muy*) very; **estar harto de** to be fed up with; **hartura** *nf* (*exceso*) surfeit; (*abundancia*) abundance; (*satisfacción*) satisfaction.

has *vb ver* **haber**.

hasta ['asta] *ad* even // *prep* (*alcanzando a*) as far as, up/down to; (*de tiempo: a tal hora*) till, until; (*antes de*) before // *conj* ~ **que** until; ~ **luego/la vista** see you soon.

hastiar [as'tjar] *vt* (*gen*) to weary; (*aburrir*) to bore; (*asquear*) to disgust; ~**se** *vr*: ~**se de** to get fed up with; **hastío** *nm* weariness; boredom; disgust.

hato ['ato], **hatillo** [a'tiʎo] *nm* belongings *pl*, kit; (*víveres*) provisions *pl*; (*banda*) gang, group; (*montón*) bundle, heap.

hay *vb ver* **haber.**

Haya ['aja] *nf*: **la ~** The Hague.

haya *etc vb ver* **haber** // ['aja] *nf* beech tree; **hayal, hayedo** *nm* beech grove.

haz [aθ] *vb ver* **hacer** // *nm* bundle, bunch; (*rayo: de luz*) beam.

hazaña [a'θaɲa] *nf* feat, exploit.

hazmerreír [aθmerre'ir] *nm* laughing stock.

he *vb ver* **haber.**

hebilla [e'βiʎa] *nf* buckle, clasp.

hebra ['eβra] *nf* thread; (*BOT: fibra*) fibre, grain; **tabaco de ~** loose tobacco.

hebreo, a [e'βreo, a] *a, nm/f* Hebrew // *nm* (*lengua*) Hebrew.

hectárea [ek'tarea] *nf* hectare.

hechizar [etʃi'θar] *vt* to cast a spell on, bewitch.

hechizo, a [e'tʃiθo, a] *a* (*gen*) false, artificial; (*removible*) detachable // *nm* witchcraft, magic; (*acto de magia*) spell, charm.

hecho, a ['etʃo, a] *pp de* **hacer** // *a* complete; (*maduro*) mature; (*costura*) ready-to-wear // *nm* deed, act; (*dato*) fact; (*cuestión*) matter; (*suceso*) event // *excl* agreed!, done!; **¡bien ~!** well done!; **de ~** in fact, as a matter of fact.

hechura [e'tʃura] *nf* making, creation; (*producto*) product; (*forma*) form, shape; (*de persona*) build; (*TEC*) craftsmanship; **~s** *nfpl* cost of making up *sg.*

hedor [e'ðor] *vi* to stink, smell; (*fig*) to l... [misprint]

hediondez [eðjon'deθ] *nf* stench, stink; (*cosa*) stinking thing;

hediondo, a *a* stinking; (*insoportable*) repulsive, unbearable.

hedor [e'ðor] *nm* stench.

helado, a [e'laðo, a] *a* frozen;

(*glacial*) icy; (*fig*) chilly, cold // *nm* ice-cream // *nf* frost.

helar [e'lar] *vt* to freeze, ice (up); (*dejar atónito*) to amaze; (*desalentar*) to discourage // *vi*, **~se** *vr* to freeze.

hélice ['eliθe] *nf* spiral; (*TEC*) propeller.

helicóptero [eli'koptero] *nm* helicopter.

hembra ['embra] *nf* (*BOT, ZOOL*) female; (*mujer*) woman; (*TEC*) nut.

hemorragia [emo'rraxja] *nf* haemorrhage.

hemorroides [emo'rroiðes] *nfpl* haemorrhoids.

hemos *vb ver* **haber.**

henchir [en'tʃir] *vt* to fill, stuff; **~se** *vr* (*llenarse de comida*) to stuff o.s. (with food); (*inflarse*) to swell (up).

hender [en'der] *vt* to cleave, split; **hendidura** *nf* crack, split; (*GEO*) fissure.

heno ['eno] *nm* hay.

herbicida [erβi'θiða] *nm* weed-killer.

heredad [ere'ðað] *nf* landed property; (*granja*) farm.

heredar [ere'ðar] *vt* to inherit; **heredero, a** *nm/f* heir/heiress.

hereje [e'rexe] *nm/f* heretic; **herejía** *nf* heresy.

herencia [e'renθja] *nf* inheritance.

herido, a [e'riðo, a] *a* injured, wounded // *nm/f* casualty // *nf* wound, injury; (*insulto*) insult.

herir [e'rir] *vt* to wound, injure; (*fig*) to offend.

hermanar [erma'nar] *vt* to match; (*unir*) to join.

hermandad [erman'dað] *nf* brotherhood.

hermano, a [er'mano, a] *nm/f* brother/sister; **~ gemelo** twin brother; **~ político** brother-in-law; **~ política** sister-in-law.

hermético, a [er'metiko, a] *a* hermetic; (*fig*) watertight.

hermoso, a [er'moso, a] *a* beautiful, lovely; (*estupendo*) splen-

did; (*guapo*) handsome; **hermosura**
nf beauty.

héroe ['eroe] *nm* hero; **heroico**, a *a*
heroic.

heroína [ero'ina] *nf* (*mujer*)
heroine; (*droga*) heroin.

heroísmo [ero'ismo] *nm* heroism.

herrador [erra'ðor] *nm* blacksmith; **herradura** *nf*: **curva en
herradura** hairpin bend.

herramienta [erra'mjenta] *nf*
tool; (*conjunto*) set of tools.

herrería [erre'ria] *nf* smithy; (*TEC*)
forge; **herrero** *nm* blacksmith.

herrumbre [e'rrumbre] *nf* rust.

hervidero [erβi'ðero] *nm* (*burbu-
jeo*) boiling, seething; (*fuente*) hot
spring.

hervir [er'βir] *vi* (*gen*) to boil;
(*burbujear*) to bubble; (*fig*): ~ **de** to
teem with; ~ **a fuego lento** to
simmer; **hervor** *nm* boiling; (*fig*)
ardour, fervour.

heterogéneo, a [etero'xeneo] *a*
heterogeneous.

heterosexual [eterosek'swal] *a*
heterosexual.

hice *etc vb ver* **hacer.**

hidráulico, a [i'ðrauliko, a] *a*
hydraulic // *nf* hydraulics *sg*.

hidro... [iðro] *pref* hydro-..., water-...;
~**ala** *nf* hovercraft; ~**avión** *nm*
seaplane; ~**eléctrico, a** a hydroelectric; ~**fobia** *nf* hydrophobia,
rabies; **hidrófugo, a** a damp-proof;
hidrógeno *nm* hydrogen.

hiedra ['jeðra] *nf* ivy.

hiel [jel] *nf* gall, bile; (*fig*) bitterness.

hiela *etc vb ver* **helar.**

hielo ['jelo] *nm* (*gen*) ice; (*escarza*)
frost; (*fig*) coldness, reserve.

hiena ['jena] *nf* hyena.

hierba ['jerβa] *nf* (*BOT*) grass; (*MED*)
herb; **mala** ~ weed; (*fig*) evil
influence; ~**buena** *nf* mint.

hierro ['jerro] *nm* (*metal*) iron;
(*objeto*) iron object; (*herramienta*)
tool; ~ **acanalado** corrugated iron;
~ **colado** *o* **fundido** cast iron.

hígado ['iɣaðo] *nm* liver.

higiene [i'xjene] *nf* hygiene;
higiénico, a *a* hygienic.

higo ['iɣo] *nm* fig; ~ **paso** *o* **seco**
dried fig; **higuera** *nf* fig tree.

hijastro, a [i'xastro, a] *nm/f*
stepson/daughter.

hijo, a ['ixo, a] *nm/f* son/daughter,
child; ~**s** *nmpl* children, sons and
daughters; ~ **de papá/mamá**
daddy's/mummy's boy; ~ **de puta**
bastard, son of a bitch.

hilado, a [i'laðo, a] a spun // *nm*
yarn.

hilandero, a [ilan'dero, a] *nm/f*
spinner.

hilar [i'lar] *vt* to spin; ~ **delgado** to
split hairs.

hilera [i'lera] *nf* row, file.

hilo ['ilo] *nm* (*gen*) thread; (*BOT*)
fibre; (*metal*) wire; (*de agua*)
trickle, thin stream; (*de luz*) beam,
ray.

hilvanar [ilβa'nar] *vt* to tack; (*fig*)
to do hurriedly.

Himalayas [ima'lajas] *nfpl*: **las** ~
the Himalayas.

himno ['imno] *nm* hymn; ~
nacional national anthem.

hincapié [inka'pje] *nm*: **hacer** ~
en to emphasize.

hincar [in'kar] *vt* to drive (in),
thrust (in); ~**se** *vr*: ~**se de rodillas**
to kneel down.

hinchado, a [in'tʃaðo, a] a (*gen*)
swollen; (*persona*) pompous.

hinchar [in'tʃar] *vt* (*gen*) to swell;
(*inflar*) to blow up, inflate; (*fig*) to
exaggerate; ~**se** *vr* (*inflarse*) to
swell up; (*fam*: *llenarse*) to stuff o.s.;
hinchazón *nf* (*MED*) swelling;
(*altivez*) arrogance.

hinojo [i'noxo] *nm* fennel.

hipar [i'par] *vi* to hiccup; (*perro*) to
pant.

hipnotismo [ipno'tismo] *nm*
hypnotism; **hipnotizar** *vt* to hypnotize.

hipo ['ipo] *nm* hiccups *pl*.

hipocresía [ipokre'sia] *nf* hypocrisy; **hipócrita** a hypocritical // nm/f hypocrite.

hipódromo [i'poðromo] nm racetrack.

hipopótamo [ipo'potamo] nm hippopotamus.

hipoteca [ipo'teka] nf mortgage.

hipótesis [i'potesis] nf hypothesis.

hiriente [i'rjente] a offensive, cutting.

hirsuto, a [ir'suto, a] a hairy; (fig) rough.

hispánico, a [is'paniko, a] a Hispanic.

hispano, a [is'pano, a] a Hispanic, Spanish, Hispano-; **H~américa** nf Spanish or Latin America; **~americano, a** a, nm/f Spanish or Latin American.

histeria [is'terja] nf hysteria.

historia [is'torja] nf (gen) history; (cuento) story, tale; **~s** nfpl (chismes) gossip sg; **dejarse de ~s** to come to the point; **pasar a la ~** to go down in history; **~dor, a** nm/f historian; **historiar** vt to chronicle, write the history of; **histórico, a** a historical; (fig) historic.

historieta [isto'rjeta] nf tale, anecdote; (dibujos) strip cartoon.

hito ['ito] nm (gen) landmark; (objetivo) goal, target.

hizo vb ver hacer.

hocico [o'θiko] nm snout; (fig) grimace; **caer o dar de ~s** to fall on one's face.

hockey ['xoki] nm hockey; **~ sobre patines** o **hielo** ice hockey.

hogar [o'ɣar] nm fireplace, hearth; (casa) home; (vida familiar) home life; **~eño, a** a home; (persona) home-loving.

hoguera [o'ɣera] nf (gen) bonfire; (llamas) blaze.

hoja ['oxa] nf (gen) leaf, (de flor) petal; (de papel) sheet; (página) page; **~ de afeitar** razor blade; **~ de estaño** tinfoil.

hojalata [oxa'lata] nf tin(plate).

hojear [oxe'ar] vt to leaf through, turn the pages of.

hola ['ola] excl hello!

Holanda [o'landa] nf Holland; **holandés, esa** a Dutch // nm/f Dutchman/woman // nm (lengua) Dutch.

holgado, a [ol'ɣaðo, a] a loose, baggy; (libre) free; (desempleado) idle; (rico) well-to-do.

holganza [ol'ɣanθa] nf (ocio) leisure; (pereza) idleness; (diversión) amusement.

holgar [ol'ɣar] vi (descansar) to rest; (sobrar) to be superfluous, **~ vt** to enjoy o.s.; **huelga decir que** it goes without saying that

holgazán, ana [olɣa'θan, ana] a idle, lazy // nm/f loafer.

holgura [ol'ɣura] nf looseness, bagginess; (TEC) play, free movement; (vida) comfortable living, luxury.

hollar [o'ʎar] vt to tread (on), trample.

hollín [o'ʎin] nm soot.

hombradía [ombra'ðia] nf manliness.

hombre ['ombre] nm (gen) man(kind); (uno) man // excl (claro) of course!; (para énfasis) man, old boy; (sorpresa) you don't say!; **~ de negocios** businessman; **~-rana** frogman; **~ de pro** o **de provecho** honest man.

hombrera [om'brera] nf shoulder strap.

hombro ['ombro] nm shoulder.

hombruno, a [om'bruno, a] a mannish.

homenaje [ome'naxe] nm (gen) homage; (lealtad) allegiance; (tributo) tribute.

homicida [omi'θiða] a homicidal // nm/f murderer; **homicidio** nm (gen) murder, homicide.

homosexual [omosek'swal] a, nm/f homosexual.

hondo, a ['ondo, a] a deep; (profundo) low // nm depth(s) (pl), bottom; ~**nada** *nf* hollow, depression; (*cañón*) ravine; (*GEO*) lowland; **honda** *nf* depth, profundity.

Honduras [on'duras] *nf* Honduras.

hondureño, a [ondu'reɲo, a] *a, nm/f* Honduran.

honestidad [onesti'ðað] *nf* purity, chastity; (*decencia*) decency; **honesto, a** *a* chaste; decent, honest; (*justo*) just.

hongo ['ongo] *nm* (*BOT: gen*) fungus; (: *comestible*) mushroom; (: *venenoso*) toadstool.

honor [o'nor] *nm* (*gen*) honour; (*gloria*) glory; **en ~ a la verdad** to be fair; **~able** *a* honourable.

honorario, a [ono'rarjo, a] *a* honorary; **~s** *nmpl* fees.

honra ['onra] *nf* (*gen*) honour; (*nombre*) reputation; **~dez** *nf* honesty; (*de persona*) integrity; **~do, a** *a* honest, upright.

honrar [on'rar] *vt* to honour; **~se** *vr*: **~se con algo/de hacer algo** to be honoured by/to do sth.

honroso, a [on'roso, a] *a* (*honrado*) honourable; (*respetado*) respectable.

hora ['ora] *nf* (*gen*) time; (*específica*) hour; **¿qué ~ es?** what time is it?; **¿a qué ~?** at what time?; **media ~** half an hour; **a la ~ de recreo** at playtime; **a primera ~** first thing (in the morning); **a última ~** at the last moment; **en las altas ~s** in the small hours; **¡a buena ~!** it's high time!; **dar la ~** to strike the hour; **~s de oficina/de trabajo** office/working hours; **~s de visita** visiting times; **~s extras** *o* **extraordinarias** overtime *sg*; **~s punta** rush hours.

horadar [ora'ðar] *vt* to drill, bore.

horario, a [o'rarjo, a] *a* hourly, hour *cpd // nm* timetable.

horca ['orka] *nf* gallows *sg*.

horcajadas [orka'xaðas]: **a ~** *ad* astride.

horda ['orða] *nf* horde.

horizontal [oriθon'tal] *a* horizontal; **horizonte** *nm* horizon.

horma ['orma] *nf* mould.

hormiga [or'miɣa] *nf* ant; **~s** *nfpl* (*MED*) pins and needles.

hormigón [ormi'ɣon] *nm* concrete; **~ armado/pretensado** reinforced/prestressed concrete.

hormigueo [ormi'ɣeo] *nm* (*comezón*) itch; (*fig*) uneasiness; (*amontonamiento*) swarming.

hormona [or'mona] *nf* hormone.

hornillo [or'niʎo] *nm* small furnace; (*cocina*) portable stove.

horno ['orno] *nm* (*CULIN*) oven; (*TEC*) furnace; **alto ~** blast furnace.

horóscopo [o'roskopo] *nm* horoscope.

horquilla [or'kiʎa] *nf* hairpin; (*AGR*) pitchfork.

horrendo, a [o'rrendo, a] *a* horrendous, frightful.

horrible [o'rriβle] *a* horrible, dreadful.

horripilante [orripi'lante] *a* hair-raising; (*espeluznante*) creepy.

horripilar [orripi'lar] *vt*: **~ a uno** to horrify sb; **~se** *vr* to be horrified.

horror [o'rror] *nm* horror, dread; (*atrocidad*) atrocity; **¡qué ~!** (*fam*) oh, my God!; **~izar** *vt* to horrify, frighten; **~izarse** *vr* to be horrified; **~oso, a** *a* horrifying, ghastly.

hortaliza [orta'liθa] *nf* vegetable.

hortelano, a [orte'lano, a] *nm/f* (market) gardener.

hosco, a ['osko, a] *a* dark; (*triste, ceñudo*) sullen, gloomy.

hospedar [ospe'ðar] *vt* to put up, lodge; **~se** *vr* to stay, lodge.

hospital [ospi'tal] *nm* hospital.

hospitalario, a [ospita'larjo, a] *a* hospitable; **hospitalidad** *nf* hospitality.

hosquedad [oske'ðað] *nf* sullenness.

hostal [os'tal] *nm* small hotel.

hostelero, a [oste'lero, a] *nm/f* innkeeper, landlord/lady.

hostería [oste'ria] *nf* hostelry.

hostia ['ostja] nf host, consecrated wafer; (fam: golpe) whack, punch // excl: ¡~s! damn it!

hostigar [osti'sar] vt to whip; (fig) to harass, pester.

hostil [os'til] a hostile; ~idad // hostility.

hotel [o'tel] nm hotel; ~ero, a a hotel cpd // nm/f hotelier.

hoy [oi] ad (este día) today; (el ahora) now(adays) // nm present time, - (en) día now(adays).

hoya ['oja] nf pit; (sepulcro) grave; (GEO) valley.

hoyo ['ojo] nm hole, pit; **hoyuelo** nm dimple.

hoz [oθ] nf sickle.

hube etc vb ver **haber.**

hucha ['utʃa] nf money box; (fig) nest egg.

hueco, a ['weko, a] a (vacío) hollow, empty; (blanco: papel blank; (resonante) booming // nm hollow, cavity.

huelga etc vb ver **holgar** // ['welsa] nf strike; **declararse en** ~ to go on strike, come out on strike; ~ **de brazos caídos/de hambre** sit-down/hunger strike; ~ **patronal** lockout.

huelgo etc vb ver **holgar** // ['welxo] nm breath; (espacio) room, space.

huelguista [wel'sista] nm/f striker.

huelo etc vb ver **oler.**

huella ['weʎa] nf (acto de pisar, pisada) tread(ing); (marca del paso) footprint, footstep; (: de animal, máquina) track; ~ **digital** fingerprint; ~ **del sonido** sound track.

huérfano, a ['werfano, a] a orphan(ed) // nm/f orphan.

huerta ['werta] nf market garden; (área de regadío) irrigated region.

huerto ['werto] nm orchard.

hueso ['weso] nm (ANAT) bone; (de fruta) stone.

huésped, a ['wespeð] nm/f (invitado) guest; (habitante) resident; (anfitrión) host.

huesudo, a [we'suðo, a] a bony, big-boned.

huevo ['weßo] nm egg; ~ **en cáscara/escalfado/estrellado** o **frito/pasado por agua** boiled/poached/fried/soft-boiled egg; ~**s revueltos** scrambled eggs

huida [u'iða] nf escape, flight.

huidizo, a [ui'ðiθo, a] a (tímido) shy; (pasajero) fleeting.

huir [u'ir] vt (escapar) to flee, escape (from); (evadir) to avoid; ~**se** vr (escaparse) to escape; (el tiempo) to fly.

hule ['ule] nm (goma) rubber; (encerado) oilskin.

humanidad [umani'ðað] nf (los hombres) man(kind); (cualidad) humanity.

humanizar [umani'θar] vt to humanize.

humano, a [u'mano, a] a (gen) human; (humanitario) humane // nm human; **ser** ~ human being.

humareda [uma'reða] nf cloud of smoke.

humear [ume'ar] vi to smoke.

humedad [ume'ðað] nf (del clima) humidity; (de pared etc) dampness; **a prueba de** ~ damp-proof; **humedecer** vt to moisten, wet; **humedecerse** vr to get wet.

húmedo, a ['umeðo, a] a (mojado) damp, wet; (tiempo etc) humid.

humildad [umil'ðað] nf humility, humbleness; **humilde** a humble, modest; (pequeño: voz) small.

humillación [umiʎaθjon] nf humiliation; **humillante** a humiliating; **humillar** vt to humiliate; **humillarse** vr to humble o.s., grovel.

humo ['umo] nm (de fuego) smoke; (gas nocivo) fumes pl; ~**s** nmpl (fig) conceit sg.

humor [u'mor] nm (disposición) mood, temper; (lo que divierte) humour; **de buen/mal** ~ in a good/bad mood; ~**ada** nf witticism.

~**ismo** *nm* humour; ~**ista** *nm/f* humorist; ~**ístico**, **a** a funny, humorous.

hundido, a [un'diðo, a] a (de mejillas) sunken; (de ojos) deep-set.

hundimiento [undi'mjento] *nm* (gen) sinking; (colapso) collapse.

hundir [un'dir] *vt* to sink; (edificio, plan) to ruin, destroy; ~**se** *vr* to sink, collapse.

húngaro, a ['ungaro, a] a, *nm/f* Hungarian.

Hungría [un'gria] *nf* Hungary.

huracán [ura'kan] *nm* hurricane.

huraño, a [u'raño, a] a shy; (antisocial) unsociable.

hurgar [ur'xar] *vt* to poke, jab; (remover) to stir (up).

hurgonear [urxone'ar] *vt* to poke.

hurón, ona [u'ron, ona] a unsociable // *nm* (ZOOL) ferret; (persona tímida) shy person; (persona arisca) unsociable person.

hurtadillas [urta'ðiʎas]: **a ~ ad** stealthily, on the sly.

hurtar [ur'tar] *vt* to steal; ~**se** *vr* to hide, withdraw; **hurto** *nm* theft, stealing.

husmear [usme'ar] *vt* (oler) to sniff out, scent; (fam) to pry into // *vi* to smell bad; **husmo** *nm* strong smell.

huyo etc *vb ver* **huir.**

I

iba etc *vb ver* **ir.**

ibérico, a [i'ßeriko, a] a Iberian.

iberoamericano, a [ißeroameri-'kano, a] a, *nm/f* Spanish American.

íbice ['ißiße] *nm* ibex.

ibicenco, a [ißi'ßenko, a] a Ibizan.

Ibiza [i'ßiθa] *nf* Ibiza.

ibón [i'ßon] *nm* lake, tarn.

iceberg ['aisßerx] *nm* iceberg.

icono ['ikono] *nm* ikon, icon.

iconoclasta [ikono'klasta] a icono-

clastic // *nm/f* iconoclast.

ictericia [ikte'riθja] *nf* jaundice.

ida ['iða] *nf* going, departure; ~ **y vuelta** round trip, return.

idea [i'ðea] *nf* idea; **darse/hacerse una ~ de...** to get an idea of... .

ideal [iðe'al] a, *nm* ideal; ~**ista** *nm/f* idealist; ~**izar** *vt* to idealize.

idear [iðe'ar] *vt* to think up; (aparato) to invent; (viaje) to plan.

ídem ['iðem] *pron* ditto.

idéntico, a [i'ðentiko, a] a identical.

identidad [iðenti'ðað] *nf* identity; **carné de ~** identity card.

identificación [iðentifika'θjon] *nf* identification; **identificar** *vt* to identify; **identificarse** *vr*: **identificarse con** to identify o.s. with.

ideología [iðeolo'xia] *nf* ideology; **ideológico, a** a ideological.

idioma [i'ðjoma] *nm* (gen) language; (giro) idiom.

idiota [i'ðjota] a idiotic // *nm/f* idiot; **idiotez** *nf* idiocy.

idólatra [i'ðolatra] *nm/f* idolater/tress; **idolatría** *nf* idolatry.

ídolo ['iðolo] *nm* idol.

idóneo, a [i'ðoneo, a] a (apto) fit; (conveniente) suitable.

iglesia [i'xlesja] *nf* church.

ignición [ixni'θjon] *nf* ignition.

ignominia [ixno'minja] *nf* ignominy; **ignominioso, a** a ignominious.

ignorado, a [ixno'raðo, a] a unknown; (dato) obscure.

ignorancia [ixno'ranθja] *nf* ignorance; **ignorante** a ignorant, uninformed // *nm/f* ignoramus.

ignorar [ixno'rar] *vt* not to know, be ignorant of.

ignoto, a [ix'noto, a] a unknown.

igual [i'xwal] a (gen) equal; (similar) like, similar; (mismo) (the) same; (constante) constant; (temperatura) even // *nm/f* equal; **al ~ que** prep, conj like, just like.

igualada [ixwa'laða] *nf* equaliser.

igualar [ixwa'lar] *vt* (gen) to equalize, make equal; (allanar) *nivelar*) to level (off), even (out); ~**se** *vr* (*platos de balanza*) to balance out; (*equivaler*) to be equal.

igualdad [iɣwal'dað] *nf* equality; (*similaridad*) sameness; (*uniformidad*) evenness, uniformity.

igualmente [iɣwal'mente] *ad* equally; (*también*) also, likewise // *excl* the same to you.

ikurriña [iku'rriɲa] *nf* Basque flag.

ilegal [ile'ɣal] *a* illegal.

legítimo, a [lle'xitimo, a] *a* illegitimate.

ileso, a [i'leso, a] *a* unhurt.

ilícito, a [i'liθito] *a* illicit.

ilimitado, a [ilimi'taðo, a] *a* unlimited.

ilógico, a [i'loxiko, a] *a* illogical.

iluminación [ilumina'θjon] *nf* (*gen*) illumination; (*alumbrado*) lighting.

iluminar [ilumi'nar] *vt* to illuminate, light (up); (*fig*) to enlighten.

ilusión [ilu'sjon] *nf* illusion; (*quimera*) delusion; (*esperanza*) hope; **ilusionado, a** *a* excited.

ilusionista [ilusjo'nista] *nm/f* conjurer.

iluso, a [i'luso, a] *a* easily deceived.

ilusorio, a [ilu'sorjo, a] *a* (*de ilusión*) illusory, deceptive; (*esperanza*) vain.

ilustración [ilustra'θjon] *nf* illustration; (*saber*) learning, erudition; **la I~** the Enlightenment; **ilustrado, a** *a* illustrated; learned.

ilustrar [ilus'trar] *vt* (*gen*) to illustrate; (*instruir*) to instruct; (*explicar*) to explain, make clear; ~**se** *vr* to acquire knowledge.

ilustre [i'lustre] *a* famous, illustrious.

imagen [i'maxen] *nf* (*gen*) image; (*dibujo*) picture; (*semejanza*) likeness.

imaginación [imaxina'θjon] *nf* imagination.

imaginar [imaxi'nar] *vt* (*gen*) to imagine; (*idear*) to think up;

(*suponer*) to suppose; ~**se** *vr* to imagine; ~**io, a** *a* imaginary; **imaginativo, a** *a* imaginative.

imán [i'man] *nm* magnet.

imbécil [im'beθil] *nm/f* imbecile, idiot; **imbecilidad** *nf* imbecility.

imbuir [imbu'ir] *vt* to imbue.

imitación [imita'θjon] *nf* imitation; **imitar** *vt* to imitate; (*parodiar*, *remedar*) to mimic, ape.

impaciencia [impa'θjenθja] *nf* impatience; **impaciente** *a* impatient; (*nervioso*) anxious.

impacto [im'pakto] *nm* impact.

impar [im'par] *a* odd.

imparcial [impar'θjal] *a* impartial, fair; ~**idad** *nf* impartiality, fairness.

impartir [impar'tir] *vt* to impart, give.

impasible [impa'siβle] *a* impassive.

impavidez [impaβi'ðeθ] *nf* fearlessness, intrepidness; **impávido, a** *a* fearless, intrepid.

impecable [impe'kaβle] *a* impeccable.

impedimento [impeði'mento] *nm* impediment, obstacle.

impedir [impe'ðir] *vt* (*obstruir*) to impede, obstruct; (*estorbar*) to prevent.

impeler [impe'ler] *vt* to drive, propel; (*fig*) to impel.

impenetrabilidad [impenetraβili'ðað] *nf* impenetrability; **impenetrable** *a* impenetrable; (*fig*) incomprehensible.

impenitente [impeni'tente] *a* unrepentant.

impensado, a [impen'saðo, a] *a* unexpected.

imperar [impe'rar] *vi* (*reinar*) to rule, reign; (*fig*) to prevail, reign; (*precio*) to be current.

imperativo, a [impera'tiβo, a] *a* (*persona*) imperious, (*urgencia*) urgent; imperative.

imperceptible [imperθep'tiβle] *a* imperceptible.

imperdible [imper'ðiβle] *nm* safety pin.

imperdonable [imperðo'naβle] *a* unforgivable, inexcusable.

imperfección [imperfek'θjon] *nf* imperfection.

imperfecto, a [imper'fekto, a] *a* imperfect.

imperial [impe'rjal] *a* imperial; ~**ismo** *nm* imperialism.

impericia [impe'riθja] *nf* (*torpeza*) unskilfulness; (*inexperiencia*) inexperience.

imperio [im'perjo] *nm* empire; (*reino, dominación*) rule, authority; (*fig*) pride, haughtiness; ~**so, a** *a* imperious; (*urgente*) urgent; (*imperativo*) imperative.

impermeable [imperme'aβle] *a* impermeable; (*a prueba de agua*) waterproof // *nm* raincoat.

impersonal [imperso'nal] *a* impersonal.

impertérrito, a [imper'territo, a] *a* undaunted.

impertinencia [imperti'nenθja] *nf* (*inoportunidad*) irrelevance; (*insolencia*) impertinence; **impertinente** *a* irrelevant; impertinent.

imperturbable [impertur'βaβle] *a* imperturbable.

ímpetu ['impetu] *nm* (*impulso*) impetus, impulse; (*impetuosidad*) impetuosity; (*violencia*) violence.

impetuosidad [impetwosi'ðað] *nf* impetuousness; (*violencia*) violence; **impetuoso, a** *a* impetuous; (*persona*) headstrong; (*río*) rushing, violent; (*acto*) hasty.

impío, a [im'pio, a] *a* impious, ungodly.

implacable [impla'kaβle] *a* implacable.

implicar [impli'kar] *vt* (*gen*) to implicate, involve; (*entrañar*) to imply.

implícito, a [im'pliθito, a] *a* (*tácito*) implicit; (*sobreentendido*) implied.

implorar [implo'rar] *vt* to beg, implore.

imponente [impo'nente] *a* (*impresionante*) impressive, imposing; (*solemne*) grand // *nm/f* investor.

imponer [impo'ner] *vt* (*gen*) to impose; (*informar*) to inform, instruct; (*exigir*) to exact, command; (*COM*) to invest; ~**se** *vr* to assert o.s.; (*prevalecer*) to prevail.

impopular [impopu'lar] *a* unpopular.

importación [importa'θjon] *nf* (*acto*) importing; (*objetos*) imports *pl*.

importancia [impor'tanθja] *nf* importance; (*valor*) value, significance; (*extensión*) size, magnitude; **importante** *a* important; valuable, significant.

importar [impor'tar] *vt* (*del extranjero*) to import; (*valer*) to amount to, be worth // *vi* to be important, matter; **me importa el rábano** I don't give a damn; **no importa** it doesn't matter.

importe [im'porte] *nm* (*total*) amount; (*valor*) value.

importunar [importu'nar] *vt* to bother, pester.

importuno, a [impor'tuno, a] *a* (*inoportuno, molesto*) inopportune; (*indiscreto*) troublesome.

imposibilidad [imposiβili'ðað] *nf* impossibility; **imposibilitar** *vt* to make impossible, prevent; (*incapacitar*) to disable, cripple.

imposible [impo'siβle] *a* (*gen*) impossible; (*insoportable*) unbearable, intolerable.

imposición [imposi'θjon] *nf* imposition; (*COM*) tax; (*enganche*) deposit.

impostor [impos'tor] *a* *nm/f* impostor; **impostura** *nf* fraud, imposture.

impotencia [impo'tenθja] *nf* impotence; **impotente** *a* impotent, powerless.

impracticable [imprakti'kaβle] *a*

(irrealizable) impracticable; *(intransitable)* impassable.

imprecar [impre'kar] *vi* to curse.

impregnar [impreɣ'nar] *vt* to impregnate; ~**se** *vr* to become impregnated.

imprenta [im'prenta] *nf (gen)* printing; *(aparato)* press; *(casa)* printer's; *(letra)* print

imprescindible [impresθin'diβle] *a* essential, indispensable.

impresión [impre'sjon] *nf (gen)* impression; *(IMPRENTA)* printing; *(edición)* edition; *(FOTO)* print; *(marca)* imprint; ~ **digital** fingerprint.

impresionable [impresjo'naβle] *a (sensible)* impressionable; *(excitable)* emotional.

impresionante [impresjo'nante] *a* impressive; *(tremendo)* tremendous; *(maravilloso)* great, marvellous

impresionar [impresjo'nar] *vt (conmover)* to move; *(afectar)* to impress, strike; *(película fotográfica)* to expose; ~**se** *vr* to be impressed; *(conmoverse)* to be moved.

impreso, a [im'preso, a] *pp de* **imprimir** // *a* printed // *nm* printed paper/book etc.

impresor [impre'sor] *nm* printer.

imprevisto, a [impre'βisto, a] *a (gen)* unforeseen; *(inesperado)* unexpected.

imprimir [impri'mir] *vt* to imprint, impress, stamp; *(textos)* to print

improbabilidad [improβaβili'ðað] *nf (sin seguridad)* improbability; *(inverosimilitud)* unlikelihood; **improbable** *a* improbable; unlikely.

improcedente [improθe'ðente] *a (incoveniente)* unsuitable; *(inadecuado)* inappropriate.

improductivo, a [improðuk'tiβo, a] *a* unproductive.

improperio [impro'perjo] *nm* insult, taunt.

impropiedad [impropje'ðað] *nf*

impropriety (of language).

impropio, a [im'propjo, a] *a* improper.

improvido, a [im'proβiðo, a] *a* improvident.

improvisación [improβisa'θjon] *nf* improvisation; **improvisado, a** *a* improvised; **improvisar** *vt* to improvise.

improviso, a [impro'βiso, a], **improvisto, a** [impro'βisto, a] *a* unexpected, unforeseen; **de** ~ unexpectedly, suddenly.

imprudencia [impru'ðenθja] *nf* imprudence; *(indiscreción)* indiscretion; *(descuido)* carelessness; **imprudente** *a* imprudent; indiscreet; *(irreflexivo)* unwise.

impúdico, a [im'puðiko, a] *a* shameless, immodest; *(lujurioso)* lecherous, lewd.

impudor [impu'ðor] *nm* shamelessness, immodesty; *(lujuria)* lechery, lewdness.

impuesto, a [im'pwesto, a] *a* imposed; *(informado)* informed // *nm* tax.

impugnar [impuɣ'nar] *vt* to oppose, contest; *(refutar)* to refute, impugn.

impulsar [impul'sar] *vt* → **impeler.**

impulsión [impul'sjon] *nf (TEC)* propulsion, *(fig)* impulse.

impulso [im'pulso] *nm* impulse; *(fuerza, empuje)* thrust, drive; *(rapto)* urge, impulse.

impune [im'pune] *a* unpunished; **impunidad** *nf* impunity.

impureza [impu'reθa] *nf* impurity; *(fig)* lewdness; **impuro, a** *a* impure; lewd.

imputación [imputa'θjon] *nf* imputation.

imputar [impu'tar] *vt (atribuir)* to attribute to; *(cargar)* to impute.

inacabable [inaka'βaβle] *a (infinito)* endless; *(interminable)* interminable.

inaccesible [inakθe'siβle] a inaccesible.

inacción [inak'θjon] nf (gen) inaction; (desocupación) inactivity; (ocio) idleness.

inaceptable [inaθep'taβle] a inaceptable.

inactividad [inaktiβi'ðað] nf inactivity; (pereza) laziness, idleness; (COM) dullness; **inactivo, a** a inactive.

inadaptación [inaðapta'θjon] nf maladjustment.

inadecuado, a [inaðe'kwaðo, a] a (insuficiente) inadequate; (inapto) unsuitable.

inadmisible [inaðmi'siβle] a inadmisible.

inadvertencia [inaðβer'tenθja] nf oversight.

inadvertido, a [inaðβer'tiðo, a] a (distraído) inattentive; (no visto) unnoticed; (descuidado) careless.

inagotable [inaɣo'taβle] a inexhaustible.

inaguantable [inaɣwan'taβle] a unbearable.

inalterable [inalte'raβle] a immutable, unchangeable; (permanente) permanent.

inanición [inani'θjon] nf starvation.

inanimado, a [inani'maðo, a] a inanimate.

inapto, a [in'apto] a unsuited.

inaudito, a [inau'ðito, a] a unheard-of.

inauguración [inauɣura'θjon] nf inauguration; (de exposición) opening; **inaugurar** vt to inaugurate; to open.

I.N.B. abr de Instituto Nacional de Bachillerato ≈ secondary school.

inca ['inka] nm/f Inca; ~ico, a a Inca.

incalculable [inkalku'laβle] a incalculable.

incandescente [inkandes'θente] a incandescent.

incansable [inkan'saβle] a tireless, untiring.

incapacidad [inkapaθi'ðað] nf incapacity; (incompetencia) incompetence; ~ física/mental physical/mental incapacity or disability.

incapacitar [inkapaθi'tar] vt (inhabilitar) to incapacitate, render unfit; (descalificar) to disqualify.

incapaz [inka'paθ] a incapable.

incautación [inkauta'θjon] nf confiscation; **incautarse** vr: **incautarse de** to seize, confiscate.

incauto, a [in'kauto, a] a (imprudente) incautious, unwary.

incendiar [inθen'djar] vt to set on fire; (fig) to inflame; ~se vr to catch fire; ~io, a a incendiary; (fig) inflammatory.

incendio [in'θendjo] nm fire.

incentivo [inθen'tiβo] nm incentive.

incertidumbre [inθerti'ðumbre] nf (inseguridad) uncertainty; (duda) doubt.

incesante [inθe'sante], **incesable** [inθe'saβle] a incessant.

incesto [in'θesto] nm incest.

incidencia [inθi'ðenθja] nf (accidente) incident; (MAT) incidence.

incidente [inθi'ðente] a incidental // nm incident.

incidir [inθi'ðir] vi (influir) to influence; (afectar) to affect; ~ en un error to fall into error.

incienso [in'θjenso] nm incense.

incierto, a [in'θjerto, a] a uncertain.

incineración [inθinera'θjon] nf incineration; (de cadáveres) cremation; **incinerar** vt to burn; to cremate.

incipiente [inθi'pjente] a incipient.

incisión [inθi'sjon] nf incision.

incisivo, a [inθi'siβo, a] a sharp, cutting; (fig) incisive.

incitación [inθita'θjon] nf incitement.

incitante [inθi'tante] a (estimulante) exciting; (provocativo) provocative; **incitar** vt to incite, rouse.

incivil [inθi'βil] a rude, uncivil.

inclemencia [inkle'menθja] *nf* (*severidad*) harshness, severity; (*del tiempo*) inclemency; **inclemente** *a* harsh, severe; inclement.

inclinación [inklina'θjon] *nf* (*gen*) inclination; (*de tierras*) slope, incline; (*de cabeza*) nod, bow; (*fig*) leaning, bent.

inclinar [inkli'nar] *vt* to incline; (*cabeza*) to nod, bow; (*tierras*) to slope; (*persuadir*) to persuade; ~se *vr* to bow; (*encorvarse*) to stoop; ~se a to take after, resemble; ~se ante to bow down to; **me inclino a pensar que** I'm inclined to think that.

ínclito, a ['inklito, a] *a* illustrious, renowned.

incluir [inklu'ir] *vt* to include; (*incorporar*) to incorporate; (*meter*) to enclose.

inclusive [inklu'siβe] *ad* inclusive // *prep* including.

incluso, a [in'kluso, a] *a* included // *ad* inclusively; (*hasta*) even.

incógnito, a [in'koɣnito, a] *a* unknown // *nm*: **de ~** incognito // *nf* unknown factor.

incoherente [inkoe'rente] *a* incoherent.

incoloro, a [inko'loro, a] *a* colourless.

incólume [in'kolume] *a* (*gen*) safe; (*indemne*) unhurt, unharmed.

incomodar [inkomo'ðar] *vt* to inconvenience; (*molestar*) to bother, trouble; (*fastidiar*) to annoy; ~se *vr* to put o.s. out; (*fastidiarse*) to get annoyed.

incomodidad [inkomoði'ðað] *nf* inconvenience; (*fastidio*, *enojo*) annoyance; (*de vivienda*) discomfort.

incómodo, a [in'komoðo, a] *a* (*inconfortable*) uncomfortable; (*molesto*) annoying; (*inconveniente*) inconvenient.

incomparable [inkompa'raβle] *a* incomparable.

incompatible [inkompa'tiβle] *a* incompatible.

incompetencia [inkompe'tenθja] *nf* incompetence; **incompetente** *a* incompetent.

incompleto, a [inkom'pleto, a] *a* incomplete, unfinished.

incomprensible [inkompren-'siβle] *a* incomprehensible.

incomunicado, a [inkomuni-'kaðo, a] *a* (*aislado*) cut off, isolated; (*confinado*) in solitary confinement.

inconcebible [inkonθe'βiβle] *a* inconceivable.

inconcluso, a [inkon'kluso, a] *a* (*inacabado*) unfinished; (*incompleto*) incomplete.

incondicional [inkondiθjo'nal] *a* unconditional; (*apoyo*) wholehearted; (*partidario*) staunch.

inconexo, a [inko'nekso, a] *a* (*gen*) unconnected; (*desunido*) disconnected.

inconfundible [inkonfun'diβle] *a* unmistakable.

incongruente [inkon'ɣrwente] *a* incongruous.

inconmensurable [inkonmensu-'raβle] *a* immeasurable, vast.

inconsciencia [inkons'θjenθja] *nf* unconsciousness; (*fig*) thoughtlessness; **inconsciente** *a* unconscious; thoughtless.

inconsecuencia [inkonse'kwen-θja] *nf* inconsistency; **inconsecuente** *a* inconsistent.

inconsiderado, a [inkonside-'raðo, a] *a* inconsiderate.

inconsistente [inkonsis'tente] *a* weak; (*tela*) flimsy.

inconstancia [inkons'tanθja] *nf* (*inconsecuencia*, *veleidad*) inconstancy; (*inestabilidad*) unsteadiness; **inconstante** *a* inconstant.

incontestable [inkontes'taβle] *a* unanswerable; (*innegable*) undeniable.

incontinencia [inkonti'nenθja] *nf* incontinence; **incontinente** *a* incontinent.

inconveniencia [inkonße'njenθja] *nf* unsuitability, inappropriateness; (*incorrección*) impoliteness; **inconveniente** *a* unsuitable; impolite // *nm* obstacle; (*desventaja*) disadvantage.

incorporación [inkorpora'θjon] *nf* incorporation; (*del cuerpo*) sitting/tanding up; **incorporar** *vt* to incorporate; **incorporarse** *vr* to sit/tand up.

incorrección [inkorrek'θjon] *nf* (*gen*) incorrectness, inaccuracy; (*descortesía*) bad-mannered behaviour; **incorrecto, a** *a* (*gen*) incorrect, wrong; (*facciones*) irregular, odd; (*comportamiento*) bad-mannered.

incorregible [inkorre'xißle] *a* incorrigible.

incorruptible [inkorrup'tißle] *a* incorruptible; ~ **a la intemperie** rustproof.

incredulidad [inkreðuli'ðað] *nf* incredulity; (*escepticismo*) scepticism; **incrédulo, a** *a* incredulous, unbelieving; sceptical.

increíble [inkre'ißle] *a* incredible.

incremento [inkre'mento] *nm* increment; (*aumento*) rise, increase.

increpar [inkre'par] *vt* to reprimand.

incruento, a [in'krwento, a] *a* bloodless.

incrustar [inkrus'tar] *vt* to incrust; (*piedras:* en *joya*) to inlay.

incubar [inku'ßar] *vt* to incubate; (*fig*) to hatch.

inculcar [inkul'kar] *vt* to inculcate.

inculpar [inkul'par] *vt* (*acusar*) to accuse; (*achacar, atribuir*) to charge, blame.

inculto, a [in'kulto, a] *a* (*persona*) uneducated, uncultured; (*terreno*) uncultivated // *nm/f* ignoramus.

incumplimiento [inkumpli'mjento] *nm* non-fulfilment; ~ **de contrato** breach of contract.

incurrir [inku'rrir] *vi*: ~ **en** to

incur; (*crimen*) to commit; ~ **en un error** to fall into error.

indagación [indaxa'θjon] *nf* investigation; (*búsqueda*) search; (*JUR*) inquest; **indagar** *vt* to investigate; to search; (*averiguar*) to ascertain.

indecente [inde'θente] *a* indecent, improper; (*lascivo*) obscene.

indecible [inde'θißle] *a* unspeakable; (*indescriptible*) indescribable.

indeciso, a [inde'θiso, a] *a* (*por decidir*) undecided; (*vacilante*) hesitant; (*resultado*) indecisive.

indefectible [indefek'tißle] *a* unfailing.

indefenso, a [inde'fenso, a] *a* defenceless.

indefinido, a [indefi'niðo, a] *a* indefinite; (*vago*) vague, undefined.

indeleble [inde'leßle] *a* indelible.

indemnizar [indemni'θar] *vt* to indemnify; (*compensar*) to compensate.

independencia [indepen'denθja] *nf* independence.

independiente [indepen'djente] *a* (*libre*) independent; (*autónomo*) self-sufficient.

indeterminado, a [indetermi'naðo, a] *a* indefinite; (*desconocido*) indeterminate.

India ['indja] *nf*: **la ~** India.

indicación [indika'θjon] *nf* indication; (*señal*) sign; (*sugerencia*) suggestion, hint; (*de termómetro*) reading.

indicador [indika'ðor] *nm* indicator; (*TEC*) gauge, meter.

indicar [indi'kar] *vt* (*mostrar*) to indicate, show; (*termómetro etc*) to read, register; (*señalar*) to point to.

índice ['indiθe] *nm* index; (*catálogo*) catalogue; (*ANAT*) index finger, forefinger; (*de cuadrante*) pointer, needle; (*de reloj*) hand.

indicio [in'diθjo] *nm* indication, sign; (*huella*) trace; (*pesquisa*) clue.

indiferencia [indife'renθja] *nf*

indifference; (*apatía*) apathy; **indiferente** *a* indifferent.

indígena [indi'xena] *a* indigenous, native; (*aborigen*) aboriginal // *nm/f* native; aborigine.

indigencia [indi'xenθja] *nf* poverty, need.

indigestión [indixes'tjon] *nf* indigestion.

indigesto, a [indi'xesto] *a* undigested; (*indigestible*) indigestible; (*fig*) turgid.

indignación [indixna'θjon] *nf* indignation; **indignado, a** *a* indignant.

indignar [indix'nar] *vt* to anger, make indignant; ~**se vr**: ~**se de o por** to get indignant about.

indignidad [indixni'ðað] *nf* (*insulto*) indignity, insult; (*ruindad*) vile act; **indigno, a** *a* (*despreciable*) low, contemptible; (*inmerecido*) unworthy.

indio, a [indjo, a] *a*, *nm/f* Indian.

indirecta [indi'rekta] *nf* insinuation, innuendo; (*sugerencia*) hint.

indirecto, a [indi'rekto, a] *a* indirect.

indiscreción [indiskre'θjon] *nf* (*imprudencia*) indiscretion; (*irreflexión*) tactlessness; (*acto*) gaffe, tactless act.

indiscreto, a [indis'kreto, a] *a* indiscreet.

indiscutible [indisku'tiβle] *a* indisputable, unquestionable.

indispensable [indispen'saβle] *a* indispensable.

indisponer [indispo'ner] *vt* to spoil, upset; (*salud*) to make ill; ~**se vr** to fall ill; ~**se con uno** to fall out with sb.

indisposición [indisposi'θjon] *nf* indisposition.

indistinto, a [indis'tinto, a] *a* indistinct; (*vago*) vague.

individual [indiβi'ðwal] *a* individual; (*habitación*) single // *nm* (*DEPORTE*) singles *sg*.

individuo, a [indi'ðiðwo, a] *a*

individual // *nm* individual; (*miembro*, *socio*) member, fellow.

indiviso, a [indi'βiso, a] *a* undivided.

índole ['indole] *nf* (*naturaleza*) nature; (*clase*) sort, kind.

indolencia [indo'lenθja] *nf* indolence, laziness.

indomable [indo'maβle] *a* indomitable; (*animal*) untameable; (*fig*) unmanageable.

indómito, a [in'domito, a] *a* indomitable.

inducir [indu'θir] *vt* to induce; (*inferir*) to infer; (*persuadir*) to persuade.

indudable [indu'ðaβle] *a* undoubted; (*incuestionable*) unquestionable.

indulgencia [indul'xenθja] *nf* indulgence.

indultar [indul'tar] *vt* (*perdonar*) to pardon, reprieve; (*librar de pago*) to exempt; **indulto** *nm* pardon; exemption.

industria [in'dustrja] *nf* industry; (*habilidad*) skill; **industrial** *a* industrial // *nm* industrialist.

industrioso, a [indus'trjoso, a] *a* industrious.

inédito, a [in'eðito, a] *a* (*libro*) unpublished; (*nuevo*) unheard-of.

inefable [ine'faβle] *a* ineffable, indescribable.

ineficaz [inefi'kaθ] *a* (*inútil*) ineffective; (*ineficiente*) inefficient.

ineludible [inelu'ðiβle] *a* inescapable, unavoidable.

ineptitud [inepti'tuð] *nf* ineptitude, incompetence; **inepto, a** *a* inept, incompetent.

inequívoco, a [ine'kiβoko, a] *a* unequivocal; (*inconfundible*) unmistakable.

inercia [in'erθja] *nf* inertia; (*fig*) passivity.

inerme [in'erme] *a* (*sin armas*) unarmed; (*indefenso*) defenceless.

inerte [in'erte] *a* inert; (*fig*) passive.

inesperado, a [inespe'raðo, a] *a*

unexpected, unforeseen.
inestable [ines'taßle] a unstable.
inevitable [ineßi'taßle] a inevitable.
inexactitud [ineksakti'tuð] nf inaccuracy; **inexacto, a** a inaccurate; (falso) untrue.
infamar [infa'mar] vt to dishonour; (calumniar) to defame, slander.
infame [in'fame] a infamous // nm/f vile person; **infamia** nf infamy; (deshonra) disgrace.
infancia [in'fanθja] nf infancy, childhood.
infante [in'fante] nm (niño) infant, child; (hijo del rey) prince.
infantería [infante'ria] nf infantry.
infantil [infan'til] a (pueril, aniñado) infantile; (cándido) childlike; (literatura) children's.
infarto [in'farto] nm heart attack.
infatigable [infati'saßle] a tireless, untiring.
infausto, a [in'fausto, a] a unlucky.
infección [infek'θjon] nf infection; **infeccioso, a** a infectious.
infectar [infek'tar] vt to infect; **~se** vr to become infected.
infelicidad [infeliθi'ðað] nf unhappiness.
infeliz [infe'liθ] a unhappy, wretched // nm/f wretch.
inferior [infe'rjor] a inferior; (situación) lower // nm/f inferior, subordinate.
inferir [infe'rir] vt (deducir) to infer, deduce; (causar) to cause.
infestar [infes'tar] vt (infectar) to infect; (apestar) to infest; (fig) to harass.
inficionar [infiθjo'nar] vt to infect; (fig) to corrupt.
infidelidad [infiðeli'ðað] nf (gen) infidelity, unfaithfulness; (REL) lack of faith.
infiel [in'fjel] a unfaithful, disloyal; (falso) inaccurate // nm/f infidel, unbeliever.
infierno [in'fjerno] nm hell.
ínfimo, a [in'fimo, a] a vile, mean.

infinidad [infini'ðað] nf infinity; (abundancia) great quantity.
infinito, a [infi'nito, a] a, nm infinite.
inflación [infla'θjon] nf (hinchazón) swelling; (monetaria) inflation; (fig) conceit; **inflacionario, a** a inflationary.
inflamar [infla'mar] vt to set on fire; (MED) to inflame; **~se** vr to catch fire; (fig) to become inflamed.
inflar [in'flar] vt (hinchar) to inflate, blow up; (fig) to exaggerate; **~se** vr to swell (up); (fig) to get conceited.
inflexible [inflek'sißle] a inflexible; (irrompible) unbending; (fig) strict.
infligir [infli'xir] vt to inflict.
influencia [influ'enθja] nf influence; **influenciar** vt to influence.
influir [influ'ir] vt to influence.
influjo [in'fluxo] nm influence.
influyente [influ'jente] a influential.
información [informa'θjon] nf information; (noticias) news sg; (JUR) inquiry.
informal [infor'mal] a (gen) irregular, incorrect; (persona) unreliable; (poco serio) frivolous; (trabajo) disorganized; (comportamiento) unconventional.
informalidad [informali'ðað] nf (impuntualidad) unpunctuality; (incorrección) bad manners pl; (ligereza) frivolity.
informante [infor'mante] nm/f informant.
informar [infor'mar] vt (gen) to inform; (revelar) to reveal, make known // vi (JUR) to plead; (denunciar) to inform; (dar cuenta de) to report on; **~se** vr to find out; **~se de** to inquire into.
informe [in'forme] a shapeless // nm report.
infortunio [infor'tunjo] nm misfortune.
infracción [infrak'θjon] nf infrac-

tion, infringement; (*transgresión*) transgression.

infranqueable [infranke'aβle] a impassable; (*impracticable*) insurmountable.

infringir [infrin'xir] vt to infringe, contravene.

infructuoso, a [infruk'twoso, a] a fruitless, unsuccessful.

infundado, a [infun'daðo, a] a groundless, unfounded.

infundir [infun'dir] vt to infuse, instil.

ingeniar [inxe'njar] vt to think up, devise; **~se** vr: **~se para** to manage to.

ingeniería [inxenje'ria] nf engineering; **ingeniero, a** nm/f engineer; **ingeniero agrónomo/de sonido** agronomist/sound engineer.

ingenio [in'xenjo] nm (*talento*) talent; (*agudeza*) wit; (*habilidad*) ingenuity, inventiveness; (*TEC*): **~ azucarero** sugar refinery.

ingenioso, a [inxe'njoso, a] a ingenious, clever; (*divertido*) witty.

ingénito, a [in'xenito, a] a innate.

ingenuidad [inxenwi'ðað] nf ingenuousness; (*candor*) candour, **ingenuo, a** a ingenuous

ingerencia [inxe'renθja] nf = **injerencia**.

ingerir [inxe'rir] vt to ingest; (*tragar*) to swallow; (*consumir*) to consume.

Inglaterra [ingla'terra] nf England.

ingle ['ingle] nf groin.

inglés, esa [in'gles, esa] a English // nm/f Englishman/woman // nm (*lengua*) English.

ingratitud [ingrati'tuð] nf ingratitude; **ingrato, a** a (*ipgit*) ungrateful; (*desagradable*) unpleasant.

ingrediente [ingre'ðjente] nm ingredient.

ingresar [ingre'sar] vt (*dinero*) to deposit // vi to come in; **~ en un** club to join a club; **~ en el hospital** to go into hospital.

ingreso [in'greso] nm (*entrada*) entry; (: *en hospital etc*) admission; (*de dinero*) income, takings pl.

inhábil [in'aβil] a unskilful, clumsy; **día ~** non-working day.

inhabitable [inaβi'taβle] a uninhabitable.

inherente [ine'rente] a inherent.

inhibir [ini'βir] vt to inhibit; (*REL*) to restrain.

inhospitalario, a [inospita'larjo, a] a inhospitable.

inhumano, a [inu'mano, a] a inhuman.

I. N. I. ['ini] nm abr de **Instituto Nacional de Industria** = National Enterprise Board.

inicial [ini'θjal] a, nf initial.

iniciar [ini'θjar] vt (*persona*) to initiate; (*estudios*) to begin, commence; (*conversación*) to start up.

iniciativa [iniθja'tiβa] nf initiative; **la ~ privada** private enterprise.

inicuo, a [in'ikwo, a] a iniquitous.

ininterrumpido, a [ininterrum'piðo, a] a uninterrupted.

injerencia [inxe'renθja] nf interference.

injertar [inxer'tar] vt to graft; (*inyectar*) to inject; **injerto** nm graft.

injuria [in'xurja] nf (*agravio*, *ofensa*) offence; (*insulto*) insult; (*daño*) harm; **injuriar** vt to insult; to harm; **injurioso, a** a offensive, insulting, harmful.

injusticia [inxus'tiθja] nf injustice.

injusto, a [in'xusto, a] a unjust, unfair.

inmadurez [inmaðu'reθ] nf immaturity.

inmarcesible [inmarθe'siβle], **inmarchitable** [inmartʃi'taβle] a imperishable.

inmediaciones [inmeðja'θjones] nfpl neighbourhood, environs.

inmediato, a [inme'ðjato, a] a immediate; (*contiguo*) adjoining;

(*rápido*) prompt; (*próximo*) close, next; **de ~** immediately.

inmejorable [inmexo'raßle] *a* unsurpassable; (*precio*) unbeatable.

inmenso, a [in'menso, a] *a* immense, huge.

inmerecido, a [inmere'θiðo, a] *a* undeserved.

inmigración [inmixra'θjon] *nf* immigration.

inmiscuirse [inmisku'irse] *vr* to interfere, meddle.

inmobiliario, a [inmoßi'ljarjo, a] *a* real-estate *cpd* // *nf* estate agency.

inmoderado, a [inmoðe'raðo, a] *a* immoderate, excessive.

inmolar [inmo'lar] *vt* to immolate, sacrifice.

inmoral [inmo'ral] *a* immoral.

inmortal [inmor'tal] *a* immortal; **~izar** *vt* to immortalize.

inmotivado, a [inmoti'ßaðo, a] *a* motiveless.

inmóvil [in'moßil] *a* immobile; (*inamovible*) immovable; (*invariable*) unchanging; (*parado*) still, stationary.

inmueble [in'mweßle] *nm* property.

inmundicia [inmun'diθja] *nf* filth; **inmundo, a** *a* filthy.

inmunidad [inmuni'ðað] *nf* immunity.

inmutar [inmu'tar] *vt* to alter; **~se** *vr* to turn pale.

innato, a [in'nato, a] *a* innate.

innecesario, a [inneθe'sarjo, a] *a* unnecessary.

innoble [in'noßle] *a* ignoble.

innocuo, a [in'nokwo, a] *a* innocuous.

innovación [innoßa'θjon] *nf* innovation; **innovar** *vt* to introduce.

inocencia [ino'θenθja] *nf* innocence.

inocentada [inoθen'taða] *nf* practical joke.

inocente [ino'θente] *a* (*ingenuo*)

naive, simple; (*inculpable*) innocent // *nm/f* simpleton.

inodoro [ino'ðoro] *nm* toilet, lavatory.

inofensivo, a [inofen'sißo, a] *a* inoffensive.

inolvidable [inolßi'ðaßle] *a* unforgettable.

inoperante [inope'rante] *a* unworkable.

inopinado, a [inopi'naðo, a] *a* unexpected.

inoportuno, a [inopor'tuno, a] *a* untimely; (*molesto*) inconvenient.

inoxidable [inoksi'ðaßle] *a*: **acero ~** stainless steel.

inquebrantable [inkeßran'taßle] *a* unbreakable.

inquietar [inkje'tar] *vt* to worry, trouble, disturb; **~se** *vr* to worry, get upset; **inquieto, a** *a* anxious, worried; **inquietud** *nf* anxiety, worry.

inquilino, a [inki'lino, a] *nm/f* tenant.

inquirir [inki'rir] *vt* to enquire into, investigate.

insaciable [insa'θjaßle] *a* insatiable.

insalubre [insa'lußre] *a* unhealthy.

inscribir [inskri'ßir] *vt* to inscribe; (*lista*) to list; (*censo*) to register; **~se** *vr* to register; (*ESCOL etc*) to enrol.

inscripción [inskrip'θjon] *nf* inscription; (*ESCOL etc*) enrolment; (*censo*) registration.

insecto [in'sekto] *nm* insect.

inseguridad [insexuri'ðað] *nf* insecurity.

inseguro, a [inse'xuro, a] *a* insecure; (*inconstante*) unsteady; (*incierto*) uncertain.

insensato, a [insen'sato, a] *a* foolish, stupid.

insensibilidad [insensißili'ðað] *nf* (*gen*) insensitivity; (*dureza de corazón*) callousness.

insensible [insen'sißle] *a* (*gen*) insensitive; (*duro*) callous; (*movi-*

miento) imperceptible; (*sin sentido*) nulup.

insertar [inser'tar] vt to insert.
inservible [inser'βiβle] a useless.
insidioso, a [insi'ðjoso, a] a insidious.
insignia [in'siɣnja] nf (*señal distintiva*) badge; (*estandarte*) flag, (*condecoración*) decoration.
insignificante [insiɣnifi'kante] a insignificant.
insinuar [insi'nwar] vt to insinuate, imply; ~se vr: ~se con uno to ingratiate o.s. with sb.
insípido, a [in'sipiðo, a] a insipid.
insistencia [insis'tenθja] nf (*obstinación*) insistence; (*porfía*) persistence.
insistir [insis'tir] vi to insist; ~ en algo to stress sth.
insolación [insola'θjon] nf (MED) sunstroke.
insolencia [inso'lenθja] nf insolence; **insolente** a insolent.
insólito, a [in'solito, a] a unusual.
insoluble [inso'luβle] a insoluble.
insolvencia [insol'βenθja] nf insolvency.
insomnio [in'somnjo] nm insomnia.
insondable [inson'daβle] a bottomless.
insoportable [insopor'taβle] a unbearable.
inspección [inspek'θjon] nf inspection, check; **inspeccionar** vt (*examinar*) to inspect, examine; (*controlar*) to check.
inspector [inspek'tor] a nm/f inspector.
inspiración [inspira'θjon] nf inspiration; **inspirar** vt to inspire; (MED) to inhale; **inspirarse** vr: **inspirarse en** to be inspired by.
instalar [insta'lar] vt (*establecer*) to instal; (*erguir*) to set up, erect; ~se vr to establish o.s.
instancia [ins'tanθja] nf (JUR) petition; (*ruego*) request; **en última ~** in the last resort.
instantáneo, a [instan'taneo, a] a

instant, instantaneous // nf snap(shot).
instante [ins'tante] nm instant, moment.
instar [ins'tar] vt to press, urge // vi to be pressing or urgent.
instigar [insti'ɣar] vt to instigate.
instinto [ins'tinto] nm instinct; **por ~** instinctively.
institución [institu'θjon] nf institution, establishment.
instituir [institu'ir] vt to establish; (*fundar*) to found; **instituto** nm (*gen*) institute; (*escuela*) high school.
instrucción [instruk'θjon] nf instruction.
instructivo, a [instruk'tiβo, a] a instructive.
instruir [instru'ir] vt (*gen*) to instruct; (*enseñar*) to teach, educate; (MIL, DEPORTE) to train.
instrumento [instru'mento] nm (*gen*) instrument; (*herramienta*) tool, implement.
insubordinarse [insuβorði'narse] vr to rebel.
insuficiencia [insufi'θjenθja] nf (*carencia*) lack; (*inadecuación*) inadequacy; **insuficiente** a (*gen*) insufficient; (*incompetente*) incompetent; (*nota*) inadequate.
insufrible [insu'friβle] a insufferable.
insular [insu'lar] a insular.
insulsez [insul'seθ] nf (*insipidez*) tastipidity; (*fig*) dullness.
insultar [insul'tar] vt to insult; **insulto** nm insult.
insuperable [insupe'raβle] a (*excelente*) unsurpassable; (*arduo*) insurmountable.
insurgente [insur'xente] a, nm/f insurgent.
insurrección [insurrek'θjon] nf insurrection, rebellion.
intacto, a [in'takto, a] a intact.
intachable [inta'tʃaβle] a irreproachable.

integral [inte'xral] *a*: **pan** ~
wholemeal bread.

integrar [inte'xrar] *vt* to make up,
compose; (COM) to repay; (MAT) to
integrate.

integridad [integri'ðað] *nf* whole-
ness; (carácter) integrity; **íntegro, a**
a whole, entire; (honrado) honest.

intelectual [intelek'twal] *a*, *nm/f*
intellectual.

inteligencia [inteli'xenθja] *nf* intelligence; (ingenio) ability; **inteligente a** intelligent.

intemperancia [intempe'ranθja] *nf*
excess, intemperance.

intemperie [intem'perje] *nf* bad
weather; **a la ~** outdoors, in the
open air.

intempestivo, a [intempes'tiβo,
a] *a* untimely.

intención [inten'θjon] *nf* (gen)
intention; (propósito) purpose; **con
segundas intenciones** maliciously;
de primera ~ provisionally; **con ~**
deliberately.

intencionado, a [intenθjo'naðo, a]
a deliberate; **bien/mal ~** well-
meaning/ill-disposed.

intendencia [inten'denθja] *nf*
management, administration.

intenso, a [in'tenso, a] *a* intense;
(impresión) vivid; (sentimiento)
profound, deep.

intentar [inten'tar] *vt* (tratar) to
try, attempt; **intento** *nm* (intención)
intention, purpose; (tentativa)
attempt.

intercalar [interka'lar] *vt* to
insert.

intercambio [inter'kambjo] *nm*
exchange, swap.

interceder [interθe'ðer] *vi* to
intercede.

intercesión [interθe'sjon] *nf*
intercession.

interés [inte'res] *nm* (gen) interest;
(parte) share, part; (pey) self-
interest; **intereses creados** vested
interests.

interesado, a [intere'saðo, a] *a*

interested; (prejuiciado) prejudiced;
(pey) mercenary, self-seeking.

interesar [intere'sar] *vt*, *vi* to
interest, be of interest to; **~se vr**
~se en o por to take an interest in.

interferir [interfe'rir] *vt* to
interfere with; (TELEC) to jam // *vi*
to interfere.

interior [inte'rjor] *a* inner, inside;
(COM) domestic, internal // *nm*
interior, inside; (fig) soul, mind;
Ministerio del I~ Home Office.

interjección [interxek'θjon] *nf*
interjection.

interlocutor, a [interloku'tor]
nm/f speaker.

intermediario, a [interme'ðjarjo,
a] *nm/f* intermediary // *nm*
middleman.

intermedio, a [inter'meðjo, a] *a*
intermediate // *nm* interval.

interminable [intermi'naβle] *a*
endless.

intermitente [intermi'tente] *a*
intermittent // *nm* indicator.

internacional [internaθjo'nal] *a*
international.

internar [inter'nar] *vt* to intern;
(loco) to commit; **~se vr** (en un
hospital) to go into hospital;
(penetrar) to penetrate.

interno, a [in'terno, a] *a* internal,
interior; (POL etc) domestic // *nm*
(alumno) boarder.

interpelar [interpe'lar] *vt* (rogar)
to implore; (hablar) to speak to.

interponer [interpo'ner] *vt* to
interpose, put in; **~se vr** to
intervene.

interposición [interposi'θjon] *nf*
insertion.

interpretación [interpreta'θjon]
nf interpretation; **interpretar** *vt* to
interpret; **intérprete** *nm/f* interpre-
ter; (traductor) translator; (músico,
TEATRO) performer, artist(e).

interrogación [interroxa'θjon] *nf*
interrogation; (LING) question mark;
interrogar *vt* to interrogate,
question.

interrumpir [interrum'pir] vt to interrupt; (ELEC) to switch off, cut off.

interrupción [interrup'θjon] nf interruption.

interruptor [interrup'tor] nm (ELEC) switch.

intersección [intersek'θjon] nf intersection.

interurbano, a [interur'ßano, a] a: **llamada ~a** trunk call.

intervalo [inter'ßalo] nm interval; (descanso) break; **a ~s** at intervals, every now and then.

intervenir [interße'nir] vt (controlar) to control, supervise; (MED) to operate on // vi (participar) to take part, participate; (mediar) to intervene.

interventor, a [interßen'tor, a] nm/f inspector; (COM) auditor.

interviú [inter'ßju] nf interview.

intestino, a [intes'tino, a] a internal; (doméstico) domestic // nm intestine.

intimar [inti'mar] vt to intimate, announce // vi to become friendly.

intimidad [intimi'ðað] nf intimacy; (confianza) confidence; (familiaridad) familiarity; (vida privada) private life; (soledad) privacy.

íntimo, a [intimo, a] a intimate.

intolerable [intole'raßle] a intolerable, unbearable.

intransitable [intransi'taßle] a impassable.

intrepidez [intrepi'ðeθ] nf courage, bravery; **intrépido, a** a intrepid.

intriga [in'triγa] nf intrigue; (plan) plot; **intrigar** vt, vi to intrigue.

intrincado, a [intrin'kaðo, a] a intricate.

intrínseco, a [in'trinseko, a] a intrinsic.

introducción [introðuk'θjon] nf introduction.

introducir [introðu'θir] vt (gen) to introduce; (hacer penetrar) to insert.

intruso, a [in'truso, a] a intrusive // nm/f intruder.

intuición [intwi'θjon] nf intuition.

inundación [inunda'θjon] nf flood(ing); **inundar** vt to flood, swamp, inundate; (fig) to swamp, inundate.

inusitado, a [inusi'taðo, a] a unusual.

inútil [in'util] a useless; (esfuerzo) vain, fruitless; **inutilidad** nf uselessness.

inutilizar [inutili'θar] vt to make useless, render useless; **~se** vr to become useless.

invadir [inßa'ðir] vt to invade.

inválido, a [in'ßaliðo, a] a invalid // nm/f invalid.

invariable [inßa'rjaßle] a invariable.

invasión [inßa'sjon] nf invasion.

invasor, a [inßa'sor, a] a invading // nm/f invader.

invención [inßen'θjon] nf invention.

inventar [inßen'tar] vt to invent.

inventario [inßen'tarjo] nm inventory.

inventiva [inßen'tißa] nf inventiveness.

inventor, a [inßen'tor, a] nm/f inventor.

inverosímil [inßero'simil] a implausible; (improbable) unlikely, improbable.

inversión [inßer'sjon] nf (COM) investment; (AUTO) reversing; **inversionista** nm/f investor.

inverso, a [in'ßerso, a] a inverse, opposite; **en el orden ~** in reverse order; **a la ~a** inversely, the other way round.

invertir [inßer'tir] vt (COM) to invest; (volcar) to turn upside down; (tiempo etc) to spend; (AUTO) to reverse.

investigación [inßestiγa'θjon] nf investigation; (estudio) research; **investigar** vt to investigate; (estudiar) to do research into.

inveterado, a [inβete'raðo, a] *a* inveterate, confirmed.

invicto, a [in'βikto, a] *a* unconquered.

invierno [in'βjerno] *nm* winter.

invitar [inβi'tar] *vt* to invite; (*incitar*) to entice; (*pagar*) to buy, pay for.

invocar [inβo'kar] *vt* to invoke, call on.

inyección [injek'θjon] *nf* injection.

inyectar [injek'tar] *vt* to inject.

ir [ir] *vi* (*gen*) to go; (*viajar*) to travel; (*ropa*) to suit; ~ **caminando** to walk; ~ **en coche/bicicleta/caballo/a pie** to drive/cycle/ride/walk; ¡voy! I'm coming!; ~ **de viaje** to travel, go away; **voy para viejo** I'm getting on (in years); ~ **por/a por algo** to go for/go and get sth; **¡qué val** (*no digas*) you don't say!; (: **¡no!**) no way!, rubbish!; **¡vamos!** come on!; **vaya susto que me has dado** what a fright you gave me; ~**se** *vr* to go away, leave; (*mano etc*) to slip; **¡vete!** go away!

ira ['ira] *nf* anger, rage.

iracundo, a [ira'kundo, a] *a* irascible; (*colérico*) irate.

Irán [i'ran] *nm* Iran; **iraní, esa** [ira'ni a, nm/f] Iranian.

iris ['iris] *nm* (*arco* ~) rainbow; (ANAT) iris.

Irlanda [ir'landa] *nf* Ireland; **irlandés, esa** *a* Irish // *nm/f* Irishman/woman.

ironía [iro'nia] *nf* irony; **irónico, a** *a* ironic(al).

irreal [irre'al] *a* unreal.

irreflexión [irreflek'sjon] *nf* thoughtlessness.

irremediable [irreme'ðjaβle] *a* incurable, hopeless.

irresoluto, a [irreso'luto, a] *a* irresolute, hesitant.

irrespetuoso, a [irrespe'twoso, a] *a* disrespectful.

irresponsable [irrespon'saβle] *a* irresponsible.

irrigar [irri'xar] *vt* to irrigate.

irrisorio, a [irri'sorjo, a] *a* derisory, ridiculous.

irritar [irri'tar] *vt* to irritate, annoy.

irrupción [irrup'θjon] *nf* irruption; (*invasión*) invasion.

isla ['isla] *nf* island.

islandés, esa [islan'des, esa] *a* Icelandic // *nm/f* Icelander.

Islandia [is'landja] *nf* Iceland.

isleño, a [is'leno, a] *a* island *cpd* // *nm/f* islander.

Israel [isra'el] *nm* Israel; **israelí** *a, nm/f* Israeli.

istmo ['istmo] *nm* isthmus.

Italia [i'talja] *nf* Italy; **italiano, a** *a, nm/f* Italian.

itinerario [itine'rarjo] *nm* itinerary, route.

izar [i'θar] *vt* to hoist.

izquierdista [iθkjer'ðista] *nm/f* left-winger, leftist.

izquierdo, a [iθ'kjerðo, a] *a* left // *nf* left; **a la** ~**a** on the left.

J

jabalí [xaβa'li] *nm* wild boar.

jabalina [xaβa'lina] *nf* javelin.

jabón [xa'βon] *nm* soap; **jabonar** *vt* to soap.

jaca ['xaka] *nf* pony.

jacinto [xa'θinto] *nm* hyacinth.

jactancia [xak'tanθja] *nf* boasting, boastfulness.

jactarse [xak'tarse] *vr* to boast, brag.

jadeante [xaðe'ante] *a* panting, gasping; **jadear** *vi* to pant, gasp for breath; **jadeo** *nm* panting, gasping.

jaez [xa'eθ] *nm* (*de caballerías*) harness; (*clase*) kind, sort.

jaguar [xa'xwar] *nm* jaguar.

jalar [xa'lar] *vt* to pull, haul.

jalbegue [xal'βexe] *nm* (*pintura*) whitewash; (*fig*) make-up.

jalea [xa'lea] *nf* jelly.

jaleo [xa'leo] nm racket, uproar; (baile) Andalusian popular dance; **estar de ~** to be having a good time; **armar un ~** to kick up a din.

Jamaica [xa'maika] nf Jamaica.

jamás [xa'mas] ad never; (sin negación) ever.

jamón [xa'mon] nm ham.

Japón [xa'pon] nm: **el ~** Japan; **japonés, esa** a, nm/f Japanese.

jaque ['xake] nm cheque; (fam) bully; **~ mate** checkmate.

jaqueca [xa'keka] nf (severe) headache, migraine.

jarabe [xa'raβe] nm syrup.

jarcia ['xarθja] nf (NAUT) ropes pl, rigging; (para pescar) (fishing) tackle; (confusión, revoltijo) jumble, mess.

jardín [xar'ðin] nm garden; **jardinería** nf gardening; **jardinero, a** nm/f gardener.

jarra ['xarra] nf jar.

jarro ['xarro] nm jug.

jaula ['xaula] nf cage.

jauría [xau'ria] nf pack of hounds.

J C. abr de **Jesucristo.**

jefatura [xefa'tura] nf: **~ de policía** police headquarters sg.

jefe ['xefe] nm (gen) chief, head; (patrón) boss; **~ de camareros** head waiter; **~ de cocina** chef; **~ de estación** stationmaster; **~ de estado** head of state; **~ supremo** commander-in-chief; **ser el ~** (fig) to be the boss.

jengibre [xen'xiβre] nm ginger.

jeque ['xeke] nm sheik.

jerarquía [xerar'kia] nf (orden) hierarchy; (rango) rank, **jerárquico, a** a hierarchic(al).

jerez [xe'reθ] nm sherry.

jerga ['xerɣa] nf (tela) coarse cloth; (lenguaje) jargon, slang.

jerigonza [xeri'ɣonθa] nf (jerga) jargon, slang; (galimatías) nonsense, gibberish.

jeringa [xe'ringa] nf syringe; (AM) annoyance, bother; **~ de engrase** grease gun; **jeringar** vt to syringe;

(inyectar) to inject; (AM) to annoy, bother.

jeroglífico [xero'slifiko] nm hieroglyphic.

jersé, jersey (pl **jerseys**) [xer'sei] nm jersey, pullover, jumper.

Jerusalén [xerusa'len] n Jerusalem.

Jesucristo [xesu'kristo] n Jesus Christ.

jesuita [xe'swita] a, nm Jesuit.

Jesús [xe'sus] nm Jesus; **¡~!** good heavens!; (al estornudar) bless you!

jícara ['xikara] nf small cup.

jifero, a [xi'fero, a] a (fam) filthy // nm butcher's knife; (matarife) butcher, slaughterer.

jinete [xi'nete] nm (horse)rider.

jipijapa [xipi'xapa] nm (AM) straw hat.

jira ['xira] nf (de tela) strip; (excursión) picnic.

jirafa [xi'rafa] nf giraffe.

jirón [xi'ron] nm rag, shred.

jocosidad [xokosi'ðað] nf humour; (chiste) joke.

jocoso, a [xo'koso, a] a humorous, jocular.

jofaina [xo'faina] nf washbasin.

jornada [xor'naða] nf day's journey; (camino o viaje entero) journey; (día de trabajo) working day; (fig) lifetime.

jornal [xor'nal] nm (day's) wage; **~ero** nm (day) labourer.

joroba [xo'roβa] nf hump, hunched back; (fam) nuisance; **~do, a** a hunchbacked // nm/f hunchback.

jota ['xota] nf letter J; (danza) Aragonese dance; (fam) iota; **no saber ~** to have no idea.

joven ['xoβen] a young // nm young man, youth // nf young woman, girl.

jovial [xo'βjal] a cheerful, jovial; **~idad** nf cheerfulness, joviality.

joya ['xoja] nf jewel, gem; (fig: persona) gem, **joyería** (joyas) jewellery; (tienda) jeweller's (shop); **joyero** nm (persona) jeweller; (caja) jewel case.

juanete [xwa'nete] *nm* bunion.

jubilación [xuβila'θjon] *nf* (*retiro*) retirement; (*alegría*) jubilation.

jubilar [xuβi'lar] *vt* to pension off, retire; (*fam*) to discard // *vi* to rejoice; ~**se** *vr* to retire.

jubileo [xuβi'leo] *nm* (*indulgencia*) jubilee; (*fam*) comings and goings *pl*.

júbilo ['xuβilo] *nm* joy, jubilation, rejoicing; ~**so, a** *a* jubilant.

judaísmo [xuða'ismo] *nm* Judaism.

judía [xu'ðia] *nf* Jewess; (*CULIN*) bean.

judicatura [xuðika'tura] *nf* (*cargo de juez*) office of judge; (*magistratura*) judicature.

judicial [xuði'θjal] *a* judicial.

judío, a [xu'ðio, a] *a* Jewish // *nm/f* Jew/ess.

juego *etc vb ver* **jugar** // ['xweɣo] *nm* (*gen*) play; (*pasatiempo, partido*) game; (*en casino*) gambling; (*conjunto*) set; **fuera de ~** (*persona*) offside; (*pelota*) out of play.

juerga ['xwerɣa] *nf* good time; (*fiesta*) party; **ir de ~** to go out on a spree.

jueves ['xweβes] *nm inv* Thursday.

juez [xweθ] *nm* judge; ~ **de línea** linesman; ~ **de salida** starter.

jugada [xu'ɣaða] *nf* play; **buena ~** good move/shot/stroke *etc*.

jugador, a [xuɣa'ðor, a] *nm/f* player; (*en casino*) gambler.

jugar [xu'ɣar] *vt, vi* to play; (*en casino*) to gamble; ~**se** *vr* to gamble (away).

juglar [xu'ɣlar] *nm* minstrel.

jugo ['xuɣo] *nm* (*BOT*) juice; (*fig*) essence, substance; ~**so, a** *a* juicy; (*fig*) substantial, important.

juguete [xu'ɣete] *nm* toy; (*TEATRO*) sketch; ~**ar** *vi* to play; ~**ría** *nf* toyshop.

juguetón, ona [xuɣe'ton, ona] *a* playful.

juicio ['xwiðjo] *nm* judgement; (*sana razón*) sanity, reason; (*opinión*)

opinion; **estar fuera de ~** to be out of one's mind; ~**so, a** *a* wise, sensible.

julio ['xuljo] *nm* July.

jumento, a [xu'mento, a] *nm/f* donkey.

junco ['xunko] *nm* rush, reed.

jungla ['xungla] *nf* jungle.

junio ['xunjo] *nm* June.

junta ['xunta] *nf ver* **junto**.

juntamente [xunta'mente] *ad* (*conjuntamente*) together; (*al mismo tiempo*) together, at the same time.

juntar [xun'tar] *vt* to join, unite; (*maquinaria*) to assemble, put together; (*dinero*) to collect; (*puerta*) to half-close, leave ajar; ~**se** *vr* to join, meet; (*reunirse: personas*) to meet, assemble; (*arrimarse*) to approach, draw closer; (*vivir juntos*) to live together; ~**se con uno** to join sb.

junto, a ['xunto, a] *a* (*unido*) joined, united; (*anexo*) near, close; (*continuo, próximo*) next, adjacent // *ad*: **todo ~** all at once // *nf* (*asamblea*) meeting, assembly; (*comité, consejo*) board, council, committee; (*articulación*) joint; ~ **a** near (to), next to; ~**s** together.

juntura [xun'tura] *nf* (*punto de unión*) join, junction; (*articulación*) joint.

jurado [xu'raðo] *nm* (*JUR*) juror; (: *conjunto de* ~**s**) jury; (*de concurso*) panel (of judges); (: *individuo*) member of a panel.

juramentar [xuramen'tar] *vt* to swear in, administer the oath to; ~**se** *vr* to be sworn in, take the oath.

juramento [xura'mento] *nm* oath; (*maldición*) oath, curse; **prestar ~** to take the oath; **tomar ~ a** to swear in, administer the oath to.

jurar [xu'rar] *vt, vi* to swear; ~ **en falso** to commit perjury; **jurárselas a uno** to have it in for sb.

jurídico, a [xu'riðiko, a] *a* legal.

jurisdicción [xurisðikˈθjon] *nf* (*poder, autoridad*) jurisdiction; (*territorio*) district.

jurisprudencia [xurispruˈðenθja] *nf* jurisprudence.

jurista [xuˈrista] *nm/f* jurist.

justamente [xustaˈmente] *ad* justly, fairly; (*precisamente*) just, precisely, exactly

justicia [xusˈtiθja] *nf* justice; (*equidad*) fairness, justice; **justiciero, a** *a* just, righteous.

justificación [xustifikaˈθjon] *nf* justification; **justificar** *vt* to justify.

justo, a [ˈxusto] *a* (*equitativo*) just, fair, right; (*preciso*) exact, correct; (*ajustado*) tight // *ad* (*exactamente*) exactly, precisely

juvenil [xuβeˈnil] *a* youthful.

juventud [xuβenˈtuð] *nf* (*adolescencia*) youth; (*jóvenes*) young people *pl*.

juzgado [xuθˈɣaðo] *nm* tribunal; (*JUR*) court.

juzgar [xuθˈɣar] *vt* to judge; **a ~ por...** to judge by..., judging by... .

K

kg *abr de* **kilogramo**.

kilo [ˈkilo] *nm* kilo // *pref*: **~gramo** *nm* kilogramme; **~litro** *nm* kilolitre; **~metraje** *nm* distance in kilometres; **~métrico** *nm* kilometre; **~vatio** *nm* kilowatt.

kiosco [ˈkjosko] *nm* = **quiosco**.

km *abr de* **kilómetro**.

kv *abr de* **kilovatio**.

L

l *abr de* **litro**.

la [la] *det* the // *pron* her; (*Ud.*) you; (*cosa*) it // *nm* (*MUS*) la; **~ del sombrero rojo** the girl in the red hat.

laberinto [laβeˈrinto] *nm* labyrinth.

labia [ˈlaβja] *nf* fluency; (*pey*) glibness.

labial [laˈβjal] *a* labial; **lectura ~** lip-reading.

labio [ˈlaβjo] *nm* lip.

labor [laˈβor] *nf* labour; (*AGR*) farm work; (*tarea*) job, task; (*costura*) needlework; **~able** *a* workable; **día ~able** working day; **~ar** *vi* to work; **~eo** *nm* (*AGR*) cultivation; (*de minas*) working; **~ioso, a** *a* (*persona*) hard-working; (*trabajo*) tough; **~ista** *a*: **Partido L~ista** Labour Party.

labrado, a [laˈβraðo, a] *a* worked; (*cincelado*) carved; (*metal*) wrought // *nm* (*AGR*) cultivated field.

labrador, a [laβraˈðor, a] *a* farming // *nm/f* farmer.

labrantío, a [laβranˈtio, a] *a* arable.

labranza [laˈβranθa] *nf* (*AGR*) cultivation.

labrar [laˈβrar] *vt* (*gen*) to work; (*madera etc*) to carve; (*fig*) to cause.

labriego, a [laˈβrjeɣo, a] *nm/f* peasant.

laca [ˈlaka] *nf* lacquer.

lacayo [laˈkajo] *nm* lackey.

lacerar [laθeˈrar] *vt* to lacerate.

lacio, a [ˈlaθjo, a] *a* (*pelo*) lank; (*movimiento*) limp; (*BOT*) withered.

lacónico, a [laˈkoniko, a] *a* laconic.

lacrar [laˈkrar] *vt* (*MED*) to injure the health of; (*fig*) to harm; (*cerrar*) to seal (*with sealing wax*); **~se** *vr* to harm o.s.; **lacre** *nm* sealing wax.

lacrimoso, a [lakri'moso, a] *a* tearful.

lactar [lak'tar] *vt, vi* to suckle.

ladear [laðe'ar] *vt* to tip, tilt; (*ciudad, colina*) to skirt // *vi* to tilt; ~**se** *vr* to lean.

ladera [la'ðera] *nf* slope.

ladino, a [la'ðino, a] *a* cunning.

lado [la'ðo] *nm* (*gen*) side; (*fig*) protection; (*MIL*) flank; **al ~ de** beside; **poner de ~** to put on its side; **poner a un ~** to put aside; **por todos ~s** on all sides, all round.

ladrar [la'ðrar] *vi* to bark; **ladrido** *nm* bark, barking.

ladrillo [la'ðriʎo] *nm* (*gen*) brick; (*azulejo*) tile; (*color*) brick red.

ladrón, ona [la'ðron, ona] *nm/f* thief.

lagar [la'xar] *nm* (wine/oil) press.

lagarto [la'xarto] *nm* (*ZOOL*) lizard; (*fig: fam*) sharp customer; ~ **de Indias** alligator.

lago ['laxo] *nm* lake.

lágrima ['laxrima] *nf* tear; **lagrimar** *vi* to weep.

laguna [la'xuna] *nf* (*lago*) lagoon; (*hueco*) gap.

laico, a ['laiko, a] *a* lay.

lamentable [lamen'taβle] *a* lamentable, regrettable; (*miserable*) pitiful.

lamentar [lamen'tar] *vt* (*sentir*) to regret; (*deplorar*) to lament; ~**se** *vr* to lament; **lamento** *nm* lament.

lamer [la'mer] *vt* to lick.

lámina ['lamina] *nf* (*plancha delgada*) sheet; (*para estampar, estampa*) plate; **laminar** *vt* (*en libro*) to laminate.

lámpara ['lampara] *nf* lamp; ~ **de alcohol/gas** spirit/gas lamp; ~ **de bolsillo** torch; ~ **de pie** standard lamp.

lampiño [lam'piɲo] *a* clean-shaven.

lana ['lana] *nf* wool.

lance ['lanθe] *nm* (*golpe*) stroke; (*suceso*) event, incident; (*riña*) quarrel; (*tirada*) throw; **libros de ~** second-hand books.

lancha ['lantʃa] *nf* launch; ~ **automóvil** motorboat; ~ **de pesca** fishing boat; ~ **salvavidas/torpedera** lifeboat/torpedo boat; **lanchero** *nm* boatman.

lanero, a [la'nero, a] *a* woollen.

langosta [lan'gosta] *nf* (*insecto*) locust; (*crustáceo*) lobster; (*fig*) plague; **langostín, langostino** *nm* prawn.

languidecer [langiðe'θer] *vi* to languish; **languidez** *nf* languor; **lánguido, a** *a* (*gen*) languid; (*sin energía*) listless.

lanilla [la'niʎa] *nf* nap.

lanudo, a [la'nuðo, a] *a* woolly.

lanza ['lanθa] *nf* (*arma*) lance, spear; (*de vagón*) pole.

lanzadera [lanθa'ðera] *nf* shuttle.

lanzamiento [lanθa'mjento] *nm* (*gen*) throwing; (*NAUT, COM*) launch, launching; ~ **de pesos** putting the shot.

lanzar [lan'θar] *vt* (*gen*) to throw; (*DEPORTE*) to bowl; (*NAUT, COM*) to launch; (*JUR*) to evict; (*MED*) to vomit; ~**se** *vr* to throw o.s.

laña ['laɲa] *nf* clamp.

lapa ['lapa] *nf* limpet.

lapicero [lapi'θero] *nm* propelling pencil.

lápida ['lapiða] *nf* stone; ~ **mortuoria** headstone; ~ **conmemorativa** memorial stone; **lapidar** *vt* to stone; **lapidario, a** *a, nm* lapidary.

lápiz ['lapiθ] *nm* pencil; ~ **de color** coloured pencil; ~ **de labios** lipstick.

lapón, ona [la'pon, ona] *nm/f* Laplander, Lapp.

lapso ['lapso] *nm* (*de tiempo*) interval; (*error*) error.

largar [lar'xar] *vt* (*soltar*) to release; (*aflojar*) to loosen; (*lanzar*) to launch; (*fam*) to let fly; (*pelota*) to throw; (*velas*) to unfurl; (*AM*) to throw; ~**se** *vr* (*fam*) to beat it; (*NAUT*) to set sail; ~**se a** (*AM*) to start to.

largo, a ['larxo, a] *a* (*longitud*) long;

(*tiempo*) lengthy; (*persona: alta*) tall; (*fig*) generous // *nm* length; (*MUS*) largo // *ad* widely; **dos años ~s** two long years; **tiene 9 metros de ~** it is 9 metres long; **a lo ~ de** along.

largueza [lar'xeθa] *nf* generosity.

lárice ['lariθe] *nm* larch.

laringe [la'rinxe] *nf* larynx; **laringitis** *nf* laryngitis.

larva ['larβa] *nf* larva.

las [las] *det* the // *pron* them; **~ que** cantan the ones/women/girls who sing.

lascivo, a [las'θiβo, a] *a* lewd.

láser ['laser] *nm* laser.

lasitud [lasi'tuð] *nf* lassitude, weariness.

lástima ['lastima] *nf* (*pena*) pity; (*queja*) complaint; **dar ~** to be pitiful; **es ~ que** it's a pity that; **¡qué ~!** what a pity!; **ella está hecha una ~** she looks pitiful.

lastimar [lasti'mar] *vt* (*herir*) to wound; (*ofender*) to offend; (*compadecer*) to pity; **~se** *vr* to hurt o.s.; **~se de** to feel sorry for; **lastimero, a, lastimoso, a** *a* pitiful, pathetic.

lastre ['lastre] *nm* (*TEC, NAUT*) ballast; (*fig*) dead weight.

lata ['lata] *nf* (*metal*) tin; (*caja*) tin, can; (*fam*) nuisance; **hoja de ~** tin(plate); **en ~** tinned; **dar (la) ~** to be a nuisance.

latente [la'tente] *a* latent.

lateral [late'ral] *a* side, lateral // *nm* (*TEATRO*) wings.

latido [la'tiðo] *nm* (*del corazón*) beat; (*de perro*) yelp.

latifundio [lati'fundjo] *nm* large estate; **latifundista** *nm/f* owner of a large estate.

latigazo [lati'γaθo] *nm* (*golpe*) lash, (*sonido*) crack; (*fig: regaño*) sharp reproof; (*fam: bebida*) swig.

látigo ['latiγo] *nm* whip.

latín [la'tin] *nm* Latin.

latino, a [la'tino, a] *a* Latin;

~americano, a *a*, *nm/f* Latin-American.

latir [la'tir] *vi* (*corazón, pulso*) to beat; (*perro*) to yelp.

latitud [lati'tuð] *nf* (*GEO*) latitude; (*fig*) breadth.

lato, a ['lato, a] *a* broad.

latón [la'ton] *nm* brass.

latoso, a [la'toso, a] *a* (*cansado*) annoying; (*aburrido*) boring.

latrocinio [latro'θinjo] *nm* robbery.

laúd [la'uð] *nm* lute.

laudo ['lauðo] *nm* (*JUR*) decision.

laureado, a [laure'aðo, a] *a* honoured // *nm* laureate.

laurel [lau'rel] *nm* (*BOT*) laurel; (*CULIN*) bay.

lava ['laβa] *nf* lava.

lavabo [la'βaβo] *nm* washbasin.

lavadero [laβa'ðero] *nm* laundry.

lavado [la'βaðo] *nm* washing; (*de ropa*) laundry; (*ARTE*) wash; **~ de cerebro** brainwashing; **~ en seco** dry cleaning.

lavadora [laβa'ðora] *nf* washing machine.

lavamanos [laβa'manos] *nm inv* washbasin.

lavandería [laβande'ria] *nf* laundry; **~ automática** launderette.

lavaplatos [laβa'platos] *nm o f inv* dishwasher.

lavar [la'βar] *vt* to wash; (*borrar*) to wipe away; **~se** *vr* to wash o.s.; **~se las manos** to wash one's hands; **~ y marcar** (*pelo*) to shampoo and set; **~ en seco** to dry clean.

lavavajillas [laβaβa'xiλas] *nm inv* dishwasher.

laxante [lak'sante] *nm* laxative.

laya ['laja] *nf* spade; **de la misma ~** (*fig*) of the same sort.

lazada [la'θaða] *nf* bow.

lazo ['laθo] *nm* knot; (*lazada*) bow; (*para animales*) lasso; (*trampa*) snare; (*de camino*) hairpin bend; (*vínculo*) tie.

lb(s) *abr de* **libra(s)**.

le [le] *pron* (*directo*) him; (: *usted*)

you; (*indirecto*) to him; (: *usted*) to you.

leal [le'al] *a* loyal; ~**tad** *nf* loyalty.

lebrel [le'βrel] *nm* greyhound.

lección [lek'θjon] *nf* lesson.

lector, a [lek'tor, a] *nm/f* reader.

lectura [lek'tura] *nf* reading.

leche ['letʃe] *nf* milk; **tener mala** ~ to be nasty; ~ **condensada/en polvo** condensed/powdered milk; ~ **desnatada** skimmed milk; ~ **de magnesia** milk of magnesia; ~**ra** *nf* (*vendedora*) milkmaid; (*para hervir*) milk pan; (*para servir*) milkjug; (*AM*) cow; ~**ría** *nf* dairy.

lecho ['letʃo] *nm* (*cama*) bed; (*de río*) bottom; (*GEO*) layer.

lechón [le'tʃon] *nm* sucking pig.

lechoso, a [le'tʃoso, a] *a* milky.

lechuga [le'tʃuɣa] *nf* lettuce.

lechuza [le'tʃuθa] *nf* owl.

leer [le'er] *vt* to read.

legación [leɣa'θjon] *nf* legation.

legado [le'ɣaðo] *nm* (*don*) bequest; (*herencia*) legacy; (*enviado*) legate.

legajo [le'ɣaxo] *nm* file.

legal [le'ɣal] *a* (*gen*) legal; (*persona*) trustworthy; ~**idad** *nf* legality; ~**izar** *vt* to legalize; (*documento*) to authenticate.

légamo ['leɣamo] *nm* (*cieno*) mud, ooze.

legar [le'ɣar] *vt* to bequeath, leave; **legatario, a** *nm/f* legatee.

legión [le'ɣjon] *nf* legion; **legionario, a** *a* legionary // *nm* legionnaire.

legislación [lexisla'θjon] *nf* legislation; **legislar** *vt* to legislate.

legitimar [lexiti'mar] *vt* to legitimize; **legítimo, a** *a* (*genuino*) authentic; (*legal*) legitimate.

lego, a ['leɣo, a] *a* (*REL*) secular; (*ignorante*) ignorant // *nm* layman.

legua [le'ɣwa] *nf* league.

leguleyo [leɣu'lejo] *nm* (*pey*) petty lawyer.

legumbre [le'ɣumbre] *nf* vegetable.

leído, a [le'iðo, a] *a* well-read.

lejanía [lexa'nia] *nf* distance; **lejano, a** *a* far-off; (*en el tiempo*) distant; (*fig*) remote.

lejía [le'xia] *nf* bleach.

lejos ['lexos] *ad* far, far away; **a lo** ~ in the distance; **de o desde** ~ from afar; ~ **de** *prep* far from.

lelo, a ['lelo, a] *a* silly; (*fig*) openmouthed // *nm/f* idiot.

lema ['lema] *nm* motto; (*POL*) slogan.

lencería [lenθe'ria] *nf* drapery.

lengua ['lengwa] *nf* tongue; ~ **moderna** modern language; **morderse la** ~ to hold one's tongue.

lenguado [len'gwaðo] *nm* sole.

lenguaje [len'gwaxe] *nm* language.

lenguaraz [lengwa'raθ] *a* talkative; (*pey*) foul-mouthed.

lengüeta [len'gweta] *nf* (*ANAT*) epiglottis; (*de balanza, zapatos, MUS*) tongue; (*herramienta*) needle.

lenidad [leni'ðað] *nf* lenience.

lente ['lente] *nm o f* lens; (*lupa*) magnifying glass; ~**s** *npl* glasses; ~**s de contacto** contact lenses.

lenteja [len'texa] *nf* lentil; **lentejuela** *nf* sequin.

lentitud [lenti'tuð] *nf* slowness; **con** ~ slowly.

lento, a ['lento, a] *a* slow.

leña ['leɲa] *nf* firewood; ~**dor, a**, ~**tero, a** *nm/f* woodcutter.

leño ['leɲo] *nm* (*trozo de árbol*) log; (*madera*) timber; (*fig*) blockhead.

Leo ['leo] *nm* Leo.

león [le'on] *nm* lion; (*AM*) puma; ~ **marino** sea lion; **leonino, a** *a* leonine.

leontina [leon'tina] *nf* watch chain.

leopardo [leo'parðo] *nm* leopard.

lepra ['lepra] *nf* leprosy; **leproso, a** *nm/f* leper.

lerdo, a ['lerðo, a] *a* (*lento*) slow; (*patoso*) clumsy.

les [les] *pron* (*directo*) them; (: *ustedes*) you; (*indirecto*) to them; (: *ustedes*) to you.

lesbiana [les'βjana] *a, nf* lesbian.

lesión [le'sjon] *nf* (*daño*) lesion;

(fig) injury; **lesionado, a** *a* injured // *nm/f* injured person.

letal [le'tal] *a* lethal.

letanía [leta'nia] *nf* litany.

letargo [le'taɾɣo] *nm* (MED) lethargy.

letra ['letɾa] *nf* letter; *(escritura)* handwriting; *(MUS)* lyrics *pl*; **~ de cambio** bill of exchange; **~ de imprenta** print; **~do, a** *a* learned; *(fam)* pedantic // *nm* lawyer; **letrero** *nm* (cartel) sign; *(etiqueta)* label.

leva ['leβa] *nf* (NAUT) weighing anchor; (MIL) levy; (TEC) lever.

levadizo [leβa'ðiθo] *a*: **puente ~** drawbridge.

levadura [leβa'ðuɾa] *nf (para el pan)* yeast; *(de la cerveza)* brewer's yeast.

levantamiento [leβanta'mjento] *nm* raising, lifting; *(rebelión)* revolt, rising; **~ de pesos** weight-lifting.

levantar [leβan'taɾ] *vt* (gen) to raise; *(del suelo)* to pick up; *(hacia arriba)* to lift (up); *(plan)* to make, draw up; *(mesa)* to clear away; *(campamento)* to strike; *(fig)* to cheer up, hearten; **~se** *vr* to get up; *(enderezarse)* to straighten up; *(rebelarse)* to rebel; **~ el ánimo** to cheer up.

levante [le'βante] *nm* east coast, **el L~** the Near East, the Levant.

levar [le'βaɾ] *vt* to weigh anchor; **~se** *vr* to set sail.

leve ['leβe] *a* light; *(fig)* trivial; **~dad** *nf* lightness.

levita [le'βita] *nf* frock coat.

léxico ['leksiko] *nm* lexicon, dictionary.

ley [lei] *nf* (gen) law; *(fig)* loyalty; *(metal)* purity, law.

leyenda [le'jenda] *nf* legend.

leyó *etc vb ver* **leer.**

liar [li'aɾ] *vt* to tie (up); *(unir)* to bind; *(envolver)* to wrap (up); *(enredar)* to confuse; *(cigarrillo)* to roll; **~se** *vr (fam)* to get involved;

~se a palos to get involved in a fight.

Líbano ['liβano] *nm*: **el ~ the** Lebanon.

libar [li'βaɾ] *vt* to suck.

libelo [li'βelo] *nm* satire, lampoon; *(JUR)* petition.

libélula [li'βelula] *nf* dragonfly.

liberación [liβeɾa'θjon] *nf* liberation; *(de la cárcel)* release.

liberal [liβe'ɾal] *a*, *nm/f* liberal; **~idad** *nf* liberality; *(lujo)* lavishness.

liberar [liβe'ɾaɾ] *vt* to liberate.

libertad [liβeɾ'tað] *nf* liberty; *(soltura)* freedom; **~ de culto/de prensa/de comercio** freedom of worship/the press/of trade; **~ condicional** probation; **~ bajo palabra** parole; **~ bajo fianza** bail.

libertar [liβeɾ'taɾ] *vt (preso)* to set free; *(de una obligación)* to release; *(eximir)* to exempt.

libertino, a [liβeɾ'tino] *a* loose-living // *nm/f* libertine.

libra ['liβɾa] *nf* pound. **L~** (ASTRO) Libra; **~ esterlina** pound sterling.

librador, a [liβɾa'ðor, a] *nm/f* drawer.

libramiento [liβɾa'mjento] *nm* rescue; *(COM)* delivery.

libranza [li'βɾanθa] *nf* (COM) draft; *(de letra de cambio)* bill of exchange.

librar [li'βɾaɾ] *vt (de peligro)* to save; *(batalla)* to wage, fight; *(de impuestos)* to exempt; *(secreto)* to reveal; *(mercancías)* to draw; *(cheque)* to make out; *(JUR)* to exempt // *vi* to give birth; **~se** *vr*: **~se de** to escape from, free o.s. from.

libre ['liβɾe] *a* (gen) free; *(lugar)* unoccupied; *(asiento)* vacant; *(de impuestos)* tax-free; *(de deudas)* free of debt; **~ de franqueo** post-free; **tiro ~** free kick; **los 100 metros ~** 100 metres free-style (race); **al aire ~** in the open air.

librería [liβɾe'ɾia] *nf (biblioteca*

library; (*comercio*) bookshop; **librero, a** nm/f bookseller.

libreta [li'βreta] nf notebook; ~ **de ahorros** savings book; ~ **de banco** bank book.

libro ['liβro] nm book; ~ **en rústica/en pasta** o **encuadernado** paperback/hardback; ~ **de bolsillo** paperback; ~ **de caja** cashbook; ~ **de cheques** cheque book; ~ **de inventario** stock-list; ~ **de pedidos** order book; ~ **de texto** textbook.

Lic. *abr de* **licenciado, a.**

licencia [li'θenθja] nf (*gen*) licence; (*permiso*) permission; ~ **por enfermedad/con goce de sueldo** sick leave/paid leave; ~ **de caza/de conductor** game/driving licence; ~ **de derecho/de letras** law/arts degree; ~ **do, a** a licensed // nm/f graduate; **licenciar** vt (*empleado*) to dismiss; (*permitir*) to permit, allow; (*soldado*) to discharge; (*estudiante*) to confer a degree upon; **licenciarse** vr: **licenciarse en letras** to graduate in arts.

licencioso, a [liθen'θjoso, a] a licentious.

liceo [li'θeo] nm (high) school.

licitador [liθita'ðor] nm bidder; (*AM*) auctioneer; **licitar** vt to bid for; (*AM*) to sell by auction.

lícito, a ['liθito, a] a (*legal*) lawful; (*justo*) fair, just; (*permisible*) permissible.

licor [li'kor] nm spirits pl; (*preparado*) liqueur.

licuadora [likwa'ðora] nf food-mixer, liquidizer; **licuar** vt to liquidize.

lid [lið] nf combat; (*fig*) controversy.

líder ['liðer] nm/f leader; **liderato** nm leadership.

lidia ['liðja] nf bullfight; **toros de** ~ fighting bulls; **lidiar** vt, vi to fight.

liebre ['ljeβre] nf hare.

lienzo ['ljenθo] nm linen; (*ARTE*) canvas; (*pañuelo*) handkerchief; (*ARQ*) wall.

liga ['liɣa] nf (*de medias*) garter, suspender; (*confederación*) league; (*venda*) band; (*aleación*) alloy; (*BOT*) mistletoe.

ligadura [liɣa'ðura] nf bond, tie; (*MED, MUS*) ligature.

ligamento [liɣa'mento] nm (*ANAT*) ligament; (*atadura*) tie; (*unión*) bond.

ligar [li'ɣar] vt (*atar*) to tie; (*unir*) to join; (*MED*) to bind up; (*MUS*) to slur; (*metales*) to alloy // vi to mix, blend; (*fam*) to pick up; (*entenderse*) to get on (well); ~**se** vr to commit o.s.

ligereza [lixe'reθa] nf lightness; (*rapidez*) swiftness; (*agilidad*) agility; (*superficialidad*) flippancy.

ligero, a [li'xero, a] a (*de peso*) light; (*tela*) thin; (*rápido*) swift, quick; (*ágil*) agile, nimble; (*de importancia*) slight; (*de carácter*) flippant, superficial // ad: **a la** ~**a** superficially.

lija ['lixa] nf (*ZOOL*) dogfish; (*papel de*) ~ sandpaper.

lila ['lila] nf lilac // nm (*fam*) twit.

lima ['lima] nf file; (*BOT*) lime; ~ **de carpintero** file; ~ **de uñas** nail-file; **limar** vt to file.

limitación [limita'θjon] nf limitation, limit.

limitar [limi'tar] vt to limit; (*reducir*) to reduce, cut down // vi: ~ **con** to border on; ~**se** vr: ~**se a** to limit o.s. to.

límite ['limite] nm (*gen*) limit; (*fin*) end; (*frontera*) border; ~ **de velocidad** speed limit.

limítrofe [li'mitrofe] a bordering, neighbouring.

limón [li'mon] nm lemon // a: **amarillo** ~ lemon-yellow; **limonada** nf lemonade; **limonero** nm lemon tree.

limosna [li'mosna] nf alms pl; **vivir de** ~ to live on charity.

limpiabotas [limpja'βotas] nm inv bootblack, shoeshine boy/girl.

limpiaparabrisas [limpjapara-

'Brisas] nm inv windscreen wiper.

limpiar [lim'pjar] vt (gen) to clean; (con trapo) to wipe; (quitar) to wipe away; (zapatos) to shine, polish; (fig) to clean up.

limpieza [lim'pjeθa] nf (estado) cleanliness; (acto) cleaning; (: de las calles) cleansing; (: de zapatos) polishing; (habilidad) skill; (fig) clean-up; (pureza) purity; (MIL): **operación de ~** mopping-up operation; **~ en seco** dry cleaning.

limpio, a ['limpjo, a] a clean; (moralmente) pure; (COM) clear, net; (fam) honest // ad: **jugar ~** to play fair // nm: **pasar en ~** to make a fair copy.

linaje [li'naxe] nm lineage, family; linajudo, a a highborn.

linaza [li'naθa] nf linseed; **aceite de ~** linseed oil.

lince ['linθe] nm lynx.

linchar [lin'tʃar] vt to lynch.

lindante [lin'dante] a adjoining; **~ con** bordering on.

lindar [lin'dar] vi to adjoin; **~ con** to border on; **linde** nm o f boundary; **lindero, a** a adjoining // nm boundary.

lindo, a ['lindo, a] a pretty, lovely // ad (AM): **nos divertimos de lo ~** we had a marvellous time; **canta muy ~** he/she sings beautifully.

línea ['linea] nf (gen) line; **~ aérea** airline; **~ delantera** (DEPORTE) forward line; **~ de meta** goal line; (de carrera) finishing line; **~ de saque** service line, base line; **~ recta** straight line.

lingüista [lin'gwista] nm/f linguist.

liniento [li'njemento] nm liniment.

lino ['lino] nm linen; (BOT) flax.

linóleo [li'noleo] nm linoleum.

linterna [lin'terna] nf lantern, lamp; **~ eléctrica** o **de pilas** torch.

lío ['lio] nm bundle; (fam) fuss; (desorden) muddle; mess: **armar un ~** to make a fuss.

liquidación [likiða'θjon] nf

liquidation; **venta de ~** clearance sale.

liquidar [liki'ðar] vt (licuar) to liquidize; (eliminar) to liquidate; (mercaderías) to sell off; (pagar) to pay off; (terminar) to wind up; (AM) to ruin; **~se** vr to liquefy.

líquido, a ['likiðo, a] a liquid; (ganancia) net; (AM) accurate // nm liquid; **~ imponible** net taxable income.

lira ['lira] nf (MUS) lyre; (moneda) lira.

lirio ['lirjo] nm (BOT) iris.

Lisboa [lis'βoa] n Lisbon.

lisiado, a [li'sjaðo, a] a injured // nm/f cripple.

lisiar [li'sjar] vt to maim; **~se** vr to injure o.s.

liso, a ['liso, a] a (terreno) flat; (cabello) straight; (superficie) even; (tela) smooth.

lisonja [li'sonxa] nf flattery; **lisonjear** vt to flatter; (fig) to please; **lisonjero, a** a (gen) flattering; (agradable) gratifying, pleasing // nm/f flatterer.

lista ['lista] nf (gen) list; (de alumnos) school register; (de libros) catalogue; (de correos) poste restante; (de platos) menu; (de precios) price list; **pasar ~** to call the roll; **~ de espera** waiting list; **tela a ~s** striped material.

listado, a [lis'taðo, a] a striped.

listo, a ['listo, a] a (perspicaz) smart, clever; (preparado) ready.

listón [lis'ton] nm (tela) ribbon; (de madera, metal) strip.

litera [li'tera] nf (en barco, tren) berth; (en dormitorio) bunk, bunk bed.

literario, a [lite'rarjo, a] a literary.

literato, a [lite'rato, a] a literary // nm/f writer.

literatura [litera'tura] nf literature.

litigar [liti'ɣar] vt to fight // vi (JUR) to go to law; (fig) to dispute, argue.

litigio [li'tixjo] *nm* (JUR) lawsuit; (*fig*): **en ~ con** in dispute with.

litografía [litoɣra'fia] *nf* lithography; (*una ~*) lithograph.

litoral [lito'ral] *a* coastal // *nm* coast, seaboard.

litro ['litro] *nm* litre.

liviano, a [li'βjano, a] *a* (*persona*) fickle; (*cosa, objeto*) trivial.

lívido, a ['liβiðo, a] *a* livid; (AM) pale.

ll... *ver bajo la letra LL, después de L.*

lo [lo] *det neuter def art*; **~ bueno** the good // *pron* (*persona*) him; (*cosa*) it.

loa ['loa] *nf* praise; **loable** *a* praiseworthy; **loar** *vt* to praise.

lobato [lo'βato] *nm* wolf cub.

lobo ['loβo] *nm* wolf; **~ de mar** sea dog; **~ marino** seal.

lóbrego, a ['loβrexo, a] *a* dark; (*fig*) gloomy.

lóbulo ['loβulo] *nm* lobe.

locación [loka'θjon] *nf* lease.

local [lo'kal] *a* local // *nm* place, site; (*oficinas*) premises *pl*; **~idad** *nf* (*barrio*) locality; (*lugar*) location; (TEATRO) seat, ticket; **~izar** *vt* (*ubicar*) to locate, find; (*restringir*) to localize; (*situar*) to place.

loco, a ['loko, a] *a* mad // *nm/f* lunatic, mad person.

locomoción [lokomo'θjon] *nf* locomotion.

locomotora [lokomo'tora] *nf* engine.

locuaz [lo'kwaθ] *a* loquacious.

locución [loku'θjon] *nf* expression.

locura [lo'kura] *nf* madness; (*acto*) crazy act.

lodo ['loðo] *nm* mud; **~s** *nmpl* (MED) mudbath *sg*.

lógico, a ['loxiko, a] *a* logical // *nf* logic.

logística [lo'xistika] *nf* logistics *pl*.

lograr [lo'xrar] *vt* to achieve; (*obtener*) to get, obtain; **~ hacer** to manage to do; **~ que uno venga** to manage to get sb to come.

logro ['loxro] *nm* achievement,

success; **prestar a ~** to lend at a high rate of interest.

loma ['loma] *nf* hillock.

lombriz [lom'briθ] *nf* worm; **~ solitaria** tapeworm.

lomo ['lomo] *nm* (*de animal*) back; (*de cerdo*) pork loin; (*de vaca*) rib steak; (*de libro*) spine.

lona ['lona] *nf* canvas.

Londres ['londres] *n* London.

longaniza [longa'niθa] *nf* pork sausage.

longitud [lonxi'tuð] *nf* length; (GEO) longitude; **tener 3 metros de ~** to be 3 metres long; **~ de onda** wavelength.

lonja ['lonxa] *nf* slice; (*de jamón*) rasher; **~ de pescado** fish market.

lontananza [lonta'nanθa] *nf* background.

loor [lo'or] *nm* praise.

loro ['loro] *nm* parrot.

los [los] *det* the // *pron* them; (*ustedes*) you; **mis libros y ~ de Ud** my books and yours.

losa ['losa] *nf* stone; **~ sepulcral** gravestone.

lote ['lote] *nm* portion; (COM) lot.

lotería [lote'ria] *nf* lottery; (*juego*) lotto.

loza ['loθa] *nf* crockery.

lozanía [loθa'nia] *nf* (*lujo*) luxuriance; (*orgullo*) pride; **lozano, a** *a* luxuriant; (*animado*) lively; (*altanero*) haughty.

lubricante [luβri'kante] *nm* lubricant; **lubricar** *vt* to lubricate.

lucero [lu'θero] *nm* (ASTRO) bright star; (*fig*) brilliance.

lucidez [luθi'ðeθ] *nf* lucidity; **lúcido, a** *a* lucid.

luciente [lu'θjente] *a* shining.

luciérnaga [lu'θjernaxa] *nf* glowworm.

lucimiento [luθi'mjento] *nm* (*brillo*) brilliance; (*éxito*) success.

lucir [lu'θir] *vt* to illuminate, light (up); (*fig*) to show off // *vi* (*brillar*) to shine; (*tener éxito*) to be successful; **~se** *vr* to dress up.

lucrarse [lu'krarse] *vr* to enrich o.s.

lucro ['lukro] *nm* profit, gain.

luctuoso, a [luk'twoso, a] *a* mournful.

lucha ['lutʃa] *nf* fight, struggle; ~ **de clases** class struggle; ~ **libre** wrestling; **luchar** *vi* to fight.

ludibrio [lu'ðiβrjo] *nm* mockery.

luego ['lweɣo] *ad* (*después*) next; (*más tarde*) later, afterwards; (*pronto*) soon; **desde** ~ of course; **tan** ~ **como** as soon as.

lugar [lu'ɣar] *nm* place; (*sitio*) spot; **en** ~ **de** instead of; **hacer** ~ to make room; **fuera de** ~ out of place; **tener** ~ to take place; ~ **común** commonplace.

lugareño, a [luɣa'reɲo, a] *a* village *cpd* // *nm/f* villager.

lúgubre ['luɣuβre] *a* mournful.

lujo ['luxo] *nm* luxury; (*fig*) profusion, abundance; ~**so, a** *a* luxurious.

lujuria [lu'xurja] *nf* lust; (*fig*) lewdness.

lumbre ['lumbre] *nf* (*gen*) light.

lumbrera [lum'brera] *nf* luminary; (*en techo*) skylight; (*de barco*) vent, port.

luminoso, a [lumi'noso, a] *a* luminous, shining.

luna ['luna] *nf* moon; (*de un espejo*) glass; (*de gafas*) lens; (*fig*) crescent; ~ **llena/nueva** full/new moon; **estar con** ~ to have one's head in the clouds.

lunar [lu'nar] *a* lunar // (*ANAT*) mole; **tela a** ~**es** spotted material.

lunes ['lunes] *nm inv* Monday.

lupa ['lupa] *nf* magnifying glass.

lustrar [lus'trar] *vt* (*mueble*) to polish; (*zapatos*) to shine; ~ *nm* polish; (*fig*) lustre; **dar lustre a** to polish; **lustroso, a** *a* shining.

luterano, a [lute'rano, a] *a* Lutheran.

luto ['luto] *nm* mourning; (*congoja*) grief, sorrow; ~**s** *nmpl* mourning.

clothes; **llevar el** *o* **vestirse de** ~ to be in mourning.

Luxemburgo [luksem'burxo] *nm* Luxembourg.

luz [luθ] (*pl* **luces**) *nf* light; **dar a** ~ **un niño** to give birth to a child; **sacar a** ~ to bring to light; (*ELEC*): **dar** ~ to switch on the light; **prender/apagar la** ~ to put the light on/off; **a todas luces** by any reckoning; **hacer la** ~ **sobre** to shed light on; **tener pocas luces** to be dim *o* stupid; ~ **roja/verde** red/green light; (*AUTO*): ~ **de costado** sidelight; ~ **de freno** brake light; ~ **del relámpago** flashlight; **luces de tráfico** traffic light's; **traje de luces** bullfighter's costume.

LL

llaga ['ʎaɣa] *nf* wound.

llama ['ʎama] *nf* flame; (*zool*) llama.

llamada [ʎa'maða] *nf* call; ~ **al orden** call to order; **toque de** ~ (*MIL*) call-up; **a pie de página** reference note.

llamamiento [ʎama'mjento] *nm* call.

llamar [ʎa'mar] *vt* to call; (*atención*) to attract // *vi* (*por teléfono*) to telephone; (*a la puerta*) to knock/ring; (*por señas*) to beckon; (*MIL*) to call up; ~**se** *vr* to be called, be named; **¿cómo se llama Usted?** what's your name?

llamarada [ʎama'raða] *nf* (*llamas*) blaze; (*rubor*) flush; (*fig*) flare-up.

llamativo, a [ʎama'tiβo, a] *a* (*color*) loud.

llamear [ʎame'ar] *vi* to blaze.

llaneza [ʎa'neθa] *nf* (*gen*) simplicity; (*honestidad*) straightforwardness, frankness.

llano, a ['ʎano, a] *a* (*superficie*) flat;

(*persona*) straightforward; (*estilo*) clear // *nm* plain, flat ground.

llanta ['ʎanta] *nf* (wheel) rim; (AM): ~ **de goma** tyre.

llanto ['ʎanto] *nm* weeping.

llanura [ʎa'nura] *nf* plain.

llave ['ʎaβe] *nf* key; (*del agua*) tap; (MECÁNICA) spanner; (*de la luz*) switch; (MUS) key; ~ **inglesa** monkey wrench; ~ **de contacto** (AUTO) ignition key; **echar** ~ **a** to lock up; ~**ro** *nm* keyring; **llavín** *nm* latchkey.

llegada [ʎe'xaða] *nf* arrival.

llegar [ʎe'xar] *vi* to arrive; (*alcanzar*) to reach; (*bastar*) to be enough; ~**se** *vr*: ~**se a** to approach; ~ **a** to manage to, succeed in; ~ **a ser** to become; ~ **a las manos de** to come into the hands of.

llenar [ʎe'nar] *vt* (*gen*) to fill; (*espacio*) to cover; (*formulario*) to fill in *or* up; (*deber*) to fulfil; (*fig*) to heap.

lleno, a ['ʎeno, a] *a* full, filled; (*repleto*) full up // *nm* (*abundancia*) abundance; (ASTRO) full moon; (TEATRO) full house; **dar de** ~ **contra un muro** to hit a wall head-on.

llevadero, a [ʎeβa'ðero, a] *a* bearable, tolerable.

llevar [ʎe'βar] *vt* (*gen*) to take; (*ropa*) to wear; (*cargar*) to carry; (*quitar*) to take away; (*conducir a alguien*) to drive; (*cargar hacia*) to transport; (*traer: dinero*) to carry; (*conducir*) to lead; (MAT) to carry; ~**se** *vr* to carry off, take away; **llevamos dos días aquí** we have been here for two days; **él me lleva 2 años** he's 2 years older than me; (COM): ~ **los libros** to keep the books; ~**se bien** to get on well (together).

llorar [ʎo'rar] *vt, vi* to weep; ~ **de risa** to cry with laughter.

lloriquear [ʎorike'ar] *vi* to snivel, whimper.

lloro ['ʎoro] *nm* weeping; **llorón,**

ona *a* tearful // *nm/f* cry-baby; ~**so, a** *a* (*gen*) weeping, tearful; (*triste*) sad, sorrowful.

llover [ʎo'βer] *vi* to rain; ~**se** *vr* (*techo*) to leak.

llovizna [ʎo'βiθna] *nf* drizzle; **lloviznar** *vi* to drizzle.

llueve *etc vb ver* **llover.**

lluvia ['ʎuβja] *nf* rain; ~ **radioactiva** radioactive fallout; **lluvioso, a** *a* rainy.

M

m *abr de* **metro; minuto.**

macarrones [maka'rrones] *nmpl* macaroni *sg*.

macerar [maθe'rar] *vt* to macerate; (*fig*) to mortify; ~**se** *vr* to mortify o.s.

maceta [ma'θeta] *nf* (*de flores*) pot of flowers; (*para plantas*) flowerpot; (*mazo pequeño*) mallet.

macilento, a [maθi'lento, a] *a* wan; (*ojeroso*) haggard.

macis ['maθis] *nf* mace.

macizo, a [ma'θiθo, a] *a* massive; (*puerta*) solid // *nm* mass, chunk; (*de edificios*) block; (AUTO) solid tyre.

mácula ['makula] *nf* stain, blemish; (ANAT) blind spot.

machacar [matʃa'kar] *vt* to crush, pound // *vi* to go on, keep on.

machamartillo [matʃamar'tiʎo]: **a** ~ *ad*: **cumplir a** ~ to carry out a task to the letter; **eran cristianos a** ~ they were totally convinced Christians.

machete [ma'tʃete] *nm* (AM) machete, (large) knife.

macho ['matʃo] *a* male; (*fig*) virile // *nm* male; (*fig*) he-man.

machucar [matʃu'kar] *vt* to pound.

madeja [ma'ðexa] *nf* (*de lana*) skein, hank; (*de pelo*) mop.

madera [ma'ðera] *nf* wood; (*fig*)

nature, character; **una ~** a piece of wood.

madero [ma'ðero] *nm* beam; (*fig*) ship.

madrastra [ma'ðrastra] *nf* stepmother.

madre ['maðre] *a* mother *cpd*; (*AM*) tremendous // *nf* mother; (*ANAT*) womb; (*AGR*) main channel; (*de vino etc*) dregs *pl*; (*de río*) bed; **~ política/soltera** mother-in-law/unmarried mother.

madreperla [maðre'perla] *nf* mother-of-pearl.

madreselva [maðre'selβa] *nf* honeysuckle.

madriguera [maðri'vera] *nf* burrow.

madrileño, a [maðri'leno, a] *a* of or from Madrid // *nm/f* native of Madrid.

madrina [ma'ðrina] *nf* (*protectora*) godmother; (*ARQ*) prop, shore; (*TEC*) brace; **~ de boda** bridesmaid.

madrugada [maðru'xaða] *nf* early morning; (*alba*) dawn, daybreak; **madrugador, a** *a* early-rising; **madrugar** *vi* to get up early; (*fig*) to get ahead.

madurar [maðu'rar] *vt*, *vi* (*fruta*) to ripen; (*fig*) to mature; **madurez** *nf* ripeness; maturity; **maduro, a** *a* ripe; mature.

maestra [ma'estra] *nf* ver **maestro**.

maestría [maes'tria] *nf* mastery; (*habilidad*) skill, expertise.

maestro, a [ma'estro, a] *a* (*perito*) skilled, expert; (*principal*) main; (*educado*) trained // *nm/f* master/mistress; (*que enseña*) teacher // *nm* (*autoridad*) authority; (*MUS*) maestro; (*AM*) skilled workman; **obra ~a** masterpiece; **~ albañil** master mason.

magia ['maxia] *nf* magic; **mágico, a** *a* magic(al) // *nm/f* magician.

magisterio [maxis'terjo] *nm* (*enseñanza*) teaching; (*profesión*)

teaching profession; (*maestros*) teachers *pl*.

magistrado [maxis'traðo] *nm* magistrate.

magistral [maxis'tral] *a* magisterial; (*fig*) masterly.

magnánimo, a [mav'nanimo, a] *a* magnanimous.

magnate [mav'nate] *nm* magnate, tycoon.

magnético, a [mav'netiko, a] *a* magnetic; **magnetizar** *vt* to magnetize.

magnetófon [mavne'tofon], **magnetófono** [mavne'tofono] *nm* tape recorder; **magnetofónico, a** *a*: **cinta magnetofónica** recording tape.

magnífico, a [mav'nifiko, a] *a* splendid, magnificent, wonderful.

magnitud [mavni'tuð] *nf* magnitude.

mago, a ['mayo, a] *nm/f* magician; **los Reyes M~s** the Magi, the Three Wise Men.

magro, a ['mayro, a] *a* (*persona*) thin, lean; (*carne*) lean.

magullar [mayu'ʎar] *vt* (*amoratar*) to bruise; (*dañar*) to damage; (*fam: golpear*) to bash, beat.

mahometano, a [maome'tano, a] *a* Mohammedan.

maíz [ma'iθ] *nm* maize, sweet corn.

majada [ma'xaða] *nf* (*abrigo*) sheepfold; (*abono*) dung.

majadero, a [maxa'ðero, a] *a* silly, stupid // *nm* (*TEC*) pestle; (*canilla*) bobbin.

majar [ma'xar] *vt* to crush, grind; (*fig*) to bother, pester.

majestad [maxes'tað] *nf* majesty; **majestuoso, a** *a* majestic.

majo, a ['maxo, a] *a* nice; (*guapo*) attractive, good-looking; (*lujoso*) smart.

mal [mal] *ad* badly; (*equivoca-damente*) wrongly; (*con dificultad*) with difficulty // *a* = **malo** // *nm* evil; (*desgracia*) misfortune; (*daño*) harm, hurt; (*MED*) illness; ¡**menos** ~! just as well!; ~ **que bien** rightly or wrongly.

malabarismo [malaβa'rismo] *nm* juggling; **malabarista** *nm/f* juggler.

malaconsejado, a [malakonse-'xaðo, a] *a* ill-advised.

malagueño, a [mala'xeɲo, a] *a* of or from Málaga.

malaria [ma'larja] *nf* malaria.

malbaratar [malβara'tar] *vt* (*malgastar*) to squander; (*malvender*) to sell off cheap.

malcontento, a [malkon'tento, a] *a* discontented.

malcriado, a [mal'krjaðo, a] *a* (*grosero*) rude, bad-mannered; (*consentido*) spoiled.

maldad [mal'dað] *nf* evil, wickedness.

maldecir [malde'θir] *vt* to curse // *vi*: ~ **de** to speak ill of.

maldición [maldi'θjon] *nf* curse.

maldito, a [mal'dito, a] *pp* de **maldecir** // *a* (*condenado*) damned; (*perverso*) wicked // *nf*: **soltar la** ~ **a** to talk too much.

maleante [male'ante] *a* wicked // *nm/f* malefactor; **malear** *vt* to spoil; (*fig*) to corrupt.

malecón [male'kon] *nm* pier, jetty.

maledicencia [maleði'θenθja] *nf* slander, scandal.

maleficiar [malefi'θjar] *vt* to harm, damage; (*hechizar*) to bewitch; **maleficio** *nm* curse, spell.

malestar [males'tar] *nm* (*gen*) discomfort; (*fig*) uneasiness; (*POL*) unrest.

maleta [ma'leta] *nf* case, suitcase; (*AUTO*) boot; **maletín** *nm* small case, bag.

malevolencia [maleβo'lenθja] *nf* malice, spite; **malévolo, a** *a* malicious, spiteful.

maleza [ma'leθa] *nf* (*hierbas malas*) weeds *pl*; (*arbustos*) thicket.

malgastar [malxas'tar] *vt* (*tiempo, dinero*) to waste; (*salud*) to ruin.

malhechor, a [male'tʃor, a] *nm/f*

malefactor; (*criminal*) criminal.

malicia [ma'liθja] *nf* (*maldad*) wickedness; (*astucia*) slyness, guile; (*mala intención*) malice, spite; (*carácter travieso*) mischievousness; ~**s** *nfpl* suspicions; **malicioso, a** *a* wicked, evil; sly, crafty; malicious, spiteful; mischievous.

malignidad [malixni'ðað] *nf* (*MED*) malignancy; (*malicia*) malice.

maligno, a [ma'lixno, a] *a* evil; (*malévolo*) malicious; (*MED*) malignant.

malo, a ['malo, a] *a* bad; (*falso*) false // *nm/f* villain // *nf* spell of bad luck; **estar** ~ to be ill; **estar de** ~ as to be in a bad mood.

malograr [malo'xrar] *vt* to spoil; (*plan*) to upset; (*tiempo, ocasión*) to waste; ~**se** *vr* (*plan etc*) to fail, come to grief; (*persona*) to die before one's time; **malogro** *nm* (*fracaso*) failure; (*pérdida*) waste; (*muerte*) early death.

malparado, a [malpa'raðo, a] *a*: **salir** ~ to come off badly.

malparir [malpa'rir] *vi* to have a miscarriage.

malquistar [malkis'tar] *vt* to estrange, cause a rift with/between.

malsano, a [mal'sano, a] *a* unhealthy.

Malta ['malta] *nf* Malta.

maltratar [maltra'tar] *vt* to ill-treat; **maltrato** *nm* ill-treatment; (*ofensa*) abuse, insults *pl*.

maltrecho, a [mal'tretʃo, a] *a* battered, damaged.

malvado, a [mal'βaðo, a] *a* evil, villainous.

malvavisco [malβa'βisko] *nm* marshmallow.

malversar [malβer'sar] *vt* to embezzle, misappropriate.

Malvinas [mal'βinas]: **Islas** ~ *nfpl* Falkland Islands.

malla ['maʎa] *nf* mesh; (*de baño*) bathing costume; ~**s** *nfpl* tights; ~ **de alambre** wire mesh; **hacer** ~ to knit.

Mallorca [ma'ʎorka] nf Majorca.

mama ['mama] nf (de animal) teat; (de persona) breast.

mamá [ma'ma] (pl ~s) nf (fam) mum, mummy.

mamar [ma'mar] vt (pecho) to suck; (fig) to absorb, assimilate // vi to suck

mamarracho [mama'rratʃo] nm sight, mess.

mampara [mam'para] nf (entre habitaciones) partition; (biombo) screen.

mampostería [mamposte'ria] nf masonry.

mampuesto [mam'pwesto] nm (piedra) rough stone; (muro) wall, parapet; de ~ spare, emergency.

mamut [ma'mut] nm mammoth.

manada [ma'naða] nf (rebaño) herd; (de ovejas) flock; (de lobos) pack.

manantial [manan'tjal] nm spring; (fuente) fountain; (fig) source.

manar [ma'nar] vt to run with, flow with // vi to run, flow; (abundar) to abound.

mancebo [man'θeβo] nm (joven) young man, (soltero) bachelor; (dependiente) assistant.

mancilla [man'θiʎa] nf stain, blemish.

manco, a ['manko, a] a one-armed, one-handed; (fig) defective, faulty.

mancomún [manko'mun]: de ~ ad jointly, together; **mancomunar** vt to unite, bring together; (recursos) to pool; (JUR) to make jointly responsible; **mancomunarse** vr to unite, merge; **mancomunidad** nf union, association; (POL) commonwealth; (JUR) joint responsibility.

mancha ['mantʃa] nf spot, mark; (boceto) sketch, outline, **manchar** vt (gen) to stain, mark; (ensuciar) to soil, dirty.

manchego, a [man'tʃexo, a] a of or from La Mancha.

mandadero [manda'ðero] nm messenger; (niño) errand boy.

mandado [man'daðo] nm (orden) order; (comisión) commission, errand.

mandamiento [manda'mjento] nm (orden) order, command; (REL) commandment; ~ judicial warrant.

mandar [man'dar] vt (ordenar) to order; (dirigir) to lead, command; (enviar) to send; (pedir) to order, ask for // vi to be in charge, (pey) to be bossy; ~se vr (MED) to get about by o.s.; ¿mande? pardon?; ~ hacer un traje to have a suit made; ~se cambiar to go away, leave.

mandarín [manda'rin] nm mandarin // nf tangerine, mandarin.

mandatario, a [manda'tarjo, a] nm/f (representante) agent; (AM) leader.

mandato [man'dato] nm (orden) order; (POL) term of office; (: territorio) mandate; ~ judicial (search) warrant.

mandíbula [man'diβula] nf jaw.

mandil [man'dil] nm (delantal) apron; (vestido) pinafore dress.

mando ['mando] nm (MIL) command; (de país) rule; (el primer lugar) lead; (POL) term of office; (TEC) control; ~ a la izquierda left-hand drive; ~ remoto remote control.

mandolina [mando'lina] nf mandolin(e).

mandón, ona [man'don, ona] a bossy, domineering.

manea [ma'nea] nf hobble.

manejable [mane'xaβle] a manageable.

manejar [mane'xar] vt (gen) to manage; (máquina) to work, operate; (idioma, caballo etc) to handle; (casa) to run, manage; (AM) to drive; ~se vr (comportarse) to behave; (arreglárselas) to manage; (MED) to get about unaided; **manejo** nm management; handling; running; driving; (MED) de trato) ease, confidence; **manejos** nmpl intrigues.

manera [ma'nera] nf way, manner, fashion; ~s nfpl manners; ~ de ser way of life; (aire) manner; de ninguna ~ no way, by no means; de otra ~ otherwise; de todas ~s at any rate; no hay ~ de persuadirle there's no way of convincing him.

manga ['manga] nf (de camisa) sleeve; (de riego) hose; (tromba) downpour; (filtro) filter; (NAUT) beam.

mangana [man'gana] nf lasso.

mango ['mango] nm handle; (BOT) mango.

mangonear [mangone'ar] vt to manage, boss about // vi (meterse) to meddle, interfere; (ser mandón) to boss people about.

manguera [man'gera] nf (de riego) hose; (tubo) pipe.

maní [ma'ni] nm (AM) peanut.

manía [ma'nia] nf (MED) mania; (capricho) rage, craze; (disgusto) dislike; (malicia) spite; maníaco, a a maniac(al) // nm/f maniac.

maniatar [manja'tar] vt to tie the hands of.

maniático, a [ma'njatiko, a] a maniac(al) // nm/f maniac.

manicomio [mani'komjo] nm asylum, mental hospital.

manifestación [manifesta'θjon] nf (declaración) statement, declaration; (demostración) show, manifestation; (POL) demonstration.

manifestar [manifes'tar] vt to show, manifest; (declarar) to state, declare; manifiesto, a a clear, manifest // nm manifesto.

manija [ma'nixa] nf handle.

manilla [ma'niʎa] nf: ~s de hierro handcuffs.

maniobra [ma'njoβra] nf manœuvring; (manejo) handling; (fig) manœuvre; (estratagema) stratagem; ~s nfpl manœuvres; maniobrar vt to manœuvre; (manejar) to handle.

manipulación [manipula'θjon] nf manipulation; **manipular** vt to

manipulate; (manejar) to handle.

maniquí [mani'ki] nm dummy // nf model.

manirroto, a [mani'rroto, a] a lavish, extravagant // nm/f spendthrift.

manivela [mani'βela] nf crank.

manjar [man'xar] nm (tasty) dish; ~ blanco blancmange.

mano ['mano] nf hand; (ZOOL) foot, paw; (de pintura) coat; (serie) lot, series; a ~ by hand; a la ~ on hand, within reach; a ~ derecha/izquierda on the right(-hand side)/left(-hand side); de primera ~ (at) first hand; de segunda ~ (at) second hand; robo a ~ armada armed robbery; de obra labour, manpower; estrechar la ~ a uno to shake sb's hand.

manojo [ma'noxo] nm handful, bunch; ~ de llaves bunch of keys.

manoseado, a [manose'aðo, a] a well-worn; manosear vt (tocar) to handle, touch; (desordenar) to mess up, rumple; (insistir en) to overwork; (AM) to caress, fondle.

manotazo [mano'taθo] nm slap, smack.

mansalva [man'salβa]: a ~ ad without rest, without any danger.

mansedumbre [manse'ðumbre] nf gentleness, meekness.

mansión [man'sjon] nf mansion.

manso, a ['manso, a] a gentle, mild, meek; (animal) tame.

manta ['manta] nf blanket; (abrigo) shawl.

manteca [man'teka] nf fat; ~ de cacahuete/cacao peanut/cocoa butter; ~ de cerdo lard.

mantecado [mante'kaðo] nm icecream.

mantel [man'tel] nm tablecloth.

mantener [mante'ner] vt (gen) to support, maintain; (alimentar) to sustain; (conservar) to keep; (TEC) to maintain, service; ~se vr (seguir de pie) to be still standing; (no ceder) to hold one's ground;

(*subsistir*) to sustain o.s., keep going; **mantenimiento** *nm* maintenance; sustenance; (*sustento*) support.

mantequera [mante'kera] *nf* (*para hacer*) churn; (*para servir*) butter dish.

mantequilla [mante'kiʎa] *nf* butter.

mantilla [man'tiʎa] *nf* mantilla; ~**s** *nfpl* baby clothes.

manto ['manto] *nm* (*capa*) cloak; (*chal*) shawl; (*de ceremonia*) robe, gown.

mantón [man'ton] *nm* shawl.

manual [ma'nwal] *a* manual // *nm* manual, handbook.

manufactura [manufak'tura] *nf* manufacture; (*fábrica*) factory.

manuscrito, a [manus'krito, a] *a* handwritten // *nm* manuscript.

manutención [manuten'θjon] *nf* maintenance; (*sustento*) support.

manzana [man'θana] *nf* apple; (*ARQ*) block.

manzanilla [manθa'niʎa] *nf* (*planta*) camomile; (*infusión*) camomile tea; (*vino*) manzanilla.

manzano [man'θano] *nm* apple tree.

maña ['maɲa] *nf* (*gen*) skill, dexterity; (*pey*) guile; (*costumbre*) habit; (*una ~*) trick, knack.

mañana [ma'ɲana] *ad* tomorrow // *nm* future // *nf* morning; **de o por la** ~ **in the morning; ¡hasta ~!** see you tomorrow!; ~ **por la** ~ tomorrow morning; **mañanero, a** *a* early-rising.

mañoso, a [ma'ɲoso, a] *a* (*hábil*) skilful; (*astuto*) smart, clever.

mapa ['mapa] *nm* map.

maque ['make] *nm* lacquer.

maqueta [ma'keta] *nf* (*scale*) model.

maquillaje [maki'ʎaxe] *nm* make-up; (*acto*) making up; **maquillar** *vt* to make up; **maquillarse** *vr* to put on (some) make-up.

máquina ['makina] *nf* machine; (*de tren*) locomotive, engine;

(*cámara*) camera; (*fig*) machinery; (*: proyecto*) plan, project; **escrito a** ~ typewritten; ~ **de afeitar** (safety) razor; ~ **de escribir** typewriter; ~ **de coser/lavar** sewing/washing machine.

maquinación [makina'θjon] *nf* machination, scheme, plot.

maquinal [maki'nal] *a* (*fig*) mechanical, automatic.

maquinaria [maki'narja] *nf* (*máquinas*) machinery; (*mecanismo*) mechanism, works *pl*.

maquinista [maki'nista] *nm* (*de tren*) engine driver; (*TEC*) operator; (*NAUT*) engineer.

mar [mar] *nm o f* sea; (*marea*) tide; ~ **adentro o afuera** out at sea; **en alta** ~ **on the high seas; la** ~ **de** (*fam*) lots of; **el M**~ **Negro/Báltico** the Black/Baltic Sea.

maraña [ma'raɲa] *nf* (*maleza*) thicket; (*confusión*) tangle.

maravilla [mara'βiʎa] *nf* marvel, wonder; (*BOT*) marigold; **maravillar** *vt* to astonish, amaze; **maravillarse** *vr* to be astonished, be amazed; **maravilloso, a** *a* wonderful, marvellous.

marca ['marka] *nf* (*gen*) mark; (*sello*) stamp; (*COM*) make, brand; **de** ~ excellent, outstanding; ~ **de fábrica** trademark.

marcado, a [mar'kaðo, a] *a* marked, strong.

marcar [mar'kar] *vt* (*gen*) to mark; (*número de teléfono*) to dial; (*gol*) to score; (*números*) to record, keep a tally of; (*el pelo*) to set; (*fig*) to indicate, point to // *vi* (*DEPORTE*) to score; (*TELEC*) to dial; ~**se** *vr* (*NAUT*) to take one's bearings; (*fig*) to make one's mark, stand out.

marcial [mar'θjal] *a* martial, military.

marciano, a [mar'θjano, a] *a* Martian.

marco ['marko] *nm* frame; (*DEPORTE*) goal-posts *pl*; (*moneda*) mark; (fig) framework; ~ de chimenea mantelpiece.

marcha [mar'tʃa] nf march; (TEC) running, working; (AUTO) gear; (velocidad) speed; (fig) progress; (dirección) course; **poner en** ~ to put into gear; **dar** ~ **atrás** to reverse, put into reverse; **estar en** ~ to be under way, be in motion.

marchante, a [mar'tʃante, a] nm/f dealer, merchant; (AM: cliente) client, customer; (: buhonero) pedlar.

marchar [mar'tʃar] vi to go; (funcionar) to work, go; ~**se** vr to go (away), leave.

marchitar [martʃi'tar] vt to wither, dry up; ~**se** vr (BOT) to wither; (fig) to go into a decline; (persona) to fade away.

marchito, a a withered, faded; (fig) in decline.

marea [ma'rea] nf tide; (llovizna) drizzle.

marear [mare'ar] vt (NAUT) to sail, navigate; (fig) to annoy, upset; (MED): ~ **a uno** to make sb feel sick; ~**se** vr (tener náuseas) to feel/be sick; (desvanecerse) to feel faint; (aturdirse) to feel dizzy; (fam: emborracharse) to get a bit drunk.

maremoto [mare'moto] nm tidal wave.

mareo [ma'reo] nm (náusea) sick feeling; (aturdimiento) dizziness; (fam: lata) nuisance.

marfil [mar'fil] nm ivory.

margarina [marxa'rina] nf margarine.

margarita [marxa'rita] nf (BOT) daisy; (perla) pearl.

margen ['marxen] nm (borde) edge, border; (fig) margin, space // nf bank; **dar** ~ **para** to give an opportunity for; **mantenerse al** ~ to keep out (of things).

marica [ma'rika] nm magpie; (fam) sissy.

maricón [mari'kon] nm (fam) queer (fam).

marido [ma'riðo] nm husband.

marijuana [mari'xwana] nf marijuana, cannabis.

marina [ma'rina] nf navy; ~ **mercante** merchant navy.

marinero, a [mari'nero, a] a sea cpd; (barco) seaworthy // nm sailor, seaman.

marino, a [ma'rino, a] a sea cpd, marine // nm sailor.

marioneta [marjo'neta] nf puppet.

mariposa [mari'posa] nf butterfly.

mariscos [ma'riskos] nmpl shellfish, seafood sg.

marisma [ma'risma] nf marsh, swamp.

marítimo, a [ma'ritimo, a] a sea cpd, maritime.

marmita [mar'mita] nf pot.

mármol ['marmol] nm marble; **marmóreo, a** a marble.

marqués, esa [mar'kes, esa] nm/f marquis/marchioness.

marrar [ma'rrar] vi to miss.

marrón [ma'rron] a brown.

marroquí [marro'ki] a Moroccan // nm Morocco (leather).

Marruecos [ma'rrwekos] nm Morocco.

Marsellas [mar'seʎas] n Marseille.

martes ['martes] nm inv Tuesday.

martillar [marti'ʎar] vt to hammer.

martillo [mar'tiʎo] nm hammer; ~ **neumático** pneumatic drill; ~ **de orejas** claw-hammer.

mártir ['martir] nm/f martyr; **martirio** nm martyrdom; (fig) torture, torment.

marxismo [mark'sismo] nm Marxism; **marxista** a/nm/f Marxist.

marzo ['marθo] nm March.

mas [mas] conj but.

más [mas] a, ad more; (superlativo) most // conj and, plus; **es** ~ **de medianoche** it's after midnight; **el libro** ~ **leído del año** the most-read book of the year; **¡qué perro** ~ **feo!** what an ugly dog!; ~ **de, ~ de lo que, ~ que** more than; ~ **bien** rather; ~ **o menos** more or less.

masa ['masa] nf (mezcla) dough; (volumen) volume, mass; (Física) mass; (Elec) earth; **en ~ en masse**; **las ~s** the masses.

masacre [ma'sakre] nm massacre.

masaje [ma'saxe] nm massage.

mascar [mas'kar] vt to chew; (fig) to mumble, mutter.

máscara ['maskara] nf (gen) mask // nm/f masked person; **mascarada** nf masquerade.

masculino, a [masku'lino, a] a masculine; (Bio) male.

mascullar [masku'ʎar] vt to mumble, mutter.

masilla [ma'siʎa] nf putty.

masivo, a [ma'siβo, a] a (enorme) massive; (en masa) mass, en masse.

masón [ma'son] nm (free)mason.

masoquista [maso'kista] nm/f masochist.

masticar [masti'kar] vt to chew; (fig) to ponder.

mástil ['mastil] nm (de navío) mast; (de guitarra) neck; (sostén) post, support.

mastín [mas'tin] nm mastiff; **~ danés** Great Dane.

masturbación [masturβa'θjon] nf masturbation; **masturbarse** vr to masturbate.

mata ['mata] nf bush, shrub; (de hierbas) tuft; (campo) field; (AM) clump (of trees).

matadero [mata'ðero] nm slaughterhouse, abattoir.

matador, a [mata'ðor, a] a killing // nm/f killer // nm (Taur) matador, bullfighter.

matanza [ma'tanθa] nf (de personas) killing; (de animales) slaughter(ing).

matar [ma'tar] vt, vi to kill; **~se** vr (suicidarse) to kill o.s., commit suicide; (por otro) to be killed; **~ el hambre** to stave off hunger.

mate ['mate] a (sin brillo: color) dull // nm (en ajedrez) (check)mate; (AM: hierba) maté; (: vasija) gourd.

matemáticas [mate'matikas] nfpl mathematics; **matemático, a** a mathematical // nm/f mathematician.

materia [ma'terja] nf (gen) matter; (Tec) material; **en ~ de** on the subject of; **~ prima** raw material; **material** a material; (dolor) physical // nm material; (Tec) equipment; **materialismo** nm materialism; **materialista** a materialist(ic); **materialmente** ad materially; (fig) absolutely.

maternal [mater'nal] a motherly, maternal.

maternidad [materni'ðað] nf motherhood, maternity; **materno, a** a motherly, maternal; (lengua) mother cpd.

matinal [mati'nal] a morning cpd.

matiz [ma'tiθ] nm shade, **~ar** vt (dar tonos de) to tinge, tint; (variar) to vary; (Arte) to blend.

matón [ma'ton] nm bully.

matorral [mato'ral] nm thicket.

matraca [ma'traka] nf rattle.

matrícula [ma'trikula] nf (registro) register; (Auto) registration number; (: placa) licence plate; **matricular** vt to register, enrol.

matrimonial [matrimo'njal] a matrimonial.

matrimonio [matri'monjo] nm (boda) wedding; (pareja) (married) couple; (unión) marriage.

matriz [ma'triθ] nf womb; (Tec) mould; **casa ~** (Com) head office.

matrona [ma'trona] nf (persona de edad) matron; (partera) midwife.

matute [ma'tute] nm contraband.

maullar [mau'ʎar] vi to mew, miaow.

mausoleo [mauso'leo] nm mausoleum.

maxilar [maksi'lar] nm jaw(bone).

máxima ['maksima] ver **máximo**.

máxime ['maksime] ad especially.

máximo, a ['maksimo, a] a

maximum; (*más alto*) highest; (*más grande*) greatest // *nm* maximum // *nf* maxim.

mayo ['majo] *nm* May.

mayonesa [majo'nesa] *nf* mayonnaise.

mayor [ma'jor] *a* (*gen*) main, chief; (*adulto*) adult; (*de edad avanzada*) elderly; (*MUS*) major; (*comparativo: de tamaño*) bigger; (: *de edad*) older; (*superlativo: de tamaño*) biggest; (: *de edad*) oldest // *nm* chief, boss; **al por ~** wholesale; **~ de edad** adult; **~es** *nmpl* ancestors.

mayoral [majo'ral] *nm* foreman.

mayordomo [major'ðomo] *nm* (*criado*) butler; (*de hotel*) steward.

mayoría [majo'ria] *nf* majority, greater part.

mayorista [majo'rista] *nm/f* wholesaler.

mayúsculo, a [ma'juskulo, a] *a* (*fig*) big, tremendous // *nf* capital (letter).

mazapán [maθa'pan] *nm* marzipan.

mazo ['maθo] *nm* (*martillo*) mallet; (*de flores*) bunch; (*fig*) bore; (*DEPORTE*) bat; (*palo*) club.

me [me] *pron* (*directo*) me; (*indirecto*) (to) me; (*reflexivo*) (to) myself; **¡démelo!** give it to me!

mecánico, a [me'kaniko, a] *a* mechanical // *nm/f* mechanic // *nf* (*estudio*) mechanics *sg*; (*mecanismo*) mechanism.

mecanismo [meka'nismo] *nm* mechanism; (*marcha*) gear.

mecanografía [mekanoɣra'fia] *nf* typewriting; **mecanógrafo, a** *nm/f* typist.

mecedor, a [meθe'ðor, a] *a* rocking // *nm* (*columpio*) swing // *nf* rocking chair.

mecer [me'θer] *vt* (*cuna*) to rock; (*líquido*) to stir; **~se** *vr* to rock; (*ramo*) to sway.

mechero [me'tʃero] *nm* (*cigarette*) lighter.

mechón [me'tʃon] *nm* (*gen*) tuft;

(*manojo*) bundle; (*de pelo*) lock.

medalla [me'ðaʎa] *nf* medal.

media ['meðja] *nf ver* **medio**.

mediado, a [me'ðjaðo, a] *a* half-full; (*trabajo*) half-complete; **a ~s de** in the middle of, halfway through.

mediano, a [me'ðjano, a] *a* (*regular*) medium, average; (*mediocre*) mediocre; (*indiferente*) indifferent.

medianoche [meðja'notʃe] *nf* midnight.

mediante [me'ðjante] *ad* by (means of), through.

mediar [me'ðjar] *vi* (*llegar a la mitad*) to get to the middle, get halfway; (*estar en medio*) to be in the middle; (*interceder*) to mediate, intervene.

medicación [meðika'θjon] *nf* medication, treatment.

medicamento [meðika'mento] *nm* medicine, drug.

medicina [meði'θina] *nf* medicine.

medición [meði'θjon] *nf* measurement.

médico, a ['meðiko, a] *a* medical // *nm/f* doctor.

medida [me'ðiða] *nf* (*gen*) measure; (*medición*) measurement; (*prudencia*) moderation, prudence; **en cierta/gran ~** up to a point/to a great extent; **un traje a ~** a made-to-measure suit; **~ de cuello** collar size; **a ~ de** in proportion to; (*de acuerdo con*) in keeping with.

medio, a ['meðjo, a] *a* half (*a*); (*punto*) mid, middle; (*promedio*) average // *ad* half // *nm* (*centro*) middle, centre; (*promedio*) average; (*DEPORTE*) half-back; (*método*) means, way; (*ambiente*) environment // *nf* (*prenda de vestir*) stocking; (*promedio*) average; **~s** *nmpl* means, resources; **~ litro** half a litre; **las tres y ~a** half past three; **M~ Oriente** Middle East; **a ~ terminar** half finished; **pagar a ~as** to share the cost; **hacer ~a** to knit.

mediocre [me'ðjokre] a middling, average; (pey) mediocre.

mediodía [meðjo'ðia] nm midday, noon.

medir [me'ðir] vt (gen) to measure; (pesar) to weigh up // vi to measure.

meditar [meði'tar] vt to ponder, think over, meditate (on); (planear) to think out.

mediterráneo, a [meðite'rraneo, a] a Mediterranean // nm: el M~ the Mediterranean.

medroso, a [me'ðroso, a] a fearful, timid.

medusa [me'ðusa] nf jellyfish.

megáfono [me'safono] nm megaphone.

megalómano, a [mexa'lomano, a] nm/f megalomaniac.

mejicano, a [mexi'kano, a] a, nm/f Mexican.

Méjico ['mexiko] nm Mexico.

mejilla [me'xiʎa] nf cheek.

mejor [me'xor] a, ad (comparativo) better; (superlativo) best; a lo ~ probably; (quizá) maybe; ~ dicho rather; tanto ~ so much the better.

mejora [me'xora] nf improvement; **mejorar** vt to improve, make better // vi, **mejorarse** vr to improve, get better.

melancólico, a [melan'koliko, a] a (triste) sad, melancholy; (soñador) dreamy.

melena [me'lena] nf (de persona) long hair; (del león) mane.

melocotón [meloko'ton] nm peach.

melodía [melo'ðia] nf melody; (aire) air.

melodrama [melo'ðrama] nm melodrama; **melodramático, a** a melodramatic.

melón [me'lon] nm melon.

meloso, a [me'loso, a] a honeyed, sweet.

mellizo, a [me'ʎiθo, a] a, nm/f twin.

membrete [mem'brete] nm letterhead.

memorable [memo'raβle] a memorable.

memorándum [memo'randum] nm (libro) notebook; (comunicación) memorandum.

memoria [me'morja] nf (gen) memory; (informe) report; ~s nfpl (de autor) memoirs.

mencionar [menθjo'nar] vt to mention.

mendigar [mendi'xar] vt to beg (for).

mendigo, a [men'dixo, a] nm/f beggar.

mendrugo [men'druxo] nm crust.

menear [mene'ar] vt to move; (fig) to handle; ~se vr to shake; (balancearse) to sway; (moverse) to move; (fig) to get a move on.

menester [menes'ter] nm (necesidad) necessity; (ocupación) job; ~es nmpl (deberes) duties; (instrumentos) tackle sg, tools; es ~ it is necessary.

mengua ['mengwa] nf (disminución) decrease; (falta) lack; (pobreza) poverty; (fig) discredit; ~do, a a cowardly, timid; (cicatero) mean.

menguante [men'gwante] a decreasing, diminishing; **menguar** vt to lessen, diminish; (fig) to discredit // vi to diminish, decrease; (fig) to decline.

menopausia [meno'pausja] nf menopause.

menor [me'nor] a (más pequeño: comparativo) smaller; (: superlativo) smallest; (más joven: comparativo) younger; (: superlativo) youngest; (Mus) minor // nm/f (joven) young person, juvenile; no tengo la ~ idea I haven't the slightest idea; al por ~ retail; de ~ edad person under age.

menos ['menos] a (comparativo: sg) less; (: pl) fewer; (superlativo: sg) least; (: pl) fewest // ad (comparativo) less; (superlativo) least // conj except // nm (Mat) minus; es lo ~ que puedo hacer it's

the least I can do; **lo ~ posible** as
little as possible; **a ~ que** unless; **te
echo de ~** I miss you; **al o por lo ~**
at least.

menoscabar [menoska'βar] vt
(*estropear*) to damage, harm;
(*acortar*) to lessen, reduce; (*fig*) to
discredit.

menospreciar [menospre'θjar] vt
to underrate, undervalue; (*despreciar*) to scorn, despise; **menosprecio**
nm underrating, undervaluation;
scorn, contempt.

mensaje [men'saxe] *nm* message;
~ro, a *nm/f* messenger.

menstruar [mens'trwar] vi to
menstruate; **menstruo** *nm* menstruation, period.

mensual [men'swal] a monthly; **100
ptas ~es** 100 ptas. a month.

menta ['menta] *nf* mint.

mental [men'tal] a mental.

mentar [men'tar] vt to mention,
name.

mente ['mente] *nf* mind.

mentecato, a [mente'kato, a] a
silly, stupid // *nm/f* fool, idiot.

mentir [men'tir] vi to lie; **~a** *nf*
(*una* **~a**) lie; (*acto*) lying;
(*invención*) fiction; **parece ~a
que...** it seems incredible that..., I
can't believe that...; **~oso, a** a lying;
(*texto*) full of errors // *nm/f* liar.

mentís [men'tis] *nm*: **dar el ~ a** to
deny.

menú [me'nu] *nm* menu.

menudeo [menu'ðeo] *nm*: **vender
al ~** to sell retail.

menudo, a [me'nuðo, a] a
(*pequeño*) small, tiny; (*sin
importancia*) petty, insignificant;
(*exacto*) exact, meticulous; **¡~
negocio!** (*fam*) some deal!; **a ~**
often, frequently; **por ~** in detail.

meñique [me'nike] *nm* little finger.

meollo [me'oʎo] *nm* (*gen*) marrow;
(*fig*) core.

mercadería [merkaðe'ria] *nf*
commodity; **~s** *nfpl* goods,
merchandise *sg*.

mercado [mer'kaðo] *nm* market;
M~ Común Common Market.

mercadotecnia [merkaðo'teknja]
nf marketing.

mercancía [merkan'θia] *nf*
commodity; **~s** *nfpl* goods,
merchandise *sg*.

mercantil [merkan'til] a
mercantile, commercial.

mercenario, a [merθe'narjo, a] a,
nm mercenary.

mercurio [mer'kurjo] *nm* mercury.

merecer [mere'θer] vt to deserve,
merit // vi to be deserving, be
worthy; **merece la pena** it's
worthwhile; **merecido, a** a (well)
deserved; **llevar su merecido** to get
one's deserts.

merendar [meren'dar] vt to have
for tea // vi to have tea; (*en el
campo*) to have a picnic.

merengue [me'renge] *nm*
meringue.

merienda [me'rjenda] *nf* (light)
tea, afternoon snack; (*de campo*)
picnic.

mérito ['merito] *nm* merit; (*valor*)
worth, value.

merluza [mer'luθa] *nf* hake.

merma ['merma] *nf* decrease;
(*pérdida*) wastage; **mermar** vt to
reduce, lessen // vi, **mermarse** vr to
decrease, dwindle; (*fig*) to waste
away.

mermelada [merme'laða] *nf* jam.

mero, a ['mero, a] a mere.

mes [mes] *nm* month; (*salario*)
month's pay.

mesa ['mesa] *nf* table; (*de trabajo*)
desk; (*GEO*) plateau; (*ARQ*) landing;
~ directiva board; **poner/quitar la
~** to lay/clear the table.

meseta [me'seta] *nf* (*GEO*) meseta,
tableland; (*ARQ*) landing.

mesón [me'son] *nm* olde-worlde
bar.

mestizo, a [mes'tiθo, a] a half-
caste, of mixed race; (*ZOOL*)

crossbred // nm/f half-caste, half-breed.

mesura [me'sura] nf (moderación) moderation, restraint; (dignidad) dignity, calm; (cortesía) courtesy, finish.

meta ['meta] nf goal; (de carrera) finish.

metáfora [me'tafora] nf metaphor.

metal [me'tal] nm (materia) metal; (MUS) brass; (fig) quality; **metálico, a** a metallic; (de metal) metal // nm cash.

metalurgia [meta'lurxja] nf metallurgy.

meteoro [mete'oro] nm meteor.

meter [me'ter] vt (colocar) to put, place; (introducir) to put in, insert; (añadir) to add; (involucrar) to involve; (causar) to make, cause; ~se vr: ~se en to go into, enter; (fig) to interfere in, meddle in; ~se a to start; ~se a escritor to become a writer; ~se con alguien to provoke sb, pick a quarrel with sb.

meticuloso, a [metiku'loso, a] a meticulous, thorough.

metódico, a [me'toðiko, a] a methodical.

metodismo [meto'ðismo] nm Methodism.

método ['metoðo] nm method.

metralleta [metra'ʎeta] nf submachine gun.

métrico, a ['metriko, a] a metric.

metro ['metro] nm metre; (tren) underground, subway.

México ['meksiko] nm Mexico.

mezcla ['meθkla] nf mixture; (Arg) mortar; **mezclar** vt to mix (up); (naipes) to shuffle; **mezclarse** vr to mix, mingle; **mezclarse en** to get mixed up in, get involved in.

mezquino, a [meθ'kino, a] a (cicatero) mean; (pobre) miserable.

mezquita [meθ'kita] nf mosque.

mi [mi] det my.

mí [mi] pron me; myself.

miaja ['mjaxa] nf crumb.

microbús [mikro'βus] nm minibus.

micrófono [mi'krofono] nm microphone.

microlentillas [mikrolen'tiʎas] nfpl contact lenses.

microscopio [mikro'skopjo] nm microscope.

miedo ['mjeðo] nm fear; (nerviosismo) apprehension, nervousness; **tener ~** to be afraid; **de ~** wonderful, marvellous; **hace un frío de ~** (fam) it's terribly cold; ~**so, a** a fearful, timid.

miel [mjel] nf honey.

miembro ['mjembro] nm limb; (socio) member; ~ **viril** penis.

mientes ['mjentes] nfpl: **no parar ~ en** to pay no attention to; **traer a las ~** to recall.

mientras ['mjentras] conj while; (duración) as long as // ad meanwhile; ~ **tanto** meanwhile; ~ **más tiene, más quiere** the more he has, the more he wants.

miércoles ['mjerkoles] nm inv Wednesday.

mierda ['mjerða] nf (fam) shit.

miga ['miɣa] nf crumb; (fig) essence; **hacer buenas ~s** (fam) to get on well.

migración [miɣra'θjon] nf migration.

mil [mil] num thousand; **dos ~ libras** two thousand pounds.

milagro [mi'laɣro] nm miracle; ~**so, a** a miraculous.

mili ['mili] nf: **hacer la ~** (fam) to do one's military service.

milicia [mi'liθja] nf (MIL) militia; (arte) art of war; (servicio militar) military service.

milímetro [mi'limetro] nm millimetre.

militante [mili'tante] a militant.

militar [mili'tar] a (del ejército) military; (guerrero) warlike // nm/f soldier // vi to serve in the army; (fig) to be a member of a party.

milla ['miʎa] nf mile.

millar [mi'ʎar] nm thousand.

millón [mi'ʎon] num million.

millonario, a nm/f millionaire.

mimar [mi'mar] vt (gen) to spoil, pamper; (al poderoso) to flatter.

mimbre ['mimbre] nm wicker.

mímica ['mimika] nf (para comunicarse) sign language; (imitación) mimicry.

mimo ['mimo] nm (caricia) affectionate caress; (de niño) spoiling; (TEATRO) mime.

mina ['mina] nf mine; **minar** vt to mine; (fig) to undermine.

mineral [mine'ral] a mineral // (GEO) mineral; (mena) ore.

minero, a [mi'nero, a] a mining // nm/f miner.

miniatura [minja'tura] a inv, nf miniature.

minifalda [mini'falda] nf miniskirt.

mínimo, a ['minimo, a] a, nm minimum.

ministerio [minis'terjo] nm Ministry; **M~ de Hacienda/del Exterior** Treasury/Foreign Office.

ministro [mi'nistro] nm minister.

minorar [mino'rar] vt to reduce.

minoría [mino'ria] nf minority.

minucioso, a [minu'θjoso, a] a thorough, meticulous; (prolijo) very detailed.

minúsculo, a [mi'nuskulo, a] a tiny, minute // nf small letter.

minuta [mi'nuta] nf (de comida) menu; (borrador) rough draft; (apunte) note.

minutero [minu'tero] nm minute hand.

minuto [mi'nuto] nm minute.

mío, a ['mio, a] pron: **el ~** mine; **un amigo ~** a friend of mine; **lo ~** what is mine.

miope [mi'ope] a short-sighted.

mira ['mira] nf (de arma) sight(s) (pl); (fig) aim, intention; **estar a la ~** to be on the look-out, keep watch; **~da** nf look, glance; (expresión) look, expression; **echar una ~da a** to glance at; **~da, a** a (sensato) sensible; (considerado) considerate;

bien/mal ~do well/not well thought of.

mirador [mira'ðor] nm viewpoint, vantage point.

mirar [mi'rar] vt to look at; (observar) to watch; (considerar) to consider, think over; (vigilar, cuidar) to watch, look after // vi to look; (ARQ) to face; **~se vr** (dos personas) to look at each other; **~bien/mal** to think highly of/have a poor opinion of; **~se al espejo** to look at o.s. in the mirror.

mirlo ['mirlo] nm blackbird.

misa ['misa] nf mass.

miserable [mise'raßle] a (avaro) mean, stingy; (nimio) miserable, paltry; (lugar) squalid; (fam) vile, despicable // nm/f (indigente) wretch, poor person; (perverso) rotter.

miseria [mi'serja] nf misery; (pobreza) poverty; (tacañería) meanness, stinginess; (condiciones) squalor; **una ~** a pittance.

misericordia [miseri'korðja] nf (compasión) compassion, pity; (piedad) mercy.

misil [mi'sil] nm missile.

misión [mi'sjon] nf mission; **misionero, a** nm/f missionary.

mismo, a ['mismo, a] a (semejante) same; (después de pronombre) -self; (para énfasis) very; **el ~ traje** the same suit; **en ese ~ momento** at that very moment; **vino el ~ Ministro** the minister himself came; **yo ~ lo vi** I saw it myself; **lo ~** the same (thing); **da lo ~** it's all the same; **quedamos en las ~as** as we're no further forward // ad: **aquí/hoy ~** right here/this very day; **ahora ~** right now // conj: **lo ~ que** just like, just as; **por lo ~** for the same reason.

misterio [mis'terjo] nm (gen) mystery; (lo secreto) secrecy.

mitad [mi'tað] nf (medio) half; (centro) middle; **a ~ de precio** (at) half-price; **en** o **a** ~ **del camino** halfway along the road; **cortar por la** ~ to cut through the middle.

mitin ['mitin] nm meeting.

mito ['mito] nm myth.

mixto, a ['miksto, a] a mixed.

mobiliario [moβi'ljarjo] nm furniture.

mocedad [moθe'ðað] nf youth.

moción [mo'θjon] nf motion.

mochila [mo'tʃila] nf rucksack.

moda ['moða] nf (gen) fashion; (estilo) style; **de** o **a la** ~ in fashion, fashionable; **pasado** o **fuera de** ~ out of fashion.

modales [mo'ðales] nmpl manners.

modalidad [moðali'ðað] nf kind, variety.

modelar [moðe'lar] vt to model.

modelo [mo'ðelo] a inv, nm/f model.

moderado, a [moðe'raðo, a] a moderate.

moderar [moðe'rar] vt to moderate; (violencia) to restrain, control; (velocidad) to reduce; ~se vr to restrain o.s., control o.s.

modernizar [moðerni'θar] vt to modernize.

moderno, a [mo'ðerno, a] a modern; (actual) present-day.

modestia [mo'ðestja] nf modesty; **modesto, a** a modest.

módico, a ['moðiko, a] a moderate, reasonable.

modificar [moðifi'kar] vt to modify.

modista [mo'ðista] nm/f dressmaker.

modo ['moðo] nm (manera, forma) way, manner; (MUS) mode; ~s nmpl manners; **de ningún** ~ in no way; **de todos** ~s at any rate; ~ **de empleo** directions pl (for use).

modorra [mo'ðorra] nf drowsiness.

modular [moðu'lar] vt to modulate.

mofa ['mofa] nf mockery, ridicule; **hacer** ~ **de** to mock; **mofar** vi to mock, scoff; **mofarse** vr: **mofarse de** to mock, scoff at.

mohino, a [mo'ino, a] a (triste) gloomy, depressed; (enojado) sulky.

moho ['moo] nm (BOT) mould; (oxidación) rust; ~**so, a** a mouldy; rusty.

mojar [mo'xar] vt to wet; (humedecer) to damp(en), moisten; (calar) to soak // vi: ~ **en** to get involved in; ~**se** vr to get wet.

mojón [mo'xon] nm (en un camino) signpost; (montón) heap, pile.

molde ['molde] nm mould; (de costura) pattern; (fig) model; **el vestido le está de** ~ the dress is just right for her; ~**ar** vt to mould.

mole ['mole] nf mass, bulk

moledora [mole'ðora] nf grinder, mill.

moler [mo'ler] vt to grind, crush; (cansar) to tire out, exhaust; (irritar) to annoy.

molestar [moles'tar] vt (gen) to bother; (fastidiar) to annoy; (incomodar) to inconvenience, put out // vi to be a nuisance; ~**se** vr to bother; (incomodarse) to go to trouble; (ofenderse) to take offence.

molestia [mo'lestja] nf (gen) bother, trouble; (incomodidad) inconvenience; (MED) discomfort, **es una** ~ it's a nuisance; **molesto, a** a (que causa molestia) annoying; (incómodo) inconvenient; (inquieto) uncomfortable, ill at ease; (enfadado) annoyed.

molinillo [moli'niʎo] nm. ~ **de carne/café** mincer/coffee grinder.

molino [mo'lino] nm (edificio) mill; (máquina) grinder.

momentáneo, a [momen'taneo, a] a momentary.

momento [mo'mento] nm (gen) moment; (TEC) momentum; **de** ~ at the moment, for the moment.

momia ['momja] nf mummy.

monarca [mo'narka] nm/f monarch, ruler; **monarquía** nf monarchy; **monarquista** nm/f royalist, monarchist.

monasterio [monas'terjo] *nm* monastery.

mondar [mon'dar] *vt* (*limpiar*) to clean; (*podar*) to prune, trim; (*pelar*) to peel; **~se** *vr*: **~ se los dientes** to pick one's teeth.

moneda [mo'neða] *nf* (*tipo de dinero*) currency, money; (*pieza*) coin; **una ~ de 5p a 5p piece**; **monedero** *nm* purse; **monetario, a** *a* monetary, financial.

monja ['monxa] *nf* nun.

monje ['monxe] *nm* monk.

mono, a ['mono, a] *a* (*bonito*) lovely, pretty; (*gracioso*) nice, charming // *nm/f* monkey, ape // *nm* (*overoles*) overalls *pl*.

monopolio [mono'poljo] *nm* monopoly; **monopolizar** *vt* to monopolize.

monoriel [mono'rjel] *nm* monorail.

monotonía [monoto'nia] *nf* (*sonido*) monotone; (*fig*) monotony.

monótono, a [mo'notono, a] *a* monotonous.

monstruo ['monstrwo] *nm* monster // *a* fantastic; **~so, a** *a* monstrous.

monta ['monta] *nf* total, sum; **de poca ~** unimportant, of little account.

montaje [mon'taxe] *nm* assembly; (*ARQ*) erection; (*TEATRO*) décor; (*CINE*) montage.

montaña [mon'taɲa] *nf* (*monte*) mountain; (*sierra*) mountains *pl*, mountainous area; (*AM*) forest; **~ rusa** roller coaster; **montañés, esa** *a* mountain *cpd* // *nm/f* highlander; (*de Santander*) native of the Santander region.

montar [mon'tar] *vt* (*subir a*) to mount, get on; (*caballo etc*) to ride; (*TEC*) to assemble, put together; (*ARQ*) to erect; (*negocio*) to set up; (*arma*) to cock; (*colocar*) to lift on // *vi* to mount, get on; (*sobresalir*) to overlap; **~ a** to amount to, come to; **~ en cólera** to get angry.

montaraz [monta'raθ] *a* mountain *cpd*, highland *cpd*; (*salvaje*) wild,

untamed; (*pey*) uncivilized.

monte ['monte] *nm* (*montaña*) mountain; (*bosque*) woodland; (*área sin cultivar*) wild area, wild country; **~ de Piedad** pawnshop; **~ alto** forest; **~ bajo** scrub(land).

monto ['monto] *nm* total, amount.

montón [mon'ton] *nm* heap, pile; (*fig*): **un ~ de** heaps of, lots of.

monumento [monu'mento] *nm* monument.

monzón [mon'θon] *nm* monsoon.

moña ['moɲa] *nf* hair ribbon.

moño ['moɲo] *nm* bun.

morado, a [mo'raðo, a] *a* purple; (*violado*) violet // *nm* bruise // *a* (*casa*) dwelling, abode; (*período*) stay.

moral [mo'ral] *a* moral // *nf* (*ética*) ethics; (*moralidad*) morals *pl*, morality; (*ánimo*) morale.

moraleja [mora'lexa] *nf* moral.

moralizar [morali'θar] *vt* to moralize.

morboso, a [mor'βoso, a] *a* morbid.

morcilla [mor'θiʎa] *nf* blood sausage, black pudding.

mordaz [mor'ðaθ] *a* biting, scathing.

mordaza [mor'ðaθa] *nf* (*para la boca*) gag; (*TEC*) clamp.

morder [mor'ðer] *vt* to bite; (*mordisquear*) to nibble; (*consumir*) to eat away, eat into; **mordisco** *nm* bite.

moreno, a [mo'reno, a] *a* (*color*) (*dark*) brown; (*de tez*) dark; (*de pelo ~*) dark-haired; (*negro*) Negro.

moretón [more'ton] *nm* (*fam*) bruise.

morfina [mor'fina] *nf* morphine.

moribundo, a [mori'βundo, a] *a* dying.

morir [mo'rir] *vi* (*gen*) to die; (*fuego*) to die down; (*luz*) to go out; **~se** *vr* (*gen*) to die; (*pierna etc*) to go to sleep, go numb; (*fig*) to be dying; **fue muerto en un accidente** he was killed in an accident; **~se**

por algo to be dying for sth.
morisco, a [mo'risko,a], **moro, a** ['moro, a] a Moorish // nm/f Moor.
morral [mo'rral] nm haversack.
morsa ['morsa] nf walrus.
mortaja [mor'taxa] nf shroud; (TEC) mortise; (AM) cigarette paper.
mortal [mor'tal] a mortal; (golpe) deadly; ~**idad, mortandad** nf mortality.
mortero [mor'tero] nm mortar.
mortífero, a [mor'tifero, a] a deadly, lethal.
mortificar [mortifi'kar] vt (MED) to damage, affect seriously; (fig) to mortify; ~**se** vr to be (very) embarrassed.
mosca ['moska] nf fly.
Moscú [mos'ku] n Moscow.
mosquitero [moski'tero] nm mosquito net.
mosquito [mos'kito] nm mosquito.
mostaza [mos'taθa] nf mustard.
mostrador [mostra'ðor] nm (de tienda) counter; (de café) bar; (de reloj) face, dial.
mostrar [mos'trar] vt (gen) to show; (exhibir) to display, exhibit; (explicar) to explain; ~**se** vr: ~se amable to be kind, to prove to be kind; no se muestra muy inteligente he doesn't seem (to be) very intelligent.
mostrenco, a [mos'trenko, a] a ownerless, unclaimed; (perro) stray; (persona) homeless; (fam) dense, slow.
mota ['mota] nf speck, tiny piece; (en diseño) dot.
mote ['mote] nm (apodo) nickname; (sentencia) motto.
motín [mo'tin] nm (del pueblo) revolt, rising, (del ejército) mutiny.
motivar [moti'βar] vt (causar) to cause, motivate; (explicar) to explain, justify, motive; **~ o** nm motive // nm reason.
moto ['moto] nf, **motocicleta** [motoθi'kleta] nf motorbike.

motoniveladora [motoniβela-'ðora] nf bulldozer.
motor [mo'tor] nm motor, engine; ~ **a chorro** o **de reacción/de explosión** jet engine/internal combustion engine.
motora [mo'tora] nf, **motorbote** [motor'βote] nm motorboat.
motosierra [moto'sjerra] nf mechanical saw.
movedizo, a [moβe'ðiθo, a] a easily moved, movable; (inseguro) unsteady; (fig) unsettled, changeable; (persona) fickle.
mover [mo'βer] vt (gen) to move; (cabeza) to shake; (accionar) to drive; (fig) to cause, provoke; ~**se** vr to move; (fig) to get a move on.
móvil ['moβil] a mobile; (pieza de máquina) moving; (mueble) movable // nm motive, **movilidad** nf mobility; **movilizar** vt to mobilize.
movimiento [moβi'mjento] nm (gen) movement; (TEC) motion; (actividad) activity; **el M~** the Falangist Movement.
mozo, a ['moθo, a] a (joven) young; (soltero) single, unmarried // nm/f (joven) youth, lad/girl; (criada) servant // nm (camarero) waiter.
muchacho, a [mu'tʃatʃo, a] a nm/f (niño) boy/girl; (criado) servant/ ervant or maid.
muchedumbre [mutʃe'ðumbre] nf crowd.
mucho, a ['mutʃo, a] a (sg) a lot of; (gen en frase negativa o interrogativa) much; (pl) many, a lot of, lots of // ad (en cantidad) a lot, a great deal, much; (después de un verbo) long; (muy) very // pron: **tengo ~ que hacer** I have a lot to do; ~**s dicen que** a lot of people say that; **ni ~ menos** far from it.
mudanza [mu'ðanθa] nf (cambio) change; (de casa) move; ~**s** nfpl (fig) moodiness sg.
mudar [mu'ðar] vt to change; (ZOOL) to shed // vi to change; ~**se**

vr (*la ropa*) to change; (*de casa*) to move (house).

mudo, a ['muðo, a] *a* dumb; (*callado, CINE*) silent.

mueble ['mweßle] *nm* piece of furniture; ~**s** *nmpl* furniture *sg*; ~**ría** *nf* furniture shop.

mueca ['mweka] *nf* face, grimace; **hacer** ~**s a** to make faces at.

muela ['mwela] *nf* (*diente*) tooth; (: *de atrás*) molar.

muelle ['mweʎe] *a* (*blando*) soft; (*elástico*) springy; (*fig*) soft, easy // *nm* spring; (*NAUT*) wharf; (*malecón*) jetty.

muero *etc vb ver* **morir.**

muerte ['mwerte] *nf* death; (*homicidio*) murder; **dar** ~ **a** to kill.

muerto, a ['mwerto, a] *pp de morir* // *a* dead; (*color*) dull // *nm/f* dead man/woman; (*difunto*) deceased; (*cadáver*) corpse; **estar** ~ **de cansancio** to be dead tired.

muestra ['mwestra] *nf* (*señal*) indication, sign; (*demostración*) demonstration; (*prueba*) proof; (*estadística*) sample; (*modelo*) model, pattern; (*testimonio*) token; **muestreo** *nm* sample, sampling.

muestro *etc vb ver* **mostrar.**

muevo *etc vb ver* **mover.**

mugir [mu'xir] *vi* (*vaca*) to moo; (*persona*) to roar, howl.

mugre ['muxre] *nf* dirt, filth; **mugriento, a** *a* dirty, filthy.

mujer [mu'xer] *nf* (*de sexo femenino*) woman; (*esposa*) wife; ~**iego** *a* womaniser.

mula ['mula] *nf* mule.

muladar [mula'ðar] *nm* dungheap, dunghill.

muleta [mu'leta] *nf* (*para andar*) crutch; (*TAUR*) stick with red cape attached; (*fig*) prop, support.

multa ['multa] *nf* fine; **multar** *vt* to fine.

multicopista [multiko'pista] *nm* duplicator.

múltiple ['multiple] *a* multiple; (*pl*) many, numerous.

multiplicar [multipli'kar] *vt* (*MAT*) to multiply; (*fig*) to increase; ~**se** *vr* (*BIO*) to multiply; (*fig*) to attend to a lot of things at one time.

multitud [multi'tuð] *nf* (*gentío, muchedumbre*) crowd; ~ **de** lots of.

mullido, a [mu'ʎiðo, a] *a* (*cama*) soft; (*hierba*) soft, springy // *nm* stuffing, filling.

mundano, a [mun'dano, a] *a* worldly; (*de moda*) fashionable.

mundial [mun'djal] *a* world-wide, universal; (*guerra, récord*) world *cpd.*

mundo ['mundo] *nm* world; **todo el** ~ everybody; **tener** ~ to be experienced, know one's way around.

munición [muni'θjon] *nf* (*MIL*) stores *pl*, supplies *pl*; (*de arma*) ammunition.

municipio [muni'θipjo] *nm* (*municipalidad*) town council, corporation; (*comuna*) town, municipality.

muñeca [mu'ɲeka] *nf* (*ANAT*) wrist; (*juguete*) doll; (*maniquí*) dummy.

muñeco [mu'ɲeko] *nm* (*figura*) figure; (*marioneta*) puppet; (*maniquí*) dummy; (*fig*) puppet, pawn.

muralla [mu'ra/a] *nf* (*city*) wall(s) (*pl*).

murciélago [mur'θjelaxo] *nm* bat.

murmullo [mur'muʎo] *nm* murmur(ing); (*cuchicheo*) whispering; (*de arroyo*) murmur, rippling.

murmuración [murmura'θjon] *nf* gossip; **murmurar** *vi* to murmur, whisper; (*criticar*) to criticize; (*cotillear*) to gossip.

muro ['muro] *nm* wall.

muscular [musku'lar] *a* muscular.

músculo ['muskulo] *nm* muscle.

museo [mu'seo] *nm* museum.

musgo ['musxo] *nm* moss.

músico, a ['musiko, a] *a* musical // *nm/f* musician // *nf* music.

musitar [musi'tar] *vt*, *vi* to mutter, mumble.

muslo ['muslo] *nm* thigh.

mustio, a ['mustjo, a] *a (persona)* depressed, gloomy; *(planta)* faded, withered.

musulmán, ana [musul'man, ana] *nm/f* Moslem.

mutación [muta'θjon] *nf (BIO)* mutation; *(cambio)* (sudden) change.

mutilar [muti'lar] *vt* to mutilate; *(a una persona)* to maim.

mutuamente [mutwa'mente] *ad* mutually; **mutuo, a** a mutual.

muy [mwi] *ad* very; *(demasiado)* too; **Muy Señor mío** Dear Sir; **~ de noche** very late at night; **eso es ~ de él** that's just like him.

N

N *abr de* norte.

n/ *abr de* nuestro, a.

nabo ['naβo] *nm* turnip; *(raíz)* root.

nácar ['nakar] *nm* mother-of-pearl.

nacer [na'θer] *vi* to be born; *(de huevo)* to hatch; *(vegetal)* to sprout; *(río)* to rise; **~ al amor** to awaken to love; **nació una sospecha en su mente** a suspicion formed in her mind; **nacido, a** born; **recién nacido** newborn; **naciente** a new, emerging; *(sol)* rising; **nacimiento** *nm* birth; *(fig)* birth, origin; *(de Navidad)* Nativity; *(linaje)* descent, family; *(de río)* source.

nación [na'θjon] *nf* nation; **nacional** a national; **nacionalismo** *nm* nationalism; **nacionalista** *nm/f* nationalist; **nacionalizar** *vt* to nationalize; **nacionalizarse** *vr* to become naturalized.

nada ['naða] *pron* nothing // *ad* not at all, in no way; **no decir ~** to say nothing, not to say anything; **de ~** don't mention it.

nadaderas [naða'ðeras] *nfpl* water-wings.

nadador, a [naða'ðor, a] *nm/f* swimmer.

nadar [na'ðar] *vi* to swim.

nadie ['naðje] *pron* nobody, no-one; **~ habló** nobody spoke; **no había ~** there was nobody there, there wasn't anybody there.

nado ['naðo]: **a ~** *ad*: **pasar a ~** to swim across.

naipe ['naipe] *nm* playing card; **~s** *nmpl* cards.

nalgas ['nalɣas] *nfpl* buttocks.

nana ['nana] *nf (fam: abuela)* grandma *(fam)*, granny *(fam)*; *(: canción)* lullaby.

naranja [na'ranxa] *a, nf* orange; **media ~** *(fam)* better half *(fam)*; **~do, a** a orange // *nf* orangeade; **naranjo** *nm* orange tree.

narciso [nar'θiso] *nm* narcissus.

narcótico, a [nar'kotiko, a] *a, nm* narcotic; **narcotizar** *vt* to drug.

nardo ['narðo] *nm* lily.

narigón, ona [nari'ɣon, ona], **narigudo, a** [nari'ɣuðo, a] a big-nosed.

nariz [na'riθ] *nf* nose; **narices** *nfpl* nostrils; **en las narices de uno** under one's (very) nose.

narración [narra'θjon] *nf* narration; **narrador, a** *nm/f* narrator.

narrar [na'rrar] *vt* to narrate, recount; **narrativa** *nf* narrative, story.

nata ['nata] *nf* cream.

natación [nata'θjon] *nf* swimming.

natal [na'tal] a natal; **ciudad ~** home town; **~icio** *nm* birthday; **~idad** *nf* birth rate.

natillas [na'tiʎas] *nfpl* custard *sg*.

natividad [natiβi'ðað] *nf* nativity.

nativo, a [na'tiβo, a] a native; **nato, a** ['nato, a] a born; **un músico ~** a born musician.

natural [natu'ral] a natural; *(fruta etc)* fresh // *nm/f* native // *nm* nature; **~eza** *nf* nature; *(género)* nature, kind; **~eza muerta** still life;

~**idad** *nf* naturalness; ~**ización** *nf* naturalization; ~**izarse** *vr* to become naturalized; (*aclimatarse*) to become acclimatized; ~**mente** *ad* naturally.

naufragar [naufra'xar] *vi* to sink; **naufragio** *nm* shipwreck; **náufrago, a** *nm/f* castaway, shipwrecked person.

náusea ['nausea] *nf* nausea; **me da** ~ it makes me feel sick; **nauseabundo, a** *a* nauseating, sickening.

náutico, a ['nautiko, a] *a* nautical.

nava [na'ßa] *nf* (*GEO*) plain.

navaja [na'ßaxa] *nf* (*cortaplumas*) clasp knife, penknife; (*de barbero, peluquero*) razor.

navarro, a [na'ßarro, a] *a* Navarrese.

nave ['naße] *nf* (*barco*) ship, vessel; (*ARQ*) nave; ~ **espacial** spaceship.

navegación [naßexa'θjon] *nf* navigation; (*viaje*) sea journey; ~ **aérea** air traffic; ~ **costera** coastal shipping; **navegante** *nm/f* navigator; **navegar** *vi* (*barco*) to sail; (*avión*) to fly // *vt* to sail; to fly; (*dirigir el rumbo*) to navigate.

navidad [naßi'ðað] *nf* Christmas; **navideño, a** *a* Christmas *cpd*.

navío [na'ßio] *nm* ship.

nazi [na'θi] *a, nm/f* Nazi.

neblina [ne'ßlina] *nf* mist.

nebuloso, a [neßu'loso, a] *a* foggy; (*calinoso*) misty; (*cielo*) cloudy; (*indefinido*) nebulous, vague // *nf* nebula.

necedad [neθe'ðað] *nf* foolishness; (*una* ~) foolish act.

necesario, a [neθe'sarjo, a] *a* necessary.

neceser [neθe'ser] *nm* vanity case; (*bolsa*) holdall; ~ **de viaje** travelling case.

necesidad [neθesi'ðað] *nf* need; (*lo inevitable*) necessity; (*miseria*) poverty, need; **en caso de** ~ in case of need or emergency; **hacer sus** ~**es** to relieve o.s.

necesitado, a [neθesi'taðo, a] *a* needy, poor; ~ **de** in need of.

necesitar [neθesi'tar] *vt* to need, require // *vi*: ~ **de** to have need of.

necio, a ['neθjo, a] *a* foolish.

necrología [nekrolo'xia] *nf* obituary.

necrópolis [ne'kropolis] *nf* cemetery.

nectarina [nekta'rina] *nf* nectarine.

nefando, a [ne'fando, a] *a* unspeakable.

nefasto, a [ne'fasto, a] *a* ill-fated, unlucky.

negación [nexa'θjon] *nf* negation; (*rechazo*) refusal, denial.

negar [ne'xar] *vt* (*renegar, rechazar*) to refuse; (*prohibir*) to refuse, deny; (*desmentir*) to deny; ~**se** *vr*: ~**se a** to refuse to.

negativo, a [nexa'tißo, a] *a, nm* negative // *nf* (*gen*) negative; (*rechazo*) refusal, denial.

negligencia [nexli'xenθja] *nf* negligence; **negligente** *a* negligent.

negociable [nexo'θjaßle] *a* (*COM*) negotiable.

negociado [nexo'θjaðo] *nm* department, section.

negociante [nexo'θjante] *nm/f* businessman/woman; (*comerciante*) merchant.

negociar [nexo'θjar] *vt, vi* to negotiate; ~ **en** to deal in, trade in.

negocio [ne'xoθjo] *nm* (*COM*) business; (*asunto*) affair, business; (*operación comercial*) deal, transaction; (*AM*) firm; (*lugar*) place of business; **los** ~**s** business *sg*; **hacer** ~ to do business.

negro, a ['nexro, a] *a* black; (*suerte*) awful // *nm* black // *nm/f* Negro/Negress, black // *nf* (*MUS*) crotchet; **negrura** *nf* blackness.

nene, a ['nene, a] *nm/f* baby, small child; (*fam*) dear.

nenúfar [ne'nufar] *nm* water lily.

neologismo [neolo'xismo] *nm* neologism.

neoyorquino, a [neojorˈkino, a] *a* (of) New York.

nepotismo [nepoˈtismo] *nm* nepotism.

nervio [ˈnerβjo] *nm* (ANAT) nerve; (*tendón*) tendon; (*fig*) vigour; **~sidad** *nf* nervousness, nerves *pl*; **~so, a, nervudo, a** *a* nervous.

neto, a [ˈneto, a] *a* clear; (*verdad etc*) pure; (*limpio*) clean; (COM) net.

neumático, a [neuˈmatiko, a] *a* pneumatic // *nm* tyre; **~ de recambio** spare tyre.

neuralgia [neuˈralxja] *nf* neuralgia.

neurastenia [neurasˈtenja] *nf* nervous exhaustion.

neuritis [neuˈritis] *nf* neuritis.

neurólogo, a [neuˈroloxo, a] *nm/f* neurologist.

neurosis [neuˈrosis] *nf inv* neurosis.

neutral [neuˈtral] *a* neutral; **~izar** *vt* to neutralize; (*contrarrestar*) to counteract.

neutro, a [ˈneutro, a] *a* (BIO) neuter, sexless; (LING) neuter.

neutrón [neuˈtron] *nm* neutron; **bomba de neutrones** neutron bomb.

nevada [neˈβaða] *nf* snowstorm, (*caída de nieve*) snowfall.

nevar [neˈβar] *vi* to snow; **nevasca** *nf* snowstorm.

nevera [neˈβera] *nf* refrigerator, icebox.

nevisca [neˈβiska] *nf* flurry of snow; (*aguanieve*) sleet; **neviscar** *vi* to snow lightly; to sleet.

ni [ni] *conj* nor, neither; (**~ siquiera** not ... even, **~ que** not even if); **blanco ~ negro** neither white nor black.

Nicaragua [nikaˈraswa] *nf* Nicaragua; **nicaragüense** *a, nm/f* Nicaraguan.

nicotina [nikoˈtina] *nf* nicotine.

nicho [ˈnitʃo] *nm* niche.

nido [ˈniðo] *nm* nest; (*fig*) hiding place; (*lugar predilecto*) haunt.

niebla [ˈnjeβla] *nf* fog; (*neblina*) mist.

niego *etc vb ver* **negar.**

nieto, a [ˈnjeto, a] *nm/f* grandson/daughter; **~s** *nmpl* grandchildren.

nieva *etc vb ver* **nevar.**

nieve [ˈnjeβe] *nf* snow.

nigromancia [niɣroˈmanθja] *nf* necromancy, black magic.

nihilismo [niiˈlismo] *nm* nihilism.

Nilo [ˈnilo] *nm*: **el ~** the Nile.

nimbo [ˈnimbo] *nm* (*aureola*) halo; (*nube*) nimbus.

nimiedad [nimjeˈðað] *nf* smallmindedness; (*prolijidad*) longwindedness; (*trivialidad*) triviality.

nimio, a [ˈnimjo, a] *a* (*insignificante*) trivial, insignificant; (*escrupuloso*) fussy, overparticular.

ninfa [ˈninfa] *nf* nymph.

ninfómana [ninˈfomana] *nf* nymphomaniac.

ninguno, a [ninˈguno, a], **ningún** [ninˈgun] *a* no // *pron* (*nadie*) nobody; (*ni uno*) none, not one; (*ni uno ni otro*) neither; **de ~a manera** by no means, not at all.

niña [ˈnina] *nf ver* **niño.**

niñera [niˈnera] *nf* nursemaid, nanny; **niñería** *nf* childish act.

niñez [niˈneθ] *nf* childhood; (*infancia*) infancy.

niño, a [ˈnino, a] *a* (*joven*) young; (*inmaduro*) immature // *nm* (*chico*) boy, child // *nf* (*chica*) girl; child; (ANAT) pupil.

nipón, ona [niˈpon, ona] *a, nm/f* Japanese.

níquel [ˈnikel] *nm* nickel; **niquelar** *vt* (TEC) to nickel-plate.

nitidez [nitiˈðeθ] *nf* (*claridad*) clarity; (*de atmósfera*) brightness; (*de imagen*) sharpness; **nítido, a** *a* clear, sharp.

nitrato [niˈtrato] *nm* nitrate.

nitrógeno [niˈtroxeno] *nm* nitrogen.

nitroglicerina [nitroɣliθeˈrina] *nf* nitroglycerine.

nivel [niˈβel] *nm* (GEO) level; (*norma*) level, standard; (*altura*) height; ~ **de aceite** oil level; ~ **de aire** spirit level; ~ **de vida** standard of living; ~**ar** vt (*terreno*) to level out; (*equilibrar: mueble*) to even up; (*COM*) to balance.

NN. UU. *nfpl abr de* **Naciones Unidas** U.N. *sg* (United Nations).

no [no] *ad* no; not; (*con verbo*) not // *excl* no!; ~ **tengo nada** I don't have anything, I have nothing; ~ **es el mío** it's not mine; **ahora** ~ not now; ¿ ~ **lo sabes?** don't you know?; ~ **mucho** not much; ~ **bien termine, lo entregaré** as soon as I finish I'll hand it over; **¡a que** ~ **lo sabes!** I bet you don't know!; **¡cuándo** *o* **cómo** ~! of course!; **los países** ~ **alineados** the non-aligned countries; **el** ~ **conformismo** non-conformism; **la** ~ **intervención** non-intervention.

NO *abr de* **noroeste**.

no. *abr de* **número.**

noble ['noβle] *a, nm/f* noble; ~**za** *nf* nobility.

noción [no'θjon] *nf* notion.

nocivo, a [no'θiβo, a] *a* harmful.

noctambulismo [noktamβu-'lismo] *nm* sleepwalking; **noctámbulo, a** *nm/f* sleepwalker.

nocturno, a [nok'turno, a] *a* (*de la noche*) nocturnal, night *cpd*; (*de la tarde*) evening *cpd* // *nm* nocturne.

noche ['notʃe] *nf* night, night-time; (*la tarde*) evening; (*fig*) darkness; **de** ~, **por la** ~ at night.

nochebuena [notʃe'βwena] *nf* Christmas Eve.

nochevieja [notʃe'βjexa] *nf* New Year's Eve.

nodriza [no'θriθa] *nf* wet nurse.

nogal [no'xal] *nm* walnut tree.

nómada ['nomaða] *a* nomadic // *nm/f* nomad.

nombradía [nombra'ðia] *nf* fame.

nombramiento [nombra'mjento] *nm* naming; (*a un empleo*) appointment.

nombrar [nom'brar] *vt* (*designar*) to name; (*mencionar*) to mention; (*dar puesto a*) to appoint.

nombre ['nombre] *nm* name; (*sustantivo*) noun; (*fama*) renown; ~ **y apellidos** name in full; ~ **común/propio** common/proper noun; ~ **de pila/de soltera** Christian/maiden name.

nomenclatura [nomenkla'tura] *nf* nomenclature.

nomeolvides [nomeol'βiðes] *nm inv* forget-me-not.

nómina [no'mina] *nf* (*lista*) list; (*COM*) payroll.

nominal [nomi'nal] *a* nominal.

nominativo, a [nomina'tiβo, a] *a* (*COM*): **cheque** ~ **a X** cheque made out to X.

non [non] *a* odd, uneven // *nm* odd number.

nonada [no'naða] *nf* trifle.

nono, a ['nono, a] *a* ninth.

nordeste [nor'ðeste] *a* north-east, north-eastern, north-easterly // *nm* north-east.

nórdico, a ['norðiko, a] *a* (*del norte*) northerly; (*escandinavo*) Nordic.

noria [no'rja] *nf* (*AGR*) waterwheel; (*de carnaval*) big wheel.

normal [nor'mal] *a* (*corriente*) normal; (*habitual*) usual, natural; (*gasolina*) ~ two-star petrol; ~**idad** *nf* normality; **restablecer la** ~**idad** to restore order; ~**izar** *vt* (*reglamentar*) to normalize; (*TEC*) to standardize; ~**izarse** *vr* to return to normal.

normando, a [nor'mando, a] *a, nm/f* Norman.

noroeste [noro'este] *a* north-west, north-western, north-westerly // *nm* north-west.

norte ['norte] *a* north, northern, northerly // *nm* north; (*fig*) guide.

norteamericano, a [norteameri-'kano, a] *a, nm/f* (North) American.

noruego, a [no'rweɣo, a] *a, nm/f* Norwegian; **N~a** *nf* Norway.

nos [nos] *pron* (*directo*) us; (*indirecto*) us; to us; for us; from us; (*reflexivo*) to ourselves; (*reci-*

proco) (to) each other; ~ **levanta-mos a las 7 we get up at 7.**

nosotros [no'sotros] *pron (sujeto)* we; *(después de prep)* us.

nostalgia [nos'talxja] *nf* nostalgia.

nota ['nota] *nf* note; *(ESCOL)* mark.

notabilidad [notaβili'ðað] *nf (persona)* notable.

notable [no'taβle] *a, nm/f* notable.

notación [nota'θjon] *nf (nota)* note; *(MAT, MUS)* notation.

notar [no'tar] *vt (advertir)* to notice, note; *(anotar, asentar)* to note (down); *(censurar)* to criticize; **~se** *vr* to be obvious.

notarial [nota'rjal] *a;* **acta ~** affidavit.

notario [no'tarjo] *nm* notary.

noticia [no'tiθja] *nf (información)* piece of news; **las ~s** the news *sg;* **tener ~s de alguien** to hear from sb.

noticiar [noti'θjar] *vt* to notify; **~ io** *nm (CINE)* newsreel; *(TV)* news bulletin; **noticioso, a** *a* well-informed.

notificación [notifika'θjon] *nf* notification; **notificar** *vt* to notify, inform.

notoriedad [notorie'ðað] *nf* fame, renown; **notorio, a** *a (público)* well-known; *(evidente)* obvious.

novato, a [no'βato, a] *a, inexperienced // nm/f* beginner.

novecientos [noβe'θjentos] *num* nine hundred.

novedad [noβe'ðað] *nf (calidad de nuevo)* newness; *(noticia)* piece of news; *(cambio)* change, (new) development.

novedoso, a [noβe'ðoso, a] *a* novel.

novel [no'βel] *a* new; *(inexperto)* inexperienced // *nm/f* beginner.

novela [no'βela] *nf* novel.

novelero, a [noβe'lero, a] *a* highly imaginative; *(voluble)* fickle; *(chismoso)* gossipy.

novelesco, a [noβe'lesko, a] *a* fictional; *(romántico)* romantic; *(fantástico)* fantastic.

noveno, a [no'βeno, a] *a* ninth.

noventa [no'βenta] *num* ninety.

novia ['noβja] *nf ver* **novio.**

noviazgo [no'βjaθɣo] *nm* engagement.

novicio, a [no'βiθjo, a] *nm/f* novice.

noviembre [no'βjembre] *nm* November.

novilla [no'βiʎa] *nf* heifer; **~da** *nf (TAUR)* bullfight with young bulls; **novillero** *nm* novice bullfighter; **novillo** *nm* young bull; **hacer novillos** *(fam)* to play truant.

novio, a [no'βjo, a] *nm/f* boyfriend/girlfriend; *(prometido)* fiancé/fiancée; *(recién casado)* bridegroom/bride; **los ~s** the newlyweds.

N. S. *abr de* Nuestro Señor.

nubarrón [nuβa'rron] *nm* storm cloud.

nube ['nuβe] *nf* cloud.

nublado, a [nu'βlaðo, a] *a* cloudy // *nm* storm cloud; **nublar** *vt (oscurecer)* to darken; *(confundir)* to cloud; **nublarse** *vr* to grow dark.

nuca ['nuka] *nf* nape of the neck.

nuclear [nukle'ar] *a* nuclear.

núcleo ['nukleo] *nm (centro)* core; *(FÍSICA)* nucleus.

nudillo [nu'ðiʎo] *nm* knuckle.

nudo ['nuðo] *nm (EGN)* knot; *(unión)* bond; *(de problema)* crux; *(de comunicaciones)* centre; **~so, a** *a* knotty.

nuera ['nwera] *nf* daughter-in-law.

nuestro, a ['nwestro, a] *adj our // pron* ours; **~ padre** our father; **un amigo ~** a friend of ours; **es el ~** it's ours.

nueva ['nweβa] *nf ver* **nuevo.**

nuevamente [nweβa'mente] *ad (otra vez)* again; *(de nuevo)* anew.

nueve ['nweβe] *num* nine.

nuevo, a ['nweβo, a] *a (gen)* new // *ad* **de ~** again; **N~a York** *n* New York; **N~a Zelandia** *nf* New Zealand.

nuez [nweθ] *(pl* **nueces)** *nf (fruto)* nut; *(del nogal)* walnut; **~ de Adán**

Adam's apple; ~ **moscada** nutmeg.

nulidad [nuli'ðað] *nf* (*incapacidad*) incompetence; (*abolición*) nullity.

nulo, a ['nulo, a] *a* (*inepto, torpe*) useless; (*inválido*) (null and void); (*DEPORTE*) drawn, tied.

núm. *abr de* **número.**

numen ['numen] *nm* inspiration.

numeración [numera'θjon] *nf* (*cifras*) numbers *pl*; (*arábiga, romana etc*) numerals *pl.*

numeral [nume'ral] *nm* numeral.

numerar [nume'rar] *vt* to number.

numerario, a [nume'rarjo] *nm* hard cash.

numérico, a [nu'meriko, a] *a* numerical.

número ['numero] *nm* (*gen*) number; (*tamaño: de zapato*) size; (*ejemplar: de diario*) number, issue; **sin ~** numberless, unnumbered; ~ **de matrícula/telefónico** registration/telephone number; ~ **atrasado** back number.

numeroso, a [nume'roso, a] *a* numerous.

nunca ['nunka] *ad* (*jamás*) never; ~ **lo pensé** I never thought it; **no vino** ~ he never came; ~ **más** never again.

nuncio ['nunθjo] *nm* (*REL*) nuncio.

nupcias ['nupθjas] *nfpl* wedding *sg*, nuptials.

nutria ['nutrja] *nf* otter.

nutrición [nutri'θjon] *nf* nutrition.

nutrido, a [nu'triðo, a] *a* (*alimentado*) nourished; (*fig: grande*) large; (*abundante*) abundant.

nutrir [nu'trir] *vt* (*alimentar*) to nourish; (*dar de comer*) to feed; (*alentar*) to encourage; (*esperanzas*) to cherish; **nutritivo, a** *a* nourishing, nutritious.

nylon [ni'lon] *nm* nylon.

Ñ

ñame ['name] *nm* yam.

ñaque ['nake] *nm* junk.

ñato, a ['nato, a] *a* (*AM*) snub-nosed.

ñoñería [none'ria], **ñoñez** [no'neθ] *nf* insipidness.

ñoño, a ['nono, a] *a* (*AM. tonto*) silly, stupid; (*soso*) insipid; (*persona*) spineless.

O

o [o] *conj* or.

O *abr de* **oeste.**

o/ *abr de* **orden.**

oasis [o'asis] *nm* oasis.

obcecar [oßθe'kar] *vt* to blind.

obedecer [oßeðe'θer] *vt* to obey; **obediencia** *nf* obedience; **obediente** *a* obedient.

obertura [oßer'tura] *nf* overture.

obesidad [oßesi'ðað] *nf* obesity; **obeso, a** *a* obese.

obispo [o'ßispo] *nm* bishop.

objeción [oßxe'θjon] *nf* objection; **objetar** *vt, vi* to object.

objetivo, a [oßxe'tißo, a] *a, nm* objective.

objeto [oß'xeto] *nm* (*cosa*) object; (*fin*) aim.

oblicuo, a [o'ßlikwo, a] *a* oblique; (*mirada*) sidelong.

obligación [oßliɣa'θjon] *nf* obligation; (*COM*) bond.

obligar [oßli'ɣar] *vt* to force; ~ **se** *vr* to bind o.s.; **obligatorio, a** *a* compulsory, obligatory.

oboe [o'ßoe] *nm* oboe.

obra ['oßra] *nf* (*gen*) work; (*hechura*) piece of work; (*ARQ*) construction, building; (*TEATRO*) play; ~ **maestra** masterpiece; (**Ministerio de**) **O~s Públicas** Ministry of Public Works; **en** ~ **de** in about; **por** ~ **de** thanks to (the efforts of); **obrar** vt to work; (tener efecto) to have an effect on // vi to act, behave; (tener efecto) to have an effect; **la carta obra en su poder** the letter is in his/her possession; **obrero, a** a working, labour cpd; **clase obrera** working class // nm/f (gen) worker; (sin oficio) labourer.

obscenidad [oβsθeni'ðað] nf obscenity; **obsceno, a** a obscene.

obscu... = oscu... .

obsequiar [oβse'kjar] vt (ofrecer) to present with; (agasajar) to make a fuss of, lavish attention on; **obsequio** nm (regalo) gift; (cortesía) courtesy, attention; **obsequioso, a** a attentive.

observación [oβserβa'θjon] nf observation; (reflexión) remark.

observancia [oβser'βanθja] nf observance.

observar [oβser'βar] vt to observe; (anotar) to notice; **~se** vr to keep to, observe.

obsesión [oβse'sjon] nf obsession; **obsesionar** vt to obsess.

obstaculizar [oβstakuli'θar] vt (dificultar) to hinder; (impedir) to stand in the way of.

obstáculo [oβs'takulo] nm (gen) obstacle; (impedimento) hindrance, drawback.

obstante [oβs'tante]: **no ~** ad nevertheless // prep in spite of.

obstar [oβs'tar] vi: **~ a** to hinder.

obstetricia [oβste'triθja] nf obstetrics sg; **obstétrico, a** a obstetric // nm/f obstetrician.

obstinado, a [oβsti'naðo, a] a (gen) obstinate; (terco) stubborn.

obstinarse [oβsti'narse] vr to be obstinate; **~ en** to persist in.

obstrucción [oβstruk'θjon] nf obstruction; **obstruir** vt to obstruct.

obtener [oβte'ner] vt (conseguir) to obtain; (ganar) to gain.

obtuso, a [oβ'tuso, a] a (filo) blunt; (MAT, fig) obtuse.

obviar [oβ'βjar] vt to clear away // vi to stand in the way.

obvio, a [oβ'βjo, a] a obvious.

ocasión [oka'sjon] nf (oportunidad) opportunity, chance; (momento) occasion, time; (causa) cause; **de ~** secondhand; **ocasionar** vt to cause.

ocaso [o'kaso] nm (oeste) west; (fig) decline.

occidente [okθi'ðente] nm west.

océano [o'θeano] nm ocean; **el ~ índico** the Indian Ocean.

O.C.E.D. nf abr de Organización de Cooperación Económica y Desarrollo OECD (Organization for Economic Cooperation and Development).

ocio ['oθjo] nm (tiempo) leisure; (pey) idleness; **~s** nmpl pastime sg; **~sidad** nf idleness; **~so,** a a (inactivo) idle; (inútil) useless.

octanaje [okta'naxe] nm: **de alto ~** high octane; **octano** nm octane.

octavín [okta'βin] nm piccolo.

octavo, a [ok'taβo, a] a eighth.

octogenario, a [oktoxe'narjo, a] a octogenarian.

octubre [ok'tuβre] nm October.

ocular [oku'lar] a ocular, eye cpd; **testigo ~** eyewitness.

oculista [oku'lista] nm/f oculist.

ocultar [okul'tar] vt (esconder) to hide; (callar) to withhold; **oculto, a** a hidden; (fig) secret.

ocupación [okupa'θjon] nf occupation.

ocupado, a [oku'paðo, a] a (persona) busy; (sitio) occupied; (teléfono) engaged; **ocupar** vt (gen) to occupy; **ocuparse** vr: **ocuparse con o de o en** (gen) to concern o.s. with; (cuidar) to look after.

ocurrencia [oku'rrenθja] nf (ocasión) occurrence; (agudeza) witticism.

ocurrir [oku'rrir] vi to happen; **~se** vr: **se me ocurre que...** it occurs to me that...

ochenta [o'tʃenta] num eighty.

oda ['oða] nm ouni sight.

odiar [o'ðjar] vt to hate; **odio** nm (gen) hate, hatred; (disgusto)

dislike; odioso, a a (gen) hateful; (malo) nasty.

O.E.A. nf abr de **Organización de Estados Americanos** O.A.S. (Organization of American States).

oeste [o'este] nm west; **una película del ~** a western.

ofender [ofen'der] vt (agraviar) to offend; (ser ofensivo a) to be offensive to; **~se** vr to take offence; **ofensa** nf offence; **ofensivo, a** a (insultante) insulting; (MIL) offensive // nf offensive.

oferta [o'ferta] nf offer; (propuesta) proposal; **la ~ y la demanda** supply and demand; **artículos en ~** goods on offer.

oficial [ofi'θjal] a official // nm official; (MIL) officer.

oficina [ofi'θina] nf office; **oficinista** nm/f clerk.

oficio [ofi'θjo] nm (profesión) profession; (puesto) post; (REL) service; **ser del ~** to be an old hand; **tener mucho ~** to have a lot of experience; **~ de difuntos** funeral service; **de ~** officially.

oficiosidad [ofiθjosi'ðað] nf helpfulness; (pey) officiousness.

oficioso, a [ofi'θjoso, a] a (diligente) attentive; (pey) officious; (no oficial) unofficial, informal.

ofrecer [ofre'θer] vt (dar) to offer; (proponer) to propose; **~se** vr (persona) to offer o.s., volunteer; (situación) to present itself; ¿**qué se le ofrece?**, ¿**se le ofrece algo?** what can I do for you?, can I get you anything?

ofrecimiento [ofreθi'mjento] nm offer, offering.

ofrendar [ofren'dar] vt to offer, contribute.

oftálmico, a [of'talmiko, a] a ophthalmic.

ofuscación [ofuska'θjon] nf, **ofuscamiento** [ofuska'mjento] nm (fig) bewilderment; **ofuscar** vt (confundir) to bewilder; (encegecer) to dazzle, blind.

oída [o'iða] nf hearing; **de ~s** by hearsay.

oído [o'iðo] nm ear; (sentido) hearing.

oigo etc vb ver **oír.**

oír [o'ir] vt (gen) to hear; (atender a) to listen to; ¡**oiga! listen!; ~ misa** to attend mass.

O.I.T. nf abr de **Organización Internacional del Trabajo** I.L.O. (International Labour Organization).

ojal [o'xal] nm buttonhole.

ojalá [oxa'la] excl if only it were so!, some hope(s)! // conj if only...!, would that...!; **~ que venga hoy** I hope he comes today.

ojeada [oxe'aða] nf glance; **ojear** vt (mirar fijo) to stare at; (examinar) to eye; (mirar de reojo) to glance at.

ojera [o'xera] nf: **tener ~s** to have rings or circles under the eyes.

ojeriza [oxe'riθa] nf ill-will.

ojeroso, a [oxe'roso, a] a haggard.

ojete [o'xete] nm eye(let).

ojo [o'xo] nm eye; (de puente) span; (de cerradura) keyhole // excl careful!; **tener ~ para** to have an eye for; **~ de buey** porthole.

ola [o'la] nf wave.

olé [o'le] excl bravo!, olé!

oleada [ole'aða] nf big wave, swell; (fig) surge.

oleaje [ole'axe] nm swell.

óleo [o'leo] nm oil; **oleoducto** nm (oil) pipeline.

oler [o'ler] vt (gen) to smell; (husmear) to pry into; (fig) to sniff out // vi: **~ a** to smell of.

olfatear [olfate'ar] vt to smell; (fig) to sniff out; (husmear) to pry into; **olfato** nm sense of smell.

oliente [o'ljente] a smelling; **bien/mal ~** sweet-/foul-smelling.

oligarquía [oligar'kia] nf oligarchy.

olimpíada [olim'piaða] nf: **las O~s** the Olympics.

oliva [o'liβa] nf (aceituna) olive;

(*árbol*) olive tree; **aceite de ~** olive oil; **olivo** *nm* olive tree.

olmo ['olmo] *nm* elm (tree).

olor [o'lor] *nm* smell; (*fig*) **~oso, a** *a* scented.

olvidadizo, a [olβiða'oiθo, a] *a* (*desmemoriado*) forgetful; (*distraído*) absent-minded.

olvidar [olβi'ðar] *vt* to forget; (*omitir*) to omit; **~se** *vr* to forget o.s.; **se me olvidó** I forgot.

olvido [ol'βiðo] *nm* oblivion.

olla ['oʎa] *nf* pan; (*comida*) stew; **~ a presión** *o* **autopresión** pressure cooker; **~ podrida** Spanish stew.

ombligo [om'blixo] *nm* navel.

ominoso, a [omi'noso, a] *a* ominous.

omisión [omi'sjon] *nf* (*abstención*) omission; (*descuido*) neglect.

omiso, a [o'miso, a] *a*: **hacer caso ~ de** to ignore, pass over.

omitir [omi'tir] *vt* to omit.

omnipotente [omnipo'tente] *a* omnipotent.

omnívoro, a [om'niβoro, a] *a* omnivorous.

omóplato [o'moplato] *nm* shoulder blade.

O.M.S. *nf abr de* **Organización Mundial de la Salud** W.H.O. (World Health Organization).

once ['onθe] *num* eleven; **las ~** (*fam*) elevenses.

onda ['onda] *nf* wave; **~ corta/larga/media** short/long/medium wave; **~s acústicas/hertzianas** acoustic/Hertzian waves; **ondear** *vt* to wave // *vi* to wave; (*tener ondas*) to be wavy; (*pelo*) to flow; (*agua*) to ripple; **ondearse** *vr* to swing, sway.

ondulación [ondula'θjon] *nf* undulation; **ondulado, a** *a* wavy // *nm* wave; **ondulante** *a* undulating; (*cartón*, *chapa*) corrugated.

ondular [ondu'lar] *vt* (*el pelo*) to wave // *vi*, **~se** *vr* to undulate.

oneroso, a [one'roso, a] *a* onerous.

ONU *nf abr de* **Organización de las Naciones Unidas** UNO (United Nations Organization).

O.P. *nfpl abr de* **Obras Públicas** Public Works.

opaco, a [o'pako, a] *a* opaque; (*fig*) dull.

opalescente [opales'θente] *a* opalescent.

ópalo ['opalo] *nm* opal.

opción [op'θjon] *nf* (*gen*) option; (*derecho*) right, option.

ópera ['opera] *nf* opera; **~ bufa** *o* **cómica** comic opera.

operación [opera'θjon] *nf* (*gen*) operation; (*COM*) transaction, deal.

operador, a [opera'ðor, a] *nm/f* operator; (*en cine*) projectionist; (*de cine*) camera operator.

opereta [ope'reta] *nf* operetta.

opinar [opi'nar] *vt* (*estimar*) to think // *vi* (*enjuiciar*) to give one's opinion; **opinión** *nf* (*creencia*) belief; (*criterio*) opinion.

opio ['opjo] *nm* opium.

oponente [opo'nente] *nm/f* opponent.

oponer [opo'ner] *vt* (*resistencia*) to put up, offer; (*negativa*) to raise; **~se** *vr* (*objetar*) to object; (*estar frente a frente*) to be opposed; (*dos personas*) to oppose each other; **A a B** to set A against B; **me opongo a pensar que...** I refuse to believe or think that...

oportunidad [oportuni'ðað] *nf* (*ocasión*) opportunity; (*posibilidad*) chance.

oportunismo [oportu'nismo] *nm* opportunism; **oportunista** *nm/f* opportunist.

oportuno, a [opor'tuno, a] *a* (*apto*) appropriate, suitable; (*en su tiempo*) opportune; (*conveniente*) convenient; **en el momento** ~ at the right moment.

oposición [oposi'θjon] *nf* opposition; **oposiciones** *nfpl* public examinations.

opositor, a [oposi'tor, a] *nm/f* (*adversario*) opponent; (*concurrente*) competitor.

opresión [opre'sjon] *nf* oppression; **opresivo, a** *a* oppressive; **opresor, a** *nm/f* oppressor.

oprimir [opri'mir] *vt* to squeeze; (*fig*) to oppress.

oprobio [o'proβjo] *nm* (*infamia*) ignominy; (*descrédito*) shame.

optar [op'tar] *vi* (*elegir*) to choose; ~ **a** o **por** to opt for.

óptico, a [a 'optiko, a] *a* optic(al) // *nm/f* optician.

optimismo [opti'mismo] *nm* optimism; **optimista** *nm/f* optimist.

óptimo, a [a 'optimo, a] *a* (*bueno*) very good; (*el mejor*) very best.

opuesto, a [o'pwesto, a] *a* (*contrario*) opposite; (*antagónico*) opposing.

opugnar [opuɣ'nar] *vt* to attack.

opulencia [opu'lenθja] *nf* opulence; **opulento, a** *a* opulent.

oquedad [oke'ðað] *nf* (*fig*) void.

ora ['ora] *ad*: ~ **tú** ~ **yo** now you, now me.

oración [ora'θjon] *nf* (*discurso*) speech; (*REL*) prayer; (*LING*) sentence.

oráculo [o'rakulo] *nm* oracle.

orador, a [a 'oraðor, a] *nm/f* (*predicador*) preacher; (*conferenciante*) speaker.

oral [o'ral] *a* oral.

orangután [orangu'tan] *nm* orangutan.

orar [o'rar] *vi* (*REL*) to pray; (*hablar*) to make a speech.

oratoria [ora'torja] *nf* oratory.

órbita ['orβita] *nf* orbit.

orden [or'ðen] *nm* order // *nf* (*gen*) order; ~ **del día** agenda; **de primer** ~ first-rate; **en** ~ **de prioridad** in order of priority.

ordenado, a [orðe'naðo, a] *a* (*metódico*) methodical; (*arreglado*) orderly.

ordenador [orðena'ðor] *nm* computer.

ordenanza [orðe'nanθa] *nf* ordinance.

ordenar [orðe'nar] *vt* (*mandar*) to order; (*poner orden*) to put in order, arrange; ~**se** *vr* (*REL*) to be ordained.

ordeñadora [orðeɲa'ðora] *nf* milking machine.

ordeñar [orðe'ɲar] *vt* to milk.

ordinario, a [orði'narjo, a] *a* (*común*) ordinary, usual; (*bajo*) vulgar, common.

orégano [o'reɣano] *nm* oregano.

oreja [o'rexa] *nf* ear; (*de zapatos*) tongue; (*MECÁNICA*) lug, flange.

orfandad [orfan'dað] *nf* orphanhood.

orfebrería [orfeβre'ria] *nf* gold/silver work.

organillo [orɣa'niʎo] *nm* barrel organ.

organismo [orɣa'nismo] *nm* (*BIO*) organism; (*POL*) organization.

organista [orɣa'nista] *nm/f* organist.

organización [orɣaniθa'θjon] *nf* organization; **organizar** *vt* to organize.

órgano ['orɣano] *nm* organ.

orgasmo [or'xasmo] *nm* orgasm.

orgía [or'xia] *nf* orgy.

orgullo [or'ɣuʎo] *nm* (*altanería*) pride; (*autorespeto*) self-respect; **orgulloso, a** *a* (*gen*) proud; (*altanero*) haughty.

orientación [orjenta'θjon] *nf* (*posición*) position; (*dirección*) direction; (*entrenamiento*) training.

orientar [orjen'tar] *vt* (*situar*) to orientate; (*señalar*) to point; (*dirigir*) to direct; (*informar*) to guide; ~**se** *vr* to get one's bearings; (*decidirse*) to decide on a course of action.

oriente [o'rjente] *nm* east; Cer-

cano/Medio/Lejano O~ Near/ Middle/Far East.

origen [o'rixen] nm (germen) origin; (nacimiento) lineage, birth.

original [orixi'nal] a (nuevo) original; (extraño) odd, strange; ~**idad** nf originality.

originar [orixi'nar] vt to originate; ~**se** vr to originate; ~**lo, a** a (nativo) native; (primordial) original.

orilla [o'riʎa] nf (borde) border; (de río) bank; (de bosque, tela) edge; (de taza etc) rim, lip; (de calle) pavement; **orillar** vt (bordear) to skirt, go round; (resolver) to wind up; (tocar: asunto) to touch briefly on.

orín [o'rin] nm rust.

orina [o'rina] nf urine; **orinal** nm (chamber) pot; **orinar** vi to urinate; **orinarse** vr to wet o.s.; **orines** nmpl urine sg.

oriundo, a [o'rjundo, a] a: ~ **de** native of.

orlar [or'lar] vt (adornar) to adorn, decorate; (encuadrar) to frame.

ornamentar [ornamen'tar] vt (adornar, ataviar) to adorn; (revestir) to bedeck.

ornamento [orna'mento] nm ornament

ornar [or'nar] vt to adorn.

oro ['oro] nm gold; ~**s** nmpl (NAIPES) hearts.

oropel [oro'pel] nm tinsel.

orozuz [oro'θuθ] nm liquorice.

orquesta [or'kesta] nf orchestra; ~ **de cámara/sinfónica** chamber/symphony orchestra.

orquídea [or'kiðea] nf orchid.

ortiga [or'tiʀa] nf nettle.

ortodoxo, a [orto'ðokso, a] a orthodox.

ortografía [ortosra'fia] nf spelling.

ortopedia [orto'peðja] nf orthopaedics sg.

oruga [o'ruʀa] nf caterpillar; (BOT) rocket.

orzuelo [or'θwelo] nm (MED) stye.

os [os] pron (gen) you; (a vosotros) to you.

osa ['osa] nf (she-)bear; **O~ Mayor/Menor** Great/Little Bear.

osadía [osa'ðia] nf daring.

osar [o'sar] vi to dare.

oscilación [osθila'θjon] nf (movimiento) oscillation; (fluctuación) fluctuation; (vacilación) hesitation; (columpio) swinging, movement to and fro; **oscilar** vi to oscillate; to fluctuate; to hesitate.

ósculo ['oskulo] nm kiss.

oscurecer [oskure'θer] vt to darken // vi to grow dark; ~**se** vr to grow or get dark.

oscuridad [oskuri'ðað] nf obscurity; (tinieblas) darkness.

oscuro, a [os'kuro, a] a dark; (fig) obscure; **a ~as** in the dark.

óseo, a [o'seo, a] a bony.

oso ['oso] nm bear; ~ **de peluche** teddy bear; ~ **hormiguero** anteater.

ostensible [osten'sißle] a obvious.

ostentación [ostenta'θjon] nf (gen) ostentation; (acto) display; **ostentar** vt (gen) to show; (pey) to flaunt, show off; (poseer) to have, possess; **ostentoso, a** a ostentatious, showy.

osteópata [oste'opata] nm/f osteopath.

ostra ['ostra] nf oyster.

ostracismo [ostra'θismo] nm ostracism.

osuno, a [o'suno, a] a bear-like.

OTAN ['otan] nf abr de **Organización del Tratado del Atlántico Norte** NATO (North Atlantic Treaty Organization).

otear [ote'ar] vt to observe; (fig) to look into.

otitis [o'titis] nf earache.

otoñal [oto'nal] a autumnal.

otoño [o'tono] nm autumn.

otorgamiento [otorxa'mjento] nm conferring, granting; (JUR) execution.

otorgar [otor'xar] *vt* (*conceder*) to concede; (*dar*) to grant.

otro, a ['otro, a] *a* (*sg*) another; (*pl*) other // *pron* another one; ~s others; ~ a cosa something else; de ~ a manera otherwise; en ~ tiempo formerly, once; ni uno ni ~ neither one nor the other; ~ tanto the same again.

ovación [oβa'θjon] *nf* ovation.

oval [o'βal], **ovalado, a** [oβa'laðo, a] *a* oval; **óvalo** *nm* oval.

oveja [o'βexa] *nf* sheep; **ovejuno, a** *a* sheep *cpd*.

overol [oβe'rol] *nm* overalls *pl*.

ovillar [oβi'ʎar] *vt* to wind (into a ball); ~se *vr* to curl up into a ball.

OVNI ['oβni] *nm abr de* **objeto volante no identificado** UFO (unidentified flying object).

ovulación [oβula'θjon] *nf* ovulation; **óvulo** *nm* ovum.

oxidación [oksiða'θjon] *nf* rusting; **oxidar** *vt* to rust; **oxidarse** *vr* to become rusty.

óxido ['oksiðo] *nm* oxide.

oxigenado, a [oksixe'naðo, a] *a* (*QUIMICA*) oxygenated; (*pelo*) bleached // *nm* peroxide.

oxígeno [ok'sixeno] *nm* oxygen.

oyente [o'jente] *nm/f* listener, hearer.

oyes, oyó *etc vb ver* **oír**.

P

P *abr de* **padre**.

pabellón [paβe'ʎon] *nm* bell tent; (*ARQ*) pavilion; (*de hospital etc*) block, section; (*bandera*) flag.

pábilo [pa'βilo] *nm* wick.

pacer [pa'θer] *vi* to graze // *vt* to graze on.

paciencia [pa'θjenθja] *nf* patience.

paciente [pa'θjente] *a, nm/f* patient.

pacificación [paθifika'θjon] *nf*

pacification; **pacificar** *vt* to pacify; (*tranquilizar*) to calm.

pacífico, a [pa'θifiko, a] *a* (*persona*) peace-loving; (*existencia*) pacific; **el (océano) P~** the Pacific (Ocean).

pacifismo [paθi'fismo] *nm* pacifism; **pacifista** *nm/f* pacifist.

pactar [pak'tar] *vt* to agree to, agree on // *vi* to come to an agreement.

pacto ['pakto] *nm* (*tratado*) pact; (*acuerdo*) agreement.

padecer [paðe'θer] *vt* (*sufrir*) to suffer; (*soportar*) to endure, put up with; (*ser víctima de*) to be a victim of; **padecimiento** *nm* suffering.

padrastro [pa'ðrastro] *nm* stepfather.

padre ['paðre] *nm* father // *a* (*fam*): **un éxito** ~ a tremendous success; ~s *nmpl* parents.

padrino [pa'ðrino] *nm* (*REL*) godfather; (*fig*) sponsor, patron; ~s *nmpl* godparents; ~ de boda best man.

padrón [pa'ðron] *nm* (*censo*) census, roll; (*de socios*) register; (*TEC*) pattern.

paella [pa'eʎa] *nf* paella, *dish of rice with meat, shellfish etc.*

paga ['paxa] *nf* (*dinero pagado*) payment; (*sueldo*) pay, wages *pl*.

pagadero, a [paxa'ðero, a] *a* payable; ~ a la entrega/a plazos payable on delivery/in instalments.

pagano, a [pa'xano, a] *a, nm/f* pagan, heathen.

pagar [pa'xar] *vt* (*gen*) to pay; (*las compras, crimen*) to pay for; (*fig: favor*) to repay // *vi* to pay; ~ al contado/a plazos to pay (in) cash/in instalments; ~se *vr*: ~se con algo to be content with sth; ~se de sí mismo to be conceited.

pagaré [paxa're] *nm* I.O.U.

página ['paxina] *nf* page.

pago ['paɣo] nm (dinero) payment; (fig) return; (barrio) district; (AM) home region, home area; **estar ~ to be even or quits; ~ anticipado/a cuenta/a la entrega/en especie** advance payment/payment on account/cash on delivery/payment in kind.

país [pa'is] nm (gen) country; (región) land; (paisaje) landscape; **los P~es Bajos** the Low Countries; **el P~ Vasco** the Basque Country; **paisaje** nm countryside, scenery.

paisano, a [pai'sano, a] a of the same country // nm/f (compatriota) fellow countryman/woman; (campesino) peasant; **vestir de ~** (soldado) to be in civvies (fam); (guardia) to be in plain clothes.

paja ['paxa] nf straw; (fig) trash, rubbish.

pájara ['paxara] nf hen bird; (cometa) kite; (mujer) thief.

pájaro ['paxaro] nm bird.

pajita [pa'xita] nf (drinking) straw.

pala ['pala] nf (de mango largo) spade; (de mango corto) shovel; (raqueta etc) bat; (: de tenis) racquet; (CULIN) slice; **~ matamoscas** fly swat.

palabra [pa'laβra] nf (gen) word; (facultad) (power of) speech; (derecho de hablar) right to speak; **palabrota** nf swearword.

palacio [pa'laθjo] nm palace; (mansión) mansion, large house; **~ de justicia** courthouse; **~ municipal** town/city hall.

paladar [pala'ðar] nm (gen) palate; **paladear** vt to taste.

palanca [pa'laŋka] nf lever; (fig) pull, influence.

palangana [palaŋ'gana] nf washbasin.

palco ['palko] nm box.

palenque [pa'leŋke] nm (cerca) stockade, fence; (área) arena, enclosure; (de gallos) pit.

Palestina [pales'tina] nf Palestine.

paliar [pa'ljar] vt (mitigar) to mitigate; (disfrazar) to conceal; **paliativo** nm palliative.

palidecer [paliðe'θer] vi to turn pale; **palidez** nf paleness; **pálido, a** a pale.

palillo [pa'liʎo] nm small stick; (para dientes) toothpick.

paliza [pa'liθa] nf beating, thrashing.

palizada [pali'θaða] nf fence; (lugar cercado) enclosure.

palma ['palma] nf (ANAT) palm; (árbol) palm tree; **batir o dar ~s to** clap, applaud; **~da** nf slap; **~s** nfpl clapping sg, applause sg.

palmear [palme'ar] vi to clap.

palmo ['palmo] nm (medida) span; (fig) small amount; **~ a ~** inch by inch.

palmotear [palmote'ar] vi to clap, applaud; **palmoteo** nm clapping, applause; (palmada) slap.

palo ['palo] nm stick; (poste) post, pole; (mango) handle, shaft; (golpe) blow, hit; (de golf) club; (de béisbol) bat; (NAUT) mast; (NAIPES) suit; **~ de tienda** tent pole.

paloma [pa'loma] nf dove, pigeon.

palomilla [palo'miʎa] nf moth; (TEC tuerca) wing nut; (: hierro) angle iron.

palomitas [palo'mitas] nfpl popcorn sg.

palpar [pal'par] vt to touch, feel; (acariciar) to caress, fondle; (caminar a tientas) to grope one's way along; (fig) to appreciate, understand; **~ a uno** to frisk sb.

palpitación [palpita'θjon] nf palpitation; **palpitante** a palpitating; (fig) burning; **palpitar** vi to palpitate; (latir) to beat.

palúdico, a [pa'luðiko, a] a marshy.

paludismo [palu'ðismo] nm malaria.

pampa ['pampa] nf (AM) pampa(s), prairie.

pan [pan] nm (en general) bread;

(*una barra*) loaf; (*trigo*) wheat; **de ～ llevar** arable; (*para la cabeza*) (head)scarf.

pana ['pana] *nf* corduroy.

panadería [pana‹e'ria] *nf* baker's (shop); **panadero, a** *nm/f* baker.

Panamá [pana'ma] *nm* Panama; **panameño, a** *a* Panamanian.

pancarta [pan'karta] *nf* placard, banner.

panda ['panda] *nf* panda.

pandereta [pande'reta] *nf* tambourine.

pandilla [pan'di‹a] *nf* (*de cine*) set, group; (*de criminales*) gang; (*pey*) clique.

pando, a ['pando, a] *a* sagging.

panel [pa'nel] *nm* panel.

pánico ['paniko] *nm* panic.

panorama [pano'rama] *nm* panorama; (*vista*) view.

pantalones [panta'lones] *nmpl* trousers.

pantalla [pan'ta‹a] *nf* (*de cine*) screen; (*cubre-luz*) lampshade.

pantano [pan'tano] *nm* (*ciénaga*) marsh, swamp; (*depósito: de agua*) reservoir; (*fig*) jam, fix, difficulty.

pantera [pan'tera] *nf* panther.

pantimedias [panti'me‹jas] *nfpl* tights.

pantomima [panto'mima] *nf* pantomime.

pantorrilla [panto'rri‹a] *nf* calf (of the leg).

pantufla [pan'tufla] *nf* slipper.

panza ['panθa] *nf* belly, paunch; **panzudo, a, panzón, ona** *a* fat, potbellied.

pañal [pa'ɲal] *nm* nappy; **～es** *nmpl* (*fig*) early stages, infancy *sg*.

pañería [paɲe'ria] *nf* drapery; **pañero, a** *nm/f* draper.

paño ['paɲo] *nm* (*tela*) cloth; (*pedazo de tela*) (piece of) cloth; (*trapo*) duster, rag; **～ higiénico** sanitary towel; **～s menores** underclothes.

pañuelo [pa'ɲwelo] *nm* handker-

chief, hanky (*fam*); (*para la cabeza*) (head)scarf.

papa ['papa] *nf* (*AM*) potato // *nm*: **el P～** the Pope.

papá [pa'pa] (*pl* **～s**) *nm* (*fam*) dad, daddy.

papagayo [papa'vajo] *nm* parrot.

papamoscas [papa'moskas] *nm inv* fly-catcher.

papanatas [papa'natas] *nm inv* (*fam*) sucker, simpleton.

papar [pa'par] *vt* to swallow, gulp (down).

paparrucha [papa'rrutʃa] *nf* (*tontería*) piece of nonsense; (*engaño*) hoax.

papaya [pa'paja] *nf* papaya.

papel [pa'pel] *nm* (*en general*) paper; (*hoja de papel*) sheet of paper; (*TEATRO*) part, role; **～ de calcar/carbón/de cartas** tracing paper/carbon paper/stationery; **～ de envolver o empapelar** brown paper, wrapping paper/wallpaper; **～ de estaño/higiénico** tinfoil/toilet paper; **～ de lija** sandpaper; **～ moneda** paper money; **～ secante** blotting paper.

papeleo [pape'leo] *nm* red tape.

papelera [pape'lera] *nf* (*cesto*) wastepaper basket; (*escritorio*) desk.

papelería [papele'ria] *nf* (*papeles*) mass of papers; (*tienda*) stationer's (shop).

papeleta [pape'leta] *nf* (*pedazo de papel*) slip or bit of paper; (*tarjeta de archivo*) index card; (*POL*) ballot paper; (*ESCOL*) report.

paperas [pa'peras] *nfpl* mumps.

paquete [pa'kete] *nm* (*caja*) packet; (*bulto*) parcel; (*AM: fam*) nuisance, bore.

par [par] *a* (*igual*) like, equal; (*MAT*) even // *nm* equal; (*de guantes*) pair; (*de veces*) couple; (*dignidad*) peer; (*GOLF, COM*) par; **abrir de ～ en ～** to open wide.

para ['para] *prep* (*gen*) for; **no es ～ comer** it's not for eating; **decir ～ sí**

to say to o.s.; ¿~ qué lo quieres? what do you want it for?; se casaron ~ separarse otra vez they married only to separate again; lo tendré ~ mañana I'll have it for tomorrow; ir ~ casa to go home, head for home; ~ profesor es muy estúpido he's very stupid for a teacher; ¿quién es usted ~ gritar así? who are you to shout like that?; tengo bastante ~ vivir I have enough to live on; estoy ~ cantar I'm about to sing.

parabién [para'βjen] nm congratulations pl.

parábola [pa'raβola] nf parable; (MAT) parabola.

parabrisas [para'βrisas] nm inv windscreen.

paracaídas [paraka'iðas] nm inv parachute; **paracaidista** nm/f parachutist; (MIL) paratrooper.

parachoques [para'tʃokes] nm inv bumper; (en auto) shock absorber.

parada [pa'raða] nf ver parado.

paradero [para'ðero] nm stopping-place; (situación) whereabouts; (fin) end.

parado, a [pa'raðo, a] a (persona) motionless, standing still; (fábrica) closed, at a standstill; (coche) stopped; (AM) standing (up); (sin empleo) unemployed, idle; (confuso) // nf (gen) stop; (acto) stopping; (de industria) shutdown, stoppage; (de pagos) suspension; (lugar) stopping-place; (apuesta) bet; ~ de autobús bus stop.

paradoja [para'ðoxa] nf paradox.

parador [para'ðor] nm (luxury) hotel.

paráfrasis [pa'rafrasis] nm inv paraphrase.

parágolpes [para'volpes] nm inv bumper.

paraguas [pa'raɣwas] nm inv umbrella.

Paraguay [para'ɣwai] nm: el ~ Paraguay.

paraíso [para'iso] nm paradise, heaven.

paraje [pa'raxe] nm place, spot.

paralelo, a [para'lelo, a] a parallel.

parálisis [pa'ralisis] nf inv paralysis; **paralítico, a** a, nm/f paralytic; **paralizar** vt to paralyse; **paralizarse** vr to become paralysed; (fig) to come to a standstill.

paramilitar [paramili'tar] a paramilitary.

páramo ['paramo] nm bleak plateau.

parangón [paran'gon] nm: sin ~ incomparable.

paranoico, a [para'noiko, a] nm/f paranoiac.

parapléjico, a [para'plexiko, a] a, nm/f paraplegic.

parar [pa'rar] vt to stop; (golpe) to ward off // vi to stop; ~se vr to stop; (AM) to stand up; ha parado de llover it has stopped raining; van a ~ en la comisaría they're going to end up in the police station; ~se en to pay attention to.

parásito, a [pa'rasito, a] nm/f parasite.

parasol [para'sol] nm parasol, sunshade.

parcela [par'θela] nf plot, piece of ground.

parcial [par'θjal] a (pago) part-; (eclipse) partial; (juez) prejudiced, biased; ~idad nf (prejuicio) prejudice, bias; (partido, facción) party, faction.

parco, a ['parko, a] a (frugal) frugal; (mezquino) mean; (moderado) moderate.

parche ['partʃe] nm (MED) sticking plaster; (gen) patch.

parear [pare'ar] vt (juntar, hacer par) to match, but (calcetines) to put into pairs; (BIO) to mate, pair.

parecer [pare'θer] nm (opinión) opinion, view; (aspecto) looks pl // vi (tener apariencia) to seem, look; (asemejarse) to look like, seem like; (aparecer, llegar) to appear; ~se vr to look alike, resemble each other;

~se a to look like, resemble; **según o a lo que parece** evidently, apparently; **me parece que** I think (that), it seems to me that; **parecido, a** a similar // nm similarity, likeness, resemblance; **bien parecido** good-looking, nice-looking.

pared [pa'reð] nf wall.

parejo, a [pa'rexo, a] a (igual) equal; (liso) smooth, even // nf (dos) pair; (: de personas) couple; (el otro: de un par) other one (of a pair); (: persona) partner.

parentela [paren'tela] nf relations pl.

parentesco [paren'tesko] nm relationship.

paréntesis [pa'rentesis] nm inv parenthesis; (digresión) digression; (en escrito) bracket.

parezco etc vb ver **parecer.**

pariente, a [pa'rjente, a] nm/f relative, relation.

parihuela [pari'wela] nf stretcher.

parir [pa'rir] vt to give birth to // vi (mujer) to give birth, have a baby.

París [pa'ris] n Paris.

parlamentar [parlamen'tar] vi (hablar) to talk, converse; (negociar) to parley.

parlamentario, a [parlamen-'tarjo, a] a parliamentary // nm/f member of parliament.

parlamento [parla'mento] nm (POL) parliament; (conversación) parley.

parlanchín, ina [parlan'tʃin, ina] a loose-tongued, indiscreet // nm/f chatterbox.

parlar [par'lar] vi to chatter (away), talk (a lot); (chismear) to gossip; **parlero, a** a talkative; gossipy; (pájaro) singing.

paro ['paro] nm (huelga) stoppage (of work), strike; (desempleo) unemployment; **subsidio de** ~ unemployment benefit; **hay** ~ **en la industria** work in the industry is at a standstill.

parodia [pa'roðja] nf parody; **parodiar** vt to parody.

parpadear [parpaðe'ar] vi (los ojos) to blink; (luz) to flicker.

párpado ['parpaðo] nm eyelid.

parque ['parke] nm (lugar verde) park; (depósito) depot; ~ **de atracciones/de estacionamiento/zoológico** fairground/car park/zoo.

parquímetro [par'kimetro] nm parking meter.

párrafo ['parrafo] nm paragraph; **echar un** ~ (fam) to have a chat.

parranda [pa'rranda] nf (fam) spree, binge.

parrilla [pa'rriʎa] nf (CULIN) grill; (de coche) grille; (carne de) ~ barbecue; ~**da** nf barbecue.

párroco ['parroko] nm parish priest.

parroquia [pa'rrokja] nf parish; (iglesia) parish church; (COM) clientele, customers pl; ~**no, a** a nm/f parishioner; client, customer.

parte ['parte] nm message; (informe) report // nf (gen) part; (lado, cara) side; (de reparto) share; (JUR) party; **en alguna** ~ **de Europa** somewhere in Europe; **en cualquier** ~ anywhere; **en gran** ~ to a large extent; **la mayor** ~ **de los españoles** most Spaniards; **de algún tiempo a esta** ~ for some time past; **de** ~ **de alguien** on sb's behalf; **por** ~ **de** on the part of; **yo por mí** ~ I for my part; **por otra** ~ on the other hand; **dar** ~ to inform; **tomar** ~ to take part.

partera [par'tera] nf midwife.

partición [parti'θjon] nf division, sharing-out; (POL) partition.

participación [partiθipa'θjon] nf (acto) participation, taking part; (parte, COM) share; (de lotería) small prize; (aviso) notice, notification.

participante [partiθi'pante] nm/f participant; **participar** vt to notify, inform // vi to take part, participate; (compartir) to share.

partícipe [par'tiθipe] nm/f participant.

particular [partiku'lar] a (especial) particular, special; (individual, personal) private, personal // nm (punto, asunto) particular, point; (individuo) individual; tiene coche ~ he has a car of his own; ~izar vt to distinguish; (especificar) to specify; (detallar) to give details about.

partida [par'tiða] nf (salida) departure; (COM) entry, item; (juego) game; (apuesta) bet; (grupo, bando) band, group; mala ~ dirty trick; ~ de nacimiento/matrimonio/defunción birth/marriage/death certificate.

partidario, a [parti'ðarjo, a] a partisan // nm/f (DEPORTE) supporter; (POL) partisan.

partido [par'tiðo] nm (POL) party; (encuentro) game, match; (apoyo) support; (equipo) team; sacar ~ de to profit from, benefit from; tomar ~ to take sides.

partir [par'tir] vt (dividir) to split, divide; (compartir, distribuir) to share (out), distribute; (romper) to break open, split open; (rebanada) to cut (off) // vi (tomar camino) to set off, set out; (comenzar) to start (off or out); ~se vr to crack or split or break (in two etc); a ~ de (starting) from.

parto ['parto] nm birth; (fig) product, creation; estar de ~ to be in labour.

parvulario [parβu'larjo] nm nursery school, kindergarten.

pasa ['pasa] nf raisin; de Corinto/de Esmirna currant/sultana.

pasada [pa'saða] nf ver pasado.

pasadizo [pasa'ðiθo] nm (pasillo) passage, corridor; (callejuela) alley.

pasado, a [pa'saðo, a] a nast; (malo: comida, fruta) bad; (muy cocido) overdone; (anticuado) out of date // nm past // nf passing, passage; (acción de pulir) rub,

polish; ~s nmpl ancestors; ~ mañana the day after tomorrow; el mes ~ last month; de ~ in passing, incidentally; una mala ~ a dirty trick.

pasador [pasa'ðor] nm (gen) bolt; (de pelo) pin, grip; ~es nmpl cufflinks.

pasaje [pa'saxe] nm (gen) passage; (pago de viaje) fare; (los pasajeros) passengers pl; (pasillo) passageway.

pasajero, a [pasa'xero, a] a passing; (calle) busy // nm/f passenger; (viajero) traveller.

pasamanos [pasa'manos] nm rail, handrail; (de escalera) banister.

pasaporte [pasa'porte] nm passport.

pasar [pa'sar] vt (gen) to pass; (tiempo) to spend; (durezas) to suffer, endure; (noticia) to give, pass on; (río) to cross; (barrera) to pass through; (falta) to overlook, tolerate; (contrincante) to surpass, do better than; (coche) to overtake // vi (gen) to pass; (terminarse) to be over; (ocurrir) to happen; ~se vr (flores) to fade; (comida) to go bad, go off; (fig) to overdo it, go too far; ~ de to go beyond, exceed; ¡pase! come in!; ~se al enemigo to go over to the enemy; se me pasó I forgot; no se le pasa nada nothing escapes him, he misses nothing; pase lo que pase come what may.

pasarela [pasa'rela] nf footbridge; (en barco) gangway.

pasatiempo [pasa'tjempo] nm pastime; (distracción) amusement.

Pascua ['paskwa] nf: ~ (de Resurrección) Easter; ~ de Navidad Christmas; ~s nfpl Christmas time; ¡felices ~s! Merry Christmas.

pase ['pase] nm pass.

pasear [pase'ar] vt to take for a walk, parade, show off // vi, ~se vr to walk, go for a walk; (holgazanear) to idle, loaf about;

en coche to go for a drive; **paseo** nm (avenida) avenue; (distancia corta) short walk; **dar un paseo** to go for a walk.

pasillo [pa'siʎo] nm passage, corridor.

pasión [pa'sjon] nf passion.

pasivo, a [pa'siβo, a] a passive; (inactivo) inactive // nm (COM) liabilities pl, debts pl.

pasmar [pas'mar] vt (asombrar) to amaze, astonish; (enfriar) to chill (to the bone); **pasmo** nm amazement, astonishment; chill; (fig) wonder, marvel; **pasmoso, a** a amazing, astonishing.

paso, a ['paso, a] a dried // nm (gen) step; (modo de andar) walk; (huella) footprint; (rapidez) speed, pace, rate; (camino accesible) way through; passage; (cruce) crossing; (pasaje) passing, passage; (GEO) pass; (estrecho) strait; **a ese ~** (fig) at that rate; **salir al ~ de** o **a** to waylay; **estar de ~** to be passing through; **~ elevado** flyover; **prohibido el ~** no entry; **ceda el ~** give way.

pasta ['pasta] nf (gen) paste; (CULIN: masa) dough; (: de bizcochos etc) pastry; (cartón) cardboard; (fam) money, dough (fam); **~s** nfpl (bizcochos) pastries, small cakes; (fideos, espaguetis etc) noodles, spaghetti sg etc; **~ de dientes** o **dentífrica** toothpaste; **~ de madera** wood pulp.

pastar [pas'tar], **pastear** [paste'ar] vt, vi to graze.

pastel [pas'tel] nm (dulce) cake; (de carne) pie; (pintura) pastel; **~ería** nf cake shop, pastry shop.

pasteurizado, a [pasteuri'θaðo, a] a pasteurized.

pastilla [pas'tiʎa] nf (de jabón, chocolate) cake, bar; (píldora) tablet, pill.

pasto ['pasto] nm (hierba) grass; (lugar) pasture, field.

pastor, a [pas'tor, a] nm/f

shepherd/ess // nm clergyman, pastor.

pata ['pata] nf (pierna) leg; (pie) foot; (de muebles) leg; **~s arriba** upside down; **meter la ~** to put one's foot in it; (TEC): **~ de cabra** crowbar; **tener buena/mala ~** to be lucky/unlucky; **~da** nf stamp; (puntapié) kick.

patalear [patale'ar] vi to stamp one's feet.

patata [pa'tata] nf potato; **~s fritas** o **a la española** chips, French fries; **~s inglesas** crisps.

patear [pate'ar] vt (pisar) to stamp on, trample (on); (pegar con el pie) to kick // vi to stamp (with rage), stamp one's foot.

patente [pa'tente] a obvious, evident; (COM) patent // nf patent; **patentizar** vt to show, reveal, make evident.

paternal [pater'nal] a fatherly, paternal; **paterno, a** a paternal.

patético, a [pa'tetiko, a] a pathetic, moving.

patillas [pa'tiʎas] nfpl sideburns.

patín [pa'tin] nm skate; (de tobogán) runner; **patinaje** nm skating; **patinar** vi to skate; (resbalarse) to skid, slip; (fam) to slip up, blunder.

patio ['patjo] nm (de casa) patio, courtyard; **~ de recreo** playground.

pato ['pato] nm duck; **pagar el ~** (fam) to take the blame, carry the can.

patológico, a [pato'loxiko, a] a pathological.

patraña [pa'traɲa] nf story, fib.

patria ['patrja] nf native land, mother country.

patrimonio [patri'monjo] nm inheritance; (fig) heritage.

patriota [pa'trjota] nm/f patriot; **patriotismo** nm patriotism.

patrocinar [patroθi'nar] vt to sponsor; (apoyar) to back, support; **patrocinio** nm sponsorship; backing, support.

patrón, ona [pa'tron, ona] nm/f

(*jefe*) boss, chief, master/mistress; (*propietario*) landlord/lady; (REL) patron saint // *nm* (TEC, *costura*) pattern; **patronal** a: **la clase patronal** management; **patronato** *nm* sponsorship; (*acto*) patronage; (COM) employers' association.

patrulla [pa'truʎa] *nf* patrol.

pausa ['pausa] *nf* pause; (*intervalo*) break; (*interrupción*) interruption.

pausado, a [pau'saðo, a] *a* slow, deliberate.

pauta ['pauta] *nf* line, guide line.

pavo ['paβo] *nm* turkey; ~ **real** peacock.

pavor [pa'βor] *nm* dread, terror.

payaso, a [pa'jaso, a] *nm/f* clown.

paz [paθ] *nf* peace; (*tranquilidad*) peacefulness, tranquility; **hacer las paces** to make peace; (*fig*) to make up.

P.C.E. *abr de* **Partido Comunista Español**.

peaje [pe'axe] *nm* toll.

peatón [pea'ton] *nm* pedestrian.

peca ['peka] *nf* freckle.

pecado [pe'kaðo] *nm* sin; **pecador, a** a sinful // *nm/f* sinner.

pecaminoso, a [pekami'noso, a] *a* sinful.

pecar [pe'kar] *vi* (REL) to sin; (*fig*): **peca de generoso** he is too generous.

peculiar [peku'ljar] *a* special, peculiar; (*característico*) typical, characteristic; ~**idad** *nf* peculiarity; special feature, characteristic.

pecho ['petʃo] *nm* (ANAT) chest (de *mujer*) breast(s) (*pl*), bosom; (*corazón*) heart, breast, (*valor*) courage, spirit; **dar el** ~ a to breastfeed; **tomar algo a** ~ to take sth to heart.

pechuga [pe'tʃuxa] *nf* breast (de chicken *etc*).

pedal [pe'ðal] *nm* pedal; ~**ear** *vi* to pedal.

pedante [pe'ðante] a pedantic // *nm/f* pedant; ~**ría** *nf* pedantry.

pedazo [pe'ðaθo] *nm* piece, bit;

hacerse ~**s** to fall to pieces; (*romperse*) to smash, shatter.

pedernal [peðer'nal] *nm* flint.

pediatra [pe'ðjatra] *nm/f* pediatrician.

pedicuro, a [peði'kuro, a] *nm/f* chiropodist.

pedido [pe'ðiðo] *nm* (COM: *mandado*) order; (*petición*) request.

pedir [pe'ðir] *vt* to ask for, request; (*comida*, COM: *mandar*) to order; (*exigir*: *precio*) to ask; (*necesitar*) to need, demand, require // *vi* to ask; **me pidió que cerrara la puerta** he asked me to shut the door; **¿cuánto piden por el coche?** how much are they asking for the car?

pegadizo, a [peɣa'ðiθo, a] a sticky; (MED) infectious // *nm/f* sponger, hanger-on (*fam*).

pegajoso, a [peɣa'xoso, a] a sticky, adhesive; (MED) infectious.

pegamento [peɣa'mento] *nm* gum, sticky stuff.

pegar [pe'ɣar] *vt* (*papel, sellos*) to stick (on); (*cartel*) to post, stick up; (*coser*) to sew (on); (*unir*: *partes*) to join, fix together; (MED) to give, infect with; (*dar*: *golpe*) to give, deal // *vi* (*adherirse*) to stick, adhere; (*prender*: *fuego*) to catch; (*ir juntos: colores*) to match, go together; (*cuadro, pear*) to hit; (*quemar*: *el sol*) to strike hot, burn (*fig*); ~**se** *vr* (*gen*) to stick; (*dos personas*) to hit each other, fight; (*fam*): ~ **un grito** to let out a yell; ~ **un salto** to jump (with fright); ~ **en to touch**; ~**se un tiro** to shoot o.s.

peinado [pei'naðo] *nm* (*en peluquería*) hairdo; (*estilo*) hair style.

peinador, a [peina'ðor, a] *nm/f* hairdresser.

peinar [pei'nar] *vt* to comb; (*hacer estilo*) to style; ~**se** *vr* to comb one's hair.

peine ['peine] *nm* comb; ~**ta** *nf* ornamental comb.

Pekín [pe'kin] *n* Pekin(g).

pelado, a [pe'laðo, a] *a* (*cabeza*) shorn; (*fruta*) peeled; (*campo*, *fig*) bare // *nm* bare patch; (*fig*) wretch, poor devil.

pelaje [pe'laxe] *nm* (*ZOOL*) fur, coat; (*fig*) appearance.

pelambre [pe'lambre] *nm* (*pelo largo*) long hair, mop; (*piel de animal cortado*) fur; (: *de oveja*) fleece; (*parte sin piel*) bare patch.

pelar [pe'lar] *vt* (*cortar el pelo a*) to cut the hair of; (*quitar la piel: animal*) to skin; ~**se** *vr* (*la piel*) to peel off; (*persona*) to lose one's hair; **voy a** ~**me** I'm going to get my hair cut.

peldaño [pel'daɲo] *nm* step.

pelea [pe'lea] *nf* (*lucha*) fight; (*discusión*) quarrel, row; **pelear** *vi* to fight; **pelearse** *vr* to fight; (*reñirse*) to fall out, quarrel.

peletería [pelete'ria] *nf* furrier's, fur shop.

pelícano [pe'likano], **pelícano** [pe'likano] *nm* pelican.

pelicorto, a [peli'korto, a] *a* short-haired.

película [pe'likula] *nf* film; (*cobertura ligera*) thin covering; (*FOTO: rollo*) roll or reel of film.

peligro [pe'liɣro] *nm* danger; (*riesgo*) risk; **correr** ~ **de** to be in danger of; ~**so, a** *a* dangerous, risky.

pelirrojo, a [peli'rroxo, a] *a* a red-haired, red-headed.

pelo ['pelo] *nm* (*cabellos*) hair; (*de barba*, *bigote*) whisker; (*de animal: pellejo*) fur; (*de perro etc*) hair, coat; **al** ~ just right; **venir al** ~ to be exactly what one needs; **un hombre de** ~ **en pecho** a brave man; **por los** ~**s** by the skin of one's teeth; **no tener** ~**s en la lengua** to be outspoken, not mince words; **tomar el** ~ **a uno** to pull sb's leg.

pelón, ona [pe'lon, ona] *a* hairless, bald; (*fig*) broke, skint (*fam*).

pelota [pe'lota] *nf* ball; (*fam*:

cabeza) nut (*fam*); **en** ~ stark naked; ~ **vasca** pelota.

pelotón [pelo'ton] *nm* (*pelota*) big ball; (*muchedumbre*) crowd; (*MIL*) squad, detachment.

peluca [pe'luka] *nf* wig.

peluche [pe'lutʃe] *nm* felt.

peludo, a [pe'luðo, a] *a* hairy, shaggy.

peluquería [peluke'ria] *nf* hairdresser's; (*para hombres*) barber's (shop); **peluquero, a** *nm/f* hairdresser; barber.

pelleja [pe'ʎexa] *nf* skin, hide; (*fam*) whore.

pellejo [pe'ʎexo] *nm* (*de animal*) skin, hide; (*de fruta*) skin, peel.

pellizcar [peʎiθ'kar] *vt* to pinch, nip.

pena ['pena] *nf* (*congoja*) grief, sadness; (*ansia*) anxiety; (*remordimiento*) regret; (*dificultad*) trouble; (*dolor*) pain; **merecer** o **valer la** ~ to be worthwhile; **a duras** ~**s** with great difficulty; ~ **de muerte** death penalty; ~ **pecuniaria** fine; ¡**qué** ~! what a shame!

penal [pe'nal] *a* penal // *nm* (*cárcel*) prison; (*FÚTBOL*) penalty.

penalidad [penali'ðað] *nf* (*problema*, *dificultad*) trouble, hardship; (*JUR*) penalty, punishment.

penar [pe'nar] *vt* to penalize; (*castigar*) to punish // *vi* to suffer; ~**se** *vr* to grieve, mourn.

pender [pen'der] *vi* (*colgar*) to hang; (*JUR*) to be pending.

pendiente [pen'djente] *a* (*colgante*) hanging; (*por resolver*) pending, unsettled // *nm* earring // *nf* hill, slope.

pene ['pene] *nm* penis.

penetración [penetra'θjon] *nf* (*acto*) penetration; (*agudeza*) sharpness, insight.

penetrante [pene'trante] *a* (*herida*) deep; (*persona*, *arma*) sharp; (*sonido*) penetrating, piercing; (mirada) searching; (viento, ironía) biting.

penetrar [pene'trar] vt to penetrate, pierce; (entender) to grasp // vi to penetrate, go in; (líquido) to soak in; (emoción) to pierce.

penicilina [peniθi'lina] nf penicillin.

península [pe'ninsula] nf peninsula; **peninsular** a peninsular.

penitencia [peni'tenθja] nf (remordimiento) penitence; (castigo) penance; **penitencial** a penitential; ~ría nf prison, penitentiary.

penoso, a [pe'noso, a] a (afligido) painful, distressing; (trabajoso) laborious, difficult.

pensador, a [pensa'ðor, a] nm/f thinker.

pensamiento [pensa'mjento] nm (gen) thought; (mente) mind; (idea) idea; (intento) intention.

pensar [pen'sar] vt to think; (considerar) to think over, think out; (proponerse) to intend, plan, propose; (imaginarse) to think up, invent // vi to think; ~ en to aim at, aspire to; **pensativo, a** a thoughtful, pensive.

pensión [pen'sjon] nf (casa) boarding house, guest house; (dinero) pension; (cama y comida) board and lodging; (beca) scholarship; **pensionista** nm/f (jubilado) (old-age) pensioner; (quien vive en pensión) lodger.

penúltimo, a [pe'nultimo, a] a penultimate, second last.

penumbra [pe'numbra] nf halflight, semi-darkness.

penuria [pe'nurja] nf shortage, want.

peña ['peɲa] nf (roca) rock; (cuesta) cliff, crag; (grupo) group, circle.

peñascal [peɲas'kal] nm rocky place; **peñasco** nm large rock, boulder.

peñón [pe'ɲon] nm mass of rock; el P~ the Rock (of Gibraltar).

peón [pe'on] nm labourer; (AM) labourer, farmhand; (eje) spindle, shaft, axle; (AJEDREZ) pawn.

peor [pe'or] a (comparativo) worse; (superlativo) worst // ad worse; worst: **de mal en** ~ from bad to worse

pepino [pe'pino] nm cucumber; (no) me importa un ~ I don't care two hoots

pepita [pe'pita] nf (BOT) pip; (MINERÍA) nugget.

pequeñez [peke'ɲeθ] nf smallness, littleness; (infancia) infancy; (trivialidad) trifle, triviality.

pequeño, a [pe'keɲo, a] a small, little.

pera ['pera] nf pear; **peral** nm pear tree.

percance [per'kanθe] nm setback, misfortune.

percatarse [perka'tarse] vr: ~ de to notice, take note of.

percepción [perθep'θjon] nf (vista) perception; (idea) notion, idea; (colecta de fondos) collection.

perceptible [perθep'tißle] a perceptible, noticeable; (COM) payable, receivable

percibir [perθi'ßir] vt to perceive, notice; (COM) to earn, receive, get.

percusión [perku'sjon] nf percussion.

percha ['pertʃa] nf (poste) pole, support; (ganchos) coat stand; (colgador) coat hanger; (de ave) perch.

perdedor, a [perðe'ðor, a] a (que pierde) losing; (olvidadizo) forgetful // nm/f loser.

perder [per'ðer] vt (gen) to lose; (tiempo, palabras) to waste; (oportunidad) to lose, miss; (tren) to miss // vi to lose; ~se vr (extraviarse) to get lost; (desaparecer) to disappear, be lost to view; (arruinarse) to be ruined; (hundirse) to sink; **echar a** ~ (comida) to spoil, ruin; (oportunidad) to waste.

perdición [perði'θjon] nf perdition, ruin.

pérdida ['perðiða] nf (gen) loss; (de tiempo) waste; ~s nfpl (COM) losses.

perdido, a [per'ðiðo, a] a lost; (incorregible) incorrigible; ~so, a a (que pierde) losing; (fácilmente ~) easily lost.

perdiz [per'ðiθ] nf partridge.

perdón [per'ðon] nm (disculpa) pardon, forgiveness; (clemencia) mercy; ¡~! sorry!, I beg your pardon!; **perdonar** vt to pardon, forgive; (la vida) to spare; (excusar) to exempt, excuse.

perdurable [perðu'raßle] a lasting; (eterno) everlasting; **perdurar** vi (resistir) to last, endure; (seguir existiendo) to stand, still exist.

perecer [pere'θer] vi (morir) to perish, die; (objeto) to shatter.

peregrinación [pereɣrina'θjon] nf long tour, travels pl; (REL) pilgrimage; **peregrino, a** a travelling; (nuevo) newly-introduced // nm/f pilgrim.

perejil [pere'xil] nm parsley.

perenne [pe'renne] a everlasting, perennial.

perentorio, a [peren'torjo, a] a (urgente) urgent, peremptory; (fijo) set, fixed.

pereza [pe'reθa] nf (flojera) laziness; (lentitud) sloth, slowness; **perezoso, a** a lazy; slow, sluggish.

perfección [perfek'θjon] nf perfection; (acto) completion; **perfeccionar** vt to perfect; (acabar) to complete, finish.

perfecto, a [per'fekto, a] a perfect; (terminado) complete, finished.

perfidia [per'fiðja] nf perfidy, treachery.

perfil [per'fil] nm (parte lateral) profile; (silueta) silhouette, outline; (ARQ) (cross) section; ~es nmpl features; (fig) social graces; **perfilado, a** a (bien formado) well-shaped; (largo: cara) long; ~ar vt (trazar) to outline; (dar carácter a) to shape, give character to.

perforación [perfora'θjon] nf perforation; (con taladro) drilling; **perforadora** nf drill.

perforar [perfo'rar] vt to perforate; (agujero) to drill, bore; (papel) to punch a hole in // vi to drill, bore.

perfumado, a [perfu'maðo, a] a scented, perfumed.

perfume [per'fume] nm perfume, scent.

pericia [pe'riθja] nf skill, expertise.

periferia [peri'ferja] nf periphery; (de ciudad) outskirts pl.

perímetro [pe'rimetro] nm perimeter.

periódico, a [pe'rjoðiko, a] a periodic(al) // nm newspaper; **periodismo** nm journalism; **periodista** nm/f journalist.

periodo [pe'rjoðo], **período** [pe'rioðo] nm period.

perito, a [pe'rito, a] a (experto) expert; (diestro) skilled, skilful // nm/f expert; skilled worker; (técnico) technician.

perjudicar [perxuði'kar] vt (gen) to damage, harm; **ese vestido le perjudica** that dress doesn't suit her; **perjudicial** a damaging, harmful; (en detrimento) detrimental; **perjuicio** nm damage, harm; (pérdidas) financial loss.

perjurar [perxu'rar] vi to commit perjury.

perla ['perla] nf pearl; **me viene de** ~ it suits me fine.

permanecer [permane'θer] vi (quedarse) to stay, remain; (seguir) to continue to be.

permanencia [perma'nenθja] nf (duración) permanence; (estancia) stay.

permanente [perma'nente] a (que queda) permanent; (constante) constant // nf perm.

permisible [permi'siβle] a permissible, allowable.

permiso [per'miso] *nm* permission; (*licencia*) permit, licence; **con ~ excuse me; estar de ~** (*MIL*) to be on leave; **~ de conducir** *o* **conductor** driving licence.

permitir [permi'tir] *vt* to permit, allow.

pernicioso, a [perni'θjoso, a] *a* (*maligno, MED*) pernicious; (*persona*) wicked.

pernio ['pernjo] *nm* hinge.

perno ['perno] *nm* bolt.

pero ['pero] *conj* but; (*aún*) yet // *nm* (*defecto*) flaw, defect; (*reparo*) objection.

perorar [pero'rar] *vi* to make a speech.

perpendicular [perpendiku'lar] *a* perpendicular; **el camino es ~ al río** the road is at right angles to the river.

perpetrar [perpe'trar] *vt* to perpetrate.

perpetuamente [perpetwa'mente] *ad* perpetually; **perpetuar** *vt* to perpetuate; **perpetuo, a** *a* perpetual.

perplejo, a [per'plexo, a] *a* perplexed, bewildered.

perra ['perra] *nf* bitch; (*fam*) ... ...

perrera [pe'rrera] *nf* kennel.

perrillo [pe'rriλo] *nm* puppy.

perro ['perro] *nm* dog; **~ caliente** hot dog.

persa ['persa] *a, nm/f* Persian.

persecución [perseku'θjon] *nf* pursuit, hunt, chase; (*REL, POL*) persecution.

perseguir [perse'xir] *vt* to pursue, hunt; (*cortejar*) to chase after; (*molestar*) to pester, annoy; (*REL, POL*) to persecute.

perseverante [perseβe'rante] *a* persevering, persistent; **perseverar** *vi* to persevere, persist; **perseverar en** to persevere in, persist with.

persiana [per'sjana] *nf* (Venetian) blind.

persignarse [persix'narse] *vr* to cross o.s.

persistente [persis'tente] *a* persistent; **persistir** *vi* to persist.

persona [per'sona] *nf* person; **10 ~s 10 people.**

personaje [perso'naxe] *nm* important person, celebrity; (*TEATRO*) character.

personal [perso'nal] *a* (*particular*) personal; (*para una persona*) single, for one person // *nm* personnel, staff; **~idad** *nf* personality.

personarse [perso'narse] *vr* to appear in person.

personificar [personifi'kar] *vt* to personify.

perspectiva [perspek'tiβa] *nf* perspective, (*vista, panorama*) view, panorama; (*posibilidad futura*) outlook, prospect.

perspicacia [perspi'kaθja] *nf* keen-sightedness; (*fig*) discernment, perspicacity.

perspicaz [perspi'kaθ] *a* (*agudo: de la vista*) keen; (*fig*) shrewd.

persuadir [perswa'ðir] *vt* (*gen*) to persuade; (*convencer*) to convince; **~se** *vr* to become convinced; **persuasión** *nf* (*acto*) persuasion; (*estado de mente*) conviction; **persuasivo, a** *a* persuasive; convincing.

pertenecer [pertene'θer] *vi* to belong; (*fig*) to concern; **pertenencia** *nf* ownership; **pertenencias** *nfpl* possessions, property *sg*; **perteneciente** *a* ... belonging to.

pertinaz [perti'naθ] *a* (*persistente*) persistent; (*terco*) obstinate.

pertinente [perti'nente] *a* relevant, pertinent; (*apropiado*) appropriate; **~ a** concerning, relevant to.

perturbación [perturβa'θjon] *nf* (*POL*) disturbance; (*MED*) upset, disturbance.

perturbado, a [pertur'βaðo, a] *a* mentally unbalanced.

perturbador, a [perturßa'ðor, a] *a* (*que perturba*) perturbing, disturbing; (*subversivo*) subversive.

perturbar [pertur'ßar] *vt* (*el orden*) to disturb; (*MED*) to upset, disturb; (*mentalmente*) to perturb.

Perú [pe'ru] *nm*: el ~ Peru; **peruano, a** *a, nm/f* Peruvian.

perversión [perßer'sjon] *nf* perversion; **perverso, a** *a* perverse; (*depravado*) depraved; **pervertido, a** *a* perverted // *nm/f* pervert; **pervertir** *vt* to pervert, corrupt; (*distorsionar*) to distort.

pesa ['pesa] *nf* weight; (*DEPORTE*) shot.

pesadez [pesa'ðeθ] *nf* (*calidad de pesado*) heaviness; (*lentitud*) slowness; (*aburrimiento*) tediousness.

pesadilla [pesa'ðiʎa] *nf* nightmare, bad dream.

pesado, a [pe'saðo, a] *a* (*gen*) heavy; (*lento*) slow; (*difícil, duro*) tough, hard; (*aburrido*) tedious, boring; (*bochornoso*) sultry.

pesadumbre [pesa'ðumbre] *nf* grief, sorrow.

pésame ['pesame] *nm* expression of condolence, message of sympathy.

pesar [pe'sar] *vt* to weigh // *vi* to weigh; (*ser pesado*) to weigh a lot, be heavy; (*fig: opinión*) to carry weight // *nm* (*sentimiento*) regret; (*pena*) grief, sorrow; a ~ de o pese a (que) in spite of, despite.

pesario [pe'sarjo] *nm* pessary.

pesca ['peska] *nf* (*acto*) fishing; (*cantidad de pescado*) catch; **ir de ~** to go fishing.

pescadería [peskaðe'ria] *nf* fish shop.

pescado [pes'kaðo] *nm* fish.

pescador, a [peska'ðor, a] *nm/f* fisherman/woman.

pescar [pes'kar] *vt* (*coger*) to catch; (*tratar de coger*) to fish for; (*conseguir: trabajo*) to manage to get // *vi* to fish, go fishing; **viene a**

~ **un marido** she's come to get a husband.

pescuezo [pes'kweθo] *nm* neck.

pesebre [pe'seßre] *nm* manger.

peseta [pe'seta] *nf* peseta.

pesimista [pesi'mista] *a* pessimistic // *nm/f* pessimist.

pésimo, a ['pesimo, a] *a* abominable, vile.

peso ['peso] *nm* weight; (*balanza*) scales *pl*; (*moneda*) peso; ~ **bruto/neto** gross/net weight; **vender a** ~ to sell by weight.

pesquero, a [pes'kero, a] *a* fishing *cpd*.

pesquisa [pes'kisa] *nf* inquiry, investigation.

pestaña [pes'taɲa] *nf* (*ANAT*) eyelash; (*borde*) rim; **pestañear, pestañar** *vi* to blink.

peste ['peste] *nf* (*gen*) plague; (*mal olor*) stink, stench.

pesticida [pesti'θiða] *nm* pesticide.

pestilencia [pesti'lenθja] *nf* (*plaga*) pestilence, plague; (*mal olor*) stink, stench.

pétalo ['petalo] *nm* petal.

petardista [petar'ðista] *nm/f* (*tramposo*) cheat; (*rompehuelgas*) blackleg.

petición [peti'θjon] *nf* (*pedido*) request, plea; (*memorial*) petition; (*JUR*) plea.

petrificar [petrifi'kar] *vt* to petrify.

petróleo [pe'troleo] *nm* oil, petroleum; **petrolero, a** *a* petroleum *cpd* // *nm* (*COM*) oil man; (*extremista*) extremist, revolutionary; (*buque*) (oil) tanker.

peyorativo, a [pejora'tiβo, a] *a* pejorative.

pez [peθ] *nm* fish.

pezón [pe'θon] *nm* teat, nipple; (*MECÁNICA*) nipple, lubrication point.

piadoso, a [pja'ðoso, a] *a* (*devoto*) pious, devout; (*misericordioso*) kind, merciful.

pianista [pja'nista] *nm/f* pianist.

piano ['pjano] *nm* piano.

piar [pi'ar] *vi* to cheep.
picadillo [pika'ðiʎo] *nm* mince, minced meat.
picado, a [pi'kaðo, a] *a* pricked, punctured; (*mar*) choppy; (*diente*) bad; (*tabaco*) cut; (*enfadado*) cross // *nf* prick; (*de abeja*) sting; (*de mosquito*) bite.
picador [pika'ðor] *nm* (TAUR) picador; (*entrenador de caballos*) horse trainer; (*minero*) faceworker.
picadura [pika'ðura] *nf* (*diente*) bad tooth; (*pinchazo*) puncture; (*de abeja*) sting; (*de mosquito*) bite; (*tabaco picado*) cut tobacco.
picante [pi'kante] *a* hot; (*comentario*) racy, spicy.
picar [pi'kar] *vt* (*agujerear, perforar*) to prick, puncture, (*abeja*) to sting; (*mosquito, serpiente*) to bite; (*incitar*) to incite, goad; (*dañar, irritar*) to annoy, bother; (*quemar: lengua*) to burn, sting // *vi* (*pez*) to bite, take the bait; (*el sol*) to burn, scorch; (*abeja, MED*) to sting; (*mosquito*) to bite; **~se** *vr* (*decaer*) to decay; (*agriarse*) to turn sour, go off; (*ofenderse*) to take offence; **~en** (*fig*) to dabble in.
picardía [pikar'ðia] *nf* villainy; (*astucia*) slyness, craftiness; (*una ~*) dirty trick; (*palabra*) rude/bad word or expression.
pícaro, a [pikaro, a] *a* (*malicioso*) villainous; (*travieso*) mischievous // *nm* (*ladrón*) crook; (*astuto*) sly sort; (*sinvergüenza*) rascal, scoundrel.
pico [piko] *nm* (*de ave*) beak; (*punta aguda*) peak, sharp point; (*TEC*) pick, pickaxe; (*GEO*) peak, summit; **y ~** and a bit.
picotear [pikote'ar] *vt* to peck // *vi* to nibble, pick; (*fam*) to chatter; **~se** *vr* to squabble.
picudo, a [pi'kuðo, a] *a* pointed, with a point.
pichón [pi'tʃon] *nm* young pigeon.
pido, pidió etc *vb ver* **pedir**.
pie [pje] (*pl* **~s**) *nm* (*gen*) foot; (*fig: motivo*) motive, basis; (:

fundamento) foothold; **ir a ~** to go on foot, walk; **estar de ~** to be standing (up); **ponerse de ~** to stand up; **al ~ de la letra** (*citar*) literally, verbatim; (*copiar*) exactly, word for word; **en ~ de guerra** on a war footing; **dar ~ a** to give cause for.
piedad [pje'ðað] *nf* (*lástima*) pity, compassion; (*clemencia*) mercy; (*devoción*) piety, devotion.
piedra [pjeðra] *nf* stone; (*roca*) rock; (*de mechero*) flint; (*METEOROLOGIA*) hailstone.
piel [pjel] *nf* (ANAT) skin; (ZOOL) skin, hide; (*de oso*) fur; (*cuero*) leather; (HORT) skin, peel, **~ de ante** o **de Suecia** suede.
pienso etc *vb ver* **pensar**.
pierdo etc *vb ver* **perder**.
pierna [pjerna] *nf* leg.
pieza [pjeθa] *nf* piece; (*habitación*) room; **~ de recambio** o **repuesto** spare (part).
pigmeo, a [piɣ'meo, a] *a, nm/f* pigmy.
pijama [pi'xama] *nm* pyjamas *pl*.
pila [pila] *nf* (ELEC) battery; (*montón*) heap, pile; (*fuente*) sink.
píldora [pildora] *nf* pill; **la ~ (anticonceptiva)** the pill.
pileta [pi'leta] *nf* basin, bowl; (AM) swimming pool.
pilón [pi'lon] *nm* pillar, post; (ELEC) pylon.
piloto [pi'loto] *nm* pilot; (*de aparato*) rear light, tail light; (AUTO) driver.
pillaje [pi'ʎaxe] *nm* pillage, plunder.
pillar [pi'ʎar] *vt* (*saquear*) to pillage, plunder; (*fam: coger*) to catch; (: *agarrar*) to grasp, seize; (: *entender*) to grasp, catch on to.
pillo, a [piʎo, a] *a* villainous; (*astuto*) sly, crafty // *nm/f* rascal, rogue, scoundrel.
pimentón [pimen'ton] *nm* (*polvo*) paprika; (*pimiento*) red pepper.
pimienta [pi'mjenta] *nf* pepper.

pimiento [pi'mjento] nm pepper, pimiento.

pinacoteca [pinako'teka] nf art gallery.

pinar [pi'nar] nm pinewood.

pincel [pin'θel] nm paintbrush.

pinchar [pin'tʃar] vt (perforar) to prick, pierce; (neumático) to puncture; (incitar) to prod; (herir) to wound.

pinchazo [pin'tʃaðo] nm (perforación) prick; (de llanta) puncture; (fig) prod.

pinchitos [pin'tʃitos] nmpl bar snacks.

pingüino [pin'gwino] nm penguin.

pino ['pino] nm pine (tree); en ~ upright, vertical.

pinta ['pinta] nf spot; (medida) spot, drop; (aspecto) appearance, look(s) (pl); ~do, a a spotted; (de muchos colores) colourful.

pintar [pin'tar] vt to paint // vi to paint; (fam) to count, be important; ~se vr to put on make-up.

pintor, a [pin'tor, a] nm/f painter.

pintoresco, a [pinto'resko, a] a picturesque.

pintura [pin'tura] nf painting; ~ a la acuarela watercolour; ~ al óleo oil painting; ~ rupestre cave painting.

pinza ['pinθa] nf (zool) claw; (para colgar ropa) clothes peg; (tec) pincers pl; ~s nfpl (para depilar) tweezers pl.

piña ['pina] nf (fruto del pino) pine cone; (fruta) pineapple; (fig) group.

pío, a ['pio, a] a (devoto) pious, devout; (misericordioso) merciful // nm cheep, chirp.

piojo [pi'poxo] nm louse.

pionero, a [pjo'nero, a] a pioneering // nm/f pioneer.

pipa ['pipa] nf pipe; (bot) edible sunflower seed.

pipí [pi'pi] nm (fam): hacer ~ to have a wee(wee).

pique ['pike] nm (resentimiento) pique, resentment; (rivalidad) rivalry, competition; irse a ~ to sink; (familia) to be ruined.

piquera [pi'kera] nf hole, vent.

piqueta [pi'keta] nf pick(axe).

piquete [pi'kete] nm (herida) prick, jab; (agujerito) small hole; (mil) squad, party; (de obreros) picket.

piragua [pi'raɣwa] nf canoe; **piragüismo** nm (deporte) canoeing.

pirámide [pi'ramiðe] nf pyramid.

pirata [pi'rata] a, nm pirate.

Pirineo(s) [piri'neo(s)] nm(pl) Pyrenees pl.

piropo [pi'ropo] nm compliment, (piece of) flattery.

pisada [pi'saða] nf (paso) footstep; (huella) footprint.

pisar [pi'sar] vt (caminar sobre) to walk on, tread on; (apretar con el pie) to press; (fig) to trample on, walk all over // vi to tread, step, walk.

piscina [pis'θina] nf swimming pool; (para peces) fishpond.

Piscis [pis'θis] nm Pisces.

piso ['piso] nm (suelo, de edificio) floor; (apartamento) flat, apartment.

pisotear [pisote'ar] vt to trample (on or underfoot).

pista ['pista] nf track, trail; (indicio) clue; ~ de aterrizaje runway; ~ de baile dance floor; ~ de tenis tennis court; ~ de hielo ice rink.

pistola [pis'tola] nf pistol; (tec) spray-gun; **pistolero, a** nm/f gunman, gangster // nf holster.

pistón [pis'ton] nm (tec) piston; (mus) key.

pitar [pi'tar] vt (hacer sonar) to blow; (rechiflar) to whistle at, boo // vi to whistle; (auto) to sound or toot one's horn; (am) to smoke.

pitillo [pi'tiʎo] nm cigarette.

pito ['pito] nm whistle; (de coche) horn.

pitón [pi'ton] nm (zool) python; (protuberancia) bump, lump; (de jarro) spout.

pitonisa [pito'nisa] *nf* fortune-teller.

pizarra [pi'θarra] *nf* (*piedra*) slate; (*encerado*) blackboard.

pizca ['piθka] *nf* pinch, spot; (*fig*) spot, speck, trace: **ni ~** not a bit.

placa ['plaka] *nf* plate; **~ de matrícula** number plate.

placentero, a [plaθen'tero, a] *a* pleasant, agreeable.

placer [pla'θer] *nm* pleasure // *vt* to please.

plácido, a ['plaθiðo, a] *a* placid.

plaga ['plaxa] *nf* pest; (*MED*) plague; (*abundancia*) abundance; **plagar** *vt* to infest, plague; (*llenar*) to fill.

plagio ['plaxjo] *nm* plagiarism.

plan [plan] *nm* (*esquema, proyecto*) plan; (*idea, intento*) idea, intention; **tener ~** (*fam*) to have a date; **tener un ~** (*fam*) to have an affair; **en ~ económico** (*fam*) on the cheap; **vamos en ~ de turismo** we're going as tourists; **si se pone en ese ~...** if that's your attitude... .

plana ['plana] *nf* ver **plano**.

plancha ['plantʃa] *nf* (*para planchar*) iron; (*rótulo*) plate; (*NAUT*) gangway; **~do** *nm* ironing; **planchar** *vt* to iron // *vi* to do the ironing.

planeador [planea'ðor] *nm* glider; **~a** *nf* bulldozer.

planear [plane'ar] *vt* to plan // *vi* to glide.

planeta [pla'neta] *nm* planet.

planicie [pla'niθje] *nf* plain.

planificación [planifika'θjon] *nf* planning; (*de familias*) family planning.

plano, a ['plano, a] *a* flat, level, even // *nm* (*MAT, TEC, AVIAT*) plane; (*foto*) shot; (*ANO*) plan; (*CEO*) map; (*de ciudad*) map, street plan // *nf* sheet (of paper), page; (*TEC*) trowel; **primer ~** close-up; **caer de ~** to fall flat; **caer primer ~ on the front page; **~a mayor** staff.

planta ['planta] *nf* (*BOT, TEC*) plant;

(*ANAT*) sole of the foot; foot; **~ baja** ground floor.

plantación [planta'θjon] *nf* (*AGR*) plantation; (*acto*) planting.

plantar [plan'tar] *vt* (*BOT*) to plant; (*levantar*) to erect, set up; **~se** *vr* to stand firm; **~ a uno en la calle** to chuck sb out; **dejar plantado a uno** (*fam*) to stand sb up.

plantear [plante'ar] *vt* (*problema*) to pose; (*dificultad*) to raise; (*planificar*) to plan; (*institución*) to set up, establish; (*reforma*) to implant.

plantilla [plan'tiʎa] *nf* (*de zapato*) insole; (*de media*) sole; (*personal*) personnel; **ser de ~** to be on the staff.

plantío [plan'tio] *nm* (*acto*) planting; (*lugar*) plot, bed, patch.

plantón [plan'ton] *nm* (*MIL*) guard, sentry; (*fam*) long wait; **dar (un) ~ a uno** to stand sb up.

plañidero, a [plaɲi'ðero, a] *a* mournful, plaintive.

plañir [pla'ɲir] *vi* to mourn.

plasmar [plas'mar] *vt* (*dar forma*) to mould, shape; (*representar*) to represent // *vi*: **~ en** to take the form of.

plasticina [plasti'θina] *nf* plasticine.

plástico, a ['plastiko, a] *a* plastic // *nf* (*art of*) sculpture, modelling // *nm* plastic.

plata ['plata] *nf* (*metal*) silver; (*cosas hechas de plata*) silverware; (*AM*) money; **hablar en ~** to speak bluntly or frankly.

plataforma [plata'forma] *nf* platform; **~ de lanzamiento/perforación** launching pad/drilling rig.

plátano ['platano] *nm* (*fruta*) banana; (*árbol*) banana tree.

platea [pla'tea] *nf* (*TEATRO*) pit.

plateado, a [plate'aðo, a] *a* silver; (*TEC*) silver-plated.

platería [plate'ria] *nf* silversmith's.

plática ['platika] *nf* talk, chat; **platicar** *vi* to talk, chat.

platillo [pla'tiʎo] *nm* saucer; **~s** *nmpl* cymbals; **~ volador** *o* **volante** flying saucer.

platino [pla'tino] *nm* platinum; **~s** *nmpl* (*AUTO*) contact points.

plato ['plato] *nm* plate, dish; (*parte de comida*) course; (*guiso*) dish.

playa ['plaja] *nf* beach; (*lugar veraniego*) seaside resort; (*costa*) seaside; **~ de estacionamiento** (*AM*) car park.

playera [pla'jera] *nf* T-shirt.

plaza ['plaθa] *nf* square; (*mercado*) market(place); (*sitio*) room, space; (*en vehículo*) seat, place; (*colocación*) post, job.

plazco *etc vb ver* **placer.**

plazo ['plaθo] *nm* (*lapso de tiempo*) time, period, term; (*fecha de vencimiento*) expiry date; (*pago parcial*) instalment; **a corto/largo ~** short-/long-term; **comprar a ~s** to buy on hire purchase, pay for in instalments.

plazoleta [plaθo'leta], **plazuela** [pla'θwela] *nf* small square.

pleamar [plea'mar] *nf* high tide.

plebe ['pleβe] *nf*: **la ~** the common people *pl*, the masses *pl*; (*pey*) the plebs *pl*; **~yo, a** *a* plebeian; (*pey*) coarse, common.

plebiscito [pleβis'θito] *nm* plebiscite.

plegable [ple'xaβle], **plegadizo, a** [plexa'ðiθo, a] *a* pliable; (*silla*) folding.

plegar [ple'xar] *vt* (*doblar*) to fold, bend; (*COSTURA*) to pleat; **~se** *vr* to yield, submit.

pleito ['pleito] *nm* (*JUR*) lawsuit, case; (*fig*) dispute, feud.

plenilunio [pleni'lunjo] *nm* full moon.

plenitud [pleni'tuð] *nf* plenitude, fullness; (*abundancia*) abundance.

pleno, a ['pleno, a] *a* (*gen*) full; (*completo*) complete // *nm* plenum; **en ~ día** in broad daylight; **en ~**

verano at the height of summer; **en ~ a cara** full in the face.

pleuresía [pleure'sia] *nf* pleurisy.

plexiglás [pleksi'xlas] *nm* perspex.

pliego ['pljeɣo] *nm* (*hoja*) sheet (of paper); (*carta*) sealed letter/document; **~ de condiciones** details *pl*, specifications *pl*.

pliegue ['pljeɣe] *nm* fold, crease; (*de vestido*) pleat.

plisado [pli'saðo] *nm* pleating; **~ de acordeón** accordion pleats *pl*.

plomero [plo'mero] *nm* plumber.

plomo ['plomo] *nm* (*metal*) lead; (*ELEC*) fuse.

pluma ['pluma] *nf* (*gen*) feather; (*para escribir*) pen.

plural [plu'ral] *a* plural; **~idad** *nf* plurality; **una ~idad de votos** a majority of votes.

plus [plus] *nm* bonus.

plutocracia [pluto'kraθja] *nf* plutocracy.

población [poβla'θjon] *nf* population; (*pueblo, ciudad*) town, city; **poblado, a** *a* inhabited // *nm* (*aldea*) village; (*pueblo*) (small) town; **densamente ~** densely populated.

poblador, a [poβla'ðor, a] *nm/f* settler, colonist; (*fundador*) founder.

poblar [po'βlar] *vt* (*colonizar*) to colonize; (*fundar*) to found; (*habitar*) to inhabit.

pobre ['poβre] *a* poor // *nm/f* poor person; **¡~!** poor thing!; **~za** *nf* poverty.

pocilga [po'θilxa] *nf* pigsty.

poción [po'θjon], **pócima** ['poθima] *nf* potion.

poco, a ['poko, a] *a* little; **~s** few // *ad* (*no mucho*) little, not much // *nm*: **un ~** a little, a bit; **tener a uno en ~** to think little or not think much of sb; **por ~** almost, nearly; **a ~** a little by little, gradually; **dentro de ~** (+ *presente o futuro*) shortly; (+ *pasado*) soon after; **hace ~** a short time ago, not long ago.

podar [po'ðar] *vt* to prune.

podenco [po'ðenko] nm hound.

poder [po'ðer] vi can; (sujeto: persona) to be able to, can; (permiso) can, may; (posibilidad, hipótesis) may // nm (gen) power; (autoridad) authority; **puede que sea así** it may be, maybe; ¿**se puede?** may I come in?; ¿**puedes con eso?** can you manage that?; **a más no** ~ to the utmost; **no** ~ **menos de hacer algo** not to be able to help doing sth; **no** ~ **más** to have had enough; **~ío** nm power; (autoridad) authority; **~oso, a** a powerful.

podrido, a [po'ðriðo, a] a rotten, bad; (fig) rotten, corrupt.

podrir [po'ðrir] = **pudrir**.

poema [po'ema] nm poem.

poesía [poe'sia] nf poetry.

poeta [po'eta] nm poet; **poético, a** a poetic(al).

póker ['poker] nm poker.

polaco, a [po'lako, a] a Polish // nm/f Pole.

polar [po'lar] a polar; **~idad** nf polarity; **~izarse** vr to polarize.

polea [po'lea] nf pulley.

polémica [po'lemika] nf (gen) polemics sg; (una ~) controversy.

policía [poli'θia] nm/f policeman/woman // nf police; ~ **de policía** police cpd; **novela ~ca** detective story.

poligamia [poli'xamja] nf polygamy.

polilla [po'liʎa] nf moth.

polio [po'lio] nf polio.

politécnico [poli'tekniko] nm polytechnic.

politene [poli'tene], **politeno** [poli'teno] nm polythene.

político, a [po'litiko, a] a political; (discreto) tactful; (de familia) in-law // nm/f politician // nf politics sg; (económica, agraria) policy; **padre** ~ father-in-law; **politicastro** nm (pey) politician, politico.

póliza [po'liθa] nf insurance policy.

polo ['polo] nm (GEO, ELEC) pole;

(helado) iced lolly; (DEPORTE) polo; (suéter) polo-neck; ~ **Norte/Sur** North/South Pole.

Polonia [po'lonja] nf Poland.

poltrona [pol'trona] nf reclining chair, easy chair.

polución [polu'θjon] nf pollution.

polvera [pol'ßera] nf powder compact, vanity case.

polvo ['polßo] nm dust; (QUÍMICA, CULIN, MED) powder; **~s** nmpl powder sg; **~ de talco** talcum powder; **estar hecho** ~ to be worn out or exhausted.

pólvora ['polßora] nf gunpowder; (fuegos artificiales) fireworks pl.

polvoriento, a [polßo'rjento, a] a (superficie) dusty; (sustancia) powdery.

pollería [poʎe'ria] nf poulterer's (shop).

pollo ['poʎo] nm chicken.

pomada [po'maða] nf pomade.

pomelo [po'melo] nm grapefruit.

pómez ['pomeθ] nf: **piedra** ~ pumice stone.

pompa ['pompa] nf (burbuja) bubble; (bomba) pump; (esplendor) pomp, splendour; **pomposo, a** a splendid, magnificent; (pey) pompous.

pómulo ['pomulo] nm cheekbone.

pon [pon] vb ver **poner**.

ponche ['pontʃe] nm punch.

poncho ['pontʃo] nm (AM) poncho, cape.

ponderado, a [ponde'raðo, a] a calm, steady, balanced.

ponderar [ponde'rar] vt (considerar) to weigh up, consider; (elogiar) to praise highly, speak in praise of.

pondré etc vb ver **poner**.

poner [po'ner] vt (gen) to put; (colocar) to place, set; (ropa) to put on; (problema, la mesa) to set; (telegrama) to send; (TELEC) to connect; (radio, TV) to switch on, turn on; (tienda) to open, set up; (nombre) to give; (añadir) to add;

(TEATRO, CINE) to put on; (+ adjetivo) to make, turn; (suponer) to suppose // vi (ave) to lay (eggs); ~se vr to put or place o.s.; (ropa) to put on; (+ adjetivo) to turn, get, become; (el sol) to set; **póngame con el Señor X** get me Mr X, put me through to Mr X; ~**se de zapatero** to take a job as a shoemaker; ~**se a bien con uno** get on good terms with sb; ~**se con uno** to quarrel with sb; ~**se rojo** to blush; ~**se a** to begin to.

pongo etc vb ver **poner.**

pontificado [pontifi'kaðo] nm papacy, pontificate; **pontífice** nm pope, pontiff.

pontón [pon'ton] nm pontoon.

ponzoña [pon'θoɲa] nf poison, venom; **ponzoñoso, a** a poisonous, venomous.

popa ['popa] nf stern.

popular [popu'lar] a popular; (del pueblo) of the people; ~**idad** nf popularity; ~**izarse** vr to become popular.

poquedad [poke'ðað] nf (escasez) scantiness; (una ~) small thing, trifle; (fig) timidity.

por [por] prep (con el fin de) in order to; (a favor de, hacia) for; (a causa de) out of, because of, from; (según) according to; (por agencia de) by; (a cambio de) for, in exchange for; (en lugar de) instead of, in place of; (durante) for; **10** ~ **10 son 100** 10 times 10 are 100; **será** ~ **poco tiempo** it won't be for long; ~ **correo/avión** by post/plane; ~ **centenares** by the hundred; **(el) 10** ~ **ciento** 10 per cent; ~ **orden** in order; **ir a Bilbao** ~ **Santander** to go to Bilbao via Santander; **pasar** ~ **Madrid** to pass through Madrid; **camina** ~ **la izquierda** walk on the left; ~ **todo el país** throughout the country; **entra** ~ **delante/detrás** come/go in by the front/back (door); ~ **la calle** along the street; ~ **la mañana** in the morning; ~ **la**

noche at night; **£2** ~ **hora** £2 an hour; ~ **allí** over there; **está** ~ **el norte** it's somewhere in the north; ~ **mucho que quisiera, no puedo** much as I would like to, I can't; ~**que** because; ¿~ **qué?** why?; ~ **(lo) tanto** so, therefore; ~ **cierto** (seguro) certainly; (a propósito) by the way; ~ **ejemplo** for example; ~ **favor** please; ~ **fuera/dentro** outside/inside; ~ **si (acaso)** just in case; ~ **sí mismo** o **sólo** by o.s.

porcelana [porθe'lana] nf porcelain; (china) china.

porcentaje [porθen'taxe] nm percentage.

porción [por'θjon] nf (parte) portion, share; (cantidad) quantity, amount.

pordiosear [porðjose'ar] vi to beg; **pordiosero, a** nm/f beggar.

porfía [por'fia] nf persistence; (terquedad) obstinacy; **porfiado, a** a persistent; obstinate; **porfiar** vi to persist, insist; (disputar) to argue stubbornly.

pormenor [porme'nor] nm detail, particular.

pornografía [pornoxra'fia] nf pornography.

poro ['poro] nm pore; ~**so, a** a porous.

porque ['porke] conj (a causa de) because; (ya que) since; (con el fin de) so that, in order that.

porqué [por'ke] nm reason, cause.

porquería [porke'ria] nf (suciedad) filth, muck, dirt; (acción) dirty trick; (objeto) small thing, trifle; (fig) rubbish.

porro, a ['porro, a] a (fam) stupid // (arma) stick, club; (TEC) large hammer; (fam) bore.

porrón, ona [po'rron, ona] a a slow, stupid // nm glass wine jar with a long spout.

portada [por'taða] nf (entrada) porch, doorway; (de revista) cover.

portador, a [porta'ðor, a] nm/f carrier, bearer.

portaequipajes [portaeki'paxes] nm inv boot; (arriba del coche) luggage rack.

portal [por'tal] nm (entrada) vestibule, hall; (portada) porch, doorway; (puerta de ciudad) gate; (DEPORTE) goal.

portaligas [porta'lixas] nm inv suspender belt.

portamaletas [portama'letas] nm inv boot.

portamonedas [portamo'neðas] nm inv purse.

portarse [por'tarse] vr to behave, conduct o.s.

portátil [por'tatil] a portable.

portaviones [porta'βjones] nm inv aircraft carrier.

portavoz [porta'βoθ] nm (megáfono) megaphone, loudhailer; (vocero) spokesman/woman.

portazo [por'taθo] nm: **dar un ~** to slam the door.

porte ['porte] nm (COM) transport; (precio) transport charges pl; (comportamiento) conduct, behaviour.

portento [por'tento] nm marvel, wonder; **~so, a** a marvellous, extraordinary.

porteño, a [por'teɲo, a] a of or from Buenos Aires.

portería [porte'ria] nf (oficina) porter's office; (gol) goal.

portero, a [por'tero, a] nm/f porter; (conserje) caretaker; (ujier) doorman // nm goalkeeper.

pórtico ['portiko] nm (patio) portico, porch; (fig) gateway; (arcada) arcade.

portilla [por'tiʎa] nf porthole.

portillo [por'tiʎo] nm (abertura) gap, opening; (OEO) narrow pass.

portorriqueño, a [portorri'keɲo, a] a Puerto Rican.

Portugal [portu'xal] nm Portugal; **portugués, esa** a, nm/f Portuguese.

porvenir [porβe'nir] nm future.

pos [pos] prep: **en ~ de** after, in pursuit of.

posada [po'saða] nf (refugio) shelter, lodging; (mesón) guest house; **dar ~ a** to give shelter to, take in.

posaderas [posa'ðeras] nfpl backside sg, buttocks.

posar [po'sar] vt (en el suelo) to lay down, put down; (la mano) to place, put gently // vi to sit, pose; **~se** vr to settle; (pájaro) to perch; (avión) to land, come down.

posdata [pos'ðata] nf postscript.

pose ['pose] nf pose.

poseedor, a [posee'ðor, a] nm/f owner, possessor; (de record, puesto) holder.

poseer [pose'er] vt to have, possess, own; (ventaja) to enjoy; (récord, puesto) to hold; **poseído, a** a possessed; **posesión** nf possession; **posesionarse** vr: **posesionarse de** to take possession of, take over; **posesivo, a** a possessive.

posibilidad [posiβili'ðað] nf possibility; (oportunidad) chance; **posibilitar** vt to make possible, permit; (hacer factible) to make feasible.

posible [po'siβle] a possible; (factible) feasible; **de ser ~** if possible; **en lo ~** as far as possible.

posición [posi'θjon] nf (gen) position; (rango social) status.

positivo, a [posi'tiβo, a] a positive // nf (FOTO) print.

poso ['poso] nm sediment.

posponer [pospo'ner] vt to put behind/below, (AM) to postpone.

posta ['posta] nf (de caballos) relay, team; (pedazo) slice // nm courier.

postal [pos'tal] a postal // nf postcard.

poste ['poste] nm (de telégrafos) post, pole; (columna) pillar; **dar ~ a una** (fam) to keep sb hanging about.

postergar [poster'xar] vt (AM: posponer) to postpone, delay.

posteridad [posteri'ðað] nf posterity.

posterior [poste'rjor] a back, rear; (*siguiente*) following, subsequent; (*más tarde*) later; ~**idad** nf: con ~**idad** later, subsequently.

postizo, a [pos'tiθo, a] a false, artificial // nm hairpiece.

postor, a [pos'tor, a] nm/f bidder.

postrado, a [pos'traðo, a] a prostrate; **postrar** vt (*derribar*) to cast down, overthrow; (*humillar*) to humble; (*MED*) to weaken, exhaust.

postre ['postre] nm sweet, dessert.

postremo, a [pos'tremo, a], **postrer, ero, a** [pos'trer, ero, a] a (*último*) last; (*que viene detrás*) rear.

postulado [postu'laðo] nm postulate; **postular** vt (*empleo*) to apply for; (*pedir*) to seek, demand; (*proponer*) to postulate.

póstumo, a ['postumo, a] a posthumous.

postura [pos'tura] nf (*del cuerpo*) posture, position; (*fig*) attitude, position.

potable [po'taßle] a drinkable.

potaje [po'taxe] nm stew; ~s nmpl mixed vegetables.

pote ['pote] nm pot, jar.

potencia [po'tenθja] nf power.

potencial [poten'θjal] a, nm potential.

potente [po'tente] a powerful.

pozo ['poθo] nm well; (*de río*) deep pool; (*de mina*) shaft.

práctica ['praktika] nf ver **práctico**.

practicable [prakti'kaßle] a practicable; (*camino*) passable, usable.

practicante [prakti'kante] nm/f (*MED*: *ayudante de doctor*) medical assistant; (: *enfermero*) male nurse; (*quien practica algo*) practitioner // a practising.

practicar [prakti'kar] vt to practise; (*deporte*) to go in for, play; (*realizar*) to carry out, perform.

práctico, a ['praktiko, a] a (*gen*) practical; (*conveniente*) handy; (*instruído*: *persona*) skilled, expert // nf (*método*) method; (*arte, capacidad*) skill; **en la** ~ **a** in practice.

pradera [pra'ðera] nf meadow; (*de Canadá*) prairie.

prado ['praðo] nm (*campo*) meadow, field; (*pastizal*) pasture.

Praga ['praxa] n Prague.

pragmático, a [prax'matiko, a] a pragmatic.

preámbulo [pre'ambulo] nm preamble, introduction.

precario, a [pre'karjo, a] a precarious.

precaución [prekau'θjon] nf (*medida preventiva*) preventive measure, precaution; (*prudencia*) caution, wariness.

precaver [preka'ßer] vt to guard against; (*impedir*) to forestall; ~**se** vr: ~**se de** o **contra algo** to (be on one's) guard against sth; **precavido, a** a cautious, wary.

precedencia [preθe'ðenθja] nf precedence; (*prioridad*) priority; (*superioridad*) greater importance, superiority; **precedente** a preceding; (*anterior*) former // nm precedent; **preceder** vt, vi to precede, go/come before.

precepto [pre'θepto] nm precept.

preciado, a [pre'θjaðo, a] a (*estimado*) esteemed, valuable; (*vanidoso*) presumptuous; **preciar** vt to esteem, value; **preciarse** vr to pride o.s. on, boast of being.

precio ['preθjo] nm (*de mercado*) price; (*costo*) cost; (*valor*) value, worth; (*de viaje*) fare; ~ **al contado/de coste/de oportunidad** cash/cost/bargain price; ~ **tope** top price.

preciosidad [preθjosi'ðað] nf (*valor*) (high) value, (great) worth; (*encanto*) charm; (*cosa bonita*) beautiful thing; **es una** ~ it's lovely, it's really beautiful; **precioso, a** _a_ precious; (_de mucho valor_) valuable; (_fam_) lovely, beautiful.

precipicio [preθi'piθjo] _nm_ cliff, precipice; (_fig_) abyss.

precipitación [preθipita'θjon] _nf_ haste; (_lluvia_) rainfall.

precipitado, a [preθipi'taðo, a] _a_ hasty, rash; (_salida_) hasty, sudden.

precipitar [preθipi'tar] _vt_ (_arrojar_) to hurl down, throw; (_apresurar_) to hasten; (_acelerar_) to speed up, accelerate; ~se _vr_ to throw o.s.; (_apresurarse_) to rush, (_actuar sin pensar_) to act rashly.

precipitoso, a [preθipi'toso, a] _a_ (_escarpado_) steep, sheer; (_a la carrera, imprudente_) hasty, rash.

precisamente [preθisa'mente] _ad_ precisely; (_justo_) precisely, exactly, just.

precisar [preθi'sar] _vt_ (_necesitar_) to need, require; (_fijar_) to determine exactly, fix; (_especificar_) to specify // _vi_ to be necessary

precisión [preθi'sjon] _nf_ (_exactitud_) precision; (_necesidad_) need, necessity.

preciso, a [pre'θiso, a] _a_ (_exacto_) precise; (_necesario_) necessary, essential.

preconcebido, a [prekonθe'βiðo, a] _a_ preconceived.

preconizar [prekoni'θar] _vt_ (_aconsejar_) to advise; (_prever_) to foresee.

precoz [pre'koθ] _a_ (_persona_) precocious; (_calvicie_) premature.

precursor, a [prekur'sor, a] _nm/f_ precursor.

predecir [preðe'θir] _vt_ to predict, foretell, forecast.

predestinado, a [preðesti'naðo, a] _a_ predestined.

predeterminar [preðetermi'nar] _vt_ to predetermine.

prédica ['preðika] _nf_ sermon; **predicador, a** _nm/f_ preacher; **predicar** _vt, vi_ to preach.

predicción [preðik'θjon] _nf_ prediction.

predilecto, a [preði'lekto, a] _a_ favourite.

predio ['preðjo] _nm_ property, estate.

predisponer [preðispo'ner] _vt_ to predispose; (_pey_) to prejudice; **predisposición** _nf_ predisposition, inclination; prejudice, bias.

predominante [preðomi'nante] _a_ predominant.

predominar [preðomi'nar] _vt_ to dominate // _vi_ to predominate; (_prevalecer_) to prevail; **predominio** _nm_ predominance; prevalence.

prefabricado, a [prefaβri'kaðo, a] _a_ prefabricated.

prefacio [pre'faθjo] _nm_ preface.

preferencia [prefe'renθja] _nf_ preference; **de ~** preferably, for preference; **preferible** _a_ preferable; **preferir** _vt_ to prefer.

prefigurar [prefixu'rar] _vt_ to foreshadow, prefigure.

pregonar [prexo'nar] _vt_ to proclaim, announce.

pregunta [pre'xunta] _nf_ question; **hacer una ~** to ask or put a question.

preguntar [prexun'tar] _vt_ to ask; (_cuestionar_) to question // _vi_ to ask; **~se** _vr_ to wonder; **~ por alguien** to ask for sb; **preguntón, ona** _a_ inquisitive.

prehistórico, a [preis'toriko, a] _a_ prehistoric.

prejuicio [pre'xwiθjo] _nm_ prejudgement; (_preconcepción_) preconception; (_pey_) prejudice, bias.

prelación [prela'θjon] _nf_ priority.

preliminar [prelimi'nar] _a_ preliminary.

preludio [pre'luðjo] _nm_ prelude.

prematuro, a [prema'turo, a] _a_ premature.

premeditación [premeðita'θjon] _nf_ premeditation; **premeditar** _vt_ to premeditate.

premiar [pre'mjar] _vt_ to reward;

(*en un concurso*) to give a prize to; **premio** *nm* reward; prize; (*COM*) premium.

premonición [premoni'θjon] *nf* premonition.

premura [pre'mura] *nf* (*aprieto*) pressure; (*prisa*) haste, urgency.

prenatal [prena'tal] *a* antenatal, prenatal.

prenda ['prenda] *nf* (*ropa*) garment, article of clothing; (*garantía*) pledge; ~s *nfpl* talents, gifts.

prendar [pren'dar] *vt* to captivate, enchant; ~**se de uno** to fall in love with sb.

prendedor [prende'ðor] *nm* brooch.

prender [pren'der] *vt* (*captar*) to catch, capture; (*detener*) to arrest; (*coser*) to pin, attach; (*sujetar*) to fasten // *vi* to catch; (*arraigar*) to take root; ~**se** (*encenderse*) to catch fire; (*engalanarse*) to dress up.

prensa ['prensa] *nf* press; **la P~** the press; **prensar** *vt* to press.

preñado, a [pre'naðo, a] *a* (*mujer*) pregnant; ~ **de** pregnant with, full of; **preñez** (*prisa*) pregnancy.

preocupación [preokupa'θjon] *nf* worry, concern; (*ansiedad*) anxiety; **preocupado, a** *a* worried, concerned; anxious.

preocupar [preoku'par] *vt* to worry; ~**se** *vr* to worry; ~**se de algo** (*hacerse cargo*) to worry about sth, take care of sth.

preparación [prepara'θjon] *nf* (*acto*) preparation; (*estado*) preparedness, readiness; (*entrenamiento*) training; **preparado, a** *a* (*dispuesto*) prepared; (*CULIN*) ready (to serve) // *nm* preparation.

preparador, a [prepara'ðor, a] *nm/f* trainer.

preparar [prepa'rar] *vt* (*disponer*) to prepare, get ready; (*TEC: tratar*) to prepare, process, treat; (*entrenar*) to teach, train; ~**se** *vr*:

~**se a** *o* **para** to prepare to *or* for, get ready to *or* for; **preparativo, a** *a* preparatory, preliminary; **preparativos** *nmpl* preparations; **preparatorio, a** *a* preparatory.

prerrogativa [prerroxa'tiβa] *nf* prerogative, privilege.

presa ['presa] *nf* (*captura*) capture, seizure; (*cosa apresada*) catch; (*víctima*) victim; (*de animal*) prey; (*de agua*) dam.

presbítero [pres'βitero] *nm* priest.

prescindible [presθin'diβle] *a* dispensable.

prescindir [presθin'dir] *vi*: ~ **de** (*privarse de*) to do without, go without; (*descartar*) to dispense with.

prescribir [preskri'βir] *vt* to prescribe; **prescripción** *nf* prescription.

presencia [pre'senθja] *nf* presence; **presencial** *a*: **testigo presencial** eyewitness; **presenciar** *vt* to be present at; (*asistir a*) to attend; (*ver*) to see, witness.

presentación [presenta'θjon] *nf* presentation; (*introducción*) introduction.

presentador, a [presenta'ðor, a] *nm/f* compère.

presentar [presen'tar] *vt* to present; (*ofrecer*) to offer; (*mostrar*) to show, display; (*a una persona*) to introduce; ~**se** *vr* (*llegar inesperadamente*) to appear, turn up; (*ofrecerse: como candidato*) to run, stand; (*aparecer*) to show, appear; (*solicitar empleo*) to apply.

presente [pre'sente] *a* present // *nm* present; **hacer** ~ to state, declare; **tener** ~ to remember, bear in mind.

presentimiento [presenti'mjento] *nm* premonition, presentiment; **presentir** *vt* to have a premonition of.

preservación [preserβa'θjon] *nf* protection, preservation; **preservar** *vt* to protect, preserve; **preserva-**

tivo *nm* sheath, condom.
presidencia [presi'ðenθja] *nf* presidency; (*de comité*) chairmanship; **presidente** *nm/f* president; chairman/woman.

presidiario [presi'ðjarjo] *nm* convict, **presidio** *nm* (*penitenciaría*) prison, penitentiary; (*trabajo forzoso*) hard labour; (*MIL*) garrison.

presidir [presi'ðir] *vt* (*dirigir*) to preside at, preside over; (*comité*) to take the chair at; (*dominar*) to dominate, rule // *vi*: **presidir** to take the chair.

presión [pre'sjon] *nf* pressure; **presionar** *vt* to press; (*fig*) to press, put pressure on // *vi*: **presionar para** *o* **por** to press for.

preso, a [preso, a] *nm/f* prisoner; **tomar** *o* **llevar ~ a uno** to arrest sb, take sb prisoner.

prestado, a [pres'taðo, a] *a* on loan; **pedir ~** to borrow.

prestamista [presta'mista] *nm/f* moneylender.

préstamo ['prestamo] *nm* loan.

prestar [pres'tar] *vt* to lend, loan; (*atención*) to pay; (*ayuda*) to give // *vi* to give, stretch.

prestatario, a [presta'tarjo, a] *nm/f* borrower.

presteza [pres'teθa] *nf* speed, promptness.

prestigio [pres'tixjo] *nm* prestige; **~so, a** *a* (*honorable*) prestigious; (*famoso, renombrado*) renowned, famous.

presto, a ['presto, a] *a* (*rápido*) quick, prompt; (*dispuesto*) ready // *ad* at once, right away.

presumir [presu'mir] *vt* to presume // *vi* (*tener aires*) to be conceited; **según cabe ~** as may be presumed, presumably; **presunción** *nf* presumption; **presunto, a** *a* (*supuesto*) supposed, presumed; (*así llamado*) so-called; **presuntuoso, a** *a* conceited, presumptuous.

presuponer [presupo'ner] *vt* to presuppose.

presupuesto [presu'pwesto] *nm* (*FINANZAS*) budget; (*estimación: de costo*) estimate.

presuroso, a [presu'roso, a] *a* (*rápido*) quick, speedy; (*que tiene prisa*) hasty.

pretencioso, a [preten'θjoso, a] *a* pretentious.

pretender [preten'der] *vt* (*intentar*) to try to, seek to; (*reivindicar*) to claim; (*buscar*) to seek, try for; (*cortejar*) to woo, court; **~ que** to expect that; **pretendiente** *nm/f* (*candidato*) candidate, applicant; (*amante*) suitor; **pretensión** *nf* (*aspiración*) aspiration; (*reivindicación*) claim; (*orgullo*) pretension.

pretexto [pre'teksto] *nm* pretext; (*excusa*) excuse.

prevalecer [preβaleθer] *vi* to prevail; **prevaleciente** *a* prevailing, prevalent.

prevalerse [preβa'lerse] *vr*: **~ de** to avail o.s. of.

prevención [preβen'θjon] *nf* (*preparación*) preparation; (*estado*) preparedness, readiness; (*el evitar*) prevention; (*previsión*) foresight, forethought; (*prejuicio*) bias, prejudice; (*precaución*) precaution.

prevenido, a [preβe'niðo, a] *a* prepared, ready; (*cauteloso*) cautious.

prevenir [preβe'nir] *vt* (*impedir*) to prevent; (*prever*) to foresee, anticipate; (*predisponer*) to prejudice, bias; (*avisar*) to warn; (*preparar*) to prepare, get ready; **~se** *vr* to get ready, prepare; **~se contra** to take precautions against; **preventivo, a** *a* preventive, precautionary.

prever [pre'βer] *vt* to foresee.

previo, a ['preβjo, a] *a* (*anterior*) previous; (*examen*) preliminary // *prep*: **~ acuerdo de los otros** subject to the agreement of the others.

previsión [preβi'sjon] *nf* (*perspicacia*) foresight; (*predicción*) fore-

cast; ~ **social** social security.
prieto, a ['prjeto, a] *a* (*oscuro*) dark; (*fig*) mean; (*comprimido*) tight, compressed.
prima ['prima] *nf ver* **primo.**
primacía [prima'θia] *nf* primacy.
primario, a [pri'marjo, a] *a* primary.
primavera [prima'βera] *nf* (*temporada*) spring; (*período*) springtime.
primer, primero, a [pri'mer, pri'mero, a] *a* first; (*fig*) prime // *ad* first; (*más bien*) sooner, rather // *nf* (*AUTO*) first gear; (*FERRO*) first class; **de ~a** (*fam*) first-class, first-rate; **~a plana** front page.
primitivo, a [primi'tiβo, a] *a* primitive; (*original*) original.
primo, a ['primo, a] *nm/f* cousin; (*fam*) fool, dupe // *pf* (*COM*) bonus; **~ hermano** first cousin; **materias ~as** raw materials.
primogénito, a [primo'xenito, a] *a* first-born.
primordial [primor'ðjal] *a* basic, fundamental.
primoroso, a [primo'roso, a] *a* exquisite, delicate.
princesa [prin'θesa] *nf* princess.
principal [prinθi'pal] *a* principal, main // *nm* (*jefe*) chief, principal.
príncipe ['prinθipe] *nm* prince.
principiante [prinθi'pjante] *nm/f* beginner; **principiar** *vt* to begin.
principio [prin'θipjo] *nm* (*comienzo*) beginning, start; (*origen*) origin; (*primera etapa*) rudiment, basic idea; (*moral*) principle; **a ~s de** at the beginning of; **tener** o **tomar en ~** to start from, to based on.
pringue ['pringe] *nm* (*grasa*) grease, fat, dripping; (*mancha*) grease stain.
prioridad [priori'ðað] *nf* priority.
prisa ['prisa] *nf* (*apresuramiento*) hurry, haste; (*rapidez*) speed; (*urgencia*) (sense of) urgency; **a** o **de ~** quickly; **correr ~** to be

urgent; **darse ~** to hurry up; **estar de** o **tener ~** to be in a hurry.
prisión [pri'sjon] *nf* (*cárcel*) prison; (*período de cárcel*) imprisonment; **prisionero, a** *nm/f* prisoner.
prismáticos [pris'matikos] *nmpl* binoculars.
privación [priβa'θjon] *nf* deprivation; (*falta*) want, privation.
privado, a [pri'βaðo, a] *a* private.
privar [pri'βar] *vt* to deprive; (*prohibir*) to forbid // *vi* (*gozar de favor*) to be in favour; (*prevalecer*) to prevail; **privativo, a** *a* exclusive.
privilegiado, a [priβile'xjaðo, a] *a* privileged; (*memoria*) very good; **privilegiar** *vt* to grant a privilege to; (*favorecer*) to favour.
privilegio [priβi'lexjo] *nm* privilege; (*concesión*) concession; **~ de invención** patent.
pro [pro] *nm* o *f* profit, advantage // *prep*: **asociación ~ ciegos** association for the blind // *pref*: **~ soviético/americano** pro-Soviet/ -American; **en ~ de** on behalf of, for; **los ~s y los contras** the pros and cons.
probabilidad [proβaβili'ðað] *nf* probability, likelihood; (*oportunidad, posibilidad*) chance, prospect; **probable** *a* probable, likely.
probanza [pro'βanθa] *nf* proof, evidence.
probar [pro'βar] *vt* (*demostrar*) to prove; (*someter a prueba*) to test, try out; (*ropa*) to try on; (*comida*) to taste // *vi* to try; **~se un traje** to try on a suit.
probeta [pro'βeta] *nf* test tube.
problema [pro'βlema] *nm* problem.
procaz [pro'kaθ] *a* insolent, impudent.
procedente [proθe'ðente] *a* (*razonable*) reasonable; (*conforme a derecho*) proper, fitting; **~ de** coming from, originating in.
proceder [proθe'ðer] *vi* (*avanzar*) to proceed; (*actuar*) to act; (*ser*

correcto) to be right (and proper), be fitting // *nm (acción)* course of action; *(comportamiento)* behaviour, conduct; **procedimiento** *nm* procedure; *(proceso)* process; *(método)* means, method.

procesado, a [proθe'saðo, a] *nm/f* accused (person); **procesar** *vt* to try, put on trial.

procesión [proθe'sjon] *nf* procession.

proceso [pro'θeso] *nm* process; (JUR) trial; *(lapso)* course (of time).

proclama [pro'klama] *nf (acto)* proclamation; *(cartel)* poster; **proclamar** *vt* to proclaim.

procreación [prokrea'θjon] *nf* procreation; **procrear** *vt, vi* to procreate.

procurador, a [prokura'ðor, a] *nm/f* attorney.

procurar [proku'rar] *vt (intentar)* to try, endeavour; *(conseguir)* to get, obtain; *(asegurar)* to secure; *(producir)* to produce.

prodigio [pro'ðixjo] *nm* prodigy; *(milagro)* wonder, marvel; ~**so, a** *a* prodigious, marvellous.

pródigo, a [pro'ðixo, a] *a*: **hijo** ~ **prodigal son**

producción [proðuk'θjon] *nf* production; *(suma de productos)* output; *(producto)* product; ~ **en serie** mass production.

producir [proðu'θir] *vt* to produce; *(generar)* to cause, bring about; ~**se** *vr (gen)* to come about, happen, *(hacerse)* to be produced, be made; *(estallar)* to break out.

productividad [proðuktiβi'ðað] *nf* productivity; **productivo, a** *a* productive; *(provechoso)* profitable.

producto [pro'ðukto] *nm* product; *(producción)* production.

productor, a [proðuk'tor, a] *a* productive, producing // *nm/f* producer.

proeza [pro'eθa] *nf* exploit, feat.

profanar [profa'nar] *vt* to desecrate, profane; **profano, a** *a*

profane // *nm/f* layman/woman.

profecía [profe'θia] *nf* prophecy.

proferir [profe'rir] *vt (palabra, sonido)* to utter; *(injuria)* to hurl, let fly.

profesar [profe'sar] *vt (declarar)* to profess; *(practicar)* to practise.

profesión [profe'sjon] *nf* profession; **profesional** *a* professional.

profesor, a [profe'sor, a] *nm/f* teacher; ~**ado** *nm* teaching profession

profeta [pro'feta] *nm/f* prophet; **profetizar** *vt, vi* to prophesy.

prófugo, a [pro'fuxo, a] *nm/f* fugitive; *(desertor)* deserter.

profundidad [profundi'ðað] *nf* depth; **profundizar** *vt (fig)* to go deeply into, *(ahondar)* to go deep; *(misterio, pensador)* profound.

progenie [pro'xenje] *nf* offspring.

progenitor [proxeni'tor] *nm* ancestor; ~**es** *nmpl (fam)* parents.

programa [pro'xrama] *nm* programme; ~**ción** *nf* programming; ~**dor, a** *nm/f* programmer; **programar** *vt* to programme.

progresar [proxre'sar] *vi* to progress, make progress; **progresista** *a, nm/f* progressive; **progresivo, a** *a* progressive; *(gradual)* gradual; *(continuo)* continuous; **progreso** *nm* progress.

prohibición [proiβi'θjon] *nf* prohibition, ban; **prohibir** *vt* to prohibit, ban, forbid; **se prohibe fumar** no smoking.

prohijar [proi'xar] *vt* to adopt.

prójimo, a ['proximo, a] *nm/f* fellow man, neighbour.

proletariado [proleta'rjaðo] *nm* proletariat; **proletario, a** *a, nm/f* proletarian.

proliferación [prolifera'θjon] *nf* proliferation; **proliferar** *vi* to proliferate; **prolífico, a** *a* prolific.

prolijo, a [pro'lixo, a] *a* long-winded, tedious

prólogo ['proloxo] *nm* prologue.

prolongación [prolonga'θjon] *nf*

extension; **prolongado, a** a (largo) long; (alargado) lengthy; **prolongar** vt (gen) to extend; (en el tiempo) to prolong; (calle, tubo) to make longer, extend.

promedio [pro'meðjo] nm average; (de distancia) middle, mid-point.

promesa [pro'mesa] nf promise.

prometer [prome'ter] vt to promise // vi to show promise; ~se vr (dos personas) to get engaged; **prometido, a** a promised; engaged // nm/f fiancé/fiancée.

prominente [promi'nente] a prominent.

promiscuo, a [pro'miskwo, a] (mezclado) mixed(-up), in disorder; (ambiguo) ambiguous.

promoción [promo'θjon] nf promotion.

promotor [promo'tor] nm promoter; (instigador) instigator.

promover [promo'ßer] vt to promote; (causar) to cause; (instigar) to instigate, stir up.

promulgar [promul'xar] vt to promulgate; (fig) to proclaim.

pronosticar [pronosti'kar] vt to predict, foretell, forecast; **pronóstico** nm prediction, forecast.

prontitud [pronti'tuð] nf speed, quickness; (de ingenio) quickness, sharpness.

pronto, a ['pronto, a] a (rápido) prompt, quick; (preparado) ready; (astuto) quick, sharp // ad quickly, promptly; (en seguida) at once, right away; (dentro de poco) soon; (temprano) early // nm: tener ~s de enojo to be quick-tempered; al ~ at first; de ~ suddenly; por lo ~ meanwhile, for the present.

pronunciación [pronunθja'θjon] nf pronunciation; **pronunciar** vt to pronounce; (discurso) to make, deliver; **pronunciarse** vr to revolt, rise, rebel; (declararse) to declare o.s.

propagación [propaxa'θjon] nf propagation.

propaganda [propa'xanda] nf (política) propaganda; (comercial) advertising.

propagar [propa'xar] vt to propagate.

propensión [propen'sjon] nf inclination, propensity; **propenso, a** a inclined to; **ser propenso a** to be inclined to, have a tendency to.

propiamente [propja'mente] ad properly; (realmente) really, exactly.

propicio, a [pro'piθjo, a] a favourable, propitious.

propiedad [propje'ðað] nf (gen) property; (posesión) possession, ownership; ~ **industrial** patent rights pl; ~ **literaria** copyright; ~ **particular** private property.

propietario, a [propje'tarjo, a] nm/f owner, proprietor.

propina [pro'pina] nf tip.

propio, a ['propjo, a] a own, of one's own; (característico) characteristic, typical; (conveniente) proper; (mismo) selfsame, very; **el ~ ministro** the minister himself; ¡**tienes casa ~a?** have you a house of your own?

proponer [propo'ner] vt to propose, put forward; (problema) to pose; ~se vr to propose, plan, intend.

proporción [propor'θjon] nf proportion; (MAT) ratio; (oportunidad) chance, opportunity; **proporciones** nfpl dimensions; (fig) size sg; **proporcionado, a** a proportionate; (regular) medium, middling; (justo) just right; **proporcionar** vt (dar) to give, supply, provide; (adaptar) to adjust, adapt.

proposición [proposi'θjon] nf proposition; (propuesta) proposal.

propósito [pro'posito] nm purpose; (intento) aim, intention // a a appropriate, suitable // ad: a ~ by the way, incidentally; a ~ de about, with regard to; de ~ on purpose, deliberately.

propuesta [pro'pwesta] *nf* proposal.

propulsar [propul'sar] *vt* to drive, propel; (*fig*) to promote, encourage; **propulsión** *nf* propulsion; **propulsión a chorro** *o* **por reacción** jet propulsion

prórroga ['prorroɣa] *nf* (*gen*) extension; (*JUR*) stay; (*COM*) deferment; **prorrogar** *vt* (*período*) to extend; (*decisión*) to defer, postpone.

prorrumpir [prorrum'pir] *vi* to burst forth, break out.

prosa ['prosa] *nf* prose.

proscribir [proskri'βir] *vt* to prohibit, ban; (*desterrar*) to exile, banish; (*partido*) to proscribe; **proscripción** *nf* prohibition, ban; banishment; proscription.

prosecución [proseku'θjon] *nf* continuation; (*persecución*) pursuit.

proseguir [prose'xir] *vt* to continue, carry on, proceed with // *vi* to continue, go on.

prospección [prospek'θjon] *nf* exploration; (*del petróleo, del oro*) prospecting.

prospecto [pros'pekto] *nm* prospectus.

prosperar [prospe'rar] *vi* to prosper, thrive, flourish; **prosperidad** *nf* prosperity; (*éxito*) success; **próspero, a** a prosperous, thriving, flourishing; (*que tiene éxito*) successful.

prostíbulo [pros'tiβulo] *nm* brothel.

prostitución [prostitu'θjon] *nf* prostitution; **prostituir** *vt* to prostitute; **prostituirse** *vr* to prostitute o.s., become a prostitute; **prostituta** *nf* prostitute.

protagonista [protaxo'nista] *nm/f* protagonist.

protección [protek'θjon] *nf* protection.

protector, a [protek'tor, a] a protective, protecting // *nm/f* protector.

proteger [prote'xer] *vt* to protect; **protegido, a** *nm/f* protégé/protégée.

proteína [prote'ina] *nf* protein.

protesta [pro'testa] *nf* protest; (*declaración*) protestation.

protestante [protes'tante] a Protestant.

protestar [protes'tar] *vt* to protest, declare, (*fe*) to protest // *vi* to protest.

protocolo [proto'kolo] *nm* protocol.

prototipo [proto'tipo] *nm* prototype.

provecho [pro'βetʃo] *nm* advantage, benefit; (*FINANZAS*) profit; **¡buen ~!** bon appétit; **en ~ de** to the benefit of; **sacar ~ de** to benefit from, profit by.

proveer [proβe'er] *vt* to provide, supply; (*preparar*) to provide, get ready; (*vacante*) to fill; (*negocio*) to transact, dispatch // *vi*: **~ a** to provide for.

provenir [proβe'nir] *vi*: **~ de** to come from, stem from.

proverbio [pro'βerβjo] *nm* proverb.

providencia [proβi'ðenθja] *nf* providence; (*previsión*) foresight; **~s** *nfpl* measures, steps.

provincia [pro'βinθja] *nf* province; **~no, a** a provincial; (*del campo*) country *cpd*.

provisión [proβi'sjon] *nf* provision; (*abastecimiento*) provision, supply; (*medida*) measure, step.

provisional [proβisjo'nal] a provisional.

provocación [proβoka'θjon] *nf* provocation; **provocar** *vt* to provoke; (*alentar*) to tempt, invite; (*causar*) to bring about, lead to; (*promover*) to promote; (*estimular*) to rouse, stir, stimulate; **provocativo, a** a provocative.

próximamente [proksima'mente] *ad* shortly, soon.

proximidad [proksimi'ðað] *nf* closeness, proximity; **próximo, a** a

near, close; (*vecino*) neighbouring; (*el que viene*) next.
proyectar [projek'tar] vt (*objeto*) to hurl, throw; (*luz*) to cast, shed; (*CINE*) to screen, show; (*planear*) to plan.
proyectil [projek'til] nm projectile, missile; (*MIL*) missile.
proyecto [pro'jekto] nm plan; (*estimación de costo*) detailed estimate.
proyector [projek'tor] nm (*CINE*) projector; (*MIL*) searchlight; (*de teatro*) spotlight.
prudencia [pru'ðenθja] nf (*sabiduría*) wisdom, prudence; (*cautela*) care; **prudente** a sensible, wise, prudent; (*conductor*) careful.
prueba [prweßa] etc vb ver **probar** // nf proof; (*ensayo*) test, trial; (*saboreo*) testing, sampling; (*de ropa*) fitting; ~s nfpl trials; a ~ on trial; a ~ de proof against; a ~ de agua/fuego waterproof/fireproof; **sala de** ~s fitting room; **someter a** ~ to put to the test.
prurito [pru'rito] nm itch; (*de bebé*) nappy rash.
psico... [siko] pref psycho...; ~**análisis** nm psychoanalysis; ~**logía** nf psychology; ~**lógico, a** a psychological; **psicólogo, a** nm/f psychologist; **psicópata** nm/f psychopath; ~**sis** nf inv psychosis.
psiquiatra [si'kjatra] nm/f psychiatrist; **psiquiátrico, a** a psychiatric.
psíquico, a ['sikiko, a] a psychic(al).
PSOE abr de **Partido Socialista Obrero Español.**
púa ['pua] nf sharp point; (*para guitarra*) plectrum; **alambre de** ~ barbed wire.
pubertad [pußer'tað] nf puberty.
publicación [pußlika'θjon] nf publication; **publicar** vt (*editar*) to publish; (*hacer público*) to publicize; (*vulgarizar*) to make public, divulge.
publicidad [pußliθi'ðað] nf pub-

licity; (*COM*) advertising; **publicitario, a** a publicity cpd; advertising cpd.
público, a ['pußliko, a] a public // nm public; (*TEATRO etc*) audience.
puchero [pu'tʃero] nm stew; **hacer** ~s to pout.
pude etc vb ver **poder.**
púdico, a ['puðiko, a] a modest.
pudiera etc vb ver **poder.**
pudor [pu'ðor] nm modesty.
pudrir [pu'ðrir] vt to rot; (*fam*) to upset, annoy; ~**se** vr to rot, decay.
pueblo ['pweßlo] nm people; (*nación*) nation; (*aldea*) village.
puedo etc vb ver **poder.**
puente ['pwente] nm (*gen*) bridge; ~ **aéreo** airlift; ~ **colgante** suspension bridge; **hacer el** ~ (*fam*) to take an extra day off work between 2 public holidays.
puerco, a ['pwerko, a] nm/f pig/sow // a (*sucio*) dirty, filthy; (*obsceno*) disgusting; ~ **de mar** porpoise; ~ **marino** dolphin.
pueril [pwe'ril] a childish.
puerro ['pwerro] nm leek.
puerta ['pwerta] nf door; (*de jardín*) gate; (*portal*) doorway; (*fig*) gateway; (*gol*) goal; a ~ **cerrada** behind closed doors; ~ **giratoria** swing door, revolving door.
puertaventana [pwertaßen'tana] nf shutter.
puerto ['pwerto] nm port; (*paso*) pass; (*fig*) haven, refuge.
Puerto Rico [pwerto'riko] nm Puerto Rico; **puertorriqueño, a** a Puerto Rican.
pues [pwes] ad (*entonces*) then; (*¡entonces!*) well, well then; (*así que*) so // conj (*ya que*) since; ~**!** (*sí*) yes!, certainly!
puesto, a ['pwesto, a] pp de **poner** // a dressed // nm (*lugar, posición*) place; (*trabajo*) post, job; (*COM*) stall // conj: ~ **que** since, as // (*apuesta*) bet, stake; ~ **a en marcha** starting; ~**a del sol** sunset.
púgil ['puxil] nm boxer.

pugna ['puɣna] nf battle, conflict; **~cidad** nf pugnacity, aggressiveness; **pugnar** vi (luchar) to struggle, fight; (pelear) to fight.

pulcro, a ['pulkro, a] a neat, tidy; (bello) exquisite.

pulga ['pulɣa] nf flea.

pulgada [pul'ɣaða] nf inch.

pulgar [pul'ɣar] nm thumb.

pulir [pu'lir], **pulimentar** [pulimen'tar] vt to polish; (alisar) to smooth; (fig) to polish up, touch up.

pulmón [pul'mon] nm lung, **pulmonía** nf pneumonia.

pulpa ['pulpa] nf pulp; (de fruta) flesh, soft part.

púlpito ['pulpito] nm pulpit.

pulpo ['pulpo] nm octopus.

pulsación [pulsa'θjon] nf beat, pulsation; (ANAT) throb(bing).

pulsador [pulsa'ðor] nm button, push button.

pulsar [pul'sar] vt (tecla) to touch, tap; (MUS) to play; (botón) to press, push // vi to pulsate; (latir) to beat, throb; (MED): ~ a uno to take sb's pulse.

pulsera [pul'sera] nf bracelet.

pulso ['pulso] nm (ANAT) pulse; (: muñeca) wrist; (fuerza) strength; (firmeza) steadiness, steady hand; (tacto) tact, good sense.

pulverizador [pulßeriða'ðor] nm spray, spray gun; **pulverizar** vt to pulverize; (líquido) to spray.

pulla ['puʎa] nf cutting remark; (expresión grosera) obscene remark.

pungir [pun'xir] vt to puncture, prick, pierce; (fig) to cause suffering to.

punición [puni'θjon] nf punishment; **punitivo, a** a punitive.

punta ['punta] nf point, tip; (extremidad) end; (fig) touch, trace; horas ~s peak hours, rush hours; **sacar ~ a** to sharpen, **estar de ~** to be edgy.

puntada [pun'taða] nf (COSTURA) stitch; (fam) hint; **no ha dado ~** he hasn't done a stroke.

puntal [pun'tal] nm prop, support.

puntapié [punta'pje] nm kick.

puntear [punte'ar] vt (marcar) to tick, mark; (coser) to stitch up.

puntería [punte'ria] nf (de arma) aim, aiming; (destreza) marksmanship.

puntiagudo, a [puntja'ɣuðo, a] a sharp, pointed.

puntilla [pun'tiʎa] nf (de pluma) point, nib; (andar) de ~s (to walk) on tiptoe.

punto ['punto] nm (gen) point; (señal diminuta) spot, dot; (lugar) spot, place; (momento) point, moment; a ~ ready; estar a ~ de to be on the point of or about to; ~ on the dot; ~ de arranque starting point; ~ muerto dead centre; (AUTO) neutral (gear); ~ y coma semicolon; ~ de interrogación question mark.

puntuación [puntwa'θjon] nf punctuation; (puntos: en examen) mark(s) (pl); (: DEPORTE) score.

puntual [pun'twal] a (a tiempo) punctual; (exacto) exact, accurate; (seguro) reliable; **~idad** nf punctuality; exactness, accuracy; reliability; **~izar** vt to fix specify; (en la memoria) to fix in one's mind/memory.

punzante [pun'θante] a (dolor) shooting, sharp; (herramienta) sharp; **punzar** vt to prick, pierce // vi to shoot, stab.

puñado [pu'ɲaðo] nm handful.

puñal [pu'ɲal] nm dagger; **~ada** nf stab; **~ada de misericordia** coup de grâce.

puñetazo [puɲe'taðo] nm punch.

puño ['puɲo] nm (ANAT) fist; (cantidad) fistful, handful; (COSTURA) cuff; (de herramienta) handle.

pupila [pu'pila] nf pupil.

pupitre [pu'pitre] nm desk.

puré [pu're] nm puree; (sopa)

(thick) soup; ~ **de patatas** mashed potatoes.

pureza [pu'reθa] nf purity.

purga ['purxa] nf purge; **purgante** a, nm purgative; **purgar** vt to purge.

purgatorio [purxa'torjo] nm purgatory.

purificar [purifi'kar] vt to purify; (refinar) to refine.

puritano, a [puri'tano, a] a (actitud) puritanical; (iglesia, tradición) puritan // nm/f puritan.

puro, a ['puro, a] a pure; (cielo) clear; (verdad) simple, plain // ad: **de ~ cansado** out of sheer tiredness // nm cigar.

púrpura ['purpura] nf purple; **purpúreo, a** a purple.

puse, pusiera etc vb ver **poner.**

pústula ['pustula] nf pimple, sore.

puta ['puta] nf whore, prostitute.

putrefacción [putrefak'θjon] nf rotting, putrefaction.

pútrido, a ['putriðo, a] a rotten.

Q

q.e.p.d. abr de **que en paz descanse.**

q.e.s.m. abr de **que estrecha su mano.**

que [ke] pron (sujeto) who, that; (: cosa) which, that; (complemento) whom, that; (: cosa) which, that // conj that; **el momento en ~ llegó** the moment he arrived; **lo ~ digo** what I say; **dar ~ hablar** to give cause to talk, cause talk; **le ruego ~ se calle** I'm asking you to keep quiet; **te digo ~ sí** I'm telling you, I assure you; **yo ~ tú** if I were you.

qué [ke] a what?, which? // pron what?; **¡~ divertido!** how funny!; **¿~ edad tiene Ud?** how old are you?; **¿de ~ me hablas?** what are you saying to me?; **¿~ tal?** how are you?, how are things?; **¿~ hay (de nuevo)?** what's new?

quebrada [ke'βraða] nf ver **quebrado.**

quebradizo, a [keβra'ðiθo, a] a fragile; (persona) frail.

quebrado, a [ke'βraðo, a] a (roto) broken; (pálido) pale; (COM) bankrupt // nm/f bankrupt // nf ravine.

quebradura [keβra'ðura] nf (fisura) fissure; (GEO) gorge; (MED) rupture.

quebrantadura [keβranta'ðura] nf, **quebrantamiento** [keβranta'mjento] nm (acto) breaking; (estado) exhaustion.

quebrantar [keβran'tar] vt (romper) to break; (infringir) to violate, transgress; ~**se** (persona) to fail in health; (deshacerse) to break.

quebranto [ke'βranto] nm damage, harm; (decaimiento) exhaustion; (debilidad) weakness; (dolor) grief, pain.

quebrar [ke'βrar] vt to break, smash; (interrumpir) to interrupt // vi to go bankrupt; ~**se** vr to break, get broken; (MED) to be ruptured.

quedar [ke'ðar] vi (permanecer) to stay; (seguir siendo) to remain; (encontrarse) to be; (restar) to remain, be left; ~**se** vr to remain, stay (behind); ~**se con** to keep; ~ **en** (acordar) to agree on/to; (acabar siendo) to end up as; ~ **por hacer** to be still to be done; ~ **ciego/mudo** to be left blind/dumb; **no te queda bien ese vestido** that dress doesn't suit you; **quedamos a las seis** we agreed to meet at six.

quedo, a ['keðo, a] a still // ad softly, gently.

quehacer [kea'θer] nm task, job; (doméstico) chore.

queja ['kexa] nf complaint; **quejarse** vr (enfermo) to moan, groan; (protestar) to complain;

quejido nm moan; **quejoso, a** a complaining.

quemado, a [ke'maðo, a] a burnt.

quemadura [kema'ðura] nf burn, scald.

quemar [ke'mar] vt to burn; (fig) to burn up, squander // vi to be burning hot; **~se** vr to burn (up); (del sol) to get sunburnt.

quemarropa [kema'rropa]: **a ~** ad point-blank.

quemazón [kema'θon] nf burn; (calor) intense heat, (sensación) itch.

quepo etc vb ver **caber**.

querella [ke're.ʎa] nf (JUR) charge; (disputa) dispute.

querer [ke'rer] vt (desear) to want, wish, (amar a?) to love, **~ hacer algo** to want to do sth; **querido, a** a dear // nf darling // nf mistress.

quesería [kese'ria] nf dairy, cheese factory.

queso ['keso] nm cheese; **~ crema** cream cheese; **~ helado** ice-cream brick.

quicio ['kiθjo] nm hinge; **sacar a uno de ~** to get on sb's nerves.

quiebra ['kjeβra] nf break, split; (COM) bankruptcy; (ECON) slump.

quiebro ['kjeβro] nm (del cuerpo) swerve.

quien [kjen] pron who; **hay ~ piensa que** there are those who think that; **no hay ~ lo haga** no-one will do it.

quién [kjen] pron who, whom; **¿~ es?** who's there?

quienquiera [kjen'kjera] (pl **quienesquiera**) pron whoever.

quiero etc vb ver **querer**.

quieto, a ['kjeto, a] a still; (carácter) placid; **quietud** nf stillness.

quijada [ki'xaða] nf jaw, jawbone.

quilate [ki'late] nm carat.

quimera [ki'mera] nf chimera; **quimérico, a** a fantastic.

químico, a ['kimiko, a] a chemical // nm/f chemist // nf chemistry.

quincalla [kin'ka.ʎa] nf hardware, ironmongery.

quince ['kinθe] num fifteen; **~na** nf fortnight; (pago) fortnightly pay; **~nal** a fortnightly.

quiniela [ki'njela] nf pools coupon; **~s** nfpl football pools.

quinientos [ki'njentos] num five hundred.

quinina [ki'nina] nf quinine.

quinqui ['kinki] nm gangster.

quinto, a ['kinto, a] a fifth // nf country house; (MIL) call-up, draft.

quiosco ['kjosko] nm (de música) bandstand; (de periódicos) news stand.

quirúrgico, a [ki'rurxiko, a] a surgical.

quise, quisiera etc vb ver **querer**.

quisquilloso, a [kiski'ʎoso, a] a touchy; (fam) pernickety.

quiste ['kiste] nm cyst.

quita ['kita] nf remission of debt; **de ~ y pon** detachable.

quitaesmalte [kitaes'malte] nm nail-polish remover.

quitamanchas [kita'mantʃas] nm inv stain remover.

quitar [ki'tar] vt to remove, take away; (ropa) to take off; (dolor) to kill, stop; **¡quita de ahí!** get away!; **~se** vr to withdraw; **se quitó el sombrero** he took off his hat.

quitasol [kita'sol] nm sunshade.

quite ['kite] nm (esgrima) parry; (evasión) dodge.

quizá(s) [ki'θa(s)] ad perhaps, maybe.

R

rábano ['raβano] nm radish; **me importa un ~** I don't give a damn.

rabia ['raβja] nf (MED) rabies; (fig) fury, rage; **rabiar** vi to have rabies; to rage, be furious; **rabiar por algo**

to be dying for or long for sth.

rabieta [ra'βjeta] nf tantrum, fit of temper.

rabino [ra'βino] nm rabbi.

rabioso, a [ra'βjoso, a] a rabid; (fig) furious.

rabo ['raβo] nm tail.

racial [ra'θjal] a racial, race cpd.

racimo [ra'θimo] nm bunch.

raciocinio [raθjo'θinjo] nm reason.

ración [ra'θjon] nf portion; **raciones** nfpl rations.

racional [raθjo'nal] a (razonable) reasonable; (lógico) rational; **~izar** vt to rationalize.

racionar [raθjo'nar] vt to ration (out).

racismo [ra'θismo] nm racialism, racism; **racista** a, nm/f racist.

racha ['ratʃa] nf gust of wind.

radar [ra'ðar] nm radar.

radiador [raðja'ðor] nm radiator.

radiante [ra'ðjante] a radiant.

radical [raði'kal] a, nm/f radical.

radicar [raði'kar] vi to take root; **~ en** to lie or consist in; **~se** vr to establish o.s., put down (one's) roots.

radio ['raðjo] nm radio; (aparato) radio (set) // nm (MAT) radius; (QUÍMICA) radium; **~activo, a** a radioactive; **~difusión** nf broadcasting; **~emisora** nf transmitter, radio station; **~escucha** nm/f listener; **~grafía** nf X-ray; **~grafiar** vt to X-ray; **~terapia** nf radiotherapy; **radioyente** nm/f listener.

raer [ra'er] vt to scrape (off).

ráfaga ['rafaxa] nf gust; (de luz) flash; (de tiros) burst.

raído, a [ra'iðo, a] a (ropa) threadbare; (persona) shameless.

raigambre [rai'xambre] nf (BOT) roots pl; (fig).

raíz [ra'iθ] (pl **raíces**) nf root; **~ cuadrada** square root; **a ~ de** as a result of.

raja ['raxa] nf (de melón etc) slice; (grieta) crack; **rajar** vt to split; (fam) to slash; (fruta etc) to slice;

rajarse vr to split, crack; (AM) to quit.

rajatabla [raxa'taβla]: **a ~ ad** (estrictamente) strictly, to the letter; (cueste lo que cueste) at all costs.

ralo, a ['ralo, a] a thin, sparse.

rallado, a [ra'ʎaðo, a] a grated; **rallador** nm grater; **rallar** vt to grate.

rama ['rama] nf branch; **~da** nf, **~je** nm branches pl, foliage; **ramal** nm (de cuerda) strand; (FERRO) branch line; (AUTO) branch (road).

rambla ['rambla] nf (de agua) stream; (avenida) avenue.

ramera [ra'mera] nf whore.

ramificación [ramifika'θjon] nf ramification; **ramificarse** vr to branch out.

ramillete [rami'ʎete] nm bouquet; (fig) select group.

ramo ['ramo] nm branch; (COM) department, section.

rampa ['rampa] nf (MED) cramp; (plano) ramp.

ramplón, ona [ram'plon, ona] a uncouth, coarse.

rana ['rana] nf frog; **~ toro** bullfrog; **salto de ~** leapfrog.

rancio, a ['ranθjo, a] a rancid; (vino) aged, mellow; (fig) ancient.

rancho ['rantʃo] nm grub (fam); (AM) farm.

rango ['rango] nm rank, standing.

ranura [ra'nura] nf groove; (de teléfono) slot.

rapacidad [rapaθi'ðað] nf rapacity.

rapar [ra'par] vt to shave; (los cabellos) to crop; (fam) to pinch, nick (fam).

rapaz [ra'paθ] a (ladrón) thieving; (ZOOL) predatory.

rapaz, a [ra'paθ, a] nm/f young boy/girl.

rape ['rape] nm quick shave; **al ~** cropped.

rapé [ra'pe] nm snuff.

rapidez [rapi'ðeθ] nf speed, rapidity; **rápido, a** a rapid, fast,

quick // ad quickly // nm (tren)
express; **rápidos** nmpl rapids.

rapiña [ra'piɲa] nm robbery; **ave de ~** bird of prey.

raptar [rap'tar] vt to kidnap; **rapto**
nm kidnapping; (impulso) sudden
impulse; (éxtasis) ecstasy, rapture.

raqueta [ra'keta] nf racquet.

raquítico, a [ra'kitiko, a] a
stunted; (fig) poor, inadequate;
raquitismo nm rickets sg.

rareza [ra'reθa] nf rarity; (fig)
eccentricity.

raro, a ['raro, a] a (poco común)
rare; (extraño) odd, strange; (excepcional) remarkable.

ras [ras] nm: **a ~ de** level with; **a ~
de tierra** at ground level.

rasar [ra'sar] vt (igualar) to level;
(frotar) to graze.

rascacielos [raska'θjelos] nm inv
skyscraper.

rascar [ras'kar] vt (con las uñas) to
scratch; (raspar) to scrape; **~se** vr
to scratch (o.s.).

rasgadura [rasɣa'ðura] nf tear,
rip; **rasgar** vt to tear, rip (up).

rasgo ['rasɣo] nm stroke; **~s** nmpl
features, characteristics; **a grandes
~s** in outline, broadly.

rasguñar [rasɣu'ɲar] vt to scratch;
rasguño nm scratch.

raso, a ['raso, a] a (liso) flat, level;
(a baja altura) very low // nm satin;
cielo ~ clear sky; **soldado ~**
private.

raspadura [raspa'ðura] nm scrape;
(marca) a mark; **~s** nfpl scrapings;
raspar vt to scrape; (arañar) to
scratch; (limar) to file.

rastra ['rastra] nf (huella) track;
(AGR) rake; **a ~s** by dragging; (fig)
unwillingly; **pescar a ~** to trawl.

rastreador [rastrea'ðor] nm
tracker; (NAUT) trawler; **~ de
minas** minesweeper; **rastrear** vt to
track; (laguna, río) to dredge, drag.

rastrero, a [ras'trero, a] a

creeping; (vestido) trailing; (fig)
despicable, mean.

rastrillar [rastri'ʎar] vt to rake;
rastrillo nm rake.

rastro ['rastro] nm (AGR) rake;
(pista) track, trail; (curso) course;
(vestigio) trace; (matadero) slaughterhouse; **el R~** the Madrid flea-market.

rastrojo [ras'troxo] nm stubble.

rasurador [rasura'ðor] nm, **rasuradora** [rasura'ðora] nf electric
shaver, **rasurarse** vr to shave.

rata ['rata] nf rat.

ratear [rate'ar] vt (robar) to steal;
(distribuir) to share out.

ratería [rate'ria] nf petty theft.

ratero, a [ra'tero, a] a light-
fingered // nm pickpocket.

ratificar [ratifi'kar] vt to ratify.

rato ['rato] nm while, short time; **a
~s** at times; **hay para ~** there's
still a long way to go; **pasar el ~** to
kill time; **pasar un buen/mal ~** to
have a good/rough time.

ratón [ra'ton] nm mouse; **ratonera**
nf mousetrap.

raudal [rau'ðal] nm torrent; **a ~es**
in abundance.

raya ['raja] nf line; (marca) scratch;
(en tela) stripe; (de pelo) parting;
(límite) boundary; **tener a ~** to
keep in check; **rayar** vt to line; to
scratch; (talón) to cross; (subrayar)
to underline // vi: **rayar en** to
border on.

rayo ['rajo] nm (del sol) ray, beam;
(de luz) shaft; (en una tormenta)
lightning, flash of lightning; **~s X**
X rays.

rayón [ra'jon] nm rayon.

raza ['raθa] nf race; **~ humana**
human race.

razón [ra'θon] nf (gen) reason;
(justicia) right, justice; (razonamiento) reasoning; (motivo) cause;
(MAT) ratio; **a ~ de 10 cada día** at
the rate of 10 a day; **"~: ..."**
"inquiries to ..."; **en ~ de** with
regard to; **dar ~ a uno** to agree with

sb is right; **tener ~ to** be right; **~ directa/inversa** direct/inverse proportion; **~ de ser** raison d'être; **razonable** *a* reasonable; (*justo, moderado*) fair; **razonamiento** *nm* (*juicio*) judgement; (*argumento*) reasoning; **razonar** *vt* to reason, argue; (*cuenta*) to itemize // *vi* to reason, argue.

reabastecer [reaβaste'θer] *vt* to refuel.

reabrir [rea'βrir] *vt* to reopen.

reacción [reak'θjon] *nf* reaction; **avión a ~** jet plane; **~ en cadena** chain reaction; **reaccionar** *vi* to react; **reaccionario, a** *a* reactionary.

reacio, a [re'aθjo, a] *a* stubborn.

reactor [reak'tor] *nm* reactor.

readaptación [readapta'θjon] *nf:* **~ profesional** industrial retraining.

reafirmar [reafir'mar] *vt* to reaffirm.

reagrupar [reaɣru'par] *vt* to regroup.

reajuste [rea'xuste] *nm* readjustment.

real [re'al] *a* real; (*del rey, fig*) royal.

realce [re'alθe] *nm* (*TEC*) embossing; (*lustre, fig*) splendour; (*ARTE*) highlight; **poner de ~** to emphasize.

realidad [reali'ðað] *nf* reality, fact; (*verdad*) truth.

realista [rea'lista] *nm/f* realist.

realización [realiθa'θjon] *nf* fulfilment; (*COM*) sale, selling-up.

realizador, a [realiθa'ðor, a] *nm/f* (*TV etc*) producer.

realizar [reali'θar] *vt* (*objetivo*) to achieve; (*plan*) to carry out; (*viaje*) to make, undertake; (*COM*) to sell up; **~se** *vr* to come about, come true.

realmente [real'mente] *ad* really, actually.

realzar [real'θar] *vt* (*TEC*) to raise; (*embellecer*) to enhance; (*acentuar*) to highlight.

reanimar [reani'mar] *vt* to revive;

(*alentar*) to encourage; **~se** *vr* to revive.

reanudar [reanu'ðar] *vt* (*renovar*) to renew; (*retomar*) to resume.

reaparición [reapari'θjon] *nf* reappearance.

rearme [re'arme] *nm* rearmament.

reata [re'ata] *nf* rope, rein; **de ~** in single file.

rebaja [re'βaxa] *nf* (*COM*) reduction; (*menoscabo*) lessening; **rebajar** *vt* (*bajar*) to lower; (*reducir*) to reduce; (*disminuir*) to lessen; (*humillar*) to humble.

rebanada [reβa'naða] *nf* slice.

rebaño [re'βaɲo] *nm* herd; (*de ovejas*) flock.

rebasar [reβa'sar] *vt* (*también ~ de*) to exceed; (*AUTO*) to overtake.

rebatir [reβa'tir] *vt* to refute; (*descontar*) to deduct.

rebato [re'βato] *nm* alarm; (*ataque*) surprise attack.

rebelarse [reβe'larse] *vr* to rebel, revolt.

rebelde [re'βelde] *a* rebellious; (*indócil*) unruly // *nm/f* rebel; **rebeldía** *nf* rebelliousness; (*desobediencia*) disobedience; **rebelión** *nf* rebellion.

reblandecer [reβlande'θer] *vt* to soften.

rebosante [reβo'sante] *a* overflowing; **rebosar** *vi* to overflow; (*abundar*) to abound, be plentiful.

rebotar [reβo'tar] *vt* to bounce; (*rechazar*) to repel; **~se** *vr* (*pelota*) to rebound; (*bala*) to ricochet; **rebote** *nm* rebound; **de rebote** on the rebound.

rebozar [reβo'θar] *vt* to wrap up; (*CULIN*) to fry in batter; **rebozo** *nm* muffler; (*AM*) shawl; **decir algo sin rebozo** to call a spade a spade.

rebuscado, a [reβus'kaðo, a] *a* affected.

rebuscar [reβus'kar] *vt* to search carefully; (*objeto*) to search for carefully.

rebuznar [reβuθ'nar] *vi* to bray.

recabar [reka'βar] vt to manage to get.

recado [re'kaðo] nm errand; (mensaje) message; **tomar un ~** (TELEC) to take a message.

recaer [reka'er] vi to relapse; **~ en** to fall to or on; **recaída** nf relapse.

recalcar [rekal'kar] vt (fig) to stress, emphasize.

recalcitrante [rekalθi'trante] a recalcitrant.

recalcitrar [rekalθi'trar] vi (echarse atrás) to step back; (resistir) to resist, be stubborn.

recalentar [rekalen'tar] vt (volver a calentar) to reheat; (demasiado) to overheat.

recambio [re'kambjo] nm spare; (de pluma) refill.

recapacitar [rekapaθi'tar] vt to think over // vi to reflect.

recargado, a [rekar'xaðo, a] a overloaded; **recargar** vt to overload; (batería) to recharge; **recargar los precios** to increase prices; **recargo** nm surcharge; (aumento) increase.

recatado, a [reka'taðo, a] a modest, demure; (prudente) cautious.

recatar [reka'tar] vt to hide; **~se** vr to hide o.s.

recato [re'kato] nm modesty, demureness; (cautela) caution.

recaudación [rekauða'θjon] nf collection; (suma) takings pl; (en deporte) gate; **recaudador** nm tax collector.

recelar [reθe'lar] vt: **~ que** (sospechar) to suspect that; (temor) to fear that // vi, **~se vr: ~(se) de** to distrust; **recelo** nm distrust, suspicion, misgiving; **receloso, a** a distrustful, suspicious.

recepción [reθep'θjon] nf reception; **recepcionista** nm/f receptionist.

receptáculo [reθep'takulo] nm receptacle.

receptivo, a [reθep'tiβo, a] a receptive.

receptor, a [reθep'tor, a] nm/f recipient // (línea) receiver.

recesión [reθe'sjon] nf recession.

receta [re'θeta] nf (CULIN) recipe; (MED) prescription.

recibidor, a [reθiβi'ðor, a] nm/f receiver, recipient.

recibimiento [reθiβi'mjento] nm (recepción) reception; (acogida) welcome.

recibir [reθi'βir] vt (gen) to receive; (dar la bienvenida) to welcome // vi to entertain; **~se vr: ~se de** to qualify as; **recibo** nm receipt.

reciedumbre [reθje'ðumbre] nf strength; (vigor) vigour.

recién [re'θjen] ad recently, newly; **~ casados** the newlyweds; **~ nacido** the newborn child.

reciente [re'θjente] a recent; (fresco) fresh.

recinto [re'θinto] nm (gen) enclosure; (área) area, place.

recio, a ['reθjo, a] a strong, tough; (voz) loud; (tiempo) harsh // ad hard; loud(ly).

recipiente [reθi'pjente] nm receptacle.

reciprocidad [reθiproθi'ðað] nf reciprocity; **recíproco, a** a reciprocal.

recital [reθi'tal] nm (MUS) recital; (LITERATURA) reading; **recitar** vt to recite.

reclamación [reklama'θjon] nf claim, demand; (queja) complaint.

reclamar [rekla'mar] vt to claim, demand // vi: **~ contra** to complain about; **~ en justicia** to take to court; **reclamo** nm (anuncio) advertisement; (tentación) attraction.

reclinar [rekli'nar] vt to recline, lean; **~se vr** to lean back.

recluir [reklu'ir] vt to intern, confine.

reclusión [reklu'sjon] nf (prisión) prison; (refugio) seclusion; **~ perpetua** life imprisonment.

recluta [reˈkluta] *nm/f* recruit // *nf* recruitment.

reclutamiento [reklutaˈmjento] *nm* recruitment.

recobrar [rekoˈβrar] *vt* (*recuperar*) to recover; (*rescatar*) to get back; ~**se** *vr* to recover.

recodo [reˈkoðo] *nm* (*de río, camino*) bend.

recogedor, a [rekoxeˈðor, a] *nm/f* picker, harvester.

recoger [rekoˈxer] *vt* (*gen*) to collect; (*AGR*) to harvest; (*levantar*) to pick up; (*juntar*) to gather; (*pasar a buscar*) to come for, fetch; (*dar asilo*) to give shelter to; (*faldas*) to gather up; (*pelo*) to put up; ~**se** *vr* (*retirarse*) to retire; **recogido, a** *a* (*lugar*) quiet, secluded; (*persona*) modest, retiring; (*pequeño*) small // *nf* (*del correo*) collection; (*AGR*) harvest.

recolección [rekolekˈθjon] *nf* (*de las mieses*) harvesting; (*colecta*) collection.

recomendación [rekomendaˈθjon] *nf* (*sugerencia*) suggestion, recommendation; (*elogio*) praise; **recomendar** *vt* to suggest, recommend; to praise; (*confiar*) to entrust.

recompensa [rekomˈpensa] *nf* reward, recompense; **recompensar** *vt* to reward, recompense; (*por pérdidas*) to compensate.

recomponer [rekompoˈner] *vt* to mend; ~**se** *vr* (*fam*) to doll up.

reconciliación [rekonθiljaˈθjon] *nf* reconciliation; **reconciliar** *vt* to reconcile; **reconciliarse** *vr* to become reconciled.

reconfortar [rekonforˈtar] *vt* to comfort; ~**se** *vr*: ~**se con** to fortify o.s. with.

reconocer [rekonoˈθer] *vt* to recognize; (*registrar*) to search; (*MED*) to examine; **reconocido, a** *a* recognized; (*agradecido*) grateful; **reconocimiento** *nm* recognition;

search; examination; gratitude; (*confesión*) admission.

reconquista [rekonˈkista] *nf* reconquest.

reconstituyente [rekonstituˈjente] *nm* tonic.

reconstruir [rekonstruˈir] *vt* to reconstruct.

recopilación [rekopilaˈθjon] *nf* (*sumario*) summary; (*compendio*) compilation; **recopilar** *vt* to compile.

récord [ˈrekorð] *a inv, nm* record.

recordar [rekorˈðar] *vt* (*acordarse de*) to remember; (*acordar a otro*) to remind // *vi* to remember.

recorrer [rekoˈrrer] *vt* (*país*) to cross, travel through; (*distancia*) to cover; (*repasar*) to go over, look over; **recorrido** *nm* run, journey; **tren de largo recorrido** main-line train.

recortado, a [rekorˈtaðo, a] *a* uneven, irregular.

recortar [rekorˈtar] *vt* to cut out; **recorte** *nm* (*acción*) cutting; (*de prensa*) cutting, clipping; (*de telas, chapas*) trimming.

recostado, a [rekosˈtaðo, a] *a* leaning; **estar** ~ to be lying down.

recostar [rekosˈtar] *vt* to lean; ~**se** *vr* to lie down.

recoveco [rekoˈβeko] *nm* bend; (*en casa*) cubby hole.

recreación [rekreaˈθjon] *nf* recreation; (*TEATRO, CINE*) interval, intermission.

recrear [rekreˈar] *vt* (*entretener*) to entertain; (*volver a crear*) to recreate; **recreativo, a** *a* recreational; **recreo** *nm* recreation; (*ESCOL*) break, playtime.

recriminar [rekrimiˈnar] *vt* to reproach // *vi* to recriminate; ~**se** *vr* to reproach each other.

recrudecer [rekruðeˈθer] *vt, vi,* ~**se** *vr* to worsen.

recrudecimiento [rekruðeθiˈmjento] *nm*, **recrudescencia** [rekruðesˈθenθja] *nf* upsurge.

recta ['rekta] *nf ver* **recto.**

rectángulo, a [rek'tangulo, a] *a* rectangular // *nm* rectangle.

rectificar [rektifi'kar] *vt* to rectify; (*volverse recto*) to straighten // *vt* to correct o.s.

rectitud [rekti'tuð] *nf* (*exactitud*) correctness; (*fig*) rectitude.

recto, a ['rekto, a] *a* straight; (*persona*) honest, upright // *nm* rectum // *nf* straight line.

rector, a [rek'tor, a] *a* governing.

recua ['rekwa] *nf* mule train.

recuento [re'kwento] *nm* inventory; **hacer el ~ de** to count or reckon up.

recuerdo [re'kwerðo] *nm* souvenir; **~s** *nmpl* memories; **¡~s a tu madre!** give my regards to your mother.

recular [reku'lar] *vi* to fall back; (*fig*) to back down.

recuperable [rekupe'raßle] *a* recoverable; **recuperación** *nf* recovery.

recuperar [rekupe'rar] *vt* to recover; (*tiempo*) to make up; **~se** *vr* to recuperate.

recurrir [reku'rrir] *vi* (*JUR*) to appeal; **~ a** to resort to; (*persona*) to turn to; **recurso** *nm* resort; (*medios*) means *nf*; **resources** *pl*; (*JUR*) appeal.

recusar [reku'sar] *vt* to reject, refuse.

rechazar [retʃa'θar] *vt* to repel, drive back; (*idea*) to reject; (*oferta*) to turn down.

rechazo [re'tʃaθo] *nm* (*retroceso*) recoil; (*rebote*) rebound; (*negación*) rebuff.

rechifla [re'tʃifla] *nf* hissing, booing; (*fig*) derision; **rechiflar** *vt* to hiss, boo; **rechiflarse** *vr* to take things as a joke.

rechinar [retʃi'nar] *vi* to creak; (*gruñir*) to grumble; (*dientes*) to grind.

rechoncho, a [re'tʃontʃo, a] *a* (*fam*) chubby, thickset.

red [reð] *nf* net, mesh; (*de ferrocarriles etc*) network; (*trampa*) trap.

redacción [reðak'θjon] *nf* editing; (*oficina*) newspaper office; (*personal*) editorial staff.

redactar [reðak'tar] *vt* to draw up, draft; (*periódico*) to edit.

redada [re'ðaða] *nf*: **~ policíaca** police raid, round up.

rededor [reðe'ðor] *nm*: **al o en ~** around, round about.

redención [reðen'θjon] *nf* redemption; **redentor, a** *a* redeeming.

redescubrir [reðesku'ßrir] *vt* to rediscover.

redicho, a [re'ðitʃo, a] *a* affected, stilted.

redil [re'ðil] *nm* sheepfold.

redimir [reði'mir] *vt* to redeem.

rédito [re'ðito] *nm* interest, yield.

redoblar [reðo'ßlar] *vt* to redouble; (*plegar*) to fold back // *vi* (*tambor*) to play a roll on the drums.

redomado, a [reðo'maðo, a] *a* sly, crafty.

redonda [re'ðonda] *nf ver* **redondo.**

redondear [reðonde'ar] *vt* to round, round off; **~se** *vr* to become wealthy.

redondel [reðon'del] *nm* (*círculo*) circle; (*TAUR*) bullring, arena.

redondo, a [re'ðondo, a] *a* (*circular*) round; (*directo*) straight; (*completo*) complete // *nf*: **a la ~a** around, round about.

reducción [reðuk'θjon] *nf* reduction; (*MED*) setting.

reducido, a [reðu'θiðo, a] *a* reduced; (*limitado*) limited; (*pequeño*) small; **reducir** *vt* to reduce; to limit; (*MED*) to set a bone; **reducirse** *vr* to diminish.

redundancia [reðun'danθja] *nf* redundancy.

reembolsar [reembol'sar] *vt* to reimburse; (*depósito*) to refund; **reembolso** *nm* reimbursement; refund.

reemplazar [reempla'θar] *vt* to replace; *nm* replacement; **de reemplazo** (*MIL*) reserve.

refacción [refak'θjon] *nf* (*AM*) repair(s) (*pl*).

refajo [re'faxo] *nm* (*enagua*) flannel underskirt; (*falda*) short skirt.

referencia [refe'renθja] *nf* reference; (*informe*) report; **con ~** a with reference to.

referente [refe'rente] *a*: **~ a** concerning, relating to.

referir [refe'rir] *vt* (*contar*) to tell, recount; (*relacionar*) to refer, relate; **~se** *vr*: **~se a** to refer to.

refilón [refi'lon]: **de ~** *ad* obliquely, aslant.

refinado, a [refi'naðo, a] *a* refined; **refinamiento** *nm* refinement; **refinar** *vt* to refine; (*fig*) to perfect, polish.

reflejar [refle'xar] *vt* (*gen*) to reflect; **reflejo, a** *a* reflected; (*movimiento*) reflex // *nm* reflection; (*ANAT*) reflex.

reflexión [reflek'sjon] *nf* reflection; **reflexionar** *vt* to reflect on // *vi* to reflect; (*detenerse*) to pause (to think).

reflexivo, a [reflek'sißo, a] *a* thoughtful; (*LING, fig*) reflexive.

reflujo [re'fluxo] *nm* ebb.

refocilar [refoθi'lar] *vt* to cheer up.

reforma [re'forma] *nf* reform; (*ARQ etc*) repair; **~ agraria** agrarian reform.

reformar [refor'mar] *vt* (*modificar*) to change, alter; (*formar de nuevo*) to reform; (*ARQ*) to repair; **~se** *vr* to mend one's ways.

reformatorio [reforma'torjo] *nm* reformatory.

reforzar [refor'θar] *vt* (*gen*) to strengthen; (*ARQ*) to reinforce; (*fig*) to encourage.

refractario, a [refrak'tarjo, a] *a* stubborn; (*TEC*) heat-resistant.

refrán [re'fran] *nm* proverb, saying.

refregar [refre'xar] *vt* to scrub.

refrenar [refre'nar] *vt* to check, restrain.

refrendar [refren'dar] *vt* (*firma*) to endorse, countersign; (*pasaporte*) to stamp; (*ley*) to approve.

refrescar [refres'kar] *vt* (*gen*) to refresh // *vi* to cool down; **~se** *vr* to get cooler; (*tomar aire fresco*) to go out for a breath of fresh air.

refresco [re'fresko] *nm* soft drink, cool drink; "**~s**" "refreshments".

refriega [re'frjexa] *nf* scuffle, brawl.

refrigeración [refrixera'θjon] *nf* refrigeration; (*de casa*) air-conditioning; **refrigerador** *nm* refrigerator; **refrigerar** *vt* to refrigerate; to air-condition.

refuerzo [re'fwerθo] *nm* reinforcement; (*TEC*) support.

refugiado, a [refu'xjaðo, a] *nm/f* refugee; **refugiarse** *vr* to take refuge, shelter; **refugio** *nm* refuge; (*protección*) shelter.

refulgencia [reful'xenθja] *nf* brilliance; **refulgir** *vi* to shine, be dazzling.

refundición [refundi'θjon] *nf* recasting, revision; **refundir** *vt* to recast.

refunfuñar [refunfu'nar] *vi* to grunt, growl; (*quejarse*) to grumble.

refutación [refuta'θjon] *nf* refutation; **refutar** *vt* to refute.

regadera [rexa'ðera] *nf* watering can.

regadío [rexa'ðio] *nm* irrigated land.

regalado, a [rexa'laðo, a] *a* comfortable, luxurious; (*gratis*) free, for nothing; (*pey*) soft.

regalar [rexa'lar] *vt* (*dar*) to give, present; (*entregar*) to give away; (*mimar*) to pamper, make a fuss of.

regalía [rexa'lia] *nf* privilege, prerogative; (*COM*) bonus; (*de autor*) royalty.

regaliz [rexa'liθ] *nm*, **regaliza** [rexa'liθa] *nf* liquorice.

regalo [re'γalo] nm (obsequio) gift, present; (gusto) pleasure; (comodidad) comfort.

regalón, ona [reγa'lon, ona] a spoiled, pampered.

regañadientes [reγaɲa'ðjentes] a ~ ad reluctantly.

regañar [reγa'ɲar] vt to scold // vi to grumble; **regaño** nm scolding, telling-off; (queja) grumble; **regañón, ona** a grumbling; (mujer) nagging.

regar [re'γar] vt to water, irrigate; (fig) to scatter, sprinkle.

regatear [reγate'ar] vt to bargain over; (guardar) to be mean with // vi to bargain, haggle; (DEPORTE) to dribble; **regateo** nm bargaining; haggling; (del cuerpo) swerve, dodge.

regazo [re'γaθo] nm lap.

regeneración [rexenera'θjon] nf regeneration; **regenerar** vt to regenerate.

regentar [rexen'tar] vt to direct, manage; **regente** nm manager; (POL) regent.

régimen ['reximen] (pl **regímenes**) nm regime; (MED) diet.

regimiento [rexi'mjento] nm regiment; (organización) administration.

regio, a ['rexjo, a] a royal, regal; (fig:suntuoso) splendid.

región [re'xjon] nf region; **regionalista** nm/f regionalist.

regir [re'xir] vt to govern, rule; (dirigir) to manage, run // vi to apply, to be in force.

registrador [rexistra'ðor] nm registrar, recorder.

registrar [rexis'trar] vt (buscar en cajón) to look through, search; (inspeccionar) to inspect; (anotar) to register, record; ~**se** vr to register; (ocurrir) to happen.

registro [re'xistro] nm registration; (MUS, libro) register; (inspección) inspection, search; ~ **civil** registry office.

regla ['reγla] nf (ley) rule, regulation; (de medir) ruler, rule; **la** ~ (MED) periods pl; **salir de** ~ to step out of line.

reglamentación [reγlamenta'θjon] nf (acto) regulation; (lista) rules pl; **reglamentar** vt to regulate; **reglamentario, a** a statutory, **reglamento** nm rules pl, regulations pl.

reglar [re'γlar] vt (papel) to rule, (actos) to regulate.

regocijado, a [reγoθi'xaðo, a] a merry; **regocijar** vt to cheer up, gladden; **regocijarse** vr to have a good time, make merry; (alegrarse) to rejoice; **regocijo** nm joy, happiness.

regodearse [reγoðe'arse] vr to be glad, be delighted; **regodeo** nm delight.

regresar [reγre'sar] vi to come/go back, return; **regresivo, a** a backward; (fig) regressive; **regreso** nm return.

reguero [re'γero] nm irrigation ditch.

regulador [reγula'ðor] nm (gen) regulator; (de radio etc) knob, control.

regular [reγu'lar] a (gen) regular; (normal) normal, usual; (común) ordinary; (organizado) regular, orderly; (mediano) average; (fam) not bad, so-so // ad so-so, alright // vt (controlar) to control, regulate; (TEC) to adjust; **por lo** ~ as a rule; ~**idad** nf regularity; ~**izar** vt to regularize.

regusto [re'γusto] nm aftertaste.

rehabilitación [reaβilita'θjon] nf rehabilitation; (ARQ) restoration; **rehabilitar** vt to rehabilitate; to restore; (reintegrar) to reinstate.

rehacer [rea'θer] vt (reparar) to mend, repair; (volver a hacer) to redo, repeat; ~**se** vr (MED) to recover; (dominarse) to pull o.s. together.

rehén [re'en] nm hostage.

rehilete [rei'lete] nm (dardo) dart; (DEPORTE) badminton, shuttlecock.

rehuir [reu'ir] vt to avoid, shun.

rehusar [reu'sar] vt, vi to refuse.

reina ['reina] nf queen; ~do nm reign; **reinante** a (fig) prevailing; **reinar** vi to reign.

reincidir [reinθi'ðir] vi to relapse.

reincorporarse [reinkorpo'rarse] vr: ~ **a** to rejoin.

reino ['reino] nm kingdom; **el R~ Unido** the United Kingdom.

reintegrar [reinte'xrar] vt (reconstituir) to reconstruct; (persona) to reinstate; (dinero) to return, pay back; **~se** vr: **~se a** to return to.

reír [re'ir] vi, **~se** vr to laugh; **~se de** to laugh at.

reiterar [reite'rar] vt to reiterate.

reivindicación [reiβindika'θjon] nf (demanda) claim, demand; (justificación) vindication; **reivindicar** vt to claim; (restaurar) to restore.

reja ['rexa] nf (de ventana) grille, bars pl; (en la calle) grating; (del arado) ploughshare.

rejilla [re'xiʎa] nf (de ventana) grille; (de silla) wickerwork; (de ventilación) vent; (de coche) luggage rack.

rejoneador [rexonea'ðor] nm mounted bullfighter.

rejuvenecer [rexuβene'θer] vt, vi to rejuvenate; **~se** vr to be rejuvenated.

relación [rela'θjon] nf relation, relationship; (MAT) ratio; (informe) report; **relaciones públicas** public relations; **con ~ a** o **en ~ con** in relation to; **relacionar** vt to relate, connect; **relacionarse** vr to be connected, be linked.

relajación [relaxa'θjon] nf relaxation; **relajado, a** a (disoluto) loose; (cómodo) relaxed; (MED) ruptured; **relajar** vt, **relajarse** vr to relax.

relamer [rela'mer] vt to lick (repeatedly); **~se** vr to lick one's lips.

relamido, a [rela'miðo, a] a (pulcro) overdressed; (afectado) affected.

relámpago [re'lampaɣo] nm flash of lightning; **visita/huelga** ~ lightning visit/strike; **relampaguear** vi to flash.

relatar [rela'tar] vt to tell, relate.

relativo, a [rela'tiβo, a] a relative; **en lo** ~ **a** concerning.

relato [re'lato] nm (narración) story, tale; (informe) report.

relegar [rele'xar] vt to relegate.

relevante [rele'βante] a eminent, outstanding.

relevar [rele'βar] vt (sustituir) to relieve; **~se** vr to relay; **~ a uno de un cargo** to relieve sb of his post.

relevo [re'leβo] nm relief; **carrera de** ~**s** relay race.

relieve [re'ljeβe] nm (ARTE, TEC) relief; (fig) prominence, importance; **~s** nmpl left-overs; **bajo** ~ bas-relief.

religión [reli'xjon] nf religion; **religiosidad** nf religiosity; **religioso, a** a religious // nm/f monk/nun // nm cleric.

relinchar [relin'tʃar] vi to neigh; **relincho** nm neigh; (acto) neighing.

reliquia [re'likja] nf relic; ~ **de familia** family heirloom.

reloj [re'lo(x)] nm watch; (de iglesia etc) clock; ~ **de pulsera** wristwatch; ~ **despertador** alarm clock; **~ero, a** nm/f watchmaker; clockmaker.

reluciente [relu'θjente] a brilliant, shining; **relucir** vi to shine; (fig) to excel.

relumbrante [relum'brante] a dazzling; **relumbrar** vi to dazzle, shine brilliantly.

rellano [re'ʎano] nm (ARQ) landing.

rellenar [reʎe'nar] vt (llenar) to fill up; (CULIN) to stuff; (COSTURA) to pad; **relleno, a** a full up; stuffed // nm stuffing; (de tapicería) padding.

remachar [rema'tʃar] *vt* to rivet; *(fig)* to hammer home, drive home; **remache** nm rivet.

remanente [rema'nente] nm remainder; *(COM)* balance; *(de producto)* surplus.

remanso [re'manso] nm pool; *(fig)* quiet place.

remar [re'mar] *vi* to row.

rematado, a [rema'taðo, a] a complete, utter.

rematar [rema'tar] *vt* to finish off; *(COM)* to sell off cheap // *vi* to end, finish off.

remate [re'mate] nm end, finish; *(punta)* tip; *(DEPORTE)* shot; *(ARQ)* top; *(COM)* auction sale; **de o para ~** to crown it all.

remedar [reme'ðar] *vt* to imitate.

remediar [reme'ðjar] *vt (gen)* to remedy; *(subsanar)* to make good, repair; *(ayudar)* to help; *(evitar)* to avoid.

remedio [re'meðjo] nm remedy; *(alivio)* relief, help; *(JUR)* recourse, remedy; **poner ~ a** to correct, stop; **no tener más ~** to have no alternative; **¡qué ~!** there's no choice; **sin ~** hopeless, incurable.

remedo [re'meðo] nm imitation; *(pey)* parody.

remendar [remen'dar] *vt* to repair; *(con parche)* to patch.

remesa [re'mesa] nf remittance; *(COM)* shipment; **remesar** *vt* to remit, send.

remiendo [re'mjendo] nm *(gen)* mend; *(con parche)* patch; *(cosido)* darn.

remilgado, a [remil'gaðo, a] a prim; *(afectado)* affected; **remilgo** nm primness; affectation.

reminiscencia [reminis'θenθja] nf reminiscence.

remisión [remi'sjon] nf *(acto)* sending, shipment.

remiso, a [re'miso, a] a remiss.

remitir [remi'tir] *vt* to remit, send; *(perdonar)* to pardon; *(posponer)* to postpone // *vi* to slacken; *(en carta):*

remite: X sender: X; remitente nm/f sender.

remo ['remo] nm *(de barco)* oar; *(deporte)* rowing.

remoción [remo'θjon] nf removal.

remojar [remo'xar] *vt* to steep, soak; *(galleta etc)* to dip.

remojo [re'moxo] nm: **dejar la ropa a ~** to leave clothes to soak.

remolacha [remo'latʃa] nf beet, beetroot.

remolcador [remolka'ðor] nm *(NAUT)* tug; *(AUTO)* breakdown lorry.

remolinar [remoli'nar] *vi* to whirl, eddy; **remolino** nm *(gen)* eddy; *(de agua)* whirlpool; *(de viento)* whirlwind; *(de gente)* throng.

remolque [re'molke] nm tow, towing; *(cuerda)* towrope; **llevar a ~** to tow.

remontar [remon'tar] *vt* to mend; **~se** *vr* to soar; **~se a** *(COM)* to amount to; **~ el vuelo** to soar.

rémora ['remora] nf hindrance.

remorder [remor'ðer] *vt* to distress, disturb; **~se** *vr* to suffer remorse; **~se la conciencia** to have a troubled conscience; **remordimiento** nm remorse.

remoto, a [re'moto, a] a remote.

remover [remo'ðer] *vt* to stir; *(tierra)* to turn over; *(objetos)* to move around; *(quitar)* to remove.

remozar [remo'θar] *vt* to rejuvenate; **~se** *vr* to be rejuvenated, look younger.

remuneración [remunera'θjon] nf remuneration; **remunerar** *vt* to remunerate; *(premiar)* to reward.

renacer [rena'θer] *vi* to be reborn; *(fig)* to revive; **renacimiento** nm rebirth; **el Renacimiento** the Renaissance.

renal [re'nal] a renal, kidney *cpd*.

rencilla [ren'θiʎa] nf quarrel.

rencor [ren'kor] nm rancour, bitterness; **~oso, a** a spiteful.

rendición [rendi'θjon] nf surrender.

rendido, a [ren'diðo, a] a *(sumiso)*

submissive; (*cansado*) worn-out.

rendimiento [rendi'mjento] *nm* (MIL) surrender; (*producción*) output; (*agotamiento*) exhaustion; (TEC, COM) efficiency.

rendir [ren'dir] *vt* (*vencer*) to defeat; (*producir*) to produce; (*dar beneficio*) to yield; (*agotar*) to exhaust; (*dominar*) to dominate // *vi* to pay; ~**se** *vr* (*someterse*) to surrender; (*cansarse*) to wear o.s. out; ~ **homenaje** *o* **culto a** to pay homage to.

renegado, a [rene'xaðo, a] *a, nm/f* renegade.

renegar [rene'xar] *vi* (*renunciar*) to renounce; (*blasfemar*) to blaspheme; (*fam*) to curse; (*quejarse*) to complain.

RENFE *nf abr de* **Red Nacional de los Ferrocarriles Españoles.**

renglón [ren'glon] *nm* (*línea*) line; (COM) item, article; **a ~ seguido** immediately after.

reniego [re'njexo] *nm* curse, oath; (*queja*) grumble, complaint.

renombrado, a [renom'braðo, a] *a* renowned; **renombre** *nm* renown.

renovación [renoβa'θjon] *nf* (*de contrato*) renewal; (ARQ) renovation; **renovar** *vt* to renew; to renovate.

renta ['renta] *nf* (*ingresos*) income; (*beneficio*) profit; (*alquiler*) rent; ~ **vitalicia** annuity; **rentable** *a* profitable; **rentar** *vt* to produce, yield.

rentero, a [ren'tero, a] *nm/f* tenant farmer.

rentista [ren'tista] *nm/f* stockholder.

renuencia [re'nwenθja] *nf* reluctance; **renuente** *a* reluctant.

renuncia [re'nunθja] *nf* (*gen*) resignation.

renunciar [renun'θjar] *vt* to renounce // *vi* to resign; ~ **a hacer algo** to give up doing sth.

reñido, a [re'niðo, a] *a* (*batalla*)

bitter, hard-fought; **estar ~ con uno** to be on bad terms with sb.

reñir [re'nir] *vt* (*regañar*) to scold // *vi* (*estar peleado*) to quarrel, fall out; (*combatir*) to fight.

reo ['reo] *nm/f* culprit, offender; ~ **de muerte** prisoner condemned to death.

reojo [re'oxo]: **de ~** *ad* out of the corner of one's eye; (*fig*) askance.

reorganizar [reorxani'θar] *vt* to reorganize.

reorientar [reorjen'tar] *vt* to reorientate; (*reajustar*) to readjust.

reparación [repara'θjon] *nf* (*acto*) mending, repairing; (TEC) repair; (*fig*) amends, reparation; **reparar** *vt* to repair; to make amends for; (*suerte*) to retrieve; (*observar*) to observe // *vi*: **reparar en** (*darse cuenta de*) to notice; (*poner atención en*) to pay attention to.

reparo [re'paro] *nm* (*reparación*) repair; (*advertencia*) observation; (*duda*) doubt; (*dificultad*) difficulty; (*resguardo*) defence.

reparón, ona [repa'ron, ona] *a* carping.

repartición [reparti'θjon] *nf* distribution; (*división*) division; **repartidor, a** *nm/f* distributor.

repartir [repar'tir] *vt* to distribute, share out; (*correo*) to deliver; **reparto** *nm* distribution; delivery; (TEATRO, CINE) cast.

repasar [repa'sar] *vt* (*sitio*) to pass by again; (*lección*) to revise; (MECÁNICA) to check; **repaso** *nm* revision; overhaul, checkup; (*de ropa*) mending.

repatriar [repa'trjar] *vt* to repatriate.

repecho [re'petʃo] *nm* steep incline; **a ~** uphill.

repelente [repe'lente] *a* repellent, repulsive; **repeler** *vt* to repel.

repensar [repen'sar] *vt* to reconsider.

repente [re'pente] *nm*: **de ~** suddenly; **un ~ de ira** a fit of anger.

repentino, a [repen'tino, a] a sudden.

repercusión [reperku'sjon] nf repercussion.

repercutir [reperku'tir] vi (sonido) to echo; ~se vr to reverberate; **en** to have repercussions on.

repertorio [reper'torjo] nm list; (TEATRO) repertoire.

repetición [repeti'θjon] nf repetition; **repetir** vt to repeat; (plato) to have a second helping // vi to repeat; **repetirse** vr (volver sobre tema) to come back.

repicar [repi'kar] vt (desmenuzar) to chop up finely; (campanas) to ring; ~se vr to boast.

repique [re'pike] nm pealing, ringing; ~teo nm pealing; (de tambor) drumming.

repisa [re'pisa] nf ledge, shelf; ~ de chimenea mantelpiece.

repito etc vb ver **repetir.**

replegar [reple'yar] vt to fold over; ~se vr to fall back, retreat.

repleto, a [re'pleto, a] a replete, full up.

réplica ['replika] nf answer; (ARTE) replica.

replicar [repli'kar] vi to answer; (objetar) to argue, answer back.

repliegue [re'pljeye] nm (MIL) withdrawal.

repoblación [repoβla'θjon] nf repopulation; (de río) restocking; ~ **forestal** reafforestation; **repoblar** vt to repopulate; to reafforest.

repollo [re'poʎo] nm cabbage.

reponer [repo'ner] vt to replace, put back; (TEATRO) to revive; ~se vr to recover; ~ que to reply that.

reportaje [repor'taxe] nm report, article.

reposacabezas [reposaka'βeθas] nm inv headrest.

reposado, a [repo'saðo, a] a (descansado) restful; (tranquilo) calm; **reposar** vi to rest, repose.

reposición [reposi'θjon] nf replacement; (CINE) remake.

repositorio [reposi'torjo] nm repository.

reposo [re'poso] nm rest.

repostar [repos'tar] vt to replenish; (AUTO) to fill up (with petrol).

repostería [reposte'ria] nf confectioner's (shop); (depósito) pantry, larder; **repostero, a** nm/f confectioner.

reprender [repren'der] vt to reprimand; **represión** nf rebuke, reprimand.

represa [re'presa] nf dam; (lago artificial) lake, pool.

represalia [repre'salja] nf reprisal.

representación [representa'θjon] nf representation; (TEATRO) performance; **representante** nm/f performer.

representar [represen'tar] vt to represent; (TEATRO) to play; (edad) to look; ~se vr to imagine; **representativo, a** a representative.

represión [repre'sjon] nf repression.

reprimir [repri'mir] vt to repress.

reprobar [repro'βar] vt to censure, reprove.

réprobo, a ['reproβo, a] nm/f reprobate.

reprochar [repro't∫ar] vt to reproach; **reproche** nm reproach.

reproducción [reproðuk'θjon] nf reproduction.

reproducir [reproðu'θir] vt to reproduce; ~se vr to breed; (situación) to recur.

reptil [rep'til] nm reptile.

república [re'puβlika] nf republic; **republicano, a** a, nm/f republican.

repudiar [repu'ðjar] vt to repudiate; (fe) to renounce; **repudio** nm repudiation.

repuesto [re'pwesto] nm (pieza de recambio) spare (part); (abastecimiento) supply; **rueda de ~** spare wheel.

repugnancia [repux'nanθja] nf repugnance; **repugnante** a repugnant, repulsive.

repugnar [repux'nar] vt to disgust // vi, ~**se** vr (contradecirse) to conflict; (dar asco) to be disgusting.

repujar [repu'xar] vt to emboss.

repulgar [repul'xar] vt to hem.

repulido, a [repu'liðo, a] a (gen) polished; (persona) dressed up, dolled up.

repulsa [re'pulsa] nf rebuff; (fig) reprimand.

repulsión [repul'sjon] nf repulsion, aversion; **repulsivo, a** a repulsive.

reputación [reputa'θjon] nf reputation.

reputar [repu'tar] vt to consider, deem.

requemado, a [reke'maðo, a] a (quemado) scorched; (bronceado) tanned.

requerimiento [rekeri'mjento] nm request; (JUR) summons.

requerir [reke'rir] vt (rogar) to ask, request; (exigir) to require; (llamar) to send for, summon.

requesón [reke'son] nm cottage cheese.

requete... ['rekete] pref extremely.

réquiem ['rekjem] nm requiem.

requisa [re'kisa] nf (inspección) survey, inspection; (MIL) requisition.

requisito [reki'sito] nm requirement, requisite.

res [res] nf beast, head of cattle.

resabio [re'saβjo] nm (maña) vice, bad habit; (dejo) aftertaste.

resaca [re'saka] nf (en el mar) undertow, undercurrent; (fig) backlash; (fam) hangover.

resalado, a [resa'laðo, a] a (fam) lively.

resaltar [resal'tar] vi to project, stick out; (persona) to stand out, be conspicuous.

resarcimiento [resarθi'mjento] nm compensation; **resarcir** vt to compensate; **resarcirse** vr to make up for.

resbaladero [resβala'ðero] nm (gen) slippery place; (en parque infantil) slide.

resbaladizo, a [resβala'ðiθo, a] a slippery.

resbalar [resβa'lar] vi, ~**se** vr to slip, slide; (fig) to slip (up).

rescatar [reska'tar] vt (heridos) to save, rescue; (objeto) to get back, recover; (cautivos) to ransom.

rescate [res'kate] nm rescue, recovery; **pagar un** ~ to pay a ransom.

rescindir [resθin'dir] vt to rescind.

rescisión [resθi'sjon] nf cancellation.

rescoldo [res'koldo] nm embers pl; (fig) scruple.

resecar [rese'kar] vt to dry thoroughly; (MED) to remove; ~**se** vr to dry up.

reseco, a [re'seko, a] a a very dry; (fig) skinny.

resentido, a [resen'tiðo, a] a resentful; **resentimiento** nm resentment, bitterness.

resentirse [resen'tirse] vr (debilitarse: persona) to suffer; ~ **con** to resent; ~ **de** (consecuencias) to feel the effects of.

reseña [re'seɲa] nf (cuenta) account; (informe) report; (LITERATURA) review; **reseñar** vt to describe; to review.

reserva [re'serβa] nf (gen) reserve; (reservación) reservation; **a** ~ **de** except for; **con toda** ~ in strictest confidence.

reservado, a [reser'βaðo, a] a reserved; (retraído) cold, distant // nm private room.

reservar [reser'βar] vt (guardar) to keep; (habitación, entrada) to reserve; (callar) to keep to o.s.; ~**se** vr to save o.s.

resfriado [resfri'aðo] nm cold; **resfriar** vt to cool; (MED) to catch (a) cold.

resguardar [resxwar'ðar] vt to protect, shield; ~**se** vr: ~**se de** to guard against; **resguardo** nm defence; (custodia) protection; (garantía) guarantee; (vale) voucher.

residencia [resi'ðenθja] nf residence.

residente [resi'ðente] a, nm/f resident.

residir [resi'ðir] vi to reside, live; ~ **en** to reside in, lie in.

residuo [re'siðwo] nm residue.

resignación [resiɣna'θjon] nf resignation; **resignar** vt to resign; **resignarse** a o con to resign o.s. to, be resigned to.

resistencia [resis'tenθja] nf (dureza) endurance, strength; (oposición, eléctrica) resistance; **resistente** a strong, hardy; resistant.

resistir [resis'tir] vt (soportar) to bear; (oponerse a) to resist, oppose, (aguantar) to put up with // vi to resist; (aguantar) to last, endure; ~**se** vr: ~**se a** to refuse to, resist.

resma ['resma] nf ream.

resol [re'sol] nm glare of the sun.

resolución [resolu'θjon] nf (gen) resolution; (decisión) decision; **resoluto, a** a resolute.

resolver [resol'ßer] vt to resolve; (solucionar) to solve, resolve; (decidir) to decide, settle; ~**se** vr to make up one's mind.

resollar [reso'ʎar] vi to breathe noisily, wheeze.

resonancia [reso'nanθja] nf (del sonido) resonance; (repercusión) repercussion; **resonante** a resonant, resounding; (fig) tremendous; **resonar** vi to ring, echo.

resoplar [reso'plar] vi to snort; **resoplido** nm heavy breathing.

resorte [re'sorte] nm (pieza) spring; (elasticidad) elasticity; (fig) lever.

respaldar [respal'dar] vt to endorse; (fig) to back (up), support; ~**se** vr to lean back; ~**se con** o **en** to take one's stand on; **respaldo** nm (de cama) headboard; (de sillón) back; (fig) support, backing.

respectivo, a [respek'tißo, a] a respective; **en lo** ~ **a** with regard to.

respecto [res'pekto] nm: **al** ~ on this matter; **con** ~ **a**, ~ **de** with regard to, in relation to.

respetable [respe'taßle] a respectable; **respetar** vt to respect; **respeto** nm respect; (acatamiento) deference; **respetos** nmpl respects; **respetuoso, a** a respectful.

respingar [respin'gar] vi to shy; **respingo** nm start, jump; (fig) gesture of disgust.

respiración [respira'θjon] nf breathing; (MED) respiration; (ventilación) ventilation; **respirar** vi to breathe; (inhalar) to inhale; **respiratorio, a** a respiratory; **respiro** nm breathing; (fig) respite.

resplandecer [resplande'θer] vi to shine; **resplandeciente** a resplendent, shining; **resplandor** nm brilliance, brightness; (del fuego) blaze.

responder [respon'der] vt to answer // vi to answer; (fig) to respond; (pey) to answer back; ~ **de** o **por** to answer for

responsabilidad [responsaßili'ðað] nf responsibility; **responsable** a responsible.

respuesta [res'pwesta] nf answer, reply.

resquebrajar [reskeßra'xar] vt, ~**se** vr to crack, split.

resquemor [reske'mor] nm resentment.

resquicio [res'kiθjo] nm chink; (hendedura) crack.

restablecer [restaßle'θer] vt to reestablish, restore; ~**se** vr to recover.

restallar [resta'ʎar] vi to crack.

restante [res'tante] a remaining; **lo** ~ the remainder.

restar [res'tar] vt (MAT) to subtract; (fig) to take away // vi to remain, be left.

restauración [restaura'θjon] nf restoration.

restaurán [restau'ran], **restaurante** [restau'rante] *nm* restaurant.

restaurar [restau'rar] *vt* to restore.

restitución [restituθ'jon] *nf* return, restitution.

restituir [restitu'ir] *vt* (*devolver*) to return, give back; (*rehabilitar*) to restore; ~**se** *vr*: ~**se a** to rejoin.

resto ['resto] *nm* (*residuo*) rest, remainder; (*apuesta*) stake; ~**s** *nmpl* remains.

restregar [restre'ɣar] *vt* to scrub, rub.

restricción [restrik'θjon] *nf* restriction.

restrictivo, a [restrik'tiβo, a] *a* restrictive.

restringir [restrin'xir] *vt* to restrict, limit.

resucitar [resuθi'tar] *vt, vi* to resuscitate, revive.

resuelto, a [re'swelto, a] *pp de* **resolver** // *a* resolute, determined.

resuello [re'sweλo] *nm* breath.

resultado [resul'taðo] *nm* (*conclusión*) outcome; (*consecuencia*) result, consequence; **resultante** *a* resulting, resultant.

resultar [resul'tar] *vi* (*llegar a ser*) to turn out to be; (*salir bien*) to turn out well; (*com*) to amount to; ~ **de** to stem from; **me resulta difícil hacerlo** it's difficult for me to do it.

resumen [re'sumen] *nm* summary, résumé; **en** ~ in short.

resumir [resu'mir] *vt* to sum up; (*cortar*) to abridge, cut down.

retablo [re'taβlo] *nm* altarpiece.

retaguardia [reta'ɣwarðja] *nf* rearguard.

retahíla [reta'ila] *nf* series, string.

retal [re'tal] *nm* remnant.

retama [re'tama] *nf* (*AM*) broom.

retar [re'tar] *vt* (*gen*) to challenge; (*desafiar*) to defy, dare.

retardar [retar'ðar] *vt* (*demorar*) to delay; (*hacer más lento*) to slow

down; (*retener*) to hold back; **retardo** *nm* delay.

retazo [re'taθo] *nm* snippet.

rete... ['rete] *pref* very, extremely.

retén [re'ten] *nm* (*TEC*) catch; (*reserva*) store, reserve.

retener [rete'ner] *vt* (*guardar*) to retain, keep; (*intereses*) to withhold.

retina [re'tina] *nf* retina.

retintín [retin'tin] *nm* jangle.

retirada [reti'raða] *nf* (*MIL, refugio*) retreat; (*de dinero*) withdrawal; (*de embajador*) recall; **retirado, a a** (*distante*) remote; (*tranquilo*) quiet; (*jubilado*) retired.

retirar [reti'rar] *vt* to withdraw; (*quitar*) to remove; (*jubilar*) to retire, pension off; ~**se** *vr* to retreat, withdraw; to retire; (*acostarse*) to retire, go to bed; **retiro** *nm* retreat; retirement; (*pago*) pension.

reto ['reto] *nm* dare, challenge.

retocar [reto'kar] *vt* (*fotografía*) to touch up, retouch.

retoño [re'toɲo] *nm* sprout, shoot; (*fig*) offspring, child.

retoque [re'toke] *nm* retouching; (*MED*) symptom.

retorcer [retor'θer] *vt* (*gen*) to twist; (*manos, lavado*) to wring; ~**se** *vr* to become twisted; (*mover el cuerpo*) to writhe.

retorcimiento [retorθi'mjento] *nm* twist, twisting; (*fig*) deviousness.

retórica [re'torika] *nf* rhetoric; (*fig*) affectedness.

retornar [retor'nar] *vt* to return, give back // *vi* to return, go/come back; **retorno** *nm* return.

retortijón [retorti'xon] *nm* twist, twisting.

retozar [reto'θar] *vi* (*juguetear*) to frolic, romp; (*saltar*) to gambol; **retozón, ona** *a* playful.

retracción [retrak'θjon] *nf*, **retractación** [retrakta'θjon] *nf* retraction.

retractar [retrak'tar] *vt* to retract; ~**se** *vr* to retract; **me retracto** I take that back.

retraer [retra'er] vt to dissuade; ~se vr to retreat, withdraw; **retraído, a** a a shy, retiring; **retraimiento** nm (gen) retirement; (timidez) shyness; (lugar) retreat.

retransmisión [retransmi'sjon] nf repeat (broadcast), **retransmitir** vt (mensaje) to relay; (TV etc) to retransmit; (: en vivo) to broadcast live.

retrasado, a [retra'saðo, a] a late; (MED) mentally retarded; (país etc) backward, underdeveloped; **retrasar** vt (demorar) to postpone, put off; (retardar) to slow down // vi, **retrasarse** vr (atrasarse) to be late; (reloj) to be slow; (producción) to fall (away); (quedarse atrás) to lag behind.

retraso [re'traso] nm (demora) delay; (lentitud) slowness; (tardanza) lateness; (atraso) backwardness; **llegar con ~** to arrive late; ~ **mental** mental deficiency.

retratar [retra'tar] vt (ARTE) to paint the portrait of; (fotografiar) to photograph; (fig) to depict; ~**se** vr to have one's portrait painted; to have one's photograph taken; **retrato** nm portrait; (fig) likeness; **retrato-robot** nm identikit picture.

retreta [re'treta] nf retreat.

retrete [re'trete] nm toilet, lavatory.

retribución [retriβu'θjon] nf (recompensa) reward; (pago) pay, payment; **retribuir** vt to reward; to pay.

retro... [retro] pref retro...

retroactivo, a [retroak'tiβo, a] a retroactive, retrospective.

retroceder [retroθe'ðer] vi (echarse atrás) to move back(wards); (tropas) to fall back, retreat; (arma de fuego) to recoil; (fig) to back down.

retroceso [retro'θeso] nm backward movement; (MIL) withdrawal, retreat; (MED) relapse; (fig) backing down.

retrógrado, a [re'troxraðo, a] a (atrasado) retrograde; (POL) reactionary.

retropropulsión [retropropul'sjon] nf jet propulsion.

retrospectivo, a [retrospek'tiβo, a] a retrospective.

retrovisor [retroβi'sor] nm driving or rear-view mirror.

retumbante [retum'bante] a resounding; **retumbar** vi to echo, resound.

reuma ['reuma] nm rheumatism; **reumático, a** a rheumatic; **reumatismo** nm rheumatism.

reunificar [reunifi'kar] vt to reunify.

reunión [reu'njon] nf (asamblea) meeting; (fiesta) party; (reencuentro) reunion.

reunir [reu'nir] vt (juntar) to reunite, join; (recoger) to gather; (personas) to assemble; (cualidades) to combine; ~**se** vr to meet, gather.

revalidar [reβali'ðar] vt to confirm, ratify.

revalorar [reβalo'rar] vt to revalue, reassess.

revancha [re'βantʃa] nf revenge.

revelación [reβela'θjon] nf revelation.

revelado [reβe'laðo] nm developing.

revelar [reβe'lar] vt to reveal; (FOTO) to develop.

revendedor, a [reβende'ðor, a] nm/f retailer; (pey) ticket tout.

reventar [reβen'tar] vt to burst, explode; (fam: plan) to ruin // vi, ~**se** vr (estallar) to burst, explode; (fam: morirse) to kick the bucket (fam); ~ **por** to be bursting to.

reventón [reβen'ton] nm burst, explosion; (AUTO) blow-out, puncture.

reverberación [reβerβera'θjon] nf reverberation; **reverberar** vi to reverberate; **reverbero** nm reverberation.

reverdecer [reβerðe'θer] vi (fig)

to revive, come to life again..

reverencia [reβe'renθja] nf reverence; **reverenciar** vt to revere.

reverendo, a [reβe'rendo, a] a reverend; **reverente** a reverent.

reversión [reβer'sjon] nf reversion.

reverso [re'βerso] nm back, wrong side; (de moneda) reverse.

revertir [reβer'tir] vi to revert.

revés [re'βes] nm back, wrong side; (fig) reverse, setback; (DEPORTE) backhand; **hacer al ~** to do sth the wrong way round; **volver algo al ~** to turn sth round; (ropa) to turn sth inside out.

revestir [reβes'tir] vt to put on; (cubrir) to cover, coat; ~ **con** o **de** to invest with.

revisar [reβi'sar] vt (examinar) to check; (rever) to revise; **revisión** nf revision.

revisor, a [reβi'sor, a] nm/f inspector; (FERRO) ticket collector.

revista [re'βista] nf magazine, review; (TEATRO) revue; (inspección) inspection; **pasar ~ a** to review, inspect.

revivir [reβi'βir] vi to revive.

revocación [reβoka'θjon] nf repeal; **revocar** vt to revoke.

revolcar [reβol'kar] vt to knock down, send flying; **~se** vr to roll about.

revolotear [reβolote'ar] vi to flutter; **revoloteo** nm fluttering.

revoltijo [reβol'tixo] nm mess, jumble.

revoltoso, a [reβol'toso, a] a (travieso) naughty, unruly; (rebelde) rebellious.

revolución [reβolu'θjon] nf revolution; **revolucionar** vt to revolutionize; **revolucionario, a** a, nm/f revolutionary.

revólver [re'βolβer] nm revolver.

revolver [reβol'βer] vt (desordenar) to disturb, mess up; (mover) to move about; (poner al revés) to turn over; (investigar) to look through;

(adentrarse en) to go into; (POL) to stir up; (hacer paquete) to wrap up // vi: ~ **en** to go through, rummage (about) in; **~se** vr to turn round; (por dolor) to writhe; (volver contra) to turn on or against.

revuelco [re'βwelko] nm fall, tumble.

revuelo [re'βwelo] nm fluttering; (fig) commotion.

revuelto, a [re'βwelto, a] pp de **revolver** // a (mezclado) mixed-up; (huevos) scrambled; (descontento) discontented; (travieso) mischievous // nf (motín) revolt; (conmoción) commotion.

revulsivo [reβul'siβo] nm enema.

rey [rei] nm king.

reyerta [re'jerta] nf quarrel, brawl.

rezagado, a [reθa'xaðo, a] nm/f straggler.

rezagar [reθa'xar] vt (dejar atrás) to leave behind; (retrasar) to delay, postpone.

rezar [re'θar] vi to pray; ~ **con** (fam) to concern, have to do with; **rezo** nm prayer.

rezongar [reθon'gar] vi to grumble.

rezumar [reθu'mar] vt to ooze // vi to leak; **~se** vr to leak out.

ría ['ria] nf estuary.

riada [ri'aða] nf flood.

ribera [ri'βera] nf (de río) bank; (: área) riverside; (del mar) shore.

ribete [ri'βete] nm (de vestido) border; (fig) addition; **~ar** vt to edge, border.

rico, a ['riko, a] a (gen) rich; (adinerado) wealthy; (lujoso) luxurious; (comida) tasty, delicious // nm/f rich person.

rictus ['riktus] nm (mueca) sneer, grin.

ridiculez [riðiku'leθ] nf absurdity; **ridiculizar** vt to ridicule.

ridículo, a [ri'ðikulo, a] a ridiculous; **hacer el ~** to make o.s. ridiculous; **poner a uno en ~** to ridicule sb.

riego ['rjexo] nm (aspersión)

watering; (*irrigación*) irrigation.

riel [rjel] *nm* rail.

rienda ['rjenda] *nf* rein; **dar ~ suelta a** to give free rein to.

riente ['rjente] *a* laughing.

riesgo ['rjesγo] *nm* risk; **correr el ~ de** to run the risk of.

rifa ['rifa] *nf* (*lotería*) raffle; (*disputa*) quarrel; **rifar** *vt* to raffle // *vi* to quarrel; **rifarse** *vr*: **rifarse algo** to fight over sth.

rifle ['rifle] *nm* rifle.

rigidez [rixi'δeθ] *nf* rigidity, stiffness; (*fig*) strictness; **rígido, a** *a* rigid, stiff; strict, inflexible.

rigor [ri'γor] *nm* strictness, rigour; (*inclemencia*) harshness, de rigueur, essential; **riguroso, a** *a* rigorous; harsh, (*severo*) severe.

rimar [ri'mar] *vi* to rhyme.

rimbombante [rimbom'bante] *a* resounding; (*fig*) pompous.

rincón [rin'kon] *nm* (inside) corner.

rinoceronte [rinoθe'ronte] *nm* rhinoceros.

riña ['rina] *nf* (*disputa*) argument; (*pelea*) brawl.

riñón [ri'non] *nm* (*gen*) kidney; **tener riñones** to have guts.

río *etc vb ver* **reír** // ['rio] *nm* river; (*fig*) torrent, stream; **~ abajo/arriba** downstream/upstream.

rioplatense [riopla'tense] *a* of the River Plate region.

ripio ['ripjo] *nm* (*residuo*) refuse, waste; (*cascotes*) rubble, debris.

riqueza [ri'keθa] *nf* wealth, riches *pl*; (*cualidad*) richness.

risa ['risa] *nf* (*una ~*) laugh; (*gen*) laughter.

risco ['risko] *nm* crag, cliff; **~so, a** *a* steep.

risible [ri'sible] *a* (*ridículo*) ludicrous; (*jocoso*) laughable.

risotada [riso'taδa] *nf* guffaw.

ristra ['ristra] *nf* string.

risueño, a [ri'sweno, a] *a* (*sonriente*) smiling; (*contento*) cheerful.

ritmo ['ritmo] *nm* rhythm; **a ~**

lento slowly; **trabajar a ~ lento** to go slow.

rito ['rito] *nm* rite.

ritual [ri'twal] *a, nm* ritual.

rival [ri'βal] *a, nm/f* rival; **~idad** *nf* rivalry; **~izar** *vi*: **~izar con** to rival, vie with.

rizado, a [ri'θaδo, a] *a* curly // *nm* curls *pl*; **rizar** *vt* to curl; **rizarse** *vr* (*el pelo*) to curl; (*el mar*) to ripple; **rizo** *nm* curl; ripple.

RNE *nf abr de* **Radio Nacional de España.**

robar [ro'βar] *vt* to rob; (*objeto*) to steal; (*casa etc*) to break into; (*NAIPES*) to draw.

roble [ro'βle] *nm* oak; **~do, ~dal** *nm* oakwood.

roblón [ro'βlon] *nm* rivet.

robo [ro'βo] *nm* robbery, theft; **~ relámpago** smash-and-grab raid.

robot [ro'βo(t)] *nm* robot.

robustecer [roβuste'θer] *vt* to strengthen.

robusto, a [ro'βusto, a] *a* robust, strong.

roca ['roka] *nf* rock.

rocalla [ro'kaʎa] *nf* pebbles *pl*.

roce ['roθe] *nm* (*caricia*) brush; (*TEC*) friction; (*en la piel*) graze; **tener ~ con** to be in close contact with.

rociada [ro'θjaδa] *nf* (*aspersión*) sprinkling; (*fig*) hail, shower; **rociar** *vt* to spray.

rocín [ro'θin] *nm* nag, hack.

rocío [ro'θio] *nm* dew.

rocoso, a [ro'koso, a] *a* rocky.

rodado, a [ro'δaδo, a] *a* (*con ruedas*) wheeled; (*redondo*) round // *nf* rut.

rodaja [ro'δaxa] *nf* (*raja*) slice; (*rueda*) small wheel.

rodaje [ro'δaxe] *nm* (*TEC*) wheels *pl*, set of wheels; (*CINE*) shooting, filming; (*AUTO*): **en ~** running in.

rodar [ro'δar] *vt* (*vehículo*) to wheel; (*escalera*) to roll down; (*viajar por*) to travel (over) // *vi* to roll; (*coche*) to go, run; (*CINE*) to shoot, film.

rodear [roðe'ar] *vt* to surround // *vi* to go round; **~se** *vr*: **~se de amigos** to surround o.s. with friends.

rodeo [ro'ðeo] *nm* (*ruta indirecta*) detour; (*evasión*) evasion; (*AM*) rodeo; **hablar sin ~s** to come to the point, speak plainly.

rodilla [ro'ðiʎa] *nf* knee; **de ~s** kneeling.

rodillo [ro'ðiʎo] *nm* roller; (*CULIN*) rolling-pin; **~ apisonador** *o* **de vapor** steamroller.

rododendro [roðo'ðendro] *nm* rhododendron.

roedor, a [roe'ðor, a] *a* gnawing // *nm* rodent.

roer [ro'er] *vt* (*masticar*) to gnaw; (*corroer, fig*) to corrode.

rogar [ro'xar] *vt, vi* (*pedir*) to ask for; (*suplicar*) to beg, plead; **se ruega no fumar** please do not smoke.

rojete [ro'xete] *nm* rouge.

rojizo, a [ro'xiθo, a] *a* reddish.

rojo, a ['roxo, a] *a* nm red; **al ~ vivo** red-hot; **~ de labios** lipstick.

rol [rol] *nm* list, roll; (*AM: papel*) role.

rollizo, a [ro'ʎiθo, a] *a* (*objeto*) cylindrical; (*persona*) plump.

rollo ['roʎo] *nm* (*gen*) roll; (*de cuerda*) coil; (*madera*) log; (*fam*) bore; **¡qué ~!** what a carry-on!

Roma ['roma] *nf* Rome.

romance [ro'manθe] *nm* Romance language; (*LITERATURA*) ballad; **hablar en ~** to speak plainly.

romántico, a [ro'mantiko, a] *a* romantic.

romería [rome'ria] *nf* (*REL*) pilgrimage; (*excursión*) trip, outing.

romero, a [ro'mero, a] *a* nm/f pilgrim // *nm* rosemary.

romo, a ['romo, a] *a* blunt; (*fig*) dull.

rompecabezas [rompeka'βeθas] *nm inv* riddle, puzzle; (*juego*) jigsaw.

rompehuelgas [rompe'welɣas]

nm inv strikebreaker, blackleg.

rompeolas [rompe'olas] *nm inv* breakwater.

romper [rom'per] *vt* (*gen*) to break; (*hacer pedazos*) to smash; (*papel etc*) to tear, rip // *vi* (*olas*) to break; (*sol, diente*) to break through; **~ un contrato** to break a contract; **~ a** to start (suddenly) to; **~ en llanto** to burst into tears; **~ con uno** to fall out with sb.

rompimiento [rompi'mjento] *nm* breaking; (*fig*) break; (*quiebra*) crack; **~ de hostilidades** outbreak of hostilities.

ron [ron] *nm* rum.

roncar [ron'kar] *vi* to snore.

ronco, a ['ronko, a] *a* (*sin voz*) hoarse; (*áspero*) raucous.

roncha ['rontʃa] *nf* weal; (*contusión*) bruise.

ronda ['ronda] *nf* (*gen*) round; (*patrulla*) patrol; **rondar** *vt* to patrol // *vi* to patrol; (*fig*) to prowl round.

rondón [ron'don]: **de ~** *ad* unexpectedly.

ronquear [ronke'ar] *vi* to be hoarse; **ronquedad** *nf* hoarseness.

ronquido [ron'kiðo] *nm* snore, snoring.

ronronear [ronrone'ar] *vi* to purr; **ronroneo** *nm* purr.

ronzal [ron'θal] *nm* halter.

roña ['roɲa] *nf* scab; (*mugre*) crust (of dirt).

roñoso, a [ro'ɲoso, a] *a* (*mugriento*) filthy; (*inútil*) useless; (*tacaño*) mean.

ropa ['ropa] *nf* clothes *pl*, clothing; **~ blanca** linen; **~ de cama** bed linen; **~ interior** underwear; **~je** *nm* gown, robes *pl*; **~; vejero, a** *nm/f* second-hand clothes dealer.

ropero [ro'pero] *nm* linen cupboard; (*guardarropa*) wardrobe.

roque ['roke] *nm* rook, castle.

roquedal [roke'ðal] *nm* rocky place.

rosa ['rosa] *a inv* pink // *nf* rose;

(ANAT) red birthmark; ~ **de los vientos** the compass; ~**s** *nfpl* popcorn *sg*.

rosado, a [roˈsaðo, a], **rosáceo, a** [roˈsaθeo, a] *a* a pink // *nm* rosé.

rosal [roˈsal] *nm* rosebush.

rosario [roˈsarjo] *nm* (REL) rosary; **rezar el ~** to say the rosary.

rosca [ˈroska] *nf* (*de tornillo*) thread; (*de humo*) coil, spiral; (*pan, postre*) ring-shaped roll/pastry.

rosetón [roseˈton] *nm* rosette; (ARQ) rose window; (AUTO) cloverleaf (junction).

rostro [ˈrostro] *nm* (*cara*) face.

rotación [rotaˈθjon] *nf* rotation; ~ **de cultivos** crop rotation.

rotativo, a [rotaˈtiβo, a] *a* a rotary.

roto, a [ˈroto, a] *pp de* **romper** // *a* broken; (*disipado*) debauched.

rótula [ˈrotula] *nf* kneecap; (TEC) ball-and-socket joint.

rotular [rotuˈlar] *vt* (*titular, encabezar*) to head, entitle; (*etiquetar*) to label; **rótulo** *nm* heading, title; label.

rotundo, a [roˈtundo, a] *a* round; (*enfático*) emphatic.

rotura [roˈtura] *nf* (*rompimiento*) breaking; (*quiebra*) crack; (MED) fracture.

roturar [rotuˈrar] *vt* to plough.

rozado, a [roˈθaðo, a] *a* a worn.

rozadura [roθaˈðura] *nf* abrasion, graze.

rozar [roˈθar] *vt* (*frotar*) to rub; (*arañar*) to scratch; (*arrugar*) to crumple; (AGR) to graze; (*tocar ligeramente*) to shave, touch lightly; ~**se** *vr* to rub (together); (*trabarse*) to trip over one's own feet; ~ **con** (*fam*) to rub shoulders with.

roznar [roθˈnar] *vi* to bray.

rte *abr de* **remite, remitente** sender.

rubí [ruˈβi] *nm* ruby.

rubicundo, a [ruβiˈkundo, a] *a* ruddy; (*de salud*) rosy with health.

rubio, a [ˈruβjo, a] *a* fair-haired // *nm/f* blond/blonde; **tabaco** ~ Virginia tobacco.

rubor [ruˈβor] *nm* (*timidez*) bashful-

ness; (*sonrojo*) blush; ~**izarse** *vr* to blush; ~**oso, a** a blushing.

rúbrica [ˈruβrika] *nf* title, heading; (*de la firma*) flourish; **rubricar** *vt* (*firmar*) to sign with a flourish; (*concluir*) to sign and seal.

rucio, a [ˈruθjo, a] a a grey.

rudeza [ruˈðeθa] *nf* (*tosquedad*) coarseness; (*sencillez*) simplicity.

rudimento [ruðiˈmento] *nm* rudiment.

rudo, a [ˈruðo, a] *a* (*sin pulir*) unpolished; (*tosco*) coarse; (*violento*) violent; (*vulgar*) common; (*estúpido*) stupid.

rueda [ˈrweða] *nf* (*gen*) wheel; (*círculo*) ring, circle; (*rodaja*) slice, round; ~ **delantera/trasera/de repuesto** front/back/spare wheel; ~ **de prensa** press conference.

ruedo [ˈrweðo] *nm* (*contorno*) edge, border; (*de vestido*) hem; (*círculo*) circle; (TAUR) arena, bullring.

ruego *etc vb ver* **rogar** // [ˈrweɣo] *nm* request.

rufián [ruˈfjan] *nm* scoundrel.

rugby [ˈruɣβi] *nm* rugby.

rugido [ruˈxiðo] *nm* roar; **rugir** *vi* to roar.

rugoso, a [ruˈɣoso, a] *a* (*arrugado*) wrinkled; (*áspero*) rough; (*desigual*) ridged.

ruibarbo [rwiˈβarβo] *nm* rhubarb.

ruido [ˈrwiðo] *nm* (*gen*) noise; (*sonido*) sound; (*alboroto*) racket, row; (*escándalo*) commotion, rumpus; ~**so, a** a noisy, loud; (*fig*) sensational.

ruin [ruˈin] a contemptible, mean.

ruina [ruˈina] *nf* (*gen*) ruin; (*colapso*) collapse; (*de persona*) ruin, downfall; (*de imperio*) decline.

ruindad [rwinˈdað] *nf* lowness, meanness; (*acto*) low or mean act.

ruinoso, a [rwiˈnoso, a] *a* (*ruinante*) (*destartalado*) dilapidated; tumbledown; (COM) disastrous.

ruiseñor [rwiseˈɲor] *nm* nightingale.

rula ['rula], **ruleta** [ru'leta] nf roulette.

Rumania [ru'manja] nf Rumania.

rumba ['rumba] nf rumba.

rumbo ['rumbo] nm (ruta) route, direction; (ángulo de dirección) course, bearing; (fig) course of events.

rumboso, a [rum'boso, a] a generous.

rumiante [ru'mjante] nm ruminant.

rumiar [rumi'nar] vt to chew; (fig) to chew over // vi to chew the cud.

rumor [ru'mor] nm (ruido sordo) low sound; (murmuración) murmur, buzz; ~**earse** vr: se ~**ea que** it is rumoured that; ~**eo** nm murmur.

rupestre [ru'pestre] a rock cpd.

ruptura [rup'tura] nf (MED) fracture; (fig) rupture.

rural [ru'ral] a rural.

Rusia ['rusja] nf Russia; **ruso, a** a, nm/f Russian.

rústico, a ['rustiko, a] a rustic; (ordinario) coarse, uncouth // nm/f yokel // nf: **libro en ~a** paperback.

ruta ['ruta] nf route.

rutina [ru'tina] nf routine; ~**rio, a** a routine.

S

S abr de santo, a; sur.

s. abr de siglo; siguiente.

sábado ['saβaðo] nm Saturday.

sábana ['saβana] nf sheet.

sabandija [saβan'dixa] nf bug, insect.

sabañón [saβa'ɲon] nm chilblain.

sabelotodo [saβelo'toðo] nm/f inv know-all.

saber [sa'βer] vt to know; (llegar a conocer) to find out, learn; (tener capacidad de) to know how to // vi: ~ **a** to taste of, taste like // nm knowledge, learning; **a** ~ namely; ¿**sabes nadar?** can you swim?; ¿**sabes ir?** do you know the way?

sabiduría [saβiðu'ria] nf (conocimientos) wisdom; (instrucción) knowledge, learning.

sabiendas [sa'βjendas]: **a** ~ ad knowingly.

sabio, a [sa'βjo,a] a (docto) learned; (prudente) wise, sensible.

sabor [sa'βor] nm taste, flavour; ~**ear** vt to savour, relish; (dar ~ a) to flavour.

sabotaje [saβo'taxe] nm sabotage; **sabotear** vt to sabotage.

sabré etc vb ver **saber**.

sabroso, a [sa'βroso, a] a tasty; (fig: fam) racy, salty.

sacacorchos [saka'kortʃos] nm inv corkscrew.

sacapuntas [saka'puntas] nm inv pencil sharpener.

sacar [sa'kar] vt (gen) to take out; (fig) to get (out); (quitar) to remove, get out; (hacer salir) to bring out; (conclusión) to draw; (novela etc) to publish, bring out; (ropa) to take off; (obra) to make; (FOTO) to take; (premio) to receive; (entradas) to get; ~ **adelante** to bring up; ~ **a alguien a bailar** to get sb up to dance; ~ **apuntes** to take notes; ~ **la cara por alguien** to stick up for sb; ~ **la lengua** to stick out one's tongue.

sacarina [saka'rina] nf saccharin(e).

sacerdote [saθer'ðote] nm priest.

saco ['sako] nm (gen) bag; (grande) sack; (su contenido) bagful; (AM) jacket; ~ **de dormir** sleeping bag.

sacramento [sakra'mento] nm sacrament.

sacrificar [sakrifi'kar] vt to sacrifice; **sacrificio** nm sacrifice.

sacrilegio [sakri'lexjo] nm sacrilege; **sacrílego, a** a a sacrilegious.

sacristía [sakris'tia] nf sacristy.

sacro, a ['sakro, a] a sacred.

sacudida [saku'ðiða] nf (zaran-

deada) shake, shaking; (*sacudimiento*) jolt, bump; ~ **eléctrica** electric shock; **sacudir** *vt* to shake; (*golpear*) to hit.

sádico, a [ˈsaðiko, a] *a* sadistic; **sadismo** *nm* sadism.

saeta [saˈeta] *nf* (*flecha*) arrow; (*do reloj*) hand; (*brújula*) magnetic needle.

sagacidad [savaθiˈðuð] *nf* shrewdness, cleverness; **sagaz** *a* shrewd, clever; (*astuto*) astute.

sagrado, a [saˈɣraðo, a] *a* sacred, holy // *nm* sanctuary, asylum.

Sáhara [ˈsaara] *nm*: **el** ~ **the** Sahara (desert).

sahumar [sauˈmar] *vt* to fumigate.

sal [sal] *vb ver* **salir** // *nf* salt; ~ **de la Higuera** Epsom salts.

sala [ˈsala] *nf* (*cuarto grande*) large room; (~ *de estar*) living room; (TEATRO) house, auditorium; (*de hospital*) ward; (*de apelación*) court; ~ **de espera** waiting room.

salado, a [saˈlaðo, a] *a* salty; (*fig*) witty, amusing; **agua** ~ **a** salt water; **salar** *vt* to salt, add salt to.

salario [saˈlarjo] *nm* wage, pay.

salchicha [salˈtʃitʃa] *nf* pork sausage; **salchichón** *nm* (salami-type) sausage.

saldar [salˈdar] *vt* to pay, (*vender*) to sell off; (*fig*) to settle, resolve; **saldo** *nm* (*pago*) settlement; (*de una cuenta*) balance; (*lo restante*) remnant(s) (*pl*), remainder.

saldré *etc vb ver* **salir**.

salero [saˈlero] *nm* salt cellar.

salgo *etc vb ver* **salir**.

salida [saˈliða] *nf* exit, way out; (*acto*) leaving, going out; (*de tren*, AVIAT) departure; (TEC) output, production; (*fig*) way out; (COM) opening; (GEO, *válvula*) outlet; (*de gas, aire*) escape, leak; **calle sin** ~ cul-de-sac; ~ **de emergencia** emergency exit.

saliente [saˈljente] *a* (ARQ) projecting; (*que se retira*) outgoing,

retiring; (*el sol*) rising; (*fig*) outstanding.

salir [saˈlir] *vi* (*gen*) to come/go out; (*resultar*) to turn out; (*partir*) to leave, depart; (*aparecer*) to appear; (*sobresalir*) to project, jut out; ~ **se** *vr* (*vasija*) to leak; (*animal*) to escape, get out; ~ **con** to go out with; ~ **a la superficie** to come to the surface; ~ **caro/barato** to work out expensive/cheap.

saliva [saˈliβa] *nf* saliva.

salmantino, a [salmanˈtino, a] *a* of Salamanca.

salmo [ˈsalmo] *nm* psalm.

salmón [salˈmon] *nm* salmon.

salmuera [salˈmwera] *nf* pickle, brine.

salón [saˈlon] *nm* (*de casa*) living-room, lounge; (*muebles*) lounge suite; ~ **de belleza** beauty parlour; ~ **de pintura** art gallery; ~ **de baile** dance hall.

salpicadero [salpikaˈðero] *nm* dashboard.

salpicar [salpiˈkar] *vt* (*rociar*) to sprinkle, spatter; (*esparcir*) to scatter.

salsa [ˈsalsa] *nf* sauce; (*con carne asada*) gravy; (*fig*) spice.

saltamontes [saltaˈmontes] *nm inv* grasshopper.

saltar [salˈtar] *vt* to jump (over), leap (over); (*dejar de lado*) to skip, miss out // *vi* to jump, leap; (*pelota*) to bounce; (*al aire*) to fly up; (*quebrarse*) to break; (*al agua*) to dive; (*fig*) to explode, blow up.

saltear [salteˈar] *vt* (*robar*) to rob (in a holdup); (*asaltar*) to assault, attack; (CULIN) to sauté.

saltimbanqui [saltimˈbanki] *nm/f* acrobat.

salto [ˈsalto] *nm* jump, leap; (*al agua*) dive; (DEPORTE) jump; ~ **de agua** waterfall.

saltón, ona [salˈton, ona] *a* (*ojos*) bulging, popping; (*dientes*) protruding.

salubre [sa'luβre] a healthy, salubrious.

salud [sa'luð] nf health; ¡(a su) ~! good health!; ~**able** a (de buena ~) healthy; (provechoso) good, beneficial.

saludar [salu'ðar] vt to greet; (MIL) to salute; **saludo** nm greeting; **saludos** (en carta) best wishes, regards, greetings.

salvación [salβa'θjon] nf (gen) salvation; (rescate) rescue.

salvaguardar [salβaɣwar'ðar] vt to safeguard.

salvaje [sal'βaxe] a wild; (tribú) savage; **salvajismo** nm, **salvajez** nf savagery.

salvar [sal'βar] vt (rescatar) to save, rescue; (resolver) to overcome, resolve; (cubrir distancias) to cover, travel; (hacer excepción) to except, exclude; (un barco) to salvage.

salvavidas [salβa'βiðas] nm inv lifebelt // a: **bote/chaleco/cinturón** ~ lifeboat/jacket/belt.

salvia [salβja] nf sage.

salvo, a ['salβo, a] a safe // ad except (for), save, a ~ out of danger; ~ **que** unless; ~**conducto** nm safe-conduct.

san [san] a saint; ~ **Juan** St. John.

sanar [sa'nar] vt (herida) to heal; (persona) to cure // vi (persona) to get well, recover; (herida) to heal.

sanatorio [sana'torjo] nm sanatorium.

sanción [san'θjon] nf sanction; **sancionar** vt to sanction.

sandalia [san'dalja] nf sandal.

sandía [san'dia] nf watermelon.

sandwich ['sandwitʃ] nm sandwich.

saneamiento [sanea'mjento] nm sanitation; (de la tierra) drainage; (indemnización) compensation; (fig) remedy; **sanear** vt to drain; to compensate; to remedy, repair; (garantizar) to guarantee; (asegurar) to insure.

sangrar [san'grar] vt, vi to bleed; **sangre** nf blood.

sangría [san'gria] nf sangria, sweetened drink of red wine with fruit.

sangriento, a [san'grjento, a] a (herido) bleeding; (batalla) bloody.

sanguinario, a [sangi'narjo, a] a bloodthirsty.

sanguíneo, a [san'gineo, a] a blood cpd.

sanidad [sani'ðað] nf sanitation; (calidad de sano) health, healthiness; ~ **pública** public health.

sanitario, a [sani'tarjo, a] a sanitary; (de la salud) health cpd.

sano, a ['sano, a] a healthy; (sin daños) sound; (comida) good; (entero) whole, intact; ~ **y salvo** safe and sound.

santidad [santi'ðað] nf holiness, sanctity; **santificar** vt to sanctify, make holy.

santiguar [santi'ɣwar] vt (fig) to slap, hit; ~**se** vr to make the sign of the cross.

santo, a ['santo, a] a holy; (fig) wonderful, miraculous // nm/f saint // nm saint's day; ~ **y seña** password.

santuario [san'twarjo] nm sanctuary, shrine.

saña ['saɲa] nf rage, fury.

sapo ['sapo] nm toad.

saque ['sake] nm (TENIS) service, serve; (FÚTBOL) throw-in; ~ **de esquina** corner (kick).

saquear [sake'ar] vt (MIL) to sack; (robar) to loot, plunder; (fig) to ransack; **saqueo** nm sacking; looting, plundering; ransacking.

sarampión [saram'pjon] nm measles sg.

sarcasmo [sar'kasmo] nm sarcasm; **sarcástico, a** a sarcastic.

sardina [sar'ðina] nf sardine.

sardónico, a [sar'ðoniko, a] a sardonic; (irónico) ironical, sarcastic.

sargento [sar'xento] nm sergeant.

sarna ['sarna] *nf* itch; (*MED*) scabies.

sartén [sar'ten] *nf* frying pan.

sastre ['sastre] *nm* tailor; **~ría** *nf* (*arte*) tailoring; (*tienda*) tailor's (shop).

satélite [sa'telite] *nm* satellite.

sátira ['satira] *nf* satire.

satisfacción [satisfak'θjon] *nf* satisfaction; **satisfacer** *vt* to satisfy; (*gastos*) to meet; (*pérdida*) to make good; **satisfacerse** *vr* to satisfy o.s., be satisfied; (*vengarse*) to take revenge; **satisfecho, a** *a* satisfied; (*contento*) content(ed), happy; (*vanidoso*) self-satisfied, smug.

saturar [satu'rar] *vt* to saturate.

sauce ['sauθe] *nm* willow; **~ llorón** weeping willow.

sauna ['sauna] *nf* sauna.

savia ['saβja] *nf* sap.

saxofón [sakso'fon], **saxófono** [sak'sofono] *nm* saxophone.

sayo ['sajo] *nm* smock.

sazonado, a [saθo'naðo, a] *a* (*fruta*) ripe; (*CULIN*) flavoured, seasoned; **sazonar** *vt* to ripen; to flavour, season.

se [se] *pron reflexivo* oneself; (*sg: m*) himself; (: *f*) herself; (: *de una cosa*) itself; (: *de Ud*) yourself; (*pl*) themselves; (: *de Uds*) yourselves; (*de una*) *cnsnsg*; *~ mira en el espejo* he looks at himself in the mirror; (*recíproco*) each other, one another; *~ ayudan* they help each other; *~ miraron* (*el uno al otro*) they looked at one another; (*uso impersonal*): *~ compró hace 3 años* it was bought 3 years ago; *en esa parte ~ habla francés* in that area French is spoken o people speak French; (*dativo*): *le daré* I'll give it to him/her/you; *él ~ ha comprado un sombrero* he has bought himself a hat.

SE *abr de* **sudeste**.

sé *vb ver* **saber, ser**.

sea *etc vb ver* **ser**.

sebo ['seβo] *nm* fat, grease.

seca ['seka] *nf ver* **seco**.

secador [seka'ðor] *nm*: **~ de cabello** *o* **para el pelo** hair-dryer.

secadora [seka'ðora] *nf* wringer; **~ centrífuga** spin-dryer.

secar [se'kar] *vt* to dry; **~se** *vr* to dry (off); (*río, planta*) to dry up.

sección [sek'θjon] *nf* section.

seco, a ['seko, a] *a* dry; (*carácter*) cold; (*respuesta*) sharp, curt; (*coñac*) straight // *a* drought; **vivir a pan ~** to live by bread alone; **habrá pan a ~as** there will be just bread; **decir algo a ~as** to say sth curtly; **parar en ~** to stop dead.

secretaría [sekreta'ria] *nf* secretariat; **secretario, a** *nm/f* secretary.

secreto, a [se'kreto, a] *a* secret; (*persona*) secretive // *nm* secret; (*calidad*) secrecy.

secta ['sekta] *nf* sect; **~rio, a** *a* sectarian.

sector [sek'tor] *nm* sector.

secuela [se'kwela] *nf* consequence.

secuestrar [sekwes'trar] *vt* to kidnap; (*bienes*) to seize, confiscate; **secuestro** *nm* kidnapping; seizure, confiscation.

secular [seku'lar] *a* secular.

secundar [sekun'dar] *vt* to second, support.

secundario, a [sekun'darjo, a] *a* secondary.

sed [seð] *nf* thirst; **tener ~** to be thirsty.

seda ['seða] *nf* silk.

sedal [se'ðal] *nm* fishing line.

sedante [se'ðante], **sedativo** [seða'tiβo] *nm* sedative.

sede ['seðe] *nf* (*de gobierno*) seat; (*de compañía*) headquarters *pl*; **Santa S~** Holy See.

sedentario, a [seðen'tarjo, a] *a* sedentary.

sedimentar [seðimen'tar] *vt* to deposit; **~se** *vr* to settle; **sedimento** *nm* sediment.

seducción [seðuk'θjon] *nf* seduction; **seducir** *vt* to seduce; (*sobornar*) to bribe; (*cautivar*) to charm, fascinate; **seductor, a** *a* seductive;

charming, fascinating; (*engañoso*) deceptive, misleading // *nm/f* seducer.

segadora-trilladora [sexa'ðora triʎa'ðora] *nf* combine harvester.

seglar [se'xlar] *a* secular, lay.

segregación [sexreɣa'θjon] *nf* segregation; ~ **racial** racial segregation; **segregar** *vt* to segregate, separate.

seguido, a [se'ɣiðo, a] *a* (*continuo*) continuous, unbroken; (*recto*) straight; ~**s** consecutive, successive // *ad* (*directo*) straight (on); (*después*) after // *nf*: **en** ~ **a** at once, right away; **5 días** ~**s** 5 days running, 5 days in a row.

seguimiento [sexi'mjento] *nm* chase, pursuit; (*continuación*) continuation.

seguir [se'xir] *vt* (*gen*) to follow; (*venir después*) to follow on, come after; (*proseguir*) to continue; (*perseguir*) to chase, pursue // *vi* (*gen*) to follow; (*continuar*) to continue, carry or go on; ~**se** *vr* to follow; **sigo sin comprender** I still don't understand; **sigue lloviendo** it's still raining.

según [se'xun] *prep* according to // *ad* according to circumstances; ~ **y conforme** it all depends; ~ **esté el tiempo** depending on the weather.

segundo, a [se'xundo, a] *a* a second // *nm* second // *nf* second meaning; **de** ~ **a mano** second hand.

segur [se'xur] *nf* (*hacha*) axe; (*hoz*) sickle.

seguramente [sexura'mente] *ad* surely; (*con certeza*) for sure, with certainty.

seguridad [sexuri'ðað] *nf* (*gen*) safety; (*del estado, de casa etc*) security; (*certidumbre*) certainty; (*confianza*) confidence; (*estabilidad*) stability; ~ **social** social security.

seguro, a [se'xuro, a] *a* (*cierto*) sure, certain; (*fiel*) trustworthy; (*libre del peligro*) safe; (*bien defendida, firme*) secure // *ad* for

sure, certainly // *nm* (*COM*) insurance; ~ **contra terceros/a todo riesgo** third party/comprehensive insurance; ~**s sociales** social security *sg*.

seis [seis] *num* six.

seismo ['seismo] *nm* tremor, earthquake.

selección [selek'θjon] *nf* selection; **seleccionar** *vt* to pick, choose, select; **selecto, a** *a* select, choice; (*escogido*) selected.

selva ['selβa] *nf* (*bosque*) forest, woods *pl*; (*jungla*) jungle.

sello ['seʎo] *nm* stamp; (*medicinal*) capsule, pill.

semáforo [se'maforo] *nm* (*AUTO*) traffic lights *pl*; (*FERRO*) signal.

semana [se'mana] *nf* week; **entre** ~ during the week; **semanal, semanario, a** *a* weekly.

semblante [sem'blante] *nm* face; (*fig*) face, appearance.

sembrar [sem'brar] *vt* to sow; (*objetos*) to sprinkle, scatter about; (*noticias*) to spread.

semejante [seme'xante] *a* (*parecido*) similar; ~**s alike**, similar // *nm* fellow man, fellow creature; **no he dicho cosa** ~ I have not said any such thing; **semejanza** *nf* similarity, resemblance.

semejar [seme'xar] *vi* to seem like, resemble; ~**se** *vr* to look alike, be similar.

semen ['semen] *nm* semen; ~**tal** *nm* stud.

semestral [semes'tral] *a* half-yearly, bi-annual.

semicírculo [semi'θirkulo] *nm* semicircle.

semiconsciente [semikons-'θjente] *a* semiconscious.

semilla [se'miʎa] *nf* seed.

seminario [semi'narjo] *nm* (*REL*) seminary; (*en universidad*) seminar.

sémola ['semola] *nf* semolina.

sempiterno, a [sempi'terno, a] *a* everlasting // *nf* evergreen.

Sena ['sena] *nm*: el ~ the (river) Seine.

senado [se'naðo] *nm* senate; **senador, a** *nm/f* senator.

sencillez [senθi'λeθ] *nf* (*gen*) simplicity; (*naturalidad*) naturalness; **sencillo, a** *a* simple: natural, unaffected.

senda ['senda] *nf*, **sendero** [sen'dero] *nm* path, track.

sendos, as ['sendos, as] *apl*: les dio ~ golpes he hit both of them.

senil [se'nil] *a* senile.

seno ['seno] *nm* (*ANAT*) bosom; bust; (*fig*) bosom; (*vacío*) hollow; ~s breasts.

sensación [sensa'θjon] *nf* (*gen*) sensation; (*sentido*) sense; (*sentimiento*) feeling

sensato, a [sen'sato, a] *a* sensible.

sensible [sen'sible] *a* sensitive; (*apreciable*) perceptible, appreciable; (*pérdida*) considerable.

sensitivo, a [sensi'tiβo, a], **sensorio, a** [sen'sorjo, a], **sensorial** [senso'rjal] *a* sensory.

sensual [sen'swal] *a* sensual.

sentado, a [sen'taðo, a] *a* (*establecido*) settled; (*carácter*) sensible; **estar** ~ to sit, be sitting (down) // *nf* sitting; **dar por** ~ to take for granted, assume

sentar [sen'tar] *vt* to sit, seat; (*fig*) to establish // *vi* (*vestido*) to suit; (*alimento*): ~ **bien/mal** a to agree/disagree with; ~**se** *vr* (*persona*) to sit, sit down; (*el tiempo*) to settle (down); (*los depósitos*) to settle.

sentencia [sen'tenθja] *nf* (*máxima*) maxim, saying; (*JUR*) sentence; **sentenciar** *vt* to sentence // *vi* to give one's opinion.

sentido, a [sen'tiðo, a] *a* (*pérdida*) regrettable; (*carácter*) sensitive // *nm* (*gen*) sense; (*sentimiento*) feeling; (*significado*) sense, meaning; (*dirección*) direction; **mi más ~ pésame** my deepest sympathy; ~

del humor sense of humour; ~ **único** one-way (street).

sentimental [sentimen'tal] *a* sentimental; **vida** ~ love life.

sentimiento [senti'mjento] *nm* (*emoción*) feeling, emotion; (*sentido*) sense; (*pesar*) regret, sorrow.

sentir [sen'tir] *vt* (*gen*) to feel; (*percibir*) to perceive, sense; (*lamentar*) to regret, be sorry for // *vi* (*tener la sensación*) to feel; (*lamentarse*) to feel sorry // *nm* opinion, judgement; ~**se bien/mal** to feel well/ill; **lo siento** I'm sorry.

seña ['seɲa] *nf* sign; (*MIL*) password; ~**s** *nfpl* address *sg*; ~**s personales** personal details.

señal [se'ɲal] *nf* (*gen*) sign; (*síntoma*) symptom; (*FERRO, TELEC*) signal; (*marca*) mark; (*COM*) deposit; **en** ~ **de** as a token of, as a sign of; ~**ar** *vt* to mark; (*indicar*) to point out, indicate; (*fijar*) to fix, settle; ~**arse** *vr* to make one's mark.

señor [se'ɲor] *nm* (*hombre*) man; (*caballero*) gentleman; (*dueño*) owner, master; (*trato: antes de nombre propio*) Mr; (: *directo*) sir; **muy** ~ **mío** Dear Sir; **el** ~ **alcalde/presidente** the mayor/president.

señora [se'ɲora] *nf* (*dama*) lady; (*trato*) Mrs; (*tratamiento de cortesía*) madam; (*fam*) wife; **Nuestra S**~ Our Lady.

señorita [seɲo'rita] *nf* (*gen*) Miss; (*mujer joven*) young lady.

señuelo [se'ɲwelo] *nm* decoy.

sepa *etc vb ver* **saber**.

separación [separa'θjon] *nf* separation; (*división*) division; (*distancia*) gap, distance.

separar [sepa'rar] *vt* to separate; (*dividir*) to divide; ~**se** *vr* (*parte*) to come away; (*partes*) to come apart; (*persona*) to leave, go away; (*matrimonio*) to separate; **separatismo** *nm* separatism.

sepia ['sepja] *nf* cuttlefish.

séptico, a ['septiko, a] *a* septic.

septiembre [sep'tjembre] *nm*
September.

séptimo, a ['septimo, a] *a, nm*
seventh.

sepultar [sepul'tar] *vt* to bury;
sepultura *nf* (*acto*) burial; (*tumba*)
grave, tomb; **sepulturero, a** *nm/f*
gravedigger.

sequedad [seke'ðað] *nf* dryness;
(*fig*) brusqueness, curtness.

sequía [se'kia] *nf* drought.

séquito ['sekito] *nm* followers *pl*,
retinue.

ser [ser] *vi* (*gen*) to be; (*devenir*) to
become // *nm* being; ~ **de** (*origen*)
to be from, come from; (*hecho de*)
to be (made) of; (*pertenecer a*) to
belong to; **es la una** it is one o'clock;
es de esperar que it is to be hoped
that; **era de ver** it was worth seeing,
you should have seen it; **a no ~ que**
unless; **de no ~ así** if it were not so,
were it not so; **o sea** that is to say;
sea como sea be that as it may.

serenarse [sere'narse] *vr* to calm
down.

sereno, a [se'reno, a] *a* (*persona*)
calm, unruffled; (*el tiempo*) fine,
settled; (*ambiente*) calm, peaceful
// *nm* night watchman.

serie ['serje] *nf* series; (*cadena*)
sequence, succession; **fuera de ~**
out of order; (*fig*) special; **fabricación en ~** mass
production.

seriedad [serje'ðað] *nf* seriousness;
(*formalidad*) reliability; (*de crisis*)
gravity, seriousness; **serio, a** *a*
serious; reliable, dependable; grave,
serious; **en serio** *ad* seriously.

sermón [ser'mon] *nm* (*REL*)
sermon.

serpentear [serpente'ar] *vi* to
wriggle; (*fig*) to wind, snake.

serpentina [serpen'tina] *nf*
streamer.

serpiente [ser'pjente] *nf* snake; ~
boa boa constrictor; ~ **pitón**
python; ~ **de cascabel** rattlesnake.

serranía [serra'nia] *nf* mountainous area; **serrano, a** *a* highland *cpd*,

hill *cpd* // *nm/f* highlander.

serrar [se'rrar] *vt* = **aserrar**.

serrín [se'rrin] *nm* = **aserrín**.

serrucho [se'rrutʃo] *nm* saw.

servicio [ser'βiθjo] *nm* service; ~**s**
toilet(s).

servidor, a [serβi'ðor, a] *nm/f*
servant; **su seguro ~ (s.s.s.)** yours
faithfully; **servidumbre** *nf*
(*sujeción*) servitude; (*criados*)
servants *pl*, staff.

servil [ser'βil] *a* servile.

servilleta [serβi'ʎeta] *nf* serviette,
napkin.

servir [ser'βir] *vt* to serve // *vi* to
serve; (*tener utilidad*) to be of use,
be useful; ~**se** *vr* to serve *or* help
o.s.; ~**se de algo** to make use of sth,
use sth; **sírvase pasar** please come
in.

sesenta [se'senta] *num* sixty.

sesgado, a [ses'saðo, a] *a* slanted,
slanting; **sesgo** *nm* slant; (*fig*) slant,
twist.

sesión [se'sjon] *nf* (*POL*) session,
sitting; (*CINE*) showing.

seso ['seso] *nm* brain; **sesudo, a** *a*
sensible, wise.

seta ['seta] *nf* mushroom.

setenta [se'tenta] *num* seventy.

seudo... ['seuðo] *pref* pseudo... .

seudónimo [seu'ðonimo] *nm*
pseudonym.

severidad [seβeri'ðað] *nf* severity;
severo, a *a* severe.

Sevilla [se'βiʎa] *n* Seville.

sexo ['sekso] *nm* sex.

sexto, a ['seksto, a] *a, nm* sixth.

sexual [sek'swal] *a* sexual; **vida** ~
sex life.

si [si] *conj* if; **me pregunto** ~... I
wonder if *or* whether... .

sí [si] *ad* yes // *nm* consent // *pron*
(*gen*) oneself; (*sg: m*) himself; (: *f*)
herself; (: *de cosa*) itself; (*de usted*)
yourself; (*pl*) themselves; (*de ustedes*) yourselves; (*recíproco*) each
other; **él no quiere pero yo ~** he
doesn't want to but I do; **ella ~ vendrá** she will certainly come, she is

sure to come; **claro que** ~ of course; **creo que** ~ I think so.

siderúrgico, a [siðe'rurxico, a] *a* iron and steel *cpd* // *nf*: **la** ~**a** the iron and steel industry.

sidra ['siðra] *nf* cider.

siembra ['sjembra] *nf* sowing.

siempre ['sjempre] *ad* (*gen*) always; (*todo el tiempo*) all the time; ~ **que** *conj* (*cada vez*) whenever; (*dado que*) provided that; **para** ~ for ever.

sien [sjen] *nf* temple.

siento *etc vb ver* **sentar, sentir.**

sierra ['sjerra] *nf* (TEC) saw; (*cadena de montañas*) mountain range.

siervo, a ['sjerβo, a] *nm/f* slave.

siesta ['sjesta] *nf* siesta, nap.

siete ['sjete] *num* seven.

sífilis ['sifilis] *nf* syphilis.

sifón [si'fon] *nm* syphon; **whisky con** ~ whisky and soda.

sigla ['sixla] *nf* symbol.

siglo ['sixlo] *nm* century; (*fig*) age.

significación [sixnifika'θjon] *nf* significance.

significado [sixnifi'kaðo] *nm* significance; (*de palabra*) meaning.

significar [sixnifi'kar] *vt* to mean, signify; (*notificar*) to make known, express; ~**se** *vr* to become known, make a name for o.s.; **significativo, a** *a* significant.

signo ['sixno] *nm* sign; ~ **de admiración** *o* **exclamación** exclamation mark; ~ **de interrogación** question mark.

sigo *etc vb ver* **seguir.**

siguiente [si'xjente] *a* next, following.

siguió *etc vb ver* **seguir.**

sílaba ['silaβa] *nf* syllable.

silbar [sil'βar] *vt, vi* to whistle; **silbato** *nm* whistle; **silbido** *nm* whistle, whistling.

silenciador [silenθja'ðor] *nm* silencer.

silenciar [silen'θjar] *vt* (*persona*) to silence; (*escándalo*) to hush up;

silencio *nm* silence, quiet; **silencioso, a** *a* silent, quiet.

silicio [si'liθjo] *nm* silicon.

silueta [si'lweta] *nf* silhouette; (*de edificio*) outline; (*figura*) figure.

silvestre [sil'βestre] *a* rustic, rural; (*salvaje*) wild.

silla ['siʎa] *nf* (*asiento*) chair, (*de jinete*) saddle.

sillón [si'ʎon] *nm* armchair, easy chair; ~ **de ruedas** wheelchair.

simbólico, a [sim'boliko, a] *a* symbolic(al); **símbolo** *nm* symbol.

simetría [sime'tria] *nf* symmetry.

simiente [si'mjente] *nf* seed.

similar [simi'lar] *a* similar.

simio ['simjo] *nm* ape.

simpatía [simpa'tia] *nf* liking; (*afecto*) affection; (*amabilidad*) kindness, (*solidaridad*) mutual support, solidarity; **simpático, a** *a* nice, pleasant; kind; **simpatizante** *nm/f* sympathiser; **simpatizar** *vi*: **simpatizar con** to get on well with.

simple ['simple] *a* (*gen*) simple; (*elemental*) simple, easy; (*mero*) mere; (*puro*) pure, sheer // *nm/f* simpleton; ~**za** *nf* simpleness; (*necedad*) silly thing; **simplicidad** *nf* simplicity; **simplificar** *vt* to simplify.

simular [simu'lar] *vt* to simulate.

simultáneo, a [simul'taneo, a] *a* simultaneous.

sin [sin] *prep* without; **la ropa está** ~ **lavar** the clothes are unwashed; ~ **que** *conj* without; ~ **embargo** however, still.

sinagoga [sina'xoxa] *nf* synagogue.

sinceridad [sinθeri'ðað] *nf* sincerity; **sincero, a** *a* sincere.

sincronizar [sinkroni'θar] *vt* to synchronize.

sindical [sindi'kal] *a* union *cpd*, trade-union *cpd*; ~**ista** *nm/f* trade-unionist; **sindicato** *nm* (*de trabajadores*) trade(s) union; (*de negociantes*) syndicate.

sinfín [sin'fin] *nm*: **un** ~ **de** a great many, no end of.

sinfonía [sinfo'nia] nf symphony.

singular [singu'lar] a singular; (fig) outstanding, exceptional; (pey) peculiar, odd; ~**idad** nf singularity, peculiarity; ~**izar** vt to single out; ~**izarse** vr to distinguish o.s., stand out.

siniestro, a [si'njestro, a] a left; (fig) sinister.

sinnúmero [sin'numero] nm = **sinfín**.

sino [sino] nm fate, destiny // conj (pero) but; (salvo) except, save.

sinónimo [si'nonimo] nm synonym.

sinrazón [sinra'θon] nf wrong, injustice.

síntesis ['sintesis] nf synthesis; **sintético, a** a synthetic; **sintetizar** vt to synthesize.

sintió vb ver **sentir**.

síntoma ['sintoma] nm symptom.

sinvergüenza [sinßer'xwenθa] nm/f shameless person.

sionismo [sjo'nismo] nm Zionism.

siquiera [si'kjera] conj even if, even though // ad at least; **ni** ~ not even.

sirena [si'rena] nf siren.

sirviente, a [sir'ßjente, a] nm/f servant.

sirvo etc vb ver **servir**.

sisear [sise'ar] vt, vi to hiss.

sismógrafo [sis'moxrafo] nm seismograph.

sistema [sis'tema] nm system; (método) method; **sistemático, a** a systematic.

sitiar [si'tjar] vt to besiege, lay seige to.

sitio ['sitjo] nm (lugar) place; (espacio) room, space; (MIL) siege.

situación [sitwa'θjon] nf situation, position; (estatus) position, standing.

situar [si'twar] vt to place, put; (edificio) to locate, situate.

slip [slip] nm pants pl, briefs pl.

smoking ['smokin] (pl ~**s**) nm dinner jacket.

so [so] prep under.

SO abr de **sudoeste**.

sobaco [so'ßako] nm armpit.

soberanía [soßera'nia] nf sovereignty; **soberano, a** a sovereign; (fig) supreme // nm/f sovereign.

soberbio, a [so'ßerßjo, a] a (orgulloso) proud; (altivo) haughty, arrogant; (fig) magnificent, superb // nf pride; haughtiness, arrogance; magnificence; (cólera) anger.

sobornar [soßor'nar] vt to bribe; **soborno** nm bribe.

sobra ['soßra] nf excess, surplus; ~**s** nfpl left-overs, scraps; **de** ~ surplus, extra; **tengo de** ~ I've more than enough; **de** ~**do, a** a (de ~) more than enough; (excesivo) excessive // ad too, exceedingly; **sobrante** a remaining, extra // nm surplus, remainder; **sobrar** vt to exceed, surpass // vi (tener de más) to be more than enough; (quedar) to remain, be left (over).

sobre ['soßre] prep (gen) on; (encima) on (top of); (por encima de, arriba de) over, above; (más que) more than; (además) in addition to, besides; (alrededor de, tratando de) about // nm envelope.

sobrecama [soßre'kama] nf bedspread.

sobrecargar [soßrekar'sar] vt (camión) to overload; (COM) to surcharge.

sobrehumano, a [soßreu'mano, a] a superhuman.

sobrellevar [soßreʎe'ßar] vt (fig) to bear, endure.

sobremarcha [soßre'martʃa] nf (AUTO) overdrive.

sobrenatural [soßrenatu'ral] a supernatural.

sobrepasar [soßrepa'sar] vt to exceed, surpass.

sobreponer [soßrepo'ner] vt (poner encima) to put on top; (añadir) to add; ~**se** vr: ~**se a** to win through, pull through.

sobreprecio [soßre'preθjo] nm surcharge.

sobresaliente [soßresa'ljente] a

projecting; (fig) outstanding, excellent; **sobresalir** vi to project, jut out; to stand out, excel.

sobresaltar [soβresal'tar] vt (asustar) to scare, frighten; (sobrecoger) to startle; **sobresalto** nm (movimiento) start; (susto) scare; (turbación) sudden shock; **de sobresalto** suddenly.

sobrescrito [soβres'krito] nm address.

sobretodo [soβre'toðo] nm overcoat.

sobreviviente [soβreβi'βjente] a surviving // nm/f survivor; **sobrevivir** vi to survive.

sobriedad [soβrje'ðað] nf sobriety, soberness; (moderación) moderation, restraint.

sobrino, a [so'βrino, a] nm/f nephew/niece.

sobrio, a ['soβrjo, a] a sober; (moderado) moderate, restrained.

socarrón, ona [soka'rron, ona] a (sarcástico) sarcastic, ironic(al); (astuto) crafty, cunning.

sociable [so'θjaβle] a (persona) sociable, friendly; (animal) social.

social [so'θjal] a social; (COM) company cpd.

socialdemócrata [soθjalðe'mokrata] nm/f social democrat.

socialista [soθja'lista] a, nm/f socialist.

socializar [soθjali'θar] vt to socialize.

sociedad [soθje'ðað] nf (gen) society; (COM) company; ~ **anónima (SA)** limited company.

socio, a ['soθjo, a] nm/f (miembro) member; (COM) partner; ~ **comanditario** sleeping partner.

sociología [soθjolo'xia] nf sociology.

socorrer [soko'rrer] vt to help; **socorro** nm (ayuda) help, aid; (MIL) relief; **¡socorro!** help!

soda ['soða] nf (sosa) soda; (bebida) soda water.

sofá [so'fa] (pl ~s) nm sofa, settee.

~**-cama** nm studio couch.

sofisticación [sofistika'θjon] nf sophistication.

sofocar [sofo'kar] vt to suffocate; (apagar) to smother, put out; ~**se** vr to suffocate; (fig) to blush, feel embarrassed; **sofoco** nm suffocation, embarrassment.

soga ['soɣa] nf rope.

sois vb ver **ser**.

sojuzgar [soxuθ'ɣar] vt to subdue, rule despotically.

sol [sol] nm sun; (luz) sunshine, sunlight; **hace** ~ it is sunny.

solamente [sola'mente] ad only, just.

solapa [so'lapa] nf (de ropa) lapel; (de libro) jacket.

solar [so'lar] a solar, sun cpd.

solaz [so'laθ] nm recreation, relaxation; (alivio) solace; ~**ar** vt (divertir) to amuse; (aliviar) to console.

soldada [sol'daða] nf pay.

soldado [sol'daðo] nm soldier.

soldador [solda'ðor] nm soldering iron; (persona) welder; **soldar** vt to solder, weld; (unir) to join, unite.

soledad [sole'ðað] nf solitude; (estado infeliz) loneliness; (nostalgia) grieving, mourning.

solemne [so'lemne] a solemn; **solemnidad** nf solemnity.

soler [so'ler] vi to be in the habit of, be accustomed to.

solfa ['solfa] nf, **solfeo** [sol'feo] nm solfa; (conjunto de signos) musical notation.

solicitación [soliθita'θjon] nf request; (de votos) canvassing; **solicitar** vt (permiso) to ask for, seek; (puesto) to apply for; (votos) to canvass; (atención) to attract; (persona) to pursue, chase after.

solícito, a [so'liθito, a] a (diligente) diligent; (cuidadoso) careful; **solicitud** nf (calidad) great care; (petición) request; (memorial) petition; (a un puesto) application.

solidaridad [soliðari'ðað] nf solidarity; **solidario, a** a (participación) joint, common; (compromiso) mutually binding.

solidez [soli'ðeθ] nf solidity; **sólido, a** a solid.

soliloquio [soli'lokjo] nm soliloquy, monologue.

solista [so'lista] nm/f soloist.

solitario, a [soli'tarjo, a] a lonely, solitary // nm/f recluse; (en la sociedad) loner // nm solitaire.

soliviar [soli'βjar] vt to lift.

solo, a ['solo, a] a (único) single, sole; (sin compañía) alone; (solitario) lonely; **hay una ~a dificultad** there is just one difficulty; **a ~as** alone, by o.s.

sólo ['solo] ad only, just.

solomillo [solo'miʎo] nm sirloin.

soltar [sol'tar] vt (dejar ir) to let go of; (desprender) to unfasten, loosen; (librar) to release, set free; (estornudo, risa) to let out.

soltero, a [sol'tero, a] a single, unmarried // nm bachelor // nf single woman, spinster.

soltura [sol'tura] nf looseness, slackness; (de los miembros) agility, ease of movement; (en el hablar) fluency, ease; (MED) diarrhoea.

soluble [so'luβle] a (QUÍMICA) soluble; (problema) solvable.

solución [solu'θjon] nf solution; **solucionar** vt (problema) to solve; (asunto) to settle.

solventar [solβen'tar] vt (pagar) to settle, pay; (resolver) to resolve.

sollozar [soʎo'θar] vi to sob; **sollozo** nm sob.

sombra ['sombra] nf shadow; (como protección) shade; **~s** nfpl darkness sg; **tener buena/mala ~** to be lucky/unlucky.

sombreador [sombrea'ðor] nm: **~ de ojos** eyeshadow.

sombrero [som'brero] nm hat.

sombrilla [som'briʎa] nf parasol, sunshade.

sombrío, a [som'brio, a] a (oscuro) dark; (sombreado) shaded; (fig)

sombre, sad; (persona) gloomy.

somero, a [so'mero, a] a superficial.

someter [some'ter] vt (país) to conquer; (persona) to subject to one's will; (informe) to present, submit; **~se** vr to give in, yield, submit; **~ a** to subject to.

somnambulismo [somnambu-'lismo] nm sleepwalking; **somnámbulo, a** nm/f sleepwalker.

somnífero [som'nifero] nm sleeping pill.

somos vb ver **ser**.

son [son] vb ver **ser** // nm sound; **en ~ de broma** as a joke.

sonar [so'nar] vt to ring // vi to sound; (hacer ruido) to make a noise; (pronunciarse) to be sounded, be pronounced; (ser conocido) to sound familiar; (campana) to ring; (reloj) to strike, chime; **~se** vr: **~se (las narices)** to blow one's nose; **me suena ese nombre** that name rings a bell.

sonda ['sonda] nf (NAUT) sounding; (TEC) bore, drill; (MED) probe; **sondear** vt to sound; to bore (into), drill; to probe, sound; (fig) to sound out; **sondeo** nm sounding; boring, drilling; (fig) poll, enquiry.

sónico, a ['soniko, a] a sonic, sound cpd.

sonido [so'niðo] nm sound.

sonoro, a [so'noro, a] a sonorous; (resonante) loud, resonant.

sonreír [sonre'ir] vi, **~se** vr to smile; **sonriente** a smiling; **sonrisa** nf smile.

sonrojo [son'roxo] nm blush.

soñador, a [soɲa'ðor, a] nm/f dreamer; **soñar** vt, vi to dream; **soñar con** to dream about, dream of.

soñoliento, a [soɲo'ljento, a] a sleepy, drowsy.

sopa ['sopa] nf soup.

soplador [sopla'ðor] nm fan, ventilator.

soplar [so'plar] vt (polvo) to blow

away, blow off; (inflar) to blow up; (vela) to blow out // vi to blow; **~se** vr (fam: ufanarse) to get conceited; **soplo** nm blow, puff; (de viento) puff, gust.

soporífero [sopo'rifero] nm sleeping pill.

soportable [sopor'taßle] a bearable; **soportar** vt to bear, carry; (fig) to bear, put up with; **soporte** nm support; (fig) pillar, support.

soprano [so'prano] nf soprano.

sorber [sor'ßer] vt (chupar) to sip; (inhalar) to inhale; (tragar) to swallow (up); (absorber) to soak up, absorb.

sorbete [sor'ßete] nm iced fruit drink.

sorbo ['sorßo] nm (trago) gulp, swallow; (chupada) sip.

sordera [sor'ðera] nf deafness.

sórdido, a ['sorðiðo, a] a dirty, squalid; (palabra) nasty, dirty; (fig) mean.

sordo, a ['sorðo, a] a (persona) deaf; (máquina) quiet // nm/f deaf person; **~as** on the quiet; **~mudo**, a a deaf and dumb.

sorprendente [sorpren'dente] a surprising; **sorprender** vt to surprise; **sorpresa** nf surprise.

sortear [sorte'ar] vt to draw lots for; (objeto) to raffle; (dificultad) to avoid; **sorteo** nm drawing lots; raffle.

sosegado, a [sose'saðo, a] a quiet, calm; **sosegar** vt to quieten, calm; (el ánimo) to reassure // vi to rest; **sosiego** nm quiet(ness), calm(ness).

soslayo [sos'lajo]: **al ~ o de ~** ad obliquely, sideways.

soso, a ['soso, a] a (CULIN) tasteless; (fig) dull, uninteresting.

sospecha [sos'petʃa] nf suspicion; **sospechar** vt to suspect; **sospechoso, a** a suspicious; (testimonio, opinión) suspect // nm/f suspect.

sostén [sos'ten] nm (apoyo) support; (prenda femenina) bra,

brassière; (alimentación) sustenance, food.

sostener [soste'ner] vt to support; (mantener) to keep up, maintain; (alimentar) to sustain, keep going; **~se** vr to support o.s.; (seguir) to continue, remain; **sostenido, a** a continuous, sustained; (prolongado) prolonged.

sótano ['sotano] nm basement.

soterrar [sote'rrar] vt to bury.

soviético, a [so'ßjetiko, a] a Soviet.

soy vb ver **ser**.

sport [sport] nm sport.

Sr abr de **Señor**.

Sra abr de **Señora**.

S.R.C. abr de **se ruega contestación** R.S.V.P.

Sta abr de **Santa**; **Señorita**.

status ['status] nm inv status.

Sto abr de **Santo**.

su [su] pron (de él) his; (de ella) her; (de una cosa) its; (de ellos, ellas) their; (de usted, ustedes) your.

suave ['swaße] a gentle; (superficie) smooth; (trabajo) easy; (música, voz) soft, sweet; **suavidad** nf gentleness; smoothness; softness, sweetness, **suavizar** vt to soften; (quitar la aspereza) to smooth (out).

subalimentado, a [sußalimen'taðo, a] a undernourished.

subasta [su'ßasta] nf auction; **subastar** vt to auction (off).

subconsciencia [sußkons'θjenθja] nf subconscious; **subconsciente** a subconscious.

subdesarrollado, a [sußðesarro-'λaðo, a] a underdeveloped; **subdesarrollo** nm underdevelopment.

súbdito, a ['sußðito, a] nm/f subject.

subdividir [sußðißi'ðir] vt to subdivide.

subestimar [sußesti'mar] vt to underestimate, underrate; (propiedad) to undervalue.

subexpuesto, a [sußeks'pwesto, a] a underexposed.

subido, a [su'βiðo, a] a (color) bright, strong; (precio) high // nf (gen) ascent, climb; (de precio) rise, increase; (camino) way up; (pendiente) slope, hill.

subir [su'βir] vt (objeto) to raise, lift up; (cuesta, calle) to go up; (montaña) to climb; (precio) to raise, put up // vi to go/come up; (a un coche) to get in; (a un autobús) to get on; (precio) to rise, go up; (río) to rise; ~se vr to get up, climb.

súbito, a ['suβito, a] a (repentino) sudden; (imprevisto) unexpected; (precipitado) hasty, rash // ad: (de) ~ suddenly.

sublevación [suβleβa'θjon] nf revolt, rising.

sublime [su'βlime] a sublime.

submarino, a [suβma'rino, a] a underwater // nm submarine.

subordinado, a [suβorði'naðo, a] a, nm/f subordinate.

subrayar [suβra'jar] vt to underline.

subrepticio, a [suβrep'tiθjo, a] a surreptitious.

subsanar [suβsa'nar] vt (reparar) to make good; (perdonar) to excuse; (sobreponerse a) to overcome.

subscribir [suβskri'βir] vt = suscribir.

subsidiario, a [suβsi'ðjarjo, a] a subsidiary.

subsidio [suβ'siðjo] nm (ayuda) aid, financial help; (subvención) subsidy, grant; (de enfermedad, paro etc) benefit.

subsistencia [suβsis'tenθja] nf subsistence; **subsistir** vi (gen) to subsist; (vivir) to live; (sobrevivir) to survive, endure.

subterráneo, a [suβte'rraneo, a] a underground, subterranean // nm underpass, underground passage.

suburbano, a [suβur'βano, a] a suburban.

suburbio [su'βurβjo] nm (barrio) slum quarter; (afueras) suburbs pl.

subvencionar [suββenθjo'nar] vt to subsidize.

subversión [suββer'sjon] nf subversion; **subversivo, a** a subversive.

subyugar [suβju'xar] vt (país) to subjugate, subdue; (enemigo) to overpower; (voluntad) to dominate.

suceder [suθe'ðer] vt, vi to happen; (seguir) to succeed, follow; lo que sucede es que... the fact is that...; **sucesión** nf succession; (serie) sequence, series.

sucesivamente [suθesiβa'mente] ad: y así ~ and so on.

sucesivo, a [suθe'siβo, a] a successive, following; en lo ~ in future, from now on.

suceso [su'θeso] nm (hecho) event, happening; (incidente) incident; (resultado) outcome.

suciedad [suθje'ðað] nf (estado) dirtiness; (mugre) dirt, filth.

sucinto, a [su'θinto, a] a (conciso) succinct, concise.

sucio, a ['suθjo, a] a dirty.

suculento, a [suku'lento, a] a succulent.

sucumbir [sukum'bir] vi to succumb.

sucursal [sukur'sal] nf branch (office).

sudamericano, a [suðameri-'kano, a] a South American.

sudar [su'ðar] vt, vi to sweat.

sudeste [su'ðeste] nm south-east; **sudoeste** nm south-west.

sudor [su'ðor] nm sweat; ~oso, a, **sudoso, a**, ~iento, a a sweaty, sweating.

Suecia ['sweθja] nf Sweden; **sueco, a** a Swedish // nm/f Swede.

suegro, a ['swexro, a] nm/f father-/mother-in-law.

suela ['swela] nf sole.

sueldo ['sweldo] nm pay, wage(s) (pl); el ~ mínimo the minimum wage.

suele etc vb ver **soler.**

suelo ['swelo] nm (tierra) ground; (de casa) floor.

suelto, a ['swelto, a] *a* loose; *(libre)* free; *(separado)* detached, individual; *(ágil)* quick, agile; *(corriente)* fluent, flowing // *nm* (loose) change, small change.

sueño *etc vb ver* **soñar** // ['sweɲo] *nm* sleep; *(somnolencia)* sleepiness, drowsiness; *(lo soñado, fig)* dream; **tener ~** to be sleepy.

suero ['swero] *nm* serum.

suerte ['swerte] *nf (fortuna)* luck; *(azar)* chance; *(destino)* fate, destiny; *(condición)* lot; *(género)* sort, kind; **tener ~** to be lucky; **de otra ~** otherwise, if not; **de ~ que** so that, in such a way that.

suéter ['sweter] *nm* sweater.

suficiente [sufi'θjente] *a* enough, sufficient; *(capaz)* capable.

sufragio [su'fraxjo] *nm (voto)* vote; *(derecho de voto)* suffrage; *(ayuda)* help, aid.

sufrimiento [sufri'mjento] *nm (dolor)* suffering; *(paciencia)* patience; *(tolerancia)* tolerance.

sufrir [su'frir] *vt (padecer)* to suffer; *(soportar)* to bear, stand, put up with; *(apoyar)* to hold up, support // *vi* to suffer.

sugerencia [suxe'renθja] *nf* suggestion; **sugerir** *vt* to suggest; *(sutilmente)* to hint.

sugestión [suxes'tjon] *nf* suggestion, *(influir)* hint; **sugestionar** *vt* to influence.

sugestivo, a [suxes'tiβo, a] *a* stimulating; *(fascinante)* fascinating.

suicida [sui'θiða] *a* suicidal // *nm/f* suicidal person; *(muerto)* suicide, person who has committed suicide; **suicidio** *nm* suicide.

Suiza ['swiθa] *nf* Switzerland; **suizo, a** *a, nm/f* Swiss.

sujeción [suxe'θjon] *nf* subjection.

sujetador [suxeta'ðor] *nm* fastener, clip; *(de papeles)* paper clip.

sujetar [suxe'tar] *vt (fijar)* to fasten; *(detener)* to hold down; *(fig)* to subject, subjugate; **~se** *vr* to

subject o.s.; **sujeto, a** *a* fastened, secure // *nm* subject; *(individuo)* individual; **sujeto a** subject to.

suma ['suma] *nf (cantidad)* total, sum; *(de dinero)* sum; *(acto)* adding (up), addition; *(resumen)* summary; *(esencia)* essence; **en ~** in short, **~dora** *nf* adding machine.

sumamente [suma'mente] *ad* extremely, exceedingly.

sumar [su'mar] *vt* to add (up); *(reunir)* to collect, gather; *(abreviar)* to summarize, sum up // *vi* to add up.

sumario, a [su'marjo, a] *a* brief, concise // *nm* summary.

sumergir [sumer'xir] *vt* to submerge; *(hundir)* to sink; *(bañar)* to immerse, dip; **sumersión** *nf* submersion; *(fig)* absorption.

sumidero [sumi'ðero] *nm* drain; *(TEC)* sump.

suministrador, a [suministra'ðor, a] *nm/f* supplier; **suministrar** *vt* to supply, provide; **suministro** *nm* supply; *(acto)* supplying, providing.

sumir [su'mir] *vt* to sink, submerge; *(fig)* to plunge.

sumisión [sumi'sjon] *nf (acto)* submission; *(calidad)* submissiveness, docility; **sumiso, a** *a* submissive, docile.

sumo, a ['sumo, a] *a* great, extreme; *(mayor)* highest, supreme.

supe *etc vb ver* **saber**.

super... [super] *pref* super..., over... // *nm* high-grade fuel.

superar [supe'rar] *vt (sobreponerse a)* to overcome; *(rebasar)* to surpass, do better than; *(pasar)* to go beyond; **~se** *vr* to excel o.s.

superávit [supe'raβit] *nm* surplus.

supercarburante [superkarβu'rante] *nm* high-grade fuel.

superestructura [superestruk'tura] *nf* superstructure.

superficial [superfi'θjal] *a* superficial, *(medida)* surface *cpd*, of the surface.

superficie [super'fiθje] nf surface; (área) area.

superfluo, a [su'perflwo, a] a superfluous.

superintendente [superinten-'dente] nm/f supervisor, superintendent.

superior [supe'rjor] a (piso, clase) upper; (temperatura, número, nivel) higher; (mejor: calidad, producto) superior, better // nm/f superior; ~ **idad** nf superiority.

supermercado [supermer'kaðo] nm supermarket.

supersónico, a [super'soniko, a] a supersonic.

superstición [supersti'θjon] nf superstition; **supersticioso, a** a superstitious.

supervisor, a [superßi'sor, a] nm/f supervisor.

supervivencia [superßi'ßenθja] nf survival.

supiera etc vb ver **saber.**

suplementario, a [suplemen-'tarjo, a] a supplementary; **suplemento** nm supplement.

suplente [su'plente] a, nm/f substitute.

súplica ['suplika] nf request; (REL) supplication.

suplicante [supli'kante] nm/f applicant.

suplicar [supli'kar] vt (cosa) to beg (for), plead for; (persona) to beg, plead with.

suplicio [su'pliθjo] nm torture.

suplir [su'plir] vt (compensar) to make good, make up for; (reemplazar) to replace, substitute // vi: ~ **a o por** to take the place of, substitute for.

suponer [supo'ner] vt to suppose // vi to have authority; **suposición** nf supposition; (autoridad) authority.

supremacía [suprema'θia] nf supremacy.

supremo, a [su'premo, a] a supreme.

supresión [supre'sjon] nf sup-

pression; (de derecho) abolition; (de dificultad) removal; (de palabra) deletion; (de restricción) cancellation, lifting.

suprimir [supri'mir] vt to suppress; (derecho, costumbre) to abolish; (dificultad) to remove; (palabra) to delete; (restricción) to cancel; lift.

supuesto, a [su'pwesto, a] a (hipotético) supposed; (falso) false // nm assumption, hypothesis; ~ **que** conj since; **por** ~ of course.

sur [sur] nm south.

surcar [sur'kar] vt to plough, furrow; (superficie) to cut, score; **surco** nm groove; (AGR) furrow.

surgir [sur'xir] vi to arise, emerge; (dificultad) to come up, crop up.

surtido, a [sur'tiðo, a] a mixed, assorted // nm (gen) selection, assortment; (abastecimiento) supply, stock.

surtir [sur'tir] vt to supply, provide // vi to spout, spurt.

susceptible [susθep'tiβle] a susceptible; (sensible) sensitive; ~ **de** capable of.

suscitar [susθi'tar] vt to cause, provoke; (interés) to arouse.

suscribir [suskri'βir] vt (firmar) to sign; (respaldar) to subscribe to, endorse; ~ **se** vr to subscribe; **suscripción** nf subscription.

suspender [suspen'der] vt (objeto) to hang (up), suspend; (trabajo) to stop, suspend; (a estudiante) to fail; **suspensión** nf suspension; (fig) stoppage, suspension.

suspenso, a [sus'penso, a] a hanging, suspended; (estudiante) failed; (admirado) astonished, amazed // nm: **quedar o estar en** ~ to be pending.

suspicacia [suspi'kaθja] nf suspicion, mistrust; **suspicaz** a suspicious, distrustful.

suspirar [suspi'rar] vi to sigh; **suspiro** nm sigh.

sustancia [sus'tanθja] nf substance.

sustentar [susten'tar] vt (alimentar) to sustain, nourish; (objeto) to hold up, support; (idea, teoría) to maintain, uphold; (fig) to sustain, keep going; **sustento** nm support; (alimento) sustenance, food.

sustituir [sustitu'ir] vt to substitute, replace; **sustituto, a** nm/f substitute, replacement.

susto ['susto] nm fright, scare.

sustraer [sustra'er] vt to remove, take away; (MAT) to subtract; **~se** vr (evitar) to avoid; (retirarse) to withdraw.

susurrar [susu'rrar] vi to whisper; **susurro** nm whisper.

sutil [su'til] a subtle; (tenue) thin; **~eza** nf subtlety; thinness.

suyo, a ['sujo, a] a (con artículo o después del verbo ser: de él) his; (: de ella) hers; (: de ellos, ellas) theirs; (: de Ud, Uds) yours; (después de un nombre: de él) of his; (: de ella) of hers; (: de ellos, ellas) of theirs; (: de Ud, Uds) of yours.

T

t abr de **tonelada.**

taba ['taβa] nf (ANAT) ankle bone; (juego) jacks sg.

tabaco [ta'βako] nm tobacco; (fam) cigarettes pl.

taberna [ta'βerna] nf bar; **tabernero, a** nm/f (encargado) publican; (camarero) barman.

tabique [ta'βike] nm (pared) thin wall; (para dividir) partition.

tabla ['taβla] nf (de madera) plank; (estante) shelf; (de anuncios) board; (lista, catálogo) list; (mostrador) counter; (de vestido) pleat; (ARTE) panel; **~s** (TAUR, TEATRO) boards; **hacer ~s** to draw; **~do** nm (plataforma) platform; (suelo) plank floor; (TEATRO) stage.

tablero [ta'βlero] nm (de madera)

plank, board; (pizarra) blackboard; (de ajedrez, damas) board; (AUTO) dashboard.

tablilla [ta'βliʎa] nf small board; (MED) splint.

tablón [ta'βlon] nm (de suelo) plank; (de techo) beam; (de anuncios) notice board.

tabú [ta'βu] nm taboo.

tabular [taβu'lar] vt to tabulate.

taburete [taβu'rete] nm stool.

tacaño, a [ta'kaɲo, a] a (avaro) mean; (astuto) crafty.

tácito, a ['taθito, a] a tacit.

taciturno, a [taθi'turno, a] a (callado) silent; (malhumorado) sullen.

taco ['tako] nm (BILLAR) cue; (libro de billetes) book; (manojo de billetes) wad; (AM) heel; (tarugo) peg; (fam: bocado) snack; (: palabrota) swear word; (: trago de vino) swig.

tacón [ta'kon] nm heel; **de ~ alto** high heeled; **taconeo** nm (heel) stamping.

táctico, a ['taktiko, a] a tactical // nf tactics pl.

tacto ['takto] nm touch; (acción) touching.

tacha ['tatʃa] nf flaw; (TEC) stud; **poner ~ a** to find fault with; **tachar** vt (borrar) to cross out; (corregir) to correct; (criticar) to criticize; **tachar de** to accuse of.

tafetán [tafe'tan] nm taffeta; **tafetanes** nmpl (fam) frills; **~ adhesivo** o **inglés** sticking plaster.

tafilete [tafi'lete] nm morocco leather.

tahona [ta'ona] nf (panadería) bakery; (molino) flourmill.

tahur [ta'ur] nm gambler; (pey) cheat.

taimado, a [tai'maðo, a] a (astuto) sly; (resentido) sullen.

taja ['taxa] nf (corte) cut; (repartición) division; **~da** nf slice; **~dera** nf (instrumento) chopper;

(*madera*) chopping block; **tajante** *a* sharp.

tajar [ta'xar] *vt* to cut; **tajo** *nm* (*corte*) cut; (*filo*) cutting edge; (*GEO*) cleft.

tal [tal] *a* such; ~ **vez** perhaps // *pron* (*persona*) someone, such a one; (*cosa*) something, such a thing; ~ **como** such as; ~ **para cual** tit for tat; (*dos iguales*) two of a kind // *ad*: ~ **como** (*igual*) just as; ~ **cual** (*como es*) just as it is; ~ **el padre, cual el hijo** like father, like son; ¿**qué** ~? how are things?; ¿**qué** ~ **te gusta?** how do you like it? // *conj*: **con** ~ **de que** provided that.

talabartero [talaβar'tero] *nm* saddler.

taladrar [tala'ðrar] *vt* to drill; **taladro** *nm* (*gen*) drill; (*hoyo*) drill hole; **taladro neumático** pneumatic drill.

talante [ta'lante] *nm* (*humor*) mood; (*voluntad*) will, willingness.

talar [ta'lar] *vt* to fell, cut down; (*fig*) to devastate.

talco ['talko] *nm* (*polvos*) talcum powder; (*MINEROLOGÍA*) talc.

talego [ta'lexo] *nm*, **talega** [ta'lexa] *nf* sack.

talento [ta'lento] *nm* talent; (*capacidad*) ability; (*don*) gift.

talidomida [taliðo'miða] *nm* thalidomide.

talismán [talis'man] *nm* talisman.

talmente [tal'mente] *ad* (*de esta forma*) in such a way; (*hasta tal punto*) to such an extent; (*exactamente*) exactly.

talón [ta'lon] *nm* (*gen*) heel; (*COM*) counterfoil.

talonario [talo'narjo] *nm* (*de cheques*) chequebook; (*de billetes*) book of tickets; (*de recibos*) receipt book.

talud [ta'luð] *nm* slope.

talla [ta'ʎa] *nf* (*estatura, fig, MED*) height, stature; (*palo*) measuring rod; (*ARTE*) carving.

tallado, a [ta'ʎaðo, a] *a* carved //

nm carving; **tallar** *vt* (*trabajar*) to work, carve; (*grabar*) to engrave; (*medir*) to measure; (*repartir*) to deal // *vi* to deal.

tallarín [taʎa'rin] *nm* noodle.

talle [ta'ʎe] *nm* (*ANAT*) waist; (*medida*) size; (*física*) build; (: *de mujer*) figure; (*física*) appearance.

taller [ta'ʎer] *nm* (*TEC*) workshop; (*de artista*) studio.

tallo [ta'ʎo] *nm* (*de planta*) stem; (*de hierba*) blade; (*brote*) shoot; (*col*) cabbage; (*CULIN*) candied peel.

tamaño, a [ta'maɲo, a] *a* such a (big/small) // *nm* size; **de** ~ **natural** full-size.

tamarindo [tama'rindo] *nm* tamarind.

tambalearse [tambale'arse] *vr* (*persona*) to stagger; (*vehículo*) to sway.

también [tam'bjen] *ad* (*igualmente*) also, too, as well; (*además*) besides.

tambor [tam'bor] *nm* drum; (*ANAT*) eardrum; ~ **del freno** brake drum.

tamiz [ta'miθ] *nm* sieve; ~**ar** *vt* to sieve.

tamo ['tamo] *nm* fluff.

tampoco [tam'poko] *ad* nor, neither; **yo** ~ **lo compré** I didn't buy it either.

tampón [tam'pon] *nm* plug; (*MED*) tampon.

tan [tan] *ad* so; ~ **es así que** so much so that.

tanda ['tanda] *nf* (*gen*) series; (*juego*) set; (*turno*) shift; (*grupo*) gang.

tangente [tan'xente] *nf* tangent.

Tánger ['tanxer] *n* Tangier(s).

tangible [tan'xiβle] *a* tangible.

tanque ['tanke] *nm* (*gen*) tank; (*AUTO, NAUT*) tanker.

tantear [tante'ar] *vt* (*calcular*) to reckon (up); (*medir*) to take the measure of; (*probar*) to test, try out; (*tomar la medida: persona*) to take the measurements of; (*considerar*) to weigh up // *vi* (*DEPORTE*) to score; **tanteo** nm (cálculo) (rough) calculation; (prueba) test, trial; (DEPORTE) scoring; (adivinanzas) guesswork; **al tanteo** by trial and error.

tanto, a ['tanto, a] a (cantidad) so much, as much; ~s so many, as many; **20 y ~s** 20-odd // al (cantidad) so much, as much; (tiempo) so long, as long; ~ **tú como yo** both you and I; ~ **como eso** it's not as bad as that; ~ **más ... cuanto que** it's all the more ... because; ~ **mejor/peor** so much the better/the worse; ~ **si viene como si va** whether he comes or whether he goes; ~ **es así que** so much so that; **por o por lo** ~ therefore; **me he vuelto ronco de o con** ~ **hablar** I have become hoarse with so much talking // conj: **con** ~ **que** provided (that); **en** ~ **que** while; **hasta** ~ **(que)** until such time as // nm (suma) certain amount; (proporción) so much; (punto) point; (gol) goal; **al** ~ up to date; **un** ~ **perezoso** somewhat lazy; **al** ~ **de que** because of the fact that // pron: **cada uno paga** ~ each one pays so much; **a** ~ **de agosto** on such and such a day in August.

tapar [ta'par] vt (cubrir) to cover; (envolver) to wrap or cover up (la vista) to obstruct; (persona, falta) to conceal; (AM) to fill; ~**se** vr to wrap o.s. up.

taparrabo [tapa'rra\u03b2o] nm (bañador) (bathing or swimming) trunks pl

tapete [ta'pete] nm table cover.

tapia ['tapja] nf (garden) wall; **tapiar** vt to wall in.

tapicería [tapi\u03b8e'ria] nf tapestry; (para muebles) upholstery; (tienda) upholsterer's (shop); **tapiz** nm (alfombra) carpet; (tela tejida) tapestry; **tapizar** vt (pared) to wallpaper; (suelo) to carpet; (muebles) to upholster.

tapón [ta'pon] nm (corcho) stopper; (TEC) plug; (MED) tampon; ~ **de rosca** o **de tuerca** screw-top.

taquigrafía [takixra'fia] nf shorthand; **taquígrafo, a** nm/f shorthand writer.

taquilla [ta'ki\u028ea] nf (donde se compra) booking office; (suma recogida) takings pl; **taquillero, a** a: **función taquillera** box office success // nm/f ticket clerk.

taquímetro [ta'kimetro] nm speedometer; (de control) tachymeter.

tara ['tara] nf (defecto) defect; (COM) tare.

tarántula [ta'rantula] nf tarantula.

tararear [tarare'ar] vi to hum.

tardanza [tar'\u00f0an\u03b8a] nf (demora) delay; (lentitud) slowness.

tardar [tar'\u00f0ar] vi (tomar tiempo) to take a long time; (llegar tarde) to be late; (demorar) to delay; **¿tarda mucho el tren?** does the train take long?; **a más** ~ at the latest; **no tardes en venir** come soon, come before long.

tarde ['tar\u00f0e] ad (hora) late; (después de tiempo) too late // nf (de día) afternoon; (al anochecer) evening; **de** ~ **en** ~ from time to time; **¡buenas** ~**s!** (de día) good afternoon!; (de noche) good evening!; **a o por la** ~ in the afternoon; in the evening.

tardío, a [tar'\u00f0io, a] a (retrasado) late; (lento) slow (to arrive).

tardo, a ['tar\u00f0o, a] a (lento) slow; (torpe) dull.

tarea [ta'rea] nf task; (ESCOL) homework; ~ **de asunto** chore.

tarifa [ta'rifa] nf (lista de precios) price list; (COM) tariff; ~ **completa** all-in cost.

tarima [ta'rima] nf (plataforma) platform; (taburete) stool; (litera) bunk.

tarjeta [tar'xeta] nf card; ~ **postal/de crédito/de Navidad** postcard/credit card/Christmas card.

tarro ['tarro] *nm* jar, pot.

tarta ['tarta] *nf* (*pastel*) cake; (*torta*) tart.

tartamudear [tartamuðe'ar] *vi* to stammer; **tartamudo, a** *a* stammering // *nm/f* stammerer.

tartana [tar'tana] *nf* (*barco*) dinghy.

tartárico, a [tar'tariko, a] *a*: **ácido ~** tartaric acid.

tártaro ['tartaro] *a, nm* Tartar.

tasa ['tasa] *nf* (*precio*) (fixed) price, rate; (*valoración*) valuation; (*medida, norma*) measure, standard; **~ de interés** rate of interest; **~ción** *nf* (*gen*) valuation; (*de oro etc*) appraisal; **~dor** *nm* valuer.

tasajo [ta'saxo] *nm* dried beef.

tasar [ta'sar] *vt* (*arreglar el precio*) to fix a price for; (*valorar*) to value, assess; (*limitar*) to limit.

tasca ['taska] *nf* (*fam*) pub.

tatarabuelo [tatara'βwelo] *nm* great-great-grandfather.

tatuaje [ta'twaxe] *nm* (*dibujo*) tattoo; (*acto*) tattooing; **tatuar** *vt* to tattoo.

taumaturgo [tauma'turxo] *nm* miracle-worker.

taurino, a [tau'rino, a] *a* a bullfighting *cpd*.

Tauro ['tauro] *nm* Taurus.

tauromaquia [tauro'makja] *nf* tauromachy.

tautología [tautolo'xia] *nf* tautology.

taxi ['taksi] *nm* taxi.

taxidermia [taksi'ðermja] *nf* taxidermy.

taxista [tak'sista] *nm/f* taxi driver.

taza ['taθa] *nf* (*de retrete*) bowl; **~ para café** coffee cup; **tazón** *nm* (**~ grande**) large cup; (*escudilla*) basin.

te [te] *pron* (*complemento de objeto*) you; (*complemento indirecto*) (to) you; (*reflexivo*) (to) yourself; ¿**~ duele mucho el brazo?** does your arm hurt a lot?; **~ equivocas** you're wrong; ¡**cálma~!** calm yourself!

té [te] *nm* tea.

tea ['tea] *nf* torch.

teatral [tea'tral] *a* theatre *cpd*; (*fig*) theatrical; **teatro** *nm* (*gen*) theatre; (*LITERATURA*) plays *pl*, drama.

tebeo [te'βeo] *nm* children's comic.

tecla ['tekla] *nf* key; **~do** *nm* keyboard; **teclear** *vi* to strum; (*fam*) to drum; **tecleo** *nm* (*MUS; sonido*) strumming; (*forma de tocar*) fingering; (*fam*) drumming.

técnico, a ['tekniko, a] *a* technical // *nm* technician; (*experto*) expert // *nf* (*procedimientos*) technique; (*arte, oficio*) craft.

tecnócrata [tek'nokrata] *nm/f* technocrat.

tecnología [teknolo'xia] *nf* technology; **tecnológico, a** *a* technological; **tecnólogo** *nm* technologist.

techo ['tet∫o] *nm* (*externo*) roof; (*interno*) ceiling; **techumbre** *nf* roof.

tedio ['teðjo] *nm* (*aburrimiento*) boredom; (*apatía*) apathy; (*fastidio*) depression; **~so, a** *a* boring; (*cansado*) wearisome, tedious.

teja ['texa] *nf* (*azulejo*) tile; (*BOT*) lime (tree); **~do** *nm* (tiled) roof.

tejanos [te'xanos] *nmpl* jeans.

tejemaneje [texema'nexe] *nm* (*bullicio*) bustle; (*lío*) fuss; (*aspaviento*) to-do; (*intriga*) intrigue.

tejer [te'xer] *vt* to weave; (*AM*) to knit; (*fig*) to fabricate; **tejido** *nm* fabric; (*telaraña*) web; (*estofa, tela*) (knitted) material; (*ANAT*) tissue; (*textura*) texture.

tel, teléf *abr de* **teléfono**.

tela ['tela] *nf* (*material*) material; (*telaraña*) web; (*de fruta, en líquido*) skin; (*del ojo*) film; **telar** *nm* (*máquina*) loom; (*de teatro*) gridiron; **telares** *nmpl* textile mill *sg*.

telaraña [tela'raɲa] *nf* cobweb.

tele ['tele] *nf* (*fam*) TV.

tele... ['tele] *pref* tele...; **~comunicación** *nf* telecommunication; **~control** *nm* remote control; **~diario** *nm* television news;

~difusión nf (television) broadcast; ~dirigido, a a remote-controlled; ~férico nm (tren) cable-railway; (de esquí) ski-lift; ~fonear vi to telephone; ~fónico, a a telephone cpd; ~fonista nm/f telephonist; teléfono nm telephone; ~foto nf telephoto; ~grafía nf telegraphy; telégrafo nm telegraph, (fam: persona) telegraph boy; ~grama nm telegram; ~impresor nm teleprinter; telémetro nm rangefinder; ~objetivo nm telephoto lens; ~pático, a a telepathic; ~scópico, a a telescopic; ~scopio nm telescope; ~silla nf chairlift; ~spectador, a nm/f viewer; ~squi nm ski-lift; ~tipista nm/f teletypist; ~tipo nm teletype; ~vidente nm/f viewer; ~visar vt to televise; ~visión nf television; ~visión en colores colour television; ~visor nm television set

telex [te'leks] nm telex.

telón [te'lon] nm curtain; ~ de boca/seguridad front/safety curtain; ~ de acero (POL) iron curtain; ~ de fondo backcloth, background.

tema ['tema] nm (asunto) subject, topic; (MUS) theme // nf (obsesión) obsession; (manía) ill-will; tener ~ a uno to have a grudge against sb; temático, a a thematic.

tembladera [tembla'ðera] nf shaking // nm.

temblar [tem'blar] vi to shake, tremble; (de frío) to shiver; tembleque a shaking // nm = tembladera; temblón, ona a shaking; temblor nm trembling; (AM: de tierra) earthquake; tembloroso, a a trembling.

temer [te'mer] vt to fear // vi to be afraid; temo que llegue tarde I am afraid he may be late.

temerario, a [teme'rarjo, a] a (descuidado) reckless; (arbitrario) hasty; temeridad nf (imprudencia) rashness; (audacia) boldness.

temeroso, a [teme'roso, a] a

(miedoso) fearful; (que inspira temor) frightful.

temible [te'miβle] a fearsome.

temor [te'mor] nm (miedo) fear; (duda) suspicion.

témpano ['tempano] nm (MUS) kettledrum; ~ de hielo ice-flow; ~ de tocino flitch of bacon.

temperamento [tempera'mento] nm temperament.

temperatura [tempera'tura] nf temperature.

temperie [tem'perje] nf state of the weather.

tempestad [tempes'taδ] nf storm; tempestuoso, a a stormy.

templado, a [tem'plaðo, a] a (moderado) moderate; (: en el comer) frugal; (: en el beber) abstemious; (agua) lukewarm; (clima) mild; (MUS) well-tuned; templanza nf moderation; abstemiousness; mildness.

templar [tem'plar] vt (moderar) to moderate; (furia) to restrain; (calor) to reduce; (solución) to dilute; (afinar) to tune (up); (acero) to temper; (fierza) to tighten up // vi to moderate; ~se vr to be restrained; temple nm (humor) mood; (ajuste) tempering; (afinación) tuning; (clima) temperature; (pintura) tempera.

templete [tem'plete] nm bandstand.

templo ['templo] nm (iglesia) church; (pagano etc) temple.

temporada [tempo'raða] nf time, period; (estación) season.

temporal [tempo'ral] a (no permanente) temporary; (REL) temporal // nm storm.

temporero, a [tempo'rero, a] (BOT) early; (persona) early-rising.

temprano, a [tem'prano, a] a early; (demasiado pronto) too soon, too early.

ten vb ver tener.

tenacidad [tenaθi'ðaδ] nf (gen)

tenacity; (*dureza*) toughness; (*terquedad*) stubbornness.

tenacillas [tena'θiλas] *nfpl* (*gen*) tongs; (*para el pelo*) curling tongs; (*MED*) forceps.

tenaz [te'naθ] *a* (*material*) tough; (*persona*) tenacious; (*pegajoso*) sticky; (*terco*) stubborn.

tenaza(s) [te'naθa(s)] *nf(pl)* (*MED*) forceps; (*TEC*) pliers; (*ZOOL*) pincers.

tendal [ten'dal] *nm* awning.

tendedero [tende'ðero] *nm* (*para ropa*) drying-place; (*cuerda*) clothes line.

tendencia [ten'denθja] *nf* tendency; (*proceso*) trend; **tener ~ a** to tend to or have a tendency to; **tendencioso, a** a tendentious.

tender [ten'der] *vt* (*extender*) to spread out; (*colgar*) to hang out; (*vía férrea, cable*) to lay; (*cuerda*) to stretch // *vi* to tend; **~se** *vr* to lie down; (*fig: dejarse llevar*) to let o.s. go; (: *dejar ir*) to let things go; **~ la cama/la mesa** (*AM*) to make the bed/lay the table.

ténder ['tender] *nm* tender.

tenderete [tende'rete] *nm* (*puesto*) stall; (*carretilla*) barrow; (*exposición*) display of goods; (*jaleo*) mess.

tendero, a [ten'dero, a] *nm/f* shopkeeper.

tendido, a [ten'diðo, a] *a* (*acostado*) lying down, flat; (*colgado*) hanging // *nm* (*ropa*) washing; (*TAUR*) front rows of seats; (*colocación*) laying; (*ARQ: enyesado*) coat of plaster; **a galope ~** flat out.

tendón [ten'don] *nm* tendon.

tendré *etc vb ver* **tener.**

tenducho [ten'dutʃo] *nm* small dirty shop.

tenebroso, a [tene'ßroso, a] *a* (*oscuro*) dark; (*fig*) gloomy; (*siniestro*) sinister.

tenedor [tene'ðor] *nm* (*CULIN*) fork; (*poseedor*) holder; **~ de libros** book-keeper.

teneduría [teneðu'ria] *nf* keeping;

~ de libros book-keeping.

tenencia [te'nenθja] *nf* (*de casa*) tenancy; (*de oficio*) tenure; (*de propiedad*) possession.

tener [te'ner] *vt* (*poseer*) to have; (*en la mano*) to hold; (*caja*) to hold, contain; (*considerar*) to consider; **~ suerte** to be lucky; **~ permiso** to have permission; **tiene 10 años** he is 10 years old; **¿cuántos años tienes?** how old are you?; **~ sed/hambre/frío/calor** to be thirsty/hungry/cold/hot; **~ ganas (de)** to want (to); **~ celos** to be jealous; **~ cuidado** to be careful; **~ razón** to be right; **~ un metro de ancho/de largo** to be one metre wide/long; **~ a bien** to see fit to; **~ en cuenta** to bear in mind, take into account; **~ a menos** to consider it beneath o.s.; **~ a uno en más (estima)** to think all the more of sb; **~ a uno por...** to think sb...; **~ por seguro** to be sure; **~ presente** to remember, bear in mind; **~ que** (*obligación*) to have to; **tiene que ser así** it has to be this way; **nos tiene preparada una sorpresa** he has prepared a surprise for us; **¿qué tiene?** what's the matter with him?; **¿ésas tenemos?** what's all this?; **tiene un mes de muerto** he has been dead for a month; **~se** *vr* (*erguirse*) to stand; (*apoyarse*) to lean (on); (*fig*) to control o.s.; (*considerarse*) to consider o.s.

tenería [tene'ria] *nf* tannery.

tengo *etc vb ver* **tener.**

tenia ['tenja] *nf* tapeworm.

teniente [te'njente] *nm* (*rango*) lieutenant; (*ayudante*) deputy.

tenis ['tenis] *nm* tennis; **~ta** *nm/f* tennis player.

tenor [te'nor] *nm* (*tono*) tone; (*sentido*) meaning; (*MUS*) tenor; **a ~ de** on the lines of.

tensar [ten'sar] *vt* to tauten; (*arco*) to draw.

tensión [ten'sjon] *nf* (*gen*) tension; (*TEC*) stress; (*MED*): **~ arterial**

blood pressure; tener la ~ alta to
have high blood pressure; **tenso, a** a
tense.
tentación [tenta'θjon] nf temptation.
tentáculo [ten'takulo] nm tentacle.
tentador, a [tenta'ðor, a] a
tempting // nm/f tempter/temptress.
tentar [ten'tar] vt (tocar) to touch,
feel; (seducir) to tempt; (atraer) to
attract; (probar) to try (out);
(lanzarse a) to venture; (MED) to
probe; **tentativa** nf attempt;
tentativa de asesinato attempted
murder.
tentempié [tentem'pje] nm (fam)
snack.
tenue ['tenwe] a (delgado) thin,
slender; (alambre) fine; (insubstancial) tenuous; (sonido) faint,
(neblina) light; (lazo, vínculo) slight;
tenuidad nf thinness, fineness;
(ligereza) lightness; (sencillez) simplicity.
teñir [te'nir] vt to dye; (fig) to tinge;
~se vr to dye; ~se el pelo to dye
one's hair.
teología [teolo'xia] nf theology.
teorema [teo'rema] nm theorem.
teoría [teo'ria] nf theory; en ~ in
theory; **teóricamente** ad theoretically; **teórico, a** a theoretic(al) //
nm/f theoretician, theorist; **teorizar**
vi to theorize.
terapéutico, a [tera'peutiko, a] a
therapeutic.
terapia [te'rapja] nf therapy; ~
laboral occupational therapy.
tercer [ter'θer] a ver tercero.
tercero [terθ'e̶ro] vi (mediación)
mediation; (arbitraje) arbitration.
tercero, tercer, a [ter'θero,
ter'θer, a] a (third) // nm (árbitro)
mediator; (JUR) third party.
terceto [ter'θeto] nm trio.
terciado, a [ter'θjaðo, a] a slanting;
azúcar ~ brown sugar.
terciar [ter'θjar] vt (MAT) to divide
into three; (inclinarse) to slope;

(llevar) to wear (across the
shoulder) // vi (participar) to take
part; (hacer de árbitro) to mediate;
~se vr to come up; ~io, a a
tertiary.
tercio ['terθjo] nm third.
terciopelo [terθjo'pelo] nm velvet.
terco, a ['terko, a] a obstinate;
(material) tough.
tergiversación [terxiβersa'θjon]
nf (deformación) distortion; (evasivas) prevarication; **tergiversar** (evtensiva) to distort // vi to prevaricate.
termas ['termas] nfpl hot springs.
terminación [termina'θjon] nf
(final) end; (conclusión) conclusion,
ending; **terminal** a, nm, nf terminal;
terminante a (final) final,
definitive; (gigante) categorical,
terminar nf (simplificar) to
complete, finish; (concluir) to end //
vi (llegar a su fin) to end; (parar) to
stop; (acabar) to finish; **terminarse**
vr to come to an end; **terminar por
hacer algo** to end up (by) doing sth;
término nm end, conclusion;
(parada) terminus; (límite)
boundary; **término medio** average;
(fig) middle way; en último término
(a fin de cuentas) in the last
analysis; (como último recurso) as a
last resort; **en términos de** in terms
of.
terminología [terminolo'xia] nf
terminology.
termodinámico, a [termoði'namiko, a] a thermodynamic.
termómetro [ter'mometro] nm
thermometer.
termonuclear [termonukle'ar] a
thermonuclear.
termo(s) ['termo(s)] nm thermos.
termostato [termo'stato] nm
thermostat.
ternero, a [ter'nero, a] nm/f
(animal) calf // nf (carne) veal.
terneza [ter'neθa] nf tenderness.
terno ['terno] nm (traje) threepiece suit; (conjunto) set of three.
ternura [ter'nura] nf (trato)

tenderness; (*palabra*) endearment; (*cariño*) fondness.

terquedad [terke'ðað] *nf* obstinacy; (*dureza*) harshness.

terrado [te'rraðo] *nm* terrace.

terraplén [terra'plen] *nm* (AGR) terrace; (FERRO) embankment; (MIL) rampart; (*cuesta*) slope.

terrateniente [terrate'njente] *nm* landowner.

terraza [te'rraθa] *nf* (*balcón*) balcony; (*techo*) flat roof; (AGR) terrace.

terremoto [terre'moto] *nm* earthquake.

terrenal [terre'nal] *a* earthly.

terreno [te'rreno] *nm* (*tierra*) land; (*parcela*) plot; (*suelo*) soil; (*fig*) field; **un ~** a piece of land.

terrero, a [te'rrero, a] *a* (*de la tierra*) earthy; (*vuelo*) low; (*fig*) humble.

terrestre [te'rrestre] *a* terrestrial; (*ruta*) land *cpd*.

terrible [te'rrißle] *a* (*espantoso*) terrible; (*aterrador*) dreadful; (*tremendo*) awful.

territorio [terri'torjo] *nm* territory.

terrón [te'rron] *nm* (*de azúcar*) lump; (*de tierra*) clod, lump; **terrones** *nmpl* land sg.

terror [te'rror] *nm* terror; **~ífico, a** a terrifying; **~ista** a, *nm/f* terrorist.

terroso, a [te'rroso, a] *a* earthy.

terruño [te'rruno] *nm* (*pedazo*) clod; (*parcela*) plot; (*fig*) native soil.

terso, a ['terso, a] *a* (*liso*) smooth; (*pulido*) polished; (*fig*: *estilo*) flowing; **tersura** *nf* smoothness; (*brillo*) shine.

tertulia [ter'tulja] *nf* (*reunión informal*) social gathering; (*grupo*) group, circle; (*sala*) cloobroom.

tesar [te'sar] *vt* to tighten up.

tesis ['tesis] *nf inv* thesis.

tesón [te'son] *nm* (*firmeza*) firmness; (*tenacidad*) tenacity.

tesorero, a [teso'rero, a] *nm/f* treasurer; **tesoro** *nm* (*gen*)

treasure; (FIN, POL) treasury.

testaferro [testa'ferro] *nm* figurehead.

testamentaría [testamenta'ria] *nf* execution of a will.

testamentario, a [testamen-'tarjo, a] *a* testamentary // *nm/f* executor/executrix; **testamento** *nm* will; **testar** *vi* to make a will.

testarudo, a [testa'ruðo, a] *a* stubborn.

testero, a [tes'tero, a] *nm/f* (*gen*) front // *nm* (ARQ) front wall.

testes ['testes] *nmpl* testes.

testículo [tes'tikulo] *nm* testicle.

testificar [testifi'kar] *vt* to testify; (*fig*) to attest // *vi* to give evidence.

testigo [tes'tivo] *nm/f* witness; **~ de cargo/descargo** witness for the prosecution/defence; **~ ocular** eye witness.

testimoniar [testimo'njar] *vt* to testify to; (*fig*) to show; **testimonio** *nm* testimony.

teta ['teta] *nf* (*de biberón*) teat; (ANAT) nipple; (*fam*) breast.

tétanos ['tetanos] *nm* tetanus.

tetera [te'tera] *nf* teapot.

tetilla [te'tiʎa] *nf* (ANAT) nipple; (*de biberón*) teat.

tétrico, a ['tetriko, a] *a* gloomy, dismal.

textil [teks'til] *a* textile; **~es** *nmpl* textiles.

texto ['teksto] *nm* text; **textual** *a* textual.

textura [teks'tura] *nf* (*de tejido*) texture; (*de mineral*) structure.

tez [teθ] *nf* (*cutis*) complexion; (*color*) colouring.

ti [ti] *pron* you; (*reflexivo*) yourself.

tía ['tia] *nf* (*pariente*) aunt; (*mujer cualquiera*) girl, bird (*col*); (*fam*: *pej*: *vieja*) old bag; (: *prostituta*) whore.

tibia ['tißja] *nf* tibia.

tibieza [ti'ßjeθa] *nf* (*temperatura*) tepidness; (*fig*) coolness; **tibio, a** *a* lukewarm.

tiburón [tißu'ron] *nm* shark.

tic [tik] *nm* (*ruido*) click; (*de reloj*) tick; (*MED*): ~ **nervioso** nervous tic.

tictac [tik'tak] *nm* (*de reloj*) tick tock.

tiempo ['tjempo] *nm* (*gen*) time; (*época, período*) age, period; (*METEOROLOGÍA*) weather; (*LING*) tense; (*edad*) age, (*de juego*) half; **a** ~ **in time; a un o al mismo** ~ **at the same time; al poco** ~ **very soon** (after); **de** ~ **en** ~ **from time to time; hace buen/mal** ~ **the weather is fine/bad; estar a** ~ **to be in time; hace** ~ **some time ago; hacer** ~ **to while away the time; motor de 2** ~ **s two-stroke engine.**

tienda ['tjenda] *nf* (*gen*) shop; (*más grande*) store; (*NAUT*) awning; ~ **de campaña** tent.

tienes *etc vb ver* **tener.**

tienta ['tjenta] *nf* (*MED*) probe; (*fig*) tact; **andar a** ~ **s** to grope one's way along.

tiento ['tjento] *nm* (*tacto*) touch; (*precaución*) wariness; (*pulso*) steady hand; (*ZOOL*) feeler; (*de ciego*) blind man's stick.

tierno, a ['tjerno, a] *a* (*blando, dulce*) tender; (*fresco*) fresh.

tierra ['tjerra] *nf* earth; (*suelo*) soil; (*mundo*) world; (*país*) country, land; ~ **adentro** inland.

tieso, a ['tjeso, a] *a* (*rígido*) rigid, (*duro*) stiff; (*fig: testarudo*) stubborn; (*fam: orgulloso*) conceited // *ad* strongly.

tiesto ['tjesto] *nm* flowerpot; (*pedazo*) piece of pottery.

tiesura [tje'sura] *nf* rigidity; (*fig*) stubbornness; (*fam*) conceit.

tifo ['tifo] *nm* typhus.

tifoidea [tifoi'ðea] *nf* typhoid.

tifón [ti'fon] *nm* (*huracán*) typhoon; (*de mar*) tidal wave.

tifus ['tifus] *nm* typhus.

tigre ['tixre] *nm* tiger.

tijera [ti'xera] *nf* (*AM*) scissors *pl*; (*ZOOL*) claw; (*persona*) gossip; **de** ~ folding; ~ **s** *nfpl* scissors; (*para*

plantas*) shears; **tijeretear** *vt* to snip // *vi* (*fig*) to meddle.

tildar [til'dar] *vt*: ~ **de** to brand as.

tilde ['tilde] *nf* (*defecto*) defect; (*trivialidad*) triviality; (*TIPOGRAFÍA*) tilde.

tilín [ti'lin] *nm* tinkle.

tilo ['tilo] *nm* lime tree.

timar [ti'mar] *vt* (*robar*) to steal; (*estafar*) to swindle; ~ **se** *vr* (*fam*) to make eyes (*con uno*) (*a uno*).

timbal [tim'bal] *nm* small drum.

timbrar [tim'brar] *vt* to stamp.

timbre ['timbre] *nm* (*sello*) stamp; (*campanilla*) bell; (*tono*) timbre; (*COM*) stamp duty.

timidez [timi'ðeθ] *nf* shyness; timidity; **tímido, a** *a* shy.

timo ['timo] *nm* swindle.

timón [ti'mon] *nm* helm, rudder; **timonel** *nm* helmsman.

tímpano ['timpano] *nm* (*ANAT*) eardrum; (*MUS*) small drum.

tina ['tina] *nf* tub; (*baño*) bathtub; **tinaja** *nf* large jar.

tinglado [tiŋ'glaðo] *nm* (*cobertizo*) shed; (*fig: truco*) trick; (*intriga*) intrigue.

tinieblas [ti'njeβlas] *nfpl* (*gen*) darkness *sg*; (*sombras*) shadows.

tino ['tino] *nm* (*habilidad*) skill; (*MIL*) marksmanship; (*juicio*) insight; (*moderación*) moderation.

tinta ['tinta] *nf* ink; (*TEC*) dye; (*ARTE*) colour.

tinte ['tinte] *nm* (*acto*) dyeing; (*carácter*) tinge; (*barniz*) veneer.

tinterillo [tinte'riʎo] *nm* pen pusher.

tintero [tin'tero] *nm* inkwell.

tintinear [tintine'ar] *vt* to tinkle.

tinto, a ['tinto, a] *a* (*teñido*) dyed; (*manchado*) stained // *nm* red wine.

tintorera [tinto'rera] *nf* shark.

tintorería [tintore'ria] *nf* dry cleaner's.

tintura [tin'tura] *nf* (*acto*) dyeing; (*QUÍMICA*) dye; (*farmacéutico*) tincture.

tío ['tio] *nm* (*pariente*) uncle; (*fam:*

viejo) old fellow; (: *individuo*), bloke, chap.

tiovivo [tio'ßißo] *nm* roundabout.

típico, a ['tipiko, a] *a* typical.

tiple ['tiple] *nm* soprano (voice) // *nf* soprano.

tipo ['tipo] *nm* (*clase*) type, kind; (*norma*) norm; (*patrón*) pattern; (*hombre*) fellow; (ANAT) build; (: *de mujer*) figure; (IMPRENTA) type; ~ **bancario/de descuento/de interés/de cambio** bank/discount/interest/exchange rate.

tipografía [tipoxra'fia] *nf* (*tipo*) printing; (*aparato*) printing press; **tipográfico, a** *a* printing; **tipógrafo, a** *nm/f* printer.

tiquismiquis [tikis'mikis] *nm* fussy person // *nmpl* (*querellas*) squabbling *sg*; (*escrúpulos*) silly scruples.

tira ['tira] *nf* strip; (*fig*) abundance; ~ **y afloja** give and take.

tirabuzón [tiraßu'θon] *nm* corkscrew.

tirado, a [ti'raðo, a] *a* (*barato*) dirtcheap; (*fam*: *fácil*) very easy // *nf* (*acto*) cast, throw; (*distancia*) distance; (*serie*) series; (TIPOGRAFÍA) printing, edition; **de una ~a** at one go.

tirador [tira'ðor] *nm* (*mango*) handle; (ELEC) flex.

tiranía [tira'nia] *nf* tyranny; **tirano, a** *a* tyrannical // *nm/f* tyrant.

tirante [ti'rante] *a* (*cuerda*) tight, taut; (*relaciones*) strained // *nm* (ARQ) brace; (TEC) stay; (*correa*) shoulder strap; ~**s** *nmpl* braces; **tirantez** *nf* tightness; (*fig*) tension.

tirar [ti'rar] *vt* (*aventar*) to throw; (*dejar caer*) to drop; (*volcar*) to upset; (*derribar*) to knock down or over; (*jalar*) to pull; (*desechar*) to throw out or away; (*disipar*) to squander; (*imprimir*) to print; (*dar*: *golpe*) to deal // *vi* (*disparar*) to shoot; (*jalar*) to pull; (*fig*) to draw; (*fam*: *andar*) to go; (*tender a, buscar realizar*) to tend to; (DEPORTE) to

tiovivo [tio'ßiß] *nm* roundabout.

shoot; ~**se** *vr* to throw o.s.; (*fig*) to cheapen o.s.; ~ **abajo** to bring down, destroy; **tira más a su padre** he takes more after his father; **ir tirando** to manage; **a todo ~** at the most.

tirita [ti'rita] *nf* (sticking) plaster.

tiritar [tiri'tar] *vi* to shiver.

tiro ['tiro] *nm* (*lanzamiento*) throw; (*disparo*) shot; (*disparar*) shooting; (DEPORTE) drive; (*alcance*) range; (*de escalera*) flight (of stairs); (*golpe*) blow; (*engaño*) hoax; ~ **al blanco** target practice; **caballo de** ~ cart-horse; **andar de ~s largos** to be all dressed up; **al** ~ (AM) at once.

tirón [ti'ron] *nm* (*sacudida*) pull, tug; **de un** ~ in one go.

tirotear [tirote'ar] *vt* to shoot at; ~**se** *vr* to exchange shots; **tiroteo** *nm* exchange of shots, shooting.

tísico, a ['tisiko, a] *a* consumptive.

títere ['titere] *nm* puppet.

titilar [titi'lar] *vi* (*luz, estrella*) to twinkle; (*parpado*) to flutter.

titiritero, a [titiri'tero, a] *nm/f* puppeteer.

titubeante [titußé'ante] *a* (*inestable*) shaky, tottering; (*farfullante*) stammering; (*dudoso*) hesitant; **titubear** *vi* to stagger; (*fig*) to hesitate; **titubeo** *nm* staggering; stammering; hesitation.

titulado, a [titu'laðo, a] *a* (*libro*) entitled; (*persona*) titled; **titular** *a* titular // *nm/f* occupant // *nm* headline // *vt* to title; **titularse** *vr* to be entitled; **título** *nm* (*gen*) title; (*de diario*) headline; (*certificado*) professional qualification; (*universitario*) university degree; (*fig*) right; **a título de** in the capacity of.

tiza ['tiθa] *nf* chalk.

tizna ['tiθna] *nf* grime; **tiznar** *vt* to blacken; (*fig*) to tarnish.

tizón [ti'θon], **tizo** ['tiθo] *nm* brand; (*fig*) stain.

toalla [to'aʎa] *nf* towel.

tobillo [to'ßiʎo] *nm* ankle.

tobogán [toβoˈxan] nm toboggan; (montaña rusa) switchback; (resbaladilla) chute, slide.

toca [ˈtoka] nf headdress.

tocadiscos [tokaˈðiskos] nm inv record player.

tocado, a [toˈkaðo, a] a rotten; (fam) touched // nm headdress.

tocador [tokaˈðor] nm (mueble) dressing table; (cuarto) boudoir; (neceser) toilet case; (fam) ladies' toilet.

tocante [toˈkante]: ~ a prep with regard to.

tocar [toˈkar] vt to touch; (MUS) to play; (topar con) to run into, strike; (referirse a) to allude to; (padecer) to suffer; (el pelo) to do // vi (a la puerta) to knock (on or at the door); (ser de turno) to fall to, be the turn of; (ser hora) to be due; (barco, avión) to call at; (atañer) to concern; ~se vr (cubrirse la cabeza) to cover one's head; (tener contacto) to touch (each other); por lo que a mí me toca as far as I am concerned; esto toca en la locura this verges on madness.

tocayo, a [toˈkajo, a] nm/f namesake.

tocino [toˈθino] nm bacon.

todavía [toðaˈβia] ad (aun) still; (aún) yet; ~ más yet more; ~ no not yet.

todo, a [ˈtoðo, a] a all; (cada) every; (entero) whole; (sentido negativo): en ~ el día lo he visto I haven't seen him all day; ~as las semanas/~s los martes every week/Tuesday // ad all, completely // pron: everything / pron: ~s/~as everyone; a ~a velocidad at full speed; estaba ~ ojos he was all eyes; puede ser ~ lo honesto que quiera he can be as honest as he likes; ante ~ above all; en un ~ as a whole; corriendo y ~, no llegaron a tiempo even though they ran, they still didn't arrive in time; con ~ ... still, even so; del ~ completely.

todopoderoso, a [toðopoðeˈroso, a] a all powerful; (REL) almighty.

toga [ˈtoɣa] nf toga; (ESCOL) gown.

Tokio [ˈtokjo] n Tokyo.

toldo [ˈtoldo] nm (para el sol) sunshade; (tienda) marquee; (fig) pride.

tole [ˈtole] nm (fam) commotion.

tolerable [toleˈraβle] a tolerable; **tolerancia** nf tolerance; **tolerar** vt to tolerate; (resistir) to endure.

toma [ˈtoma] nf (gen) taking; (MED) dose.

tomar [toˈmar] vt (gen) to take; (aspecto) to take on; (beber) to drink // vi to take; (AM) to drink; ~se vr por to consider o.s. to be; ~ a bien/a mal to take well/badly; ~ en serio to take seriously; ~ el pelo a alguien to pull sb's leg; ~la con uno to pick a quarrel with sb.

tomate [toˈmate] nm tomato; ~ra nf tomato plant.

tomillo [toˈmiʎo] nm thyme.

tomo [ˈtomo] nm (libro) volume; (tamaño) size; (fig) importance.

ton [ton] abr de **tonelada** // nm: sin ~ ni son without rhyme or reason.

tonada [toˈnaða] nf tune.

tonalidad [tonaliˈðað] nf tone.

tonel [toˈnel] nm barrel.

tonelada [toneˈlaða] nf ton; **tonelaje** nm tonnage.

tonelero [toneˈlero] nm cooper.

tónico, a [ˈtoniko, a] a tonic // nm (MED) tonic // nf (MUS) tonic; (fig) keynote.

tonificar [tonifiˈkar] vt to tone up.

tonillo [toˈniʎo] nm monotonous voice.

tono [ˈtono] nm tone; fuera de ~ inappropriate; darse ~ to put on airs.

tontería [tonteˈria] nf (cualidad) foolishness; (una ~) stupid remark; ~s nfpl rubbish sg, nonsense sg.

tonto, a [ˈtonto, a] a stupid; (sentimental) silly // nm/f fool; (payaso) clown.

topacio [to'paθjo] nm topaz.

topar [to'par] vt (tropezar) to bump into; (encontrar) to find, come across; (ZOOL) to butt // vi: ~ **contra** o en to run into; ~ **con** to run up against; **el problema topa en eso** that's where the problem lies.

tope ['tope] a maximum // nm (fin) end; (límite) limit; (riña) quarrel; (FERRO) buffer; (AUTO) bumper; **al** ~ end to end.

tópico, a ['topiko, a] a topical // nm platitude.

topo ['topo] nm (ZOOL) mole; (fig) blunderer.

topografía [topoxra'fia] nf topography; **topógrafo, a** nm/f topographer.

toque ['toke] nm touch; (MUS) beat; (de campana) peal; (fig) crux; **dar un** ~ a to test; ~ **de queda** curfew; ~**tear** vt to handle.

toquilla [to'kiʎa] nf (bufanda) headscarf; (chal) shawl.

torbellino [torbe'ʎino] nm whirlwind; (fig) whirl.

torcedura [torθe'ðura] nf twist; (MED) sprain.

torcer [tor'θer] vt to twist; (la esquina) to turn; (MED) to sprain; (cuerda) to plait; (ropa, manos) to wring; (persona) to corrupt // vi (desviar) to turn off; (pelota) to spin; ~**se** vr (ladearse) to bend; (desviarse) to go astray; (fracasar) to go wrong; **torcido, a** a twisted // (fig) crooked // nm curl.

tordo [a 'torðo, a] a dappled // nm thrush.

torear [tore'ar] vt (fig: evadir) to avoid; (jugar con) to toy with // vi to fight bulls; **toreo** nm bullfighting; **torero, a** nm/f bullfighter.

tormenta [tor'menta] nf storm; (fig: confusión) turmoil; (desgracia) misfortune.

tormento [tor'mento] nm torture; (fig) anguish.

tornar [tor'nar] vt (devolver) to return, give back; (transformar) to

transform // vi to go back; ~**se** vr (ponerse) to become; (volver) to return.

tornasol [torna'sol] nm (BOT) sunflower; **papel de** ~ litmus paper; ~**ado, a** a (brillante) iridescent; (reluciente) shimmering.

torneo [tor'neo] nm tournament.

tornero, a [tor'nero, a] nm/f machinist.

tornillo [tor'niʎo] nm screw.

torniquete [torni'kete] nm (puerta) turnstile; (MED) tourniquet.

torno ['torno] nm (TEC) winch; (tambor) drum; **en** ~ (a) round, about.

toro ['toro] nm bull; (fam) he-man; **los** ~**s** bullfighting.

toronja [to'ronxa] nf grapefruit.

torpe ['torpe] a (poco hábil) clumsy, awkward; (necio) dim; (lento) slow; (indecente) crude; (no honrado) dishonest.

torpedo [tor'peðo] nm torpedo.

torpeza [tor'peθa] nf (falta de agilidad) clumsiness; (lentitud) slowness; (rigidez) stiffness; (error) mistake; (crudeza) obscenity.

torre ['torre] nf tower; (de petróleo) derrick.

torrente [to'rrente] nm torrent.

tórrido, a ['torriðo, a] a torrid.

torrija [to'rrixa] nf fried bread; ~**s** French toast sg.

torsión [tor'sjon] nf twisting.

torso ['torso] nm torso.

torta ['torta] nf cake; (fam) slap.

tortícolis [tor'tikolis] nm stiff neck.

tortilla [tor'tiʎa] nf omelette; (AM) maize pancake; ~ **francesa/española** plain/potato omelette.

tórtola ['tortola] nf turtledove.

tortuga [tor'tuxa] nf tortoise.

tortuoso, a [tor'twoso, a] a winding.

tortura [tor'tura] nf torture; **torturar** vt to torture.

tos [tos] nf cough; ~ **ferina** whooping cough.

tosco, a ['tosko, a] a coarse.

toser [to'ser] *vi* to cough.

tostado, a [tos'taðo, a] *a* toasted; *(por el sol)* dark brown; *(piel)* tanned // *nf* tan; **tostador** *nm* toaster; **tostar** *vt* to toast; *(café)* to roast; *(al sol)* to tan; **tostarse** *vr* to get brown.

total [to'tal] *a* total // *ad* in short, *(al fin y al cabo)* when all is said and done // *nm* total; **~ que** to cut a long story short.

totalidad [totali'ðað] *nf* whole.

totalitario, a [totali'tarjo, a] *a* totalitarian.

tóxico, a ['toksiko, a] *a* toxic // *nm* poison.

tozudo, a [to'θuðo, a] *a* obstinate.

traba ['traβa] *nf* bond, tie; *(cadena)* fetter.

trabajador, a [traβaxa'ðor, a] *nm/f* worker // *a* hard-working.

trabajar [traβa'xar] *vt* to work; *(arar)* to till; *(empeñarse en)* to work at; *(empujar: persona)* to push; *(convencer)* to persuade // *vi* to work; *(esforzarse)* to strive; **trabajo** *nm* work; *(tarea)* task; *(POL)* labour; *(fig)* effort; **tomarse el trabajo de** to take the trouble to; **trabajo por turno/a destajo** shift work/piecework; **trabajoso, a** *a* hard; *(MED)* pale.

trabalenguas [traβa'lengwas] *nm inv* tongue twister.

trabar [tra'βar] *vt* (juntar) to join, unite; *(atar)* to tie down, fetter; *(agarrar)* to seize; *(amistad)* to strike up; **~se** *vr* to become entangled; *(reñir)* to squabble; **trabazón** *nf* (TEC) joining, assembly; *(fig)* bond, link.

trabucar [traβu'kar] *vt* (confundir) to confuse, mix up; *(palabras)* to misplace.

tracción [trak'θjon] *nf* traction; **~ delantera/trasera** front wheel/rear wheel drive.

tractor [trak'tor] *nm* tractor.

tradición [traði'θjon] *nf* tradition; **tradicional** *a* traditional.

traducción [traðuk'θjon] *nf* translation; **traducir** *vt* to translate; **traductor, a** *nm/f* translator.

traer [tra'er] *vt* (gen) to bring; *(llevar)* to carry; *(ropa)* to wear; *(imán)* to draw; *(incluir)* to carry; *(fig)* to cause; **~se** *vr*: **~se algo** to be up to sth; **~se bien/mal** to dress well/badly.

traficar [trafi'kar] *vi* to trade.

tráfico ['trafiko] *nm* (COM) trade, (AUTO) traffic.

tragaluz [traɣa'luθ] *nm* skylight.

tragamonedas [traɣamo'neðas] *nm inv*, **tragaperras** [traɣa'perras] *nm inv* slot machine.

tragar [tra'ɣar] *vt* to swallow; *(devorar)* to devour, bolt down; **~se** *vr* to swallow.

tragedia [tra'xeðja] *nf* tragedy; **trágico, a** *a* tragic.

trago ['traɣo] *nm* (líquido) drink; *(comida de golpe)* gulp; *(fam: de bebida)* swig; *(desgracia)* blow.

traición [trai'θjon] *nf* treachery; *(JUR)* treason; *(una ~)* act of treachery; **traicionar** *vt* to betray; **traidor, a, traicionero, a** *a* treacherous // *nm/f* traitor.

traigo etc vb ver **traer**.

traje ['traxe] *vb ver* **traer** // *nm* (gen) dress; *(de hombre)* suit; *(vestimenta típica)* costume; *(fig)* garb; **~ de baño** swimsuit; **~ de luces** bullfighter's costume.

trajera etc vb ver **traer**.

trajín [tra'xin] *nm* haulage; *(fam: movimiento)* bustle; **trajines** *nmpl* goings-on; **trajinar** *vt* (llevar) to carry, transport // *vi* (moverse) to bustle about; *(viajar)* to travel around.

trama ['trama] *nf* (fig) link; *(: intriga)* plot; *(de tejido)* weft; **tramar** *vt* to plot; *(TEC)* to weave.

tramitar [trami'tar] *vt* (asunto) to transact; *(negociar)* to negotiate; *(manejar)* to handle; **trámite** *nm* (paso) step; *(JUR)* transaction; **trámites** *nmpl* (burocracia) paperwork *sg*, procedures; (*JUR*) proceedings.

tramo ['tramo] *nm* (*de tierra*) plot; (*de escalera*) flight; (*de vía*) section.

tramoya [tra'moja] *nf* (*TEATRO*) piece of stage machinery; (*fig*) trick; **tramoyista** *nm/f* scene shifter; (*fig*) trickster.

trampa ['trampa] *nf* (*gen*) trap; (*en el suelo*) trapdoor; (*prestidigitación*) conjuring trick; (*engaño*) trick; (*fam*) fiddle; (*de pantalón*) fly; **trampear** *vt, vi* to cheat; **trampista** *nm/f* = **tramposo**.

trampolín [trampo'lin] *nm* trampoline; (*de piscina etc*) diving board.

tramposo, a [tram'poso, a] *a* crooked, cheating // *nm/f* crook, cheat.

tranca ['tranka] *nf* (*palo*) stick; (*viga*) beam; (*de puerta, ventana*) bar; **trancar** *vt* to bar // *vi* to stride along.

trance ['tranθe] *nm* (*momento difícil*) difficult moment; (*situación crítica*) critical situation; (*estado hipnotizado*) trance.

tranco ['tranko] *nm* stride.

tranquilidad [trankili'ðað] *nf* (*calma*) calmness, stillness; (*paz*) peacefulness; **tranquilizar** *vt* (*calmar*) to calm (down); (*asegurar*) to reassure; **tranquilo, a** *a* (*calmado*) calm; (*apacible*) peaceful; (*mar*) calm; (*mente*) untroubled.

transacción [transak'θjon] *nf* transaction.

transar [tran'sar] *vt* = **transigir**.

transbordador [transβorða'ðor] *nm* ferry.

transbordar [transβor'ðar] *vt* to transfer; **~se** *vr* to change; **transbordo** *nm* transfer; **hacer transbordo** to change (trains).

transcurrir [transku'rrir] *vi* (*tiempo*) to pass; (*hecho*) to turn out.

transcurso [trans'kurso] *nm:* ~

del tiempo lapse (of time).

transeúnte [transe'unte] *a* transient // *nm/f* passer-by.

transferencia [transfe'renθja] *nf* transference; (*COM*) transfer; **transferir** *vt* to transfer; (*de tiempo*) to postpone.

transfigurar [transfixu'rar] *vt* to transfigure.

transformador [transforma'ðor] *nm* transformer.

transformar [transfor'mar] *vt* to transform; (*convertirse*) to convert.

tránsfuga ['transfuxa] *nm/f* (*MIL*) deserter; (*POL*) turncoat.

transgresión [transxre'sjon] *nf* transgression.

transición [transi'θjon] *nf* transition.

transido, a [tran'siðo, a] *a* overcome.

transigir [transi'xir] *vi* to compromise, make concessions.

transistor [transis'tor] *nm* transistor.

transitar [transi'tar] *vi* to go (from place to place); **tránsito** *nm* transit; (*AUTO*) traffic; (*parada*) stop; **transitorio, a** *a* transitory.

transmisión [transmi'sjon] *nf* (*TEC*) transmission; (*transferencia*) transfer; ~ **en directo/exterior** live/outside broadcast; **transmitir** *vt* (*gen*) to transmit; (*RADIO, TV*) to broadcast.

transparencia [transpa'renθja] *nf* transparency; (*claridad*) clearness, clarity; (*foto*) slide; **transparentar** *vt* to reveal // *vi* to be transparent; **transparente** *a* transparent; clear; (*ligero*) diaphanous // *nm* curtain.

transpirar [transpi'rar] *vi* to perspire; (*fig*) to transpire.

transponer [transpo'ner] *vt* to transpose; (*cambiar de sitio*) to change the place of // *vi* (*desaparecer*) to disappear; (*ir más allá*) to go beyond; **~se** *vr* to change places; (*ocultarse*) to hide; (*sol*) to go down.

transportación [transporta'θjon] *nf* transportation; **transportar** *vt* to transport; (*llevar*) to carry; **transporte** *nm* transport; (*COM*) haulage.

tranvía [tran'βia] *nm* tram.

trapecio [tra'peθjo] *nm* trapeze; **trapecista** *nm/f* trapeze artist.

trapero, a [tra'pero, a] *nm/f* ragman.

trapicheos [trapi'tʃeos] *nmpl* (*fam*) schemes, fiddles.

trapisonda [trapi'sonda] *nf* (*jaleo*) row; (*estafa*) swindle.

trapo ['trapo] *nm* (*tela*) rag; (*de cocina*) cloth.

traquetео [trake'teo] *nm* (*crujido*) crack; (*golpeteo*) rattling.

tras [tras] *prep* (*detrás*) behind; (*después*) after; ~ de besides.

trascendencia [trasθen'denθja] *nf* (*importancia*) importance; (*filosofía*) transcendence; **trascendental** *a* important; transcendental; **trascender** *vi* (*oler*) to smell; (*evocar*) to evoke, suggest; (*noticias*) to come out; (*suceso*) to have a wide effect; **trascender a** to smack of.

trasegar [trase'ɣar] *vt* (*moverse*) to move about; (*vino*) to decant.

trasero, a [tra'sero, a] *a* back // *nm* (*ANAT*) bottom; ~s *nmpl* ancestors.

trasfondo [tras'fondo] *nm* background.

trasgredir [trasɣre'ðir] *vt* to contravene.

trashumante [trasu'mante] *a* migrating.

trasladar [trasla'ðar] *vt* (*gen*) to move; (*persona*) to transfer; (*posergar*) to postpone; (*copiar*) to copy; (*interpretar*) to interpret; **traslado** *nm* (*gen*) move; (*mudanza*) move, removal; (*copia*) copy.

traslucir [traslu'θir] *vt* to show; ~se *vr* to be translucent; (*fig*) to be revealed.

trasluz [tras'luθ] *nm* reflected light; **al ~** against *or* up to the light.

trasnochar [trasno'tʃar] *vi* (*acos-*

tarse tarde) to stay up late; (*no dormir*) to have a sleepless night; (*pasar la noche*) to stay the night.

traspasar [traspa'sar] *vt* (*bala*) to pierce, go through; (*propiedad*) to sell, transfer; (*calle*) to cross over; (*límites*) to go beyond; (*ley*) to break; **traspaso** *nm* transfer; (*fig*) anguish.

traspié [tras'pje] *nm* (*caída*) stumble; (*tropezón*) trip; (*fig*) blunder.

trasplantar [trasplan'tar] *vt* to transplant.

traste ['traste] *nm* (*MUS*) fret; **dar al ~ con algo** to ruin sth.

trastienda [tras'tjenda] *nf* backshop; **obtener algo por la ~** to get sth by underhand means.

trasto ['trasto] *nm* (*mueble*) piece of furniture; (*jarro viejo*) old pot; (*pey: cosa*) piece of junk, (: *persona*) dead loss; ~s *nmpl* (*TEATRO*) scenery *sg*.

trastornado, a [trastor'naðo, a] *a* (*loco*) mad; (*agitado*) crazy; **trastornar** *vt* to overturn, upset; (*fig: ideas*) to confuse; (: *nervios*) to shatter; (: *persona*) to drive crazy; **trastornarse** *vr* (*plan*) to fall through; **trastorno** *nm* (*acto*) overturning; (*confusión*) confusion.

trasunto [tra'sunto] *nm* copy.

tratable [tra'taβle] *a* friendly.

tratado [tra'taðo] *nm* (*POL*) treaty; (*COM*) agreement.

tratamiento [trata'mjento] *nm* treatment.

tratar [tra'tar] *vt* (*ocuparse de*) to treat; (*manejar, TEC*) to handle; (*MED*) to treat; (*calle*) to address // *vi*: ~ de (*hablar sobre*) to deal with, be about; (*intentar*) to try to; ~ con (*com*) to trade in; (*negociar*) to negotiate with; (*tener contactos*) to have dealings with; ~se *vr* to treat each other; **trato** *nm* dealings *pl*; (*relaciones*) relationship; (*comportamiento*) manner; (*COM*) agreement; (*título*) (form of) address.

trauma ['trauma] nm trauma.

través [tra'ßes] nm (fig) reverse; al ~ ad across, crossways; a ~ de prep across; (sobre) over; (por) through.

travesaño [traße'saɲo] nm (ARQ) crossbeam; (DEPORTE) crossbar.

travesía [traße'sia] nf (calle) cross-street; (NAUT) crossing.

travesura [traße'sura] nf (broma) prank; (ingenio) wit; **travieso, a** a (niño) naughty; (adulto) restless; (ingenioso) witty // nf crossing; (ARQ) crossbeam.

trayecto [tra'jekto] nm (ruta) road, way; (viaje) journey; (tramo) stretch; (curso) course; ~ria nf trajectory; (fig) path.

traza ['traθa] nf (plan, design; (aspecto) looks pl; (señal) sign; (engaño) trick; (habilidad) skill; ~do, a a: bien ~do shapely, well-formed // nm (ARQ) plan, design; (fig) outline; **trazar** vt (ARQ) to plan; (ARTE) to sketch; (fig) to trace; (plan) to follow; **trazo** nm (línea) line; (bosquejo) sketch.

trébol ['treßol] nm (BOT) clover.

trece ['treθe] num thirteen.

trecho ['tretʃo] nm (distancia) distance; (de tiempo) while; (fam) piece; de ~ en ~ at intervals.

tregua ['trexwa] nf (MIL) truce; (fig) lull.

treinta ['treinta] num thirty.

tremendo, a [tre'mendo, a] a (terrible) terrible; (imponente: cosa) imposing; (fam: fabuloso) tremendous; (divertido) entertaining.

trémulo, a ['tremulo, a] a quivering.

tren [tren] nm train; ~ de aterrizaje undercarriage.

trenza ['trenθa] nf (de pelo) plait; **trenzar** vt (el pelo) to plait // vi (en baile) to weave in and out; **trenzarse** vr (AM) to become involved with.

trepadora [trepa'ðora] nf (BOT)

climber; **trepar** vt, vi to climb; (TEC) to drill.

trepidación [trepiða'θjon] nf shaking, vibration; **trepidar** vi to shake, vibrate.

tres [tres] num three.

tresillo [tre'siʎo] nm three-piece suite; (MUS) triplet.

treta ['treta] nf (COM etc) gimmick; (fig) trick.

triángulo [tri'angulo] nm triangle.

tribu ['trißu] nf tribe.

tribuna [tri'ßuna] nf (plataforma) platform; (DEPORTE) stand; (fig) public speaking.

tribunal [trißu'nal] nm (juicio) court; (comisión, fig) tribunal.

tributar [trißu'tar] vt to pay; (las gracias) to give; (cariño) to show; **tributo** nm (COM) tax.

trigal [tri'xal] nm wheat field; **trigo** nm wheat; **trigos** nmpl wheat field(s) (pl).

trigueño, a [tri'xeɲo, a] a (pelo) corn-coloured; (piel) olive-skinned.

trillado, a [tri'ʎaðo, a] a threshed; (fig) trite, hackneyed; **trilladora** nf threshing machine; **trillar** vt (fig) to frequent; (AGR) to thresh.

trimestral [trimes'tral] a quarterly; (ESCOL) termly; **trimestre** nm (ESCOL) term.

trincar [trin'kar] vt (atar) to tie up; (NAUT) to lash; (agarrar) to pinion.

trinchar [trin'tʃar] vt to carve.

trinchera [trin'tʃera] nf (fosa) trench; (para vía) cutting; (impermeable) trench-coat.

trineo [tri'neo] nm sledge.

trinidad [trini'ðað] nf trio; (REL): el T~ the Trinity.

trino ['trino] nm trill.

trinquete [trin'kete] nm (TEC) pawl; (NAUT) foremast.

tripa ['tripa] nf (ANAT) intestine; (fam) insides pl.

triple ['triple] a triple.

triplicado, a [tripli'kaðo] a: por ~ in triplicate.

tripulación [tripula'θjon] nf crew;

tripulante *nm/f* crewman/woman;
tripular *vt* (*barco*) to man; (*AUTO*)
to drive.
triquiñuela [triki'ŋwela] *nf* trick.
tris [tris] *nm* crack; **en un ~** in an
instant.
triste ['triste] *a* (*afligido*) sad;
(*sombrío*) melancholy, gloomy;
(*desolado*) desolate; (*lamentable*)
sorry, miserable; (*viejo*) old; **~za** *nf*
(*aflicción*) sadness; (*melancolía*)
melancholy.
triturar [tritu'rar] *vt* (*moler*) to
grind; (*mascar*) to chew.
triunfar [trjun'far] *vi* (*tener éxito*)
to triumph; (*ganar*) to win; **triunfo**
nm triumph.
trivial [tri'βjal] *a* trivial; **~izar** *vt*
to minimize, play down.
triza ['triθa] *nf* bit, piece, hacer **~s**
to smash to bits; **trizar** *vt* to smash
to bits.
trocar [tro'kar] *vt* (*COM*) to
exchange; (*dinero, de lugar*) to
change; (*palabras*) to exchange;
(*confundir*) to confuse; (*vomitar*) to
vomit.
trocha ['trotʃa] *nf* (*sendero*) by-
path; (*atajo*) short cut.
troche ['trotʃe]: **a ~ y moche**
ad helter-skelter, pell-mell.
trofeo [tro'feo] *nm* (*premio*) trophy;
(*éxito*) success.
troje ['troxe] *nf* granary.
tromba ['tromba] *nf* whirlwind.
trombón [trom'bon] *nm* trombone.
trombosis [trom'bosis] *nf* thrombosis.
trompa ['trompa] *nf* horn; (*trompo*)
humming top; (*hocico*) snout; (*fam*):
cogerse una ~ to get tight.
trompeta [trom'peta] *nf* trumpet;
(*clarín*) bugle.
trompo ['trompo] *nm* spinning top.
trompón [trom'pon] *nm* bump.
tronado, a [tro'naðo, a] *a* broken-
down.
tronar [tro'nar] *vt* (*AM*) to shoot //
vi to thunder; (*fig*) to rage; (*fam*) to
go broke.

tronco ['tronko] *nm* (*de árbol,
ANAT*) trunk; (*de planta*) stem.
tronchar [tron'tʃar] *vt* (*árbol*) to
chop down; (*fig: vida*) to cut short;
(*esperanza*) to shatter; (*persona*) to
tire out; **~se** *vr* to fall down.
tronera [tro'nera] *nf* (*MIL*) loop-
hole; (*ARQ*) small window.
trono ['trono] *nm* throne.
tropa ['tropa] *nf* (*MIL*) troop;
(*soldados*) soldiers *pl*; (*gentío*) mob.
tropel [tro'pel] *nm* (*muchedumbre*)
crowd; (*prisa*) rush; (*montón*)
throng.
tropelía [trope'lia] *nm* outrage.
tropezar [trope'θar] *vi* to trip,
stumble; (*fig*) to slip up; **~ con**
(*encontrar*) to run into; (*topar con*)
to bump into; (*reñir*) to fall out with;
tropezón *nm* trip; (*fig*) blunder.
tropical [tropi'kal] *a* tropical;
trópico *nm* tropic.
tropiezo [tro'pjeθo] *nm* (*error*) slip,
blunder; (*desgracia*) misfortune;
(*obstáculo*) snag; (*discusión*)
quarrel.
trotamundos [trota'mundos] *nm
inv* globetrotter.
trotar [tro'tar] *vi* to trot; **trote** *nm*
trot; (*fam*) travelling, de **mucho
trote** hard-wearing.
trozo ['troθo] *nm* bit, piece.
truco ['truko] *nm* (*habilidad*) knack;
(*engaño*) trick; **~s** *nmpl* billiards *sg*.
trucha ['trutʃa] *nf* (*pez*) trout; (*TEC*)
crane.
trueno ['trweno] *nm* (*gen*) thunder;
(*estampido*) boom; (*de arma*) bang.
trueque ['trweke] *nm* exchange;
(*COM*) barter.
trufa ['trufa] *nf* (*BOT*) truffle; (*fig:
fam*) fib.
truhán, ana [tru'an, ana] *nm/f*
rogue.
truncado, a [trun'kaðo, a] *a*
truncated; **truncar** *vt* (*cortar*) to
truncate; (*la vida etc*) to cut short;
(*el desarrollo*) to stunt.
tu [tu] *a* your.
tú [tu] *pron* you.

tubérculo [tu'βerkulo] *nm* (BOT) tuber.

tuberculosis [tußerku'losis] *nf* tuberculosis.

tubería [tuße'ria] *nf* pipes *pl*; (*conducto*) pipeline; **tubo** *nm* tube, pipe; **tubo de ensayo** test-tube; **tubo de escape** exhaust (pipe).

tuerca ['twerka] *nf* nut.

tuerto, a ['twerto, a] *a* (*torcido*) twisted; (*ciego*) blind in one eye // *nm* one-eyed person; (*ofensa*) wrong; **a ~as** upside-down.

tuétano ['twetano] *nm* (*gen*) marrow; (BOT) dish.

tufo ['tufo] *nm* vapour; (*fig: pey*) stench.

tul [tul] *nm* tulle.

tulipán [tuli'pan] *nm* tulip.

tullido, a [tu'ʎiðo, a] *a* crippled; (*cansado*) exhausted.

tumba ['tumba] *nf* (*sepultura*) tomb; (*sacudida*) shake; (*voltereta*) somersault.

tumbar [tum'bar] *vt* to knock down; (*doblar*) to knock over; (*fam: suj: olor*) to overpower // *vi* to fall down; **~se** *vr* (*echarse*) to lie down; (*extenderse*) to stretch out.

tumbo ['tumbo] *nm* (*caída*) fall; (*de vehículo*) jolt; (*momento crítico*) critical moment.

tumido, a [tu'miðo, a] *a* swollen.

tumor [tu'mor] *nm* tumour.

tumulto [tu'multo] *nm* turmoil.

tuna ['tuna] *nf* ver **tuno**.

tunante [tu'nante] *a* rascally.

tunda ['tunda] *nf* (*de tela*) shearing; (*golpeo*) beating; **tundir** *vt* (*tela*) to shear; (*hierba*) to mow; (*fig*) to exhaust; (*fam: golpear*) to beat.

túnel ['tunel] *nm* tunnel.

Túnez [tuneθ] *nm* Tunisia; (*ciudad*) Tunis.

tuno, a ['tuno, a] *nm/f* (*fam*) rogue // *nf* (BOT) prickly pear; (MUS) student music group.

tuntún [tun'tun]: **al ~** *ad* thoughtlessly.

tupido, a [tu'piðo, a] *a* (*denso*) dense; (*fig*) dim; (*tela*) close-woven.

turba ['turßa] *nf* crowd.

turbación [turßa'θjon] *nf* (*molestia*) disturbance; (*preocupación*) worry; **turbado, a** *a* (*molesto*) disturbed; (*preocupado*) worried; **turbar** *vt* (*molestar*) to disturb; (*incomodar*) to upset; **turbarse** *vr* to be disturbed.

turbina [tur'ßina] *nf* turbine.

turbio, a ['turßjo, a] *a* cloudy; (*lenguaje*) confused // *ad* indistinctly.

turbión [tur'ßjon] *nf* (*fig*) shower.

turbohélice [turßo'eliße] *nm* turboprop.

turbulencia [turßu'lenθja] *nf* turbulence; (*fig*) restlessness; **turbulento, a** *a* turbulent; (*fig: intranquilo*) restless; (*: ruidoso*) noisy.

turco, a ['turko, a] *a* Turkish.

turismo [tu'rismo] *nm* tourism; (*coche*) saloon car; **turista** *nm/f* tourist; **turístico, a** *a* tourist *cpd*.

turnar [tur'nar] *vi*, **~se** *vr* to take (it in) turns; **turno** *nm* (INDUSTRIA) shift; (*oportunidad, orden de prioridad*) opportunity; (DEPORTE *etc*) turn.

turquesa [tur'kesa] *nf* turquoise.

Turquía [tur'kia] *nf* Turkey.

turrón [tu'rron] *nm* (*dulce*) nougat; (*fam*) sinecure.

tutear [tute'ar] *vt* to address as familiar 'tú'; **~se** *vr* to be on familiar terms.

tutela [tu'tela] *nf* (*legal*) guardianship; (*instrucción*) guidance; **tutelar** *a* tutelary // *vt* to protect.

tutor, a [tu'tor, a] *nm/f* (*legal*) guardian; (ESCOL) tutor.

tuve, tuviera *etc vb ver* **tener**.

tuyo, a [tu'jo, a] *a* yours, of yours // *pron* yours; **los ~s** (*fam*) your relations, your family.

TVE *nf abr de* **Televisión Española**.

U

u [u] *conj* or.

ubérrimo, a [u'ßerrimo, a] *a* very rich, fertile.

ubicar [uβi'kar] *vt* (*AM*) to place, situate, (*, fig*) to install in a post; **~se** *vr* to lie, be located.

ubicuo, a [u'ßikwo, a] *a* ubiquitous.

ubre [u'ßre] *nf* udder.

U.C.D. *abr de* **Unión del Centro Democrático.**

Ud(s) *abr de* **usted(es).**

ufanarse [ufa'narse] *vr* to boast; **~ de** to pride o.s. on; **ufano, a** *a* (*arrogante*) arrogant; (*presumido*) conceited.

U.G.T. *abr de* **Unión General de Trabajadores.**

ujier [u'xjer] *nm* usher; (*portero*) doorkeeper.

úlcera [' ulθera] *nf* ulcer; **ulcerar** *vt* to make sore; **ulcerarse** *vr* to ulcerate.

ulterior [ulte'rjor] *a* (*más allá*) farther, further; (*subsecuente, siguiente*) subsequent; **~mente** *ad* later, subsequently.

últimamente [ultima'mente] *ad* (*recientemente*) lately, recently; (*finalmente*) finally; (*como último recurso*) as a last resort.

ultimar [ulti'mar] *vt* to finish; (*finalizar*) to finalize; (*AM: rematar*) to finish off.

último, a [' ultimo, a] *a* last; (*más reciente*) latest, most recent; (*más bajo*) bottom; (*más alto*) top; (*fig*) final, extreme; **en las ~as** on one's last legs; **por ~** finally.

ultra [' ultra] *a* ultra // *nm/f* extreme right-winger.

ultrajar [ultra'xar] *vt* (*escandalizar*) to outrage; (*insultar*) to insult, abuse; **ultraje** *nm* outrage; insult.

ultramar [ultra'mar] *nm*: **de** o **en ~** abroad, overseas; **~ino, a** *a* overseas, foreign; **~inos** *nmpl*

groceries; **tienda de ~inos** grocer's (shop).

ultranza [ul'tranθa]: **a ~** *ad* to the death; (*a todo trance*) at all costs; (*completo*) outright.

ultrasónico, a [ultra'soniko, a] *a* ultrasonic.

ulular [ulu'lar] *vi* to howl; (*búho*) to hoot.

umbral [um'bral] *nm* (*gen*) threshold.

umbroso, a [um'broso, a], **umbrío, a** [um'brio, a] *a* shady.

un, una [un, 'una] *det a* // *num* one; *ver* **uno.**

unánime [u'nanime] *a* unanimous; **unanimidad** *nf* unanimity.

unción [un'θjon] *nf* anointing; **extrema ~** Extreme Unction.

undécimo, a [un'deθimo, a] *a* eleventh.

undular [undu'lar] *vi ver* **ondular.**

ungir [un'xir] *vt* to rub with ointment; (*REL*) to anoint.

ungüento [un'gwento] *nm* ointment; (*fig*) salve, balm.

únicamente [' unikamente] *ad* solely, (*solamente*) only; **único, a** *a* only; (*solo*) sole, single; (*sin par*) unique.

unidad [uni'ðað] *nf* unity; (*TEC*) unit.

unido, a [u'niðo, a] *a* joined, linked; (*fig*) united.

unificar [unifi'kar] *vt* to unite, unify.

uniformar [uniфor'mar] *vt* to make uniform, level up; (*persona*) to put into uniform; **uniforme** *a* uniform, equal, (*superficie*) even // *nm* uniform; **uniformidad** *nf* uniformity; (*llaneza*) levelness, evenness.

unilateral [unilate'ral] *a* unilateral.

unión [u'njon] *nf* (*gen*) union; (*acto*) uniting, joining; (*calidad*) unity; (*TEC*) joint; (*fig*) closeness, togetherness; **la U~ Soviética** the Soviet Union.

unir [u'nir] *vt* (*juntar*) to join, unite;

(*atar*) to tie, fasten; (*combinar*) to combine // *vi* to mix well; **~se** *vr* to join together, unite; (*empresas*) to merge.

unísono [u'nisono] *nm*: **al ~** in unison.

universal [uniβer'sal] *a* universal; (*mundial*) world *cpd*.

universidad [uniβersi'ðað] *nf* university.

universo [uni'βerso] *nm* universe.

uno ['uno] *num, det* one // *pron* one; (*alguien*) someone, somebody; **~s** some, a few; **~ a ~, ~ por ~** one by one; **cada ~** each or every one; **estar en ~** to be at one; **~s que otro** some, a few; **~s y otros** all of them; **~ y otro** both.

untar [un'tar] *vt* (*gen*) to rub; (*engrasar*) to grease, oil; (*MED*) to rub with ointment; (*fig*) to bribe; **~se** *vr* to be crooked; **unto** *nm* animal fat; (*MED*) ointment; (*fam*) slush fund.

uña ['uṇa] *nf* (*ANAT*) nail; (*garra*) claw; (*casco*) hoof; (*arrancaclavos*) claw.

uranio [u'ranjo] *nm* uranium.

urbanidad [urβani'ðað] *nf* courtesy, politeness.

urbanismo [urβa'nismo] *nm* town planning.

urbanización [urβaniθa'θjon] *nf* housing scheme.

urbano, a [ur'βano, a] *a* (*de ciudad*) urban; (*cortés*) courteous, polite.

urbe ['urβe] *nf* large city.

urdimbre [ur'ðimbre] *nf* (*de tejido*) warp; (*intriga*) intrigue; **urdir** *vt* to warp; (*fig*) to plot, contrive.

urgencia [ur'xenθja] *nf* urgency; (*prisa*) haste, rush; **servicios de ~** emergency services; **urgente** *a* urgent; (*insistente*) insistent; **urgir** *vi* to be urgent.

urinario, a [uri'narjo, a] *a* urinary // *nm* urinal.

urna ['urna] *nf* urn; (*POL*) ballot box.

urraca [u'rraka] *nf* magpie.

URSS *nf*: **la ~** the USSR.

Uruguay [uru'ɣwai] *nm*: **el ~** Uruguay; **uruguayo, a** *a, nm/f* Uruguayan.

usado, a [u'saðo, a] *a* (*gen*) used; (*ropa etc*) worn.

usanza [u'sanθa] *nf* custom, usage.

usar [u'sar] *vt* to use; (*ropa*) to wear; (*tener costumbre*) to be in the habit of; **~se** *vr* to be used; **uso** *nm* use; wear; (*costumbre*) usage, custom; (*moda*) fashion; **al uso** in keeping with custom; **al uso de** in the style of.

usted [us'teð] *pron* you.

usual [u'swal] *a* usual.

usuario, a [usu'arjo, a] *nm/f* user.

usura [u'sura] *nf* usury; **usurero, a** *nm/f* usurer.

usurpar [usur'par] *vt* to usurp.

utensilio [uten'siljo] *nm* tool; (*CULIN*) utensil.

útero ['utero] *nm* uterus, womb.

útil ['util] *a* useful // *nm* tool; **utilidad** *nf* usefulness; (*COM*) profit; **utilizar** *vt* to use, utilize.

utopía [uto'pia] *nf* Utopia; **utópico, a** *a* Utopian.

uva ['uβa] *nf* grape.

V

v *abr de* **voltio.**

va *vb ver* **ir.**

vaca ['baka] *nf* (*animal*) cow; (*carne*) beef; (*cuero*) cowhide.

vacaciones [baka'θjones] *nfpl* holidays.

vacante [ba'kante] *a* vacant, empty // *nf* vacancy.

vacar [ba'kar] *vi* to fall vacant; **~ a** *o* **en** to devote o.s. to.

vaciado, a [ba'θjaðo, a] *a* (*hecho en molde*) cast in a mould; (*hueco*) hollow // *nm* cast.

vaciar [ba'θjar] *vt* to empty out;

(*ahuecar*) to hollow out; (*moldear*) to cast // *vi* (*río*) to flow (en into); ~**se** *vr* to empty; (*fig*) to blab, spill the beans.

vaciedad [baθje'ðað] *nf* emptiness.

vacilación [baθila'θjon] *nf* hesitation; **vacilante** *a* unsteady; (*habla*) faltering; (*fig*) hesitant; **vacilar** *vi* to be unsteady; to falter; to hesitate, waver; (*persona*) to stagger, stumble; (*memoria*) to fail.

vacío, a [ba'θio, a] *a* empty, (*puesto*) vacant; (*desocupado*) idle; (*vano*) vain // *nm* emptiness; (*FISICA*) vacuum; (*un* ~) (empty) space.

vacuna [ba'kuna] *nf* vaccine; **vacunar** *vt* to vaccinate.

vacuno, a [ba'kuno, a] *a* bovine.

vacuo, a [ba'kwo, a] *a* empty.

vadear [baðe'ar] *vt* (*río*) to ford; (*problema*) to overcome; (*persona*) to sound out; **vado** *nm* ford; (*solución*) solution; (*descanso*) respite.

vagabundo, a [baɣa'βundo, a] *a* wandering; (*pey*) vagrant // *nm* tramp.

vagamente [baɣa'mente] *ad* vaguely.

vagancia [ba'ɣanθja] *nf* vagrancy; **vagar** *vi* (*gen*) to wander; (*no hacer nada*) to idle // *nm* leisure.

vagido [ba'xiðo] *nm* wail.

vagina [ba'xina] *nf* vagina.

vago, a ['baɣo, a] *a* vague; (*perezoso*) lazy; (*ambulante*) wandering // *nm/f* (*vagabundo*) tramp; (*flojo*) lazybones *sg*, idler.

vagón [ba'ɣon] *nm* (*de pasajeros*) carriage; (*de mercancías*) wagon.

vaguedad [baɣe'ðað] *nf* vagueness.

vaho ['bao] *nm* (*vapor*) vapour, steam; (*olor*) smell; (*respiración*) breath.

vaina ['baina] *nf* sheath.

vainilla [bai'ni.ʎa] *nf* vanilla.

vais *vb ver* **ir.**

vaivén [bai'βen] *nm* to-and fro movement; (*de tránsito*) coming

and going; **vaivenes** *nmpl* (*fig*) ups and downs.

vajilla [ba'xiʎa] *nf* crockery, dishes *pl.*

val, valdré *etc vb ver* **valer.**

vale ['bale] *nm* voucher; (*recibo*) receipt; (*pagaré*) I.O.U.

valedero, a [bale'ðero, a] *a* valid.

valenciano, a [balen'θjano, a] *a* Valencian.

valentía [balen'tia] *nf* courage, bravery; (*pey*) boastfulness; (*acción*) heroic deed; **valentón, ona** *a* blustering.

valer [ba'ler] *vt* to aid, protect; (*MAT*) to equal // *vi* to be worth; (*costar*) to cost; (*ser útil*) to be useful; (*ser válido*) to be valid; ~**se** *vr* to defend o.s.; ~**se de** to make use of, take advantage of // *nm* worth, value; ~ **la pena** to be worthwhile; ¿**vale**? O. K.?

valgo *etc vb ver* **valer.**

validar [bali'ðar] *vt* to validate; **validez** *nf* validity; **válido, a** *a* valid.

valiente [ba'ljente] *a* brave, valiant; (*pey*) boastful // *nm* hero.

valija [ba'lixa] *nf* case; (*mochila*) satchel.

valioso, a [ba'ljoso, a] *a* valuable; (*rico*) wealthy.

valor [ba'lor] *nm* value, worth; (*precio*) price; (*valentía*) valour, courage; (*importancia*) importance; ~**es** *nmpl* (*COM*) securities; ~**ación** *nf* valuation; ~**ar** *vt* to value.

vals [bals] *nm* waltz.

válvula ['balβula] *nf* valve.

valla ['baʎa] *nf* fence; (*DEPORTE*) hurdle; (*fig*) barrier; **vallar** *vt* to fence in.

valle ['baʎe] *nm* valley, vale.

vamos *vb ver* **ir.**

vampiro, resa [bam'piro, i'resa] *nm/f* vampire.

van *vb ver* **ir.**

vanagloriarse [banaɣlo'rjarse] *vr* to boast.

vándalo, a ['bandalo, a] *nm/f* vandal; **vandalismo** *nm* vandalism.

vanguardia [ban'gwarðja] nf vanguard; (ARTE) avant-garde.

vanidad [bani'ðað] nf vanity; (irrealidad) unreality; **vanidoso, a** a vain, conceited.

vano, a ['bano, a] a (irreal) unreal; (irracional) unreasonable; (inútil) useless; (persona) vain, conceited; (frívolo) frivolous.

vapor [ba'por] nm vapour; (vaho) steam; (neblina) mist; **~es** nmpl (MED) hysterics; **al ~** (CULIN) steamed; **~izar** vt to vaporize; **~oso, a** a vaporous; (vahoso) steamy.

vaquero, a [ba'kero, a] a cattle cpd // nm cowboy; **~s** nmpl jeans.

vara ['bara] nf stick, wand; (TEC) rod.

varear [bare'ar] vt to hit, beat.

variable [ba'rjaßle] a, nf variable; **variación** nf variation; **variar** vt to vary; (modificar) to modify; (cambiar de posición) to switch around // vi to vary; **variedad** nf variety.

varilla [ba'riʎa] nf stick; (BOT) twig; (TEC) rod; (de rueda) spoke.

vario, a ['barjo, a] a (variado) varied; (multicolor) motley; (cambiable) changeable; **~s** various, several.

varón [ba'ron] nm male, man; **varonil** a manly.

Varsovia [bar'soßja] n Warsaw.

vas vb ver **ir**.

vascongado, a [baskon'gaðo, a], **vascuence** [bas'kwenθe], **vasco, a** ['basko, a] a Basque; **las Vascongadas** the Basque Country.

vaselina [base'lina] nf vaseline.

vasija [ba'sixa] nf container, vessel.

vaso ['baso] nm glass, tumbler; (ANAT) vessel.

vástago ['bastaɣo] nm (BOT) shoot; (TEC) rod; (fig) offspring.

vasto, a ['basto, a] a vast, huge.

Vaticano [bati'kano] nm: **el ~** the Vatican.

vaticinio [bati'θinjo] nm prophecy.

vatio ['batjo] nm (ELEC) watt.

vaya etc vb ver **ir**.

Vd(s) abr de usted(es).

ve vb ver **ir, ver**.

vecindad [beθin'dað] nf, **vecindario** [beθin'darjo] nm neighbourhood; (habitantes) residents pl; **vecino, a** a neighbouring // nm/nf neighbour; (residente) resident.

veda ['beða] nf prohibition.

vedado [be'ðaðo] nm preserve.

vedar [be'ðar] vt (prohibir) to ban, prohibit; (impedir) to stop, prevent.

vegetación [bexeta'θjon] nf vegetation.

vegetal [bexe'tal] a, nm vegetable.

vehemencia [bee'menθja] nf (insistencia) vehemence; (pasión) passion; (fervor) fervour; (violencia) violence; **vehemente** a vehement; passionate; fervent.

vehículo [be'ikulo] nm vehicle; (MED) carrier.

veía etc vb ver **ver**.

veinte ['beinte] num twenty.

vejación [bexa'θjon] nf vexation; (humillación) humiliation.

vejamen [be'xamen] nm satire.

vejar [be'xar] vt (irritar) to annoy, vex; (humillar) to humiliate.

vejez [be'xeθ] nf old age.

vejiga [be'xiɣa] nf (ANAT) bladder.

vela ['bela] nf (de cera) candle; (NAUT) sail; (insomnio) sleeplessness; (vigilia) vigil; (MIL) sentry duty; (fam) snot; **estar a dos ~s** (fam) to be skint (fam).

velado, a [be'laðo, a] a veiled; (sonido) muffled; (FOTO) blurred // nf soirée.

velador [bela'ðor] nm watchman; (candelero) candlestick.

velar [be'lar] vt (hacer guardia) to keep watch over; (cubrir) to veil // vi to stay awake; **~ por** to watch over, look after.

veleidad [belei'ðað] nf (ligereza) fickleness; (capricho) whim.

velero [be'lero] nm (NAUT) sailing ship; (AVIAT) glider.

veleta [be'leta] nf weather vane.

velo ['belo] nm veil.

velocidad [beloθi'ðað] nf speed; (TEC, AUTO) gear.

velocímetro [beloθimetro] nm speedometer.

velódromo [be'loðromo] nm cycle track

veloz [bc'loθ] a fast.

vello ['beʎo] nm down, fuzz; **vellón** nm fleece; ~**so, a** a fuzzy; **velludo, a** a shaggy // nm plush, velvet.

ven vb ver **venir**.

vena ['bena] nf vein.

venablo [be'naβlo] nm javelin.

venado [be'naðo] nm deer.

venal [be'nal] a (ANAT) venous; (pey) venal, ~**idad** nf venality.

vencedor, a [benθe'ðor, a] a victorious // nm/f victor, winner.

vencer [ben'θer] vt (dominar) to defeat, beat; (derrotar) to vanquish; (superar, controlar) to overcome, master // vi (triunfar) to win (through), triumph; (plazo) to expire; **vencido, a** a (derrotado) defeated, beaten; (COM) due // ad: **pagar vencido** to pay in arrears; **vencimiento** nm collapse; (COM) maturity.

venda ['benda] nf bandage; ~**je** nm bandage, dressing; **vendar** vt to bandage; **vendar los ojos** to blindfold.

vendaval [benda'βal] nm (viento) gale; (huracán) hurricane.

vendedor, a [bende'ðor, a] nm/f seller.

vender [ben'der] vt to sell; ~ **al contado/al por mayor/al por menor** to sell for cash/wholesale/retail.

vendimia [ben'dimja] nf grape harvest.

vendré etc vb ver **venir**.

veneno [be'neno] nm poison, venom; ~**so, a** a poisonous.

venerable [bene'raβle] a venerable; **veneración** nf veneration;

venerar vt (reconocer) to venerate; (adorar) to worship.

venéreo, a [be'nereo, a] a venereal.

venero [be'nero] nm (veta) seam, lode; (fuente) spring.

venezolano, a [beneθo'lano, a] a Venezuelan.

Venezuela [bene'θwela] nf Venezuela.

venganza [ben'ganθa] nf vengeance, revenge; **vengar** vt to avenge; **vengarse** vr to take revenge; **vengativo, a** a (persona) vindictive.

vengo etc vb ver **venir**.

venia ['benja] nf (perdón) pardon; (permiso) consent

venial [be'njal] a venial.

venida [be'niða] nf (llegada) arrival; (regreso) return; (fig) rashness.

venidero, a [beni'ðero, a] a coming, future.

venir [be'nir] vi to come; (llegar) to arrive; (fig) to stem from; (ocurrir) to happen; ~ **bien/mal** to be suitable/unsuitable; **el año que viene** next year; ~**se abajo** to collapse.

venta ['benta] nf (COM) sale; ~ **a plazos** hire purchase; ~ **al contado/al por mayor/al por menor o al detalle** cash sale/wholesale/retail; ~ **de liquidación** clearance sale.

ventaja [ben'taxa] nf advantage; **ventajoso, a** a advantageous.

ventana [ben'tana] nf window; ~ **de guillotina/saledizo** sash/bay window; **ventanilla** nf (de taquilla) window (of booking office etc).

ventear [bente'ar] vt (ropa) to hang out to dry; (oler) to sniff // vi (investigar) to investigate; (soplar) to blow; ~**se** vr (romperse) to crack; (ANAT) to break wind.

ventilación [bentila'θjon] nf ventilation; (corriente) draught; **ventilar** vt to ventilate; (a secar) to put out to dry; (fig) to air, discuss.

ventisca [ben'tiska] nf, **ventis-quero** [bentis'kero] nm blizzard; (nieve amontonada) snowdrift.

ventosear [bentose'ar] vi to break wind.

ventoso, a [ben'toso, a] a windy.

ventrílocuo, a [ben'trilokwo, a] nm/f ventriloquist; **ventriloquia** nf ventriloquism.

ventura [ben'tura] nf (felicidad) happiness; (buena suerte) luck; (destino) fortune; **a la (buena)** ~ at random; **venturoso, a** a happy; (afortunado) lucky, fortunate.

veo etc vb ver **ver.**

ver [ber] vt, vi to see; (mirar) to look at, watch; (investigar) to look into; ~se vr (encontrarse) to meet; (dejarse ~) to be seen; (hallarse: en un apuro) to find o.s., be // vi to see // (mirar) looks pl, appearance; **a** ~ let's see; **dejarse** ~ to become apparent; **no tener nada que** ~ **con** to have nothing to do with; **a mi modo de** ~ as I see it.

vera ['bera] nf edge, verge; (de río) bank.

veracidad [beraθi'ðað] nf truthfulness.

veranear [berane'ar] vi to spend the summer; **veraneo** nm summer holiday; **veraniego, a** a summer cpd; **verano** nm summer.

veras ['beras] nfpl truth sg; **de** ~ really, truly.

veraz [be'raθ] a truthful.

verbal [ber'βal] a verbal.

verbena [ber'βena] nf street party.

verbigracia [berβi'xraθja] ad for example.

verbo ['berβo] nm verb; ~**so, a** a verbose.

verdad [ber'ðað] nf (lo verídico) truth; (fiabilidad) reliability // ad really; **de** ~ a real, proper; **a decir** ~ to tell the truth; ~**ero, a** a (veraz) true, truthful; (fiable) reliable; (fig) real.

verde ['berðe] a green; (sucio) blue, dirty // nm green; **viejo** ~ dirty old

man; ~**ar**, ~**cer** vi to turn green; **verdor** nm (lo ~) greenness; (BOT) verdure; (fig) youthful vigour.

verdugo [ber'ðuxo] nm executioner; (BOT) shoot; (cardenal) weal.

verdulero, a [berðu'lero, a] nm/f greengrocer.

verdura [ber'ðura] nf greenness; ~**s** nfpl (CULIN) greens.

vereda [be'reða] nf path.

veredicto [bere'ðikto] nm verdict.

vergonzoso, a [berxon'θoso, a] a shameful; (tímido) timid, bashful.

vergüenza [ber'xwenθa] nf shame, sense of shame; (timidez) bashfulness; (pudor) modesty.

verídico, a [be'riðiko, a] a true, truthful.

verificar [berifi'kar] vt to check; (corroborar) to verify; (llevar a cabo) to carry out; ~**se** vr to occur, happen.

verja ['berxa] nf grating.

vermut [ber'mut] nm vermouth.

verosímil [bero'simil] a likely, probable; (relato) credible.

verruga [be'rruxa] nf wart.

versado, a [ber'saðo, a] a: ~ **en** versed in.

versar [ber'sar] vi to go round, turn.

versátil [ber'satil] a versatile.

versión [ber'sjon] nf version; (traducción) translation.

verso ['berso] nm (gen) verse; **un** ~ a line of poetry.

vértebra ['berteβra] nf vertebra.

verter [ber'ter] vt (vaciar) to empty, pour (out); (tirar) to dump // vi to flow.

vertical [berti'kal] a vertical.

vértice ['bertiθe] nm vertex, apex.

vertiente [ber'tjente] nf slope.

vertiginoso, a [bertixi'noso, a] a giddy, dizzy; **vértigo** nm vertigo; (mareo) dizziness.

vesícula [be'sikula] nf blister.

vespertino, a [besper'tino, a] a evening cpd.

vestíbulo [bes'tiβulo] nm hall; (de teatro) foyer.

vestido [bes'tiðo] nm (ropa) clothes pl, clothing; (de mujer) dress, frock.

vestigio [bes'tixjo] nm (traza) trace; (señal) sign; ~s nmpl remains.

vestimenta [besti'menta] nf clothing.

vestir [bes'tir] vt (poner: ropa) to put on; (llevar: ropa) to wear; (cubrir) to clothe, cover; (pagar: la ropa) to pay for the clothing of; (sastre) to make clothes for // vi (ponerse: ropa) to dress; (verse bien) to look good; ~se vr to get dressed, dress o.s.

vestuario [bes'twarjo] nm clothes pl, wardrobe; (TEATRO) dressing room; (DEPORTE) changing room.

veta ['beta] nf (vena) vein, seam; (raya) streak; (de madera) grain.

vetar [be'tar] vt to veto.

veterano, a [bete'rano, a] a, nm veteran.

veterinario, a [beteri'narjo, a] nm/f vet(erinary surgeon) // nf veterinary science.

veto ['beto] nm veto.

vetusto, a [be'tusto, a] a ancient.

vez [beθ] nf (gen) time; (turno) turn; a la ~ que at the same time as; a su ~ in its turn; cada ~ más/menos more and more/less and less; una ~ once; de una ~ in one go; de una ~ para siempre once and for all; en ~ de instead of; a veces sometimes; una y otra ~ repeatedly; de ~ en cuando from time to time; 7 veces 9 7 times 9; hacer las veces de to stand in for; tal ~ perhaps.

v. g., v. gr. abr de verbigracia.

vía ['bia] nf track, route; (FERRO) line; (fig) way; (ANAT) passage, tube // prep vía, by way of; por ~ judicial by legal means; por ~ oficial through official channels; por ~ de by way of; en ~s de in the process of; ~ aérea airway.

viaducto [bja'ðukto] nm viaduct.

viajante [bja'xante] nm commercial traveller.

viajar [bja'xar] vi to travel; **viaje** nm journey; (gira) tour; (NAUT) voyage; **estar de viaje** to be on a journey; **viaje de ida y vuelta** round trip; **viaje de novios** honeymoon; **viajero, a** a travelling, (ZOOL) migratory // nm/f (quien viaja) traveller; (pasajero) passenger.

vial [bjal] a road cpd, traffic cpd.

víbora ['biβora] nf viper.

vibración [biβra'θjon] nf vibration; **vibrador** nm vibrator; **vibrante** a vibrant; **vibrar** vt, vi to vibrate.

vicario [bi'karjo] nm curate.

vicepresidente [biθepresi'ðente] nm/f vice-president.

viciado, a [bi'θjaðo, a] a (corrompido) corrupt; (contaminado) foul, contaminated; **viciar** vt (pervertir) to pervert; (adulterar) to adulterate; (falsificar) to falsify; (JUR) to nullify; (estropear) to spoil; (sentido) to twist; **viciarse** vr to become corrupted.

vicio ['biθjo] nm (libertinaje) vice; (mala costumbre) bad habit; (mimo) spoiling; (alabeo) warp, warping; **~so, a** (muy malo) vicious; (corrompido) depraved; (mimado) spoiled // nm/f depraved person.

vicisitud [biθisi'tuð] nf vicissitude.

víctima ['biktima] nf victim.

victoria [bik'torja] nf victory; **victorioso, a** a victorious.

vicuña [bi'kuɲa] nf vicuña.

vid [bið] nf vine.

vida ['biða] nf (gen) life; (duración) lifetime; **de por ~** for life; **en la/mi ~** never; **estar con ~** to be still alive; **ganarse la ~** to earn one's living.

vidriero, a [bi'ðrjero, a] nm/f glazier // nf (ventana) stained-glass window; (puerta) glass door.

vidrio ['biðrjo] nm glass; **~so, a** a glassy; (frágil) fragile, brittle; (resbaladizo) slippery.

viejo, a ['bjexo, a] a old // nm/f old man/woman.

vienes etc vb ver **venir.**

vienés, esa [bje'nes, esa] a Viennese.

viento ['bjento] nm wind; (olfato) scent.

vientre ['bjentre] nm belly; (matriz) womb; ~s nmpl bowels.

viernes ['bjernes] nm inv Friday.

Vietnam [bjet'nam] nm: **el** ~ Vietnam; **vietnamita** a Vietnamese.

viga ['biɣa] nf beam, rafter.

vigencia [bi'xenθja] nf validity; **estar en** ~ to be in force; **vigente** a valid, in force; (imperante) prevailing.

vigésimo, a [bi'xesimo, a] a twentieth.

vigía [bi'xia] nm look-out // nf (atalaya) watchtower; (acción) watching.

vigilancia [bixi'lanθja] nf vigilance; **vigilar** vt to watch over // vi (gen) to be vigilant; (hacer guardia) to keep watch.

vigilia [vi'xilja] nf wakefulness, being awake; (REL) fast; **comer de** ~ to fast.

vigor [bi'vor] nm vigour, vitality; **en** ~ in force; **entrar/poner en** ~ to take/put into effect; ~**oso, a** a vigorous.

vil [bil] a vile, low; ~**eza** nf vileness; (acto) base deed.

vilipendiar [bilipen'djar] vt to vilify, revile.

vilo ['bilo]: **en** ~ ad in the air, suspended.

villa ['bi/a] nf (pueblo) small town; (municipalidad) municipality.

villorrio [bi'λorrjo] nm one-horse town, dump (fam).

vinagre [bi'naɣre] nm vinegar.

vinculación [binkula'θjon] nf (lazo) link, bond; (acción) linking; **vincular** vt to link, bind; **vínculo** nm link, bond.

vindicar [bindi'kar] vt to vindicate; (vengar) to avenge; (JUR) to claim.

vine etc vb ver **venir.**

vinicultura [binikul'tura] nf wine growing.

viniera etc vb ver **venir.**

vino ['bino] nm wine.

viña ['biɲa] nf, **viñedo** [bi'ɲeðo] nm vineyard.

violación [bjola'θjon] nf violation; ~ (sexual) rape; **violar** vt to violate; to rape.

violencia [bjo'lenθja] nf (fuerza) violence, force; (embarazo) embarrassment; (acto injusto) unjust act; **violentar** vt to force; (casa) to break into; (agredir) to assault; (violar) to violate; **violento, a** a violent; (furioso) furious; (situación) embarrassing; (acto) forced, unnatural; (difícil) awkward.

violeta [bjo'leta] nf violet.

violín [bjo'lin] nm violin.

violón [bjo'lon] nm double bass.

viraje [bi'raxe] nm turn; (de vehículo) swerve; (de carretera) bend; (fig) change of direction; **virar** vt, vi to change direction.

virgen ['birxen] a, nf virgin.

Virgo ['birɣo] nm Virgo.

viril [bi'ril] a virile; ~**idad** nf virility.

virtualmente [birtwal'mente] ad virtually.

virtud [bir'tuð] nf virtue; **virtuoso, a** a virtuous // nm/f virtuoso.

viruela [bi'rwela] nf smallpox; ~**s** nfpl pockmarks; ~**s locas** chickenpox.

virulento, a [biru'lento, a] a virulent.

virus ['birus] nm virus.

visado [bi'saðo] nm visa.

viscoso, a [bis'koso, a] a viscous.

visera [bi'sera] nf visor.

visibilidad [bisiβili'ðað] nf visibility; **visible** a visible; (fig) obvious.

visión [bi'sjon] nf (ANAT) vision, (eye)sight; (fantasía) vision, fantasy; (panorama) view; **visionario, a** a (que preve) visionary; (alucinado) deluded // nm/f visionary; (chalado) lunatic.

visita [bi'sita] nf call, visit; (persona) visitor; **visitar** vt to visit, call on; (inspeccionar) to inspect.

vislumbrar [bislum'brar] vt to glimpse, catch a glimpse of; **vislumbre** nf glimpse, (centelleo) gleam; (idea vaga) glimmer.

viso ['biso] nm (del metal) glint, gleam; (de tela) sheen; (aspecto) appearance.

visón [bi'son] nm mink.

visor [bi'sor] nm (FOTO) viewfinder.

víspera ['bispera] nf eve, day before.

vista ['bista] nf sight, vision; (capacidad de ver) (eye)sight; (mirada) look(s) (pl) // nm customs officer; a primera ~ at first glance; hacer la ~ gorda to turn a blind eye; volver la ~ to look back; está a la ~ que it's obvious that; en ~ de in view of; en ~ de que in view of the fact that; ¡hasta la ~! so long!, see you!; con ~s a with a view to; ~zo nm glance; dar o echar un ~zo to glance at.

visto etc vb ver **vestir**.

visto, a ['bisto, a] pp de ver // a seen; (considerado) considered // nm: ~ bueno approval; '~ bueno' approved; por lo ~ evidently, para que it's clear that; está bien/mal ~ it's acceptable/unacceptable; ~ que conj since, considering that.

vistoso, a [bis'toso, a] a colourful; (alegre) gay; (pey) gaudy.

vital [bi'tal] a life cpd, living cpd; (fig) vital; (persona) lively, vivacious; **~icio, a** a for life.

vitamina [bita'mina] nf vitamin.

viticultor, a [bitikul'tor, a] nm/f vine grower; **viticultura** nf vine growing.

vitorear [bitore'ar] vt to cheer, acclaim.

vítreo, a ['bitreo, a] a vitreous.

vitrina [bi'trina] nf glass case.

vituperar [bitupe'rar] vt to

condemn; **vituperio** nm (condena) condemnation; (censura) censure; (insulto) insult.

viudo, a ['bjuðo, a] nm/f widower/widow; **viudez** nf widowhood.

vivacidad [biβaθi'ðað] nf (vigor) vigour; (vida) vivacity.

vivaracho, a [biβa'ratʃo, a] a jaunty, lively; (ojos) bright, twinkling.

vivaz [bi'βaθ] a (que dura) enduring; (vigoroso) vigorous, (vivo) lively.

víveres ['biβeres] nmpl provisions.

viveza [bi'βeθa] nf liveliness; (agudeza) sharpness.

vivienda [bi'βjenda] nf (alojamiento) housing; (morada) dwelling.

viviente [bi'βjente] a living.

vivificar [biβifi'kar] vt to give life to.

vivir [bi'βir] vt, vi to live // nm life, living.

vivo, a ['biβo, a] a living, live, alive; (fig) vivid; (astuto) smart, clever; llegar a lo ~ to cut to the quick.

vocablo [bo'kaβlo] nm (palabra) word; (término) term.

vocabulario [bokaβu'larjo] nm vocabulary.

vocación [boka'θjon] nf vocation.

vocal [bo'kal] a vocal // nf vowel; **~izar** vt to vocalize.

vocear [boθe'ar] vt (para vender) to cry; (aclamar) to acclaim; (fig) to proclaim // vi to yell; **vocerío** nm, **vocería** nf shouting.

vocero [bo'θero] nm/f spokesman/woman.

vociferar [boθife'rar] vt to shout; (jactarse) to proclaim boastfully // vi to yell.

vocinglero, a [boθin'glero, a] a vociferous; (gárrulo) garrulous; (fig) blatant.

vodka ['boðka] nf vodka.

vol abr de **volumen**.

volador, a [bola'ðor, a] a flying.

volante [bo'lante] a flying // nm

(de máquina, coche) steering wheel; (de reloj) balance.

volar [bo'lar] vt (demolir) to blow up, demolish // vi to fly.

volátil [bo'latil] a volatile; (fig) changeable.

volcán [bol'kan] nm volcano; **~ico, a** a volcanic.

volcar [bol'kar] vt to upset, overturn; (tumbar, derribar) to knock over; (vaciar) to empty out // vi to overturn; **~se** vr to tip over.

volibol [boli'βol] nm volleyball.

volición [boli'θjon] nf volition.

voltaje [bol'taxe] nm voltage.

volteador, a [boltea'ðor, a] nm/f acrobat.

voltear [bolte'ar] vt to turn over; (volcar) to turn upside down; (doblar) to peal // vi to roll over.

voltio ['boltjo] nm volt.

voluble [bo'luβle] a fickle.

volumen [bo'lumen] nm volume; **voluminoso, a** a voluminous; (enorme) massive.

voluntad [bolun'tað] nf will, willpower; (deseo) desire, wish; (afecto) fondness.

voluntario, a [bolun'tarjo, a] a voluntary // nm/f volunteer.

voluntarioso, a [bolunta'rjoso, a] a headstrong.

voluptuoso, a [bolup'twoso, a] a voluptuous.

volver [bol'βer] vt (gen) to turn; (dar vuelta) to turn (over); (voltear) to turn round, turn upside down; (poner al revés) to turn inside out; (devolver) to return; (transformar) to change, transform // vi to return, go/come back; **~se** vr to turn round; (llegar a ser) to become; **~ la espalda** to turn one's back; **~ bien por mal** to return good for evil; **~ a hacer** to do again; **~ en sí** to come to; **~se loco** to go mad.

vomitar [bomi'tar] vt, vi to vomit; **vómito** nm (acto) vomiting; (resultado) vomit.

voraz [bo'raθ] a voracious; (fig) fierce.

vórtice ['bortiθe] nm whirlpool; (de aire) whirlwind.

vosotros [bo'sotros] pron you.

votación [bota'θjon] nf (acto) voting; (voto) vote; **votar** vi to vote; **voto** nm vote; (promesa) vow; (maldición) oath, curse; **votos** (good) wishes.

voy vb ver **ir.**

voz [boθ] nf voice; (grito) shout; (chisme) rumour; (LING) word; **dar voces** to shout, yell; **a media ~** in a low voice; **a ~ en cuello** or **grito** at the top of one's voice; **de viva ~** verbally; **en ~ alta** aloud; **~ de mando** command.

vuelco ['bwelko] nm spill, over-turning; (fig) collapse.

vuelo ['bwelo] vb ver **voler** // nm flight; (encaje) lace, frill; (fig) importance; **coger al ~** to catch in flight.

vuelta ['bwelta] nf (gen) turn; (curva) bend, curve; (regreso) return; (revolución) revolution; (paseo) stroll; (circuito) lap; (de papel, tela) reverse; (cambio) change; **V~ de Francia** Tour de France; **~ cerrada** hairpin bend; **a la ~** on one's return; **a ~ de correo** by return of post; **dar ~s** to turn, revolve; **dar ~s a una idea** to turn over an idea (in one's head); **estar de ~** (fam) to be back; **dar una ~** to go for a walk.

vuelto pp de **volver.**

vuelvo etc vb ver **volver.**

vuestro, a ['bwestro, a] a your; **un amigo ~** a friend of yours // pron: **el ~/la ~/los ~s/las ~s** yours.

vulgar [bul'xar] a (ordinario) vulgar; (común) common; **~idad** nf commonness; (acto) vulgarity; (expresión) coarse expression; **~idades** nfpl banalities; **~izar** vt to popularize.

vulgo ['bulxo] nm common people.

vulnerable [bulne'raßle] a vulnerable.

vulnerar [bulne'rar] vt to harm, damage.

vulpino, a [bul'pino, a] a vulpine; (fig) foxy.

(BOT) leaf bud; (fig) best part; ~ del dedo fingertip.

yergo etc vb ver **erguir**.

yermo, a [ˈjermo, a] a uninhabited // nm waste land.

yerno [ˈjerno] nm son-in-law.

yerro etc vb ver **errar**.

yerto, a [ˈjerto, a] a stiff.

yesca [ˈjeska] nf tinder.

yeso [ˈjeso] nm (GEO) gypsum; (ARQ) plaster.

W

wáter [ˈbater] nm lavatory.

wátman [ˈwatman] a inv (fam) cool.

whisky [ˈwiski] nm whisky.

X

xenofobia [kseno'foßja] nf xenophobia.

xilófono [ksi'lofono] nm xylophone.

Y

y [i] conj and.

ya [ja] ad (gen) already; (ahora) now; (en seguida) at once; (pronto) soon // excl all right! // conj (ahora que) now that; ~ lo sé I know; ~ dice que sí, ~ dice que no first he says yes, then he says no; ~ que since.

yacer [ja'θer] vi to lie.

yacimiento [jaθi'mjento] nm bed deposit.

yanqui [ˈjanki] a Yankee.

yate [ˈjate] nm yacht.

yazco etc vb ver **yacer**.

yedra [ˈjeðra] nf ivy.

yegua [ˈjeɣwa] nf mare.

yema [ˈjema] nf (del huevo) yoke;

yodo [ˈjoðo] nm iodine.

yugo [ˈjuxo] nm yoke.

Yugoslavia [juɣos'laßja] nf Yugoslavia.

yugular [juɣu'lar] a jugular.

yunque [ˈjunke] nm anvil.

yunta [ˈjunta] nf yoke; **yuntero** nm ploughman.

yute [ˈjute] nm jute.

yuxtaponer [jukstapo'ner] vt to juxtapose; **yuxtaposición** nf juxtaposition.

Z

zafar [θa'far] vt (soltar) to untie; (superficie) to clear; ~se vr (escaparse) to escape; (ocultarse) to hide o.s. away; (TEC) to slip off.

zafio, a [ˈθafjo, a] a coarse.

zafiro [θa'firo] nm sapphire.

zaga [ˈθaɣa] nf rear; a la ~ behind, in the rear.

zagal, a [θa'ɣal, a] nm/f boy/girl, lad/lass.

zaguán [θa'ɣwan] nm hallway.

zahareño, a [θaa'reɲo, a] a (salvaje) wild; (arisco) unsociable.

zaherir [θae'rir] vt (criticar) to criticise; (fig: herir) to wound.

zahorí [θao'ri] nm clairvoyant.

zaino, a [ˈθaino, a] a (color de caballo) chestnut; (pérfido) treacherous; (animal) vicious.

zalameria [θala'merja] nf flattery;

zalamero, a a flattering; (relamido) suave.

zamarra [θa'marra] nf (piel) sheepskin; (saco) sheepskin jacket.

zambra [θambra] nf gypsy dance.

zambullirse [θambu'λirse] vr to dive; (ocultarse) to hide o.s.

zampar [θam'par] vt (esconder) to hide or put away (hurriedly); (comer) to gobble; (arrojar) to hurl // vi to eat voraciously; **~se** vr (chocar) to bump; (fig) to gatecrash.

zanahoria [θana'orja] nf carrot.

zancada [θan'kaða] nf stride.

zancadilla [θanka'ðiλa] nf trip; (fig) stratagem.

zancajo [θan'kaxo] nm (ANAT) heel; (fig) dwarf.

zanco [θanko] nm stilt.

zancudo, a [θan'kuðo, a] a long-legged // nm (AM) mosquito.

zángano [θangano] nm drone.

zanja [θanxa] nf (fosa) ditch; (tumba) grave; **zanjar** vt (fosa) to ditch, trench; (problema) to surmount; (conflicto) to resolve.

zapapico [θapa'piko] nm pick, pickaxe.

zapata [θa'pata] nf half-boot; (MECÁNICA) shoe.

zapatear [θapate'ar] vt (tocar) to tap with one's foot; (patear) to kick; (fam) to ill-treat // vi to tap with one's feet.

zapatería [θapate'ria] nf (oficio) shoemaking; (tienda) shoe-shop; (fábrica) shoe factory; **zapatero, a** nm/f shoemaker.

zapatilla [θapa'tiλa] nf slipper.

zapato [θa'pato] nm shoe.

zarabanda [θara'βanda] nf saraband; (fig) whirl.

zaranda [θa'randa] nf sieve; **zarandear** vt to sieve; (fam) to shake vigorously.

zarcillo [θar'θiλo] nm earring.

zarpa [θarpa] nf (garra) claw.

zarpar [θar'par] vi to weigh anchor.

zarza [θarθa] nf (BOT) bramble; **zarzal** nm (matorral) bramble patch.

zarzamora [θarθa'mora] nf blackberry.

zarzuela [θar'θwela] nf Spanish light opera.

zigzag [θiɣ'θax] a zigzag; **zigzaguear** vi to zigzag.

zinc [θink] nm zinc.

zócalo [θokalo] nm (ARQ) plinth, base.

zona [θona] nf zone; **~ fronteriza** border area.

zoología [θoolo'xia] nf zoology; **zoológico, a** a zoological // nm zoo; **zoólogo, a** nm/f zoologist.

zopilote [θopi'lote] nm (AM) buzzard.

zoquete [θo'kete] nm (madera) block; (pan) crust; (fam) blockhead.

zorro, a [θorro, a] a crafty // nm/f fox/vixen.

zozobra [θo'θoβra] nf (fig) anxiety; **zozobrar** vi (hundirse) to capsize; (fig) to fail.

zueco [θweko] nm clog.

zumbar [θum'bar] vt (burlar) to tease; (golpear) to hit // vi to buzz; (fam) to be very close; **~se** vr: **~se de** to tease; **zumbido** nm buzzing; (fam) punch.

zumo [θumo] nm juice; (ganancia) profit.

zurcir [θur'θir] vt (coser) to darn; (fig) to put together.

zurdo, a [θurðo, a] a (mano) left; (persona) left-handed.

zurrar [θu'rrar] vt (TEC) to dress; (fam: pegar duro) to wallop; (: aplastar) to flatten; (: criticar) to criticize harshly.

zurriago [θu'rrjaxo] nm whip, lash.

zurrón [θu'rron] nm pouch.

zutano, a [θu'tano, a] nm/f so-and-so.

A

a, an [ei, ə, ən, æn, n] *det* un(a); 3 a day/week 3 por día/semana; 10 km an hour 10 km por hora.

A.A. *n abbr of* **Automobile Association; Alcoholics Anonymous.**

aback [ə'bæk] *ad:* to be taken ~ quedar desconcertado.

abandon [ə'bændən] *vt* abandonar; (renounce) renunciar a // *n* abandono; (wild behaviour) desenfreno.

abashed [ə'bæʃt] *a* avergonzado, confuso.

abate [ə'beit] *vi* moderarse; (lessen) disminuir; (calm down) calmarse.

abattoir ['æbətwɑ:*] *n* matadero.

abbey ['æbi] *n* monasterio.

abbot ['æbət] *n* abad *m.*

abbreviate [ə'bri:vieit] *vt* abreviar; **abbreviation** [-'eiʃən] *n* (short form) abreviatura; (act) abreviación *f.*

abdicate ['æbdikeit] *vt, vi* abdicar; **abdication** ['-keiʃən] *n* abdicación *f.*

abdomen ['æbdəmən] *n* abdomen *m*

abduct [æb'dʌkt] *vt* raptar, secuestrar; ~**ion** [-'dʌkʃən] *n* rapto, secuestro.

aberration [æbə'reiʃən] *n* aberración *f.*

abet [ə'bet] *vt* (incite) incitar; (aid) ser cómplice de.

abeyance [ə'beiəns] *n:* in ~ (law) en desuso; (matter) en suspenso.

abhor [əb'hɔ:*] *vt* aborrecer, abominar de; ~**rent** [əb'hɔrənt] *a* aborrecible, detestable.

abide [ə'baid] *vt, pp* abode *or* **abided** *vt* aguantar, soportar; to ~ **by** *vt fus* atenerse a.

ability [ə'biliti] *n* habilidad *f,* capacidad *f;* (talent) talento.

ablaze [ə'bleiz] *a* en llamas, ardiendo.

able ['eibl] *a* capaz; (skilled) hábil; to be ~ to do sth poder hacer algo; ~-**bodied** *a* sano; **ably** *ad* hábilmente.

abnormal [æb'nɔ:məl] *a* anormal; ~**ity** [-'mæliti] *n* anormalidad *f.*

aboard [ə'bɔ:d] *ad* a bordo // *prep* a bordo de.

abode [ə'bəud] *pt, pp of* **abide** // *n* domicilio.

abolish [ə'bɔliʃ] *vt* suprimir, abolir; **abolition** [æbəu'liʃən] *n* supresión *f,* abolición *f.*

abominable [ə'bɔminəbl] *a* abominable.

aborigine [æbə'ridʒini] *n* aborigen *m.*

abort [ə'bɔ:t] *vt* abortar; ~**ion** [ə'bɔ:ʃən] *n* aborto (provocado); to have an ~**ion** abortarse, hacerse abortar; ~**ive** *a* fracasado.

abound [ə'baund] *vi* abundar.

about [ə'baut] *prep* (subject) acerca de, sobre; (place) alrededor de, por // *ad* casi, más o menos, a eso de; to **walk ~ the town** andar por la ciudad; **it takes ~ 10 hours** es cosa de 10 horas más o menos; at ~ **2 o'clock** a eso de las 2; to be ~ to estar a punto de; **what or how ~ doing this?** ¿qué tal si hacemos esto?; ~ **turn** *n* media vuelta.

above [ə'bʌv] *ad* encima, por encima, arriba // *prep* encima de; **mentioned** ~ susodicho; ~ **all** sobre todo; ~ **board** a legítimo.

abrasion [ə'breiʒən] *n* (on skin) abrasión *f,* **abrasive** [ə'breiziv] *a* abrasivo.

abreast [ə'brest] *ad* de frente; to **keep** ~ mantenerse al corriente de.

abridge [ə'brɪdʒ] vt abreviar.
abroad [ə'brɔːd] ad (to be) en el extranjero; (to go) al extranjero.
abrupt [ə'brʌpt] a (sudden) brusco; (gruff) áspero.
abscess ['æbsɪs] n absceso.
abscond [əb'skɔnd] vi fugarse.
absence ['æbsəns] n ausencia.
absent ['æbsənt] a ausente; **~ee** [-'tiː] n ausente m/f; **~eeism** [-'tiːɪzəm] n absentismo; **~-minded** a distraído.
absolute ['æbsəluːt] a absoluto; **~ly** [-'luːtlɪ] ad absolutamente.
absolve [əb'zɔlv] vt: to **~ sb (from)** absolver a alguien (de).
absorb [əb'zɔːb] vt absorber; to be **~ed in a book** estar absorto en un libro; **~ent** a absorbente; **~ing** a absorbente.
abstain [əb'steɪn] vi: to **~ (from)** abstenerse (de).
abstention [əb'stɛnʃən] n abstención f.
abstinence ['æbstɪnəns] n abstinencia.
abstract ['æbstrækt] a abstracto.
absurd [əb'sɔːd] a absurdo; **~ity** n absurdo.
abundance [ə'bʌndəns] n abundancia; **abundant** [-dənt] a abundante.
abuse [ə'bjuːs] n (insults) improperios mpl, injurias fpl; (misuse) abuso // vt [ə'bjuːz] (ill-treat) maltratar; (take advantage of) abusar de; **abusive** a ofensivo.
abysmal [ə'bɪzməl] a abismal; (ignorance etc) profundo.
abyss [ə'bɪs] n abismo.
academic [ækə'dɛmɪk] a académico, universitario; (pej: issue) puramente teórico.
academy [ə'kædəmɪ] n (learned body) academia; (school) instituto, colegio.
accede [æk'siːd] vi: to **~ to** (request) consentir en; (throne) subir a.
accelerate [æk'sɛləreɪt] vt acelerar // vi acelerarse; accelera-

tion [-'reɪʃən] n aceleración f;
accelerator n acelerador m.
accent ['æksənt] n acento.
accept [æk'sɛpt] vt aceptar; (approve) aprobar; (permit) admitir; **~able** a aceptable; admisible; **~ance** n aceptación f, aprobación f.
access ['æksɛs] n acceso; to have **~ to** tener libre acceso a; **~ible** ['sɛsəbl] a accesible.
accessory [æk'sɛsərɪ] n accesorio; **toilet accessories** npl artículos mpl de tocador.
accident ['æksɪdənt] n accidente m; (chance) casualidad f; by **~** (unintentionally) sin querer; (by coincidence) por casualidad; **~al** [-'dɛntl] a accidental, fortuito; **~ally** ['dɛntəlɪ] ad sin querer; por casualidad; **~-prone** a con tendencia a sufrir/causar accidentes.
acclaim [ə'kleɪm] vt aclamar, aplaudir // n aclamación f, aplausos mpl.
acclimatize [ə'klaɪmətaɪz] vt: to **become ~** d aclimatarse.
accommodate [ə'kɔmədeɪt] vt alojar, hospedar; (reconcile) componer; (oblige, help) complacer; (adapt): to **~ one's plans to** acomodar sus proyectos a; **accommodating** a servicial, complaciente.
accommodation [əkɔmə'deɪʃən] n alojamiento; (space) sitio.
accompaniment [ə'kʌmpənɪmənt] n acompañamiento;
accompany [-nɪ] vt acompañar.
accomplice [ə'kʌmplɪs] n cómplice m/f.
accomplish [ə'kʌmplɪʃ] vt (finish) acabar, alcanzar; (achieve) realizar, llevar a cabo; **~ed** a experto, hábil; **~ment** n (ending) conclusión f; (bringing about) realización f; (skill) talento.
accord [ə'kɔːd] n acuerdo // vt concordar; **of his own ~** espontáneamente; **~ance** n: in

~ance with de acuerdo con; ~ing to prep según; (in accordance with) conforme a; ~ingly ad (thus) por consiguiente.

accordion [ɔ'kɔːdiɔn] n acordeón m.

accost [ɔ'kɔst] vt abordar, dirigirse a.

account [ɔ'kaunt] n (COMM) cuenta, factura; (report) informe m; of little ~ de poca importancia; on ~ a cuenta, on no ~ de ninguna manera, bajo ningún concepto; on ~ of a causa de, por motivo de; to take into ~, take ~ of tomar o tener en cuenta; to ~ for vt (answer for) responder de; (explain) dar cuenta o razón de; ~able a responsable.

accountancy [ɔ'hauntɔnsɪ] n contabilidad f; **accountant** [-tnt] n contador/a m/f.

accumulate [ɔ'kjuːmjuleɪt] vt acumular // vi acumularse; **accumulation** [-'leɪʃɔn] n acumulación f.

accuracy ['ækjurɔsɪ] n exactitud f, precisión f; **accurate** [-rɪt] a (number) exacto; (answer) acertado; (shot) certero.

accusation [ækju'zeɪʃɔn] n acusación f; **accuse** [ɔ'kjuːz] vt acusar; (blame) echar la culpa a; **accused** [ɔ'kjuːzd] n acusado/a.

accustom [ɔ'kʌstɔm] vt acostumbrar; ~ed a: ~ed to acostumbrado a.

ace [eɪs] n as m.

ache [eɪk] n dolor m // vi doler; my head ~s me duele la cabeza.

achieve [ɔ'tʃiːv] vt (reach) alcanzar; (realize) llevar a cabo; (victory, success) lograr, conseguir; ~ment n (completion) realización f; (success) éxito.

acid ['æsɪd] a ácido; (bitter) agrio // n ácido; ~ity [ɔ'sɪdɪtɪ] n acidez f; (MED) acedía.

acknowledge [ɔk'nɔlɪdʒ] vt (letter) acusar recibo de; (fact)

reconocer; ~ment n acuse m de recibo; reconocimiento.

acne ['æknɪ] n acné m.

acorn ['eɪkɔːn] n bellota.

acoustic [ɔ'kuːstɪk] a acústico; ~s n, npl acústica sg.

acquaint [ɔ'kweɪnt] vt: to ~ sb with sth (warn) avisar a uno de algo; (inform) poner a uno al corriente de algo; to be ~ed with (person) conocer; (fact) estar al corriente de; ~ance n conocimiento; (person) conocido/a.

acquiesce [ækwɪ'es] vi: to ~ in consentir en, conformarse con.

acquire [ɔ'kwaɪɔ*] vt adquirir; (achieve) conseguir; **acquisition** [ækwɪ'zɪʃɔn] n adquisición f; **acquisitive** [ɔ'kwɪzɪtɪv] a codicioso.

acquit [ɔ'kwɪt] vt absolver, exculpar; to ~ o.s. well defenderse, salir con éxito; ~tal n absolución f, exculpación f.

acre ['eɪkɔ*] n acre m.

acrimonious [ækrɪ'mɔunɪɔs] a (remark) mordaz, (argument) reñido.

acrobat ['ækrɔbæt] n acróbata m/f; ~ics [ækrɔ'bætɪks] n, npl acrobacia sg.

across [ɔ'krɔs] prep (on the other side of) al otro lado de, del otro lado de; (crosswise) a través de // ad de un lado a otro, de una parte a otra; a través, al través; to run/swim ~ atravesar corriendo/nadando; ~ from enfrente de.

act [ækt] n acto, acción f; (THEATRE) acto; (in music-hall etc) número; (LAW) decreto, ley f // vi (machine) funcionar, marchar; (person) actuar, comportarse; (THEATRE) actuar, trabajar; (pretend) fingir; (take action) obrar // vt (part) hacer el papel de, representar; to ~ as actuar o hacer de; ~ing a suplente // n: to do some ~ing ser actor/actriz.

action ['ækʃɔn] n acción f; acto; (MIL) acción f, batalla; (LAW) proceso, demanda; **to take** ~ tomar medidas.

activate ['æktɪveɪt] vt (mechanism) activar.

active ['æktɪv] a activo, enérgico; (volcano) en actividad; **activity** [-'tɪvɪtɪ] n actividad f.

actor ['æktə*] n actor m; **actress** [-trɪs] n actriz f.

actual ['æktjuəl] a verdadero, real; ~**ly** ad realmente, en realidad.

acupuncture ['ækjupʌŋktʃə*] n acupuntura.

acute [ə'kju:t] a (gen) agudo.

ad [æd] n abbr of **advertisement**.
A.D. ad abbr of **Anno Domini** A.C. (año de Cristo).

Adam ['ædəm] n Adán; ~'s **apple** n nuez f de la garganta.

adamant ['ædəmənt] a firme, inflexible.

adapt [ə'dæpt] vt adaptar; (reconcile) acomodar // vi: **to** ~ **(to)** adaptarse (a), ajustarse (a); ~**able** a (device) adaptable; (person) que se adapta; ~**ation** [ædæp'teɪʃən] n adaptación f; ~**er** n (ELEC) adaptador m.

add [æd] vt añadir, agregar; (figures: also: ~ **up**) sumar // vi: **to** ~ **to** (increase) aumentar, acrecentar; **it doesn't** ~ **up** no tiene sentido.

adder ['ædə*] n víbora.

addict ['ædɪkt] n (enthusiast) entusiasta m/f; (to drugs etc) adicto/a; ~**ed** [ə'dɪktɪd] a: **to be** ~**ed to** ser aficionado de; ser adicto a; **addiction** [ə'dɪkʃən] n (enthusiasm) afición f; (dependence) hábito morboso.

adding machine ['ædɪŋməʃi:n] n calculadora.

addition [ə'dɪʃən] n (adding up) adición f; (thing added) añadidura, añadido; **in** ~ además, por añadidura; **in** ~ **to** además de; ~**al** a adicional.

additive ['ædɪtɪv] n aditivo.

address [ə'drɛs] n dirección f, señas fpl; (speech) discurso // vt

(letter) dirigir; (speak to) dirigirse a, dirigir la palabra a; ~**ee** [ædrɛ'si:] n destinatario/a.

adenoids ['ædɪnɔɪdz] npl vegetaciones fpl adenoideas.

adept ['ædɛpt] a: ~ **at** experto o hábil en.

adequate ['ædɪkwɪt] a (apt) adecuado; (enough) suficiente.

adhere [əd'hɪə*] vi: **to** ~ **to** pegarse a; (fig: abide by) observar; (: hold to) adherirse a; **adherent** n partidario/a.

adhesive [əd'hi:zɪv] a, n adhesivo.

adjacent [ə'dʒeɪsənt] a: ~ **to** contiguo a, inmediato a.

adjective ['ædʒɛktɪv] n adjetivo.

adjoining [ə'dʒɔɪnɪŋ] a contiguo, vecino.

adjourn [ə'dʒə:n] vt aplazar; (session) suspender, levantar // vi suspenderse.

adjudicate [ə'dʒu:dɪkeɪt] vi sentenciar; **adjudicator** n juez m, árbitro.

adjust [ə'dʒʌst] vt (change) modificar; (arrange) arreglar; (machine) ajustar // vi: **to** ~ **(to)** adaptarse (a); ~**able** a ajustable; ~**ment** n modificación f, arreglo; (of prices, wages) ajuste m.

adjutant ['ædʒətənt] n ayudante m.

ad-lib [æd'lɪb] vt, vi improvisar; **ad lib** ad a voluntad, a discreción.

administer [əd'mɪnɪstə*] vt proporcionar; (justice) administrar; **administration** [-'treɪʃən] n administración f; (government) gobierno; **administrative** [-trətɪv] a administrativo; **administrator** [-treɪtə*] n administrador/a m/f.

admirable ['ædmərəbl] a admirable.

admiral ['ædmərəl] n almirante m; **A**~**ty** n Ministerio de Marina, Almirantazgo.

admiration [ædmə'reɪʃən] n admiración f.

admire [əd'maɪə*] vt admirar; **admirer** [əd'maɪərə*] n admirador/a m/f.

(suitor) pretendiente *m*.

admission [ədˈmɪʃən] *n* *(entry)* entrada; *(enrolment)* ingreso; *(confession)* confesión *f*.

admit [ədˈmɪt] *vt* dejar entrar, dar entrada a; *(permit)* admitir; *(acknowledge)* reconocer; *(accept)* aceptar; **to ~ to** confesarse culpable de; **~tance** *n* entrada; **~tedly** *ad* de acuerdo que.

admonish [ədˈmɒnɪʃ] *vt* amonestar; *(advise)* aconsejar.

ado [əˈduː] *n*: **without (any) more ~** sin más (ni más).

adolescence [ædəʊˈlesns] *n* adolescencia; **adolescent** [-ˈlesnt] *a*, *n* adolescente *m/f*.

adopt [əˈdɒpt] *vt* adoptar; **~ion** [əˈdɒpʃən] *n* adopción *f*; **~ed** *a* adoptivo.

adore [əˈdɔː*] *vt* adorar.

adorn [əˈdɔːn] *vt* adornar.

adrenalin [əˈdrenəlɪn] *n* adrenalina.

Adriatic [eɪdrɪˈætɪk] *n*: **the ~ (Sea)** el (Mar) Adriático.

adrift [əˈdrɪft] *ad* a la deriva; **to come ~** desprenderse.

adult [ˈædʌlt] *n* (gen) adulto.

adulterate [əˈdʌltəreɪt] *vt* adulterar.

adultery [əˈdʌltərɪ] *n* adulterio.

advance [ədˈvɑːns] *n* (gen) adelanto, progreso; *(money)* anticipo, préstamo; *(MIL)* avance *m* // *vt* avanzar, adelantar; anticipar; prestar // *vi* avanzar, adelantarse; **in ~** por adelantado; **~d** *a* avanzado; *(SCOL: studies)* adelantado; **~d in years** entrado en años; **~ment** *n* progreso; *(in rank)* ascenso.

advantage [ədˈvɑːntɪdʒ] *n* (also TENNIS) ventaja; **to take ~ of** (use) aprovecharse de; *(gain by)* sacar provecho de; **~ous** [ædvənˈteɪdʒəs] *a* ventajoso, provechoso.

advent [ˈædvənt] *n* advenimiento; **A~** Adviento.

adventure [ədˈventʃə*] *n* aventura;

(suitor) pretendiente *m*.

adventurous [-tʃərəs] *a* aventurero.

adverb [ˈædvɜːb] *n* adverbio.

adversary [ˈædvəsərɪ] *n* adversario, contrario.

adverse [ˈædvɜːs] *a* adverso, contrario; **~ to** adverso a.

adversity [ədˈvɜːsɪtɪ] *n* infortunio.

advert [ˈædvɜːt] *n* abbr of **advertisement**.

advertise [ˈædvətaɪz] *vi* hacer propaganda; *(in newspaper etc)* poner un anuncio // *vt* anunciar; **~ment** [ədˈvɜːtɪsmənt] *n* (COMM) anuncio; **advertising** *n* publicidad *f*, propaganda; anuncios *mpl*.

advice [ədˈvaɪs] *n* consejo, consejos *mpl*; *(notification)* aviso; **to take legal ~** consultar a un abogado.

advisable [ədˈvaɪzəbl] *a* aconsejable, conveniente.

advise [ədˈvaɪz] *vt* aconsejar; *(inform)* avisar; **adviser** *n* consejero; *(business adviser)* asesor *m*; **advisory** *a* consultivo.

advocate [ˈædvəkeɪt] *vt* (argue for) abogar por; *(give support to)* ser partidario de // *n* [-kɪt] abogado.

aerial [ˈeərɪəl] *n* antena // *a* aéreo.

aeroplane [ˈeərəpleɪn] *n* avión *m*.

aerosol [ˈeərəsɒl] *n* aerosol *m*.

aesthetic [iːsˈθetɪk] *a* estético.

afar [əˈfɑː*] *ad*: **from ~** desde lejos.

affable [ˈæfəbl] *a* afable.

affair [əˈfeə*] *n* asunto; *(also: love ~)* aventura o relación *f* (amorosa).

affect [əˈfekt] *vt* afectar, influir en; *(move)* conmover; **~ation** [æfekˈteɪʃən] *n* afectación *f*; **~ed** *a* afectado.

affection [əˈfekʃən] *n* afecto, cariño; **~ate** *a* afectuoso, cariñoso.

affiliated [əˈfɪlɪeɪtɪd] *a* afiliado.

affinity [əˈfɪnɪtɪ] *n* afinidad *f*.

affirmation [æfəˈmeɪʃən] *n* afirmación *f*.

affirmative [əˈfɜːmətɪv] *a* afirmativo.

affix [əˈfɪks] *vt* (signature) poner, añadir; *(stamp)* pegar.

afflict [əˈflɪkt] *vt* afligir; **~ion**

affluence [ˈæfluəns] n opulencia, riqueza; **affluent** [-ənt] a opulento, acaudalado.

afford [əˈfɔːd] vt (provide) dar, proporcionar; **can we ~ it?** ¿tenemos bastante dinero para comprarlo?

affront [əˈfrʌnt] n afrenta, ofensa.

afield [əˈfiːld] ad: **far ~** muy lejos.

afloat [əˈflout] ad (floating) a flote; (at sea) en el mar.

afoot [əˈfut] ad: **there is something ~** algo se está tramando.

aforesaid [əˈfɔːsed] a susodicho.

afraid [əˈfreid] a: **to be ~ of** (person) tener miedo a; (thing) tener miedo de; **to be ~** to tener miedo de temer; **I am ~ that** me temo que.

afresh [əˈfreʃ] ad de nuevo, otra vez.

Africa [ˈæfrikə] n África; **~n** a, n africano/a.

aft [ɑːft] ad (to be) en popa; (to go) a popa.

after [ˈɑːftə*] prep (time) después de; (place, order) detrás de, tras // ad (behind) // conj después que; **what/who are you ~?** ¿qué/a quién busca Usted?; **to ask ~** sb preguntar por alguien; **~ all** después de todo, al fin y al cabo; **~ you!** ¡pase Usted!; **~birth** n secundinas fpl; **~-effects** npl consecuencias fpl, efectos mpl; **~life** n vida futura; **~math** n consecuencias fpl, resultados mpl; **~noon** n tarde f; **~-shave (lotion)** n loción f para después del afeitado; **~thought** n ocurrencia (tardía); **~wards** ad después, más tarde.

again [əˈgen] ad otra vez, de nuevo; **to do sth ~** volver a hacer algo; **~ and ~** una y otra vez; **now and ~** de vez en cuando.

against [əˈgenst] prep (opposed) contra, en contra de; (close to) contra, junto a.

age [eidʒ] n (gen) edad f; (old ~)

vejez f; (period) época // vi envejecer(se) // vt envejecer; **to come of ~** llegar a la mayoría de edad; **it's been ~s since** hace muchísimo tiempo que; **~d** a [ˈeidʒid] viejo, anciano // a [eidʒd]: **~d 10** de 10 años de edad; **~ group** n: **to be in the same ~ group** tener la misma edad; **~less** a (eternal) eterno; (ever young) siempre joven; **~ limit** n edad mínima/máxima.

agency [ˈeidʒənsi] n agencia; **through** or **by the ~ of** por medio de.

agenda [əˈdʒendə] n orden m del día.

agent [ˈeidʒənt] n (gen) agente m/f; (representative) representante m/f, delegado/a.

aggravate [ˈægrəveit] vt agravar; (annoy) irritar, exasperar; **aggravation** [-ˈveiʃən] n agravación f.

aggregate [ˈægrigeit] n (whole) conjunto; (collection) agregado.

aggression [əˈgreʃən] n agresión f; **aggressive** [əˈgresiv] a agresivo; (zealous) enérgico.

aggrieved [əˈgriːvd] a ofendido, agraviado.

aghast [əˈgɑːst] a horrorizado; **to be ~** pasmarse.

agile [ˈædʒail] a ágil.

agitate [ˈædʒiteit] vt (shake) agitar; (trouble) inquietar; **to ~ for** hacer campaña pro o en favor de; **agitator** n agitador/a m/f.

ago [əˈgou] ad: **2 days ~** hace 2 días; **not long ~** hace poco; **how long ~?** ¿hace cuánto tiempo?

agog [əˈgɔg] a (anxious) ansiado; (excited) emocionado.

agonizing [ˈægənaiziŋ] a (pain) atroz, agudo; (suspense) angustioso.

agony [ˈægəni] n (pain) dolor m agudo; (distress) angustia; **to be in ~** sufrir atrozmente.

agree [əˈgriː] vt (price) acordar, quedar en // vi (statements etc) coincidir, concordar; **to ~ (with)** (person) estar de acuerdo (con, ponerse de acuerdo (con); **to ~ to do** aceptar hacer; **to ~ to sth** consentir en algo; **to ~ that** (*admit*) estar de acuerdo en que; **garlic doesn't ~ with me** el ajo no me sienta bien; **~able** *a* agradable; (*person*) simpático; (*willing*) de acuerdo, conforme; **~d** *a* (*time, place*) convenido; **~ment** *n* acuerdo, (*COMM*) contrato; **in ~ment** de acuerdo, conforme.

agricultural [ægrɪˈkʌltʃərəl] *a* agrícola; **agriculture** [ˈægrɪkʌltʃə*] *n* agricultura.

aground [əˈgraund] *ad*: **to run ~** encallar, embarrancar.

ahead [əˈhed] *ad* delante; **~ of** delante de; (*fig: schedule etc*) antes de; **~ of time** antes de la hora; **to be ~ of sb** (*fig*) llevar la ventaja a alguien; **go right** *or* **straight ~** ¡siga adelante!

aid [eɪd] *n* ayuda, auxilio // *vt* ayudar, auxiliar; **in ~ of** a beneficio de; **to ~ and abet** (*LAW*) ser cómplice de.

aide [eɪd] *n* (*person*) edecán *m*.

ailment [ˈeɪlmənt] *n* enfermedad *f*, achaque *m*.

aim [eɪm] *vt* (*gun, camera*) apuntar; (*missile, remark*) dirigir; (*blow*) asestar // *vi* (*also*: **take ~**) apuntar // *n* puntería; (*objective*) propósito, meta; **to ~ at** (*objective*) aspirar a, pretender; **to ~ to do** tener la intención de hacer; **~less** *a* sin propósito, sin objeto; **~lessly** *ad* a la ventura, a la deriva.

air [ɛə*] *n* aire *m*; (*appearance*) aspecto *m* // *vt* ventilar; (*grievances, ideas*) airear // *cpd* (*currents, attack etc*) aéreo, aeronáutico; **~borne** *a* (*in the air*) en el aire; (*MIL*) aerotransportado; **~-conditioned** *a* con aire acondicionado; **~conditioning** *n* aire acondicionado; **~craft** *n, pl inv* avión *m*; **~craft carrier** *n* (na)viones *m inv*; **A~ Force** *n* Fuerzas Aéreas *fpl*, aviación *f*; **~gun** *n* escopeta de aire

comprimido; **~ hostess** *n* azafata; **~ letter** *n* carta aérea; **~lift** *n* puente *m* aéreo; **~line** *n* línea aérea; **~liner** *n* avión *m* de pasajeros; **~lock** *n* esclusa de aire; **~mail** *n*: **by ~mail** por avión; **~port** *n* aeropuerto; **~ raid** *n* ataque *m* aéreo; **~sick** *a*: **to be ~sick** marearse (en un avión); **~strip** *n* pista de aterrizaje; **~tight** *a* hermético; **~y** *a* (*room*) bien ventilado; (*manners*) ligero.

aisle [aɪl] *n* (*of church*) nave *f*, (*of theatre*) pasillo.

ajar [əˈdʒɑː*] *a* entreabierto.

akin [əˈkɪn] *a*: **~ to** relacionado con.

alarm [əˈlɑːm] *n* alarma; (*anxiety*) inquietud *f* // *vt* asustar, inquietar; **~ clock** *n* despertador *m*.

Albania [ælˈbeɪnɪə] *n* Albania.

album [ˈælbəm] *n* álbum *m*; (*L.P.*) elepé *m*.

alcohol [ˈælkəhɒl] *n* alcohol *m*; **~ic** [-ˈhɒlɪk] *a, n* alcohólico/a; **~ism** *n* alcoholismo.

alcove [ˈælkəʊv] *n* nicho, hueco.

alderman [ˈɔːldəmən] *n, pl* **-men** concejal *m*.

ale [eɪl] *n* cerveza.

alert [əˈlɜːt] *a* alerta; (*sharp*) despierto, despabilado // *n* alerta *m* alarma // *vt* poner sobre aviso; **to be on the ~** estar alerta *o* sobre aviso.

algebra [ˈældʒɪbrə] *n* álgebra.

Algeria [ælˈdʒɪərɪə] *n* Argelia; **~n** *a, n* argelino/a.

alias [ˈeɪlɪəs] *ad* alias, por otro nombre // *n* alias *m*.

alibi [ˈælɪbaɪ] *n* coartada.

alien [ˈeɪlɪən] *n* extranjero/a // *a*: **~ to** distinto de, ajeno a; **~ate** *vt* enajenar, alejar; **~ation** [-ˈneɪʃən] *n* enajenación *f*.

alight [əˈlaɪt] *a* ardiendo, quemando // *vi* apearse, bajar.

align [əˈlaɪn] *vt* alinear; **~ment** *n* alineación *f*.

alike [əˈlaɪk] *a* semejantes, iguales

// ad igualmente, del mismo modo; **to look ~** parecerse.

alimony ['ælɪmənɪ] *n* (*payment*) alimentos *mpl*.

alive [ə'laɪv] *a* (*gen*) vivo; (*lively*) activo, enérgico.

alkali ['ælkəlaɪ] *n* álcali *m*.

all [ɔːl] *a* todo; (*pl*) todos(as) **// pron** todo; (*pl*) todos(as) **// pron** completamente, del todo; **~ alone** completamente solo; **at ~** en absoluto, del todo; **~ the time/his** life todo el tiempo/toda su vida; **~ five** todos los cinco; **~ of them** todos (ellos); **~ of us went** fuimos todos; **not as hard as ~ that** no tan difícil; **~ in ~** con todo, así y todo.

allay [ə'leɪ] *vt* (*fears*) aquietar; (*pain*) aliviar.

allegation [ælɪ'ɡeɪʃən] *n* aseveración *f*, alegación *f*.

allege [ə'ledʒ] *vt* afirmar, pretender.

allegiance [ə'liːdʒəns] *n* lealtad *f*.

allegory ['ælɪɡərɪ] *n* alegoría *f*.

allergic [ə'lɜːdʒɪk] *a*: **~ to** alérgico a; **allergy** ['ælədʒɪ] *n* alergia *f*.

alleviate [ə'liːvɪeɪt] *vt* aliviar, mitigar.

alley ['ælɪ] *n* (*street*) callejuela *f*; (*in garden*) paseo.

alliance [ə'laɪəns] *n* alianza *f*, **allied** ['ælaɪd] *a* aliado; (*related*) relacionado.

alligator ['ælɪɡeɪtə*] *n* caimán *m*.

all-in ['ɔːlɪn] *a* (*also ad*: *charge*) todo incluido; **~ wrestling** *n* lucha libre.

alliteration [əlɪtə'reɪʃən] *n* aliteración *f*.

all-night ['ɔːl'naɪt] *a* (*café*) abierto toda la noche; (*party*) que dura toda la noche.

allocate ['æləkeɪt] *vt* (*share out*) repartir, distribuir; (*devote*) asignar; **allocation** ['-'keɪʃən] *n* (*of money*) ración *f*, cuota; (*distribution*) reparto.

allot [ə'lɒt] *vt* asignar; **~ment** *n*

// ad igualmente, del mismo modo; **to look ~** parecerse.

ración *f*, porción *f*; (*garden*) parcela.

all-out ['ɔːl'aut] *a* (*effort etc*) máximo; **all out** *ad* con todas sus fuerzas; (*speed*) a la máxima velocidad.

allow [ə'lau] *vt* (*practice, behaviour*) permitir, dejar; (*sum to spend etc*) pagar, dar; (*a claim*) admitir; (*sum, time estimated*) dar, conceder; (*concede*): **to ~ that** reconocer que; **to ~ sb to do** permitir a alguien hacer; **to ~ for** *vt fus* tener en cuenta, tomar en consideración; **~ance** *n* (*gen*) concesión *f*; (*payment*) subvención *f*, pensión *f*; (*discount*) descuento, rebaja; **family ~ance** subsidio familiar; **to make ~ances for** ser indulgente con; tener en cuenta.

alloy ['ælɔɪ] *n* (*mix*) mezcla.

all: **~ right** *ad* (*well*) bien; (*correct*) correcto; (*as answer*) ¡conforme!, ¡está bien!; **~-round** *a* (*gen*) completo; (*view*) amplio; (*person*) que hace de todo; **~-time** *a* (*record*) de todos los tiempos.

allude [ə'luːd] *vi*: **to ~ to** aludir a.

alluring [ə'ljuərɪŋ] *a* seductor(a), atractivo.

allusion [ə'luːʒən] *n* referencia, alusión *f*.

ally ['ælaɪ] *n* aliado/a **// vr** [ə'laɪ]: **to ~ o.s. with** aliarse con.

almighty [ɔːl'maɪtɪ] *a* todopoderoso, omnipotente.

almond ['ɑːmɒnd] *n* (*fruit*) almendra; (*tree*) almendro.

almost ['ɔːlməust] *ad* casi, por poco.

alms [ɑːmz] *npl* limosna *sg*.

aloft [ə'lɒft] *ad* arriba, en alto.

alone [ə'ləun] *a* solo **// ad** sólo, solamente; **to leave sb ~** dejar a uno solo o en paz; **to leave sth ~** no tocar algo, dejar algo sin tocar; **~ let** ~ sin hablar de.

along [ə'lɒŋ] *prep* a lo largo de, por **// ad**: **is he coming ~ with us?** ¿nos acompaña?; **he was limping ~** iba cojeando; **~ with** junto con, además de; ~**side** *prep* junto a, al lado de // *ad* (NAUT) al costado.

aloof [ə'lu:f] *a* reservado // *ad*: **to stand** ~ mantenerse a distancia.

aloud [ə'laud] *ad* en voz alta.

alphabet ['ælfəbet] *n* alfabeto; ~**ical** [-'betikəl] *a* alfabético.

alpine ['ælpaɪn] *a* alpino, alpestre.

Alps [ælps] *npl*: **the** ~ los Alpes.

already [ɔːl'redɪ] *ad* ya.

alright ['ɔːl'raɪt] *ad* = **all right.**

also ['ɔːlsəu] *ad* también, además.

altar ['ɔːltə*] *n* altar *m*.

alter ['ɔːltə*] *vt* cambiar, modificar // *vi* cambiarse, mudarse; (**worsen**) alterarse, ~**ation** [ɔːltə'reɪʃən] *n* cambio, modificación *f*, alteración *f*.

alternate [ɔl'tə:nɪt] *a* alterno, alternativo // *vi* [ɔl'tə:neɪt] alternarse; **on** ~ **days** un día sí y otro no; ~**ly** *ad* alternativamente, por turno; **alternating** ['-neɪtɪŋ] *a* (**current**) alterno.

alternative [ɔl'tə:nətɪv] *a* alternativo // *n* alternativa; ~**ly** *ad*: ~**ly one could...** por otra parte se podría....

alternator ['ɔltə:neɪtə*] *n* (AUT) alternador *m*.

although [ɔːl'ðəu] *conj* aunque; (**given that**) si bien.

altitude ['æltɪtjuːd] *n* altitud *f*, altura.

alto ['æltəu] *n* (**female**) contralto *f*; (**male**) alto.

altogether [ɔːltə'geðə*] *ad* enteramente, del todo; (**on the whole, in all**) en total, en conjunto.

aluminium [ælju'mɪnɪəm], **aluminum** [ə'luːmɪnəm] (US) *n* aluminio.

always ['ɔːlweɪz] *ad* siempre.

am [æm] *vb see* **be.**

a.m. *ad abbr of* **ante meridiem** de la mañana, antes de mediodía.

amalgamate [ə'mælgəmeɪt] *vi* amalgamarse, unirse // *vt* amalgamar, unir; **amalgamation** ['-meɪʃən] *n* (COMM) amalgamación *f*, unión *f*.

amass [ə'mæs] *vt* amontonar, acumular.

amateur ['æmətə*] *n* aficionado/a, amateur *m/f*.

amaze [ə'meɪz] *vt* asombrar, pasmar; ~**ment** *n* asombro, sorpresa.

Amazon ['æməzən] *n* (GEO) Amazonas *m*.

ambassador [æm'bæsədə*] *n* embajador/a.

amber ['æmbə*] *n* ámbar *m*; **at** ~ (AUT) en el amarillo.

ambidextrous [æmbɪ'dekstrəs] *a* ambidextro.

ambiguity [æmbɪ'gjuɪtɪ] *n* ambigüedad *f*, (**of meaning**) doble sentido; **ambiguous** [-'bɪgjuəs] *a* ambiguo.

ambition [æm'bɪʃən] *n* ambición *f*; **ambitious** [-ʃəs] *a* ambicioso; (**plan**) grandioso.

ambivalent [æm'bɪvələnt] *a* ambivalente; (*pej*) equívoco.

amble ['æmbl] *vi* (**gen**: ~ **along**) deambular, andar sin prisa.

ambulance ['æmbjuləns] *n* ambulancia.

ambush ['æmbuʃ] *n* emboscada // *vt* tender una emboscada a; (*fig*) coger por sorpresa.

amenable [ə'miːnəbl] *a*: ~ **to** (**advice etc**) sensible a.

amend [ə'mend] *vt* (**law, text**) enmendar; (**habits**) corregir, mejorar; **to make** ~**s** compensar, dar satisfacción por; ~**ment** *n* enmienda.

amenities [ə'miːnɪtɪz] *npl* conveniencias *fpl*, comodidades *fpl*.

America [ə'merɪkə] *n* Estados Unidos *mpl*; ~**n** *a, n* norteamericano/a.

amiable ['eɪmɪəbl] *a* (**kind**) amable, simpático; (**hearty**) bonachón(ona).

amicable ['æmɪkəbl] *a* amistoso, amigable.

amid(st) [ə'mɪd(st)] *prep* entre, en medio de.

amiss [ə'mɪs] *ad*: **to take sth ~**
tomar algo a mal.

ammonia [ə'məʊnɪə] *n* amoníaco.

ammunition [æmjʊ'nɪʃən] *n*
municiones *fpl*.

amnesia [æm'niːzɪə] *n* amnesia.

amnesty [ˈæmnɪstɪ] *n* amnistía.

amok [ə'mɔk] *ad*: **to run ~**
enloquecerse, desbocarse.

among(st) [ə'mʌŋ(st)] *prep* entre,
en medio de.

amoral [æ'mɔrəl] *a* amoral.

amorous [ˈæmərəs] *a* amoroso; *(in
love)* enamorado.

amount [ə'maʊnt] *n (gen)* cantidad
f, *(of bill etc)* suma, importe *m* // *vi*:
to ~ to *(reach)* alcanzar; *(total)*
sumar; *(be same as)* equivaler a,
significar.

amp(ère) [ˈæmp(eə*)] *n* amperio.

amphibian [æm'fɪbɪən] *n* anfibio;
amphibious [-bɪəs] *a* anfibio.

amphitheatre [ˈæmfɪθɪətə*] *n*
anfiteatro.

ample [ˈæmpl] *a (spacious)* amplio,
ancho; *(abundant)* abundante;
(enough) bastante, suficiente.

amplifier [ˈæmplɪfaɪə*] *n* amplificador *m*.

amplify [ˈæmplɪfaɪ] *vt* amplificar,
aumentar; *(explain)* explicar.

amputate [ˈæmpjʊteɪt] *vt* amputar.

amuck [ə'mʌk] *ad* = **amok**.

amuse [ə'mjuːz] *vt* divertir;
(distract) distraer, entretener;
~ment *n* diversión *f*, *(pastime)*
pasatiempo; *(laughter)* risa.

an [æn, ən, n] *det* see **a**.

anaemia [ə'niːmɪə] *n* anemia;
anaemic [-mɪk] *a* anémico; *(fig)*
soso, insípido.

anaesthetic [ænɪs'θetɪk] *n* anes-
tesia; **anaesthetist** [æ'niːsθɪtɪst] *n*
anestesista *m/f*.

analgesic [ænæl'dʒiːsɪk] *a*, *n*
analgésico.

analogy [ə'nælədʒɪ] *n* analogo.

analyse [ˈænəlaɪz] *vt* analizar;
analysis [ə'nælɪsɪs], *pl* **-ses** [-siːz] *n*
análisis *m inv*; **analyst** [-ɪst] *n (US)*

analista *m/f*; **analytic(al)** [-'lɪtɪk(əl)]
a analítico.

anarchist [ˈænəkɪst] *a*, *n*
anarquista *m/f*; **anarchy** [-kɪ] *n*
anarquía, desorden *m*.

anatomy [ə'nætəmɪ] *n* anatomía.

ancestor [ˈænsɪstə*] *n* antepasado;
ancestry [-trɪ] *n* ascendencia,
abolengo.

anchor [ˈæŋkə*] *n* ancla, áncora //
vi anclar // *vt* *(fig)* sujetar,
asegurar; **to weigh ~** levar anclas;
~age *n* ancladero.

anchovy [ˈæntʃəvɪ] *n* anchoa.

ancient [ˈeɪnʃənt] *a* antiguo.

and [ænd] *conj* y; *(before i, hi)* e; **~
so on** etcétera, y así sucesivamente;
try ~ come procure o intente venir;
better ~ better cada vez mejor.

Andes [ˈændiːz] *npl*: **the ~** los
Andes.

anecdote [ˈænɪkdəʊt] *n* anécdota.

anew [ə'njuː] *ad* de nuevo, otra vez.

angel [ˈeɪndʒəl] *n* ángel *m*.

anger [ˈæŋgə*] *n* cólera, ira // *vt*
enojar, provocar.

angina [æn'dʒaɪnə] *n* angina (de
pecho).

angle [ˈæŋgl] *n* ángulo; **from their
~** desde su punto de vista.

angler [ˈæŋglə*] *n* pescador/a *m/f*
(de caña).

Anglican [ˈæŋglɪkən] *a*, *n*
anglicano/a.

angling [ˈæŋglɪŋ] *n* pesca con caña.

Anglo- [ˈæŋgləʊ] *pref* anglo... .

angrily [ˈæŋgrɪlɪ] *ad* con enojo,
airadamente.

angry [ˈæŋgrɪ] *a* enfadado, enojado;
to be ~ with sb/at sth estar
enfadado con alguien/por algo; **to
get ~** enfadarse, enojarse.

anguish [ˈæŋgwɪʃ] *n (physical)*
dolor *m* agudo; *(mental)* angustia.

angular [ˈæŋgjʊlə*] *a (shape)*
angular; *(features)* anguloso.

animal [ˈænɪməl] *n* animal *m*,
bestia; *(insect)* bicho // *a* animal.

animate [ˈænɪmeɪt] *vt (enliven)*
animar; *(encourage)* estimular,

alentar; ~ **d** a vivo, animado.

animosity [æni'mɔsiti] n animosidad f, rencor m.

aniseed ['ænisi:d] n anís m.

ankle ['æŋkl] n tobillo m.

annex [ə'neks] n (also: **annexe**) (edificio) anexo, dependencia // vt [æ'neks] (territory) anexar; (document) adjuntar.

annihilate [ə'naiəleit] vt aniquilar.

anniversary [æni'və:səri] n aniversario.

annotate ['ænəuteit] vt anotar, comentar.

announce [ə'nauns] vt comunicar, anunciar; ~**ment** n anuncio, aviso, declaración f; (RADIO, TV) locutor/a m/f.

annoy [ə'nɔi] vt molestar, fastidiar, irritar; **don't get ~ed!** ¡no se enfade!; ~**ance** n enojo; (thing) molestia; ~**ing** a molesto, fastidioso; (person) pesado.

annual ['ænjuəl] a anual // n (BOT) anual m; (book) anuario; ~**ly** ad anualmente, cada año.

annuity [ə'nju:iti] n renta o pensión f vitalicia.

annul [ə'nʌl] vt anular, cancelar; (law) revocar; ~**ment** n anulación f, cancelación f.

annum ['ænəm] n see **per**.

anoint [ə'nɔint] vt ungir.

anomaly [ə'nɔməli] n anomalía.

anonymity [ænə'nimiti] n anonimato; **anonymous** [ə'nɔniməs] a anónimo.

anorak ['ænəræk] n anorak m.

anorexia [ænə'reksiə] n (MED) anorexia

another [ə'nʌðə*] a: ~ **book** (one more) otro libro; (a different one) un libro distinto // pron otro; see also **one**.

answer ['ɑ:nsə*] n contestación f, respuesta; (to problem) solución f // vi contestar, responder // vt (reply to) contestar a, responder a; (problem) resolver; to ~ **the phone** contestar el teléfono; **in ~ to your**

letter contestando o en contestación a su carta; to ~ **the bell** o **the door** acudir a la puerta; to ~ **back** vi replicar, ser respondón(ona); to ~ **for** vt fus responder o por; to ~ **to** vt fus (description) corresponder a; (needs) satisfacer; ~**able** a: ~**able to sb for sth** responsable ante uno de algo.

ant [ænt] n hormiga.

antacid [ænt'æsid] a antiácido.

antagonist [æn'tægənist] n antagonista m/f, adversario/a; ~**ic** [-'nistik] a antagónico; (opposed) contrario, opuesto; **antagonize** [-naiz] vt enemistarse con.

Antarctic [ænt'ɑ:ktik] n: the ~ el Antártico; ~ a Antártida.

antelope ['æntiləup] n antílope m.

antenatal [ænti'neitl] a antenatal, prenatal; ~ **clinic** n clínica prenatal.

antenna [æn'tenə], pl ~ **e** [-ni:] n antena.

anthem ['ænθəm] n: **national** ~ himno nacional.

anthology [æn'θɔlədʒi] n antología.

anthropologist [ænθrə'pɔlədʒist] n antropólogo; **anthropology** [-dʒi] n antropología.

anti... [ænti] pref anti...; ~**aircraft** a antiaéreo.

antibiotic [æntibai'ɔtik] a, n antibiótico.

anticipate [æn'tisipeit] vt (foresee) prever; (expect) esperar, contar con; (forestall) anticiparse a, adelantarse a; (look forward to) prometerse; **anticipation** [-'peiʃən] n previsión f, esperanza, anticipación f, prevención f.

anticlimax [ænti'klaimæks] n decepción f.

anticlockwise [ænti'klɔkwaiz] ad en dirección contraria a la de las agujas del reloj.

antics ['æntiks] npl payasadas fpl; (of child) travesuras fpl.

anticyclone [ænti'saikləun] n anticiclón m.

antidote ['æntɪdəʊt] n antídoto.

antifreeze ['æntɪfriːz] n anticongelante m, solución f anticongelante.

antihistamine [æntɪ'hɪstəmiːn] n antihistamínico.

antiquated ['æntɪkweɪtɪd] a anticuado.

antique [æn'tiːk] n antigüedad f, antigualla // a antiguo, anticuado; ~ **dealer** n anticuario; ~ **shop** n tienda de antigüedades.

antiquity [æn'tɪkwɪtɪ] n antigüedad f.

antiseptic [æntɪ'septɪk] a, n antiséptico.

antisocial [æntɪ'səʊʃəl] a antisocial.

antlers ['æntləz] npl cuernas fpl.

anus ['eɪnəs] n ano.

anvil ['ænvɪl] n yunque m.

anxiety [æŋ'zaɪətɪ] n (worry) inquietud f; (eagerness) ansia, anhelo; (MED) ansiedad f.

anxious ['æŋkʃəs] a (worried) inquieto; (keen) deseoso; ~ly ad con inquietud, de manera angustiada.

any ['enɪ] a (in negative and interrogative sentences = some) algún, alguno, alguna; (negative sense) ningún, ninguno, ninguna; (no matter which) cualquier(a); (each and every) todo; I haven't ~ money/books no tengo dinero/ libros; have you ~ butter/ children? ¿tiene mantequilla/ hijos?; at ~ moment en cualquier momento; in ~ case de todas formas, de todas maneras; at ~ rate de todas formas, sea como sea // pron alguno; ninguno; (anybody) cualquiera; (in negative and interrogative sentences): I haven't ~ no tengo ninguno; have you got ~? ¿tiene algunos?; can ~ of you sing? ¿alguno de Ustedes sabe cantar? // ad (in negative sentences) nada; (in interrogative and conditional constructions) algo; I can't hear him ~ more no le oigo

más; do you want ~ more soup? ¿quiere más sopa?; ~body pron cualquiera, cualquier persona; (in interrogative sentences) alguien; (in negative sentences): I don't see ~body no veo a nadie; ~how ad de todos modos, de todas maneras; (carelessly) de cualquier manera; ~one = ~body; ~thing pron (see ~body) algo, cualquier cosa; algo; (in negative sentences) nada; (everything) todo; ~time ad (at any moment) en cualquier momento, de un momento a otro; (whenever) no importa cuándo, cuando quiera; ~way ad de todas maneras; (in any case) de todos modos; ~where ad (see ~body) dondequiera; en algún sitio; (negative sense) en ningún sitio; (everywhere) en o por todas partes; I don't see him ~where no le veo en ningún sitio.

apart [ə'pɑːt] ad aparte, separadamente; 10 **miles** ~ separados por 10 millas; ~ **from** prep aparte de.

apartheid [ə'pɑːteɪt] n apartheid m.

apartment [ə'pɑːtmənt] n (US) piso, apartamento; (room) cuarto.

apathetic [æpə'θetɪk] a apático, indiferente; **apathy** ['æpəθɪ] n apatía, indiferencia.

ape [eɪp] n mono // vt imitar, remedar.

aperitif [ə'perɪtɪv] n aperitivo.

aperture ['æpətʃʊə*] n rendija, resquicio; (PHOT) abertura.

apex ['eɪpeks] n ápice m; (fig) cumbre f.

aphrodisiac [æfrəʊ'dɪzɪæk] a, n afrodisíaco.

apiece [ə'piːs] ad cada uno.

apologetic [əpɔlə'dʒetɪk] a (tone, letter) lleno de disculpas.

apologize [ə'pɔlədʒaɪz] vi: to ~ (for sth to sb) disculparse (con alguien de algo); **apology** [-dʒɪ] n disculpa, excusa.

apostle [ə'pɔsl] n apóstol m/f.

apostrophe [ə'pɔstrəfi] n apóstrofe m.

appal [ə'pɔːl] vt horrorizar, espantar; **~ling** a espantoso; (awful) pésimo.

apparatus [æpə'reitəs] n aparato.

apparent [ə'pærənt] a aparente; (obvious) manifiesto, claro; ~ly ad por lo visto, al parecer.

apparition [æpə'riʃən] n aparición f, (ghost) fantasma m.

appeal [ə'piːl] vi (LAW) apelar // n (LAW) apelación f; (request) llamamiento; (plea) súplica, ruego; (charm) atractivo, encanto; **to ~ for** suplicar, reclamar; **to ~ to** (subj: person) rogar a, suplicar a; (subj: thing) atraer, interesar; **to ~ to sb for mercy** rogarle misericordia a alguien; **it doesn't ~ to me** no me atrae, no me llama la atención; **~ing** a (nice) atrayente, atractivo; (touching) conmovedor(a), emocionante.

appear [ə'piə*] vi aparecer, presentarse; (LAW) comparecer; (publication) salir (a luz), publicarse; (seem) parecer; **it would ~ that** parecería que; **~ance** n aparición f; (look, aspect) apariencia, aspecto.

appease [ə'piːz] vt (pacify) apaciguar; (satisfy) satisfacer, saciar.

appendicitis [əpendi'saitis] n apendicitis f.

appendix [ə'pendiks], pl **-dices** [-disiːz] n apéndice m.

appetite ['æpitait] n apetito; (fig) deseo, anhelo.

appetizing ['æpitaizɪŋ] a apetitoso.

applaud [ə'plɔːd] vt, vi aplaudir.

applause [-ɔːz] n aplausos mpl.

apple ['æpl] n manzana; **~ tree** n manzano.

appliance [ə'plaiəns] n aparato.

applicable [ə'plikəbl] a aplicable, pertinente.

applicant ['æplikənt] n candidato/a, solicitante m/f.

application [æpli'keiʃən] n aplicación f; (for a job, a grant etc) solicitud f, petición f; **~ form** n formulario.

apply [ə'plai] vt: **to ~ (to)** aplicar (a); (fig) emplear (para) // vi: **to ~ to** (ask) presentarse a, ser candidato a; (be suitable for) aplicable a; (be relevant to) tener que ver con; **to ~ for** (permit, grant, job) solicitar; **to ~ the brakes** aplicar los frenos; **to ~ o.s. to** aplicarse a, dedicarse a.

appoint [ə'pɔint] vt (to post) nombrar; (date, place) fijar, señalar; **~ment** n (engagement) cita; (date) compromiso; (act) nombramiento; (post) puesto.

apportion [ə'pɔːʃən] vt repartir, distribuir; (blame) dar.

appraisal [ə'preizl] n tasación f, valoración f.

appreciable [ə'priːʃəbl] a sensible.

appreciate [ə'priːʃieit] vt (like) apreciar, tener en mucho; (be grateful for) agradecer; (assess) valorar, apreciar; (be aware of) comprender, percibir // vi (COMM) aumentar(se) en valor, subir; **appreciation** [-'eiʃən] n aprecio; reconocimiento; agradecimiento; aumento en valor.

appreciative [ə'priːʃiətiv] a (person) agradecido; (comment) elogioso.

apprehend [æpri'hend] vt percibir, comprender; (arrest) detener.

apprehension [æpri'henʃən] n (fear) recelo, aprensión f; **apprehensive** [-'hensiv] a aprensivo.

apprentice [ə'prentis] n aprendiz/a m/f; **~ship** n aprendizaje m.

approach [ə'prəutʃ] vi acercarse // vt acercarse a; (be approximate) aproximarse a; (ask, apply to) dirigirse a // n acercamiento; aproximación f; (access) acceso; (proposal) proposición f; **~able** a (person) abordable; (place) accesible.

appropriate [ə'prəuprıeıt] *vt* (*take*) apropiarse; (*allot*): **to ~ sth for** destinar algo a // à [-rııt] (*apt*) apropiado, conveniente; (*relevant*) competente.

approval [ə'pru:vəl] *n* aprobación *f*, visto bueno; **on ~** (*COMM*) a prueba.

approve [ə'pru:v] *vt* aprobar; **~d school** *n* correccional *m*.

approximate [ə'prɒksımıt] *a* aproximado // *vt* [-meıt] aproximarse a, acercarse a; **approximation** [-'meıʃən] *n* aproximación *f*.

apricot ['eıprıkɒt] *n* albaricoque *m*.

April ['eıprəl] *n* abril *m*; **~ Fool's Day** *n* Día *m* de los Inocentes.

apron ['eıprən] *n* delantal *m*.

apt [æpt] *a* (*suitable*) acertado, oportuno; (*appropriate*) conveniente; (*likely*): **~ to do** con tendencia a hacer.

aptitude ['æptıtju:d] *n* aptitud *f*, capacidad *f*.

aqualung ['ækwəlʌŋ] *n* aparato de buceo autónomo.

aquarium [ə'kwεərıəm] *n* acuario.

Aquarius [ə'kwεərıəs] *n* Acuario.

aquatic [ə'kwætık] *a* acuático.

aqueduct ['ækwıdʌkt] *n* acueducto.

Arab ['ærəb] *n* árabe *m/f*.

Arabia [ə'reıbıə] *n* Arabia; **~n a** árabe.

Arabic ['ærəbık] *n* árabe *m*.

arable ['ærəbl] *a* cultivable.

arbitrary ['ɑ:bıtrərı] *a* arbitrario.

arbitrate ['ɑ:bıtreıt] *vi* arbitrar; **arbitration** [-'treıʃən] *n* arbitraje *m*; **arbitrator** *n* juez *m* árbitro.

arc [ɑ:k] *n* arco.

arcade [ɑ:'keıd] *n* arcada; (*round a square*) soportales *mpl*; (*passage with shops*) galería, pasaje *m*.

arch [ɑ:tʃ] *n* arco; (*vault*) bóveda; (*of foot*) empeine *m* // *vt* arquear.

archaeology [ɑ:kı'ɒlədʒıst] *n* arqueólogo; **archaeology** [-dʒı] *n* arqueología.

archaic [ɑ:'keıık] *a* arcaico.

archbishop [ɑ:tʃ'bıʃəp] *n* arzobispo.

arch-enemy ['ɑ:tʃ'εnımı] *n* enemigo jurado.

archer ['ɑ:tʃə*] *n* arquero; **~y n** tiro con arco.

archetype ['ɑ:kıtaıp] *n* arquetipo.

archipelago [ɑ:kı'pεlıgəu] *n* archipiélago.

architect ['ɑ:kıtεkt] *n* arquitecto; **~ural** [-'tεktʃərəl] *a* arquitectónico; **~ure** *n* arquitectura.

archives ['ɑ:kaıvz] *npl* archivo *sg*.

archway ['ɑ:tʃweı] *n* arco, arcada.

Arctic ['ɑ:ktık] *a* ártico // *n*: **the ~** el Ártico.

ardent ['ɑ:dənt] *a* (*passionate*) ardiente, apasionado; (*fervent*) fervoroso; **ardour** ['ɑ:də*] *n* ardor *m*; fervor *m*.

arduous ['ɑ:djuəs] *a* (*gen*) arduo; (*journey*) penoso.

are [ɑ:*] *vb* see **be**.

area ['εərıə] *n* (*gen*) área; (*MATH etc*) superficie *f*, extensión *f*; (*zone*) región *f*, zona.

arena [ə'ri:nə] *n* arena; (*of circus*) pista; (*for bullfight*) plaza, ruedo.

aren't [ɑ:nt] = **are not**.

Argentina [ɑ:dʒən'ti:nə] *n* Argentina; **Argentinian** [-'tınıən] *a, n* argentino/a.

argue ['ɑ:gju:] *vi* (*quarrel*) discutir; (*reason*) argüir, discurrir; **to ~ that** sostener que; **argument** *n* (*reasons*) argumento; (*quarrel*) discusión *f*; (*debate*) debate *m*, disputa; **argumentative** [-mεntətıv] *a* discutidor(a).

aria ['ɑ:rıə] *n* (*MUS*) aria.

arid ['ærıd] *a* árido.

Aries ['εərız] *n* Aries *m*.

arise [ə'raız], *pt* **arose**, *pp* **arisen** [ə'rızn] *vi* (*rise up*) levantarse, alzarse; (*emerge*) surgir, presentarse; **to ~ from** resultar de.

aristocracy [ærıs'tɒkrəsı] *n* aristocracia; **aristocrat** ['ærıstəkræt] *n* aristócrata *m/f*.

arithmetic [ə'rıθmətık] *n* aritmética.

ark [ɑ:k] *n*: **Noah's A~** Arca de Noé.

arm [ɑːm] n (ANAT) brazo; (weapon, MIL: branch) arma // vt armar; ~s npl (weapons) armas fpl; (HERALDRY) escudo sg; ~s race carrera de armamentos; ~ in ~ cogidos del brazo; ~band n brazalete m; ~chair n sillón m; ~ed a armado; ~ed robbery n robo a mano armada; ~ful n brazado, brazada.

armistice ['ɑːmistis] n armisticio.

armour ['ɑːmə*] n armadura; ~ed car n coche m blindado; ~y n armería, arsenal m.

armpit ['ɑːmpit] n sobaco, axila.

army ['ɑːmi] n ejército.

aroma [ə'rəumə] n aroma m, fragancia; ~tic [ærə'mætik] a aromático, fragante.

arose [ə'rəuz] pt of arise.

around [ə'raund] ad alrededor; (in the area) a la redonda // prep alrededor de, en torno de; (fig: about) alrededor de.

arouse [ə'rauz] vt despertar.

arrange [ə'reindʒ] vt arreglar, ordenar; (programme) organizar; ~ment n arreglo; (agreement) acuerdo; ~ments npl (plans) planes mpl, medidas fpl; (preparations) preparativos m.

arrears [ə'rɪəz] npl atrasos mpl; to be in ~ with one's rent atrasarse en el arriendo.

arrest [ə'rest] vt detener; (sb's attention) llamar // n detención f; under ~ detenido.

arrival [ə'raivl] n llegada; new ~ recién llegado.

arrive [ə'raiv] vi llegar.

arrogance ['æragəns] n arrogancia; **arrogant** [-gənt] a arrogante.

arrow ['ærəu] n flecha.

arsenal ['ɑːsinl] n arsenal m.

arsenic ['ɑːsnik] n arsénico.

arson ['ɑːsn] n delito de incendiar.

art [ɑːt] n arte m; (craft) artes fpl y oficios mpl; (skill) destreza; (technique) técnica; A~s npl (SCOL)

Letras fpl; ~ gallery n museo de bellas artes; (small and private) galería de arte.

artery ['ɑːtəri] n (MED) arteria; (fig) vía principal.

arthritis [ɑː'θraitis] n artritis f.

artichoke ['ɑːtitʃəuk] n alcachofa; **Jerusalem** ~ aguaturma.

article ['ɑːtikl] n artículo, objeto, cosa; (in newspaper) artículo; (for training) ~s npl contrato sg de aprendizaje.

articulate [ɑː'tikjulit] a claro o distinto en el hablar // vt [-leit] articular; ~d lorry n camión m articulado.

artificial [ɑːti'fiʃəl] a artificial; (teeth etc) postizo; ~ respiration n respiración f artificial.

artillery [ɑː'tiləri] n artillería.

artisan ['ɑːtizæn] n artesano.

artist ['ɑːtist] n artista m/f; (MUS) intérprete m/f; ~ic [ɑː'tistik] a artístico; ~ry n arte m, habilidad f artística.

artless ['ɑːtlis] a (innocent) natural, sencillo; (clumsy) desmañado.

as [æz, əz] conj (cause) como, ya que; (time: moment) como, cuando; (: duration) mientras; (manner) como, lo mismo que, tal como; (in the capacity of) como; ~ big ~ tan grande como; twice ~ big ~ dos veces más grande que...; she said ~ como ella dijo; ~ if o though como si; ~ for o to that en cuanto a eso, en lo que a eso se refiere; ~ or so long ~ conj mientras (que); ~ much/many ~ tanto(s)... como; ~ soon ~ conj tan pronto como; ~ such ad como tal, ~ well ad también, además; ~ well ~ conj así como; see also such.

asbestos [æz'bestəs] n asbesto, amianto.

ascend [ə'send] vt subir; ~ancy n ascendiente m, dominio.

ascent [ə'sent] n subida; (slope) cuesta, pendiente m; (promotion) ascenso.

ascertain [æsə'teɪn] *vt* averiguar, determinar.

ascetic [ə'sɛtɪk] *a* ascético.

ascribe [ə'skraɪb] *vt*: to ~ sth to atribuir algo a.

ash [æʃ] *n* ceniza; (*tree*) fresno.

ashamed [ə'feɪmd] *a* avergonzado; to be ~ of avergonzarse de.

ashen ['æʃn] *a* ceniciendo, pálido.

ashore [ə'ʃɔː*] *ad* en tierra.

ashtray ['æʃtreɪ] *n* cenicero.

Asia ['eɪʃə] *n* Asia; ~n, ~tic [eɪsɪ'ætɪk] *a, n* asiático/a.

aside [ə'saɪd] *ad* aparte, a un lado.

ask [ɑːsk] *vt* (*question*) preguntar; (*demand*) pedir; (*invite*) invitar; to ~ sb sth/to do sth preguntar algo a alguien/pedir a alguien que haga algo; to ~ sb about sth preguntar algo a alguien; to ~ (sb) a question hacer una pregunta (a alguien); to ~ sb out to dinner invitar a comer a uno; to ~ for *vt fus* pedir.

askance [ə'skɑːns] *ad*: to look ~ at sb mirar con recelo a uno.

askew [ə'skjuː] *ad* sesgado, ladeado, oblicuamente.

asleep [ə'sliːp] *a* dormido; to fall ~ dormirse, quedarse dormido.

asparagus [əs'pærəgəs] *n* espárragos *mpl*.

aspect ['æspɛkt] *n* aspecto, apariencia; (*direction in which a building etc faces*) orientación *f*.

aspersions [əs'pɜːʃənz] *npl*: to cast ~ on difamar a, calumniar a.

asphalt ['æsfælt] *n* asfalto; (*place*) pista asfaltada.

asphyxiate [æs'fɪksɪeɪt] *vt* asfixiar // *vi* asfixiarse; **asphyxiation** [-'eɪʃən] *n* asfixia.

aspiration [æspə'reɪʃən] *n* (*fig*) anhelo, deseo, ambición *f*.

aspire [əs'paɪə*] *vi*: to ~ to aspirar a, ambicionar.

aspirin ['æsprɪn] *n* aspirina.

ass [æs] *n* asno, burro; (*col*) imbécil *m*.

assailant [ə'seɪlənt] *n* asaltador/a *m/f*, agresor/a *m/f*.

assassin [ə'sæsɪn] *n* asesino; ~ate *vt* asesinar; ~ation [-'neɪʃən] *n* asesinato.

assault [ə'sɔːlt] *n* (*gen*: *attack*) asalto, ataque *m* // *vt* asaltar, atacar; (*sexually*) violar.

assemble [ə'sɛmbl] *vt* reunir, juntar; (*TECH*) montar // *vi* reunirse, juntarse.

assembly [ə'sɛmblɪ] *n* (*meeting*) reunión *f*, asamblea; (*people*) concurrencia *f*; (*construction*) montaje *m*; ~ line *n* línea de producción.

assent [ə'sɛnt] *n* asentimiento, aprobación *f* // *vi* consentir, asentir.

assert [ə'sɜːt] *vt* afirmar; (*claim etc*) hacer valer; ~ion [ə'sɜːʃən] *n* afirmación *f*.

assess [ə'sɛs] *vt* valorar, calcular; (*tax, damages*) fijar; (*property etc: for tax*) gravar; ~ment *n* valoración *f*; gravamen *m*; ~or *n* asesor/a *m/f*; (*of tax*) tasador/a *m/f*.

asset ['æsɛt] *n* posesión *f*; (*quality*) ventaja *sg*; ~s *npl* (*funds*) activo *sg*, fondos *mpl*.

assiduous [ə'sɪdjuəs] *a* asiduo.

assign [ə'saɪn] *vt* (*date*) fijar; (*task*) asignar; (*resources*) destinar; (*property*) traspasar; ~ment *n* asignación *f*; (*task*) tarea.

assimilate [ə'sɪmɪleɪt] *vt* asimilar.

assist [ə'sɪst] *vt* ayudar; (*progress etc*) fomentar; ~ance *n* ayuda, auxilio; (*welfare*) subsidio; ~ant *n* ayudante *m/f*, auxiliar *m/f*; (*also: shop* ~**ant**) dependiente/a *m/f*.

assizes [ə'saɪzɪz] *npl* sesión *f* de un tribunal.

associate [ə'səuʃɪt] *a* asociado // *n* asociado, colega *m*; (*in crime*) cómplice *m/f*; (*member*) miembro *m/f* // (*vb*: [-ʃɪeɪt]) *vt* asociar, relacionar // *vi*: to ~ with sb tratar con alguien.

association [əsəusɪ'eɪʃən] *n* asociación *f*; (*COMM*) sociedad *f*.

assorted [ə'sɔːtɪd] *a* surtido, variado.

assortment [ə'sɔːtmənt] *n* surtido.

assume [ə'sjuːm] *vt* (*suppose*) suponer, dar por sentado; (*responsibilities etc*) asumir; (*attitude name*) adoptar, tomar.

assumption [ə'sʌmpʃən] *n* (*supposition*) suposición *f*, presunción *f*; (*act*) asunción *f*.

assurance [ə'ʃuərəns] *n* garantía, promesa; (*confidence*) confianza, aplomo; (*certainty*) certeza; (*insurance*) seguro.

assure [ə'ʃuə*] *vt* asegurar.

asterisk ['æstərɪsk] *n* asterisco.

astern [ə'stəːn] *ad* a popa, por la popa.

asteroid ['æstərɔɪd] *n* asteroide *m*.

asthma ['æsmə] *n* asma; ~tic [æs'mætɪk] *a*, asmático/a.

astonish [ə'stɔnɪʃ] *vt* asombrar, pasmar; ~ment *n* asombro, sorpresa.

astound [ə'staund] *vt* asombrar, pasmar.

astray [ə'streɪ] *ad*: **to go** ~ extraviarse; **to lead** ~ llevar por mal camino.

astride [ə'straɪd] *ad* a horcajadas // *prep* a caballo o horcajadas sobre.

astrologer [əs'trɔlədʒə*] *n* astrólogo; **astrology** *[-dʒɪ]* *n* astrología.

astronaut ['æstrənɔːt] *n* astronauta *m/f*.

astronomer [əs'trɔnəmə*] *n* astrónomo; **astronomical** [æstrə'nɔmɪkəl] *a* astronómico; (*fig*) tremendo, enorme; **astronomy** *[-mɪ]* *n* astronomía.

astute [əs'tjuːt] *a* astuto.

asunder [ə'sʌndə*] *ad*: **to tear** ~ romper en dos, hacer pedazos.

asylum [ə'saɪləm] *n* (*refuge*) asilo; (*hospital*) manicomio.

at [æt] *prep* en, a; ~ **the top** en la cumbre; ~ **4 o'clock** a las cuatro; ~ **£1 a kilo** a libra el kilo; ~ **night** de noche, por la noche; ~ **a stroke** de un golpe; **two** ~ **a time** de dos en dos; ~ **times** a veces.

ate [eɪt] *pt of* eat.

atheist ['eɪθɪɪst] *n* ateo/a.

Athens ['æθɪnz] *n* Atenas *f*.

athlete ['æθliːt] *n* atleta *m/f*.

athletic [æθ'letɪk] *a* atlético; ~**s** *n* atletismo.

Atlantic [ət'læntɪk] *n*: **the** ~ (**Ocean**) el (Océano) Atlántico.

atlas ['ætləs] *n* atlas *m*.

atmosphere ['ætməsfɪə*] *n* atmósfera, (*fig*) ambiente *m*.

atom ['ætəm] *n* átomo; ~**ic** [ə'tɔmɪk] *a* atómico; ~(**ic**) **bomb** *n* bomba atómica; ~**izer** ['ætəmaɪzə*] *n* atomizador *m*.

atone [ə'təun] *vi*: **to** ~ **for** expiar.

atrocious [ə'trəuʃəs] *a* (*very bad*) atroz; (*fig*) horrible, infame.

atrocity [ə'trɔsɪtɪ] *n* atrocidad *f*.

attach [ə'tætʃ] *vt* (*gen*) sujetar, pegar; (*document, letter*) adjuntar; **to be** ~**ed to sb/sth** (*to like*) tener cariño a alguien/algo.

attaché [ə'tæʃeɪ] *n* agregado; ~ **case** *n* maletín *m*.

attachment [ə'tætʃmənt] *n* (*tool*) accesorio; (*love*): ~ (**to**) cariño (a).

attack [ə'tæk] *vt* (*MIL*) atacar; (*criminal*) agredir, asaltar; (*task etc*) emprender // *n* ataque *m*, asalto; (*on sb's life*) atentado; **heart** ~ ataque al corazón o cardíaco; ~**er** *n* agresor/a *m/f*, asaltante *m/f*.

attain [ə'teɪn] *vt* (*also*: ~ **to**) alcanzar; (*achieve*) lograr, conseguir; ~**ments** *npl* dotes *fpl*, talento *sg*.

attempt [ə'tempt] *n* tentativa, intento; (*attack*) atentado // *vt* intentar, tratar de.

attend [ə'tend] *vt* asistir a; (*patient*) atender; **to** ~ **to** *vt fus* (*needs, affairs etc*) ocuparse de; (*speech etc*) prestar atención a; (*customer*) atender a; ~**ance** *n* asistencia, presencia; (*people present*) concurrencia; ~**ant** *n* sirviente/a *m/f*, mozo/a; (*THEATRE*) acomodador/a *m/f* // *a* concomitante.

attention [ə'tenʃən] *n* atención *f* //

excl (MIL) ¡firme(s)!; **for the ~ of...** (ADMIN) atención... .

attentive [ə'tɛntɪv] *a* atento; (*polite*) cortés.

attest [ə'tɛst] *vi:* **to ~ to** dar fe de.

attic [ˈætɪk] *n* desván *m*, ático.

attitude [ˈætɪtjuːd] *n* (*gen*) actitud *f*, (*disposition*) disposición *f*.

attorney [ə'tɜːnɪ] *n* (*lawyer*) abogado; (*having proxy*) apoderado; **A~ General** *n* (*Brit*) fiscal *m* de la corona; (*US*) procurador *m* general.

attract [ə'trækt] *vt* atraer; (*attention*) llamar; **attraction** [ə'trækʃən] *n* (*gen pl*) encantos *mpl*; (*amusements*) diversiones *fpl*; (*PHYSICS*) atracción *f*, (*fig: towards sth*) atractivo; **~ive** *a* atractivo; (*interesting*) atrayente; (*pretty*) guapo, mono.

attribute [ˈætrɪbjuːt] *n* atributo // *vt* [ə'trɪbjuːt]: **to ~ sth to** atribuir *o* achacar algo a.

aubergine [ˈoʊbəʒiːn] *n* berenjena.

auburn [ˈɔːbən] *a* castaño rojizo.

auction [ˈɔːkʃən] *n* (*also:* **sale by ~**) subasta // *vt* subastar; **~eer** [-ˈnɪə*] *n* subastador/a *m/f*.

audacious [ɔː'deɪʃəs] *a* audaz, atrevido; (*pej*) descarado; **audacity** [ɔː'dæsɪtɪ] *n* audacia, atrevimiento; (*pej*) descaro.

audible [ˈɔːdɪbl] *a* audible, que se puede oír.

audience [ˈɔːdɪəns] *n* auditorio, público; (*interview*) audiencia.

audio-visual [ˈɔːdɪəʊˈvɪzjuəl] *a* audiovisual.

audit [ˈɔːdɪt] *vt* revisar, intervenir.

audition [ɔː'dɪʃən] *n* audición *f*.

auditor [ˈɔːdɪtə*] *n* interventor/a *m/f*, censor/a *m/f* de cuentas.

auditorium [ɔːdɪ'tɔːrɪəm] *n* auditorio.

augment [ɔːg'mɛnt] *vt* aumentar // *vi* aumentarse.

augur [ˈɔːgə*] *vi:* **it ~s well** es de buen agüero.

August [ˈɔːgəst] *n* agosto.

aunt [ɑːnt] *n* tía; **~ie, ~y** *n* diminutive of aunt.

au pair [ˈəʊ'pɛə*] *n* (*also:* **~ girl**) au pair *f*.

aura [ˈɔːrə] *n* emanación *f*, (*atmosphere*) ambiente *m*.

auspices [ˈɔːspɪsɪz] *npl:* **under the ~ of** bajo los auspicios de.

auspicious [ɔːs'pɪʃəs] *a* propicio, de buen augurio.

austere [ɒs'tɪə*] *a* austero; (*manner*) adusto; **austerity** [ɔ'stɛrɪtɪ] *n* austeridad *f*.

Australia [ɒs'treɪlɪə] *n* Australia; **~n** *a, n* australiano/a.

Austria [ˈɒstrɪə] *n* Austria; **~n** *a, n* austríaco/a.

authentic [ɔː'θɛntɪk] *a* auténtico.

author [ˈɔːθə*] *n* autor/a *m/f*.

authoritarian [ɔːθɒrɪ'tɛərɪən] *a* autoritario.

authoritative [ɔː'θɒrɪtətɪv] *a* autorizado; (*manner*) autoritario.

authority [ɔː'θɒrɪtɪ] *n* autoridad *f*, **the authorities** *npl* las autoridades.

authorize [ˈɔːθəraɪz] *vt* autorizar.

auto [ˈɔːtəʊ] *n* (*US*) coche *m*, automóvil *m*.

autobiography [ɔːtəbaɪ'ɒgrəfɪ] *n* autobiografía.

autocratic [ɔːtə'krætɪk] *a* autocrático.

autograph [ˈɔːtəgrɑːf] *n* autógrafo // *vt* firmar; (*photo etc*) dedicar.

automatic [ɔːtə'mætɪk] *a* automático // *n* (*gun*) pistola automática.

automation [ɔːtə'meɪʃən] *n* automatización *f*.

automaton [ɔː'tɒmətən], *pl* **-mata** [-tə] *n* autómata *m/f*.

automobile [ˈɔːtəməbiːl] *n* (*US*) coche *m*, automóvil *m*.

autonomous [ɔː'tɒnəməs] *a* autónomo.

autopsy [ˈɔːtɒpsɪ] *n* autopsia.

autumn [ˈɔːtəm] *n* otoño.

auxiliary [ɔːg'zɪlɪərɪ] *a* auxiliar.

Av. *abbr of* avenue.

avail [ə'veɪl] *vt:* **to ~ o.s. of**

aprovechar(se) de, valerse de // n: to no ~ en vano, sin resultado.

availability [ə'veɪlə'bɪlɪtɪ] n disponibilidad f.

available [ə'veɪləbl] a disponible; (usable) asequible.

avalanche ['ævəlɑːnʃ] n alud m, avalancha.

avant-garde ['ævãŋˈɡɑːd] a de vanguardia.

avaricious [ævəˈrɪʃəs] a avaro, avariento.

Ave. abbr of **avenue**.

avenge [ə'vendʒ] vt vengar.

avenue ['ævənjuː] n avenida; (path) camino.

average ['ævərɪdʒ] n promedio, término medio // a (mean) medio, de término medio; (ordinary) regular, corriente // vt calcular el promedio de, prorratear; **on ~** por regla general; **to ~ out** vi: **to ~ out at** resultar por promedio, ser por regla general.

averse [ə'vɜːs] a: **to be ~ to sth/doing** sentir aversión o antipatía por algo/por hacer; **aversion** [ə'vɜːʃən] n aversión f, repugnancia.

avert [ə'vɜːt] vt prevenir; (blow) desviar; (one's eyes) apartar.

aviary ['eɪvɪərɪ] n pajarera, aviario.

aviation [eɪvɪ'eɪʃən] n aviación f.

avid ['ævɪd] a ávido, ansioso.

avocado [ævə'kɑːdəʊ] n (also: ~ pear) aguacate m.

avoid [ə'vɔɪd] vt evitar, eludir; **~able** a evitable, eludible; **~ance** n el evitar, evitación f.

await [ə'weɪt] vt esperar, aguardar.

awake [ə'weɪk] a despierto // (vb: pt awoke, pp awoken or awaked) vt despertar // vi despertarse; **~ning** n el despertar.

award [ə'wɔːd] n (prize) premio, condecoración f; (LAW) fallo, sentencia; (act) concesión f // vt (prize) otorgar, conceder; (LAW: damages) adjudicar, decretar.

aware [ə'wɛə*] a consciente;

(awake) despierto; (informed) enterado; **to become ~ of** darse cuenta de, enterarse de; **~ness** n conciencia, conocimiento.

awash [ə'wɒʃ] a inundado.

away [ə'weɪ] ad (gen) fuera; (far ~) lejos, **two kilometres ~** a dos kilómetros de distancia, **two hours ~ by car** a dos horas en coche; **the holiday was two weeks ~** faltaba dos semanas para las vacaciones; **~ from** lejos de, fuera de; **he's ~ for a week** estará ausente una semana; **to take ~** vt llevar(se); **to work/pedal ~** seguir trabajando/pedaleando; **to fade ~** desvanecerse; (sound) apagarse; **~ match** n (SPORT) partido de fuera.

awe [ɔː] n pavor m, respeto, temor m reverencial; **~-inspiring, ~some** a imponente, pasmoso; **~-struck** a pasmado.

awful ['ɔːfəl] a tremendo, terrible, pasmoso; **~ly** ad (very) terriblemente.

awhile [ə'waɪl] ad durante un rato, un rato, algún tiempo.

awkward ['ɔːkwəd] a (clumsy) desmañado, torpe; (shape) incómodo; (problem) difícil (embarrassing) delicado, desagradable.

awning ['ɔːnɪŋ] n (of shop) toldo; (of window etc) marquesina.

awoke [ə'wəʊk], **awoken** [-kən] pt, pp of **awake**.

awry [ə'raɪ] ad: **to be ~** estar de través o al sesgo; **to go ~** salir mal, fracasar.

axe, ax (US) [æks] n hacha // vt (employee) despedir; (project etc) parar, cortar; (jobs) reducir.

axiom ['æksɪəm] n axioma m.

axis ['æksɪs], pl **axes** [-siːz] n eje m.

axle ['æksl] n eje m, árbol m.

aye(e) [aɪ] excl (yes) sí; **the ayes** npl los que votan a favor.

Aztec ['æztɛk] n azteca m/f.

B

B.A. *abbr of* **Bachelor of Arts** licenciado en letras.

babble ['bæbl] *vi* barbullar.

baboon [bə'bu:n] *n* mandril *m*.

baby ['beɪbɪ] *n* nene/a *m/f*; ~ **carriage** *n* (*US*) cochecito; ~**ish** *a* infantil; ~**sit** *vi* hacer de canguro; ~**sitter** *n* canguro *m/f*.

bachelor ['bætʃələ*] *n* soltero.

back [bæk] *n* (*of person*) espalda; (*of animal*) lomo; (*of hand*) dorso; (*of house, car, train*) parte *f* de atrás; (*of chair*) respaldo; (*of page*) reverso; (FOOTBALL) defensa *m* // *vt* (*candidate: also*: ~ **up**) respaldar, apoyar; (*horse: at races*) apostar a; (*car*) dar marcha atrás a o con // *vi* (*car etc*) dar marcha atrás // *a* (*in compounds*) tras; ~ **seats/wheels** (AUT) asientos *mpl*/ruedas *fpl* de atrás; ~ **payments** pagos *mpl* con efecto retroactivo; ~ **rent** renta atrasada // *ad* (*not forward*) (hacia) atrás; (*returned*) he's ~ está de vuelta, ha vuelto; **he ran** ~ retrocedió corriendo; (*restitution*): **throw the ball** ~ devuelve la pelota; **can I have it** ~? ¿me lo devuelve?; (*again*): **he called** ~ llamó de nuevo; **to** ~ **down** *vi* echarse atrás; **to** ~ **out** *vi* (*of promise*) volverse atrás.

back: ~**ache** *n* dolor *m* de espalda; ~**bencher** *n* miembro *m* del parlamento sin portafolio; ~**biting** *n* murmuración *f*; ~**bone** *n* columna vertebral; ~**cloth** *n* telón *m* de foro; ~**date** *vt* (*letter*) poner fecha atrasada a; ~**dated pay rise** alza de sueldo con efecto retroactivo; ~**er** *n* partidario; (COMM) promotor *m*; ~**fire** *vi* (AUT) petardear; (*plans*) fallar, salir al revés; ~**gammon** *n* backgammon *m*; ~**ground** *n* fondo; (*of events*) antecedentes *mpl*; (*basic knowledge*) bases *fpl*; (*experience*) conocimientos *mpl*, educación *f*;

family ~**ground** origen *m*, antecedentes *mpl*; ~**hand** *n* (TENNIS: *also*: ~**hand stroke**) revés *m*; ~**handed** *a* (*fig*) ambiguo, equívoco; ~**hander** *n* (*bribe*) soborno; ~**ing** *n* (*fig*) apoyo, respaldo; ~**lash** *n* reacción *f*, resaca; ~**log** *n*: ~**log of work** atrasos *mpl*; ~ **number** *n* (*of magazine etc*) número atrasado; ~ **pay** *n* pago atrasado; ~**side** *n* (*col*) trasero, culo; ~**stage** *ad* entre bastidores; ~**stroke** *n* braza de espaldas; ~**ward** *a* (*movement*) hacia atrás; (*person, country*) atrasado; (*shy*) tímido; ~**wards** *ad* (*move, go*) hacia atrás; (*read a list*) al revés; (*fall*) de espaldas; ~**water** *n* (*fig*) lugar *m* atrasado o apartado; ~**yard** *n* traspatio.

bacon ['beɪkən] *n* tocino.

bacteria [bæk'tɪərɪə] *npl* bacteria *sg*.

bad [bæd] *a* malo; (*serious*) grave; (*meat, food*) podrido, pasado; **to go** ~ echarse a perder.

badge [bædʒ] *n* insignia; (*of policeman*) chapa, placa.

badger ['bædʒə*] *n* tejón *m*.

badly ['bædlɪ] *ad* (*work, dress etc*) mal; ~ **wounded** gravemente herido; **he needs it** ~ le hace gran falta; **to be** ~ **off (for money)** andar mal de dinero.

badminton ['bædmɪntən] *n* badminton *m*.

bad-tempered ['bæd'tempəd] *a* de mal genio o carácter; (*temporary*) de mal humor.

baffle ['bæfl] *vt* (*puzzle*) desconcertar, confundir.

bag [bæg] *n* bolsa, saco; (*handbag*) bolso; (*satchel*) mochila; (*case*) maleta; (*of hunter*) caza // *vt* (*col: take*) coger, pescar; ~**ful** *n* saco (lleno); ~**gage** *n* equipaje *m*; ~**gy** *a* que hace bolsas; ~**pipes** *npl* gaita *sg*.

bail [beɪl] *n* fianza, caución *f* // *vt* (*prisoner: gen: give* ~ **to**) poner en libertad bajo fianza; (*boat: also:* ~ out) achicar; **to ~ sb out** obtener la libertad de uno bajo fianza; *see also* **bale**.

bailiff ['beɪlɪf] *n* alguacil *m*.

bait [beɪt] *n* cebo // *vt* cebar, poner el cebo en.

bake [beɪk] *vt* cocer (al horno) // *vi* (*cook*) cocerse; (*be hot*) hacer un calor terrible; **~d beans** *npl* judías *fpl* en salsa de tomate; **baker** *n* panadero; **~ry** *n* (*for bread*) panadería; (*for cakes*) pastelería; **baking** *n* (*act*) cocción *f*; (*batch*) hornada; **baking powder** *n* polvos *mpl* de levadura.

balaclava [bælə'klɑːvə] *n* (*also:* ~ **helmet**) pasamontañas *m inv*.

balance ['bæləns] *n* equilibrio, (*COMM. sum*) balance *m*; (*remainder*) resto; (*scales*) balanza // *vt* equilibrar; (*budget*) nivelar; (*account*) saldar; (*compensate*) contrapesar; **~ of trade/payments** balanza de comercio/pagos; **~d** *a* (*personality, diet*) equilibrado; **~ sheet** *n* balance *m*.

balcony ['bælkənɪ] *n* (*open*) balcón *m*; (*closed*) galería.

bald [bɔːld] *a* calvo; **~ness** *n* calvicie *f*.

bale [beɪl] *n* (*AGR*) paca, fardo; **to ~ out** (*of a plane*) lanzarse en paracaídas; **to ~ sb out of a difficulty** sacar a uno de un problema.

baleful ['beɪlful] *a* (*look*) triste; (*sinister*) funesto, siniestro.

ball [bɔːl] *n* bola; (*football*) balón *m*; (*for tennis, golf*) pelota; (*dance*) baile *m*.

ballad ['bæləd] *n* balada, romance *m*.

ballast ['bæləst] *n* lastre *m*.

ballerina [bælə'riːnə] *n* bailarina.

ballet ['bæleɪ] *n* ballet *m*, baile *m*; **~ dancer** *n* bailarín/ina *m/f*.

balloon [bə'luːn] *n* globo; **~ist** *n* ascensionista *m/f*.

ballot ['bælət] *n* votación *f*; **~ box** *n*

urna (electoral); **~ paper** *n* papeleta.

ball-point pen ['bɔːlpɔɪnt-] *n* bolígrafo.

ballroom ['bɔːlrum] *n* salón *m* de baile.

balmy ['bɑːmɪ] *a* (*breeze, air*) suave, fragante; (*col*) = **barmy**.

Baltic ['bɔːltɪk] *n*: **the ~ (Sea)** el (Mar) Báltico.

balustrade ['bæləstreɪd] *n* barandilla.

bamboo [bæm'buː] *n* bambú *m*.

ban [bæn] *n* prohibición *f*, proscripción *f* // *vt* prohibir, proscribir; (*exclude*) excluir.

banal [bə'nɑːl] *a* banal, vulgar.

banana [bə'nɑːnə] *n* plátano.

band [bænd] *n* (*group*) banda; (*gang*) pandilla; (*strip*) faja, tira; (*at a dance*) orquesta; (*MIL*) banda; **to ~ together** *vi* juntarse, asociarse.

bandage ['bændɪdʒ] *n* venda, vendaje *m* // *vt* vendar.

bandit ['bændɪt] *n* bandido; **one-armed ~** máquina tragaperras.

bandstand ['bændstænd] *n* quiosco.

bandwagon ['bændwægən] *n*: **to jump on the ~** (*fig*) seguir la corriente o la moda.

bandy ['bændɪ] *vt* (*jokes, insults*) cambiar.

bandy-legged ['bændɪ'legd] *a* estevado.

bang [bæŋ] *n* estallido; (*of door*) portazo; (*blow*) golpe *m* // *vt* hacer estallar; (*door*) cerrar de golpe // *vi* estallar.

banger ['bæŋə*] *n* (*car: gen: old* ~) chatarra.

bangle ['bæŋgl] *n* ajorca.

banish ['bænɪʃ] *vt* desterrar.

banister(s) ['bænɪstə(z)] *n(pl)* pasamanos *m inv*.

banjo ['bændʒəu], *pl* **~es** *or* **~s** *n* banjo.

bank [bæŋk] *n* (*COMM*) banco; (*of river, lake*) ribera, orilla; (*of earth*) terraplén *m* // *vi* (*AVIAT*) ladearse; **to ~ on** *vt fus* contar con; **to ~ with**

tener la cuenta con; ~ **account** n cuenta de banco; ~ **er** n banquero; **B~ holiday** n día m festivo; ~**ing** n banca; ~**note** n billete m de banco; ~ **rate** n tipo de interés bancario.

bankrupt ['bæŋkrʌpt] n quebrado/a // a quebrado, insolvente; **to go** ~ quebrar; **to be** ~ estar en quiebra; ~**cy** n quiebra; (fraudulent) bancarrota.

banner ['bænə*] n bandera; (in demonstration) pancarta.

banns [bænz] npl amonestaciones fpl.

banquet ['bæŋkwɪt] n banquete m.

baptism ['bæptɪzəm] n bautismo.

baptize [bæp'taɪz] vt bautizar.

bar [ba:*] n barra; (of window etc) tranca; (of soap) pastilla; (fig: hindrance) obstáculo; (prohibition) proscripción f; (pub) bar m; (counter: in pub) mostrador m; (MUS) barra // vt (road) obstruir; (person) excluir; (activity) prohibir; **behind** ~**s** en la cárcel; **the B~** (LAW: profession) la abogacía; (people) el cuerpo de abogados; ~ **none** sin excepción.

barbaric [ba:'bærɪk] a bárbaro.

barbarous ['ba:bərəs] a bárbaro.

barbecue ['ba:bɪkju:] n barbacoa.

barbed wire ['ba:bd-] n alambre m de púas.

barber ['ba:bə*] n peluquero, barbero.

barbiturate [ba:'bɪtjurɪt] n barbitúrico.

bare [bɛə*] a desnudo; (head) descubierto // vt desnudar; **to** ~ **one's teeth** enseñar los dientes; ~**back** ad sin montura; ~**faced** a descarado; ~**foot** a, ad descalzo; ~**ly** ad apenas.

bargain ['ba:gɪn] n pacto, negocio; (good buy) ganga // vi negociar; (haggle) regatear; **into the** ~ además, por añadidura.

barge [ba:dʒ] n barcaza; **to** ~ **in** vi

irrumpir, entrar sin permiso; **to** ~ **into** vt fus dar contra.

baritone ['bærɪtəun] n barítono.

bark [ba:k] n (of tree) corteza; (of dog) ladrido // vi ladrar.

barley ['ba:lɪ] n cebada.

barmaid ['ba:meɪd] n camarera.

barman ['ba:mən] n camarero, barman m.

barmy ['ba:mɪ] a (col) chiflado, lelo.

barn [ba:n] n granero.

barnacle ['ba:nəkl] n percebe m.

barometer [bə'rɔmɪtə*] n barómetro.

baron ['bærən] n barón m; ~**ess** n baronesa.

barracks ['bærəks] npl cuartel m.

barrage ['bæra:ʒ] n (MIL) descarga, bombardeo; (dam) presa.

barrel ['bærəl] n tonel m, barril m; (of gun) cañón m.

barren ['bærən] a estéril, árido.

barricade [bærɪ'keɪd] n barricada // vt levantar barricadas.

barrier ['bærɪə*] n barrera.

barring ['ba:rɪŋ] prep excepto, salvo.

barrister ['bærɪstə*] n abogado m/f.

barrow ['bærəu] n (cart) carretilla (de mano).

bartender ['ba:tɛndə*] n (US) camarero, barman m.

barter ['ba:tə*] vt: **to** ~ **sth for sth** trocar algo por algo.

base [beɪs] n base f // vt: **to** ~ **sth on** basar o fundar algo en // a bajo, infame; ~**ball** n béisbol m; ~**ment** n sótano.

bash [bæʃ] vt (col) golpear.

bashful ['bæʃful] a tímido, vergonzoso.

bashing ['bæʃɪŋ] n (col) tunda.

basic ['beɪsɪk] a básico; ~**ally** ad fundamentalmente, en el fondo.

basil ['bæzl] n albahaca.

basin ['beɪsn] n (vessel) cuenco, tazón m; (GEO) cuenca; (also: **wash~**) palangana, jofaina.

basis ['beisis], pl -ses [-si:z] n base f.

bask [bɑːsk] vi: to ~ in the sun tomar el sol.

basket ['bɑːskɪt] n cesta, cesto; (with handle) canasta; ~ball n baloncesto; ~work n cestería.

Basque [bæsk] a, n vasco/a; ~ Country Euskadi m, País m Vasco.

bass [beis] n (MUS) contrabajo.

bassoon [bə'suːn] n bajón m.

bastard ['bɑːstəd] n bastardo.

baste [beist] vt (CULIN) pringar.

bastion ['bæstiən] n baluarte m.

bat [bæt] n (ZOOL) murciélago; (for ball games) palo; (for cricket, baseball) bate m; (for table tennis) raqueta; he didn't ~ an eyelid ni pestañeó.

batch [bætʃ] n (of bread) hornada; (of papers) colección f lote m.

bated ['beitid] a: with ~ breath sin respiración.

bath [bɑːθ, pl bɑːðz] n (~tub) baño, bañera; (also: ~s pl) baño, piscina // vt bañar; to have a ~ bañarse, tomar un baño; ~chair n silla de ruedas.

bathe [beið] vi bañarse // vt bañar; bather n bañista m/f.

bathing ['beiðiŋ] n el bañarse; ~ cap n gorro de baño; ~ costume n traje m de baño; ~ trunks npl bañador m.

bath: ~mat n estera de baño; ~room n (cuarto de) baño; ~s npl piscina sg; ~ towel n toalla de baño.

baton ['bætən] n (MUS) batuta.

battalion [bə'tæliən] n batallón m.

batter ['bætə*] vt apalear, azotar // n batido; ~ed a (hat, pan) estropeado.

battery ['bætəri] n batería, (of torch) pila.

battle ['bætl] n batalla; (fig) lucha // vi luchar; ~field n campo m de batalla; ~ments npl almenas fpl; ~ship n acorazado.

bawdy ['bɔːdɪ] a indecente; (joke) verde.

bawl [bɔːl] vi chillar, gritar.

bay [bei] n (GEO) bahía; (BOT) laurel m // vi aullar; to hold sb at ~ mantener a alguien a raya.

bayonet ['beiənit] n bayoneta.

bay window ['bei-] n ventana salediza.

bazaar [bə'zɑː*] n bazar m.

bazooka [bə'zuːkə] n bazuca.

b. & b., B. & B. abbr of bed and breakfast cama y desayuno.

BBC n abbr of British Broadcasting Corporation.

B.C. ad abbr of before Christ a. de J.C. (antes de Jesucristo).

be [biː], pt was, were, pp been vi (of state) ser; (of place, temporary condition) estar, I am English soy inglés; I am tired estoy cansado, how are you? ¿cómo está Usted?; who is it? ¿quién es?; it is raining está lloviendo; I am warm tengo calor; it is cold hace frío; how much is it? ¿cuánto es o cuesta?; he is four (years old) tiene cuatro años; 2 and 2 are 4 dos más dos son cuatro; where have you been? ¿dónde has estado?, ¿de dónde vienes?

beach [biːtʃ] n playa // vt varar.

beacon ['biːkən] n (lighthouse) faro; (marker) guía.

bead [biːd] n cuenta, abalorio; (of sweat) gota.

beak [biːk] n pico.

beaker ['biːkə*] n jarra.

beam [biːm] n (ARCH) viga, travesaño; (of light) rayo, haz m de luz // vi brillar; (smile) sonreír; ~ing a (sun, smile) radiante.

bean [biːn] n judía; runner/broad ~ habichuela/haba; coffee ~ grano de café.

bear [bɛə*] n oso // vb: pt bore, pp borne) vt (weight etc) llevar; (cost) pagar; (responsibility) tener; (endure) soportar, aguantar; (stand up to) resistir a; (children) parir // vi: to ~ right/left torcer a la derecha/izquierda; ~able *a* soportable.

beard [biəd] *n* barba; ~ed *a* barbado.

bearing ['bɛəriŋ] *n* porte *m*, comportamiento; (*connection*) relación *f*; (*ball*) ~s *npl* cojinetes *mpl* a bolas; **to take a** ~ marcarse; **to find one's** ~s orientarse.

beast [bi:st] *n* bestia; (*col*) bruto, salvaje *m*; ~**ly** *a* bestial; (*awful*) horrible.

beat [bi:t] *n* (*of heart*) latido; (*MUS*) ritmo, compás *m*; (*of policeman*) ronda // (*vb: pt* **beat**, *pp* **beaten**) *vt* (*hit*) golpear; (*eggs*) batir; (*defeat*) vencer, derrotar; (*better*) sobrepasar; (*drum*) tocar; (*rhythm*) marcar // *vi* (*heart*) latir; **to** ~ **about the bush** ir por rodeos; **to** ~ **it** largarse; **to** ~ **off** rechazar; **to** ~ **up** *vt* (*col: person*) dar una paliza a; ~**er** *n* (*for eggs, cream*) batidora; ~**ing** *n* golpeo.

beautiful ['bju:tiful] *a* hermoso, bello; ~**ly** *ad* maravillosamente; **beautify** [-fai] *vt* embellecer.

beauty ['bju:ti] *n* belleza, hermosura; (*person*) belleza; ~ **salon** *n* salón *m* de belleza; ~ **spot** *n* lunar *m* postizo; (*TOURISM*) lugar *m* de excepcional belleza.

beaver ['bi:və*] *n* castor *m*.

becalmed [bi'ka:md] *a* encalmado.

became [bi'keim] *pt of* **become**.

because [bi'kɔz] *conj* porque; ~ **of** *prep* debido a, a causa de.

beck [bɛk] *n*: **to be at the** ~ **and call of** estar a disposición de.

beckon ['bɛkən] *vt* (*also:* ~ **to**) llamar con señas.

become [bi'kʌm] (*irg: like* **come**) *vt* (*suit*) favorecer, sentar a // *vi* (+ *noun*) hacerse, llegar a ser; (+ *adj*) ponerse, volverse; **to** ~ **fat** engordarse.

becoming [bi'kʌmiŋ] *a* (*behaviour*) decoroso; (*clothes*) favorecedor(a).

bed [bɛd] *n* cama; (*of flowers*) macizo; (*of coal, clay*) capa; **to go to**

~ acostarse; **single/double** ~ **cama** individual/matrimonial; ~**clothes** *npl* ropa *sg* de cama; ~**ding** *n* ropa de cama.

bedlam ['bɛdləm] *n* confusión *f.*

bedraggled [bi'drægld] *a* mojado, ensuciado.

bed: ~**ridden** *a* postrado (en cama); ~**room** *n* dormitorio, alcoba; ~**side** *n*: **at sb's** ~**side** a la cabecera de alguien; ~**sit(ter)** *n* apartamento; ~**spread** *n* sobrecama *m*, colcha.

bee [bi:] *n* abeja.

beech [bi:tʃ] *n* haya.

beef [bi:f] *n* carne *f* de vaca; **roast** ~ rosbif *m.*

bee: ~**hive** *n* colmena; ~**line** *n*: **to make a** ~**line for** ir derecho a.

been [bi:n] *pp of* **be**.

beer [biə*] *n* cerveza.

beetle [bi'tl] *n* escarabajo.

beetroot ['bi:tru:t] *n* remolacha.

before [bi'fɔ:*] *prep* (*of time*) antes de; (*of space*) delante de // *conj* antes (de) que // *ad* (*time*) antes, anteriormente; (*space*) delante, adelante; **the week** ~ **la semana anterior; I've never seen it** ~ no lo he visto nunca.

befriend [bi'frɛnd] *vt* ofrecer amistad a, ayudar.

beg [bɛg] *vi* pedir, rogar; (*as beggar*) pedir limosna // *vt* pedir, rogar; (*entreat*) suplicar.

began [bi'gæn] *pt of* **begin**.

beggar ['bɛgə*] *n* mendigo.

begin [bi'gin], *pt* **began**, *pp* **begun** *vt, vi* empezar, comenzar; ~**ner** *n* principiante *m/f*; ~**ning** *n* principio, comienzo.

begrudge [bi'grʌdʒ] *vt*: **to** ~ **sb sth** tenerle envidia a alguien por algo.

begun [bi'gʌn] *pp of* **begin**.

behalf [bi'hɑ:f] *n*: **on** ~ **of** en nombre de, por.

behave [bi'heiv] *vi* (*person*) portarse, comportarse; (*thing*) funcionar; (*well: also:* ~ **o.s.**) portarse bien; **behaviour, behavior** (*US*) *n* comportamiento, conducta.

behind [bɪ'haɪnd] prep detrás de // ad detrás, por detrás, atrás // n trasero; ~ **time** atrasado.

behold [bɪ'həuld] (irg: like hold) vt contemplar.

beige [beɪʒ] a beige.

being ['biːɪŋ] n ser m; **to come into** ~ nacer, aparecer.

belated [bɪ'leɪtɪd] a atrasado, tardío.

belch [beltʃ] vi eructar // vt (gen: ~ **out**: smoke etc) arrojar.

belfry ['belfrɪ] n campanario.

Belgian ['beldʒən] a, n belga m/f.

Belgium ['beldʒəm] n Bélgica.

belie [bɪ'laɪ] vt desmentir, contradecir.

belief [bɪ'liːf] n (opinion) opinión f; (trust, faith) fe f; (acceptance as true) creencia.

believable [bɪ'liːvəbl] a creíble.

believe [bɪ'liːv] vt, vi creer; **believer** n creyente m/f, fiel m/f; (POL) partidario/a.

belittle [bɪ'lɪtl] vt minimizar, despreciar.

bell [bel] n campana; (small) campanilla; (on door) timbre m; (animal's) cencerro; (on toy etc) cascabel m.

belligerent [bɪ'lɪdʒərənt] a (at war) beligerante; (fig) agresivo.

bellow ['beləu] vi bramar; (person) rugir // vt (orders) gritar, vociferar.

bellows ['beləuz] npl fuelle m.

belly ['belɪ] n barriga, panza.

belong [bɪ'lɒŋ] vi: **to** ~ **to** pertenecer a; (club etc) ser socio de; ~**ings** npl pertenencias fpl.

beloved [bɪ'lʌvɪd] a, n querido/a, amado/a.

below [bɪ'ləu] prep bajo, debajo de // ad abajo, (por) debajo; **see** ~ véase más abajo.

belt [belt] n cinturón m; (MED) faja; (TECH) correa, cinta // vt (thrash) golpear con correa.

bench [bentʃ] n banco; **the B**~

(LAW) tribunal m; (people) judicatura.

bend [bend] pt, pp bent vt doblar, inclinar; (leg, arm) torcer // vi doblarse, inclinarse // n (in road) recodo, vuelta; (in pipe, river) ángulo; curva; **to** ~ **down** vi inclinar, doblar; **to** ~ **over** vi inclinarse.

beneath [bɪ'niːθ] prep bajo, debajo de; (unworthy of) indigno de // ad abajo, (por) debajo.

benefactor ['benɪfæktə*] n bienhechor m.

beneficial [benɪ'fɪʃəl] a provechoso, beneficioso.

benefit ['benɪfɪt] n beneficio, provecho; (profit) utilidad f; (money) subsidio // vt beneficiar, aprovechar // vi: **he'll** ~ **from it** le sacará provecho.

Benelux ['benɪlʌks] n Benelux m.

benevolent [bɪ'nevələnt] a benévolo.

bent [bent] pt, pp of **bend** // n inclinación f // a: **to be** ~ **on** estar empeñado en.

bequeath [bɪ'kwiːð] vt legar.

bequest [bɪ'kwest] n legado.

bereaved [bɪ'riːvd] n: **the** ~ los afligidos mpl; **bereavement** [-'riːvmənt] n aflicción f.

beret ['bereɪ] n boina.

berry ['berɪ] n baya.

berserk [bə'sɜːk] a: **to go** ~ perder los estribos.

berth [bɜːθ] n (bed) litera; (cabin) camarote m; (for ship) amarradero // vi atracar, amarrar.

beseech [bɪ'siːtʃ] pt, pp **besought** [-'sɔːt] vt suplicar.

beset [bɪ'set] pt, pp **beset** vt rodear; (person) acosar.

beside [bɪ'saɪd] prep junto a, al lado de; **to be** ~ **o.s. (with anger)** estar fuera de sí.

besides [bɪ'saɪdz] ad además // prep (as well as) además de; (except) fuera de, excepto.

besiege [bɪ'si:dʒ] vt (town) sitiar; (fig) asediar.

best [best] a (el/la) mejor // ad (lo) mejor; **the ~ part of** (quantity) la mayor parte de; **at ~** en el mejor de los casos; **to make the ~ of sth** sacar el mejor partido de algo; **to the ~ of my knowledge** que yo sepa; **to the ~ of my ability** como mejor puedo; **~ man** n padrino de boda.

bestow [bɪ'stəu] vt otorgar; (affection) ofrecer.

bestseller ['best'selə*] n éxito de librería, bestseller m.

bet [bet] n apuesta // vt, vi, pt, pp **bet** or **betted** apostar, jugar.

betray [bɪ'treɪ] vt traicionar; (denounce) delatar; **~al** n traición f.

better ['betə*] a mejor // ad mejor // vt mejorar; (go above) superar // n: **to get the ~ of** quedar por encima de alguien; **you had ~ do it** más vale que lo haga; **he thought ~ of it** cambió de parecer; **to get ~** mejorar(se); (MED) reponerse; **~ off** a más acomodado.

betting ['betɪŋ] n juego, el apostar; **~ shop** n agencia de apuestas.

between [bɪ'twi:n] prep entre // ad en medio.

beverage ['bevərɪdʒ] n bebida.

bevy ['bevɪ] n: **a ~ of** una bandada de.

beware [bɪ'weə*] vi: **to ~ (of)** precaverse de, tener cuidado de // excl ¡cuidado!

bewildered [bɪ'wɪldəd] a aturdido, perplejo.

bewitching [bɪ'wɪtʃɪŋ] a hechicero, encantador(a).

beyond [bɪ'jɔnd] prep (in space) más allá de; (exceeding) además de, fuera de; (above) superior a // ad más allá, más lejos; **~ doubt** fuera de toda duda; **~ repair** irreparable.

bias ['baɪəs] n (prejudice) prejuicio, pasión f; (preference) predisposición f; **~(s)ed** a (against) con prejuicios; (towards) partidario a.

bib [bɪb] n babero.

Bible ['baɪbl] n Biblia.

bibliography [bɪblɪ'ɔgrəfɪ] n bibliografía.

bicker ['bɪkə*] vi reñir.

bicycle ['baɪsɪkl] n bicicleta.

bid [bɪd] n (at auction) oferta, postura; (attempt) tentativa, conato // (vb: pt **bade** [bæd] or **bid**, pp **bidden** ['bɪdn] or **bid**) vi hacer una oferta // vt mandar, ordenar; **to ~ sb good day** dar a uno los buenos días; **~der** n: **the highest ~** el mejor postor; **~ding** n (at auction) ofertas fpl; (order) orden f, mandato.

bide [baɪd] vt: **to ~ one's time** esperar el momento adecuado.

bidet [bi:'deɪ] n bidet m.

bier [bɪə*] n féretro.

big [bɪg] a grande.

bigamy ['bɪgəmɪ] n bigamia.

bigheaded ['bɪg'hedɪd] a engreído.

bigot ['bɪgət] n fanático, intolerante m/f; **~ed** a fanático, intolerante; **~ry** n fanatismo, intolerancia.

bike [baɪk] n bici f.

bikini [bɪ'ki:nɪ] n bikini m.

bile [baɪl] n bilis f.

bilingual [baɪ'lɪŋgwəl] a bilingüe.

bill [bɪl] n (account) cuenta; (invoice) factura; (POL) proyecto de ley; (US: banknote) billete m; (of bird) pico; **stick no ~s** prohibido fijar carteles.

billet ['bɪlɪt] n alojamiento.

billfold ['bɪlfəuld] n (US) cartera.

billiards ['bɪljədz] n billar m.

billion ['bɪljən] n (Brit) billón m; (US) mil millones.

billy goat ['bɪlɪ-] n macho cabrío.

bin [bɪn] n (gen) cubo; **bread/litter ~** nasa/papelera.

bind [baɪnd], pt, pp **bound** vt atar, liar; (wound) vendar; (book) encuadernar; (oblige) obligar; **~ing** a (contract) obligatorio.

binge [bɪndʒ] n borrachera, juerga.

bingo ['bɪŋgəu] n bingo m.

binoculars [bɪ'nɔkjuləz] npl

gemelos *mpl*, prismáticos *mpl*.
bio... [baɪə] *pref*: ~**chemistry** *n*
bioquímica; ~**graphy** [baɪˈɒgrəfɪ] *n*
biografía; ~**logical** *a* biológico;
~**logy** [baɪˈɒlədʒɪ] *n* biología.
birch [bəːtʃ] *n* abedul *m*, (cane)
vara.
bird [bəːd] *n* ave *f*, pájaro; (col: *girl*)
chica; (cage *n* jaula); ~**'s eye view**
n vista de pájaro; ~ **watcher** *n*
ornitólogo.
birth [bəːθ] *n* nacimiento; (MED)
parto; **to give** ~ **to** parir, dar a luz;
~ **certificate** *n* partida de
nacimiento; ~ **control** *n* control de
natalidad; (methods) métodos
mpl anticonceptivos; ~**day** *n*
cumpleaños *m*; ~**place** *n* lugar *m*
de nacimiento; ~ **rate** (tasa de)
natalidad *f*.
biscuit ['bɪskɪt] *n* galleta.
bisect [baɪˈsɛkt] *vt* bisecar.
bishop ['bɪʃəp] *n* obispo.
bit [bɪt] *pt of* **bite** // *n* trozo, pedazo,
pedacito; (of *horse*) freno, bocado; **a**
~ **of** un poco de; **a** ~ **mad** algo
loco; ~ **by** ~ poco a poco.
bitch [bɪtʃ] *n* (dog) perra.
bite [baɪt], *pt* **bit**, *pp* **bitten** *vt*, *vi*
morder; (insect *etc*) picar // *n*
mordedura; (insect) picadura;
(mouthful) bocado; **let's have a** ~
(to eat) comamos algo.
biting ['baɪtɪŋ] *a* penetrante,
cortante; (sharp) mordaz.
bitten ['bɪtn] *pp of* **bite**.
bitter ['bɪtə*] *a* amargo; (wind,
criticism) cortante, penetrante;
(battle) encarnizado // *n* (beer)
cerveza clara; ~**ness** *n* amargura,
(anger) rencor *m*.
bizarre [bɪˈzɑː*] *a* raro,
estrafalario.
blab [blæb] *vi* chismear, soplar // *vt*
(also: ~ **out**) revelar, contar.
black [blæk] *a* (colour) negro;
(dark) oscuro // *n* negro; (colour)
color *m* negro // *vt* (shoes) lustrar;
(INDUSTRY) boicotear; **to give sb a**
~ **eye** darle a uno una bofetada (en

el ojo); ~ **and blue** *a* amoratado;
~**berry** *n* zarzamora; ~**bird** *n*
mirlo; ~**board** *n* pizarra; ~**currant**
n grosella negra; ~**en** *vt*
ennegrecer; (fig) denigrar; ~ **leg** *n*
esquirol *m*, rompehuelgas *m inv*;
~**list** *n* lista negra; ~**mail**
chantaje *m* // *vt* chantajear;
~**mailer** *n* chantajista *m/f*;
~ **market** *n* mercado negro; ~**out** *n*
apagón *m*; (fainting) desmayo,
pérdida de conocimiento; ~**smith** *n*
herrero.
bladder ['blædə*] *n* vejiga.
blade [bleɪd] *n* hoja; (cutting *edge*)
filo; **a** ~ **of grass** una brizna de
hierba
blame [bleɪm] *n* culpa // *vt*: **to** ~
sb for sth echar a uno la culpa de
algo; **to be to** ~ tener la culpa de;
~**less** *a* (person) inocente.
bland [blænd] *a* suave; (taste) soso.
blank [blæŋk] *a* en blanco; (shot) sin
bala; (look) sin expresión // *n*
blanco, espacio en blanco; cartucho
sin bala *o* de fogueo.
blanket ['blæŋkɪt] *n* manta // *vt*
envolver.
blare [blɛə*] *vi* (brass *band*, horns,
radio) resonar.
blasé ['blɑːzeɪ] *a* hastiado.
blasphemy ['blæsfɪmɪ] *n*
blasfemia.
blast [blɑːst] *n* (of *wind*) ráfaga,
soplo; (of *whistle*) toque *m*; (of
explosive) carga explosiva; (force)
choque *m* // *vt* (blow *up*) volar;
(blow *open*) abrir con carga
explosiva; ~**-off** *n* (SPACE)
lanzamiento.
blatant ['bleɪtənt] *a* descarado.
blaze [bleɪz] *n* (fire) fuego, (flames)
llamarada, (fig) arranque *m* // *vi*
(fire) arder en llamas; (fig) brillar //
vt: **to** ~ **a trail** (fig) abrir (un)
camino.
blazer ['bleɪzə*] *n* chaqueta ligera.
bleach [bliːtʃ] *n* (also: household
~) lejía // *vt* (linen) blanquear;
~**ed** *a* (hair) decolorado.

bleak [bliːk] a (countryside) desierto; (prospect) poco prometedor(a).

bleary-eyed ['blɪərɪ'aɪd] a de ojos legañosos.

bleat [bliːt] vi balar.

bleed [bliːd], pt, pp **bled** [bled] vt, vi sangrar.

blemish ['blemɪʃ] n mancha, tacha.

blend [blend] n mezcla // vt mezclar // vi (colours etc) combinarse, mezclarse.

bless [bles], pt, pp **blessed** or **blest** [blest] vt bendecir; **~ing** n bendición f; (advantage) beneficio, ventaja.

blew [bluː] pt of **blow**.

blight [blaɪt] vt (hopes etc) frustrar, arruinar.

blimey ['blaɪmɪ] excl (col) ¡caray!

blind [blaɪnd] a ciego // n (for window) persiana // vt cegar; (dazzle) deslumbrar; **~ alley** n callejón m sin salida; **~ corner** n esquina escondida; **~fold** n venda // a, ad con los ojos vendados // vt vendar los ojos a; **~ly** ad a ciegas, ciegamente; **~ness** n ceguera; **~ spot** n mácula.

blink [blɪŋk] vi parpadear, pestañear; (light) oscilar; **~ers** npl anteojeras fpl.

blinking ['blɪŋkɪŋ] a (col): this **~...** este condenado...

bliss [blɪs] n felicidad f; (fig) éxtasis m.

blister ['blɪstə*] n (on skin) ampolla // vi (paint) ampollarse; **~ing** n (heat) abrasador(a).

blithe [blaɪð] a alegre.

blithering ['blɪðərɪŋ] a (col): this **~ idiot** este tonto perdido.

blitz [blɪts] n bombardeo aéreo.

blizzard ['blɪzəd] n ventisca.

bloated ['bləʊtɪd] a hinchado.

blob [blɒb] n (drop) gota; (stain, spot) mancha.

block [blɒk] n bloque m; (in pipes) obstáculo; (of buildings) manzana // vt (gen) obstruir, cerrar; (progress)

estorbar; **~ade** [-'keɪd] n bloqueo // vt bloquear; **~age** n estorbo, obstrucción f; **~ of flats** n bloque m de pisos; **~ letters** npl letras fpl de molde.

bloke [bləʊk] n (col) tipo, tío.

blond(e) [blɒnd] a, n rubio/a.

blood [blʌd] n sangre f; **~ donor** n donador/a m/f de sangre; **~ group** n grupo sanguíneo; **~ hound** n sabueso; **~ pressure** n presión f sanguínea; **~shed** n matanza; **~shot** a inyectado en sangre; **~stained** a manchado de sangre; **~stream** n corriente f sanguínea; **~thirsty** a sanguinario; **~ transfusion** n transfusión f de sangre; **~y** a sangriento; (col!): this **~y...** este condenado/puñetero...; **~y strong/good** (col!) terriblemente fuerte/bueno; **~y-minded** a (col) malintencionado.

bloom [bluːm] n floración f; (fig) perfección f, plenitud f // vi florecer; **~ing** a (col): this **~ing...** este condenado... .

blossom ['blɒsəm] n flor f // vi florecer; (fig) desarrollarse.

blot [blɒt] n borrón m // vt secar; (ink) manchar; **to ~ out** vt (view) oscurecer, hacer desaparecer.

blotchy ['blɒtʃɪ] a (complexion) enrojecido, lleno de manchas.

blotting paper ['blɒtɪŋ-] n papel m secante.

blouse [blauz] n blusa.

blow [bləʊ] n golpe m // (vb: pt **blew**, pp **blown** [bləʊn]) vi soplar // vt (glass) soplar; (fuse) quemar; (instrument) tocar; **to ~ one's nose** sonarse; **to ~ away** vt llevarse, arrancar; **to ~ down** vt derribar; **to ~ off** vt arrebatar; **to ~ out** vi apagarse; **to ~ over** vi pasar, quedar olvidado; **to ~ up** vi estallar // vt volar; (tyre) inflar; (PHOT) ampliar; **~lamp** n soplete m, lámpara de soldar; **~out** n (of tyre) pinchazo.

blubber ['blʌbə*] n grasa de

ballena // vi (pej) lloriquear.

blue [blu:] a azul; to have the ~s estar melancólico; ~**bell** n campanilla, campánula azul; ~**bottle** n moscarda, mosca azul; ~**jeans** npl bluejean m inv, vaqueros mpl; ~**print** n (fig) anteproyecto.

bluff [blʌf] vi hacer un bluff, farolear // n bluff m, farol m.

blunder ['blʌndə*] n error m garrafal, metedura de pata // vi cometer un error, meter la pata.

blunt [blʌnt] a embotado, desafilado; (person) franco, directo // vt embotar, desafilar; ~**ness** n (of person) franqueza, brusquedad f.

blur [blə:*] n aspecto borroso // vt hacer borroso.

blurt [blə:t]: ~ **out** vt (say) descuidar con, dejar escapar.

blush [blʌʃ] vi ruborizarse, ponerse colorado // n rubor m.

blustering ['blʌstərɪŋ] a (person) fanfarrón(ona).

blustery ['blʌstərɪ] a (weather) tempestuoso, tormentoso.

board [bɔ:d] n tabla, tablero, (on wall) tablón m; (for chess etc) tablero; (committee) junta, consejo; (in firm) mesa o junta directiva // n (ship) embarcarse en; (train) vt subir a; full ~ pensión f completa; to go by the ~ (fig) ser abandonado/olvidado; to ~ up vt (door) entablar, enmaderar; ~ **and lodging** n pensión f; ~**er** n huésped/a m/f; (SCOL) interno; ~**ing house** n casa de huéspedes; ~**ing school** n internado; ~**room** n sala de juntas.

boast [bəust] vi jactarse, presumir // vt ostentar // n alarde m, baladronada; ~**ful** a presumido, jactancioso.

boat [bəut] n barco, buque m; (small) barca, bote m; ~**er** n (hat) sombrero de paja; ~**ing** n canotaje m; ~**man** n barquero; ~**swain** ['bəusn] n contramaestre m.

bob [bɔb] vi (boat, cork on water: also: ~ **up and down**) menearse, balancearse; to ~ **up** vi aparecer, levantarse // n (col) = **shilling**.

bobbin ['bɔbɪn] n (of sewing machine) carrete m, bobina.

bobby ['bɔbɪ] n (col) poli m/f.

bobsleigh ['bɔbsleɪ] n bob m.

bodice ['bɔdɪs] n corpiño.

bodily ['bɔdɪlɪ] a corpóreo, corporal // ad (in person) en persona; (lift) en peso.

body ['bɔdɪ] n cuerpo; (corpse) cadáver m; (of car) caja, carrocería; (fig: society) conjunto; (fig: quantity) parte f principal; in a ~ en bloque, en conjunto; ~**guard** n guardaespaldas m inv; ~**work** n carrocería.

bog [bɔg] n pantano, ciénaga // vt: to get ~**ged down** (fig) empantanarse, atascarse.

boggle ['bɔgl] vi: the mind ~s le deja boquiabierto a uno.

bogus ['bəugəs] a falso, fraudulento; (person) fingido.

boil [bɔɪl] vt cocer; (eggs) pasar por agua // vi hervir // n (MED) furúnculo, divieso; to come to the ~ comenzar a hervir; to ~ **down to** (fig) reducirse a; to ~**er** n caldera; ~**er suit** n mono; ~**ing point** n punto de ebullición.

boisterous ['bɔɪstərəs] a (noisy) bullicioso; (excitable) exuberante; (crowd) tumultuoso.

bold [bəuld] a (brave) valiente, audaz; (excessively) atrevido; (pej) descarado; (outline, colour) fuerte; ~**ness** n valor m, audacia; (cheek) descaro.

Bolivia [bə'lɪvɪə] n Bolivia.

bollard ['bɔləd] n (AUT) poste m.

bolster ['bəulstə*] n travesero, cabezal m; to ~ **up** vt reforzar; (fig) alentar.

bolt [bəult] n (lock) cerrojo; (with nut) perno, tornillo // vt (door) echar el cerrojo a; (food) engullir // vi fugarse; (horse) desbocarse.

bomb [bɒm] n bomba // vt bombardear; ~**ard** [-'bɑːd] vt bombardear; ~**ard** [-'bɑːd] (fig) asediar; ~**ardment** [-'bɑːdmənt] n bombardeo.

bombastic [bɒm'bæstɪk] a rimbombante; (person) farolero.

bomb: ~ **disposal** n desmontaje m de explosivos; ~**er** n (AVIAT) bombardero; ~**shell** n obús m, granada; (fig) bomba.

bona fide ['bəunə'faɪdɪ] a genuino, auténtico.

bond [bɒnd] n (binding promise) fianza; (FINANCE) bono; (link) vínculo, lazo.

bondage [bɒndɪdʒ] n esclavitud f.

bone [bəun] n hueso; (of fish) espina // vt deshuesar; quitar las espinas a; ~**-dry** a completamente seco; ~**idle** a gandul.

bonfire ['bɒnfaɪə*] n hoguera, fogata.

bonnet ['bɒnɪt] n gorra; (Brit: of car) capó m.

bonus ['bəunəs] n sobrepaga, prima.

bony ['bəunɪ] a (arm, face, MED: tissue) huesudo; (meat) lleno de huesos; (fish) lleno de espinas.

boo [buː] vt abuchear, rechiflar.

booby trap ['buːbɪ-] n trampa explosiva.

book [buk] n libro; (notebook) libreta; (of stamps etc) librito; (COMM): ~**s** las cuentas, el balance // vt (ticket) sacar; (seat, room) reservar; (driver) fichar; ~**case** n librería, estante m para libros; ~**ing office** n (RAIL) despacho de billetes; (THEATRE) taquilla; ~**keeping** n teneduría de libros; ~**let** n folleto; ~**maker** n corredor m de apuestas; ~**seller** n librero; ~**shop** n librería; ~**stall** n quiosco de libros.

boom [buːm] n (noise) trueno, estampido; (in prices etc) alza rápida; (ECON) boom m, prosperidad f repentina.

boomerang ['buːməræŋ] n bumerang m.

boon [buːn] n favor m, beneficio.

boost [buːst] n estímulo, empuje m // vt estimular, empujar; ~**er** n (MED) reinyección f.

boot [buːt] n bota; (Brit: of car) maleta, maletero // vt dar un puntapié a; **to ~** (in addition) además, por añadidura.

booth [buːð] n (at fair) barraca; (telephone ~, voting ~) cabina.

booty ['buːtɪ] n botín m.

booze [buːz] (col) n bebida, trago // vi emborracharse.

border ['bɔːdə*] n borde m, margen m, orilla; (of a country) frontera // a fronterizo; **the B~s** región fronteriza entre Escocia e Inglaterra; **to ~ on** vt fus lindar con; (fig) rayar en; ~**line** n (fig) frontera.

bore [bɔː*] pt of **bear** // vt (hole) taladrar, agujerear; (person) aburrir // n (person) pelmazo, pesado; (of gun) calibre m // ~**dom** n aburrimiento.

boring [bɔːrɪŋ] a aburrido.

born [bɔːn] a: **to be ~** nacer; **I was ~ in 1960** nací en 1960.

borne [bɔːn] pp of **bear**.

borough ['bʌrə] n municipio.

borrow ['bɔrəu] vt: **to ~ sth (from sb)** pedir algo prestado a alguien.

borstal ['bɔːstl] n reformatorio (de menores).

bosom ['buzəm] n pecho; (fig) seno; ~ **friend** n amigo del alma o íntimo.

boss [bɔs] n jefe m; (employer) patrón/ona m/f; (political etc) cacique m // vt regentar, dar órdenes a; ~**y** a mandón(ona).

bosun ['bəusn] n contramaestre m.

botanist ['bɔtənɪst] n botanista m/f; **botany** [-nɪ] n botánica.

botch [bɔtʃ] vt (also: ~ **up**) arruinar, estropear.

both [bəuθ] a, pron ambos(as), los dos; ~ **of us went, we ~ went** fuimos los dos, ambos fuimos // ad: ~ **A and B** tanto A como B.

bother ['bɔðə*] vt (worry)

preocupar; (disturb) molestar, fastidiar // vi (gen: ~ o.s.) molestarse; to ~ doing tomarse la molestia de hacer // n: what a ~! ¡qué lata!

bottle ['bɒtl] n botella; (small) frasco; (baby's) biberón m // vt embotellar; to ~ up vt embotellar, contener; ~neck n embotellamiento; ~opener n destapador m, abrebotellas m inv.

bottom ['bɒtəm] n (of box, sea) fondo; (buttocks) trasero, culo; (of page, list) pie m // a (low) inferior, más bajo; (last) último; ~less a sin fondo, insondable.

bough [bau] n rama.

bought [bɔːt] pt, pp of **buy**.

boulder ['bəuldə*] n canto rodado.

bounce [bauns] vi (ball) (re)botar; (cheque) ser rechazado o incobrable // vt hacer (re)botar // n (rebound) (re)bote m.

bound [baund] pt, pp of **bind** // n (leap) salto; (gen: pl: limit) límite m // vi (leap) saltar // a: ~ by (limited by) rodeado de, confinado con; to be ~ to do sth (obliged) tener el deber de hacer algo; (likely) estar seguro de hacer algo; out of ~s prohibido el paso; ~ for con destino a.

boundary ['baundri] n límite m, lindero.

boundless ['baundlis] a ilimitado.

bouquet [buˈkeɪ] n (of flowers) ramo; (of wine) aroma m.

bout [baut] n (of malaria etc) ataque m; (BOXING etc) combate m o encuentro.

bow [bəu] n (knot) lazo; (weapon, MUS) arco // n [bau] (of the body) reverencia; (NAUT) proa // vi [bau] inclinarse, hacer una reverencia; (yield): to ~ to or before ceder ante, someterse a.

bowels [bauəlz] npl intestinos mpl, vientre m.

bowl [bəul] n tazón m, cuenco; (for washing) palangana, jofaina; (ball)

bola // vi (CRICKET) arrojar la pelota; ~s n juego de las bochas, bolos mpl.

bow-legged ['bəuˈlegɪd] a estevado.

bowler ['bəulə*] n (CRICKET) lanzador m (de la pelota); (also: ~ hat) hongo, hombín m.

bowling ['bəulɪŋ] n (game) bochas fpl, bolos mpl; ~ alley n bolera; ~ green n pista para bochas.

bow tie ['bəu-] n corbata de lazo.

box [bɒks] n (also: cardboard ~) caja, cajón m; (for jewels) estuche m; (for money) cofre m; (THEATRE) palco // vt encajonar // vi (SPORT) boxear; ~er n (person) boxeador m; (dog) boxer m; ~ing n (SPORT) boxeo; B~ing Day n Día de San Esteban, 26 de diciembre; ~ing gloves npl guantes mpl de boxeo; ~ing ring n ring m, cuadrilátero; ~office n taquilla; ~room n trastero.

boy [bɔɪ] n (young) niño; (older) muchacho; (servant) criado.

boycott ['bɔɪkɒt] n boicot m // vt boicotear.

boyfriend ['bɔɪfrend] n novio.

boyish ['bɔɪɪʃ] a muchachil.

B.R. abbr of **British Rail**.

bra [brɑː] n sostén m.

brace [breɪs] n refuerzo, abrazadera; (on teeth) aparato; (tool) barrquín m // vt asegurar, reforzar; ~s npl tirantes mpl; to ~ o.s. (fig) fortalecer el ánimo.

bracelet ['breɪslɪt] n pulsera, brazalete m.

bracing ['breɪsɪŋ] a vigorizante, tónico.

bracken ['brækən] n helecho.

bracket ['brækɪt] n (TECH) soporte m, puntal m; (group) clase f, categoría; (also: brace ~) soporte m, abrazadera; (also: round ~) paréntesis m inv; (also: square ~) corchete m // vt (group) agrupar.

brag [bræg] vi jactarse.

braid [breɪd] n (trimming) galón m; (of hair) trenza.

Braille [breɪl] n Braille m.

brain [breɪn] n cerebro; ~**s** npl
sesos mpl; ~**child** n parto del
ingenio; ~**wash** vt lavar el cerebro
a; ~**wave** n idea luminosa; ~**y** a
muy listo o inteligente.

braise [breɪz] vt cocer a fuego
lento.

brake [breɪk] n (on vehicle) freno
// vt, vi frenar; ~ **drum** n tambor m
de freno; ~ **fluid** n líquido para
freno.

bramble ['bræmbl] n zarza.

branch [brɑ:ntʃ] n rama; (fig)
ramo; (road) ramal m; (COMM)
sucursal f // vi (also: ~ **out**)
ramificarse; (: fig) extenderse.

brand [brænd] n marca; (iron)
hierro de marcar // vt (cattle)
marcar con hierro candente.

brandish ['brændɪʃ] vt blandir.

brand-new ['brænd'nju:] a fla-
mente, completamente nuevo.

brandy ['brændɪ] n coñac m,
brandy m.

brash [bræʃ] a (rough) tosco;
(cheeky) descarado.

brass [brɑ:s] n latón m; ~ **band** n
banda de metal.

brassière ['bræsɪə*] n sostén m.

brat [bræt] n (pej) mocoso.

bravado [brə'vɑ:dəʊ] n
baladronada.

brave [breɪv] a valiente, valeroso //
n valiente m // vt (challenge)
desafiar; (resist) aguantar; ~**ry** n
valor m, valentía.

brawl [brɔ:l] n pendencia, reyerta
// vi pelearse.

brawn [brɔ:n] n fuerza; (meat)
carne f en gelatina; ~**y** a fornido,
musculoso.

bray [breɪ] n rebuzno // vi rebuznar.

brazen ['breɪzn] a descarado, cínico
// vt: to ~ **it out** defenderse con
descaro.

brazier ['breɪzɪə*] n brasero.

Brazil [brə'zɪl] n (el) Brasil; ~**ian** a,
n brasileño/a.

breach [bri:tʃ] vt abrir brecha en //
n (gap) brecha; (breaking): ~ **of**

contract infracción f de contrato; ~
of the peace perturbación f del
orden público.

bread [bred] n pan m; ~ **and butter**
n pan m con mantequilla; (fig) pan
(de cada día) // a común y
corriente; ~**crumbs** npl migajas
fpl; (CULIN) pan molido.

breadth [bretθ] n anchura; (fig)
amplitud f.

breadwinner ['bredwɪnə*] n
sostén m de la familia.

break [breɪk], pt **broke**, pp
broken vt (gen) romper;
(promise) faltar a; (fall)
amortiguar; (journey) interrumpir;
(law) violar, infringir; (record)
batir; (news) comunicar // vi
romperse, quebrarse; (storm)
estallar // n (gap) abertura; (crack)
grieta; (fracture) fractura;
(breakdown) ruptura, rompimiento;
(rest) descanso; (time) intérvalo; ~
at school (período de) recreo;
(chance) oportunidad f; (escape)
evasión f, fuga; **to ~ down** vt
(figures, data) analizar, descomponer; (undermine) acabar con // vi
estropearse; (MED) sufrir un
colapso; (AUT) averiarse; (person)
romper a llorar; **to ~ even** vi salir
sin ganar ni perder; **to ~ free** or
loose vi abrirse paso; **to ~ in** vt
(horse etc) domar // vi (burglar)
forzar una entrada; **to ~ into** vt fus
(house) forzar; **to ~ off** vi (speaker)
pararse, detenerse; (branch) partir;
to ~ open vt (door etc) abrir por la
fuerza, forzar; **to ~ out** vi estallar;
to ~ out in spots salir con granos;
to ~ up vi romperse // vt romper,
intervenir en; ~**able** a quebradizo;
~**age** n rotura; ~**down** n (AUT)
avería; (in communications)
interrupción f; (MED also: **nervous**
~**down**) colapso, crisis f nerviosa;
~**down lorry** n grúa, camión m
grúa; ~**er** n rompiente m, ola
grande.

breakfast ['brekfəst] n desayuno.

break: ~through n ruptura; (fig) avance m, adelanto; ~water n rompeolas m inv.

breast [brest] n (of woman) pecho, seno; (chest) pecho; (of bird) pechuga; ~-stroke n braza de pecho.

breath [breθ] n aliento, respiración f; out of ~ sin aliento, sofocado; ~alyser n prueba de alcohol por el aliento.

breathe [bri:ð] vt, vi respirar; (noisily) resollar; **breather** n respiro.

breath: ~less a sin aliento, jadeante; ~taking a imponente, pasmoso.

breed [bri:d] pt, pp **bred** [bred] vt criar, engendrar // vi reproducirse procrear // n raza, casta; ~er n (person) criador/a m/f; ~ing n (of person) educación f.

breeze [bri:z] n brisa.

breezy ['bri:zi] a de mucho viento, ventoso; (person) despreocupado.

brevity ['breviti] n brevedad f.

brew [bru:] vt (tea) hacer; (beer) elaborar // vi hacerse, prepararse; (fig) amenazar; ~er n cervecero; ~ery n fábrica de cerveza.

bribe [braib] n soborno // vt sobornar, cohechar; ~ry n soborno, cohecho.

brick [brik] n ladrillo; ~layer n albañil m; ~works n ladrillar m.

bridal ['braidl] a nupcial.

bride [braid] n novia; ~groom n novio; **bridesmaid** n dama de honor.

bridge [bridʒ] n puente m; (NAUT) puente m de mando; (of nose) caballete m; (CARDS) bridge m // vt (river) tender un puente sobre; ~head n cabeza de puente.

bridle ['braidl] n brida, freno // vt poner la brida a, (fig) reprimir, refrenar; ~ path n camino de herradura.

brief [bri:f] a breve, corto // n (LAW) escrito // vt (inform) informar; (instruct) dar órdenes a;

~s npl (for men) calzoncillos mpl; (for women) bragas fpl; ~case n cartera; ~ing n (PRESS) informe m.

brigade [bri'geid] n (MIL) brigada.

brigadier [brigə'diə*] n general m de brigada.

bright [brait] a claro, luminoso; (weather) de sol; (person) clever) listo, inteligente; (: lively) alegre, animado; (colour) vivo; ~en vi (room) hacer más alegre // vi (weather) despejarse; (person: gen: ~en up) animarse, alegrarse.

brilliance ['briljəns] n brillo, brillantez f; **brilliant** [-ənt] a brillante; (clever) genial.

brim [brim] n borde m; (of hat) ala; ~ful a lleno hasta el borde; (fig) rebosante (de).

brine [brain] n (CULIN) salmuera.

bring [briŋ] pt, pp **brought** vt (thing) traer; (person) conducir; to ~ about vt ocasionar, producir; to ~ back vt volver a traer; (return) devolver; to ~ down vt bajar; (price) rebajar; to ~ forward vt adelantar; to ~ in vt (harvest) recoger; to ~ off vt (task, plan) lograr, conseguir; to ~ out vt (object) sacar; to ~ round vt (unconscious person) hacer volver en sí; (convince) convencer, ganar; to ~ up vt (person) educar, criar; (carry up) subir; (question) sacar a colación.

brink [briŋk] n borde m.

brisk [brisk] a enérgico, vigoroso; (speedy) rápido; (trade) activo.

brisket ['briskit] n carne f de vaca para asar.

bristle ['brisl] n cerda // vi erizarse.

Britain ['britən] n Gran Bretaña.

British ['britiʃ] a británico; the ~ npl los británicos; the ~ Isles npl las Islas Británicas.

Briton ['britən] n británico/a.

brittle ['britl] a quebradizo, frágil.

broach [brəutʃ] vt (subject) abordar.

broad [brɔːd] a ancho, amplio; (accent) cerrado; **in ~ daylight** en pleno día; **~cast** n emisión f // (vb: pt, pp **~cast**) vt (RADIO) emitir; (TV) transmitir // vi hablar o tocar por la radio; **~casting** n radiodifusión f, difusión f; **~en** vt ensanchar // vi ensancharse; **~ly** ad en general; **~minded** a tolerante, liberal.

brochure ['brəʊʃjʊə*] n folleto.

broke [brəʊk] pt of **break** // a (col) pelado, sin blanca.

broken ['brəʊkən] pp of **break** // a: **~ leg** pierna rota; **in ~ English** en un inglés imperfecto; **~hearted** con el corazón partido.

broker ['brəʊkə*] n agente m/f, bolsista m/f.

bronchitis [brɔŋ'kaɪtɪs] n bronquitis f.

bronze [brɔnz] n bronce m.

brooch [brəʊtʃ] n prendedor m.

brood [bruːd] n camada, cría; (children) progenie f; (: pej) prole f // vi (hen) empollar; (obsessively) darle vueltas (a).

brook [bruk] n arroyo.

broom [brum] n escoba; (BOT) retama; **~stick** n palo de escoba.

Bros. abbr of **Brothers.**

broth [brɔθ] n caldo.

brothel ['brɔθl] n burdel m.

brother ['brʌðə*] n hermano; **~in-law** n cuñado.

brought [brɔːt] pt, pp of **bring.**

brow [brau] n ceja; (forehead) frente m; (of hill) cumbre f.

brown [braun] a moreno; (hair) castaño; (tanned) bronceado // n (colour) color m moreno o pardo // vt poner moreno; (tan) broncear; (CULIN) dorar; **~ie** n niña Girl Guide.

browse [brauz] vi (among books) hojear libros.

bruise [bruːz] n cardenal n, contusión f // vt magullar.

brunette [bruː'net] n morena.

brunt [brʌnt] n: **the ~ of** lo más fuerte de, lo peor de.

brush [brʌʃ] n cepillo; (large) escoba; (for painting, shaving etc) brocha; (artist's) pincel m; (BOT) maleza; (quarrel) escaramuza, encuentro // vt cepillar; (gen: ~ past, ~ against) rozar al pasar; **to ~ aside** vt rechazar, no hacer caso a; **to ~ up** vt (knowledge) repasar, refrescar; **~wood** n (bushes) maleza; (sticks) leña.

brusque [bruːsk] a brusco, áspero.

Brussels [brʌslz] n Bruselas; **~ sprout** n colecilla de Bruselas.

brutal ['bruːtl] a brutal; **~ity** [-'tælɪtɪ] n brutalidad f.

brute [bruːt] n bruto; (person) bestia.

B.Sc. abbr of **Bachelor of Science** licenciado en ciencias.

bubble ['bʌbl] n burbuja, ampolla // vi burbujear, borbotar; **~ gum** n chicle m de globo.

buck [bʌk] n macho; (US: col) dólar m // vi corcovear; **to pass the ~ (to sb)** echar (a uno) el muerto; **to ~ up** vi (cheer up) animarse, cobrar ánimo.

bucket ['bʌkɪt] n cubo, balde m.

buckle ['bʌkl] n hebilla // vt abrochar con hebilla // vi torcerse, combarse.

bud [bʌd] n brote m, yema; (of flower) capullo // vi brotar, echar brotes; (fig) florecer.

Buddhism ['budɪzm] n Budismo.

budding ['bʌdɪŋ] a en ciernes, en embrión.

buddy ['bʌdɪ] n (US) compañero, compinche m.

budge [bʌdʒ] vt mover; (fig) hacer ceder // vi moverse.

budgerigar ['bʌdʒərɪgaː*] n periquito.

budget ['bʌdʒɪt] n presupuesto.

budgie ['bʌdʒɪ] n = **budgerigar.**

buff [bʌf] a (colour) color m de ante // n (enthusiast) entusiasta m/f.

buffalo ['bʌfələu], pl **~** or **~es** n búfalo.

buffer ['bʌfə*] n amortiguador m.

buffet ['bufeɪ] n (*bar*) bar m, cafetería; (*food*) buffet m // vt ['bʌfɪt] (*strike*) abofetear; (*wind etc*) golpear; ~ **car** n coche-comedor m.

buffoon [bə'fu:n] n bufón m.

bug [bʌg] n (*insect*) chinche m; (: *gen*) bicho, sabandija; (: *fig: germ*) microbio, bacilo; (*spy device*) micrófono oculto; (*tap*) intervención f; (*machine for tapping*) aparato de intervención // vt (*fam*) fastidiar; (*spy on*) poner micrófono oculto en.

bugle ['bju:gl] n corneta, clarín m.

build [bɪld] n (*of person*) talle m, tipo // vt, pt, pp built construir, edificar; ~**er** n constructor m; (*contractor*) contratista m/f; ~**ing** n (*act of construction*) construcción f; (*habitation, offices*) edificio; ~**ing society** n sociedad f inmobiliaria, cooperativa de construcciones; **to ~ up** vt (*MED*) fortalecer; (*stocks*) acumular.

built [bɪlt] pt, pp of **build** // a: ~-**in** (*cupboard*) empotrado; (*device*) interior, incorporado; ~-**up** (*area*) urbanizado.

bulb [bʌlb] n (*BOT*) bulbo; (*ELEC*) bombilla.

Bulgaria [bʌl'geərɪə] n Bulgaria; ~**n** a, n búlgaro/a.

bulge [bʌldʒ] n bombeo, pandeo // vi bombearse, pandearse; (*pocket etc*) hacer bulto.

bulk [bʌlk] n (*mass*) bulto, volumen m; (*major part*) grueso; **in** (*COMM*) a granel; **the ~ of** la mayor parte de; ~**head** n mamparo; ~**y** a voluminoso, abultado.

bull [bʊl] n toro; ~**dog** n dogo.

bulldozer ['bʊldəʊzə*] n aplanadora, motoniveladora.

bullet ['bʊlɪt] n bala; ~**proof** a a prueba de balas; ~ **wound** n balazo.

bulletin ['bʊlɪtɪn] n anuncio, parte m.

bullfight ['bʊlfaɪt] n corrida de toros; ~**er** n torero; ~**ing** n los toros mpl, el toreo; (*art of* ~**ing**) tauromaquia.

bullion ['bʊljən] n oro o plata en barras.

bullock ['bʊlək] n novillo.

bull's-eye ['bʊlzaɪ] n centro del blanco.

bully ['bʊlɪ] n valentón m, matón m // vt intimidar, tiranizar.

bum [bʌm] n (*col: backside*) culo, trasero; (*tramp*) vagabundo.

bumblebee ['bʌmblbi:] n (*ZOOL*) abejorro.

bump [bʌmp] n (*blow*) tope m, choque m; (*jolt*) sacudida; (*on road etc, on head*) bollo, abolladura // vt (*strike*) chocar contra, topetar // vi dar sacudidas; **to ~ into** vt fus chocar contra, tropezar con; (*person*) topar; ~**er** n (*Brit*) parachoques m inv // a: ~**er crop/harvest** cosecha abundante.

bumpy ['bʌmpɪ] a (*road*) lleno de baches; (*journey*) zarandeado.

bun [bʌn] n (*of bread*) bollo; (*of hair*) moño.

bunch [bʌntʃ] n (*of flowers*) ramo; (*of keys*) manojo; (*of bananas*) piña; (*of people*) grupo; (*pej*) pandilla.

bundle ['bʌndl] n (*gen*) bulto, fardo; (*of sticks*) haz f; (*of papers*) legajo // vt (*also*: ~ **up**) atar, envolver; (*put*) ~ **sth/sb into** meter algo/a alguien precipitadamente en.

bung [bʌŋ] n tapón m, bitoque m // vt (*throw: gen*: ~ **into**) arrojar.

bungalow ['bʌŋgələʊ] n bungalow m, chalé m.

bungle ['bʌŋgl] vt chapucear

bunion ['bʌnjən] n juanete m.

bunk [bʌŋk] n tonterías fpl; ~ **beds** npl literas fpl.

bunker ['bʌŋkə*] n (*coal store*) carbonera; (*MIL*) refugio; (*GOLF*) búnker m.

bunny ['bʌnɪ] n (*also*: ~ **rabbit**) conejito.

bunting ['bʌntɪŋ] n empavesada, banderas fpl.

buoy [bɔɪ] n boya; **to ~ up** vt

mantener a flote; *(fig)* animar; **~ant a** boyante.

burden ['bə:dn] n carga // vt cargar.

bureau [bjuə'rəu], pl **~x** [-z] n *(furniture)* escritorio, buró m; *(office)* oficina, agencia.

bureaucracy [bjuə'rɔkrəsi] n burocracia; **bureaucrat** [bjuərəkræt] n burócrata m/f.

burglar ['bə:glə*] n ladrón/ona m/f; **~ alarm** n alarma f de ladrones; **~y** n robo con allanamiento, robo de una casa; **burgle** ['bə:gl] vt robar (con allanamiento).

burial ['beriəl] n entierro; **~ ground** n cementerio.

burlesque [bə:'lesk] n parodia.

burly ['bə:li] a fornido, membrudo.

Burma ['bə:mə] n Birmania.

burn [bə:n], pt, pp **burned** or **burnt** vt quemar; *(house)* incendiar // vi quemarse, arder; incendiarse; *(sting)* escocer // n quemadura; **to ~ down** vt incendiar; **~er** n *(gas)* quemador m, fuego; **~ing** a ardiente.

burp [bə:p] *(col)* n eructo // vi eructar.

burrow ['bʌrəu] n madriguera // vt hacer una madriguera.

bursar ['bə:sə*] n tesorero; *(student)* becario; **~y** n beca.

burst [bə:st], pt, pp **burst** vt *(balloon, pipe)* reventar; *(banks etc)* romper // vi reventarse; romperse; *(tyre)* pincharse; *(bomb)* estallar // n *(gen)* reventón m; *(explosion)* estallido; *(shots)* ráfaga de tiros; **a ~ of energy** una explosión f de energía; **to ~ into flames** estallar en llamas; **to ~ into laughter** soltar la carcajada; **to ~ into tears** deshacerse en lágrimas; **to be ~ing with** reventar por o de; **to ~ into** vt fus *(room etc)* irrumpir en; **to ~ open** vi abrirse de golpe.

bury ['beri] vt enterrar; *(body)* enterrar, sepultar.

bus [bʌs] n autobús m.

bush [buʃ] n arbusto; *(scrub land)* monte m; **to beat about the ~** ir por rodeos; **~y** a *(thick)* espeso, poblado.

busily ['bizili] ad atareadamente, afanosamente.

business ['biznis] n *(matter)* negocio; *(trading)* comercio, negocios mpl; *(firm)* empresa, casa; *(occupation)* oficio; *(affair)* asunto; **it's my ~ to...** me toca o corresponde...; **it's none of my ~** no tengo nada que ver; **he means ~** habla en serio; **~like a** formal, metódico; **~man** n hombre m de negocios.

bus-stop ['bʌsstɔp] n parada de autobús.

bust [bʌst] n *(ANAT)* pecho // a *(broken)* roto, estropeado; **to go ~** quebrarse.

bustle ['bʌsl] n bullicio, movimiento // vi menearse, apresurarse; **bustling** a *(town)* animado, bullicioso.

busy ['bizi] a ocupado, atareado; *(shop, street)* concurrido, animado // vt: **to ~ o.s. with** ocuparse en; **~body** n entrometido.

but [bʌt] conj pero // prep excepto, menos; **nothing ~** nada más que; **~ for** a no ser por, si no fuera por; **all ~ finished** casi terminado.

butane ['bju:tein] n butano.

butcher ['butʃə*] n carnicero // vt hacer una carnicería con; *(cattle etc for meat)* matar; **~'s (shop)** n carnicería.

butler ['bʌtlə*] n mayordomo.

butt [bʌt] n *(cask)* tonel m; *(for rain)* tina; *(thick end)* cabo, extremo; *(of gun)* culata; *(of cigarette)* colilla; *(fig: target)* blanco // vt dar cabezadas contra, topetar.

butter ['bʌtə*] n mantequilla // vt untar con mantequilla; **~ bean** n judía blanca; **~cup** n ranúnculo.

butterfly ['bʌtəflai] n mariposa.

buttocks ['bʌtəks] npl nalgas fpl.

button ['bʌtn] n botón m // vt abotonar, abrochar; ~ vi abrocharse; ~**hole** n ojal m; (flower) flor f que se lleva en el ojal // vt obligar a escuchar.

buttress ['bʌtrɪs] n contrafuerte m; (fig) apoyo, sostén m.

buxom ['bʌksəm] a (baby) rollizo; (woman) frescachona.

buy [baɪ], pt, pp **bought** vt comprar // n compra; **to ~ sb sth/sth from sb** comprar algo para alguien/comprarle algo a alguien; ~**er** n comprador/a m/f.

buzz [bʌz] n zumbido; (col: phone call) llamada (por teléfono) // vi zumbar.

buzzard ['bʌzəd] n águila ratonera.

buzzer ['bʌzə*] n zumbador m, vibrador m.

by [baɪ] prep por; (beside) junto a, cerca de; (according to) según, de acuerdo con; (before): ~ **4 o'clock** para las cuatro // ad: see **pass, go** etc; ~ **bus/car** en autobús/coche; **paid ~ the hour** pagado por horas; ~ **night/day** de noche/día; (all) ~ **oneself** (completamente) solo, ~ **the way** a propósito, por cierto; **and large** en general; ~ **and luego**, más tarde.

bye(-bye) ['baɪ('baɪ)] excl adiós, hasta luego.

by(e)-law ['baɪlɔ] n ordenanza municipal.

by-election ['baɪɪlekʃən] n elección f parcial.

bygone ['baɪgɔn] a pasado, del pasado // n: **let ~s be ~s** lo pasado pasado está.

bypass ['baɪpɑs] n carretera de circunvalación // vt evitar.

by-product ['baɪprɔdʌkt] n subproducto, derivado.

bystander ['baɪstændə*] n espectador/a m/f.

byword ['baɪwɜd] n: **to be a ~ for** ser conocidísimo por.

C

C. abbr of **centigrade.**

C.A. abbr of **chartered accountant.**

cab [kæb] n taxi m; (of truck) cabina.

cabaret ['kæbəreɪ] n cabaret m.

cabbage ['kæbɪdʒ] n col m, berza.

cabin ['kæbɪn] n cabaña; (on ship) camarote m; ~ **cruiser** n yate m de motor.

cabinet ['kæbɪnɪt] n (POL) consejo de ministros; (furniture) armario; (also: display ~) vitrina; ~-**maker** n ebanista m.

cable ['keɪbl] n cable m // vt cablegrafiar; ~-**car** n coche m de teleférico, tren m aéreo.

cackle ['kækl] vi cacarear.

cactus ['kæktəs] pl **-ti** [-taɪ] n cacto.

caddie ['kædɪ] n cadi m.

cadet [kə'det] n (MIL) cadete m.

cadge [kædʒ] vt gorronear; **cadger** n gorrón/ona m/f.

Caesarean (section) [si'zeərɪən] n cesárea.

café ['kæfeɪ] n café m. **cafeteria** [kæfɪ'tɪərɪə] n café m

caffein(e) ['kæfin] n cafeína.

cage [keɪdʒ] n jaula // vt enjaular.

cagey ['keɪdʒɪ] a (col) cauteloso, reservado.

Cairo ['kaɪərəu] n el Cairo.

cajole [kə'dʒəul] vt engatusar.

cake [keɪk] n (large) pastel m; (small) pasta, bizcocho; (of soap) pastilla. ~**d with** cubierta de.

calamitous [kə'læmɪtəs] a calamitoso; **calamity** [-ɪtɪ] n calamidad f.

calcium ['kælsɪəm] n calcio.

calculate ['kælkjuleɪt] vt calcular; **calculating** a (clever) astuto; (devious) calculador(a); **calculation** [-'leɪʃən] n cálculo, cómputo; **calculator** n calculadora.

calculus ['kælkjuləs] n cálculo.

calendar ['kæləndə*] n calendario.

~ **month/year** mes m/año civil.

calf [kɑ:f], pl **calves** n (of cow) ternero, becerro; (of other animals) cría; (also: ~**skin**) piel m de becerro; (ANAT) pantorrilla.

calibre, caliber (US) ['kælɪbə*] n calibre m.

call [kɔ:l] vt (gen, also TEL) llamar // vi (shout) llamar; (telephone) llamar por teléfono; (visit: also: ~ **in,** ~ **round**) hacer una visita // n (shout, TEL) llamada; (of bird) canto; (appeal) llamamiento; **to ~ for** vt fus (demand) pedir, exigir; (fetch) venir por; **to ~ off** vt suspender; (cancel) cancelar; **to ~ on** vt fus (visit) visitar; (turn to) acudir a; **to ~ out** vi gritar, dar voces; **to ~ up** vt (MIL) llamar al servicio militar; ~**box** n cabina telefónica; ~**er** n visita m/f; (TEL) usuario; ~ **girl** n prostituta; ~**ing** n vocación f, profesión f.

callous ['kæləs] a insensible, cruel.

calm [kɑ:m] n calma, tranquilidad f // vt calmar, tranquilizar // a (gen) tranquilo; (sea) liso, en calma; ~**ly** ad tranquilamente, con calma; ~**ness** n calma; **to ~ down** vi calmarse, tranquilizarse // vt calmar, tranquilizar.

calorie ['kælərɪ] n caloría.

calve [kɑ:v] vi parir.

calves [kɑ:vz] pl of **calf.**

camber ['kæmbə*] n (of road) combadura, comba.

Cambodia [kæm'bəudjə] n Camboya.

came [keɪm] pt of **come.**

camel ['kæməl] n camello.

cameo ['kæmɪəu] n camafeo.

camera ['kæmərə] n máquina fotográfica; (CINEMA, TV) cámara; **in ~** en secreto; ~**man** n cámara m, cámara m/f.

camouflage ['kæməflɑ:ʒ] n camuflaje m // vt camuflar.

camp [kæmp] n campo, campamento // vi acampar // a afectado, afeminado.

campaign [kæm'peɪn] n (MIL, POL etc) campaña // vi hacer campaña.

camp: ~**bed** n cama de campaña; ~**er** n campista m/f; (vehicle) caravana; ~**ing** n camping m; **to go ~ing** hacer camping; ~**site** n camping m.

campus ['kæmpəs] n ciudad f universitaria.

can [kæn] auxiliary vb (gen) poder; (know how to) saber; **I ~ swim** sé nadar // n (of oil, water) lata, bote m // vt enlatar; (preserve) conservar en lata.

Canada ['kænədə] n el Canadá; **Canadian** [kə'neɪdɪən] a, n canadiense m/f.

canal [kə'næl] n canal m.

canary [kə'neərɪ] n canario; **C~ Islands** npl las (Islas) Canarias fpl.

cancel ['kænsəl] vt cancelar; (train) suprimir; (appointment) anular; (cross out) tachar, borrar; ~**lation** [-'leɪʃən] n cancelación f; supresión f.

cancer ['kænsə*] n cáncer m; **C~** (ASTRO) Cáncer m.

candid ['kændɪd] a franco, abierto.

candidate ['kændɪdeɪt] n candidato.

candle ['kændl] n vela; (in church) cirio; ~**stick** n (also: ~ **holder**) (single) candelero; (low) palmatoria; (bigger, ornate) candelabro.

candour ['kændə*] n franqueza.

candy ['kændɪ] n azúcar m cande; (US) dulce m, caramelo.

cane [keɪn] n (BOT) caña; (stick) vara, palmeta // vt (SCOL) castigar (con palmeta).

canine ['kænaɪn] a canino.

canister ['kænɪstə*] n bote m, lata.

cannabis ['kænəbɪs] n cáñamo, marijuana.

canned ['kænd] a en lata, de lata.

cannibal ['kænɪbəl] n caníbal m/f; ~**ism** n canibalismo.

cannon ['kænən], pl ~ or ~**s** n cañón m; ~**ball** n bala (de cañón).

cannot ['kænɔt] = **can not.**

canny ['kænɪ] a astuto.

canoe [kə'nu:] n canoa; (SPORT) piragua; ~**ing** n (SPORT) piragüismo; ~**ist** n piragüista m/f.

canon ['kænən] n (clergyman) canónigo; (standard) canon m.

canonize ['kænənaɪz] vt canonizar.

can opener ['kænˌəʊpnə*] n abrelatas m inv.

canopy ['kænəpɪ] n dosel m, toldo; (ARCH) baldaquín m.

can't [kænt] = **can not**.

cantankerous [kæn'tæŋkərəs] a arisco, malhumorado.

canteen [kæn'ti:n] n cantina; (bottle) cantimplora; (of cutlery) juego m de cubiertos.

canter ['kæntə*] n medio galope // vi ir a medio galope.

canvas ['kænvəs] n (gen) lona; (painting) lienzo; (NAUT) velas fpl; **under** ~ (camping) bajo lona.

canvass ['kænvəs] vt (POL) solicitar votos de.

canyon ['kænjən] n cañón m.

cap [kæp] n gorra; (of pen) capuchón m; (of bottle) tapa, cápsula; (MED) diafragma m // vt coronar, poner remate a; (outdo) superar; (FOOTBALL) seleccionar (para el equipo nacional).

capability [keɪpə'bɪlɪtɪ] n capacidad f; **capable** ['keɪpəbl] a capaz.

capacity [kə'pæsɪtɪ] n capacidad f; (position) calidad f.

cape [keɪp] n capa; (GEO) cabo.

caper ['keɪpə*] n (CULIN: gen: ~s) alcaparra; (prank) travesura.

capital ['kæpɪtl] n (also: ~ city) capital f; (money) capital m; (also: ~ letter) mayúscula; ~**ism** n capitalismo; ~**ist** a, n capitalista m/f; ~ **punishment** n pena de muerte.

capitulate [kə'pɪtjuleɪt] vi capitular, rendirse; **capitulation** [-'leɪʃən] n capitulación f, rendición f.

capricious [kə'prɪʃəs] a caprichoso.

Capricorn ['kæprɪkɔ:n] n Capricornio.

capsize [kæp'saɪz] vt volcar, hacer zozobrar // vi volcarse, zozobrar.

capstan ['kæpstən] n cabrestante m.

capsule ['kæpsju:l] n cápsula.

captain ['kæptɪn] n capitán m // vt capitanear, ser el capitán de.

caption ['kæpʃən] n (heading) título; (to picture) leyenda.

captivate ['kæptɪveɪt] vt cautivar, encantar.

captive ['kæptɪv] a, n cautivo/a; **captivity** [-'tɪvɪtɪ] n cautiverio.

capture ['kæptʃə*] vt prender, apresar; (place) tomar; (attention) captar, llamar // n apresamiento; toma, (thing taken) presa.

car [ka:*] n coche m, automóvil m, (RAIL) vagón m.

carafe [kə'ræf] n garrafa.

caramel ['kærəməl] n caramelo.

carat ['kærət] n quilate m.

caravan ['kærəvæn] n caravana, rulota; (of camels) caravana.

caraway ['kærəweɪ] n: ~ **seed** carvi m.

carbohydrate [ka:bəʊ'haɪdreɪt] n hidrato de carbono; (food) fécula.

carbon ['ka:bən] n carbono; ~ **copy** n copia al carbón; ~ **paper** n papel m carbón.

carburettor [ka:bju'retə*] n carburador m.

carcass ['ka:kəs] n cadáver m de animal.

card [ka:d] n carta, naipe m; (visiting ~, post~ etc) tarjeta; **board** n cartón m, cartulina; ~ **game** n juego de naipes.

cardiac ['ka:dɪæk] a cardíaco.

cardigan ['ka:dɪgən] n rebeca.

cardinal ['ka:dɪnl] a cardinal // n cardenal m.

card index n fichero.

care [keə*] n (gen) cuidado; (worry) inquietud f, solicitud f; (charge) cargo, custodia // vi: **to** ~ **about** preocuparse de, tener interés en;

sb's ~ a cargo de alguien; **to take ~ to** cuidarse o tener cuidado de; **to take ~ of** vt cuidar; **to ~ for** vt fus cuidar a; (*like*) querer; **I don't ~** no me importa.

career [kə'rɪə*] n carrera // vi (*also*: ~ **along**) correr a toda velocidad.

carefree ['kɛəfriː] a despreocupado.

careful ['kɛəful] a cuidadoso; (*cautious*) cauteloso; (**be**) ~! ¡tenga cuidado!; ~**ly** ad con cuidado, cuidadosamente.

careless ['kɛəlɪs] a descuidado; (*heedless*) poco atento; ~**ly** ad sin cuidado, a la ligera; ~**ness** n descuido, falta de atención.

caress [kə'rɛs] n caricia // vt acariciar.

caretaker ['kɛəteɪkə*] n portero, conserje m/f.

car-ferry ['kɑːfɛrɪ] n transbordador m para coches.

cargo ['kɑːgəu], pl ~**es** n cargamento, carga.

Caribbean [kærɪ'biːən] a: **the ~ (Sea)** el Caribe.

caricature ['kærɪkətjuə*] n caricatura.

carnal ['kɑːnl] a carnal.

carnation [kɑː'neɪʃən] n clavel m.

carnival ['kɑːnɪvəl] n fiesta, feria, carnaval m.

carnivore ['kɑːnɪvɔː*] n carnívoro.

carol ['kærəl] n: (**Christmas**) ~ villancico.

carp [kɑːp] n (*fish*) carpa; **to ~ at** vt fus quejarse de.

car park n aparcamiento, parking m.

carpenter ['kɑːpɪntə*] n carpintero; **carpentry** [-trɪ] n carpintería.

carpet ['kɑːpɪt] n alfombra // vt alfombrar; ~ **slippers** npl zapatillas fpl.

carriage ['kærɪdʒ] n coche m; (*RAIL*) vagón m; (*for goods*) transporte m; (*bearing*) porte m; ~**way** n (*part of road*) carretera;

dual ~**way** carretera de doble calzada.

carrier ['kærɪə*] n trajinista m/f; (*company*) empresa de transportes; ~ **bag** n bolsa (de papel).

carrot ['kærət] n zanahoria.

carry ['kærɪ] vt (*gen*) llevar; (*transport*) transportar; (*a motion, bill*) aprobar; (*involve: responsibilities etc*) entrañar, implicar // vi (*sound*) oírse; **to ~ on** vi (*continue*) seguir (adelante), continuar; (*fam: complain*) quejarse, protestar // vt proseguir, continuar; **to ~ out** vt (*orders*) cumplir; (*investigation*) llevar a cabo, realizar.

cart [kɑːt] n carro, carreta // vt acarrear, llevar (en carro).

cartilage ['kɑːtɪlɪdʒ] n cartílago.

cartographer [kɑː'tɔgrəfə*] n cartógrafo.

carton ['kɑːtən] n (*box*) caja (de cartón); (*of yogurt*) pote m.

cartoon [kɑː'tuːn] n (*PRESS*) caricatura; (*comic strip*) tira cómica; (*film*) dibujos mpl animados; ~**ist** n caricaturista m/f; dibujante m/f.

cartridge ['kɑːtrɪdʒ] n cartucho.

carve [kɑːv] vt (*meat*) trinchar; (*wood, stone*) cincelar, esculpir; (*on tree*) grabar; **to ~ up** dividir, repartir; **carving** n (*in wood etc*) escultura, (obra de) talla; **carving knife** n trinchante m.

car wash n lavado de coches.

cascade [kæs'keɪd] n salto de agua, cascada; (*fig*) chorro // vi caer a chorros o en forma de cascada.

case [keɪs] n (*container*) caja; (*MED*) caso; (*for jewels etc*) estuche m; (*LAW*) causa, proceso; (*also: suit~*) maleta; **in ~ of** en caso de (que); **in any ~** en todo caso; **just in ~** por si acaso; **to make a good ~** tener buenos argumentos.

cash [kæʃ] n (dinero en) efectivo, dinero contante // vt cobrar, hacer efectivo; **to pay (in) ~** pagar al contado; ~ **on delivery** cóbrese al entregar; ~**book** n libro de caja; ~**desk** n caja.

cashew [kæˈʃuː] n (also: ~ **nut**) anacardo.

cashier [kæˈʃɪə*] n cajero.

cashmere [kæʃˈmɪə*] n casimir m, cachemira.

cash register n caja.

casing [ˈkeɪsɪŋ] n envoltura; (of boiler etc) revestimiento.

casino [kəˈsiːnəu] n casino.

cask [kɑːsk] n tonel m, barril m.

casket [ˈkɑːskɪt] n cofre m, estuche m; (US: coffin) ataúd m.

casserole [ˈkæsərəul] n cacerola; (food) cazuela.

cassette [kæˈset] n cassette m; ~ **player** n tocacassettes m inv.

cassock [ˈkæsək] n sotana.

cast [kɑːst] pt, pp **cast** vt (throw) echar, arrojar, lanzar; (skin) mudar, perder; (metal) fundir; (THEATRE) hacer el reparto de // (FISHING) lanzar // n (THEATRE) reparto; (mould) forma, molde m; (also: plaster ~) vaciado; **to ~ away** vt desechar; **to ~ down** vt derribar; **to ~ loose** soltar; **to ~ one's vote** dar el voto; **to ~ off** vi (NAUT) desamarrar.

castanets [kæstəˈnets] npl castañuelas fpl.

castaway [ˈkɑːstəweɪ] n náufrago.

caste [kɑːst] n casta.

casting vote [ˈkɑːstɪŋ-] n voto decisivo.

cast iron n hierro fundido.

castle [ˈkɑːsl] n castillo; (CHESS) torre f.

castor [ˈkɑːstə*] n (wheel) ruedecilla; ~ **oil** n aceite m de ricino; ~ **sugar** n azúcar m extrafino.

castrate [kæsˈtreɪt] vt castrar.

casual [ˈkæʒjul] a (by chance) fortuito; (irregular: work etc) eventual, temporero; (unconcerned) despreocupado; (informal: clothes) de sport; ~**ly** ad por casualidad; de

manera despreocupada.

casualty [ˈkæʒjultɪ] n víctima m/f, herido; (dead) muerto; (MIL) baja; **casualties** npl pérdidas fpl.

cat [kæt] n gato.

Catalan [ˈkætəlæn] a, n Catalán/ana m/f.

catalogue, **catalog** (US) [ˈkætəlog] n catálogo // vt catalogar.

Catalonia [kætəˈləunɪə] n Cataluña.

catalyst [ˈkætəlɪst] n catalizador m.

catapult [ˈkætəpʌlt] n tirador m.

cataract [ˈkætərækt] n (also MED) catarata.

catarrh [kəˈtɑː*] n catarro.

catastrophe [kəˈtæstrəfɪ] n catástrofe m; **catastrophic** [kætəˈstrɒfɪk] a catastrófico.

catch [kætʃ] pt, pp **caught** vt (gen) coger; (arrest) detener; (grasp) asir; (breath) suspender; (person, by surprise) sorprender; (attract: attention) ganar; (MED) contagiarse de, coger; (also: ~ **up**) alcanzar // vi (fire) encenderse; (in branches etc) enredarse // n (fish etc) pesca; (act of catching) cogida; (trick) trampa; (of lock) pestillo, cerradura; **to ~ on** vi (understand) caer en la cuenta; (grow popular) hacerse popular; **to ~ sight of** divisar; **to ~ up** vi (fig) ponerse al día.

catch: ~**ing** a (MED) contagioso; ~**ment area** n zona de captación; ~ **phrase** n lema m, slogan m; ~**y** a (tune) pegadizo.

catechism [ˈkætɪkɪzəm] n (REL) catequismo.

categoric(al) [kætɪˈgorɪk(əl)] a categórico, terminante.

categorize [ˈkætɪgəraɪz] vt clasificar; **category** [-rɪ] n categoría, clase f.

cater [ˈkeɪtə*] vi: **to ~ for** abastecer a; (needs) atender a; (consumers) proveer a; ~**er** n abastecedor m, proveedor m; ~**ing** n servicio de comidas; (trade) abastecimiento.

caterpillar ['kætəpɪlə*] n oruga, gusano; ~ **track** n rodado de oruga.

cathedral [kə'θi:drəl] n catedral f.

catholic ['kæθəlɪk] a católico; **C~** a, n (REL) católico/a.

cattle ['kætl] npl ganado sg.

catty ['kætɪ] a malicioso, rencoroso.

Caucasus ['kɔ:kəsəs] n Cáucaso.

caught [kɔ:t] pt, pp of **catch**.

cauliflower ['kɔlɪflauə*] n coliflor f.

cause [kɔ:z] n causa, motivo, razón f // vt causar; (provoke) provocar.

causeway ['kɔ:zweɪ] n (road) carretera elevada; (embankment) terraplén m.

caustic ['kɔ:stɪk] a cáustico; (fig) mordaz.

caution ['kɔ:ʃən] n cautela, prudencia; (warning) advertencia, amonestación f // vt amonestar.

cautious ['kɔ:ʃəs] a cauteloso, prudente, precavido; ~**ly** ad con cautela; ~**ness** n cautela.

cavalier [kævə'lɪə*] a arrogante, desdeñoso.

cavalry ['kævəlrɪ] n caballería.

cave [keɪv] n cueva, caverna; **to ~ in** vi (roof etc) derrumbarse, hundirse; ~**man** n cavernícola m/f, troglodita m.

cavern ['kævən] n caverna.

caviar(e) ['kævɪɑ:*] n caviar m.

cavity ['kævɪtɪ] n hueco, cavidad f.

cavort [kə'vɔ:t] vi dar cabriolades.

caw [kɔ:] vi graznar.

CBI n abbr of **Confederation of British Industries**.

cc abbr of **cubic centimetres**; **carbon copy**.

cease [si:s] vt, vi cesar; ~**fire** n cese m de hostilidades o fuego; ~**less** a incesante; ~**lessly** ad sin cesar.

cedar ['si:də*] n cedro.

cede [si:d] vt ceder.

ceiling ['si:lɪŋ] n techo; (fig) límite m.

celebrate ['selɪbreɪt] vt celebrar; (marriage) solemnizar // vi divertirse; ~**d** a célebre; **celebration** [-'breɪʃən] n fiesta, celebración f.

celebrity [sɪ'lebrɪtɪ] n celebridad f.

celery ['selərɪ] n apio.

celestial [sɪ'lestɪəl] a (of sky) celeste; (divine) celestial.

celibacy ['selɪbəsɪ] n celibato.

cell [sel] n celda; (BIOL) célula; (ELEC) elemento.

cellar ['selə*] n sótano; (for wine) bodega.

'**cello** ['tʃeləu] n violoncelo.

cellophane ['seləfeɪn] n celofán m.

cellular ['seljulə*] a celular.

cellulose ['seljuləus] n celulosa.

Celt [kelt, selt] a, n celta m/f; ~**ic** a celta.

cement [sə'ment] n cemento // vt cementar; (fig) cimentar, fortalecer.

cemetery ['semɪtrɪ] n cementerio.

cenotaph ['senətɑ:f] n cenotafio.

censor ['sensə*] n censor m // vt (cut) tachar, suprimir; ~**ship** n censura.

censure ['senʃə*] vt censurar.

census ['sensəs] n censo.

cent [sent] n (US: coin) centavo, céntimo; see also **per**.

centenary [sen'ti:nərɪ] n centenario.

centi... [sentɪ] pref: ~**grade** a centígrado; ~**litre** n centilitro; ~**metre** n centímetro; ~**pede** n ciempiés m.

central ['sentrəl] a central; (of town) céntrico; **C~ American** a centroamericano; ~ **heating** n calefacción f central; ~**ize** vt centralizar.

centre ['sentə*] n centro; ~-**forward** n (SPORT) delantero centro; ~-**half** n (SPORT) medio centro.

century ['sentjurɪ] n siglo; **20th** ~ siglo veinte.

ceramic [sɪ'ræmɪk] a cerámico; ~**s** n cerámica.

cereal ['sɪərɪəl] n cereal m.

ceremony ['serɪmənɪ] n ceremonia.

certain ['sɜːtən] a (gen) seguro; (correct) cierto; (person) seguro; (a particular) cierto; **for ~** a ciencia cierta; **~ly** ad desde luego, por cierto; **~ty** n certeza, certidumbre f, seguridad f.

certificate [sə'tɪfɪkɪt] n certificado.

certify ['sɜːtɪfaɪ] vt certificar.

cervix ['sɜːvɪks] n cerviz f.

cessation [sə'seɪʃən] n cesación f, suspensión f.

cf. abbr = **compare** cfr.

chafe [tʃeɪf] vt (rub) rozar; (wear) desgastar; (irritate) irritar.

chaffinch ['tʃæfɪntʃ] n pinzón m vulgar.

chagrin ['ʃægrɪn] n disgusto, desazón f.

chain [tʃeɪn] n (gen) cadena // vt (also: ~ **up**) encadenar; **~ reaction** n reacción f en cadena; **store** n tienda de una cadena.

chair [tʃeə*] n silla; (armchair) sillón m; (of university) cátedra f // vt (meeting) presidir; **~lift** n telesilla; **~man** n presidente m.

chalet ['ʃæleɪ] n chalet m.

chalice ['tʃælɪs] n cáliz m.

chalk [tʃɔːk] n (GEO) creta; (for writing) tiza.

challenge ['tʃælɪndʒ] n desafío, reto // vt desafiar, retar; (statement, right) poner en duda, cuestionar; **to ~ sb to do sth** retar a uno a que haga algo; **challenger** n (SPORT) contrincante m/f; **challenging** a desafiante; (tone) de desafío.

chamber ['tʃeɪmbə*] n cámara, sala; **~ of commerce** cámara de comercio; **~maid** n camarera; **~ music** n música de cámara.

chamois ['ʃæmwɑː] n gamuza.

champagne [ʃæm'peɪn] n champaña m, champán m.

champion ['tʃæmpɪən] n campeón/ona m/f; **~ship** n campeonato.

chance [tʃɑːns] n (luck) casualidad f, suerte f; (fate) azar m; (opportunity) ocasión f, oportunidad f; (likelihood) posibilidad f; (risk) riesgo // vt arriesgar, probar / a fortuito, casual; **to ~ it** aventurarse, arriesgarse; **to take a ~** arriesgarse; **by ~** por casualidad.

chancel ['tʃɑːnsəl] n coro y presbiterio.

chancellor ['tʃɑːnsələ*] n canciller m; **C~ of the Exchequer** n Ministro de Hacienda.

chandelier [ʃændə'lɪə*] n araña (de luces).

change [tʃeɪndʒ] vt (gen) cambiar; (replace) reemplazar; (gear, clothes, house) cambiar de, mudar de; (exchange) trocar; (transform) transformar // vi (gen) cambiar(se), mudar; (trains) hacer transbordo; **to ~ into** transformarse en / n cambio, modificación f, transformación f; (coins) moneda suelta, suelto; (money returned) vuelta; **for a ~** para variar; **~able** a (weather) cambiable, mudable; **~less** a inmutable; **~ over to** (to new system) cambio.

changing ['tʃeɪndʒɪŋ] a cambiante; **~ room** n vestuario.

channel ['tʃænl] n (TV) canal m; (of river) cauce m; (of sea) estrecho; (groove, fig: medium) conducto, medio // vt canalizar, encauzar; **the (English) C~** el Canal de la Mancha; **the C~ Islands** las Islas Normandas fpl.

chant [tʃɑːnt] n canto // vt cantar; (fig) recitar en tono monótono.

chaos ['keɪɒs] n caos m; **chaotic** [keɪ'ɒtɪk] a caótico, desordenado.

chap [tʃæp] n (col: man) tío, tipo // vi (skin) agrietarse.

chapel ['tʃæpəl] n capilla.

chaperon ['ʃæpərəʊn] n carabina.

chaplain ['tʃæplɪn] n capellán m.

chapter ['tʃæptə*] n capítulo.

char [tʃɑː*] vt (burn) carbonizar, chamuscar // n = **charlady**.

character ['kærɪktə*] n carácter

m, naturaleza, índole *f*, calidad *f*; (*in novel, film*) personaje *m*; (*role*) papel *m*; ~**istic** [-'rıstık] *a* característico // *n* característica; ~**ize** *vt* caracterizar.

charade [ʃəˈrɑːd] *n* charada.

charcoal ['tʃɑːkəul] *n* carbón *m* vegetal; (ART) carboncillo.

charge [tʃɑːdʒ] *n* carga; (LAW) cargo, acusación *f*; (*cost*) precio, coste *m*; (*responsibility*) cargo; (*task*) encargo // *vt* (LAW) acusar (*with de*); (*gun, battery, MIL: enemy*) cargar; (*price*) pedir; (*customer*) cobrar; (*sb with task*) encargar // *vi* cargar, precipitarse; (*make pay*) cobrar; ~**s** *npl*: **bank** ~**s** suplemento cobrado por el banco; **free of** ~ gratis; **to reverse the** ~**s** (TEL) poner una conferencia por cobrar; **to take** ~ **of** hacerse cargo de, encargarse de; **to be in** ~ **of** estar a cargo de o encargado de; **how much do you** ~? ¿cuánto cobra Usted?; **to** ~ **an expense (up) to sb's account** cargar algo a cuenta de alguien.

charitable ['tʃærıtəbl] *a* caritativo.

charity ['tʃærıtı] *n* (*gen*) caridad *f*; (*sympathy*) compasión *f*; (*organization*) sociedad *f* benéfica.

charlady ['tʃɑːleıdı] *n* mujer *f* de la limpieza.

charm [tʃɑːm] *n* encanto, atractivo; (*spell*) hechizo; (*object*) amuleto // *vt* encantar; hechizar; ~**ing** *a* encantador(a), simpático.

chart [tʃɑːt] *n* cuadro; (*graph*) gráfica; (*map*) carta de navegación // *vt* (*course*) trazar.

charter ['tʃɑːtə*] *vt* (*plane*) alquilar; (*ship*) fletar // *n* (*document*) carta; ~**ed accountant** *n* perito contable; ~**flight** *n* vuelo charter.

charwoman ['tʃɑːwumən] *n* = **charlady**.

chase [tʃeıs] *vt* (*follow*) perseguir; (*hunt*) cazar // *n* persecución *f*, caza; **to** ~ **after** correr tras.

chasm ['kæzəm] *n* abismo.

chassis ['ʃæsı] *n* chasis *m*.

chaste [tʃeıst] *a* casto; **chastity** ['tʃæstıtı] *n* castidad *f*.

chat [tʃæt] *vi* (*also*: **have a** ~) charlar // *n* charla.

chatter ['tʃætə*] *vi* (*person*) charlar; (*teeth*) castañetear // *n* (*of birds*) parloteo; (*of people*) charla, cháchara; ~**box** *n* parlanchín/ina *m/f*.

chatty ['tʃætı] *a* (*style*) familiar; (*person*) hablador(a), locuaz.

chauffeur ['ʃəufə*] *n* chófer *m*.

cheap [tʃiːp] *a* barato; (*trick*) malo; (*poor quality*) barato, de poca calidad // *ad* barato; ~**en** *vt* rebajar el precio, abaratar; **to** ~**en o.s.** rebajarse; ~**ly** *ad* barato, a bajo precio.

cheat [tʃiːt] *vi* hacer trampa // *vt* defraudar, timar // *n* trampa, fraude *m*; (*person*) tramposo; ~**ing** *n* trampa, fraude *m*.

check [tʃɛk] *vt* (*examine*) controlar; (*facts*) comprobar; (*count*) contar; (*halt*) parar, detener; (*restrain*) refrenar, restringir // *n* (*inspection*) control *m*, inspección *f*; (*curb*) freno; (*bill*) nota, cuenta; (*obstacle*) impedimento, estorbo; (*token*) ficha; (*pattern*: *gen pl*) cuadro; **to** ~ **in** *vi* (*in hotel, airport*) registrarse // *vt* (*luggage*) facturar; **to** ~ **out** *vi* (*of hotel*) pagar la cuenta y marcharse; **to** ~ **up** *vi*: **to** ~ **up on sth** comprobar algo; **to** ~ **up on sb** investigar a una persona; ~**mate** *n* jaque *m* mate; ~**out** *n* caja; ~**point** *n* (punto de) control *m*; ~**up** *n* (MED) reconocimiento general; (*of machine*) repaso.

cheek [tʃiːk] *n* mejilla; (*impudence*) descaro; ~**bone** *n* pómulo; ~**y** *a* fresco, descarado.

cheer [tʃıə*] *vt* vitorear, aplaudir; (*gladden*) alegrar, animar // *vi* aplaudir, gritar con entusiasmo // *n* grito (de entusiasmo); ~**s** *npl* aplausos *mpl*; ~**s**! ¡salud!; **to** ~ **up**

vi animarse, cobrar ánimos // *vt* alegrar, animar; **~ful** *a* alegre; **~fulness** *n* alegría; **cheerio** *excl* ¡hasta luego!; **~less** *a* triste, sombrío.

cheese [tʃiːz] *n* queso.

chef [ʃef] *n* jefe/a *m/f* de cocina.

chemical ['kemɪkəl] *a* químico // *n* elemento químico.

chemist ['kemɪst] *n* farmacéutico; (*scientist*) químico; **~ry** *n* química; **~'s (shop)** *n* farmacia.

cheque [tʃek] *n* cheque *m*; **~book** *n* libro de cheques, chequera.

chequered ['tʃekəd] *a* (*fig*) variado, accidentado.

cherish ['tʃerɪʃ] *vt* (*love*) querer, apreciar; (*protect*) cuidar, (*hope etc*) abrigar.

cherry ['tʃerɪ] *n* cereza.

chess [tʃes] *n* ajedrez *m*; **~board** *n* tablero (de ajedrez); **~man** *n* pieza, trebejo.

chest [tʃest] *n* (*ANAT*) pecho; (*box*) cofre *m*, cajón *m*; **~ of drawers** *n* cómoda.

chestnut ['tʃesnʌt] *n* castaña; **~ (tree)** *n* castaño.

chew [tʃuː] *vt* mascar, masticar; **~ing gum** *n* chicle *m*.

chic [ʃiːk] *a* elegante.

chick [tʃɪk] *n* pollito, polluelo; (*fam*) chica.

chicken ['tʃɪkɪn] *n* gallina, pollo; (*food*) pollo; **~pox** *n* varicela.

chickpea ['tʃɪkpiː] *n* garbanzo.

chicory ['tʃɪkərɪ] *n* (*for coffee*) achicoria; (*salad*) escarola.

chief [tʃiːf] *n* jefe/a *m/f* // *a* principal; **~ly** *ad* principalmente.

chiffon ['ʃɪfɒn] *n* gasa.

chilblain ['tʃɪlbleɪn] *n* sabañón *m*.

child [tʃaɪld], *pl* **~ren** ['tʃɪldrən] *n* niño/a; (*offspring*) hijo/a; **~birth** *n* parto; **~hood** *n* niñez *f*, infancia; **~ish** *a* pueril, aniñado; **~like** *a* como (de) niño; **~ minder** *n* cuidadora de niños.

Chile ['tʃɪlɪ] *n* Chile *m*; **~an** *a*, *n* chileno/a.

chill [tʃɪl] *n* frío; (*MED*) escalofrío, resfriado // *vt* enfriar; (*CULIN*) congelar; **~y** *a* frío.

chime [tʃaɪm] *n* (*peal*) repique *m*, campanada // *vi* repicar, sonar.

chimney ['tʃɪmnɪ] *n* chimenea; **~ sweep** *n* deshollinador *m*.

chimpanzee [tʃɪmpæn'ziː] *n* chimpancé *m*.

chin [tʃɪn] *n* barba, barbilla.

china ['tʃaɪnə] *n* porcelana; (*gen*) loza.

China ['tʃaɪnə] *n* China; **Chinese** [tʃaɪ'niːz] *a* chino // *n* chino/a; (*LING*) el chino.

chink [tʃɪŋk] *n* (*opening*) grieta, hendedura; (*noise*) tintineo.

chip [tʃɪp] *n* (*gen pl: CULIN*) patata frita; (*of wood*) astilla; (*of glass, stone*) lasca; (*at poker*) ficha // *vt* (*cup*) desportillar; **to ~ in** *vi* interrumpir; (*contribute*) compartir los gastos.

chiropodist [kɪ'rɒpədɪst] *n* pedicuro.

chirp [tʃəːp] *vi* gorjear, piar; (*cricket*) chirriar.

chisel ['tʃɪzl] *n* (*for wood*) formón *m*; (*for stone*) cincel *m*.

chit [tʃɪt] *n* nota.

chitchat ['tʃɪttʃæt] *n* chismes *mpl*, habladurías *fpl*.

chivalrous ['ʃɪvəlrəs] *a* caballeroso; **chivalry** [-rɪ] *n* caballerosidad *f*.

chives [tʃaɪvz] *npl* cebollino *sg*.

chlorine ['klɔːriːn] *n* cloro.

chock [tʃɒk]: **~-a-block**, **~-full** *a* de bote en bote, atestado.

chocolate ['tʃɒklɪt] *n* chocolate *m*.

choice [tʃɔɪs] *n* elección *f*, selección *f*; (*preference*) preferencia // *a* selecto, elegido.

choir ['kwaɪə*] *n* coro; **~boy** *n* corista *m*.

choke [tʃəʊk] *vi* sofocarse; (*on food*) atragantarse // *vt* ahogar, sofocar; (*block*) obstruir *m*, (*n* (*AUT*) estrangulador *m*; **choker** *n* (*necklace*) gargantilla.

cholera [ˈkɔlərə] n cólera m.

choose [tʃuːz], pt **chose**, pp **chosen** vt escoger, elegir; (team) seleccionar.

chop [tʃɔp] vt (wood) cortar, tajar; (CULIN: also: ~ up) desmenuzar; (meat) picar // n golpe m cortante; (CULIN) chuleta; ~s npl (jaws) boca sg, labios mpl; ~py a (sea) picado, agitado; ~sticks npl palillos mpl.

choral [ˈkɔːrəl] a coral.

chord [kɔːd] n (MUS) acorde m.

chore [tʃɔːʳ] n faena, tarea; (routine task) trabajo rutinario.

choreographer [kɔrɪˈɔgrəfəʳ] n coreógrafo.

chorister [ˈkɔrɪstəʳ] n corista m/f.

chortle [ˈtʃɔːtl] vi reír entre dientes.

chorus [ˈkɔːrəs] n coro; (repeated part of song) estribillo.

chose [tʃəuz], **chosen** [ˈtʃəuzn] pt, pp of **choose**.

Christ [kraɪst] n Cristo.

christen [ˈkrɪsn] vt bautizar; ~ing n bautizo.

Christian [ˈkrɪstɪən] a, n cristiano/a; ~ity [-ˈænɪtɪ] n cristianismo; ~ name n nombre m de pila.

Christmas [ˈkrɪsməs] n Navidad f; **Merry ~!** ¡Felices Pascuas!; ~ **Eve** n Nochebuena.

chrome [krəum], **chromium** [ˈkrəumɪəm] n cromo.

chromosome [ˈkrəuməsəum] n cromosoma m.

chronic [ˈkrɔnɪk] a crónico.

chronicle [ˈkrɔnɪkl] n crónica.

chronological [krɔnəˈlɔdʒɪkəl] a cronológico.

chrysanthemum [krɪˈsænθəməm] n crisantemo.

chubby [ˈtʃʌbɪ] a rechoncho.

chuck [tʃʌk] vt lanzar, arrojar; to ~ **out** vt echar (fuera), tirar; to ~ (up) vt abandonar.

chuckle [ˈtʃʌkl] vi reírse entre dientes.

chug [tʃʌg] vi resoplar; to ~ **along** vi (fig) ir tirando.

chum [tʃʌm] n compinche m, compañero.

chunk [tʃʌŋk] n pedazo, trozo.

church [tʃəːtʃ] n iglesia; ~**yard** n campo santo.

churlish [ˈtʃəːlɪʃ] a grosero, hosco.

churn [tʃəːn] n (for butter) mantequera; (for milk) lechera // vt revolver, agitar.

chute [ʃuːt] n (also: **rubbish** ~) vertedero; (children's slide) tobogán m.

chutney [ˈtʃʌtnɪ] n salsa picante.

CID n abbr of **Criminal Investigation Department** B.I.C. (Brigada de Investigación Criminal).

cider [ˈsaɪdəʳ] n sidra.

cigar [sɪˈgɑːʳ] n puro.

cigarette [sɪgəˈret] n cigarrillo; (fam) pitillo; ~ **case** n pitillera; ~ **end** n colilla; ~ **holder** n boquilla.

Cinderella [sɪndəˈrelə] n la Cenicienta.

cinders [ˈsɪndəz] npl cenizas fpl.

cine [sɪnɪ]: ~**camera** n cámara cinematográfica; ~**film** n película cinematográfica.

cinema [ˈsɪnəmə] n cine m.

cinnamon [ˈsɪnəmən] n canela.

cipher [ˈsaɪfəʳ] n cifra.

circle [ˈsəːkl] n círculo; (in cinema) anfiteatro // vi dar vueltas // vt (surround) rodear, cercar; (move round) dar la vuelta a.

circuit [ˈsəːkɪt] n circuito; (tour) gira; (track) pista; (lap) vuelta; ~**ous** [səːˈkjuɪtəs] a tortuoso, indirecto.

circular [ˈsəːkjuləʳ] a circular // n circular f.

circulate [ˈsəːkjuleɪt] vi circular // vt poner en circulación, hacer circular; **circulation** [-ˈleɪʃən] n circulación f; (of newspaper) tirada.

circumcise [ˈsəːkəmsaɪz] vt circuncidar.

circumference [səˈkʌmfərəns] n circunferencia.

circumspect [ˈsəːkəmspekt] a circunspecto, prudente.

circumstances ['sɜːkəmstənsɪz] *npl* circunstancias *fpl*; *(financial condition)* situación *f* económica.

circus ['sɜːkəs] *n* circo; *(roundabout)* glorieta.

cistern ['sɪstən] *n* tanque *m*, depósito; *(in toilet)* cisterna.

cite [saɪt] *vt* citar.

citizen ['sɪtɪzn] *n* (POL) ciudadano/a; *(resident)* vecino/a, habitante *m/f*; ~**ship** *n* ciudadanía.

citrus fruit ['sɪtrəs] *n* agrios *mpl*.

city ['sɪtɪ] *n* ciudad *f*; the C~ *n* centro financiero de Londres.

civic ['sɪvɪk] *a* cívico, municipal.

civil ['sɪvɪl] *a* civil; *(polite)* atento, cortés; *(defence)* pasivo; *(well-bred)* educado; ~ **engineer** *n* ingeniero civil, C ~ **Service** administración *f* pública; ~**ian** [sɪ'vɪlɪən] *a* civil, de paisano // *n* civil *m/f*, paisano.

civilization [sɪvɪlaɪ'zeɪʃən] *n* civilización *f*.

civilized ['sɪvɪlaɪzd] *a* civilizado.

claim [kleɪm] *vt* exigir, reclamar; *(rights etc)* reivindicar; *(assert)* pretender // *vi* (*for insurance*) reclamar // *n* reclamación *f*; (LAW) demanda; *(pretension)* pretensión *f*; ~**ant** *n* (ADMIN, LAW) demandante *m/f*.

clairvoyant [klɛə'vɔɪənt] *n* clarividente *m/f*.

clam [klæm] *n* almeja.

clamber ['klæmbə*] *vi* subir gateando, trepar.

clammy ['klæmɪ] *a* *(cold)* frío y húmedo; *(sticky)* pegajoso.

clamp [klæmp] *n* abrazadera, grapa // *vt* afianzar (con abrazadera); to ~ **down on** *vt fus* suprimir, restringir.

clan [klæn] *n* clan *m*.

clang [klæŋ] *n* sonido metálico // *vi* sonar, hacer estruendo.

clap [klæp] *vi* aplaudir // *vt* *(hands)* batir; *(put)* poner // *n* *(of hands)* palmada; *(of thunder)* estampido (de trueno); ~**ping** *n* aplausos *mpl*.

claret ['klærət] *n* clarete *m*.

clarification [klærɪfɪ'keɪʃən] *n* aclaración *f*, **clarify** ['klærɪfaɪ] *vt* aclarar.

clarinet [klærɪ'net] *n* clarinete *m*.

clarity ['klærɪtɪ] *n* claridad *f*.

clash [klæʃ] *n* *(fig)* choque *m* // *vi* *(meet)* encontrarse; *(battle)* chocar; *(disagree)* estar en desacuerdo.

clasp [klɑːsp] *n* broche *m*; *(on jewels)* cierre *m* // *vt* abrochar; *(hand)* apretar, estrechar; *(embrace)* abrazar.

class [klɑːs] *n* *(gen)* clase *f* // *a* clasista, de clase // *vt* clasificar.

classic ['klæsɪk] *a* clásico // *n* *(work)* obra clásica; ~**al** *a* clásico.

classification [klæsɪfɪ'keɪʃən] *n* clasificación *f*, **classify** ['klæsɪfaɪ] *vt* clasificar.

class: ~**-mate** *n* compañero de clase; ~**room** *n* aula.

clatter ['klætə*] *n* ruido, estruendo; *(of hooves)* trápala // *vi* hacer ruido o estruendo.

clause [klɔːz] *n* cláusula; (LING) oración *f*.

claustrophobia [klɔːstrə'fəubɪə] *n* claustrofobia.

claw [klɔː] *n* *(of cat)* uña; *(of bird of prey)* garra; *(of lobster)* pinza; (TECH) garfio // *vt*: to ~ **at** *vt* arañar; *(tear)* desgarrar.

clay [kleɪ] *n* arcilla.

clean [kliːn] *a* limpio; *(clear)* neto, bien definido // *vt* limpiar; to ~ **out** *vt* limpiar; to ~ **up** *vt* limpiar, asear; ~**cut** *a* *(person)* de buen parecer; *(clear)* nítido; ~**er** *n* *(person)* asistenta; ~**ing** *n* *(gen)* limpieza; *(clothes)* limpieza en seco, ~**liness** ['klɛnlɪnɪs] *n* limpieza; ~**shaven** *a* sin barba, lampiño.

cleanse [klɛnz] *vt* limpiar; **cleanser** *n* crema de limpieza; *(for face)* desmaquillador *m*; **cleansing department** *n* departamento de limpieza.

clear [klɪə*] *a* claro; *(road, way)* limpio, libre; *(complete)* completo

// vt (space) despejar, limpiar; (LAW: suspect) absolver; (obstacle) salvar, saltar por encima de; (debt) liquidar // vi (gen) aclararse; (fog etc) despejarse // ad: ~ of a distancia de; to ~ up vt limpiar; (mystery) aclarar, resolver; ~ance n (removal) despeje m; (permission) acreditación f; ~cut a bien definido, nítido; ~ing n (in wood) claro; ~ing bank n cámara de compensación; ~ly ad claramente; ~way n (Brit) carretera donde no se puede aparcar.

cleaver ['kli:və] n cuchilla (de carnicero).

clef [klef] n (MUS) clave f.

clemency ['klɛmənsɪ] n clemencia.

clench [klɛntʃ] vt apretar, cerrar.

clergy ['klə:dʒɪ] n clero; ~man n clérigo.

clerical ['klɛrɪkəl] a oficinista; (REL) clerical.

clerk [kla:k, (US) klə:rk] n empleado, oficinista m/f.

clever ['klɛvə*] a (mentally) inteligente, listo; (deft, crafty) hábil; (device, arrangement) ingenioso.

cliché ['kli:ʃeɪ] n cliché m, frase f hecha.

click [klɪk] vt (tongue) chasquear; (heels) taconear.

client ['klaɪənt] n cliente m/f; ~ele [kli:ɑ:n'tɛl] n clientela.

cliff [klɪf] n acantilado.

climate ['klaɪmɪt] n clima m; (fig) ambiente m.

climax ['klaɪmæks] n colmo, punto culminante; (sexual) clímax m.

climb [klaɪm] vi subir, trepar // vt (stairs) subir; (tree) trepar a; (hill) escalar // n subida; ~er n alpinista m/f, montañista m/f; ~ing n alpinismo.

clinch [klɪntʃ] vt (deal) cerrar; (argument) remachar.

cling [klɪŋ], pt, pp **clung** [klʌŋ] vi: to ~ to pegarse a, quedar pegado a; (of clothes) ajustarse a.

clinic ['klɪnɪk] n clínica; ~al a clínico.

clink [klɪŋk] vi tintinar.

clip [klɪp] n (for hair) prendido; (also: paper ~) sujetapapeles m inv; (clamp) grapa // vt (cut) cortar; (shorten) acortar; (clamp) sujetar; ~pers npl (for gardening) tijeras fpl; (for hair) maquinilla sg; (for nails) cortaúñas m inv; ~ping n recorte m.

clique [kli:k] n camarilla, pandilla.

cloak [kləʊk] n capa, manto // vt (fig) encubrir, disimular; ~room n guardarropa; (in station) consigna; (WC) lavabo, aseos mpl.

clock [klɒk] n reloj m; (in taxi) taxímetro; (fam) cara; ~wise ad en el sentido de las agujas del reloj; ~work n aparato de relojería // a de cuerda.

clog [klɒg] n zueco, chanclo // vt atascar // vi atascarse.

cloister ['klɔɪstə*] n claustro.

close a, ad and derivatives [kləʊs] a cercano, próximo; (print, weave) tupido, compacto; (friend) íntimo; (connection) estrecho; (examination) detallado, minucioso; (weather) bochornoso; (atmosphere) sofocante; (room) mal ventilado // ad cerca // vb and derivatives [kləʊz] vt (shut) cerrar; (end) concluir, terminar // vi (shop etc) cerrarse; (end) concluirse, terminarse // n (end) fin m, final m, conclusión f; to ~ down vi cerrarse definitivamente; to ~ up vi (crowd) arrimarse; ~d a (shop etc) cerrado; ~d shop n acuerdo de emplear sólo trabajadores sindicados; ~ly ad (exactly) fielmente; (carefully) atentamente.

closet ['klɔzɪt] n (cupboard) armario; (WC) lavabo.

close-up ['kləʊsʌp] n primer plano.

closure ['kləʊʒə*] n (close-down) cierre m, clausura; (end) fin m.

clot [klɔt] n (gen: blood ~) embolia; (fam: idiot) imbécil m/f // vi *(blood)* cuajarse, coagularse.

cloth [klɔθ] n *(material)* tela, paño; *(rag)* trapo.

clothe [kləuð] vt vestir; *(fig)* revestir; ~**s** npl ropa sg; ~**s brush** n cepillo (para la ropa); ~**s line** n cuerda (para tender la ropa); ~**s peg** n pinza; **clothing** n = **clothes**.

cloud [klaud] n nube f; *(storm~)* nubarrón m; **burst** n chaparrón m; ~**y** a nublado, nubloso; *(liquid)* turbio.

clout [klaut] vt dar un tortazo a.

clove [kləuv] n clavo; ~ **of garlic** diente m de ajo.

clover ['kləuvə*] n trébol m.

clown [klaun] n payaso // vi *(also: ~ about, ~ around)* hacer el payaso.

club [klʌb] n *(society)* club m; *(weapon)* porra, cachiporra; *(also: golf ~)* palo // vt aporrear // vi: to ~ **together** hacer una colecta; ~**s** npl *(CARDS)* tréboles mpl; ~**house** n sala de reunión.

cluck [klʌk] vi cloquear.

clue [klu:] n pista; *(in crosswords)* indicación f; **I haven't a** ~ no tengo idea.

clump [klʌmp] n *(of trees)* grupo.

clumsy ['klʌmzɪ] a *(person)* torpe, desmañado; *(movement)* pesado.

cluster ['klʌstə*] n grupo; *(BOT)* racimo // vi agruparse, apiñarse.

clutch [klʌtʃ] n *(grip, grasp)* apretón m, agarro; *(AUT)* embrague m; *(pedal)* pedal m de embrague // vt sujetar, empuñar.

clutter ['klʌtə*] vt atestar, llenar desordenadamente.

Co. abbr of **county**; **company**.

c/o abbr of **care of** c/a (en casa de), a/c (a cuidado de).

coach [kəutʃ] n *(bus)* autocar m; *(horse-drawn)* coche m; *(of train)* vagón m, coche m; *(SPORT)* entrenador m, instructor m // vt *(SPORT)* entrenar; *(student)* preparar, enseñar.

coagulate [kəu'æɡjuleɪt] vi coagularse.

coal [kəul] n carbón m; ~ **face** n frente m de carbón; ~**field** n yacimiento de carbón.

coalition [kəuə'lɪʃən] n coalición f.

coal. **man**, ~ **merchant** n carbonero; ~**mine** n mina de carbón.

coarse [kɔ:s] a basto, burdo; *(vulgar)* grosero, ordinario.

coast [kəust] n costa, litoral m // vi *(AUT)* ir en punto muerto; ~**al** a costero, costanero; ~**er** n buque m costero, barco de cabotaje; ~**guard** n guardacostas m inv; ~**line** n litoral m.

coat [kəut] n *(jacket)* chaqueta; *(overcoat)* abrigo; *(of animal)* pelo, lana; *(of paint)* mano f, capa // vt cubrir, revestir; ~ **of arms** n escudo de armas; ~ **hanger** n percha; ~**ing** n capa, baño.

coax [kəuks] vt engatusar.

cob [kɔb] n see **corn**.

cobbler ['kɔblə] n zapatero remendón.

cobbles ['kɔblz] **cobblestones** ['kɔblstəunz] npl guijarros mpl.

cobra ['kəubrə] n cobra

cobweb ['kɔbweb] n telaraña.

cocaine [kə'keɪn] n cocaína.

cock [kɔk] n *(rooster)* gallo; *(male bird)* macho // vt *(gun)* amartillar; ~**atoo** n cacatúa; ~**erel** n gallito.

cockle ['kɔkl] n berberecho.

cockney ['kɔknɪ] n habitante m/f de ciertos barrios bajos de Londres.

cockpit ['kɔkpɪt] n *(in aircraft)* carlinga, cabina.

cockroach ['kɔkrəutʃ] n cucaracha.

cocktail ['kɔkteɪl] n combinado, cóctel m; ~ **cabinet** n mueble-bar m; ~ **party** n cóctel m, cóctel m.

cocoa ['kəukəu] n cacao; *(drink)* chocolate m.

coconut ['kəukənʌt] n coco.

cocoon [kə'ku:n] n capullo.

cod [kɔd] n bacalao.

code [kəud] *n* código; (*cipher*) clave *f*; **codify** *vt* codificar.

coerce [kəu'ə:s] *vt* forzar, obligar; **coercion** [-'ə:ʃən] *n* coacción *f*.

coexistence ['kəuig'zistəns] *n* coexistencia.

coffee ['kɒfi] *n* café *m*; ~ **bean** *n* grano de café; ~ **grounds** *npl* heces *fpl* de café; ~**pot** *n* cafetera.

coffin ['kɒfin] *n* ataúd *m*.

cog [kɔg] *n* diente *m*; ~**wheel** *n* rueda dentada.

cognac ['kɒnjæk] *n* coñac *m*.

coherent [kəu'hiərənt] *a* coherente.

coil [kɔil] *n* rollo; (*rope*) adujada; (*ELEC*) bobina, carrete *m*; (*contraceptive*) espiral *f* // *vi* enrollarse, arrollarse.

coin [kɔin] *n* moneda // *vt* (*word*) inventar, idear; ~**age** *n* moneda; ~**-box** *n* caja recaudadora.

coincide [kəuin'said] *vi* coincidir; (*agree*) estar de acuerdo; **coincidence** [kəu'insidəns] *n* casualidad *f*.

coke [kəuk] *n* (*coal*) coque *m*; (*drink*) Coca Cola *f*.

colander ['kɒləndə*] *n* colador *m*, escurridor *m*.

cold [kəuld] *a* frío // *n* frío; (*MED*) resfriado; **it's** ~ hace frío; **to be** ~ tener frío; **to catch** ~ resfriarse, acatarrarse; **to** ~**shoulder** tratar con frialdad; ~**ly** *ad* fríamente; ~ **sore** *n* herpes *m* labial.

coleslaw ['kəulslɔ:] *n* ensalada de col.

colic ['kɒlik] *n* cólico.

collaborate [kə'læbəreit] *vi* colaborar; **collaboration** [-'reiʃən] *n* colaboración *f*.

collage [kɒ'lɑ:ʒ] *n* collage *m*.

collapse [kə'læps] *vi* (*gen*) hundirse, derrumbarse; (*MED*) sufrir colapso // *n* (*gen*) hundimiento; (*MED*) colapso; **collapsible** *a* plegable.

collar ['kɒlə*] *n* (*of coat, shirt*) cuello; ~**bone** *n* clavícula.

collate [kə'leit] *vt* cotejar.

colleague ['kɒli:g] *n* colega *m/f*.

collect [kə'lekt] *vt* reunir; (*as a hobby*) coleccionar; (*call and pick up*) recoger; (*wages*) cobrar; (*debts*) recaudar; (*donations, subscriptions*) colectar // *vi* reunirse; coleccionar; ~**ion** [kə'lekʃən] *n* colección *f*, cobro; (*of people*) grupo; (*of donations*) recaudación *f*; (*of post*) recogida.

collective [kə'lektiv] *a* colectivo.

collector [kə'lektə*] *n* coleccionista *m/f*; (*of taxes etc*) recaudador *m*.

college ['kɒlidʒ] *n* colegio.

collide [kə'laid] *vi* chocar.

collie ['kɒli] *n* perro pastor.

collision [kə'liʒən] *n* choque *m*.

colloquial [kə'ləukwiəl] *a* familiar, coloquial.

colon ['kəulən] *n* (*sign*) dos puntos; (*MED*) colón *m*.

colonel ['kə:nl] *n* coronel *m*.

colonial [kə'ləuniəl] *a* colonial.

colonize ['kɒlənaiz] *vt* colonizar.

colony ['kɒləni] *n* colonia.

colossal [kə'lɒsl] *a* colosal.

colour, color (*US*) ['kʌlə*] *n* color *m* // *vt* color(e)ar; (*with crayons*) pintar; (*dye*) teñir // *vi* (*blush*) sonrojarse; ~**s** *npl* (*of party, club*) colores *mpl*; ~**-blind** *a* daltoniano; ~**ed** *a* de color; (*photo*) a colores; ~**eds** *npl* gente *f* de color; ~**film** *n* película en colores; ~**ful** *a* lleno de color; (*personality*) animado; ~**ing** *n* colorido; ~**less** *a* incoloro, sin color; ~ **scheme** *n* combinación *f* de colores; ~ **television** *n* televisión *f* en color(es).

colt [kəult] *n* potro.

column ['kɒləm] *n* columna; ~**ist** ['kɒləmnist] *n* columnista *m/f*.

coma ['kəumə] *n* coma *m*.

comb [kəum] *n* peine *m*; (*ornamental*) peineta // *vt* (*hair*) peinar; (*area*) registrar.

combat ['kɒmbæt] *n* combate *m* // *vt* combatir.

combination [kɔmbɪ'neɪʃən] n (gen) combinación f.

combine [kəm'baɪn] vt combinar; (qualities) reunir // vi combinarse // n ['kɔmbaɪn] (ECON) asociación f; (pej) monopolio; ~ (harvester) n cosechadora.

combustion [kəm'bʌstʃən] n combustión f.

come [kʌm], pt **came**, pp **come** vi venir; to ~ about vi suceder, ocurrir; to ~ across vt fus (person) topar; (thing) dar con; to ~ away vi marcharse; to ~ back vi volver; to ~ by vt fus (acquire) conseguir; to ~ down vi bajar; (plane) aterrizarse; (crash) estrellarse; (buildings) despiomarse; to ~ forward vi presentarse; to ~ in vi entrar; (train) llegar; (fashion) ponerse de moda; to ~ in for vt fus (criticism etc) merecer; to ~ into vt fus (money) heredar; to ~ off vi (button) soltarse, desprenderse; (attempt) tener lugar; to ~ on vi (pupil, undertaking) crecer, desarrollarse // vt (find) encontrar; ~ on! ¡vamos!; to ~ out vi salir, aparecer; (be revealed) salir a luz; to ~ out for/against declararse por/contra; to ~ to vi volver en sí; (total) sumar; to ~ up vi subir; (sun) salir; (problem) surgir; to ~ up against vt fus (resistance, difficulties) tropezar con; to ~ up with vt fus (idea) sugerir, proponer; to ~ upon vt fus dar con; ~back n (THEATRE) reaparición f.

comedian [kə'miːdɪən] n cómico; **comedienne** [-'en] n cómica.

comedown ['kʌmdaʊn] n (fam) revés m, bajón m.

comedy ['kɔmɪdɪ] n comedia.

comet ['kɔmɪt] n cometa m.

comfort ['kʌmfət] n comodidad f, confort m; (well-being) bienestar m; (solace) consuelo; (relief) alivio // vt consolar, aliviar; ~able a cómodo.

comic ['kɔmɪk] a (also: ~al)

cómico // n (magazine) tebeo; ~ strip n tira cómica.

coming ['kʌmɪŋ] n venida, llegada // a que viene; ~(s) and going(s) n(pl) ir y venir m, ajetreo.

comma ['kɔmə] n coma.

command [kə'mɑːnd] n orden f, mandato; (MIL: authority) mando; (mastery) dominio // vt (troops) mandar; (give orders to) mandar, ordenar; (dispose of) disponer de; (deserve) merecer; ~eer [kɔmən'dɪə*] vt requisar; ~er n (MIL) comandante m/f, jefe/a m/f.

commando [kə'mɑːndəʊ] n comando.

commemorate [kə'meməreɪt] vt conmemorar; **commemoration** [-'reɪʃən] n conmemoración f; **commemorative** [-rətɪv] a conmemorativo.

commence [kə'mens] vt, vi comenzar, empezar.

commend [kə'mend] vt (praise) elogiar, alabar; (recommend) recomendar; (entrust) encomendar; ~ation [kɔmen'deɪʃən] n elogio, encomio; recomendación f.

commensurate [kə'menʃərɪt] a equivalente (with a).

comment ['kɔment] n comentario // vi hacer comentarios; ~ary ['kɔmentərɪ] n comentario; ~ator ['kɔmenteɪtə*] n comentador m.

commerce ['kɔmə:s] n comercio.

commercial [kə'mə:ʃəl] a comercial // n (TV) anuncio (comercial); ~ break n emisión f publicitaria; ~ize vt comercializar.

commiserate [kə'mɪzəreɪt] vi: to ~ with compadecerse de, condolerse de.

commission [kə'mɪʃən] n (fee) comisión f; (act) perpetración f // vt (MIL) nombrar; (work of art) encargar; out of ~ inutilizado; ~aire [kəmɪʃə'nɛə*] n portero; ~er n comisario; (POLICE) jefe/a m/f de policía.

commit [kə'mɪt] vt (act) cometer;

(to sb's care) entregar; **to ~ o.s. (to do)** comprometerse (a hacer); **to ~ suicide** suicidarse; **~ment** n compromiso.

committee [kə'mɪtɪ] n comité m.

commodity [kə'mɔdɪtɪ] n mercancía.

common ['kɔmən] a *(gen)* común; *(pej)* ordinario // n campo común; **the C~s** npl (la Cámara de) los Comunes; **in ~** en común; **~er** n plebeyo; **~ law** n ley f consuetudinaria; **~ly** ad comúnmente; **C~ Market** n Mercado Común; **~place** a vulgar, trivial; **~room** n salón m común; **~ sense** n sentido común; **the C~wealth** n la Mancomunidad.

commotion [kə'məʊʃən] n tumulto, confusión f.

communal ['kɔmju:nl] a comunal.

commune ['kɔmju:n] n *(group)* comuna // vi [kə'mju:n]: **to ~ with** comulgar o conversar con.

communicate [kə'mju:nɪkeɪt] vt comunicar // vi: **to ~ (with)** comunicarse (con).

communication [kəmju:nɪ'keɪʃən] n comunicación f; **~ cord** n timbre m de alarma.

communion [kə'mju:nɪən] n *(also: Holy C~)* comunión f.

communiqué [kə'mju:nɪkeɪ] n comunicado, parte m.

communism ['kɔmjunɪzəm] n comunismo; **communist** a, n comunista m/f.

community [kə'mju:nɪtɪ] n comunidad f; *(large group)* colectividad f; *(locals)* vecindario; **~ centre** n centro social.

commute [kə'mju:t] vi viajar a diario // vt conmutar; **commuter** n persona que viaja a menudo.

compact [kəm'pækt] a compacto; *(style)* conciso; *(packed)* apretado // n ['kɔmpækt] *(pact)* pacto; *(for powder)* polvera.

companion [kəm'pænɪən] n

compañero; **~ship** n compañerismo.

company ['kʌmpənɪ] n *(gen)* compañía; *(COMM)* sociedad f, compañía; **to keep sb ~** acompañar a uno; **limited ~** sociedad f anónima.

comparable ['kɔmpərəbl] a comparable.

comparative [kəm'pærətɪv] a relativo.

compare [kəm'pɛə*] vt comparar; *(set side by side)* cotejar // vi: **to ~ (with)** compararse (con); **comparison** [-'pærɪsn] n comparación f; cotejo; **in comparison (with)** en comparación (con).

compartment [kəm'pɑ:tmənt] n *(also RAIL)* departamento.

compass ['kʌmpəs] n brújula; **~es** npl compás m.

compassion [kəm'pæʃən] n compasión f; **~ate** a compasivo.

compatible [kəm'pætɪbl] a compatible.

compel [kəm'pel] vt obligar; **~ling** a *(fig: argument)* convincente.

compendium [kəm'pendɪəm] n compendio.

compensate ['kɔmpənseɪt] vt compensar // vi: **to ~ for** compensar; **compensation** [-'seɪʃən] n *(for loss)* indemnización f.

compère ['kɔmpɛə*] n presentador m.

compete [kəm'pi:t] vi *(take part)* tomar parte, concurrir; *(vie with)* competir, hacer competencia.

competence ['kɔmpɪtəns] n capacidad f, aptitud f; **competent** [-ənt] a competente, capaz.

competition [kɔmpɪ'tɪʃən] n *(contest)* concurso; *(ECON)* competencia; *(rivalry)* competencia f.

competitive [kəm'petɪtɪv] a *(ECON)* competidor(a); *(spirit)* competidor(a), de competencia.

competitor [kəm'petɪtə*] n *(rival)* competidor/a m/f; *(participant)* concursante m/f.

compile [kəm'paɪl] vt recopilar, compilar.

complacency [kəm'pleɪsnsɪ] n satisfacción f de sí mismo; **complacent** [-sənt] a complacido.

complain [kəm'pleɪn] vi (gen) quejarse; ~t n (gen) queja; (JUR) demanda, querella; (MED) enfermedad f.

complement ['kɒmplɪmənt] n complemento; (esp ship's crew) dotación f; ~ary [kɒmplɪ'mɛntərɪ] a complementario.

complete [kəm'pliːt] a (full) completo; (finished) acabado // vt (fulfil) completar; (finish) acabar; (a form) llenar; ~ly ad completamente; **completion** n (gen) conclusión f, terminación f, (of contract etc) realización f.

complex ['kɒmplɛks] a complejo // n (gen) complejo.

complexion [kəm'plɛkʃən] n (of face) tez f, cutis m; (fig) aspecto.

complexity [kəm'plɛksɪtɪ] n complejidad f.

compliance [kəm'plaɪəns] n (submission) sumisión f; (agreement) conformidad f; in ~ with de acuerdo con; **compliant** [-ənt] a sumiso; conforme.

complicate ['kɒmplɪkeɪt] vt complicar; ~d a complicado; **complication** [-'keɪʃən] n complicación f.

compliment n ['kɒmplɪmənt] (formal) cumplido; (lovers') piropo; ~s npl saludos mpl; to pay sb a ~ (amorously) piropear, echar piropos a alguien; ~ary [-'mɛntərɪ] a lisonjero; (free) de favor.

comply [kəm'plaɪ] vi: to ~ with cumplir con.

component [kəm'pəʊnənt] a componente // n (TECH) pieza.

compose [kəm'pəʊz] vt componer; to be ~d of componerse de, constar de; to ~ o.s. tranquilizarse; ~d a sosegado; **composer** n (MUS) compositor m.

composite ['kɒmpəzɪt] a compuesto.

composition [kɒmpə'zɪʃən] n composición f.

compost ['kɒmpɒst] n abono compuesto.

composure [kəm'pəʊʒə*] n serenidad f, calma.

compound n ['kɒmpaʊnd] n (CHEM, LING) compuesto; (enclosure) recinto // a (gen) compuesto; (fracture) complicado.

comprehend [kɒmprɪ'hɛnd] vt comprender; **comprehension** [-'hɛnʃən] n comprensión f.

comprehensive [kɒmprɪ'hɛnsɪv] a (broad) extenso; (general) de conjunto; (INSURANCE) contra todo riesgo; ~ (school) n integrado.

compress [kəm'prɛs] vt comprimir // n ['kɒmprɛs] (MED) compresa; ~ion [-'prɛʃən] n compresión f.

comprise [kəm'praɪz] vt (also: be ~d of) comprender, constar de.

compromise ['kɒmprəmaɪz] n (agreement) componenda, arreglo; (midpoint) término medio // vt comprometer // vi transigir.

compulsion [kəm'pʌlʃən] n obligación f.

compulsive [kəm'pʌlsɪv] a compulsivo; (novel) absorbente.

compulsory [kəm'pʌlsərɪ] a obligatorio.

computer [kəm'pjuːtə*] n ordenador m, computador m, computadora; ~ize vt computerizar; ~ programmer n programador/a m/f; ~ programming n programación f; ~ science n ciencia de computadoras.

comrade ['kɒmrɪd] n camarada m/f; ~ship n camaradería, compañerismo.

con [kɒn] vt estafar // n estafa.

concave ['kɒn'keɪv] a cóncavo.

conceal [kən'siːl] vt ocultar.

concede [kən'siːd] vt conceder // vi ceder, darse por vencido.

conceit [kən'si:t] *n* presunción *f*; **~ed** *a* presumido.

conceivable [kən'si:vəbl] *a* concebible.

conceive [kən'si:v] *vt, vi* concebir.

concentrate ['kɔnsəntreɪt] *vi* concentrarse // *vt* concentrar.

concentration [kɔnsən'treɪʃən] *n* concentración *f*; **~ camp** *n* campo de concentración.

concept ['kɔnsept] *n* concepto.

conception [kən'sepʃən] *n* (*idea*) concepto, idea; (*BIOL*) concepción *f*.

concern [kən'sɜːn] *n* (*matter*) asunto; (*COMM*) empresa; (*anxiety*) preocupación *f* // *vt* tener que ver con; **to be ~ed** (*about*) interesarse (por), preocuparse (por); **~ing** *prep* sobre, acerca de.

concert ['kɔnsət] *n* concierto; **~ hall** *n* sala de conciertos.

concertina [kɔnsə'ti:nə] *n* concertina.

concerto [kən'tʃɑːtəu] *n* concierto.

concession [kən'seʃən] *n* concesión *f*; **tax ~** privilegio fiscal.

conciliation [kənsɪlɪ'eɪʃən] *n* conciliación *f*; **conciliatory** [-'sɪlɪətrɪ] *a* conciliador(a).

concise [kən'saɪs] *a* conciso.

conclude [kən'klu:d] *vt* (*finish*) concluir; (*treaty etc*) firmar; (*agreement*) llegar a; (*decide*) llegar a la conclusión de; **conclusion** [-'klu:ʒən] *n* conclusión *f*; **conclusive** [-'klu:sɪv] *a* decisivo, concluyente.

concoct [kən'kɔkt] *vt* (*gen*) confeccionar; (*plot*) tramar.

concrete ['kɔnkri:t] *n* hormigón *m* // *a* concreto.

concur [kən'kɜː*] *vi* estar de acuerdo, asentir.

concurrently [kən'kʌrntlɪ] *ad* al mismo tiempo.

concussion [kən'kʌʃən] *n* conmoción *f* cerebral.

condemn [kən'dem] *vt* condenar; **~ation** [kɔndem'neɪʃən] *n* (*gen*) condenación *f*; (*blame*) censura.

condensation [kɔnden'seɪʃən] *n* condensación *f*.

condense [kən'dens] *vi* condensarse // *vt* condensar, abreviar; **~d milk** *n* leche *f* condensada.

condescend [kɔndɪ'send] *vi* condescender, dignarse; **~ing** *a* condescendiente.

condition [kən'dɪʃən] *n* condición *f* // *vt* condicionar; **on ~ that** a condición (de) que.

condolences [kən'dəulənsɪz] *npl* pésame *m*.

condone [kən'dəun] *vt* condonar.

conducive [kən'dju:sɪv] *a*: **~ to** conducente a.

conduct ['kɔndʌkt] *n* conducta, comportamiento // *vt* [kən'dʌkt] (*lead*) conducir; (*manage*) llevar, dirigir; (*MUS*) dirigir // *vi* (*MUS*) llevar la batuta; **to ~ o.s.** comportarse; **~or** *n* (*of orchestra*) director *m*; (*on bus*) cobrador *m*; (*ELEC*) conductor *m*; **~ress** *n* (*on bus*) cobradora.

cone [kəun] *n* cono; (*for ice-cream*) barquillo.

confectioner [kən'fekʃənə*] *n* pastelero; **~'s (shop)** *n* pastelería (*sweet shop*) confitería; **~y** *n* (*cakes*) pasteles *mpl*; (*sweets*) dulces *mpl*.

confederation [kənfedə'reɪʃən] *n* confederación *f*.

confer [kən'fɜː*] *vt* otorgar (*on* a) // *vi* conferenciar.

conference ['kɔnfərns] *n* (*meeting*) congreso.

confess [kən'fes] *vt* confesar // *vi* confesarse; **~ion** [-'feʃən] *n* confesión *f*; **~ional** [-'feʃənl] *n* confesionario; **~or** *n* confesor *m*.

confetti [kən'fetɪ] *n* confeti *m*.

confide [kən'faɪd] *vi*: **to ~ in** confiar en, fiarse de.

confidence ['kɔnfɪdns] *n* (*gen*) confianza; (*secret*) confidencia; **~ trick** *n* timo; **confident** *a* seguro de sí mismo; **confidential** [kɔnfɪ'denʃəl] *a* confidencial; (*secretary*) de confianza.

confine [kən'faɪn] *vt* (*limit*) limitar; (*shut up*) encerrar; ~**d** *a* (*space*) reducido; ~**ment** *n* (*prison*) prisión *f*; (*enclosure*) encierro *m*; (*MED*) parto, sobreparto; ~**s** ['kɒnfaɪnz] *npl* confines *mpl*.

confirm [kən'fɜːm] *vt* confirmar; ~**ation** [kɒnfə'meɪʃən] *n* confirmación *f*; ~**ed** *a* empedernido.

confiscate ['kɒnfɪskeɪt] *vt* confiscar; **confiscation** [-'keɪʃən] *n* incautación *f*.

conflict ['kɒnflɪkt] *n* conflicto // [kɒn'flɪkt] (*opinions*) chocar; ~**ing** *a* contrario.

conform [kən'fɔːm] *vi* conformarse; to ~ ajustarse a, cuadrar con; ~**ist** *n* conformista *m/f*.

confound [kən'faʊnd] *vt* confundir; ~**ed** *a* condenado.

confront [kən'frʌnt] *vt* (*problems*) encararse con; (*enemy, danger*) enfrentarse con; ~**ation** [kɒnfrən'teɪʃən] *n* enfrentamiento *m*.

confuse [kən'fjuːz] *vt* (*perplex*) aturdir, desconcertar; (*mix up*) confundir; ~**d** *a* confuso; (*person*) perplejo, desplstado, **confusing** *a* confuso; **confusion** [-'fjuːʒən] *n* confusión *f*.

congeal [kən'dʒiːl] *vi* (*freeze*) congelarse; (*coagulate*) coagularse.

congenial [kən'dʒiːnɪəl] *a* simpático, agradable.

congenital [kən'dʒenɪtl] *a* congénito.

congested [kən'dʒestɪd] *a* (*gen*) lleno; (*area*) superpoblado; **congestion** [-'dʒestʃən] *n* congestión *f*.

conglomeration [kənglɒmə'reɪʃən] *n* conglomeración *f*.

congratulate [kən'grætjuleɪt] *vt* felicitar; **congratulations** [-'leɪʃənz] *npl* felicidades *fpl*.

congregate ['kɒŋgrɪgeɪt] *vi* congregarse; **congregation** [-'geɪʃən] *n* (*in church*) fieles *mpl*; (*assembly*) reunión *f*.

congress ['kɒŋgres] *n* congreso; ~**man** *n* (*US*) diputado.

conical ['kɒnɪkl] *a* cónico.

conifer ['kɒnɪfə*] *n* conífera; ~**ous** [kə'nɪfərəs] *a* (*forest*) conífero.

conjecture [kən'dʒektʃə*] *n* conjetura.

conjugal ['kɒndʒugl] *a* conyugal.

conjugate ['kɒndʒugeɪt] *vt* conjugar.

conjunction [kən'dʒʌŋkʃən] *n* conjunción *f*.

conjure ['kʌndʒə*] *vi* hacer juegos de manos; to ~ **up** *vt* (*ghost, spirit*) hacer aparecer; (*memories*) evocar; ~**r** *n* ilusionista *m/f*; **conjuring trick** *n* ilusionismo, juego de manos.

conk [kɒŋk]: to ~ **out** *vi* (*col*) estropearse.

con man [kɒn-] *n* timador *m*.

connect [kə'nekt] *vt* juntar, unir; (*ELEC*) conectar; (*fig*) relacionar, asociar // *vi*: to ~ **with** (*train*) enlazar con; ~**ion** [-ʃən] *n* juntura, unión *f*; (*ELEC*) conexión *f*; (*RAIL*) correspondencia; (*TEL*) comunicación *f*; (*fig*) relación *f*.

connive [kə'naɪv] *vi*: to ~ **at** hacer la vista gorda con.

connoisseur [kɒnɪ'sə*] *n* experto, entendido.

connotation [kɒnə'teɪʃən] *n* connotación *f*.

conquer ['kɒŋkə*] *vt* (*gen*) conquistar; (*enemy*) vencer; (*feelings*) dominar; ~**or** *n* conquistador *m*.

conquest ['kɒŋkwest] *n* conquista.

cons [kɒnz] *npl* see **pro.**

conscience ['kɒnʃəns] *n* conciencia.

conscientious [kɒnʃɪ'enʃəs] *a* concienzudo; (*objection*) de conciencia.

conscious ['kɒnʃəs] *a* consciente; ~**ness** *n* conciencia; (*MED*) conocimiento.

conscript ['kɒnskrɪpt] *n* recluto

m/f; ~**ion** [kɔn'skrɪpʃən] *n* servicio militar (obligatorio).

consecrate ['kɔnsɪkreɪt] *vt* consagrar.

consecutive [kɔn'sekjʊtɪv] *a* sucesivo, seguido.

consensus [kɔn'sensəs] *n* consenso.

consent [kɔn'sent] *n* consentimiento // *vi*: **to ~ to** consentir en.

consequence ['kɔnsɪkwəns] *n* consecuencia.

consequently ['kɔnsɪkwəntlɪ] *ad* por consiguiente.

conservation [kɔnsə'veɪʃən] *n* conservación *f*.

conservative [kɔn'sɔːvətɪv] *a* conservador(a); (*cautious*) cauteloso; **C~** *a, n* conservador/a *m/f*.

conservatory [kɔn'sɔːvətrɪ] *n* (*greenhouse*) invernadero.

conserve [kɔn'sɔːv] *vt* conservar // *n* conserva.

consider [kɔn'sɪdə*] *vt* (*gen*) considerar; (*take into account*) tomar en cuenta; (*study*) estudiar, examinar; ~**able** *a* considerable; (*sum*) importante.

considerate [kɔn'sɪdərɪt] *a* considerado; **consideration** [-'reɪʃən] *n* consideración *f*; (*reward*) retribución *f*.

considering [kɔn'sɪdərɪŋ] *prep* en consideración a.

consign [kɔn'saɪn] *vt* consignar; ~**ment** *n* envío.

consist [kɔn'sɪst] *vi*: **to ~ of** consistir en.

consistency [kɔn'sɪstənsɪ] *n* (*of person etc*) consecuencia; (*thickness*) consistencia.

consistent [kɔn'sɪstənt] *a* (*person*) consecuente; (*even*) constante.

consolation [kɔnsə'leɪʃən] *n* consuelo.

console [kɔn'səʊl] *vt* consolar // *n* ['kɔnsəʊl] consola.

consolidate [kɔn'sɔlɪdeɪt] *vt* consolidar.

consommé [kɔn'sɔmeɪ] *n* consomé *m*, caldo.

consonant ['kɔnsənənt] *n* consonante *f*.

consortium [kɔn'sɔːtɪəm] *n* consorcio.

conspicuous [kɔn'spɪkjuəs] *a* (*visible*) visible; (*garish*) llamativo; (*outstanding*) notable.

conspiracy [kɔn'spɪrəsɪ] *n* conjura, complot *m*.

conspire [kɔn'spaɪə*] *vi* conspirar.

constable ['kʌnstəbl] *n* policía *m/f*; **chief ~** jefe *m* de policía.

constabulary [kɔn'stæbjʊlərɪ] *n* policía.

constant ['kɔnstənt] *a* (*gen*) constante; (*loyal*) leal, fiel.

constellation [kɔnstə'leɪʃən] *n* constelación *f*.

consternation [kɔnstə'neɪʃən] *n* consternación *f*.

constipated ['kɔnstɪpeɪtəd] *a* estreñido.

constituency [kɔn'stɪtjuənsɪ] *n* (*POL*) distrito electoral; **constituent** [-ənt] *n* (*POL*) elector/a *m/f*; (*part*) componente *m*.

constitute ['kɔnstɪtjuːt] *vt* constituir.

constitution [kɔnstɪ'tjuːʃən] *n* constitución *f*; ~**al** *a* constitucional.

constrain [kɔn'streɪn] *vt* obligar; ~**ed** *a*: **to feel** ~**ed to...** sentirse en la necesidad de...; ~**t** *n* (*force*) fuerza; (*confinement*) encierro; (*shyness*) reserva.

constrict [kɔn'strɪkt] *vt* apretar, estrechar.

construct [kɔn'strʌkt] *vt* construir; ~**ion** [-ʃən] *n* construcción *f*; ~**ive** *a* constructivo.

construe [kɔn'struː] *vt* interpretar.

consul ['kɔnsl] *n* cónsul *m/f*; ~**ate** ['kɔnsjʊlɪt] *n* consulado.

consult [kɔn'sʌlt] *vt, vi* consultar; ~**ant** *n* (*MED*) especialista *m/f*; (*other specialist*) asesor *m*; ~**ation** [kɔnsəl'teɪʃən] *n* consulta; ~**ing room** *n* consultorio.

consume [kən'sju:m] *vt* (*eat*)
comerse; (*drink*) beberse; (*fire etc,
COMM*) consumir; **consumer** *n*
consumidor/a *m/f*; **consumer goods**
npl bienes *mpl* de consumo;
consumer society *n* sociedad *f* de
consumo.

consummate ['kɒnsʌmeɪt] *vt*
consumar.

consumption [kən'sʌmpʃən] *n*
consumo.

cont. *abbr of* **continued.**

contact ['kɒntækt] *n* contacto, (*pej*)
enchufe *m* // *vt* ponerse en
contacto con; **he has good ~s** tiene
buenas relaciones; **~ lenses** *npl*
lentes *fpl* de contacto, microlentillas
fpl.

contagious [kən'teɪdʒəs] *a* contagioso.

contain [kən'teɪn] *vt* contener; **to
~ o.s.** contenerse; **~er** *n* recipiente
m; (*for shipping etc*) contenedor *m*.

contaminate [kən'tæmɪneɪt] *vt*
contaminar; **contamination** [-'neɪ-
ʃən] *n* contaminación *f*.

cont'd *abbr of* **continued.**

contemplate ['kɒntəmpleɪt] *vt*
(*gen*) contemplar; (*expect*) contar
con; (*intend*) pensar; **contemplation**
[-'pleɪʃən] *n* contemplación *f*.

contemporary [kən'tempərərɪ] *a,
n* contemporáneo/a.

contempt [kən'tempt] *n* desprecio;
~ible *a* despreciable; **~uous** *a*
despectivo, desdeñoso.

contend [kən'tend] *vt* (*argue*)
afirmar // *vi* (*struggle*) luchar; **~er**
n contendiente *m/f*.

content [kən'tent] *a* (*happy*)
contento; (*satisfied*) satisfecho // *vt*
contentar; satisfacer // *n* ['kɒntent]
contenido; **~s** *npl*
contenido *sg*; **~ed** *a* contento,
satisfecho.

contention [kən'tenʃən] *n* contienda; (*argument*) argumento.

contentment [kən'tentmənt] *n*
contento.

contest ['kɒntest] *n* contienda;

(*competition*) concurso // *vt*
[kən'test] (*dispute*) impugnar; (*legal
case*) defender; (*POL*) ser candidato
en; **~ant** [kən'testənt] *n* concursante
m/f; (*in fight*) contendiente *m/f*.

context ['kɒntekst] *n* contexto.

continent ['kɒntɪnənt] *n* continente
m; **the C~** el continente europeo;
~al [-'nentl] *a* continental.

contingency [kən'tɪndʒənsɪ] *n*
contingencia; **contingent** [-ənt] *n*
contingente *m*.

continual [kən'tɪnjuəl] *a* continuo;
~ly *ad* constantemente.

continuation [kəntɪnju'eɪʃən] *n*
prolongación *f*; (*after interruption*)
continuación *f*.

continue [kən'tɪnju:] *vi* seguir,
continuar // *vt* seguir, continuar;
(*start again*) proseguir.

continuity [kɒntɪ'njuɪtɪ] *n* continuidad *f*.

continuous [kən'tɪnjuəs] *a* continuo.

contort [kən'tɔ:t] *vt* retorcer; **~ion**
[-'tɔ:ʃən] *n* contorsión *f*; **~ionist**
[-'tɔ:ʃənɪst] *n* contorsionista *m/f*.

contour ['kɒntuə*] *n* contorno;
(*also: ~ line*) curva de nivel.

contraband ['kɒntrəbænd] *n*
contrabando.

contraception [kɒntrə'sepʃən] *n*
contracepción *f*; **contraceptive**
[-'septɪv] *a, n* anticonceptivo.

contract ['kɒntrækt] *n* contrato //
(*vb*: [kən'trækt]) *vi* (*COMM*): **to ~ to
do sth** comprometerse por contrato
a hacer algo; (*become smaller*)
contraerse, encogerse // *vt*
contraer; **~ion** [-ʃən] *n* contracción
f; **~or** *n* contratista *m/f*.

contradict [kɒntrə'dɪkt] *vt* (*deny*)
desmentir; (*be contrary to*)
contradecir; **~ion** [-ʃən] *n* contradicción *f*.

contralto [kən'træltəu] *n* contralto.

contraption [kən'træpʃən] *n* (*pej*)
armatoste *m*.

contrary ['kɒntrərɪ] *a, n* a contrario.

contrast ['kɒntrɑ:st] *n* contraste *m*

// vt [kɔn'trɑːst] comparar; ~ing a opuesto.

contravene [kɔntrə'viːn] vt oponerse a; (law) contravenir.

contribute [kɔn'trɪbjuːt] vi contribuir // vt: to ~ to (gen) contribuir a; (newspaper) escribir para; **contribution** [kɔntrɪ'bjuːʃən] n (money) aportación f; (to debate) intervención f; (to journal) colaboración f; **contributor** n (to newspaper) colaborador m.

contrive [kɔn'traɪv] vt (invent) idear; (carry out) efectuar; (plot) tramar // vi: to ~ to do lograr hacer.

control [kɔn'trəul] vt (gen) controlar; (traffic etc) dirigir; (machinery) regular; (temper) dominar // n (command) control m; (of car) conducción f; (check) freno; ~s npl mando sg; ~ panel n tablero de instrumentos; ~ room n sala de mando; ~ tower n (AVIAT) torre f de control.

controversial [kɔntrə'vɜːʃl] a discutible; **controversy** ['kɔntrəvɜːsi] n controversia.

convalesce [kɔnvə'les] vi convalecer; **convalescence** n convalecencia; **convalescent** a, n convaleciente m/f.

convector [kɔn'vektə*] n (heater) calentador m de convección.

convene [kɔn'viːn] vt convocar // vi reunirse.

convenience [kɔn'viːnɪəns] n (comfort) comodidad f; (advantage) ventaja; **at your** ~ cuando le sea conveniente; **public** ~ aseos públicos mpl; **convenient** [-ənt] a cómodo; (useful) útil; (place) accesible; (time) oportuno, conveniente.

convent ['kɔnvənt] n convento; ~ school n colegio de monjas.

convention [kɔn'venʃən] n convención f; (meeting) asamblea; ~al a convencional.

converge [kɔn'vɜːdʒ] vi converger.

conversant [kɔn'vɜːsnt] a: **to be** ~ **with** ser enterado de.

conversation [kɔnvə'seɪʃən] n conversación f; ~al a (familiar) familiar; (talkative) locuaz.

converse ['kɔnvɜːs] n inversa // [kɔn'vɜːs] conversar; ~ly [-'vɜːslɪ] ad a la inversa.

conversion [kɔn'vɜːʃən] n conversión f; ~ **table** n tabla de conversión.

convert [kɔn'vɜːt] vt (REL, COMM) convertir; (alter) transformar // n [kɔn'vɜːt] converso/a; ~**ible** a convertible // n descapotable m.

convex ['kɔn'veks] a convexo.

convey [kɔn'veɪ] vt (gen) llevar; (thanks) comunicar; (idea) expresar; ~**or belt** n cinta transportadora.

convict [kɔn'vɪkt] vt (gen) condenar; (sentence) declarar culpable // n ['kɔnvɪkt] presidiario; ~**ion** [-ʃən] n condena; (belief) creencia, convicción f.

convince [kɔn'vɪns] vt convencer; **convincing** a convincente.

convoy ['kɔnvɔɪ] n convoy m.

convulse [kɔn'vʌls] vt convulsionar; (laughter) hacer morir de risa; **convulsion** [-'vʌlʃən] n convulsión f; (laughter) paroxismo.

coo [kuː] vi arrullar.

cook [kuk] vt (gen) cocinar; (stew etc) guisar; (meal) preparar // vi cocer; (person) cocinar // n cocinero; ~**ery** n cocina; ~**ery book** n (US) libro de cocina; ~**ie** n (US) bizcocho; ~**ing** n cocina.

cool [kuːl] a fresco; (not hot) tibio; (not afraid) tranquilo; (unfriendly) frío // vt enfriar // vi enfriarse; ~**ness** n frescura; tranquilidad f; (hostility) frialdad f; (indifference) falta de entusiasmo.

coop [kuːp] n gallinero // vt: to ~ **up** (fig) encerrar.

co-op ['kəuɔp] n abbr of

Cooperative (Society).

cooperate [kəu'ɔpəreɪt] *vi* cooperar, colaborar; **cooperation** [-'reɪʃən] *n* cooperación *f*, colaboración *f*; **cooperative** [-rətɪv] *a* cooperativo // *n* cooperativa.

coordinate [kəu'ɔːdɪneɪt] *vt* coordinar; **coordination** [-'neɪʃən] *n* coordinación *f*.

cop [kɔp] *n* (col) poli m.

cope [kəup] *vi*: to ~ **with** poder con; (*problem*) hacer frente a.

co-pilot ['kəu'paɪlət] *n* copiloto.

copious ['kəupɪəs] *a* copioso, abundante.

copper ['kɔpə*] *n* (*metal*) cobre m; (*col: policeman*) poli m; ~**s** npl monedas fpl de poco valor.

coppice ['kɔpɪs], **copse** [kɔps] *n* bosquecillo.

copulate ['kɔpjuleɪt] *vi* copularse; **copulation** [-'leɪʃən] *n* cópula.

copy ['kɔpɪ] *n* copia *f*; (*of book etc*) ejemplar m; (*of writing*) original m // *vt* copiar; ~**right** *n* derechos mpl de autor.

coral ['kɔrəl] *n* coral m; ~ **reef** *n* arrecife m (de coral).

cord [kɔːd] *n* cuerda; (*ELEC*) cordón m; (*fabric*) pana.

cordial ['kɔːdɪəl] *a* afectuoso // *n* cordial m.

cordon ['kɔːdn] *n* cordón m; to ~ **off** *vt* acordonar.

corduroy ['kɔːdərɔɪ] *n* pana.

core [kɔː*] *n* (*gen*) centro, núcleo; (*of fruit*) corazón m // *vt* quitar el corazón de.

coriander [kɔrɪ'ændə*] *n* culantro.

cork [kɔːk] *n* corcho; (*tree*) alcornoque m; ~**screw** *n* sacacorchos m inv.

cormorant ['kɔːmərnt] *n* cormorán m grande.

corn [kɔːn] *n* (*wheat*) trigo; (*US: maize*) maíz m; (*cereals*) granos mpl; (*on foot*) callo; ~ **on the cob** (*CULIN*) maíz m en la mazorca.

corned beef ['kɔːnd-] *n* carne *f* de vaca acecinada.

corner ['kɔːnə*] *n* (*gen*) ángulo; (*outside*) esquina; (*inside*) rincón m; (*in road*) curva; (*FOOTBALL*) córner m // *vt* (*trap*) arrinconar; (*COMM*) acaparar // *vi* (*in car*) tomar una curva; ~**stone** *n* piedra angular.

cornet ['kɔːnɪt] *n* (*MUS*) corneta; (*of ice-cream*) barquillo.

cornflour ['kɔːnflauə*] *n* harina de maíz.

Cornwall ['kɔːnwəl] *n* Cornualles m.

corny ['kɔːnɪ] *a* (*col*) viejo, gastado.

corollary [kə'rɔlərɪ] *n* corolario.

coronary ['kɔrənərɪ] *n*: ~ (**thrombosis**) trombosis *f* coronaria.

coronation [kɔrə'neɪʃən] *n* coronación *f*.

coroner ['kɔrənə*] *n* juez m de primera instancia.

coronet ['kɔrənɪt] *n* corona.

corporal ['kɔːpərl] *n* cabo // *a* corporal.

corporate ['kɔːpərɪt] *a* corporativo.

corporation [kɔːpə'reɪʃən] *n* (*of town*) ayuntamiento; (*COMM*) corporación *f*.

corps [kɔː*], *pl* **corps** [kɔːz] *n* cuerpo.

corpse [kɔːps] *n* cadáver m.

corpuscle ['kɔːpʌsl] *n* corpúsculo m.

corral [kɔ'rɑːl] *n* corral m.

correct [kə'rekt] *a* (*accurate*) justo, exacto; (*proper*) correcto // *vt* corregir; (*exam*) calificar; ~**ion** [-ʃən] *n* rectificación *f*; (*erasure*) tachadura.

correlate ['kɔrɪleɪt] *vt* correlacionar.

correspond [kɔrɪs'pɔnd] *vi* (*write*) escribirse; (*be equal to*) corresponder; ~**ence** *n* correspondencia; ~**ence course** *n* curso por correspondencia; ~**ent** *n* corresponsal m/f; ~**ing** *a* correspondiente.

corridor ['kɔrɪdɔː*] *n* pasillo.

corroborate [kə'rɔbəreɪt] *vt* corroborar.

corrode [kə'rəud] *vt* corroer // *vi*

corroerse; **corrosion** [-'rəʊʒən] *n* corrosión *f.*

corrugated ['kɒrəgeɪtɪd] *a* ondulado; ~ **iron** *n* chapa ondulada.

corrupt [kə'rʌpt] *a* corrompido; (person) venal // *vt* corromper; (bribe) sobornar; ~**ion** [-ʃən] *n* corrupción *f.*

corset ['kɔːsɪt] *n* faja.

Corsica ['kɔːsɪkə] *n* Córcega.

cortège [kɔː'teːʒ] *n* cortejo, desfile *m.*

cortisone ['kɔːtɪzəʊn] *n* cortisona.

cosh [kɒʃ] *n* cachiporra.

cosiness ['kəʊzɪnɪs] *n* comodidad *f*; (atmosphere) lo holgado.

cos lettuce [kɒs-] *n* lechuga cos.

cosmetic [kɒz'metɪk] *n* cosmético.

cosmic ['kɒzmɪk] *a* cósmico.

cosmonaut ['kɒzmənɔːt] *n* cosmonauta *m/f.*

cosmopolitan [kɒzmə'pɒlɪtn] *a* cosmopolita.

cosmos ['kɒzmɒs] *n* cosmos *m.*

cost [kɒst] *n* (gen) coste *m*, costo; (price) precio; ~**s** *npl* costes *mpl* // *vi*, *pt*, *pp* **cost** costar, valer // *vt* preparar el presupuesto de; **at the ~ of** a costa de; **how much does it ~?** ¿cuánto cuesta?

co-star ['kəʊstɑ:*] *n* colega *m/f* de reparto.

Costa Rican ['kɒstə'riːkən] *a* costarriqueño.

costly ['kɒstlɪ] *a* (expensive) costoso; (valuable) suntuoso.

cost price *n* precio de coste.

costume ['kɒstjuːm] *n* traje *m*; (also: swimming ~) traje de baño.

cosy ['kəʊzɪ] *a* cómodo; (atmosphere) acogedor(a); (life) holgado.

cot [kɒt] *n* (child's) cuna.

cottage ['kɒtɪdʒ] *n* casita de campo; (rustic) barraca; ~ **cheese** *n* requesón *m.*

cotton ['kɒtn] *n* algodón *m*; (thread) hilo; **to ~ on to** *vt* (col) caer en la cuenta de; ~ **wool** *n* algodón *m* (hidrófilo).

couch [kaʊtʃ] *n* sofá *m.*

cough [kɒf] *vi* toser // *n* tos *f*; **to ~ up** *vt* escupir; ~ **drop** *n* pastilla para la tos.

could [kud] *pt of* **can**; ~**n't = could not.**

council ['kaʊnsl] *n* consejo; **city** *or* **town** ~ consejo municipal; ~ **estate** *n* polígono de renta limitada; ~ **house** *n* vivienda de renta limitada; ~**lor** *n* concejal *m/f.*

counsel ['kaʊnsl] *n* (advice) consejo; (lawyer) abogado // *vt* aconsejar; ~**lor** *n* consejero.

count [kaʊnt] *vt* (gen) contar; (include) incluir // *vi* contar // *n* (gen) cuenta; (of votes) escrutinio; (nobleman) conde *m*; (sum) total *m*, suma; **to ~ on** *vt fus* contar con; **that doesn't ~!** ¡eso no vale!; ~**down** *n* cuenta hacia atrás.

counter ['kaʊntə*] *n* (in shop) mostrador *m*; (in games) ficha *f* // *vt* contrarrestar; (blow) parar; (attack) contestar a // *ad*: ~ **to** contrario a; ~**act** *vt* contrarrestar; ~**attack** *n* contraataque *m* // *vi* contratacar; ~**balance** *n* contrapeso; ~**-espionage** *n* contraespionaje *m.*

counterfeit ['kaʊntəfɪt] *n* moneda falsa // *vt* falsificar // *a* falso, falsificado.

counterfoil ['kaʊntəfɔɪl] *n* talón *m.*

counterpart ['kaʊntəpɑːt] *n* (of person) colega *m/f.*

counter-revolution [kaʊntərevə-'luːʃən] *n* contrarrevolución *f.*

countersign ['kaʊntəsaɪn] *vt* refrendar.

countess ['kaʊntɪs] *n* condesa.

countless ['kaʊntlɪs] *a* incontable.

country ['kʌntrɪ] *n* país *m*; (native land) patria; (as opposed to town) campo; (region) región *f*, tierra; ~ **dancing** *n* baile *m* regional; ~ **house** *n* quinta, finca; ~**side** *n* campo.

county ['kaʊntɪ] *n* condado; ~ **town** *n* cabeza de partido.

coup [kuː] *pl* ~**s** [-z] *n* golpe *m*; ~

d'état/de grâce golpe de estado/de gracia.

coupé ['ku:pei] n cupé m.

couple ['kʌpl] n (of things) par m; (of people) pareja; (married ~) matrimonio // vt (ideas, names) unir, juntar; (machinery) acoplar; a ~ of un par de.

coupling ['kʌplɪŋ] n (RAIL) enganche m.

coupon ['ku:pon] n cupón m; (pools ~) boleto.

courage ['kʌrɪdʒ] n valor m, valentía; ~ous [kə'reɪdʒəs] a valiente.

courier ['kurɪə*] n estafeta; (diplomatic) correo; (for tourists) agente m/f de turismo.

course [kɔ:s] n (direction) dirección f, (of river, ESCOL) curso; (of ship) rumbo, derrota; (of bullet) trayectoria; (fig) proceder m; (GOLF) campo; (part of meal) plato; of ~ ad desde luego, naturalmente; of ~! ¡claro!; in due ~ en el momento oportuno.

court [kɔ:t] n (royal) corte m; (LAW) tribunal m, juzgado, (TENNIS) pista, cancha // vt (woman) cortejar; (danger etc) buscar; to take to ~ demandar.

courteous ['kə:tɪəs] a cortés.

courtesan [kɔ:tɪ'zæn] n cortesana.

courtesy ['kə:tɪsɪ] n cortesía; by ~ of con permiso de.

court-house ['kɔ:thaus] n (US) palacio de justicia.

courtier ['kɔ:tɪə*] n cortesano.

court: ~-martial, pl ~s martial n consejo de guerra // vt someter a consejo de guerra; ~-room n sala de justicia; ~yard n patio.

cousin ['kʌzn] n primo/a; first ~ primo carnal.

cove [kəuv] n cala, ensenada.

covenant ['kʌvənənt] n convenio.

cover ['kʌvə*] vt (gen) cubrir; (with lid) tapar; (chairs etc) revestir; (distance) recorrer; (include) abarcar; (protect) abrigar;

(journalist) investigar; (issues) tratar // n (gen) cubierta; (lid) tapa; (for chair etc) funda; (for bed) cobertor m; (envelope) sobre m; (for book) forro; (of magazine) portada; (shelter) abrigo; (insurance) cobertura; under ~ (indoors) bajo techo; under ~ of al abrigo de; (fig) so capa de; to ~ up for sb encubrir a uno; ~age n alcance m; ~ charge n precio del cubierto; ~ing n cubierta, envoltura; ~ing letter n carta explicatoria.

covet ['kʌvɪt] vt codiciar.

cow [kau] n vaca // vt intimidar.

coward ['kauəd] n cobarde m/f; ~ice [-ɪs] n cobardía; ~ly a cobarde.

cowboy ['kauboi] n vaquero.

cower ['kauə*] vi encogerse (de miedo).

cowshed ['kaufed] n establo.

coxswain ['kɒksn] n (abbr: cox) timonel m/f.

coy [kɔi] a tímido.

coyote [kɔi'əuti] n coyote m.

crab [kræb] n cangrejo; ~ apple n manzana silvestre.

crack [kræk] n grieta; (noise) crujido; (: of whip) chasquido; (fam) chiste m // vt agrietar, romper; (nut) cascar; (safe) forzar; (whip etc) chasquear; (knuckles) crujir; (joke) contar // a (expert) experto; to ~ up vi (MED) sufrir un colapso nervioso; ~er n (biscuit) cracker m; (Christmas cracker) sorpresa.

crackle ['krækl] vi crepitar; crackling n (of fire) crepitación f; (of leaves etc) crujido; (of pork) chicharrón m.

cradle ['kreɪdl] n cuna.

craft [krɑ:ft] n (skill) arte m; (trade) oficio; (cunning) astucia; (boat) barco.

craftsman ['krɑ:ftsmən] n artesano; ~ship n artesanía.

crafty ['krɑ:ftɪ] a astuto.

crag [kræg] n peñasco; ~**gy** a escarpado.

cram [kræm] vt (fill) llenar, henchir; ~**med** a atestado.

cramp [kræmp] n (MED) calambre m; (TECH) grapa // vt (limit) restringir; (annoy) estorbar; ~**ed** a apretado, estrecho.

crampon ['kræmpən] n crampón m.

cranberry ['krænbərı] n arándano agrio.

crane [kreɪn] n (TECH) grúa; (bird) grulla.

crank [kræŋk] n manivela; (person) chiflado; ~**shaft** n eje m del cigüeñal.

cranky ['kræŋkɪ] a (eccentric) maniático; (bad-tempered) irritable.

cranny ['krænɪ] n see **nook**.

crash [kræʃ] n (noise) estruendo; (of cars etc) choque m; (of plane) accidente m de avión; (COMM) quiebra // (of plane) estrellar // vi (plane) estrellarse; (two cars) chocar; (fall noisily) caer con estrépito; ~ **course** n curso acelerado; ~ **helmet** n casco (protector); ~ **landing** n aterrizaje m forzoso.

crate [kreɪt] n cajón m de embalaje; (fam) armatoste m.

crater ['kreɪtə*] n cráter m.

cravat(e) [krə'væt] n pañuelo.

crave [kreɪv] vt: **to ~ for** ansiar, anhelar; **craving** n (of pregnant woman) antojo.

crawl [krɔːl] vi (gen) arrastrarse; (child) andar a gatas, gatear; (vehicle) avanzar a paso de tortuga // n (SWIMMING) crol m.

crayfish ['kreɪfɪʃ] n, pl inv langostino.

crayon ['kreɪən] n pastel m, lápiz m de color.

craze [kreɪz] n manía; (fashion) moda.

crazy ['kreɪzɪ] a (person) loco; (idea) disparatado.

creak [kriːk] vi chirriar, rechinar; (door etc) crujir.

cream [kriːm] n (of milk) nata; (gen) crema; (fig) flor y nata // a (colour) color m (de) crema; ~ **cake** n pastel m de nata; ~ **cheese** n queso de nata; ~**y** a cremoso.

crease [kriːs] n (fold) pliegue m; (in trousers) raya; (wrinkle) arruga // vt (fold) doblar, plegar; (wrinkle) arrugar // vi (wrinkle up) arrugarse.

create [kriː'eɪt] vt crear; **creation** [-ʃən] n creación f; **creative** a creador(a); **creator** n creador m.

creature ['kriːtʃə*] n (animal) animal m, bicho; (living thing) criatura.

crèche, creche [krɛʃ] n guardería infantil.

credentials [krɪ'dɛnʃlz] npl credenciales fpl.

credibility [krɛdɪ'bɪlɪtɪ] n credibilidad f.

credible ['krɛdɪbl] a creíble.

credit ['krɛdɪt] n (gen) crédito; (merit) honor m, mérito // vt (COMM) abonar; (believe) creer, prestar fe a // a (to crediticio); ~**s** npl (CINEMA) fichas técnicas; ~**able** a estimable, digno de elogio; ~ **card** n tarjeta de crédito; ~**or** n acreedor m.

credulity [krɪ'djuːlɪtɪ] n credulidad f.

creed [kriːd] n credo.

creek [kriːk] n cala, ensenada; (US) riachuelo.

creep [kriːp] pt, pp **crept** vi (animal) deslizarse; (gen) arrastrarse; (plant) trepar; ~**er** n enredadera; ~**y** a (frightening) horripilante.

cremate [krɪ'meɪt] vt incinerar; **cremation** [-ʃən] n incineración f.

crematorium [krɛmə'tɔːrɪəm], pl **-ria** [-rɪə] n (horno) crematorio.

creosote ['krɪəsəut] n creosota.

crêpe [kreɪp] n (fabric) crespón m;

(*rubber*) crepé m; ~ **bandage** n venda de crepé.

crept [krept] *pt, pp of* **creep.**

crescent ['krɛsnt] n media luna; (*street*) calle f en semicírculo.

cress [krɛs] n mastuerzo.

crest [krɛst] n (*of bird*) cresta; (*of hill*) cima, cumbre f; (*of helmet*) cimera; (*of coat of arms*) blasón m; ~**fallen** a alicaído.

Crete [kriːt] n Creta.

crevasse [krɪˈvæs] n grieta.

crevice ['krɛvɪs] n grieta, hendedura.

crew [kruː] n (*of ship etc*) tripulación f; (*gang*) banda; (MIL) dotación f; ~**-cut** n corte m al rape; ~**-neck** n cuello llano.

crib [krɪb] n pesebre m // vt (*col*) plagiar.

crick [krɪk] n (*in neck*) tortícolis m.

cricket ['krɪkɪt] n (*insect*) grillo; (*game*) criquet m.

crime [kraɪm] n crimen m; (*less serious*) delito; **criminal** ['krɪmɪnl] a criminal m, delincuente m // a criminal, delictivo; (*law*) penal; the **Criminal Investigation Department (CID)** Brigada de Investigación Criminal (B.I.C.)

crimson ['krɪmzn] a carmesí.

cringe [krɪndʒ] vi agacharse, encogerse.

crinkle ['krɪŋkl] vt arrugar.

cripple ['krɪpl] n lisiado, mutilado // vt lisiar, tullir.

crisis ['kraɪsɪs], pl **-ses** [-siːz] n crisis f.

crisp [krɪsp] a (*fresh*) fresco; (*cooked*) tostado; (*hair*) crespo; (*manner*) seco; ~**s** npl papas fritas fpl.

criss-cross ['krɪskrɔs] a entrelazado.

criterion [kraɪˈtɪərɪən], pl **-ria** [-rɪə] n criterio.

critic ['krɪtɪk] n (*gen*) crítico/ona m/f; (*paper*) crítico; ~**al** a (*gen*) crítico; (*illness*) grave; ~**ally** ad (*ill*) gravemente; ~**ism** ['krɪtɪsɪzm] n crítica; ~**ize** ['krɪtɪsaɪz] vt criticar.

croak [krəuk] vi (*frog*) croar; (*raven*) graznar // n graznido.

crochet ['krəuʃeɪ] n ganchillo.

crockery ['krɔkərɪ] n loza, vajilla.

crocodile ['krɔkədaɪl] n cocodrilo.

crocus ['krəukəs] n azafrán m.

croft [krɔft] n granja pequeña; ~**er** n pequeño granjero.

croissant ['krwasã] n croissant m, medialuna.

crone [krəun] n bruja.

crony ['krəunɪ] n compinche m/f.

crook [kruk] n (*fam*) maleante m/f; (*of shepherd*) cayado; (*of arm*) pliegue m; ~**ed** ['krukɪd] a torcido; (*path*) tortuoso; (*action*) poco limpio.

crop [krɔp] n (*species*) cultivo; (*quantity*) cosecha // vt cortar, recortar; **to ~ up** vi surgir, presentarse.

croquet ['krəukeɪ] n croquet m.

croquette [krɔ'kɛt] n croqueta.

cross [krɔs] n cruz f // vt (*street etc*) cruzar, atravesar // a de mal humor, malhumorado; **to ~ o.s.** santiguarse; **to ~ out** vt tachar; **to ~ over** vi cruzar; ~**bar** n travesaño; (SPORT) larguero; ~**country** (*race*) n carrera a campo traviesa, cross m; ~**examination** n repregunta, interrogatorio; ~**examine** vt repreguntar; ~**eyed** a bizco; ~**ing** n (*road*) cruce m; (*rail*) paso a nivel; (*sea-passage*) travesía; (*also:* **pedestrian ~**) paso para peatones; ~ **purposes** npl: **to be at ~ purposes** malentenderse uno a otro; ~**reference** n contrarreferencia; ~**roads** n cruce m encrucijada; ~ **section** n corte m transversal; (*of population*) sección f representativa; ~**wind** n viento de costado; ~**word** n crucigrama m.

crotch [krɔtʃ] n (*of garment*) entrepierna.

crotchet ['krɔtʃɪt] n (MUS) negra.

crotchety ['krɔtʃɪtɪ] a (*person*) arisco.

crouch [krautʃ] vi agacharse, acurrucarse.

croupier ['kru:pɪə] n crupier m/f.

crow [krəu] n (bird) cuervo; (of cock) canto, cacareo // vi (cock) cantar, cacarear.

crowbar ['krəuba:*] n palanca.

crowd [kraud] n muchedumbre f; (SPORT) público; (unruly) tropel m; (common herd) vulgo // vt (gather) amontonar; (fill) llenar // vi (gather) reunirse; (pile up) amontonarse; ~ed a (full) atestado; (well-attended) concurrido.

crown [kraun] n corona; (of head) coronilla; (of hat) copa; (of hill) cumbre f // vt coronar; ~ jewels npl joyas fpl reales; ~ prince n príncipe m heredero.

crucial ['kru:ʃl] a decisivo.

crucifix ['kru:sɪfɪks] n crucifijo; ~ion [-'fɪkʃən] n crucifixión f; **crucify** [-faɪ] vt crucificar.

crude [kru:d] a (materials) bruto; (fig: basic) tosco; (: vulgar) ordinario; ~ (oil) n aceite m crudo.

cruel ['kruəl] a cruel; ~ty n crueldad f.

cruet ['kru:ɪt] n angarillas fpl.

cruise [kru:z] n crucero, viaje m por mar // vi (ship) hacer un crucero; (car) circular lentamente; **cruiser** n crucero.

crumb [krʌm] n miga, migaja.

crumble ['krʌmbl] vt desmenuzar // vi (gen) desmenuzarse; (building) desmoronarse; **crumbly** a desmenuzable.

crumpet ['krʌmpɪt] n bollo blando.

crumple ['krʌmpl] vt (paper) estrujar; (material) arrugar.

crunch [krʌntʃ] vt (food etc) mascar; (underfoot) hacer crujir // n (fig) crisis f; ~y a crujiente.

crusade [kru:'seɪd] n cruzada.

crush [krʌʃ] n (people) agolpamiento; (crowd) aglomeración f; (drink): **lemon** ~ limonada // vt (gen) aplastar; (paper) estrujar; (cloth) arrugar; (fruit) exprimir;

~ing a aplastante; (burden) agobiador(a).

crust [krʌst] n corteza; (MED) costra.

crutch [krʌtʃ] n muleta.

crux [krʌks] n lo esencial.

cry [kraɪ] vi llorar; (shout) gritar // n grito.

crypt [krɪpt] n cripta.

cryptic ['krɪptɪk] a enigmático, secreto.

crystal ['krɪstl] n cristal m; ~-clear a transparente, claro como el agua; **crystallize** vt cristalizar // vi cristalizarse.

cub [kʌb] n cachorro.

Cuba ['kju:bə] n Cuba; ~n a, n cubano/a.

cubbyhole ['kʌbɪhəul] n chiribitil m.

cube [kju:b] n cubo; (of sugar) terrón m // vt (MATH) cubicar; ~ **root** n raíz f cúbica; **cubic** a cúbico.

cubicle ['kju:bɪkl] n (at pool) caseta; (for bed) camarilla.

cuckoo ['kuku:] n cuco; ~ **clock** n reloj m de cuclillo.

cucumber ['kju:kʌmbə*] n pepino.

cuddle ['kʌdl] vt abrazar amorosamente // vi abrazarse; **cuddly** a mimoso.

cue [kju:] n (snooker) taco; (THEATRE etc) entrada, apunte m.

cuff [kʌf] n (of shirt, coat etc) puño; (blow) bofetada; **off the** ~ ad de improviso; ~**links** npl gemelos mpl.

cuisine [kwɪ'zi:n] n cocina.

cul-de-sac ['kʌldəsæk] n callejón m sin salida.

culinary ['kʌlɪnərɪ] a culinario.

cull [kʌl] vt (flowers) coger; (select) entresacar.

culminate ['kʌlmɪneɪt] vi: to ~ in terminar en; **culmination** [-'neɪʃən] n culminación f, colmo.

culpable ['kʌlpəbl] a culpable.

culprit ['kʌlprɪt] n (person) delincuente m/f.

cult [kʌlt] n culto.

cultivate ['kʌltɪveɪt] vt (also fig)

cultivar; **cultivation** [-'veɪʃən] n cultivo; (fig) cultura.

cultural ['kʌltʃərəl] a cultural.

culture ['kʌltʃə*] n (also fig) cultura; ~d a culto.

cumbersome ['kʌmbəsəm] a molesto, incómodo.

cumulative ['kju:mjulətɪv] a cumulativo.

cunning ['kʌnɪŋ] n astucia // a astuto.

cup [kʌp] n taza; (prize, event) copa.

cupboard ['kʌbəd] n armario; (on wall) alacena.

Cupid ['kju:pɪd] n Cupido.

cupola ['kju:pələ] n cúpula.

cup-tie ['kʌptaɪ] n partido de copa.

cur [kə:] n perro de mala raza; (person) canalla m/f.

curable ['kjuərəbl] a curable.

curate ['kjuərɪt] n cura m.

curator [kjuə'reɪtə*] n director m.

curb [kə:b] vt refrenar // n freno.

curdle ['kə:dl] vi cuajarse.

curds [kə:dz] npl requesón m.

cure [kjuə*] vt curar // n cura, curación f.

curfew ['kə:fju:] n toque m de queda.

curio ['kjuərɪəu] n curiosidad f.

curiosity [kjuərɪ'ɒsɪtɪ] n curiosidad f, curiosa [kjuərɪəs] a curioso.

curl [kə:l] n rizo, bucle m // vt (hair) rizar; (paper) arrollar; (lip) fruncir // vi rizarse; arrollarse; to ~ **up** vi arrollarse; (person) hacer un ovillo; (fam) morirse de risa; ~**er** n bigudí m, chincho; ~**y** a rizado.

currant ['kʌrnt] n pasa; (black, red) grosella.

currency ['kʌrnsɪ] n moneda.

current ['kʌrnt] n corriente f // a corriente, actual; ~ **account** n cuenta corriente; ~ **affairs** npl actualidades fpl; ~**ly** ad actualmente.

curriculum [kə'rɪkjuləm] pl ~**s** or -la [-lə] n plan m de estudios; ~ **vitae** n currículum m.

curry ['kʌrɪ] n curry m // vt: to ~ **favour with** buscar favores con; ~ **powder** n polvos mpl de curry.

curse [kə:s] vi echar pestes // vt maldecir, echar pestes de // n maldición f; (swearword) palabrota.

cursory ['kə:sərɪ] a rápido, superficial.

curt [kə:t] a corto, seco.

curtail [kə:'teɪl] vt (visit etc) acortar; (expenses etc) restringir.

curtain ['kə:tn] n cortina; (THEATRE) telón m; ~ **ring** n anilla.

curts(e)y ['kə:tsɪ] n reverencia // vi hacer una reverencia.

curve [kə:v] n curva // vt encorvar, torcer // vi encorvarse, torcerse; (road) hacer (una) curva.

cushion ['kuʃən] n cojín m; (SNOOKER) banda // vt (seat) acolchar; (shock) amortiguar.

custard ['kʌstəd] n (for pouring) natilla.

custodian [kʌs'təudiən] n custodio.

custody ['kʌstədɪ] n custodia; to take into ~ detener.

custom ['kʌstəm] n costumbre f; (COMM) clientela; ~**ary** a acostumbrado.

customer ['kʌstəmə*] n cliente m/f.

custom-made ['kʌstəm'meɪd] a hecho a la medida.

customs ['kʌstəmz] npl aduana sg; ~ **duty** n derechos mpl de aduana; ~ **officer** n aduanero.

cut [kʌt], pt, pp cut vt cortar; (price) rebajar; (record) grabar; (reduce) reducir // n corte m; (in skin) cortadura; (with sword) tajo; (of knife) cuchillada; (in salary etc) rebaja; (of meat) tajada; (power) apagón m; to ~ **a tooth** salirle a uno un diente, to ~ **down** vt (tree) derribar; (reduce) reducir; to ~ **off** vt (gen) cortar; (retreat) impedir; (troops) cercar; to ~ **out** vt (shape) recortar; (delete) suprimir; to ~

through *vi* abrirse camino; **~back** *n* reducción *f*.

cute [kju:t] *a* lindo; (*shrewd*) listo.

cuticle ['kju:tikl] *n* cutícula.

cutlery ['kʌtləri] *n* cubiertos *mpl*.

cutlet ['kʌtlit] *n* chuleta.

cut: **~out** *n* recortable *m*; **~-price** *a* a precio reducido; **~throat** *n* asesino *a* intenso.

cutting ['kʌtiŋ] *a* (*gen*) cortante; (*remark*) mordaz // *n* (*PRESS*) recorte *m*; (*RAIL*) desmonte *m*.

cwt *abbr of* **hundredweight(s).**

cyanide ['saiənaid] *n* cianuro.

cyclamen ['sikləmən] *n* ciclamen *m*.

cycle ['saikl] *n* ciclo; (*bicycle*) bicicleta // *vi* ir en bicicleta; **cycling** *n* ciclismo; **cyclist** *n* ciclista *m/f*.

cyclone ['saikləun] *n* ciclón *m*.

cygnet ['signit] *n* pollo de cisne.

cylinder ['silində*] *n* cilindro; **~ block** *n* bloque *m* de cilindros; **~ capacity** *n* cilindrada; **~ head** *n* culata de cilindro; **~-head gasket** *n* junta de culata.

cymbals ['simblz] *npl* platillos *mpl*.

cynic ['sinik] *n* cínico; **~al** *a* cínico; **~ism** ['sinisizəm] *n* cinismo.

cypress ['saiprəs] *n* ciprés *m*.

Cypriot ['sipriət] *a*, *n* chipriota *m/f*.

Cyprus ['saiprəs] *n* Chipre *f*.

cyst [sist] *n* quiste *m*; **~ itis** *n* cistitis *f*.

czar [zɑ:*] *n* zar *m*.

Czech [tʃek] *a*, *n* checo/a.

Czechoslovakia [tʃekəslə'vækiə] *n* Checoslovaquia.

D

dab [dæb] *vt* (*eyes, wound*) tocar (ligeramente); (*paint, cream*) mojar ligeramente // *n* (*of paint*) brochazo; (*of liquid*) gota; (*amount*) pequeña cantidad *f*.

dabble ['dæbl] *vi*: **to ~ in** interesarse por.

dad [dæd], **daddy** ['dædi] *n* papá *m*; **daddy-long-legs** *n* típula.

daffodil ['dæfədil] *n* narciso trompón.

daft [dɑ:ft] *a* estúpido, tonto.

dagger ['dægə*] *n* puñal *m*, daga; **to look ~s at sb** apuñalar a alguien con la mirada.

daily ['deili] *a* diario, cotidiano // *n* (*paper*) diario; (*domestic help*) asistenta // *ad* a diario, cada día.

dainty ['deinti] *a* delicado; (*tasteful*) elegante, primoroso.

dairy ['dɛəri] *n* (*shop*) lechería; (*on farm*) vaquería // *a* lechero; **~ farm** *n* granja; **~ produce** *n* productos *mpl* lácteos.

daisy ['deizi] *n* margarita.

dale [deil] *n* valle *m*.

dam [dæm] *n* presa // *vt* represar.

damage ['dæmidʒ] *n* daño, perjuicio; (*to machine*) avería // *vt* dañar, perjudicar; averiar; **~s** *npl* (*LAW*) daños y perjuicios.

damn [dæm] *vt* condenar; (*curse*) maldecir // *n* (*col*): **I don't give a ~** me trae sin cuidado // *a* (*col*) maldito; (**it)!** ¡mecachis!; **~ing** *a* (*evidence*) irrecusable.

damp [dæmp] *a* húmedo, mojado // *n* humedad *f* // *vt* (*also*: **~en**) (*cloth, rag*) mojar; (*enthusiasm etc*) desalentar; **~ness** *n* humedad *f*.

damson ['dæmzən] *n* ciruela damascena.

dance [dɑ:ns] *n* baile *m* // *vi* bailar; **~ hall** *n* salón *m* de baile; **dancer** *n* bailador/a *m/f*; (*professional*) bailarín/ina *m/f*; **dancing** *n* baile *m*.

dandelion ['dændilaiən] *n* diente *m* de león.

dandruff ['dændrəf] *n* caspa.

Dane [dein] *n* danés/esa *m/f*.

danger ['deindʒə*] *n* peligro; (*risk*) riesgo; **~!** (*on sign*) ¡peligro de muerte!; **to be in ~ of** correr riesgo de; **~ous** *a* peligroso; **~ously** *ad* peligrosamente.

dangle ['dæŋgl] vt colgar // vi pender, estar colgado.

Danish ['deɪnɪʃ] a, n danés/esa m/f.

dare [dɛə*] vt: **to ~ sb to do** desafiar a uno a hacer algo // vi: **to ~ (to) do sth** atreverse a hacer algo; **~devil** n temerario, atrevido; **daring** a atrevido, osado // n atrevimiento, osadía.

dark [dɑːk] a (gen) oscuro; (hair, complexion) moreno; (cheerless) triste, sombrío; (fig) secreto, escondido // n (gen) oscuridad f; (night) tinieblas fpl; **to be left in the ~ about** (fig) quedar sin saber nada de; **after ~** después del anochecer; **~en** vt oscurecer; (colour) hacer más oscuro // vi oscurecerse; (sky) anublarse; **~ glasses** npl gafas fpl oscuras; **~ness** n oscuridad f, tinieblas fpl; **~ room** n cuarto oscuro.

darling ['dɑːlɪŋ] a, n querido/a.

darn [dɑːn] vt zurcir.

dart [dɑːt] n dardo; (in game) rehilete m; (in sewing) sisa // vi precipitarse; **to ~ away/along** irse/seguir precipitado; **~board** n blanco; **~s** n juego de rehiletes.

dash [dæʃ] n (sign) guión m, (: long) raya; (rush) carrera // vt (break) romper, estrellar; (hopes) defraudar // vi precipitarse, ir de prisa; **to ~ away or off** vi marcharse apresuradamente; **~board** n tablero de instrumentos; **~ing** a gallardo.

data ['deɪtə] npl datos mpl; **~ processing** n procesamiento de datos.

date [deɪt] n (day) fecha; (with friend) cita; (fruit) dátil m; (tree) palmera // vt fechar; citar; **to ~ ad** hasta la fecha; **out of ~** fuera de moda; **up to ~** moderno, al día; **~d** a anticuado.

daub [dɔːb] vt manchar.

daughter ['dɔːtə*] n hija; **~-in-law** n nuera, hija política.

daunting ['dɔːntɪŋ] a desalentador(a).

dawdle ['dɔːdl] vi (waste time) perder el tiempo; (go slow) andar muy despacio.

dawn [dɔːn] n alba, amanecer m // vi (day) amanecer; (fig): **it ~ed on him that...** cayó en la cuenta de que....

day [deɪ] n día m; (working ~) jornada; **the ~ before** el día anterior; **the following ~** el día siguiente; **by ~** de día; **~break** n amanecer m; **~dream** n ensueño // vi soñar despierto; **~light** n luz f (del día); **~time** n día m // a de día.

daze [deɪz] vt (stun) aturdir // n: **in a ~** aturdido.

dazzle ['dæzl] vt deslumbrar; **dazzling** a deslumbrante.

dead [dɛd] a (gen) muerto; (deceased) difunto; (telephone) cortado; (ELEC) sin corriente // ad (gen) totalmente; (exactly) justo; **~ tired** muerto de cansancio; **to stop ~** parar en seco; **the ~** los muertos; **~en** vt (blow, sound) amortiguar; (make numb) calmar, aliviar; **~ end** n callejón m sin salida; **~ heat** n (SPORT) empate m; **~line** n fecha o hora tope; **~lock** n punto muerto; **~ly** a mortal, fatal; **~pan** a sin expresión.

deaf [dɛf] a sordo; **~-aid** n audífono; **~en** vt ensordecer; **~ening** a ensordecedor(a); **~ness** n sordera; **~mute** n sordomudo/a.

deal [diːl] n (agreement) pacto, convenio; (business) negocio, trato; (CARDS) reparto // vt, pt, pp **dealt** [dɛlt] (gen) dar; **a great ~ (of)** bastante, mucho; **to ~ in** tratar en, comerciar en; **to ~ with** vt fus (people) tratar con; (problem) ocuparse de; (subject) tratar de; (punish) castigar; **~er** n comerciante m; (CARDS) mano f; **~ings** npl transacciones fpl; (relations) relaciones fpl.

dear [dɪə*] a querido; (*expensive*) caro // n: my ~; ~ querido/a // excl: ~ me! ¡Dios mío!; D~ Sir/Madam (*in letter*) Muy Señor Mío, estimado Señor/estimada Señora; ~ly ad (*love*) tiernamente; (*pay*) caro.

death [deθ] n muerte f; ~bed n lecho de muerte; ~ certificate n partida de defunción; ~ duties npl (*Brit*) derechos mpl de herencia; ~ly a mortal; (*silence*) profundo; ~ penalty n pena de muerte; ~ rate n mortalidad f.

debar [dɪˈbɑː*] vt (*exclude*) excluir.

debase [dɪˈbeɪs] vt degradar.

debate [dɪˈbeɪt] n debate m // vt discutir.

debauchery [dɪˈbɔːtʃərɪ] n libertinaje m.

debit ['debɪt] n debe m // vt: to ~ a sum to sb or to sb's account cargar una suma en cuenta a alguien.

debris ['debrɪ] n escombros mpl.

debt [det] n deuda; to be in ~ tener deudas; ~or n deudor/a m/f.

début ['deɪbjuː] n presentación f.

decade ['dekeɪd] n decenio.

decadence ['dekədəns] n decadencia.

decay [dɪˈkeɪ] n decadencia; (*of building*) desmoronamiento; (*fig*) deterioro; (*rotting*) pudrición f; (*of tooth*) caries f // vi (*rot*) pudrirse; (*fig*) decaer.

deceased [dɪˈsiːst] a difunto.

deceit [dɪˈsiːt] n engaño; ~ful a engañoso.

deceive [dɪˈsiːv] vt engañar.

decelerate [diːˈseləreɪt] vt moderar la marcha de // vi decelerar.

December [dɪˈsembə*] n diciembre.

decency ['diːsənsɪ] n decencia.

decent ['diːsənt] a (*proper*) decente; (*person*) amable, bueno.

decentralize [diːˈsentrəlaɪz] vt descentralizar.

deception [dɪˈsepʃən] n engaño;

deceptive [-tɪv] a engañoso.

decibel ['desɪbel] n decibel(io) m.

decide [dɪˈsaɪd] vt (*person*) decidir; (*question, argument*) resolver // vi decidir; **to** ~ **on sth** decidir por algo; ~d a (*resolute*) decidido; (*clear, definite*) indudable; ~dly [-dlɪ] ad decididamente.

deciduous [dɪˈsɪdjuəs] a de hoja caduca.

decimal ['desɪməl] a decimal // n decimal f; ~ **point** n coma de decimales.

decimate ['desɪmeɪt] vt diezmar.

decipher [dɪˈsaɪfə*] vt descifrar.

decision [dɪˈsɪʒən] n decisión f.

decisive [dɪˈsaɪsɪv] a decisivo; (*conclusive*) terminante; (*manner*) tajante.

deck [dek] n (NAUT) cubierta; (*of bus*) piso; (*of cards*) baraja; ~**chair** n tumbona, hamaca.

declaration [dekləˈreɪʃən] n declaración f; **declare** [dɪˈklɛə*] vt (*gen*) declarar.

decline [dɪˈklaɪn] n decaimiento, decadencia; (*lessening*) disminución f // vt rehusar // vi decaer; disminuir; (*fall*) bajar.

declutch ['diːˈklʌtʃ] vi desembragar.

decode [diːˈkəud] vt descifrar.

decompose [diːkəmˈpəuz] vi descomponerse; **decomposition** [diːkɔmpəˈzɪʃən] n descomposición f.

decontaminate [diːkənˈtæmɪneɪt] vt descontaminar.

décor ['deɪkɔː*] n decoración f; (THEATRE) decorado.

decorate ['dekəreɪt] vt adornar, decorar; (*paint*) pintar; (*paper*) empapelar; **decoration** [-ˈreɪʃən] n adorno; (*act*) decoración f; (*medal*) condecoración f; **decorator** n (*painter*) pintor m.

decoy ['diːkɔɪ] n señuelo.

decrease ['diːkriːs] n disminución f // [diːˈkriːs] vt disminuir, reducir // vi reducirse.

decree [dɪˈkriː] n decreto; ~ **nisi** n

orden f provisional de divorcio.
decrepit [dɪ'krepɪt] a decrépito.
dedicate ['dedɪkeɪt] vt dedicar; **dedication** [-'keɪʃən] n (devotion) dedicación f; (in book) dedicatoria.
deduce [dɪ'djuːs] vt deducir.
deduct [dɪ'dʌkt] vt restar; (from wage etc) descontar; **~ion** [dɪ'dʌkʃən] n descuento; (conclusion) deducción f, conclusión f.
deed [diːd] n hecho, acto; (feat) hazaña; (LAW) escritura.
deem [diːm] vt juzgar.
deep [diːp] a (gen) profundo; (voice) bajo; (breath) profundo, a pleno pulmón; (person) insondable // ad: **the spectators stood 20** — los espectadores se formaron de 20 en fondo, to be 4 metres ~ tener 4 metros de profundo; **~en** vt ahondar, profundizar // vi (darkness) intensificarse; **~freeze** n congelador; **~fry** vt freír en aceite abundante; **~sea diving** n buceo de altura; **~seated** a (beliefs) (profundamente) arraigado; **~set** a (eyes) hundido.
deer [dɪə*] n, pl inv ciervo; **~skin** n gamuza, piel f de ciervo.
deface [dɪ'feɪs] vt desfigurar, mutilar.
defamation [defə'meɪʃən] n difamación f.
default [dɪ'fɔːlt] vi no pagar; (SPORT) dejar de presentarse // n: **by** — (LAW) en rebeldía; (SPORT) por no presentarse al adversario; **~er** n (in debt) moroso/a.
defeat [dɪ'fiːt] n derrota // vt derrotar, vencer; (fig: efforts) frustrar; **~ist** a, n derrotista m/f.
defect [dɪ'fiːkt] n defecto // vi [dɪ'fɛkt] desertar; **~ive** [dɪ'fɛktɪv] a (gen) defectuoso; (person) anormal.
defence [dɪ'fɛns] n defensa; **~less** a indefenso.
defend [dɪ'fɛnd] vt defender; **~ant** n acusado/a; (in civil case) demandado/a; **~er** n defensor m.
defensive [dɪ'fɛnsɪv] a defensivo;

on the ~ a la defensiva.
defer [dɪ'fɜː*] vt (postpone) aplazar; **to** — **to** diferir a; **~ence** ['defərəns] n deferencia, respeto.
defiance [dɪ'faɪəns] n desafío; **in** — **of** en contra de; **defiant** [-ənt] a (insolent) insolente; (challenging) retador(a).
deficiency [dɪ'fɪʃənsɪ] n (lack) falta; (defect) defecto; **deficient** [-ənt] a (lacking) insuficiente; (incomplete) incompleto; (defective) defectuoso, (mentally) anormal; **deficient in** falto de.
deficit ['defɪsɪt] n déficit m.
defile [dɪ'faɪl] vt manchar, deshonrar.
define [dɪ'faɪn] vt definir.
definite ['defɪnɪt] a (fixed) determinado; (clear, obvious) claro, categórico; **he was** — **about it** no dejó lugar a dudas (sobre ello); **~ly** ad claramente.
definition [defɪ'nɪʃən] n definición f.
definitive [dɪ'fɪnɪtɪv] a definitivo.
deflate [diː'fleɪt] vt (gen) desinflar; (person) quitar los humos a.
deflect [dɪ'flɛkt] vt desviar.
deform [dɪ'fɔːm] vt deformar; **~ed** a deformado; **~ity** n deformación f.
defraud [dɪ'frɔːd] vt estafar; **to** — **sb of sth** estafar algo a uno.
defrost [diː'frɔst] vt (fridge) deshelar, descongelar.
deft [dɛft] a diestro, hábil.
defunct [dɪ'fʌŋkt] a difunto.
defuse [diː'fjuːz] vt quitar el fusible a.
defy [dɪ'faɪ] vt (resist) oponerse resueltamente a; (challenge) desafiar; (order) contravenir.
degenerate [dɪ'dʒenəreɪt] vi degenerar // a [dɪ'dʒenərɪt] degenerado.
degradation [degrə'deɪʃən] n degradación f; **degrading** [dɪ'greɪdɪŋ] a degradante.
degree [dɪ'griː] n grado; (SCOL)

título; ~ **in maths** licencia en matemáticas.
dehydrated [diː'haɪ'dreɪtɪd] a deshidratado; (*milk*) en polvo.
de-ice [diː'aɪs] vt (*windscreen*) deshelar.
deign [deɪn] vi: **to ~ to do** dignarse hacer.
deity ['diːɪtɪ] n deidad f, divinidad f.
dejected [dɪ'dʒɛktɪd] a abatido, desanimado; (*face*) cariacontecido; **dejection** [-ʃən] n abatimiento.
delay [dɪ'leɪ] vt demorar, aplazar; (*person*) entretener; (*trains*) retrasar // vi tardar // n (*gen*) dilación f; (*a ~*) demora, retraso; **without ~** en seguida, sin tardar.
delegate ['dɛlɪgɪt] n delegado/a // vt ['dɛlɪgeɪt] delegar; **delegation** [-'geɪʃən] n delegación f.
delete [dɪ'liːt] vt suprimir, tachar.
deliberate [dɪ'lɪbərɪt] a (*intentional*) intencionado; (*slow*) pausado, lento // vi [dɪ'lɪbəreɪt] deliberar; **~ly** ad (*on purpose*) a propósito; (*slowly*) pausadamente.
delicacy ['dɛlɪkəsɪ] n delicadeza; (*choice food*) golosina.
delicate ['dɛlɪkɪt] a (*gen*) delicado; (*fragile*) frágil; (*skilled*) fino.
delicatessen [dɛlɪkə'tɛsn] n tienda especializada en comida exótica.
delicious [dɪ'lɪʃəs] a delicioso, rico.
delight [dɪ'laɪt] n (*feeling*) placer m, deleite m; (*object*) encanto, delicia // vt encantar, deleitar; **to take ~ in** deleitarse con; **~ful** a encantador(a), delicioso.
delinquency [dɪ'lɪŋkwənsɪ] n delincuencia; **delinquent** [-ənt] a, n delincuente m/f.
delirious [dɪ'lɪrɪəs] a delirante; **delirium** [-ɪəm] n delirio.
deliver [dɪ'lɪvə*] vt (*distribute*) repartir; (*hand over*) entregar; (*message*) comunicar; (*speech*) pronunciar; (*blow*) lanzar, dar; (*MED*): **to be ~ed** dar a luz; **~y** n reparto; entrega; (*distribution*) distribución f; (*of speaker*) modo de

expresarse; (*MED*) parto, alumbramiento; (*saving*) liberación f; **to take ~y of** recibir.
delta ['dɛltə] n delta m.
delude [dɪ'luːd] vt engañar.
deluge ['dɛljuːdʒ] n diluvio // vt inundar.
delusion [dɪ'luːʒən] n ilusión f, engaño.
de luxe [də'lʌks] a de lujo.
delve [dɛlv] vi: **to ~ into** ahondar en.
demand [dɪ'mɑːnd] vt (*gen*) exigir; (*rights*) reclamar // n (*gen*) exigencia; (*claim*) reclamación; (*ECON*) demanda; **to be in ~** ser muy solicitado; **on ~** a solicitud; **~ing** a (*boss*) exigente; (*work*) absorbente.
demarcation [diːmɑː'keɪʃən] n demarcación f.
demean [dɪ'miːn] vt: **to ~ o.s.** rebajarse.
demeanour [dɪ'miːnə*] n porte m, conducta.
demented [dɪ'mɛntɪd] a demente.
demister [diː'mɪstə*] n (*AUT*) des(s)fumador m de vapores.
democracy [dɪ'mɒkrəsɪ] n democracia; **democrat** ['dɛməkræt] n demócrata m/f; **democratic** [dɛmə'krætɪk] a democrático.
demolish [dɪ'mɒlɪʃ] vt derribar, demoler; **demolition** [dɛmə'lɪʃən] n derribo, demolición f.
demonstrate ['dɛmənstreɪt] vt demostrar // vi manifestarse; **demonstration** [-'streɪʃən] n (*POL*) manifestación f; (*proof*) prueba, demostración f; **demonstrator** n (*POL*) manifestante m/f.
demoralize [dɪ'mɒrəlaɪz] vt desmoralizar.
demote [dɪ'məut] vt degradar.
demure [dɪ'mjuə*] a recatado.
den [dɛn] n (*of animal*) guarida; (*study*) estudio.
denial [dɪ'naɪəl] n (*refusal*) negativa; (*of report etc*) desmentimiento; **self-~** abnegación f.

denim ['dɛnɪm] n dril m; ~s npl vaqueros mpl.

Denmark ['dɛnmɑːk] n Dinamarca.

denomination [dɪnɒmɪ'neɪʃən] n valor m; (REL) confesión f.

denominator [dɪ'nɒmɪneɪtə*] n denominador m.

denote [dɪ'nəut] vt indicar, significar.

denounce [dɪ'nauns] vt denunciar.

dense [dɛns] a (thick) espeso; (: foliage etc) tupido; (stupid) torpe, duro de mollera; ~ly ad: ~ly populated con gran densidad de población.

density ['dɛnsɪtɪ] n densidad f.

dent [dɛnt] n abolladura // vt (also: make a ~ in) abollar.

dental ['dɛntl] a dental; ~ surgeon n odontólogo.

dentist ['dɛntɪst] n dentista m/f; ~ry n odontología.

dentures ['dɛntʃəz] npl dentadura sg (postiza).

deny [dɪ'naɪ] vt (gen) negar; (charge) rechazar; (report) desmentir; to ~ o.s. privarse (de).

deodorant [diː'əudərənt] n desodorante m.

depart [dɪ'pɑːt] vi irse, marcharse; (train) salir; to ~ from (fig. differ from) apartarse de.

department [dɪ'pɑːtmənt] n (COMM) sección f; (SCOL) ramo; (POL) ministerio; ~ store n gran almacén m.

departure [dɪ'pɑːtʃə*] n partida, ida; (of train) salida; a new ~ un nuevo rumbo.

depend [dɪ'pɛnd] vi: to ~ on depender de; (rely on) contar con; it ~s depende, según; ~able a (person) formal, serio; (car etc) seguro; ~ant, ~ent n dependiente m/f.

depict [dɪ'pɪkt] vt (in picture) pintar; (describe) representar.

depleted [dɪ'pliːtɪd] a reducido.

deplorable [dɪ'plɔːrəbl] a lamentable, deplorable; **deplore** [dɪ'plɔː*] vt lamentar, deplorar.

deploy [dɪ'plɔɪ] vt desplegar.

depopulation ['diːpɒpju'leɪʃən] n despoblación f.

deport [dɪ'pɔːt] vt deportar; ~ation [-'teɪʃən] n deportación f; ~ment n comportamiento.

depose [dɪ'pəuz] vt deponer.

deposit [dɪ'pɒzɪt] n (gen) depósito; (CHEM) sedimento; (of ore, oil) yacimiento // vt (gen) depositar; ~ account n cuenta de ahorros; ~or n cuentacorrentista m/f.

depot ['dɛpəu] n (storehouse) depósito; (for vehicles) parque m.

depraved [dɪ'preɪvd] a depravado, vicioso; **depravity** [-'prævɪtɪ] n depravación f, vicio.

depreciate [dɪ'priːʃɪeɪt] vi depreciarse, perder valor; **depreciation** ['ɪʃ'eɪʃən] n depreciación f.

depress [dɪ'prɛs] vt deprimir; (press down) presionar; ~ed a deprimido; ~ing a deprimente; ~ion [dɪ'prɛʃən] n depresión f.

deprivation [dɛprɪ'veɪʃən] n privación f; (loss) pérdida.

deprive [dɪ'praɪv] vt: to ~ sb of privar a alguien de; ~d a pobre.

depth [dɛpθ] n (gen) profundidad f; (of room etc) fondo; in the ~s of en lo más hondo de.

deputation [dɛpju'teɪʃən] n delegación f.

deputize ['dɛpjutaɪz] vi: to ~ for sb sustituir por uno.

deputy ['dɛpjutɪ] a: ~ head subdirector/a m/f sustituto/a, suplente m; (POL) diputado; (agent) representante m.

derail [dɪ'reɪl] vt: to be ~ed descarrilarse; ~ment n descarrilamiento.

deranged [dɪ'reɪndʒd] a (person) vuelto loco, trastornado (mentalmente).

derelict ['dɛrɪlɪkt] a abandonado.

deride [dɪ'raɪd] vt ridiculizar,

mofarse de; **derision** [-'rɪʒən] n irrisión f, mofas fpl.

derivative [dɪ'rɪvətɪv] n derivado // a derivado; (work) poco original.

derive [dɪ'raɪv] vt derivar // vi: to ~ **from** derivarse de.

dermatitis [dɔ:mə'taɪtɪs] n dermatitis f; **dermatology** [-'tɔlədʒɪ] n dermatología.

derogatory [dɪ'rɔgətərɪ] a despectivo.

derrick ['derɪk] n torre f de perforación.

descend [dɪ'sɛnd] vt, vi descender, bajar; **to** ~ **from** descender de; ~**ant** n descendiente m/f.

descent [dɪ'sɛnt] n descenso; (GEO) pendiente m, declive m; (origin) descendencia.

describe [dɪs'kraɪb] vt describir; **description** [-'krɪpʃən] n descripción f; (sort) clase f, género; **descriptive** [-'krɪptɪv] a descriptivo.

desecrate ['desɪkreɪt] vt profanar.

desert ['dezət] n desierto // (vb: [dɪ'zɔ:t]) vt abandonar, desamparar // vi (MIL) desertar; ~**er** n desertor m; ~**ion** [dɪ'zɔ:ʃən] n deserción f.

deserve [dɪ'zɔ:v] vt merecer, ser digno de; **deserving** a (person) digno; (action, cause) meritorio.

design [dɪ'zaɪn] n (sketch) bosquejo; (layout, shape) diseño; (pattern) dibujo; (intention) propósito, intención f // vt (gen) diseñar; (plan) proyectar.

designate ['dezɪgneɪt] vt (point to) señalar; (appoint) nombrar; (destine) designar // a ['dezɪgnɪt] designado; **designation** [-'neɪʃən] n (appointment) nombramiento; (name) denominación f.

designer [dɪ'zaɪnə*] n (ART) dibujante m; (TECH) diseñador m; (fashion ~) modista m/f.

desirable [dɪ'zaɪərəbl] a (proper) deseable; (attractive) atractivo.

desire [dɪ'zaɪə*] n deseo // vt desear.

desk [desk] n (in office) escritorio;

(for pupil) pupitre m; (in hotel, at airport) recepción f.

desolate ['desəlɪt] a (place) desierto; (person) afligido; **desolation** [-'leɪʃən] n (of place) desolación f; (of person) aflicción f.

despair [dɪs'peə*] n desesperación f // vi: **to** ~ **of** desesperarse de.

despatch [dɪs'pætʃ] n, vt = **dispatch**.

desperate ['despərɪt] a desesperado; (fugitive) peligroso; ~**ly** ad desesperadamente; (very) terriblemente, gravemente.

desperation [despə'reɪʃən] n desesperación f; **in** ~ desesperado.

despicable [dɪs'pɪkəbl] a vil, despreciable.

despise [dɪs'paɪz] vt despreciar.

despite [dɪs'paɪt] prep a pesar de, pese a.

despondent [dɪs'pɔndənt] a deprimido, abatido.

dessert [dɪ'zɔ:t] n postre m; ~**spoon** n cuchara de (postre).

destination [destɪ'neɪʃən] n destino.

destiny ['destɪnɪ] n destino.

destitute ['destɪtju:t] a desamparado, indigente.

destroy [dɪs'trɔɪ] vt (gen) destruir; (finish) acabar con; ~**er** n (NAUT) destructor m.

destruction [dɪs'trʌkʃən] n destrucción f; (fig) ruina; **destructive** [-tɪv] a destructivo, destructor(a).

detach [dɪ'tætʃ] vt separar; (unstick) despegar; ~**able** a separable; (TECH) desmontable; ~**ed** a (attitude) objetivo, imparcial; (house) independiente, solo; ~**ment** n (gen) separación f; (MIL) destacamento; (fig) objetividad f, imparcialidad f.

detail ['di:teɪl] n detalle m // vt (gen) detallar; (MIL) destacar; **in** ~ en detalle; ~**ed** a detallado.

detain [dɪ'teɪn] vt retener; (in captivity) detener.

detect [dɪ'tekt] vt (gen) descubrir;

(MED, POLICE) identificar; _(MIL, RADAR, TECH)_ detectar; ~**ion** [dɪ'tɛkʃən] n descubrimiento; identificación f; ~**ive** _n_ detective m; ~**ive story** _n_ novela policíaca; ~ **or** n detector m.

détente [deɪ'tɑːnt] n détente f.

detention [dɪ'tenʃən] n detención f, arresto.

deter [dɪ'tɜː*] vt _(discourage)_ desalentar; _(dissuade)_ disuadir; _(prevent)_ impedir.

detergent [dɪ'tɜːdʒənt] n detergente.

deteriorate [dɪ'tɪərɪəreɪt] vi deteriorarse; **deterioration** [-'reɪʃən] n deterioro.

determination [dɪtɜːmɪ'neɪʃən] n _(gen)_ determinación f; _(resolve)_ resolución f.

determine [dɪ'tɜːmɪn] vt _(gen)_ determinar; _(limits etc)_ definir; _(dispute)_ resolver; ~**d** a _(person)_ resuelto.

deterrent [dɪ'terənt] n fuerza de disuasión.

detest [dɪ'test] vt aborrecer; ~**able** a aborrecible.

detonate [dɪ'təuneɪt] vi estallar // vt hacer detonar; **detonator** n detonador m, fulminante m.

detour [dɪ'tuə*] n rodeo.

detract [dɪ'trækt] vt: to ~ from quitar mérito a, desvirtuar.

detriment [dɪ'detrɪmənt] n: to the ~ of en perjuicio de; ~**al** a [detrɪ'mentl] a perjudicial _(to a)._

devaluation [dɪvæljʊ'eɪʃən] n devaluación f; **devalue** [-'væljuː] vt devaluar.

devastate ['devəsteɪt] vt devastar; he was ~**d by the news** las noticias le dejaron desolado; **devastating** a devastador(a); _(fig)_ arrollador(a).

develop [dɪ'veləp] vt _(gen)_ desarrollar; _(PHOT)_ revelar; _(disease)_ coger; _(engine trouble)_ empezar a tener // vi desarrollarse; _(advance)_ progresar; _(appear)_ aparecer; ~**ing country** país m en

desarrollo; ~**ment** n desarrollo; _(advance)_ progreso; _(of affair, case)_ desenvolvimiento; _(of land)_ urbanización f.

deviate ['diːvɪeɪt] vi desviarse; **deviation** [-'eɪʃən] n desviación f.

device [dɪ'vaɪs] n _(scheme)_ estratagema f, recurso; _(apparatus)_ aparato, mecanismo.

devil ['devl] n diablo, demonio, ~**ish** a diabólico.

devious ['diːvɪəs] a intricado, enrevesado; _(person)_ taimado.

devise [dɪ'vaɪz] vt idear, inventar.

devoid [dɪ'vɔɪd] a: ~ **of** desprovisto de.

devote [dɪ'vəut] vt: to ~ **sth to** dedicar algo a; ~**d** a _(loyal)_ leal, fiel; **the book is** ~**d to politics** el libro trata de la política; **devotee** [devəu'tiː] n devoto/a.

devotion [dɪ'vəuʃən] n dedicación f; _(REL)_ devoción f.

devour [dɪ'vauə*] vt devorar.

devout [dɪ'vaut] a devoto.

dew [djuː] n rocío.

dexterity [dɛks'terɪtɪ] n destreza.

diabetes [daɪə'biːtiːz] n diabetes f; **diabetic** ['betɪk] a, n diabético/a.

diagnose [daɪəg'nəuz] vt diagnosticar; **diagnosis** [-'nəusɪs] pl -**ses** [-'nəusiːz] n diagnóstico.

diagonal [daɪ'ægənl] a diagonal // n diagonal f.

diagram ['daɪəgræm] n diagrama m, esquema m.

dial ['daɪəl] n esfera, cuadrante m // vt _(number)_ marcar; ~**ling tone** n tono de marcar.

dialect ['daɪəlekt] n dialecto.

dialogue ['daɪəlɒg] n diálogo.

diameter [daɪ'æmɪtə*] n diámetro.

diamond ['daɪəmənd] n diamante m; ~**s** npl _(CARDS)_ oros mpl.

diaper ['daɪəpə*] n _(US)_ pañal m.

diaphragm ['daɪəfræm] n diafragma m.

diarrhoea, diarrhea _(US)_ [daɪə'rɪə] n diarrea.

diary ['daɪərɪ] n _(daily account)_

diario; (*book*) agenda *m*.

dice [daɪs] *n*, *pl inv* dados *mpl* // (*CULIN*) cortar en cuadritos.

dictate [dɪk'teɪt] *vt* dictar; **~s** ['dɪkteɪts] *npl* dictados *mpl*; **dictation** [-'teɪʃən] *n* dictado *m*.

dictator [dɪk'teɪtə*] *n* dictador *m*; **~ship** *n* dictadura *f*.

diction ['dɪkʃən] *n* dicción *f*.

dictionary ['dɪkʃənrɪ] *n* diccionario.

did [dɪd] *pt of* do.

die [daɪ] *vi* morir; **to ~ away** *vi* (*sound, light*) extinguirse lentamente; **to ~ down** *vi* (*gen*) apagarse; (*wind*) amainar; **to ~ out** *vi* desaparecer, extinguirse.

diesel ['diːzəl]: **~ engine** *n* motor *m* Diesel; **~ (oil)** *n* gas-oil *m*.

diet ['daɪət] *n* dieta; (*restricted food*) régimen *m* // *vi* (*also*: **be on a ~**) estar a dieta, hacer régimen.

differ ['dɪfə*] *vi* (*be different*) ser distinto, diferenciarse; (*disagree*) discrepar; **~ence** *n* diferencia; (*quarrel*) desacuerdo; **~ent** *a* diferente, distinto; **~entiate** [-'renʃɪeɪt] *vt* distinguir // *vi* diferenciarse; **to ~entiate between** distinguir entre; **~ently** *ad* de otro modo, en forma distinta.

difficult ['dɪfɪkəlt] *a* difícil; **~y** *n* dificultad *f*.

diffidence ['dɪfɪdəns] *n* timidez *f*; **diffident** [-ənt] *a* tímido.

diffuse [dɪ'fjuːs] *a* difuso // *vt* [dɪ'fjuːz] difundir.

dig [dɪg], *pt, pp* dug *vt* (*hole*) cavar; (*garden*) cultivar; (*coal*) extraer; (*nails etc*) hincar // *n* (*prod*) empujón *m*; (*archaeological*) excavación *f*; (*remark*) indirecta; **to ~ in** *vi* atrincherarse; **to ~ into** *vt* (*savings*) consumir; **to ~ out** *vt* (*hole*) excavar; (*fig*) sacar; **to ~ up** *vt* desenterrar; (*plant*) desarraigar.

digest [daɪ'dʒest] *vt* (*food*) digerir; (*facts*) asimilar // *n* ['daɪdʒest] resumen *m*; **~ion** [dɪ'dʒestʃən] *n* digestión *f*.

digital ['dɪdʒɪtəl] *a* digital.

dignified ['dɪgnɪfaɪd] *a* grave, solemne; (*action*) decoroso.

dignity ['dɪgnɪtɪ] *n* dignidad *f*.

digress [daɪ'gres] *vi*: **to ~ from** apartarse de; **~ion** [daɪ'greʃən] *n* digresión *f*.

digs [dɪgz] *npl* (*Brit: col*) pensión *f*, alojamiento.

dilapidated [dɪ'læpɪdeɪtɪd] *a* desmoronado, ruinoso.

dilate [daɪ'leɪt] *vt* dilatar // *vi* dilatarse.

dilemma [daɪ'lemə] *n* dilema *m*.

diligent ['dɪlɪdʒənt] *a* diligente.

dilute [daɪ'luːt] *vt* diluir // *a* diluido.

dim [dɪm] *a* (*light*) débil; (*sight*) turbio; (*outline*) indistinto; (*stupid*) lerdo; (*room*) oscuro // *vt* (*light*) bajar; (*AUT*) poner a media luz.

dime [daɪm] *n* (*US*) moneda de diez centavos.

dimension [dɪ'menʃən] *n* dimensión *f*.

diminish [dɪ'mɪnɪʃ] *vi* disminuirse.

diminutive [dɪ'mɪnjutɪv] *a* diminuto // *n* (*LING*) diminutivo.

dimly ['dɪmlɪ] *ad* débilmente; (*not clearly*) indistintamente.

dimple ['dɪmpl] *n* hoyuelo.

din [dɪn] *n* estruendo, estrépito.

dine [daɪn] *vi* cenar; **diner** *n* (*person*) comensal *m/f*; (*RAIL*) = **dining car**.

dinghy ['dɪŋgɪ] *n* bote *m*; **rubber ~** lancha (neumática).

dingy ['dɪndʒɪ] *a* (*room*) sombrío; (*dirty*) sucio; (*dull*) deslucido.

dining ['daɪnɪŋ]: **~ car** *n* coche-comedor *m*; **~ room** *n* comedor *m*.

dinner ['dɪnə*] *n* (*evening meal*) cena; (*lunch*) comida; (*public*) cena, banquete *m*; **~ jacket** *n* smoking *m*; **~ party** *n* cena; **~ time** *n* hora de cenar o comer.

diocese ['daɪəsɪs] *n* diócesis *f*.

dip [dɪp] *n* (*slope*) pendiente *m*; (*in sea*) baño // *vt* (*in water*) mojar; (*ladle etc*) meter; (*AUT: lights*) poner a media luz // vi inclinarse hacia abajo.

diphtheria [dɪfˈθɪərɪə] n difteria.

diploma [dɪˈpləʊmə] n diploma m.

diplomacy [dɪˈpləʊməsɪ] n diplomacia; **diplomat** [ˈdɪpləmæt] n diplomático; **diplomatic** [dɪpləˈmætɪk] a diplomático.

dipstick [ˈdɪpstɪk] n (AUT) varilla graduada, indicador m de nivel (del aceite).

dire [daɪə*] a calamitoso.

direct [daɪˈrɛkt] a (gen) directo //, vt dirigir; **can you ~ me to..?** ¿puede indicarme dónde está..?

direction [dɪˈrɛkʃən] n dirección f; **~s** npl (advice) órdenes fpl, instrucciones fpl; **~s for use** modo de empleo.

directly [dɪˈrɛktlɪ] ad (in straight line) directamente; (at once) en seguida.

director [dɪˈrɛktə*] n director m; **managing ~** director gerente.

directory [dɪˈrɛktərɪ] n (TEL) guía (telefónica).

dirt [dɜːt] n suciedad f; **~-cheap** a tirado, muy barato; **~-y** a sucio; (joke) verde // vt ensuciar; (stain) manchar; **~y trick** n juego sucio.

disability [dɪsəˈbɪlɪtɪ] n incapacidad f; **disabled** [dɪsˈeɪbld] a disminuido, minusválido.

disadvantage [dɪsədˈvɑːntɪdʒ] n desventaja, inconveniente m.

disagree [dɪsəˈɡriː] vi (differ) discrepar; (be against, think otherwise) **to ~ (with)** no estar de acuerdo (con); **~able** a desagradable; **~ment** n (gen) desacuerdo; (quarrel) riña.

disallow [dɪsəˈlaʊ] vt (goal) anular.

disappear [dɪsəˈpɪə*] vi desaparecer; **~ance** n desaparición f.

disappoint [dɪsəˈpɔɪnt] vt decepcionar; (hopes) defraudar; **~ing** a decepcionante; **~ment** n decepción f.

disapproval [dɪsəˈpruːvəl] n desaprobación f.

disapprove [dɪsəˈpruːv] vi: **to ~ of** desaprobar.

disarm [dɪsˈɑːm] vt desarmar; **~ament** n desarme m; **~ing** a encantador(a).

disaster [dɪˈzɑːstə*] n desastre m; **disastrous** a desastroso.

disband [dɪsˈbænd] vt disolver // vi desbandarse.

disbelief [dɪsbəˈliːf] n incredulidad f.

disc [dɪsk] n disco.

discard [dɪsˈkɑːd] vt (old things) tirar; (fig) descartar.

discern [dɪˈsɜːn] vt percibir, discernir; **~ing** a perspicaz.

discharge [dɪsˈtʃɑːdʒ] vt (duties) cumplir, desempeñar; (ship etc) descargar; (patient) dar de alta; (employee) despedir; (soldier) licenciar; (defendant) poner en libertad // n [ˈdɪstʃɑːdʒ] (ELEC) descarga; (dismissal) despedida; (of duty) desempeño; (of debt) pago, descargo.

disciple [dɪˈsaɪpl] n discípulo.

discipline [ˈdɪsɪplɪn] n disciplina // vt disciplinar.

disclaim [dɪsˈkleɪm] vt negar.

disclose [dɪsˈkləʊz] vt revelar; **disclosure** [-ˈkləʊʒə*] n revelación f.

disco [ˈdɪskəʊ] n abbr of discothèque.

discoloured [dɪsˈkʌləd] a descolorado.

discomfort [dɪsˈkʌmfət] n incomodidad f; (unease) inquietud f; (physical) malestar m.

disconcert [dɪskənˈsɜːt] vt desconcertar.

disconnect [dɪskəˈnekt] vt (gen) separar; (ELEC etc) desconectar.

discontent [dɪskənˈtent] n descontento; **~ed** a descontento.

discontinue [dɪskənˈtɪnjuː] vt interrumpir; (payments) suspender.

discord [ˈdɪskɔːd] n discordia; (MUS)

disonancia; ~ant [dɪsˈkɔːdənt] *a* disonante.

discothèque [ˈdɪskəʊtɛk] *n* discoteca.

discount [ˈdɪskaunt] *n* descuento // *vt* [dɪsˈkaunt] descontar.

discourage [dɪsˈkʌrɪdʒ] *vt* desalentar; *(oppose)* oponerse a; **discouraging** *a* desalentador(a).

discourteous [dɪsˈkɔːtɪəs] *a* descortés.

discover [dɪsˈkʌvə*] *vt* descubrir; ~y *n* descubrimiento.

discredit [dɪsˈkrɛdɪt] *vt* desacreditar.

discreet [dɪsˈkriːt] *a (tactful)* discreto; *(careful)* circunspecto, prudente; ~ly *ad* discretamente.

discrepancy [dɪsˈkrɛpənsɪ] *n (difference)* diferencia; *(disagreement)* discrepancia.

discretion [dɪsˈkrɛʃən] *n (tact)* discreción *f*; *(care)* prudencia, circunspección *f*.

discriminate [dɪsˈkrɪmɪneɪt] *vi*: to ~ between distinguir entre; to ~ against discriminar contra; **discriminating** *a* perspicaz; **discrimination** [-ˈneɪʃən] *n (discernment)* perspicacia; *(bias)* discriminación *f*.

discuss [dɪsˈkʌs] *vt (gen)* discutir; *(a theme)* tratar; ~ion [dɪsˈkʌʃən] *n* discusión *f*.

disdain [dɪsˈdeɪn] *n* desdén *m* // *vt* desdeñar.

disease [dɪˈziːz] *n* enfermedad *f*.

disembark [dɪsɪmˈbɑːk] *vt, vi* desembarcar.

disengage [dɪsɪnˈgeɪdʒ] *vt* soltar; *(clutch)* desembragar.

disentangle [dɪsɪnˈtæŋgl] *vt* desenredar.

disfigure [dɪsˈfɪgə*] *vt* desfigurar.

disgrace [dɪsˈgreɪs] *n* ignominia; *(downfall)* caída; *(shame)* vergüenza, escándalo // *vt* deshonrar; ~ful *a* vergonzoso; *(behaviour)* escandaloso.

disgruntled [dɪsˈgrʌntld] *a* disgustado, malhumorado.

disguise [dɪsˈgaɪz] *n* disfraz *m* // *vt* disfrazar; **in** ~ disfrazado.

disgust [dɪsˈgʌst] *n* repugnancia // *vt* repugnar, dar asco a; ~**ing** *a* repugnante, asqueroso.

dish [dɪʃ] *n (gen)* plato; **to do** o **wash the** ~**es** fregar los platos; **to** ~ **up** *vt* servir; **to** ~ **out** *vt* repartir; ~**cloth** *n* paño de cocina, bayeta.

dishearten [dɪsˈhɑːtn] *vt* desalentar.

dishevelled [dɪˈʃevəld] *a* despeinado, desmelenado.

dishonest [dɪsˈɔnɪst] *a (person)* poco honrado, tramposo; *(means)* fraudulento; ~y *n* falta de honradez.

dishonour [dɪsˈɔnə*] *n* deshonra; ~**able** *a* deshonroso.

dishwasher [ˈdɪʃwɔʃə*] *n* lavaplatos *m inv*; *(person)* friegaplatos *m/f inv*.

disillusion [dɪsɪˈluːʒən] *vt* desilusionar.

disinfect [dɪsɪnˈfɛkt] *vt* desinfectar; ~**ant** *n* desinfectante *m*.

disintegrate [dɪsˈɪntɪgreɪt] *vi* disgregarse, desintegrarse.

disinterested [dɪsˈɪntrəstɪd] *a* desinteresado.

disjointed [dɪsˈdʒɔɪntɪd] *a* inconexo.

disk [dɪsk] *n* = **disc.**

dislike [dɪsˈlaɪk] *n* antipatía, aversión *f* // *vt* tener antipatía a.

dislocate [ˈdɪsləkeɪt] *vt* dislocar.

dislodge [dɪsˈlɔdʒ] *vt* sacar; *(enemy)* desalojar.

disloyal [dɪsˈlɔɪəl] *a* desleal.

dismal [ˈdɪzml] *a (dark)* sombrío; *(depressing)* triste; *(depressed)* abatido; *(very bad)* fatal.

dismantle [dɪsˈmæntl] *vt* desmontar, desarmar.

dismay [dɪsˈmeɪ] *n* consternación *f* // *vt* consternar.

dismiss [dɪsˈmɪs] *vt (worker)* despedir; *(official)* destituir; *(idea, LAW)* rechazar; *(possibility)* descartar // vi (MIL) romper filas; ~**al** n despedida; destitución f.

dismount [dis'maunt] vi apearse.

disobedience [diso'bi:dions] n desobediencia; **disobedient** [-ənt] a desobediente.

disobey [diso'bei] vt desobedecer.

disorder [dis'ɔ:də*] n desorden m; (rioting) disturbio; (MED) trastorno; (disease) enfermedad f; ~**ly** a (untidy) desordenado; (meeting) alborotado; (conduct) escandaloso.

disorganized [dis'ɔ:gənaizd] a desorganizado.

disorientated [dis'ɔ:rientitd] a desorientado.

disown [dis'əun] vt desconocer.

disparaging [dis'pæridʒiŋ] a despreciativo.

disparity [dis'pæriti] n disparidad f.

dispatch [dis'pætʃ] vt enviar; (kill) despachar // n (sending) envío; (speed) prontitud f, (PRESS) informe m; (MIL) parte m.

dispel [dis'pel] vt disipar, dispersar.

dispensary [dis'pensəri] n dispensario, farmacia.

dispense [dis'pens] vt dispensar, repartir; **to ~ with** vt fus prescindir de; **dispenser** n (container) distribuidor m automático; **dispensing chemist** n farmacéutico.

dispersal [dis'pə:sl] n dispersión f; **disperse** [-'pə:s] vt dispersar // vi dispersarse.

displace [dis'pleis] vt (shift) sacar de su sitio; ~**d** (POL) desplazado/a; ~**ment** n cambio de sitio.

display [dis'plei] n (exhibition) exposición f; (MIL) alarde m; (of feeling) manifestación f; (pej) aparato, pompa // vt exponer; manifestar; (ostentatiously) lucir.

displease [dis'pli:z] vt (offend) ofender; (annoy) enojar, enfadar; (be unpleasant to) desagradar; ~**d with** disgustado con; **displeasure** [-'pleʒə*] n disgusto

disposable [dis'pəuzəbl] a para (usar y) tirar.

disposal [dis'pəuzl] n (sale) venta; (of house) traspaso; (arrangement) colocación f; (of rubbish) destrucción f; **at one's ~** a disposición de uno.

dispose [dis'pəuz] vt: **to ~ of** (time, money) disponer de; (unwanted goods) deshacerse de; (throw away) tirar; ~**d a**: **~d to do** dispuesto a hacer; **disposition** [-'ziʃən] n disposición f.

disproportionate [dispra'pɔ:ʃənət] a desproporcionado.

disprove [dis'pru:v] vt refutar.

dispute [dis'pju:t] n disputa; (verbal) discusión f; (also: industrial ~) conflicto (laboral) // vt (argue) disputar; (question) cuestionar.

disqualification [diskwɔlifi'keiʃən] n inhabilitación f; (SPORT, from driving) descalificación f.

disqualify [dis'kwɔlifai] vt (SPORT) descalificar; **to ~ sb for sth/from doing sth** inhabilitar a alguien para algo/hacer algo.

disregard [disri'ga:d] vt desatender; (ignore) no hacer caso de.

disrepair [disri'peə*] n: **to fall into ~** desmoronarse.

disreputable [dis'repjutəbl] a (person) de mala fama; (behaviour) vergonzoso.

disrespectful [disri'spektful] a irrespetuoso.

disrupt [dis'rʌpt] vt (plans) desbaratar; (conversation) interrumpir; ~**ion** [-'rʌpʃən] n trastorno; desbaratamiento, interrupción f.

dissatisfaction [dissætis'fækʃən] n disgusto, descontento; **dissatisfied** [-'sætisfaid] a insatisfecho.

dissect [di'sekt] vt disecar.

dissent [di'sent] n disensión f.

disservice [dis'sə:vis] n: **to do sb a ~** perjudicar a alguien.

dissident ['disidnt] a, n disidente m/f.

dissipate ['dɪsɪpeɪt] vt disipar; (waste) desperdiciar.

dissociate [dɪ'səʊʃɪeɪt] vt disociar.

dissolute ['dɪsəluːt] a disoluto.

dissolve [dɪ'zɒlv] vt disolver // vi disolverse.

dissuade [dɪ'sweɪd] vt: to ~ sb (from) disuadir a alguien (de).

distance ['dɪstns] n distancia; in the ~ a lo lejos.

distant ['dɪstnt] a lejano; (manner) reservado, frío.

distaste [dɪs'teɪst] n repugnancia; ~ful a repugnante, desagradable.

distil [dɪs'tɪl] vt destilar; ~lery n destilería.

distinct [dɪs'tɪŋkt] a (different) distinto; (clear) claro; (unmistakable) inequívoco; as ~ from a diferencia de; ~ion [dɪs'tɪŋkʃən] n distinción f; (in exam) sobresaliente m; ~ive a distintivo; ~ly ad claramente.

distinguish [dɪs'tɪŋgwɪʃ] vt distinguir; ~ed a (eminent) distinguido; ~ing a (feature) distintivo.

distort [dɪs'tɔːt] vt torcer, retorcer; ~ion [dɪs'tɔːʃən] n deformación f; (of sound) distorsión f.

distract [dɪs'trækt] vt distraer; (attention) apartar; (bewilder) aturdir; ~ed a distraído; ~ion [dɪs'trækʃən] n distracción f; (confusion) aturdimiento; (amusement) diversión f.

distraught [dɪs'trɔːt] a turbado, enloquecido.

distress [dɪs'tres] n (anguish) angustia; (misfortune) desgracia; (want) miseria; (pain) dolor m; (danger) peligro // vt (cause anguish) apenar, afligir; (pain) doler; ~ing a doloroso; ~ signal n señal f de socorro.

distribute [dɪs'trɪbjuːt] vt (gen) distribuir; (share out) repartir; **distribution** [-'bjuːʃən] n distribución f, **distributor** n (AUT) distribuidor m; (COMM) distribuidora.

district ['dɪstrɪkt] n (of country) zona, región f; (of town) barrio; (ADMIN) distrito; ~ **attorney** n (US) fiscal m/f; ~ **nurse** n (Brit) enfermera que asiste a barrios.

distrust [dɪs'trʌst] n desconfianza // vt desconfiar de.

disturb [dɪs'tɜːb] vt (gen) perturbar; (bother) molestar; (interrupt) interrumpir; (upset) trastornar; (disorganize) desordenar; ~ance n (gen) perturbación f; (political etc) disturbio; (violence) alboroto; (of mind) trastorno; ~ing a inquietante, perturbador(a).

disuse [dɪs'juːs] n: to fall into ~ caer en desuso.

disused [dɪs'juːzd] a abandonado.

ditch [dɪtʃ] n zanja; (irrigation ~) acequia // vt (col) deshacerse de.

dither ['dɪðə*] vi vacilar.

ditto ['dɪtəu] ad ídem, lo mismo.

divan [dɪ'væn] n diván m.

dive [daɪv] n (from board) salto; (underwater) buceo; (of submarine) sumersión f; (AVIAT) picada // vi saltar; bucear; sumergirse; picar; **diver** n (SPORT) saltador/a m/f; (underwater) buzo.

diverge [daɪ'vɜːdʒ] vi divergir.

diverse [daɪ'vɜːs] a diversos(as), varios(as).

diversify [daɪ'vɜːsɪfaɪ] vt diversificar.

diversion [daɪ'vɜːʃən] n (AUT) desviación f; (distraction, MIL) diversión f.

diversity [daɪ'vɜːsɪti] n diversidad f.

divert [daɪ'vɜːt] vt (turn aside) desviar; (amuse) divertir.

divest [daɪ'vest] vt: to ~ sb of sth despojar a alguien de algo.

divide [dɪ'vaɪd] vt dividir; (separate) separar // vi dividirse; (road) bifurcarse.

dividend ['dɪvɪdend] n dividendo; (fig) beneficio.

divine [dɪ'vaɪn] a divino.

diving ['daɪvɪŋ] n (SPORT) salto;

(*underwater*) buceo; ~ **board** n trampolín m; ~ **suit** n escafandra.
divinity [dɪ'vɪnɪtɪ] n divinidad f; (*SCOL*) teología f.
division [dɪ'vɪʒən] n división f; (*sharing out*) repartimiento m; (*disagreement*) discordia; (*POL*) votación f.
divorce [dɪ'vɔːs] n divorcio // vt divorciarse de; ~**d a** divorciado; **divorcee** [-'siː] n divorciado/a.
divulge [daɪ'vʌldʒ] vt divulgar, revelar.
D.I.Y. a, n abbr of **do-it-yourself**.
dizziness ['dɪzɪnɪs] n vértigo.
dizzy ['dɪzɪ] a (*person*) mareado; (*height*) vertiginoso; **to feel** ~ marearse, estar mareado.
DJ n abbr of **disc jockey**.
do [duː] pt **did**, pp **done** vt, vi (*gen*) hacer; (*speed*) ir a; (*THEATRE*) representar // n (*col*) fiesta; **he didn't laugh so no se rió; she swims better than I** ~ **nada mejor que yo; he laughed, didn't he?** se rió ¿no?; **that will** ~! ¡basta!; **to make do with contentarse con; ~ you agree?** ¿está Usted de acuerdo?; **to** ~ **one's hair** (*comb*) peinarse; (*style*) arreglarse el pelo; **will it** ~? ¿sirve?; ¿conviene?; **to** ~ **well** prosperar, tener éxito; **to** ~ **without** sth prescindir de algo; **to** ~ **away with** vt fus (*kill*) exterminar; (*suppress*) suprimir; **to** ~ **up** vt (*laces*) liar, atar; (*room*) renovar.
docile ['dəʊsaɪl] a dócil.
dock [dɔk] n (*NAUT*) muelle m; (*LAW*) banquillo m (de los acusados); ~**s** npl muelles mpl, puerto // vi (*arrive*) llegar; (*enter* ~) atracar al muelle; (*pay etc*) rebajar; ~**er** n trabajador m portuario, estibador m; ~**yard** n astillero m.
doctor ['dɔktə*] n médico; (*Ph.D. etc*) doctor/a m/f // vt (*fig*) arreglar, falsificar; (*drink etc*) adulterar.
doctrine ['dɔktrɪn] n doctrina f.

document ['dɔkjʊmənt] n documento; ~**ary** [-'mɛntərɪ] a documental // n documental m; ~**ation** [-'teɪʃən] n documentación f.
dodge [dɔdʒ] n (*of body*) regate m; (*fig*) truco // vt (*gen*) evadir; (*blow*) esquivar.
dodgems ['dɔdʒəmz] npl coches mpl de choque.
dog [dɔg] n perro // vt seguir los pasos de; ~ **biscuits** npl galletas fpl de perro; ~ **collar** n collar m de perro; (*fig*) cuello de cura.
dogged ['dɔgɪd] a tenaz, obstinado.
dogma ['dɔgmə] n dogma m; ~**tic** [-'mætɪk] a dogmático.
doings ['duːɪŋz] npl (*events*) sucesos mpl, (*acts*) hechos mpl.
do-it-yourself [duːɪtjɔː'self] n bricolaje m.
doldrums ['dɔldrəmz] npl: **to be in the** ~ (*person*) estar abatido, (*business*) estar encalmado.
dole [dəʊl] n (*Brit*) (*payment*) subsidio de paro; **on the** ~ parado; **to** ~ **out** vt repartir.
doleful ['dəʊlful] a triste, lúgubre.
doll [dɔl] n muñeca; **to** ~ **o.s. up** ataviarse.
dollar ['dɔlə*] n dólar m.
dolphin ['dɔlfɪn] n delfín m.
domain [də'meɪn] n campo, competencia; (*empire*) dominio.
dome [dəʊm] n (*ARCH*) cúpula; (*shape*) bóveda.
domestic [də'mɛstɪk] a (*gen*) doméstico; (*national*) nacional; (*home-loving*) hogareño; (*internal: trade*) interior; (*: strife*) interno; ~**ated** a domesticado; (*home-loving*) casero, hogareño.
dominant ['dɔmɪnənt] a dominante.
dominate ['dɔmɪneɪt] vt dominar; **domination** [-'neɪʃən] n dominación f.
domineering [dɔmɪ'nɪərɪŋ] a dominante.
dominion [də'mɪnɪən] n dominio.
domino ['dɔmɪnəʊ], pl ~**es** n ficha

de dominó; ~es n (game) dominó.
donate [dəʊˈneɪt] vt donar; **donation** [dəʊˈneɪʃən] n donativo.
done [dʌn] pp of do.
donkey [ˈdɒŋkɪ] n burro.
donor [ˈdəʊnə*] n donante m/f.
don't [dəʊnt] = do not.
doom [duːm] n (fate) suerte f; (death) muerte f // vt: to be ~ed to failure ser condenado al fracaso.
door [dɔː*] n puerta; (entry) entrada; **next** ~ en la casa del lado; ~**bell** n timbre m; ~ **handle** n tirador m; (of car) manija; ~ **knocker** n aldaba; ~**man** n (in hotel) portero; ~**mat** n felpudo, estera; ~**step** n peldaño.
dope [dəʊp] n (col: person) imbécil m/f // vt (horse etc) drogar.
dopey [ˈdəʊpɪ] a (dizzy) mareado.
dormant [ˈdɔːmənt] a inactivo; (latent) latente.
dormitory [ˈdɔːmɪtrɪ] n dormitorio.
dormouse [ˈdɔːmaʊs], pl **-mice** [-maɪs] n lirón m.
dosage [ˈdəʊsɪdʒ] n dósis f inv.
dose [dəʊs] n dósis f inv // vt: to ~ o.s. medicinarse.
doss house [ˈdɒs-] n pensión f de mala muerte.
dot [dɒt] n punto; ~**ted with** salpicado de; **on the** ~ en punto.
dote [dəʊt]: to ~ **on** vt fus adorar, idolatrar.
double [ˈdʌbl] a doble // ad (twice): **to cost** ~ costar el doble // n (gen) doble m // vt doblar; (efforts) redoblar // vi doblarse; **at the** ~ corriendo; ~**s** n (TENNIS) juego de dobles; ~ **bass** n contrabajo; ~ **bed** n cama matrimonial; ~ **bend** n doble curva; ~-**breasted** a cruzado; ~**cross** vt (trick) engañar; (betray) traicionar; ~**decker** n autobús m de dos pisos; ~ **room** n cuarto para dos; **doubly** ad doblemente.
doubt [daʊt] n duda // vt dudar; (suspect) dudar de; **to ~ that** dudar que; **there is no** ~ **that** no cabe duda de que; ~**ful** a dudoso;

(person) sospechoso; ~**less** ad sin duda.
dough [dəʊ] n masa, pasta; ~**nut** n buñuelo.
dove [dʌv] n paloma; ~**tail** vi (fig) encajar.
dowdy [ˈdaʊdɪ] a desaliñado; (inelegant) poco elegante.
down [daʊn] n (fluff) pelusa; (feathers) plumón m, flojel m // ad (~wards) abajo, hacia abajo; (on the ground) por/en tierra // prep abajo // vt (col: drink) beberse; (: food) devorar; **the D~s** zona de colinas del sur de Inglaterra;; ~ **with X!** ¡abajo X!; ~-**at-heel** a venido a menos; (appearance) desaliñado; ~**cast** a abatido; ~**fall** n caída, ruina; ~**hearted** a desanimado; ~**hill** ad: **to go** ~hill ir cuesta abajo; ~ **payment** n enganche m, pago al contado; ~**pour** n aguacero; ~**right** a (clear) manifiesto; (out-and-out) terminante, definitivo; ~**stairs** ad (below) (en la casa) de abajo; (~wards) escaleras abajo; ~**stream** ad aguas o río abajo; ~-**to-earth** a práctico; ~**town** ad en el centro de la ciudad; ~**ward** a, ad, ~**wards** ad hacia abajo.
dowry [ˈdaʊrɪ] n dote f.
doz. abbr of dozen.
doze [dəʊz] vi dormitar; **to** ~ **off** vi quedarse medio dormido.
dozen [ˈdʌzn] n docena.
Dr. abbr of doctor; drive.
drab [dræb] a gris, monótono.
draft [drɑːft] n (first copy) borrador m; (COMM) giro; (US: call-up) quinta // vt (plan) redactar; (send) mandar; (conscript) quintar; (write roughly) hacer un borrador de; see also **draught**.
drag [dræg] vt arrastrar; (river) dragar, rastrear // vi arrastrarse por el suelo // n (col) lata; **to** ~ **on** vi ser interminable.
dragonfly [ˈdrægənflaɪ] n libélula.
drain [dreɪn] n desaguadero; (in

street sumidero; (source of loss) desagüe m; (loss) pérdida; (on resources) sumidero // vt (land, marshes) desaguar; (MED) drenar; (reservoir) desecar, (fig) agotar // vi escurrirse; ~age n (act) desagüe m; (MED, AGR) drenaje m; (sewage) alcantarillado; ~ing board, ~board (US) n escurridera; escurridor m; ~pipe n tubo de desagüe.

dram [dræm] n (drink) trago.

drama ['drɑ:mə] n (art) teatro; (play) drama m; ~tic [drə'mætik] a dramático; ~tist ['dræmətist] n dramaturgo.

drank [dræŋk] pt of drink.

drape [dreip] vt cubrir, ~s npl (US) cortinas fpl; draper n pañero.

drastic ['dræstik] a (measure) severo; (change) radical; (forceful) enérgico.

draught [drɑ:ft] n (of air) corriente f; (drink) trago; (NAUT) calado; ~s n juego de damas; on ~ (beer) de barril; ~board n tablero de damas.

draughtsman ['drɑ:ftsmən] n proyectista m, delineante m.

draw [drɔ:] pt drew, pp drawn vt (pull) tirar; (take out) sacar; (attract) atraer; (picture) dibujar; (money) retirar // vi (SPORT) empatar // n (SPORT) empate m; (lottery) sorteo; (attraction) atracción f; to ~ near vi acercarse; to ~ out vi (lengthen) alargar; to ~ up (stop) pararse // vt (document) redactar; ~back n inconveniente m, desventaja; ~bridge n puente m levadizo.

drawer [drɔ:*] n cajón m.

drawing ['drɔ:iŋ] n dibujo; ~ board n tablero (de dibujante); ~ pin n chinche m; ~ room n salón m.

drawl [drɔ:l] n habla lenta y cansina.

drawn [drɔ:n] pp of draw.

dread [dred] n pavor m, terror m // vt temer, tener miedo o pavor a; ~ful a espantoso.

dream [dri:m] n sueño // a, vi, pt, pp dreamed or dreamt [dremt] soñar; ~er n soñador/a m/f; ~y a (distracted) soñador(a), distraído; (music) de sueño.

dreary ['drɪərɪ] a monótono, aburrido.

dredge [dredʒ] vt dragar; dredger n (ship) draga; (also: sugar dredger) espolvoreador m.

dregs [dregz] npl heces fpl.

drench [drentʃ] vt empapar, to get ~ed mojarse hasta los huesos.

dress [dres] n vestido; (clothing) ropa f // vt vestir; (wound) vendar; (CULIN) aliñar // vi vestirse; to ~ up vi vestirse de etiqueta; (in fancy dress) disfrazarse; ~ circle n principal m; ~er n (furniture) aparador m; (: US) cómoda con espejo, ~ing n (MED) vendaje m; (CULIN) aliño; ~ing gown n bata; ~ing room n (THEATRE) camarín m; (SPORT) vestidor m; ~ing table n tocador m; ~maker n modista, costurera; ~making n costura; ~ rehearsal n ensayo general; ~shirt n camisa de frac.

drew [dru:] pt of draw.

dribble ['dribl] vi gotear, caer gota a gota; (baby) babear // vt (ball) regatear.

dried [draid] a (fruit) seco; (milk) en polvo.

drift [drift] n (of current etc) velocidad f; (of sand etc) montón m; (distance off course) deriva; (meaning) significado // vi (boat) ir a la deriva; (sand, snow) amontonarse; ~wood n madera de deriva.

drill [dril] n taladro; (bit) broca; (of dentist) fresa; (for mining etc) perforadora, barrena; (MIL) instrucción f // vt perforar, taladrar // vi (for oil) perforar.

drink [driŋk] n bebida // vt, vi, pt drank, pp drunk beber; to have a ~ tomar; ~er n bebedor/a m/f; ~ing water n agua potable.

drip [drɪp] n (act) goteo, gotea; (one ~) gota; (MED) gota a gota m // vi gotear, caer gota a gota; ~**-dry** a (shirt) de lava y pon; ~**ping** n pringue m; ~**ping wet** a calado.

drive [draɪv] n paseo (en coche); (journey) viaje m; (also: ~**way**) entrada; (energy) energía, vigor m; (PSYCH) impulso; (SPORT) ataque m // (vb: pt **drove**, pp **driven** ['drɪvn]) vt (car) conducir; (urge) hacer trabajar; (by power) mover; (nail) clavar; (push) empujar; (TECH: motor) impulsar // vi (AUT: at controls) conducir; (: travel) pasearse en coche; **left-/right-hand** ~ conducción f a la izquierda/derecha.

driver ['draɪvə*] n conductor m; (of taxi, bus) chofer m; ~**'s license** n (US) permiso de conducir.

driving ['draɪvɪŋ] n el conducir, automovilismo; ~ **instructor** n instructor m de conducción; ~ **lesson** n clase f de conducción; ~ **licence** n (Brit) permiso de conducir; ~ **mirror** n retrovisor m; ~ **school** n autoescuela; ~ **test** n examen m de conducción.

drizzle ['drɪzl] n llovizna // vi lloviznar.

drone [drəun] n zumbido; (male bee) zángano.

drool [druːl] vi babear; **to ~ over sth** extasiarse ante algo.

droop [druːp] vi colgar; (fig) decaer, desanimarse.

drop [drɔp] n (of water) gota; (lessening) baja; (fall) caída; (of cliff) pendiente m, declive m // vt (allow to fall) dejar caer; (voice, eyes, price) bajar; (set down from car) dejar; (omit) omitir // vi caer; (price, temperature) bajar; (wind) amainar; **to ~ off** vi (sleep) dormirse // vt (passenger) bajar; **to ~ out** vi (withdraw) retirarse; ~**-out** n marginado; ~**per** n cuentagotas m inv; ~**pings** npl excremento sg (de animal).

drought [draut] n sequía.

drove [drəuv] pt of **drive**.

drown [draun] vt ahogar // vi ahogarse.

drowsy ['drauzɪ] a soñoliento; **to be ~** tener sueño.

drudgery ['drʌdʒərɪ] n trabajo monótono.

drug [drʌg] n medicamento; (narcotic) droga // vt drogar; ~ **addict** n drogadicto/a; ~**gist** n (US) farmacéutico; ~**store** n (US) farmacia.

drum [drʌm] n tambor m; (large) bombo; (for oil, petrol) bidón m; ~s npl batería sg // vi tocar el tambor; (with fingers) tamborilear; ~**mer** n tambor m; ~**stick** n (MUS) palillo; (of chicken) muslo.

drunk [drʌŋk] pp of **drink** // a borracho // n (also: ~**ard**) borracho/a; ~**en** a borracho; ~**enness** n embriaguez f.

dry [draɪ] a seco; (day) sin lluvia; (climate) árido, seco // vt secar; (tears) enjugar // vi secarse; **to ~ up** vi agotarse; (in speech) atascarse; ~**-cleaner's** n tintorería; ~**-cleaning** n lavado en seco; ~**er** n lavadora; ~**ness** n sequedad f; ~**rot** n putrefacción f fungoide.

dual ['djuəl] a doble; ~**-control** a de doble mando; ~**-nationality** n doble nacionalidad f; ~**-purpose** a de doble uso.

dubbed [dʌbd] a (CINEMA) doblado.

dubious ['djuːbɪəs] a dudoso; (reputation, company) sospechoso.

duchess ['dʌtʃɪs] n duquesa.

duck [dʌk] n pato // vi agacharse; ~**ling** n patito.

duct [dʌkt] n conducto, canal m.

dud [dʌd] n (shell) obús m que no estalla; (object, tool): **it's a ~** es una filfa // a: ~ **cheque** cheque m sin fondos.

due [djuː] a (proper) debido; (expected) esperado; (fitting) conveniente, oportuno // n (debt) deuda; (desert) lo que merece uno

// ad: ~ **north** derecho al norte; ~**s** npl (for club, union) cuota sg; (in harbour) derechos mpl; **in** ~ **course** a su debido tiempo; ~ **to** debido a.

duel ['djuəl] n duelo.

duet [dju:'ɛt] n dúo.

dug [dʌg] pt, pp of **dig**.

duke [dju:k] n duque m.

dull [dʌl] a (light) apagado; (slow) torpe; (boring) pesado; (sound, pain) sordo; (weather, day) gris // vt (pain, grief) aliviar; (mind, senses) entorpecer.

duly ['dju:lɪ] ad debidamente; (on time) a su debido tiempo.

dumb [dʌm] a mudo; (stupid) estúpido; ~**founded** [dʌm'faundɪd] a pasmado.

dummy ['dʌmɪ] n (tailor's model) maniquí m; (for baby) chupete m // a falso, postizo.

dump [dʌmp] n (heap) montón m; (place) basurero, vaciadero; (col) casucha; (MIL) depósito // vt (put down) verter, vaciar; (get rid of) deshacerse de; (goods) inundar el mercado con; ~**ing** n (ECON) dumping m; (of rubbish) 'no ~**ing**' 'prohibido verter basura'.

dumpling ['dʌmplɪŋ] n bola de masa hervida.

dunce [dʌns] n zopenco.

dune [dju:n] n duna.

dung [dʌŋ] n estiércol m.

dungarees [dʌŋgə'ri:z] npl mono sg.

dungeon ['dʌndʒən] n calabozo.

dupe [dju:p] n (victim) víctima // vt engañar.

duplicate ['dju:plɪkət] n duplicado // vt ['dju:plɪkeɪt] duplicar; (on machine) multicopiar; **in** ~ por duplicado; **duplicator** n multicopista m.

durable ['djuərəbl] a duradero.

duration [djuə'reɪʃən] n duración f.

duress [djuə'rɛs] n: **under** ~ por compulsión.

during ['djuərɪŋ] prep durante.

dusk [dʌsk] n crepúsculo, anochecer m.

dust [dʌst] n polvo // vt (furniture) desempolvorar; (cake etc): **to** ~ **with** espolvorear de; ~**bin** n (Brit) cubo de la basura; ~**er** n paño, trapo, bayeta; (feather ~) plumero; ~ **jacket** n sobrecubierta; ~**man** n (Brit) basurero; ~**y** a polvoriento.

Dutch [dʌtʃ] a holandés(esa) // n (LING) holandés m; ~**man/woman** n holandés/esa m/f.

duty ['dju:tɪ] n deber m; (tax) derechos mpl de aduana; **on** ~ de servicio; (at night etc) de guardia; **off** ~ libre (de servicio); ~**-free** a libre de derechos de aduana.

dwarf [dwɔ:f], pl **dwarves** [dwɔ:vz] n enano // vt empequeñecer.

dwell [dwɛl] pt, pp **dwelt** [dwɛlt] vi morar; **to** ~ **on** vt fus explayarse en; ~**ing** n vivienda.

dwindle ['dwɪndl] vi menguar, disminuir.

dye [daɪ] n tinte m // vt teñir.

dying ['daɪɪŋ] a moribundo, agonizante; (moments) final; (words) último.

dynamic [daɪ'næmɪk] a dinámico; ~**s** n, npl dinámica sg.

dynamite ['daɪnəmaɪt] n dinamita.

dynamo ['daɪnəməu] n dínamo f.

dynasty ['dɪnəstɪ] n dinastía.

E

each [i:tʃ] det cada inv // pron cada uno; ~ **other** el uno al otro; **they hate** ~ **other** se odian (entre ellos o mutuamente); **they have 2 books** ~ tiene 2 libros por persona.

eager ['i:gə*] a (gen) impaciente; (hopeful) ilusionado; (ambitious) ambicioso; **to be** ~ **to do sth** ansiar hacer algo, impacientarse por hacer algo; **to be ~ for** ansiar, anhelar.

eagle [ˈiːgl] n águila.

ear [ɪə*] n oreja; (MUS) oído; (of corn) espiga; **~ache** n dolor m de oídos; **~drum** n tímpano.

earl [ɜːl] n conde m.

early [ˈəːlɪ] ad (gen) temprano; (before time) con tiempo, con anticipación // a (gen) temprano; (reply) pronto; (first) primero, (work) juvenil; **have an ~ night** acuéstate temprano; **in the ~ or ~ in the spring/19th century** a principios de primavera/del siglo diez y nueve; **as ~ as possible** cuánto antes, lo más pronto posible.

earmark [ˈɪəmɑːk] vt reservar (for para), destinar (for a).

earn [əːn] vt (gen) ganar; (salary) percibir; (interest) devengar; (praise) merecerse.

earnest [ˈəːnɪst] a serio, formal; **in ~** ad en serio.

earnings [ˈəːnɪŋz] npl (personal) sueldo, ingresos mpl; (company) ganancias fpl.

ear: ~phones npl auriculares mpl; **~ring** n pendiente m, arete m; **~shot** n: **within ~shot** al alcance del oído.

earth [əːθ] n (gen) tierra; (ELEC) cable m de toma de tierra // vt (ELEC) conectar a tierra; **~enware** n loza de barro; **~quake** n terremoto; **~y** a (fig: vulgar) grosero; (: sensual) sensual.

earwig [ˈɪəwɪg] n tijereta.

ease [iːz] n (gen) facilidad f; (relief) alivio; (calm) tranquilidad f; (relaxed state) comodidad f // vt facilitar; (pain) aliviar; tranquilizar; (loosen) soltar; (relieve: pressure) aflojar; (weight) aligerar; (help pass): **to ~ sth in/out** meter/sacar con cuidado; at **~!** (MIL) ¡descanso!; **to ~ off** or **up** vi (gen) suavizarse; (at work) dejar de trabajar tanto; (wind) amainar; (rain) moderarse.

easel [ˈiːzl] n caballete m.

east [iːst] n este m, oriente m // a del este, oriental // ad al este, hacia el este; **the E~** el Oriente.

Easter [ˈiːstə*] n Pascua (de Resurrección).

easterly [ˈiːstəlɪ] a (to the east) al este; (from the east) del este.

eastern [ˈiːstən] a del este, oriental.

East Germany n Alemania Oriental.

eastward(s) [ˈiːstwəd(z)] ad hacia el este.

easy [ˈiːzɪ] a (gen) fácil; (simple) sencillo; (slow) lento, pausado; (comfortable) holgado, cómodo; (relaxed) natural, llano // ad: **to take it** or **things ~** (not worry) tomarlo con calma; (go slowly) ir despacio; (rest) descansar; **~ chair** n sillón m; **~-going** a acomodadizo.

eat [iːt] vt ate, pp eaten [ˈiːtn] vt (gen) comer; (supper) cenar; **to ~ into, to ~ away at** vt fus corroer; **~able** a comestible.

eau de Cologne [əudəkəˈləun] n (agua de) Colonia.

eaves [iːvz] npl alero sg.

eavesdrop [ˈiːvzdrɒp] vi escuchar a escondidas (on sb a uno).

ebb [ɛb] n reflujo // vi bajar; (fig: also: ~ away) decaer; **~ tide** n marea menguante.

ebony [ˈɛbənɪ] n ébano.

eccentric [ɪkˈsɛntrɪk] a, n excéntrico/a.

ecclesiastical [ɪkliːzɪˈæstɪkəl] a eclesiástico.

echo [ˈɛkəu], pl **~es** n eco m // vt (sound) repetir // vi resonar, hacer eco.

eclipse [ɪˈklɪps] n eclipse m // vt eclipsar.

ecology [ɪˈkɒlədʒɪ] n ecología.

economic [iːkəˈnɒmɪk] a económico; (business etc) rentable; **~al** a económico; **~s** n (ie) la economía.

economist [ɪˈkɒnəmɪst] n economista m/f.

economize [ɪˈkɒnəmaɪz] vi economizar, ahorrar.

economy [ɪ'kɒnəmɪ] n economía.

ecstasy ['ekstəsɪ] n éxtasis m; **ecstatic** [-'tætɪk] a extático.

ecumenical [i:kju'menɪkl] a ecuménico.

eczema ['eksɪmə] n eczema m.

edge [edʒ] n (of knife etc) filo; (of object) borde m; (of lake etc) orilla // it (SEWING) ribetear; on ~ (fig) = edgy, to ~ away from alejarse poco a poco; ~ways ad: he couldn't get a word in ~ways no pudo meter baza; **edging** n (SEWING) ribete m; (of path) borde m.

edgy ['edʒɪ] a nervioso, inquieto.

edible ['edɪbl] a comestible.

edict ['i:dɪkt] n edicto.

edifice ['edɪfɪs] n edificio.

edit ['edɪt] vt (be editor of) dirigir; (cut) cortar; ~**ion** [ɪ'dɪʃən] n (gen) edición f; (number printed) tirada; ~**or** n (of newspaper) director m; (of book) autor m de la edición; ~**orial** [-'tɔ:rɪəl] a editorial, de la dirección // n editorial m.

educate ['edjukeɪt] vt (gen) educar; (instruct) instruir.

education [edju'keɪʃən] n educación f; (schooling) enseñanza; (SCOL) pedagogía; ~**al** a (policy etc) educacional; (teaching) docente; (instructive) educativo.

EEC n abbr of European Economic Community CEE (Comunidad Económica Europea).

eel [i:l] n anguila.

eerie ['ɪərɪ] a (strange) extraño; (mysterious) misterioso.

effect [ɪ'fekt] n efecto // vt efectuar, llevar a cabo; ~s npl efectos mpl; to take ~ (drug) surtir efecto; in ~ en realidad; ~**ive** a (gen) eficaz; (striking) impresionante; (real) efectivo; to become ~**ive** entrar en vigor; ~**iveness** n eficacia.

effeminate [ɪ'femɪnɪt] a afeminado.

effervescent [efə'vesnt] a efervescente.

efficiency [ɪ'fɪʃənsɪ] n (gen) eficiencia; (of machine) rendimiento.

efficient [ɪ'fɪʃənt] a eficiente.

effigy ['efɪdʒɪ] n efigie f.

effort ['efət] n esfuerzo; to make an ~ to esforzarse por; ~**less** a sin esfuerzo (alguno).

effrontery [ɪ'frʌntərɪ] n descaro.

effusive [ɪ'fju:sɪv] a efusivo.

e.g. ad abbr of exempli gratia p. ej. (por ejemplo).

egg [eg] n huevo; **hard-boiled/poached/soft-boiled ~** huevo duro/escalfado/pasado por agua; **scrambled ~s** huevos revueltos; to ~ on vt incitar; ~**cup** n huevera; ~**shell** n cáscara de huevo.

ego ['i:gəu] n ego; ~**ism** n egoísmo; ~**ist** n egoísta m/f.

Egypt ['i:dʒɪpt] n Egipto; ~**ian** [ɪ'dʒɪpʃən] a, n egipcio/a.

eiderdown ['aɪdədaun] n edredón m.

eight [eɪt] num ocho; **eighteen** num diez y ocho, dieciocho; **eighth** a, n octavo; ~**y** num ochenta.

Eire ['eɪrə] n Eire m.

either ['aɪðə*] det cualquier ... de los dos; (both, each) uno u otro; on ~ side en ambos lados // pron: (of them) cualquiera (de los dos); I don't like ~ no me gusta ni uno ni otro // ad tampoco; no, I don't ~ no, yo tampoco // conj: ~ yes or no sí o no.

eject [ɪ'dʒekt] vt echar; (tenant) desahuciar; ~**or seat** n asiento proyectable.

eke [i:k] to ~ out vt (make last) escatimar; (add to) suplir las deficiencias de.

elaborate [ɪ'læbərɪt] a complicado; (decorated) rebuscado // (vb: [ɪ'læbəreɪt]) vt elaborar // vi explicarse con muchos detalles.

elapse [ɪ'læps] vi transcurrir.

elastic [ɪ'læstɪk] a, n elástico; ~**band** n gomita.

elated [ɪˈleɪtɪd] *a*: to be ~ regocijarse; **elation** [ɪˈleɪʃən] *n* regocijo.

elbow [ˈelbəu] *n* codo.

elder [ˈeldə*] *a* mayor // *n* (*tree*) saúco; (*person*) mayor; (*of tribe*) anciano; ~ly a de edad, mayor // *a*: the ~ly la gente mayor.

eldest [ˈeldɪst] *a, n* el/la mayor.

elect [ɪˈlekt] *vt* elegir; to ~ to do optar por hacer // *a*: the president ~ el presidente electo; ~**ion** [ɪˈlekʃən] *n* elección *f*; ~**ioneering** [ɪlekʃəˈnɪərɪŋ] *n* campaña electoral; ~**or** *n* elector/a *m/f*; ~**oral** *a* electoral; ~**orate** *n* electorado.

electric [ɪˈlektrɪk] *a* eléctrico; ~al *a* eléctrico; ~ **blanket** *n* manta eléctrica; ~ **chair** *n* silla eléctrica; ~ **cooker** *n* cocina eléctrica; ~ **fire** *n* estufa eléctrica.

electrician [ɪlekˈtrɪʃən] *n* electricista *m/f*.

electricity [ɪlekˈtrɪsɪtɪ] *n* electricidad *f*.

electrify [ɪˈlektrɪfaɪ] *vt* (*RAIL*.) electrificar; (*audience*) electrizar.

electro... [ɪlektrəu] *pref*: ~**cute** [-kjuːt] *vt* electrocutar; **electrode** [ɪˈlektrəud] *n* electrodo; ~**magnetic** *a* electromagnético.

electron [ɪˈlektrɔn] *n* electrón *m*.

electronic [ɪlekˈtrɔnɪk] *a* electrónico; ~**s** *n* electrónica *f*.

elegance [ˈelɪgəns] *n* elegancia; **elegant** [-gənt] *a* elegante.

element [ˈelɪmənt] *n* (*gen*) elemento; to brave the ~s salir a la intemperie; ~**ary** [ˈmentəri] *a* (*gen*) elemental; (*primitive*) rudimentario; (*school, education*) de primera enseñanza.

elephant [ˈelɪfənt] *n* elefante *m*.

elevate [ˈelɪveɪt] *vt* (*gen*) elevar; (*in rank*) ascender.

elevation [elɪˈveɪʃən] *n* elevación *f*; (*rank*) ascenso; (*height*) altura.

elevator [ˈelɪveɪtə*] *n* (*US*) ascensor *m*.

eleven [ɪˈlevn] *num* once; ~**ses** *npl*

las once; ~**th** *a* undécimo.

elf [elf], *pl* **elves** [elvz] *n* duende *m*.

elicit [ɪˈlɪsɪt] *vt*: to ~ (from) sacar (de).

eligible [ˈelɪdʒəbl] *a* elegible; to be ~ for sth llenar los requisitos para algo.

eliminate [ɪˈlɪmɪneɪt] *vt* eliminar; (*strike out*) suprimir; (*suspect*) descartar; **elimination** [-neɪʃən] *n* eliminación *f*; supresión *f*.

élite [eɪˈliːt] *n* élite *f*.

elm [elm] *n* olmo.

elocution [eləˈkjuːʃən] *n* elocución *f*.

elongated [ˈiːlɔŋgeɪtɪd] *a* alargado, estirado.

elope [ɪˈləup] *vi* fugarse con su amante; ~**ment** *n* fuga.

eloquence [ˈeləkwəns] *n* elocuencia; **eloquent** [-wənt] *a* elocuente.

else [els] *ad* lo(s) demás; **something** ~ otra cosa; **somewhere** ~ en otra parte; **everywhere** ~ en todas partes (menos aquí); **where** ~? ¿dónde más?, ¿en qué otra parte?; **there was little** ~ **to do** apenas quedaba otra cosa que hacer; **nobody** ~ **spoke** no habló nadie más; ~**where** *ad* (*be*) en otra parte; (*go*) a otra parte.

elucidate [ɪˈluːsɪdeɪt] *vt* aclarar, elucidar.

elude [ɪˈluːd] *vt* (*gen*) eludir; (*blow*) esquivar; (*pursuer*) escaparse de, zafarse de.

elusive [ɪˈluːsɪv] *a* esquivo; (*answer*) difícil de encontrar.

emaciated [ɪˈmeɪsɪeɪtɪd] *a* demacrado.

emanate [ˈeməneɪt] *vi* emanar, proceder.

emancipate [ɪˈmænsɪpeɪt] *vt* emancipar; ~**d** *a* liberado; **emancipation** [-ˈpeɪʃən] *n* emancipación *f*, liberación *f*.

embalm [ɪmˈbɑːm] *vt* embalsamar.

embankment [ɪmˈbæŋkmənt] *n* terraplén *m*; (*riverside*) dique *m*.

embargo [ɪmˈbɑːgəu], *pl* **~es** *n* prohibición *f*.

embark [ɪmˈbɑːk] *vi* embarcarse // *vt* embarcar; **to ~ on** *(fig)* emprender, lanzarse a; **~ation** [embɑːˈkeɪʃən] *n (people)* embarco; *(goods)* embarque *m*.

embarrass [ɪmˈbærəs] *vt* desconcertar, azorar; *(financially etc)* poner en un aprieto; **~ing** *a* embarazoso; **~ment** *n* desconcierto, azoramiento; *(financial)* apuros *mpl*.

embassy [ˈembəsɪ] *n* embajada.

embed [ɪmˈbed] *vt (gen)* empotrar; *(teeth etc)* clavar.

embellish [ɪmˈbelɪʃ] *vt* embellecer; *(fig)* adornar.

embers [ˈembəz] *npl* rescoldo *sg*, ascua *sg*.

embezzle [ɪmˈbezl] *vt* desfalcar, malversar; **~ment** *n* desfalco, malversación *f*.

embitter [ɪmˈbɪtə*] *vt* amargar; *(fig)* envenenar; **~ed** *a* resentido, amargado.

emblem [ˈembləm] *n* emblema *m*.

embody [ɪmˈbɔdɪ] *vt (features)* encarnar; *(ideas)* expresar.

embossed [ɪmˈbɔst] *a* realzado; **~ with** con grabado en relieve.

embrace [ɪmˈbreɪs] *vt* abrazar, dar un abrazo a; *(include)* abarcar; *(adopt: idea)* adherirse a // *vi* abrazarse // *n* abrazo.

embroider [ɪmˈbrɔɪdə*] *vt* bordar; *(fig: story)* adornar, embellecer; **~y** *n* bordado.

embryo [ˈembrɪəu] *n (also fig)* embrión *m*.

emerald [ˈemərəld] *n* esmeralda.

emerge [ɪˈmɜːdʒ] *vi (gen)* salir, aparecer; *(arise)* surgir: **emergence** *n* salida, aparición *f*, surgimiento.

emergency [ɪˈmɜːdʒənsɪ] *n (event)* emergencia; *(crisis)* crisis *f*; *(need)* necesidad *f* urgente; **in an ~** en caso de urgencia; **state of ~** estado de emergencia; **~ exit** *n* salida de emergencia; **~ landing** *n* aterrizaje

m forzoso; **~ meeting** *n* reunión *f* extraordinaria.

emery [ˈemərɪ]: **~ board** *n* lima de uñas; **~ paper** *n* papel *m* de esmeril.

emetic [ɪˈmetɪk] *n* emético.

emigrant [ˈemɪgrənt] *n* emigrante *m/f*.

emigrate [ˈemɪgreɪt] *vi* emigrarse; **emigration** [-ˈgreɪʃən] *n* emigración *f*.

eminence [ˈemɪnəns] *n* eminencia; **eminent** [-ənt] *a* eminente.

emission [ɪˈmɪʃən] *n* emisión *f*.

emit [ɪˈmɪt] *vt (gen)* emitir; *(smoke)* arrojar; *(smell)* despedir; *(sound)* producir.

emotion [ɪˈməuʃən] *n* emoción *f*; **~al** *a (person)* sentimental; *(scene)* conmovedor(a), emocionante; **~ally** *ad* con emoción.

emotive [ɪˈməutɪv] *a* emotivo.

emperor [ˈempərə*] *n* emperador *m*.

emphasis [ˈemfəsɪs], *pl* **-ses** [-siːz] *n* énfasis *m inv*.

emphasize [ˈemfəsaɪz] *vt (word, point)* subrayar, recalcar; *(feature)* hacer resaltar.

emphatic [emˈfætɪk] *a (strong)* enérgico; *(unambiguous, clear)* enfático; **~ally** *ad* con énfasis.

empire [ˈempaɪə*] *n* imperio.

empirical [emˈpɪrɪkl] *a* empírico.

employ [ɪmˈplɔɪ] *vt* emplear; **~ee** [-ˈiː] *n* empleado/a; **~er** *n* patrón/ona *m/f*, empresario; **~ment** *n (gen)* empleo; *(work)* trabajo; **full ~ment** pleno empleo; **~ment agency** *n* agencia de colocaciones; **~ment exchange** *n* bolsa de trabajo.

empower [ɪmˈpauə*] *vt*: **to ~ sb to do sth** autorizar a uno a hacer algo.

empress [ˈemprɪs] *n* emperatriz *f*.

emptiness [ˈemptɪnɪs] *n (gen)* vacío; *(of life etc)* vaciedad *f*.

empty [ˈemptɪ] *a* vacío; *(place)* desierto; *(house)* desocupado; *(threat)* vano // *n (bottle)* envase *m*

// vt vaciar; (place) dejar vacío // vi vaciarse; (house) quedar desocupado; (place) quedar desierto; ~-handed a con las manos vacías.

emulate ['emjuleɪt] vt emular.

emulsion [ɪ'mʌlʃən] n emulsión f.

enable [ɪ'neɪbl] vt: to ~ sb to do sth (allow) permitir a uno hacer algo; (prepare) capacitar a uno para hacer algo.

enact [ɪn'ækt] vt (law) promulgar; (play) representar; (role) hacer.

enamel [ɪ'næməl] n esmalte m.

enamoured [ɪ'næməd] a: to be ~ of (person) estar enamorado de; (activity etc) tener gran afición a; (idea) aferrarse a.

encased [ɪn'keɪst] a: ~ in (enclosed) encerrado en; (covered) revestido de.

enchant [ɪn'tʃɑːnt] vt encantar; ~ing a encantador(a).

encircle [ɪn'sɜːkl] vt (gen) rodear; (waist) ceñir.

encl. abbr of enclosed adj. (adjunto).

enclose [ɪn'kləuz] vt (land) cercar; (with letter etc) adjuntar; (in receptacle) encerrar; **please find** ~d le adjunto.

enclosure [ɪn'kləuʒə*] n cercado, recinto, (COMM) carta adjunta.

encore [ɔŋ'kɔː*] excl ¡otra!, ¡bis! // n bis m.

encounter [ɪn'kauntə*] n encuentro // vt encontrar, encontrarse con; (difficulty) tropezar con.

encourage [ɪn'kʌrɪdʒ] vt alentar, animar; (growth) estimular; ~ment n estímulo; (of industry) fomento.

encroach [ɪn'krəutʃ] vi: to ~ (up)on (gen) invadir; (time) ocupar.

encrusted [ɪn'krʌstəd] a: ~ with incrustado de.

encumber [ɪn'kʌmbə*] vt: to be ~ed with (carry) tener que cargar con; (debts) estar gravado de.

encyclo(a)edia [ɛnsaɪkləu'piːdɪə] n enciclopedia.

end [ɛnd] n (gen, also aim) fin m; (of

table) extremo; (of street) final m; (SPORT) final // vt terminar, acabar; (also: bring to an ~, put an ~ to) acabar con // vi terminar, acabar; **in the** ~ al fin, por fin, finalmente; **on** ~ (object) de punta, de cabeza; **to stand on** ~ (hair) erizarse; **for hours on** ~ horas seguidas; **to** ~ **up** vi: **to** ~ **up in** terminar en; (place) ir a parar en.

endanger [ɪn'deɪndʒə*] vt poner en peligro.

endear [ɪn'dɪə*] vr: **to** ~ **o.s.** to hacerse querer de; ~ing a simpático, atractivo; ~ment n cariño, palabra cariñosa.

endeavour [ɪn'dɛvə*] n esfuerzo; (attempt) tentativa; (striving) empeño // vt: **to do** esforzarse por hacer; (try) procurar hacer.

ending ['ɛndɪŋ] n fin m, conclusión f, (of book) desenlace m; (LING) terminación f.

endless ['ɛndlɪs] a interminable, inacabable.

endorse [ɪn'dɔːs] vt (cheque) endosar; (approve) aprobar; ~ment n (on driving licence) nota de inhabilitación.

endow [ɪn'dau] vt (provide with money) dotar; (: institution) fundar; **to be** ~ed with estar dotado de.

endurance [ɪn'djuərəns] n resistencia; **endure** vt (bear) aguantar, soportar; (resist) resistir // vi (last) durar; (resist) resistir.

enemy ['ɛnəmɪ] a, n enemigo/a.

energetic [ɛnə'dʒɛtɪk] a enérgico.

energy ['ɛnədʒɪ] n energía.

enforce [ɪn'fɔːs] vt (LAW) hacer cumplir; ~d a forzoso, forzado.

engage [ɪn'geɪdʒ] vt (attention) llamar; (in conversation) abordar; (worker) contratar; (taxi) alquilar; (clutch) embragar // vi (TECH) engranar con; **to** ~ **in** dedicarse a, ocuparse en; ~d a (busy, in use) ocupado; (betrothed) prometido; **to get** ~d prometerse; **he is** ~d **in research** se dedica a la investigación; ~d tone n señal f de comunicando; ~ment n (appointment) compromiso, cita; (battle) combate m; (to marry) compromiso; (period) noviazgo; ~ment ring n alianza, anillo de prometida.

engaging [ɪn'geɪdʒɪŋ] a atractivo, simpático.

engender [ɪn'dʒɛndə*] vt engendrar.

engine ['ɛndʒɪn] n (AUT) motor m; (RAIL) locomotora; ~ driver n maquinista m.

engineer [ɛndʒɪ'nɪə*] n ingeniero; (US: RAIL) maquinista m; ~ing n ingeniería.

England ['ɪŋglənd] n Inglaterra.

English ['ɪŋglɪʃ] a inglés(esa) // n (LING) el inglés; the ~ los ingleses; ~man/woman n inglés/esa m/f.

engrave [ɪn'greɪv] vt grabar; **engraving** n grabado.

engrossed [ɪn'grəust] a: ~ in absorto en.

engulf [ɪn'gʌlf] vt sumergir, hundir.

enhance [ɪn'hɑːns] vt (gen) intensificar, aumentar; (beauty) realzar.

enigma [ɪ'nɪgmə] n enigma m; ~tic [enɪg'mætɪk] a enigmático.

enjoy [ɪn'dʒɔɪ] vt (possess) poseer; (have: health, fortune) disfrutar de, gozar de; (food) comer con gusto; to ~ o.s. divertirse, pasarlo bien; ~able a (pleasant) agradable; (amusing) divertido; ~ment n (use) disfrute m; (joy) placer m.

enlarge [ɪn'lɑːdʒ] vt aumentar; (broaden) extender; (PHOT) ampliar // vi: to ~ on (subject) tratar con más detalles; ~ment n (PHOT) ampliación f.

enlighten [ɪn'laɪtn] vt (inform) informar, instruir; ~ed a (cultured) culto; (knowledgeable) bien informado; (tolerant) comprensivo; ~ment n (HISTORY): the E~ment n la Ilustración, el Siglo de las Luces.

enlist [ɪn'lɪst] vt alistar; (support) conseguir // vi alistarse.

enmity ['ɛnmɪtɪ] n enemistad f.

enormity [ɪ'nɔːmɪtɪ] n enormidad f; **enormous** [-məs] a enorme.

enough [ɪ'nʌf] a: ~ time/books bastante tiempo/bastantes libros // n: have you got ~? ¿tiene Usted bastante? // ad: big ~ bastante grande; he has not worked ~ no ha trabajado bastante; ~! ¡basta ya!; that's ~, thanks con eso basta, gracias; I've had ~ of him estoy harto de él; ... which, funnily ~ ... ... lo que, por extraño que parezca...

enquire [ɪn'kwaɪə*] vt, vi = **inquire**.

enrage [ɪn'reɪdʒ] vt enfurecer, hacer rabiar.

enrich [ɪn'rɪtʃ] vt enriquecer.

enrol [ɪn'rəul] vt inscribir; (SCOL) matricular // vi inscribirse; matricularse; ~ment n inscripción f, matriculación f.

en route [ɔn'ruːt] ad (on the way to) camino de; (on the way) en camino.

ensign ['ɛnsaɪn] n (flag) bandera; (MIL) alférez m.

enslave [ɪn'sleɪv] vt esclavizar.

ensue [ɪn'sjuː] vi seguirse; (result) resultar; (happen) sobrevenir.

ensure [ɪn'ʃuə*] vt asegurar.

entail [ɪn'teɪl] vt (imply) suponer; (result in) acarrear.

entangle [ɪn'tæŋgl] vt enredar, enmarañar; ~ment n enredo.

enter ['ɛntə*] vt (room) entrar en; (club) hacerse socio de; (army) alistarse en; (sb for a competition) inscribir; (write down) anotar, apuntar // vi entrar; to ~ for vt fus presentarse para; to ~ into vt fus (relations) establecer; (plans) formar parte de; (debate) tomar parte en; (agreement) llegar a, firmar; to ~ (up)on vt fus (career) emprender.

enteritis [ɛntə'raɪtɪs] n enteritis f.

enterprise ['ɛntəpraɪz] n empresa; (spirit) iniciativa; **free ~** la libre empresa; **private ~** la iniciativa privada; **enterprising** a emprendedor(a).

entertain [entə'teɪn] vt (amuse) divertir; (receive: guest) recibir (en casa); (idea) abrigar; (plan) estudiar; **~er** n artista m/f; **~ing** a divertido, entretenido; **~ment** n (amusement) diversión f; (show) espectáculo; (party) fiesta.

enthralled [ɪn'θrɔːld] a encantado, cautivado.

enthusiasm [ɪn'θuːzɪæzəm] n entusiasmo.

enthusiast [ɪn'θuːzɪæst] n entusiasta m/f; **~ic** [-'æstɪk] a entusiasta inv; **to be ~ic about** entusiasmarse por.

entice [ɪn'taɪs] vt tentar; (seduce) seducir; **enticing** a atractivo, tentador(a).

entire [ɪn'taɪə*] a entero, completo; (in total) total, todo; **~ly** ad totalmente; **~ty** [ɪn'taɪərətɪ] n: **in its ~ty** en su totalidad.

entitle [ɪn'taɪtl] vt: **to ~ sb to sth** dar a uno derecho a algo; **~d** a (book) que se titula; **to be ~d to** do tener derecho a hacer.

entourage [ɔntuˈrɑːʒ] n séquito.

entrails ['entreɪlz] npl entrañas fpl.

entrance ['entrəns] n entrada // vt [ɪn'trɑːns] encantar, hechizar; **to gain ~ to** (university etc) ingresar en; **~ examination** n examen m de ingreso; **~ fee** n cuota.

entrant ['entrənt] n participante m/f.

entreat [en'triːt] vt rogar, suplicar; **~y** n ruego, súplica.

entrée ['ɔntreɪ] n (CULIN) entrada.

entrenched [en'trentʃd] a atrincherado.

entrepreneur [ɔntrəprəˈnəː] n empresario; (of works) contratista m/f.

entrust [ɪn'trʌst] vt: **to ~ sth to sb** confiar algo a uno.

entry ['entrɪ] n entrada; (permission to enter) acceso; (in register) apunte m; (in account) partida; **~**

form n boleto de inscripción; **no ~** prohibido el paso; (AUT) dirección prohibida.

enumerate [ɪ'njuːməreɪt] vt enumerar.

enunciate [ɪ'nʌnsɪeɪt] vt pronunciar; (principle etc) enunciar.

envelop [ɪn'vɛləp] vt envolver.

envelope ['ɛnvələʊp] n sobre m.

envious ['ɛnvɪəs] a envidioso; (look) de envidia.

environment [ɪn'vaɪərnmənt] n medio ambiente; **~al** [-'mɛntl] a ambiental.

envisage [ɪn'vɪzɪdʒ] vt (foresee) prever; (imagine) concebir, representarse.

envoy ['ɛnvɔɪ] n enviado.

envy ['ɛnvɪ] n envidia // vt tener envidia a; **to ~ sb sth** envidiar algo a uno.

enzyme ['ɛnzaɪm] n enzima.

ephemeral [ɪ'fɛmərl] a efímero.

epic ['ɛpɪk] n épica // a épico.

epidemic [ɛpɪ'dɛmɪk] n epidemia.

epilepsy ['ɛpɪlɛpsɪ] n epilepsia; **epileptic** [-'lɛptɪk] a, n epiléptico/a.

episode ['ɛpɪsəʊd] n episodio.

epistle [ɪ'pɪsl] n epístola.

epitaph ['ɛpɪtɑːf] n epitafio.

epitome [ɪ'pɪtəmɪ] n epítome m; **epitomize** vt epitomar, resumir.

epoch ['iːpɔk] n época.

equable ['ɛkwəbl] a uniforme, igual; (character) tranquilo, afable.

equal ['iːkwl] a (gen) igual; (treatment) equitativo // a igual m/f // vt ser igual a; **to be ~ to** (task) estar a la altura de; **~ity** [iː'kwɔlɪtɪ] n igualdad f; **~ize** vt, vi igualar; (SPORT) lograr el empate; **~izer** n (igualada, el) igual; **~ly** ad igualmente; (share etc) por igual.

equanimity [ɛkwəˈnɪmɪtɪ] n ecuanimidad f.

equate [ɪ'kweɪt] vt: **to ~ sth with** considerar algo equivalente a; **equation** [ɪ'kweɪʃən] n (MATH) ecuación f.

equator [ɪ'kweɪtə*] n ecuador m.

~ial [ɛkwə'tɔːrɪəl] a ecuatorial.

equilibrium [iːkwɪ'lɪbrɪəm] n equilibrio.

equinox ['iːkwɪnɒks] n equinoccio.

equip [ɪ'kwɪp] vt (gen) equipar; (person) proveer; **to be well ~ped** estar bien dotado; ~ment n equipo; (tools) avíos mpl.

equitable ['ɛkwɪtəbl] a equitativo.

equivalent [ɪ'kwɪvələnt] a equivalente; **to be ~ to** equivaler a // n equivalente m.

equivocal [ɪ'kwɪvəkl] a equívoco; (open to suspicion) ambiguo.

era ['ɪərə] n era, época.

eradicate [ɪ'rædɪkeɪt] vt erradicar, extirpar.

erase [ɪ'reɪz] vt borrar; **eraser** n goma de borrar.

erect [ɪ'rɛkt] a erguido // vt erigir, levantar; (assembly) montar.

erection [ɪ'rɛkʃən] n construcción f; (assembly) montaje m; (structure) edificio; (MED) erección f.

ermine ['əːmɪn] n armiño.

erode [ɪ'rəud] vt (GEO) erosionar; (metal) corroer, desgastar; **erosion** [ɪ'rəuʒən] n erosión f; desgaste m.

erotic [ɪ'rɒtɪk] a erótico; ~ism [ɪ'rɒtɪsɪzm] n erotismo.

err [əː] vi errar, equivocarse; (REL) pecar.

errand ['ɛrnd] n recado, mandado; ~ boy n recadero.

erratic [ɪ'rætɪk] a irregular; (uneven) desigual, poco uniforme.

erroneous [ɪ'rəunɪəs] a erróneo.

error ['ɛrə*] n error m, equivocación f.

erupt [ɪ'rʌpt] vi estar en erupción; (MED) hacer erupción; (fig) estallar; ~ion [ɪ'rʌpʃən] n erupción f; (fig) explosión f.

escalate ['ɛskəleɪt] vi extenderse, intensificarse; **escalation** [-'leɪʃən] n escalamiento, intensificación f.

escalator ['ɛskəleɪtə*] n escalera móvil.

escapade [ɛskə'peɪd] n travesura.

escape [ɪ'skeɪp] n (gen) fuga; (from duties) escapatoria; (from chase) fuga, evasión f // vi (gen) escaparse, (flee) huir, evadirse; (leak) fugarse // vt evitar, eludir; (consequences) escapar a; **to ~ from** (place) escaparse de; (person) escapar a; (clutches) librarse de; **escapism** n escapismo.

escort ['ɛskɔːt] n acompañante m/f; (MIL) escolta; (NAUT) convoy m // vt [ɪ'skɔːt] acompañar; (MIL, NAUT) escoltar.

Eskimo ['ɛskɪməu] n esquimal m/f.

especially [ɪ'spɛʃlɪ] ad (gen) especialmente; (above all) sobre todo; (particularly) en particular.

espionage ['ɛspɪənɑːʒ] n espionaje m.

esplanade [ɛsplə'neɪd] n (by sea) paseo marítimo.

espouse [ɪ'spauz] vt adherirse a.

Esquire [ɪ'skwaɪə*] n (abbr Esq.): **J. Brown, ~ Sr. Don J. Brown**.

essay ['ɛseɪ] n (SCOL) ensayo.

essence ['ɛsns] n esencia.

essential [ɪ'sɛnʃl] a (necessary) imprescindible; (basic) esencial; ~ly ad esencialmente.

establish [ɪ'stæblɪʃ] vt establecer; (facts) verificar; (proof) demostrar; (relations) entablar; ~ed a (business) de buena reputación, (staff) de plantilla; ~ment n establecimiento; **the E~ment** la clase dirigente.

estate [ɪ'steɪt] n (land) finca, hacienda; (property) propiedad f; (inheritance) herencia; (POL) estado; **housing ~** urbanización f; **industrial ~** polígono industrial; ~ **agent** n agente m/f inmobiliario; ~ **car** n (Brit) furgoneta.

esteem [ɪ'stiːm] n: **to hold sb in high ~** estimar en mucho a uno // vt estimar.

estimate ['ɛstɪmət] n estimación f, apreciación f; (assessment) tasa, cálculo; (COMM) presupuesto // vt [-meɪt] estimar, tasar, calcular; **estimation** [-'meɪʃən] n opinión f, juicio; (*esteem*) aprecio.

estrange [ɪ'streɪndʒ] vt enajenar.

estuary ['estjuərɪ] n estuario, ría.

etching ['etʃɪŋ] n aguafuerte f.

eternal [ɪ'tə:nl] a eterno.

eternity [ɪ'tə:nɪtɪ] n eternidad f.

ether ['i:θə*] n éter m.

ethical ['eθɪkl] a ético; (*honest*) honrado; **ethics** ['eθɪks] n ética // npl moralidad f.

ethnic ['eθnɪk] a étnico.

etiquette ['etɪket] n etiqueta.

eucalyptus [ju:kə'lɪptəs] n eucalipto.

euphemism ['ju:fəmɪzm] n eufemismo.

euphoria [ju:'fɔ:rɪə] n euforia.

Europe ['juərəp] n Europa; **European** [-'pi:ən] a, n europeo/a.

euthanasia [ju:θə'neɪzɪə] n eutanasia.

evacuate [ɪ'vækjueɪt] vt desocupar; **evacuation** [-'eɪʃən] n evacuación f.

evade [ɪ'veɪd] vt evadir, eludir.

evaluate [ɪ'væljueɪt] vt evaluar; (*value*) tasar; (*evidence*) interpretar.

evangelist [ɪ'vændʒəlɪst] n evangelizador m, evangelista m/f.

evaporate [ɪ'væpəreɪt] vi evaporarse, desvanecerse // vt evaporar; **~d milk** n leche f evaporada; **evaporation** [-'reɪʃən] n evaporación f.

evasion [ɪ'veɪʒən] n evasiva, evasión f; **evasive** [-sɪv] a evasivo.

eve [i:v] n: **on the ~ of** en vísperas de.

even ['i:vn] a (*level*) llano; (*smooth*) liso; (*speed, temperature*) uniforme; (*number*) par; (*nature*) ecuánime; (*SPORT*) igual(es) // ad hasta aun, siquiera; ~ **more** aun más; ~ **so** aun así; **not** ~ ni siquiera; ~ **he was there** hasta él estuvo allí; ~ **on Sundays** incluso los domingos; **to ~ out** vi nivelarse; **to get ~ with sb** ajustar cuentas con uno.

evening ['i:vnɪŋ] n tarde f; (*dusk*) atardecer m; (*night*) noche f;

(*event*) velada; **in the ~** por la tarde; ~ **class** n clase f nocturna; ~ **dress** n (*man's*) traje m de etiqueta; (*woman's*) traje m de noche.

event [ɪ'vent] n suceso, acontecimiento; (*SPORT*) prueba; **in the ~ of** en caso de que; **~ful** a accidentado; (*game etc*) lleno de emoción.

eventual [ɪ'ventʃuəl] a (*last*) final; (*resulting*) consiguiente; **~ity** ['ælɪtɪ] n eventualidad f; **~ly** ad (*finally*) finalmente, al fin y al cabo; (*in time*) a la larga.

ever ['evə*] ad nunca, jamás; (*at all times*) alguna vez; **the best ~** el/la mejor que se ha visto jamás; **have you ~ seen it?** ¿lo ha visto Usted jamás?; **better than ~** mejor que nunca; ~ **since** ad desde entonces // conj después de que; **~green** n árbol m de hoja perenne; **~lasting** a eterno, perpetuo.

every ['evrɪ] det (*each*) cada; (*all*) todo; ~ **day** cada día; ~ **other car** cada dos coches; ~ **now and then** de vez en cuando; **~body** pron todos pl, todo el mundo; **~day** a (*daily*) diario, cotidiano; (*usual*) corriente; (*common*) vulgar; (*routine*) rutinario; **~one** = **~body**; **~thing** pron todo; **~where** ad (be) en todas partes; (go) a o por todas partes.

evict [ɪ'vɪkt] vt desahuciar; **~ion** [ɪ'vɪkʃən] n desahucio.

evidence ['evɪdəns] n (*proof*) prueba; (*of witness*) testimonio; (*facts*) datos mpl, hechos mpl; **to give ~** prestar declaración, dar testimonio.

evident ['evɪdənt] a evidente, manifiesto; **~ly** ad naturalmente.

evil ['i:vl] a malo; (*influence*) funesto; (*smell*) horrible // n mal m, maldad f; **~doer** n malhechor/a m/f.

evocative [ɪ'vɔkətɪv] a sugestivo, evocador(a).

evoke [ɪ'vəuk] vt evocar.

evolution [i:vəˈluːʃən] n evolución f, desarrollo.

evolve [ɪˈvɔlv] vt desarrollar // vi evolucionar, desarrollarse.

ewe [juː] n oveja.

ex-... [eks] pref ex.

exact [ɪgˈzækt] a exacto // vt: to ~ sth (from) exigir algo (de); ~ing a exigente; (conditions) arduo, ~itude n exactitud f; ~ly ad exactamente; (time) en punto.

exaggerate [ɪgˈzædʒəreɪt] vt, vi exagerar, **exaggeration** [-ˈreɪʃən] n exageración f.

exalted [ɪgˈzɔːltɪd] a exaltado, elevado.

exam [ɪgˈzæm] n abbr of **examination**.

examination [ɪgzæmɪˈneɪʃən] n (gen) examen m; (LAW) interrogación f; (inquiry) investigación f.

examine [ɪgˈzæmɪn] vt (gen) examinar; (inspect) inspeccionar, escudriñar; (SCOL, LAW: person) interrogar; (at customs: luggage) registrar; **examiner** n inspector m.

example [ɪgˈzɑːmpl] n ejemplo; (copy) ejemplar m; **for** ~ por ejemplo.

exasperate [ɪgˈzɑːspəreɪt] vt exasperar, irritar, **exasperating** a irritante.

excavate [ˈekskəveɪt] vt excavar; **excavation** [-ˈveɪʃən] n excavación f.

exceed [ɪkˈsiːd] vt exceder; (number) pasar de; (speed limit) sobrepasar; (limits) rebasar; (powers) excederse en; (hopes) superar; ~ingly ad sumamente, sobremanera.

excel [ɪkˈsel] vi sobresalir.

excellence [ˈeksələns] n excelencia.

Excellency [ˈeksələnsɪ] n: His ~ Su Excelencia.

excellent [ˈeksələnt] a excelente.

except [ɪkˈsept] prep (also: ~ for, ~ing) excepto, salvo, con excepción de // vt exceptuar;

~ if/when excepto si/cuando; ~ that salvo que; ~ion [ɪkˈsepʃən] n excepción f; to take ~ion to ofenderse por; ~ional [ɪkˈsepʃənl] a excepcional.

excerpt [ˈeksɜːpt] n extracto.

excess [ɪkˈses] n exceso; (COMM) excedente m; ~ baggage n exceso de equipaje; ~ fare n suplemento m; ~ive a excesivo.

exchange [ɪksˈtʃeɪndʒ] n cambio; (of goods) canje m; (of ideas) intercambio; (also: telephone ~) central f (telefónica) // vt cambiar, canjear.

exchequer [ɪksˈtʃekə*] n hacienda.

excise [ˈeksaɪz] n impuestos mpl sobre el comercio exterior // vt [ɛkˈsaɪz] suprimir.

excite [ɪkˈsaɪt] vt (stimulate) excitar; (awaken) despertar; (move) entusiasmar; to get ~d emocionarse; ~ment n emoción f; (anticipation) ilusión f, (agitation) agitación f; **exciting** a emocionante.

exclaim [ɪkˈskleɪm] vi exclamar; **exclamation** [ekskləˈmeɪʃən] n exclamación f; **exclamation mark** n punto de admiración.

exclude [ɪkˈskluːd] vt excluir; (except) exceptuar; **exclusion** [ɪkˈskluːʒən] n exclusión f.

exclusive [ɪkˈskluːsɪv] a exclusivo; (club, district) selecto; ~ of tax excluyendo impuestos; ~ly ad únicamente.

excommunicate [ekskəˈmjuːnɪkeɪt] vt excomulgar.

excrement [ˈekskrəmənt] n excremento.

excrete [ɪkˈskriːt] vi excretar.

excruciating [ɪkˈskruːʃieɪtɪŋ] a agudísimo, atroz.

excursion [ɪkˈskɜːʃən] n excursión f.

excusable [ɪkˈskjuːzəbl] a perdonable.

excuse [ɪkˈskjuːs] n disculpa, excusa; (evasion) pretexto // vt [ɪkˈskjuːz] disculpar, perdonar; to ~

sb from doing sth dispensar a uno de hacer algo; ~ **me** ¡perdón!; **if you will** ~ **me** con su permiso.

execute ['eksɪkjuːt] vt (plan) realizar; (order) cumplir; (person) ajusticiar, ejecutar; **execution** n realización f; cumplimiento; ejecución f; **executioner** n verdugo.

executive [ɪg'zekjutɪv] n (COMM, POL) ejecutivo /a // a ejecutivo.

executor [ɪg'zekjutə*] n albacea m, testamentario.

exemplary [ɪg'zempləri] a ejemplar.

exemplify [ɪg'zemplɪfaɪ] vt ejemplificar.

exempt [ɪg'zempt] a: ~ **from** exento de // vt: **to** ~ **sb from** eximir a uno de; ~**ion** [ɪg'zempʃən] n exención f; (immunity) inmunidad f.

exercise ['eksəsaɪz] n ejercicio // vt ejercer; (right) valerse de; (dog) llevar de paseo // vi hacer ejercicio(s); ~ **book** n cuaderno.

exert [ɪg'zəːt] vt ejercer; **to** ~ **o.s.** esforzarse, afanarse; (overdo things) trabajar demasiado; ~**ion** n esfuerzo.

exhaust [ɪg'zɔːst] n (pipe) escape m; (fumes) gases mpl de escape // vt agotar; ~**ion** n agotamiento; **nervous** ~**ion** postración f nerviosa; ~**ive** a exhaustivo.

exhibit [ɪg'zɪbɪt] n (ART) obra expuesta; (LAW) objeto expuesto // vt (show) manifestar; (emotion) acusar; (film) presentar; (paintings) exponer; ~**ion** [eksɪ'bɪʃən] n exposición f; (exhibiting) demostración f; ~**ionist** [eksɪ'bɪʃənɪst] n exhibicionista m/f.

exhilarating [ɪg'zɪləreɪtɪŋ] a estimulante, tónico.

exhort [ɪg'zɔːt] vt exhortar.

exile ['eksaɪl] n exilio; (person) exiliado/a // vt desterrar, exiliar.

exist [ɪg'zɪst] vi existir; ~**ence** n existencia // (life) vida; ~**ing** a existente, actual.

exit ['eksɪt] n salida.

exonerate [ɪg'zɔnəreɪt] vt: **to** ~ **from** exculpar de.

exorcize ['eksɔːsaɪz] vt exorcizar.

exotic [ɪg'zɔtɪk] a exótico.

expand [ɪk'spænd] vt (widen) ensanchar; (number) aumentar // vi (trade etc) expandirse; (gas, metal) dilatarse.

expanse [ɪk'spæns] n extensión f; (of wings) envergadura f.

expansion [ɪk'spænʃən] n (of town) ensanche m; (of trade) expansión f.

expatriate [eks'pætrɪət] n expatriado/a.

expect [ɪk'spekt] vt (gen) esperar; (count on) contar con; (suppose) suponer // vi: **to be** ~**ing** estar encinta; ~**ant mother** n mujer f encinta; ~**ation** [ekspek'teɪʃən] n esperanza, expectativa.

expedience [ek'spiːdɪəns], **expediency** [ek'spiːdɪənsɪ] n conveniencia; **expedient** a conveniente, oportuno // n recurso, expediente m.

expedition [ekspə'dɪʃən] n expedición f.

expel [ɪk'spel] vt arrojar; (SCOL) expulsar.

expend [ɪk'spend] vt gastar; (use up) consumir; ~**able** a prescindible; ~**iture** n gastos mpl, desembolso.

expense [ɪk'spens] n gasto, gastos mpl; (high cost) costa; ~**s** npl (COMM) gastos mpl; **at the** ~ **of** a costa o expensas de; ~ **account** n cuenta de gastos.

expensive [ɪk'spensɪv] a caro, costoso.

experience [ɪk'spɪərɪəns] n experiencia // vt experimentar; (suffer) sufrir; ~**d** a experimentado.

experiment [ɪk'sperɪmənt] n experimento // vi hacer experimentos; ~**al** [-'mentl] a experimental.

expert ['ekspəːt] a experto, perito // n experto, perito; (specialist) especialista *m/f*; **~ise** [-'ti:z] *n* pericia.

expire [ɪk'spaɪə*] *vi* (gen) expirar; (end) terminar; (run out) caducar, vencerse; **expiry** *n* expiración *f*; terminación *f*; vencimiento.

explain [ɪk'spleɪn] *vt* explicar; (clarify) aclarar; (demonstrate) exponer; **explanation** [ekspləˈneɪʃən] *n* explicación *f*; aclaración *f*; **explanatory** [ɪk'splænətrɪ] *a* explicativo; aclaratorio.

explicit [ɪk'splɪsɪt] *a* explícito.

explode [ɪk'spləud] *vi* estallar, explotar; (with anger) reventar // *vt* volar, explotar.

exploit ['eksplɔɪt] *n* hazaña // *vt* [ɪk'splɔɪt] explotar; **~ation** [-'teɪʃən] *n* explotación *f*.

exploration [ekspləˈreɪʃən] *n* exploración *f*; **exploratory** [ɪk'splɔrətrɪ] *a* (fig: talks) exploratorio, de sondaje.

explore [ɪk'splɔ:*] *vt* explorar; (fig) examinar, sondar; **explorer** *n* explorador *m*.

explosion [ɪk'spləuʒən] *n* explosión *f*; **explosive** [-sɪv] *a, n* explosivo.

exponent [ɪk'spəunənt] *n* exponente *m/f*, intérprete *m/f*.

export [ek'spɔ:t] *vt* exportar // *n* ['ekspɔ:t] exportación *f* // *cpd* de exportación; **~ation** [-'teɪʃən] *n* exportación *f*; **~er** *n* exportador *m*.

expose [ɪk'spəuz] *vt* exponer; (unmask) desenmascarar; **~d** *a* expuesto; (position) desabrigado.

exposure [ɪk'spəuʒə*] *n* exposición *f*; (PHOT) revelación *f*; (: shot) fotografía; **to die from ~** (MED) morir de frío; **~ meter** *n* fotómetro.

expound [ɪk'spaund] *vt* exponer, explicar.

express [ɪk'spres] *a* (definite) expreso, explícito; (letter etc) urgente // *n* (train) rápido // *ad* (send) por carta urgente // *vt* expresar; (squeeze) exprimir; **~ion** [ɪk'spreʃən] *n* expresión *f*; **~ive** *a* expresivo; **~ly** *ad* expresamente.

expulsion [ɪk'spʌlʃən] *n* expulsión *f*.

exquisite [ek'skwɪzɪt] *a* exquisito.

extend [ɪk'stend] *vt* (visit, street) prolongar; (building) ensanchar; (offer) ofrecer // *vi* (land) extenderse.

extension [ɪk'stenʃən] *n* extensión *f*; (building) ampliación *f*; (TEL: line) línea derivada; (: telephone) extensión *f*; (of deadline) prórroga.

extensive [ɪk'stensɪv] *a* (gen) extenso; (broad) vasto, ancho; (frequent) general, común; **he's travelled ~ly** ha viajado por muchos países.

extent [ɪk'stent] *n* (breadth) extensión *f*; (scope) alcance *m*; **to some ~** hasta cierto punto; **to the ~ of...** hasta el punto de...; **to such an ~ that...** hasta tal punto que...; **to what ~?** ¿hasta qué punto?

exterior [ek'stɪərɪə*] *a* exterior, externo // *n* exterior *m*; (appearance) aspecto.

exterminate [ek'stɜ:mɪneɪt] *vt* exterminar; **extermination** [-'neɪʃən] *n* exterminación *f*.

external [ek'stɜ:nl] *a* externo, exterior; **~ly** *ad* por fuera.

extinct [ɪk'stɪŋkt] *a* extinto; **~ion** [ɪk'stɪŋkʃən] *n* extinción *f*.

extinguish [ɪk'stɪŋgwɪʃ] *vt* extinguir, apagar; **~er** *n* extintor *m*.

extort [ɪk'stɔ:t] *vt* sacar a la fuerza (from sb de uno); **~ion** [ɪk'stɔ:ʃən] *n* exacción *f*; **~ionate** [ɪk'stɔ:ʃnət] *a* excesivo, prohibitivo.

extra ['ekstrə] *a* adicional; (excessive) de más, de sobra; (bonus: payment) extraordinario // *ad* (in addition) especialmente // *n* (addition) extra *m*, suplemento; (THEATRE) extra *m/f*, comparsa *m/f*; (newspaper) edición *f* extraordinaria.

extra... ['ekstrə] pref extra...

extract [ɪk'strækt] *vt* sacar; extraer; (confession) arrancar, obtener // *n* ['ekstrækt] extracto.

extradite ['ekstrədaɪt] *vt* (from

country) conceder la extradición de; (*to country*) obtener la extradición de; **extradition** [-'dɪʃən] *n* extradición *f*.

extramarital [ekstrə'mærɪtl] *a* extramatrimonial.

extramural [ekstrə'mjuərl] *a* de extramuros.

extraordinary [ɪk'strɔːdnrɪ] *a* extraordinario; (*odd*) raro.

extravagant [ɪk'strævəgənt] *a* (*lavish*) pródigo, (*wasteful*) derrochador(a); (*price*) exorbitante; (*praise*) excesivo; (*odd*) raro.

extreme [ɪk'striːm] *a* extremo; (*poverty etc*) extremado; (*case*) excepcional // *n* extremo, extremidad *f*; **~ly** *ad* sumamente, extremadamente; **extremist** *a, n* extremista *m/f*.

extremity [ɪk'stremɪtɪ] *n* extremidad *f*, punta; (*need*) apuro, necesidad *f*.

extricate ['ekstrɪkeɪt] *vt* librar.

extrovert ['ekstrəvəːt] *n* extrovertido/a.

exuberant [ɪg'zjuːbərnt] *a* (*person*) eufórico; (*style*) exuberante.

exude [ɪg'zjuːd] *vt* rezumar, sudar.

exult [ɪg'zʌlt] *vi* regocijarse.

eye [aɪ] *n* ojo // *vt* mirar de soslayo, ojear; **to keep an ~ on** vigilar, estar pendiente de; **~ball** *n* globo del ojo; **~bath** *n* ojera; **~brow** *n* ceja; **~brow pencil** *n* lápiz *m* de cejas; **~-catching** *a* llamativo; **~drops** *npl* gotas *fpl* para los ojos; **~lash** *n* pestaña; **~lid** *n* párpado; **~opener** *n* revelación *f*, gran sorpresa; **~shadow** *n* sombreador *m* de ojos; **~sight** *n* vista; **~sore** *n* monstruosidad *f*; **~wash** *n* (*fig*) disparates *mpl*, tonterías *fpl*; **~witness** *n* testigo *m/f* presencial.

eyrie ['ɪərɪ] *n* aguilera.

F

F. *abbr of* **Fahrenheit.**

fable ['feɪbl] *n* fábula.

fabric ['fæbrɪk] *n* tejido, tela.

fabrication [fæbrɪ'keɪʃən] *n* invención *f*.

fabulous ['fæbjuləs] *a* fabuloso.

façade [fə'sɑːd] *n* fachada.

face [feɪs] *n* cara; (*ANAT*) cara, rostro; (*of clock*) esfera; (*side, surface*) superficie *f* // *vt* (*person*) encararse con; (*building*) dar a; **to lose ~** desprestigiarse; **in the ~ of** (*difficulties etc*) en vista de; **on the ~ of it** a primera vista; **~ to ~** cara a cara; **to ~ up to** *vt fus* hacer frente a, arrostrar; **~ cloth** *n* paño; **~ cream** *n* crema (de belleza); **~ lift** *n* cirugía estética; **~ powder** *n* polvos *mpl*; **~-saving** *a* para salvar las apariencias.

facet ['fæsɪt] *n* faceta.

facetious [fə'siːʃəs] *a* chistoso.

face value ['feɪs'væljuː] *n* (*of stamp*) valor *m* nominal; **to take sth at ~** (*fig*) tomar algo en sentido literal, aceptar las apariencias de algo.

facial ['feɪʃəl] *a* de la cara.

facile ['fæsaɪl] *a* superficial, ligero.

facilitate [fə'sɪlɪteɪt] *vt* facilitar.

facilities [fə'sɪlɪtɪz] *npl* facilidades *fpl*.

facing ['feɪsɪŋ] *prep* frente a // *a* de enfrente.

fact [fækt] *n* hecho; **in ~** en realidad.

faction ['fækʃən] *n* facción *f*.

factor ['fæktə*] *n* factor *m*.

factory ['fæktərɪ] *n* fábrica.

factual ['fæktjuəl] *a* objetivo.

faculty ['fækəltɪ] *n* facultad *f*; (*US: teaching staff*) profesorado.

fade [feɪd] *vi* desteñirse; (*sound, hope*) desvanecerse; (*light*) apagarse; (*flower*) marchitarse.

fag [fæg] *n* (*col: cigarette*) pitillo; **~**

end *n* colilla; ~**ged out** *a* (col) agotado.

fail [feil] *vt* (candidate) suspender; (exam) no aprobar // *vi* acabarse; (engine) fallar; (voice) desfallecer; (patient) debilitarse; to ~ **to do sth** (neglect) dejar de hacer algo; (be unable) no poder hacer algo; **without** ~ sin falta; ~**ing** *n* falta, defecto // *prep* a falta de; ~**ure** ['feiljə*] *n* fracaso; (person) fracasado/a; (mechanical etc) fallo.

faint [feint] *a* débil; (recollection) vago; (mark) apenas visible // *n* desmayo // *vi* desmayarse; **to feel** ~ estar mareado, marearse; ~**-hearted** *a* pusilánime; ~**ly** *ad* débilmente; vagamente; ~**ness** *n* debilidad f.

fair [feə*] *a* justo, (colour) rubio; (weather) bueno; (good enough) suficiente; (sizeable) considerable // *ad* (play) limpio // *n* feria; (funfair) parque *m* de atracciones; ~**ly** *ad* (justly) con justicia; (equally) equitativamente; (quite) bastante; ~**ness** *n* justicia, (impartiality) imparcialidad f.

fairy ['feəri] *n* hada; ~ **tale** *n* cuento de hadas.

faith [feiθ] *n* fe f, (trust) confianza; (sect) religión f; ~**ful** *a* fiel; ~**fully** *ad* fielmente; **yours** ~**fully** le saluda atentamente.

fake [feik] *n* (painting etc) falsificación f; (person) impostor *m* // *a* falso // *vt* fingir; (painting etc) falsificar; **his illness is a** ~ su enfermedad es una invención.

falcon ['fɔːlkən] *n* halcón *m*.

fall [fɔːl] *n* caída; (US: autumn) otoño // *vi*, *pt* **fell**, *pp* **fallen** ['fɔːlən] caer, caerse; (price) bajar; ~**s** *npl* (waterfall) cascada, salto de agua; **to** ~ **flat** *vi* (on one's face) caerse (boca abajo); (plan) fracasar; **to** ~ **back** *vi* retroceder; **to** ~ **back on** *vt* fus (remedy etc) recurrir a; **to** ~ **backwards** *vi* caer de espaldas; **to** ~ **behind** *vi* quedarse atrás; **to** ~

down *vi* (person) caerse; (building, hopes) derrumbarse; **to** ~ **for** *vt fus* (trick) dejarse engañar por; (person) enamorarse de; **to** ~ **in** *vi* (roof) hundirse; (MIL) alinearse; **to** ~ **off** *vi* caerse; (diminish) disminuir; **to** ~ **out** *vi* (friends etc) reñir; (MIL) romper filas; **to** ~ **through** *vi* (plan, project) fracasar.

fallacy ['fæləsi] *n* (error) error *m*; (lie) mentira.

fallible ['fæləbl] *a* falible.

fallout ['fɔːlaut] *n* lluvia radioactiva; ~ **shelter** *n* refugio contra ataques nucleares.

false [fɔːls] *a* (gen) falso; (hair, teeth etc) postizo; (disloyal) desleal, traidor(a); **under** ~ **pretences** con engaños; ~**hood** *n* (lie) mentira, (falseness) falsedad f; ~**ly** *ad* (accuse) falsamente; ~ **teeth** *npl* dentadura postiza *sg*.

falter ['fɔːltə*] *vi* vacilar.

fame [feim] *n* fama.

familiar [fə'miliə*] *a* familiar; (well-known) conocido; (tone) de confianza; **to be** ~ **with** (subject) estar enterado de; ~**ity** [fəmili'æriti] *n* familiaridad f; ~**ize** [fə'miliəraiz] *vt*; **to** ~**ize o.s. with** familiarizarse con.

family ['fæmili] *n* familia; ~ **business** *n* negocio familiar; ~ **doctor** *n* médico de cabecera.

famine ['fæmin] *n* hambre f.

famished ['fæmiʃt] *a* hambriento.

famous ['feiməs] *a* famoso, célebre; ~**ly** *ad* (get on) estupendamente.

fan [fæn] *n* abanico; (ELEC) ventilador *m*; (person) aficionado/a // *vt* abanicar; (fire, quarrel) atizar; **to** ~ **out** *vi* desparramarse.

fanatic [fə'nætik] *n* fanático/a; ~**al** *a* fanático.

fan belt ['fænbelt] *n* correa de ventilador.

fanciful ['fænsiful] *a* (gen) fantástico; (imaginary) imaginario.

fancy ['fænsi] *n* (whim) capricho, antojo; (taste) afición f, gusto;

(*imagination*) imaginación *f*; (*delusion*) quimera *f* // *a* (*decorative*) hermoso; (*luxury*) de lujo; (*as decoration*) de adorno // *vt* (*feel like*, *want*) tener ganas de; (*imagine*) imaginarse; (*think*) creer; **to take a ~ to** encapricharse por, tomar afición a; **it took** *or* **caught my ~** me cayó en gracia; **to ~ that...** imaginarse que...; **he fancies her** le gusta (ella); **~ dress** *n* disfraz *m*; **~-dress ball** *n* baile *m* de disfraces.

fang [fæŋ] *n* colmillo.

fantastic [fæn'tæstɪk] *a* fantástico.

fantasy ['fæntəzɪ] *n* fantasía.

far [fɑ:*] *a* (*distant*) lejano // *ad* lejos; **~ away**, **~ off** (a lo) lejos; **~ better** mucho mejor; **~ from** lejos de; **by ~** con mucho; **go as ~ as the farm** vaya hasta la granja; **as ~ as I know** que yo sepa; **how ~?** ¿hasta dónde?; (*fig*) ¿hasta qué punto?; **the F~ East** el Extremo Oriente; **~away** *a* remoto.

farce [fɑ:s] *n* farsa; **farcical** *a* absurdo.

fare [feə*] *n* (*on trains*, *buses*) precio (del billete); (*in taxi*: *cost*) tarifa; (: *passenger*) pasajero; (*food*) comida.

farewell [feə'wel] *excl*, *n* adiós *m*.

farm [fɑ:m] *n* granja, finca, estancia (*AM*) // *vt* cultivar; **~er** *n* granjero, estanciero (*AM*); **~hand** *n* peón *m*; **~house** *n* casa de labranza; **~ing** *n* (*gen*) agricultura; (*tilling*) cultivo; **~land** *n* tierra de cultivo; **~ worker** *n* = **~hand**; **~yard** *n* corral *m*.

far-sighted ['fɑ:'saɪtɪd] *a* previsor(a).

fart [fɑ:t] (*col!*) *n* pedo // *vi* tirarse un pedo.

farther ['fɑ:ðə*] *ad* más lejos, más allá.

farthest ['fɑ:ðɪst] *superlative of* **far**.

fascinate ['fæsɪneɪt] *vt* fascinar; **fascination** [-'neɪʃən] *n* fascinación *f*.

fascism ['fæʃɪzəm] *n* fascismo;

fascist [-ɪst] *a*, *n* fascista *m/f*.

fashion ['fæʃən] *n* moda; (*manner*) manera // *vt* formar; **in ~** a la moda; **out of ~** pasado de moda; **~able** *a* de moda; **~ show** *n* desfile *m* de modelos.

fast [fɑ:st] *a* rápido; (*dye*, *colour*) sólido; (*clock*): **to be ~** estar adelantado // *ad* rápidamente, de prisa; (*stuck*, *held*) firmemente // *n* ayuno // *vi* ayunar; **~ asleep** profundamente dormido.

fasten ['fɑ:sn] *vt* asegurar, sujetar; (*coat*, *belt*) abrochar // *vi* cerrarse; **~er**, **~ing** *n* (*gen*) cierre *m*; (*of door etc*) cerrojo; **zip ~er** cremallera.

fastidious [fæs'tɪdɪəs] *a* (*fussy*) delicado; (*demanding*) exigente.

fat [fæt] *a* gordo; (*meat*) con mucha grasa; (*greasy*) grasiento // *n* grasa; (*on person*) carnes *fpl*; (*lard*) manteca.

fatal ['feɪtl] *a* (*gen*) fatal; (*injury*) mortal; (*consequence*) funesto; **~ism** *n* fatalismo; **~ity** [fə'tælɪtɪ] *n* (*road death etc*) víctima *m/f*; **~ly** *ad*: **~ly injured** herido a muerte.

fate [feɪt] *n* destino; (*of person*) suerte *f*; **~ful** *a* fatídico.

father ['fɑ:ðə*] *n* padre; **~hood** *n* paternidad *f*; **~-in-law** *n* suegro; **~ly** *a* paternal.

fathom ['fæðəm] *n* braza // *vt* (*NAUT*) sondear; (*unravel*) desentrañar; (*understand*) lograr comprender.

fatigue [fə'ti:g] *n* fatiga, cansancio.

fatten ['fætn] *vt*, *vi* engordar.

fatty ['fætɪ] *a* (*food*) graso // *n* (*fam*) gordito/a, gordinflón/ona *m/f*.

faucet ['fɔ:sɪt] *n* (*US*) grifo.

fault [fɔ:lt] *n* (*error*) falta; (*blame*) culpa; (*defect*: *in character*) defecto; (*in manufacture*) desperfecto; (*GEO*) falla // *vt* tachar; **it's my ~** es culpa mía; **to find ~ with** criticar, poner peros a; **at ~** culpable; **~less** *a* (*action*) intachable; (*person*) sin defectos; ~y a defectuoso.

fauna ['fɔ:nə] n fauna.

faux pas ['fəu'pɑ:] n paso en falso; (gaffe) plancha.

favour, favor (US) ['feɪvə*] n favor m; (support) apoyo; (approval) aprobación f // vt (proposition) estar a favor de, aprobar; (person etc) favorecer; (assist) ser propicio a; to ask a ~ of pedir un favor a; to do sb a ~ hacer un favor a uno; to find ~ with caer en gracia de; in ~ of a favor de; ~able a favorable; ~ite [-rɪt] a, n favorito, preferido // n favoritismo.

fawn [fɔ:n] n cervato a (also: ~-coloured) color de cervato, leonado.

fear [fɪə*] n miedo, temor m // vt tener miedo a o de, temer; for ~ of por temor a; ~ful a temeroso, miedoso; (cowardly) tímido; (awful) terrible; ~less a (gen) sin miedo o temor; (bold) audaz.

feasible ['fi:zəbl] a factible.

feast [fi:st] n banquete m; (REL: also: ~ day) fiesta // vt, vi banquetear.

feat [fi:t] n hazaña.

feather ['feðə*] n pluma; ~weight n (BOXING) peso pluma.

feature ['fi:tʃə*] n (gen) característica; (ANAT) rasgo; (article) crónica // vt (subj: film) presentar // vi figurar; ~s npl (of face) facciones fpl; ~ film n película (de largo metraje).

February ['februəri] n febrero.

fed [fed] pt, pp of **feed**.

federal ['fedərəl] a federal; **federation** [-'reɪʃən] n federación f.

fed-up [fed'ʌp] a: to be ~ estar harto.

fee [fi:] n derechos mpl, honorarios mpl; (of school) matrícula; (of club) cuota.

feeble ['fi:bl] a débil; ~-minded a imbécil.

feed [fi:d] n (gen) comida; (of baby) alimento infantil; (of animal) pienso // vt, pt, pp **fed** (gen) alimentar; (baby: breastfeed) dar el pecho a; (animal) dar de comer a, (data, information): to ~ into suministrar a; on vt fus alimentarse de; ~ing bottle n biberón m.

feel [fi:l] n (sensation) sensación f; (sense of touch) tacto // vt, pt, pp **felt** tocar, palpar; (cold, pain etc) sentir; (think, believe) creer; to ~ hungry/cold tener hambre/frío; to ~ lonely/better sentirse solo/mejor; it ~a soft es suave al tacto; to ~ like (want) tener ganas de; to ~ about or around tantear; ~er n (of insect) antena; to put out ~ers (fig) sondear; ~ing n (sense) sensación f; (foreboding) presentimiento; (opinion) opinión f; (emotion) sentimiento.

feet [fi:t] pl of **foot**.

feign [feɪn] vt fingir.

feline ['fi:laɪn] a felino.

fell [fel] pt of **fall** // vt (tree) talar.

fellow ['feləu] n (gen) tipo; (fam) tío; (of learned society) socio // cpd: ~ citizen n conciudadano; ~ countryman n compatriota m/f; ~ men npl semejantes mpl; ~ship n compañerismo; (grant) beca.

felony ['feləni] n crimen m.

felt [felt] pt, pp of **feel** // n fieltro; ~-tip pen n rotulador m.

female ['fi:meɪl] n (woman) mujer f; (zool) hembra // a femenino.

feminine ['femɪnɪn] a femenino.

feminist ['femɪnɪst] n feminista.

fence [fens] n valla, cerca // vt (also: ~ in) cercar // vi hacer esgrima; **fencing** n esgrima.

fend [fend] vi: to ~ for o.s. arreglárselas por su cuenta.

fender ['fendə*] n guardafuego; (US: AUT) parachoques m inv; (: RAIL) trompa.

ferment [fə'ment] vi fermentar // n ['fɜ:ment] (fig) agitación f; ~ation

[-'teɪʃən] n fermentación f.

fern [fəːn] n helecho.

ferocious [fə'rəuʃəs] a feroz; **ferocity** [-'rɔsɪtɪ] n ferocidad f.

ferret ['ferɪt] n hurón m // vt: **to ~ out** descubrir.

ferry ['ferɪ] n (small) barca (de pasaje), balsa; (large: also: **~boat**) transbordador m // vt transportar.

fertile ['fəːtaɪl] a fértil; (BIOL) fecundo; **fertility** [fə'tɪlɪtɪ] n fertilidad f; fecundidad f; **fertilize** ['fəːtɪlaɪz] vt fertilizar; fecundar; (AGR) abonar; **fertilizer** n fertilizante m.

fervent ['fəːvənt] a ardiente, apasionado.

fester ['festə*] vi ulcerarse.

festival ['festɪvəl] n (REL) fiesta; (ART, MUS) festival m.

festive ['festɪv] a festivo; **the ~ season** (Christmas) las Navidades.

festivities [fes'tɪvɪtɪz] npl fiestas fpl.

fetch [fetʃ] vt ir a buscar; (sell for) venderse por.

fetching ['fetʃɪŋ] a atractivo.

fête [feɪt] n fiesta.

fetish ['fetɪʃ] n fetiche m.

fetters ['fetəz] npl grillos mpl.

feud [fjuːd] n (hostility) enemistad f; (quarrel) disputa.

feudal ['fjuːdl] a feudal; **~ism** n feudalismo.

fever ['fiːvə*] n fiebre f; **~ish** a febril.

few [fjuː] a (not many) pocos; (some) algunos, unos; **a ~** a unos pocos // pron algunos; **~er** a menos; **~est** a los/las menos.

fiancé [fɪ'ãːseɪ] n novio, prometido; **~e** n novia, prometida.

fiasco [fɪ'æskəu] n fiasco.

fibre, fiber (US) ['faɪbə*] n fibra; **~-glass** n fibra de vidrio.

fickle ['fɪkl] a inconstante.

fiction ['fɪkʃən] n (gen) ficción f; **~al** a novelesco; **fictitious** [fɪk'tɪʃəs] a ficticio.

fiddle ['fɪdl] n (MUS) violín m;

(cheating) trampa; (swindle) estafa // vt (accounts) falsificar; **to ~ with** vt fus jugar con; **fiddler** n violinista m/f.

fidelity [fɪ'delɪtɪ] n fidelidad f.

fidget ['fɪdʒɪt] vi moverse nerviosamente; **~y** a nervioso.

field [fiːld] n campo; (ELEC) prado; (fig) esfera, especialidad f; (competitors) competidores mpl; (entrants) concurrentes mpl; **~ glasses** npl gemelos mpl; **~ marshal** n mariscal m; **~work** n trabajo de campo.

fiend [fiːnd] n demonio; **~ish** a diabólico.

fierce [fɪəs] a feroz; (wind, attack) violento; (heat) intenso; (fighting, enemy) encarnizado.

fiery ['faɪərɪ] a (burning) ardiente; (temperament) apasionado.

fifteen [fɪf'tiːn] num quince.

fifth [fɪfθ] a, n quinto.

fiftieth ['fɪftɪɪθ] a quincuagésimo.

fifty ['fɪftɪ] num cincuenta.

fig [fɪg] n higo.

fight [faɪt] n (gen) pelea; (MIL) combate m; (struggle) lucha // (vb: pt, pp fought) vt luchar contra; (cancer, alcoholism) combatir // vi pelear, luchar; **~er** n combatiente m/f; (fig) luchador a m/f; (plane) caza; **~ing** n (gen) el luchar; (battle) combate m.

figment ['fɪgmənt] n: **a ~ of the imagination** una quimera.

figurative ['fɪgjurətɪv] a figurado.

figure ['fɪgə*] n (DRAWING, GEOM) figura, dibujo; (number, cipher) cifra; (body, outline) talle m, tipo // vt (esp US) imaginar // vi (appear) figurar; **to ~ out** vt (understand) comprender; **~head** n mascarón m de proa; **~ skating** n patinaje m de figuras.

file [faɪl] n (tool) lima; (dossier) expediente m; (folder) carpeta; (row) fila // vt limar; (papers) clasificar; (LAW: claim) presentar; (store) archivar; **to ~ in/out** vi entrar/salir en fila; **to ~** *past vt fus* desfilar ante; **filing** *n* el archivar; **filing cabinet** *n* fichero, archivo.

fill [fɪl] *vt* llenar // *n*: **to eat one's ~** llenarse; **to ~ in** *vt* rellenar; **to ~ up** *vt* llenar (hasta el borde) // *vi* (AUT) poner gasolina.

fillet ['fɪlɪt] *n* filete *m*.

filling ['fɪlɪŋ] *n* (CULIN) relleno; (for tooth) empaste *m*; **~ station** *n* estación *f* de servicio.

film [fɪlm] *n* película // *vt* (scene) filmar // *vi* rodar (una película); **~ star** *n* astro, estrella de cine; **~strip** *n* tira de película.

filter ['fɪltə*] *n* filtro // *vt* filtrar; **~ tip** *n* boquilla.

filth [fɪlθ] *n* suciedad *f*; **~y** *a* sucio; (language) obsceno.

fin [fɪn] *n* (gen) aleta.

final ['faɪnl] *a* (last) final, último; (definitive) definitivo, terminante // *n* (SPORT) final *f*; **~s** *npl* (SCOL) exámenes *mpl* finales.

finale [fɪ'nɑːlɪ] *n* final *m*.

final: **~ist** *n* (SPORT) finalista *m/f*; **~ize** *vt* concluir, completar; **~ly** *ad* (lastly) por último, finalmente; (eventually) por fin; (irrevocably) de modo definitivo.

finance [faɪ'næns] *n* (money) fondos *mpl*; **~s** *npl* finanzas *fpl* // *vt* financiar; **financial** ['naɪ∫əl] *a* financiero; (economic) económico; **financier** *n* (gen) financiero; (investor) inversionista *m/f*.

find [faɪnd] *pt, pp* **found** *vt* (gen) encontrar, hallar; (come upon) descubrir // *n* hallazgo; descubrimiento; **to ~ sb guilty** (LAW) declarar culpable a uno; **to ~ out** *vt* averiguar; (truth, secret) descubrir; **to ~ out about** (by chance) enterarse de // *n* (LAW) veredicto *sg*, fallo *sg*; (of report) recomendaciones *fpl*.

fine [faɪn] *a* (delicate) fino; (good) bueno; (beautiful) bonito // *ad* (well) bien; (small) delgado // *n* (LAW) multa // *vt* (LAW) multar; **to**

be ~ (weather) hacer buen tiempo; **~ arts** *npl* bellas artes *fpl*.

finery ['faɪnərɪ] *n* adornos *mpl*.

finesse [fɪ'nes] *n* sutileza.

finger ['fɪŋgə*] *n* dedo // *vt* (touch) manosear; (MUS) tocar (distraídamente); **little/index ~** dedo meñique/índice; **~nail** *n* uña; **~print** *n* huella dactilar; **~tip** *n* yema del dedo.

finicky ['fɪnɪkɪ] *a* (fussy) delicado.

finish ['fɪnɪʃ] *n* (end) fin *m*; (goal) meta; (polish etc) acabado // *vt, vi* terminar; **to ~ off** *vt* acabar, terminar; (kill) acabar con; **to ~ third** llegar el tercero; **~ing line** *n* línea de llegada o meta.

finite ['faɪnaɪt] *a* finito.

Finland ['fɪnlənd] *n* Finlandia.

Finn [fɪn] *n* finlandés/esa *m/f*; **~ish** *a* finlandés(esa) // *n* (LING) finlandés *m*.

fiord [fjɔːd] *n* fiordo.

fir [fɜː*] *n* abeto.

fire ['faɪə*] *n* (gen) fuego; (accidental) incendio // *vt* (gun) disparar; (set fire to) incendiar; (excite) exaltar; (interest) despertar; (dismiss) despedir // *vi* encenderse; **on ~** ardiendo, en llamas; **~ alarm** *n* alarma de incendios; **~arm** *n* arma de fuego; **~ brigade** *n* (cuerpo de) bomberos *mpl*; **~ engine** *n* coche *m* de bomberos; **~ escape** *n* escalera de incendios; **~ extinguisher** *n* extintor *m* (de fuego); **~man** *n* bombero; **~place** *n* chimenea; **~proof** *a* a prueba de fuego; **~side** *n* hogar *m*; **~ station** *n* parque *m* de bomberos; **~wood** *n* leña; **~works** *npl* fuegos *mpl* artificiales.

firing ['faɪərɪŋ] *n* (MIL) disparos *mpl*, tiroteo; **~ squad** *n* pelotón *m* de ejecución.

firm [fɜːm] *a* firme // *n* firma; **~ly** *ad* firmemente; **~ness** *n* firmeza.

first [fɜːst] *a* primero // *ad* (before others) primero; (when listing reasons etc) en primer lugar, primeramente // n (person: in race) primero; (AUT) primera; at ~ al principio; ~ of all ante todo; ~-aid kit n botiquín m; ~-class a de primera clase; ~-hand a de primera mano; ~-ly ad en primer lugar; ~ name n nombre m de pila; ~-rate a de primera clase.

fir tree n abeto.

fiscal ['fɪskəl] a fiscal.

fish [fɪʃ] n, pl inv pez m; (food) pescado // vt, vi pescar; to go ~ing ir de pesca; ~erman n pescador m; ~ery n pesquería; ~ fingers npl dedos mpl de pescado; ~ing boat n barca de pesca; ~ing line n sedal m; ~ing rod n caña (de pescar); ~ing tackle n aparejo (de pescar); ~ market n mercado de pescado; ~monger n pescadero; ~monger's (shop) n pescadería; ~y a (fig) sospechoso.

fission ['fɪʃən] n fisión f.

fissure ['fɪʃə*] n fisura.

fist [fɪst] n puño.

fit [fɪt] a (MED, SPORT) en (buena) forma; (proper) adecuado, apropiado // vt (clothes) sentar bien a; (try on: clothes) probar; (facts) cuadrar o corresponder con; (accommodate) ajustar, adaptar; (correspond exactly) encajar en // vi (clothes) entallar; (in space, gap) caber; (correspond) corresponder // n (MED) ataque m; ~ to apto para; ~ for apropiado para; this dress is a good ~ este vestido me sienta bien; to ~ in vi (gen) encajarse; (fig: person) llevarse bien (con todos); to ~ out (also: ~ up) vt equipar; ~ful a espasmódico, intermitente; ~ment n mueble m; ~ness n (MED) salud f; (of remark) conveniencia; ~ter n ajustador m; ~ting a apropiado // n (of dress) prueba; ~tings npl instalaciones fpl.

five [faɪv] num cinco; ~r n (Brit: col) billete m de cinco libras.

fix [fɪks] vt (secure) fijar, asegurar;

(mend) arreglar // n: to be in a ~ estar en un aprieto; ~ed [fɪkst] a (prices etc) fijo; ~ture ['fɪkstʃə*] n cosa fija; (furniture) mueble m fijo; (SPORT) partido.

fizz [fɪz] vi hacer efervescencia.

fizzle ['fɪzl]: ~ out vi apagarse.

fizzy ['fɪzɪ] a (drink) gaseoso; (gen) efervescente.

fjord [fjɔːd] n = **fiord**.

flabbergasted ['flæbəgɑːstɪd] a pasmado.

flabby ['flæbɪ] a flojo; (fat) gordo.

flag [flæg] n bandera; (stone) losa // vi acabarse, decaer; to ~ sb down hacer signos a uno para que se detenga; ~pole n asta de bandera.

flagrant ['fleɪgrənt] a flagrante.

flair [fleə*] n aptitud f especial.

flake [fleɪk] n (of rust, paint) escama; (of snow, soap powder) copo // vi (also: ~ off) desprenderse en escamas.

flamboyant [flæm'bɔɪənt] a (dress) vistoso; (person) extravagante.

flame [fleɪm] n llama.

flamingo [flə'mɪŋgəu] n flamenco.

flammable ['flæməbl] a inflamable.

flan [flæn] n tarta.

flank [flæŋk] n flanco; (of person) costado // vt flanquear.

flannel ['flænl] n (also: face ~) paño; (fabric) franela; (col) coba; ~s npl pantalones mpl de franela.

flap [flæp] n (of pocket) cartera; (of envelope) solapa; (of table) hoja (plegadiza); (wing movement) aletazo // vt (wings) aletear // vi (sail, flag) ondear.

flare [fleə*] n llamarada; (MIL) bengala; (in skirt etc) vuelo; to ~ up vi encenderse; (fig: person) encolerizarse; (: revolt) estallar.

flash [flæʃ] n relámpago; (also: news ~) noticias fpl de última hora; (PHOT) flash m // vt (light, headlights) encender y apagar (la luz); (torch) encender // vi brillar, relampaguear; **in a ~** en un instante; **he ~ed by** or **past** pasó como un rayo; **~back** n flashback m; **~ bulb** n bombilla fusible; **~er** n (AUT) intermitente m.

flashy ['flæʃɪ] a (pej) ostentoso.

flask [flɑːsk] n frasco; (also: **vacuum ~**) termo.

flat [flæt] a llano; (smooth) liso; (tyre) desinflado; (beer) muerto; (MUS) desafinado // n (apartment) piso, apartamento; (MUS) bemol m; (AUT) pinchazo; **~ly** ad terminantemente, de plano; **~ness** n (of land) llanura, lo llano; **~ten** vt (also: **~ten out**) allanar; (smooth out) alisar; (demolish) aplastar.

flatter ['flætə*] vt adular, halagar; **~er** n adulador/a m/f; **~ing** a halagüeño; **~y** n adulación f.

flatulence ['flætjuləns] n flatulencia.

flaunt [flɔːnt] vt ostentar, lucir.

flavour, flavor (US) ['fleɪvə*] n sabor m, gusto // vt sazonar, condimentar; **~ed with con** sabor a; **~ing** n condimento.

flaw [flɔː] n defecto; **~less** a intachable.

flax [flæks] n lino; **~en** a rubio.

flea [fliː] n pulga; **~ market** n mercado de baja categoría.

flee [fliː], pt, pp **fled** [fled] vt huir de, abandonar // vi huir, fugarse.

fleece [fliːs] n vellón m; (wool) lana // vt (col) pelar.

fleet [fliːt] n (gen) flota; (of lorries etc) escuadra.

fleeting ['fliːtɪŋ] a fugaz.

Flemish ['flemɪʃ] a flamenco.

flesh [fleʃ] n carne f; (of fruit) pulpa; **of ~ and blood** de carne y hueso.

flew [fluː] pt of **fly**.

flex [fleks] n cordón m // vt (muscles) tensar; **~ibility** [-'bɪlɪtɪ] n flexibilidad f; **~ible** a flexible.

flick [flɪk] n golpecito; (with finger) capirotazo; (with whip) chasquido // vt dar un golpecito a; **~ through** vt fus hojear.

flicker ['flɪkə*] vi (light) parpadear; (flame) vacilar // n parpadeo.

flier ['flaɪə*] n aviador/a m/f.

flight [flaɪt] n vuelo; (escape) huida, fuga; (also: **~ of steps**) tramo (de escaleras); **to take ~** huir, darse a la fuga, fugarse; **to put to ~** ahuyentar; **~ deck** n (AVIAT) cabina.

flimsy ['flɪmzɪ] a (thin) muy ligero; (weak) débil.

flinch [flɪntʃ] vi acobardarse.

fling [flɪŋ], pt, pp **flung** vt arrojar.

flint [flɪnt] n pedernal m; (in lighter) piedra.

flip [flɪp] vt dar la vuelta a; (coin) echar a cara o cruz.

flippant ['flɪpənt] a poco serio.

flirt [flɜːt] vi coquetear flirtear // n coqueta m/f; **~ation** [-'teɪʃən] n coqueteo, flirteo.

flit [flɪt] vi revolotear.

float [fləʊt] n flotador m; (in procession) carroza // vi flotar; (swimmer) hacer la plancha // vt (gen) hacer flotar; (company) lanzar.

flock [flɒk] n (of sheep) rebaño; (of birds) bandada; (of people) multitud f.

flog [flɒg] vt azotar; (col) vender.

flood [flʌd] n inundación f; (of words tears etc) torrente m // vt inundar; **~ing** n inundación f; **~light** n foco.

floor [flɔː*] n suelo; (storey) piso; (of sea) fondo; (dance ~) pista // vt (fig) dejar sin respuesta; **ground ~** (Brit), **first ~** (US) planta baja, primer piso; **first ~** (Brit), **second ~** (US) primer piso; **~board** n tabla; **~ show** n cabaret m.

flop [flɒp] n fracaso // vi (fail) fracasar.

floppy ['flɒpɪ] a flojo.

flora ['flɔːrə] n flora; **floral** ['flɔːrl] a floral.

florid ['flɒrɪd] a (style) florido.

florist ['flɒrɪst] n florista m/f; **~'s (shop)** n florería.

flounce [flauns] n volante m; **to ~ out** vi salir enfadado.

flounder ['flaundə*] vi tropezar.

flour ['flauə*] n harina.

flourish ['flʌrɪʃ] vi florecer; **~ing** a floreciente.

flout [flaut] vt burlarse de.

flow [fləu] n (movement) flujo; (direction) curso; (tide) corriente f // vi correr, fluir; (blood) derramarse.

flower ['flauə*] n flor f // vi florecer; **~ bed** n macizo; **~pot** n tiesto; **~y** a florido.

flown [fləun] pp of **fly**.

flu [fluː] n gripe f.

fluctuate ['flʌktjueit] vi fluctuar; **fluctuation** [-'eɪʃən] n fluctuación f.

fluent ['fluːənt] a (speech) elocuente; **he speaks ~ French, he's ~ in French** domina el francés; **~ly** ad con fluidez.

fluff [flʌf] n pelusa; **~y** a velloso.

fluid ['fluːɪd] a, n fluido, líquido.

fluke [fluːk] n (col) chiripa.

flung [flʌŋ] pt, pp of **fling**.

fluorescent [fluə'resnt] a fluorescente.

fluoride ['fluəraid] n fluoruro.

flurry ['flʌrɪ] n (of snow) ráfago; (haste) agitación f; **~ of activity** frenesí m de actividad.

flush [flʌʃ] n (on face) rubor m; (plenty) plenitud f, abundancia // vt limpiar con agua // vi ruborizarse // a: **~ with** a ras de; **to ~ the toilet** hacer funcionar el WC; **~ed** a ruborizado.

flustered ['flʌstəd] a aturdido.

flute [fluːt] n flauta.

flutter ['flʌtə*] n emoción f; (of wings) revoloteo, aleteo; (fam: bet) apuesta // vi revolotear.

flux [flʌks] n flujo; **in a state of ~** cambiando continuamente.

fly [flaɪ] n (insect) mosca; (on trousers: also: **flies**) bragueta // vb: pt **flew**, pp **flown** vt (gen) hacer volar; (plane) pilot(e)ar; (cargo) transportar en avión; (distances)

recorrer (en avión) // vi volar; (passengers) ir o subir en avión; (escape) evadirse; (flag) ondear; **to let ~** desahogarse; **~ing** n (activity) (el) volar // a: **~ing visit** visita relámpago; **with ~ing colours** con lucimiento; **~ing saucer** n platillo volante; **~over** n (Brit: bridge) paso a desnivel o superior; **~past** n desfile m aéreo; **~sheet** n (for tent) doble techo.

foal [fəul] n potro.

foam [fəum] n espuma // vi echar espuma; **~ rubber** n espuma de caucho.

fob [fɔb] vt: **to ~ sb off** deshacerse de alguien con excusas.

focal ['fəukəl] a focal.

focus ['fəukəs], pl **~es** n foco // vt (field glasses etc) enfocar; **to ~ on** enfocar a; **in/out of ~** enfocado/desenfocado.

fodder ['fɔdə*] n pienso.

foe [fəu] n enemigo.

foetus ['fiːtəs] n feto.

fog [fɔg] n niebla; **~gy** a: **it's ~gy** hay niebla, está brumoso.

foil [fɔil] vt frustrar // n hoja; (also: **kitchen ~**) papel m (de aluminio); (FENCING) florete m.

fold [fəuld] n (bend, crease) pliegue m; (of skin) arruga; (AGR) redil m // vt doblar; **to ~ up** vi (map etc) plegarse, doblarse; (business) quebrar // vt (map etc) plegar; **~er** n (for papers) carpeta; (brochure) folleto; **~ing** a (chair, bed) plegable.

foliage ['fəulɪɪdʒ] n follaje m.

folk [fəuk] npl gente f // a popular, folklórico; **~s** npl familia, parientes mpl; **~lore** ['fəuklɔː*] n folklore m; **~song** n canción f popular o folklórica.

follow ['fɔləu] vt seguir // vi seguir; (result) resultar; **he ~ed suit** hizo lo mismo; **to ~ up** vt (letter, offer) responder a; (case) investigar; **~er** n seguidor/a m/f; (POL) partidario/a; **~ing** a siguiente // n afición f, partidarios mpl.

folly ['fɔli] n locura.

fond [fɔnd] a (loving) cariñoso; **to be ~ of** tener cariño a.

fondle ['fɔndl] vt acariciar.

fondness ['fɔndnis] n (for things) gusto; (for people) cariño.

font [fɔnt] n pila bautismal.

food [fu:d] n comida; **~ mixer** n hatidora; **~ poisoning** n botulismo; **~stuffs** npl comestibles mpl.

fool [fu:l] n tonto/a; (CULIN) puré m de frutas con nata // vt engañar // vi (gen: **~ around**) bromear; (waste time) perder el tiempo; **~hardy** a temerario; **~ish** a tonto; (stupid) estúpido; (careless) imprudente; **~proof** a (plan etc) infalible.

foot [fut], pl **feet** n pie m; (measure) pie m (= 304 mm); (of animal) pata // vt (bill) pagar; **on ~** a pie; **~ball** n balón m; (game) fútbol m; **~baller** n futbolista m; **~brake** n freno de pie; **~bridge** n puente m para peatones; **~hills** npl estribaciones fpl; **~hold** n pie m firme; **~ing** n (fig) posición f; **to lose one's ~ing** perder el pie; **on an equal ~ing** en pie de igualdad; **~lights** npl candilejas fpl; **~man** n lacayo; **~note** n nota de pie; **~path** n sendero; (pavement) acera; **~sore** a con los pies adoloridos; **~step** n paso; **~wear** n calzado.

for [fɔ:] prep (gen) para; (as, in exchange for, because of) por; (during) durante; (in spite of) a pesar de // conj (since, as: rather) pues; **what ~?** ¿para qué? (reason); **he was sold ~ 100 pesetas** se vendió por 100 pesetas; **what ~?** ¿para qué?; **what's it ~?** ¿para qué sirve?; **he was away ~ 2 years** estuvo fuera 2 años; **he went ~ the paper** fue a buscar el periódico; **~ only ~ sale** se vende.

forage ['fɔridʒ] n forraje m.

foray ['fɔrei] n incursión f.

forbid [fə'bid], pt **forbad(e)** [fə'bæd], pp **forbidden** [fə'bidn] vt prohibir; **~ding** a (gloomy) lúgubre; (severe) severo.

force [fɔ:s] n fuerza // vt forzar; **to ~ o.s. to** hacer un esfuerzo por; **the F~s** npl las Fuerzas Armadas; **in ~** en vigor; **~d** [fɔ:st] a forzado; **~ful** a enérgico.

forceps ['fɔ:seps] npl fórceps m inv.

forcibly ['fɔ:səbli] ad a la fuerza.

ford [fɔ:d] n vado // vt vadear.

forearm ['fɔ:rɑ:m] n antebrazo.

foreboding [fɔ:'bəudiŋ] n presagio.

forecast ['fɔ:kɑ:st] n pronóstico // vt (irg: like cast) pronosticar.

forefathers ['fɔ:fɑ:ðəz] npl antepasados mpl.

forefinger ['fɔ:fiŋgə*] n (dedo) índice m.

forego = forgo.

foregone ['fɔ:gɔn] a: **it's a ~ conclusion** es una conclusión inevitable.

foreground ['fɔ:graund] n primer plano.

forehead ['fɔrid] n frente f.

foreign ['fɔrin] a extranjero; (trade) exterior; **~er** n extranjero; **~ exchange** n divisas fpl; **F~ Minister** n Ministro de Asuntos Exteriores; **F~ Office** n Ministerio de Asuntos Exteriores.

foreleg ['fɔ:leg] n pata de lantero.

foreman ['fɔ:mən] n capataz m; (in construction) maestro de obras.

foremost ['fɔ:məust] a principal.

forensic [fə'rensik] a forense.

forerunner ['fɔ:rʌnə*] n precursor/a m/f.

foresee [fɔ:'si:] (irg: like see) vt prever; **~able** a previsible.

foresight ['fɔ:sait] n previsión f.

forest ['fɔrist] n bosque m.

forestall [fɔ:'stɔ:l] vt prevenir.

forestry ['fɔristri] n silvicultura.

foretaste ['fɔ:teist] n (gen) anticipo; (sample) muestra.

foretell [fɔ:'tel] (irg: like tell) vt predecir, pronosticar.

forever [fə'revə*] ad para siempre.

foreword ['fɔ:wə:d] n prefacio.

forfeit ['fɔːfɪt] n pérdida; (fine) multa // vt perder (derecho a).

forgave [fə'geɪv] pt of forgive.

forge [fɔːdʒ] n fragua; (smithy) herrería // vt (signature, money) falsificar; (metal) forjar; to ~ ahead vi avanzar constantemente; **forger** n falsificador/a m/f; ~ry n falsificación f.

forget [fə'get], pt **forgot**, pp **forgotten** vt olvidar // vi olvidarse; ~**ful** a olvidadizo; ~**fulness** n (gen) olvido; (thoughtlessness) descuido; (oblivion) falta de memoria.

forgive [fə'gɪv], pt **forgave**, pp **forgiven** vt perdonar; to ~ sb for sth perdonar algo a uno; ~**ness** n perdón m.

forgo [fɔː'gəʊ] (irg: like go) vt (give up) renunciar a; (go without) privarse de.

forgot [fə'gɒt] pt of forget.

forgotten [fə'gɒtn] pp of forget.

fork [fɔːk] n (for eating) tenedor m; (for gardening) horca; (of roads) bifurcación f; (in tree) horcadura // vi (road) bifurcarse; to ~ out (col: pay) desembolsar; ~ed [fɔːkt] a (lightning) en zigzag; ~**-lift truck** n elevadora-transportadora de horquilla.

form [fɔːm] n forma; (SCOL) clase f; (questionnaire) formulario // vt formar; **in top** ~ en plena forma.

formal ['fɔːməl] a (offer, receipt) oficial; (person etc) ceremonioso; (occasion, dinner) oficial, protocolario; (dress) de etiqueta; ~**ity** [-'mælɪtɪ] n ceremonia; ~**ities** npl formalidades fpl; ~**ly** ad oficialmente.

format ['fɔːmæt] n formato.

formation [fɔː'meɪʃən] n formación f.

formative ['fɔːmətɪv] a (years) formativo.

former ['fɔːmə*] a anterior; (earlier) antiguo; (ex) ex; **the ~ ...**

the latter ... aquél ... éste ...; ~**ly** ad antiguamente.

formidable ['fɔːmɪdəbl] a formidable.

formula ['fɔːmjʊlə] n fórmula.

formulate ['fɔːmjʊleɪt] vt formular.

forsake [fə'seɪk], pt **forsook** [fə'sʊk], pp **forsaken** [fə'seɪkən] vt (gen) abandonar; (plan) renunciar a.

fort [fɔːt] n fuerte m.

forte ['fɔːtɪ] n fuerte m.

forth [fɔːθ] ad en adelante; **back and** ~ de acá para allá; **and so** ~ y así sucesivamente; ~**coming** a próximo, venidero; (character) comunicativo; ~**right** a franco.

fortieth ['fɔːtɪɪθ] a cuadragésimo.

fortification [fɔːtɪfɪ'keɪʃən] n fortificación f; **fortify** ['fɔːtɪfaɪ] vt fortalecer.

fortitude ['fɔːtɪtjuːd] n fortaleza.

fortnight ['fɔːtnaɪt] n quincena; ~**ly** a quincenal // ad quincenalmente.

fortress ['fɔːtrɪs] n fortaleza.

fortuitous [fɔː'tjuːɪtəs] a fortuito.

fortunate ['fɔːtʃənɪt] a: **to be** ~ tener suerte; **it is** ~ **that...** es afortunado que...; ~**ly** ad afortunadamente.

fortune ['fɔːtʃən] n suerte f; (wealth) fortuna; ~**-teller** n adivina.

forty ['fɔːtɪ] num cuarenta.

forum ['fɔːrəm] n foro.

forward ['fɔːwəd] a (movement, position) avanzado; (front) delantero; (not shy) atrevido // n (SPORT) delantero // vt (letter) remitir; (career) progresar; **to move** ~ avanzar; ~**(s)** ad (hacia) adelante.

fossil ['fɔsl] n fósil m.

foster ['fɔstə*] vt fomentar; ~ **brother** n hermano de leche; ~ **child** n hijo adoptivo; ~ **mother** n madre f adoptiva.

fought [fɔːt] pt, pp of fight.

foul [faʊl] a (gen) sucio, puerco; (weather) horrible; (smell etc) asqueroso // n (FOOTBALL) falta (en contra) // vt (dirty) ensuciar; (block) atascar; (football player) cometer una falta contra; ~ play n (SPORT) mala jugada; (LAW) muerte f violenta.

found [faund] pt, pp of **find** // vt (establish) fundar; ~ation [-'deiʃən] n (act) fundación f; (basis) base f; (also: ~ation cream) crema base; ~ations npl (of building) cimientos mpl.

founder ['faundə*] n fundador/a m/f // vi hundirse.

foundry ['faundri] n fundición f.

fountain ['fauntin] n fuente f, ~ pen n pluma-fuente f.

four [fɔ:*] num cuatro; on all ~s a gatas; ~poster n cama de columnas; ~some ['fɔ:səm] n grupo de cuatro personas; ~teen num catorce; ~teenth a decimocuarto; ~th a cuarto.

fowl [faul] n ave f (de corral).

fox [fɔks] n zorro // vt confundir; ~ trot n fox m.

foyer ['fɔiei] n vestíbulo.

fracas ['fræka:] n gresca, riña.

fraction ['frækʃən] n fracción f

fracture ['fræktʃə*] n fractura // vt fracturar.

fragile ['frædʒail] a frágil.

fragment ['frægmənt] n fragmento; ~ary a fragmentario.

fragrance ['freigrəns] n fragancia; **fragrant** [-ənt] a fragante, oloroso.

frail [freil] a (fragile) frágil, quebradizo; (weak) delicado.

frame [freim] n (gen) estructura; (body) talle m; (TECH) armazón m; (of picture, door etc) marco; (of spectacles: also: ~s) montura // vt (picture) enmarcar; (reply) formular; (fam) incriminar; ~ of mind n estado de ánimo; ~work n marco.

France [fra:ns] n Francia.

franchise ['fræntʃaiz] n (POL) derecho de votar, sufragio.

frank [fræŋk] a franco // vt (letter)

franquear; ~ly ad francamente; ~ness n franqueza.

frantic ['fræntik] a frenético.

fraternal [frə'tə:nl] a fraterno; **fraternity** [-niti] n (club) fraternidad f; (US) club m de estudiantes; (guild) cofradía; **fraternize** ['frætənaiz] vi confraternizar.

fraud [frɔd] n fraude m; (person) impostor/a; ~ulent a fraudulento.

fraught [frɔ:t] a: ~ with cargado de.

fray [frei] n combate m, lucha // vi deshilacharse; **tempers were** ~ tenían los nervios a punto.

freak [fri:k] n (person) fenómeno; (event) suceso anormal; (thing) cosa insólita.

freckle ['frekl] n peca.

free [fri:] a (gen) libre; (not fixed) suelto; (gratis) gratuito; (unoccupied) desocupado; (liberal) generoso // vt (prisoner etc) poner en libertad; (jammed object) soltar; ~ (of charge) ad gratis; ~dom ['fri:dəm] n libertad f; ~-for-all n riña general; ~ kick n tiro libre; ~lance a independiente; ~ly ad libremente; generosamente; ~mason n francmasón m; ~ trade n libre comercio; ~way n (US) autopista; ~wheel vi ir en punto muerto; ~ will n libre albedrío f; of one's own ~ will por su propia voluntad.

freeze [fri:z] n, pt **froze**, pp **frozen** vi helarse, congelarse // vt helar; (prices, food, salaries) congelar // n helada; congelación f; **freezer** n congelador m.

freezing ['fri:ziŋ] a helado; ~ point n punto de congelación; 3 degrees below ~ tres grados bajo cero.

freight [freit] n (goods) carga; (money charged) flete m; ~ car n (US) vagón m de mercancías.

French [frentʃ] a francés(esa) // n (LING) francés m; **the** ~ los franceses; ~ **fried (potatoes)** npl patatas *fpl* fritas; ~**man/woman** *n* francés/esa *m/f*; ~ **window** *n* puertaventana.

frenzy ['frenzı] *n* frenesí *m*.

frequency ['fri:kwǝnsı] *n* frecuencia; **frequent** [-ǝnt] *a* frecuente // *vt* [frɪ'kwent] frecuentar; **frequently** [-ǝntlı] *ad* frecuentemente, a menudo.

fresco ['freskǝu] *n* fresco.

fresh [freʃ] *a* (*gen*) fresco; (*new*) nuevo; (*water*) dulce; ~**en** *vi* (*wind, air*) soplar más recio; **to** ~**en up** *vi* (*person*) lavarse, arreglarse; ~**ly** *ad* (*newly*) nuevamente; (*recently*) recientemente; ~**ness** *n* frescura.

fret [fret] *vi* inquietarse.

friar ['fraɪǝ*] *n* fraile *m*; (*before name*) fray.

friction ['frɪkʃǝn] *n* fricción *f*.

Friday ['fraɪdı] *n* viernes *m*.

fridge [frɪdʒ] *n* nevera.

friend [frend] *n* amigo/a; ~**liness** *n* simpatía; ~**ly** *a* simpático; ~**ship** *n* amistad *f*.

frieze [fri:z] *n* friso.

frigate ['frɪgɪt] *n* fragata.

fright [fraɪt] *n* susto; **to take** ~ asustarse; ~**en** *vt* asustar; ~**ening** *a* espantoso; ~**ful** *a* espantoso, horrible; ~**fully** *ad* terriblemente.

frigid ['frɪdʒɪd] *a* (*MED*) frígido, frío; ~**ity** [frɪ'dʒɪdɪtɪ] *n* frialdad *f*, (*MED*) frigidez *f*.

frill [frɪl] *n* volante *m*.

fringe [frɪndʒ] *n* flequillo; (*edge: of forest etc*) borde *m*, margen *m*; ~ **benefits** *npl* ventajas *fpl* supletorias.

frisky ['frɪskı] *a* juguetón(ona), fogoso.

fritter ['frɪtǝ*] *n* buñuelo; **to** ~ **away** *vt* desperdiciar.

frivolous ['frɪvǝlǝs] *a* frívolo.

frizzy ['frɪzı] *a* rizado.

fro [frǝu] see **to**.

frock [frɔk] *n* vestido.

frog [frɔg] *n* rana; ~**man** *n* hombre-rana *m*.

frolic ['frɔlɪk] *vi* juguetear.

from [frɔm] *prep* de; ~ **January**

(*on*) a partir de enero; ~ **what he says** por lo que dice.

front [frʌnt] *n* (*foremost part*) parte *f* delantera; (*of house*) fachada; (*promenade: also: sea* ~) paseo marítimo; (*MIL, POL, METEOROLOGY*) frente *m*; (*fig: appearances*) apariencias *fpl* // *a* delantero, primero; **in** ~ (**of**) delante (de); ~**al** *a* frontal; ~ **door** *n* puerta principal; ~**ier** ['frʌntɪǝ*] *n* frontera; ~ **page** *n* primera plana; ~ **room** *n* (*Brit*) salón *m*, sala; ~**wheel drive** *n* tracción *f* delantera.

frost [frɔst] *n* (*gen*) helada; (*visible*) escarcha; ~**bite** *n* congelación *f*; ~**ed** *a* (*glass*) deslustrado; ~**y** *a* (*window*) cubierto de escarcha; (*welcome*) glacial.

froth [frɔθ] *n* espuma.

frown [fraun] *n* ceño // *vi* fruncir el ceño.

froze [frǝuz] *pt of* **freeze**.

frozen ['frǝuzn] *pp of* **freeze**.

frugal ['fru:gǝl] *a* frugal.

fruit [fru:t] *n* (*gen*) *inv* fruta; ~**erer** *n* frutero; ~**erer's** (**shop**) *n* frutería; ~**ful** *a* provechoso; ~**ion** [fru:'ɪʃǝn] *n*: **to come to** ~**ion** realizarse; ~ **machine** *n* máquina tragaperras.

frustrate [frʌs'treɪt] *vt* frustrar; ~**d** *a* frustrado; **frustration** [-'treɪʃǝn] *n* frustración *f*.

fry [fraɪ] *pt, pp* **fried** *vt* freír; **small** ~ *gente f menuda*; ~**ing pan** *n* sartén *f*.

ft. *abbr of* **foot, feet**.

fuchsia ['fju:ʃǝ] *n* fucsia.

fudge [fʌdʒ] *n* (*CULIN*) dulce *m* de azúcar, manjar *m*.

fuel [fjuǝl] *n* (*for heating*) combustible *m*; (*coal*) carbón *m*; (*wood*) leña; (*for propelling*) carburante *m*; ~ **oil** *n* aceite *m* combustible; ~ **tank** *n* depósito de combustible.

fugitive ['fju:dʒɪtɪv] *n* fugitivo.

fulfil [ful'fɪl] *vt* (*function*) cumplir con; (*condition*) satisfacer; (*wish,*

desire) realizar; ~**ment** *n*
satisfacción *f*; realización *f*.
full [ful] *a* lleno; (*fig*) pleno;
(*complete*) completo; (*information*)
detallado // *ad*: ~ **well**
perfectamente; I'm ~ estoy lleno;
~ **employment** pleno empleo; ~
fare pasaje *m* completo; a ~ **two
hours** dos horas completas; at ~
speed a máxima velocidad; **in** ~
(*reproduce, quote*) íntegramente;
~**length** *a* (*portrait*) de cuerpo
entero; ~ **moon** *n* luna llena;
~**sized** *a* (*portrait etc*) de tamaño
natural; ~ **stop** *n* punto; ~**time** *a*
(*work*) de tiempo completo // *n*
(*SPORT*) final *m*, ~**y** *ad*
completamente; ~**y-fledged** *a*
(*teacher, barrister*) diplomado.
fumble ['fʌmbl] **to** ~ **with** *vt fus*
revolver, manosear.
fume [fju:m] *vi* humear, echar
humo; ~**s** *npl* humo *sg*, gases *mpl*.
fumigate ['fju:mɪgeɪt] *vt* fumigar.
fun [fʌn] *n* (*amusement*) diversión *f*,
(*joy*) alegría *f*; **to have** ~ divertirse;
for ~ en broma; **to make** ~ **of** *vt
fus* burlarse de.
function ['fʌŋkʃən] *n* función *f* // *vi*
funcionar; ~**al** *a* funcional.
fund [fʌnd] *n* fondo; (*source, store*)
fuente *f*; ~**s** *npl* fondos *mpl*.
fundamental [fʌndə'mentl] *a*
fundamental.
funeral ['fju:nərəl] *n* (*burial*)
entierro; (*ceremony*) funerales *mpl*;
~ **service** *n* misa *f* de difuntos.
funfair ['fʌnfeə*] *n* parque *m* de
atracciones.
fungus ['fʌŋgəs], *pl* -**gi** [-gaɪ] *n*
hongo.
funnel ['fʌnl] *n* embudo; (*of ship*)
chimenea.
funnily ['fʌnɪlɪ] *ad* de modo
divertido.
funny ['fʌnɪ] *a* gracioso, divertido;
(*strange*) curioso, raro.
fur [fə:*] *n* piel *f*; (*in kettle etc*)
sarro; ~ **coat** *n* abrigo de pieles.
furious ['fjuərɪəs] *a* furioso; (*effort*)

violento; ~**ly** *ad* con furia.
furlong ['fə:lɔŋ] *n* octava parte de
una milla.
furlough ['fə:ləu] *n* (US) licencia.
furnace ['fə:nɪs] *n* horno.
furnish ['fə:nɪʃ] *vt* amueblar;
(*supply*) suministrar; ~**ings** *npl*
muebles *mpl*.
furniture ['fə:nɪtʃə*] *n* muebles
mpl; **piece of** ~ mueble *m*; ~
polish *n* cera de lustrar.
furrier ['fʌrɪə*] *n* peletero.
furrow ['fʌrəu] *n* surco.
furry ['fə:rɪ] *a* peludo.
further ['fə:ðə*] *a* (*new*) nuevo,
adicional; (*place*) más lejano // *ad*
más lejos; (*more*) más; (*moreover*)
además // *vt* promover, adelantar;
~ **education** *n* educación *f* superior;
~**more** [fə:ðə'mɔ:*] *ad* además.
furthest ['fə:ðɪst] *superlative of*
far.
furtive ['fə:tɪv] *a* furtivo.
fury ['fjuərɪ] *n* furia.
fuse, fuze (US) [fju:z] *n* fusible *m*;
(*for bomb etc*) mecha // *vt* (*metal*)
fundir; (*fig*) fusionar // *vi* fundirse;
fusionarse; (*ELEC*): **to** ~ **the lights**
fundir los plomos; ~ **box** *n* caja de
fusibles.
fuselage ['fju:zəla:ʒ] *n* fuselaje *m*.
fusion ['fju:ʒən] *n* fusión *f*.
fuss [fʌs] *n* (*noise*) bulla; (*dispute*)
lío, (*complaining*) protesta; (*ceremony*) ceremonias *fpl*; **to make** ~
~ armar un lío o jaleo; ~**y** *a*
(*person*) exigente.
futile ['fju:taɪl] *a* vano; **futility**
[-'tɪlɪtɪ] *n* inutilidad *f*.
future ['fju:tʃə*] *a* (*gen*) futuro;
(*coming*) venidero // *n* futuro;
futuristic [-'rɪstɪk] *a* futurístico.
fuzzy ['fʌzɪ] *a* (*PHOT*) borroso; (*hair*)
muy rizado.

G

gabble ['gæbl] *vi* hablar atropelladamente; (*gossip*) cotorrear.

gable ['geɪbl] *n* aguilón *m*.

gadget ['gædʒɪt] *n* aparato.

Gaelic ['geɪlɪk] *a* (*LING*) gaélico.

gag [gæg] *n* (*joke*) chiste *m* // *vt* amordazar.

gaiety ['geɪtɪ] *n* alegría.

gaily ['geɪlɪ] *ad* alegremente.

gain [geɪn] *n* ganancia // *vt* ganar // *vi* (*watch*) adelantarse; **to ~ by sth** sacar provecho de algo; **to ~ on sb** ir ganando terreno a uno.

gait [geɪt] *n* modo de andar.

gala ['gɑːlə] *n* fiesta.

galaxy ['gæləksɪ] *n* galaxia.

gale [geɪl] *n* (*wind*) vendaval *m*.

gallant ['gælənt] *a* valiente; (*towards ladies*) atento; **~ry** *n* valentía; (*courtesy*) cortesía.

gall-bladder ['gɔːlblædə*] *n* vesícula biliar.

gallery ['gælərɪ] *n* galería; (*also: art ~*) museo.

galley ['gælɪ] *n* (*ship's kitchen*) cocina; (*ship*) galera.

gallon ['gælən] *n* galón *m* (4.543 litros).

gallop ['gæləp] *n* galope *m* // *vi* galopar.

gallows ['gæləuz] *n* horca.

gallstone ['gɔːlstəun] *n* cálculo biliario.

gamble ['gæmbl] *n* (*risk*) riesgo; (*bet*) apuesta // *vt*: **to ~ on apostar a**; (*fig*) confiar en que // *vi* jugar; (*COMM*) especular; **gambler** *n* jugador/a *m/f*; **gambling** *n* el juego.

game [geɪm] *n* (*gen*) juego; (*match*) partido; (*of cards*) partida; (*HUNTING*) caza // *a* valiente; (*ready*): **to be ~ for anything** atreverse a todo; **~ bird** *n* ave *f* de caza; **~keeper** *n* guardabosques *m inv*.

gammon ['gæmən] *n* (*bacon*) tocino ahumado; (*ham*) jamón *m* ahumado.

gang [gæŋ] *n* pandilla; (*of workmen*) brigada // *vi*: **to ~ up on sb** conspirar contra uno.

gangrene ['gæŋgriːn] *n* gangrena.

gangster ['gæŋstə*] *n* gángster *m*.

gangway ['gæŋweɪ] *n* (*in theatre etc*) pasillo; (*on ship*) pasarela; (*on dock*) pasadera.

gaol [dʒeɪl] = **jail**.

gap [gæp] *n* vacío, hueco; (*in trees, traffic*) claro; (*in time*) intervalo.

gape [geɪp] *vi* estar o quedarse boquiabierto; **gaping** (*a hole*) muy abierto.

garage ['gærɑːʒ] *n* garaje *m*.

garbage ['gɑːbɪdʒ] *n* basura; **~ can** *n* (*US*) cubo de la basura.

garbled ['gɑːbld] *a* (*distorted*) falsificado, amañado.

garden ['gɑːdn] *n* jardín *m*; **~er** *n* jardinero; **~ing** *n* jardinería.

gargle ['gɑːgl] *vi* hacer gárgaras.

gargoyle ['gɑːgɔɪl] *n* gárgola.

garish ['gɛərɪʃ] *a* chillón *m*.

garland ['gɑːlənd] *n* guirnalda.

garlic ['gɑːlɪk] *n* ajo.

garment ['gɑːmənt] *n* prenda (de vestir).

garnish ['gɑːnɪʃ] *vt* adornar; (*CULIN*) aderezar.

garrison ['gærɪsn] *n* guarnición *f* // *vt* guarnecer.

garrulous ['gærjuləs] *a* gárrulo.

garter ['gɑːtə*] *n* liga; **~ belt** *n* portaligas *m inv*.

gas [gæs] *n* gas *m*; (*US: gasoline*) gasolina // *vt* asfixiar con gas; **~ cooker** *n* cocina de gas; **~ cylinder** *n* bombona de gas; **~ fire** *n* estufa de gas.

gash [gæʃ] *n* raja; (*on face*) cuchillada // *vt* (*gen*) rajar; (*with knife*) acuchillar.

gasket ['gæskɪt] *n* (*AUT*) junta.

gas: ~mask *n* careta antigás; **~ meter** *n* contador *m* de gas.

gasoline ['gæsəliːn] *n* (*US*) gasolina.

gasp [gɑːsp] n grito sofocado // vi (pant) jadear; **to ~ out** vt (say) decir con voz entrecortada.

gas: ~ ring n hornillo de gas; **~ stove** n cocina de gas; **~sy** a gaseoso; **~ tap** n llave f del gas.

gastric ['gæstrɪk] a gástrico; **~ ulcer** n úlcera gástrica.

gate [geɪt] n puerta; (RAIL) barrera; **~crash** vt colarse de gorra en; **~way** n puerta.

gather ['gæðə*] vt (flowers, fruit) coger; (assemble) reunir; (pick up) recoger; (SEWING) fruncir; (understand) entender // vi (assemble) reunirse; **~ing** n reunión f, asamblea.

gauche [gəuʃ] a torpe.

gaudy ['gɔːdɪ] a chillón(ona).

gauge [geɪdʒ] n medida; (RAIL) entrevía; (instrument) indicador m // vt medir.

gaunt [gɔːnt] a descarnado; (grim, desolate) desolado.

gauntlet ['gɔːntlɪt] n (fig): **to run the ~** correr baquetas; **to throw down the ~** arrojar el guante.

gauze [gɔːz] n gasa.

gave [geɪv] pt of **give**.

gay [geɪ] a (person) alegre, (colour) vistoso, vivo; (homosexual) gay.

gaze [geɪz] n mirada fija; **to ~ at** sth mirar algo con fijeza.

gazelle [gə'zel] n gacela.

gazetteer [gæzə'tɪə*] n diccionario geográfico.

G.B. abbr of **Great Britain**.

G.C.E. n abbr of **General Certificate of Education**.

gear [gɪə*] n equipo, herramientas fpl; (TECH) engranaje m; (AUT) velocidad f, marcha; **top/low** n torcera (o cuarta)/primera velocidad; **in ~** en marcha; **~ box** n caja de cambios; **~ lever, ~ shift** (US) n palanca de velocidades; **~ wheel** n rueda dentada.

geese [giːs] pl of **goose**.

gelatin(e) ['dʒelətiːn] n gelatina.

gelignite ['dʒelɪgnaɪt] n gelignita.

gem [dʒem] n joya.

Gemini ['dʒemɪnaɪ] n Géminis m, Gemelos mpl.

gender ['dʒendə*] n género.

general ['dʒenərl] n general m // a general; **in ~** en general; **~ election** n elecciones fpl generales; **~ization** [-aɪ'zeɪʃən] n generalización f; **~ize** vi generalizar; **~ly** ad generalmente, en general; **~ practitioner (G.P.)** n médico general.

generate ['dʒenəreɪt] vt (ELEC) generar; (fig) producir.

generation [dʒenə'reɪʃən] n generación f.

generator ['dʒenəreɪtə*] n generador m.

generosity [dʒenə'rɒsɪtɪ] n generosidad f; **generous** ['dʒenərəs] a generoso; (helping etc) abundante.

genetics [dʒɪ'netɪks] n genética.

Geneva [dʒɪ'niːvə] n Ginebra.

genial ['dʒiːnɪəl] a afable, simpático.

genitals ['dʒenɪtlz] npl órganos mpl genitales.

genius ['dʒiːnɪəs] n genio.

genocide ['dʒenəusaɪd] n genocidio.

gent [dʒent] n abbr of **gentleman**.

genteel [dʒen'tiːl] a fino, elegante.

gentle ['dʒentl] a (sweet) amable, dulce; (touch etc) ligero, suave; (animal) manso.

gentleman ['dʒentlmən] n señor m; (well-bred man) caballero.

gentleness ['dʒentlnɪs] n dulzura; (of touch) suavidad f; (of animal) mansedumbre f.

gently ['dʒentlɪ] ad suavemente.

gentry ['dʒentrɪ] n alta burguesía.

gents [dʒents] n (aseos de) caballeros mpl.

genuine ['dʒenjuɪn] a auténtico; (person) sincero.

geographic(al) [dʒɪə'græfɪk(l)] a geográfico; **geography** [dʒɪ'ɒgrəfɪ] n geografía.

geological [dʒɪəˈlɔdʒɪkl] a geológico; **geologist** [dʒɪˈɔlədʒɪst] n geólogo; **geology** [dʒɪˈɔlədʒɪ] n geología.

geometric(al) [dʒɪəˈmetrɪk(l)] a geométrico; **geometry** [dʒɪˈɔmətrɪ] n geometría.

geranium [dʒɪˈreɪnjəm] n geranio.

germ [dʒə:m] n (gen) microbio, bacteria; (BIO, fig) germen m.

German [ˈdʒə:mən] a alemán(ana) // n alemán/ana m/f; (LING) alemán m; ~ **measles** n rubéola.

Germany [ˈdʒə:mənɪ] n Alemania.

germination [dʒə:mɪˈneɪʃən] n germinación f.

gesticulate [dʒesˈtɪkjuleɪt] vi gesticular.

gesture [ˈdʒestʃə*] n gesto.

get [get], pt, pp **got**, pp **gotten** (US) vt (obtain) obtener; (receive) recibir; (achieve) conseguir; (find) encontrar; (catch) coger; (fetch) traer, ir a buscar; (understand) entender // vi (become) hacerse, volverse; to ~ **old** hacerse viejo, envejecer; to ~ **to** (place) llegar a; **he got under the fence** pasó por debajo de la barrera; to ~ **ready/washed** preparase/lavarse; to ~ **sb to do sth** hacer que alguien haga algo; to ~ **sth done** hacer algo de algo; to ~ **about** vi salir mucho, viajar mucho; (news) divulgarse; to ~ **along** vi (agree) entenderse; (depart) marcharse; (manage) = to ~ **by**; to ~ **at** vt fus (attack) atacar; (reach) llegar a; (the truth) descubrir; to ~ **away** vi marcharse; (on holiday) irse de vacaciones; (escape) escaparse; to ~ **away with** vt fus hacer impunemente; to ~ **back** vi (return) volver // vt recobrar; to ~ **by** vi (pass) lograr pasar; (manage) arreglárselas; to ~ **down** vi bajarse // vt (object) bajar; (depress) deprimir; to ~ **down to** vt fus (work) ponerse a (hacer); to ~ **in** vi (train) llegar; (arrive home)

volver a casa, regresar; to ~ **off** vi (from train etc) bajar; (depart: person, car) marcharse // vt fus (train, bus) bajar de; to ~ **on** vi (at exam etc) tener éxito; (agree) entenderse // vt (horse) subir; to ~ **out** vi salir; (of vehicle) bajar; (news) saberse // vt (take out) sacar; to ~ **out of** vt fus (duty etc) escaparse de; to ~ **over** vt (illness) recobrarse de; (put across) hacer comprender; to ~ **round** vt fus rodear; (fig: person) engatusar a; to ~ **through** vt fus (TEL) comunicar con; to ~ **together** vi reunirse; to ~ **up** vi (rise) levantarse // vt fus levantar; to ~ **up to** vt fus (reach) llegar a; (prank etc) hacer; ~**away** n fuga, escape m.

geyser [ˈgi:zə*] n calentador m de agua; (GEO) géiser m.

Ghana [ˈgɑ:nə] n Ghana.

ghastly [ˈgɑ:stlɪ] a horrible; (pale) pálido.

gherkin [ˈgɔ:kɪn] n pepinillo.

ghetto [ˈgetəu] n ghetto.

ghost [gəust] n fantasma m; ~**ly** a fantasmal.

giant [ˈdʒaɪənt] n gigante m // a gigantesco, gigante.

gibberish [ˈdʒɪbərɪʃ] n galimatías m.

gibe [dʒaɪb] n pulla.

giblets [ˈdʒɪblɪts] npl menudillos mpl.

giddiness [ˈgɪdɪnɪs] n vértigo; **giddy** a (dizzy) mareado; (speed) vertiginoso; (frivolous) atolondrado; **it makes me giddy** me marea.

gift [gɪft] n (gen) regalo; (offering) obsequio; (ability) talento; ~**ed** a dotado.

gigantic [dʒaɪˈgæntɪk] a gigantesco.

giggle [ˈgɪgl] vi reírse con risa tonta // n risilla tonta.

gill [dʒɪl] n (measure) = 0.14 l // n [gɪl] (of fish) agalla, branquia.

gilt [gɪlt] a, n dorado; **~-edged** a (COMM) del Estado.

gimmick ['gɪmɪk] n truco.

gin [dʒɪn] n (liquor) ginebra.

ginger ['dʒɪndʒə*] n jengibre m; ~ ale n cerveza de jengibre; ~bread n pan m de jengibre; ~-haired a pelirrojo.

gingerly ['dʒɪndʒəlɪ] ad con pies de plomo.

gipsy ['dʒɪpsɪ] n gitano/a.

giraffe [dʒɪ'rɑːf] n jirafa.

girder ['gɜːdə*] n viga.

girdle ['gɜːdl] n (corset) faja // vt ceñir.

girl [gɜːl] n (small) niña; (young woman) chica, joven f, muchacha; an English ~ una (chica) inglesa; ~friend n (of girl) amiga; (of boy) novia; ~ish a de niña.

girth [gɜːθ] n circunferencia; (stoutness) gordura.

gist [dʒɪst] n lo esencial.

give [gɪv], pt gave, pp given n (gen) dar; (deliver) entregar; (as gift) regalar // vi (break) romperse; (stretch: fabric) dar de sí; to ~ sth sth, ~ sth to sb dar algo a uno; to ~ away vt (give free) regalar; (betray) traicionar; (disclose) revelar; to ~ back vi devolver; to ~ in vi ceder // vt entregar; to ~ off vt despedir; to ~ out vt renunciar, darse por vencido // vi renunciar a; to ~ up smoking dejar de fumar; to ~ way vi ceder; (AUT) ceder el paso.

glacier ['glæsɪə*] n glaciar m.

glad [glæd] a contento; ~den vt alegrar.

gladioli [glædɪ'əʊlaɪ] npl gladíolos mpl.

gladly ['glædlɪ] ad con mucho gusto.

glamorous ['glæmərəs] a encantador(a), atractivo; **glamour** n encanto, atractivo.

glance [glɑːns] n ojeada, mirada // vi: to ~ at echar una ojeada a; to ~

off (bullet) rebotar; **glancing** a (blow) oblicuo.

gland [glænd] n glándula.

glare [glɛə*] n luz f deslumbradora, brillo // vi deslumbrar; to ~ at mirar ferozmente a; **glaring** a (mistake) notorio.

glass [glɑːs] n vidrio, cristal m; (for drinking) vaso; (: with stem) copa; (also: looking ~) espejo; ~es fpl gafas fpl; ~house n invernadero; ~ware n cristalería; ~y a (eyes) vidrioso.

glaze [gleɪz] vt (door) poner cristal a; (pottery) barnizar // n barniz m; ~d a (eye) vidrioso; (pottery) barnizado.

glazier ['gleɪzɪə*] n vidriero.

gleam [gliːm] n destello // vi brillar; ~ing a reluciente.

glee [gliː] n alegría, regocijo.

glen [glɛn] n cañada, valle m estrecho.

glib [glɪb] a de mucha labia; ~ness n labia.

glide [glaɪd] vi deslizarse; (AVIAT, birds) planear // n deslizamiento, (AVIAT) vuelo sin motor; **glider** n (AVIAT) planeador m; **gliding** n (AVIAT) vuelo sin motor.

glimmer ['glɪmə*] n luz f trémula.

glimpse [glɪmps] n vista momentánea, vislumbre m // vt vislumbrar, entrever.

glint [glɪnt] n destello; (in the eye) chispa // vi centellear.

glisten ['glɪsn] vi relucir, brillar.

glitter ['glɪtə*] vi relucir, brillar // n brillo.

gloat [gləʊt] vi: to ~ (over) recrearse en, saborear.

global ['gləʊbl] a mundial; (sum) global.

globe [gləʊb] n globo, esfera.

gloom [gluːm] n tinieblas fpl, oscuridad f; (sadness) tristeza, melancolía; ~y a (dark) oscuro; (sad) triste; (pessimistic) pesimista.

glorify ['glɔːrɪfaɪ] vt glorificar; (praise) alabar.

glorious ['glɔːrɪəs] a glorioso; **glory** n gloria.

gloss [glɔs] n (shine) brillo; (paint) pintura brillante o esmalte; **to ~ over** vt fus encubrir.

glossary ['glɔsərɪ] n glosario.

glossy ['glɔsɪ] a lustroso.

glove [glʌv] n guante m; **~ compartment** n (AUT) guantera.

glow [gləu] vi (shine) brillar; (fire) arder // n brillo.

glower ['glauə*] vi: **to ~ at** mirar con ceño.

glucose ['gluːkəus] n glucosa.

glue [gluː] n goma (de pegar) // vt pegar.

glum [glʌm] a (mood) abatido; (person, tone) melancólico.

glut [glʌt] n superabundancia.

glutton ['glʌtn] n glotón/ona m/f; **a ~ for work** un trabajador incansable; **~y** n gula, glotonería.

glycerin(e) ['glɪsərɪn] n glicerina.

gnarled [nɑːld] a nudoso.

gnat [næt] n mosquito.

gnaw [nɔː] vt roer.

gnome [nəum] n gnomo.

go [gəu], pt **went**, pp **gone** vi ir; (travel) viajar; (depart) irse, marcharse; (work) funcionar, marchar; (be sold) venderse; (time) pasar; (fit, suit): **to ~ with** hacer juego con; (become) ponerse; (break etc) estropearse, romperse // n, pl **~es: to have a ~ (at)** probar suerte (con); **to be on the ~** moverse, estar trabajando; **whose ~ is it?** ¿a quién le toca?; **he's going to do it** va a hacerlo; **to ~ for a walk** ir de paseo; **to ~ dancing** ir a bailar; **how did it ~?** ¿qué tal salió o resultó?; ¿cómo ha ido?; **to ~ about** vi (rumour) propagarse // vt fus: **how do I ~ about this?** ¿cómo me las arreglo para hacer esto?; **to ~ ahead** vi (make progress) avanzar; (get going) seguir; **to ~ along** vi ir // vt fus bordear; **to ~ along with** estar de acuerdo con; **to ~ away** vi irse, marcharse; **to ~ back** vi

volver; (fall back) retroceder; **to ~ back on** vt fus (promise) faltar a; **to ~ by** vi (years, time) pasar // vt fus guiarse por; **to ~ down** vi bajar; (ship) hundirse; (sun) ponerse // vt fus bajar por; **to ~ for** vt fus (fetch) ir por; (like) gustar; (attack) atacar; **to ~ in** vi entrar; **to ~ in for** vt fus (competition) presentarse a; **to ~ into** vt fus entrar en; (investigate) investigar; (embark on) embarcarse en; **to ~ off** vi irse, marcharse; (food) pasarse; (explode) estallar; (event) realizarse // vt fus dejar de gustar; **to ~ on** vi seguir, continuar; (happen) pasar, ocurrir; **to ~ on doing sth** seguir haciendo algo; **to ~ out** vi salir; (fire, light) apagarse; **to ~ over** vi (ship) zozobrar // vt fus (check) repasar; **to ~ through** vt fus (town etc) atravesar; **to ~ up** vi subir; **to ~ without** vt fus pasarse sin.

goad [gəud] vt aguijonear.

go-ahead ['gəuəhed] a emprendedor(a) // n luz f verde.

goal [gəul] n meta; (score) gol m; **~keeper** n portero; **~-post** n poste m de la portería.

goat [gəut] n cabrío, cabra m/f.

gobble ['gɔbl] vt (also: **~ down, ~ up**) engullir(se) (ávidamente).

goblet ['gɔblɪt] n copa.

goblin ['gɔblɪn] n duende m.

go-cart ['gəukɑːt] n go-cart m.

god [gɔd] n dios m; **G~** n Dios m; **~child** n ahijado/a; **~dess** n diosa; **~father** n padrino; **~-forsaken** a dejado de la mano de Dios; **~mother** n madrina; **~send** n don m del cielo; **~son** n ahijado.

goggles ['gɔglz] npl gafas fpl submarinas.

going ['gəuɪŋ] n (conditions) estado del terreno // a: **the ~ rate** la tarifa corriente o en vigor.

gold [gəuld] n oro // a: de oro; **~ en** a (made of ~) de oro; (in colour) dorado; **~fish** n pez m de colores; **~mine** n mina de oro.

golf [gɔlf] n golf m; ~ **club** n club m de golf; (stick) palo (de golf); ~ **course** n campo de golf; ~**er** n jugador a m/f de golf.

gondola ['gɔndələ] n góndola.

gone [gɔn] pp of **go**.

gong [gɔŋ] n gong m.

gonorrhea [gɔnə'riə] n gonorrea.

good [gud] a (gen) bueno; (kind) bueno, amable; (well-behaved) educado; (useful) útil // n bien m, provecho; ~**s** npl bienes mpl; (COMM) mercancías fpl; **to be** ~ **at** tener aptitud para; **to be** ~ **for** servir para; **it's** ~ **for you** te hace bien; **would you be** ~ **enough to...?** ¿podría hacerme el favor de...?; ¿sería tan amable de...?; **a** ~ **deal (of)** mucho; **a** ~ **many** muchos; **to make** ~ vt reparar; **for** ~ para siempre, definitivamente; ~ **morning/afternoon!** ¡buenos días/buenas tardes!; ~ **evening!** ¡buenas noches!; ~ **night!** ¡buenas noches!; ~**bye!** ¡adiós!; **to say** ~**bye** despedirse; **G**~ **Friday** n Viernes m Santo; ~**-looking** a guapo; ~**ness** n (of person) bondad f; **for** ~**ness sake!** ¡Por Dios!; ~**ness gracious!** ¡Dios mío!; ~**will** n buena voluntad f.

goose [gu:s], pl **geese** n ganso, oca.

gooseberry ['guzbəri] n grosella espinosa.

gooseflesh ['gu:sfleʃ] n, **goose pimples** npl carne f de gallina.

gore [gɔ:*] vt cornear // n sangre f.

gorge [gɔ:dʒ] n barranco // vr: **to** ~ **o.s. (on)** atracarse (de).

gorgeous ['gɔ:dʒəs] a magnífico, maravilloso.

gorilla [gə'rɪlə] n gorila m.

gorse [gɔ:s] n aulaga.

gory ['gɔ:ri] a sangriento.

go-slow ['gəu'sləu] n huelga de trabajo lento.

gospel ['gɔspl] n evangelio.

gossip ['gɔsip] n (scandal) chismorreo, chismes mpl; (chat) charla; (scandalmonger) chismoso/a;

(talker) hablador/a m/f // vi cotillear.

got [gɔt] pt, pp of **get**; ~**ten** (US) pp of **get**.

gout [gaut] n gota.

govern ['gʌvn] vt (gen) gobernar; (dominate) dominar.

governess ['gʌvənis] n institutriz f.

government ['gʌvnmənt] n gobierno; ~**al** [-'mentl] a gubernamental.

governor ['gʌvənə*] n gobernador m; (of jail) director/a m/f.

gown [gaun] n traje m; (of teacher, judge) toga.

G.P. n abbr of **general practitioner**.

GPO n abbr of **General Post Office.**

grab [græb] vt coger, arrebatar.

grace [greis] n (REL) gracia; (gracefulness) elegancia, finura // vt (favour) honrar; (adorn) adornar; **5 days'** ~ un plazo de 5 días; **to say** ~ bendecir la mesa; ~**ful** a elegante, gracioso; **gracious** ['greiʃəs] a amable.

grade [greid] n (quality) clase f, calidad f; (degree) grado; (US: SCOL) clase f // vt clasificar.

gradient ['greidiənt] n pendiente f

gradual ['grædjuəl] a paulatino; ~**ly** ad paulatinamente.

graduate ['grædjuit] n graduado, licenciado // vi ['grædjueit] graduarse, licenciarse; **graduation** [-'eiʃən] n graduación f.

graft [gra:ft] n (AGR, MED) injerto; (bribery) corrupción f // vt injertar.

grain [grein] n grano; (corn) granos mpl, cereales mpl; (in wood) fibra.

gram [græm] n gramo.

grammar ['græmə*] n gramática; **grammatical** [grə'mætikl] a gramatical.

gramme [græm] n = **gram**.

gramophone ['græməfəun] n tocadiscos m inv.

granary ['grænəri] n granero, troj f.

grand [grænd] *a* magnífico, imponente; ~**children** *npl* nietos *mpl*; ~**dad** *n* yayo, abuelito; ~**daughter** *n* nieta; ~**eur** ['grændjə*] *n* magnificencia, lo grandioso; ~**father** *n* abuelo; ~**lose** ['grændɪʌuz] *a* grandioso, (*pej*) pomposo; ~**ma** *n* yaya, abuelita; ~**mother** *n* abuela; ~**pa** *n* = ~**dad**; ~ **piano** *n* piano de cola; ~**son** *n* nieto; ~**stand** *n* (SPORT) tribuna.

granite ['grænɪt] *n* granito.

granny ['grænɪ] *n* abuelita, yaya.

grant [grɑːnt] *vt* (*concede*) conceder; (*admit*) asentir // *n* (SCOL) beca; **to take sth for** ~**ed** dar algo por sentado.

granulated sugar ['grænju-leɪtɪd] *a* azúcar *m* granulado.

granule ['grænjuːl] *n* gránulo.

grape [greɪp] *n* uva; **sour** ~**s** (*fig*) envidia.

grapefruit ['greɪpfruːt] *n* pomelo, toronja (AM).

graph [grɑːf] *n* gráfica; ~**ic** *a* gráfico.

grapple ['græpl] *vi*: **to** ~ **with sth** esforzarse por resolver algo.

grasp [grɑːsp] *vt* agarrar, asir, (*understand*) comprender // *n* (*grip*) asimiento; (*reach*) alcance *m*; (*understanding*) comprensión *f*; ~**ing** *a* avaro.

grass [grɑːs] *n* hierba; (*lawn*) césped *m*; ~**hopper** *n* saltamontes *m inv*; ~**land** *n* pradera; ~**roots** *a* popular; ~ **snake** *n* culebra; ~**y** *a* cubierto de hierba.

grate [greɪt] *n* (*fireplace*) chimenea; (*of iron*) parrilla // *vi* rechinar // *vt* (CULIN) rallar.

grateful ['greɪtful] *a* agradecido.

grater ['greɪtə*] *n* rallador *m*.

gratify ['grætɪfaɪ] *vt* complacer; (*whim*) satisfacer; ~**ing** *a* grato.

grating ['greɪtɪŋ] *n* (*iron bars*) rejilla // *a* (*noise*) áspero.

gratitude ['grætɪtjuːd] *n* agradecimiento.

gratuity [grə'tjuːɪtɪ] *n* gratificación *f*.

grave [greɪv] *n* tumba // *a* serio, grave; ~**digger** *n* sepulturero.

gravel ['grævl] *n* grava.

grave: ~**stone** *n* lápida; ~**yard** *n* cementerio, camposanto.

gravity ['grævɪtɪ] *n* gravedad *f*; (*seriousness*) seriedad *f*.

gravy ['greɪvɪ] *n* salsa.

gray [greɪ] *a* = **grey**.

graze [greɪz] *vi* pacer // *vt* (*touch lightly*) rozar; (*scrape*) raspar // *n* (MED) rasguño.

grease [griːs] *n* (*fat*) grasa; (*lubricant*) lubricante *m* // *vt* engrasar; ~**proof** *a* a prueba de grasa; (*paper*) apergaminado; **greasy** *a* grasiento.

great [greɪt] *a* grande; (*col*) magnífico, estupendo; G~ **Britain** *n* Gran Bretaña; ~**grandfather**/**mother** *n* bisabuelo/a; ~**ly** *ad* sumamente, mucho, muy; ~**ness** *n* grandeza.

Greece [griːs] *n* Grecia.

greed [griːd] *n* (*also*: ~**iness**) codicia, avaricia; (*for food*) gula; ~**ily** *ad* con avidez; ~**y** *a* avaro; (*for food*) glotón(ona).

Greek [griːk] *a* griego *a* // *n* griego/a; (LING) griego.

green [griːn] *a* verde; (*inexperienced*) novato // *n* verde *m*; (*stretch of grass*) césped *m*; ~**s** *npl* verduras *fpl*; ~**gage** *n* claudia; ~**grocer** *n* verdulero; ~**house** *n* invernadero; ~**ish** *a* verdoso.

Greenland ['griːnlənd] *n* Groenlandia.

greet [griːt] *vt* saludar; (*welcome*) dar la bienvenida a; ~**ing** *n* (*gen*) saludo; (*welcome*) bienvenida.

gregarious [grə'gɛərɪəs] *a* gregario.

grenade [grə'neɪd] *n* granada.

grew [gruː] *pt of* **grow**.

grey [greɪ] *a* gris; ~**haired** *a* canoso; ~**hound** *n* galgo.

grid [grɪd] *n* reja; (ELEC) red *f*.

grief [griːf] n dolor m, pena.

grievance ['griːvəns] n motivo de queja, agravio.

grieve [griːv] vi afligirse, acongojarse // vt dar pena a; **to ~ for** llorar por.

grievous ['griːvəs] a penoso.

grill [grɪl] n (on cooker) parrilla // vt asar a la parrilla; (question) interrogar duramente.

grille [grɪl] n reja; (AUT) rejilla.

grim [grɪm] a siniestro, (fam) horrible.

grimace [grɪ'meɪs] n mueca // vi hacer muecas.

grime [graɪm] n mugre f; **grimy** a mugriento.

grin [grɪn] n sonrisa abierta // vi sonreír abiertamente.

grind [graɪnd], pt, pp **ground** vt (coffee, pepper etc) moler; (make sharp) afilar // n (work) trabajo pesado y aburrido; **to ~ one's teeth** rechinar los dientes.

grip [grɪp] n (hold) asimiento; (of hands) apretón m; (handle) asidero; (of racquet etc) mango; (holdall) maletín m; (understanding) comprensión f // vt agarrar; **to come to ~s with** luchar a brazo partido con; **~ping** a absorbente.

grisly ['grɪzli] a horripilante, horrible.

gristle ['grɪsl] n cartílago.

grit [grɪt] n gravilla; (courage) valor m // vt (road) poner gravilla en; **to ~ one's teeth** apretar los dientes.

groan [grəun] n gemido, quejido // vi gemir, quejarse.

grocer ['grəusə*] n tendero de ultramarinos; **~ies** npl comestibles mpl; **~'s (shop)** n tienda de ultramarinos.

groggy ['grɔgi] a atontado, (BOXING) grogui.

groin [grɔɪn] n ingle f.

groom [gruːm] n mozo de caballos; (also: **bride~**) novio // vt (horse) cuidar; **well-~ed** a acicalado.

groove [gruːv] n ranura, surco.

grope [grəup] vi ir a tientas; **to ~ for** vt fus buscar a tientas.

gross [grəus] a grueso; (COMM) bruto; **~ly** ad (greatly) enormemente.

grotesque [grə'tɛsk] a grotesco.

grotto ['grɔtəu] n gruta.

ground [graund] pt, pp of **grind** // n suelo, tierra; (SPORT) campo, terreno; (reason: gen pl) causa, razón f // vt (plane) mantener en tierra; (US. ELEC) conectar con tierra // vi (ship) varar, encallar; **~s** npl (of coffee etc) poso sg; (gardens etc) jardines mpl, parque m; **on the ~** en el suelo; **to the ~** al suelo; **~ floor** n planta baja; **~ing** n (in education) conocimientos mpl básicos; **~less** a infundado; **~sheet** n tela impermeable; **~ staff** n personal m de tierra; **~work** n preparación f.

group [gruːp] n grupo; (musical) conjunto // (vb: also: **~ together**) vt agrupar // vi agruparse.

grouse [graus] n, pl inv (bird) urogallo // vi (complain) quejarse.

grove [grəuv] n arboleda.

grovel ['grɔvl] vi (fig) humillarse.

grow [grəu], pt **grew**, pp **grown** vi (gen) crecer; (plant) cultivarse; (increase) aumentar; (spread) extenderse, desarrollarse; (become) volverse; **to ~ rich/weak** enriquecerse/debilitarse // vt cultivar, dejar crecer; **to ~ up** vi crecer, hacerse hombre/mujer; **~er** n cultivador/a m/f, productor/a m/f; **~ing** a creciente.

growl [graul] vi gruñir.

grown [grəun] pp of **grow**; **~-up** n adulto, persona mayor.

growth [grəuθ] n crecimiento, desarrollo; (what has grown) brote m; (MED) acceso, tumor m.

grub [grʌb] n gusano; (col: food) comida.

grubby ['grʌbi] a sucio, mugriento.

grudge [grʌdʒ] n motivo de rencor // vt: **to ~ sb sth** dar algo a uno de mala gana, escatimar algo a uno; **to bear sb a ~** guardar rencor a uno; **he ~s (giving) the money** da el dinero de mala gana.

gruelling [ˈgruəlɪŋ] a penoso, duro.

gruesome [ˈgruːsəm] a horrible.

gruff [grʌf] a (voice) bronco; (manner) brusco.

grumble [ˈgrʌmbl] vi refunfuñar, quejarse.

grumpy [ˈgrʌmpɪ] a gruñón(ona).

grunt [grʌnt] vi gruñir // n gruñido.

guarantee [gærənˈtiː] n garantía // vt garantizar.

guarantor [gærənˈtɔː*] n garante m/f, fiador/a m/f.

guard [gɑːd] n guardia; (RAIL) jefe m de tren // vt guardar; **~ed** a (fig) cauteloso; **~ian** n guardián/ana m/f, (of minor) tutor/a m/f; **~'s van** n furgón m.

guerrilla [gəˈrɪlə] n guerrillero; **~ warfare** n guerra de guerrillas.

guess [gɛs] vi, vt (gen) adivinar; (suppose) suponer // n suposición f, conjetura; **to take o have a ~** tratar de adivinar; **~work** n conjeturas fpl.

guest [gɛst] n invitado/a; (in hotel) huésped/a m/f; **~house** n casa de huéspedes, pensión f; **~ room** n cuarto de huéspedes.

guffaw [gʌˈfɔː] n carcajada // vi reírse a carcajadas.

guidance [ˈgaɪdəns] n (gen) dirección f; (advice) consejos mpl.

guide [gaɪd] n (person) guía m/f; (book, fig) guía // vt guiar; (girl) **~** n exploradora; **~book** n guía; **~ dog** n perro guía; **~ lines** npl (fig) principios mpl generales.

guild [gɪld] n gremio; **~hall** n (Brit) ayuntamiento.

guile [gaɪl] n astucia; **~less** a cándido.

guillotine [ˈgɪlətiːn] n guillotina.

guilt [gɪlt] n culpabilidad f; **~y** a culpable.

guinea pig [ˈgɪnɪpɪg] n conejillo de Indias.

guise [gaɪz] n: in or under the ~ of so capa de.

guitar [gɪˈtɑː*] n guitarra; **~ist** n guitarrista m/f.

gulf [gʌlf] n golfo; (abyss) abismo.

gull [gʌl] n gaviota.

gullet [ˈgʌlɪt] n esófago; (fam) garganta.

gullible [ˈgʌlɪbl] a crédulo.

gully [ˈgʌlɪ] n barranco.

gulp [gʌlp] vi tragar saliva // (also: ~ **down**) tragarse // n: **at one ~** de un trago.

gum [gʌm] n (ANAT) encía; (glue) goma; (sweet) caramelo de goma; (also: chewing-~) chiclé m // vt engomar, pegar con goma; **~boots** npl botas fpl de goma.

gun [gʌn] n (gen) arma de fuego; (small) pistola; (shotgun) escopeta; (rifle) fusil m; (cannon) cañón m; **~boat** n cañonero; **~fire** n fuego, disparos mpl; **~man** n pistolero; **~ner** n artillero; **at ~point** bajo la amenaza de un arma; **~powder** n pólvora; **~shot** n escopetazo, cañonazo; **~smith** n armero.

gurgle [ˈgəːgl] vi gorgotear.

gush [gʌʃ] vi chorrear; (fig) deshacerse en efusiones.

gusset [ˈgʌsɪt] n escudete m.

gust [gʌst] n (of wind) ráfaga.

gusto [ˈgʌstəu] n entusiasmo.

gut [gʌt] n intestino, tripa; (MUS etc) cuerda de tripa; **~s** npl (courage) valor m.

gutter [ˈgʌtə*] n (of roof) canalón m; (in street) arroyo.

guttural [ˈgʌtərl] a gutural.

guy [gaɪ] n (also: **~rope**) cuerda; (col: man) tío, tipo.

guzzle [ˈgʌzl] vi tragar // vt engullir.

gym [dʒɪm] n (also: **gymnasium**) gimnasio; (also: **gymnastics**) gimnasia; **~nast** n gimnasta m/f; **~nastics** n gimnasia; **~ shoes** npl zapatillas fpl de gimnasia; **~ slip** n túnica de colegiala.

gynaecologist, gynecologist

(US) [gaɪnɪ'kɔlɔdʒɪst] n ginecólogo;
gynaecology, gynecology (US)
[-nɪ'kɔlɔdʒɪ] n ginecología.
gypsy ['dʒɪpsɪ] n = **gipsy.**
gyrate [dʒaɪ'reɪt] vi girar.

H

haberdashery ['hæbə'dæʃərɪ] n
mercería.
habit ['hæbɪt] n hábito, costumbre f,
(costume) hábito.
habitable ['hæbɪtəbl] a habitable.
habitual [hə'bɪtjuəl] a acostumbrado, habitual; (drinker, liar)
empedernido; ~**ly** ad por
costumbre.
hack [hæk] vt (cut) cortar; (slice)
tajar // n corte m; (axe blow)
hachazo.
hackneyed ['hæknɪd] a trillado,
gastado.
had [hæd] pt, pp of **have.**
haddock ['hædək] pl ~ or ~s n
especie de merluza.
hadn't ['hædnt] = **had not.**
haemorrhage, hemorrhage
(US) ['hemərɪdʒ] n hemorragia.
haemorrhoids, hemorrhoids
(US) ['hemərɔɪdz] npl hemorroides
fpl.
haggard ['hægəd] a ojeroso.
haggle ['hægl] vi (argue) discutir;
(bargain) regatear.
Hague [heɪg] n: **The ~** La Haya.
hail [heɪl] n (weather) granizo // vt
saludar; (call) llamar a // vi
granizar; ~**stone** n (piedra de)
granizo.
hair [hɛə*] n (gen) pelo, cabellos
mpl; (one ~) pelo, cabello; (head of
~) cabellera; (on legs) vello; **grey**
~**s** fpl canas fpl; ~**brush** n cepillo (del
pelo); ~**cut** n corte m de pelo; to
have a ~**cut** pelarse; ~**do** n
peinado; ~**dresser** n peluquero;
~**dresser's** n peluquería; ~**drier** n
secador m de pelo; ~**net** n

redecilla; ~**piece** n trenza postiza;
~**pin** n horquilla; ~**pin bend** n
curva de horquilla; ~**raising** a
espeluznante; ~ **remover** n
depilador m; (cream) crema
depilatoria; ~ **spray** n laca; ~**style**
n peinado; ~**y** a peludo; velludo.
half [hɑ:f], pl **halves** n mitad f // a
medio // ad medio, a medias; ~ **an
hour** media hora; **two and a ~** dos y
media; ~ **a pound** media libra; **to
cut sth in** ~ cortar algo por la
mitad; ~ **asleep** medio dormido;
~**price** a mitad de precio; ~**back**
n (SPORT) medio; ~**breed, ~caste**
n mestizo; ~**hearted** a indiferente,
poco entusiasta; ~**hour** n media
hora; ~**penny** ['heɪpnɪ] n medio
penique; ~**time** n medio tiempo;
~**way** ad a medio camino.
halibut ['hælɪbət] n, pl inv halibut
m.
hall [hɔ:l] n (for concerts) sala;
(entrance way) hall m, vestíbulo,
town ~ palacio municipal; ~ **of
residence** n residencia (universitaria).
hallmark ['hɔ:lmɑ:k] n (mark)
marca; (seal) sello.
hallo [hə'ləʊ] excl = **hello.**
hallucination [həlu:sɪ'neɪʃən] n
alucinación f
halo ['heɪləʊ] n (of saint) aureola.
halt [hɔ:lt] n (stop) alto, parada;
(RAIL) apeadero // vt parar // vi
pararse; (process) interrumpirse.
halve [hɑ:v] vt partir por la mitad.
halves [hɑ:vz] pl of **half.**
ham [hæm] n jamón m (cocido);
(actor) comicastro.
hamburger ['hæmbɜ:gə*] n hamburguesa.
hamlet ['hæmlɪt] n aldea.
hammer ['hæmə*] n martillo // vt
martillar; (nail) vi (on door) golpear.
hammock ['hæmək] n hamaca.
hamper ['hæmpə*] vt estorbar // n
cesto.
hand [hænd] n mano f; (of clock)
manecilla; (writing) letra;

(*applause*) aplausos *mpl*; (*worker*) obrero; (*measure*) palmo // *vt* (*give*) dar, pasar; (*deliver*) entregar; **to give sb a ~** dar una mano a uno, ayudar a uno; **at ~** a la mano; **in ~** entre manos; **on the one ~ ..., on the other ~ ...** por una parte ... por otra (parte) ...; **to ~ in** *vt* entregar; **to ~ out** *vt* distribuir; **to ~ over** *vt* (*deliver*) entregar; (*surrender*) ceder; **~bag** *n* bolso; **~basin** *n* lavabo; **~book** *n* manual *m*; **~brake** *n* freno de mano; **~cuffs** *npl* esposas *fpl*; **~ful** *n* puñado.

handicap ['hændikæp] *n* handicap *m*, desventaja // *vt* estorbar; **mentally/physically ~ped** incapacitado mentalmente/físicamente.

handicraft ['hændikrɑːft] *n* artesanía.

handkerchief ['hæŋkətʃif] *n* pañuelo.

handle ['hændl] *n* (*of door etc*) tirador *m*, manija; (*of cup etc*) asa; (*of knife etc*) mango; (*for winding*) manivela; (*fam: name*) título // *vt* (*touch*) tocar; (*deal with*) encargarse de; (*treat: people*) manejar; **'~ with care'** 'tratar con cuidado'; **to fly off the ~** perder los estribos; **~bar(s)** *n(pl)* manillar *m*.

hand-luggage ['hændlʌgidʒ] *n* equipaje *m* de mano.

handmade ['hændmeid] *a* hecho a mano.

handout ['hændaut] *n* (*distribution*) repartición *f*; (*charity*) limosna; (*leaflet*) folleto.

handshake ['hændʃeik] *n* apretón *m* de manos.

handsome ['hænsəm] *a* guapo.

handwriting ['hændraitiŋ] *n* letra.

handy ['hændi] *a* (*close at hand*) a mano; (*convenient*) práctico; (*skilful*) hábil, diestro; **~man** *n* (*hombre*) mañoso.

hang [hæŋ], *pt, pp* **hung** *vt* colgar; (*criminal: pt, pp* **hanged**) ahorcar; (*head*) bajar // *vi* colgar; **to ~**

about *vi* haraganear; **to ~ on** *vi* (*wait*) esperar; **to ~ up** *vi* (*TEL*) colgar.

hangar ['hæŋəʳ] *n* hangar *m*.

hanger ['hæŋəʳ] *n* percha; **~-on** *n* parásito.

hangover ['hæŋəuvəʳ] *n* (*after drinking*) resaca.

hang-up ['hæŋʌp] *n* complejo.

hanker ['hæŋkəʳ] *vi*: **to ~ after** (*miss*) echar de menos; (*long for*) añorar.

hankie, hanky ['hæŋki] *n abbr of* **handkerchief.**

haphazard [hæp'hæzəd] *a* fortuito.

happen ['hæpən] *vi* suceder, ocurrir; (*take place*) tener lugar, realizarse; **to ~ upon** tropezar con; **~ing** *n* suceso, acontecimiento.

happily ['hæpili] *ad* (*luckily*) afortunadamente; (*cheerfully*) alegremente.

happiness ['hæpinis] *n* (*gen*) felicidad *f*; (*joy*) alegría.

happy ['hæpi] *a* feliz, alegre; **to be ~ (with)** estar contento (con); **to be ~** ser feliz.

harass ['hærəs] *vt* acosar, hostigar; **~ment** *n* persecución *f*; (*worry*) preocupación *f*.

harbour, harbor (*US*) ['hɑːbəʳ] *n* puerto // *vt* (*hope etc*) abrigar; (*hide*) esconder.

hard [hɑːd] *a* (*gen*) duro; (*difficult*) difícil, arduo; (*work*) penoso; (*person*) severo // *ad* (*work*) mucho, duro, duramente; (*think, try*) seriamente; **to look ~ at** mirar fijo o fijamente; **no ~ feelings!** sin rencor; **to be ~ of hearing** ser duro de oído; **to be ~ done by** ser tratado injustamente; **~back** *n* libro encuadernado; **~board** *n* chapa de madera; **~en** *vt* endurecer; (*fig*) curtir // *vi* endurecerse; **~-headed** *a* poco sentimental, práctico; **~ labour** *n* trabajos *mpl* forzados.

hardly ['hɑːdli] *ad* (*scarcely*) apenas; **that can ~ be true**

dificilmente puede ser cierto; ~ ever casi nunca.

hardness ['hɑːdnɪs] n dureza.

hardship ['hɑːdʃɪp] n (troubles) penas fpl; (financial) apuro.

hard-up [hɑːd'ʌp] a (col) pelado.

hardware ['hɑːdwɛə*] n ferretería; (COMPUTERS) material m; ~ shop n ferretería.

hard-wearing [hɑːd'wɛərɪŋ] a resistente, duradero.

hard-working [hɑːd'wəːkɪŋ] a trabajador(a).

hardy ['hɑːdɪ] a fuerte; (plant) resistente.

hare [hɛə*] n liebre f; ~-brained a casquivano.

harem [hɑː'riːm] n harén m.

haricot (bean) ['hærɪkəu] n alubia.

harm [hɑːm] n daño, mal m // vt (person) hacer daño a, perjudicar; (thing) dañar; out of ~'s way a salvo; ~ful a perjudicial; (pest) dañino; ~less a inofensivo.

harmonica [hɑː'mɔnɪkə] n armónica.

harmonious [hɑː'məunɪəs] a armonioso; **harmonize** ['hɑːmənaɪz] vt, vi armonizar; **harmony** ['hɑːmənɪ] n armonía.

harness ['hɑːnɪs] n arreos mpl // vt (horse) enjaezar; (resources) aprovechar.

harp [hɑːp] n arpa // vi: to ~ on about hablar constantemente de; ~ist n arpista m/f.

harpoon [hɑː'puːn] n arpón m.

harrowing ['hærəuɪŋ] a horroroso.

harsh [hɑːʃ] a (hard) duro, cruel; (severe) severo; (unpleasant) desagradable; (: colour) chillón(ona); (contrast) violento; ~ness n dureza.

harvest ['hɑːvɪst] n cosecha; (of grapes) vendimia // vt, vi cosechar; ~er n (machine) cosechadora.

has [hæz] vb see have.

hash [hæʃ] n (CULIN) picadillo; (fig: mess) lío.

hashish ['hæʃɪʃ] n hachís m, hachich m.

hasn't ['hæznt] = has not.

hassle ['hæsl] n pelea // vt molestar a.

haste [heɪst] n prisa; **hasten** ['heɪsn] vt acelerar // vi darse prisa; **hastily** ad de prisa, hasty a apresurado.

hat [hæt] n sombrero.

hatch [hætʃ] n (NAUT: also: ~way) escotilla // vi salir del cascarón // vt incubar; (plot) tramar.

hatchback ['hætʃbæk] n (AUT) coche m con puerta trasera.

hatchet ['hætʃɪt] n hacha.

hate [heɪt] vt odiar, aborrecer // n odio; ~ful a odioso; **hatred** n odio.

hat trick ['hættrɪk] n (SPORT, also fig) tres triunfos seguidos.

haughty ['hɔːtɪ] a altanero, arrogante.

haul [hɔːl] vt tirar; (by lorry) transportar // n (of fish) redada; (of stolen goods etc) botín m; ~age n transporte m; (costs) gastos mpl de transporte; ~ier n contratista m de transportes.

haunch [hɔːntʃ] n anca; (of meat) pierna.

haunt [hɔːnt] vt (subj: ghost) aparecer en; (frequent) frecuentar; (obsess) obsesionar // n guarida; ~ed house casa de fantasmas.

have [hæv], pt, pp had vt (gen) tener; (possess) poseer; (meal, shower) tomar; to ~ sth done hacer hacer algo; she has to do it tiene que hacerlo; I had better leave más vale que me marche; I won't ~ it no lo tolero, he has gone se ha ido; to ~ it out with sb ajustar cuentas con alguien; to ~ a baby parir, dar a luz.

haven ['heɪvn] n puerto; (fig) refugio.

haven't ['hævnt] = have not.

haversack ['hævəsæk] n mochila.

havoc ['hævək] n estragos mpl.

hawk [hɔːk] n halcón m.

hay [heɪ] n heno; ~ fever n fiebre f

del heno; ~**stack** n almiar m.

haywire ['heɪwaɪə*] a (col): **to go ~** (person) volverse loco; (plan) embarullarse.

hazard ['hæzəd] n riesgo m // vt aventurar; ~**ous** a (dangerous) peligroso; (risky) arriesgado.

haze [heɪz] n neblina.

hazelnut ['heɪzlnʌt] n avellana.

hazy ['heɪzi] a brumoso; (idea) vago.

he [hi:] pron él; ~ **who...** él que..., quien...; ~**man** a macho.

head [hed] n cabeza; (leader) jefe/a m/f // (list) encabezar; (group) capitanear; ~**s (or tails)** cara (o cruz); ~ **first** de cabeza; ~ **over heels** patas arriba; **to ~ the ball** cabecear (la pelota); **to ~ for** vt fus dirigirse a; ~**ache** n dolor m de cabeza; ~**ing** n título; ~**lamp** n faro; ~**land** n promontorio; ~**light** = ~**lamp**; ~**line** n titular m; ~**long** ad (fall) de cabeza; (rush) precipitadamente; ~**master/ mistress** n director/a m/f (de escuela); ~**office** n oficina central, central f; ~**-on** a (collision) de frente; ~**phones** npl auriculares mpl; ~**quarters (HQ)** npl sede f central; (MIL) cuartel m general; ~**rest** n reposa-cabezas m inv; ~**room** n (in car) espacio para la cabeza; (under bridge) luz f; ~**scarf** n pañuelo (de cabeza); ~**stone** n lápida mortuoria; ~**strong** a voluntarioso; ~**waiter** n jefe m de camareros; ~**way** n progreso; **to make ~way** avanzar; ~**wind** n viento contrario.

heal [hi:l] vt curar // vi cicatrizarse.

health [helθ] n salud f; **good ~!** ¡salud y pesetas!; ~ **food** n comida natural; **H~ Service** n Seguro de Enfermedad; ~**y** a (gen) sano.

heap [hi:p] n montón m // vt amontonar; (plate) colmar.

hear [hɪə*], pt, pp **heard** [hɜːd] vt oír; (perceive) sentir; (listen to) escuchar; (lecture) asistir a // vi oír; **to ~ about** oír hablar de; **to ~**

from sb tener noticias de alguien; ~**ing** n (sense) oído; (LAW) vista; ~**ing aid** n audífono; ~**say** n rumores mpl, hablillas fpl.

hearse [hɜːs] n coche m fúnebre.

heart [hɑːt] n corazón m; ~**s** npl (CARDS) corazones mpl; **at ~** en el fondo; **by ~** (learn, know) de memoria; ~ **attack** n ataque m cardíaco; ~**beat** n latido (del corazón); ~**breaking** a desgarrador(a); **to be ~broken** estar angustiado; ~**burn** n acedía; ~ **failure** n fallo cardíaco; ~**felt** a (cordial) cordial; (deeply felt) más sentido.

hearth [hɑːθ] n (gen) hogar m; (fireplace) chimenea.

heartily ['hɑːtɪlɪ] ad sinceramente, cordialmente; (laugh) a carcajadas; (eat) con buen apetito.

heartless ['hɑːtlɪs] a cruel.

hearty ['hɑːtɪ] a cordial.

heat [hi:t] n (gen) calor m; (ardour) ardor m; (SPORT. also: qualifying ~) prueba eliminatoria // vt calentar; (fig) aclorar; **to ~ up** vi (gen) calentarse; ~**ed** a caliente; (fig) acalorado; ~**er** n calentador m.

heath [hi:θ] n (Brit) brezal m.

heathen ['hi:ðn] a, n pagano/a.

heather ['heðə*] n brezo.

heating ['hi:tɪŋ] n calefacción f.

heatstroke ['hi:tstrəuk] n insolación f.

heatwave ['hi:tweɪv] n ola de calor.

heave [hi:v] vt (pull) tirar de; (push) empujar con esfuerzo; (lift) levantar (con esfuerzo) // vi (water) agitarse // n tirón m; empujón m; (effort) esfuerzo; (throw) echada.

heaven ['hevn] n cielo; (REL) paraíso; ~**ly** a celestial; (REL) divino.

heavily ['hevɪlɪ] ad pesadamente; (drink, smoke) con exceso; (sleep, sigh) profundamente.

heavy ['hevɪ] a pesado; (work) duro;

(sea, rain, meal) fuerte; *(drinker, smoker)* gran; *(eater)* comilón(ona); ~**weight** n *(SPORT)* peso pesado.

Hebrew ['hi:bru:] a hebreo.

heckle ['hekl] vt interrumpir.

hectic ['hektik] a febril, agitado.

he'd [hi:d] = **he would; he had.**

hedge [hedʒ] n seto // vt cercar (con un seto) // vi contestar con evasivas; **to ~ one's bets** *(fig)* cubrirse.

hedgehog ['hedʒhɔg] n erizo.

heed [hi:d] vt *(also:* **take ~** *of)* *(attend to)* hacer caso de; *(bear in mind)* tener en cuenta; ~**less** a desatento.

heel [hi:l] n talón m // vt *(shoe)* poner tacón a.

hefty ['heftɪ] a *(person)* fornido; *(piece)* grande; *(price)* gordo.

heifer ['hefə*] n novilla, ternera.

height [haɪt] n *(of person)* talle m, *(of building)* altura; *(high ground)* cerro; *(altitude)* altitud f; ~**en** vt elevar; *(fig)* aumentar.

heir [eə*] n heredero; ~**ess** n heredera; ~**loom** n reliquia de familia.

held [held] pt, pp of **hold.**

helicopter ['helɪkɔptə*] n helicóptero.

hell [hel] n infierno; ~! *(demonios!*

he'll [hi:l] = **he will; he shall.**

hellish ['helɪʃ] a infernal; *(fam)* horrible.

hello [hə'ləu] excl ¡hola!; *(surprise)* ¡caramba!

helm [helm] n *(NAUT)* timón m.

helmet ['helmɪt] n casco.

help [help] n ayuda; *(charwoman)* criada, asistenta; *(assistant etc)* empleado // vt ayudar; ~! ¡socorro!, **~ yourself** sírvete; **he can't ~ it** no es culpa suya; ~**er** n ayudante m/f; ~**ful** a útil, servicial; ~**ing** n ración f; ~**less** a *(incapable)* incapaz; *(defenceless)* indefenso.

hem [hem] n dobladillo; **to ~ in** vt cercar.

hemisphere ['hemɪsfɪə*] n hemisferio.

hen [hen] n gallina.

hence [hens] ad *(therefore)* por lo tanto; **2 years ~** de aquí a 2 años; ~**forth** ad de hoy en adelante.

henchman ['hentʃmən] n *(pej)* secuaz m.

henpecked ['henpekt] a dominado por su mujer.

her [hə:*] pron *(direct)* la; *(indirect)* le; *(stressed, after prep)* ella // a su.

herald ['herəld] n *(forerunner)* precursor/a m/f // vt anunciar.

heraldry ['herəldrɪ] n heráldica.

herb [hə:b] n hierba.

herd [hə:d] n rebaño.

here [hɪə*] ad aquí; ~! *(present)* presente; **~ she is** aquí está; ~**after** ad en el futuro // n: **the ~after** *(a vida de)* ultratumba; ~**by** ad *(in letter)* por la presente.

hereditary [hɪ'redɪtrɪ] a hereditario; **heredity** [-tɪ] n herencia.

heresy ['herəsɪ] n herejía.

heretic ['herətɪk] n hereje m/f; ~**al** [hɪ'retɪkl] a herético.

heritage ['herɪtɪdʒ] n *(gen)* herencia; *(fig)* patrimonio.

hermit ['hə:mɪt] n ermitaño.

hernia ['hə:nɪə] n hernia.

hero ['hɪərəu], pl ~es n héroe m; *(in book, film)* protagonista m; ~**ic** [hɪ'rəuɪk] a heroico.

heroin ['herəuɪn] n heroína.

heroine ['herəuɪn] n heroína; *(in book, film)* protagonista.

heroism ['herəuɪzm] n heroísmo.

heron ['herən] n garza.

herring ['herɪŋ] n arenque m.

hers [hə:z] pron el suyo/(la) suya etc.

herself [hə:'self] pron *(reflexive)* se; *(emphatic)* ella misma; *(after prep)* sí (misma).

he's [hi:z] = **he is; he has.**

hesitant ['hezɪtənt] a vacilante, dudoso.

hesitate ['hezɪteɪt] vi dudar,

vacilar; **hesitation** ['-teɪʃən] n indecisión f.

hew [hju:] vt cortar con hacha.

hexagon ['heksəgən] n hexágono; ~**al** ['-sægənl] a hexagonal.

hi [haɪ] excl ¡oye!, ¡hola!

hibernate ['haɪbəneɪt] vi invernar.

hiccough, hiccup ['hɪkʌp] vi hipar; ~s npl hipo sg.

hid [hɪd] pt of hide.

hidden ['hɪdn] pp of hide.

hide [haɪd] n (skin) piel f // (vb: pt **hid**, pp **hidden**) vt esconder, ocultar // vi: to ~ (from sb) esconderse o ocultarse (de alguien); ~**-and-seek** n escondite m; ~**away** n escondite m.

hideous ['hɪdɪəs] a horrible.

hiding ['haɪdɪŋ] n (beating) paliza; **to be in** ~ (concealed) estar escondido; ~ **place** n escondrijo.

hierarchy ['haɪərɑːkɪ] n jerarquía.

high [haɪ] a (gen) alto; (speed, number) grande; (price) elevado; (wind) fuerte; (voice) agudo // ad alto, a gran altura; **it is 20 m** ~ tiene 20 m de altura; ~ **in the air** en las alturas; ~**brow** a culto; ~**chair** n silla alta; ~**-handed** a despótico; ~**-heeled** a de tacón alto; ~**jack** = **hijack**; ~ **jump** n (SPORT) salto de altura; ~**light** n (fig: of event) punto culminante // vt subrayar; ~**ly** ad sumamente; ~**ly strung** a hipertenso; **H**~ **Mass** n misa mayor; ~**ness** n altura; **Her H**~**ness** Su Alteza; ~**-pitched** a agudo; ~**-rise block** n torre f de pisos; ~ **school** n colegio de segunda enseñanza, Instituto; ~ **street** n calle f mayor; ~**way** n carretera.

hijack ['haɪdʒæk] vt secuestrar; ~**er** n secuestrador/a m/f.

hike [haɪk] vi (go walking) ir de excursión; (tramp) caminar // n caminata; **hiker** n excursionista m/f.

hilarious [hɪ'lɛərɪəs] a (behaviour, event) regocijante.

hill [hɪl] n colina; (high) montaña; (slope) cuesta; ~**side** n ladera; ~**y** a montañoso; (uneven) accidentado.

hilt [hɪlt] n (of sword) empuñadura; **to the** ~ completamente.

him [hɪm] pron (direct) le, lo; (indirect) se; (stressed, after prep) él; ~**self** pron (reflexive) se; (emphatic) él mismo; (after prep) sí (mismo).

hind [haɪnd] a posterior // n cierva.

hinder ['hɪndə*] vt estorbar, impedir; **hindrance** ['hɪndrəns] n estorbo, obstáculo.

Hindu ['hɪndu:] n hindú m/f.

hinge [hɪndʒ] n bisagra, gozne m // vi (fig): **to** ~ **on** depender de.

hint [hɪnt] n indirecta; (advice) consejo // vt: **to** ~ **that** insinuar que // vi soltar indirectas; **to** ~ **at** hacer una alusión a.

hip [hɪp] n cadera; ~ **pocket** n bolsillo de atrás.

hippopotamus [hɪpə'pɒtəməs], pl ~**es** or ~**mi** [-maɪ] n hipopótamo.

hire ['haɪə*] vt (car, equipment) alquilar; (worker) contratar // n alquiler m; (of person) salario; **for** ~ se alquila; (taxi) libre; ~ **purchase (H.P.)** n compra a plazos.

his [hɪz] pron (el) suyo/(la) suya etc // a su.

Hispanic [hɪs'pænɪk] a hispánico.

hiss [hɪs] vi silbar, sisear // n silbido, siseo.

historian [hɪ'stɔːrɪən] n historiador/a m/f.

historic(al) [hɪ'stɒrɪk(l)] a histórico.

history ['hɪstərɪ] n historia.

hit [hɪt], pt, pp **hit** vt (strike) golpear, pegar; (reach: target) alcanzar; (collide with: car) chocar contra // n golpe m; (success) éxito, sensación f; **to** ~ **it off with sb** hacer buenas migas con alguien.

hitch [hɪtʃ] vt (fasten) atar, amarrar; (also: ~ **up**) alzar // n (difficulty) dificultad f; **to** ~ **a lift** hacer autostop.

hitch-hike ['hɪtʃhaɪk] vi hacer autostop, hitch-hiker n autostopista m/f.

hive [haɪv] n colmena.

hoard [hɔːd] n acumulación f // vt acumular; ~ing n acumulación f; (for posters) cartelera.

hoarfrost ['hɔːfrɒst] n escarcha.

hoarse [hɔːs] a ronco.

hoax [həʊks] n trampa.

hobble ['hɒbl] vi cojear // vt (horse) manear.

hobby ['hɒbɪ] n pasatiempo, afición f; ~-horse n (fig) tema, manía.

hobo ['həʊbəʊ] n (US) vagabundo.

hockey ['hɒkɪ] n hockey m.

hoe [həʊ] n azadón m // vt azadonar.

hog [hɒg] n cerdo, puerco // vt (fig) acaparar; to go the whole ~ liarse la manta a la cabeza.

hoist [hɔɪst] n (lift) montacargas m inv; (crane) grúa.

hold [həʊld], pt, pp **held** vt tener; (contain) contener; (keep back) retener; (believe) sostener; (take — of) coger; (take weight) soportar; (meeting) celebrar // vi (withstand pressure) resistir; (be valid) valer; (stick) pegarse // n (handle) asidero; (grasp) asimiento; (fig) dominio; (WRESTLING) presa; (NAUT) bodega; ~ the line! (TEL) no cuelgue; to ~ one's own (fig) defenderse; to catch or get (a) ~ of agarrarse, asirse de; to ~ back vt retenerse; (secret) guardar; to ~ down vt (person) sujetar; (job) conservar; to ~ off vt (enemy) rechazar; to ~ on vi agarrarse bien; (wait) esperar; ~ on! (TEL) no cuelgue; to ~ on to vt fus agarrarse a; (keep) guardar; to ~ out vt alargar // vi (resist) resistir; to ~ up vt (raise) levantar; (support) apoyar; (delay) atrasar; (rob) asaltar; ~all n funda, neceser m; ~er n (of ticket, record) poseedor/a m/f; (of office, title etc) titular m/f; ~ing n (share) interés

m; ~up n (robbery) atraco; (delay) parada; (in traffic) embotellamiento.

hole [həʊl] n agujero // vt agujerear.

holiday ['hɒlədɪ] n vacaciones fpl; (day off) (día de) fiesta, feriado; ~-maker n veraneante m/f; ~ resort n punto de veraneo.

holiness ['həʊlɪnɪs] n santidad f.

Holland ['hɒlənd] n Holanda.

hollow ['hɒləʊ] a hueco, vacío; (eyes) hundido; (sound) sordo; (doctrine) falso // n (gen) hueco; (in ground) hoyo // vt: to ~ out ahuecar.

holly ['hɒlɪ] n acebo; ~hock n malva loca.

holster ['həʊlstə*] n pistolera.

holy ['həʊlɪ] a (gen) santo, sagrado; (water) bendito; H~ Ghost or Spirit n Espíritu m Santo.

homage ['hɒmɪdʒ] n homenaje m; to pay ~ to rendir homenaje a.

home [həʊm] n casa; (country) patria; (institution) asilo // a (domestic) casero, de casa; (ECON, pol) nacional // ad (direction) a casa; at ~ en casa; to go/come ~ ir/volver a casa; make yourself at ~ ¡estás en tu casa!; ~ address n señas fpl; ~land n tierra natal; ~less a sin hogar, sin casa; ~ly a (domestic) casero; (simple) sencillo; ~made a hecho en casa; ~ rule n autonomía; H~ Secretary n (Brit) Ministro del Interior; ~sick a: to be ~sick tener morriña, tener nostalgia; ~ town n ciudad f natal; ~ward ['həʊmwəd] a (journey) hacia casa; ~work n tarea.

homicide ['hɒmɪsaɪd] n (US) homicidio.

homosexual [hɒməʊ'sɛksjuəl] a, n homosexual m.

honest ['ɒnɪst] a honrado; (sincere) franco, sincero; ~ly ad honradamente; francamente; ~y n honradez f.

honey ['hʌnɪ] n miel f; ~comb

panal m; (*pattern*) nido de abejas; **~moon** n luna de miel; (*trip*) viaje m de novios.

honk [hɔŋk] vi (AUT) tocar la bocina.

honorary [ˈɔnərərɪ] a no remunerado; (*duty, title*) honorario.

honour, honor (US) [ˈɔnə*] vt honrar // n honor m, honra; **~able** a honorable; **~s degree** n (SCOL) título universitario.

hood [hud] n capucha; (*Brit: AUT*) capota; (*US: AUT*) capó m.

hoodlum [ˈhuːdləm] n matón m.

hoof [huːf], pl **hooves** n pezuña.

hook [huk] n gancho; (*on dress*) corchete m, broche m; (*for fishing*) anzuelo // vt enganchar.

hooligan [ˈhuːligən] n gamberro.

hoop [huːp] n aro.

hoot [huːt] vi (AUT) tocar la bocina; (*siren*) tocar la sirena // n bocinazo; toque m de sirena; to **~ with laughter** morirse de risa; **~er** n (AUT) bocina; (NAUT) sirena.

hooves [huːvz] pl of **hoof**.

hop [hɔp] vi saltar, brincar; (*on one foot*) saltar con un pie // n salto, brinco.

hope [həup] vt, vi esperar // n esperanza; **I ~ so/not** espero que sí/no; **~ful** a (*person*) optimista, lleno de esperanzas; (*situation*) prometedor(a); **~fully** ad con optimismo, con esperanza; **~less** a desesperado.

hops [hɔps] npl lúpulo sg.

horde [hɔːd] n horda.

horizon [həˈraɪzn] n horizonte m; **~tal** [hɔrɪˈzɔntl] a horizontal.

hormone [ˈhɔːməun] n hormona.

horn [hɔːn] n cuerno; (MUS) trompa; (AUT) bocina; **~rimmed** de concha; **~ed** a (*animal*) con cuernos.

hornet [ˈhɔːnɪt] n avispón m.

horny [ˈhɔːnɪ] a (*material*) córneo; (*hands*) calloso.

horoscope [ˈhɔrəskəup] n horóscopo.

horrible [ˈhɔrɪbl] a horrible.

horrid [ˈhɔrɪd] a horrible, horroroso.

horrify [ˈhɔrɪfaɪ] vt horrorizar.

horror [ˈhɔrə*] n horror m; **~ film** n película de horror.

hors d'œuvre [ˈɔːˈdəːvrə] n entremeses mpl.

horse [hɔːs] n caballo; **on ~back** a caballo; **~man/woman** n jinete m/amazona; **~power (h.p.)** n caballo (de fuerza); **~racing** n carreras fpl de caballos; **~radish** n rábano picante; **~shoe** n herradura.

horticulture [ˈhɔːtɪkʌltʃə*] n horticultura.

hose [həuz] n (*also*: **~pipe**) manga.

hosiery [ˈhəuʒɪərɪ] n calcetería.

hospitable [ˈhɔspɪtəbl] a hospitalario.

hospital [ˈhɔspɪtl] n hospital m.

hospitality [hɔspɪˈtælɪtɪ] n hospitalidad f.

host [həust] n anfitrión m; (*in hotel etc*) huésped m; (*large number*): **a ~ of** multitud de; (REL) hostia.

hostage [ˈhɔstɪdʒ] n rehén m.

hostel [ˈhɔstl] n hostal m; **youth ~** n albergue m de juventud.

hostess [ˈhəustɪs] n anfitriona; (*air ~*) azafata; (*in night-club*) cabaretera.

hostile [ˈhɔstaɪl] a hostil; **hostility** [-ˈstɪlɪtɪ] n hostilidad f.

hot [hɔt] a caliente; (*weather*) caluroso, de calor; (*as opposed to only warm*) muy caliente; (*spicy*) picante; (*fig*) ardiente, acalorado; **~ dog** n perro caliente.

hotel [həuˈtel] n hotel m; **~ier** n hotelero.

hot: ~headed a exaltado; **~house** n invernadero; **~ly** ad con pasión, apasionadamente; **~-water bottle** n bolsa de agua caliente.

hound [haund] vt acosar // n perro de caza.

hour [ˈauə*] n hora; **~ly** ad cada hora.

house [haus, pl: ˈhauzɪz] n (*also: firm*) casa; (POL) cámara; (THEATRE) sala // vt [hauz] (person) alojar; **on the ~** (fig) la casa invita; **~ arrest** n arresto domiciliario; **~boat** n casa flotante; **~breaking** n robo (en una casa); **~coat** n bata; **~hold** n familia; **~keeper** n ama de llaves; **~keeping** n (work) trabajos domésticos mpl; **~keeping (money)** dinero para gastos domésticos; **~warming party** n fiesta de estreno de casa; **~wife** n ama de casa; **~work** n faenas fpl (de la casa).

housing ['hauziŋ] n (act) alojamiento; (houses) viviendas fpl; **~ estate** n bloque m de viviendas.

hovel n ['hɔvl] n pocilga.

hover ['hɔvə] vi flotar (en el aire); **~craft** n hidroala m, aerodeslizador m.

how [hau] ad cómo; **~ are you?** ¿cómo está Vd?, ¿cómo estás?; **~ long have you been here?** ¿cuánto tiempo hace que estás aquí?; **~ lovely!** ¡qué bonito!; **~ many/much?** ¿cuántos/cuánto?; **~ old are you?** ¿cuántos años tienes?; **~ ever** ad de cualquier manera; (+ adjective) por muy ... que; (in questions) cómo // conj sin embargo, no obstante.

howl [haul] n aullido // vi aullar.

h.p., **H.P.** abbr of hire purchase; horse power.

HQ abbr of headquarters.

hub [hʌb] n (of wheel) centro.

hubbub ['hʌbʌb] n barahúnda, barullo.

hubcap ['hʌbkæp] n tapacubo.

huddle ['hʌdl] vi: **to ~ together** amontonarse.

hue [hju:] n color m, matiz m; **~ and cry** n alarma.

huff [hʌf] n: **in a ~** con rabieta.

hug [hʌg] vt abrazar // n abrazo.

huge [hju:dʒ] a enorme.

hulk [hʌlk] n (wreck) barco viejo; (hull) casco.

hull [hʌl] n (of ship) casco.

hullo [hə'ləu] excl = hello.

hum [hʌm] vt tararear, canturrear // vi tararear, canturrear; (insect) zumbar // n zumbido.

human ['hju:mən] a, n humano.

humane [hju:'mein] a humano, humanitario.

humanity [hju:'mæniti] n humanidad f.

humble ['hʌmbl] a humilde // vt humillar; **humbly** ad humildemente.

humbug ['hʌmbʌg] n embustes mpl; (sweet) caramelo de menta.

humdrum ['hʌmdrʌm] a (boring) monótono, aburrido; (routine) rutinario.

humid ['hju:mid] a húmedo; **~ity** [-'miditi] n humedad f.

humiliate [hju:'milieit] vt humillar; **humiliation** [-'eiʃən] n humillación f.

humility [hju:'militi] n humildad f.

humorist ['hju:mərist] n humorista m/f.

humorous ['hju:mərəs] a gracioso, divertido.

humour, humor (US) ['hju:mə *] n humorismo, sentido del humor; (mood) humor m // vt (person) complacer.

hump [hʌmp] n (in ground) montículo; (camel's) giba.

hunch [hʌntʃ] n (premonition) presentimiento; **~back** n joroba; **~ed a** jorobado.

hundred ['hʌndrəd] num ciento; (before a) cien; **~weight** n (Brit) = 50.8 kg; 112 lb; (US) = 45.3 kg; 100 lb.

hung [hʌŋ] pt, pp of hang.

Hungarian [hʌŋ'gɛəriən] a, n húngaro/a.

Hungary ['hʌŋgəri] n Hungría.

hunger ['hʌŋgə] n hambre f // vi: **to ~ for** (gen) tener hambre de; (desire) anhelar; **~ strike** n huelga de hambre; **hungrily** [-grəli] ad ávidamente, con ganas; **hungry** [-gri] a hambriento; **to be hungry** tener hambre.

hunt [hʌnt] vt (seek) buscar; (SPORT) cazar // vi cazar // n caza, cacería;

~er n cazador m; ~ing n caza.
hurdle ['hə:dl] n (SPORT) valla; (fig) obstáculo.
hurl [hə:l] vt lanzar, arrojar.
hurrah [hu'rɑ:], **hurray** [hu'reɪ] n ¡viva!, ¡vítor!
hurricane ['hʌrɪkən] n huracán m.
hurried ['hʌrɪd] a (fast) apresurado; (rushed) hecho de prisa; ~ly ad con prisa, apresuradamente.
hurry ['hʌrɪ] n prisa // vi apresurarse, darse prisa // vt (person) dar prisa a; (work) apresurar; to be in a ~ tener prisa.
hurt [hə:t], pt, pp hurt vt hacer daño a // vi doler a // a lastimado; ~ful a (gen) dañoso; (remark) hiriente.
hurtle ['hə:tl] vi: to ~ past pasar como un rayo; to ~ down caer con violencia.
husband ['hʌzbənd] n marido.
hush [hʌʃ] n silencio // vt hacer callar; (cover up) encubrir; ~! ¡chitón!, ¡cállate!
husk [hʌsk] n (of wheat) cáscara.
husky ['hʌskɪ] a ronco; (burly) fornido // n perro esquimal.
hustle ['hʌsl] vt (push) empujar; (hurry) dar prisa a // n bullicio, actividad f febril; ~ and bustle n vaivén m.
hut [hʌt] n cabaña; (shed) cobertizo.
hutch [hʌtʃ] n conejera.
hyacinth ['haɪəsɪnθ] n jacinto.
hybrid ['haɪbrɪd] a, n híbrido.
hydrant ['haɪdrənt] n (also: fire ~) boca de incendios.
hydraulic [haɪ'drɔ:lɪk] a hidráulico.
hydroelectric [haɪdrəu'lektrɪk] a hidroeléctrico.
hydrogen ['haɪdrədʒən] n hidrógeno.
hyena [haɪ'i:nə] n hiena.
hygiene ['haɪdʒi:n] n higiene f; **hygienic** [-'dʒi:nɪk] a higiénico.
hymn [hɪm] n himno.
hyphen ['haɪfn] n guión m.
hypnosis [hɪp'nəusɪs] n hipnosis f; **hypnotic** [-'nɔtɪk] a hipnótico;

hypnotism ['hɪpnətɪzm] n hipnotismo; **hypnotist** ['hɪpnətɪst] n hipnotista m/f; **hypnotize** ['hɪpnətaɪz] vt hipnotizar.
hypocrisy [hɪ'pɔkrɪsɪ] n hypocresía; **hypocrite** ['hɪpəkrɪt] n hipócrita m/f; **hypocritical** [hɪpə'krɪtɪkl] a hipócrita.
hypothesis [haɪ'pɔθɪsɪs], pl -ses [-si:z] n hipótesis f; **hypothetic(al)** [-pəu'θetɪk(l)] a hipotético.
hysteria [hɪ'stɪərɪə] n histeria; **hysterical** [-'sterɪkl] a histérico; **hysterics** [-'sterɪks] npl histeria sg, histerismo sg.

I

I [aɪ] pron yo.
ice [aɪs] n hielo // vt (cake) alcorzar; (drink) helar // vi (also: ~ over, ~ up) helarse; ~ age n período glacial; ~ axe n piolet m; ~berg n iceberg m; ~box n (US) nevera; ~-cold a helado; ~ cream n helado; ~ cube n cubito de hielo; ~ hockey n hockey m sobre hielo.
Iceland ['aɪslənd] n Islandia; ~er n islandés/esa m/f; ~ic [-'lændɪk] a islandés(esa).
ice: ~ rink n pista de hielo; ~ skating n patinaje m sobre hielo.
icicle ['aɪsɪkl] n carámbano.
icing ['aɪsɪŋ] n (CULIN) alcorza, garapiña; (AVIAT etc) formación f de hielo; ~ sugar n azúcar m de alcorza.
icon ['aɪkɔn] n ícono.
icy ['aɪsɪ] a (road) helado; (fig) glacial.
I'd [aɪd] = **I would; I had.**
idea [aɪ'dɪə] n idea.
ideal [aɪ'dɪəl] n ideal m // a ideal; ~ist n idealista m/f.
identical [aɪ'dentɪkl] a idéntico.
identification [aɪdentɪfɪ'keɪʃən] n identificación f; **means of**

documentos *mpl* personales.
identify [ar'dentıfaı] *vt* identificar.
identikit picture [ar'dentıkıt-] *n* retrato-robot *m*.
identity [ar'dentıtı] *n* identidad *f*.
ideological [aıdıə'lɒdʒıkəl] *a* ideológico; **ideology** [aıdı'ɒlədʒı] *n* ideología.
idiocy ['ıdıəsı] *n* idiotez *f*; (*stupid act*) estupidez *f*.
idiom ['ıdıəm] *n* modismo; (*style of speaking*) lenguaje *m*.
idiosyncrasy [ıdıəu'sıŋkrəsı] *n* idiosincrasia.
idiot ['ıdıət] *n* (*gen*) idiota *m/f*; (*fool*) tonto/a; **~ic** [-'ɒtık] *a* idiota; tonto.
idle ['aıdl] *a* (*gen*) ocioso; (*lazy*) holgazán(ana); (*unemployed*) desocupado; (*pointless*) inútil // *vi* (*machine*) marchar en vacío // *vt*: **to ~ away the time** malgastar el tiempo; **~ness** *n* ociosidad *f*; holgazanería; desocupación *f*.
idol ['aıdl] *n* ídolo; **~ize** *vt* idolatrar.
if [ıf] *conj* si.
igloo ['ıglu:] *n* iglú *m*.
ignite [ıg'naıt] *vt* encender; (*set fire to*) incendiar // *vi* encenderse.
ignition [ıg'nıʃən] *n* (*AUT*) encendido; **to switch on/off the ~** encender/apagar el motor; **~ key** *n* (*AUT*) llave *f* de contacto.
ignorance ['ıgnərəns] *n* ignorancia; **ignorant** [-ənt] *a* ignorante; **to be ignorant of** ignorar.
ignore [ıg'nɔ:*] *vt* (*person*) no hacer caso de; (*fact*) pasar por alto.
I'll [aıl] = **I will, I shall.**
ill [ıl] *a* enfermo, malo; (*bad*) malo // *n* mal *m*; (*fig*) infortunio // *ad* mal; **to take** or **be taken ~** ponerse enfermo, enfermar; **~-advised** *a* poco recomendable; (*misled*) mal aconsejado; **~-at-ease** *a* incómodo.
illegal [ı'li:gl] *a* ilegal.
illegible [ı'ledʒıbl] *a* ilegible.
illegitimate [ılı'dʒıtımət] *a* ilegítimo.

ill: **~-fated** *a* malogrado; **~ feeling** *n* rencor *m*.
illicit [ı'lısıt] *a* ilícito.
illiterate [ı'lıtərət] *a* analfabeto.
ill-mannered [ıl'mænəd] *a* mal educado.
illness ['ılnıs] *n* enfermedad *f*.
illogical [ı'lɒdʒıkl] *a* ilógico.
ill-treat [ıl'tri:t] *vt* maltratar.
illuminate [ı'lu:mıneıt] *vt* (*room, street*) iluminar, alumbrar; (*subject*) aclarar; **illumination** [-'neıʃən] *n* alumbrado; **illuminations** *npl* luminarias *fpl*.
illusion [ı'lu:ʒən] *n* ilusión *f*; **to be under the ~ that...** estar bajo la ilusión de que...; **illusory** [-sərı] *a* ilusorio.
illustrate ['ıləstreıt] *vt* (*gen*) ilustrar; (*subject*) aclarar; (*point*) poner ejemplos a; **illustration** [-'streıʃən] *n* (*example*) ejemplo; (*explanation*) aclaración *f*; (*in book*) lámina.
illustrious [ı'lʌstrıəs] *a* ilustre.
ill will [ıl'wıl] *n* rencor *m*.
I'm [aım] = **I am.**
image ['ımıdʒ] *n* imagen *f*.
imaginary [ı'mædʒınərı] *a* imaginario; **imagination** [-'neıʃən] *n* imaginación *f*; (*inventiveness*) inventiva; (*illusion*) fantasía; **imaginative** [-ətıv] *a* imaginativo; **imagine** *vt* imaginarse; (*delude o.s.*) hacerse la ilusión (de que).
imbalance [ım'bæləns] *n* (*gen*) desequilibrio; (*inequality*) falta de correspondencia.
imbecile ['ımbəsi:l] *n* imbécil *m/f*.
imbue [ım'bju:] *vt*: **to ~ sth with** imbuir algo de.
imitate ['ımıteıt] *vt* imitar; **imitation** [-'teıʃən] *n* imitación *f*; (*copy*) copia; (*mimicry*) mímica.
immaculate [ı'mækjulət] *a* perfectamente limpio; (*REL*) inmaculado.
immaterial [ımə'tıərıəl] *a* incorpóreo; **it is ~ whether...** no importa si... .
immature [ımə'tjuə*] *a* (*person*)

poco maduro; (*of one's youth*) juvenil.

immediate [ı'miːdıət] *a* inmediato; (*pressing*) urgente, apremiante; **~ly** *ad* (*at once*) en seguida; **~ly next to** muy junto a.

immense [ı'mɛns] *a* inmenso, enorme.

immerse [ı'mɔːs] *vt* (*submerge*) sumergir; (*sink*) hundir; **to be ~d in** (*fig*) estar absorto en.

immersion heater [ı'mɔːʃən-] *n* calentador *m* de inmersión.

immigrant ['ımıgrənt] *n* inmigrante *m/f*; **immigrate** [-greıt] *vi* inmigrar; **immigration** [-'greıʃən] *n* inmigración *f*.

imminent ['ımınənt] *a* inminente.

immobile [ı'məubaıl] *a* inmóvil; **immobilize** [-bılaız] *vt* inmovilizar.

immoral [ı'mɔrl] *a* inmoral; **~ity** [-'rælıtı] *n* inmoralidad *f*.

immortal [ı'mɔːtl] *a* inmortal; **~ize** *vt* inmortalizar.

immune [ı'mjuːn] *a*: **~ (to)** inmune (contra); **immunity** (*MED*) inmunidad *f*; (*COMM*) exención *f*.

immunization [ımjunaı'zeıʃən] *n* inmunización *f*; **immunize** ['ımjunaız] *vt* inmunizar.

imp [ımp] *n* diablillo.

impact ['ımpækt] *n* (*gen*) impacto.

impair [ım'pɛə*] *vt* perjudicar.

impale [ım'peıl] *vt* atravesar.

impart [ım'pɑːt] *vt* comunicar.

impartial [ım'pɑːʃl] *a* imparcial; **~ity** [ımpɑːʃı'ælıtı] *n* imparcialidad *f*.

impassable [ım'pɑːsəbl] *a* (*barrier*) infranqueable; (*river*) invadeable; (*road*) intransitable.

impatience [ım'peıʃəns] *n* impaciencia; **impatient** [-ənt] *a* impaciente; **to get** *or* **grow impatient** impacientarse.

impeccable [ım'pɛkəbl] *a* impecable.

impede [ım'piːd] *vt* estorbar, dificultar.

impediment [ım'pɛdımənt] *n*

obstáculo, estorbo; (*also:* **speech ~**) defecto (del habla).

impending [ım'pɛndıŋ] *a* (*near*) próximo.

impenetrable [ım'pɛnıtrəbl] *a* (*gen*) impenetrable; (*unfathomable*) insondable.

imperative [ım'pɛrətıv] *a* (*tone*) imperioso; (*necessary*) indispensable; (*pressing*) urgente // *n* (*LING*) imperativo.

imperceptible [ımpə'sɛptıbl] *a* imperceptible, insensible.

imperfect [ım'pɔːfıkt] *a* imperfecto; (*goods etc*) defectuoso; **~ion** [-'fɛkʃən] *n* (*blemish*) desperfecto; (*state*) imperfección *f*.

imperial [ım'pıərıəl] *a* imperial; **~ism** *n* imperialismo.

imperil [ım'pɛrıl] *vt* arriesgar, poner en peligro.

impersonal [ım'pɔːsənl] *a* impersonal.

impersonate [ım'pɔːsəneıt] *vt* hacerse pasar por; (*THEATRE*) imitar.

impertinent [ım'pɔːtınənt] *a* impertinente, insolente.

impervious [ım'pɔːvıəs] *a* impermeable; (*fig*:) **~ to** insensible a.

impetuous [ım'pɛtjuəs] *a* impetuoso, irreflexivo.

impetus ['ımpətəs] *n* ímpetu *m*; (*fig*) impulso.

impinge [ım'pındʒ]: **to ~ on** *vt fus* invadir, abusar de; (*affect*) afectar a.

implausible [ım'plɔːzıbl] *a* inverosímil.

implement ['ımplımənt] *n* instrumento, herramienta // *vt* ['ımplımənt] hacer efectivo; (*carry out*) realizar.

implicate ['ımplıkeıt] *vt* (*compromise*) comprometer; (*involve*) enredar; **implication** [-'keıʃən] *n* consecuencia, implicancia (*AM*).

implicit [ım'plısıt] *a* (*gen*) implícito; (*complete*) absoluto.

implore [ɪm'plɔ:*] vt (person) suplicar.

imply [ɪm'plaɪ] vt (involve) implicar; (mean) significar; (hint) dar a entender que; **it is implied** se sobreentiende.

impolite [ɪmpə'laɪt] a mal educado.

import [ɪm'pɔ:t] vt importar // n ['ɪmpɔ:t] (COMM) importación f; (: article) artículo importado; (meaning) significado, sentido.

importance [ɪm'pɔ:təns] n importancia; **important** [-ənt] a importante; **it's not important** no importa, no tiene importancia.

importer [ɪm'pɔ:tə*] n importador/a m/f.

impose [ɪm'pəuz] vt imponer // vi: **to ~ on sb** abusar de uno; **imposing** a imponente, impresionante.

impossible [ɪm'pɒsɪbl] a imposible; (person) insoportable.

impostor [ɪm'pɒstə*] n impostor/a m/f.

impotence ['ɪmpətəns] n impotencia; **impotent** [-ənt] a impotente.

impound [ɪm'paund] vt embargar.

impoverished [ɪm'pɒvərɪʃt] a necesitado, (land) agotado.

impracticable [ɪm'præktɪkəbl] a no factible, irrealizable.

impractical [ɪm'præktɪkl] a (person) poco práctico.

imprecise [ɪmprɪ'saɪs] a impreciso.

impregnable [ɪm'pregnəbl] a invulnerable; (castle) inexpugnable.

impregnate ['ɪmpregneɪt] vt (gen) impregnar; (soak) empapar; (fertilize) fecundar.

impresario [ɪmprɪ'sɑ:rɪəu] n empresario.

impress [ɪm'pres] vt impresionar; (mark) estampar // vi hacer buena impresión; **to ~ sth on sb** convencer a uno de algo; **it ~ed itself on me** se me grabó (en la memoria).

impression [ɪm'preʃən] n impresión f; (footprint etc) huella; (print

run) edición f; **to be under the ~ that** tener la impresión de que; **~able** a influenciable; (sensitive) sensible; **~ist** n impresionista m/f.

impressive [ɪm'presɪv] a impresionante.

imprint ['ɪmprɪnt] n impresión f, huella.

imprison [ɪm'prɪzn] vt encarcelar; **~ment** n encarcelamiento, cárcel f.

improbable [ɪm'prɒbəbl] a improbable, inverosímil.

impromptu [ɪm'prɒmptju:] a improvisado // ad de improviso.

improper [ɪm'prɒpə*] a (incorrect) impropio; (unseemly) indecoroso; (indecent) indecente.

impropriety [ɪmprə'praɪətɪ] n falta de decoro; (indecency) indecencia; (of language) impropiedad f.

improve [ɪm'pru:v] vt mejorar // vi mejorarse; (become perfect) perfeccionarse; (pupils) hacer progresos, **~ment** n mejoramiento; perfección f; progreso.

improvise ['ɪmprəvaɪz] vt, vi improvisar.

imprudent [ɪm'pru:dnt] a imprudente.

impudent ['ɪmpjudnt] a descarado, insolente.

impulse ['ɪmpʌls] n impulso, to act on ~ obrar sin reflexión; **impulsive** [-'pʌlsɪv] a irreflexivo.

impunity [ɪm'pju:nɪtɪ] n: **with ~** impunemente.

impure [ɪm'pjuə*] a (adulterated) adulterado; (not pure) impuro; **impurity** n (gen) impureza.

in [ɪn] prep en, (within) dentro de; (with time: during, within) ~ 2 **days** en 2 días; (: after) ~ 2 **weeks** dentro de 2 semanas; (with town, country): It's ~ **France** está en Francia // ad dentro, adentro; (fashionable) de moda; **is he ~?** ¿está en casa?; ~ **the country** en el campo; ~ **the distance** a lo lejos; ~ **town** en el centro (de la ciudad);

the sun al sol, bajo el sol; ~ the
rain bajo la lluvia; ~ **French** en
francés; **1 ~ 10** uno sobre 10, uno de
cada 10; ~ **hundreds** por
centenares; **the best pupil ~ the
class** el mejor alumno de la clase;
written ~ pencil escrito con lápiz;
~ **saying this** al decir esto; **their
party is** ~ su partido ha llegado al
poder; **to ask sb** ~ invitar a uno a
entrar; **to run/limp** ~ entrar
corriendo/cojeando; **the ~s and
outs** los recovecos.

in., ins *abbr of* **inch(es).**

inability [ɪnə'bɪlɪtɪ] *n* incapacidad *f*.

inaccessible [ɪnæk'sesɪbl] *a*
inaccesible.

inaccuracy [ɪn'ækjurəsɪ] *n* inexactitud *f*; **inaccurate** [-rət] *a* inexacto,
incorrecto.

inactivity [ɪnæk'tɪvɪtɪ] *n* inactividad *f*.

inadequate [ɪn'ædɪkwət] *a (insufficient)* insuficiente; *(unsuitable)*
inadecuado; *(person)* incapaz.

inadvertently [ɪnəd'vɜːtntlɪ] *ad*
por equivocación *o* descuido.

inadvisable [ɪnəd'vaɪzəbl] *a* no
aconsejable.

inane [ɪ'neɪn] *a* necio, fatuo.

inanimate [ɪn'ænɪmət] *a* inanimado.

inapplicable [ɪn'æplɪkəbl] *a* in-
aplicable.

inappropriate [ɪnə'prəuprɪət] *a*
inoportuno, inconveniente; *(word,
expression)* impropio.

inapt [ɪn'æpt] *a* impropio; ~**itude**
n incapacidad *f*.

inarticulate [ɪnɑː'tɪkjulət] *a
(person)* incapaz de expresarse;
(speech) inarticulado.

inasmuch as [ɪnəz'mʌtʃəz] *ad
(given that)* puesto que; *(since)* ya
que.

inattentive [ɪnə'tentɪv] *a* distraído.

inaudible [ɪn'ɔːdɪbl] *a* inaudible.

inaugural [ɪ'nɔːgjurəl] *a (speech)*
de apertura; **inaugurate** [-reɪt] *vt*

inaugurar; **inauguration** [-'reɪʃən] *n*
ceremonia de apertura.

in-between [ɪnbɪ'twiːn] *a* intermedio, de entre medio.

inborn [ɪn'bɔːn] *a (feeling)* innato.

inbred [ɪn'bred] *a* innato; *(family)*
engendrado por endogamia.

incalculable [ɪn'kælkjuləbl] *a*
incalculable.

incapable [ɪn'keɪpəbl] *a* incapaz.

incapacitate [ɪnkə'pæsɪteɪt] *vt:* **to**
~ **sb** incapacitar a uno.

incapacity [ɪnkə'pæsɪtɪ] *n (inability)* incapacidad *f*.

incarcerate [ɪn'kɑːsəreɪt] *vt*
encarcelar.

incarnate [ɪn'kɑːnɪt] *a* en persona
// [ɪn'kɑːneɪt] encarnar; **incarnation** [-'neɪʃən] *n* encarnación *f*.

incendiary [ɪn'sendɪərɪ] *a* incen-
diario.

incense ['ɪnsens] *n* incienso // [ɪn'sens] *(anger)* indignar,
encolerizar.

incentive [ɪn'sentɪv] *n* incentivo,
estímulo.

incessant [ɪn'sesnt] *a* incesante,
continuo; ~**ly** *ad* constantemente.

incest ['ɪnsest] *n* incesto.

inch [ɪntʃ] *n* pulgada *f*; **to be within
an** ~ **of** estar a dos dedos de; **he
didn't give an** ~ no dio concesión
alguna; **to** ~ **forward** avanzar
palmo a palmo.

incidence ['ɪnsɪdns] *n (of crime,
disease)* frecuencia.

incident ['ɪnsɪdnt] *n* incidente *m*,
suceso; *(in book)* episodio.

incidental [ɪnsɪ'dentl] *a* no
esencial, accesorio; *(unplanned)*
fortuito; ~ **to** al margen de; ~**ly**
[-'dentəlɪ] *ad (by the way)* a
propósito.

incinerator [ɪn'sɪnəreɪtə*] *n*
incinerador *m*.

incipient [ɪn'sɪpɪənt] *a* incipiente.

incision [ɪn'sɪʒən] *n* corte *m*.

incisive [ɪn'saɪsɪv] *a (mind)*
penetrante; *(tone)* mordaz; *(remark
etc)* tajante.

incite [ɪn'saɪt] vt provocar.
inclination [ɪnklɪ'neɪʃən] n (tendency) tendencia, inclinación f.
incline ['ɪnklaɪn] n pendiente m, cuesta // (vb: [ɪn'klaɪn]) vt (slope) inclinar; (head) poner de lado // vi inclinarse; **to be ~d to** (tend) ser propenso a; (be willing) estar dispuesto a.
include [ɪn'kluːd] vt incluir, comprender; (in letter) adjuntar; **including** prep incluso, inclusive.
inclusion [ɪn'kluːʒən] n inclusión f, inclusive [-sɪv] a inclusivo // **all inclusive**.
incognito [ɪnkɒg'niːtəʊ] ad de incógnito.
incoherent [ɪnkəʊ'hɪərənt] a incoherente.
income ['ɪŋkʌm] n (personal) ingresos mpl; (from property etc) renta, (profit) rédito; ~ **tax** n impuesto sobre la renta; ~ **tax inspector** n inspector/a m/f fiscal; ~ **tax return** n registro fiscal.
incoming ['ɪnkʌmɪŋ] a: ~ **flight** vuelo entrante.
incomparable [ɪn'kɒmpərəbl] a incomparable, sin par.
incompatible [ɪnkəm'pætɪbl] a incompatible.
incompetence [ɪn'kɒmpɪtəns] n incompetencia; **incompetent** [-ənt] a incompetente.
incomplete [ɪnkəm'pliːt] a incompleto; (unfinished) sin terminar.
incomprehensible [ɪnkɒmprɪ'hɛnsɪbl] a incomprensible.
inconceivable [ɪnkən'siːvəbl] a inconcebible.
inconclusive [ɪnkən'kluːsɪv] a sin resultado (definitivo); (argument) poco convincente.
incongruous [ɪn'kɒŋgrʊəs] a (foolish) absurdo, estrafalario; (remark, act) disonante, nada lógico.
inconsiderate [ɪnkən'sɪdərət] a desconsiderado; **how ~ of him!** ¡qué falta de consideración (de su parte)!

inconsistent [ɪnkən'sɪstnt] a inconsecuente; ~ **with** (que) no concuerda con.
inconspicuous [ɪnkən'spɪkjʊəs] a poco llamativo, modesto; **to make o.s. ~** no llamar la atención.
inconstant [ɪn'kɒnstnt] a inconstante.
incontinent [ɪn'kɒntɪnənt] a incontinente.
inconvenience [ɪnkən'viːnjəns] n (gen) inconvenientes mpl; (trouble) molestia, incomodidad f // vt incomodar; **inconvenient** [-ənt] a incómodo, poco práctico; (time, place) inoportuno.
incorporate [ɪn'kɔːpəreɪt] vt incorporar; (contain) comprender; (add) agregar; ~**d** a: ~**d company** (US: abbr **Inc.**) Sociedad Anónima (S.A.).
incorrect [ɪnkə'rɛkt] a incorrecto.
incorruptible [ɪnkə'rʌptɪbl] a (gen) incorruptible; (not open to bribes) insobornable.
increase ['ɪnkriːs] n aumento // vi [ɪn'kriːs] aumentarse; (grow) crecer; (price) subir; **increasing** a (number) creciente, en aumento; **increasingly** ad de más en más, cada vez más.
incredible [ɪn'krɛdɪbl] a increíble.
incredulous [ɪn'krɛdjʊləs] a incrédulo.
increment ['ɪnkrɪmənt] n aumento, incremento.
incriminate [ɪn'krɪmɪneɪt] vt incriminar.
incubation [ɪnkjʊ'beɪʃən] n incubación f; **incubator** ['ɪnkjʊbeɪtə*] n incubadora.
incumbent [ɪn'kʌmbənt] n ocupante m/f // a: **it is ~ on him to...** le incumbe...
incur [ɪn'kəː*] vt (expenses) contraer; (gen) incurrir en.
incurable [ɪn'kjʊərəbl] a incurable; (fig) irremediable.
incursion [ɪn'kəːʃən] n incursión f.

indebted [ɪnˈdetɪd] a: to be ~ to sb estar en deuda con uno.

indecent [ɪnˈdiːsnt] a indecente; ~ **assault** n atentado contra el pudor; ~ **exposure** n exhibicionismo.

indecisive [ɪndɪˈsaɪsɪv] a indeciso; (discussion) no resuelto, inconcluyente.

indeed [ɪnˈdiːd] ad de hecho, realmente; **yes** ~! claro que sí.

indefinite [ɪnˈdefɪnɪt] a indefinido; (uncertain) incierto; ~**ly** ad (wait) indefinidamente.

indelible [ɪnˈdelɪbl] a imborrable.

indemnify [ɪnˈdemnɪfaɪ] vt indemnizar, resarcir.

indentation [ɪndenˈteɪʃən] n mella; (TYP) sangría.

independence [ɪndɪˈpendns] n independencia; **independent** [-ənt] a independiente; **to become independent** independizarse.

index [ˈɪndeks] n (pl: ~**es**: in book) índice m; (: in library etc) catálogo; (pl: **indices** [ˈɪndɪsiːz]: ratio, sign) exponente m; ~ **card** n ficha; ~ **finger** n índice m; ~-**linked** a vinculado al índice del coste de la vida.

India [ˈɪndɪə] n la India; ~**n** a, n indio/a; **Red** ~ n piel roja m/f.

indicate [ˈɪndɪkeɪt] vt indicar; **indication** [-ˈkeɪʃən] n indicio, señal f; **indicator** n (gen) indicador m.

indices [ˈɪndɪsiːz] pl of **index.**

indict [ɪnˈdaɪt] vt acusar; ~**ment** n acusación f.

indifference [ɪnˈdɪfrəns] n indiferencia; **indifferent** [-ənt] a indiferente; (poor) regular.

indigenous [ɪnˈdɪdʒɪnəs] a indígena inv.

indigestion [ɪndɪˈdʒestʃən] n indigestión f, empacho.

indignant [ɪnˈdɪɡnənt] a: **to be ~ about sth** indignarse por algo; **indignation** [-ˈneɪʃən] n indignación f.

indignity [ɪnˈdɪɡnɪtɪ] n indignidad f; (insult) ultraje m, afrenta.

indigo [ˈɪndɪɡəʊ] a color de añil // n añil m.

indirect [ɪndɪˈrekt] a indirecto; ~**ly** ad indirectamente.

indiscreet [ɪndɪsˈkriːt] a indiscreto; (rash) imprudente; **indiscretion** [-ˈkreʃən] n indiscreción f; imprudencia.

indiscriminate [ɪndɪsˈkrɪmɪnət] a indistinto.

indispensable [ɪndɪsˈpensəbl] a indispensable, imprescindible.

indisposed [ɪndɪsˈpəʊzd] a (unwell) indispuesto.

indisputable [ɪndɪsˈpjuːtəbl] a incontestable.

indistinct [ɪndɪsˈtɪŋkt] a indistinto; (memory, noise) confuso.

individual [ɪndɪˈvɪdjʊəl] n individuo // a (single) individual; (personal) personal; (for/of one only) particular; ~**ist** n individualista m/f; ~**ity** [-ˈælɪtɪ] n individualidad f; ~**ly** ad individualmente, particularmente.

indoctrinate [ɪnˈdɒktrɪneɪt] vt adoctrinar; **indoctrination** [-ˈneɪʃən] n adoctrinamiento.

indolent [ˈɪndələnt] a indolente, perezoso.

indoor [ˈɪndɔː*] a (inner) interior; (household) de casa; (inside) de puertas adentro; (swimming-pool) cubierto; (games) de salón; (sport) bajo cubierta; ~**s** [ɪnˈdɔːz] ad dentro; (at home) en casa.

induce [ɪnˈdjuːs] vt inducir; (bring about) producir; (provoke) provocar; ~**ment** n (incentive) incentivo, aliciente m.

induction [ɪnˈdʌkʃən] n (MED: of birth) inducción f; ~ **course** n curso de inducción.

indulge [ɪnˈdʌldʒ] vt (desire) dar rienda suelta a; (whim) condescender con; (person) complacer; (child) consentir // vi: **to** ~ **in** darse el lujo de; **indulgence** n (of desire) gratificación f, (leniency) complacencia; **indulgent** a indulgente.

industrial [ɪnˈdʌstrɪəl] a industrial; ~ **action** n huelga; ~ **estate** n zona industrial; ~**ist** n industrial m/f; ~**ize** vt industrializar.

industrious [ɪnˈdʌstrɪəs] a (gen) trabajador(a); (student) aplicado.

industry [ˈɪndəstrɪ] n industria; (diligence) aplicación f.

inebriated [ɪˈniːbrɪeɪtɪd] a borracho.

inedible [ɪnˈedɪbl] a incomible; (plant etc) no comestible.

ineffective [ɪnɪˈfektɪv] a ineficaz, inútil.

inefficiency [ɪnɪˈfɪʃənsɪ] n ineficacia; **inefficient** [-ənt] a ineficaz, ineficiente.

ineligible [ɪnˈelɪdʒɪbl] a (candidate) inelegible; **to be ~ for** sth no tener derecho a algo.

inept [ɪˈnept] a incompetente, incapaz.

inequality [ɪnɪˈkwɔlɪtɪ] n desigualdad f.

inert [ɪˈnɜːt] a inerte, inactivo; (immobile) inmóvil; ~**ia** [ɪˈnɜːʃə] n inercia; (laziness) pereza

inescapable [ɪnɪˈskeɪpəbl] a ineludible.

inestimable [ɪnˈestɪməbl] a inestimable.

inevitable [ɪnˈevɪtəbl] a inevitable; (necessary) forzoso.

inexcusable [ɪnɪksˈkjuːzəbl] a imperdonable.

inexhaustible [ɪnɪgˈzɔːstɪbl] a inagotable.

inexorable [ɪnˈeksərəbl] a inexorable, implacable.

inexpensive [ɪnɪksˈpensɪv] a económico.

inexperience [ɪnɪksˈpɪərɪəns] n falta de experiencia; ~**d** a inexperto.

inexplicable [ɪnɪksˈplɪkəbl] a inexplicable.

inextricable [ɪnɪksˈtrɪkəbl] a inextricable.

infallible [ɪnˈfælɪbl] a infalible.

infamous [ˈɪnfəməs] a infame; **infamy** [-mɪ] n infamia.

infancy [ˈɪnfənsɪ] n infancia.

infant [ˈɪnfənt] n (baby) criatura; (young child) niño/a; ~**ile**, a infantil; (pej) aniñado; ~ **school** n escuela de párvulos.

infantry [ˈɪnfəntrɪ] n infantería; ~**man** n soldado de (infantería).

infatuated [ɪnˈfætjueɪtɪd] a: ~ **with** (gen) encaprichado por; (in love) enamorado de; **infatuation** [-ˈeɪʃən] n encaprichamiento; enamoramiento.

infect [ɪnˈfekt] vt (wound) infectar; (person) contagiar; (fig: pej) corromper; ~**ed with** (illness) contagiado de; ~**ion** [ɪnˈfekʃən] n infección f; (fig) contagio; ~**ious** [ɪnˈfekʃəs] a contagioso; (also; fig) infeccioso.

infer [ɪnˈfɜː*] vt deducir, inferir; ~**ence** [ˈɪnfərəns] n deducción f, inferencia.

inferior [ɪnˈfɪərɪə*] a, n inferior m/f; ~**ity** [-rɪˈɔrɪtɪ] n inferioridad f; ~**ity complex** n complejo de inferioridad.

infernal [ɪnˈfɜːnl] a infernal.

inferno [ɪnˈfɜːnəu] n infierno; (fig) hoguera.

infertile [ɪnˈfɜːtaɪl] a estéril; infecundo; **infertility** [-ˈtɪlɪtɪ] n esterilidad f, infecundidad f.

infested [ɪnˈfestɪd] a: ~ (**with**) plagado (de).

infidelity [ɪnfɪˈdelɪtɪ] n infidelidad f

in-fighting [ˈɪnfaɪtɪŋ] n (ˌl) luchas fpl internas.

infiltrate [ˈɪnfɪltreɪt] vt (troops etc) infiltrarse en // vi infiltrarse.

infinite [ˈɪnfɪnɪt] a infinito.

infinitive [ɪnˈfɪnɪtɪv] n infinitivo.

infinity [ɪnˈfɪnɪtɪ] n (also MATH) infinito; (an ~) infinidad f.

infirm [ɪnˈfɜːm] a enfermo, débil; ~**ary** n hospital m; ~**ity** n debilidad *f*; (*illness*) enfermedad *f*, achaque *m*.

inflame [ɪn'fleɪm] *vt* inflamar.

inflammable [ɪn'flæməbl] *a* inflamable; (*explosive*) explosivo.

inflammation [ɪnfləˈmeɪʃən] *n* inflamación *f*.

inflate [ɪn'fleɪt] *vt* (*tyre, balloon*) inflar; (*fig*) hinchar; ~d *a* (*style*) exagerado; (*value*) excesivo.

inflation [ɪn'fleɪʃən] *n* (*ECON*) inflación *f*; **inflationary** [ɪn'fleɪʃnərɪ] *a* inflacionario.

inflexible [ɪn'fleksɪbl] *a* inflexible.

inflict [ɪn'flɪkt] *vt*: **to ~ on** infligir en; (*tax etc*) imponer a; **~ion** [ɪn'flɪkʃən] *n* imposición *f*.

inflow ['ɪnfləu] *n* afluencia.

influence ['ɪnfluəns] *n* influencia // *vt* influir en, influenciar; (*persuade*) sugestionar; **under the ~ of alcohol** en estado de embriaguez; **influential** [-'enʃl] *a* influyente.

influenza [ɪnfluˈenzə] *n* gripe *f*.

influx ['ɪnflʌks] *n* afluencia.

inform [ɪn'fɔːm] *vt*: **to ~ sb of sth** informar a uno sobre o de algo; (*warn*) avisar a uno de algo; (*communicate*) comunicar algo a uno // *vi* soplar; **to ~ on sb** delatar a uno.

informal [ɪn'fɔːml] *a* (*person, manner*) desenvuelto; (*tone*) familiar; (*visit, discussion*) extraoficial; (*intimate*) de confianza; **~ity** [-'mælɪtɪ] *n* falta de ceremonia; (*intimacy*) intimidad *f*; (*familiarity*) familiaridad *f*; (*ease*) afabilidad *f*.

information [ɪnfəˈmeɪʃən] *n* información *f*, informes *mpl*; (*news*) noticias *fpl*; (*knowledge*) conocimientos *mpl*; (*LAW*) delatación *f*; **a piece of ~** un dato.

informative [ɪn'fɔːmətɪv] *a* informativo.

informer [ɪn'fɔːmə*] *n* delator/a *m/f*; (*also*: **police ~**) soplón/ona *m/f*.

infra-red [ɪnfrə'rɛd] *a* infrarrojo.

infrequent [ɪn'friːkwənt] *a* infrecuente.

infringe [ɪn'frɪndʒ] *vt* infringir, violar // *vi*: **to ~ on** invadir, abusar de; **~ment** *n* infracción *f*; (*of rights*) invasión *f*; (*SPORT*) falta.

infuriate [ɪn'fjuərɪeɪt] *vt* enfurecer; **infuriating** *a* enloquecedor(a).

ingenious [ɪn'dʒiːnjəs] *a* ingenioso; **ingenuity** [-dʒɪ'njuːɪtɪ] *n* ingeniosidad *f*.

ingenuous [ɪn'dʒɛnjuəs] *a* ingenuo.

ingot ['ɪŋgət] *n* lingote *m*, barra.

ingrained [ɪn'greɪnd] *a* arraigado.

ingratiate [ɪn'greɪʃɪeɪt] *vt*: **to ~ o.s. with** congraciarse con.

ingratitude [ɪn'grætɪtjuːd] *n* ingratitud *f*.

ingredient [ɪn'griːdɪənt] *n* ingrediente *m*.

inhabit [ɪn'hæbɪt] *vt* habitar, vivir en; (*occupy*) ocupar; **~ant** *n* habitante *m/f*.

inhale [ɪn'heɪl] *vt* inhalar // *vi* (*in smoking*) aspirar.

inherent [ɪn'hɪərənt] *a*: **~ in** *or* **to** inherente a.

inherit [ɪn'herɪt] *vt* heredar; **~ance** *n* herencia; (*fig*) patrimonio *m*.

inhibit [ɪn'hɪbɪt] *vt* inhibir, impedir; **to ~ sb from doing sth** impedir a uno hacer algo; **~ion** [-'bɪʃən] *n* inhibición *f*.

inhospitable [ɪnhɔs'pɪtəbl] *a* (*person*) inhospitalario; (*place*) inhóspito.

inhuman [ɪn'hjuːmən] *a* inhumano.

inimitable [ɪ'nɪmɪtəbl] *a* inimitable.

iniquity [ɪ'nɪkwɪtɪ] *n* inicuidad *f*; (*injustice*) injusticia.

initial [ɪ'nɪʃl] *a* inicial; (*first*) primero // *n* inicial *f* // *vt* firmar con las iniciales; **~s** *npl* iniciales *fpl*; (*abbreviation*) siglas *fpl*; **~ly** *ad* al principio, en primer lugar.

initiate [ɪ'nɪʃɪeɪt] *vt* (*start*) iniciar, dar comienzo a; **to ~ sb into a secret** iniciar a uno en un secreto; **to ~ proceedings against sb** (*LAW*) entablar proceso contra uno; **initiation** [-'eiʃən] n (into secret etc) iniciación f; (beginning) comienzo.

initiative [ɪ'nɪʃɪtɪv] n iniciativa.

inject [ɪn'dʒekt] vt (liquid) inyectar; (fig) injertar; ~ion [ɪn'dʒekʃən] n inyección f.

injunction [ɪn'dʒʌŋkʃən] n interdicto.

injure ['ɪndʒə*] vt herir, lastimar; (fig) perjudicar; (offend) ofender; **injury** n herida, lesión f; (wrong) perjuicio, daño; **injury time** n (SPORT) descuento.

injustice [ɪn'dʒʌstɪs] n injusticia.

ink [ɪŋk] n tinta.

inkling ['ɪŋklɪŋ] n sospecha; (idea) idea, atisbo.

inlaid ['ɪnleɪd] a taraceado, entarimado.

inland ['ɪnlənd] a interior, del interior // ad [ɪn'lænd] tierra adentro; **I~ Revenue** n (Brit) el fisco.

in-laws ['ɪnlɔːz] npl parientes mpl políticos.

inlet ['ɪnlet] n (GEO) ensenada, cala; (TECH) admisión f, entrada.

inmate ['ɪnmeɪt] n (in prison) presidiario; (in asylum) internado/a.

inn [ɪn] n posada, mesón m.

innate ['ɪneɪt] a innato.

inner ['ɪnə*] a interior, interno; ~ **city** n centro de la ciudad; ~ **tube** n (of tyre) cámara.

innocence ['ɪnəsns] n inocencia; **innocent** [-nt] a inocente.

innocuous ['ɪnɔkjuəs] a innocuo.

innovation [ɪnəu'veɪʃən] n novedad f.

innuendo [ɪnju'endəu], pl ~es a indirecta.

innumerable ['ɪnju:mrəbl] a innumerable.

inoculation [ɪnɔkju'leɪʃən] n inoculación f.

inopportune [ɪn'ɔpətju:n] a inoportuno.

inordinately [ɪ'nɔ:dɪnɪtlɪ] ad desmesuradamente.

inorganic [ɪnɔ:'gænɪk] a inorgánico.

in-patient ['ɪnpeɪʃənt] n paciente m/f interno/a.

input ['ɪnput] n (ELEC) entrada; (COMM) inversión f.

inquest ['ɪnkwest] n pesquisa judicial; (coroner's) encuesta judicial.

inquire [ɪn'kwaɪə*] vi pedir informes // vt (ask) preguntar; (seek information about) pedir informes sobre; **to ~ about** vi fus (person) preguntar por; (fact) informarse de; **to ~ into** vt fus investigar, indagar; **inquiring** a (mind) penetrante; (look) interrogativo; **inquiry** n pregunta; (LAW) investigación f, pesquisa; (commission) comisión f investigadora; **inquiry office** n oficina de informaciones.

inquisitive [ɪn'kwɪzɪtɪv] a (curious) activo, inquiridor(a); (prying) preguntón(ona), fisgón(ona).

inroad ['ɪnrəud] n incursión f; (fig) invasión f.

insane [ɪn'seɪn] a loco; (MED) demente.

insanitary [ɪn'sænɪtərɪ] a insalubre.

insanity [ɪn'sænɪtɪ] n demencia, locura.

insatiable [ɪn'seɪʃəbl] a insaciable.

inscribe [ɪn'skraɪb] vt inscribir; (book etc); **to ~ (to sb)** dedicar (a uno).

inscription [ɪn'skrɪpʃən] n (gen) inscripción f; (in book) dedicatoria.

inscrutable [ɪn'skru:təbl] a inescrutable, insondable.

insect ['ɪnsekt] n insecto; ~**icide** [ɪn'sektɪsaɪd] n insecticida m.

insecure [ɪnsɪ'kjuə*] a inseguro; **insecurity** n inseguridad f.

insensible [ɪn'sensɪbl] a impasible, insensible; (unconscious) inconsciente.

insensitive [ɪnˈsɛnsɪtɪv] a insensible.

inseparable [ɪnˈsɛprəbl] a inseparable; **they were ~ friends** les unía una estrecha amistad.

insert [ɪnˈsɜːt] vt (between things) intercalar; (into sth) introducir; (in paper) publicar; (: advert) poner // n [ˈɪnsɜːt] hoja suelta (intercalada); **~ion** [ɪnˈsɜːʃən] n inserción f; (publication) publicación f; (of pages) materia añadida.

inshore [ɪnˈʃɔː*] a cercano a la orilla o costa // ad (be) cerca de la orilla; (move) hacia la orilla.

inside [ˈɪnˈsaɪd] n interior m; (lining) forro f, interior, interno; (secret) secreto // ad (within) (por) dentro; (with movement) hacia dentro; (fam: in prison) en la cárcel // prep dentro de; (of time): **~ 10 minutes** en menos de 10 minutos; **~s** npl (col) tripas fpl; **~ forward** n (SPORT) delantero interior; **~ lane** n (AUT: in Britain) el carril izquierdo; (: US) el carril derecho; **~ out** ad (turn) al revés; (know) a fondo.

insidious [ɪnˈsɪdɪəs] a insidioso; (underground) clandestino.

insight [ˈɪnsaɪt] n perspicacia.

insignificant [ɪnsɪɡˈnɪfɪknt] a insignificante.

insincere [ɪnsɪnˈsɪə*] a poco sincero; **insincerity** [-ˈsɛrɪtɪ] n falta de sinceridad, doblez f.

insinuate [ɪnˈsɪnjʊeɪt] vt insinuar; **insinuation** [-ˈeɪʃən] n insinuación f; (hint) indirecta.

insipid [ɪnˈsɪpɪd] a soso, insulso.

insist [ɪnˈsɪst] vi insistir; **to ~ on doing** empeñarse en hacer; **to ~ that** insistir en que; (claim) exigir que; **~ence** n insistencia; (stubbornness) empeño, porfía; **~ent** a insistente; empeñado.

insole [ˈɪnsəʊl] n plantilla.

insolence [ˈɪnsələns] n insolencia, descaro; **insolent** [-ənt] a insolente, descarado.

insoluble [ɪnˈsɒljʊbl] a insoluble.

insolvent [ɪnˈsɒlvənt] a insolvente.

insomnia [ɪnˈsɒmnɪə] n insomnio.

inspect [ɪnˈspɛkt] vt inspeccionar, examinar; (troops) pasar revista a; **~ion** [ɪnˈspɛkʃən] n inspección f, examen m; **~or** n inspector/a m/f, (RAIL) revisor m.

inspiration [ɪnspəˈreɪʃən] n inspiración f; **inspire** [ɪnˈspaɪə*] vt inspirar.

instability [ɪnstəˈbɪlɪtɪ] n inestabilidad f.

install [ɪnˈstɔːl] vt instalar; **~ation** [ɪnstəˈleɪʃən] n instalación f.

instalment, installment (US) [ɪnˈstɔːlmənt] n plazo; (of story) entrega; (of TV serial etc) episodio.

instance [ˈɪnstəns] n ejemplo, caso; **for ~** por ejemplo; **in the first ~** en primer lugar.

instant [ˈɪnstənt] n instante m, momento // a instantáneo, inmediato; (coffee) en polvo; **~ly** ad en seguida.

instead [ɪnˈstɛd] ad en cambio; **~ of** en lugar de, en vez de.

instep [ˈɪnstɛp] n empeine m.

instigation [ɪnstɪˈɡeɪʃən] n instigación f.

instil [ɪnˈstɪl] vt: **to ~ into** infundir, inculcar en.

instinct [ˈɪnstɪŋkt] n instinto; **~ive** [-ˈstɪŋktɪv] a instintivo; **~ively** [-ˈstɪŋktɪvlɪ] ad por instinto.

institute [ˈɪnstɪtjuːt] n instituto; (professional body) colegio // vt (inquiry) iniciar, empezar; (proceedings) entablar.

institution [ɪnstɪˈtjuːʃən] n (gen) institución f; (beginning) iniciación f; (organization) instituto; (MED: home) asilo; (asylum) manicomio; (custom) costumbre f.

instruct [ɪnˈstrʌkt] vt: **to ~ sb in sth** instruir a uno en o sobre algo; **to ~ sb to do sth** dar instrucciones a uno de hacer algo; **~ion** [ɪnˈstrʌkʃən] n (teaching) instrucción f; **~ions** npl órdenes fpl; **~ions (for use)** modo sg de empleo; **~ive a**

aleccionador(a); **~or** *n* instructor/a *m/f.*

instrument ['instrumənt] *n* instrumento; **~al** [-'mentl] *a* (MUS) instrumental; **to be ~al in** contribuir materialmente a; **~ panel** *n* tablero (de instrumentos).

insubordinate [insə'bɔːdənit] *a* insubordinado; **insubordination** [-'neiʃən] *n* insubordinación *f*; (*disobedience*) desobediencia.

insufferable [in'sʌfrəbl] *a* insufrible.

insufficient [insə'fiʃənt] *a* insuficiente.

insular ['insjulə*] *a* insular; (*outlook*) de miras estrechas.

insulate ['insjuleit] *vt* aislar; **insulating tape** *n* cinta aislante; **insulation** [-'leiʃən] *n* aislamiento.

insulin ['insjulin] *n* insulina.

insult ['insʌlt] *n* insulto; (*offence*) ofensa // *vt* [in'sʌlt] insultar, injuriar; ofender; **~ing** *a* insultante; ofensivo.

insuperable [in'sjuːprəbl] *a* insuperable.

insurance [in'ʃuərəns] *n* seguro; **fire/life ~** seguro sobre la vida/contra incendios; **~ agent** *n* agente *m/f* de seguros; **~ policy** *n* póliza (de seguros).

insure [in'ʃuə*] *vt* asegurar.

insurrection [insə'rekʃən] *n* insurrección *f*.

intact [in'tækt] *a* íntegro; (*unharmed*) ileso, sano.

intake ['inteik] *n* (TECH) entrada, toma, (: *pipe*) tubo de admisión; (*of food*) cantidad admitida; (SCOL): an **~ of 200 a year** 200 matriculados al año.

intangible [in'tændʒibl] *a* intangible.

integral ['intigrəl] *a* (*whole*) íntegro; (*part*) integrante.

integrate ['intigreit] *vt* integrar // *vi* integrarse.

integrity [in'tegriti] *n* honradez *f*, rectitud *f.*

intellect ['intəlekt] *n* intelecto; **~ual** [-'lektjuəl] *a*, *n* intelectual *m/f.*

intelligence [in'tɛlidʒəns] *n* inteligencia; (MIL etc) informes *mpl*; **I~ Service** *n* Servicio de Inteligencia; **intelligent** [-ənt] *a* inteligente.

intelligible [in'tɛlidʒibl] *a* inteligible, comprensible.

intend [in'tend] *vt* (*gift etc*): **to ~ sth for** destinar algo a; **to ~ to do sth** tener intención de o proponerse hacer algo; **~ed** *a* (*effect*) deseado // *n* prometido/a.

intense [in'tens] *a* intenso; (*person*) nervioso; **~ly** *ad* intensamente; (*very*) sumamente.

intensify [in'tensifai] *vt* intensificar; (*increase*) aumentar.

intensity [in'tensiti] *n* intensidad *f*; (*strength*) fuerza.

intensive [in'tensiv] *a* intensivo; **~ care unit** *n* centro de cuidados intensivos.

intent [in'tent] *n* propósito // *a* (*absorbed*) absorto; (*attentive*) atento; **to all ~s and purposes** prácticamente; **to be ~ on doing sth** estar resuelto a hacer algo.

intention [in'tenʃən] *n* intento, propósito, (*plan*) proyecto; **~al** *a* intencional, deliberado; **~ally** *ad* a propósito.

intently [in'tentli] *ad* atentamente, fijamente.

inter [in'təː*] *vt* enterrar.

interact [intər'ækt] *vi* influirse mutuamente, **~ion** [-'ækʃən] *n* influencia mútua, acción *f* recíproca.

intercede [intə'siːd] *vi*: **to ~ (with)** interceder (con).

intercept [intə'sept] *vt* interceptar; (*stop*) detener; **~ion** [-'sepʃən] *n* interceptación *f*, detención *f*

interchange *n* ['intətʃeindʒ] intercambio; (*exchange*) canje *m*; (*on motorway*) paso a desnivel // *vt* [intə'tʃeindʒ] intercambiar; canjear; **~able** *a* intercambiable.

intercom ['ɪntəkɔm] n sistema m de intercomunicación.

interconnect [ɪntəkə'nekt] vi (rooms) conectarse.

intercourse ['ɪntəkɔ:s] n (sexual) relaciones fpl; (social) trato.

interest ['ɪntrɪst] n (also COMM) interés m; (profit) ventaja, provecho // vt interesar; **to be ~ed in** interesarse por; **~ing** a interesante.

interfere [ɪntə'fɪə*] vi: **to ~ in** (quarrel, other people's business) entrometerse o mezclarse en; **to ~ with** (hinder) estorbar; (damage) estropear; (radio) interferir con.

interference [ɪntə'fɪərəns] n (gen) intromisión f; (RADIO, TV) interferencia.

interim ['ɪntərɪm] n: **in the ~** entretanto, en el interino.

interior [ɪn'tɪərɪə*] n interior m // a interior.

interject [ɪntə'dʒekt] vt interponerse; **~ion** [-'dʒekʃən] n interyección f.

interlock [ɪntə'lɔk] vi entrelazarse; (wheels etc) endentarse.

interloper ['ɪntələupə*] n intruso.

interlude ['ɪntəluːd] n intérvalo; (rest) descanso; (THEATRE) intermedio.

intermarry [ɪntə'mærɪ] vi casarse (parientes).

intermediary [ɪntə'miːdɪərɪ] n intermediario.

intermediate [ɪntə'miːdɪət] a intermedio, medio.

intermission [ɪntə'mɪʃən] n (THEATRE) descanso.

intermittent [ɪntə'mɪtnt] a intermitente.

intern [ɪn'tɔːn] vt internar; (enclose) encerrar // n ['ɪntɔːn] (US) interno.

internal [ɪn'tɔːnl] a interno, interior; **~ly** ad interiormente; **'not to be taken ~ly'** 'uso externo'; **~ revenue** n (US) rentas fpl públicas.

international [ɪntə'næʃənl] a

internacional; **~ game** partido internacional; **~ player** jugador/a m/f internacional.

interplay ['ɪntəpleɪ] n interacción f.

interpret [ɪn'tɔːprɪt] vt interpretar; (translate) traducir; (understand) entender // vi hacer de intérprete; **~ation** [-'teɪʃən] n interpretación f; traducción f; entendimiento; **~er** n intérprete m/f.

interrelated [ɪntərɪ'leɪtɪd] a interrelacionado.

interrogate [ɪn'terəugeɪt] vt interrogar; **interrogation** [-'geɪʃən] n interrogatorio; **interrogative** [ɪntə'rɔgətɪv] a interrogativo.

interrupt [ɪntə'rʌpt] vt, vi interrumpir; **~ion** [-'rʌpʃən] n interrupción f.

intersect [ɪntə'sekt] vt cruzar // vi (roads) cruzarse; **~ion** [-'sekʃən] n intersección f; (of roads) cruce m.

intersperse [ɪntə'spɔːs] vt esparcir, entremezclar.

intertwine [ɪntə'twaɪn] vt entrelazar // vi entrelazarse.

interval ['ɪntəvl] n intérvalo; (SCOL) recreo; (THEATRE, SPORT) descanso; **at ~s** a ratos, de vez en cuando.

intervene [ɪntə'viːn] vi (gen) intervenir; (take part) participar; (occur) sobrevenir; **intervention** [-'venʃən] n intervención f.

interview ['ɪntəvjuː] n (RADIO, TV etc) entrevista // vt entrevistarse con; **~ee** [-'iː] n entrevistado/a; **~er** n entrevistador/a m/f.

intestine [ɪn'testɪn] n: **large/small ~** intestino grueso/delgado.

intimacy ['ɪntɪməsɪ] n intimidad f; (relations) relaciones fpl íntimas.

intimate ['ɪntɪmət] a íntimo; (friendship) estrecho; (knowledge) profundo // vt ['ɪntɪmeɪt] (announce) dar a entender.

intimidate [ɪn'tɪmɪdeɪt] vt intimidar, amedrentar; **intimidation** [-'deɪʃən] n intimidación f.

into ['ɪntu] prep (gen) en; (towards)

a; (*inside*) hacia el interior de; ~ **3 pieces/French** en 3 pedazos/francés.

intolerable [ɪn'tɔlərəbl] *a* intolerable, insufrible; **intolerance** [-rəns] *n* intolerancia; **intolerant** [-rənt] *a*: **intolerant of** intolerante con *o* para.

intonation [ɪntəu'neɪʃən] *n* entonación *f*.

intoxicate [ɪn'tɔksɪkeɪt] *vt* embriagar; **~d** *a* embriagado; **intoxication** [-'keɪʃən] *n* embriaguez *f*.

intractable [ɪn'træktəbl] *a* (*child*) intratable; (*material*) difícil de trabajar; (*problem*) espinoso.

intransigent [ɪn'trænsɪdʒənt] *a* intransigente.

intransitive [ɪn'trænsɪtɪv] *a* intransitivo.

intravenous [ɪntrə'viːnəs] *a* intravenoso.

intrepid [ɪn'trepɪd] *a* intrépido.

intricate ['ɪntrɪkət] *a* intrincado; (*complex*) complejo.

intrigue [ɪn'triːg] *n* intriga // *vi* interesar, fascinar // *vi* andar en intrigas; **intriguing** *a* intrigante.

intrinsic [ɪn'trɪnsɪk] *a* intrínseco.

introduce [ɪntrə'djuːs] *vt* introducir, meter; to ~ **sb** (**to sb**) presentar uno (a otro); to ~ **sb to** (*pastime, technique*) introducir a uno a; **introduction** [-'dʌkʃən] *n* introducción *f*; (*of person*) presentación *f*; **introductory** [-'dʌktərɪ] *a* preliminar.

introspective [ɪntrəu'spektɪv] *a* introspectivo.

introvert ['ɪntrəuvəːt] *a, n* introvertido/a.

intrude [ɪn'truːd] *vi* (*person*) entrometerse; to ~ **on** *o* **into** estorbar; **intruder** *n* intruso/a; **intrusion** [-ʒən] *n* invasión *f*; **intrusive** [-sɪv] *a* intruso.

intuition [ɪntjuː'ɪʃən] *n* intuición *f*; **intuitive** [-'tjuːɪtɪv] *a* intuitivo.

inundate ['ɪnʌndeɪt] *vt*: to ~ **with** inundar de.

invade [ɪn'veɪd] *vt* invadir; **invader** *n* invasor/a *m/f*.

invalid ['ɪnvəlɪd] *n* inválido/a // *a* [ɪn'vælɪd] (*not valid*) inválido, nulo; **~ate** [ɪn'vælɪdeɪt] *vt* invalidar, anular.

invaluable [ɪn'væljuəbl] *a* inestimable.

invariable [ɪn'veərɪəbl] *a* invariable.

invasion [ɪn'veɪʒən] *n* invasión *f*.

invent [ɪn'vent] *vt* inventar; **~ion** [ɪn'venʃən] *n* invento, (*inventiveness*) inventiva; (*lie*) ficción *f*, mentira; **~ive** *a* ingenioso; **~iveness** *n* ingenio, inventiva; **~or** *n* inventor/a *m/f*.

inventory ['ɪnvəntrɪ] *n* inventario.

inverse [ɪn'vəːs] *a* inverso; **~ly** *ad* a la inversa.

invert [ɪn'vəːt] *vt* invertir, volver al revés; **~ed commas** *npl* comillas *fpl*.

invertebrate [ɪn'vəːtɪbrət] *n* invertebrado.

invest [ɪn'vest] *vt, vi* invertir.

investigate [ɪn'vestɪgeɪt] *vt* investigar; (*study*) estudiar, examinar; **investigation** [-'geɪʃən] *n* investigación *f*, pesquisa; examen *m*; **investigator** *n* investigador/a *m/f*.

investiture [ɪn'vestɪtʃə*] *n* investidura.

investment [ɪn'vestmənt] *n* inversión *f*.

investor [ɪn'vestə*] *n* inversionista *m/f*.

inveterate [ɪn'vetərət] *a* empedernido.

invigorating [ɪn'vɪgəreɪtɪŋ] *a* vigorizante.

invincible [ɪn'vɪnsɪbl] *a* invencible.

inviolate [ɪn'vaɪələt] *a* inviolado.

invisible [ɪn'vɪzɪbl] *a* invisible; ~ **ink** *n* tinta simpática.

invitation [ɪnvɪ'teɪʃən] *n* invitación *f*.

invite [ɪn'vaɪt] *vt* (*gen*) invitar; (*to drink, food*) convidar; (*opinions etc*)

solicitar, pedir; (*trouble*) buscarse;
inviting *a* atractivo; (*look*)
incitante; (*food*) apetitoso.
invoice ['ɪnvɔɪs] *n* factura // *vt*
facturar.
invoke [ɪn'vəʊk] *vt* invocar; (*aid*)
implorar; (*law*) recurrir a.
involuntary [ɪn'vɒləntrɪ] *a*
involuntario.
involve [ɪn'vɒlv] *vt* (*entail*)
suponer, implicar; to ~ **sb** (**in**)
comprometer a uno (con); ~**d** *a*
complicado; ~**ment** *n* (*gen*)
enredo; (*obligation*) compromiso;
(*difficulty*) apuro.
invulnerable [ɪn'vʌlnərəbl] *a*
invulnerable.
inward ['ɪnwəd] *a* (*movement*)
interior, interno; (*thought, feeling*)
íntimo; ~**ly** *ad* (*feel, think etc*) para
sí, para dentro; ~(**s**) *ad* hacia
dentro.
iodine ['aɪəʊdiːn] *n* yodo.
iota [aɪ'əʊtə] *n* (*fig*) jota, ápice *m*.
IOU *n abbr* of **I owe you** pagaré *m*.
IQ *n abbr* of **intelligence quotient**
cociente *m* intelectual.
Iran [ɪ'rɑːn] *n* Irán *m*; ~**ian**
[ɪ'reɪnɪən] *a, n* iraní *m/f*.
Iraq [ɪ'rɑːk] *n* El Irak; ~**i** *a, n* iraki
m/f.
irascible [ɪ'ræsɪbl] *a* irascible.
irate [aɪ'reɪt] *a* enojado, indignado.
Ireland ['aɪələnd] *n* Irlanda.
iris ['aɪrɪs], *pl* ~**es** *n* (*ANAT*) iris *m*;
(*BOT*) lirio.
Irish ['aɪrɪʃ] *a* irlandés(esa) // *npl*:
the ~ los irlandeses; ~**man/
woman** *n* irlandés/esa *m/f*.
irk [ɜːk] *vt* fastidiar; ~**some** *a*
fastidioso.
iron ['aɪən] *n* hierro; (*for clothes*)
plancha // *a* de hierro // *vt*
(*clothes*) planchar; ~**s** *npl* (*chains*)
grillos *mpl*; to ~ **out** *vt* (*crease*)
quitar; (*fig*) allanar.
ironic(al) [aɪ'rɒnɪk(l)] *a* irónico.
ironing ['aɪənɪŋ] *n* (*act*) planchado;
(*ironed clothes*) ropa planchada; (*to
be ironed*) ropa por planchar. ~

board *n* tabla de planchar.
ironmonger ['aɪənmʌŋɡə*] *n*
ferretero; ~'**s** (**shop**) *n* ferretería,
quincallería.
iron ore ['aɪən'ɔː*] *n* mineral *m* de
hierro.
irony ['aɪrənɪ] *n* ironía; the ~ **of
it is that**... lo-irónico es que...
irrational [ɪ'ræʃənl] *a* irracional.
irreconcilable [ɪrekən'saɪləbl] *a*
inconciliable, irreconciliable.
irrefutable [ɪrɪ'fjuːtəbl] *a* irrefutable.
irregular [ɪ'regjʊlə*] *a* irregular;
(*surface*) desigual; (*illegal*) ilegal;
~**ity** [-'lærɪtɪ] *n* irregularidad *f*;
desigualdad *f*.
irrelevant [ɪ'reləvənt] *a* fuera de
lugar, inoportuno.
irreparable [ɪ'repərəbl] *a* irreparable.
irreplaceable [ɪrɪ'pleɪsəbl] *a*
irremplazable.
irrepressible [ɪrɪ'presəbl] *a*
irrefrenable.
irreproachable [ɪrɪ'prəʊtʃəbl] *a*
irreprochable.
irresistible [ɪrɪ'zɪstɪbl] *a* irresistible.
irresolute [ɪ'rezəluːt] *a* indeciso.
irrespective [ɪrɪ'spektɪv]: ~ **of**
prep sin tener en cuenta, no
importa.
irresponsible [ɪrɪ'spɒnsɪbl] *a*
(*act*) irresponsable; (*person*) poco
serio.
irreverent [ɪ'revərənt] *a* irreve-
rente, irrespetuoso.
irrevocable [ɪ'revəkəbl] *a* irrevocable.
irrigate ['ɪrɪgeɪt] *vt* regar;
irrigation [-'geɪʃən] *n* riego.
irritable ['ɪrɪtəbl] *a* irritable;
(*mood*) de mal humor.
irritate ['ɪrɪteɪt] *vt* irritar; (*MED*)
picar; **irritation** [-'teɪʃən] *n* irritación
f, enojo; picazón *m*, picor *m*.
Islam ['ɪzlɑːm] *n* Islam *m*.
island ['aɪlənd] *n* isla; (*also*: **traffic**

~) refugio; ~**er** n isleño/a.

isle [aɪl] n isla.

isn't ['ɪznt] = **is not.**

isolate ['aɪsəleɪt] vt aislar; ~**d** a aislado; **isolation** [-'leɪʃən] n aislamiento.

isotope ['aɪsəʊtəʊp] n isótopo.

Israel ['ɪzreɪl] n Israel m; ~**i** [ɪz'reɪlɪ] a, n israelí m/f.

issue ['ɪsjuː] n cuestión f, asunto; (outcome) resultado; (of banknotes etc) emisión f; (of newspaper etc) número; (offspring) sucesión f, descendencia // vt (rations, equipment) distribuir, repartir; (orders) dar; (certificate) expedir; (decree) promulgar; (book) publicar; (cheques) extender; (banknotes, stamps) emitir.

isthmus ['ɪsməs] n istmo.

it [ɪt] pron (subject) él/ella; (direct object) lo/la; (indirect object) le; (impersonal) ello; (after prep) él/ella/ello; ~**'s raining** llueve, está lloviendo; **where is** ~ ? ¿dónde está?; **he's proud of** ~ se enorgullece; **he agreed to** ~ está de acuerdo (con ello).

Italian [ɪ'tæljən] a italiano // n italiano/a; (LING) el italiano.

italic [ɪ'tælɪk] a cursivo; ~**s** npl cursiva ag.

Italy ['ɪtəlɪ] n Italia.

itch [ɪtʃ] n comezón m; (fig) prurito // vi (person) sentir o tener comezón; (part of body) picar; **I'm ~ing to do sth** rabio por hacer algo; ~**ing** n comezón m; ~**y** a: **to be** ~**y** picar.

it'd ['ɪtd] = **it would; it had.**

item ['aɪtəm] n (gen) artículo; (detail) detalle m; (on agenda) asunto a tratar; (in programme) número; (also: **news** ~) noticia; ~**ize** vt detallar.

itinerant [ɪ'tɪnərənt] a ambulante.

itinerary [aɪ'tɪnərərɪ] n itinerario.

it'll ['ɪtl] = **it will, it shall.**

its [ɪts] a su // pron (de) suyo/(la) suya.

it's [ɪts] = **it is; it has.**

itself [ɪt'self] pron (reflexive) sí mismo/a; (emphatic) él mismo/ella misma.

ITV n abbr of **Independent Television.**

I.U.D. n abbr of Intra-uterine device DIU.

I've [aɪv] = **I have.**

ivory ['aɪvərɪ] n marfil m; ~ **tower** n (fig) torre f de marfil.

ivy ['aɪvɪ] n hiedra.

J

jab [dʒæb] vt (elbow) dar un codazo a; (punch) dar un golpe rápido a; **to** ~ **sth into sth** clavar algo en algo // n codazo; golpe m (rápido); (MED: col) pinchazo.

jabber ['dʒæbə*] vt, vi farfullar.

jack [dʒæk] n (AUT) gato; (BOWLS) boliche m; (CARDS) sota; **to** ~ **up** vt (AUT) alzar con gato.

jackdaw ['dʒækdɔː] n grajilla.

jacket ['dʒækɪt] n chaqueta, americana; (of boiler etc) camisa; (of book) sobrecubierta; **potatoes in their** ~**s** patatas con su piel.

jack-knife ['dʒæknaɪf] n navaja.

jackpot ['dʒækpɒt] n premio gordo.

jade [dʒeɪd] n (stone) jade m.

jaded ['dʒeɪdɪd] a (tired) cansado; (fed-up) hastiado.

jagged ['dʒægɪd] a dentado.

jail [dʒeɪl] n cárcel f; ~**break** n fuga o evasión f (de la cárcel); ~**er** n carcelero.

jam [dʒæm] n mermelada; (also: **traffic** ~) embotellamiento; (difficulty) apuro // vt (passage etc) obstruir, cerrar; (mechanism, drawer etc) atascar; (RADIO) interferir // vi atascarse, trabarse; **to** ~ **sth into sth** meter algo por la fuerza en algo.

Jamaica [dʒə'meɪkə] n Jamaica.

jangle ['dʒæŋgl] *vi* sonar (de manera) discordante.

janitor ['dʒænɪtə*] *n* (*caretaker*) portero, conserje *m*.

January ['dʒænjuərɪ] *n* enero.

Japan [dʒə'pæn] *n* (el) Japón; ~ese [dʒæpə'niːz] *a* japonés(esa) // *n*, *pl inv* japonés/esa *m/f*; (*LING*) japonés *m*.

jar [dʒɑ:*] *n* (*glass: large*) jarra; (: *small*) tarro // *vi* (*sound*) chirriar; (*colours*) desentonar.

jargon ['dʒɑ:gən] *n* jerga.

jasmin(e) ['dʒæzmɪn] *n* jazmín *m*.

jaundice ['dʒɔ:ndɪs] *n* ictericia; ~d *a* (*fig: embittered*) amargado; (: *disillusioned*) desilusionado.

jaunt [dʒɔ:nt] *n* excursión *f*; ~y *a* alegre.

javelin ['dʒævlɪn] *n* jabalina.

jaw [dʒɔ:] *n* mandíbula.

jaywalker ['dʒeɪwɔ:kə*] *n* peatón *m* imprudente.

jazz [dʒæz] *n* jazz *m*; to ~ up *vt* (*liven up*) animar, avivar; ~y *a* de colores llamativos.

jealous ['dʒeləs] *a* (*gen*) celoso; (*envious*) envidioso; to be ~ tener celos; ~y *n* celos *mpl*; envidia.

jeans [dʒi:nz] *npl* (pantalones) vaqueros *o* tejanos *mpl*.

jeep [dʒi:p] *n* jeep *m*.

jeer [dʒɪə*] *vi*: to ~ (at) (*boo*) abuchear; (*mock*) mofarse (de).

jelly ['dʒelɪ] *n* jalea, gelatina; ~fish *n* medusa.

jeopardize ['dʒepədaɪz] *vt* arriesgar, poner en peligro; **jeopardy** ['-dɪ] *n*: to be in jeopardy estar en peligro *o* a riesgo.

jerk [dʒə:k] *n* (*jolt*) sacudida; (*wrench*) tirón *m* // *vt* dar una sacudida a // *vi* (*vehicle*) traquetear.

jerkin ['dʒə:kɪn] *n* cazadora.

jerky ['dʒə:kɪ] *a* espasmódico.

jersey ['dʒə:zɪ] *n* jersey *m*.

jest [dʒest] *n* broma.

jet [dʒet] *n* (*of gas, liquid*) chorro; (*AVIAT*) avión *m* a reacción; ~-**black** *a* de azabache; ~ **engine** *n* motor *m* a reacción.

jettison ['dʒetɪsn] *vt* desechar.

jetty ['dʒetɪ] *n* muelle *m*, embarcadero.

Jew [dʒu:] *n* judío; ~**ess** *n* judía.

jewel ['dʒu:əl] *n* joya; (*in watch*) rubí *m*; ~**ler**, (*US*) ~**ler's** (*shop*) *n* joyería; ~**lery** *n* joyas *fpl*, alhajas *fpl*.

Jewish ['dʒu:ɪʃ] *a* judío.

jibe [dʒaɪb] *n* pulla.

jiffy ['dʒɪfɪ] *n* (*col*): **in a ~** en un instante.

jig [dʒɪg] *n* jiga.

jigsaw ['dʒɪgsɔ:] *n* (*also*: ~ **puzzle**) rompecabezas *m inv*.

jilt [dʒɪlt] *vt* dar calabazas a.

jingle ['dʒɪŋgl] *n* (*advert*) estribillo // *vi* tintinear.

jinx [dʒɪŋks] *n* (*col*) gafe *m*, maldición *f*.

jitters ['dʒɪtəz] *npl* (*col*): **to get the ~** ponerse nervioso.

job [dʒɔb] *n* (*gen*) trabajo; (*task*) tarea; (*duty*) deber *m*; (*post*) empleo; (*fam: difficulty*) dificultad *f*; **it's a good ~ that...** menos mal que...; **just the ~!** ¡estupendo!; ~**less** *a* sin trabajo.

jockey ['dʒɔkɪ] *n* jockey *m* // *vi*: **to ~ for position** maniobrar para conseguir una posición.

jocular ['dʒɔkjulə*] *a* (*humorous*) jocoso; (*merry*) alegre.

jog [dʒɔg] *vt* empujar (ligeramente) // *vi* (*run*) hacer footing; **to ~ along** ir tirando; **to ~ sb's memory** refrescar la memoria a uno; ~**ging** *n* footing *m*.

join [dʒɔɪn] *vt* (*things*) juntar, unir; (*become member of*) inscribirse en, afiliarse a; (*meet: people*) reunirse *o* encontrarse con // *vi* (*roads, rivers*) confluir // *n* juntura; **to ~ up** *vi* unirse; (*MIL*) alistarse.

joiner ['dʒɔɪnə*] *n* carpintero; ~**y** *n* carpintería.

joint [dʒɔɪnt] *n* (*TECH*) junta, unión *f*; (*wood*) ensambladura; (*ANAT*) articulación f; (CULIN) asado; (col: place) garito // a (common) común; (combined) combinado; (committee) mixto; **by ~ agreement** por común acuerdo; **~ly** ad (gen) mutuamente, en común; (collectively) colectivamente; (together) conjuntamente.

joke [dʒəuk] n chiste m; (also: **practical ~**) broma // vi bromear; **to play a ~ on** gastar una broma a; **joker** n chistoso/a, bromista m/f; (CARDS) comodín m.

jolly ['dʒɔlɪ] a (merry) alegre; (enjoyable) divertido // ad (col) muy, terriblemente.

jolt [dʒəult] n (shake) sacudida; (blow) golpe m; (shock) susto // vt sacudir; asustar.

Jordan ['dʒɔːdən] n Jordania.

jostle ['dʒɔsl] vt dar empellones a, codear.

jot [dʒɔt] n: **not one ~** ni jota, ni pizca; **to ~ down** vt apuntar; **~ter** n bloc m; (SCOL) cuaderno.

journal ['dʒəːnl] n (paper) periódico; (magazine) revista; (diary) diario; **~ese** [-'liːz] n (pej) lenguaje m periodístico; **~ism** n periodismo; **~ist** n periodista m/f.

journey ['dʒəːnɪ] n viaje m; (distance covered) trayecto // vi viajar; **return ~** viaje de regreso.

joy [dʒɔɪ] n alegría; **~ful, ~ous** a alegre; **~ ride** n paseo en coche; (illegal) paseo en coche robado.

J.P. n abbr of **Justice of the Peace.**

Jr, Jun, Junr abbr of **junior.**

jubilant ['dʒuːbɪlnt] a jubiloso; **jubilation** [-'leɪʃən] n júbilo.

jubilee ['dʒuːbɪliː] n aniversario.

judge [dʒʌdʒ] n juez m // vt (gen) juzgar; (estimate) considerar; **judg(e)ment** n juicio; (punishment) sentencia, fallo.

judicial [dʒuː'dɪʃl] a judicial.

judicious [dʒuː'dɪʃəs] a juicioso.

judo ['dʒuːdəu] n judo.

jug [dʒʌg] n jarro.

juggernaut ['dʒʌgənɔːt] n (huge truck) mastodonte m.

juggle ['dʒʌgl] vi hacer juegos malabares; **juggler** n malabarista m/f.

Jugoslav ['juːgəu'slɑːv] a, n = **Yugoslav.**

juice [dʒuːs] n zumo, jugo; **juicy** a jugoso.

jukebox ['dʒuːkbɔks] n rocola.

July [dʒuː'laɪ] n julio.

jumble ['dʒʌmbl] n revoltijo // vt (also: **~ up**: mix up) revolver; (: disarrange) mezclar; **~ sale** n (Brit) venta de objetos usados.

jumbo (jet) ['dʒʌmbəu] n jumbo-jet m.

jump [dʒʌmp] vi saltar, dar saltos; (start) asustarse, sobresaltarse; (increase) aumentar // vt saltar // n salto; aumento; **to ~ the queue** colarse.

jumper ['dʒʌmpə*] n suéter m, jersey m.

jumpy ['dʒʌmpɪ] a nervioso.

junction ['dʒʌŋkʃən] n (of roads) cruce m; (RAIL) empalme m.

juncture ['dʒʌŋktʃə*] n: **at this ~** en este momento, en esta coyuntura.

June [dʒuːn] n junio.

jungle ['dʒʌŋgl] n selva, jungla.

junior ['dʒuːnɪə*] a (in age) menor, más joven; (competition) juvenil; (position) subalterno // n menor m/f, joven m/f; **~ school** n escuela primaria.

junk [dʒʌŋk] n (cheap goods) baratijas fpl; (lumber) trastos viejos mpl; (rubbish) basura; (ship) junco; **~shop** n tienda de objetos usados.

jurisdiction [dʒuərɪs'dɪkʃən] n jurisdicción f.

jurisprudence [dʒuərɪs'pruːdəns] n jurisprudencia.

jury ['dʒuərɪ] n jurado.

just [dʒʌst] a justo // ad (exactly) exactamente; (only) sólo, solamente; **he's ~ done it/left** acaba de hacerlo/irse; **~ right** perfecto, perfectamente; ~ **two o'clock** las dos en punto; ~ **as well that...** menos mal que...; ~ **as he was** leaving en el momento en que se marchaba; ~ **before/enough** justo antes/lo suficiente; ~ **here** aquí mismo; **he** ~ **missed** ha fallado por poco; ~ **listen** escucha (solamente).

justice ['dʒʌstɪs] n justicia; **J~ of the Peace (J.P.)** n juez m de paz.

justifiable [dʒʌstɪ'faɪəbl] a justificable; **justifiably** ad justificadamente.

justification [dʒʌstɪfɪ'keɪʃən] n justificación f, **justify** ['dʒʌstɪfaɪ] vt justificar.

justly ['dʒʌstlɪ] ad (gen) justamente, (with reason) con razón.

justness ['dʒʌstnɪs] n justicia.

jut [dʒʌt] vi (also: ~ out) sobresalir.

juvenile ['dʒuːvənaɪl] a juvenil; (court) de menores; (books) para jóvenes // n joven m/f, menor m/f de edad.

juxtapose ['dʒʌkstəpəʊz] vt yuxtaponer.

K

kaleidoscope [kə'laɪdəskəʊp] n calidoscopio.

kangaroo [kæŋgə'ruː] n canguro.

keel [kiːl] n quilla; **on an even** ~ (fig) en equilibrio.

keen [kiːn] a (interest, desire) grande, vivo; (eye, intelligence) agudo; (competition) intenso; (edge) afilado; (eager) entusiasta inv; **to be** ~ **to do** or **on doing sth** tener muchas ganas de hacer algo; **to be** ~ **on sth/sb** interesarse por algo/alguien; ~**ness** n (eagerness) entusiasmo, interés m.

keep [kiːp], pt, pp **kept** vt (retain, preserve) guardar; (hold back) quedarse con; (shop, diary) llevar;

(feed: family etc) mantener; (promise) cumplir; (chickens, bees etc) criar // vi (food) conservarse; (remain) seguir, continuar // n (of castle) torreón m; (food etc) comida, subsistencia; **to** ~ **doing sth** seguir haciendo algo; **to** ~ **sb from doing sth** impedir a alguien hacer algo; **to** ~ **sth from happening** impedir que algo ocurra; **to** ~ **sb happy** hacer a alguien feliz; **to** ~ **a place tidy** mantener un lugar limpio; **to** ~ **sth to o.s.** guardar algo para sí mismo; **to** ~ **sth (back) from sb** ocultar algo a alguien; **to** ~ **time** (clock) mantener la hora exacta; **to** ~ **on** vi seguir, continuar; **to** ~ **out** vi (stay out) permanecer fuera; **'** ~ **out'** prohibida la entrada; **to** ~ **up** vt mantener, conservar // vi no retrasarse; **to** ~ **up with** (pace) ir al paso de; (level) mantenerse a la altura de; ~**er** n guardián m; ~**ing** n (care) cuidado; **in** ~**ing with** de acuerdo con; ~**sake** n recuerdo.

keg [keg] n barrilete m, barril m.

kennel ['kenl] n perrera; ~**s** npl criadero sg de perros.

Kenya ['kenjə] n Kenia.

kept [kept] pt, pp of **keep**.

kerb [kɜːb] n bordillo.

kernel ['kɜːnl] n almendra.

kerosene ['kerəsiːn] n keroseno.

ketchup ['ketʃəp] n salsa de tomate, catsup m.

kettle ['ketl] n hervidor m, olla.

key [kiː] n (gen) llave f; (MUS) tono; (of piano, typewriter) tecla; ~**board** n teclado; ~**hole** n ojo (de la cerradura), ~**note** n (MUS) tónica; ~**ring** n llavero; ~**stone** n piedra clave.

khaki ['kɑːkɪ] n caqui.

kick [kɪk] vt (person) dar una patada a; (ball) dar un puntapié a // vi (horse) dar coces // n patada; puntapié m; (of rifle) culetazo; (thrill): **he does it for** ~**s** lo hace para divertirse; **to** ~ **off** vi (SPORT)

hacer el saque inicial; ~-off *n*
(*SPORT*) saque *m* inicial.

kid [kɪd] *n* (*child*) chiquillo; (*animal*)
cabrito; (*leather*) cabritilla // *vi*
(*col*) bromear.

kidnap ['kɪdnæp] *vt* secuestrar;
~per *n* secuestrador/a *m/f*; ~ping
n secuestro.

kidney ['kɪdnɪ] *n* riñón *m*.

kill [kɪl] *vt* (*gen*) matar; (*murder*)
asesinar; (*destroy*) destruir; (*finish
off*) acabar con // *n* acto de matar;
~er *n* asesino; ~ing *n* (*one*)
asesinato; (*several*) matanza // *a*
(*funny*) divertido.

kiln [kɪln] *n* horno.

kilo ['ki:ləu] *n* kilo; ~gram(me)
['kɪləugræm] *n* kilo, kilogramo;
~metre, ~meter (*US*) ['kɪləmi:tə*]
n kilómetro, ~watt ['kɪləuwɔt] *n*
kilovatio.

kilt [kɪlt] *n* falda escocesa.

kimono [kɪ'məunəu] *n* quimono.

kin [kɪn] *n* parientes *mpl*.

kind [kaɪnd] *a* (*generous*)
bondadoso; (*good*) bueno, amable //
n clase *f*, especie *f*; (*species*)
género; **in** ~ (*COMM*) en especie; *a*
~ **of** una especie de; **two of a** ~ dos
de la misma especie.

kindergarten ['kɪndəgɑ:tn] *n*
jardín *m* de infancia.

kind-hearted [kaɪnd'hɑ:tɪd] *a*
bondadoso, de buen corazón.

kindle ['kɪndl] *vt* encender.

kindly ['kaɪndlɪ] *a* (*gen*) bondadoso;
(*good*) bueno; (*gentle*) cariñoso // *ad*
bondadosamente, amablemente;
will you ~... sea Usted tan amable
de... .

kindness ['kaɪndnɪs] *n* bondad *f*,
amabilidad *f*.

kindred ['kɪndrɪd] *n* familia,
parientes *mpl* // *a*: ~ **spirit** espíritu
m afín.

king [kɪŋ] *n* rey *m*; ~dom *n* reino;
~fisher *n* martín *m* pescador;
~-size *a* de tamaño extra.

kink [kɪŋk] *n* (*of rope*) enroscadura;

kinky ['kɪŋkɪ] *a* (*odd*) excéntrico;
(*pej*) pervertido.

kiosk ['ki:ɔsk] *n* quiosco; (*TEL*)
cabina.

kipper ['kɪpə*] *n* arenque *m*
ahumado.

kiss [kɪs] *n* beso // *vt* besar; **to** ~
(**each other**) besarse.

kit [kɪt] *n* (*gen*) avíos *mpl*;
(*equipment*) equipo; (*set of tools etc*)
(caja de) herramientas *fpl*; (*for
assembly*) mecano.

kitchen ['kɪtʃɪn] *n* cocina;
~**garden** *n* huerto; ~ **sink** *n*
fregadero; ~**ware** *n* batería de
cocina.

kite [kaɪt] *n* (*toy*) cometa.

kitten ['kɪtn] *n* gatito.

kitty ['kɪtɪ] *n* (*pool of money*) fondo
común; (*CARDS*) polla.

kleptomaniac [kleptəu'meɪniæk]
n cleptómano/a.

knack [næk] *n*: **to have the** ~ **of
doing sth** tener el don de hacer
algo.

knapsack ['næpsæk] *n* mochila.

knead [ni:d] *vt* amasar.

knee [ni:] *n* rodilla; ~**cap** *n* rótula.

kneel [ni:l], *pt*, *pp* **knelt** *vi*
arrodillarse.

knell [nel] *n* toque *m* de difuntos.

knelt [nelt] *pt*, *pp* of **kneel**.

knew [nju:] *pt* of **know**.

knickers ['nɪkəz] *npl* bragas *fpl*.

knife [naɪf], *pl* **knives** *n* cuchillo
// *vt* acuchillar.

knight [naɪt] *n* caballero; (*CHESS*)
caballo; ~**hood** *n* caballería; (*title*):
to get a ~**hood** recibir el título de
sir.

knit [nɪt] *vt* hacer a punto; (*brows*)
fruncir // *vi* hacer punto; (*bones*)
soldarse; **to** ~ **together** (*fig*) unir,
juntar; ~**ting** *n* labor *f* de punto;
~**ting machine** *n* máquina de
tricotar; ~**ting needle** *n* aguja de
hacer punto; ~**wear** *n* géneros *mpl*
de punto.

knives [naɪvz] *pl* of **knife**.

knob [nɔb] *n* (*of door*) tirador *m*; (*of*

stick) puño; (*lump*) bulto; (*fig*): a ~ **of butter** una porción de mantequilla.

knock [nɔk] *vt* (*strike*) golpear; (*bump into*) chocar contra; (*fig: col*) denigrar // *n* golpe *m*; (*on door*) llamada; **to ~ at** or **on the door** llamar a la puerta; **to ~ down** *vt* atropellar; **to ~ off** *vi* (*col: finish*) despachar // *vt* (*col: steal*) birlar; **to ~ out** *vt* dejar sin sentido; (*BOXING*) poner fuera de combate, dejar K.O.; **~er** *n* (*on door*) aldaba; **~-kneed** a patizambo; **~out** *n* (*BOXING*) K.O. *m*, knockout *m*.

knot [nɔt] *n* (*gen*) nudo // *vt* anudar; **~ty** a (*fig*) complicado.

know [nəu], *pt* **knew**, *pp* **known** *vt* (*gen*) saber; (*person, author, place*) conocer; **to ~ that...** saber que...; **to ~ how to swim** saber nadar; **~-all** *n* sabelotodo *m/f*; **~-how** *n* habilidad *f*; **~ing** a (*look: of complicity*) de complicidad; (*spiteful*) malicioso; **~ingly** *ad* (*purposely*) adrede; (*spitefully*) maliciosamente.

knowledge ['nɔlidʒ] *n* (*gen*) conocimiento; (*range of learning*) saber *m*, conocimientos *mpl*; (*learning*) erudición *f*, ciencia; **~able** a entendido, erudito.

known [nəun] *pp* of **know**.

knuckle ['nʌkl] *n* nudillo.

K.O. *n abbr of* **knockout.**

Koran [kɔ'rɑːn] *n* Corán *m*.

L

l. *abbr of* **litre.**

lab [læb] *n abbr of* **laboratory.**

label ['leibl] *n* etiqueta; (*brand: of record*) marca // *vt* poner etiqueta a.

laboratory [lə'bɔrətəri] *n* laboratorio.

laborious [lə'bɔːriəs] a penoso.

labour, labor (*US*) ['leibə*] *n* (*task*) trabajo; (*~ force*) mano *f* de obra; (*workers*) trabajadores *mpl*; (*MED*) (dolores *mpl* del) parto // *vi*: **to ~** (**at**) trabajar en; **to insistir en; in ~** (*MED*) de parto; **L~, the L~ party** el partido laborista; **hard ~** trabajos *mpl* forzados; **~ed** a (*movement*) penoso; (*style*) pesado; **~er** *n* peón *m*; (*on farm*) peón *m*, bracero; (*day ~er*) jornalero.

labyrinth ['læbirinθ] *n* laberinto.

lace [leis] *n* encaje *m*; (*of shoe etc*) cordón *m* // *vt* (*shoe*) atar.

lack [læk] *n* (*absence*) falta; (*scarcity*) escasez *f* // *vt* no tener, carecer de; **through** or **for ~ of** por falta de; **to be ~ing** faltar, no haber.

lackadaisical [lækə'deizikl] a (*careless*) descuidado; (*indifferent*) indiferente.

laconic [lə'kɔnik] a lacónico.

lacquer ['lækə*] *n* laca.

lad [læd] *n* muchacho, chico; (*in stable etc*) mozo.

ladder ['lædə*] *n* escalera (de mano); (*in tights*) carrera // *vt* (*tights*) hacer una carrera en.

laden ['leidn] a: **~ (with)** cargado (de).

ladle ['leidl] *n* cucharón *m*.

lady ['leidi] *n* señora; (*distinguished, noble*) dama; **young ~** señorita; **'ladies' (toilets)** 'señoras'; **~bird, ~bug** (*US*) *n* mariquita; **~-in-waiting** *n* dama de honor; **~like** a fina.

lag [læg] *vi* (*also: ~ behind*) retrasarse, quedarse atrás // *vt* (*pipes*) calorifugar.

lager ['lɑːgə*] *n* cerveza (rubia).

lagging ['lægiŋ] *n* revestimiento.

lagoon [lə'guːn] *n* laguna.

laid [leid] *pt, pp* of **lay.**

lain [lein] *pp* of **lie.**

lair [lɛə*] *n* guarida.

lake [leik] *n* lago.

lamb [læm] *n* cordero; (*meat*) carne *f* de cordero; **~ chop** *n* chuleta de cordero; **lambswool** n lana de cordero.

lame [leɪm] a cojo; (*weak*) débil, poco convincente.

lament [lə'mɛnt] n lamento // vt lamentarse de; **~able** ['læmɛntəbl] a lamentable.

laminated ['læmɪneɪtɪd] a laminado.

lamp [læmp] n lámpara.

lampoon [læm'puːn] vt satirizar.

lamp: **~post** n farol m; **~shade** n pantalla.

lance [lɑːns] n lanza // vt (*MED*) abrir con lanzeta; **~ corporal** n soldado de primera clase.

lancet ['lɑːnsɪt] n lanceta.

land [lænd] n (*gen*) tierra; (*country*) país m; (*piece of ~*) tierra f, (*estate*) tierras fpl, finca; (*AGR*) campo // vi (*from ship*) desembarcar; (*AVIAT*) aterrizar (*tb: fall*) caer, terminar // vt (*obtain*) conseguir; (*passengers, goods*) desembarcar; **to ~ up in** ir a parar a/en; **~ing** n desembarco; aterrizaje m; (*of staircase*) rellano; **~ing craft** n barca de desembarco; **~ing gear** n tren m de aterrizaje; **~ing stage** n desembarcadero; **~ing strip** n pista de aterrizaje; **~lady** n (*of boarding house*) patrona; (*owner*) dueña; **~locked** a cercado de tierra; **~lord** n propietario; (*of pub etc*) patrón m; **~lubber** n hombre m de tierra; **~mark** n lugar m conocido; (*fig*) hacer época; **~owner** n terrateniente m/f.

landscape ['lænskeɪp] n paisaje m; **~d** a reformado artísticamente.

landslide ['lændslaɪd] n (*GEO*) corrimiento de tierras; (*fig: POL*) victoria arrolladora.

lane [leɪn] n (*in country*) vereda; (*in town*) callejón m; (*AUT*) carril m; (*in race*) calle f; (*for air or sea traffic*) ruta.

language ['læŋgwɪdʒ] n lenguaje m; (*national tongue*) idioma m,

lengua; **bad ~** lenguaje indecente.

languid ['læŋgwɪd] a lánguido.

languish ['læŋgwɪʃ] vi languidecer.

lank [læŋk] a (*hair*) lacio.

lanky ['læŋkɪ] a larguirucho.

lantern ['læntn] n linterna; (*NAUT*) farol m.

lap [læp] n (*of track*) vuelta; (*of body*): **to sit on sb's ~** sentarse en las rodillas de uno // vt (*also: ~ up*) lamer // vi (*waves*) chapotear; **~dog** n perro faldero.

lapel [lə'pɛl] n solapa.

Lapland ['læplænd] n Laponia; **Lapp** [læp] a, n lapón/ona m/f.

lapse [læps] n error m, equivocación f; (*moral*) desliz m // vi (*expire*) caducar; (*LAW*) equivocarse (*morally*) caer en un desliz; (*time*) pasar, transcurrir; **to ~ into bad habits** volver a las andadas; **~ of time** lapso, período.

larceny ['lɑːsənɪ] n latrocinio; **petty ~** robo de menor cuantía.

lard [lɑːd] n manteca (de cerdo).

larder ['lɑːdə*] n despensa.

large [lɑːdʒ] a (*gen*) grande; (*fat*) gordo; **at ~** (*free*) en libertad; (*generally*) en general; **~ly** ad en gran parte; **~scale** a (*map*) en gran escala; (*fig*) importante.

lark [lɑːk] n (*bird*) alondra; (*joke*) travesura, broma // **~ about** vi bromear, divertirse tontamente.

larva ['lɑːvə], pl **-vae** [-viː] n larva.

laryngitis [lærɪn'dʒaɪtɪs] n laringitis f.

larynx ['lærɪŋks] n laringe f.

lascivious [lə'sɪvɪəs] a lascivo.

laser ['leɪzə*] n laser m.

lash [læʃ] n latigazo; (*punishment*) azote m; (*gen: eyelash*) pestaña // vt azotar; (*tie*) atar, sujetar; **~ out** vi: **to ~ out at o against sb** atacar violentamente a alguien; **to ~ out** (*col: spend*) gastar generosamente.

lass [læs] n chica.

lasso [læ'suː] n lazo // vt coger con lazo.

last [lɑːst] a (*gen*) último; (*final*)

último, final // *ad* por último // *vi* (*endure*) durar; (*continue*) continuar, seguir; ~ **week** la semana pasada; ~ **night** anoche; **at** ~ por fin; ~ **but one** penúltimo; ~**ing** *a* duradero; ~**minute** *a* de última hora.

latch [lætʃ] *n* picaporte *m*, pestillo; ~**key** *n* llavín *m*.

late [leɪt] *a* (*not on time*) tarde, atrasado; (*far on in day etc*) tardío; (*hour*) avanzado; (*recent*) reciente; (*former*) antiguo, ex; (*dead*) fallecido // *ad* tarde; (*behind time, schedule*) con retraso; *of* ~ últimamente; **in** ~ **May** hacia fines de mayo; the ~ **Mr X** el difunto Sr X; ~**comer** *n* recién llegado; ~**ly** *ad* últimamente; ~**ness** *n* (*of person*) retraso; (*of event*) lo tardío.

latent [leɪtnt] *a* latente.

later [leɪtə*] *a* (*date etc*) posterior; (*version etc*) más reciente // *ad* más tarde, después.

lateral [lætərl] *a* lateral.

latest [leɪtɪst] *a* último; **at the** ~ **a** más tardar.

lathe [leɪð] *n* torno.

lather [lɑːðə*] *n* espuma (de jabón) // *vt* enjabonar // *vi* hacer espuma.

Latin [lætɪn] *n* latín *m* // *a* latino; ~ **America** *n* América latina; ~**American** *a* latinoamericano.

latitude [lætɪtjuːd] *n* latitud *f*.

latrine [lətriːn] *n* letrina.

latter [lætə*] *a* último; (*of two*) segundo // *n*: **the** ~ el último, éste; ~**ly** *ad* últimamente.

lattice [lætɪs] *n* enrejado; (*on window*) reja.

laudable [lɔːdəbl] *a* loable.

laugh [lɑːf] *n* risa; (*loud*) carcajada // *vi* reírse, reír; reírse a carcajadas; **to** ~ **at** *vt fus* reírse de; **to** ~ **off** *vt* tomar algo a risa; ~**able** *a* risible, ridículo; **to be the laughing stock of the town** ser el hazmerreír de la ciudad; ~**ter** *n* risa.

launch [lɔːntʃ] *n* (*boat*) lancha; *see also* ~**ing** // *vt* (*ship, rocket, plan*)

lanzar; ~**ing** *n* (*of rocket etc*) lanzamiento; (*inauguration*) estreno; ~(**ing**) **pad** *n* plataforma de lanzamiento.

launder [lɔːndə*] *vt* lavar.

launderette [lɔːndrɛt] *n* lavandería (automática).

laundry [lɔːndrɪ] *n* lavandería; (*clothes*) ropa sucia; **to do the** ~ hacer la colada.

laureate [lɔːrɪət] *a see* poet.

laurel [lɔrl] *n* laurel *m*.

lava [lɑːvə] *n* lava.

lavatory [lævətərɪ] *n* lavabo; **lavatories** *npl* servicios *mpl*, aseos *mpl*.

lavender [lævəndə*] *n* lavanda.

lavish [lævɪʃ] *a* abundante; (*giving freely*): ~ **with** pródigo en // *vt*: **to** ~ **sth on sb** colmar a uno de algo.

law [lɔː] *n* ley *f*; (*study*) derecho; (*of game*) regla; ~**abiding** *a* que cumple la ley; ~ **and order** *n* órden *m* público; ~**breaker** *n* infractor *m* (de la ley); ~ **court** *n* tribunal *m* (de justicia); ~**ful** *a* legítimo, lícito; ~**fully** *ad* legalmente; ~**less** *a* (*act*) ilegal; (*person*) rebelde; (*country*) desordenado.

lawn [lɔːn] *n* césped *m*; ~**mower** *n* cortacésped *m*; ~ **tennis** [-ˈtɛnɪs] *n* tenis *m*.

law: ~ **school** *n* facultad *f* de derecho; ~ **student** *n* estudiante *m/f* de derecho.

lawsuit [lɔːsuːt] *n* pleito.

lawyer [lɔːjə*] *n* abogado; (*for sales, wills etc*) notario.

lax [læks] *a* flojo; (*negligent*) negligente.

laxative [læksətɪv] *n* laxante *m*.

laxity [læksɪtɪ] *n* flojedad *f*; (*moral*) relajamiento; (*negligence*) negligencia.

lay [leɪ] *pt of* lie // *a* laico; (*not expert*) profano // *vt, pt, pp* laid (*place*) colocar; (*eggs, table*) poner; (*trap*) tender; **to** ~ **aside** *or* **by** *vt* dejar a un lado; **to** ~ **down** *vt* (*pen etc*) dejar; (~ **flat**) acostar; (*arms*) rendir; (*policy*) asentar; **to ~ down the law** imponer la ley; **to ~ off** vt (*workers*) despedir, poner en paro; **to ~ on** vt (*water, gas*) instalar; (*provide*) proveer; **to ~ up** vt (*design*) diseñar; (*display*) disponer; (*spend*) gastar; **to ~ up** vt (*subj: illness*) obligar a guardar cama; ~**about** n vago/a; ~**-by** n apartadero.

layer ['lɛɪə*] n capa.

layette [leɪ'et] n canastilla, ajuar m (de niño).

layman ['leɪmən] n persona no experta; (*REL*) lego.

layout ['leɪaut] n (*design*) plan m, trazado; (*disposition*) disposición f; (*PRESS*) composición f.

laze [leɪz] vi no hacer nada; (*pej*) holgazanear; **laziness** n pereza; **lazy** a perezoso, vago.

lb. *abbr of* **pound** (*weight*).

lead [liːd] n (*front position*) delantera, (*SPORT*) liderato; (*distance, time ahead*) ventaja; (*clue*) pista; (*ELEC*) cable m; (*for dog*) correa; (*THEATRE*) papel m principal // n [led] plomo; (*in pencil*) mina // vb: pt, pp led) vt conducir; (*induce*) llevar; (*be leader of*) dirigir; (*SPORT*) ir en cabeza de // vi primero; **to ~ to** llevar a, salir a; **to ~ astray** vt llevar por mal camino; **to ~ away** vt llevar; **to ~ back** vt hacer volver; **to ~ on** vt (*tease*) coquetear con; **to ~ on to** vt (*induce*) incitar a; **to ~ up to** vt conducir a.

leader ['liːdə*] n (*gen*) jefe m, líder m; (*of union etc*) dirigente m/f; (*of gang*) cabecilla m (*guide*) guía m/f; (*of newspaper*) artículo de fondo; ~**ship** n dirección f; (*quality*) dotes fpl de mando.

leading ['liːdɪŋ] a (*main*) principal; (*outstanding*) destacado; (*first*) primero; (*front*) delantero; ~ **lady** n (*THEATRE*) primera actriz f; ~ **light** n (*person*) figura principal.

leaf [liːf], *pl* **leaves** n hoja // vi: **to ~ through** hojear; **to turn over a new ~** reformarse.

leaflet ['liːflɪt] n folleto.

league [liːg] n sociedad f; (*FOOTBALL*) liga; **to be in ~ with** estar de manga con.

leak [liːk] n (*of liquid, gas*) escape m, fuga; (*hole*) agujero; (*in roof*) gotera; (*of money*) filtración f // vi (*shoes, ship*) hacer agua; (*pipe*) tener (un) escape; (*roof*) gotear; (*container*) salirse; (*gas*) escaparse; (*fig: news*) filtrarse // vt (*gen*) dejar escapar; (*exude*) rezumar; **the information was ~ed to the enemy** las informaciones se pasaron al enemigo; **the news ~ed out** trascendió la noticia.

lean [liːn] a (*thin*) flaco; (*meat*) magro // vb: pt, pp **leaned** or **leant** [lent]) vt: **to ~ sth on** apoyar algo en // vi (*slope*) inclinarse; (*rest*): **to ~ against** apoyarse contra; **to ~ on** apoyarse en; (*fig: rely on*) contar con (el apoyo de); **to ~ back/forward** vi inclinarse hacia atrás/hacia adelante; **to ~ over** vi ladearse; ~**ing** a inclinado // n: ~**ing (towards)** inclinación f (hacia); ~**to** n colgadizo.

leap [liːp] n salto // vi, pt, pp **leaped** or **leapt** [lept] saltar; ~**frog** n pídola; ~ **year** n año bisiesto.

learn [ləːn], pt, pp **learned** or **learnt** vt (*gen*) aprender; (*come to know of*) enterarse de // vi aprender; **to ~ how to do sth** aprender a hacer algo; ~**ed** ['ləːnɪd] a erudito; ~**er** n principiante m/f; ~**ing** n el saber m, conocimientos mpl.

lease [liːs] n arriendo // vt arrendar.

leash [liːʃ] n cuerda.

least [liːst] a (*slightest*) menor; (*smallest*) más pequeño; (*smallest amount of*) mínimo // ad menos // n: **the ~** lo menos; **the ~ possible effort** el mínimo de esfuerzo posible; **at ~** por lo menos, al menos; **not in the ~** en absoluto.

leather ['leðə*] n cuero.

leave [li:v], pt, pp **left** vt dejar; (go away from) abandonar // vi irse; (train) salir // n permiso; **to be left** quedar, sobrar; **there's some milk left over** sobra o queda algo de leche; **on ~** de permiso; **to take one's ~ of** despedirse de; **to ~ out** omitir.

leaves [li:vz] pl of **leaf.**

Lebanon ['lebənən] n Líbano.

lecherous ['letʃərəs] a lascivo.

lecture ['lektʃə*] n conferencia; (scol) clase f // vi dar una clase // vt (scold) sermonear; **to give a ~ on** dar una conferencia sobre; **lecturer** n conferenciante m/f; (at university) profesor adjunto/profesora adjunta m/f.

led [led] pt, pp of **lead.**

ledge [ledʒ] n (of window, on wall) repisa, reborde m; (of mountain) plataforma.

ledger ['ledʒə*] n libro mayor.

lee [li:] n sotavento.

leek [li:k] n puerro.

leer [lɪə*] vi: **to ~ at sb** mirar impúdicamente a alguien.

leeway ['li:weɪ] n (fig): **to have some ~** tener cierta libertad de acción.

left [left] pt, pp of **leave** // a izquierdo; (POL) de izquierda // n izquierda // ad a la izquierda; **the L~** (POL) la izquierda; **~-handed** a zurdo; **the ~-hand side** n la izquierda; **~-luggage** (office) n consigna; **~-overs** npl sobras fpl; **~-wing** a (POL) de izquierdas, izquierdista.

leg [leg] n pierna; (of animal) pata; (of chair) pie m; (CULIN: of meat) pierna; (of journey) etapa; **1st/2nd ~** (SPORT) partido de ida/de vuelta; **to pull sb's ~** bromear con uno.

legacy ['legəsɪ] n legado.

legal ['li:gl] a (gen) lícito, (of law) legal; (enquiry etc) jurídico; **~ize** vt

legalizar; **~ly** ad legalmente; **~ tender** n moneda corriente.

legend ['ledʒənd] n leyenda; **~ary** a legendario.

legible ['ledʒəbl] a legible.

legion ['li:dʒən] n legión f.

legislate ['ledʒɪsleɪt] vi legislar; **legislation** [-'leɪʃən] n legislación f; **legislative** [-lətɪv] a legislativo; **legislature** [-lətʃə*] n cuerpo legislativo.

legitimacy [lɪ'dʒɪtɪməsɪ] n legitimidad f; **legitimate** [-mət] a legítimo.

leg-room ['legru:m] n espacio para las piernas.

leisure ['leʒə*] n ocio, tiempo libre; **at ~** con tranquilidad; **~ centre** n centro de diversiones; **~ly** a pausado, lento.

lemon ['lemən] n limón m; **~ade** [-'neɪd] n (fruit juice) limonada; (fizzy) gaseosa.

lend [lend], pt, pp **lent** vt: **to ~ sth to sb** prestar algo a alguien; **~er** n prestador/a m/f; **~ing library** n biblioteca circulante.

length [leŋθ] n largo, longitud f; (section: of road, pipe etc) tramo; **at ~** (at last) por fin, finalmente; (lengthily) largamente; **~en** vt alargar // vi alargarse; **~ways** ad de largo; **~y** a largo, extenso; (meeting) prolongado.

leniency ['li:nɪənsɪ] n indulgencia; **lenient** [-ənt] a indulgente.

lens [lenz] n (of spectacles) lente f; (of camera) objetivo.

lent [lent] pt, pp of **lend.**

Lent [lent] n Cuaresma.

lentil ['lentɪl] n lenteja.

Leo ['li:əu] n Leo.

leopard ['lepəd] n leopardo.

leotard ['li:ətɑ:d] n leotardo.

leper ['lepə*] n leproso/a; **leprosy** [-prəsɪ] n lepra.

lesbian ['lezbɪən] n lesbiana.

less [les] det a (in size, degree etc) menor; (in quantity) menos // pron, ad menos; **~ than half** menos de la mitad; ~ **and** ~ cada vez menos; **the** ~ **he works...** cuanto menos trabaja... .

lessen ['lesn] vi disminuir, menguar // vt disminuir, reducir.

lesson ['lesn] n lección f; **a maths** ~ una clase o una lección de matemáticas.

lest [lest] conj: ~ **it happen** para que no pase.

let [let], pt, pp **let** vt (allow) dejar, permitir; (lease) alquilar; ~'s **go** ¡vamos!; ~ **him come** que venga; 'to ~' 'se alquila'; **to** ~ **down** vt (lower) bajar; (dress) alargar; (tyre) desinflar; (hair) soltar; (disappoint) defraudar; **to** ~ **go** vi soltar; (fig) dejarse ir // vt abandonar; **to** ~ **in** vt dejar entrar; (visitor etc) hacer pasar; **to** ~ **off** vt dejar libre; (firework etc) disparar; (smell etc) despedir, tirar; **to** ~ **on** vi (col) divulgar (that que); **to** ~ **out** vt dejar salir; (dress) ensanchar; **to** ~ **up** vi amainar, disminuir.

lethal ['li:θl] a mortífero; (wound) mortal.

lethargic [le'θɑ:dʒɪk] a letárgico; **lethargy** ['leθədʒɪ] n letargo.

letter ['letə*] n (of alphabet) letra; (correspondence) carta; ~ **bomb** n carta con bomba explosiva; ~**box** n buzón m; ~**ing** n letras fpl.

lettuce ['letɪs] n lechuga.

let-up ['letʌp] n descanso, tregua.

leukaemia, leukemia (US) [lu:'ki:mɪə] n leucemia.

level ['levl] a (flat) llano; (flattened) nivelado; (uniform) igual // ad a nivel // n nivel m; (flat place) llano // vt nivelar, allanar; **to be** ~ **with** estar a nivel de; **'A' ~s** npl Bachillerato Superior, B.U.P.; **'O' ~s** npl bachillerato elemental, octavo de básica; **on the** ~ (fig: honest) en serio; **to** ~ **off** or **out** vi (prices etc) estabilizarse; ~ **crossing** n paso a nivel; ~**headed** a sensato.

lever ['li:və*] n palanca // vt: **to** ~

up alzar con palanca; ~**age** n (fig: influence) influencia.

levity ['levɪtɪ] n frivolidad f, informalidad f.

levy ['levɪ] n impuesto // vt exigir, recaudar.

lewd [lu:d] a impúdico, obsceno.

liability [laɪə'bɪlətɪ] n responsabilidad f; (handicap) desventaja; (risk) riesgo; **liabilities** npl obligaciones fpl; (COMM) deudas fpl, pasivo sg.

liable ['laɪəbl] a (subject): ~ **to** sujeto a; **to be** ~ **for** ser responsable de; **to be** ~ **to** (likely) tener tendencia a.

liaison [li:'eɪzɔn] n (coordination) enlace m; (affair) relaciones fpl amorosas.

liar ['laɪə*] n mentiroso/a.

libel ['laɪbl] n calumnia // vt calumniar.

liberal ['lɪbərl] a (gen) liberal; (generous): ~ **with** generoso con.

liberate ['lɪbəreɪt] vt liberar; **liberation** [-'reɪʃən] n liberación f.

liberty ['lɪbətɪ] n libertad f; **to be at** ~ tener permiso para; **to take the** ~ **of doing sth** tomarse la libertad de hacer algo.

Libra ['li:brə] n Libra.

librarian [laɪ'brεərɪən] n bibliotecario/a; **library** ['laɪbrərɪ] n biblioteca.

libretto [lɪ'bretəu] n libreto.

Libya ['lɪbɪə] n Libia; ~n a, n libio/a.

lice [laɪs] pl of **louse**.

licence, license (US) ['laɪsns] n (gen) licencia; (permit) permiso; (also: **driving** ~) carnet m de conducir; (excessive freedom) libertinaje m; ~ **number** n matrícula; ~ **plate** n placa (de matrícula).

license ['laɪsns] n (US) = **licence** // vt autorizar, licenciar; ~**d** a (for alcohol) autorizado para la venta de bebidas alcohólicas.

licensee [laɪsənˈsi:] n (in a pub) patrón/ona m/f.

licentious [laɪˈsenʃəs] a licencioso.

lichen [ˈlaɪkən] n líquen m.

lick [lɪk] vt lamer // n lamedura; a ~ of paint una mano de pintura.

licorice [ˈlɪkərɪs] n = liquorice.

lid [lɪd] n (of box, case) tapa; (of pan) cobertera.

lido [ˈlaɪdəu] n piscina.

lie [laɪ] n mentira // vi mentir // ti, pt lay, pp lain (act) echarse; (state) estar echado, estar acostado; (of object: be situated) estar, encontrarse; to ~ low (fig) esconderse; to ~ about vi (things) estar en desorden; (people) gandulear; to have a ~down echarse (una siesta); to have a ~-in quedarse pegado a las sábanas.

lieu [lu:]: in ~ of prep en lugar de.

lieutenant [lefˈtenənt] n lugar- teniente m; (MIL) teniente m.

life [laɪf, pl lives] n (gen) vida; (way of living) modo de vivir; (of licence etc) vigencia; ~ assurance n seguro de vida; ~belt n salvavidas m salvavidas; ~boat n bote m salvavidas; ~guard n vigilante m; ~ jacket n chaleco salvavidas; ~less a sin vida; (dull) soso; ~like a natural; ~line n cuerda salvavidas; ~long a de toda la vida; ~saver n bañero, socorrista m/f; ~ sentence n condena perpetua; ~sized a de tamaño natural; ~ span n vida; ~ support system n (MED) respirador m artificial; ~time n: in his ~time durante su vida; once in a ~time una vez en la vida.

lift [lɪft] vt levantar; (steal) robar // vi (fog) levantarse, disiparse // n (elevator) ascensor m; to give sb a ~ llevar a uno en el coche; ~-off n despegue m.

ligament [ˈlɪgəmənt] n ligamento.

light [laɪt] n (gen) luz f; (flame) lumbre f; (lamp) luz f, lámpara;

(daylight) luz del día; (headlight) faro; (rear ~) luz trasera; (for cigarette etc): have you got a ~? ¿tiene fuego? // vt, pt, pp lighted or lit (candle, cigarette, fire) encender; (room) alumbrar // a (colour) claro; (not heavy, also fig) ligero; (room) alumbrado; to ~ up vi (smoke) encender un cigarrillo; (face) iluminarse // vt (illuminate) iluminar, alumbrar; ~ bulb n bombilla; ~en vi (grow ~) clarear // vt (give light to) iluminar; (make lighter) aclarar; (make less heavy) aligerar; ~er n (also: cigarette ~er) encendedor m, mechero; ~-headed a (dizzy) mareado; (excited) exaltado; (by nature) casquivano; ~-hearted a alegre; ~house n faro; ~ing n (act) iluminación f; (system) alumbrado; ~ly ad (touch) ligeramente; (thoughtlessly) a la ligera; (slightly) levemente; (not seriously) con poca seriedad; to get off ~ly ser castigado con poca severidad; ~ meter n (PHOT) fotómetro; ~ness n (in weight) ligereza.

lightning [ˈlaɪtnɪŋ] n relámpago, rayo; ~ conductor n pararrayos m inv.

light: ~weight a (suit) ligero // n (BOXING) peso ligero; ~ year n año luz.

like [laɪk] vt (person) querer, tener cariño a; (things) gustarle a uno // prep como // a parecido, semejante // n: the ~ semejante m/f; his ~s and dislikes sus gustos y aversiones; I would ~, I'd ~ me gustaría; (for purchase) quisiera; would you ~ a coffee? ¿te apetece un café?; to be or look ~ sb/sth parecerse a alguien/algo; that's just ~ him es muy de él, es característico de él; it is nothing ~... no tiene parecido alguno con...; ~able a simpático, agradable.

likelihood [ˈlaɪklɪhud] n proba- bilidad f; **likely** [-lɪ] a probable; he's likely to leave es probable que se vaya.

like-minded [laɪk'maɪndɪd] a de la misma opinión.

liken ['laɪkən] vt: to ~ sth to sth comparar algo con algo.

likewise ['laɪkwaɪz] ad igualmente.

liking ['laɪkɪŋ] n: to his ~ para su gusto.

lilac ['laɪlək] n lila // a (colour) de color lila.

lily ['lɪlɪ] n lirio, azucena; ~ of the valley n lirio de los valles.

limb [lɪm] n miembro.

limber ['lɪmbə*]: to ~ up vi (fig) entrenarse; (SPORT) desentumecerse.

limbo ['lɪmbəu] n: to be in ~ (fig) caer en el olvido.

lime [laɪm] n (tree) limero; (fruit) lima; (GEO) cal f.

limelight ['laɪmlaɪt] n: to be in the ~ (fig) ser el centro de atención.

limerick ['lɪmərɪk] n quintilla humorística.

limestone ['laɪmstəun] n piedra caliza.

limit ['lɪmɪt] n límite m // vt limitar; ~ation [-'teɪʃən] n limitación f; ~ed a limitado; to be ~ed to limitarse a; ~ed (liability) company (Ltd) n sociedad f anónima; ~less a sin límites.

limousine ['lɪməziːn] n limusina.

limp [lɪmp] n: to have a ~ tener cojera // vi cojear // a flojo.

limpet ['lɪmpɪt] n lapa.

limpid ['lɪmpɪd] a límpido, cristalino.

line [laɪn] n (gen) línea; (straight ~) raya; (rope) cuerda; (for fishing) sedal m; (wire) hilo; (row, series) fila, hilera, (of writing) renglón m; (on face) arruga; (specialty) rama // vt (SEWING) forrar (with de); to ~ the streets ocupar las aceras; in ~ with de acuerdo con; to ~ up vi hacer cola // vt alinear, poner en fila; ~d a (face) arrugado; (paper) rayado.

linear ['lɪnɪə*] a lineal.

linen ['lɪnɪn] n ropa blanca; (cloth) lino.

liner ['laɪnə*] n vapor m de línea, transatlántico.

linesman ['laɪnzmən] n (SPORT) juez m de línea.

line-up ['laɪnʌp] n alineación f.

linger ['lɪŋgə*] vi retrasarse, tardar en marcharse; (smell, tradition) persistir.

lingerie ['lænʒəriː] n ropa interior (de mujer).

lingering ['lɪŋgərɪŋ] a persistente; (death) lento.

lingo ['lɪŋgəu], pl ~es n (pej) jerga.

linguist ['lɪŋgwɪst] n lingüista m/f; ~ic a lingüístico; ~ics n lingüística.

lining ['laɪnɪŋ] n forro.

link [lɪŋk] n (of a chain) eslabón m; (connection) conexión f; (bond) vínculo, lazo // vt vincular, unir; ~s npl campo sg de golf; to ~ up vt acoplar // vi unirse; ~-up n (gen) unión f; (in space) acoplamiento.

lino ['laɪnəu], **linoleum** [lɪ'nəuliəm] n linóleo.

lintel ['lɪntl] n dintel m.

lion ['laɪən] n león m; ~ess n leona.

lip [lɪp] n labio; (of jug) pico; (of cup etc) borde m; ~-read vi leer los labios; ~ service n: to pay ~ service to sth alabar algo pero sin hacer nada; ~stick n lápiz m labial, barra de labios.

liquefy ['lɪkwɪfaɪ] vt liquidar.

liqueur [lɪ'kjuə*] n licor m.

liquid ['lɪkwɪd] a, n líquido.

liquidate ['lɪkwɪdeɪt] vt liquidar; **liquidation** [-'deɪʃən] n liquidación f; **liquidator** n liquidador/a m/f.

liquidize ['lɪkwɪdaɪz] vt (CULIN) licuar.

liquor ['lɪkə*] n licor m, bebidas alcohólicas fpl.

liquorice ['lɪkərɪs] n regaliz m.

lisp [lɪsp] n ceceo.

list [lɪst] n lista; (of ship) inclinación f // vt (write down) hacer una lista

de; (*enumerate*) catalogar // *vi*
(*ship*) inclinarse.

listen ['lɪsn] *vi* escuchar, oír; (*pay attention*) atender; **~er** *n* oyente *m/f*.

listless ['lɪstlɪs] *a* apático, indiferente.

lit [lɪt] *pt, pp of* **light.**

litany ['lɪtənɪ] *n* letanía.

literacy ['lɪtərəsɪ] *n* capacidad *f* de leer y escribir; **~ campaign** campaña de alfabetización.

literal ['lɪtərl] *a* literal; **~ly** *ad* literalmente.

literary ['lɪtərərɪ] *a* literario.

literate ['lɪtərət] *a* que sabe leer y escribir; (*fig*) culto.

literature ['lɪtrɪtʃə*] *n* literatura; (*brochures etc*) folletos *mpl*.

lithe [laɪð] *a* ágil.

litigation [lɪtɪ'geɪʃən] *n* litigio.

litre, liter (*US*) ['li:tə*] *n* litro.

litter ['lɪtə*] *n* (*rubbish*) basura; (*paper*) papel *m* tirado; (*young animals*) camada, cría; (*stretcher*) camilla; **~ bin** *n* papelera; **~ed with** (*scattered*) esparcido con; (*covered with*) lleno de.

little ['lɪtl] *a* (*small*) pequeño; (*not much*) poco; *often translated by suffix: eg* **~ house** casita // *ad* poco; **a ~** un poco (de); **~ by ~** poco a poco.

liturgy ['lɪtədʒɪ] *n* liturgia.

live [lɪv] *vi* vivir // *vt* (*a life*) llevar; (*experience*) vivir // *a* [laɪv] (*animal*) vivo; (*wire*) conectado; (*broadcast*) en directo; (*shell*) cargado; **to ~ down** *vt* hacer olvidar; **to ~ on** *vt fus* (*food*) vivirse de, alimentarse de; **to ~ up to** *vt fus* (*fulfil*) cumplir con; (*justify*) justificar.

livelihood ['laɪvlɪhud] *n* sustento.

lively ['laɪvlɪ] *a* (*gen*) vivo; (*talk*) animado; (*pace*) rápido; (*party, tune*) alegre.

liver ['lɪvə*] *n* (*ANAT*) hígado; **~ish** *a* (*fig*) rezongón(ona).

livery ['lɪvərɪ] *n* librea.

lives [laɪvz] *pl of* **life.**

livestock ['laɪvstɔk] *n* ganado.

livid ['lɪvɪd] *a* lívido; (*furious*) furioso.

living ['lɪvɪŋ] *a* (*alive*) vivo // *n*: **to earn** *or* **make a ~** ganarse la vida; **~ conditions** *npl* condiciones *fpl* de vida; **~ room** *n* sala (de estar); **~ standards** *npl* nivel *m* de vida; **~ wage** *n* sueldo suficiente para vivir.

lizard ['lɪzəd] *n* lagartija.

llama ['lɑːmə] *n* llama.

load [ləud] *n* (*gen*) carga; (*weight*) peso // *vt*: **to ~ (with)** cargar (con); (*fig*) colmar de; **a ~ of, ~s of** (*fig*) (gran) cantidad de, montones de; **~ed** *a* (*dice*) cargado; (*question, word*) intencionado; (*col: rich*) forrado (de dinero); (*: drunk*) trompa.

loaf [ləuf] *pl* **loaves** *n* (barra de) pan *m* // *vi* (*also:* **~ about, ~ around**) holgazanear.

loan [ləun] *n* préstamo; (*COMM*) empréstito // *vt* prestar; **on ~** prestado.

loath [ləuθ] *a*: **to be ~ to do sth** estar poco dispuesto a hacer algo.

loathe [ləuð] *vt* aborrecer; (*person*) odiar; **loathing** *n* aversión *f*; odio; **it fills me with loathing** me da asco.

loaves [ləuvz] *pl of* **loaf.**

lobby ['lɔbɪ] *n* vestíbulo, sala de espera; (*POL: pressure group*) grupo de presión // *vt* presionar.

lobe [ləub] *n* lóbulo.

lobster ['lɔbstə*] *n* langosta; (*large*) bogavante *m*.

local ['ləukl] *a* local // *n* (*pub*) bar *m*; **the ~s** *npl* los vecinos, los del lugar; **~ity** [-'kælɪt] *n* localidad *f*; **~ly** [-kəlɪ] *ad* en la vecindad.

locate [ləu'keɪt] *vt* (*find*) localizar; (*situate*) colocar.

location [ləu'keɪʃən] *n* situación *f*; **on ~** (*CINEMA*) en exteriores, fuera del estudio.

loch [lɔx] *n* lago.

lock [lɔk] *n* (*of door, box*) cerradura; (*of canal*) esclusa; (*stop*) tope *m*; (*of* hair) mechón m // vt (with key) cerrar con llave; (immobilize) inmovilizar // vi (door etc) cerrarse con llave; (wheels) bloquearse, trabarse.

locker ['lɔkə*] n casillero.

locket ['lɔkɪt] n medallón m.

lockout ['lɔkaut] n paro patronal, lockout m.

locomotive [ləukə'məutɪv] n locomotora.

locum ['ləukəm] n (MED) (médico) interino.

locust ['ləukəst] n langosta.

lodge [lɔdʒ] n casa del guarda; (porter's) portería; (FREEMASONRY) logia // vi (person): to ~ (with) alojarse (en casa de) // vt (complaint) presentar; **lodger** n huésped/a m/f.

lodgings ['lɔdʒɪŋz] npl alojamiento sg; (house) casa sg de huéspedes.

loft [lɔft] n desván m.

lofty ['lɔftɪ] a alto; (haughty) orgulloso.

log [lɔg] n (of wood) leño, tronco; (book) = logbook.

logarithm ['lɔgərɪðəm] n logaritmo.

logbook ['lɔgbuk] n (NAUT) diario de a bordo, (AVIAT) libro de vuelo; (of car) documentación f (del coche).

loggerheads ['lɔgəhedz] npl: at ~ (with) de pique (con).

logic ['lɔdʒɪk] n lógica; ~al a lógico.

logistics [lɔ'dʒɪstɪks] n logística.

loin [lɔɪn] n (CULIN) lomo, solomillo; ~s npl lomos mpl; ~ **cloth** n taparrabo.

loiter ['lɔɪtə*] vi perder el tiempo; (pej) merodear.

loll [lɔl] vi (also: ~ **about**) repantigarse.

lollipop ['lɔlɪpɔp] n pirulí m; (iced) polo, **man/lady** n persona encargada de ayudar a los niños a cruzar la calle.

London ['lʌndən] n Londres; ~ **er** n londinense m/f.

lone [ləun] a solitario.

loneliness ['ləunlɪnɪs] n soledad f, aislamiento; **lonely** [-lɪ] a solitario, solo.

loner ['ləunə*] n solitario.

long [lɔŋ] a largo // ad mucho tiempo, largamente // vi: to ~ for sth anhelar o suspirar por algo; in the ~ run a la larga; so or as ~ as mientras, con tal que; don't be ~! ¡no tardes!; ¡vuelve pronto!; how ~ is the street? ¿cuánto tiene la calle de largo?; how ~ is the lesson? ¿cuánto dura la lección?; 6 metres ~ que mide 6 metros; 6 metros de largo; 6 months ~ que dura 6 meses, de 6 meses de duración; all night ~ toda la noche; ~ before mucho antes; before ~ (+ future) dentro de poco; (+ past) poco tiempo después; at ~ last al fin, por fin; ~distance a (race) de larga distancia; (call) interurbano; ~haired a de pelo largo; ~hand n escritura (corriente); ~ing n anhelo, ansia; (nostalgia) nostalgia // a anhelante.

longitude ['lɔŋgɪtjuːd] n longitud f.

long: ~ **jump** n salto de longitud; ~**lost** a desaparecido hace mucho tiempo; ~ **playing record** (L.P.) n elepé m, disco de larga duración; ~**range** a de gran alcance; ~**sighted** a (fig) previsor(a); ~**standing** a de mucho tiempo; ~**suffering** a sufrido; ~**term** a a largo plazo; ~ **wave** a de onda larga; ~**winded** a prolijo.

loo [luː] n (col) wáter m.

loofah ['luːfə] n esponja de lufa.

look [luk] vi mirar; (seem) parecer; (building etc): to ~ south/on to the sea dar al sur/al mar // n mirada; (glance) vistazo; (appearance) aire m, aspecto; ~s npl físico, apariencia; to ~ **like** sb parecerse a alguien; to ~ **after** vt fus cuidar a; to ~ **at** vt fus mirar; (consider) considerar; to ~ **back** vi mirar hacia atrás; to ~ **down on** vt fus (fig) despreciar, mirar con desprecio; **to ~ for** *vt fus* buscar; **to ~ forward to** *vt fus* esperar con ilusión; **to ~ into** *vt* investigar; **to ~ on** *vi* mirar (como espectador); **to ~ out** *vi* (*beware*): **to ~ out** for sth tener cuidado de; **to ~ out for** *vt fus* (*seek*) buscar; (*await*) esperar; **to ~ round** *vi* volver la cabeza; **to ~ to** *vt fus* ocuparse de; (*rely on*) contar con; **to ~ up** *vi* mirar hacia arriba; (*improve*) mejorar // *vt* (*word*) buscar; (*friend*) visitar; **to ~ up to** *vt fus* admirir; **~out** *n* (*place etc*) puesto de observación; (*person*) vigía *m*; **to be on the ~-out for sth** estar al acecho de algo.

loom [lu:m] *n* telar *m* // *vi* asomarse; (*threaten*) amenazar.

loony ['lu:nɪ] *n* (*col*) loco/a; **~ bin** *n* (*col*) manicomio.

loop [lu:p] *n* lazo; (*bend*) vuelta, recodo; (*contraceptive*) espiral *f*; **~hole** *n* escapatoria.

loose [lu:s] *a* (*gen*) suelto; (*not tight*) flojo; (*wobbly etc*) movedizo; (*clothes*) ancho; (*morals, discipline*) relajado; **to be at a ~ end** no saber qué hacer; **~ly** *ad* libremente, aproximadamente; **loosen** *vt* (*free*) soltar; (*untie*) desatar; (*slacken*) aflojar.

loot [lu:t] *n* botín *m* // *vt* saquear; **~ing** *n* pillaje *m*.

lop [lɔp]: **to ~ off** *vt* cortar; (*branches*) podar.

lop-sided ['lɔp'saɪdɪd] *a* desequilibrado.

lord [lɔːd] *n* señor *m*; **L~ Smith** Lord Smith; **the L~** el Señor; (**the House of**) **L~s** la Cámara de los Lores; **~ly** *a* señorial; (*arrogant*) arrogante; **~ship** *n*: **your L~ship** su señoría.

lore [lɔː*] *n* saber *m* popular, tradiciones *fpl*.

lorry ['lɔrɪ] *n* camión *m*; **~ driver** *n* camionero.

lose [lu:z], *pt, pp* **lost** *vt* perder // *vi* perder, ser vencido; **to ~ (time)**

(*clock*) atrasarse; **loser** *n* perdedor/a *m/f*.

loss [lɔs] *n* pérdida; **to be at a ~** no saber qué hacer; **to be a dead ~** ser completamente inútil.

lost [lɔst] *pt, pp* of **lose** // *a* perdido; **~ property** *n* objetos *mpl* perdidos.

lot [lɔt] *n* (*at auctions*) lote *m*; (*destiny*) suerte *f*; **the ~** el todo, todos; **a ~** mucho, bastante; **a ~ of, ~s of** mucho(s) (*pl*); **to draw ~s (for sth)** echar suertes (para decidir algo); **I read a ~** leo bastante.

lotion ['ləuʃən] *n* loción *f*.

lottery ['lɔtərɪ] *n* lotería.

loud [laud] *a* (*voice*) alto; (*shout*) fuerte; (*noisy*) estrepitoso; (*gaudy*) chillón(ona) // *ad* (*speak etc*) en alta voz; **~hailer** *n* megáfono; **~ly** *ad* (*noisily*) ruidosamente; (*aloud*) en alta voz; **~speaker** *n* altavoz *m*.

lounge [laundʒ] *n* salón *m*, sala (de estar) // *vi* reposar, holgazanear; **~ suit** *n* traje *m* de calle.

louse [laus], *pl* **lice** *n* piojo.

lousy ['lauzɪ] *a* (*fig*) vil, asqueroso.

lout [laut] *n* gamberro.

lovable ['lʌvəbl] *a* amable, simpático.

love [lʌv] *n* amor *m* // *vt* amar, querer; **to ~ to do** gustar(le a uno) mucho hacer; **to be in ~ with** estar enamorado de; **to make ~** hacer el amor; **for the ~ of** por amor de; **'15 ~'** (*TENNIS*) 15 a cero; **I ~ paella** me gusta mucho la paella; **'with ~' con cariño; ~ affair** *n* aventura sentimental; **~ letter** *n* carta de amor; **~ life** *n* vida sentimental.

lovely ['lʌvlɪ] *a* (*delightful*) precioso, encantador(a); (*beautiful*) hermoso.

lover ['lʌvə*] *n* amante *m/f*; (*amateur*): **a ~ of** un aficionado a o un amante de.

lovesong ['lʌvsɔŋ] *n* canción *f* de amor.

loving ['lʌvɪŋ] *a* amoroso, cariñoso.

low [ləu] *a, ad* bajo // *n* (*METEOROLOGY*) área de baja presión // vi (cow) mugir; **to feel ~** sentirse deprimido; **to turn (down) ~** vt bajar; **~cut** a (dress) escotado.

lower ['ləuə*] vt bajar; (reduce) reducir // vr: **to ~ o.s. to** (fig) rebajarse a.

low: **~-grade** a de baja calidad; **~ly** a humilde; **~-lying** a de bajo nivel.

loyal ['lɔɪəl] a leal; **~ty** n lealtad f.

lozenge ['lɔzɪndʒ] n (MED) pastilla.

L.P. n abbr of **long-playing record.**

L-plates ['elpleɪts] npl placa de aprendiz de conductor.

Ltd abbr of **limited company** S.A.

lubricant ['lu:brɪkənt] n lubricante m; **lubricate** ['-keɪt] vt lubricar, engrasar.

lucid ['lu:sɪd] a lúcido; **~ity** [-'sɪdɪtɪ] n lucidez f.

luck [lʌk] n suerte f; **bad ~** mala suerte; **good ~!** ¡que tengas suerte! ¡suerte!; **~ily** ad afortunadamente; **~y** a afortunado.

lucrative ['lu:krətɪv] a lucrativo.

ludicrous ['lu:dɪkrəs] a absurdo.

ludo ['lu:dəu] n parchís m.

lug [lʌg] vt (drag) arrastrar; (pull) tirar de.

luggage ['lʌgɪdʒ] n equipaje m; **~ rack** n (in train) rejilla, redecilla; (on car) vaca, portaequipajes m inv.

lukewarm ['lu:kwɔ:m] a tibio, templado.

lull [lʌl] n tregua // vt (child) acunar; (person, fear) calmar.

lullaby ['lʌləbaɪ] n canción f de cuna.

lumbago [lʌm'beɪgəu] n lumbago.

lumber ['lʌmbə*] n (junk) trastos viejos mpl; (wood) maderos mpl; **~jack** n maderero.

luminous ['lu:mɪnəs] a luminoso.

lump [lʌmp] n terrón m; (fragment) trozo; (in sauce) grumo; (in throat) nudo; (swelling) bulto // vt (also: **~ together**) amontonar; **a ~ sum**

suma global; **~y** a (sauce) lleno de grumos.

lunacy ['lu:nəsɪ] n locura.

lunar ['lu:nə*] a lunar.

lunatic ['lu:nətɪk] a, n loco/a; **~ asylum** n manicomio.

lunch [lʌntʃ] n almuerzo, comida // vi almorzar; **~ time** n hora del almuerzo o de comer.

luncheon ['lʌntʃən] n almuerzo; **~ meat** n pastel m de carne.

lung [lʌŋ] n pulmón m; **~ cancer** n cáncer m de pulmón.

lunge [lʌndʒ] vi (also: **~ forward**) abalanzarse; **to ~ at** arremeter contra.

lurch [lə:tʃ] vi dar sacudidas // n sacudida; **to leave sb in the ~** dejar a uno plantado.

lure [luə*] n (bait) cebo; (decoy) señuelo // vt atraer, seducir.

lurid ['luərɪd] a (light) misterioso; (dress) chillón(ona); (account) sensacional; (detail) horrible.

lurk [lə:k] vi (hide) esconderse; (wait) estar al acecho.

luscious ['lʌʃəs] a delicioso.

lush [lʌʃ] a exuberante.

lust [lʌst] n lujuria; (greed) codicia; **to ~ after** vt fus codiciar; **~ful** a lascivo, lujurioso.

lustre, luster (US) ['lʌstə*] n lustre m, brillo.

lusty ['lʌstɪ] a robusto, fuerte.

lute [lu:t] n laúd m.

Luxembourg ['lʌksəmbə:g] n Luxemburgo.

luxuriant [lʌg'zjuərɪənt] a exuberante.

luxurious [lʌg'zjuərɪəs] a lujoso; **luxury** ['lʌkʃərɪ] n lujo // cpd de lujo.

lying ['laɪɪŋ] n mentiras fpl // a mentiroso.

lynch [lɪntʃ] vt linchar; **~ing** n linchamiento.

lynx [lɪŋks] n lince m.

lyre ['laɪə*] n lira.

lyric ['lɪrɪk] a lírico; **~s** npl (of song) letra sg; **~al** a lírico.

M

m. abbr of **metre**; **mile**; **million**.

M.A. abbr of **Master of Arts** licenciado en letras.

mac [mæk] n impermeable m.

macaroni [mækəˈrəʊnɪ] n macarrones mpl.

mace [meɪs] n (BOT) macis f.

machine [məˈʃiːn] n máquina // vt (dress etc) coser a máquina; ~ **gun** n ametralladora; ~**ry** n maquinaria; (fig) mecanismo; **machinist** n operario (de máquina).

mackerel [ˈmækrl] n, pl inv caballa.

mackintosh [ˈmækɪntɔʃ] n impermeable m.

mad [mæd] a (gen) loco; (crazed) demente; (angry) furioso.

madam [ˈmædəm] n señora.

madden [ˈmædn] vt volver loco.

made [meɪd] pt, pp of **make**; ~**to-measure** a hecho a la medida.

madly [ˈmædlɪ] ad locamente.

madman [ˈmædmən] n loco.

madness [ˈmædnɪs] n locura.

magazine [mægəˈziːn] n revista; (MIL: store) almacén m; (of firearm) recámara.

maggot [ˈmægət] n gusano.

magic [ˈmædʒɪk] n magia // a mágico; ~**al** a mágico; ~**ian** [məˈdʒɪʃən] n mago; (conjurer) prestidigitador m.

magistrate [ˈmædʒɪstreɪt] n juez m/f (municipal).

magnanimous [mægˈnænɪməs] a magnánimo.

magnate [ˈmægneɪt] n magnate m.

magnet [ˈmægnɪt] n imán m; ~**ic** [-ˈnetɪk] a magnético; ~**ism** n magnetismo.

magnification [mægnɪfɪˈkeɪʃən] n aumento.

magnificence [mægˈnɪfɪsns] n magnificencia; **magnificent** [-nt] a magnífico.

magnify [ˈmægnɪfaɪ] vt aumentar; (fig) exagerar; ~**ing glass** n lupa.

magnitude [ˈmægnɪtjuːd] n magnitud f.

magnolia [mægˈnəʊlɪə] n magnolia.

magpie [ˈmægpaɪ] n urraca.

mahogany [məˈhɔgənɪ] n caoba // cpd de caoba.

maid [meɪd] n criada; (pej) solterona.

maiden [ˈmeɪdn] n doncella // a (aunt etc) solterona; (speech, voyage) inaugural; ~ **name** n nombre m de soltera.

mail [meɪl] n correo; (letters) cartas fpl // vt (post) echar al correo; (send) mandar por correo; ~**box** n (US) buzón m; ~**order** n pedido postal; (business) venta por correo.

maim [meɪm] vt mutilar, lisiar.

main [meɪn] a principal, mayor // n (pipe) cañería maestra; the ~**s** (ELEC) la red eléctrica; **in the** ~ en general; ~**land** n continente m; ~**stay** n (fig) pilar m; ~**stream** n corriente f principal.

maintain [meɪnˈteɪn] vt mantener; (keep up) conservar (en buen estado); (affirm) sostener; **maintenance** [ˈmeɪntənəns] n mantenimiento.

maisonette [meɪzəˈnet] n apartamento de dos pisos.

maize [meɪz] n maíz m.

majestic [məˈdʒestɪk] a majestuoso; **majesty** [ˈmædʒɪstɪ] n majestad f.

major [ˈmeɪdʒə*] n (MIL) comandante m // a principal; (MUS) mayor.

Majorca [məˈjɔːkə] n Mallorca.

majority [məˈdʒɔrɪtɪ] n mayoría.

make [meɪk] pt, pp **made** vt hacer; (manufacture) hacer, fabricar; (cause to be): **to** ~ **sb sad** hacer o poner triste a alguien; (force): **to** ~ **sb do sth** obligar a uno a hacer algo; (equal): **2 and 2** ~ **4** 2 y 2 son 4 // n marca; **to** ~ **do with** contentarse con; **to** ~ **for** vt fus (place) dirigirse a; **to ~ out** vt (decipher) descifrar; (understand) entender; (see) distinguir; **to ~ up** vt (invent) inventar; (parcel) envolver // vi reconciliarse; (with cosmetics) maquillarse; **to ~ up for** vt fuo compensar; **~believe** a fingido; **maker** n fabricante m/f; **~shift** a improvisado; **~-up** n maquillaje m.

making ['meɪkɪŋ] n (fig.): **in the ~** en vías de formación.

malaise [mæ'leɪz] n malestar m.

malaria [mə'lɛərɪə] n malaria.

Malay ['meɪleɪ] a, n malayo/a.

Malaysia [mə'leɪzɪə] n Malaysia.

male [meɪl] n (BIOL, ELEC) macho // a (sex, attitude) masculino; (child etc) varón.

malevolent [mə'levələnt] a malévolo.

malfunction [mæl'fʌŋkʃən] n funcionamiento defectuoso.

malice ['mælɪs] n (ill will) malevolencia; (rancour) rencor m; **malicious** [mə'lɪʃəs] a malévolo; rencoroso.

malign [mə'laɪn] vt difamar, calumniar // a maligno.

malignant [mə'lɪgnənt] n (MED) maligno.

malingerer [mə'lɪŋgərə*] n enfermo fingido.

malleable ['mælɪəbl] a maleable.

mallet ['mælɪt] n mazo.

malnutrition [mælnju:'trɪʃən] n desnutrición f.

malpractice [mæl'præktɪs] n falta profesional.

malt [mɔ:lt] n malta.

Malta ['mɔ:ltə] n Malta; **Maltese** [-'ti:z] a, n, pl inv maltés/esa m/f.

maltreat [mæl'tri:t] vt maltratar.

mammal ['mæml] n mamífero.

mammoth ['mæməθ] n mamut m // a gigantesco.

man [mæn], pl men n hombre m; (CHESS) pieza // vt (NAUT) tripular; (MIL) guarnecer; **an old ~** un viejo; **~ and wife** marido y mujer.

manacle ['mænəkl] n manilla; **~s** npl grillos mpl.

manage ['mænɪdʒ] vi arreglárselas, ir tirando // vt (be in charge of) dirigir; (person etc) manejar; **~able** a manejable; **~ment** n dirección f, administración f; **manager/ess** n director/a m/f; (SPORT) entrenador/a m/f; **managerial** [-ə'dʒɪərɪəl] a directivo; **managing director** n director m general.

mandarin ['mændərɪn] n (also: ~ orange) mandarina; (person) mandarín m.

mandate ['mændeɪt] n mandato.

mandatory ['mændətərɪ] a obligatorio.

mandolin(e) ['mændəlɪn] n mandolina.

mane [meɪn] n (of horse) crin f; (of lion) melena.

manfully ['mænfəlɪ] ad violentamente.

mangle ['mæŋgl] vt mutilar, magullar // n rodillo.

mango ['mæŋgəʊ], pl **~es** n mango.

mangy ['meɪndʒɪ] a roñoso, sarnoso.

manhandle ['mænhændl] vt maltratar.

manhole ['mænhəʊl] n pozo de visita.

manhood ['mænhʊd] n edad f viril.

man-hour ['mæn'aʊə*] n hora-hombre f.

manhunt ['mænhʌnt] n caza de hombre.

mania ['meɪnɪə] n manía, maniac ['meɪnɪæk] n maníaco; (fig) maníatico.

manicure ['mænɪkjʊə*] n manicura // vt (person) hacer la manicura a; **~ set** n estuche m de manicura.

manifest ['mænɪfest] vt manifestar, mostrar // a manifiesto; **~ation** [-'teɪʃən] n manifestación f.

manifesto [mænɪ'festəʊ] n manifiesto.

manipulate [mə'nɪpjuleɪt] vt manipular, manejar.

mankind [mæn'kaɪnd] n la humanidad, el género humano.

manly ['mænlɪ] a varonil.

man-made ['mæn'meɪd] a artificial.

manner ['mænə*] n manera, modo; (behaviour) conducta, manera de ser; (type) clase f; ~s npl modales mpl, educación f; bad ~s mala educación; ~ism n hábito, peculiaridad f.

manoeuvre, maneuver (US) [mə'nu:və*] vt, vi maniobrar // n maniobra.

manor ['mænə*] n (also: ~ house) casa solariega.

manpower ['mænpauə*] n mano f de obra.

mansion ['mænʃən] n palacio, casa grande.

manslaughter ['mænslɔ:tə*] n homicidio no premeditado.

mantelpiece ['mæntlpi:s] n repisa, chimenea.

mantle ['mæntl] n manto; (fig) capa.

manual ['mænjuəl] a manual // n manual m; (MUS) teclado.

manufacture [mænju'fæktʃə*] vt fabricar // n fabricación f; **manufacturer** n fabricante m/f.

manure [mə'njuə*] n estiércol m, abono.

manuscript ['mænjuskrɪpt] n manuscrito.

Manx [mæŋks] a de la Isla de Man.

many ['menɪ] det muchos(as) // pron muchos/as; **a great ~** muchísimos, buen número de; **~ a time** muchas veces.

map [mæp] n mapa m // vt trazar el mapa de; to **~ out** vt proyectar.

maple ['meɪpl] n arce m.

mar [mɑ:*] vt estropear.

marathon ['mærəθən] n maratón m.

marauder [mə'rɔ:də*] n merodeador m; (intruder) intruso.

marble ['mɑ:bl] n mármol m; (toy) canica.

March [mɑ:tʃ] n marzo.

march [mɑ:tʃ] vi (MIL) marchar; (fig) caminar con resolución // n marcha; (demonstration) manifestación f, marcha; **~-past** n desfile m.

mare [meə*] n yegua.

margarine [mɑ:dʒə'ri:n] n margarina.

margin ['mɑ:dʒɪn] n margen m; **~al** a marginal.

marigold ['mærɪgəuld] n caléndula.

marijuana [mærɪ'wɑ:nə] n marijuana.

marina [mə'ri:nə] n marina.

marine [mə'ri:n] a marino // n soldado de marina.

marital ['mærɪtl] a matrimonial; **~ status** estado civil.

maritime ['mærɪtaɪm] a marítimo.

marjoram ['mɑ:dʒərəm] n orégano.

mark [mɑ:k] n marca, señal f; (imprint) huella; (stain) mancha; (SCOL) puntuación f, nota; (currency) marco // vt marcar; manchar; (SCOL) calificar; to **~ time** marcar el paso; to **~ out** vt trazar; **~ed** a marcado, acusado; **~er** n (sign) marcador m; (bookmark) registro.

market ['mɑ:kɪt] n mercado // vt (COMM) vender; **black ~** mercado negro; **Common M~** Mercado Común; **~ day** n día de mercado; **~ garden** n (Brit) huerto; **~ing** n márketing m, mercadotecnia; **~-place** n mercado; **~ research** n análisis m inv de mercados.

marksman ['mɑ:ksmən] n tirador m; **~ship** n puntería.

marmalade ['mɑ:məleɪd] n mermelada (de naranjas).

maroon [mə'ru:n] vt (fig): to be **~ed** (shipwrecked) naufragarse; (fig) quedar abandonado // a marrón.

marquee [mɑ:'ki:] n entoldado.

marquess, marquis ['mɑːkwɪs] n marqués m.

marriage ['mærɪdʒ] n (state) matrimonio; (wedding) boda; (act) casamiento; (~ bureau) n agencia matrimonial; ~ **certificate** n partida de casamiento.

married ['mærɪd] a casado; (life, love) conyugal.

marrow ['mærəʊ] n médula; (vegetable) calabacín m.

marry ['mærɪ] vt casarse con; (subj: father, priest etc) casar // vi (also: **get married**) casarse.

marsh [mɑːʃ] n pantano; (salt ~) marisma.

marshal ['mɑːʃl] n (MIL) mariscal m; (at sports meeting etc) oficial m // vt (facts) ordenar; (soldiers) formar.

marshmallow [mɑːʃ'mæləʊ] n malvavisco.

marshy ['mɑːʃɪ] a pantanoso.

martial ['mɑːʃl] a marcial; ~ **law** n ley f marcial.

martyr ['mɑːtə*] n mártir m/f // vt martirizar; ~**dom** n martirio.

marvel ['mɑːvl] n maravilla, prodigio // vi: **to** ~ (**at**) maravillarse (de); ~**lous**, ~**ous** (US) a maravilloso.

Marxism ['mɑːksɪzm] n marxismo, Marxist [-sɪst] a. n marxista m/f.

marzipan ['mɑːzɪpæn] n mazapán m.

mascara [mæs'kɑːrə] n rímel m.

mascot ['mæskət] n mascota.

masculine ['mæskjʊlɪn] a masculino; **masculinity** [-'lɪnɪtɪ] n masculinidad f.

mash [mæʃ] n (mix) mezcla; (pulp) amasijo; ~**ed potatoes** puré m de patatas.

mask [mɑːsk] n máscara // vt enmascarar.

masochist ['mæsəʊkɪst] n masoquista m/f.

mason ['meɪsn] n (also: **stone~**) albañil m; (also: **free~**) masón m; ~**ic** [mə'sɒnɪk] a masónico; ~**ry** n masonería; (building) mampostería.

masquerade [mæskə'reɪd] n baile m de máscaras; (fig) farsa // vi: **to** ~ **as** disfrazarse de, hacerse pasar por.

mass [mæs] n (people) muchedumbre f; (PHYSICS) masa; (REL) misa; (great quantity) montón m // vi reunirse; (MIL) concentrarse; **the** ~**es** las masas.

massacre ['mæsəkə*] n masacre f // vt masacrar.

massage ['mæsɑːʒ] n masaje m // vt dar masaje a.

masseur [mæ'sə:*] n masajista m; **masseuse** [-'sə:z] n masajista f.

massive ['mæsɪv] a (solid) sólido; (head etc) grande; (support, intervention) masivo.

mass media ['mæs'miːdɪə] npl medios mpl de comunicación masiva.

mass-production ['mæsprə-'dʌkʃən] n fabricación f en serie.

mast [mɑːst] n (NAUT) mástil m; (RADIO etc) torre f.

master ['mɑːstə*] n maestro; (landowner) señor m, amo; (in secondary school) profesor m; (title for boys): **M~ X** Señorito X // vt dominar; (learn) aprender a fondo; ~ **key** n llave f maestra; ~**ly** a magistral; ~**mind** n inteligencia superior // vt dirigir, planear; **M~ of Arts** n Licenciado en Letras; ~**piece** n obra maestra; ~ **plan** n plan m rector; ~ **stroke** n golpe m maestro; ~**y** n maestría.

masturbate ['mæstəbeɪt] vi masturbarse; **masturbation** [-'beɪʃən] n masturbación f.

mat [mæt] n estera; (also: **door~**) felpudo // a = **matt**.

match [mætʃ] n cerilla; (game) partido; (fig) igual m/f // vt emparejar; (go well with) hacer juego con; (equal) igualar, parecerse a // vi hacer juego; **to be a good** ~ hacer una buena pareja; ~**box** n caja de cerillas; ~ing a que hace juego; ~less a sin par, incomparable.

mate [meɪt] n compañero; (assistant) ayudante m/f; (CHESS) mate m; (in merchant navy) segundo de a bordo // vi acoplarse, parearse // vt acoplar, parear.

material [mə'tɪərɪəl] n (substance) materia; (equipment) material m; (cloth) tela, tejido; (data) datos mpl // a material; (important) importante; ~s npl materiales mpl; ~istic [-ə'lɪstɪk] a materialista; ~ize vi materializarse.

maternal [mə'tə:nl] a maternal.

maternity [mə'tə:nɪtɪ] n maternidad f; ~ dress vestido premamá; ~ hospital n hospital m de maternidad.

mathematical [mæθə'mætɪkl] a matemático; **mathematician** [-mə'tɪʃən] n matemático; **mathematics** [-tɪks], **maths** [mæθs] n matemáticas fpl.

matinée ['mætɪneɪ] n función f de tarde.

mating ['meɪtɪŋ] n aparejamiento; ~ call n llamada del macho; ~ season n época de celo.

matriarchal [meɪtrɪ'ɑ:kl] a matriarcal.

matrices ['meɪtrɪsi:z] pl of **matrix**.

matrimonial [mætrɪ'məʊnɪəl] a matrimonial.

matrimony ['mætrɪmənɪ] n matrimonio.

matrix ['meɪtrɪks], pl **matrices** n matriz f.

matron ['meɪtrən] n (in hospital) enfermera jefe; (in school) ama de llaves; ~ly a de matrona; (fig: figure) corpulento.

matt [mæt] a mate.

matted ['mætɪd] a enmarañado.

matter ['mætə*] n cuestión f, asunto; (PHYSICS) sustancia, materia; (content) contenido; (MED: pus) pus m // vi importar; **it doesn't ~** no

importa; **what's the ~?** ¿qué pasa?; **no ~ what** pase lo que pase; **as a ~ of course** por rutina; **as a ~ of fact** de hecho; **~-of-fact** a prosaico, práctico.

mattress ['mætrɪs] n colchón m.

mature [mə'tjuə*] a maduro // vi madurar; **maturity** n madurez f.

maudlin ['mɔ:dlɪn] a llorón(ona).

maul [mɔ:l] vt magullar.

mausoleum [mɔ:sə'lɪəm] n mausoleo.

mauve [məʊv] a de color malva.

maxim ['mæksɪm] n máxima.

maxima ['mæksɪmə] pl of **maximum**.

maximum ['mæksɪməm] a máximo // n, pl **maxima** máximo.

May [meɪ] n mayo.

may [meɪ] vi (conditional: might) (indicating possibility): **he ~ come** puede que venga; (be allowed to): ~ **I smoke?** ¿puedo fumar?; (wishes): ~ **God bless you!** que Dios le bendiga.

maybe ['meɪbi:] ad quizá(s).

mayday ['meɪdeɪ] n S.O.S. m (llamada de socorro internacional).

mayhem ['meɪhem] n mutilación f criminal.

mayonnaise [meɪə'neɪz] n mayonesa.

mayor [meə*] n alcalde m; ~ess n alcaldesa.

maypole ['meɪpəʊl] n mayo.

maze [meɪz] n laberinto.

M.D. abbr of **Doctor of Medicine**.

me [mi:] pron me; (stressed, after prep) mí; **with** ~ conmigo; **it's** ~ soy yo.

meadow ['medəʊ] n prado, pradera.

meagre, meager (US) ['mi:gə*] a escaso, pobre.

meal [mi:l] n comida; (flour) harina; ~ **time** n hora de comer.

mean [mi:n] a (with money) tacaño; (unkind) mezquino, malo; (shabby) humilde, vil; (of poor quality) inferior; (average) medio // vt, pt, pp meant (signify) querer decir, significar; (intend): to ~ to do sth pensar o pretender hacer algo // n medio, término medio; ~ful medio sg, manera sg; (resource) recursos mpl, medios mpl; by ~s of mediante, por medio de; by all ~s! ¡naturalmente!, ¡claro que sí!; do you ~ it? ¿lo dices en serio?; what do you ~? ¿qué quiere decir?

meander [mɪ'ændə*] vi (river) serpentear; (person) vagar.

meaning ['mi:nɪŋ] n significado, sentido; ~ful a significativo; ~less a sin sentido.

meanness ['mi:nnɪs] n (with money) tacañería; (shabbiness) vileza, bajeza; (unkindness) maldad f, mezquindad f.

meant [ment] pt, pp of mean.

meantime ['mi:ntaɪm], meanwhile ['mi:nwaɪl] ad (also: in the ~) mientras tanto.

measles ['mi:zlz] n sarampión m; German ~ rubéola.

measly ['mi:zlɪ] a (col) miserable.

measure ['meʒə*] vt medir; (for clothes etc) tomar las medidas a. (consider) pesar // vi medir // n medida; (ruler) regla; ~d a moderado; (tone) mesurado; ~ments npl medidas fpl.

meat [mi:t] n carne f; cold ~ fiambre m; ~ball n albóndiga; ~ pie n pastel m de carne; ~y a carnoso; (fig) sustancioso.

mechanic [mɪ'kænɪk] n mecánico; ~s n mecánica // npl mecanismo sg; ~al a mecánico.

mechanism ['mekənɪzəm] n mecanismo.

mechanization [mekənaɪ'zeɪʃən] n mecanización f.

medal ['medl] n medalla; ~lion [mɪ'dælɪən] n medallón m; ~list, ~ist (US) n (SPORT) ganador/a m/f.

meddle ['medl] vi: to ~ in entrometerse en; to ~ with sth

manosear algo; ~some a entrometido.

media ['mi:dɪə] npl medios mpl de comunicación.

mediaeval [medɪ'i:vl] a = medieval.

mediate ['mi:dɪeɪt] vi mediar; mediation [-'eɪʃən] n mediación f; mediator n intermediario, mediador/a m/f.

medical ['medɪkl] a médico // n reconocimiento médico.

medicated ['medɪkeɪtɪd] a medicinal.

medicinal [me'dɪsɪnl] a medicinal.

medicine ['medsɪn] n medicina; (drug) medicamento; ~ chest n botiquín m.

medieval [medɪ'i:vl] a medieval.

mediocre [mi:dɪ'əʊkə*] a mediocre; mediocrity [-'ɔkrɪtɪ] n mediocridad f.

meditate ['medɪteɪt] vi meditar; meditation [-'teɪʃən] n meditación f.

Mediterranean [medɪtə'reɪnɪən] a mediterráneo; the ~ (Sea) el (Mar) Mediterráneo.

medium ['mi:dɪəm] a mediano, regular // n (pl media: means) medio, (pl mediums: person) médium m/f.

medley ['medlɪ] n mezcla; (MUS) popurrí m.

meek [mi:k] a manso, dócil.

meet [mi:t] pt, pp met vt (gen) encontrar; (accidentally) encontrarse con, tropezar con; (by arrangement) reunirse con; (for the first time) conocer; (go and fetch) ir a buscar; (opponent) enfrentarse con; (obligations) cumplir // vi encontrarse, (in session) reunirse; (join: objects) unirse; (get to know) conocerse; to ~ with vt fus reunirse con; (face: difficulty) tropezar con; ~ing n encuentro; (session: of club etc) reunión f; (interview) entrevista f; (COMM) junta, sesión f; (POL) mitin m.

megalomaniac [megələʊ'meɪniæk] a, n megalómano/a.

megaphone ['megəfəun] n megáfono.

melancholy ['melənkəlı] n melancolía // a melancólico.

melee ['melei] n refriega.

mellow ['meləu] a (sound) dulce; (colour) suave; (fruit) maduro // vi (person) madurar.

melodious [mı'ləudıəs] a melodioso.

melodrama ['meləudrɑ:mə] n melodrama m.

melody ['melədı] n melodía.

melon ['melən] n melón m.

melt [melt] vi (metal) fundirse; (snow) derretirse; (fig) ablandarse // vt (also: ~ down) fundir; to ~ away vi desvanecerse; ~ing point n punto de fusión; ~ing pot n (fig) crisol m.

member ['membə*] n (gen) miembro; (of club) socio; M~ of Parliament (M.P.) n diputado; ~ship n (members) número de miembros; to seek ~ship of pedir el ingreso a; ~ship card n carnet m de socio.

membrane ['membreın] n membrana.

memento [mə'mentəu] n recuerdo.

memo ['meməu] n apunte m, nota.

memoirs ['memwɑ:z] npl memorias fpl.

memorable ['memərəbl] a memorable.

memorandum [memə'rændəm] pl -da [-də] n apunte m, nota; (POL) memorándum m.

memorial [mı'mɔ:rıəl] n monumento conmemorativo // a conmemorativo.

memorize ['meməraız] vt aprender de memoria.

memory ['memərı] n memoria; (recollection) recuerdo.

men [men] pl of **man**.

menace ['menəs] n amenaza // vt amenazar; **menacing** a amenazador(a).

menagerie [mı'nædʒərı] n casa de fieras.

mend [mend] vt reparar, arreglar; (darn) zurcir // vi reponerse // (gen) remiendo; (darn) zurcido; to be on the ~ ir mejorando; ~ing n reparación f; (clothes) ropa por remendar.

menial ['mi:nıəl] a doméstico; (pej) bajo // n criado.

meningitis [menın'dʒaıtıs] n meningitis f.

menopause ['menəupɔ:z] n menopausia.

menstruate ['menstrueıt] vi menstruar; **menstruation** [-'eıʃən] n menstruación f.

mental ['mentl] a mental; ~ity [-'tælıtı] n mentalidad f.

mention ['menʃən] n mención f // vt mencionar; (speak of) hablar de; don't ~ it! ¡de nada!

menu ['menju:] n (set ~) menú m; (printed) carta.

mercenary ['mɜ:sınərı] a, n mercenario.

merchandise ['mɜ:tʃəndaız] n mercancías fpl.

merchant ['mɜ:tʃənt] n comerciante m/f; ~ bank n banco comercial; ~ navy n marina mercante.

merciful ['mɜ:sıful] a compasivo; (fortunate) afortunado.

merciless ['mɜ:sılıs] a despiadado.

mercury ['mɜ:kjurı] n mercurio.

mercy ['mɜ:sı] n compasión f; (REL) misericordia; **at the** ~ **of** a la merced de.

mere [mıə*] a simple, mero; ~ly ad simplemente, sólo.

merge [mɜ:dʒ] vt (join) unir; (mix) mezclar; (fuse) fundir // vi unirse; (COMM) fusionarse; **merger** n (COMM) fusión f.

meridian [mə'rıdıən] n meridiano m.

meringue [mə'ræŋ] n merengue m.

merit ['merıt] n mérito // vt merecer.

mermaid ['mɜ:meıd] n sirena.

merriment ['merɪmənt] n alegría.
merry ['merɪ] a alegre; ~**-go-round** n tiovivo.
mesh [meʃ] n malla; (TECH) engranaje m // vi (gears) engranar.
mesmerize ['mezməraɪz] vt hipnotizar.
mess [mes] n (gen) confusión f; (of objects) revoltijo; (tangle) lío, (MIL) comedor m; **to ~ about** vi (col) perder el tiempo; (pass the time) entretenerse; **to ~ about with** vt fus (col) (play with) divertirse con; (handle) manosear; **to ~ up** vt (disarrange) desordenar; (spoil) estropear; (dirty) ensuciar.
message ['mesɪdʒ] n recado, mensaje m.
messenger ['mesɪndʒə*] n mensajero/a.
messy ['mesɪ] a (dirty) sucio; (untidy) desordenado.
met [met] pt, pp of **meet**.
metabolism [me'tæbolɪzəm] n metabolismo.
metal ['metl] n metal m; ~**lic** [-'tælɪk] a metálico; ~**lurgy** [-'tælədʒɪ] n metalurgia.
metamorphosis [metə'mɔːfəsɪs], pl **-ses** [-siːz] n metamorfosis f (inv).
metaphor ['metəfə*] n metáfora.
metaphysics [metə'fɪzɪks] n metafísica.
mete [miːt]: **to ~ out** vt fus (gen) repartir; (punishment) imponer.
meteor ['miːtɪə*] n meteoro.
meteorological [miːtɪərə'lɒdʒɪkl] a meteorológico; **meteorology** [-'rɒlədʒɪ] n meteorología.
meter ['miːtə*] n (instrument) contador m; (US) = **metre**.
method ['meθəd] n método; ~**ical** [mɪ'θɒdɪkl] a metódico.
Methodist ['meθədɪst] a, n metodista m/f.
meths [meθs], **methylated spirit** ['meθɪleɪtɪd-] n alcohol m metilado o desnaturalizado.
meticulous [me'tɪkjuləs] a meticuloso.

metre, meter (US) ['miːtə*] n metro.
metric ['metrɪk] a métrico.
metronome ['metrənəum] n metrónomo.
metropolis [mɪ'trɒpəlɪs] n metrópoli f.
mettle ['metl] n (spirit) valor m, ánimo; (tone) temple m.
mew [mjuː] vi (cat) maullar.
mews [mjuːz] n: ~ **cottage** casa acondicionada en antiguos establos o cocheras.
Mexican ['meksɪkən] a, n mejicano/a, mexicano/a (AM).
Mexico ['meksɪkəu] n Méjico, México (AM).
mezzanine ['metsəniːn] n entresuelo.
miaow [miː'au] vi maullar.
mice [maɪs] pl of **mouse**.
microbe ['maɪkrəub] n microbio.
micro... [maɪkrəu] pref micro...; ~**film** n microfilm m; ~**phone** n micrófono; ~**processor** n microprocesador m; ~**scope** n microscopio; ~**scopic** ['skɒpɪk] a microscópico; ~**wave** n de microonda.
mid [mɪd] a: **in May** a mediados de mayo; **in ~ afternoon** a media tarde; **in ~ air** en el aire; ~**day** n mediodía m.
middle ['mɪdl] n medio, centro; (half) mitad f; (waist) cintura // a medio; (quantity, size) mediano; ~**-aged** a de mediana edad; **the M~ Ages** npl la Edad Media; ~**-class** a de clase media; **M~ East** n Oriente m Medio; ~**man** n intermediario; ~**name** n segundo nombre.
middling ['mɪdlɪŋ] a mediano.
midge [mɪdʒ] n mosca.
midget ['mɪdʒɪt] n enano // a minúsculo.
Midlands ['mɪdləndz] npl la región central de Inglaterra.
midnight ['mɪdnaɪt] n medianoche f.

midriff ['mɪdrɪf] *n* diafragma *m*.

midst [mɪdst] *n*: **in the ~ of** entre, en medio de.

midsummer [mɪd'sʌmə*] *n*: **a ~ day** un día de pleno verano.

midway [mɪd'weɪ] *a, ad*: **~ (between)** a mitad de camino, a medio camino (entre).

midweek [mɪd'wi:k] *ad* entre semana.

midwife ['mɪdwaɪf], *pl* **-wives** [-waɪvz] *n* comadrona, partera; **~ry** [-wɪfrɪ] *n* partería.

midwinter [mɪd'wɪntə*] *n*: **in ~** en pleno invierno.

might [maɪt] *vb*: **he ~ be there** podría estar allí, puede que está allí; **I ~ as well go** más vale que vaya; **you ~ like to try** podría intentar // *n* fuerza, poder *m*; **~y** a fuerte, poderoso.

migraine ['mi:greɪn] *n* jaqueca.

migrant ['maɪgrənt] *n* (*bird*) ave *f* migratoria; (*person*) emigrante *m/f*; (*fig*) nómada *m/f* // *a* migratorio; (*worker*) emigrante.

migrate [maɪ'greɪt] *vi* emigrar; **migration** [-'greɪʃən] *n* emigración *f*.

mike [maɪk] *n* *abbr* **of microphone** micro.

mild [maɪld] *a* (*character*) pacífico; (*climate*) templado; (*slight*) ligero; (*taste*) suave; (*illness*) benigno, leve.

mildew ['mɪldju:] *n* moho.

mildness ['maɪldnɪs] *n* (*softness*) suavidad *f*; (*gentleness*) dulzura; (*quiet character*) apacibilidad *f*.

mile [maɪl] *n* milla; **~age** *n* número de millas; (*AUT*) kilometraje *m*; **~stone** *n* mojón *m*.

milieu ['mi:ljə:] *n* medio, medio ambiente.

militant ['mɪlɪtnt] *a, n* militante *m/f*.

military ['mɪlɪtərɪ] *n* militar.

militate ['mɪlɪteɪt] *vi*: **to ~ against** militar contra.

militia [mɪ'lɪʃə] *n* milicia.

milk [mɪlk] *n* leche *f* // *vt* (*cow*) ordeñar; (*fig*) chupar; **~man** *n*

lechero; **~ shake** *n* batido de leche; **~y** a lechoso; **M~y Way** *n* Vía Láctea.

mill [mɪl] *n* (*windmill etc*) molino; (*coffee ~*) molinillo; (*factory*) fábrica; (*spinning ~*) hilandería // *vt* moler // *vi* (*also: ~ about*) moverse por todas partes, apiñarse.

millennium [mɪ'lenɪəm], *pl* **~s** *or* **-ia** [-nɪə] *n* milenio, milenario.

miller ['mɪlə*] *n* molinero.

millet ['mɪlɪt] *n* mijo.

milli... ['mɪlɪ] *pref*: **~gram(me)** *n* miligramo; **~litre** *n* mililitro; **~metre** *n* milímetro.

milliner ['mɪlɪnə*] *n* modista de sombreros; **~y** *n* sombrerería.

million ['mɪljən] *n* millón *m*; **a ~ times** un millón de veces; **~aire** *n* millonario.

millstone ['mɪlstəun] *n* piedra de molino.

milometer [maɪ'lɔmɪtə*] *n* cuentakilómetros *m inv*.

mime [maɪm] *n* mímica; (*actor*) mimo // *vt* remedar // *vi* actuar de mimo.

mimic ['mɪmɪk] *n* imitador/a *m/f* // *a* mímico // *vt* remedar, imitar; **~ry** *n* imitación *f*.

min. *abbr* **of minute(s)**; **minimum**.

minaret [mɪnə'ret] *n* alminar *m*.

mince [mɪns] *vt* picar // *vi* (*in walking*) andar con pasos menudos // *n* (*CULIN*) carne *f* picada, picadillo; **~meat** *n* conserva de fruta picada; **~ pie** *n* empanadilla rellena de fruta picada; **mincer** *n* máquina de picar carne.

mind [maɪnd] *n* (*gen*) mente *f*; (*intellect*) inteligencia; (*contrasted with matter*) espíritu // *vt* (*attend to, look after*) ocuparse de, cuidar; (*be careful of*) tener cuidado con; (*object to*): **I don't ~ the noise** no me importa el ruido; **it is on my ~** me preocupa; **to my ~** en mi opinión; **to be out of one's ~** estar fuera de juicio; **never ~!** ¡es igual!;

¡no importa!; (don't worry) ¡no se preocupe!; **to bear sth in ~** tomar o tener algo en cuenta; **to make up one's ~** decidirse; '**~ the step'** cuidado con el escalón; **~ful a:** **~ful of** consciente de; **~less a** estúpido.

mine [main] pron (el) mío/(la) mía etc // a: **this book is ~** este libro es mío // n mina // vt (coal) extraer, explotar; (ship, beach) minar; **~field** n campo de minas; **miner** n minero.

mineral ['minərəl] a mineral // n mineral m; **~s** npl (soft drinks) aguas fpl minerales, gaseosa sg.

minesweeper ['mainswi:pə*] n dragaminas m inv.

mingle ['mingl] vi: **to ~ with** mezclarse con.

mingy ['mindʒi] a (col) tacaño.

miniature ['minitʃə*] a (en) miniatura // n miniatura.

minibus ['minibʌs] n microbús m.

minicab ['minikæb] n microtaxi m.

minim ['minim] n (MUS) blanca.

minimal ['miniml] a mínimo.

minimize ['minimaiz] vt minimizar.

minimum ['miniməm] n, pl **minima** ['minimə] mínimo // a mínimo.

mining ['mainiŋ] n explotación f minera // a minero.

miniskirt ['miniskə:t] n minifalda.

minister ['ministə*] n (POL) ministro; (REL) pastor m // vi **to ~ to** atender; **~ial** [-'tiəriəl] a (POL) ministerial.

ministry ['ministri] n ministerio.

mink [miŋk] n visón m; **~ coat** n abrigo de visón.

minnow ['minou] n pececillo (de agua dulce).

minor ['mainə*] a menor; (unimportant) sin importancia; (inferior) secundario; (MUS) menor // n (LAW) menor m/f de edad.

minority [mai'noriti] n minoría; (age) minoridad f.

minster ['minstə*] n catedral f.

minstrel ['minstrəl] n juglar m.

mint [mint] n (plant) menta, hierbabuena; (sweet) caramelo de menta // vt (coins) acuñar; **the (Royal) M~** la (Real) Casa de la Moneda; **in ~ condition** en perfecto estado.

minuet [minju'et] n minué m.

minus ['mainəs] n (also: **~ sign**) signo de menos // prep menos.

minute ['minit] n minuto; (fig) momento; **~s** npl actas fpl // a [mai'nju:t] diminuto; (search) minucioso; **at the last ~** a última hora.

miracle ['mirəkl] n milagro; **miraculous** [mi'rækjuləs] a milagroso.

mirage ['mira:ʒ] n espejismo.

mirror ['mirə*] n espejo; (in car) retrovisor m // vt reflejar.

mirth [mə:θ] n alegría; (laughter) risa, risas fpl.

misadventure [misəd'ventʃə*] n desgracia, accidente m.

misanthropist [mi'zænθrəpist] n misántropo.

misapprehension ['misæpri-'henʃən] n equivocación f.

misbehave [misbi'heiv] vi portarse mal; **misbehaviour** n mala conducta.

miscalculate [mis'kælkjuleit] vt calcular mal; **miscalculation** ['-'leiʃən] n error m (de cálculo).

miscarriage ['miskæridʒ] n (MED) aborto; (failure) fracaso; **~ of justice** error m judicial.

miscellaneous [misi'leiniəs] a vario(s), diverso(s).

mischance [mis'tʃɑ:ns] n desgracia, mala suerte f.

mischief ['mistʃif] n (naughtiness) travesura; (harm) mal m, daño; (maliciousness) malicia; **mischievous** [-ivəs] a travieso; dañoso; (playful) malicioso.

misconception ['miskən'sepʃən] n concepto erróneo, equivocación f.

misconduct [mɪsˈkɒndʌkt] n mala conducta; **professional** ~ falta profesional.

miscount [mɪsˈkaunt] vt, vi contar mal.

misdeed [mɪsˈdiːd] n delito.

misdemeanour, **misdemeanor** (US) [mɪsdɪˈmiːnəˀ] n delito, ofensa.

misdirect [mɪsdɪˈrekt] vt (person) informar mal; (letter) poner señas incorrectas en.

miser [ˈmaɪzəˀ] n avaro/a.

miserable [ˈmɪzərəbl] a (unhappy) triste, desgraciado; (wretched) miserable; (despicable) despreciable.

miserly [ˈmaɪzəlɪ] a avariento, tacaño.

misery [ˈmɪzərɪ] n (unhappiness) tristeza, sufrimiento; (wretchedness) miseria, desdicha.

misfire [mɪsˈfaɪəˀ] vi fallar.

misfit [ˈmɪsfɪt] n (person) inadaptado/a, desplazado/a.

misfortune [mɪsˈfɔːtʃən] n desgracia.

misgiving(s) [mɪsˈgɪvɪŋ(z)] n(pl) (mistrust) recelo; (apprehension) presentimiento.

misguided [mɪsˈgaɪdɪd] a equivocado.

mishandle [mɪsˈhændl] vt (treat roughly) maltratar; (mismanage) manejar mal.

mishap [ˈmɪshæp] n desgracia, contratiempo.

mishear [mɪsˈhɪəˀ] (irg: like hear) vt oír mal.

misinform [mɪsɪnˈfɔːm] vt informar mal.

misinterpret [mɪsɪnˈtɜːprɪt] vt interpretar mal.

misjudge [mɪsˈdʒʌdʒ] vt juzgar mal.

mislay [mɪsˈleɪ] (irg: like lay) vt extraviar, perder.

mislead [mɪsˈliːd] vt llevar a conclusiones erróneas; ~**ing** a engañoso, erróneo.

mismanage [mɪsˈmænɪdʒ] vt administrar mal; ~**ment** n mala administración f.

misnomer [mɪsˈnəuməˀ] n nombre m inapropiado o equivocado.

misogynist [mɪˈsɒdʒɪnɪst] n misógino.

misplace [mɪsˈpleɪs] vt (lose) extraviar, perder.

misprint [ˈmɪsprɪnt] n errata, error m de imprenta.

mispronounce [mɪsprəˈnauns] vt pronunciar mal.

misread [mɪsˈriːd] (irg: like read) vt leer mal.

misrepresent [mɪsreprɪˈzent] vt falsificar.

miss [mɪs] vt (train etc) perder; (fail to hit) errar, fallar; (regret the absence of): **I ~ him** (yo) le echo de menos o a faltar // n (shot) tiro fallido o perdido; (fig): **that was a near ~** (near accident) faltó poco para que chocáramos; **to ~ out** vt omitir.

Miss [mɪs] n Señorita

missal [ˈmɪsl] n misal m.

misshapen [mɪsˈʃeɪpən] a deforme.

missile [ˈmɪsaɪl] n (AVIAT) misil m; (object thrown) proyectil m.

missing [ˈmɪsɪŋ] a (pupil) ausente; (thing) perdido; (MIL) desaparecido; **to go ~** desaparecer.

mission [ˈmɪʃən] n misión f; ~**ary** n misionero.

misspent [ˈmɪsˈspent] a: **his ~ youth** su juventud disipada.

mist [mɪst] n (light) neblina; (heavy) niebla; (at sea) bruma // vi (also: ~ **over**, ~ **up**) empañarse.

mistake [mɪsˈteɪk] n error m // vt (irg: like take) entender mal, equivocarse sobre; **to ~ A for B** confundir A con B; **mistaken** a (idea etc) equivocado; **to be mistaken** equivocarse, engañarse.

mister [ˈmɪstəˀ] n (col) señor m; see **Mr**.

mistletoe [ˈmɪsltəu] n muérdago.

mistook [mɪsˈtuk] pt of **mistake**.

mistreat [mɪs'triːt] vt maltratar; ~**ment** n maltrato.

mistress ['mɪstrɪs] n (lover) amante f; (of house) señora (de la casa); (in primary school) maestra; (in secondary school) profesora; see **Mrs**.

mistrust [mɪs'trʌst] vt desconfiar de, dudar de.

misty ['mɪstɪ] a nebuloso, brumoso; (day) de niebla; (glasses) empañado.

misunderstand [mɪsʌndə'stænd] (irg: like **understand**) vt, vi entender mal; ~**ing** n malentendido.

misuse [mɪs'juːs] n mal uso; (of power) abuso // vt [mɪs'juːz] abusar de; (funds) malversar.

mitigate ['mɪtɪgeɪt] vt mitigar.

mitre, miter (US) ['maɪtə*] n mitra; (CARPENTRY) inglete m.

mitt(en) ['mɪt(n)] n mitón m.

mix [mɪks] vt (gen) mezclar; (combine) unir // vi mezclarse; (people) llevarse bien // n mezcla; **to ~ up** vt mezclar; (confuse) confundir; ~**ed** a (assorted) variado, surtido; (school etc) mixto; **~ed-up** a (confused) confuso, revuelto; ~**er** n (for food) licuadora; (person) persona sociable; ~**ture** n mezcla; **~up** n confusión f.

moan [məʊn] n gemido // vi gemir; (col: complain): **to ~** (about) quejarse (de).

moat [məʊt] n foso.

mob [mɒb] n multitud f; (pej): **the ~** el populacho // vt acosar.

mobile ['məʊbaɪl] a móvil // n móvil m; ~ **home** n caravana.

mobility [məʊ'bɪlɪtɪ] n movilidad f.

mobilize ['məʊbɪlaɪz] vt movilizar.

moccasin ['mɒkəsɪn] n mocasín m.

mock [mɒk] vt (make ridiculous) ridiculizar; (laugh at) burlarse de // a fingido; ~**ery** n burla; ~**ing** a burlón(ona); ~**up** n maqueta.

mode [məʊd] n modo; (fashion) moda.

model ['mɒdl] n (gen) modelo; (ARCH) maqueta; (person: for fashion, ART) modelo m/f // a modelo // vt modelar // vi servir de modelo; ~ **railway** ferrocarril m de juguete; **to ~ clothes** pasar modelos, ser modelo.

moderate ['mɒdərət] a, n moderado/a // (vb: [-reit]) vi moderarse, calmarse // vt moderar; **moderation** [-'reɪʃən] n moderación f.

modern ['mɒdən] a moderno; ~**ize** vt modernizar.

modest ['mɒdɪst] a modesto; ~**y** n modestia.

modicum ['mɒdɪkəm] n: **a ~ of** un mínimo de.

modification [mɒdɪfɪ'keɪʃən] n modificación f; **modify** ['mɒdɪfaɪ] vt modificar.

modulation [mɒdju'leɪʃən] n modulación f.

mohair ['məʊhɛə*] n moer m.

moist [mɔɪst] a húmedo; ~**en** ['mɔɪsn] vt humedecer; ~**ure** ['mɔɪstʃə*] n humedad f; ~**urizer** ['mɔɪstʃəraɪzə*] n crema hidratante.

molar ['məʊlə*] n muela.

molasses [məʊ'læsɪz] n melaza.

mole [məʊl] n (animal) topo; (spot) lunar m.

molecule ['mɒlɪkjuːl] n molécula.

molehill ['məʊlhɪl] n topera.

molest [məʊ'lɛst] vt importunar.

mollusc ['mɒləsk] n molusco.

mollycoddle ['mɒlɪkɒdl] vt mimar.

molten ['məʊltən] a fundido; (lava) líquido.

moment ['məʊmənt] n momento; ~**ary** a momentáneo; ~**ous** ['-mɛntəs] a trascendental, importante.

momentum [məʊ'mɛntəm] n momento; (fig) ímpetu m; **to gather ~** cobrar velocidad.

monarch ['mɒnək] n monarca m/f; ~**y** n monarquía.

monastery ['mɒnəstəri] n monasterio.

monastic [mə'næstɪk] a monástico.

Monday ['mʌndɪ] n lunes m.

monetary ['mʌnɪtərɪ] a monetario.

money ['mʌnɪ] n dinero; **to make ~** ganar dinero; **~lender** n prestamista m/f; **~ order** n giro.

mongol ['mɒŋgəl] a, n (MED) mongólico.

mongrel ['mʌŋgrəl] n (dog) perro cruzado.

monitor ['mɒnɪtə*] n (SCOL) monitor m; (also: **television ~**) receptor m de control // vt controlar.

monk [mʌŋk] n monje m.

monkey ['mʌŋkɪ] n mono; **~ nut** n cacahuete m; **~ wrench** n llave f inglesa.

mono- [mɒnəʊ] pref: **~chrome** a monocromo.

monocle ['mɒnəkl] n monóculo.

monogram ['mɒnəgræm] n monograma m.

monologue ['mɒnəlɒg] n monólogo.

monopoly [mə'nɒpəlɪ] n monopolio.

monorail ['mɒnəʊreɪl] n monorriel m.

monosyllabic [mɒnəʊsɪ'læbɪk] a monosilábico.

monotone ['mɒnətəʊn] n monotonía; **to speak in a ~** hablar en un solo tono.

monotonous [mə'nɒtənəs] a monótono; **monotony** [-nɪ] n monotonía.

monsoon [mɒn'suːn] n monzón m.

monster ['mɒnstə*] n monstruo.

monstrosity [mɒns'trɒsɪtɪ] n monstruosidad f.

monstrous ['mɒnstrəs] a (huge) enorme; (atrocious) monstruoso.

montage [mɒn'tɑːʒ] n montaje m.

month [mʌnθ] n mes m; **~ly** a mensual // ad mensualmente // n (magazine) revista mensual.

monument ['mɒnjʊmənt] n monumento; **~al** [-'mɛntl] a monumental.

moo [muː] vi mugir.

mood [muːd] n humor m; **to be in a good/bad ~** estar de buen/mal humor; **~y** a (variable) de humor variable; (sullen) melancólico.

moon [muːn] n luna; **~beam** n rayo de luna; **~light** n luz f de la luna; **~lit** a: **a ~lit night** una noche de luna.

moor [mʊə*] n páramo // vt (ship) amarrar // vi echar las amarras.

Moor [mʊə*] n moro/a.

moorings ['mʊərɪŋz] npl (chains) amarras fpl; (place) amarradero m.

Moorish ['mʊərɪʃ] a moro; (architecture) árabe, morisco.

moorland ['mʊələnd] n páramo, brezal m.

moose [muːs] n, pl inv alce m.

mop [mɒp] n fregona; (of hair) greña, melena // vt fregar; **to ~ up** vt limpiar.

mope [məʊp] vi estar o andar deprimido.

moped ['məʊpɛd] n (Brit) ciclomotor m.

moral ['mɒrl] a moral // n moraleja; **~s** npl moralidad f, moral f.

morale [mɒ'rɑːl] n moral f.

morality [mə'rælɪtɪ] n moralidad f.

morass [mə'ræs] n pantano.

morbid ['mɔːbɪd] a (depressed) melancólico; (MED) mórbido; **don't be ~!** ¡no seas morboso!

more [mɔː*] det, ad más; **once ~** otra vez, una vez más; **I want ~** quiero más; **~ dangerous than** más peligroso que; **~ or less** más o menos; **~ than ever** más que nunca.

moreover [mɔː'rəʊvə*] ad además, por otra parte.

morgue [mɔːg] n depósito de cadáveres.

moribund ['mɒrɪbʌnd] a moribundo.

Mormon ['mɔːmən] n mormón/ona m/f.

morning ['mɔːnɪŋ] n (gen) mañana; (early ~) madrugada;

good ~ buenas días; in the ~ por la mañana; 7 o'clock in the ~ las 7 de la mañana; tomorrow ~ mañana por la mañana.
Moroccan [mə'rɔkən] a, n marroquí m/f.
Morocco [mə'rɔkəu] n Marruecos m.
moron ['mɔːrɔn] n imbécil m/f; **~ic** [mə'rɔnɪk] a imbécil.
morose [mə'rəus] a hosco, malhumorado.
morphine ['mɔːfiːn] n morfina.
Morse [mɔːs] n (also: ~ code) (alfabeto) morse.
morsel ['mɔːsl] n (of food) bocado.
mortal ['mɔːtl] a, n mortal m/f; **~ity** [ˈtælɪtɪ] n mortalidad f.
mortar ['mɔːtə*] n argamasa; (mil) mortero.
mortgage ['mɔːgɪdʒ] n hipoteca // vt hipotecar.
mortify ['mɔːtɪfaɪ] vt mortificar, humillar.
mortuary ['mɔːtjuərɪ] n depósito de cadáveres.
mosaic [məu'zeɪɪk] n mosaico.
Moscow ['mɔskəu] n Moscú m.
Moslem ['mɔzləm] a, n = **Muslim**.
mosque [mɔsk] n mezquita.
mosquito [mɔsˈkiːtəu] pl ~es n mosquito.
moss [mɔs] n musgo.
most [məust] det la mayor parte de, la mayoría de // pron la mayor parte, la mayoría // ad el más; (very) muy; the ~ (also: + adjective) el más; ~ of them la mayor parte de ellos; I saw the ~ yo vi el que más; at the (very) ~ a lo sumo, todo lo más; to make the ~ of aprovechar (al máximo); ~ly ad en su mayor parte, principalmente; ~ Interesting book un libro interesantísimo.
MOT n abbr of Ministry of Transport; the ~ (test) inspección (anual) obligatoria de coches y camiones.

motel [mɔu'tɛl] n motel m.
moth [mɔθ] n mariposa nocturna; (clothes ~) polilla; **~ball** n bola de naftalina; **~-eaten** a apolillado.
mother ['mʌðə*] n madre f // a materno // vt (care for) cuidar (como una madre); **~hood** n maternidad f; **~-in-law** n suegra; **~ly** a maternal; **~-of-pearl** n nácar m; **~-to-be** n futura madre; **~ tongue** n lengua materna.
motif [məu'tiːf] n motivo; (theme) tema m.
motion ['məuʃən] n movimiento; (gesture) ademán m, señal f; (at meeting) moción f // vt, vi: to ~ (to) sb to do sth hacer señas a uno para que haga algo; **~less** a inmóvil; **~ picture** n película.
motivated ['məutɪveɪtɪd] a motivado; **motivation** [ˈveɪʃən] n motivación f.
motive ['məutɪv] n motivo // a motor (f: motora, motriz).
motley ['mɔtlɪ] a variado.
motor ['məutə*] n motor m; (col: vehicle) coche m, automóvil m // a motor (f: motora, motriz); **~bike** n moto f; **~boat** n lancha motora; **~car** n coche m, automóvil m; **~cycle** n motocicleta; **cyclist** n motorista m/f; **~ing** n automovilismo; **~ist** n conductor/a m/f, automovilista m/f; **~ oil** n aceite m de coche; **~ racing** n carreras fpl de coches, automovilismo; **~ scooter** n moto f; **~ vehicle** n automóvil m; **~way** n (Brit) autopista.
mottled ['mɔtld] a abigarrado, multicolor.
motto ['mɔtəu] pl ~es n lema m; (watchword) consigna.
mould, mold (US) [məuld] n molde m; (mildew) moho // vt moldear; (fig) formar; **~er** vi (decay) decaer; **~ing** n moldura; **~y** a enmohecido.
moult, molt (US) [məult] vi mudar (la piel/la pluma).

mound [maund] n montón m, montículo.

mount [maunt] n monte m; (horse) montura; (for jewel etc) engaste m; (for picture) marco m // vt montar, subir a // vi (also: ~ up) subirse, montarse.

mountain ['mauntin] n montaña // cpd de montaña; ~**eer** [-'nıə*] n alpinista m/f, montañero/a; ~**eering** [-'nıərıŋ] n alpinismo, montañismo; **to go ~eering** hacer alpinismo; ~**ous** a montañoso; ~**side** n ladera de la montaña.

mourn [mɔːn] vt llorar, lamentar // vi: **to ~ for** llorar la muerte de, lamentarse por; ~**er** n pariente m/f/amigo del difunto; ~**ful** a triste, lúgubre; ~**ing** n luto // cpd (dress) de luto; **in ~ing** de luto.

mouse [maus], pl **mice** n ratón m; ~**trap** n ratonera.

moustache [məs'tɑːʃ] n bigote m.

mousy ['mausı] a (person) tímido; (hair) pardusco.

mouth [mauθ], pl ~**s** [-ðz] n boca; (of river) desembocadura; ~**ful** n bocado; ~ **organ** n armónica; ~**piece** n (of musical instrument) boquilla; (spokesman) portavoz m; ~**wash** n enjuague m; ~**watering** a apetitoso.

movable ['muːvəbl] a movible.

move [muːv] n (movement) movimiento; (in game) jugada; (: turn to play) turno; (change of house) mudanza // vt mover; (emotionally) conmover; (POL: resolution etc) proponer // vi (gen) moverse; (traffic) circular; (also: ~ house) trasladarse, mudarse; **to ~ sb to do sth** mover a uno a hacer algo; **to get ~ on** darse prisa; **to ~ about** vi ir de acá para allá; (travel) viajar; **to ~ along** vi avanzar, adelantarse; **to ~ away** vi alejarse, irse; **to ~ back** vi retroceder; **to ~ forward** vi avanzar // vt adelantar; **to ~ in** vi (to a house) instalarse (en una casa); **to ~ on** vi

ponerse en camino; **to ~ out** vi (of hous) abandonar (una casa); **to ~ up** vi subir; (employee) ser ascendido.

movement ['muːvmənt] n movimiento; (TECH) mecanismo.

movie ['muːvı] n película; **to go to the ~s** ir al cine; ~ **camera** n cámara cinematográfica.

moving ['muːvıŋ] a (emotional) conmovedor(a); (that moves) móvil.

mow [məu], pt **mowed**, pp **mowed** or **mown** vt (grass) cortar; (corn: also: ~ **down**) segar; ~**er** n segadora; (for lawn) cortacéspedes m inv.

M.P. n abbr of **Member of Parliament**.

m.p.h. abbr of **miles per hour**.

Mr ['mıstə*] n: ~ **Smith** (el) Sr. Smith.

Mrs ['mısız] n: ~ **Smith** (la) Sra. Smith.

Ms [mız] n = **Miss** or **Mrs**: ~ **Smith** (la) Sa. Smith.

M.Sc. abbr of **Master of Science**.

much [mʌtʃ] det mucho // ad, n or pron mucho; (before pp) muy; **how ~ is it?** ¿cuánto es?, ¿cuánto cuesta?; **too ~** demasiado; **it's not ~** no es mucho; **as ~ as** tanto como; **however ~ he** tries por mucho que se esfuerce.

muck [mʌk] n (dirt) suciedad f; (fig) porquería; **to ~ about** vi (col) perder el tiempo; (enjoy o.s.) entretenerse; **to ~ up** vt (col: ruin) arruinar, estropear; ~**y** a (dirty) sucio.

mucus ['mjuːkəs] n moco.

mud [mʌd] n barro, lodo.

muddle ['mʌdl] n desorden m, confusión f; (mix-up) embrollo, lío // vt (also: ~ up) embrollar, confundir; **to ~ through** vi salir del paso sin saber cómo.

mud: ~**dy** a fangoso, cubierto de lodo; ~**guard** n guardabarros m inv; ~**pack** n mascarilla (de belleza).

~-slinging n injurias fpl, difamación f.

muff [mʌf] n manguito // vt (chance) desperdiciar; (lines) estropear.

muffin ['mʌfin] n mollete m.

muffle ['mʌfl] vt (sound) amortiguar; (against cold) embozar; **~d** a sordo, apagado.

mufti ['mʌfti] n: **in ~** vestido de paisano.

mug [mʌg] n (cup) taza (alta, sin platillo); (: for beer) jarra; (col: face) jeta; (: fool) bobo // vt (assault) asaltar; **~ging** n asalto.

muggy ['mʌgi] a bochornoso.

mule [mju:l] n mula.

mull [mʌl]: **to ~ over** vt meditar sobre.

mulled [mʌld] a: **~ wine** vino calentado y con especias.

multi... ['mʌlti] pref multi...; **~coloured, ~colored** (US) a multicolor.

multifarious [mʌlti'fɛəriəs] a múltiple.

multiple ['mʌltipl] a, n múltiplo; **~ sclerosis** n esclerosis f múltiple; **~ store** n (cadena de) grandes almacenes.

multiplication [mʌltipli'keiʃən] n multiplicación f; **multiply** ['mʌltiplai] vt multiplicar // vi multiplicarse.

multitude ['mʌltitju:d] n multitud f.

mum [mʌm] n mamá // a: **to keep ~** callarse.

mumble ['mʌmbl] vt, vi hablar entre dientes, refunfuñar.

mummy ['mʌmi] n (mother) mamá, (embalmed) momia.

mumps [mʌmps] n paperas fpl.

munch [mʌntʃ] vt, vi mascar.

mundane [mʌn'dein] a mundano.

municipal [mju:'nisipl] a municipal; **~ity** [-'pæliti] n municipio.

munitions [mju:'niʃənz] npl municiones fpl.

mural ['mjuərl] n (pintura) mural m.

murder ['mə:də*] n asesinato; (in law) homicidio // vt asesinar, matar; (spoil) estropear; **~er** n asesino; **~ess** n asesina; **~ous** a homicida.

murky ['mə:ki] a oscuro; (fig) tenebroso.

murmur ['mə:mə*] n murmullo // vt, vi murmurar.

muscle ['mʌsl] n músculo; (fig: strength) fuerza (muscular); **to ~ in** vi introducirse por fuerza, **muscular** ['mʌskjulə*] a muscular; (person) musculoso.

muse [mju:z] vi meditar // n musa.

museum [mju:'ziəm] n museo.

mushroom ['mʌʃrum] n (gen) seta, hongo, (food) champiñón m // vi (fig) crecer de la noche a la mañana.

mushy ['mʌʃi] a triturado; (pej) sensiblero.

music ['mju:zik] n música; **~al** a melodioso; (person) musical // n (show) (comedia) musical; **~al instrument** n instrumento musical; **~ hall** n teatro de variedades; **~ian** [-'ziʃən] n músico/a.

musket ['mʌskit] n mosquete m.

Muslim ['mʌzlim] a, n musulmán/ana m/f.

muslin ['mʌzlin] n muselina.

mussel ['mʌsl] n mejillón m.

must [mʌst] auxiliary vb (obligation): **I ~ do it** debo hacerlo, tengo que hacerlo; (probability): **he ~ be there by now** ya debe estar allí // n necesidad f; **it's a ~** es imprescindible.

mustard ['mʌstəd] n mostaza.

muster ['mʌstə*] vt juntar, reunir.

mustn't ['mʌsnt] = **must not**.

musty ['mʌsti] a mohoso, que huele a humedad.

mute [mju:t] a, n mudo/a.

muted ['mju:tid] a callado; (MUS) apagado.

mutilate ['mju:tileit] vt mutilar; **mutilation** [-'leiʃən] n mutilación f.

mutinous ['mju:tinəs] a (troops)

amotinado; (*attitude*) rebelde.
mutiny ['mjuːtɪnɪ] *n* motín *m* // *vi* amotinarse.
mutter ['mʌtə*] *vt, vi* murmurar, hablar entre dientes.
mutton ['mʌtn] *n* carne *f* de cordero.
mutual ['mjuːtʃuəl] *a* mutuo; (*gen: shared*) común; **~ly** *ad* mutuamente.
muzzle ['mʌzl] *n* hocico; (*protective device*) bozal *m*; (*of gun*) boca // *vt* amordazar; (*dog*) poner un bozal a.
my [maɪ] *a* mi // *interj*: **~!** ¡caramba!
mynah bird ['maɪnə] *n* mainat *m*.
myopic [maɪ'ɔpɪk] *a* miope.
myself [maɪ'sɛlf] *pron* (*reflexive*) me; (*emphatic*) yo mismo; (*after prep*) mí (mismo).
mysterious [mɪs'tɪərɪəs] *a* misterioso; **mystery** ['mɪstərɪ] *n* misterio.
mystic ['mɪstɪk] *a, n* místico/a; **~al** *a* místico.
mystify ['mɪstɪfaɪ] *vt* (*perplex*) dejar perplejo; (*disconcert*) desconcertar.
myth [mɪθ] *n* mito; **~ical** *a* mítico; **~ological** [mɪθə'lɔdʒɪkl] *a* mitológico; **~ology** [mɪ'θɔlədʒɪ] *n* mitología.

N

nab [næb] *vt* (*col: grab*) coger; (: *catch out*) pillar.
nag [næg] *n* (*pej: horse*) rocín *m* // *vt* (*scold*) regañar; (*annoy*) fastidiar; **~ging** *a* (*doubt*) persistente; (*pain*) continuo // *n* quejas *fpl*.
nail [neɪl] *n* (*human*) uña; (*metal*) clavo // *vt* clavar; (*fig: catch*) coger, pillar; **to ~ sb down to doing sth** comprometer a uno a que haga algo; **~brush** *n* cepillo para las

uñas; **~file** *n* lima para las uñas; **~ polish** *n* esmalte *m* o laca para las uñas; **~ scissors** *npl* tijeras *fpl* para las uñas.
naïve [naɪ'iːv] *a* ingenuo; (*simple*) sencillo.
naked ['neɪkɪd] *a* (*nude*) desnudo; (*fig*) inerme, indefenso; (*flame*) expuesto al aire; **~ness** *n* desnudez *f*.
name [neɪm] *n* (*gen*) nombre *m*; (*surname*) apellido; (*reputation*) fama, renombre *m* // *vt* (*child*) poner nombre a; (*criminal*) dar el nombre de; (*appoint*) nombrar; **by ~ de nombre**; (*maiden*) **~ nombre de soltera**; **in the ~ of** en nombre de; **what's your ~?** ¿cómo se llama?; **to give one's ~ and address** dar las señas; **~less** *a* anónimo, sin nombre; **~ly** *ad* a saber; **~sake** *n* tocayo/a.
nanny ['nænɪ] *n* niñera; **~ goat** *n* cabra.
nap [næp] *n* (*sleep*) sueñecito, siesta.
napalm ['neɪpɑːm] *n* nápalm *m*.
nape [neɪp] *n*: **the ~ of the neck** la nuca, el cogote.
napkin ['næpkɪn] *n* (*also*: table ~) servilleta; (*Brit: for baby*) pañal *m*.
nappy ['næpɪ] *n* pañal *m*; **~ liner** *n* gasa; **~ rash** *n* prurito.
narcissus [nɑː'sɪsəs], *pl* **-si** [-saɪ] *n* narciso.
narcotic [nɑː'kɔtɪk] *a, n* narcótico.
narrate [nə'reɪt] *vt* narrar, contar; **narrative** ['nærətɪv] *n* narrativa // *a* narrativo; **narrator** *n* narrador/a *m/f*.
narrow ['nærəu] *a* estrecho, angosto; (*fig*) de miras estrechas, intolerante // *vi* estrecharse, angostarse; (*diminish*) reducirse; **to ~ down the possibilities** to reducir las posibilidades a; **~ly** *ad* (*miss*) por poco; **~-minded** *a* de miras estrechas.
nasal ['neɪzl] *a* nasal.
nastiness ['nɑːstɪnɪs] *n* (*malice*)

malevolencia; (*rudeness*) grosería.

nasty ['nɑːsti] *a* (*unpleasant:*
remark) feo, horrible; (: *person*)
antipático; (*malicious*) rencoroso;
(*rude*) grosero; (*revolting:* taste,
smell) asqueroso, repugnante;
(*wound, disease etc*) peligroso,
grave.

nation ['neɪʃən] *n* nación f.

national ['næʃənl] *a, n* nacional
m/f; ~**ism** *n* nacionalismo; ~**ist** *a,
n* nacionalista *m/f*; ~**ity** [-'nælɪtɪ] *n*
nacionalidad f; ~**ization** [-aɪ'zeɪʃən]
n nacionalización f; ~**ize** *vt*
nacionalizar; ~**ly** *ad* (*nationwide*)
en escala nacional; (*as a nation*)
nacionalmente, como nación.

nationwide ['neɪʃənwaɪd] *a* en
escala o a nivel nacional.

native ['neɪtɪv] *n* (*local inhabitant*)
natural *m/f*, nacional *m/f*; (*in
colonies*) indígena *m/f*, nativo/a //
a (*indigenous*) indígena; (*of one's
birth*) natal; (*innate*) natural,
innato.

NATO ['neɪtəu] *n abbr of* North
Atlantic Treaty Organization
OTAN (Organización del Tratado
del Atlántico del Norte).

natter ['nætə*] *vi* charlar.

natural ['nætʃrəl] *a* natural;
(*unaffected manner*) infectado sin
afectación; ~**ist** *n* naturalista *m/f*;
~**ize** *vt:* **to become** ~**ized** (*person*)
naturalizarse; (*plant*) aclimatarse;
~**ly** *ad* naturalmente; (*of course*)
desde luego, por supuesto;
(*instinctively*) por instinto, por
naturaleza; ~**ness** *n* naturalidad f.

nature ['neɪtʃə*] *n* naturaleza;
(*group, sort*) género, clase f;
(*character*) carácter *m*, genio; **by** ~
por *o* de naturaleza.

naughty ['nɔːtɪ] *a* (*child*) travieso;
(*story, film*) verde, escabroso.

nausea ['nɔːsɪə] *n* náusea; nauseate
[-sɪeɪt] *vt* dar náuseas a; (*fig*) dar
asco a; **nauseating** [-sɪeɪtɪŋ] *a*
nauseabundo; (*fig*) asqueroso.

nautical ['nɔːtɪkl] *a* náutico,

marítimo; (*mile*) marino.

naval ['neɪvl] *a* naval, de marina; ~
officer *n* oficial *m/f* de marina.

nave [neɪv] *n* nave f.

navel ['neɪvl] *n* ombligo.

navigable ['nævɪgəbl] *a* navegable.

navigate ['nævɪgeɪt] *vt* (*guide*)
gobernar; (*sail along*) navegar por;
(*fig*) guiar // *vi* navegar; **navigation**
[-'geɪʃən] *n* (*action*) navegación f;
(*science*) navegación f; **navigator** *n*
navegador/a *m/f*, navegante *m/f*.

navvy ['nævɪ] *n* peón *m* caminero.

navy ['neɪvɪ] *n* marina de guerra;
(*ships*) armada, flota; ~**(-blue)** *a*
azul marino.

Nazi ['nɑːtsɪ] *n* nazi *m/f*; **nazism** *n*
nazismo.

neap tide [niːp-] *n* marea muerta.

near [nɪə*] *a* (*place*) cercano,
vecino; (*time*) próximo; (*relation*)
estrecho, íntimo // *ad* cerca // *prep*
(*also:* ~ **to**) (*space*) cerca de, junto
a; (*time*) cerca de, casi // *vt*
acercarse a, aproximarse a; ~**by**
[nɪə'baɪ] *a* cercano, próximo // *ad*
cerca; N~ **East** *n* Cercano Oriente
m; ~**ly** *ad* casi, por poco; **I** ~**ly fell**
por poco me caigo; ~ **miss** *n* tiro
cercano, fallo por poco; ~**ness** *n*
proximidad f,
cercanía; (*relationship*) intimidad f;
~**side** *n* (*aut in Britain*) lado
izquierdo; (: *in Spain*) lado derecho;
~**sighted** *a* miope, corto de vista.

neat [niːt] *a* (*place*) bien arreglado *o*
cuidado; (*person*) pulcro, esmerado;
(*skilful*) diestro; (: *plan*) hábil,
ingenioso; (*spirits*) solo.

nebulous ['nebjuləs] *a* nebuloso,
(*fig*) vago, confuso.

necessarily ['nesɪsrɪlɪ] *ad* nece-
sariamente.

necessary ['nesɪsrɪ] *a* necesario,
preciso; **he did all that was** ~ hizo
todo lo necesario.

necessitate [nɪ'sesɪteɪt] *vt*
necesitar, exigir.

necessity [nɪ'sesɪtɪ] *n* (*thing
needed*) necesidad f, requisito;
(*compelling circumstances*) la

necesidad; **necessities** npl artículos mpl de primera necesidad.

neck [nɛk] n (ANAT) cuello; (of animal) pescuezo // vi besuquearse, abrazarse; **~ and ~** parejos; **to stick one's ~ out** arriesgarse.

necklace ['nɛklɪs] n collar m.

neckline ['nɛklaɪn] n escote m.

necktie ['nɛktaɪ] n corbata.

née [neɪ] a: **~ Scott** de soltera Scott.

need [niːd] n (lack) escasez f, falta; (necessity) necesidad f; (thing needed) requisito, necesidad f // vt (require) necesitar; **I ~ to do it** tengo que o debo hacerlo, hay que hacerlo; **you don't ~ to go** no hace falta que vayas.

needle ['niːdl] n aguja // vt (fig: fam) picar, fastidiar.

needless ['niːdlɪs] a innecesario, inútil; **~ to say** huelga decir que.

needlework ['niːdlwɔːk] n (activity) costura, labor f de aguja.

needy ['niːdɪ] a necesitado.

negation [nɪ'geɪʃən] n negación f.

negative ['nɛgətɪv] n (PHOT) negativo; (answer) negativa // a negativo.

neglect [nɪ'glɛkt] vt (one's duty) faltar a, no cumplir con; (child) descuidar, desatender // n (gen) negligencia, abandono; (personal) dejadez f; (of duty) incumplimiento.

negligee ['nɛglɪʒeɪ] n (nightdress) salto de cama; (housecoat) bata.

negligence ['nɛglɪdʒəns] n negligencia, descuido; **negligent** [-ənt] a (careless) descuidado, negligente; (forgetful) olvidadizo.

negligible ['nɛglɪdʒɪbl] a insignificante, despreciable.

negotiable [nɪ'gəuʃɪəbl] a (cheque) negociable; (road) transitable.

negotiate [nɪ'gəuʃɪeɪt] vi negociar // vt (treaty) negociar; (transaction) gestionar, tramitar; (obstacle) franquear; **negotiation** [-'eɪʃən] n negociación f, gestión f; **negotiator** n negociador/a m/f.

Negress ['niːgrɪs] n negra.

Negro ['niːgrəu] a, n negro.

neigh [neɪ] n relincho // vi relinchar.

neighbour, neighbor (US) ['neɪbə*] n vecino/a; **~hood** n (place) vecindad f, barrio; (people) vecindario; **~ing** a vecino; **~ly** a amistoso, de buen vecino.

neither ['naɪðə*] a ni // conj: **I didn't move and ~ did John** no me he movido, ni Juan tampoco // pron ninguno // ad: **~ good nor bad** ni bueno ni malo.

neo... [niːəu] pref neo-.

neon ['niːɔn] n neón m; **~ light** n lámpara de neón.

nephew ['nɛvjuː] n sobrino.

nerve [nəːv] n (ANAT) nervio; (courage) valor m; (impudence) descaro, frescura; **~-racking** a que crispa los nervios; **~s** npl (fig: anxiety) nerviosidad f, nerviosismo.

nervous ['nəːvəs] a (anxious, ANAT) nervioso; (timid) tímido, miedoso; **~ breakdown** n crisis f nerviosa; **~ly** ad nerviosamente; tímidamente; **~ness** n nerviosidad f, nerviosismo; timidez f.

nest [nɛst] n (of bird) nido; (of wasp) avispero // vi anidar.

nestle ['nɛsl] vi: **to ~ up to sb** arrimarse a uno.

net [nɛt] n (gen) red f; (fig) trampa // a (COMM) neto, líquido // vt coger con red; (SPORT) marcar; **~ball** n básquet m.

Netherlands ['nɛðələndz] npl: **the ~** los Países Bajos.

nett [nɛt] a = **net**.

netting ['nɛtɪŋ] n red f, redes fpl.

nettle ['nɛtl] n ortiga.

network ['nɛtwɔːk] n red f.

neurosis [njuə'rəusɪs], pl **-ses** [-siːz] n neurosis f; **neurotic** [-'rɔtɪk] a, n neurótico/a.

neuter ['njuːtə*] a (sexless) castrado, sin sexo; (LING) neutro // vt castrar, capar.

neutral ['njuːtrəl] a (person) neutral; (colour etc, ELEC) neutro // n

n (*AUT*) punto muerto; ~ity
['træliti] *n* neutralidad *f*.

neutron ['nju:trɔn] *n* neutrón *m*; ~
bomb *n* bomba de neutrones.

never ['nevə*] *ad* nunca, jamás; I ~
went no fui nunca; ~ **in my life**
jamás en la vida; ~~-**ending** *a*
interminable, sin fin; ~**theless**
[nevəðə'les] *ad* sin embargo, no
obstante.

new [nju:] *a* (*brand* ~) nuevo;
(*recent*) reciente; (*different*) nuevo,
distinto; (*inexperienced*) tierno,
nuevo; ~**born** *a* recién
nacido; ~**comer** ['nju:kʌmə*] *n* recién
venido *o* llegado; ~**ly** *ad* nuevamente, recién; ~ **moon** *n* luna
nueva; ~**ness** *n* novedad *f*, (*fig*)
inexperiencia.

news [nju:z] *n* noticias *fpl*; **a piece
of** ~ una noticia, the ~ (*RADIO, TV*)
las noticias *fpl*, telediario; ~ **agency**
n agencia de noticias; ~**agent** *n*
vendedor *m/f* de periódicos;
~**caster** *n* presentador *a m/f* de
noticias; ~ **flash** *n* noticia de última
hora; ~**letter** *n* hoja informativa,
boletín *m*; ~**paper** *n* periódico,
diario; ~**reel** *n* noticiario; ~ **stand**
n quiosco *o* puesto de periódicos.

New Year ['nju:'jɪə*] *n* Año Nuevo;
~**'s Day** *n* Día *m* de Año Nuevo;
~**'s Eve** *n* Nochevieja.

New York ['nju:'jɔ:k] *n* Nueva
York.

New Zealand [nju:'zi:lənd] *n*
Nueva Zelanda.

next [nekst] *a* (*in space*) próximo,
vecino; (*in time*) próximo, siguiente
// *ad* (*place*) después; (*time*)
después luego; ~ **time** la próxima
vez; ~ **year** el año próximo *o* que
viene; ~ **door** *ad* en la casa de al
lado // *a* vecino, de al lado; ~~-**of-
kin** *n* pariente(s) *m(pl)* cercano(s);
~ **to** *prep* junto a, al lado de.

N.H.S. *n abbr of* **National
Health Service.**

nib [nib] *n* plumilla.

nibble ['nibl] *vt* mordisquear,
mordiscar; (*ZOOL*) roer.

nice [nais] *a* (*likeable*) simpático,
majo; (*kind*) amable; (*pleasant*)
agradable; (*attractive*) bonito,
mono; (*subtle*) fino, preciso;
~~-**looking** *a* atractivo, guapo; ~-**ly**
ad amablemente, bien.

niche [ni:ʃ] *n* nicho.

nick [nik] *n* (*wound*) rasguño; (*cut,
indentation*) mella, muesca // *vt*
(*col*) birlar, robar; **in the** ~ **of time**
a última hora.

nickel ['nikl] *n* níquel *m*.

nickname ['nikneim] *n* apodo,
mote *m* // *vt* apodar.

nicotine ['nikəti:n] *n* nicotina.

niece [ni:s] *n* sobrina.

Nigeria [nai'dʒiəriə] *n* Nigeria; ~**n**
a, n nigeriano/a.

niggardly ['nigədli] *a* (*person*)
avaro, tacaño; (*amount*) miserable.

niggling ['niglin] *a* (*trifling*) nimio,
insignificante; (*annoying*) molesto.

night [nait] *n* (*gen*) noche *f*;
(*evening*) tarde *f*; **last** ~ anoche;
the ~ **before last** anteanoche; **good
~!** ¡buenas noches!; **at** *o* **by** ~ de
noche, por la noche; ~**cap** *n* (*drink*)
resopón *m*; ~**club** *n* cabaret *m*;
~**dress** *n* camisón *m*; ~**fall** *n*
anochecer *m*; ~**gown, ~ie** ['naiti] *n* camisón
m.

nightingale ['naitingeil] *n*
ruiseñor *m*.

nightly ['naitli] *a* de noche,
nocturno // *ad* todas las noches,
cada noche.

night: ~**mare** *n* pesadilla; ~
school *n* clase(s) *f(pl)* nocturno(s);
~ **shift** *n* turno nocturno *o* de
noche; ~**time** *n* noche *f*; ~
watchman *n* sereno.

nil [nil] *n* cero, nada.

nimble ['nimbl] *a* (*agile*) ágil,
ligero; (*skilful*) diestro.

nine [nain] *num* nueve; ~**teen** *num*
diecinueve, diez y nueve; ~**ty** *num*
noventa.

ninth [nainθ] *a* noveno.

nip [nɪp] *vt* (*pinch*) pellizcar; (*bite*) morder // *n* (*drink*) trago, gota.

nipple ['nɪpl] *n* (ANAT) pezón *m*; (*of bottle*) tetilla; (TECH) boquilla, manguito.

nippy ['nɪpɪ] *a* (*person*) ágil, rápido; (*taste*) picante.

nitrate ['naɪtreɪt] *n* nitrato.

nitrogen ['naɪtrədʒən] *n* nitrógeno.

no [nəʊ] *ad* no // *a* ninguno, no ... alguno // *n* no.

nobility [nəʊ'bɪlɪtɪ] *n* nobleza.

noble ['nəʊbl] *a* (*person*) noble; (*title*) de nobleza; (*generous*) noble; **~man** *n* noble *m*, aristócrata *m*.

nobody ['nəʊbədɪ] *pron* nadie.

nod [nɒd] *vi* saludar con la cabeza; (*in agreement*) decir que sí con la cabeza; (*doze*) cabecear // *vt* inclinar // *n* inclinación *f* de cabeza; **to ~ off** *vi* cabecear.

noise [nɔɪz] *n* ruido; (*din*) escándalo, estrépito; **noisily** *ad* ruidosamente; **noisy** *a* (*gen*) ruidoso; (*child*) escandaloso.

nomad ['nəʊmæd] *n* nómada *m/f*; **~ic** [-'mædɪk] *a* nómada.

nominal ['nɒmɪnl] *a* nominal.

nominate ['nɒmɪneɪt] *vt* (*propose*) proponer; (*appoint*) nombrar; **nomination** [-'neɪʃən] *n* propuesta; nombramiento.

nominee [nɒmɪ'niː] *n* candidato/a.

non... [nɒn] *pref* no, des..., in...; **~alcoholic** *a* no alcohólico; **~aligned** *a* no alineado; **~committal** *a* (*reserved*) reservado; (*uncommitted*) evasivo; **~conformist** *a* no conformista; **~descript** [nɒndɪs'krɪpt] *a* indeterminado; (*pej*) mediocre.

none [nʌn] *pron* (*person*) nadie; (*thing*) ninguno, nada // *a* de ninguna manera.

nonentity [nɒ'nentɪtɪ] *n* cero a la izquierda, nulidad *f*.

nonetheless [nʌnðə'les] *ad* sin embargo, no obstante.

non: **~fiction** *n* literatura no novelesca; **~plussed** *a* perplejo.

nonsense ['nɒnsəns] *n* tonterías *fpl*, disparates *fpl*.

non-stop ['nɒn'stɒp] *a* continuo; (RAIL) directo // *ad* sin parar.

noodles ['nuːdlz] *npl* tallarines *mpl*.

nook [nʊk] *n* rincón *m*; **~s and crannies** escondrijos *mpl*.

noon [nuːn] *n* mediodía *m*.

no-one ['nəʊwʌn] *pron* = **nobody**.

noose [nuːs] *n* lazo corredizo; (*hangman's*) dogal *m*.

nor [nɔː*] *conj* = **neither** // *ad see* **neither**.

norm [nɔːm] *n* norma.

normal ['nɔːml] *a* (*usual*) normal; (*ordinary*) corriente, regular; **~ly** *ad* normalmente.

north [nɔːθ] *n* norte *m* // *a* del norte, norteño // *ad* al o hacia el norte; **N~ America** *n* América del Norte; **~east** *n* nor(d)este *m*; **~ern** ['nɔːðən] *a* norteño, del norte; **N~ern Ireland** *n* Irlanda del Norte; **N~ Pole** *n* Polo Norte; **N~ Sea** *n* Mar *m* del Norte; **~ward(s)** ['nɔːθwəd(z)] *ad* hacia el norte; **~west** *n* nor(d)oeste *m*.

Norway ['nɔːweɪ] *n* Noruega; **Norwegian** [-'wiːdʒən] *a, n* noruego/a.

nose [nəʊz] *n* (ANAT) nariz *f*; (ZOOL) hocico; (*sense of smell*) olfato // *vi*: **to ~ about** curiosear; **~bleed** *n* hemorragia nasal; **~dive** *n* (*deliberate*) picado vertical; (*involuntary*) caída de narices; **~y** *a* curioso, fisgón(ona).

nostalgia [nɒs'tældʒɪə] *n* nostalgia; **nostalgic** *a* nostálgico.

nostril ['nɒstrɪl] *n* ventana de la nariz; **~s** *npl* narices *fpl*.

nosy ['nəʊzɪ] *a* = **nosey**.

not [nɒt] *ad* no; **~ at all** no ... en absoluto; **~ that...** no es que...; **~ yet** todavía no; **~ now** ahora no; **why ~?** ¿por qué no?

notable ['nəʊtəbl] *a* notable.

notary ['nəʊtərɪ] *n* notario.

notch [nɒtʃ] *n* muesca, corte *m*.

note [nəʊt] *n* (MUS) nota; (*banknote*)

billete m; (letter) nota, carta; (record) nota, apunte m; (fame) importancia, renombre m; (tone) tono // vt (observe) notar, observar; (write down) apuntar, anotar; ~book n libreta, cuaderno; ~case n cartera, billetero; ~d ['nəʊtid] a célebre, conocido; ~paper n papel m para cartas.

nothing ['nʌθɪŋ] n nada; (zero) cero; for ~ (free) gratis, sin pago; (in vain) en balde.

notice ['nəʊtis] n (announcement) anuncio; (attention) atención f, interés n; (warning) aviso; (dismissal) despido; (resignation) dimisión f; (period of time) plazo // vt (observe) notar, observar; to take ~ of tomar nota de, prestar atención a; at short ~ a corto plazo, con poco anticipación; until further ~ hasta nuevo aviso; ~able a evidente, obvio; ~ board n (Brit) tablón m de anuncios.

notification [nəʊtɪfɪˈkeɪʃən] n aviso; **notify** ['nəʊtɪfaɪ] vt avisar, notificar.

notion ['nəʊʃən] n noción f, concepto; (opinion) opinión f.

notorious [nəʊˈtɔːrɪəs] a notorio, célebre.

notwithstanding [nɒtwɪθˈstændɪŋ] ad no obstante, sin embargo; ~ this a pesar de esto.

nougat ['nuːgɑː] n turrón m.

nought [nɔːt] n cero.

noun [naʊn] n nombre m, sustantivo.

nourish ['nʌrɪʃ] vt nutrir, alimentar; (fig) fomentar, nutrir; ~ing a nutritivo, rico; ~ment n alimento, sustento.

novel ['nɒvl] n novela // a (new) nuevo, original; (unexpected) insólito; ~ist n novelista m/f; ~ty n novedad f.

November [nəʊˈvɛmbə*] n noviembre m.

novice ['nɒvɪs] n principiante m/f, novato/a; (REL) novicio/a.

now [naʊ] ad (at the present time) ahora; (these days) actualmente, hoy día; right ~ ahora mismo; ~ and then, ~ and again de vez en cuando; from ~ on de ahora en adelante; ~adays ['naʊədeɪz] ad hoy (en) día, actualmente.

nowhere ['nəʊwɛə*] ad (direction) a ninguna parte; (location) en ninguna parte.

nozzle ['nɒzl] n (gen) boquilla; (TECH) tobera, inyector m.

nuance ['njuːɑːns] n matiz m.

nuclear ['njuːklɪə*] a nuclear.

nucleus ['njuːklɪəs], pl -lei [-laɪ] n núcleo.

nude [njuːd] a, n desnudo/a; in the ~ desnudo.

nudge [nʌdʒ] vt dar un codazo a.

nudist ['njuːdɪst] n nudista m/f.

nudity ['njuːdɪtɪ] n desnudez f.

nuisance ['njuːsns] n molestia; fastidio; (person) pesado, latoso; what a ~! ¡qué lata!

null [nʌl] a: ~ and void nulo y sin efecto; ~ify ['nʌlɪfaɪ] vt anular, invalidar.

numb [nʌm] a entumecido, (fig) insensible // vt entumecer, entorpecer.

number ['nʌmbə*] n número; (numeral) número, cifra // vt (pages etc) numerar, poner número a; (amount to) sumar, ascender a; to be ~ed among figurar entre; a ~ of varios, algunos; they were ten in ~ eran diez; ~ plate n placa de matrícula.

numbness ['nʌmnɪs] n entumecimiento; (fig) insensibilidad f.

numeral ['njuːmərəl] n número, cifra.

numerical ['njuːˈmɛrɪkl] a numérico.

numerous ['njuːmərəs] a numeroso, muchos.

nun [nʌn] n monja, religiosa.

nurse [nɜːs] n enfermero/a; (nanny) niñera // vt (patient) cuidar, atender; (baby) criar, amamantar;

(fig) guardar; **wet ~** nodriza.
nursery ['nɜːsərɪ] *n (institution)*
guardería infantil; *(room)* cuarto de
los niños; *(for plants)* criadero,
semillero; **~ rhyme** *n* canción *f*
infantil; **~ school** *n* parvulario,
escuela de párvulos; **~ slope** *n (SKI)*
cuesta para principiantes.
nursing ['nɜːsɪŋ] *n (profession)*
profesión *f* de enfermera; *(care)*
asistencia, cuidado; **~ home** *n*
clínica de reposo.
nut [nʌt] *n (TECH)* tuerca; *(BOT)* nuez
f; **~s** *a (col)* loco; **~case** *n (col)*
loco/a, chalado/a; **~crackers** *npl*
cascanueces *m inv;* **~meg**
['nʌtmeg] *n* nuez *f* moscada.
nutrient ['njuːtrɪənt] *n* nutrimento.
nutrition [njuːˈtrɪʃən] *n* nutrición *f,*
alimentación *f;* **nutritious** [-ʃəs] *a*
nutritivo, rico.
nutshell ['nʌtʃɛl] *n* cáscara de nuez;
in a ~ en resumidas cuentas.
nylon ['naɪlɒn] *n* nilón *m // a* de
nilón; **~s** *npl* medias *fpl* (de nilón).
nymph [nɪmf] *n* ninfa.

O

oaf [əuf] *n* zoquete *m.*
oak [əuk] *n* roble *m // a* de roble.
O.A.P. *abbr of* **old-age
pensioner.**
oar [ɔː*] *n* remo; **oarsman** *n* remero.
oasis [əuˈeɪsɪs], *pl* **-ses** [-siːz] *n* oasis
m.
oath [əuθ] *n* juramento; *(swear
word)* palabrota; **on ~** bajo
juramento.
oatmeal ['əutmiːl] *n* harina de
avena.
oats [əuts] *n* avena.
obedience [əˈbiːdɪəns] *n*
obediencia; **in ~ to** de acuerdo con;
obedient [-ənt] *a* obediente.
obesity [əuˈbiːsɪtɪ] *n* obesidad *f.*
obey [əˈbeɪ] *vt* obedecer; *(instruc-*

tions, regulations) cumplir.
obituary [əˈbɪtjuərɪ] *n* necrología.
object ['ɒbdʒɪkt] *n (gen)* objeto;
(purpose) objeto, propósito; *(LING)*
complemento *// vi* [əbˈdʒɛkt]: **to ~
to** *(attitude)* protestar contra;
(proposal) oponerse a; **I ~!** ¡yo
protesto!; **~ion** [əbˈdʒɛkʃən] *n*
protesta; **I have no ~ion to...** no
tengo inconveniente en que...;
~ionable [əbˈdʒɛkʃənəbl] *a (gen)*
desagradable; *(conduct)* censurable;
~ive *a,* *n* objetivo; **~ivity**
[ɒbdʒɪkˈtɪvɪtɪ] *n* objetividad *f;* **~or** *n*
objetor/a *m/f.*
obligation [ɒblɪˈgeɪʃən] *n* obligación *f; (debt)* deber *m;* **without ~**
sin compromiso.
obligatory [əˈblɪgətərɪ] *a* obligatorio.
oblige [əˈblaɪdʒ] *vt (force)*: **to ~ sb
to do sth** forzar *o* obligar a uno a
hacer algo; *(do a favour for)*
complacer, hacer un favor a; **I
should be ~d if...** le agradecería
que...; **obliging** *a* servicial, atento.
oblique [əˈbliːk] *a* oblicuo; *(allusion)*
indirecto.
obliterate [əˈblɪtəreɪt] *vt* borrar.
oblivion [əˈblɪvɪən] *n* olvido;
oblivious [-ɪəs] *a*: **oblivious of**
inconsciente de.
oblong ['ɒblɒŋ] *a* rectangular *// n*
rectángulo.
obnoxious [əbˈnɒkʃəs] *a* odioso,
detestable; *(smell)* nauseabundo.
oboe ['əubəu] *n* oboe *m.*
obscene [əbˈsiːn] *a* obsceno;
obscenity [-ˈsɛnɪtɪ] *n* obscenidad *f.*
obscure [əbˈskjuə*] *a* oscuro *// vt*
oscurecer; *(hide: sun)* esconder; **obscurity** *n* oscuridad *f.*
obsequious [əbˈsiːkwɪəs] *a* obsequioso.
observance [əbˈzɜːvns] *n* observancia, cumplimiento; *(ritual)* práctica.
observant [əbˈzɜːvnt] *a* obser-
vador(a).
observation [ɒbzəˈveɪʃən] *n*

observación f; (by police etc) vigilancia, (MED) examen m.

observatory [ɔb'zɜ:vətri] n observatorio.

observe [əb'zɜ:v] vt (gen) observar; (rule) cumplir; **~er** n observer, observador/a m/f.

obsess [əb'sɛs] vt obsesionar; **~ion** [əb'sɛʃən] n obsesión f, idea fija; **~ive** a obsesivo, obsesionante.

obsolescence [ɔbsə'lɛsns] n caída en desuso; **obsolete** ['ɔbsəli:t] a (que está) en desuso.

obstacle ['ɔbstəkl] n obstáculo; (nuisance) estorbo; **~ race** n carrera de obstáculos.

obstetrician [ɔbstə'trɪʃən] n obstétrico; **obstetrics** [ɔb'stɛtrɪks] n obstetricia.

obstinate ['ɔbstɪnɪt] a terco, porfiado; (determined) tenaz.

obstruct [əb'strʌkt] vt (block) obstruir; (hinder) estorbar, obstaculizar; **~ion** [əb'strʌkʃən] n obstrucción f; estorbo, obstáculo.

obtain [əb'teɪn] vt (get) obtener; (achieve) conseguir; **~able** a asequible.

obtrusive [əb'tru:sɪv] a (person) importuno, entrometido; (building etc) demasiado visible.

obvious ['ɔbvɪəs] a (clear) obvio, evidente; (unsubtle) poco sutil; **~ly** ad evidentemente, naturalmente.

occasion [ə'keɪʒən] n (gen) oportunidad f, ocasión f; (reason) motivo; (time) ocasión f, vez f; (event) acontecimiento // vt ocasionar, causar; **~al** a de vez en cuando.

occult [ɔ'kʌlt] a (gen) oculto.

occupant ['ɔkjupənt] n (of house) inquilino/a; (of car) ocupante m/f.

occupation [ɔkju'peɪʃən] n (of house) tenencia; (job) trabajo; (: calling) oficio; **unfit for ~** unfit for = inhabitable; **~al hazard** n riesgo profesional.

occupier ['ɔkjupaɪə*] n inquilino/a.

occupy ['ɔkjupaɪ] vt (gen) ocupar;

(house) habitar, vivir en; (time) emplear, pasar; (attention) entretener; **to ~ o.s. with or by doing (as job)** dedicarse a hacer; (to pass time) pasar el tiempo haciendo.

occur [ə'kɜ:*] vi pasar, suceder; **to ~ to sb** ocurrírsele a uno; **it ~s to me that...** se me ocurre que...; **~rence** n (event) acontecimiento; (existence) existencia.

ocean ['əuʃən] n océano; **~-going** a de alta mar; **~ liner** n transatlántico.

o'clock [ə'klɔk] ad: **it is 5 ~** son las 5.

octagonal [ɔk'tægənl] a octagonal.

octane ['ɔktein] n octano.

octave ['ɔktɪv] n octava.

October [ɔk'təubə*] n octubre m.

octopus ['ɔktəpəs] n pulpo.

odd [ɔd] a (strange) extraño, raro; (number) impar; (left over) sobrante, suelto; **60 ~** 60 y pico; **at ~ times** de vez en cuando; **to be the one out** estar de más; **~ity** n rareza; (person) excéntrico; **~-job man** n hombre m que hace de todo; **~ jobs** npl bricolaje m; **~ly** ad curiosamente, extrañamente; **~ments** npl (COMM) restos npl, **~s** npl (in betting) puntos mpl de ventaja; **it makes no ~s** no importa, lo mismo da; **at ~s** reñidos(as).

ode [əud] n oda.

odious ['əudɪəs] a odioso.

odour, odor (US) ['əudə*] n olor m; (perfume) perfume m; **~less** a inodoro.

of [ɔv, əv] prep de; **a friend ~ ours** un amigo nuestro; **3 ~ them** 3 de ellos; **the 5th ~ July** el 5 de julio; **a boy ~ 10** un niño de 10 años; **made ~ wood** hecho de madera.

off [ɔf] a, ad (engine) desconectado; (light) apagado; (tap) cerrado; (food: bad) pasado, malo; (milk) cortado; (cancelled) anulado // prep de; **to be ~ (to leave)** irse, marcharse; **to be 5 km ~** estar a 5 kilómetros; **a day ~** un día libre *o* sin trabajar; **to have an ~ day** tener un día malo; **he had his coat ~** se había quitado el abrigo; **10% ~** (*COMM*) (con el) 10% de descuento; **5 km ~ (the road)** a 5 km de (la carretera); **~ the coast** frente a la costa; **on the ~ chance** por si acaso.

offal ['ɔfl] *n* (*CULIN*) menudencias *fpl*.

off-colour ['ɔf'kʌlə*] *a* (*ill*) indispuesto.

offence, offense (*US*) [ə'fɛns] *n* (*crime*) delito; (*insult*) ofensa; **to take ~ at** ofenderse por.

offend [ə'fɛnd] *vt* (*person*) ofender; **~er** *n* delincuente *m/f*; (*against regulations*) infractor/a *m/f*.

offensive [ə'fɛnsɪv] *a* ofensivo; (*smell etc*) repugnante // *n* (*MIL*) ofensiva.

offer ['ɔfə*] *n* (*gen*) oferta, ofrecimiento; (*proposal*) propuesta // *vt* ofrecer; (*opportunity*) facilitar; **'on ~'** (*COMM*) 'en oferta'; **~ing** *n* ofrenda; **~tory** *n* (*REL*) ofertorio.

offhand [ɔf'hænd] *a* informal // *ad* de improviso.

office ['ɔfɪs] *n* (*place*) oficina; (*room*) despacho; (*position*) carga, oficio; **to take ~** entrar en funciones; **~ block** *n* bloque *m* de oficinas; **~ boy** *n* mozo (de oficina); **~r** *n* (*MIL etc*) oficial *m*; (*of organization*) director *m*; (*also*: **police officer**) agente *m/f* de policía; **~ worker** *n* oficinista *m/f*.

official [ə'fɪʃl] *a* (*authorized*) oficial, autorizado // *n* funcionario, oficial *m*; **~dom** *n* burocracia.

officious [ə'fɪʃəs] *a* oficioso.

offing ['ɔfɪŋ] *n*: **in the ~** (*fig*) en perspectiva.

off: **~-licence** *n* (*Brit*: *shop*) bodega, tienda de vinos y bebidas alcohólicas; **~-peak** *a* de temporada de poca actividad; **~-putting** *a* que desanima; **~-season** *a*, *ad* fuera de temporada.

offset ['ɔfsɛt] (*irg*: *like* **set**) *vt* (*counteract*) contrarrestar, compensar // *n* (*also*: **~ printing**) offset *m*.

offshore [ɔf'ʃɔ:*] *a* (que está) cerca de la costa.

offside ['ɔf'saɪd] *a* (*SPORT*) fuera de juego.

offspring ['ɔfsprɪŋ] *n* descendencia, descendientes *mpl* or *fpl*.

off: **~-stage** *ad* entre bastidores; **~-the-peg** *ad* confeccionado; **~-white** *a* blanco grisáceo.

often ['ɔfn] *ad* a menudo, con frecuencia.

ogle ['əugl] *vt* echar miradas a.

oil [ɔɪl] *n* aceite *m*; (*petroleum*) petróleo // *vt* (*machine*) engrasar; **~can** *n* lata de aceite; **~field** *n* campo petrolífero; **~-fired** *a* que quema aceite combustible; **~ painting** *n* pintura de óleo; **~ refinery** *n* refinería de petróleo; **~ rig** *n* torre *f* de perforación; **~skins** *npl* impermeables *mpl* de hule, chubasquero *sg*; **~ tanker** *n* petrolero; **~ well** *n* pozo (de petróleo); **~y** *a* aceitoso; (*food*) grasiento.

ointment ['ɔɪntmənt] *n* ungüento.

O.K., okay ['əu'keɪ] *excl* O.K., ¡está bien!, ¡vale! // *a* bien // *vt* dar el visto bueno a.

old [əuld] *a* viejo; (*former*) antiguo; **how ~ are you?** ¿cuántos años tienes?, ¿qué edad tienes?; **he's 10 years ~** tiene 10 años; **~er brother** hermano mayor; **~ age** *n* la vejez; **~-age pensioner (O.A.P.)** *n* jubilado/a; **~-fashioned** *a* anticuado, pasado de moda.

olive ['ɔlɪv] *n* (*fruit*) aceituna; (*tree*) olivo // *a* (*also*: **~-green**) verde oliva; **~ oil** *n* aceite *m* de oliva.

Olympic [əu'lɪmpɪk] *a* olímpico; **the ~ Games, the ~s** los Juegos Olímpicos.

omelet(te) ['ɔmlɪt] *n* tortilla (de huevo).

omen ['əumən] *n* presagio.

ominous ['ɔminəs] a de mal
agüero, amenazador(a).

omission [əu'miʃən] n omisión f;
(error) descuido.

omit [əu'mit] vt omitir; (by mistake)
olvidar, descuidar.

on [ɔn] prep en, sobre // ad
(machine) conectado; (light, radio)
encendido; (tap) abierto; **is the
meeting still ~?** ¿todavía hay
reunión?; **when is this film ~?**
¿cuándo van a poner esta película?;
~ the wall en la pared, colgado de
la pared; **~ television** en la
televisión; **~ horseback** a caballo;
~ seeing this al ver esto; **~ arrival**
al llegar; **~ the left** a la izquierda;
~ Friday el viernes; **a week ~
Friday** el viernes en ocho días; **to
have one's coat ~** tener el abrigo
puesto; **to go ~** seguir adelante; **it's
not ~!** ¡eso no se hace!

once [wʌns] ad una vez; (formerly)
antiguamente // conj una vez que;
at ~ en seguida, inmediatamente;
(simultaneously) a la vez; **~ a week**
una vez por semana; **~ more** otra
vez; **~ and for all** de una vez por
todas; **~ upon a time** érase una vez.

oncoming ['ɔnkʌmiŋ] a (traffic)
que viene de frente.

one [wʌn] det, num un, uno, una //
pron uno; (impersonal) se // a (sole)
único; (same) mismo; **this ~** éste;a;
that ~ ése;a, aquél;aquella; **~ by
~** uno por uno; **~ never knows**
nunca se sabe; **~ another** el uno al
otro; **~ness** a (business) individual;
~-man band n un hombre-orquesta;
~self pron uno mismo, (after prep,
also emphatic) sí (mismo;a);
'~-way' 'dirección única'.

ongoing ['ɔngəuiŋ] a continuo.

onion ['ʌnjən] n cebolla.

onlooker ['ɔnlukə*] n espectador;a
m/f.

only ['əunli] ad solamente, sólo // a
único, sólo // conj solamente que,
pero; **an ~ child** un hijo único; **not**

~ ... but also... no sólo ... sino
también... .

onset ['ɔnset] n (beginning)
comienzo m; (attack) ataque m.

onslaught ['ɔnslɔ:t] n ataque m,
embestida.

onto ['ɔntu] prep = **on to**

onus ['əunəs] n responsabilidad f.

onward(s) ['ɔnwəd(z)] ad (move)
(hacia) adelante; **from this time ~**
de ahora en adelante.

onyx ['ɔniks] n ónice m, onyx m.

ooze [u:z] vi rezumar.

opal ['əupl] n ópalo.

opaque [əu'peik] a opaco.

open ['əupn] a abierto; (car)
descubierto; (road, view) despejado;
(meeting) público; (admiration)
manifiesto // vi abrir // vi (flower,
eyes, door, debate) abrirse; (book
etc: commence) comenzar; **to ~ on
to** vt fus (subj: room, door) dar a; **to
~ up** vt abrir; (blocked road)
despejar // vi abrirse, empezar; **in
the ~ (air)** al aire libre; **~ing** n
abertura, comienzo; (opportunity)
oportunidad f; (job) puesto vacante,
vacante f; **~ly** ad abiertamente;
~minded a imparcial; **~necked** a
sin corbata.

opera ['ɔpərə] n ópera; **~ glasses**
npl gemelos mpl; **~ house** n teatro
de la ópera.

operate ['ɔpəreit] vt (machine)
hacer funcionar; (company) dirigir
// vi funcionar; (drug) hacer efecto;
to ~ on sb (MED) operar a uno.

operatic [ɔpə'rætik] a de ópera.

operating ['ɔpəreitiŋ] a: **~ table** n
mesa de operaciones; **~ theatre** n
sala de operaciones.

operation [ɔpə'reiʃən] n (gen)
operación f; (of machine) funcionamiento; **to be in ~** estar en funcionamiento o funcionando; **~al** a
operacional, en buen estado.

operative ['ɔpərətiv] a (measure)
en vigor.

operator ['ɔpəreitə*] n (of
machine) maquinista m/f, operario

(TEL) operador/a m/f, telefonista m/f.

operetta [ɔpəˈrɛtə] n opereta; (in Spain) zarzuela.

ophthalmic [ɔfˈθælmɪk] a oftálmico.

opinion [əˈpɪnjən] n (gen) opinión f; (point of view) parecer m, juicio; ~ated a testarudo; ~ poll n encuesta, sondeo.

opium [ˈəupɪəm] n opio.

opponent [əˈpəunənt] n adversario/a, contrincante m/f.

opportune [ˈɔpətjuːn] a oportuno; **opportunist** [-ˈtjuːnɪst] n oportunista m/f.

opportunity [ɔpəˈtjuːnɪtɪ] n oportunidad f.

oppose [əˈpəuz] vt oponerse a; **to be ~d to sth** oponerse a algo, resistirse a aceptar algo; **opposing** a (side) opuesto, contrario.

opposite [ˈɔpəzɪt] a opuesto; (house etc) de enfrente // ad en frente de // prep en frente de, frente a // n lo contrario.

opposition [ɔpəˈzɪʃən] n oposición f.

oppress [əˈprɛs] vt oprimir; ~ion [əˈprɛʃən] n opresión f; ~ive a opresivo.

opt [ɔpt] vi: **to ~ for** elegir; **to ~ to do** optar por hacer; **to ~ out of** optar por no hacer.

optical [ˈɔptɪkl] a óptico.

optician [ɔpˈtɪʃən] n óptico.

optimism [ˈɔptɪmɪzəm] n optimismo.

optimist [ˈɔptɪmɪst] n optimista m/f; ~ic [-ˈmɪstɪk] a optimista.

optimum [ˈɔptɪməm] a óptimo.

option [ˈɔpʃən] n opción f; **to keep one's ~s open** (fig) mantener las opciones abiertas; ~al a facultativo, discrecional.

opulent [ˈɔpjulənt] a opulento.

or [ɔː*] conj o; (before o, ho) u; (with negative): **he hasn't seen ~ heard anything** no ha visto ni oído nada; ~ **else** si no.

oracle [ˈɔrəkl] n oráculo.

(TEL) oral // n examen m oral.

orange [ˈɔrɪndʒ] n (fruit) naranja // a color naranja.

oration [ɔːˈreɪʃən] n oración f; **orator** [ˈɔrətə*] n orador/a m/f.

orbit [ˈɔːbɪt] n órbita // vt, vi orbitar.

orchard [ˈɔːtʃəd] n huerto.

orchestra [ˈɔːkɪstrə] n orquesta; **orchestral** [ɔːˈkɛstrəl] a orquestal.

orchid [ˈɔːkɪd] n orquídea.

ordain [ɔːˈdeɪn] vt (REL) ordenar, decretar; (decide) mandar.

ordeal [ɔːˈdiːl] n experiencia penosa.

order [ˈɔːdə*] n orden m; (command) orden f; (type, kind) clase f; (state) estado; (COMM) pedido, encargo // vt (also: **put in ~**) arreglar, poner en orden; (COMM) encargar, pedir; (command) mandar, ordenar; **in ~** (of document) en regla; **in ~ to do** para hacer; **to ~ sb to do sth** mandar a uno hacer algo; ~**ly** n (MIL) ordenanza m; (MED) enfermero (auxiliar) // a (room) en orden, ordenado; (person) ordenado.

ordinary [ˈɔːdnrɪ] a corriente, normal; (pej) ordinario, vulgar; **out of the** ~ fuera de lo común.

ordnance [ˈɔːdnəns] n (MIL: unit) artillería; **O~ Survey** n servicio oficial de topografía y cartografía.

ore [ɔː*] n mineral m.

organ [ˈɔːgən] n órgano; ~**ic** [ɔːˈgænɪk] a orgánico.

organism [ˈɔːgənɪzəm] n organismo.

organist [ˈɔːgənɪst] n organista m/f.

organization [ɔːgənaɪˈzeɪʃən] n organización f; **organize** [ˈɔːgənaɪz] vt organizar; **organizer** [ˈɔːgənaɪzə*] n organizador/a m/f.

orgasm [ˈɔːgæzəm] n orgasmo.

orgy [ˈɔːdʒɪ] n orgía.

Orient [ˈɔːrɪənt] n Oriente m; **oriental** [-ˈɛntl] a oriental.

orientate [ˈɔːrɪənteɪt] vt orientar.

origin ['ɒrɪdʒɪn] n origen m; (point of departure) procedencia.

original [ə'rɪdʒɪnl] a original; (first) primero; (earlier) primitivo // n original m; ~ity [-'nælɪtɪ] n originalidad f, ~ly ad (at first) al principio; (with originality) con originalidad.

originate [ə'rɪdʒɪneɪt] vi: to ~ from or in surgir de, tener su origen en.

ornament ['ɔːnəmənt] n adorno; (trinket) chuchería; ~al [-'mentl] a decorativo, de adorno.

ornate [ɔː'neɪt] a muy ornado, vistoso.

ornithologist [ɔːnɪ'θɒlədʒɪst] n ornitólogo; **ornithology** [-dʒɪ] n ornitología.

orphan ['ɔːfn] n huérfano // vt: to be ~ed quedar huérfano; ~age n orfelinato.

orthodox ['ɔːθədɒks] a ortodoxo; ~y n ortodoxia.

orthopaedic, orthopedic (US) [ɔːθə'piːdɪk] a ortopédico; ~s n ortopedia.

oscillate ['ɒsɪleɪt] vi oscilar; (person) vacilar.

ostensibly [ɒs'tensɪblɪ] ad aparentemente.

ostentation [ɒsten'teɪʃən] n ostentación f; pretencioso, aparatoso; (person) ostentativo.

osteopath ['ɒstɪəpæθ] n osteópata m/f.

ostracize ['ɒstrəsaɪz] vt condenar al ostracismo.

ostrich ['ɒstrɪtʃ] n avestruz m.

other ['ʌðə*] a otro; ~ than además de; (in another way) de otra manera que; (apart from) aparte de; ~wise ad, conj de otra manera; (if not) si no.

otter ['ɒtə*] n nutria.

ought [ɔːt] pt ought auxiliary vb: I ~ to do it debería hacerlo; this ~ to have been corrected esto debiera de haberse corregido; he ~ to win (probability) debe o debiera ganar.

ounce [auns] n onza (28.35g).

our ['auə*] a nuestro; ~s pron (el) nuestro/(la) nuestra etc; ~selves pron pl (reflexive, after prep) nosotros, (emphatic) nosotros mismos.

oust [aust] vt desalojar.

out [aut] ad fuera, afuera; (not at home) fuera (de casa); (light, fire) apagado; ~ there allí, allí fuera; he's ~ (absent) no está, ha salido; to be ~ in one's calculations equivocarse (en sus cálculos); to run ~ salir corriendo; ~ loud en alta voz; ~ of (outside) fuera de; (because of: anger etc) por; ~ of petrol sin gasolina; "~ of order" "no funciona"; ~-of-the-way (fig) insólito.

outback ['autbæk] n interior m.

outboard ['autbɔːd] a: ~ motor motor m de fuera de borda.

outbreak ['autbreɪk] n (of war) comienzo; (of disease) epidemia; (of violence etc) arranque m.

outburst ['autbɜːst] n explosión f, arranque m.

outcast ['autkɑːst] n paria m/f.

outcome ['autkʌm] n resultado.

outcry ['autkraɪ] n protesta ruidosa.

outdated [aut'deɪtɪd] a anticuado, fuera de moda.

outdo [aut'duː] vt (irg: like do) vi exceder.

outdoor [aut'dɔː*] a, ~s ad al aire libre.

outer ['autə*] a exterior, externo; ~ space n el espacio.

outfit ['autfit] n equipo; (clothes) traje m; ~ter's n camisería.

outgoing ['autgəuɪŋ] a (character) extrovertido; ~s npl gastos mpl.

outgrow [aut'grəu] (irg: like grow) vt: he has ~n his clothes su ropa le queda pequeña ya.

outing ['autɪŋ] n excursión f, paseo

outlandish [aut'lændɪʃ] a estrafalario.

outlaw ['autlɔː] n proscrito // vt (person) declarar fuera de la ley; (practice) declarar ilegal.

outlay ['autleɪ] n inversión f.

outlet ['autlet] n salida; (of pipe) desagüe m; (for emotion) desahogo; (also: retail ~) lugar m de venta.

outline ['autlaɪn] n (shape) contorno, perfil m; (of plan) trazado; (sketch) esbozo, idea general.

outlive [aut'lɪv] vt sobrevivir.

outlook ['autluk] n perspectiva; (opinion) punto de vista.

outlying ['autlaɪɪŋ] a remoto, aislado.

outmoded [aut'məudɪd] a anticuado, pasado de moda.

outnumber [aut'nʌmbə*] vt exceder en número.

outpatient ['autpeɪʃənt] n paciente m/f de consulta externa.

outpost ['autpəust] n puesto avanzado.

output ['autput] n (volumen m de) producción f, rendimiento.

outrage ['autreɪdʒ] n (scandal) escándalo; (atrocity) atrocidad f // vt ultrajar; ~ous [-'reɪdʒəs] a monstruoso.

outright [aut'raɪt] ad completamente // a ['autraɪt] completo.

outset ['autset] n principio.

outside [aut'saɪd] n exterior m; (surface) superficie f; (aspect) aspecto // a exterior, externo // ad fuera // prep fuera de; (fig) a lo sumo; ~ lane n (AUT: in Britain) carril m de la derecha; ~-left (FOOTBALL) extremo izquierdo; **outsider** n (stranger) extraño, forastero.

outsize ['autsaɪz] a (clothes) de talla grande.

outskirts ['autskəts] npl alrededores mpl, afueras fpl.

outspoken [aut'spəukən] a muy franco.

outstanding [aut'stændɪŋ] a excepcional, destacado; (unfinished) pendiente.

outstay [aut'steɪ] vt: to ~ one's

welcome quedarse más tiempo de lo indicado.

outstretched [aut'stretʃt] a (hand) extendido.

outward ['autwəd] a (sign, appearances) externo; (journey) de ida; ~ly ad por fuera.

outweigh [aut'weɪ] vt pesar más que.

outwit [aut'wɪt] vt ser más listo que, burlar.

oval ['əuvl] a ovalado // n óvalo.

ovary ['əuvərɪ] n ovario.

ovation [əu'veɪʃən] n ovación f.

oven ['ʌvn] n horno; ~proof a refractario.

over ['əuvə*] ad encima, por encima // a (of age) (finished) terminado // prep (por) encima de; (above) sobre; (on the other side of) al otro lado de; (more than) más de; (during) durante; ~ here por aquí; ~ there (por) allí o allá; all ~ (everywhere) por todas partes; ~ and ~ (again) una y otra vez; ~ and above más de; to ask sb ~ invitar a uno; to bend ~ inclinarse.

over... ['əuvə*] pref sobre..., super...; ~abundant a superabundante.

overall ['əuvərɔ:l] a (length) total; (study) de conjunto // ad [əuvər'ɔ:l] en conjunto; ~s npl mono sg o bata sg (de trabajo).

overbalance [əuvə'bæləns] vi perder el equilibrio.

overbearing [əuvə'bɛərɪŋ] a autoritario, imperioso.

overboard ['əuvəbɔ:d] ad (NAUT) por la borda; man ~! ¡hombre al agua!

overcast ['əuvəkɑ:st] a encapotado.

overcharge [əuvə'tʃɑ:dʒ] vt: to ~ sb cobrar un precio excesivo a uno.

overcoat ['əuvəkəut] n abrigo, sobretodo.

overcome [əuvə'kʌm] (irg: like come) vt (gen) vencer; (difficulty) superar.

overcrowded [əuvə'kraudɪd] a

atestado de gente; (country) superpoblado.

overdo [əuvə'du:] (irg: like do) vt exagerar; (overcook) cocer demasiado.

overdose ['əuvədəus] n dosis f excesiva.

overdraft ['əuvədrɑːft] n saldo deudor.

overdrawn [əuvə'drɔːn] a (account) en descubierto.

overdue [əuvə'djuː] a retrasado; (recognition) tardío.

overestimate [əuvər'estimeit] vt sobreestimar.

overexcited [əuvərik'saitid] a sobreexcitar.

overexpose [əuvərik'spəuz] vt (PHOT) sobreexponer.

overflow [əuvə'fləu] vi desbordarse // n ['əuvəfləu] (excess) exceso; (of river) desbordamiento; (also: ~ pipe) (cañería) de desagüe m.

overgrown [əuvə'grəun] a (garden) cubierto de hierba.

overhaul [əuvə'hɔːl] vt revisar, repasar // n ['əuvəhɔːl] revisión f.

overhead [əuvə'hed] ad por lo alto // a ['əuvəhed] de arriba; (railway) elevado, aéreo; ~s npl gastos mpl generales.

overhear [əuvə'hiə*] (irg: like hear) vt oír por casualidad.

overjoyed [əuvə'dʒɔid] a encantado, lleno de alegría.

overland ['əuvəlænd] a, ad por tierra.

overlap [əuvə'læp] vi traslaparse // n ['əuvəlæp] traslapo.

overleaf [əuvə'liːf] ad al dorso.

overload [əuvə'ləud] vt sobrecargar.

overlook [əuvə'luk] vt (have view on) dar a, tener vistas a; (miss: by mistake) pasar por alto; (: deliberately) no hacer caso de; (forgive) perdonar.

overnight [əuvə'nait] ad durante la noche; (fig) de la noche a la

mañana // a de noche; **to stay ~** pasar la noche.

overpass ['əuvəpɑːs] n paso superior.

overpower [əuvə'pauə*] vt dominar; **~ing** a (heat, stench) abrumador(a).

overrate [əuvə'reit] vt sobreestimar.

override [əuvə'raid] (irg: like ride) vt (order, objection) no hacer caso de; **overriding** a predominante.

overrule [əuvə'ruːl] vt (decision) anular; (claim) denegar.

overseas [əuvə'siːz] ad en ultramar; (abroad) en el extranjero // a (trade) exterior; (visitor) extranjero.

overseer ['əuvəsiə*] n (in factory) superintendente m/f; (foreman) capataz m.

overshadow [əuvə'ʃædəu] vt (fig) eclipsar.

overshoot [əuvə'ʃuːt] (irg: like shoot) vt excederse.

oversight ['əuvəsait] n descuido.

oversleep [əuvə'sliːp] (irg: like sleep) vi despertarse (muy) tarde.

overspend [əuvə'spend] (irg: like spend) vi gastar demasiado.

overspill ['əuvəspil] n exceso de población.

overstate [əuvə'steit] vt exagerar; **~ment** n exageración f.

overt [əu'vəːt] a abierto.

overtake [əuvə'teik] (irg: like take) vt sobrepasar; (AUT) adelantar; **overtaking** n (AUT) adelantamiento.

overthrow [əuvə'θrəu] (irg: like throw) vt (government) derrocar.

overtime ['əuvətaim] n horas fpl extraordinarias.

overtone ['əuvətəun] n (fig) sugestión f, alusión f.

overture ['əuvətʃuə*] n (MUS) obertura; (fig) propuesta.

overturn [əuvə'təːn] vt, vi volcar.

overweight [əuvə'weit] a demasiado gordo o pesado.

overwhelm [əuvə'welm] vt aplastar; ~**ing** *a* (*victory, defeat*) arrollador(a); (*desire*) irresistible.

overwork [ɔuvə'wə:k] *n* trabajo excesivo // *vt* hacer trabajar demasiado // *vi* trabajar demasiado.

overwrought [ɔuvə'rɔ:t] *a* sobreexcitado.

owe [əu] *vt* deber; **to ~ sb sth, to ~ sth to sb** deber algo a uno; **owing to** *prep* debido a, por causa de.

owl [aul] *n* búho, lechuza.

own [əun] *vt* tener, poseer // *a* propio; **a room of my ~** una habitación propia; **to get one's ~ back** tomar revancha; **on one's ~** solo, a solas; **to ~ up** *vi* confesar; **~er** *n* dueño; **~ership** *n* posesión *f*.

ox [ɔks], *pl* **~en** ['ɔksn] *n* buey *m*.

oxide ['ɔksaid] *n* óxido.

oxtail ['ɔksteil] *n*: **~ soup** sopa de rabo de buey.

oxygen ['ɔksidʒən] *n* oxígeno; **~ mask/tent** máscara/tienda de oxígeno.

oyster ['ɔistə*] *n* ostra.

oz. *abbr of* **ounce(s).**

ozone ['əuzəun] *n* ozono.

P

p [pi:] *abbr of* **penny, pence.**

p.a. *abbr of* **per annum.**

pa [pɑ:] *n* (*col*) papá *m*.

pace [peis] *n* paso; (*rhythm*) ritmo // *vi*: **to ~ up and down** pasarse de un lado a otro; **to keep ~ with** llevar el mismo paso que; (*events*) mantenerse a la altura de *o* al corriente de; **~maker** *n* (*MED*) regulador *m* cardíaco, marcapasos *m inv*.

pacific [pə'sifik] *a* pacífico // *n*: **the P~** (**Ocean**) el (Océano) Pacífico.

pacifist ['pæsifist] *n* pacifista *m/f*.

pacify ['pæsifai] *vt* (*soothe*) apaciguar; (*country*) pacificar.

pack [pæk] *n* (*gen*) paquete *m*; (*of hounds*) jauría; (*of thieves etc*) manada, bando; (*of cards*) baraja; (*bundle*) fardo; (*back ~*) mochila // *vt* (*wrap*) empaquetar; (*fill*) llenar; (*in suitcase etc*) meter *o* poner en maleta); (*cram*) llenar, atestar; (*fig: meeting etc*) llenar de partidarios; **to ~ sb off** despachar a uno; **~ it in!** (*col*) ¡déjalo!; **to ~ one's case** hacerse la maleta.

package ['pækidʒ] *n* paquete *m*; (*bulky*) bulto; (*also: ~ deal*) acuerdo global; **~ tour** *n* viaje *m* todo incluido.

packet ['pækit] *n* paquete *m*; (*NAUT*) paquebote *m*.

packing ['pækiŋ] *n* embalaje *m*; (*external*) envase *m*; (*internal*) relleno; **~ case** *n* cajón *m* de embalaje.

pact [pækt] *n* pacto.

pad [pæd] *n* (*of paper*) bloc *m*; (*cushion*) cojinete *m*; (*launching ~*) plataforma (de lanzamiento); (*foot*) pata; (*col: flat*) casa // *vi* andar sin hacer ruido; **~ding** *n* relleno; (*fig*) paja.

paddle ['pædl] *n* (*oar*) canalete *m* // *vt* impulsar con canalete // *vi* (*with feet*) chapotear; **~ steamer** *n* vapor *m* de ruedas; **paddling pool** *n* estanque *m* de juegos.

paddock ['pædək] *n* corral *m*.

paddy field ['pædi-] *n* arrozal *m*.

padlock ['pædlɔk] *n* candado // *vt* cerrar con candado.

padre ['pɑ:dri] *n* capellán *m*.

paediatrics, pediatrics (US) [pi:di'ætriks] *n* pediatría.

pagan ['peigən] *a, n* pagano/a.

page [peidʒ] *n* (*of book*) página *m*; (*of newspaper*) plana; (*also: ~ boy*) paje *m* // *vt* (*in hotel etc*) buscar (a uno) llamando su nombre.

pageant ['pædʒənt] *n* (*procession*) desfile *m*; (*show*) espectáculo; **~ry** *n* pompa.

pagoda [pə'gəudə] *n* pagoda.

paid [peid] *pt, pp of* **pay** // *a* (*work*)

remunerado; (official) asalariado; to
put ~ to acabar con.

pail [peil] n cubo, balde m.

pain [pein] n dolor m; to be in ~
sufrir; on ~ of death so pena de
muerte; to take a to do sth
tomarse trabajo en hacer algn; ~ful
a (expression) afligido; ~ful a
doloroso; (difficult) penoso; ~dis-
agreeable) desagradable; ~fully ad
(fig. very) terriblemente; ~killer n
calmante m; ~less a que no causa
dolor; painstaking [ˈpeinzteikiŋ] a
(person) concienzudo, esmerado.

paint [peint] n pintura // vt pintar;
to ~ one's face pintarse (la cara);
to ~ the door blue pintar la puerta
de azul; ~brush n (artist's) pincel
m, (decorator's) brocha; ~er n
pintor/a m/f; ~ing n pintura.

pair [peə*] n (of shoes, gloves etc)
par m; (of people) pareja; a ~ of
scissors unas tijeras; a ~ of
trousers unos pantalones, un
pantalón.

pajamas [pɪˈdʒɑːməz] npl (US)
pijama m.

Pakistan [pɑːkiˈstɑːn] n Paquistán
m ~i a, n paquistaní.

pal [pæl] n (col) compinche m/f,
compañero/a.

palace [ˈpæləs] n palacio m.

palatable [ˈpælitəbl] a sabroso;
(acceptable) aceptable.

palate [ˈpælit] n paladar m.

palaver [pəˈlɑːvə*] n (fuss) lío;
(hindrances) molestias fpl.

pale [peil] a (gen) pálido; (colour)
claro; to grow ~ palidecer; to be
beyond the ~ estar excluido;
~ness n palidez f.

Palestine [ˈpælistain] n Palestina;
Palestinian [-ˈtinian] a, n pales-
tino/a.

palette [ˈpælit] n paleta.

paling [ˈpeiliŋ] n (stake) estaca;
(fence) valla.

palisade [pæliˈseid] n palizada.

pall [pɔːl] n (of smoke) capa (de
humo) // vi perder el sabor.

pallid [ˈpælid] a pálido.

palm [pɑːm] n (gen) palma; (also:
~ tree) palmera, palma // vt: to ~
sth off on sb (col) encajar algo a
uno; ~ist n quiromántico/a; P~
Sunday n Domingo de Ramos.

palpable [ˈpælpəbl] a palpable.

palpitation [pælpiˈteiʃən] n pal
pitación f; to have ~s tener
vahídos.

paltry [ˈpɔːltri] a (insignificant)
baladí; (miserable) vil.

pamper [ˈpæmpə*] vt mimar.

pamphlet [ˈpæmflit] n folleto.

pan [pæn] n (also: sauce~)
cacerola, cazuela; (also: frying ~)
sartén m; (of lavatory) taza // vi
(CINEMA) tomar una vista
panorámica.

panacea [pænəˈsiə] n panacea.

Panama [ˈpænəmɑː] n Panamá m.

pancake [ˈpænkeik] n canapé m.

panda [ˈpændə] n panda m/f; ~ car
n coche m de la policía.

pandemonium [pændiˈməuniəm]
n (noise) estruendo; (mess) caos m.

pander [ˈpændə*] vi: to ~ to
complacer a.

pane [pein] n cristal m.

panel [ˈpænl] n (of wood) panel m;
(of cloth) paño; (RADIO, TV) tablero;
~ling, (US) ~ing n paneles mpl,
entropaños mpl.

pang [pæŋ] n: ~s of conscience
remordimiento sg; ~s of hunger
dolores mpl del hambre.

panic [ˈpænik] n (terror) pánico //
vi aterrarse; ~ky a (person)
asustadizo; ~stricken a preso de
pánico.

pannier [ˈpæniə*] n (on bicycle)
cartera; (on mule etc) alforja.

panorama [pænəˈrɑːmə] n panorama m.

pansy [ˈpænzi] n (BOT) pensamiento,
(col) marición m.

pant [pænt] vi jadear.

panther [ˈpænθə*] n pantera.

panties [ˈpæntiz] npl bragas fpl,
pantis mpl.

pantomime ['pæntəmaɪm] n
revista musical representada en
Navidad, basada en cuentos de hadas.
pantry ['pæntrɪ] n despensa.
pants [pænts] n (woman's) bragas
fpl; (man's) calzoncillos mpl; (US:
trousers) pantalones mpl.
papal ['peɪpəl] a papal.
paper ['peɪpə*] n papel m; (also:
news~) periódico, diario; (study,
article) artículo; (exam) examen m
// a de papel // vt empapelar;
(identity) ~s npl papeles mpl,
documentos mpl; ~back n libro de
bolsillo; ~ bag n saco de papel;
~ clip n grapa; ~ hankie n pañuelo de
papel; ~ money n papel moneda;
~weight n pisapapeles m inv;
~work n trabajo administrativo;
(pej) papeleo.
papier-mâché ['pæpɪeɪ'mæʃeɪ] n
cartón m piedra.
paprika ['pæprɪkə] n pimienta
húngara o roja.
par [pɑ:*] n par f; (GOLF) par m; to
be on a ~ with correr parejas con.
parable ['pærəbl] n parábola.
parachute ['pærəʃu:t] n paracaídas
m inv // vi lanzarse en paracaídas;
~ jump n salto en paracaídas.
parade [pə'reɪd] n desfile m // vt
(gen) recorrer, desfilar por; (show
off) hacer alarde de // vi desfilar;
(MIL) pasar revista.
paradise ['pærədaɪs] n paraíso.
paradox ['pærədɔks] n paradoja;
~ical [-'dɔksɪkl] a paradójico.
paraffin ['pærəfɪn] n: ~ (oil)
petróleo.
paragraph ['pærəgrɑ:f] n párrafo.
parallel ['pærəlel] a en paralelo;
(fig) semejante // n (line) paralela;
(fig, GEO) paralelo.
paralysis [pə'rælɪsɪs] n parálisis f;
paralyze ['pærəlaɪz] vt paralizar.
paramount ['pærəmaunt] a: of ~
importance de la mayor
importancia, primordial.
paranoia [pærə'nɔɪə] n paranoia;
paranoiac a paranoico.

paraphernalia [pærəfə'neɪlɪə] n
(gear) avíos mpl.
paraplegic [pærə'pli:dʒɪk] n
parapléjico.
parasite ['pærəsaɪt] n parásito.
parasol [pærə'sɔl] n sombrilla,
quitasol m.
paratrooper ['pærətru:pə*] n
paracaidista m/f.
parcel ['pɑ:sl] n paquete m // vt
(also: ~ up) empaquetar, embalar.
parch [pɑ:tʃ] vt secar, resecar; ~ed
a (person) muerto de sed.
parchment ['pɑ:tʃmənt] n
pergamino.
pardon ['pɑ:dn] n perdón m; (LAW)
indulto // vt perdonar; indultar; ~!
¡perdone!; ~ me!, I beg your ~!
¡perdone Usted!; (I beg your) ~?
¿cómo?
parent ['pɛərənt] n padre m/madre
f; ~s npl padres mpl; ~al [pə'rentl]
a paternal/maternal.
parenthesis [pə'renθɪsɪs], pl
-theses [-θɪsiːz] n paréntesis m inv.
Paris ['pærɪs] n París.
parish ['pærɪʃ] n parroquia; ~ioner
[pə'rɪʃənə*] n feligrés/esa m/f.
Parisian [pə'rɪzɪən] a, n parisino/a,
parisiense m/f.
parity ['pærɪtɪ] n paridad f, igualdad
f.
park [pɑ:k] n parque m // vt
estacionar // vi aparcar,
estacionarse; ~ing n aparcamiento,
estacionamiento; 'no ~ing'
'prohibido estacionarse'; ~ing lot n
(US) parking m; ~ing meter n
parquímetro.
parliament ['pɑ:ləmənt] n parlamento; (Spanish) Cortes mpl; ~ary
[-'mentəri] a parlamentario.
parlour, parlor (US) ['pɑ:lə*] n
sala de recibo, salón m.
parochial [pə'rəukɪəl] a parroquial;
(pej) de miras estrechas.
parody ['pærədɪ] n parodia // vt
parodiar.
parole [pə'rəul] n: on ~ libre bajo
palabra.

parquet ['pɑ:keɪ] n: ~ **floor(ing)** parquet m.

parrot ['pærət] n loro, papagayo; ~ **fashion** ad mecánicamente.

parry ['pæri] vt parar.

parsimonious [pɑːsɪ'məʊnɪəs] a parco.

parsley ['pɑːslɪ] n perejil m.

parsnip ['pɑːsnɪp] n chirivía.

parson ['pɑːsn] n (parish) párroco; (gen) cura m.

part [pɑːt] n (gen, MUS) parte f; (bit) trozo; (of machine) pieza; (THEATRE etc) papel m; (of serial) entrega f // ad = **partly** // vt dividir; (break) partir // vi (people) separarse; (roads) bifurcarse; (crowd) apartarse; (break) romperse; **to take ~ in** participar o tomar parte en; **to take sth in good ~** tomar algo en buena parte; **to take sb's ~** defender a uno; **for my ~** por mi parte; **for the most ~** en la mayor parte; **to ~ with** vi fus ceder, entregar; (money) pagar; (get rid of) deshacerse de // **in ~ exchange** como parte del pago; **spare ~** pieza de recambio.

partial ['pɑːʃl] a parcial; **to be ~ to** ser aficionado a; ~**ly** ad en parte.

participant [pɑː'tɪsɪpənt] n (in competition) concursante m/f; **participate** [-peɪt] vi: **to participate in** participar en; **participation** [-'peɪʃən] n participación f.

participle ['pɑːtɪsɪpl] n participio.

particle ['pɑːtɪkl] n partícula; (of dust) grano; (fig) pizca.

particular [pə'tɪkjʊlə*] a (special) particular; (concrete) concreto; (given) determinado; (detailed) detallado, minucioso; (fussy) quisquilloso, exigente; ~**s** npl (information) datos mpl, detalles mpl; (details) pormenores mpl; ~**ly** ad especialmente, en particular.

parting ['pɑːtɪŋ] n (act of separation) separación f; (farewell) despedida; (in hair) raya // a de despedida.

partisan [pɑːtɪ'zæn] a, n partidario/a.

partition [pɑː'tɪʃən] n (POL) división f; (wall) tabique m // vt dividir; dividir con tabiques.

partly ['pɑːtlɪ] ad en parte.

partner ['pɑːtnə*] n (COMM) socio/a; (SPORT, at dance) pareja; (spouse) cónyuge m/f; (friend etc) compañero/a // vt acompañar; ~**ship** n (gen) asociación f; (COMM) sociedad f.

partridge ['pɑːtrɪdʒ] n perdiz f.

part-time ['pɑːt'taɪm] a, ad de medio tiempo o media jornada.

party ['pɑːtɪ] n (POL) partido; (celebration) fiesta; (group) grupo; (LAW) parte f, interesado // a POL de partido; (dress etc) de fiesta, de gala.

pass [pɑːs] vt (time, object) pasar; (place) pasar por; (exam) aprobar; (overtake, surpass) rebasar; (approve) aprobar // vi pasar; (SCOL) aprobar, ser aprobado // n (permit) permiso; (membership card) carnet m; (in mountains) puerto, desfiladero; (SPORT) pase m; (STU also) ~ **mark**; **to get a ~ in** aprobar en; ~ **with through** vt fus pasar algo por algo; **to ~ away** vi fallecer; **to ~ by** vi pasar // vt (ignore) pasar por alto; **to ~ for** pasar por; **to ~ out** vi desmayarse; **to ~ up** vt renunciar a; ~**able** a (road) transitable; (work) pasable.

passage ['pæsɪdʒ] n (also: ~**way**) pasillo; (act of passing) tránsito; (fare, in book) pasaje m; (by boat) travesía; (MECH, MED) tubo.

passenger ['pæsɪndʒə*] n pasajero, viajero.

passer-by [pɑːsə'baɪ] n transeúnte m/f.

passing ['pɑːsɪŋ] a (fleeting) pasajero; **in** ~ de paso.

passion ['pæʃən] n pasión f; (anger) cólera; ~**ate** a apasionado; colérico.

passive ['pæsɪv] a (also LING) pasivo.

Passover ['pɑːsəuvə*] n Pascua (de los judíos).

passport ['pɑːspɔːt] n pasaporte m.

password ['pɑːswɜːd] n santo y seña.

past [pɑːst] prep (further than) más allá de; (later than) después de // a pasado; (president etc) ex, antiguo // n el pasado; (antecedents) antecedentes mpl; **he's ~ forty** tiene más de cuarenta años; **for the ~ few/3 days** durante los últimos/3 días; **to run ~** pasar a la carrera por.

pasta ['pæstə] n pastas fpl.

paste [peist] n (gen) pasta; (glue) engrudo // vt (stick) pegar; (glue) engomar.

pastel ['pæstl] a pastel; (painting) al pastel.

pasteurized ['pæstəraizd] a pasteurizado.

pastille ['pæstl] n pastilla.

pastime ['pɑːstaim] n pasatiempo.

pastor ['pɑːstə*] n pastor m.

pastoral ['pɑːstərl] a pastoral.

pastry ['peistri] n pasta; (cakes) pastas fpl, pasteles mpl.

pasture ['pɑːstʃə*] n (grass) pasto; (land) prado, pasto.

pasty ['pæsti] n empanada // a ['peisti] pastoso; (complexion) pálido.

pat [pæt] vt dar una palmadita a; (dog etc) acariciar // n (of butter) pastelillo; **to give sb a ~ on the back** felicitar a uno.

patch [pætʃ] n (of material) parche m; (piece) pedazo; (mend) remiendo; (of land) terreno // vt (clothes) remendar; **to ~ up** vt (mend temporarily) componer de modo provisional; (quarrel) hacer las paces con; **~work** n labor m de retazos; **~y** a desigual.

pâté ['pætei] n pastel m de carne.

patent ['peitnt] n patente f // vt patentar // a patente, evidente; **~ leather** n charol m.

paternal [pə'tɜːnl] a paternal;

(relation) paterno; **paternity** [-niti] n paternidad f.

path [pɑːθ] n senda, sendero; (trail, track) pista; (of missile) trayectoria.

pathetic [pə'θetik] a (pitiful) patético, lastimoso; (very bad) malísimo; (moving) conmovedor(a).

pathologist [pə'θɔlədʒist] n patólogo; **pathology** [-dʒi] n patología.

pathos ['peiθɔs] n patetismo, lo patético.

pathway ['pɑːθwei] n sendero, vereda.

patience ['peiʃns] n paciencia; (CARDS) solitario.

patient ['peiʃnt] n paciente m/f // a paciente, sufrido.

patio ['pætiəu] n patio.

patriot ['peitriət] n patriota m/f; **~ic** [pætri'ɔtik] a patriótico.

patrol [pə'trəul] n patrulla // vt patrullar por; **~ car** n coche m patrulla; **~man** n (US) policía m.

patron ['peitrən] n (in shop) cliente m/f; (of charity) patrocinador/a m/f; **~ of the arts** mecenas m; **~age** ['pætrənidʒ] n mecenazgo, protección f; **~ize** ['pætrənaiz] vt (shop) ser cliente de; (business) patrocinar; (look down on) tratar con condescendencia; **~ saint** n patrono.

patter ['pætə*] n golpeteo; (of feet) pasos mpl ligeros; (sales talk) jerga // vi andar con pasos ligeros; (rain) tamborilear.

pattern ['pætən] n modelo; (SEWING) patrón m; (design) dibujo; (sample) muestra.

paunch [pɔːntʃ] n panza, barriga.

pauper ['pɔːpə*] n pobre m/f.

pause [pɔːz] n pausa; (interval) intérvalo // vi hacer una pausa.

pave [peiv] vt pavimentar; **to ~ the way for** preparar el terreno para.

pavement ['peivmənt] n (Brit) acera.

pavilion [pə'viliən] n pabellón m; (for band etc) quiosco; (SPORT) caseta.

paving ['peɪvɪŋ] n pavimento, enlosado; ~ **stone** n losa.

paw [pɔː] n pata; (of cat) garra // vt tocar con la pata; (touch) tocar, manosear; (amorously) sobar.

pawn [pɔːn] n (CHESS) peón m; (fig) instrumento // vt empeñar; ~ **broker** n prestamista m/f; ~**shop** n monte m de piedad.

pay [peɪ] n paga; (wage etc) sueldo // (vb: pt, pp **paid**) vt pagar; (debt) liquidar; (visit) hacer; (respect) ofrecer // vi pagar; (be profitable) rendir; **to** ~ **attention** (**to**) prestar atención (a); **to** ~ **back** vt (money) devolver; (person) pagar; **to** ~ **for** vt fus pagar; **to** ~ **in** vt ingresar; **to** ~ **off** vt liquidar; **to** ~ **up** vi pagar (de mala gana); ~**able** a pagadero; ~ **day** n día m de paga; ~**ee** n portador(a) m/f; ~**ing** a provechoso; ~**ment** n pago; **advance** ~**ment** anticipo; **monthly** ~**ment** mensualidad f; ~ **packet** n sobre m de paga; ~**roll** n nómina; ~ **slip** n hoja de paga.

p.c. abbr of **per cent.**

pea [piː] n guisante m, **sweet** ~ guisante de olor.

peace [piːs] n paz f; (calm) paz f, tranquilidad f; ~**able** a pacífico; ~**ful** a (gentle) pacífico; (calm) tranquilo, sosegado; ~**keeping** n offering n prenda de paz.

peach [piːtʃ] n melocotón m, durazno (AM).

peacock ['piːkɔk] n pavo real.

peak [piːk] n (of mountain: top) cumbre f, cima; (: point) pico; (of cap) visera; (fig) cumbre f; ~ **hours** npl horas fpl punta.

peal [piːl] n (of bells) repique m, toque m de campanas; ~ **of laughter** carcajada.

peanut ['piːnʌt] n cacahuete m, maní m (AM); ~ **butter** n manteca de cacahuete.

pear [peə*] n pera; ~ **tree** n peral m.

pearl [pɜːl] n perla; **mother-of-**~ n nácar m.

peasant ['peznt] n campesino/a.

peat [piːt] n turba.

pebble ['pebl] n guijarro.

peck [pek] vt (also: ~ **at**) picotear; (food) comer sin ganas // n picotazo; (kiss) beso ligero; ~**ing order** n orden m de jerarquía; ~**ish** a (col) con hambre.

peculiar [pɪ'kjuːlɪə*] a (odd) extraño, raro; (typical) propio, característico; (marked) especial; ~ **to** propio de; ~**ity** [pɪkjuːlɪ'ærɪtɪ] n peculiaridad f; (feature) característica; (oddity) rareza, singularidad f.

pedal ['pedl] n pedal m // vi pedalear.

pedantic [pɪ'dæntɪk] a pedante.

peddle ['pedl] vt vender (de puerta en puerta); **peddler** n vendedor/a m/f ambulante.

pedestal ['pedɪstl] n pedestal m.

pedestrian [pɪ'destrɪən] n peatón m // a pedestre; ~ **crossing** n paso de peatones.

pedigree ['pedɪgriː] n genealogía; (of animal) raza // cpd (animal) de raza, de casta.

peek [piːk] vi mirar a hurtadillas.

peel [piːl] n piel f; (of orange, lemon) peladuras fpl // vt pelar // vi (paint etc) desconcharse; (wallpaper) despegarse, desprenderse.

peep [piːp] n (look) mirada furtiva; (sound) pío // vi piar; **to** ~ **out** vi asomar la cabeza; ~**hole** n mirilla.

peer [pɪə*] vi: **to** ~ **at** mirar con ojos de miope // n (noble) par m; (equal) igual m; ~**age** n nobleza; ~**less** a sin par.

peeved [piːvd] a enojado.

peevish ['piːvɪʃ] a malhumorado.

peg [peg] n clavija; (for coat etc) gancho, colgadero; (also: **clothes** ~) pinza; (tent ~) estaca // vt (prices) fijar; **off the** ~ ad de confección.

pejorative [pɪˈdʒɔrətɪv] a peyorativo.

pekingese [piːkɪˈniːz] n pequinés/esa m/f.

pelican [ˈpelɪkən] n pelícano.

pellet [ˈpelɪt] n bolita; (bullet) perdigón m.

pelmet [ˈpelmɪt] n galería.

pelt [pelt] vt: to ~ sb with sth tirar algo a uno // vi (rain) llover a cántaros // n pellejo.

pelvis [ˈpelvɪs] n pelvis f.

pen [pen] n pluma; (for sheep) redil m; **play~** parque m de niño; ~ **name** n seudónimo.

penal [ˈpiːnl] a penal; **~ize** vt penar; (SPORT) castigar.

penalty [ˈpenltɪ] n (gen) pena; (fine) multa; (SPORT) castigo; ~ (kick) n (FOOTBALL) penalty m.

penance [ˈpenəns] n penitencia.

pence [pens] pl of **penny**.

pencil [ˈpensl] n lápiz m; (for eyebrows) lápiz de cejas; **propelling** ~ lapicero; ~ **sharpener** n sacapuntas m inv.

pendant [ˈpendnt] n pendiente m.

pending [ˈpendɪŋ] prep antes de // a pendiente.

pendulum [ˈpendjuləm] n péndulo.

penetrate [ˈpenɪtreɪt] vt penetrar; **penetrating** a penetrante; **penetration** [-ˈtreɪʃən] n penetración f.

penfriend [ˈpenfrend] n amigo/a por correspondencia.

penguin [ˈpeŋgwɪn] n pingüino.

penicillin [penɪˈsɪlɪn] n penicilina.

peninsula [pəˈnɪnsjulə] n península.

penis [ˈpiːnɪs] n pene m.

penitence [ˈpenɪtns] n penitencia; **penitent** [-nt] a (gen) arrepentido; (REL) penitente.

penitentiary [penɪˈtenʃərɪ] n (US) cárcel f, presidio.

penknife [ˈpennaɪf] n navaja.

pennant [ˈpenənt] n banderola.

penniless [ˈpenɪlɪs] a sin dinero.

penny [ˈpenɪ], pl **pennies** [ˈpenɪz] or **pence** [pens] n penique m.

pension [ˈpenʃən] n (gen) pensión f; (old-age) jubilación f; (MIL) retiro; **~er** n jubilado; **~ fund** n caja de jubilaciones.

pensive [ˈpensɪv] a pensativo; (withdrawn) preocupado.

pentagon [ˈpentəgən] n pentágono.

Pentecost [ˈpentɪkɔst] n Pentecostés m.

penthouse [ˈpenthaus] n ático.

pent-up [ˈpentʌp] a (feelings) reprimido.

penultimate [peˈnʌltɪmət] a penúltimo.

people [ˈpiːpl] n gente f; (citizens) pueblo sg, ciudadanos mpl // n (nation, race) pueblo, nación // vt poblar; **several ~ came** vinieron varias personas; **~ say that...** dice la gente que....

pep [pep] n (col) energía; **to ~ up** vt animar.

pepper [ˈpepə*] n pimienta; (vegetable) pimiento // vt (fig) salpicar; **~mint** n menta; (sweet) pastilla de menta.

peptalk [ˈpeptɔːk] n (col) palabras fpl para levantar los ánimos.

per [pɜː*] prep por; **~ day/person** por día/persona; **~ cent** por ciento; **~ annum** al año.

perceive [pəˈsiːv] vt percibir; (realize) darse cuenta de.

percentage [pəˈsentɪdʒ] n porcentaje m.

perception [pəˈsepʃən] n percepción f; (insight) perspicacia; **perceptive** [-ˈseptɪv] a perspicaz.

perch [pɜːtʃ] n (fish) perca; (for bird) percha // vi posarse.

percolator [ˈpɜːkəleɪtə*] n cafetera filtradora.

percussion [pəˈkʌʃən] n percusión f.

peremptory [pəˈremptərɪ] a perentorio; (person: imperious) imperioso.

perennial [pəˈrenɪəl] a perenne.

perfect [ˈpɜːfɪkt] a perfecto // n (also: ~ **tense**) perfecto // vt [pə'fɛkt] perfeccionar; ~ion [-'fɛkʃən] n perfección f, ~ionist n perfeccionista m/f.

perforate ['pə:fəreɪt] vt perforar; ~d a (stamp) dentado; **perforation** [-'reɪʃən] n perforación f.

perform [pə'fɔ:m] vt (carry out) realizar, cumplir; (concert etc) representar; (piece of music) interpretar // vi (animal) hacer trucos; (THEATRE) actuar; (TECH) funcionar; ~ance n (of task) cumplimiento, realización f; (of an artist) representación f; (of player etc) actuación f; (of car, engine) funcionamiento; (of function) desempeño; ~er n (actor) actor/actriz m/f, (MUS) intérprete m/f; ~ing a (animal) amaestrado.

perfume ['pə:fju:m] n perfume m // vt perfumar.

perhaps [pə'hæps] ad quizá(s), tal vez.

peril ['pɛrɪl] n peligro, riesgo.

perimeter [pə'rɪmɪtə*] n perímetro.

period ['pɪərɪəd] n período; (HISTORY) época; (time limit) plazo; (SCOL) clase f; (full stop) punto; (MED) regla, reglas fpl // a (costume, furniture) de época; ic [-'ɔdɪk] a periódico, ~ical [-'ɔdɪkl] a periódico; ~ically [-'ɔdɪklɪ] ad de vez en cuando, cada cierto tiempo.

peripheral [pə'rɪfərəl] a periférico; **periphery** [-rɪ] n periferia.

periscope ['pɛrɪskəup] n periscopio.

perish ['pɛrɪʃ] vi perecer; (decay) echarse a perder, deteriorarse; ~able a perecedero; ~ing a (col: cold) helado, glacial.

perjure ['pə:dʒə*] vt: to ~ o.s. perjurarse; **perjury** n (LAW) perjurio.

perk [pə:k] n pago encima del sueldo; to ~ up vi (cheer up) animarse; (in health) sentirse mejor; ~y a (cheerful) alegre, despabilado.

perm [pə:m] n permanente f.

permanent ['pə:mənənt] a permanente.

permissible [pə'mɪsɪbl] a permisible, lícito.

permission [pə'mɪʃən] n permiso; (authorization) licencia.

permissive [pə'mɪsɪv] a permisivo.

permit ['pə:mɪt] n permiso, licencia // vt [pə'mɪt] permitir; (authorize) autorizar; (accept) tolerar.

permutation [pə:mju'teɪʃən] n permutación f.

pernicious [pə:'nɪʃəs] a nocivo; (MED) pernicioso.

perpendicular [pə:pən'dɪkjulə*] a perpendicular n perpendicular.

perpetrate ['pə:pɪtreɪt] vt cometer.

perpetual [pə'pɛtjuəl] a perpetuo.

perpetuate [pə'pɛtjueɪt] vt perpetuar.

perplex [pə'plɛks] vt dejar perplejo.

persecute ['pə:sɪkju:t] vt (pursue) perseguir; (harass) acosar; **persecution** [-'kju:ʃən] n persecución f.

persevere [pə:sɪ'vɪə*] vi persistir.

Persian ['pə:ʃən] a, n persa m/f.

persist [pə'sɪst] vi: to ~ (in doing sth) persistir (en hacer algo), ~ence n empeño; (of disease) pertinacia; ~ent a persistente; (determined) porfiado; (disease) pertinaz.

person ['pə:sn] n persona; ~able a atractivo; ~al a personal; (private) particular; (visit) en persona; (TEL) persona a persona; (column) de anuncios personales; ~ality [-'nælɪtɪ] n personalidad f; ~ally ad personalmente; ~ify ['-'sɔnɪfaɪ] vt encarnar.

personnel [pə:sə'nɛl] n personal m.

perspective [pə'spɛktɪv] n perspectiva.

perspex ['pə:spɛks] n plexiglás m.

perspiration [pə:spɪ'reɪʃən] n transpiración f, sudor m; **perspire** [-'spaɪə*] vi transpirar, sudar.

persuade [pə'sweɪd] vt persuadir;

persuasion [-'sweɪʒən] n persuasión f; (persuasiveness) persuasiva; (creed) creencia; **persuasive** [-'sweɪsɪv] a persuasivo.

pert [pəːt] a impertinente, fresco.

pertaining [pəː'teɪnɪŋ]: ~ to prep relacionado con.

pertinent ['pəːtɪnənt] a pertinente, a propósito.

perturb [pə'təːb] vt perturbar.

Peru [pə'ruː] n el Perú.

peruse [pə'ruːz] vt leer con detención, examinar.

Peruvian [pə'ruːvjən] a, n peruano/a.

pervade [pə'veɪd] vt impregnar, saturar.

perverse [pə'vəːs] a perverso; (stubborn) terco; (wayward) travieso; **perversion** [-'vəːʃən] n perversión f.

pervert ['pəːvəːt] n pervertido/a // vt [pə'vəːt] pervertir.

pessary ['pesərɪ] n pesario.

pessimism ['pesɪmɪzəm] n pesimismo; **pessimist** [-mɪst] n pesimista m/f; **pessimistic** [-'mɪstɪk] a pesimista.

pest [pest] n plaga; (insect) insecto nocivo; (fig) lata, molestia.

pester ['pestə*] vt molestar, acosar.

pesticide ['pestɪsaɪd] n pesticida m.

pet [pet] n animal doméstico; (favourite) favorito // vt acariciar // vi (col) besuquearse, sobarse.

petal ['petl] n pétalo.

peter ['piːtə*]: to ~ out vi agotarse, acabarse.

petite [pə'tiːt] a chiquita.

petition [pə'tɪʃən] n petición f.

petrified ['petrɪfaɪd] a (fig) pasmado, horrorizado; **petrify** vt petrificar; (frighten) pasmar.

petrol ['petrəl] n (Brit) gasolina; (for lighter) bencina.

petroleum [pə'trəulɪəm] n petróleo.

petrol: ~ **pump** n (in car) bomba de gasolina; (in garage) surtidor m de gasolina; ~ **station** n gasolinera;

~ **tank** n depósito de gasolina.

petticoat ['petɪkəut] n enagua; (slip) combinación f.

pettiness ['petɪnɪs] n mezquindad f.

petty ['petɪ] a (mean) mezquino; (unimportant) nimio; ~ **cash** n dinero suelto; ~ **officer** n contramaestre m.

petulant ['petjulənt] a malhumorado.

pew [pjuː] n banco.

pewter ['pjuːtə*] n peltre m.

phallic ['fælɪk] a fálico.

phantom ['fæntəm] n fantasma m.

Pharaoh ['fɛərəu] n Faraón m.

pharmacist ['fɑːməsɪst] n farmacéutico; **pharmacy** [-sɪ] n farmacia f.

phase [feɪz] n fase f // vt: to ~ sth in/out introducir/reducir algo por etapas.

Ph.D. abbr of **Doctor of Philosophy.**

pheasant ['feznt] n faisán m.

phenomenon [fə'nɔmɪnən], pl **-mena** [-mɪnə] n fenómeno.

phial ['faɪəl] n ampolla.

philanthropist [fɪ'lænθrəpɪst] n filántropo/a.

philately [fɪ'lætəlɪ] n filatelia.

Philippines ['fɪlɪpiːnz] npl (also: Philippine Islands) (Islas) Filipinas fpl.

philosopher [fɪ'lɔsəfə*] n filósofo; **philosophical** [fɪlə'sɔfɪkl] a filosófico; **philosophy** [-fɪ] n filosofía.

phlegm [flem] n flema; ~**atic** [fleg'mætɪk] a flemático.

phobia ['fəubjə] n fobia.

phone [fəun] n teléfono // vt telefonear, llamar (por teléfono); **to be on the** ~ tener teléfono; (be calling) estar llamando; **to** ~ **back** vt, vi devolver la llamada.

phonetics [fə'netɪks] n fonética.

phoney ['fəunɪ] a falso; (person) insincero // n (person) farsante m/f.

phosphate ['fɔsfeɪt] n fosfato.

phosphorus ['fɔsfərəs] n fósforo.

photo ['fəutəu] n fotografía.

photo... ['fəutəu] *pref*: ~**copier** *n* fotocopiador *m*; ~**copy** *n* fotocopia // *vt* fotocopiar; ~**genic** [-'dʒenɪk] *a* fotogénico; ~**graph** *n* fotografía // *vt* fotografiar; ~**grapher** [fə-'tɔgrəfə*] *n* fotógrafo; ~**graphic** [-'græfɪk] *a* fotográfico; ~**graphy** [fə'tɔgrəfɪ] *n* fotografía; ~**stat** ['fəutəustæt] *n* fotóstato.

phrase [freɪz] *n* frase *f* // *vt* expresar; ~**book** *n* libro de frases.

physical ['fɪzɪkl] *a* físico.

physician [fɪ'zɪʃən] *n* médico.

physicist ['fɪzɪsɪst] *n* físico.

physics ['fɪzɪks] *n* física.

physiology [fɪzɪ'ɔlədʒɪ] *n* fisiología.

physiotherapy [fɪzɪəu'θerəpɪ] *n* fisioterapia.

physique [fɪ'ziːk] *n* físico.

pianist ['pɪːənɪst] *n* pianista *m/f*.

piano [pɪ'ænəu] *n* piano; **grand** ~ piano de cola.

pick [pɪk] *n* (*tool: also:* ~**axe**) pico, piqueta // *vt* (*select*) elegir, escoger; (*gather*) recoger; (*lock*) forzar; **take your** ~ escoja lo que quiera; **the** ~ **of** lo mejor de; **to** ~ **one's teeth** limpiarse los dientes; **to** ~ **pockets** ratear, ser carterista; **to** ~ **off** *vt* (*kill*) matar de un tiro; **to** ~ **on** *vt fus* (*person*) meterse con; **to** ~ **out** *vt* (*distinguish*) lograr ver; **to** ~ **up** *vi* (*improve*) reponerse // *vt* (*from floor*) recoger; (*telephone*) descolgar; (*buy*) comprar; (*find*) encontrar; (*learn*) aprender; **to** ~ **up speed** acelerarse; **to** ~ **o.s. up** levantarse.

picket ['pɪkɪt] *n* (*in strike*) guardia, piquete *m* // *vt* piquetear; ~ **line** *n* línea de huelguistas.

pickle ['pɪkl] *n* (*also:* ~**s**: *as condiment*) escabeche *m*; (*fig: mess*) apuro *m* // *vt* conservar en vinagre.

pickpocket ['pɪkpɔkɪt] *n* carterista *m/f*.

pickup ['pɪkʌp] *n* (*on record player*) pickup *m*; (*small truck*) furgoneta.

picnic ['pɪknɪk] *n* picnic *m*,

merienda de campo // *vi* merendar en el campo.

pictorial [pɪk'tɔːrɪəl] *a* pictórico, (*magazine etc*) ilustrado.

picture ['pɪktʃə*] *n* cuadro; (*painting*) pintura; (*photograph*) fotografía; (*film*) película // *vt* pintar; **the** ~**s** el cine; ~ **book** *n* libro de imágenes.

picturesque [pɪktʃə'resk] *a* pintoresco.

pidgin ['pɪdʒɪn] *a*: ~ **English** el inglés macarrónico.

pie [paɪ] *n* pastel *m*; (*open*) tarta; (*of meat*) empanada.

piebald ['paɪbɔːld] *a* pío.

piece [piːs] *n* pedazo, trozo; (*of land*) terreno; (*of cake*) porción *f*, (*item*): **a** ~ **of furniture/advice** un mueble/un consejo // *vt*: **to** ~ **together** juntar; (*TECH*) montar; **to take to** ~**s** desmontar; ~**meal** *ad* poco a poco; ~**work** *n* trabajo a destajo.

pier [pɪə*] *n* muelle *m*; (*jetty*) embarcadero, malecón *m*.

pierce [pɪəs] *vt* penetrar, atravesar; (*puncture*) pinchar.

piercing ['pɪəsɪŋ] *a* (*cry*) penetrante.

piety ['paɪətɪ] *n* piedad *f*.

pig [pɪg] *n* cerdo, puerco, (*fig*) cochino.

pigeon ['pɪdʒən] *n* paloma; (*as food*) pichón *m*; ~**hole** *n* casilla.

piggy bank ['pɪgɪbæŋk] *n* hucha en forma de cerdito.

pigheaded ['pɪg'hedɪd] *a* terco, testarudo.

pigment ['pɪgmənt] *n* pigmento; ~**ation** [-'teɪʃən] *n* pigmentación *f*.

pigmy ['pɪgmɪ] *n* = **pygmy**.

pigsty ['pɪgstaɪ] *n* pocilga.

pigtail ['pɪgteɪl] *n* (*girl's*) trenza; (*Chinese*) coleta.

pike [paɪk] *n* (*spear*) pica; (*fish*) lucio.

pilchard ['pɪltʃəd] *n* sardina arenque.

pile [paɪl] *n* (*heap*) montón *m*; (*of*

carpet) pelo; (*of cloth*) pelillo // (*vb: also:* ~ **up**) *vt* amontonar; (*fig*) acumular // *vi* amontonarse.

piles [pailz] *npl* (MED) almorranas *fpl*, hemorroides *mpl*.

pile-up ['pailʌp] *n* (AUT) accidente *m* múltiple.

pilfer ['pilfə*] *vt* ratear; ~**ing** *n* ratería.

pilgrim ['pilgrim] *n* peregrino/a; ~**age** *n* peregrinaje *m*, romería.

pill [pil] *n* píldora; **the** ~ la píldora.

pillage ['pilidʒ] *n* saqueo, pillaje *m*.

pillar ['pilə*] *n* (*gen*) pilar *m*; (*concrete*) columna; ~ **box** *n* (Brit) buzón *m*.

pillion ['piljən] *n* (*of motor cycle*) asiento de atrás.

pillory ['piləri] *vt* poner en ridículo.

pillow ['piləu] *n* almohada; ~**case** *n* funda.

pilot ['pailət] *n* piloto // *a* (*scheme etc*) piloto // *vt* pilotar; (*fig*) guiar, conducir; ~ **light** *n* piloto.

pimp [pimp] *n* alcahuete *m*, chulo.

pimple ['pimpl] *n* grano.

pin [pin] *n* alfiler *m*; (TECH) perno; (: *wooden*) clavija // *vt* prender (con alfiler); sujetar con perno; ~**s and needles** hormigueo *sg*; **rolling/ safety** ~ rodillo/imperdible *m*; **to** ~ **sb down** (*fig*) hacer que uno concrete; **to** ~ **sth on sb** (*fig*) acusar (falsamente) a uno de algo.

pinafore ['pinəfɔː*] *n* delantal *m*; ~ **dress** *n* mandil *m*.

pinball ['pinbɔːl] *n* billar *m* automático.

pincers ['pinsəz] *npl* pinzas *fpl*, tenazas *fpl*.

pinch [pintʃ] *n* pellizco; (*of salt etc*) pizca // *vt* pellizcar; (*col: steal*) birlar; (: *arrest*) coger, pescar // *vi* (*shoe*) apretar; **to feel the** ~ pasar apuros.

pincushion ['pinkuʃən] *n* acerico.

pine [pain] *n* (*also:* ~ **tree**) pino // *vi*: **to** ~ **for** suspirar por; **to** ~ **away** languidecer.

pineapple ['painæpl] *n* piña, ananás *m*.

ping [piŋ] *n* (*noise*) tintineo; (*of bullet through air*) subido; ~-**pong** *n* pingpong *m*.

pink [piŋk] *a* rosado, color de rosa // *n* (*colour*) color *m* de rosa; (BOT) clavel *m*, clavellina.

pinnacle ['pinəkl] *n* cumbre *f*.

pinpoint ['pinpɔint] *vt* poner el dedo en.

pint [paint] *n* pinta (*0.57 litros*); **to go for a** ~ ir a tomar una cerveza.

pin-up ['pinʌp] *n* fotografía de mujer bonita.

pioneer [paiə'niə*] *n* pionero.

pious ['paiəs] *a* piadoso, devoto.

pip [pip] *n* (*seed*) pepita; (*time signal on radio*) señal *f*.

pipe [paip] *n* tubo, caño; (*for smoking*) pipa // *vt* conducir en cañerías; ~**s** *npl* (*gen*) cañería *sg*; (*also:* **bag**~**s**) gaita *sg*; **to** ~ **down** *vi* (*col*) callarse; ~ **dream** *n* sueño imposible; ~**line** *n* tubería, cañería; (*for oil*) oleoducto; (*for gas*) gasoducto; **piper** *n* (*gen*) flautista *m/f*; (*with bagpipes*) gaitero.

piping ['paipiŋ] *ad*: ~ **hot** bien caliente.

piquant ['piːkənt] *a* picante.

pique [piːk] *n* pique *m*, resentimiento.

pirate ['paiərət] *n* pirata *m*; ~ **radio** *n* emisora ilegal.

pirouette [piruˈet] *n* pirueta // *vi* piruetear.

Pisces ['paisiːz] *n* Piscis *m*.

piss [pis] *vi* (*col*) mear; ~**ed** *a* (*col: drunk*) trompa.

pistol ['pistl] *n* pistola.

piston ['pistən] *n* pistón *m*, émbolo.

pit [pit] *n* hoyo; (*also:* **coal** ~) mina; (*in garage*) foso de inspección; (*also:* **orchestra** ~) platea; (*quarry*) cantera // *vt*: **to** ~ **A against B** oponer A a B; ~**s** *npl* (AUT) box *m*.

pitch [pitʃ] *n* (*throw*) lanzamiento; (MUS) tono; (SPORT) campo, terreno; (*tar*) brea; (*in market etc*) puesto *m*;

vt (throw) arrojar, lanzar // *vi (fall)* caer(se); *(NAUT)* cabecear; to ~ **a tent** armar una tienda (de campaña); ~**black a** negro como boca de lobo; ~**ed battle** *n* batalla campal.

pitcher ['pɪtʃə*] *n* cántaro, jarro.

pitchfork ['pɪtʃfɔːk] *n* horca.

piteous ['pɪtɪəs] *a* lastimoso.

pitfall ['pɪtfɔːl] *n* escollo, peligro.

pith [pɪθ] *n (of orange)* médula; *(fig)* meollo.

pithy ['pɪθɪ] *a* jugoso.

pitiable ['pɪtɪəbl] *a* lastimoso.

pitiful ['pɪtɪful] *a (touching)* lastimoso, conmovedor(a); *(contemptible)* lamentable, miserable.

pitiless ['pɪtɪlɪs] *a* despiadado.

pittance ['pɪtns] *n* miseria.

pity ['pɪtɪ] *n (compassion)* compasión *f*, piedad *f*; *(shame)* lástima // *vt* tener lástima a, compadecer(se de); **what a ~!** ¡qué lástima!

pivot ['pɪvət] *n* eje *m* // *vi*: **to ~ on** girar sobre; *(fig)* depender de.

pixie ['pɪksɪ] *n* duende *m*.

placard ['plækɑːd] *n (sign)* letrero; *(in march etc)* pancarta.

placate [pla'keɪt] *vt* apaciguar.

place [pleɪs] *n (gen)* lugar *m*, sitio; *(rank)* rango; *(seat)* plaza, asiento; *(post)* puesto; *(home)*: **at/to his ~** en/a su casa // *vt (object)* poner, colocar; *(identify)* reconocer, ubicar; *(find a post for)* dar un puesto a, colocar; **to take ~** tener lugar; **to be ~d** *(in race, exam)* colocarse; **out of ~** *(not suitable)* fuera de lugar; **in the first ~** en primer lugar; **to change ~s with sb** trocarse con uno.

placid ['plæsɪd] *a* apacible.

plagiarism ['pleɪdʒjərɪzm] *n* plagio.

plague [pleɪg] *n* plaga; *(MED)* peste *f* // *vt (fig)* acosar, atormentar; **to ~ sb** fastidiar a uno.

plaice [pleɪs] *n, pl inv* platija.

plaid [plæd] *n (material)* tela a cuadros; *(pattern)* plaid *m*.

plain [pleɪn] *a (clear)* claro, evidente; *(simple)* sencillo, llano; *(frank)* franco, abierto; *(not handsome)* sin atractivo; *(pure)* natural, puro // *ad* claro, claramente // *n* llano, llanura; **in ~ clothes** *(police)* de paisano; ~**ly** *ad* claramente, evidentemente; *(frankly)* francamente, con franqueza; ~**ness** *n* claridad *f*; sencillez *f*, franqueza.

plaintiff ['pleɪntɪf] *n* demandante *m/f*.

plait [plæt] *n* trenza // *vt* trenzar.

plan [plæn] *n (drawing)* plano; *(scheme)* plan *m*, proyecto; *(schedule)* programa *m* // *vt (think in advance)* proyectar; *(prepare)* planear, planificar // *vi* hacer proyectos; **to ~ to do** proponerse hacer.

plane [pleɪn] *n (AVIAT)* avión *m*; *(tree)* plátano; *(tool)* cepillo; *(MATH)* plano.

planet ['plænɪt] *n* planeta *m*; ~**arium** [-'tɛərɪəm] *n* planetario.

plank [plæŋk] *n* tabla; *(POL)* punto.

planner ['plænə*] *n* planificador/a *m/f*.

planning ['plænɪŋ] *n* planificación *f*; **family ~** planificación familiar.

plant [plɑːnt] *n* planta; *(machinery)* maquinaria; *(factory)* fábrica // *vt* plantar; *(field)* sembrar; *(bomb)* colocar; *(fam)* colocar a escondidas.

plantation [plæn'teɪʃən] *n* plantación *f*; *(estate)* hacienda.

plaque [plæk] *n* placa.

plasma ['plæzmə] *n* plasma *m*.

plaster ['plɑːstə*] *n (for walls)* yeso; *(also: sticking ~)* curitas *m inv*, parche *m* // *vt* enyesar; *(cover)*: **to ~ with** llenar ó cubrir de; ~**ed** *a (col)* trompa; ~**er** *n* yesero.

plastic ['plæstɪk] *n* plástico // *a* de plástico.

plasticine ['plæstɪsiːn] *n* plasticina.

plastic surgery [plæstɪk'sɜːdʒərɪ] *n* cirujía plástica.

plate [pleɪt] *n (dish)* plato; *(metal, in*

book) lámina; (*PHOT, dental*) placa.

plateau ['plætəu], *pl* **~s** *or* **~x**
[-z] *n* meseta, altiplanicie *f*.

plateful ['pleɪtful] *n* plato.

plate glass ['pleɪt'glɑːs] *n* vidrio
cilindrado.

platform ['plætfɔːm] *n* (*RAIL*)
andén *m*; (*stage*) plataforma; (*at
meeting*) tribuna; (*POL*) programa *m*
electoral; **~ ticket** *n* billete *m* de
andén.

platinum ['plætɪnəm] *n* platino.

platitude ['plætɪtjuːd] *n* lugar *m*
común, tópico.

platoon [plə'tuːn] *n* pelotón *m*.

platter ['plætə*] *n* fuente *f*, platón
m.

plausible ['plɔːzɪbl] *a* verosímil,
admisible; (*person*) convincente.

play [pleɪ] *n* (*gen*) juego; (*also:
~time*) recreo; (*THEATRE*) obra,
comedia // *vt* (*game*) jugar;
(*instrument*) tocar; (*THEATRE*)
representar; (: *part*) hacer el papel
de); (*fig*) desempeñar // *vi* jugar;
(*amuse o.s.*) divertirse; (*frolic*)
juguetear; **to ~ down** *vt* quitar
importancia a; **to ~ up** *vt* (*cause
trouble to*) fastidiar a; **~acting** *n*
teatro; **~er** *n* jugador/a *m/f*;
(*THEATRE*) actor/actriz *m/f*; (*MUS*)
músico/a; **~ful** *a* juguetón(ona);
~ground *n* (*in park*) parque *m* de
juegos; (*in school*) patio de recreo;
~group *n* jardín *m* de niños; **~ing
card** *n* naipe *m*, carta; **~ing field** *n*
campo de deportes; **~mate** *n*
compañero de juego; **~off** *n*
(*SPORT*) partido de desempate;
~pen *n* corral *m*; **~thing** *n* juguete
m; **~wright** *n* dramaturgo.

plea [pliː] *n* (*request*) súplica,
petición *f*; (*excuse*) pretexto,
disculpa; (*LAW*) alegato, defensa.

plead [pliːd] *vt* (*LAW*) interceder;
(*give as excuse*) poner como
pretexto // *vi* (*LAW*) declarar; (*beg*):
to ~ with sb suplicar o rogar a uno.

pleasant ['plɛznt] *a* agradable;
(*surprise*) grato; (*person*) simpático;

book) lámina; (*PHOT, dental*) placa.

~ness *n* (*of person*) simpatía,
amabilidad *f*; (*of place*) lo
agradable; **~ries** *npl* (*polite
remarks*) cortesías *fpl*.

please [pliːz] *vt* (*give pleasure to*)
dar gusto a, agradar; (*get on well
with*) caer en gracia a // *vi* (*think
fit*): **do as you ~** haga lo que quiera
o lo que le da la gana; **~!** ¡por
favor!; **~ yourself!** ¡como Usted
guste!, ¡como quiera!; **~d** *a* (*happy*)
alegre, contento; **~d (with**)
satisfecho (de); **pleasing** *a* (*gen*)
agradable; (*surprise*) grato;
(*flattering*) halagüeño.

pleasure ['plɛʒə*] *n* placer *m*,
gusto; (*will*) voluntad *f* // *cpd* de
recreo; **'it's a ~'** el gusto es mío; **it's
a ~** se lo agradezco.

pleat [pliːt] *n* pliegue *m*.

plebs [plɛbz] *npl* (*pej*) la plebe.

plectrum ['plɛktrəm] *n* plectro.

pledge [plɛdʒ] *n* (*object*) prenda;
(*promise*) promesa, voto // *vt*
(*pawn*) empeñar; (*promise*) prometer.

plentiful ['plɛntɪful] *a* copioso,
abundante.

plenty ['plɛntɪ] *n* abundancia; **~ of**
(*enough*) bastante; (*many*) muchos.

pleurisy ['pluərɪsɪ] *n* pleuresía.

pliable ['plaɪəbl] *a* flexible; (*fig*)
manejable.

pliers ['plaɪəz] *npl* alicates *mpl*,
tenazas *fpl*.

plight [plaɪt] *n* condición *f*, situación
f difícil.

plimsolls ['plɪmsɔlz] *npl* zapatos
mpl de tenis.

plod [plɔd] *vi* caminar penosamente;
(*fig*) trabajar laboriosamente;
~der *n* empollón/ona *m/f*; **~ding** *a*
laborioso.

plonk [plɔŋk] (*col*) *n* (*wine*) vino
corriente // *vt*: **to ~ sth down** dejar
caer algo (pesadamente).

plot [plɔt] *n* (*scheme*) complot *m*,
conjura; (*of story, play*) argumento;
(*of land*) terreno // *vt* (*mark out*)
trazar; (*conspire*) tramar, urdir //

vi conspirar; **~ter** *n* conspirador/a *m/f*.

plough, plow (*US*) [plau] *n* arado *m* // *vt* (*earth*) arar; **to ~ back** *vt* (*COMM*) reinvertir; **to ~ through** *vt fus* (*crowd*) abrirse paso por la fuerza.

ploy [ploi] *n* truco, estratagema.

pluck [plʌk] *vt* (*fruit*) coger; (*musical instrument*) puntear; (*bird*) desplumar // *n* valor *m*, ánimo; **to ~ up courage** hacer de tripas corazón; **~y** *a* valiente, valeroso.

plug [plʌg] *n* tapón *m*; (*ELEC*) enchufe *m*, clavija; (*AUT: also: **sparking ~**) bujía // *vt* (*hole*) tapar; (*col: advertise*) dar publicidad a.

plum [plʌm] *n* (*fruit*) ciruela // *a* (*col: job*) breva, chollo.

plumage ['plu:midʒ] *n* plumaje *m*.

plumb [plʌm] *ad* (*exactly*) exactamente, en punto // *vt* sondar, sondear.

plumber ['plʌmə*] *n* fontanero;

plumbing [-miŋ] *n* (*trade*) fontanería; (*piping*) instalación *f* de cañerías.

plume [plu:m] *n* (*gen*) pluma; (*on helmet*) penacho.

plummet ['plʌmɪt] *vi*: **to ~ (down)** caer a plomo.

plump [plʌmp] *a* rechoncho, rollizo // *vt*: **to ~ sth (down) on** dejar caer algo en; **to ~ for** (*col: choose*) optar por.

plunder ['plʌndə*] *n* pillaje *m*; (*loot*) botín *m* // *vt* pillar, saquear; (*tomb*) robar.

plunge [plʌndʒ] *n* (*dive*) salto; (*submersion*) zambullida; (*bath*) baño // *vt* sumergir, hundir // *vi* (*fall*) caer; (*dive*) saltar; (*person*) arrojarse; (*sink*) hundirse; **to take the ~** resolverse; **plunger** *n* émbolo; **plunging** *a* (*neckline*) escotado.

pluperfect [plu:'pə:fikt] *n* pluscuamperfecto.

plural ['pluərl] *n* plural *m*.

plus [plʌs] *n* (*also: ~ sign*) signo más // *prep* más, y, además de; **ten/twenty ~** diez/veinte y pico.

plush [plʌʃ] *a* de felpa.

ply [plai] *vt* (*a trade*) ejercer // *vi* (*ship*) ir y venir; (*for hire*) ofrecerse (para alquilar); **three ~** (*wool*) de tres cordones; **to ~ sb with drink** ofrecer bebidas a alguien muchas veces; **~wood** *n* madera contrachapada.

P.M. *abbr of* **Prime Minister.**

p.m. *ad abbr of* post meridiem de la tarde o noche.

pneumatic [nju:'mætik] *a* neumático.

pneumonia [nju:'mounɪə] *n* pulmonía.

poach [poutʃ] *vt* (*cook*) escalfar; (*steal*) cazar en vedado // *vi* cazar/pescar en finca ajena; **~ed** *a* (*egg*) escalfado; **~er** *n* cazador *m* furtivo; **~ing** *n* caza/pesca furtiva.

pocket ['pɔkit] *n* bolsillo; (*of air, geol, fig*) bolsa; (*BILLIARDS*) tronera // *vt* meter en el bolsillo; (*steal*) embolsar; (*BILLIARDS*) entronerar; **to be out of ~** salir perdiendo; **~book** *n* (*US: wallet*) cartera; **~ knife** *n* navaja; **~ money** *n* dinero para gastos personales.

pod [pɔd] *n* vaina.

podgy ['pɔdʒi] *a* gordinflón(ona).

poem ['pouim] *n* poema *m*.

poet ['pouit] *n* poeta *m/f*; **~ess** *n* poetisa; **~ic** [-'etik] *a* poético; **~ laureate** *n* poeta laureado; **~ry** *n* poesía.

poignant ['poinjənt] *a* conmovedor(a); (*sharp*) agudo.

point [point] *n* (*gen*) punto; (*tip*) punta; (*purpose*) fin *m*, finalidad *f*; (*use*) utilidad *f*; (*significant part*) lo significativo; (*characteristic*) rasgo; (*also: decimal ~*) **2 ~ 3** (**2.3**) dos punto tres // *vt* (*show*) subrayar; (*gun etc*): **to ~ sth at** apuntar algo a uno // *vi* señalar con el dedo; **~s** *npl* (*AUT*) contactos *mpl*; (*RAIL*) agujas *fpl*; **to make a ~ of** no dejar de; **to get the ~** comprender; **to come to the ~** ir al grano; **there's no ~ (in doing)** no hay para qué (hacer); **to ~ out** vt señalar; **to ~ to** indicar con el dedo; (fig) indicar, señalar; **~-blank** ad (also: at **~-blank range**) a quemarropa; **~ed** a (shape) puntiagudo, afilado; (remark) directo, enfático; **~edly** ad directamente, con énfasis; **~er** n (stick) puntero; (needle) aguja, indicador m; **~less** a (useless) inútil; (senseless) sin sentido; (motiveless) sin motivo; **~ of view** n punto de vista.

poise [pɔɪz] n (balance) equilibrio; (of head, body) aire m, porte m; (calmness) confianza.

poison [pɔɪzn] n veneno // vt envenenar; **~ing** n envenenamiento; **~ous** a venenoso; (fumes etc) tóxico; (fig) pernicioso.

poke [pəʊk] vt (fire) hurgar, atizar; (jab with finger, stick etc) empujar; (put): **to ~ sth in(to)** introducir algo en // n (to fire) hurgonada; (push) empujón m; (with elbow) codazo; **to ~ about** vi fisgar.

poker [pəʊkə*] n badila, atizador m; (CARDS) póker m; **~-faced** a de cara impasible.

poky [pəʊkɪ] a estrecho.

Poland [pəʊlənd] n Polonia.

polar [pəʊlə*] a polar; **~ bear** n oso polar.

polarize [pəʊləraɪz] vt polarizar.

pole [pəʊl] n palo; (GEO) polo m; (TEL) poste m; (flag~) asta; (tent ~) mástil m.

Pole [pəʊl] n polaco/a.

pole vault [pəʊlvɔːlt] n salto con pértiga.

police [pəˈliːs] n policía // vt mantener el orden en; **~ car** n coche-patrulla m; **~man** n policía m, guardia m; **~ state** n estado policíaco; **~ station** n comisaría; **~woman** n mujer f policía.

policy [pɒlɪsɪ] n política; (also: insurance ~) póliza.

polio [pəʊlɪəʊ] n polio f.

Polish [pəʊlɪʃ] a, n polaco.

polish [pɒlɪʃ] n (for shoes) betún m; (for floor) cera (de lustrar); (for nails) esmalte m; (shine) brillo, lustre m; (fig: refinement) cultura, urbanidad f // vt (shoes) limpiar; (make shiny) pulir, sacar brillo a; (fig: improve) refinar, repasar; **to ~ off** vt (work) terminar; (food) despachar; **~ed** a (fig: person) culto, (: manners) fino.

polite [pəˈlaɪt] a cortés, atento; (formal) correcto; **~ness** n cortesía.

politic [pɒlɪtɪk] a prudente; **~al** [pəˈlɪtɪkl] a político; **~ian** [-ˈtɪʃən] n político; **~s** npl política sg.

polka [pɒlkə] n polca; **~ dot** n punto.

poll [pəʊl] n (votes) votación f, votos mpl; (also: opinion ~) sondeo, encuesta f // vt (votes) recibir, obtener.

pollen [pɒlən] n polen m.

pollination [pɒlɪˈneɪʃən] n polinización f.

polling [pəʊlɪŋ]: **~ booth** n cabina de votar; **~ day** n día m de elecciones; **~ station** n centro electoral.

pollute [pəˈluːt] vt contaminar; **pollution** [-ˈluːʃən] n polución f, contaminación f.

polo [pəʊləʊ] n (sport) polo; **~-neck** a de cuello vuelto.

polyester [pɒlɪˈestə*] n poliester m.

polygamy [pəˈlɪɡəmɪ] n poligamia.

Polynesia [pɒlɪˈniːzɪə] n Polinesia.

polytechnic [pɒlɪˈteknɪk] n politécnico, escuela de formación profesional.

polythene [pɒlɪθiːn] n politeno.

pomegranate [pɒmɪˈɡrænɪt] n granada.

pommel [pɒml] n pomo // vt dar de puñetazos.

pomp [pɒmp] n pompa.

pompous [pɒmpəs] a pomposo.

pond [pɔnd] n (natural) charca; (artificial) estanque m.

ponder ['pɔndə*] vt meditar; ~ous a pesado.

pontiff ['pɔntif] n pontífice m.

pontificate [pɔn'tifikeit] vi (fig): to ~ (about) pontificar (sobre).

pontoon [pɔn'tu:n] n pontón m; (card game) veintiuna.

pony ['pəuni] n poney m, jaca; ~tail n cola de caballo; ~ trekking n excursión f a caballo.

poodle ['pu:dl] n perro de lanas.

pool [pu:l] n (of rain) charca; (pond) estanque m; (also: swimming ~) piscina; (billiards) trucos mpl // vt juntar; (football) ~s npl quinielas fpl.

poor [puə*] a pobre; (bad) de baja calidad // npl: the ~ los pobres; ~ly a mal, enfermo.

pop [pɔp] n ¡pum!, (sound) ruido seco; (MUS) pop m; (US: col: father) papá m; (lemonade) gaseosa f // vt (put) poner // vi reventar; (cork) saltar; to ~ in vi entrar de sopetón; to ~ out vi salir un momento; to ~ up vi aparecer inesperadamente; ~concert n concierto pop; ~corn n palomitas fpl.

pope [pəup] n papa m.

poplar ['pɔplə*] n álamo.

poplin ['pɔplin] n popelina.

poppy ['pɔpi] n amapola.

populace ['pɔpjuləs] n pueblo, plebe f.

popular ['pɔpjulə*] a popular; (fashionable) de moda; ~ity [-'læriti] n popularidad f; ~ize vt popularizar; (disseminate) vulgarizar.

populate ['pɔpjuleit] vt poblar.

population [pɔpju'leiʃən] n población f.

populous ['pɔpjuləs] a populoso.

porcelain ['pɔ:slin] n porcelana.

porch [pɔ:tʃ] n pórtico, entrada.

porcupine ['pɔ:kjupain] n puerco espín.

pore [pɔ:*] n poro // vi: to ~ over estar absorto en.

pork [pɔ:k] n carne f de cerdo.

pornographic [pɔ:nə'græfik] a pornográfico; **pornography** [-'nɔ-grafi] n pornografía.

porous ['pɔ:rəs] a poroso.

porpoise ['pɔ:pəs] n marsopa.

porridge ['pɔridʒ] n avena.

port [pɔ:t] n (harbour) puerto; (NAUT: left side) babor m; (wine) (vino de) oporto.

portable ['pɔ:təbl] a portátil.

portend [pɔ:'tend] vt presagiar, anunciar; **portent** ['pɔ:tent] n presagio, augurio.

porter ['pɔ:tə*] n (for luggage) mozo; (doorkeeper) portero, conserje m.

porthole ['pɔ:thəul] n portilla.

portion ['pɔ:ʃən] n porción f; (helping) ración f.

portly ['pɔ:tli] a corpulento.

portrait ['pɔ:treit] n retrato.

portray [pɔ:'trei] vt retratar; (in writing) describir, representar; ~al n representación f.

Portugal ['pɔ:tjugl] n Portugal m.

Portuguese [pɔ:tju'gi:z] a portugués/esa // n, pl inv portugués/esa m/f; (LING) portugués m.

pose [pəuz] n postura, actitud f; (pej) afectación f, pose f // vi posar; (pretend) to ~ as darse el tono de // vt (question) plantear.

posh [pɔʃ] a (col) elegante, de lujo.

position [pə'ziʃən] n posición f; (job) puesto // vt colocar.

positive ['pɔzitiv] a positivo; (certain) seguro; (definite) definitivo.

posse ['pɔsi] n (US) pelotón m.

possess [pə'zes] vt poseer; ~ion [pə'zeʃən] n posesión f; ~ive a posesivo.

possibility [pɔsi'biliti] n posibilidad f; **possible** ['pɔsibl] a posible; as big as possible lo más grande posible; **possibly** ['pɔsibli] ad (perhaps) posiblemente, tal vez; I cannot possibly come me es imposible venir.

post [pəust] n (letters, delivery) correo; (job, situation) puesto; (pole) poste *m* // *vt* (*send by post*) echar al correo; (*MIL*) apostar; (*bills*) fijar, pegar; (*appoint*): to ~ to enviar a; ~**age** *n* porte *m*, franqueo; ~**al** *a* postal, de correos; ~**al order** *n* giro postal; ~**box** *n* buzón *m*; ~**card** *n* tarjeta postal.

postdate [poust'dett] *vt* (*cheque*) poner fecha adelantada a.

poster ['pousto*'] *n* cartel *m*.

posterior [pos'tiorio*'] *n* (*col*) culo, trasero.

posterity [pos'teriti] *n* posteridad *f*.

postgraduate ['poust'grædjuot] *n* postgraduado.

posthumous ['postjumos] *a* póstumo.

post: ~**man** *n* cartero; ~**mark** *n* matasellos *m* inv; ~**master** *n* administrador/a *m/f* de correos.

post-mortem [poust'mo:tom] *n* autopsia.

post office ['poustofis] *n* (*building*) correos *f*; (*organization*) Administración General de Correos; ~ **box** (**P.O. box**) *n* apartado postal.

postpone [pos'poun] *vt* aplazar; ~**ment** *n* aplazamiento.

postscript ['poustskript] *n* posdata.

postulate ['postjuleit] *vt* postular.

posture ['postʃo*'] *n* postura, actitud *f*.

postwar [poust'wo:*] *a* de posguerra.

posy ['pouzi] *n* ramillete *m* (de flores).

pot [pot] *n* (*for cooking*) olla; (*for flowers*) maceta; (*for jam*) tarro, pote *m*; (*col: marijuana*) mota // *vt* (*plant*) poner en tiesto; (*conserve*) conservar.

potato [po'teitou], *pl* ~**es** *n* patata, papa (*AM*).

potent ['poutnt] *a* potente, poderoso; (*drink*) fuerte.

potential [po'tɛnʃl] *a* potencial, en potencia // *n* potencial *m*, potencialidad *f*.

pothole ['pothoul] *n* (*in road*) bache *m*; (*underground*) caverna; **potholer**

n espeleólogo; **potholing** *n*: **to go potholing** dedicarse a la espeleología.

potion ['pouʃon] *n* poción *f*, pócima.

potluck [pot'lʌk] *n*: **to take** ~ contentarse con lo que haya.

potshot ['potʃot] *n*: **to take a** ~ **at sth** tirar a algo sin apuntar.

potted ['potid] *a* (*food*) en conserva; (*plant*) en tiesto o maceta.

potter ['poto*'] *n* (*artistic*) ceramista *m/f*; (*artisan*) alfarero // *vi*: **to** ~ **around**, ~ **about** ocuparse en fruslerías; ~**y** *n* cerámica; alfarería.

potty ['poti] *a* (*col: mad*) chiflado // *n* orinal *m* de niño.

pouch [pautʃ] *n* (*ZOOL*) bolsa; (*for tobacco*) petaca.

pouf(fe) [pu:f] *n* pouf *m*.

poultice ['poultis] *n* cataplasma, emplasto.

poultry ['poultri] *n* aves *fpl* de corral; (*dead*) pollos *mpl*; ~ **farm** *n* granja avícola.

pounce [pauns] *vi*: **to** ~ **on** precipitarse sobre // *n* salto, ataque *m*.

pound [paund] *n* (*gen*) libra; (*for dogs*) corral *m*; (*for cars*) depósito // *vt* (*beat*) golpear; (*crush*) machacar // *vi* (*beat*) dar golpes; ~ **sterling** *n* (libra) esterlina.

pour [po:*] *vt* echar; (*tea*) servir // *vi* correr, fluir; (*rain*) llover a cántaros; **to** ~ **away** o **off** *vt* vaciar, verter; **to** ~ **in** *vi* (*people*) entrar en tropel; **to** ~ **out** *vi* (*people*) salir en tropel // *vt* (*drink*) echar, servir; ~**ing** *a*: ~**ing rain** *n* lluvia torrencial.

pout [paut] *vi* hacer pucheros.

poverty ['povoti] *n* pobreza, miseria; (*fig*) falta, escasez *f*, ~**stricken** *a* necesitado.

powder ['paudo*'] *n* polvo; (*face* ~) polvos *mpl*; (*gun* ~) pólvora // *vt* polvorear; **to** ~ **one's face** empolvarse; ~ **compact** *n* polvera,

~ **room** n aseos mpl; ~**y** a polvoriento.

power ['pauə*] n (gen) poder m; (strength) fuerza; (nation) potencia; (ability, POL: of party, leader) poder m, poderío m; (drive) empuje m; (TECH) potencia; (ELEC) fuerza, energía // vt impulsar; ~ **cut** n apagón m; ~**ed** a: **~ed by** impulsado por; ~**ful** a poderoso; (engine) potente; (build) fuerte; (emotion) intenso; ~**less** a impotente, ineficaz; ~ **line** n línea de conducción eléctrica; ~ **point** n enchufe m; ~ **station** n central f eléctrica.

p.p. abbr of per procurationem: ~ **J. Smith** p.p. (por poder de) J. Smith.

practicable ['præktɪkəbl] a (scheme) factible.

practical ['præktɪkl] a práctico; ~ **joke** n broma pesada; ~**ly** ad (almost) prácticamente.

practice ['præktɪs] n (habit) costumbre f; (exercise) práctica, ejercicio; (training) adiestramiento; (MED) clientela // vt, vi (US) = **practise**; **in** ~ (in reality) en la práctica; **out of** ~ desentrenado.

practise, **practice** (US) ['præktɪs] vt (carry out) practicar, (be in the habit of) tener por costumbre; (profession) ejercer; (train at) hacer ejercicios de // vi ejercer (profesión); (train) entrenar, adiestrarse; **practising** a (Christian etc) practicante; (lawyer) que ejerce.

practitioner [præk'tɪʃənə*] n practicante m/f; (MED) médico/a.

pragmatic [præg'mætɪk] a pragmático.

prairie ['preərɪ] n pradera, pampa.

praise [preɪz] n alabanza, elogio, alabanzas fpl, elogios mpl; ~**worthy** a loable, digno de elogios.

pram [præm] n cochecito de niño.

prance [prɑːns] vi (horse) hacer cabriolas.

prank [præŋk] n travesura.

prattle ['prætl] vi parlotear; (child) balbucear.

prawn [prɔːn] n gamba; (small) quisquilla.

pray [preɪ] vi rezar; ~**er** n oración f, rezo; (entreaty) ruego, súplica; ~**er book** n devocionario, misal m.

preach [priːtʃ] vi predicar; ~**er** n predicador/a m/f; (US) pastor m.

preamble [prɪ'æmbl] n preámbulo.

prearranged [priːə'reɪndʒd] a arreglado de antemano.

precarious [prɪ'keərɪəs] a precario.

precaution [prɪ'kɔːʃən] n precaución f.

precede [prɪ'siːd] vt, vi preceder.

precedence ['presɪdəns] n precedencia; (priority) prioridad f; **precedent** [-ənt] n precedente m.

preceding [prɪ'siːdɪŋ] a precedente.

precept ['priːsept] n precepto.

precinct ['priːsɪŋkt] n recinto; ~**s** npl contornos mpl; **pedestrian** ~ zona reservada para peatones; **shopping** ~ zona comercial.

precious ['preʃəs] a precioso; (stylised) afectado.

precipice ['presɪpɪs] n precipicio, despeñadero.

precipitate [prɪ'sɪpɪtɪt] a (hasty) precipitado, apresurado // [prɪ'sɪpɪteɪt] (hasten) acelerar; (bring about) causar; **precipitation** [ˈreɪʃən] a precipitación f.

precipitous [prɪ'sɪpɪtəs] a (steep) escarpado.

precise [prɪ'saɪs] a preciso, exacto, (person) escrupuloso, ~**ly** ad exactamente, precisamente; **precision** [-'sɪʒən] n precisión f.

preclude [prɪ'kluːd] vt excluir.

precocious [prɪ'kəuʃəs] a precoz.

preconceived [priːkən'siːvd] a (idea) preconcebido.

precursor [priː'kɜːsə*] n precursor/a m/f.

predator ['predətə*] n animal m de

rapiña; ~y a rapaz, de rapiña.

predecessor ['pri:dɪsɛsə*] n antecesor/a m/f.

predestination [pri:dɛstɪ'neɪʃən] n predestinación f.

predetermine [pri:dɪ'tɜːmɪn] vt predeterminar.

predicament [prɪ'dɪkəmənt] n apuro.

predict [prɪ'dɪkt] vt pronosticar; ~ion [-'dɪkʃən] n pronóstico.

predominant [prɪ'dɒmɪnənt] a predominante; **predominate** [-neɪt] vi predominar.

pre-eminent [pri:'ɛmɪnənt] a preeminente.

pre-empt [pri:'ɛmt] vt apropiarse de antemano.

preen [pri:n] vt: to ~ itself (bird) limpiarse (las plumas); to ~ o.s. pavonearse.

prefab ['pri:fæb] n casa prefabricada.

prefabricated [pri:'fæbrɪkeɪtɪd] a prefabricado.

preface ['prɛfəs] n prefacio.

prefect ['pri:fɛkt] n (Brit: in school) tutor m, monitor m.

prefer [prɪ'fɜː*] vt preferir; ~able ['prɛfrəbl] a preferible; ~ably ['prɛfrəblɪ] ad de preferencia; ~ence ['prɛfrəns] n preferencia, prioridad f; ~ential [prɛfə'rɛnʃəl] a preferente.

prefix ['pri:fɪks] n prefijo.

pregnancy ['prɛɡnənsɪ] n embarazo; **pregnant** [-ənt] a embarazada; **to be pregnant** estar encinta; **pregnant with** preñado de.

prehistoric [pri:hɪs'tɒrɪk] a prehistórico.

prejudge [pri:'dʒʌdʒ] vt prejuzgar.

prejudice ['prɛdʒudɪs] n (bias) prejuicio; (harm) perjuicio // vt (predispose) predisponer; (harm) perjudicar; ~d a (person) predispuesto, con prejuicios; (view) parcial, interesado.

prelate ['prɛlət] n prelado.

preliminary [prɪ'lɪmɪnərɪ] a preliminar.

prelude ['prɛljuːd] n preludio.

premarital ['pri:'mærɪtl] a pre-marital.

premature ['prɛmətʃuə*] a prematuro.

premeditated [pri:'mɛdɪteɪtɪd] a premeditado.

premier ['prɛmɪə*] a primero, principal // n (POL) primer ministro.

première ['prɛmɪə*] n estreno.

premise ['prɛmɪs] n premisa; ~s npl local m; (house) casa sg; (shop) tienda sg; on the ~s en el local.

premium ['pri:mɪəm] n premio; (COMM) prima; **to be at a** ~ ser muy solicitado.

premonition [prɛmə'nɪʃən] n presentimiento.

preoccupation [pri:ɔkju'peɪʃən] n preocupación f; **preoccupied** [-'ɔkjupaɪd] a (worried) preocupado; (absorbed) absorto.

prep [prɛp] n (SCOL: study) deberes mpl; ~ **school** n = **preparatory school**.

prepaid [pri:'peɪd] a con porte pagado.

preparation [prɛpə'reɪʃən] n preparación f; ~s npl preparativos mpl.

preparatory [prɪ'pærətərɪ] a preparatorio, preliminar; ~ **to** con miras a; ~ **school** n escuela preparatoria.

prepare [prɪ'pɛə*] vt preparar, disponer // vi: to ~ **for** prepararse o disponerse para; (make preparations) hacer preparativos para; ~d to dispuesto a.

preponderance [prɪ'pɒndərns] n preponderancia, predominio.

preposition [prɛpə'zɪʃən] n pre-posición f.

preposterous [prɪ'pɒstərəs] a absurdo, ridículo.

prerequisite [pri:'rɛkwɪzɪt] n requisito (previo).

prerogative [pri'rɔgətiv] n prerrogativa.

presbyterian [prezbi'tiəriən] a, n presbiteriano/a.

preschool ['pri:sku:l] a preescolar.

prescribe [pri'skraib] vt prescribir; (MED) recetar.

prescription [pri'skripʃən] n prescripción f; (MED) receta.

presence ['prezns] n presencia; (attendance) asistencia; ~ of mind n presencia de ánimo.

present ['preznt] a (in attendance) presente; (current) actual // n (gift) regalo; (actuality) actualidad f, presente m // vt [pri'zent] (introduce) presentar; (expound) exponer; (give) presentar, dar, ofrecer; (THEATRE) representar; at ~ actualmente; ~able [pri'zentəbl] a presentable; ~ation [-'teiʃən] n presentación f; (gift) obsequio; (of case) exposición f; (THEATRE) representación f; ~-day a actual; ~-ly ad (soon) dentro de poco.

preservation [prezə'veiʃən] n conservación f.

preservative [pri'zə:vətiv] n preservativo.

preserve [pri'zə:v] vt (keep safe) preservar, proteger; (maintain) conservar; (food) hacer una conserva de; (in salt) salar // n (for game) coto, vedado; (often pl: jam) conserva, confitura.

preside [pri'zaid] vi presidir.

presidency ['prezidənsi] n presidencia; **president** [-ənt] n presidente m/f; ~ial [-'denʃl] a presidencial.

press [pres] n (tool, machine, newspapers) prensa; (printer's) imprenta; (crowd) apiñamiento, agolpamiento; (of hand) apretón m // vt (push) empujar; (squeeze) apretar; (clothes: iron) planchar; (TECH) prensar; (hurry) acosar; (insist): to ~ sth on sb insistir en que uno acepte algo // vi (squeeze) apretar; (pressurize) ejercer

presión; we are ~ed for time tenemos poco tiempo; to ~ on vi avanzar; (hurry) apretar el paso; ~ agency n agencia de prensa; ~ conference n conferencia de prensa; ~ cutting n recorte m (de periódico); ~ing a apremiante; ~ stud n botón m de presión.

pressure ['preʃə*] n presión f; (urgency) apremio, urgencia; (influence) influencia; (MED) tensión f nerviosa; ~ cooker n olla a presión; ~ gauge n manómetro; ~ group n grupo de presión; **pressurized** a presurizado.

prestige [pres'ti:ʒ] n prestigio; **prestigious** [-'tidʒəs] a prestigioso.

presumably [pri'zju:məbli] ad se supone que, cabe presumir que.

presume [pri'zju:m] vt presumir, suponer; to ~ to do (dare) atreverse a; (set out to) pretender.

presumption [pri'zʌmpʃən] n suposición f; (pretension) pretensión f, (boldness) atrevimiento.

presuppose [pri:sə'pəuz] vt presuponer.

pretence, pretense (US) [pri'tens] n (claim) pretensión f; (display) ostentación f, (pretext) pretexto; (make-believe) fingimiento, on the ~ of so pretexto de.

pretend [pri'tend] vt (feign) fingir // vi (feign) fingir; (claim): to ~ to sth pretender a algo.

pretension [pri'tenʃən] n (presumption) presunción f; (claim) pretensión f.

pretentious [pri'tenʃəs] a presumido; (ostentatious) ostentoso, aparatoso.

pretext ['pri:tekst] n pretexto.

pretty ['priti] a (gen) hermoso; (person) guapo; (dress) bonito; (sum) importante // ad (quite) bastante; (nearly) casi.

prevail [pri'veil] vi (win) imponerse; (be current) imperar; (be in fashion) estar de moda; (be usual) prevalecer; (persuade): to ~

(up)on sb to do sth persuadir a uno a hacer algo; ~**ing** a (*dominant*) imperante; (*usual*) corriente.

prevalent ['prevələnt] a (*dominant*) predominante; (*usual*) corriente; (*fashionable*) en boga; (*present-day*) actual.

prevent [pri'vent] vt: **to ~** (sb) **from doing sth** impedir a (uno) hacer algo; ~**able** a evitable; ~**ative** a preventivo; ~**ion** ['-'venʃən] n prevención f; ~**ive** a preventivo.

preview ['pri:vju:] n (*of film*) preestreno; (*fig*) anticipo.

previous ['pri:viəs] a previo, anterior; (*hasty*) prematuro; ~**ly** ad previamente, con anticipación; (*in earlier times*) antes.

prewar [pri:'wɔ:*] a de preguerra, prebélico.

prey [prei] n presa // vi: **to ~ on** vivir a costa de; (*feed on*) alimentarse de; (*plunder*) robar, pillar; **it was ~ing on his mind** le agobiaba, le preocupaba.

price [prais] n precio // vt (*goods*) fijar el precio de; ~**less** a inapreciable.

prick [prik] n pinchazo; (*with pin*) alfilerazo; (*sting*) picadura // vt pinchar; picar; **to ~ up one's ears** aguzar el oído.

prickle ['prikl] n (*sensation*) escozor m; (*BOT*) espina; (*ZOOL*) púa; **prickly** a espinoso; (*fig: person*) malhumorado; (: *touchy*) quisquilloso.

pride [praid] n orgullo; (*pej*) soberbia // vt: **to ~ o.s. on** enorgullecerse de, ufanarse de.

priest [pri:st] n sacerdote m; ~**ess** n sacerdotisa; ~**hood** n (*practice*) sacerdocio; (*priests*) clero.

prig [prig] n presumido/a, pedante m/f.

prim [prim] a (*formal*) estirado; (*affected*) remilgado; (*prudish*) gazmoño.

primarily ['praimərili] ad (*above*

all) ante todo; (*firstly*) en primer lugar.

primary ['praiməri] a primario; (*first in importance*) principal; ~ **school** n escuela primaria.

primate ['praimit] n (*REL*) primado // n ['praimeit] (*ZOOL*) primate m.

prime [praim] a primero, principal; (*basic*) fundamental; (*excellent*) selecto, de primera clase // vt (*gun, pump*) cebar; (*fig*) preparar, aprestar; **in the ~ of life** en la flor de la vida; **~ minister** n primer ministro; **primer** n (*book*) libro de texto; (*paint*) pintura de base.

primitive ['primitiv] a primitivo; (*crude*) rudimentario; (*uncivilized*) inculto.

primrose ['primrəuz] n primavera, prímula.

primus (stove) ['praiməs] a hornillo de campaña a presión.

prince [prins] n príncipe m.

princess [prin'ses] n princesa.

principal ['prinsipl] a principal, mayor // n director/a m/f.

principality [prinsi'pæliti] n principado.

principle ['prinsipl] n principio.

print [print] n (*impression*) marca, impresión f; (*letters*) letra de molde; (*fabric*) estampado; (*ART*) estampa, grabado; (*PHOT*) positiva // vt (*gen*) imprimir; (*on mind*) grabar; (*write in capitals*) escribir en letras de molde; **out of ~** agotado; ~**ed matter** n impresos mpl; ~**er** n impresor a m/f; ~**ing** n (*art*) imprenta; (*act*) impresión f; (*quantity*) tirada; ~**ing press** n (prensa de) imprenta.

prior ['praiə*] a anterior, previo // n prior m; ~ **to doing** antes de o hasta hacer.

priority [prai'ɔriti] n prioridad f.

prise [praiz] vt: **to ~ open** abrir con palanca.

prism ['prizəm] n prisma m.

prison ['prizn] n cárcel f, prisión f // a carcelario; ~**er** n (*in prison*) preso; (*under arrest*) detenido; (*in dock*) acusado.

privacy ['prɪvəsɪ] n (*seclusion*) aislamiento, soledad f; (*intimacy*) intimidad f.

private ['praɪvɪt] a (*personal*) particular; (*confidential*) secreto, reservado; (*intimate*) privado, íntimo; (*sitting etc*) a puertas cerradas // n soldado raso; '~' (*on envelope*) 'privado'; (*on door*) 'uso particular o privado'; in ~ en privado; ~ enterprise la empresa privada; ~ eye n detective m privado; ~ly ad en privado; (*in o.s.*) en el fondo.

privet ['prɪvɪt] n alheña.

privilege ['prɪvɪlɪdʒ] n privilegio; (*prerogative*) prerrogativa; ~d a privilegiado.

privy ['prɪvɪ] a: to be ~ to estar enterado de; P~ Council n Consejo Privado.

prize [praɪz] n premio // a premiado, (*first class*) de primera clase // vt apreciar, estimar; ~-giving n distribución f de premios; ~winner n premiado/a.

pro [prəu] n (*SPORT*) profesional m/f; the ~s and cons los pros y los contras.

probability [prɔbə'bɪlɪtɪ] n probabilidad f; **probable** ['prɔbəbl] a probable; (*plausible*) verosímil; **probably** ['prɔbəblɪ] ad probablemente.

probation [prə'beɪʃən] n: on ~ (*employee*) de prueba; (*LAW*) en libertad condicional.

probe [prəub] n (*MED, SPACE*) sonda; (*enquiry*) encuesta, sondeo // vt sondar; (*investigate*) indagar.

problem ['prɔbləm] n problema m; ~atic [-'mætɪk] a problemático.

procedure [prə'siːdʒə*] n (*ADMIN, LAW*) procedimiento; (*method*) proceder m; (*bureaucratic*) trámites mpl.

proceed [prə'siːd] vi proceder; (*continue*): to ~ (with) continuar o

seguir (con); ~ings npl acto sg, actos mpl; (*LAW*) medidas fpl; (*meeting*) función f; (*records*) actas fpl; ~s ['prəusiːdz] npl ganancias fpl, ingresos mpl.

process ['prəuses] n proceso; (*method*) método, sistema m; (*proceeding*) procedimiento // vt tratar, elaborar; in ~ en curso; ~ing n elaboración f.

procession [prə'seʃən] n desfile m; funeral ~ cortejo fúnebre.

proclaim [prə'kleɪm] vt proclamar; (*announce*) anunciar; **proclamation** [prɔklə'meɪʃən] n proclamación f; (*written*) proclama f.

procreation [prəukrɪ'eɪʃən] n procreación f.

procure [prə'kjuə*] vt conseguir, obtener.

prod [prɔd] vt (*push*) empujar; (*with elbow*) dar un codazo a; (*jab*) pinchar // n empuje m; codazo; pinchazo.

prodigal ['prɔdɪgl] a pródigo.

prodigious [prə'dɪdʒəs] a prodigioso.

prodigy ['prɔdɪdʒɪ] n prodigio.

produce ['prɔdjuːs] n (*AGR*) productos mpl agrícolas // vt [prə'djuːs] (*gen*) producir; (*profit*) rendir; (*show*) presentar, mostrar; (*THEATRE*) presentar, poner en escena; (*offspring*) dar a luz; **producer** n (*THEATRE*) director/a m/f; (*AGR, CINEMA*) productor/a m/f.

product ['prɔdʌkt] n (*thing*) producto; (*result*) fruto, resultado.

production [prə'dʌkʃən] n (*act*) producción f; (*thing*) producto; (*THEATRE*) representación f, obra; ~ line n línea o cadena de montaje.

productive [prə'dʌktɪv] a productivo; **productivity** [prɔdʌk'tɪvɪtɪ] n productividad f.

profane [prə'feɪn] a profano; (*language etc*) fuerte.

profess [prə'fes] vt profesar; (*regret*) manifestar.

profession [prə'feʃən] n profesión

f; ~**al** *n* profesional *m/f*; (*expert*) perito // *a* profesional; perito, experto; (*by profession*) de oficio.

professor [prə'fesə*] *n* catedrático/a.

proficiency [prə'fɪʃənsɪ] *n* pericia, habilidad *f*; **proficient** [-ənt] *a* perito, hábil.

profile ['prəufaɪl] *n* perfil *m*.

profit ['prɒfɪt] *n* (*COMM*) ganancia; (*fig*) provecho *f*; // *vi*: **to ~ by** *o* **from** aprovechar *o* sacar provecho de; ~**ability** [-ə'bɪlɪtɪ] *n* rentabilidad *f*; ~**able** *a* (*ECON*) rentable; (*useful*) provechoso; ~**eering** [-'tɪərɪŋ] *n* (*pej*) ganancias *fpl* excesivas.

profound [prə'faund] *a* profundo.

profuse [prə'fjuːs] *a* profuso, pródigo; ~**ly** *ad* profusamente, pródigamente; **profusion** [-'fjuːʒən] *n* profusión *f*, abundancia *f*.

progeny ['prɒdʒɪnɪ] *n* progenie *f*, prole *f*.

programme, program (*US*) ['prəugræm] *n* programa *m* // *vt* programar; **programming, programing** (*US*) *n* programación *f*.

progress ['prəugres] *n* progreso; (*development*) desarrollo // *vi* [prə'gres] progresar, avanzar; desarrollarse; **in ~** en marcha; ~**ion** [-'greʃən] *n* progresión *f*; ~**ive** [-'gresɪv] *a* progresivo; (*person*) progresista *m/f*.

prohibit [prə'hɪbɪt] *vt* prohibir; **to ~ sb from doing sth** prohibir a uno hacer algo; ~**ion** [prəuɪ'bɪʃən] *n* (*US*) prohibicionismo; ~**ive** *a* (*price etc*) excesivo.

project ['prɒdʒekt] *n* proyecto // (*vb*: [prə'dʒekt]) *vt* proyectar // *vi* (*stick out*) salir, sobresalir.

projectile [prə'dʒektaɪl] *n* proyectil *m*.

projection [prə'dʒekʃən] *n* proyección *f*; (*overhang*) saliente *m*.

projector [prə'dʒektə*] *n* proyector *m*.

proletarian [prəulɪ'tɛərɪən] *a, n*

proletario/a; **proletariat** [-rɪət] *n* proletariado.

proliferate [prə'lɪfəreɪt] *vi* proliferar, multiplicarse; **proliferation** [-'reɪʃən] *n* proliferación *f*.

prolific [prə'lɪfɪk] *a* prolífico.

prologue ['prəulɒg] *n* prólogo.

prolong [prə'lɒŋ] *vt* prolongar, extender.

prom [prɒm] *n abbr of* **promenade** baile *m* de gala.

promenade [prɒmə'nɑːd] *n* (*by sea*) paseo marítimo; ~ **concert** *n* concierto (con parte del público permanece de pie).

prominence ['prɒmɪnəns] *n* (*fig*) eminencia, importancia; **prominent** [-ənt] *a* (*standing out*) saliente; (*important*) eminente, importante.

promiscuous [prə'mɪskjuəs] *a* (*sexually*) libertino.

promise ['prɒmɪs] *n* promesa // *vi* prometer; **promising** *a* prometedor(a).

promontory ['prɒməntrɪ] *n* promontorio.

promote [prə'məut] *vt* (*gen*) promover; (*new product*) hacer propaganda por; (*MIL*) ascender; **promoter** *n* (*of sporting event*) promotor/a *m/f*; **promotion** [-'məuʃən] *n* (*gen*) promoción *f*; (*MIL*) ascenso.

prompt [prɒmpt] *a* pronto // *ad* (*punctually*) puntualmente // *vt* (*urge*) mover, incitar; (*THEATRE*) apuntar; **to ~ sb to do sth** mover a uno a hacer algo; ~**er** *n* (*THEATRE*) apuntador/a *m/f*; ~**ly** *ad* (*punctually*) puntualmente; (*rapidly*) rápidamente; ~**ness** *n* puntualidad *f*; rapidez *f*.

prone [prəun] *a* (*lying*) postrado; ~ **to** propenso a.

prong [prɒŋ] *n* diente *m*, púa.

pronoun ['prəunaun] *n* pronombre *m*.

pronounce [prə'nauns] *vt* pronunciar; (*declare*) declarar // *vi*: **to ~ (up)on** pronunciarse sobre;

~d a (marked) marcado; ~ment n declaración f.

pronunciation [prənʌnsɪˈeɪʃən] n pronunciación f.

proof [pru:f] n prueba; (of alcohol) graduación f normal // a: ~ against a prueba de; ~reader n corrector/a m/f de pruebas.

prop [prop] n apoyo; (fig) sostén m // vt (also: ~ up: support) apoyar; (lean): to ~ sth against apoyar algo contra.

propaganda [propəˈgændə] n propaganda.

propagate [ˈpropəgeɪt] vt propagar.

propel [prəˈpel] vt impulsar, propulsar; ~ler n hélice f; ~ling pencil n lapicero.

proper [ˈpropə*] a (suited, right) propio; (exact) justo; (apt) apropiado, conveniente; (timely) oportuno; (seemly) correcto, decente; (authentic) verdadero; (col: real) auténtico.

property [ˈpropətɪ] n (gen) propiedad f; (goods) bienes mpl; (estate) hacienda; it's their ~ es suyo, les pertenece.

prophecy [ˈprofɪsɪ] n profecía; **prophesy** [-saɪ] vt profetizar; (fig) predecir.

prophet [ˈprofɪt] n profeta m/f, ~ic [prəˈfetɪk] a profético.

proportion [prəˈpɔ:ʃən] n proporción f, (share) parte f, porción f; ~al a proporcional; ~ate a proporcionado.

proposal [prəˈpəuzl] n propuesta; (offer) oferta; (plan) proyecto; (of marriage) declaración f; (suggestion) sugerencia

propose [prəˈpəuz] vt proponer; (offer) ofrecer // vi declararse; to ~ to do proponerse hacer.

proposition [propəˈzɪʃən] n propuesta, proposición f.

proprietor [prəˈpraɪətə*] n propietario, dueño.

propulsion [prəˈpʌlʃən] n propulsión f.

pro rata [prəuˈrɑ:tə] ad a prorrateo.

prosaic [prəuˈzeɪɪk] a prosaico.

prose [prəuz] n prosa.

prosecute [ˈprosɪkju:t] vt (LAW) procesar; **prosecution** [-ˈkju:ʃən] n proceso, causa; (accusing side) parte f actora; **prosecutor** n acusador/a m/f; (also: public prosecutor) fiscal m.

prospect [ˈprospekt] n (view) vista; (chance) posibilidad f; (outlook) perspectiva; (hope) esperanza f; (vb: [prəˈspekt]) vt explorar // vi buscar; ~s npl (for work etc) perspectivas fpl; ~ing n prospección f; ~ive [prəˈspektɪv] a (possible) probable, esperado; (certain) futuro; (legislation) en perspectiva; ~or n explorador/a m/f.

prospectus [prəˈspektəs] n prospecto.

prosper [ˈprospə*] vi prosperar; ~ity [-ˈsperɪtɪ] n prosperidad f; ~ous a próspero.

prostitute [ˈprostɪtju:t] n prostituta.

prostrate [ˈprostreɪt] a postrado, (fig) abatido.

protagonist [prəˈtægənɪst] n protagonista m/f.

protect [prəˈtekt] vt proteger; ~ion n protección f; ~ive a protector(a); ~or n protector/a m/f.

protégé [ˈprəuteʒeɪ] n protegido.

protein [ˈprəuti:n] n proteína.

protest [ˈprəutest] n protesta // (vb: [prəˈtest]) vi protestar // vt (affirm) afirmar, declarar.

Protestant [ˈprotɪstənt] a, n protestante m/f.

protocol [ˈprəutəkol] n protocolo.

prototype [ˈprəutətaɪp] n prototipo.

protracted [prəˈtræktɪd] a prolongado.

protrude [prəˈtru:d] vi salir fuera, sobresalir.

proud [praud] a orgulloso; (pej) soberbio, altanero; (imposing) imponente.

prove [pru:v] vt probar; (verify)

comprobar; (show) demostrar // vi:
to ~ **correct** resultar correcto; to
~ **o.s.** ponerse a prueba.
proverb ['prɒvə:b] n refrán m; ~**ial**
[prə'və:biəl] a proverbial.
provide [prə'vaid] vt proporcionar,
dar; to ~ **sb with sth** proveer a uno
de algo; to ~ **for** vt (person)
mantener a; (emergency) prevenir;
~**d** (that) conj con tal que, siempre
que.
providing [prə'vaidiŋ] conj a
condición de que, siempre que.
province ['prɒvins] n provincia;
(fig) esfera; **provincial** [prə'vinʃəl] a
de provincia; (pej) provinciano.
provision [prə'viʒən] n (gen)
provisión f; (supply) suministro;
(supplying) abastecimiento; ~**s** npl
(food) comestibles mpl; ~**al** a
provisional; (temporary) interino.
proviso [prə'vaizəu] n condición f,
estipulación f.
provocation [prɒvə'keiʃən] n
provocación f.
provocative [prə'vɒkətiv] a provocativo; (stimulating) sugestivo.
provoke [prə'vəuk] vt (arouse)
provocar, incitar; (cause) causar,
producir; (anger) irritar.
prow [prau] n proa.
prowess ['prauis] n (skill) destreza,
habilidad f; (courage) valor m.
prowl [praul] vt (also: ~ **about**, ~
around) rondar // n: **on the** ~ **de**
ronda; ~**er** n rondador/a m/f;
(thief) ladrón/ona m/f.
proximity [prɒk'simiti] n
proximidad f.
proxy ['prɒksi] n poder m; (person)
apoderado/a; **by** ~ por poder o
poderes.
prudence ['pru:dns] n prudencia;
prudent [-ənt] a prudente.
prudish ['pru:diʃ] a gazmoño.
prune [pru:n] n ciruela pasa // vt
podar.
pry [prai] vi: to ~ **into**
entrometerse en.
psalm [sɑ:m] n salmo.

pseudo- [sju:dəu] pref seudo...;
~**nym** n seudónimo.
psychiatric [saiki'ætrik] a
psiquiátrico; **psychiatrist** [-'kaiə-
trist] n psiquiatra m/f; **psychiatry**
[-'kaiətri] n psiquiatría.
psychic ['saikik] a (also: ~**al**)
psíquico // n medium m/f.
psychoanalyse [saikəu'ænəlaiz]
vt psicoanalizar; **psychoanalysis**
[-kəuə'næləsis] n psicoanálisis m inv;
psychoanalyst [-'ænəlist] n
psicoanalista m/f.
psychological [saikə'lɒdʒikl] a
psicológico.
psychologist [sai'kɒlədʒist] n
psicólogo; **psychology** [-dʒi] n
psicología.
psychopath ['saikəupæθ] n
psicópata m/f.
psychosomatic [saikəusə'mætik]
a psicosomático.
psychotic [sai'kɒtik] a, n psicótico.
pub [pʌb] n abbr of **public house** pub
m, taberna.
puberty ['pju:bəti] n pubertad f.
public ['pʌblik] a, n público.
publican ['pʌblikən] n tabernero.
publication [pʌbli'keiʃən] n publicación f.
public: ~ **convenience** n aseos mpl
públicos; ~ **house** n bar m, pub m.
publicity [pʌb'lisiti] n publicidad f.
publicly ['pʌblikli] ad pública-
mente, en público.
public: ~ **opinion** n opinión f
pública; ~ **relations** n relaciones fpl
públicas; ~ **school** n (Brit) escuela
privada; ~**-spirited** a de buen
ciudadano.
publish ['pʌbliʃ] vt publicar; ~**er** n
editor/a m/f; ~**ing** n (industry) la
industria editorial.
puce [pju:s] a de color pardo rojizo.
pucker ['pʌkə*] vt (pleat) arrugar;
(brow etc) fruncir.
pudding ['pudiŋ] n pudín m;
(sweet) postre m; **black** ~ morcilla.
puddle ['pʌdl] n charco.
puff [pʌf] n soplo; (from mouth)

bocanada; (sound) resoplido; (also:
powder ~) borla // vi (gen)
soplar; (pant) jadear; to ~ out
smoke echar humo; to ~ up vt
hinchar, inflar; ~ed a (col: out of
breath) sin aliento.

puffin ['pʌfɪn] n frailecillo.

puffy ['pʌfɪ] a hinchado.

pull [pul] n (tug): to give sth a ~
dar un tirón a algo; (fig: advantage)
ventaja; (: influence) influencia //
tirar de; (tug: also) (muscle)
torcerse; (haul) tirar, arrastrar // vi
tirar, dar un tirón, to ~ a face
hacer muecas; to ~ to pieces hacer
pedazos; to ~ one's punches no
emplear toda la fuerza; to ~ one's
weight hacer su parte; to ~ o.s.
together serenarse; to ~ sb's leg
tomarle el pelo a uno; to ~ apart vt
(break) romper (en dos); to ~
down vt (house) derribar; to ~ in vi
(AUT: at the kerb) parar (junto a la
acera), (RAIL) llegar (al andén); to
~ off vt (deal etc) cerrar, concluir
con éxito, to ~ out vi tree,
marcharse; (AUT: from kerb) salir //
vt sacar, arrancar; to ~ through vi
salir (de un apuro); (MED) recobrar
la salud; to ~ up vi (stop) parar //
vt (uproot) arrancar, desarraigar;
(stop) parar.

pulley ['pulɪ] n polea.

pullover ['puləuvə*] n jersey m.

pulp [pʌlp] n (of fruit) pulpa; (for
paper) pasta.

pulpit ['pulpɪt] n púlpito.

pulsate [pʌl'seɪt] vi pulsar, latir.

pulse [pʌls] n (ANAT) pulso; (of
music, engine) pulsación f; (BOT)
legumbre f.

pulverize ['pʌlvəraɪz] vt pulverizar;
(fig) hacer polvo.

puma ['pju:mə] n puma.

pummel ['pʌml] vt dar de
puñetazos.

pump [pʌmp] n bomba; (shoe)
zapato de tenis // vt sacar con una

bomba; (fig: col) sonsacar; to ~ up
vt inflar.

pumpkin ['pʌmpkɪn] n calabaza.

pun [pʌn] n juego de palabras.

punch [pʌntʃ] n (blow) golpe m,
puñetazo; (tool) punzón m; (for
tickets) taladro; (drink) ponche m
// vi (hit): to ~ sb/sth dar un
puñetazo o golpear a uno/algo;
(make a hole in) punzar; ~card n
tarjeta perforada; ~line n palabras
que rematan un chiste; ~-up n (col)
riña.

punctual ['pʌŋktjuəl] a puntual;
~ity [-'æliti] n puntualidad f.

punctuate ['pʌŋktjueɪt] vt
interrumpir; **punctuation** ['eɪʃən] n
puntuación f.

puncture ['pʌŋktʃə*] n pinchazo //
vt pinchar.

pundit ['pʌndɪt] n sabio.

pungent ['pʌndʒənt] a acre.

punish ['pʌnɪʃ] vt castigar; ~ment
n castigo.

punt [pʌnt] n (boat) batea.

punter ['pʌntə*] n (gambler)
jugador/a m/f.

puny ['pju:nɪ] a débil.

pup [pʌp] n cachorro.

pupil ['pju:pl] n alumno/a.

puppet ['pʌpɪt] n títere m.

puppy ['pʌpɪ] n cachorro, perrito.

purchase ['pə:tʃɪs] n compra; (grip)
pie m firme // vt comprar;
purchaser n comprador/a m/f.

pure [pjuə*] a puro.

purée ['pjuəreɪ] n puré m.

purge [pə:dʒ] n (MED) purgante m;
(POL) purga // vt purgar.

purification [pjuərɪfɪ'keɪʃən] n
purificación f, depuración f; **purify**
['pjuərɪfaɪ] vt purificar, depurar.

purist ['pjuərɪst] n purista m/f.

puritan ['pjuərɪtən] n puritano/a;
~ical [-'tænɪkl] a puritano.

purity ['pjuərɪtɪ] n pureza.

purl [pə:l] n punto del revés.

purple ['pə:pl] a purpúreo; (bruise)
morado.

purport [pə:'pɔ:t] vi: to ~ to be/do

dar a entender que es/hace.

purpose ['pɔːpəs] n propósito; **on ~** a propósito, adrede; **~ful** a resuelto, determinado.

purr [pɜː*] n ronroneo // vi ronronear.

purse [pɜːs] n monedero; (bag) bolsa // vt fruncir.

purser ['pɜːsə*] n (NAUT) contador m de navío.

pursue [pə'sjuː] vt seguir, perseguir; (profession) ejercer; **pursuer** n perseguidor/a m/f.

pursuit [pə'sjuːt] n (chase) caza; (persecution) persecución f; (occupation) carrera; (pastime) pasatiempo.

purveyor [pə'veɪə*] n proveedor/a m/f.

pus [pʌs] n pus m.

push [puʃ] n (gen) empuje m; (shove) empujón m; (attack) ataque m; (advance) avance m // vt empujar; (button) apretar; (promote) promover; (thrust): to ~ sth (into) meter algo a la fuerza (en) // vi empujar; (fig) hacer esfuerzos; to ~ **aside** vt apartar con la mano; to ~ **off** vi (col) largarse; to ~ **on** vi (continue) seguir adelante; to ~ **through** vt (measure) despachar; to ~ **up** vt (total, prices) hacer subir; **~chair** n sillita de ruedas; **~ing** a emprendedor/a, enérgico; **~over** n (col): **it's a ~over** está tirado; **~y** a (pej) agresivo.

puss [pus], **pussy(-cat)** ['pusi(kæt)] n minino.

put [put], pt, pp **put** vt (place) poner, colocar; (~ into) meter; (say) declarar, expresar; (a question) hacer; (estimate) calcular; to ~ **about** vi (NAUT) virar // vt (rumour) diseminar; to ~ **across** vt (ideas etc) comunicar; to ~ **away** vt (store) guardar; to ~ **back** vt (replace) devolver a su lugar; (postpone) posponer; to ~ **by** vt (money) guardar; to ~ **down** vt (on

ground) poner en el suelo; (animal) sacrificar; (in writing) apuntar; (suppress: revolt etc) sofocar; (attribute) atribuir; to ~ **forward** vt (ideas) presentar, proponer; (date) adelantar; to ~ **in** vt (application, complaint) presentar; to ~ **off** vt (postpone) aplazar; (discourage) desanimar; to ~ **on** vt (clothes, lipstick etc) ponerse; (light etc) encender; (play etc) presentar; (weight) ganar; (brake) echar; (attitude) adoptar postura de; to ~ **out** vt (fire, light) apagar; (one's hand) alargar; (news, rumour) sacar a luz, diseminar; (tongue etc) sacar; (person: inconvenience) molestar, fastidiar; to ~ **up** vt (raise) levantar, alzar; (hang) colgar; (build) construir; (increase) aumentar; (accommodate) alojar; to ~ **up with** vt fus aguantar.

putrid ['pjuːtrɪd] a podrido.

putt [pʌt] vt golpear con poca fuerza // n put m, golpe m corto; **~er** n (GOLF) putter m; **~ing green** n campo de golf en miniatura.

putty ['pʌtɪ] n masilla.

puzzle ['pʌzl] n (riddle) acertijo; (jigsaw) rompecabezas m inv; (crossword) crucigrama m; (mystery) misterio, problema m // vt dejar perplejo, confundir // vi devanarse los sesos; **puzzling** a misterioso, enigmático.

pygmy ['pɪgmɪ] n pigmeo.

pyjamas [pɪ'dʒɑːməz] npl pijama m.

pylon ['paɪlən] n pilón m, poste m.

pyramid ['pɪrəmɪd] n pirámide m.

python ['paɪθən] n pitón m.

Q

quack [kwæk] n (of duck) graznido; (pej: doctor) curandero // vi graznar.

quad [kwɔd] *abbr of* **quadrangle; quadruplet.**

quadrangle ['kwɔdræŋgl] *n (courtyard: abbr:* quad) patio.

quadruple [kwə'drupl] *a* cuádruple // *n* cuádruplo *m* // *vt, vi* cuadruplicar.

quadruplets [kwɔ:'dru:plɪts] *npl* cuatrillizos *mpl*.

quagmire ['kwægmaɪə*] *n* lodazal *m*, cenegal *m*.

quail [kweɪl] *n (bird)* codorniz *f* // *vi* amedrentarse.

quaint [kweɪnt] *a* curioso; *(picturesque)* pintoresco.

quake [kweɪk] *vi* temblar // *n abbr of* **earthquake.**

Quaker ['kweɪkə*] *n* cuáquero/a.

qualification [kwɔlɪfɪ'keɪʃən] *n (reservation)* reserva; *(modification)* modificación *f; (act)* calificación *f; (degree)* título; **qualified** ['kwɔlɪfaɪd] *a (trained)* cualificado; *(fit)* apto, competente, *(limited)* limitado; *(professionally)* con título.

qualify ['kwɔlɪfaɪ] *vt* calificar; *(capacitate)* capacitar; *(modify)* moderar // *vi (sport)* clasificarse, to ~ *(as)* calificarse (de), graduarse (en); to ~ *(for)* reunir los requisitos (para).

quality ['kwɔlɪtɪ] *n* calidad *f, (moral)* cualidad *f.*

qualm [kwɑːm] *n* escrúpulo.

quandary ['kwɔndrɪ] *n;* **to be in a** ~ estar en un dilema.

quantity ['kwɔntɪtɪ] *n* cantidad *f.*

quarantine ['kwɔrəntiːn] *n* cuarentena.

quarrel ['kwɔrl] *n (argument)* riña; *(fight)* pelea // *vi* reñir; pelearse; ~**some** *a* pendenciero.

quarry ['kwɔrɪ] *n (for stone)* cantera; *(animal)* presa.

quart [kwɔːt] *n* cuarto de galón = 1.136 litros.

quarter ['kwɔːtə*] *n* cuarto, cuarta parte *f; (of year)* trimestre *m; (district)* barrio // *vt* dividir en cuartos; *(MIL: lodge)* alojar; ~**s** *npl*

(barracks) cuartel *m; (living* ~s*)* alojamiento sg; **a** ~ **of an hour** un cuarto de hora; ~ **final** *n* cuarto de final; ~**ly** *a* trimestral // *ad* cada 3 meses, trimestralmente; // ~**master** *n (MIL)* comisario, intendente *m* militar.

quartet(te) [kwɔː'tet] *n* cuarteto.

quartz [kwɔːts] *n* cuarzo.

quash [kwɔʃ] *vt (verdict)* anular.

quasi- ['kweɪzaɪ] *pref* cuasi.

quaver ['kweɪvə*] *n (MUS)* corchea // *vi* temblar.

quay [kiː] *n (also;* ~**side**) muelle *m.*

queasy ['kwiːzɪ] *a (sickly)* delicado.

queen [kwiːn] *n (gen)* reina; *(CARDS etc)* dama; ~ **mother** *n* reina madre.

queer [kwɪə*] *a (odd)* raro, extraño; *(suspect)* sospechoso // *n (col)* maricón *m.*

quell [kwel] *vt* calmar; *(put down)* sofocar.

quench [kwentʃ] *vt* apagar.

query ['kwɪərɪ] *n (question)* pregunta; *(doubt)* duda, *(fig)* interrogante *f* // *vt* preguntar; poner en duda.

quest [kwest] *n* busca, búsqueda.

question ['kwestʃən] *n* pregunta; *(matter)* asunto, cuestión *f* // *vt (gen)* preguntar; *(doubt)* dudar de; *(interrogate)* interrogar, hacer preguntas a; **beyond** ~ fuera de toda duda; **out of the** ~ imposible, ni hablar; ~**able** *a* discutible; *(doubtful)* dudoso; ~ **mark** *n* punto de interrogación; ~**naire** [-'nɛə*] *n* cuestionario.

queue [kjuː] *n* cola // *vi* hacer cola.

quibble ['kwɪbl] *vi* sutilizar.

quick [kwɪk] *a* rápido; *(temper)* vivo; *(agile)* ágil; *(mind)* listo; *(eye)* agudo; *(ear)* fino; **be** ~! ¡date prisa!; ~**en** *vt* apresurar // *vi* apresurarse, darse prisa; ~**ly** *ad* rápidamente, de prisa; ~**ness** *n* rapidez *f;* agilidad *f; (liveliness)* viveza; ~**sand** *n* arenas *fpl* movedizas; ~**step** *n (dance)* fox-trot *m,* quickstep m; ~-witted a perspicaz.

quid [kwɪd] n, pl inv (Brit: col) libra.

quiet ['kwaɪət] a tranquilo; (silent) callado; (ceremony) discreto // n silencio, tranquilidad f; (calm) silencio m; (of town) tranquilidad f; ¡cállate!, ¡silencio!; ~en (also: ~en down) vi (grow calm) calmarse; (grow silent) callarse // vt calmar; hacer callar; ~ly ad (gen) tranquilamente; (silently) silenciosamente; ~ness n (silence) silencio; (calm) tranquilidad f.

quilt [kwɪlt] n edredón m; (continental) ~ n edredón m.

quin [kwɪn] abbr of quintuplet.

quinine [kwɪ'ni:n] n quinina.

quintet(te) [kwɪn'tet] n quinteto.

quintuplets [kwɪn'tju:plɪts] npl quintillizos mpl.

quip [kwɪp] n pulla.

quirk [kwɜːk] n peculiaridad f.

quit [kwɪt], pt, pp quit or quitted vt dejar, abandonar; (premises) desocupar // vi (give up) retirarse; (go away) irse; (resign) dimitir; (stop work) abandonar (una empresa).

quite [kwaɪt] ad (rather) bastante; (entirely) completamente; ~ a few of them un buen número de ellos; ~ (so)! ¡así es!, ¡exactamente!

quits [kwɪts] a: ~ (with) en paz (con).

quiver ['kwɪvə*] vi estremecerse // n (for arrows) carcaj m.

quiz [kwɪz] n (game) concurso; (questioning) interrogatorio // vt interrogar; ~zical a burlón(ona).

quoits [kwɔɪts] npl juego de aros.

quorum ['kwɔːrəm] n quórum n.

quota ['kwəʊtə] n cuota.

quotation [kwəʊ'teɪʃən] n cita; (estimate) presupuesto; ~ marks npl comillas fpl.

quote [kwəʊt] n cita // vt (sentence) citar; (price) fijar // vi: to ~ from citar de.

quotient ['kwəʊʃənt] n cociente m.

R

rabbi ['ræbaɪ] n rabino.

rabbit ['ræbɪt] n conejo; ~ hole n hura (de conejos); ~ hutch n conejera.

rabble ['ræbl] n (pej) chusma, populacho.

rabies ['reɪbiːz] n rabia.

RAC n abbr of Royal Automobile Club.

raccoon [rə'ku:n] n mapache m.

race [reɪs] n (gen) carrera; (species) raza, estirpe f // vt (horse) presentar (en carrera); (engine) acelerar // vi (compete) competir; (run) correr; (pulse) latir a ritmo acelerado; ~course n hipódromo; ~horse n caballo de carreras; ~track n hipódromo; (for cars) autódromo.

racial ['reɪʃl] a racial; ~ism n racismo; ~ist a, n racista m/f.

racing ['reɪsɪŋ] n carreras fpl; ~ car n coche m de carreras; ~ driver n corredor/a m/f de coches.

racist ['reɪsɪst] a, n (pej) racista m/f.

rack [ræk] n (also: luggage ~) rejilla; (shelf) estante m; (also: roof ~) baca, portaequipajes m (also: (clothes) ~) percha // vt (cause pain to) atormentar.

racket ['rækɪt] n (for tennis) raqueta; (noise) ruido, estrépito; (swindle) estafa, timo.

racoon [rə'ku:n] n = raccoon.

racquet ['rækɪt] n raqueta.

racy ['reɪsɪ] a picante, salado.

radar ['reɪdɑ:*] n radar m.

radiance ['reɪdɪəns] n brillantez f, resplandor m; **radiant** [-ənt] a brillante, resplandeciente.

radiate ['reɪdɪeɪt] vt (heat) radiar, irradiar // vi (lines) extenderse.

radiation [reɪdɪ'eɪʃən] n radiación f.

radiator ['reɪdɪeɪtə*] n radiador m; ~ cap n tapón m de radiador.

radical ['rædɪkl] a radical.
radio ['reɪdɪəʊ] n radio f; **on the ~** por radio; **~ station** n emisora.
radio... [reɪdɪəʊ] pref: **~active** a radioactivo; **~activity** n radioactividad f; **~controlled** a teledirigido; **~graphy** ['-ɒɡrəfɪ] n radiografía; **~logy** ['-ɒlədʒɪ] n radiología; **~telephone** n radioteléfono; **~therapy** n radioterapia.
radish ['rædɪʃ] n rábano.
radius ['reɪdɪəs], pl **radii** [-ɪaɪ] n radio.
raffia ['ræfɪə] n rafia.
raffle ['ræfl] n rifa, sorteo // vt rifar.
raft [rɑːft] n (also: life ~) balsa.
rafter ['rɑːftə*] n viga.
rag [ræɡ] n (piece of cloth) trapo; (torn cloth) harapo; (pej: newspaper) periodicucho; (for charity) actividades estudiantiles benéficas // vt tomar el pelo a; **~s** npl harapos mpl; **~-and-bone man** n trapero; **~ doll** n muñeca de trapo.
rage [reɪdʒ] n (fury) rabia, furor m; (fashion) boga // vi (person) rabiar, estar furioso; (storm) bramar.
ragged ['ræɡɪd] a (edge) desigual, mellado; (cuff) roto; (appearance) andrajoso, harapiento; (coastline) accidentado.
raid [reɪd] n (MIL) incursión f; (criminal) asalto; (attack) ataque m; (by police) redada // vt invadir, atacar; asaltar; **~er** n invasor/a m/f; (criminal) asaltante m/f.
rail [reɪl] n (on stair) barandilla, pasamanos m inv; (on bridge, balcony) pretil m; (of ship) borda; (for train) riel m, carril m; **~s** npl vía f; **by ~** por ferrocarril; **~ing(s)** n(pl) verja sg, enrejado sg; **~road** (US), **~way** n ferrocarril m, vía férrea; **~wayman** n ferroviario; **~way station** n estación f de ferrocarril.
rain [reɪn] n lluvia // vi llover; **in the ~** bajo la lluvia; **it's ~ing** llueve, está lloviendo; **~bow** n arco

iris; **~coat** n impermeable m; **~drop** n gota de lluvia; **~fall** n lluvia; **~y** a lluvioso.
raise [reɪz] n aumento // vt (lift) levantar; (build) erigir, edificar; (increase) aumentar; (doubts) suscitar; (a question) plantear; (cattle, family) criar; (crop) cultivar; (army) reclutar; (funds) reunir; (loan) obtener; **to ~ one's voice** alzar la voz.
raisin ['reɪzn] n pasa de Corinto.
rake [reɪk] n (tool) rastrillo; (person) libertino // vt (garden) rastrillar; (fire) hurgar; (with machine gun) barrer.
rakish ['reɪkɪʃ] a gallardo; **at a ~ angle** echado al lado.
rally ['rælɪ] n (POL etc) reunión f, mitin m; (AUT) rallye m; (TENNIS) peloteo // vt reunir; (encourage) reanimar // vi reunirse; (sick person, Stock Exchange) recuperarse; **to ~ round** vt fus (fig) dar apoyo a.
ram [ræm] n carnero; (TECH) pisón m // vt (crash into) dar contra, chocar con; (tread down) apisonar.
ramble ['ræmbl] n caminata, excursión f en el campo // vi (pej: also: **~ on**) divagar; **rambler** n excursionista m/f; (BOT) trepadora; **rambling** a (speech) divagador/a; (BOT) trepador(a) // n excursionismo.
ramp [ræmp] n rampa.
rampage [ræm'peɪdʒ] n: **to be on the ~** desbocarse // vi: **they went rampaging through the town** corrieron como locos por la ciudad.
rampant ['ræmpənt] a (disease etc) violento.
rampart ['ræmpɑːt] n terraplén m; (wall) muralla.
ramshackle ['ræmʃækl] a destartalado.
ran [ræn] pt of **run**.
ranch [rɑːntʃ] n hacienda, estancia; **~er** n ganadero.
rancid ['rænsɪd] a rancio.

rancour, rancor (US) ['ræŋkə*] n rencor m.

random ['rændəm] a fortuito, sin orden // n: at ~ al azar.

randy ['rændɪ] a (col) cachondo.

rang [ræŋ] pt of **ring**.

range [reɪndʒ] n (of mountains) cadena, cordillera; (of missile) alcance m; (of voice) extensión f; (series) serie f; (of products) surtido; (MIL: also: **shooting** ~) campo de tiro; (also: **kitchen** ~) fogón m // vi: **to** ~ **over** (wander) recorrer; (extend) extenderse por; **to** ~ **from ... to...** oscilar entre ... y...; **ranger** n guardabosques m inv.

rank [ræŋk] n (row) fila; (MIL) rango; (status) categoría; (also: **taxi** ~) parada // vi: **to** ~ **among** figurar entre // a (stinking) fétido, rancio; **the** ~ **and file** (fig) la base.

rankle ['ræŋkl] vi (insult) doler.

ransack ['rænsæk] vt (search) registrar; (plunder) saquear.

ransom ['rænsəm] n rescate m; **to hold sb to** ~ (fig) poner a uno entre la espada y la pared.

rant [rænt] vi divagar, desvariar; ~**ing** n lenguaje m declamatorio.

rap [ræp] n golpecito, golpe m seco // vt tocar, dar un golpecito en.

rape [reɪp] n violación f // vt violar.

rapid ['ræpɪd] a rápido; ~**s** npl (GEO) rápidos mpl; ~**ity** [rə'pɪdɪtɪ] n rapidez f.

rapist ['reɪpɪst] n violador m.

rapport [ræ'pɔ:*] n armonía, relación f amistosa.

rapture ['ræptʃə*] n éxtasis m, rapto; **rapturous** a extático; (applause) entusiasta.

rare [rɛə*] a raro, poco común; (CULIN: steak) poco hecho.

rarely ['rɛəlɪ] ad rara vez.

rarity ['rɛərɪtɪ] n rareza f.

rascal ['rɑːskl] n pillo, pícaro.

rash [ræʃ] a imprudente, precipitado // n (MED) salpullido, erupción f (cutánea).

rasher ['ræʃə*] n lonja.

rasp [rɑːsp] n (tool) escofina.

raspberry ['rɑːzbərɪ] n frambuesa; ~ **bush** n frambueso.

rasping ['rɑːspɪŋ] a: **a** ~ **noise** un ruido áspero.

rat [ræt] n rata.

ratchet ['rætʃɪt] n (TECH) trinquete m.

rate [reɪt] n (ratio) razón f; (percentage) tanto por ciento; (price) precio; (: of hotel) tarifa; (of interest) tipo; (speed) velocidad f // vt (value) tasar; (estimate) estimar; **to** ~ **as** ser considerado como; ~**s** npl (Brit) impuesto sg municipal; (fees) tarifa sg; ~**able value** n valor m impuesto; ~**payer** n contribuyente m/f.

rather ['rɑːðə*] ad antes, más bien; (in speech) mejor dicho; **it's** ~ **expensive** es algo caro; (too much) es demasiado caro; **there's** ~ **a lot** hay bastante; **I would** or **I'd** ~ **go** preferiría ir.

ratify ['rætɪfaɪ] vt ratificar.

rating ['reɪtɪŋ] n (valuation) tasación f; (value) valor m; (standing) posición f; (NAUT: category) clase f; (: sailor) marinero.

ratio ['reɪʃɪəu] n razón f; **in the** ~ **of 100 to 1** a razón de 100 a 1.

ration ['ræʃən] n ración f; ~**s** npl víveres mpl // vt racionar.

rational ['ræʃənl] a racional; (solution, reasoning) lógico, razonable; (person) cuerdo, sensato; **rationale** [-'nɑːl] n razón f fundamental; ~**ize** vt organizar lógicamente, racionalizar; ~**ly** ad racionalmente; (logically) lógicamente.

rationing ['ræʃnɪŋ] n racionamiento.

rattle ['rætl] n golpeteo; (of train etc) traqueteo; (of hail) tamborileo; (object: of baby) sonaja, sonajero; (: of sports fan) matraca; (of snake) cascabel m // vi sonar, golpear; traquetear; tamborilear; (small objects) castañetear // vt agitar, sacudir; ~snake n serpiente f de cascabel.

raucous ['rɔːkəs] a estridente, ronco.

ravage ['rævidʒ] vt hacer estragos, destrozar; ~s npl estragos mpl.

rave [reiv] vi (in anger) encolerizarse; (with enthusiasm) entusiasmarse; (MED) delirar, desvariar.

raven ['reivən] n cuervo.

ravenous ['rævənəs] a hambriento, famélico.

ravine [rə'viːn] n barranco.

raving ['reiviŋ] a: ~ lunatic loco de atar.

ravioli [rævi'əuli] n ravioli mpl.

ravish ['ræviʃ] vt encantar; ~ing a encantador(a).

raw [rɔː] a (uncooked) crudo; (not processed) bruto; (sore) vivo; (inexperienced) novato, inexperto; ~ material n materia prima.

ray [rei] n rayo; ~ of hope (rayo de) esperanza.

rayon ['reiɔn] n rayón m.

raze [reiz] vt arrasar.

razor ['reizə*] n (open) navaja; (safety ~) máquina de afeitar; ~ blade n hoja de afeitar.

Rd abbr of road.

re [riː] prep con referencia a.

reach [riːtʃ] n alcance m; (BOXING) envergadura; (of river etc) extensión f entre dos recodos // vt alcanzar, llegar a; (achieve) lograr; (stretch out) alargar, extender // vi alcanzar, extenderse; within (object) al alcance (de la mano); out of ~ fuera del alcance; to ~ out for sth alargar o tender la mano para tomar algo.

react [riː'ækt] vi reaccionar; ~ion [-'ækʃən] n reacción f; ~ionary [-'ækʃənri] a, n reaccionario(a).

reactor [riː'æktə*] n reactor m.

read [riːd], pt, pp read [red] vi leer // vt leer; (understand) entender; (study) estudiar; to ~ out vt leer en

alta voz; ~able a (writing) legible; (book) que merece leerse; ~er n lector/a m/f; (book) libro de lecturas; (at university) profesor/a m/f; ~ership n (of paper etc) número de lectores.

readily ['rɛdili] ad (willingly) de buena gana; (easily) fácilmente; (quickly) en seguida.

readiness ['rɛdinis] n buena voluntad; (preparedness) preparación f; in ~ (prepared) listo, preparado.

reading ['riːdiŋ] n lectura; (understanding) comprensión f; (on instrument) indicación f.

readjust [riːə'dʒʌst] vt reajustar // vi (person); to ~ to reorientarse a.

ready ['rɛdi] a listo, preparado; (willing) dispuesto; (available) disponible // ad: ~-cooked listo para comer // n: at the ~ (MIL) listo para tirar; ~-made a confeccionado; ~ reckoner n libro de cálculos hechos.

reaffirm [riːə'fəːm] vt reafirmar.

real [riəl] a verdadero, auténtico; in ~ terms en términos reales; ~ estate n bienes mpl raíces; ~ism n (also ART) realismo; ~ist n realista m/f; ~istic [-'listik] a realista.

reality [riː'æliti] n realidad f; in ~ en realidad.

realization [riːəlai'zeiʃən] n comprensión f, (COMM) realización f.

realize ['riːəlaiz] vt (understand) darse cuenta de; (a project, COMM: asset) realizar.

really ['riːəli] ad verdaderamente, realmente; ~? ¿de veras?

realm [rɛlm] n reino; (fig) esfera.

reap [riːp] vt segar; (fig) cosechar, recoger; ~er n segadora.

reappear [riːə'piə*] vi reaparecer; ~ance n reaparición f.

reapply [riːə'plai] vi: to ~ for aplicar de nuevo.

rear [riə*] a trasero // n parte f trasera // vt (cattle, family) criar // vi (also: ~ up) (animal) encabritarse; ~**-engined** a (AUT) con motor trasero; ~**guard** n retaguardia.

rearm [ri:'ɑːm] vt, vi rearmar; ~**ament** n rearme m.

rearrange [ri:ə'reɪndʒ] vt ordenar o arreglar de nuevo.

rear-view ['rɪəvju:] a: ~ **mirror** (AUT) espejo retrovisor.

reason ['ri:zn] n (gen) razón f; (cause) motivo, causa; (sense) sensatez f // vi: to ~ **with sb** alegar razones para convencer a uno; **it stands to ~ that** es lógico que; ~**able** a razonable; (sensible) sensato; ~**ably** ad razonablemente; ~**ed** a (argument) razonado; ~**ing** n razonamiento, argumentos mpl.

reassemble [ri:ə'sɛmbl] vt (machine) montar de nuevo // vi reunirse de nuevo.

reassure [ri:ə'ʃuə*] vt tranquilizar, alentar; to ~ **sb of** tranquilizar a uno diciendo que; **reassuring** a alentador(a).

rebate ['ri:beit] n (on product) rebaja; (on tax etc) descuento.

rebel ['rɛbl] n rebelde m/f // vi [rɪ'bɛl] rebelarse, sublevarse; ~**lion** n rebelión f, sublevación f; ~**lious** a rebelde; (child) revoltoso.

rebirth [ri:'bə:θ] n renacimiento.

rebound [rɪ'baund] vi (ball) rebotar // n ['ri:baund] rebote m.

rebuff [rɪ'bʌf] n desaire m, rechazo // vt rechazar.

rebuild [ri:'bɪld] (irg: like build) vt reconstruir.

rebuke [rɪ'bju:k] n reprimenda // vt reprender.

recalcitrant [rɪ'kælsɪtrənt] a reacio.

recall [rɪ'kɔ:l] vt (remember) recordar; (ambassador etc) retirar // n aviso, llamada.

recant [rɪ'kænt] vi retractarse.

recap ['ri:kæp] vt, vi recapitular.

recapture [ri:'kæptʃə*] vt (town) reconquistar; (atmosphere) hacer revivir.

recede [rɪ'si:d] vi retroceder; **receding** a (forehead, chin) huidizo.

receipt [rɪ'si:t] n (document) recibo; (act of receiving) recepción f; ~**s** npl (COMM) ingresos mpl.

receive [rɪ'si:v] vt recibir; (guest) acoger; (wound) sufrir; **receiver** n (TEL) auricular m; (of stolen goods) receptador m/f; (COMM) recibidor/a m/f.

recent ['ri:snt] a reciente; ~**ly** ad recién, recientemente.

receptacle [rɪ'sɛptɪkl] n receptáculo.

reception [rɪ'sɛpʃən] n (gen) recepción f; (welcome) acogida; ~ **desk** n recepción f; ~**ist** n recepcionista m/f.

receptive [rɪ'sɛptɪv] a receptivo.

recess [rɪ'sɛs] n (in room) hueco; (for bed) nicho; (secret place) escondrijo; (POL etc: holiday) vacaciones fpl; ~**ion** n recesión f.

recharge [ri:'tʃɑ:dʒ] vt (battery) recargar.

recipe ['rɛsɪpɪ] n receta.

recipient [rɪ'sɪpɪənt] n recibidor/a m/f; (of letter) destinatario/a.

reciprocal [rɪ'sɪprəkl] a recíproco.

recital [rɪ'saɪtl] n recital m.

recite [rɪ'saɪt] vt (poem) recitar; (complaints etc) enumerar.

reckless ['rɛkləs] a temerario, imprudente; (speed) excesivo, peligroso; ~**ly** ad imprudentemente; de modo peligroso.

reckon ['rɛkən] vt (count) contar; (consider) considerar; (think): **I ~ that...** me parece que...; ~**ing** n (calculation) cálculo; **the day of ~ing** el día del juicio (final).

reclaim [rɪ'kleɪm] vt (land) recuperar; (: from sea) rescatar; (demand back) reclamar; **reclamation** [rɛklə'meɪʃən] n recuperación f, rescate m.

recline [rɪ'klaɪn] vi reclinarse; (lean) apoyarse; **reclining** a (seat) reclinable.

recluse [rɪ'klu:s] n recluso.

recognition [rɛkəgˈnɪʃən] n reconocimiento; **transformed beyond ~** tan transformado que resulta irreconocible.

recognizable [ˈrɛkəgnaɪzəbl] a: **~ (by)** reconocible (por).

recognize [ˈrɛkəgnaɪz] vt reconocer, conocer; **to ~ by/as** reconocer de/por.

recoil [rɪˈkɔɪl] vi (gun) retroceder; (person): **to ~ from doing sth** sentir repugnancia por hacer algo.

recollect [rɛkəˈlɛkt] vt recordar, acordarse de; **~ion** [-ˈlɛkʃən] n recuerdo.

recommend [rɛkəˈmɛnd] vt recomendar; **~ation** [-ˈdeɪʃən] n recomendación f.

recompense [ˈrɛkəmpɛns] vt recompensar // n recompensa.

reconcile [ˈrɛkənsaɪl] vt (two people) reconciliar; (two facts) conciliar; **to ~ o.s. to sth** resignarse a algo, conformarse a algo; **reconciliation** [-sɪlɪˈeɪʃən] n reconciliación f.

reconnaissance [rɪˈkɔnɪsns] n (MIL) reconocimiento.

reconnoitre, reconnoiter (US) [rɛkəˈnɔɪtə*] vi, vt (MIL) reconocer.

reconsider [riːkənˈsɪdə*] vt repensar.

reconstitute [riːˈkɔnstɪtjuːt] vt reconstituir.

reconstruct [riːkənˈstrʌkt] vt reconstruir; **~ion** [-kʃən] n reconstrucción f.

record [ˈrɛkɔːd] n (MUS) disco; (of meeting etc) relación f; (register) registro, partida; (file) archivo; (also: police ~) antecedentes mpl; (written) expediente m; (SPORT) récord m // vt [rɪˈkɔːd] (set down) registrar; (relate) hacer constar; (MUS: song etc) grabar; **in ~ time** en un tiempo récord; **off the ~** a no oficial // ad confidencialmente; **~ card** n (in file) ficha; **~er** n (MUS) flauta de pico; (TECH) contador m; **~ holder** n (SPORT) recordman m;

~ing n (MUS) grabación f; **~ player** n tocadiscos m inv.

recount [rɪˈkaʊnt] vt contar.

re-count [ˈriːkaʊnt] n (POL: of votes) segundo escrutinio // vt [riːˈkaʊnt] volver a contar.

recoup [rɪˈkuːp] vt: **to ~ one's losses** recuperar las pérdidas.

recourse [rɪˈkɔːs] n recurso; **to have ~ to** recurrir a.

recover [rɪˈkʌvə*] vt recobrar, recuperar; (rescue) rescatar // vi (from illness) reponerse; (from shock) sobreponerse; **~y** n recuperación f; rescate m; (MED) mejora.

recreate [riːkrɪˈeɪt] vt recrear.

recreation [rɛkrɪˈeɪʃən] n recreación f; (play) recreo; **~al** a de recreo.

recrimination [rɪkrɪmɪˈneɪʃən] n recriminación f.

recruit [rɪˈkruːt] n recluta m/f // vt reclutar; **~ment** n reclutamiento.

rectangle [ˈrɛktæŋgl] n rectángulo; **rectangular** [-ˈtæŋgjulə*] a rectangular.

rectify [ˈrɛktɪfaɪ] vt rectificar.

rector [ˈrɛktə*] n (REL) párroco; (SCOL) rector/a m/f; **~y** n casa del párroco.

recuperate [rɪˈkuːpəreɪt] vi reponerse, restablecerse.

recur [rɪˈkɜː*] vi repetirse; (opportunity) producirse de nuevo; **~rence** n repetición f; **~rent** a repetido.

red [rɛd] n rojo // a rojo; **to be in the ~** deber dinero; **R~ Cross** n Cruz f Roja; **~currant** n grosella; **~den** vt enrojecer // vi enrojecerse; **~dish** a (hair) rojizo.

redecorate [riːˈdɛkəreɪt] vt decorar de nuevo; **redecoration** [-ˈreɪʃən] n renovación f.

redeem [rɪˈdiːm] vt (gen) redimir; (sth in pawn) desempeñar; (fig, also REL) rescatar; **~ing** a: **~ing feature** rasgo bueno o favorable.

redeploy [riːdɪ'plɔɪ] vt (resources) disponer de nuevo.

red: ~-**haired** a pelirrojo; ~-**handed** a: **to be caught** ~-**handed** coger las con las manos en la masa; ~-**head** n pelirrojo/a; ~-**hot** a candente.

redirect [riːdaɪ'rɛkt] vt (mail) reexpedir.

redness ['rɛdnɪs] n lo rojo; (of hair) rojez f.

redo [riː'duː] (irg: like do) vt rehacer.

redouble [riː'dʌbl] vt: **to ~ one's efforts** intensificar los esfuerzos.

redress [rɪ'drɛs] n reparación f // vt reajustar.

red tape n (fig) trámites mpl, papeleo.

reduce [rɪ'djuːs] vt reducir; (lower) rebajar; '~ **speed now'** (AUT) 'reduzca la velocidad'; **at a ~d price** (of goods) (a precio) rebajado; **reduction** [rɪ'dʌkʃən] n reducción f; (of price) rebaja; (discount) descuento.

redundancy [rɪ'dʌndənsɪ] n desempleo.

redundant [rɪ'dʌndnt] a (worker) parado, sin trabajo; (detail, object) superfluo; **to be made ~** quedarse sin trabajo.

reed [riːd] n (BOT) junco, caña; (MUS: of clarinet etc) lengüeta.

reef [riːf] n (at sea) arrecife m.

reek [riːk] vi: **to ~ (of)** oler o heder a.

reel [riːl] n (gen) carrete m, bobina; (of film) rollo, película // vt (TECH) devanar; (also: ~ **in**) cobrar // vi (sway) tambalear.

re-election [riːɪ'lɛkʃən] n reelección f.

re-enter [riː'ɛntə*] vt reingresar en; **re-entry** n reingreso.

ref [rɛf] n (col) abbr of **referee**.

refectory [rɪ'fɛktərɪ] n refectorio, comedor m.

refer [rɪ'fəː*] vt (send) remitir; (ascribe) referir a, relacionar con

// vi: **to ~ to** (allude to) referirse a, aludir a; (apply to) relacionar con; (consult) remitirse a.

referee [rɛfə'riː] n árbitro; (for job application) persona que recomienda a otro // vt arbitrar.

reference ['rɛfrəns] n (mention) referencia; (sending) remisión f; (relevance) relación f; (for job application: letter) referencia, carta de recomendación; **with ~ to** con referencia a; (COMM: in letter) me remito a; ~ **book** n libro de consulta.

referendum [rɛfə'rɛndəm], pl -**da** [-də] n referéndum m.

refill [riː'fɪl] vt rellenar // n ['riːfɪl] repuesto, recambio.

refine [rɪ'faɪn] vt (sugar, oil) refinar; ~**d** a (person, taste) refinado, culto; ~**ment** n (of person) cultura, educación f; ~**ry** n refinería.

reflect [rɪ'flɛkt] vt (light, image) reflejar // vi (think) reflexionar, pensar; **it ~s badly/well on him** le perjudica/le hace honor; ~**ion** [-'flɛkʃən] n (act) reflexión f; (image) reflejo; (criticism) reproche m, crítica; **on ~ion** pensándolo bien; ~**or** n (also AUT) captafaros m inv, reflector m.

reflex ['riːflɛks] a, n reflejo; ~**ive** [rɪ'flɛksɪv] a (LING) reflexivo.

reform [rɪ'fɔːm] n reforma // vt reformar; **the R~ation** [rɛfə-'meɪʃən] n la Reforma; ~**er** n reformador/a m/f; ~**ist** n reformista m/f.

refrain [rɪ'freɪn] vi: **to ~ from doing** abstenerse de hacer // n estribillo.

refresh [rɪ'frɛʃ] vt refrescar; ~**er course** n curso de repaso; ~**ments** npl (drinks) refrescos mpl.

refrigeration [rɪfrɪdʒə'reɪʃən] n refrigeración f; **refrigerator** [-'frɪdʒəreɪtə*] n refrigeradora, nevera.

refuel [riːˈfjuəl] vi repostar combustible.

refuge [ˈrefjuːdʒ] n refugio, asilo; **to take ~ in** refugiarse en.

refugee [refjuˈdʒiː] n refugiado/a.

refund [ˈriːfʌnd] n reembolso // vt [riˈfʌnd] devolver, reembolsar.

refurbish [riːˈfɜːbiʃ] vt restaurar, renovar.

refusal [riˈfjuːzəl] n negativa; **first ~** primera opción.

refuse [ˈrefjuːs] n basura // (vb: [riˈfjuːz]) vt (reject) rehusar, (say no to) negarse a // vi negarse; (horse) rehusar; **~ bin** n cubo de la basura; **~ tip** n vertedero.

refute [riˈfjuːt] vt refutar, rebatir.

regain [riˈgein] vt recobrar, recuperar.

regal [ˈriːgl] a regio, real.

regalia [riˈgeiliə] n, npl insignias fpl reales.

regard [riˈgɑːd] n (gaze) mirada; (aspect) respecto; (attention) atención f; (esteem) respeto, consideración f // vt (consider) considerar; (look at) mirar; **with kindest ~s** con muchos recuerdos; **~ing, as ~s, with ~ to** en lo respecto a en cuanto a, **as ~s** lo que respecta a; **loss nd a** pesar de todo.

regatta [riˈgætə] n regata.

regent [ˈriːdʒənt] n regente m/f.

régime [reiˈʒiːm] n régimen m.

regiment [ˈredʒimənt] n regimiento // vt reglamentar; **~al** [-ˈmentl] a militar; **~ation** [-ˈteiʃən] n regimentación f.

region [ˈriːdʒən] n región f, **in the ~ of** (fig) alrededor de; **~al** a regional.

register [ˈredʒistə*] n (gen) registro; (list) lista // vt registrar; (birth) declarar; (letter) certificar; (subj: instrument) marcar, indicar // vi (at hotel) registrarse; (sign on) inscribirse; (make impression) producir impresión; **~ed** a (design) registrado; (letter) certificado.

registrar [ˈredʒistrɑː*] n secretario (del registro civil).

registration [redʒisˈtreiʃən] n (act) inscripción f; (AUT: also: **~ number**) matrícula.

registry [ˈredʒistri] n registro, archivo, **~ office** n registro civil; **to get married in a ~ office** casarse por lo civil.

regret [riˈgret] n sentimiento, pesar m; (remorse) remordimiento // vt sentir, lamentar; (repent of) arrepentirse de; **~fully** ad con pesar, sentidamente; **~table** a lamentable; (loss) sensible.

regroup [riːˈgruːp] vt reagrupar // vi reagruparse.

regular [ˈregjulə*] a (gen) regular; (usual) corriente, normal; (soldier) de línea; (intensive) verdadero // n (client etc) cliente m/f habitual; **~ity** [-ˈlæriti] n regularidad f; **~ly** ad con regularidad.

regulate [ˈregjuleit] vt regular, (machine) arreglar, ajustar; **regulation** [-ˈleiʃən] n (rule) regla, reglamento; (adjustment) ajuste m.

rehabilitation [ˈriːhəbiliˈteiʃən] n rehabilitación f.

rehearsal [riˈhɜːsəl] n ensayo; **rehearse** vt ensayar.

reign [rein] n reinado; (fig) dominio // vi reinar; (fig) imperar; **~ing** a (monarch) reinante, actual; (pre-dominant) imperante.

reimburse [riːimˈbɜːs] vt reembolsar; **~ment** n reembolso.

rein [rein] n (for horse) rienda; **to give ~ to** dar rienda suelta a.

reincarnation [ˈriːinkɑːˈneiʃən] n reencarnación f.

reindeer [ˈreindiə*] n, pl inv reno.

reinforce [riːinˈfɔːs] vt reforzar; **~d** a (concrete) armado; **~ment** n (action) reforzamiento; **~ments** npl (MIL) refuerzos mpl.

reinstate [riːinˈsteit] vt (worker) reintegrar a su puesto.

reiterate [riːˈitəreit] vt reiterar, repetir.

reject ['ri:dʒekt] n (COMM) artículo defectuoso // vt [ri'dʒekt] rechazar; (plan) desechar; (solution) descartar; ~ion [ri'dʒekʃən] n rechazo.

rejoice [ri'dʒɔis] vi: to ~ at or over regocijarse o alegrarse de.

rejuvenate [ri'dʒu:vəneit] vt rejuvenecer.

rekindle [ri:'kindl] vt reencender; (fig) despertar.

relapse [ri'læps] n (MED) recaída; (into crime) reincidencia.

relate [ri'leit] vt (tell) contar, relatar; (connect) relacionar // vi relacionarse; ~d a afín, conexo; (person) emparentado; ~d to con referencia a, relacionado con; **relating to** prep acerca de.

relation [ri'leiʃən] n (person) pariente m/f; (link) relación f; ~ship n relación f; (personal ties) relaciones fpl; (also: family ~ship) parentesco.

relative ['relətiv] n pariente m/f, familiar m/f // a relativo.

relax [ri'læks] vi descansar; (person: unwind) relajarse // vt relajar; (mind, person) descansar; ~ation [ri:læk'seiʃən] n (rest) descanso; (ease) relajación f, relax m; (amusement) recreo; (entertainment) diversión f; ~ed a relajado; ~ing a enervante.

relay ['ri:lei] n (race) carrera de relevos // vt (message) retransmitir.

release [ri'li:s] n (from prison, obligation) liberación f, libertad f; (of shot) disparo; (of gas etc) escape m; (of film etc) estreno // vt (prisoner) poner en libertad; (book, film) estrenar; (report, news) publicar; (gas etc) despedir, arrojar; (free: from wreckage etc) soltar; (TECH: catch, spring etc) desenganchar; (let go) soltar, aflojar.

relegate ['reləgeit] vt relegar; (SPORT): **to be ~d** descender.

relent [ri'lent] vi ablandarse, ceder; ~**less** a implacable.

relevance ['reləvəns] n relación f; **relevant** [-ənt] a relacionado; (fact) pertinente; (apt) oportuno.

reliable [ri'laiəbl] a (person, firm) de confianza, de fiar; (method, machine) seguro; (news) fidedigno; **reliably** ad: **to be reliably informed that...** saber de fuente fidedigna que...

reliance [ri'laiəns] n: ~ (on) dependencia (de).

relic ['relik] n (REL) reliquia; (of the past) vestigio.

relief [ri'li:f] n (from pain, anxiety) alivio, desahogo; (help, supplies) socorro, ayuda; (ART, GEO) relieve m.

relieve [ri'li:v] vt (pain, patient) aliviar; (bring help to) ayudar, socorrer; (burden) aligerar; (take over from: gen) sustituir a; (: guard) relevar; **to ~ sb of sth** quitar algo a uno; **to ~ o.s.** hacer sus necesidades.

religion [ri'lidʒən] n religión f; **religious** a religioso.

relinquish [ri'liŋkwiʃ] vt abandonar; (plan, habit) renunciar a.

relish ['reliʃ] n (CULIN) salsa, condimento; (enjoyment) entusiasmo; (flavour) sabor m, gusto // vt (food etc) saborear; **to ~ doing** gustar de hacer.

reload [ri:'ləud] vt recargar.

reluctance [ri'lʌktəns] n renuencia; **reluctant** [-ənt] a renuente; **reluctantly** [-əntli] ad con renuencia.

rely [ri'lai]: **to ~ on** vt fus confiar en, fiarse de; (be dependent on) depender de.

remain [ri'mein] vi (survive) quedar; (be left) sobrar; (continue) quedar(se), permanecer; ~**der** n resto; ~**ing** a sobrante; ~**s** npl restos mpl; (leftovers) desperdicios mpl.

remand [rɪ'mɑːnd] n: **on ~** detenido (en espera del juicio) // vt: **to ~ in custody** reencarcelar, mantener bajo custodia; **~ home** n reformatorio.

remark [rɪ'mɑːk] n comentario // vt comentar; (notice) observar, notar; **~able** a notable; (outstanding) extraordinario.

remarry [rɪ'mærɪ] vi casarse por segunda vez

remedial [rɪ'miːdɪəl] a (tuition, classes) de niños atrasados.

remedy ['remədɪ] n remedio // vt remediar, curar.

remember [rɪ'membə*] vt recordar, acordarse de; (bear in mind) tener presente; **remembrance** n (memory) memoria; (souvenir) recuerdo.

remind [rɪ'maɪnd] vt: **to ~ sb to do sth** recordar a uno que haga algo; **to ~ sb of sth** recordar algo a uno; **she ~s me of her mother** me recuerda a su madre; **~er** n advertencia; (souvenir) recuerdo.

reminisce [remɪ'nɪs] vi recordar viejas historias; **reminiscent** a: **to be reminiscent of sth** recordar algo.

remiss [rɪ'mɪs] a descuidado; **it was ~ of him** fue un descuido suyo.

remission [rɪ'mɪʃən] n remisión f; (of debt, sentence) perdón m.

remit [rɪ'mɪt] vt (send: money) remitir, enviar; **~tance** n remesa, envío.

remnant ['remnənt] n resto; (of cloth) retazo.

remorse [rɪ'mɔːs] n remordimientos mpl; **~ful** a arrepentido; **~less** a (fig) implacable, despiadado.

remote [rɪ'məut] a (distant) lejano; (person) distante; **~ control** n telecontrol m; **~ly** ad remotamente; (slightly) levemente; **~ness** n alejamiento; distancia.

remould ['riː'məuld] vt (tyre) recauchutar.

removable [rɪ'muːvəbl] a (detachable) amovible, separable.

removal [rɪ'muːvəl] n (taking away) el quitar; (from house) mudanza; (from office: sacking) destitución f; (MED) extirpación f; **~ van** n camión m de mudanzas.

remove [rɪ'muːv] vt quitar; (employee) destituir; (name: from list) tachar, borrar; (doubt, abuse) disipar; (TECH) retirar, separar; (MED) extirpar; **removers** npl (company) agencia de mudanzas.

remuneration [rɪmjuːnə'reɪʃən] n remuneración f.

rend [rend], pt, pp **rent** vt rasgar, desgarrar.

render ['rendə*] vt (give) dar, prestar; (hand over) entregar; (reproduce) reproducir; (make) hacer, volver; (return) devolver; **~ing** n (MUS etc) interpretación f.

rendez-vous ['rɔndɪvuː] n cita.

renegade ['renɪgeɪd] n renegado.

renew [rɪ'njuː] vt renovar; (resume) reanudar; (loan etc) prorrogar; (negotiations) volver a; (acquaintance) entablar de nuevo; **~al** n renovación f; reanudación f; prórroga

renounce [rɪ'nauns] vt renunciar a; (disown) renunciar.

renovate ['renəveɪt] vt renovar; **renovation** [-'veɪʃən] n renovación f.

renown [rɪ'naun] n renombre m; **~ed** a renombrado.

rent [rent] n, pt, pp of **rend** // n alquiler m, arriendo // vt alquilar; **~al** n (for television, car) alquiler m.

renunciation [rɪnʌnsɪ'eɪʃən] n renuncia.

reorganize [riː'ɔːgənaɪz] vt reorganizar.

rep [rep] n abbr of **representative; repertory**.

repair [rɪ'peə*] n reparación f, compostura; (patch) remiendo // vt reparar, componer; (shoes) remendar; **in good/bad ~** en buen/mal estado; ~ **kit** n caja de herramientas para reparaciones.

repartee [repɑ:'ti:] n dimes y diretes.

repay [ri:'peɪ] (irg: like pay) vt (money) devolver, reembolsar; (person) pagar; (debt) liquidar; (sb's efforts) devolver, corresponder a; ~**ment** n reembolso, devolución f; (of debt) pago.

repeal [rɪ'pi:l] n (of law) abrogación f; (of sentence) anulación f // vt abrogar, revocar.

repeat [rɪ'pi:t] n (RADIO, TV) retransmisión f // vt repetir // i repetirse; ~**edly** ad repetidas veces.

repel [rɪ'pel] vt (lit, fig) repugnar; ~**lent** a repugnante // n: **insect** ~**lent** crema/loción f anti-insectos.

repent [rɪ'pent] vi: to ~ (of) arrepentirse (de); ~**ance** n arrepentimiento.

repercussion [ri:pə'kʌʃən] n (consequence) repercusión f; to have ~**s** repercutir.

repertoire ['repətwɑ:*] n repertorio.

repertory ['repətəri] n (also: ~ theatre) teatro de repertorio.

repetition [repɪ'tɪʃən] n repetición f.

repetitive [rɪ'petɪtɪv] a (movement, work) reiterativo; (speech) lleno de repeticiones.

replace [rɪ'pleɪs] vt (put back) devolver a su sitio; (take the place of) reemplazar, sustituir; ~**ment** n (gen) reemplazo; (act) reposición f; (person) suplente m/f.

replenish [rɪ'plenɪʃ] vt (glass) rellenar; (stock etc) reponer; (with fuel) repostar.

replete [rɪ'pli:t] a repleto; (well-fed) lleno.

replica ['replɪkə] n copia, reproducción f.

reply [rɪ'plaɪ] n respuesta, contestación f // vi contestar, responder.

report [rɪ'pɔ:t] n informe m; (PRESS etc) reportaje m; (also: school ~) nota; (of gun) estallido // vt informar sobre; (PRESS etc) hacer un reportaje sobre; (bring to notice: occurrence) dar cuenta de // vi (make a report) presentar un informe; (present o.s.): to ~ (to sb) presentarse (ante uno); ~**er** n periodista m/f.

reprehensible [reprɪ'hensɪbl] a reprensible, censurable.

represent [reprɪ'zent] vt representar; (fig) hablar en nombre de; (COMM) ser agente de; ~**ation** [-'teɪʃən] n representación f; (petition) petición f; ~**ations** npl (protest) quejas fpl; ~**ative** n representante m/f // a representativo.

repress [rɪ'pres] vt reprimir; ~**ion** [-'preʃən] n represión f; ~**ive** a represivo.

reprieve [rɪ'pri:v] n (LAW) indulto; (fig) alivio // vt indultar, suspender la pena de.

reprimand ['reprɪmɑ:nd] n reprimenda // vt reprender.

reprint ['ri:prɪnt] n reimpresión f // vt [ri:'prɪnt] reimprimir.

reprisal [rɪ'praɪzl] n represalia.

reproach [rɪ'prəʊtʃ] n reproche m // vt: to ~ **sb with sth** reprochar algo a uno; **beyond** ~ intachable; ~**ful** a lleno de reproches.

reproduce [ri:prə'dju:s] vt reproducir // vi reproducirse; **reproduction** [-'dʌkʃən] n reproducción f; **reproductive** [-'dʌktɪv] a reproductor(a).

reprove [rɪ'pru:v] vt: to ~ **sb for sth** reprender algo a uno.

reptile ['reptaɪl] n reptil m.

republic [rɪ'pʌblɪk] n república; ~**an** a, n republicano/a.

repudiate [rɪ'pju:dɪeɪt] vt (accusation) rechazar; (friend) repudiar; (obligation) desconocer.

repugnant [rɪ'pʌgnənt] a repugnante.

repulse [ri'pʌls] vt rechazar, repulsar; **repulsive** a repulsivo.

reputable ['repjutəbl] a (make etc) de toda confianza; (person) formal.

reputation [repju'teiʃən] n reputación f.

repute [ri'pju:t] n reputación f, fama; **~d** a supuesto; **~dly** ad según dicen o se dice.

request [ri'kwest] n petición f; (formal) solicitud f // vt: to **~ sth of** or **from sb** pedir algo a uno; (formally) solicitar algo a uno.

requiem ['rekwiəm] n réquiem m.

require [ri'kwaiə*] vt (need: subj: person) necesitar, tener necesidad de; (: thing, situation) exigir; (want) pedir; (order) insistir en que; **~ment** n requisito; (need) necesidad f.

requisite ['rekwizit] n requisito f // a preciso, imprescindible; **toilet ~s** artículos mpl de aseo personal.

requisition [rekwi'ziʃən] n: **~ (for)** solicitud f (de) // vt (MIL.) requisar.

reroute [ri:'ru:t] vt (train etc) desviar.

resale ['ri:'seil] n reventa.

rescue ['reskju:] n rescate m // vt rescatar; **~ from** librar de; **~ party** n expedición f de salvamento; **rescuer** n salvador/a m/f.

research [ri'sə:tʃ] n investigaciones fpl // vt investigar; **~er** n investigador/a m/f; **~ work** n investigación f.

resell [ri:'sel] vt revender.

resemblance [ri'zembləns] n parecido; **to bear a ~ to** parecerse a; **resemble** vt parecerse a.

resent [ri'zent] vt resentirse de; **~ful** a resentido; **~ment** n resentimiento.

reservation [rezə'veiʃən] n (gen) reserva; (on road: also: **central ~**) faja intermedia.

reserve [ri'zə:v] n (gen) reserva; (SPORT) suplente m/f; (game ~) coto // vt (seats etc) reservar; **~s** npl (MIL.)

reserva sg; **in ~** de reserva; **~d** a reservado.

reservoir ['rezəvwa:*] n (large) embalse m; (small) depósito.

reshape [ri:'ʃeip] vt (policy) reformar, rehacer.

reshuffle [ri:'ʃʌfl] n: **Cabinet ~** (POL) reconstrucción f del gabinete.

reside [ri'zaid] vi residir, vivir.

residence ['rezidəns] n residencia, (formal: home) domicilio; (length of stay) permanencia; **resident** [-ənt] n vecino, (in hotel) huésped/a m/f // a (population) permanente; (doctor) interno; **residential** [-'denʃəl] a residencial.

residue ['rezidju:] n resto, residuo; (COMM) saldo.

resign [ri'zain] vt (one's post) renunciar a // vi dimitir; **to ~ o.s. to** (endure) resignarse a; **~ation** [rezig'neiʃən] n renuncia; (state of mind) resignación f; **~ed** a resignado.

resilience [ri'ziliəns] n (of material) elasticidad f, (of person) resistencia; **resilient** [-ənt] a (person) resistente.

resin ['rezin] n resina.

resist [ri'zist] vt resistir, oponerse a; **~ance** n resistencia.

resolute ['rezəlu:t] a resuelto.

resolution [rezə'lu:ʃən] n (gen) resolución f; (purpose) propósito.

resolve [ri'zɔlv] n resolución f; (purpose) propósito m // vi resolverse; **to ~ to do** resolver hacer; **~d** a resuelto.

resonant ['rezənənt] a resonante.

resort [ri'zɔ:t] n (town) centro de turismo; (recourse) recurso // vi: **to recurrir a**; **in the last ~** en último caso.

resound [ri'zaund] vi resonar, retumbar; **the room ~ed with shouts** los gritos resonaron en el cuarto; **~ing** a sonoro; (fig) clamoroso.

resource [ri'sɔ:s] n recurso; **~s** npl

recursos *mpl*; ~**ful** *a* inventivo, ingenioso.
respect [rɪs'pɛkt] *n* (*consideration*) respeto; (*relation*) respecto; ~ **recuerdos** *mpl*, saludos *mpl* // *vt* respetar; **with** ~ **to** con respecto a; **in this** ~ en cuanto a eso; ~**ability** [-ə'bɪlɪti] *n* respetabilidad *f*; ~**able** *a* respetable; (*large*) apreciable; (*passable*) tolerable; ~**ful** *a* respetuoso.
respective [rɪs'pɛktɪv] *a* respectivo; ~**ly** *ad* respectivamente.
respiration [rɛspɪ'reɪʃən] *n* respiración *f*.
respiratory [res'pɪrətəri] *a* respiratorio.
respite ['rɛspaɪt] *n* respiro; (*LAW*) prórroga.
resplendent [rɪs'plɛndənt] *a* resplandeciente.
respond [rɪs'pɔnd] *vi* responder; (*react*) reaccionar; **response** [-'pɔns] *n* respuesta; reacción *f*.
responsibility [rɪspɔnsɪ'bɪlɪti] *n* responsabilidad *f*.
responsible [rɪs'pɔnsɪbl] *a* (*liable*): ~ (**for**) responsable (de); (*character*) serio, formal; (*job*) de confianza.
responsive [rɪs'pɔnsɪv] *a* sensible.
rest [rest] *n* descanso, reposo; (*MUS*) pausa, silencio; (*support*) apoyo; (*remainder*) resto // *vi* descansar; (*be supported*): **to** ~ **on** posar(se) en // *vt* (*lean*): **to** ~ **sth on/against** apoyar algo en o contra/contra.
restart [ri:'stɑːt] *vt* (*engine*) volver a arrancar; (*work*) volver a empezar.
restaurant ['rɛstərɔŋ] *n* restorán *m*, restaurante *m*; ~ **car** *n* coche-comedor *m*.
restful ['rɛstful] *a* descansado, reposado.
rest home *n* residencia para jubilados.
restitution [rɛstɪ'tjuːʃən] *n*: **to make** ~ **to sb for sth** indemnizar a uno por algo.

restive ['rɛstɪv] *a* inquieto; (*horse*) rebelón(ona).
restless ['rɛstlɪs] *a* inquieto; ~**ly** *ad* inquietamente.
restoration [rɛstə'reɪʃən] *n* restauración *f*; **restore** [rɪs'tɔː*] *vt* (*building*) restaurar; (*sth stolen*) devolver; (*health*) restablecer.
restrain [rɪs'treɪn] *vt* (*feeling*) contener, refrenar; (*person*): **to** ~ (**from doing**) disuadir (de hacer); ~**ed** *a* (*style*) moderado; ~**t** *n* (*restriction*) freno, control *m*; (*moderation*) moderación *f*; (*of style*) reserva.
restrict [rɪs'trɪkt] *vt* restringir, limitar; ~**ion** [-kʃən] *n* restricción *f*, limitación *f*; ~**ive** *a* restrictivo.
rest room *n* (*US*) aseos *mpl*.
result [rɪ'zʌlt] *n* resultado // *vi*: **to** ~ **in** terminar en, dar por resultado; **as a** ~ **of** a consecuencia de.
resume [rɪ'zjuːm] *vt*, *vi* (*work*, *journey*) reanudar.
résumé ['reɪzjuːmeɪ] *n* resumen *m*.
resumption [rɪ'zʌmpʃən] *n* reanudación *f*.
resurgence [rɪ'sɔːdʒəns] *n* resurgimiento.
resurrection [rɛzə'rɛkʃən] *n* resurrección *f*.
resuscitate [rɪ'sʌsɪteɪt] *vt* (*MED*) resucitar; **resuscitation** [-'teɪʃn] *n* resucitación *f*.
retail ['riːteɪl] *n* venta al por menor // *cpd* al por menor // *vt* vender al por menor *o* al detalle; ~**er** *n* detallista *m/f*.
retain [rɪ'teɪn] *vt* (*keep*) retener, conservar; (*employ*) contratar; ~**er** *n* (*servant*) criado; (*fee*) anticipo.
retaliate [rɪ'tælɪeɪt] *vi*: **to** ~ (**against**) tomar represalias (contra); **retaliation** [-'eɪʃən] *n* represalias *fpl*.
retarded [rɪ'tɑːdɪd] *a* retrasado.
retch [rɛtʃ] *vi* dar arcadas.
retentive [rɪ'tɛntɪv] *a* (*memory*) retentivo.

reticent ['rɛtɪsnt] a reservado.

retina ['rɛtɪnə] n retina.

retinue ['rɛtɪnju:] n séquito, comitiva.

retire [rɪ'taɪə*] vi (give up work) jubilarse; (withdraw) retirarse; (go to bed) (ir a) acostarse; ~d a (person) jubilado; ~ment n (state) retiro; (act) jubilación f; retiring a (leaving) saliente; (shy) retraído.

retort [rɪ'tɔ:t] n (reply) réplica // vi contestar.

retrace [ri:'treɪs] vt: to ~ one's steps volver sobre sus pasos, desandar lo andado.

retract [rɪ'trækt] vt (statement) retirar; (claws) retraer; (undercarriage, aerial) replegar // vi retractarse; ~able a replegable.

retrain [ri:'treɪn] vt reeducar; ~ing n readaptación f profesional.

retreat [rɪ'tri:t] n (place) retiro, (act) retraimiento; (MIL) retirada // vi retirarse; (flood) bajar

retribution [rɛtrɪ'bju:ʃən] n desquite m.

retrieve [rɪ'tri:v] vt (gen) recobrar; (situation, honour) salvar; (error, loss) recuperar; retriever n perro cobrador, perdiguero.

retrospect ['rɛtrəspɛkt] n: in ~ retrospectivamente, mirando hacia atrás; ~ive [-'spɛktɪv] a (law) retroactivo.

return [rɪ'tə:n] n (going or coming back) vuelta, regreso; (of sth stolen etc) devolución f; (recompense) recompensa; (FINANCE from land shares) ganancia, ingresos mpl; (report) informe m // cpd (journey) de regreso; (ticket) de ida y vuelta; (match) de vuelta // vi (person etc: come or go back) volver, regresar; (symptoms etc) reaparecer // vt devolver; (favour, love etc) corresponder a; (verdict) declarar; (POL: candidate) elegir; ~s npl (COMM) ingresos mpl; in ~ en cambio; many happy ~s (of the day)! ¡muchas felicidades!, ¡feliz cumpleaños!

reunion [ri:'ju:nɪən] n reunión f.

reunite [ri:ju:'naɪt] vt reunir; (reconcile) reconciliar.

rev [rɛv] n abbr of revolution (AUT) // (vb: also: ~ up) vt girar (el motor de) // vi acelerarse

reveal [rɪ'vi:l] vt (make known) revelar; ~ing a revelador(a).

reveille [rɪ'vælɪ] n (MIL) diana.

revel ['rɛvl] vi: to ~ in sth/in doing sth deleitarse en algo/en hacer algo.

revelation [rɛvə'leɪʃən] n revelación f.

reveller ['rɛvlə*] n jaranero, juergista m/f; **revelry** [-rɪ] n jarana, juerga.

revenge [rɪ'vɛndʒ] n venganza; (in sport) revancha, to take ~ on vengarse de.

revenue ['rɛvənju:] n ingresos mpl, renta; (on investment) rédito; (profit) ganancia.

reverberate [rɪ'və:bəreɪt] vi (sound) resonar, retumbar; **reverberation** [-'reɪʃən] n retumbo, eco.

revere [rɪ'vɪə*] vt reverenciar, venerar; **reverence** ['rɛvərəns] n reverencia; **reverent** ['rɛvərənt] a reverente.

reverie ['rɛvərɪ] n ensueño.

reversal [rɪ'və:sl] n (of order) inversión f; (of direction) cambio completo; (of decision) revocación f.

reverse [rɪ'və:s] n (opposite) contrario; (back: of cloth) revés m; (: of coin) reverso; (: of paper) dorso; (AUT: also: ~ gear) marcha atrás, contramarcha // a (order) inverso; (direction) contrario // vt (turn over) volver al revés, (invert) invertir; (change: opinion) cambiar (completamente) de // vi (AUT) poner en marcha atrás.

revert [rɪ'və:t] vi: to ~ to volver a.

review [rɪ'vju:] n (magazine, MIL) revista; (of book, film) reseña; (examination) repaso, examen m //

vt repasar, examinar; *(MIL)* pasar revista a; *(book, film)* reseñar; **~er** *n* crítico/a.

revile [rɪ'vaɪl] *vt* injuriar, vilipendiar.

revise [rɪ'vaɪz] *vt* *(manuscript)* corregir; *(opinion)* modificar; *(study: subject)* repasar; *(look over)* revisar; **revision** [rɪ'vɪʒən] *n* corrección *f*; modificación *f*; repaso; revisión *f*.

revitalize [riː'vaɪtəlaɪz] *vt* revivificar.

revival [rɪ'vaɪvəl] *n* *(recovery)* restablecimiento; *(of interest)* renacimiento; *(THEATRE)* reestreno; *(of faith)* despertar *m*.

revive [rɪ'vaɪv] *vt* *(gen)* resucitar; *(custom)* restablecer; *(hope, courage)* reanimar; *(play)* reestrenar // *vi* *(person)* volver en sí, restablecerse; *(from faint)* revivir; *(activity)* recobrarse.

revoke [rɪ'vəuk] *vt* revocar.

revolt [rɪ'vəult] *n* rebelión *f*, sublevación *f* // *vi* rebelarse, sublevarse // *vt* dar asco a, repugnar; **~ing** *a* asqueroso, repugnante.

revolution [revə'luːʃən] *n* revolución *f*; **~ary** *a*, *n* revolucionario/a; **~ize** *vt* revolucionar.

revolve [rɪ'vɒlv] *vi* dar vueltas, girar.

revolver [rɪ'vɒlvə*] *n* revólver *m*.

revolving [rɪ'vɒlvɪŋ] *a* *(chair etc)* giratorio; **~ door** *n* puerta giratoria.

revue [rɪ'vjuː] *n* *(THEATRE)* revista.

revulsion [rɪ'vʌlʃən] *n* asco, repugnancia.

reward [rɪ'wɔːd] *n* premio, recompensa // *vt*: **to ~** *(for)* recompensar *o* premiar (por); **~ing** *a* *(fig)* provechoso, valioso.

rewire ['riː'waɪə*] *vt* *(house)* renovar el alambrado de.

reword [riː'wɜːd] *vt* expresar en otras palabras.

rewrite [riː'raɪt] *(irg: like write)* *vt* volver a escribir *o* redactar.

rhapsody ['ræpsədɪ] *n* *(MUS)* rapsodia; *(fig)* transporte *m* (de admiración).

rhetoric ['retərɪk] *n* retórica; **~al** [rɪ'tɒrɪkl] *a* retórico.

rheumatic [ruː'mætɪk] *a* reumático; **rheumatism** ['ruːmətɪzəm] *n* reumatismo, reúma.

Rhine [raɪn] *n*: **the ~** el (río) Rin.

rhinoceros [raɪ'nɒsərəs] *n* rinoceronte *m*.

rhododendron [rəudə'dendrn] *n* rododendro.

Rhone [rəun] *n*: **the ~** el (río) Ródano.

rhubarb ['ruːbɑːb] *n* ruibarbo.

rhyme [raɪm] *n* rima; *(verse)* poesía.

rhythm ['rɪðm] *n* ritmo; **~ method** método de Ojino; **~ic(al)** *a* rítmico.

rib [rɪb] *n* *(ANAT)* costilla // *vt* *(mock)* tomar el pelo a.

ribald ['rɪbəld] *a* escabroso.

ribbon ['rɪbən] *n* cinta; **in ~s** *(torn)* hecho trizas.

rice [raɪs] *n* arroz *m*; **~field** *n* arrozal *m*; **~ pudding** *n* arroz *m* con leche.

rich [rɪtʃ] *a* rico; *(banquet)* suntuoso; *(soil)* fértil; *(food)* fuerte; (: *sweet)* empalagoso; **the ~** los ricos; **~es** *npl* riqueza *sg*; **~ness** *n* riqueza; suntuosidad *f*; fertilidad *f*.

rickets ['rɪkɪts] *n* raquitismo.

rickety ['rɪkɪtɪ] *a* desvencijado; *(shaky)* tambaleante.

rickshaw ['rɪkʃɔː] *n* rikisha.

ricochet ['rɪkəʃeɪ] *n* rebote *m* // *vi* rebotar.

rid [rɪd], *pt*, *pp* **rid** *vt*: **to ~ sb of sth** librar a uno de algo; **to get ~ of** deshacerse o desembarazarse de.

ridden ['rɪdn] *pp* of **ride**.

riddle ['rɪdl] *n* *(conundrum)* acertijo; *(mystery)* enigma *m*, misterio; *(sieve)* criba // *vt*: **to be ~d with** ser lleno o plagado de.

ride [raɪd] *n* *(gen)* paseo; *(on horse)* cabalgata; *(distance covered)* viaje *m*, recorrido // *(vb: pt* **rode**, *pp*

ridden vi (as sport) montar; (go somewhere: on horse, bicycle) dar un paseo, pasearse; (journey: on bicycle, motor cycle, bus) viajar // vt (a horse) montar a; (distance) viajar; **to ~ a bicycle** ir en bicicleta; **to take sb for a** ~ (fig) engañar a uno; **rider** n (on horse) jinete m; (on bicycle) ciclista m/f; (on motorcycle) motociclista m/f.

ridge [rɪdʒ] n (of hill) cresta; (of roof) caballete m; (wrinkle) arruga.

ridicule [ˈrɪdɪkjuːl] n irrisión f, mofa // vt poner en ridículo, mofarse de; **ridiculous** [ˈdɪkjuləs] a ridículo.

riding [ˈraɪdɪŋ] n montar m a caballo; ~ **school** n escuela de equitación.

rife [raɪf] a: **to be ~** ser muy común; **to be ~ with** abundar en.

riffraff [ˈrɪfræf] n gentuza.

rifle [ˈraɪfl] n rifle m, fusil m // vt saquear; ~ **range** n campo de tiro; (at fair) tiro al blanco.

rift [rɪft] n (fig: disagreement; between friends) desavenencia; (: in party) escisión f.

rig [rɪg] n (also: oil ~) torre f de perforación // vt (election etc) falsificar los resultados de; **to ~ out** vt ataviar de; **to ~ up** vt armar; ~**ging** [ˈrɪgɪŋ] n (NAUT) aparejo.

right [raɪt] a (true, correct (suitable) indi- cado, debido; (proper) apropiado, propio; (just) justo; (morally good) bueno; (not left) derecho // n (title, claim) derecho; (not left) derecha // ad (correctly) bien, correcta- mente; (straight) derecho, directa- mente; (not on the left) a la derecha; (to the ~) hacia la derecha // vt enderezar // excl ¡bueno!, ¡está bien!; **to be ~** (per- son) tener razón; all ~! ¡está bien!; (enough) ¡basta!; ~ **now** ahora mismo; ~ **in the middle** justo en

medio, en pleno centro; ~ **away** en seguida; **by ~s** en justicia; **on the ~** a la derecha; ~ **angle** n ángulo recto; ~**eous** [ˈraɪtʃəs] a justado, honrado; (anger) justificado; ~**eousness** [ˈraɪtʃəsnɪs] n justicia; ~**ful** a (heir) legítimo; ~**-hand** n por la derecha; ~**-handed** a (per- son) que usa la mano derecha; ~**ly** ad correctamente, debidamente; (with reason) con razón; ~**-wing** a (POL) derechista.

rigid [ˈrɪdʒɪd] a rígido; (principle) inflexible; ~**ity** [rɪˈdʒɪdɪti] n rigidez f, inflexibilidad f.

rigmarole [ˈrɪgmərəʊl] n galimatías m.

rigorous [ˈrɪgərəs] a riguroso.

rigour, rigor (US) [ˈrɪgəˀ] n rigor m, severidad f.

rig-out [ˈrɪgaʊt] n (col) atuendo.

rile [raɪl] vt irritar.

rim [rɪm] n borde m; (of spectacles) aro; (of wheel) aro, llanta.

rind [raɪnd] n (of bacon) piel f; (of lemon etc) cáscara; (of cheese) costra.

ring [rɪŋ] n (of metal) aro; (on finger) anillo; (of people, objects) círculo, grupo; (of spies) camarilla; (for boxing) cuadrilátero; (of circus) pista; (bull~) ruedo, plaza; (sound of bell) toque m; (telephone call) llamada // (vb: pt rang, pp rung) vi (on telephone) llamar por teléfono; (large bell) repicar; (also: ~ **out:** voice, words) sonar; (ears) zumbar // vt (TEL also: ~ **up)** llamar; (bell etc) hacer sonar; (doorbell) tocar; **to ~ back** vi, vt (TEL) devolver la llamada; **to ~ off** vi (TEL) colgar, cortar la comunicación; ~**ing** n (of large bell) repique m; (in one's ears) zumbido; ~**leader** n (of gang) cabecilla m/f.

ringlets [ˈrɪŋlɪts] npl rizos mpl, tirabuzones mpl.

ring road n carretera periférica o de circunvalación.

rink [rɪŋk] n (also: **ice** ~) pista.

rinse [rɪns] n (of dishes) enjuague m; (of hair) reflejo // vt enjuagar; dar reflejos a.

riot ['raɪət] n motín m, disturbio // vi amotinarse; **to run ~** desmandarse; **~er** n amotinado/a; **~ous** a (per) alborotado; (party) bullicioso; (uncontrolled) desenfrenado.

rip [rɪp] n rasgón m, rasgadura // vt rasgar, desgarrar // vi correr; **~cord** n cabo de desgarre.

ripe [raɪp] a (fruit) maduro; (ready) listo; **~n** vt madurar // vi madurarse; **~ness** n madurez f.

ripple ['rɪpl] n onda, rizo; (sound) murmullo // vi rizarse // vt rizar.

rise [raɪz] n (slope) cuesta, pendiente m; (hill) altura; (increase: in wages) aumento; (: in prices, temperature) subida, alza; (fig: to power etc) ascenso // vi, pt **rose**, pp **risen** ['rɪzn] (gen) elevarse; (prices) subir; (waters) crecer; (river) nacer; (sun) salir; (person: from bed etc) levantarse; (also: **~ up**: rebel) sublevarse; (in rank) ascender; **to give ~ to** dar lugar o origen a; **to the occasion** ponerse a la altura de las circunstancias.

risk [rɪsk] n riesgo, peligro // vt (gen) arriesgar; (dare) atreverse a; **to take** o **run the ~ of doing** correr el riesgo de hacer; **at ~** en peligro; **at one's own ~** bajo su propia responsabilidad; **~y** a arriesgado, peligroso.

risqué ['riːskeɪ] a (joke) subido de color.

rissole ['rɪsəʊl] n croqueta.

rite [raɪt] n rito; **funeral ~s** exequias fpl.

ritual ['rɪtjuəl] a ritual // n ritual m, rito.

rival ['raɪvl] n rival m/f; (in business) competidor/a m/f // a rival, opuesto // vt competir con; **~ry** n rivalidad f, competencia.

river ['rɪvə*] n río; **up/down ~** río arriba/abajo; **~bank** n orilla (del río); **~bed** n lecho, cauce m; **~side**

n ribera, orilla // cpd (port, traffic) de río, del río.

rivet ['rɪvɪt] n roblón m, remache m // vt remachar; (fig) clavar.

Riviera [rɪvɪ'eərə] n: **the (French) ~** la Costa Azul (Francesa).

road [rəʊd] n (gen) camino; (motorway etc) carretera; (in town) calle f; **~block** n barricada; **~hog** n loco del volante; **~map** n mapa m de carreteras; **~side** n borde m (del camino) // cpd al lado de la carretera; **~sign** n señal f (de carretera o calle); **~ user** n usuario de la vía pública; **~way** n calzada; **~worthy** a (car) listo para conducir.

roam [rəʊm] vi vagar // vt vagar por.

roar [rɔː*] n (of animal) rugido, bramido; (of crowd) rugido; (of vehicle, storm) estruendo; (of laughter) carcajada // vi rugir, bramar; hacer estruendo; **to ~ with laughter** reírse a carcajadas; **to do a ~ing trade** hacer buen negocio.

roast [rəʊst] n carne f asada, asado // vt (meat) asar; (coffee) tostar.

rob [rɒb] vt robar; **to ~ sb of sth** robar algo a uno; (fig: deprive) quitarle algo a uno; **~ber** n ladrón/ona m/f; **~bery** n robo.

robe [rəʊb] n (for ceremony etc) toga; (also: **bath ~**) bata.

robin ['rɒbɪn] n petirrojo.

robot ['rəʊbɒt] n robot m.

robust [rəʊ'bʌst] a robusto, fuerte.

rock [rɒk] n (gen) roca; (boulder) peña, peñasco; (sweet) pirulí // vt (swing gently: cradle) balancear, mecer; (: child) arrullar; (shake) sacudir // vi mecerse, balancearse; sacudirse; **on the ~s** (drink) sobre las rocas; (marriage etc) en ruinas; **to ~ the boat** (fig) causar perturbaciones; **~ and roll** n rocanrol m; **~-bottom** a (fig) con los suelos; **~ery** n cuadro alpino.

rocket ['rɒkɪt] n cohete m.

rocking ['rɒkɪŋ]: **~ chair** n

mecedora; ~ **horse** *n* caballo de balancín.

rocky ['rɔki] *a* (*gen*) rocoso; (*unsteady: table*) débil.

rod [rɔd] *n* vara, varilla; (*TECH*) barra; (*also:* **fishing ~**) caña.

rode [rəud] *pt of* **ride**.

rodent ['rəudnt] *n* roedor *m*.

rodeo ['rəudiəu] *n* rodeo.

roe [rəu] *n* (*species: also:* **~ deer**) corzo; (*of fish*): **hard/soft ~** hueva/lecha.

rogue [rəug] *n* pícaro, pillo; **roguish** *a* pícaro.

role [rəul] *n* papel *m*, rol *m*.

roll [rəul] *n* rollo; (*of banknotes*) fajo; (*also:* **bread ~**) panecillo, bollo; (*register*) lista, nómina; (*sound: of drums etc*) redoble *m*; (*movement: of ship*) balanceo // *vt* hacer rodar; (*also:* **~ up: string**) enrollar; (: *sleeves*) arremangar; (*cigarettes*) liar; (*also:* **~ out: pastry**) aplanar // *vi* (*gen*) rodar; (*drum*) redoblar; (*in walking*) bambolearse; (*ship*) balancearse; **to ~ by** *vi* (*time*) pasar; **to ~ in** *vi* (*mail, cash*) entrar a raudales; **to ~ over** *vi* dar una vuelta; **to ~ up** *vi* (*col: arrive*) presentarse, aparecer // *vt* (*carpet*) arrollar; **~ call** *n* acto de pasar lista; **~er** *n* rodillo; (*wheel*) rueda; **~er skates** *npl* patines *mpl* de rueda.

rollicking ['rɔlikiŋ] *a* alegre, divertido.

rolling ['rəuliŋ] *a* (*landscape*) ondulado; **~ pin** *n* rodillo (de cocina); **~ stock** *n* (*RAIL*) material *m* rodante.

Roman ['rəumən] *a*, *n* romano/a; **~ Catholic** *a*, *n* católico (romano).

romance [rə'mæns] *n* (*love affair*) amorío *mpl*, aventura sentimental; (*charm*) lo romántico.

Romanesque [rəumə'nesk] *a* románico.

Romania [rəu'meiniə] *n* = **Rumania**.

romantic [rə'mæntik] *a* romántico;

romanticism [-tisizəm] *n* romanticismo.

romp [rɔmp] *n* retozo, juego // *vi* (*also:* **~ about**) jugar, brincar.

rompers ['rɔmpəz] *npl* pelele *m*.

roof [ru:f], *pl* **~s** *n* (*gen*) techo; (*of house*) techo, tejado; (*of car*) baca // *vt* techar, poner techo a, the ~ of the mouth *n* el paladar, el cielo de la boca; **~ing** *n* techumbre *f*; **~ rack** *n* (*AUT*) baca, portaequipajes *m inv*.

rook [ruk] *n* (*bird*) graja; (*CHESS*) torre *f*.

room [ru:m] *n* (*in house*) cuarto, habitación *f*, pieza; (*also:* **bed~**) dormitorio; (*in school etc*) sala; (*space*) sitio, cabida; **~s** *npl* (*lodging*) alojamiento *sg*; **'~s to let'** se alquilan pisos *o* cuartos'; **single/double ~** habitación individual/doble *o* para dos personas; **~mate** *n* compañero/a de cuarto; **~ service** *n* servicio de habitaciones; **~y** *a* espacioso.

roost [ru:st] *n* percha *f* // *vi* pasar la noche.

rooster ['ru:stə*] *n* gallo.

root [ru:t] *n* (*BOT, MATH*) raíz *f* // *vi* (*plant, belief*) arraigarse; **to ~ about** *vi* (*fig*) andar buscando; **to ~ for** *vt fus* apoyar a; **to ~ out** *vt* desarraigar.

rope [rəup] *n* cuerda; (*NAUT*) cable *m* // *vt* (*box*) atar *o* amarrar con (una) cuerda; (*climbers: also:* **~ together**) encordarse; **to ~ sb in** (*fig*) persuadir a uno a tomar parte; **to know the ~s** (*fig*) conocer un negocio a fondo; **~ ladder** *n* escala de cuerda.

rosary ['rəuzəri] *n* rosario.

rose [rəuz] *pt of* **rise** // *n* rosa; (*also:* **~bush**) rosal *m*; (*on watering can*) roseta // *a* color de rosa.

rosé ['rəuzei] *n* vino rosado, clarete *m*.

rose: **~bed** *n* rosaleda; **~bud** *n* capullo de rosa; **~bush** *n* rosal *m*.

rosemary ['rəuzməri] *n* romero.

rosette [rəu'zet] *n* rosetón *m*.

roster ['rɔstə*] n: duty ~ lista de deberes.

rostrum ['rɔstrəm] n tribuna.

rosy ['rəuzi] a rosado, sonrosado; **a ~ future** un futuro prometedor.

rot [rɔt] n (decay) putrefacción f, podredumbre f; (fig: pej) decadencia // vt, vi pudrirse, corromperse.

rota ['rəutə] n lista de tandas.

rotary ['rəutəri] a rotativo.

rotate [rəu'teit] vt (revolve) hacer girar, dar vueltas a; (change round: crops) cultivar en rotación (: jobs) alternar // vi (revolve) girar, dar vueltas; **rotating** a (movement) rotativo; **rotation** [-'teiʃən] n rotación f; **in rotation** por turno.

rotor ['rəutə*] n rotor m.

rotten ['rɔtn] a (decayed) podrido; (: wood) carcomido; (fig) corrompido; (col: bad) vil, miserable; **to feel ~** (ill) sentirse muy mal.

rotting ['rɔtiŋ] a podrido.

rotund [rəu'tʌnd] a rotundo.

rouble, ruble (US) ['ruːbl] n rublo.

rouge [ruːʒ] n colorete m.

rough [rʌf] a (skin, surface) áspero; (terrain) quebrado; (road) desigual; (voice) bronco; (person, manner: coarse) tosco, grosero; (weather) borrascoso; (treatment) brutal; (sea) bravo; (cloth) basto; (plan) preliminar; (guess) aproximado; (violent) violento // n (person) matón m; (GOLF): **in the ~** en las hierbas altas; **to ~ it** vivir sin comodidades; **to sleep ~** pasar la noche al raso; **~-and-ready** a improvisado; **~en** vt (a surface) poner áspero; **~ly** ad (handle) torpemente; (make) toscamente; (approximately) aproximadamente; **~ness** n aspereza; tosquedad f, brutalidad f.

roulette [ruː'let] n ruleta.

Roumania [ruːˈmeiniə] n = **Rumania**.

round [raund] a redondo // n

círculo; (of toast) rodaja; (of policeman) ronda; (of milkman) recorrido; (of doctor) visitas fpl; (game: of cards, in competition) partida; (of ammunition) cartucho; (BOXING) asalto; (of talks) ronda // vt (corner) doblar // prep alrededor de // ad: **all ~** por todos lados; **the long way ~** por el camino menos directo; **all the year ~** durante todo el año; **it's just ~ the corner** (fig) está a la vuelta de la esquina; **to go ~ to sb's (house)** ir a casa de uno; **to go ~ the back** pasar por atrás; **to go ~ a house** visitar una casa; **to go the ~s** (story) divulgarse; **to ~ off** vt (speech etc) acabar, poner término a; **to ~ up** vt (cattle) acorralar; (people) reunir; (prices) redondear; **~about** n (AUT) glorieta, redondel m; (at fair) tiovivo // a (route, means) indirecto; **a ~ of applause** una salva de aplausos; **a ~ of drinks** una ronda de bebidas; **~ed** a redondeado; (style) expresivo; **~ly** ad (fig) rotundamente; **~-shouldered** a cargado de espaldas; **~ trip** n viaje m de ida y vuelta; **~up** n rodeo; (of criminals) redada.

rouse [rauz] vt (wake up) despertar; (stir up) suscitar; **rousing** a emocionado, entusiasta.

rout [raut] n (MIL) derrota; (flight) fuga // vt derrotar.

route [ruːt] n ruta, camino; (of bus) recorrido; (of shipping) rumba, derrota; **~ map** n (for journey) mapa m de carreteras.

routine [ruːˈtiːn] a (work) rutinario // n rutina; (THEATRE) número.

roving ['rəuviŋ] a (wandering) errante; (salesman) ambulante.

row [rəu] n (line) fila, hilera; (KNITTING) pasada // n [rau] (noise) estrépito, estruendo; (racket) escándalo; (dispute) bronca, pelea; (fuss) jaleo, follón m; (scolding) regaño // vi (in boat) remar // vi

[rau] reñir(se) // vt (boat) conducir remando.

rowdy ['raudɪ] a (person: noisy) ruidoso; (: quarrelsome) pendenciero; (occasion) alborotado // n pendenciero/a.

rowing ['rauɪŋ] n remo; ~ **boat** n bote m de remos.

royal ['rɔɪəl] a real; ~**ist** a // n monárquico/a; ~**ty** n (~ persons) familia real; (payment to author) derechos mpl de autor.

R.S.V.P. abbr of répondez s'il vous plaît SRC (Se Ruega Contestación).

rub [rʌb] vt (gen) frotar; (hard) restregar; (polish) sacar brillo a // n fi (gen) frotamiento; (touch) roce m; to ~ **sb up the wrong way** coger a uno a contrapelo; to ~ **off** vi borrarse; to ~ **off on** influir en; to ~ **out** vt borrar.

rubber ['rʌbə*] n caucho, goma; (Brit: eraser) goma de borrar; ~ **band** n goma, gomita; ~ **plant** n árbol m del caucho, gomero; ~**y** a elástico.

rubbish ['rʌbɪʃ] n (from household) basura; (waste) desperdicios mpl; (fig: pej) tonterías fpl; (trash) pacotilla; ~ **bin** n cubo de la basura; ~ **dump** n (in town) vertedero, basurero.

rubble ['rʌbl] n escombros mpl.

ruby ['ru:bɪ] n rubí m.

rucksack ['rʌksæk] n mochila.

ructions ['rʌkʃənz] npl lío sg, jaleo sg.

rudder ['rʌdə*] n timón m.

ruddy ['rʌdɪ] a (face) rubicundo, fresco(te; (col: damned) condenado.

rude [ru:d] a (impolite: person) grosero; (: word, manners) rudo, grosero; (sudden) repentino; (shocking) indecente, ~**ly** ad groseramente, toscamente; repentinamente; ~**ness** n grosería, tosquedad f.

rudiment ['ru:dɪmənt] n rudimento; ~**ary** [-'mentərɪ] a rudimentario.

rue [ru:] vt arrepentirse de; ~**ful** a arrepentido.

ruffian ['rʌfɪən] n matón m, criminal m.

ruffle ['rʌfl] vt (hair) despeinar; (clothes) arrugar; (fig: person) agitar.

rug [rʌg] n alfombra; (on knees) manta.

rugby ['rʌgbɪ] n (also: ~ football) rugby m.

rugged ['rʌgɪd] a (landscape) accidentado; (features, character) fuerte.

rugger ['rʌgə*] n (col) rugby m.

ruin ['ru:ɪn] n ruina // vt arruinar; (spoil) estropear; ~**s** npl ruinas fpl, restos mpl; ~**ous** a ruinoso.

rule [ru:l] n (norm) norma, costumbre f; (regulation) regla; (government) dominio; (ruler) metro // vt (country, person) gobernar; (decide) disponer; (draw: lines) trazar // vi regir; (LAW) fallar; to ~ **out** excluir; as a ~ por regla general; ~**d** a (paper) rayado; **ruler** n (sovereign) soberano; (for measuring) regla; **ruling** a (party) gobernante; (class) dirigente // n (LAW) fallo, decisión f.

rum [rʌm] n ron m.

Rumania [ru:'meɪnɪə] n Rumania; ~**n** a, n rumano/a.

rumble ['rʌmbl] n retumbo, ruido sordo; (of thunder) redoble m // vi retumbar, hacer un ruido sordo; (stomach, pipe) sonar.

rummage ['rʌmɪdʒ] vi revolverlo todo.

rumour, rumor (US) ['ru:mə*] n rumor m // vt: **it is** ~**ed that...** se rumorea que...

rump [rʌmp] n (of animal) ancas fpl, grupa; ~**steak** n filete m de lomo.

rumpus ['rʌmpəs] n (col) lío, jaleo; (quarrel) pelea, riña.

run [rʌn] n carrera; (outing) paseo, excursión f; (distance travelled) trayecto; (series) serie f; (THEATRE) temporada; (SKI) pista // (vb: pt ran, pp run) vt (operate: business) dirigir; (: competition, course) organizar; (: hotel, house) administrar, llevar; (to pass: hand) pasar; (water, bath) abrir el grifo (del baño) // vi (gen) correr; (work: machine) funcionar, marchar; (bus, train: operate) circular, ir; (: travel) ir; (continue: play) seguir; (: contract) ser válido; (flow: river, bath) fluir; (colours, washing) desteñirse; (in election) ser candidato; **there was a ~ on** (meat, tickets) hubo mucha demanda en; **in the long ~** a la larga, a largo plazo; **on the ~** en fuga; **I'll ~ you to** the station te llevaré a la estación en coche; **to ~ about** vi (children) correr por todos lados; **to ~ across** vt fus (find) dar con, toparse con; **to ~ away** vi huir; **to ~ down** vi (clock) parar // vt (AUT) atropellar; (criticize) criticar; **to be ~ down** estar debilitado; **to ~ off** vt (water) dejar correr // vi huir corriendo; **to ~ out** vi (person) salir corriendo; (liquid) irse; (lease) caducar, vencer; (money) acabarse; **to ~ out of** vt fus quedar sin; **to ~ over** vt sep (AUT) atropellar // vt fus (revise) repasar; **to ~ through** vt fus (instructions) repasar; **to ~ up** vt (debt) incurrir en; **to ~ up against** (difficulties) tropezar con; **~away** a (horse) desbocado; (truck) sin frenos; (person) fugitivo.

rung [rʌŋ] pp of **ring** // n (of ladder) escalón m, peldaño.

runner ['rʌnə*] n (in race: person) corredor/a m/f; (: horse) caballo; (on sledge) patín m; (on curtain) anillo; (wheel) ruedecilla; **~ bean** n (BOT) judía escarlata; **~-up** n subcampeón/ona m/f.

running ['rʌnɪŋ] n (sport) atletismo; (race) carrera // a (water) corriente; (commentary) continuo; **6 days ~** 6 días seguidos; **~ board** n estribo.

runny ['rʌnɪ] a derretido.

run-of-the-mill ['rʌnəvðə'mɪl] a común y corriente.

runt [rʌnt] n (also: pej) redrojo, enano.

runway ['rʌnweɪ] n (AVIAT) pista de aterrizaje.

rupee [ruː'piː] n rupia.

rupture ['rʌptʃə*] n (MED) hernia // vt: **to ~ o.s.** causarse una hernia, quebrarse.

rural ['ruərl] a rural.

ruse [ruːz] n ardid m.

rush [rʌʃ] n ímpetu m; (hurry) prisa; (COMM) demanda repentina; (BOT) junco; (current) corriente f fuerte, ráfaga // vt apresurar; (work) hacer de prisa; (attack: town etc) asaltar // vi correr, precipitarse; **~ hour** n horas fpl punta.

rusk [rʌsk] n bizcocho tostado.

Russia ['rʌʃə] n Rusia; **~n** a, n ruso/a.

rust [rʌst] n herrumbre f, moho // vi oxidarse.

rustic ['rʌstɪk] a rústico.

rustle ['rʌsl] vi susurrar // vt (paper) hacer crujir; (US: cattle) hurtar, robar.

rustproof ['rʌstpruːf] a inoxidable, a prueba de herrumbre.

rusty ['rʌstɪ] a oxidado, mohoso.

rut [rʌt] n rodera, carril m; (ZOOL) celo; **to be in a ~** ir encarrilado.

ruthless ['ruːθlɪs] a despiadado; **~ness** n crueldad f, implacabilidad f.

rye [raɪ] n centeno; **~ bread** n pan de centeno.

S

sabbath ['sæbəθ] n domingo; (Jewish) sábado.

sabbatical [sə'bætɪkl] a: **~ year** año de licencia.

sabotage ['sæbəta:ʒ] n sabotaje m // vt sabotear.

saccharin(e) ['sækərɪn] n sacarina.

sack [sæk] n (bag) saco, costal m // vt (dismiss) despedir; (plunder) saquear; **to get the ~** ser despedido; **~ing** n (material) harpillera.

sacrament ['sækrəmənt] n sacramento.

sacred ['seɪkrɪd] a sagrado, santo.

sacrifice ['sækrɪfaɪs] n sacrificio // vt sacrificar.

sacrilege ['sækrɪlɪdʒ] n sacrilegio.

sacrosanct ['sækrousæŋkt] a sacrosanto.

sad [sæd] a (unhappy) triste; (deplorable) lamentable, **~den** vt entristecer.

saddle ['sædl] n silla (de montar); (of cycle) sillín m // vt (horse) ensillar; **to be ~d with sth** (col) quedar cargado con algo; **~bag** n alforja.

sadism ['seɪdɪzm] n sadismo; **sadist** n sadista m/f; **sadistic** [sə'dɪstɪk] a sádico.

sadly ['sædlɪ] ad tristemente; **lacking (in)** muy deficiente (en).

sadness ['sædnɪs] n tristeza.

safari [sə'faːrɪ] n safari m.

safe [seɪf] a (out of danger) fuera de peligro; (not dangerous, sure) seguro; (unharmed) a salvo, ileso; (trustworthy) digno de confianza // n caja de caudales, caja fuerte; **~ and sound** sano y salvo; (just) **to be on the ~ side** por mayor seguridad; **~guard** n protección f, garantía // vt proteger, defender; **~keeping** n custodia; **~ly** ad seguramente, con seguridad; (without mishap) sin peligro.

safety ['seɪftɪ] n seguridad f // a de seguridad; **~ first!** ¡precaución!; **~ belt** n cinturón m (de seguridad); **~ pin** n imperdible m.

saffron ['sæfrən] n azafrán m.

sag [sæg] vi aflojarse.

sage [seɪdʒ] n (herb) salvia; (man) sabio.

Sagittarius [sædʒɪ'tɛərɪəs] n Sagitario.

sago ['seɪgou] n sagú m.

said [sed] pt, pp of **say**.

sail [seɪl] n (on boat) vela; (trip:) **to go for a ~** tomar un paseo en barco // vt (boat) gobernar // vi (travel: ship) navegar; (: passenger) pasear en barco; (set off) zarpar; **they ~ed into Copenhagen** llegaron a Copenhague; **to ~ through** vi, vt fus (fig) hacer con facilidad; **~boat** n (US) velero, barco de vela; **~ing** n (SPORT) balandrismo; **to go ~ing** salir en balandro; **~ing ship** n barco de vela; **~or** n marinero, marino.

saint [seɪnt] n santo; **S~ John San** Juan; **S~** ...

sake [seɪk] n: **for the ~ of** por (motivo de).

salad ['sæləd] n ensalada; **~ bowl** n ensaladera; **~ cream** n mayonesa; **~ dressing** n aliño; **~ oil** n aceite m para ensaladas.

salami [sə'laːmɪ] n salami m.

salary ['sælərɪ] n sueldo.

sale [seɪl] n venta; (at reduced prices) liquidación f, saldo; **"grand ~"** grandes rebajas; **"for ~"** "se vende"; **on ~** en venta; **room** n sala de subastas; **salesman/woman** n vendedor/a m/f; (in shop) dependiente/a m/f; (representative) viajante m/f; **salesmanship** n arte m de vender.

saliva [sə'laɪvə] n saliva.

sallow ['sælou] a cetrino.

salmon ['sæmən] n, pl inv salmón m.

saloon [sə'luːn] n (US) bar m, taberna; (AUT) (coche m de) turismo; (ship's lounge) cámara, salón m.

salt [sɔlt] n sal f // vt salar; (put on) poner sal en; **~ cellar** n salero; **~water** n de agua salada; **~y** a salado.

salutary ['sæljutərɪ] a saludable.

salute [sə'lu:t] n saludo; (of guns) salva // vt saludar.

salvage ['sælvɪdʒ] n (saving) salvamento, recuperación f; (things saved) objetos mpl salvados // vt salvar.

salvation [sæl'veɪʃən] n salvación f; S~ **Army** n Ejército de Salvación.

salve [sælv] n (cream etc) ungüento, bálsamo.

salver ['sælvə*] n bandeja.

same [seɪm] a mismo // ad de la misma forma, igual // pron: the ~ el mismo/la misma; the ~ book as el mismo libro que; all or just the ~ sin embargo, aun así; to do the ~ (as sb) hacer lo mismo (que otro); the ~ to you! ¡igualmente!

sample ['sɑ:mpl] n muestra // vt (food, wine) probar.

sanatorium [sænə'tɔ:rɪəm], pl -ria [-rɪə] n sanatorio.

sanctify ['sæŋktɪfaɪ] vt santificar.

sanctimonious [sæŋktɪ'məunɪəs] a santurrón(ona).

sanction ['sæŋkʃən] n sanción f // vt sancionar.

sanctity ['sæŋktɪtɪ] n (gen) santidad f; (inviolability) inviolabilidad f.

sanctuary ['sæŋktjuərɪ] n (gen) santuario; (refuge) asilo, refugio.

sand [sænd] n arena; (beach) playa // vt enarenar.

sandal ['sændl] n sandalia; (wood) sándalo.

sand: ~**bag** n saco de arena; ~**bank** n banco de arena; ~**castle** n castillo de arena; ~**dune** n duna; ~**paper** n papel m de lija; ~**pit** n (for children) cajón m de arena; ~**stone** n piedra arenisca.

sandwich ['sænwɪtʃ] n bocadillo, sándwich m // vt (also: ~ **in**) intercalar; ~**ed between** apretujado entre; **cheese/ham** ~ sándwich de queso/jamón; ~**board** n cartelón m; ~ **course** n curso de medio tiempo.

sandy ['sændɪ] a arenoso; (colour) rojizo.

sane [seɪn] a cuerdo, sensato; (sensible) prudente.

sang [sæŋ] pt of **sing**.

sanitarium [sænɪ'tɛərɪəm] (US) = **sanatorium**.

sanitary ['sænɪtərɪ] a (system, arrangements) sanitario; (clean) higiénico; ~ **towel**, ~ **napkin** (US) n paño higiénico, compresa higiénica.

sanitation [sænɪ'teɪʃən] n (in house) saneamiento; (in town) sanidad f, higiene f.

sanity ['sænɪtɪ] n cordura; (common sense) juicio, sentido común.

sank [sæŋk] pt of **sink**.

Santa Claus [sæntə'klɔ:z] n San Nicolás, Papá Noel.

sap [sæp] n (of plants) savia // vt (strength) minar, agotar.

sapling ['sæplɪŋ] n árbol nuevo o joven.

sapphire ['sæfaɪə*] n zafiro.

sarcasm ['sɑ:kæzm] n sarcasmo; **sarcastic** [-'kæstɪk] a sarcástico.

sardine [sɑ:'di:n] n sardina.

Sardinia [sɑ:'dɪnɪə] n Cerdeña.

sari ['sɑ:rɪ] n sari m.

sash [sæʃ] n faja.

sat [sæt] pt, pp of **sit**.

Satan ['seɪtn] n Satanás m.

satchel ['sætʃl] n bolsa; (child's) cartera.

satellite ['sætəlaɪt] n satélite m.

satin ['sætɪn] n raso // a de raso.

satire ['sætaɪə*] n sátira; **satirical** [sə'tɪrɪkl] a satírico; **satirize** ['sætɪraɪz] vt satirizar.

satisfaction [sætɪs'fækʃən] n satisfacción f; (of debt) liquidación f; **satisfactory** [-'fæktərɪ] a satisfactorio.

satisfy ['sætɪsfaɪ] vt satisfacer; (pay) liquidar; (convince) convencer; ~**ing** a satisfactorio.

saturate ['sætʃəreɪt] vt: to ~ (with) empapar o saturar (de); **saturation** [-'reɪʃən] n saturación f.

Saturday ['sætədɪ] n sábado.
sauce [sɔːs] n salsa; (sweet) crema; (fig: cheek) frescura; ~**pan** n perola.
saucer ['sɔːsə*] n platillo.
saucy ['sɔːsɪ] a fresco, descarado; (flirtatious) coqueta.
sauna ['sɔːnə] n sauna.
saunter ['sɔːntə*] vi deambular.
sausage ['sɒsɪdʒ] n salchicha; (cold meat) embutido; ~ **roll** n empanadita.
sauté ['səʊteɪ] a salteado.
savage ['sævɪdʒ] a (cruel, fierce) feroz, furioso; (primitive) salvaje // n salvaje m/f // vt (attack) embestir; ~**ry** n ferocidad f; salvajismo.
save [seɪv] vt (rescue) salvar, rescatar; (money, time) ahorrar; (put by) guardar; (avoid: trouble) evitar // vi (also: ~ up) ahorrar // n (SPORT) parada // prep salvo, excepto.
saving ['seɪvɪŋ] a (on price etc) económica // a: the ~ **grace** of el único mérito de; ~**s** npl ahorros mpl; ~**s bank** n caja de ahorros.
saviour ['seɪvjə*] n salvador/a m/f.
savour, savor (US) ['seɪvə*] n sabor m, gusto // vt saborear; ~**y** a sabroso; (dish: not sweet) no dulce (: salted) salado.
saw [sɔː] pt of **see** // n (tool) sierra // vt, pt **sawed**, pp **sawed** or **sawn** serrar; ~**dust** n (a)serrín m, ~**mill** n aserradero.
saxophone ['sæksəfəʊn] n saxófono.
say [seɪ] n. to have one's ~ expresar su opinión; to have a or some ~ in sth tener voz o que ver en algo // vt, pt, pp **said** decir; to ~ yes/no decir que sí/no; that is to ~ es decir; that goes without ~**ing** eso va sin decir; ~**ing** n dicho, refrán m
scab [skæb] n costra; (pej) esquirol/a m/f; ~**by** a costroso, lleno de costras.

scaffold ['skæfəʊld] n (for execution) cadalso, patíbulo; ~**ing** n andamios mpl, andamiaje m.
scald [skɔːld] n escaldadura // vt escaldar; ~**ing** a (hot) hirviendo.
scale [skeɪl] n (gen, MUS) escala; (of fish) escama, (of salaries, fees etc) escalafón m; (of map, also: size, on tent) escala // vt (mountain) escalar; (tree) trepar; ~**s** npl (small) balanza sg; (large) báscula sg; **on a large** ~ a gran escala; ~ **of charges** tarifa, lista de precios; **social** ~ escala social; ~ **drawing** n dibujo a escala; ~ **model** n modelo a escala.
scallop ['skɒləp] n (ZOOL) venera; (SEWING) festón m.
scalp [skælp] n cabellera // vt escalpar.
scalpel ['skælpl] n escalpelo.
scamp [skæmp] n diablillo, travieso.
scamper ['skæmpə*] vi: to ~ **away**, ~ **off** lise corriendo.
scan [skæn] vt (examine) escudriñar; (glance at quickly) dar un vistazo a; (TV, RADAR) explorar, registrar.
scandal ['skændl] n escándalo; (gossip) chismes mpl; ~**ize** vt escandalizar; ~**ous** a escandaloso; (libellous) calumnioso.
Scandinavia [skændɪ'neɪvɪə] n Escandinavia; ~**n** a escandinavo.
scant [skænt] a escaso; ~**y** a escaso.
scapegoat ['skeɪpgəʊt] n cabeza de turco, chivo expiatorio.
scar [skɑː] n cicatriz f // vt marcar con una cicatriz // vi cicatrizarse.
scarce [skɛəs] a escaso, ~**ly** ad apenas; **scarcity** n escasez f; (shortage) carestía.
scare [skɛə*] n susto, sobresalto; (panic) pánico // vt asustar, espantar; **to** ~ **sb stiff** dejar muerto de miedo a uno; **bomb** ~ amenaza de bomba; ~**crow** n espantapájaros

m inv; ~**d a: to be** ~**d** asustarse, estar asustado.

scarf [skɑ:f], *pl* **scarves** *n* (*long*) bufanda; (*square*) pañuelo.

scarlet ['skɑ:lɪt] *a* escarlata; ~ **fever** *n* escarlatina.

scarves [skɑ:vz] *pl of* **scarf**.

scary ['skɛərɪ] *a* (*col*) de miedo.

scathing ['skeɪðɪŋ] *a* mordaz.

scatter ['skætə*] *vt* (*spread*) esparcir, desparramar; (*put to flight*) dispersar // *vi* desparramarse; dispersarse; ~**brained** *a* ligero de cascos; (*forgetful*) olvidadizo.

scavenger ['skævəndʒə*] *n* (*refuse collector*) basurero; (*ZOOL*) animal *m*/ave *f* que se alimenta de la carroña.

scene [si:n] *n* (*THEATRE, fig etc*) escena; (*of crime, accident*) escenario; (*sight, view*) vista, perspectiva; (*fuss*) escándalo; ~**ry** *n* (*THEATRE*) decorado; (*landscape*) paisaje *m*; **scenic** *a* (*picturesque*) pintoresco.

scent [sent] *n* perfume *m*, olor *m*; (*fig: track*) rastro, pista; (*sense of smell*) olfato // *vt* perfumar; (*smell*) oler; (*sniff out*) husmear; (*suspect*) sospechar.

sceptic, skeptic (*US*) ['skeptɪk] *n* escéptico/a; ~**al** *a* escéptico/a; ~**ism** ['skeptɪsɪzm] *n* escepticismo.

sceptre, scepter (*US*) ['septə*] *n* cetro.

schedule ['ʃedju:l] *n* (*of trains*) horario; (*of events*) programa *m*; (*plan*) plan *m*; (*list*) lista // *vt* (*timetable*) establecer el horario de; (*list*) catalogar; (*visit*) fijar la hora de; **on** ~ a la hora, sin retraso; **to be ahead of/behind** ~ estar adelantado/en retraso.

scheme [ski:m] *n* (*plan*) plan *m*, proyecto; (*method*) esquema *m*; (*plot*) intriga; (*trick*) ardid *m*; (*arrangement*) disposición *f* // *vt* proyectar // *vi* (*plan*) hacer

proyectos; (*intrigue*) intrigar; **scheming** *a* intrigante.

schism ['skɪzəm] *n* cisma *m*.

schizophrenia [skɪtsəʊ'fri:nɪə] *n* esquizofrenia; **schizophrenic** [-'frɛnɪk] *a* esquizofrénico.

scholar ['skɒlə*] *n* (*pupil*) alumno/a, estudiante *m*/f; (*learned person*) sabio, erudito; ~**ly** *a* erudito; ~**ship** *n* erudición *f*; (*grant*) beca.

school [sku:l] *n* (*gen*) escuela, colegio; (*in university*) facultad *f* // *vt* (*animal*) amaestrar; ~ **age** *n* edad *f* escolar; ~**book** *n* libro de texto; ~**boy** *n* alumno; ~**days** *npl* años *mpl* del colegio; ~**girl** *n* alumna; ~**ing** *n* enseñanza; ~**master/mistress** *n* (*primary*) maestro/a; (*secondary*) profesor/a *m*/f; ~**room** *n* clase f; ~**teacher** *n* maestro/a.

schooner ['sku:nə*] *n* (*ship*) goleta; (*glass*) jarra.

sciatica [saɪ'ætɪkə] *n* ciática.

science ['saɪəns] *n* ciencia; ~ **fiction** *n* ciencia-ficción f; **scientific** [-'tɪfɪk] *a* científico; **scientist** *n* científico.

scimitar ['sɪmɪtə*] *n* cimitarra.

scintillating ['sɪntɪleɪtɪŋ] *a* brillante, ingenioso.

scissors ['sɪzəz] *npl* tijeras *fpl*; **a pair of** ~ unas tijeras.

scoff [skɒf] *vt* (*col: eat*) engullir // *vi*: **to** ~ (**at**) (*mock*) mofarse (de).

scold [skəʊld] *vt* regañar.

scone [skɒn] *n* panecillo.

scoop [sku:p] *n* cucharón *m*; (*for flour etc*) pala; (*PRESS*) exclusiva; **to** ~ **out** *vt* excavar; **to** ~ **up** *vt* recoger.

scooter ['sku:tə*] *n* (*motor cycle*) moto f; (*toy*) patinete *m*.

scope [skəʊp] *n* (*of plan, undertaking*) ámbito; (*reach*) alcance *m*; (*of person*) competencia; (*opportunity*) campo (de acción).

scorch [skɔ:tʃ] *vt* (*clothes*) chamuscar; (*earth, grass*) quemar, secar; ~er n (col: hot day) día m abrasador; ~ing a abrasador(a).

score [skɔ:*] n (points etc) puntuación f; (MUS) partitura; (reckoning) cuenta; (twenty) veinte m, veintena f // vt (goal, point) ganar; (mark) rayar // vi marcar un tanto; (FOOTBALL) marcar un gol; (keep score) llevar el tanteo; on that — en lo que se refiere a eso; to ~ 6 out of 10 obtener una puntuación de 6 sobre 10; ~board n marcador m; ~card n (SPORT) tanteador m; ~r n marcador m; (keeping score) tanteador m.

scorn [skɔ:n] n desprecio // vt despreciar; ~ful a desdeñoso, despreciativo.

Scorpio ['skɔ:pɪəu] n Escorpión m.

scorpion ['skɔ:pɪən] n escorpión m.

Scot [skɔt] n escocés/esa m/f.

scotch [skɔtʃ] vt (rumour) desmentir; (plan) abandonar; S~ n whisky m escocés.

Scotland ['skɔtlənd] n Escocia.

Scots [skɔts] a escocés(esa); ~man/woman n escocés/esa m/f; **Scottish** ['skɔtɪʃ] a escocés(esa).

scoundrel ['skaundrl] n canalla m/f, sinvergüenza m/f.

scour ['skauə*] vt (clean) fregar, estregar; (search) recorrer, registrar; ~er n estropajo m.

scourge [skə:dʒ] n azote m.

scout [skaut] n (MIL, also: boy ~) explorador m; to ~ around reconocer el terreno.

scowl [skaul] vi fruncir el ceño; to ~ at sb mirar con ceño a uno.

scraggy ['skrægɪ] a flaco, descarnado.

scram [skræm] vi (col) largarse.

scramble ['skræmbl] n (climb) subida f; (struggle) pelea // vi: to ~ out/through salir/abrirse paso con dificultad; to ~ for pelear por; ~d eggs npl huevos mpl revueltos.

scrap [skræp] n (bit) pedacito m; (fig) pizca f; (fight) riña, bronca; (also: ~

iron) chatarra, hierro viejo // vt reducir a chatarra; (discard) desechar, descartar // vi reñir, armar (una) bronca; ~s npl (waste) sobras fpl, desperdicios mpl; ~book n álbum m de recortes.

scrape [skreip] n (fig) lío, apuro // vt raspar; (skin etc) rasguñar (~ against) rozar // vi: to ~ through pasar con dificultad; ~r n raspador m.

scrap: ~ heap n (fig): on the ~ heap desperdiciado; ~ merchant n chatarrero; ~ paper n pedazos mpl de papel; ~py a (poor) pobre; (speech) inconexo; (bitty) fragmentario.

scratch [skrætʃ] n rasguño m; (from claw) arañazo // a: ~ team equipo improvisado // vt (record) rayar; (with claw, nail) rasguñar, arañar // vi rascarse; to start from ~ partir de cero, empezar desde el principio; to be up to ~ estar a la altura de las circunstancias.

scrawl [skrɔ:l] n garabatos mpl // vi hacer garabatos.

scream [skri:m] n chillido // vi chillar.

screech [skri:tʃ] vi chirriar.

screen [skri:n] n (CINEMA, TV) pantalla; (movable) biombo; (wall) tabique m; (also: wind ~) parabrisas m inv; (from wind etc) cortina // vt (conceal) tapar; (from the wind etc) proteger; (film) proyectar; (candidate etc) investigar a; ~ing n (MED) investigación f médica; ~ test n prueba de pantalla.

screw [skru:] n tornillo; (propeller) hélice f // vt atornillar; (also: ~ in) apretar; ~driver n destornillador m; ~y a (col) chiflado.

scribble ['skrɪbl] n garabatos mpl // vt escribir con prisa.

script [skrɪpt] n (CINEMA etc) guión m; (writing) escritura, letra.

Scripture ['skrɪptʃə*] n Sagrada Escritura.

scriptwriter ['skrɪptraɪtɔ*] n guionista m/f.

scroll [skrəul] n rollo.

scrounge [skraundʒ] vt (col): to ~ sth off or from sb obtener algo de otro por gorronería // vi: to ~ on sb vivir a costa de uno; **scrounger** n gorrón/ona m/f.

scrub [skrʌb] n (clean) fregado; (land) maleza // vt fregar, restregar; (reject) cancelar, anular.

scruff [skrʌf] n: by the ~ of the neck por el pescuezo.

scruffy ['skrʌfɪ] a desaliñado, piojoso.

scruple ['skru:pl] n escrúpulo; **scrupulous** a escrupuloso.

scrutinize ['skru:tɪnaɪz] vt escudriñar; (votes) escrutar; **scrutiny** [-nɪ] n escrutinio, examen m.

scuff [skʌf] vt desgastar, restregar.

scuffle ['skʌfl] n refriega.

scullery ['skʌlərɪ] n fregadero, trascocina.

sculptor ['skʌlptɔ*] n escultor m; **sculpture** ['skʌlptʃɔ*] n escultura.

scum [skʌm] n (on liquid) nata; (pej: people) canalla; (fig) heces fpl.

scurry ['skʌrɪ] vi: to ~ off escabullirse.

scurvy ['skɜ:vɪ] n escorbuto.

scuttle ['skʌtl] n (also: coal ~) cubo, carbonera // vt (ship) barrenar // vi (scamper): to ~ away, ~ off escabullirse.

scythe [saɪð] n guadaña.

sea [si:] n mar m or f; on the ~ (boat) en el mar; (town) junto al mar; **to be all at** ~ (fig) estar despistado; **out** to **or** at ~ en alta mar; ~ **bird** n ave f marina; ~**board** n litoral m; ~ **breeze** n brisa de mar; ~**farer** n marinero; ~**food** n mariscos mpl; ~ **front** n (beach) playa; (prom) paseo marítimo; ~**going** a (ship) de alta mar; ~**gull** n gaviota.

seal [si:l] n (animal) foca; (stamp) sello // vt (close) cerrar; (: with ~) sellar; **to** ~ **off** obturar; **it** ~**ed his fate** decidió su destino.

sea level ['si:lɛvl] n nivel m del mar.

sealing wax ['si:lɪŋwæks] n lacre m.

sea lion ['si:laɪən] n león m marino.

seam [si:m] n costura; (of metal) juntura; (of coal) veta, filón m.

seaman ['si:mən] n marinero.

seamless ['si:mlɪs] a sin costura.

seamstress ['sɛmstrɪs] n costurera.

seance ['seɪɔns] n sesión f de espiritismo.

sea: ~**plane** n hidroavión m; ~**port** n puerto de mar.

search [sɜ:tʃ] n (for person, thing) busca, búsqueda; (of drawer, pockets) registro; (inspection) reconocimiento // vt (look in) buscar en; (examine) examinar; (person, place) registrar // vi: to ~ for buscar; **to** ~ **through** vt fus registrar; **in** ~ **of** en busca de; ~**ing** a penetrante; ~**light** n reflector m; ~ **party** n pelotón m de salvamento; ~ **warrant** n mandamiento (judicial).

sea: ~**shore** n playa, orilla del mar; ~**sick** a mareado; ~**side** n playa, orilla del mar; ~**side resort** n playa.

season ['si:zn] n (of year) estación f; (sporting etc) temporada; (gen) época, periodo // vt (food) sazonar; ~**al** a estacional; ~**ing** n condimento, aderezo; ~ **ticket** n billete m de abono.

seat [si:t] n (in bus, train: place) asiento; (chair) silla; (PARLIAMENT) escaño; (buttocks) culo, trasero; (of government) sede f // vt sentar; (have room for) tener asientos para; **to be** ~**ed** sentarse; ~ **belt** n cinturón m de seguridad.

sea: ~ **water** n agua m del mar; ~**weed** n alga marina; ~**worthy** a marinero, en condiciones de navegar.

sec. abbr of **second(s)**.

secede [sɪ'si:d] vi separarse.

secluded [sɪ'klu:dɪd] a retirado; **seclusion** [-'klu:ʒən] n retiro.

second ['sɛkənd] a segundo // ad (in race etc) en segundo lugar // n (gen) segundo; (AUT: also: ~ **gear**) segunda; (COMM) artículo con algún desperfecto // vt (motion) apoyar; ~**ary** a secundario; ~**ary school** n escuela secundaria; ~**class** a de segunda clase; ~**hand** a de segunda mano, usado; ~**hand** n (on clock) segundero; ~**ly** ad en segundo lugar; ~**ment** [sɪ'kɒndmənt] n traslado temporal; ~**rate** a de segunda categoría.

secrecy ['si:krəsɪ] n secreto; **secret** ['si:krɪt] a, n secreto.

secretarial [sɛkrɪ'tɛərɪəl] a de secretario/a.

secretariat [sɛkrɪ'tɛərɪət] n secretaría.

secretary ['sɛkrətrɪ] n secretario/a; **S~ of State** (Brit: POL) Ministro (con cartera).

secretive ['si:krətɪv] a reservado, sigiloso.

sect [sɛkt] n secta; ~**arian** [-'tɛərɪən] a sectario/a.

section ['sɛkʃən] n sección f; (part) parte f; (of document) artículo; (of opinion) sector m; ~**al** a (drawing) en corte.

sector ['sɛktə*] n sector m.

secular ['sɛkjulə*] a secular, seglar.

secure [sɪ'kjuə*] a (free from anxiety) seguro; (firmly fixed) firme, fijo // vt (fix) asegurar, afianzar; (get) conseguir.

security [sɪ'kjuərɪtɪ] n seguridad f; (for loan) fianza; (object) prenda.

sedate [sɪ'deɪt] a (calm) tranquilo; (formal) serio, formal // vt tratar con calmantes.

sedation [sɪ'deɪʃən] n (MED) sedación f; **sedative** ['sɛdɪtɪv] a sedante m, sedativo.

sedentary ['sɛdntrɪ] a sedentario.

sediment ['sɛdɪmənt] n sedimento.

seduce [sɪ'dju:s] vt (gen) seducir; **seduction** [-'dʌkʃən] n seducción f; **seductive** [-'dʌktɪv] a seductor(a).

see [si:], pt **saw**, pp **seen** vt (gen) ver; (accompany) acompañar; to ~ **sb** to the **door** acompañar a uno a una puerta; (understand) ver, comprender; (look at) mirar // vi ver // n sede f; to ~ **that** (ensure) asegurar que; to ~ **about** vt atender a, encargarse de; to ~ **off** vt despedirse de; to ~ **through** vt penetrar (con la vista) // vt fus llevar a cabo; to ~ **to** vt fus atender a, encargarse de.

seed [si:d] n semilla; (in fruit) pepita; (sperm) semen m, simiente f; (fig) germen m; (TENNIS) preseleccionado/a; ~**ling** n planta de semillero; ~**y** a (shabby) desaseado, raído.

seeing ['si:ɪŋ] conj: ~ (that) visto que, en vista de que.

seek [si:k], pt, pp **sought** vt (gen) buscar; (post) solicitar.

seem [si:m] vi parecer; ~**ingly** ad aparentemente, según parece.

seen [si:n] pp of **see**.

seep [si:p] vi filtrarse.

seesaw ['si:sɔ:] n balancín m, columpio.

seethe [si:ð] vi hervir; to ~ **with anger** enfurecerse.

segment ['sɛgmənt] n segmento.

segregate ['sɛgrɪgeɪt] vt segregar; **segregation** [-'geɪʃən] n segregación f.

seismic ['saɪzmɪk] a sísmico.

seize [si:z] vt (grasp) agarrar, asir; (take possession of) secuestrar; (: territory) apoderarse de; (opportunity) aprovecharse de; to ~ **(up)on** vt fus valerse de; to ~ **up** vi (TECH) agarrotarse.

seizure ['si:ʒə*] n (MED) ataque m; (LAW) incautación f.

seldom ['sɛldəm] ad rara vez.

select [sɪ'lɛkt] a selecto, escogido // vt escoger, elegir; (SPORT) seleccionar; ~**ion** [-'lɛkʃən] n selección f, elección f; (COMM) surtido; ~**ive** a selectivo; **~or** n (person) seleccionador/a m/f.

self [sɛlf] pron se; (after prep) sí mismo // n, pl **selves** uno mismo; **him~/her~** él mismo/ella misma; **the ~** el yo.

self... pref auto...; **~-appointed** a autonombrado; **~-assured** a seguro de sí mismo; **~-catering** a sin pensión; **~-centred** a egocéntrico; **~-coloured** a de color natural; (of one colour) de un color; **~-confidence** n confianza en sí mismo; **~-conscious** a cohibido; **~-contained** a (gen) independiente; (flat) con entrada particular; **~-control** n autodominio; **~-defence** n defensa propia; **~-discipline** n autodisciplina; **~-employed** a que trabaja por cuenta propia; **~-evident** a patente; **~-governing** a autónomo; **~-important** a presumido; **~-indulgent** a inmoderado; **~-interest** n egoísmo; **~-ish** a egoísta; **~-ishness** n egoísmo; **~-lessly** ad desinteresadamente; **~-pity** n autocompasión f; **~-portrait** n autorretrato; **~-possessed** a sereno, dueño de sí mismo; **~-preservation** n propia conservación f; **~-reliant** a independiente, seguro de sí mismo; **~-respect** n amor m propio; **~-righteous** a santurrón(ona); **~-sacrifice** n abnegación f; **~-satisfied** a satisfecho de sí mismo; **~-service** a de autoservicio; **~-sufficient** a autosuficiente; **~-taught** a autodidacta.

sell [sɛl], pt, pp **sold** vt vender // vi venderse; **to ~ at** or **for £10** vender a 10 libros; **to ~ off** vt liquidar; **to ~ out** vi transigir, transar (AM); **~er** n vendedor/a m/f; **~ing price** n precio de venta.

sellotape ['sɛləuteɪp] n celo.

sellout ['sɛlaut] n traición f; (of tickets): **it was a ~** fue un éxito de taquilla.

selves [sɛlvz] pl of **self.**

semaphore ['sɛməfɔ:*] n semáforo.

semen ['si:mən] n semen m.

semi... [sɛmɪ] pref semi..., medio...; **~circle** n semicírculo; **~colon** n punto y coma; **~conscious** a semiconsciente; **~detached** (house) n (casa) semiseparada; **~final** n semi-final m.

seminar ['sɛmɪnɑ:*] n seminario.

semitone ['sɛmɪtəun] n (MUS) semitono.

semolina [sɛmə'li:nə] n sémola.

senate ['sɛnɪt] n senado; **senator** n senador/a m/f.

send [sɛnd], pt, pp **sent** vt mandar, enviar; (dispatch) despachar; (telegram) poner; **to ~ away** vt (letter, goods) despachar; **to ~ away for** vt fus despachar por; **to ~ back** vt devolver; **to ~ for** vt fus mandar traer; **to ~ off** vt (goods) despachar; (SPORT: player) expulsar; **to ~ out** vt (invitation) mandar; (signal) emitir; **to ~ up** vt (person, price) hacer subir; (parody) parodiar; **~er** n remitente m/f; **~-off** n: **a good ~-off** una buena despedida.

senile ['si:naɪl] a senil; **senility** [sɪ'nɪlɪtɪ] n senilidad f.

senior ['si:nɪə*] a (older) mayor, más viejo; (: on staff) más antiguo; (of higher rank) superior // n mayor m; (in service) miembro más antiguo; **~ity** [-'ɔrɪtɪ] n antigüedad f.

sensation [sɛn'seɪʃən] n sensación f; **~al** a sensacional; **~alism** n sensacionalismo.

sense [sɛns] n sentido; (feeling) sensación f; (good ~) sentido común, juicio; (sentiment) opinión f // vt sentir, percibir; **it makes ~** tiene sentido; **~less** a estúpido, insensato; (unconscious) sin sentido.

sensibility [sɛnsɪ'bɪlɪtɪ] n sensibilidad f; **sensibilities** npl delicadeza sg.

sensible ['sensibl] a sensato, juicio; (cautious) prudente; (reasonable) razonable, lógico; (perceptible) apreciable

sensitive ['sensitiv] a sensible; (touchy) susceptible; **sensitivity** [-'tiviti] n sensibilidad f; susceptibilidad f.

sensual ['sensjuəl] a sensual.

sensuous ['sensjuəs] a sensual.

sent [sent] pt, pp of **send**.

sentence ['sentns] n (LING) frase f, oración f; (LAW) sentencia, fallo // vt: **to ~ sb to death/to 5 years** condenar a uno a muerte/a 5 años de cárcel.

sentiment ['sentimənt] n sentimiento; (opinion) opinión f; **~al** [-'mentl] a sentimental; **~ality** [-'tæliti] n sentimentalismo.

sentry ['sentri] n centinela m.

separate ['seprit] a separado; (distinct) distinto // [vb: 'sepəreit] vt separar; (part) dividir // vi separarse, ~ly ad por separado, a ~s npl (clothes) coordinados mpl; **separation** [-'reiʃən] n separación f.

September [sep'tembə*] n se(p)tiembre m.

septic ['septik] a séptico.

sequel ['si:kwl] n consecuencia, resultado; (of story) continuación f.

sequence ['si:kwəns] n sucesión f, serie f; (CINEMA) secuencia.

sequin ['si:kwin] n lentejuela.

serenade [serə'neid] n serenata // vt dar serenata a

serene [si'ri:n] a sereno, tranquilo; **serenity** [sə'reniti] n serenidad f, tranquilidad f.

sergeant ['sɑ:dʒənt] n sargento.

serial ['siəriəl] n novela por entregas; **~ize** vt publicar por entregas; **~ number** n número de serie.

series ['siəri:z] n serie f.

serious ['siəriəs] a serio; (grave) grave; **~ly** ad en serio; gravemente;

~ness n seriedad f; gravedad f.

sermon ['sə:mən] n sermón m.

serrated [si'reitid] a serrado, dentellado.

serum ['siərəm] n suero.

servant ['sə:vənt] n (gen) servidor/a m/f; (house ~) criado/a; **civil ~** funcionario.

serve [sə:v] vt (gen) servir; (in shop: goods) servir, despachar; (: customer) atender; (subj: train) pasar por; (treat) tratar; (apprenticeship) hacer; (prison term) cumplir // vi (also TENNIS) sacar; (be useful): **to ~ as/for/to do** servir de/para/para hacer // n (TENNIS) saque m; **to ~ out, ~ up** vt (food) servir.

service ['sə:vis] n (gen) servicio; (REL) misa; (AUT) mantenimiento; (of dishes) vajilla, juego // vt (car, washing machine) mantener; (: repair) reparar; **the S~s** las fuerzas armadas; **to be of ~ to sb** ser útil a uno; **~able** a servible, utilizable; **~ area** n (on motorway) servicios mpl; **~man** n militar m; **~ station** n estación f de servicio.

serviette [sə:vi'et] n servilleta.

servile ['sə:vail] a servil.

session ['seʃən] n (sitting) sesión f; **to be in ~** estar celebrando sesión.

set [set] n juego; (RADIO) aparato; (TV) televisor m; (of utensils) batería; (of cutlery) cubierto; (of books) colección f; (TENNIS) set m; (group of people) grupo; (CINEMA) plató m; (THEATRE) decorado; (HAIRDRESSING) marcado // a (fixed) fijo; (ready) listo; (resolved) resuelto, decidido // (vb: pt, pp set) vt (place) poner, colocar; (fix) fijar; (: a time) señalar; (adjust) ajustar, arreglar; (decide: rules etc) establecer, decidir // vi (sun) ponerse; (jam, jelly) cuajarse; (concrete) fraguar; **to be ~ on doing sth** estar empeñado en hacer algo; **to ~ to music** poner música a; **to ~ on fire** incendiar, poner fuego a; to ~ free poner en libertad; to ~ sth going poner algo en marcha; to ~ sail zarpar, hacerse a la vela; to ~ about vt fus (task) ponerse a; to ~ aside vt poner aparte, dejar de lado; to ~ back vi (in time): to ~ back (by) retrasar (por); to ~ off vi partir // vt (bomb) hacer estallar; (cause to start) poner en marcha; (show up well) hacer resaltar; to ~ out vi: to ~ out to do sth ponerse a hacer algo // vt (arrange) disponer; (state) exponer; to ~ up vt (organization, record) establecer; to ~ up shop (fig) establecerse; ~back n (hitch) revés m, contratiempo.

settee [se'ti:] n sofá m.

setting ['setiŋ] n (frame) marco; (placing) colocación f; (of sun) puesta; (of jewel) engaste m, montadura.

settle ['setl] vt (argument, matter) componer; (accounts) ajustar, liquidar; (land) colonizar; (MED: calm) calmar, sosegar // vi (dust etc) depositarse; (weather) serenarse; (also: ~ down) instalarse, establecerse; to ~ for sth convenir en aceptar algo; to ~ in vi instalarse; to ~ on sth quedar en algo; to ~ up with sb ajustar cuentas con uno; ~ment n (payment) liquidación f; (agreement) acuerdo, convenio; (village etc) pueblo; **settler** n colono/a, colonizador/a m/f.

setup ['setʌp] n (arrangement) plan m; (situation) situación f.

seven ['sevn] num siete; ~teen num diez y siete, diecisiete; ~th a séptimo; ~ty num setenta.

sever ['sevə*] vt cortar; (relations) romper.

several ['sevərl] a, pron varios mpl, algunos mpl; ~ of us varios de nosotros.

severance ['sevərəns] n (of relations) ruptura; ~ pay n pago de despedida.

severe [si'viə*] a severo; (serious) grave; (hard) duro; (pain) intenso; **severity** [si'veriti] n severidad f; gravedad f, intensidad f.

sew [səu], pt **sewed**, pp **sewn** vt, vi coser; to ~ up vt coser, zurcir.

sewage ['su:idʒ] n (effluence) aguas fpl residuales; (system) alcantarillado.

sewer ['su:ə*] n alcantarilla, cloaca.

sewing ['səuiŋ] n costura; ~ machine n máquina de coser.

sewn [səun] pp of **sew**.

sex [seks] n sexo; to have ~ with sb tener sexo con alguien; ~ act n acto sexual.

sextet [seks'tet] n sexteto.

sexual ['seksjuəl] a sexual.

sexy ['seksi] a sexy.

shabby ['ʃæbi] a (person) desharrapado; (clothes) raído, gastado.

shack [ʃæk] n choza, chabola.

shackles ['ʃæklz] npl grillos mpl, grilletes mpl.

shade [ʃeid] n sombra; (for lamp) pantalla; (for eyes) visera; (of colour) matiz m, tonalidad f // vt dar sombra a; **in the** ~ en la sombra.

shadow ['ʃædəu] n sombra // vt (follow) seguir y vigilar; ~ cabinet n (POL) gabinete paralelo formado por el partido de oposición; ~y a oscuro; (dim) indistinto.

shady ['ʃeidi] a sombreado; (fig: dishonest) sospechoso; (: deal) turbio.

shaft [ʃɑ:ft] n (of arrow, spear) astil m; (AUT, TECH) eje m, árbol m; (of mine) pozo; (of lift) hueco, caja; (of light) rayo.

shaggy ['ʃægi] a peludo.

shake [ʃeik], pt **shook**, pp **shaken** ['ʃeikn] vt sacudir; (building) hacer temblar; (perturb) inquietar, perturbar; (weaken) debilitar; (surprise) sorprender, pasmar // vi estremecerse; (tremble) temblar // n (movement) sacudida; to ~ hands with sb estrechar la mano con uno; **to ~ off** vt sacudirse; (fig) deshacerse de; **to ~ up** vt agitar; **shaky** a (hand, voice) trémulo; (building) inestable.

shall [ʃæl] auxiliary vb. **I ~ go** iré.

shallot [ʃəˈlɔt] n chalote m.

shallow [ˈʃæləu] a poco profundo; (fig) superficial.

sham [ʃæm] n fraude m, engaño // a falso, fingido // vt fingir, simular.

shambles [ˈʃæmblz] n confusión f.

shame [ʃeim] n vergüenza; (pity) lástima // vt avergonzar; **it is a ~** that/to do es una lástima que/hacer; **what a ~!** ¡qué lástima!; **~faced** a avergonzado; **~ful** a vergonzoso; **~less** a descarado; (immodest) impúdico.

shampoo [ʃæmˈpuː] n champú m // vt lavar el pelo (con champú).

shamrock [ˈʃæmrɔk] n trébol m.

shandy [ˈʃændi] n mezcla de cerveza con gaseosa.

shan't [ʃɑːnt] = **shall not**.

shanty town [ˈʃænti-] n barrio de chabolas.

shape [ʃeip] n forma // vt formar, dar forma a; (sb's ideas) formar; (sb's life) determinar // vi (also: **~ up**) (events) desarrollarse; (person) formarse; **to take ~** tomar forma; **-shaped** suff: **heart-shaped** en forma de corazón; **~less** a informe, sin forma definida; **~ly** a bien formado o proporcionado.

share [ʃɛə*] n (part) parte f, porción f; (contribution) cuota; (COMM) acción f // vt dividir; (have in common) compartir; **to ~ out** (among o between) repartir (entre); **~holder** n accionista m/f.

shark [ʃɑːk] n tiburón m.

sharp [ʃɑːp] a (razor, knife) afilado; (point) puntiagudo; (outline) definido; (pain) intenso; (MUS) desafinado; (contrast) marcado; (voice) agudo; (person: quick-witted) astuto; (dishonest) poco escrupuloso // n (MUS) sostenido // ad: **at 2 o'clock ~** a las 2 en punto; **~en** vt

afilar; (pencil) sacar punta a; (fig) agudizar; **~ener** n (also: **pencil ~ener**) afilador m; **~-eyed** a de vista aguda; **~-witted** a listo, perspicaz.

shatter [ˈʃætə*] vt hacer añicos o pedazos; (fig: ruin) destruir, acabar con // vi hacerse añicos.

shave [ʃeiv] vt afeitar, rasurar // vi afeitarse // n: **to have a ~** afeitarse; **shaver** n (also: **electric shaver**) máquina de afeitar (eléctrica).

shaving [ˈʃeiviŋ] n (action) el afeitarse, rasurado; **~s** npl (of wood etc) virutas fpl; **~ brush** n brocha (de afeitar); **~ cream** n crema de afeitar.

shawl [ʃɔːl] n chal m.

she [ʃiː] pron ella; **~-cat** n gata; NB: **for ships, countries follow the gender of your translation.**

sheaf [ʃiːf], pl **sheaves** n (of corn) gavilla; (of arrows) haz m; (of papers) fajo.

shear [ʃiə*], pt **sheared**, pp **sheared** or **shorn** vt (sheep) esquilar, trasquilar; **to ~ off** vt cercenar; **~s** npl (for hedge) tijeras fpl de jardín.

sheath [ʃiːθ] n vaina; (contraceptive) preservativo.

sheaves [ʃiːvz] pl of **sheaf**.

shed [ʃed] n cobertizo // vt, pt, pp **shed** (gen) desprenderse de; (skin) mudar; (tears) derramar.

she'd [ʃiːd] = **she had**; **she would**.

sheep [ʃiːp] n, pl inv oveja; **~dog** n perro pastor; **~ish** a tímido, vergonzoso; **~skin** n piel f de carnero.

sheer [ʃiə*] a (utter) puro, completo; (steep) escarpado; (almost transparent) diáfano // ad verticalmente.

sheet [ʃiːt] n (on bed) sábana; (of paper) hoja; (of glass, metal) lámina.

sheik(h) [ʃeik] n jeque m.

shelf [ʃelf], pl **shelves** n estante m.

shell [ʃel] n (on beach) concha; (of egg, nut etc) cáscara; (explosive) proyectil m, obús m; (of building) armazón m // vt (peas) desenvainar; (MIL) bombardear.

she'll [ʃiːl] = **she will**; **she shall**.

shellfish [ˈʃelfɪʃ] n, pl inv crustáceo; (pl: as food) mariscos mpl.

shelter [ˈʃeltə*] n abrigo, refugio // vt (aid) amparar, proteger; (give lodging to) abrigar; (hide) esconder // vi abrigarse, refugiarse; ~**ed** a (life) protegido; (spot) abrigado.

shelve [ʃelv] vt (fig) aplazar; ~**s** pl of **shelf**.

shepherd [ˈʃepəd] n pastor m // vt (guide) guiar, conducir; ~**ess** n pastora f; ~**'s pie** n pastel m de carne y patatas.

sheriff [ˈʃerɪf] n sheriff m.

sherry [ˈʃerɪ] n jerez m.

she's [ʃiːz] = **she is**; **she has**.

shield [ʃiːld] n escudo; (TECH) blindaje m // vt: **to** ~ (**from**) proteger (contra).

shift [ʃɪft] n (change) cambio; (of place) traslado; (of workers) turno // vt trasladar; (remove) quitar // vi moverse; (change place) cambiar de sitio; ~ **work** n trabajo por turno; ~**y** a tramposo; (eyes) furtivo.

shilling [ˈʃɪlɪŋ] n chelín m.

shimmer [ˈʃɪmə*] n reflejo trémulo // vi relucir.

shin [ʃɪn] n espinilla.

shine [ʃaɪn] n brillo, lustre m // (vb: pt, pp **shone**) vi brillar, relucir // vt (shoes) lustrar, sacar brillo a; **to** ~ **a torch on sth** dirigir una linterna hacia algo.

shingle [ˈʃɪŋgl] n (on beach) guijarras fpl; ~**s** n (MED) herpes mpl o fpl.

shiny [ˈʃaɪnɪ] a brillante, lustroso.

ship [ʃɪp] n buque m, barco // vt (goods) embarcar; (oars) desarmar; (send) transportar o enviar (por vía marítima); ~**building** n construcción f de barcos; ~**ment** n (act) embarque m; (goods) envío; ~**per** n exportador a m/f; ~**ping** n (act) embarque m; (traffic) buques mpl; ~**shape** a en regla; ~**wreck** n naufragio; ~**yard** n astillero.

shire [ˈʃaɪə*] n condado.

shirk [ʃəːk] vt eludir, esquivar; (obligations) faltar a.

shirt [ʃəːt] n camisa; **in** ~ **sleeves** en mangas de camisa.

shiver [ˈʃɪvə*] n temblor m, estremecimiento // vi temblar, estremecerse.

shoal [ʃəul] n (of fish) banco.

shock [ʃɔk] n (impact) choque m; (ELEC) descarga (eléctrica); (emotional) conmoción f; (start) sobresalto, susto; (MED) postración f nerviosa // vt dar un susto a; (offend) escandalizar; ~ **absorber** n amortiguador m; ~**ing** a (awful) espantoso; (improper) escandaloso; ~**proof** a a prueba de choques.

shod [ʃɔd] pt, pp of **shoe** // a calzado.

shoddy [ˈʃɔdɪ] a de pacotilla, de bajísima calidad.

shoe [ʃuː] n zapato; (for horse) herradura; (brake ~) zapata // vt, pt, pp **shod** (horse) herrar; ~**brush** n cepillo para zapatos; ~**horn** n calzador m; ~**lace** n cordón m; ~**maker** n zapatero; ~ **polish** n betún m; ~**shop** n zapatería.

shone [ʃɔn] pt, pp of **shine**.

shook [ʃuk] pt of **shake**.

shoot [ʃuːt] n (on branch, seedling) retoño, vástago // (vb: pt, pp **shot**) vt disparar; (kill) matar (con arma de fuego); (wound) herir (con arma de fuego); (execute) fusilar; (film) rodar, filmar // vi (with gun, bow): **to** ~ (**at**) tirar (a); (FOOTBALL) chutar; **to** ~ **down** vt (plane) derribar; **to** ~ **in/out** vi entrar corriendo/salir disparado; **to** ~ **up** vi (fig) subir (vertiginosamente); ~**ing** n (shots) tiros mpl; (HUNTING) caza con escopeta; ~ing star n estrella fugaz.

shop [ʃɔp] n tienda; (workshop) taller m // vi (also: go ~ping) ir de compras; ~ assistant n dependiente/a m/f; ~ floor a (fig) de la base; ~keeper n tendero/a; ~lifter n mechero/a; ~lifting n mechería; ~per n comprador/a m/f; ~ping n (goods) compras fpl; ~ping bag n bolsa (de compras); ~ping centre, ~ping center (US) n zona comercial o de tiendas; ~-soiled a usado; ~ steward n (INDUSTRY) enlace m/f; ~ window n escaparate m.

shore [ʃɔ:*] n (of sea, lake) orilla // vt: to ~ (up) reforzar.

shorn [ʃɔ:n] pp of shear.

short [ʃɔ:t] a (not long) corto; (in time) breve, de corta duración; (person) bajo; (curt) brusco, seco; (insufficient) insuficiente // vi (ELEC) ponerse en cortocircuito // n (also: ~ film) cortometraje m; (a pair of) ~s (unos) pantalones mpl cortos; to be ~ of sth estar falto de algo; in ~ en pocas palabras; it is ~ for es la forma abreviada de; to cut ~ (speech, visit) interrumpir, terminar inesperadamente; to fall ~ of resultar (ser) insuficiente; to stop ~ parar en seco; to stop ~ of detenerse antes de; ~age n escasez f, falta; ~bread n torta seca y quebradiza; ~-circuit n cortocircuito // vt poner en cortocircuito // vi ponerse en cortocircuito; ~coming n defecto, deficiencia; ~(crust) pastry n pasta quebradiza; ~cut n atajo; ~en vt acortar, (visit) interrumpir; ~hand n taquigrafía; ~hand typist n taquimecanógrafo/a; ~ list n (for job) lista de candidatos escogidos; ~-lived a efímero; ~ly ad en breve, dentro de poco; ~ness n (of distance) cortedad f; (of time) brevedad f; (manner) brusquedad f; ~-sighted a corto de vista, miope;

(fig) imprudente; ~ story n cuento; ~-tempered a enojadizo; ~-term a (effect) a corto plazo; ~wave n (RADIO) onda corta.

shot [ʃɔt] pt, pp of shoot // n (sound) tiro, disparo; (person) tirador/a m/f; (try) tentativa; (injection) inyección f; (PHOT) toma, fotografía; ~gun n escopeta.

should [ʃud] auxiliary vb: I ~ go now debo irme ahora; he ~ be there now debe de haber llegado (ya); I ~ go if I were you yo en tu lugar me iría; I ~ like to me gustaría.

shoulder ['ʃəuldə*] n hombro; (of road): hard ~ andén m // vt (fig) cargar con; ~ blade n omóplato.

shouldn't ['ʃudnt] = should not.

shout [ʃaut] n grito // vt gritar // vi gritar, dar voces; to ~ down vt hundir a gritos; ~ing n gritería.

shove [ʃʌv] n empujón m // vt empujar; (col: put): to ~ sth in meter algo; to ~ off vi (NAUT) alejarse del muelle; (fig: col) largarse.

shovel ['ʃʌvl] n pala; (mechanical) excavadora // vt mover con pala.

show [ʃəu] n (of emotion) demostración f; (semblance) apariencia; (exhibition) exposición f; (THEATRE) función f espectáculo // (vb: pt showed, pp shown) vt mostrar, enseñar; (courage etc) mostrar, manifestar; (exhibit) exponer; (film) proyectar // vi mostrarse; (appear) aparecer; to ~ sb in hacer pasar a uno; to ~ off vi (pej) presumir // vt (display) lucir; (pej) hacer gala de; to ~ sb out acompañar a uno a la puerta; to ~ up vi (stand out) destacar; (col: turn up) presentarse // vt descubrir; (unmask) desenmascarar; ~ business n el mundo del espectáculo; ~down n crisis f, momento decisivo.

shower ['ʃauə*] n (rain) chaparrón m, chubasco; (of stones etc) lluvia;

(*also*: ~**bath**) ducha // *vi* llover // *vt*: **to** ~ **sb with sth** colmar a uno de algo; ~**proof** *a* impermeable; ~**y** *a* (*weather*) lluvioso.

showing ['ʃəʊɪŋ] *n* (*of film*) proyección *f*.

show jumping ['ʃəʊdʒʌmpɪŋ] *n* hipismo.

shown [ʃəʊn] *pp of* **show**.

show: ~**off** *n* (*col*: *person*) presumido; ~**piece** *n* (*of exhibition etc*) obra más importante *o* central; ~**room** *n* sala de muestras.

shrank [ʃræŋk] *pt of* **shrink**.

shrapnel ['ʃræpnl] *n* metralla.

shred [ʃred] *n* (*gen pl*) triza, jirón *m* // *vt* hacer trizas; (*CULIN*) desmenuzar.

shrewd [ʃruːd] *a* astuto; ~**ness** *n* astucia.

shriek [ʃriːk] *n* chillido // *vt*, *vi* chillar.

shrill [ʃrɪl] *a* agudo, estridente.

shrimp [ʃrɪmp] *n* camarón *m*.

shrine [ʃraɪn] *n* santuario, sepulcro.

shrink [ʃrɪŋk], *pt* **shrank**, *pp* **shrunk** *vi* encogerse; (*be reduced*) reducirse // *vt* encoger; **to** ~ **from doing sth** no atreverse a hacer algo; ~**age** *n* encogimiento; reducción *f*.

shrivel ['ʃrɪvl] (*also*: ~ **up**) *vi* (*dry*) secar; (*crease*) arrugar // *vi* secarse; arrugarse.

shroud [ʃraʊd] *n* sudario // *vt*: ~**ed in mystery** envuelto en el misterio.

Shrove Tuesday ['ʃrəʊv'tjuːzdɪ] *n* martes *m* de carnaval.

shrub [ʃrʌb] *n* arbusto; ~**bery** *n* arbustos *mpl*.

shrug [ʃrʌg] *n* encogimiento de hombros // *vt*, *vi*: **to** ~ (**one's shoulders**) encogerse de hombros; **to** ~ **off** *vt* negar importancia a.

shrunk [ʃrʌŋk] *pp of* **shrink**.

shudder ['ʃʌdə*] *n* estremecimiento, escalofrío // *vi* estremecerse.

shuffle ['ʃʌfl] *vt* (*cards*) barajar; **to** ~ (**one's feet**) arrastrar los pies.

shun [ʃʌn] *vt* rehuir, esquivar.

shunt [ʃʌnt] *vt* (*RAIL*) maniobrar // *vi*: **to** ~ **to and fro** mandar de aquí para allá.

shut [ʃʌt], *pt*, *pp* **shut** *vt* cerrar // *vi* cerrarse; **to** ~ **down** *vt*, *vi* cerrarse, parar; **to** ~ **off** *vt* (*supply etc*) interrumpir, cortar; **to** ~ **up** *vi* (*col*: *keep quiet*) callarse // *vt* (*silence*) cerrar; (*silence*) callar; ~**ter** *n* contraventana; (*PHOT*) obturador *m*.

shuttle ['ʃʌtl] *n* lanzadera; (*also*: ~ **service**) servicio de transporte entre dos estaciones.

shuttlecock ['ʃʌtlkɒk] *n* volante *m*.

shy [ʃaɪ] *a* tímido; (*reserved*) reservado, cohibido; (*unsociable*) huraño; ~**ness** *n* timidez *f*; reserva; lo huraño.

Siamese [saɪə'miːz] *a*: ~ **cat** gato siamés.

Sicily ['sɪsɪlɪ] *n* Sicilia.

sick [sɪk] *a* (*ill*) enfermo; (*nauseated*) mareado; (*humour*) negro; (*vomiting*): **to be** ~ vomitar; **to feel** ~ estar mareado; **to be** ~ **of** (*fig*) estar harto de; ~ **bay** *n* enfermería; ~**en** *vt* dar asco a // *vi* enfermar; ~**ening** *a* (*fig*) asqueroso.

sickle ['sɪkl] *n* hoz *f*.

sick: ~ **leave** *n* baja por enfermedad; ~**ly** *a* enfermizo; (*causing nausea*) nauseabundo; ~**ness** *n* enfermedad *f*, mal *m*; (*vomiting*) náuseas *fpl*; ~ **pay** *n* subsidio de enfermedad.

side [saɪd] *n* (*gen*) lado; (*of body*) costado; (*of lake*) orilla; (*aspect*) aspecto; (*team*) equipo; (*of hill*) ladera // *a* (*door, entrance*) accesorio // *vi*: **to** ~ **with sb** tomar el partido de uno; **by the** ~ **of** al lado de; ~ **by** ~ juntos(as), lado a lado; **from all** ~**s** de todos lados; **to take** ~**s** (**with**) tomar partido (con); ~**board** *n* aparador *m*; ~**boards**, ~**burns** *npl* patillas *fpl*; ~ **effect** *n* efecto secundario; ~**light** *n* (*AUT*) luz *f* lateral; ~**line** *n* (*SPORT*) línea lateral; (*fig*) empleo suplementario;

~long a de soslayo; ~ road n calle f lateral; ~saddle ad a mujeriegas, a la inglesa; ~ show n (stall) caseta; (fig) atracción f secundaria; ~step vt (fig) esquivar; ~track n (fig) desviar (de su propósito); ~walk n (US) acera; ~ways ad de lado.

siding ['saidɪŋ] n (RAIL) apartadero, vía muerta.

sidle ['saidl] vi: ~ up (to) acercarse furtivamente (a).

siege [siːdʒ] n cerco, sitio.

sieve [sɪv] n coladura // vt cribar.

sift [sɪft] vt cribar; (fig: information) escudriñar.

sigh [sai] n suspiro // vi suspirar.

sight [sait] n (faculty) vista, visión f; (spectacle) espectáculo; (on gun) mira, alza // vt ver, divisar; in ~ a la vista; out of ~ fuera de (la) vista; ~seeing n excursionismo, turismo; to go ~seeing visitar monumentos.

sign [sain] n (with hand) señal f, seña; (indication) indicio; (trace) huella, rastro; (notice) letrero; (written) signo // vt firmar; to ~ sth over to sb firmar el traspaso de algo a uno; to ~ up vi (MIL) alistarse // vt (contract) contratar.

signal ['sɪɡnl] n señal f // vi (AUT) señalizar // vt (person) hacer señas a uno; (message) transmitir.

signature ['sɪɡnətʃə*] n firma.

signet ring ['sɪɡnətrɪŋ] n anillo de sello.

significance [sɪɡ'nɪfɪkəns] n significado; (importance) trascendencia; **significant** [-ənt] a significativo; trascendente.

signify ['sɪɡnɪfai] vt significar.

sign: ~ language n la mímica, lenguaje m por señas o de señas; ~post n indicador m.

silence ['sailns] n silencio // vt hacer callar; (guns) reducir al silencio; **silencer** n (on gun, AUT) silenciador m.

silent ['sailnt] a (gen) silencioso; (not speaking) callado; (film) mudo;

to remain ~ guardar silencio.

silhouette [sɪluːˈet] n silueta; ~d against destacado sobre o contra.

silicon chip ['sɪlikən'tʃɪp] n plata de silicio, astilla de silicona.

silk [sɪlk] n seda // a de seda; ~y a sedoso.

silly ['sɪli] a (person) tonto, (idea) absurdo.

silt [sɪlt] n sedimento

silver ['sɪlvə*] n plata; (money) moneda suelta // a de plata, plateado; ~ paper n papel m de plata; ~-plated a plateado; ~smith n platero; ~y a plateado.

similar ['sɪmilə*] a: ~ to parecido o semejante a; ~ity [-'lærɪti] n parecido, semejanza; ~ly ad del mismo modo.

simmer ['sɪmə*] vi hervir a fuego lento.

simpering ['sɪmpərɪŋ] a afectado; (foolish) bobo.

simple ['sɪmpl] a (easy) sencillo; (foolish, comm) simple; ~ton n inocentón/ona m/f; **simplicity** [-'plɪsiti] n sencillez f; (foolishness) ingenuidad f; **simplify** ['sɪmplɪfai] vt simplificar.

simulate ['sɪmjuleit] vt simular; **simulation** [-'leiʃən] n simulación f.

simultaneous [sɪml'teiniəs] a simultáneo; ~ly ad simultáneamente.

sin [sɪn] n pecado // vi pecar.

since [sɪns] ad desde entonces, después // prep desde // conj (time) desde que; (because) ya que, puesto que; ~ then desde entonces.

sincere [sɪn'siə*] a sincero; yours ~ly le saluda (afectuosamente); **sincerity** [-'seriti] n sinceridad f.

sinful ['sɪnful] a (thought) pecaminoso; (person) pecador(a).

sing [sɪŋ], pt **sang**, pp **sung** vt cantar // vi (gen) cantar; (bird) trinar; (ears) zumbar.

singe [sɪndʒ] vt chamuscar.

singer ['sɪŋə*] n cantante m/f.

singing ['sɪŋɪŋ] n (gen) canto;

(songs) canciones fpl; (in the ears) zumbido.

single ['sɪŋgl] a único, solo; (unmarried) soltero; (not double) simple, sencillo; (bed, room) individual // n (also: ~ ticket) billete m sencillo; (record) single m; ~s npl (TENNIS) individual m; to ~ out vt (choose) escoger; (point out) singularizar; ~ bed n cama individual; in ~ file en fila de uno; ~-handed a sin ayuda; ~-minded a resuelto, firme; ~ room n cuarto individual.

singular ['sɪŋgjulə*] a (odd) raro, extraño; (LING) singular // n (LING) singular m.

sinister ['sɪnɪstə*] a siniestro.

sink [sɪŋk] n fregadero // (vb: pt **sank**, pp **sunk**) vt (ship) hundir, echar a pique; (foundations) excavar; (piles etc) to ~ **sth** fijar algo bajo tierra // vi (gen) hundirse; to ~ **in** vi (fig) penetrar, calar; a ~ing feeling un sentimiento de que todo se acaba.

sinner ['sɪnə*] n pecador/a m/f.

sinus ['saɪnəs] n (ANAT) seno.

sip [sɪp] n sorbo // vt sorber, beber a sorbitos.

siphon ['saɪfən] n sifón m; to ~ **off** vt quitar poco a poco.

sir [sə*] n señor m; S~ **John Smith** el Señor John Smith; **yes** ~ sí, señor.

siren ['saɪərn] n sirena.

sirloin ['sɜːlɔɪn] n solomillo.

sister ['sɪstə*] n hermana; (nurse) enfermera jefe; ~-**in-law** n cuñada.

sit [sɪt], pt, pp **sat** vi sentarse; (be sitting) estar sentado; (assembly) reunirse // vt (exam) presentarse a; to ~ **down** vi sentarse; to ~ **in** on asistir a; to ~ **up** vi incorporarse, (not go to bed) velar.

site [saɪt] n sitio; (also: building ~) solar m // vt situar.

sit-in ['sɪtɪn] n (demonstration) manifestación f de brazos caídos.

sitting ['sɪtɪŋ] n (of assembly etc)

sesión f; (in canteen) turno; ~ **room** n sala de estar.

situated ['sɪtjueɪtɪd] a situado.

situation [sɪtju'eɪʃən] n situación f.

six [sɪks] num seis; ~**teen** num diez y seis, dieciséis; ~**th** a sexto; ~**ty** num sesenta.

size [saɪz] n (gen) tamaño m; (extent) extensión f; (of clothing) talla; (of shoes) número; (glue) cola, apresto; to ~ **up** vt formarse una idea de; ~**able** a importante, considerable.

sizzle ['sɪzl] vi crepitar.

skate [skeɪt] n patín m; (fish: pl inv) raya // vi patinar; ~**board** n skateboard m; ~**r** n patinador/a m/f; ~**ing** n patinaje m; **skating rink** n pista de patinaje.

skeleton ['skelɪtn] n esqueleto; (TECH) armazón m; (outline) esquema m; ~ **key** n llave f maestra; ~ **staff** n personal m reducido.

sketch [sketʃ] n (drawing) dibujo; (outline) esbozo, bosquejo; (THEATRE) pieza corta // vt dibujar; esbozar; ~ **book** n libro de dibujos; ~ **pad** n bloc m de dibujo; ~**y** a incompleto.

skewer ['skjuːə*] n broqueta.

ski [skiː] n esquí m // vi esquiar; ~ **boot** n bota de esquí.

skid [skɪd] n patinazo // vi patinar; ~**mark** n huella de patinazo.

ski: ~**er** n esquiador/a m/f; ~**ing** n esquí m; ~ **jump** n pista para salto de esquí.

skilful ['skɪlful] a diestro, experto.

ski lift n telesilla.

skill [skɪl] n destreza, pericia; ~**ed** a hábil, diestro; (worker) cualificado.

skim [skɪm] vt (milk) desnatar; (glide over) rozar, rasar // vi: to ~ **through** (book) hojear.

skimp [skɪmp] vt (work) chapucear; (cloth etc) escatimar; ~**y** a (meagre) escaso; (skirt) muy corto.

skin [skɪn] n (gen) piel f;

(*complexion*) cutis *m* // *vt* (*fruit etc*) pelar; (*animal*) despellejar; ~**deep** *a* superficial; ~ **diving** *n* natación *f* submarina; ~**ny** *a* flaco, magro; ~**tight** *a* (*dress etc*) muy ajustado.

skip [skɪp] *n* brinco, salto; (*container*) cuba // *vi* brincar; (*with rope*) saltar a la comba // *vt* (*pass over*) omitir, saltar.

ski pants *npl* pantalones *mpl* de esquí.

skipper ['skɪpə*] *n* (NAUT, SPORT) capitán *m*.

skipping rope ['skɪpɪŋ-] *n* cuerda (de saltar).

skirmish ['skə:mɪʃ] *n* escaramuza.

skirt [skə:t] *n* falda // *vt* (*surround*) ceñir, rodear; (*go round*) ladear; ~**ing board** *n* rodapié *m*.

skit [skɪt] *n* sátira, parodia.

skittle ['skɪtl] *n* bolo; ~**s** *n* (*game*) boliche *m*.

skive [skaɪv] *vi* (*Brit: col*) gandulear.

skull [skʌl] *n* calavera; (ANAT) cráneo.

skunk [skʌŋk] *n* mofeta; (*fig: person*) canalla *m/f*.

sky [skaɪ] *n* cielo; ~-**blue** *a* azul celeste; ~**light** *n* tragaluz *m*, claraboya; ~**scraper** *n* rascacielos *m* inv.

slab [slæb] *n* (*stone*) bloque *m*; (*flat*) losa; (*of cake*) porción *f* gruesa.

slack [slæk] *a* (*loose*) flojo; (*slow*) de poca actividad; (*careless*) descuidado; ~**s** *npl* pantalones *mpl*; ~**en** (*also*: ~**en off**) *vi* aflojarse // *vt* aflojar; (*speed*) disminuir.

slag [slæg] *n* escoria, escombros *mpl*; ~ **heap** *n* escorial *m*, escombrera.

slalom ['sla:ləm] *n* slalom *m*.

slam [slæm] *vt* (*door*) cerrar de golpe; (*throw*) arrojar (violentamente); (*criticize*) hablar mal de // *vi* cerrarse de golpe.

slander ['sla:ndə*] *n* calumnia, difamación *f* // *vt* calumniar,

difamar; ~**ous** *a* calumnioso, difamatorio.

slang [slæŋ] *n* argot *m*; (*jargon*) jerga; (*private language*) caló.

slant [sla:nt] *n* sesgo, inclinación *f*; (*fig*) punto de vista; ~**ed**, ~**ing** *a* inclinado.

slap [slæp] *n* palmada; (*in face*) bofetada; (*fig*) palmetazo // *vt* dar una palmada/bofetada a // *ad* (*directly*) exactamente, directamente; ~**dash** *a* descuidado; ~**stick** *n* (*comedy*) payasadas *fpl*.

slash [slæʃ] *vt* acuchillar; (*fig: prices*) quemar.

slate [sleɪt] *n* pizarra // *vt* (*fig: criticize*) criticar duramente.

slaughter ['slɔ:tə*] *n* (*of animals*) matanza; (*of people*) carnicería *f* // *vt* matar; ~**house** *n* matadero.

Slav [slɑ:v] *a* eslavo.

slave [sleɪv] *n* esclavo // *vi* (*also*: ~ **away**) sudar tinta; ~**ry** *n* esclavitud *f*. **slavish** *a* servil.

Slavonic [slə'vɔnɪk] *a* eslavo.

slay [sleɪ] *vt* matar.

sleazy ['sli:zɪ] *a* (*fig: place*) de mala fama.

sledge [sledʒ] *n* trineo; ~**hammer** *n* mazo.

sleek [sli:k] *a* (*gen*) lustroso; (*neat*) pulido.

sleep [sli:p] *n* sueño // *vi*, *pt*, *pp* slept dormir; **to go to** ~ dormirse; ~ **in** *vi* (*oversleep*) dormir tarde; ~**er** *n* (*person*) durmiente *m/f*; (*RAIL: on track*) traviesa; (: *train*) coche-cama *m*; ~**ily** *ad* soñolientamente; ~**ing bag** *n* saco de dormir; ~**ing car** *n* coche-cama *m*; ~**ing pill** *n* somnífero; ~**lessness** *n* insomnio; ~**walker** *n* sonámbulo/a; ~**y** *a* soñoliento.

sleet [sli:t] *n* nevisca.

sleeve [sli:v] *n* manga; (TECH) manguito; ~**less** *a* (*garment*) sin mangas.

sleigh [sleɪ] *n* trineo.

sleight [slaɪt] *n*: ~ **of hand** escamoteo.

slender ['slɛndə*] a delgado; (*means*) escaso.

slept [slɛpt] pt, pp of **sleep**.

slice [slaɪs] n (*of meat*) tajada; (*of bread*) rebanada; (*of lemon*) rodaja; (*utensil*) pala // vt cortar, tajar; rebanar.

slick [slɪk] a (*skilful*) hábil, diestro; (*quick*) rápido; (*astute*) astuto // n (*also*: oil ~) masa flotante.

slid [slɪd] pt, pp of **slide**.

slide [slaɪd] n (*in playground*) tobogán m; (PHOT) diapositiva; (*also*: hair ~) pasador m // (vb: pt, pp **slid**) vt correr, deslizar // vi (*slip*) resbalarse; (*glide*) deslizarse; **sliding** a (*door*) corredizo.

slight [slaɪt] a (*slim*) delgado; (*frail*) delicado; (*pain etc*) leve; (*trifling*) sin importancia; (*small*) pequeño // n desaire m // vt (*offend*) ofender, desairar; **not in the** ~**est** (ni) en lo más mínimo, en absoluto; ~**ly** ad ligeramente, un poco.

slim [slɪm] a delgado, esbelto // vi adelgazar.

slime [slaɪm] n limo, cieno; **slimy** a limoso.

slimming ['slɪmɪŋ] n adelgazamiento; a ~ **diet** un régimen.

sling [slɪŋ] n (MED) cabestrillo; (*weapon*) honda // vt, pt, pp **slung** tirar, arrojar.

slip [slɪp] n (*slide*) resbalón m; (*fall*) tropezón m; (*mistake*) descuido; (*underskirt*) combinación f; (*of paper*) trozo // vt (*slide*) deslizar // vi (*slide*) deslizarse; (*stumble*) resbalar(se); (*decline*) decaer; **to give sb the** ~ eludir o escaparse de uno; **to** ~ **away** vi escabullirse; **to** ~ **in** vt meter // vi meterse; **to** ~ **out** vi (*go out*) salir (un momento).

slipper ['slɪpə*] n zapatilla.

slippery ['slɪpərɪ] a resbaladizo.

slip: ~ **road** n carretera de acceso; ~**shod** a descuidado; ~**up** n (*error*) equivocación f; (*by neglect*) descuido; ~**way** n grada, gradas fpl.

slit [slɪt] n raja; (*cut*) corte m // vt, pt, pp **slit** rajar, cortar.

slither ['slɪðə*] vi deslizarse.

slob [slɒb] n (col) patán m.

slog [slɒg] vi sudar tinta; **it was a** ~ costó trabajo (hacerlo).

slogan ['sləugən] n slogan m, lema m.

slop [slɒp] vi (*also*: ~ **over**) derramarse, desbordarse // vt derramar, verter.

slope [sləup] n (up) cuesta, pendiente m; (down) declive m; (*side of mountain*) falda, vertiente m // vi: **to** ~ **down** estar en declive; **to** ~ **up** inclinarse; **sloping** a en pendiente, en declive.

sloppy ['slɒpɪ] a (*work*) descuidado; (*appearance*) desaliñado.

slot [slɒt] n ranura // vt: **to** ~ **into** encajar en; ~ **machine** n máquina tragaperras.

slouch [slautʃ] vi: **to** ~ **about** (*laze*) gandulear.

slovenly ['slʌvənlɪ] a (*dirty*) desaliñado, desaseado; (*careless*) descuidado.

slow [sləu] a lento; (*watch*): **to be** ~ atrasarse // ad lentamente, despacio // vt, vi (*also*: ~ **down**, ~ **up**) retardar; **'~'** (*road sign*) 'disminuir velocidad'; ~**ly** ad lentamente, despacio; **in** ~ **motion** a cámara lenta; ~**ness** n lentitud f.

sludge [slʌdʒ] n lodo, fango.

slug [slʌg] n babosa; (*bullet*) posta; ~**gish** a (*slow*) lento; (*lazy*) perezoso.

sluice [sluːs] n (*gate*) esclusa; (*channel*) canal m.

slum [slʌm] n (*area*) tugurios mpl; (*house*) casucha.

slumber ['slʌmbə*] n sueño.

slump [slʌmp] n (*economic*) depresión f // vi hundirse.

slung [slʌŋ] pt, pp of **sling**.

slur [sləː*] n calumnia // vt calumniar, difamar; (*word*) pronunciar indistintamente.

slush [slʌʃ] n nieve f a medio

derretir; ~**y** a (*snow*) a medio derretir; (*street*) fangoso; (*fig*) sentimental, sensiblero.

slut [slʌt] *n* marrana.

sly [slaɪ] a (*clever*) astuto, (*nasty*) malicioso.

smack [smæk] *n* (*slap*) manotada; (*blow*) golpe *m* // *vt* dar una manotada a, golpear con la mano // *vi*: **to ~ of** saber a, oler a.

small [smɔːl] a pequeño; ~**holder** *n* granjero, parcelero; ~**ish** a más bien pequeño; ~**pox** *n* viruela; ~**talk** *n* cháchara.

smart [smɑːt] a elegante; (*clever*) listo, inteligente; (*quick*) rápido, vivo // *vi* escocer, picar, ~**en up** *vi* arreglarse // *vt* arreglar.

smash [smæʃ] *n* (*also*: ~**-up**) choque *m* // *vt* (*break*) hacer pedazos; (*car etc*) estrellar; (*SPORT: record*) romper // *vi* (*collide*) chocar; (*against wall etc*) estrellarse; ~**ing** a (*col*) cojonudo.

smattering ['smætərɪŋ] *n*: **a ~ of** ligeros conocimientos *mpl* de.

smear [smɪə*] *n* mancha; (*MED*) citología // *vt* untar; (*fig*) calumniar, difamar.

smell [smel] *n* olor *m*; (*sense*) olfato // (*vb: pt, pp* **smelt** or **smelled**) *vt, vi* oler; **it ~s good/of garlic** huele bien/a ajo; ~**y** a que huele mal.

smile [smaɪl] *n* sonrisa // *vi* sonreír; **smiling** a sonriente.

smirk [smɜːk] *n* sonrisa falsa o afectada.

smith [smɪθ] *n* herrero; ~**y** ['smɪðɪ] *n* herrería.

smock [smɒk] *n* blusa; (*children's*) delantal *m*.

smoke [sməʊk] *n* humo // *vi* fumar; (*chimney*) echar humo // *vt* (*cigarettes*) fumar; ~**d** a (*bacon, glass*) ahumado; **smoker** *n* (*person*) fumador *a m/f*; (*RAIL*) coche *m* fumador; ~ **screen** *n* cortina de humo; **smoking** *n*: '**no smoking**' (*sign*) 'prohibido fumar'; **smoky** a

(*gen*) humeante; (*room*) lleno de humo.

smooth [smuːð] a (*gen*) liso; (*sea*) tranquilo; (*flat*) llano; (*flavour, movement*) suave; (*person*) culto, refinado; (: *pej*) meloso // *vt* alisar; (*also*: ~ **out**) (*creases, difficulties*) allanar.

smother ['smʌðə*] *vt* sofocar; (*repress*) ahogar.

smoulder ['sməʊldə*] *vi* arder sin llama.

smudge [smʌdʒ] *n* mancha // *vt* manchar.

smug [smʌg] a presumido.

smuggle ['smʌgl] *vt* pasar de contrabando; **smuggler** *n* contrabandista *m/f*; **smuggling** *n* contrabando.

smutty ['smʌtɪ] a (*fig*) verde, obsceno.

snack [snæk] *n* bocado; ~ **bar** *n* cafetería.

snag [snæg] *n* dificultad *f*, pero.

snail [sneɪl] *n* caracol *m*.

snake [sneɪk] *n* (*gen*) serpiente *f*; (*harmless*) culebra; (*poisonous*) víbora.

snap [snæp] *n* (*sound*) castañetazo; (*of whip*) chasquido; (*click*) golpe *m* seco; (*photograph*) foto *f* // a repentino // *vt* (*fingers etc*) castañetear; (*whip*) chasquear; (*break*) quebrar; (*photograph*) tomar una foto de // *vi* (*break*) quebrarse; (*fig: person*) contestar bruscamente; (*sound*) hacer un ruido seco; **to ~ shut** cerrarse de golpe; **to ~ at** *vt fus* (*subj: dog*) intentar morder; **to ~ off** *vi* (*break*) romperse (y separarse); **to ~ up** *vt* aprovecharse de, agarrar; ~**shot** *n* foto *f* (instantánea).

snare [snɛə*] *n* trampa // *vt* cazar con trampa, (*fig*) engañar.

snarl [snɑːl] *n* gruñido // *vi* gruñir.

snatch [snætʃ] *n* (*fig*) robo; (*small amount*): ~**es of** trocitos *mpl* de // *vt* (~ **away**) arrebatar; (*grasp*) coger, agarrar.

sneak [sni:k] vi: to ~ in/out entrar/salir a hurtadillas // n (fam) soplón/ona m/f; ~y a furtivo.

sneer [snɪə*] n sonrisa de desprecio // vi sonreír con desprecio; (mock) mofarse.

sneeze [sni:z] n estornudo // vi estornudar.

sniff [snɪf] n (of dog) husmeo; (of person) sorbo (por las narices) // vi sorber (por la nariz) // vt husmear, oler.

snigger ['snɪgə*] n risa disimulada // vi reírse con disimulo.

snip [snɪp] n tijeretazo; (piece) recorte m; (bargain) ganga // vt tijeretear.

sniper ['snaɪpə*] n francotirador/a m/f.

snippet ['snɪpɪt] n retazo.

snivelling ['snɪvlɪŋ] a (whimpering) llorón(ona).

snob [snɔb] n snob m/f; ~bery n snobismo; ~bish a snob.

snooker ['snu:kə*] n especie de billar.

snoop [snu:p] vi: to ~ about fisgonear; ~er n fisgón/ona m/f.

snooty ['snu:tɪ] a presumido.

snooze [snu:z] n siesta // vi echar una siesta.

snore [snɔ:*] vi // n roncar // n ronquido.

snorkel ['snɔ:kl] n tubo snorkel.

snort [snɔ:t] n bufido // vi bufar.

snout [snaut] n hocico, morro.

snow [snəu] n nieve // vi nevar; ~ball n bola de nieve // vi acumularse; ~bound a bloqueado por la nieve; ~drift n ventisquero; ~drop n campanilla; ~fall n nevada; ~flake n copo de nieve; ~man n figura de nieve; ~plough, ~plow (US) n quitanieves m inv; ~storm n nevada, nevasca; S~ White n Blanca Nieves.

snub [snʌb] vt rechazar con desdén // n desaire m, repulsa.

snuff [snʌf] n rapé m.

snug [snʌg] a (sheltered) abrigado; (fitted) ajustado.

snuggle ['snʌgl] vi: to ~ up to sb arrimarse a uno.

so [səu] ad (degree) tan; (manner: thus) así, de este modo // conj así que, por tanto; ~ that (purpose) para que, a fin de que; (result) de modo que; ~ do I yo también; if ~ de ser así, si es así; I hope ~ espero que sí; 10 or ~ 10 más o menos; ~ far hasta aquí; ~ long! ¡hasta luego!; ~ many tantos(as); ~ much ad, det tanto; ~ and ~ n Fulano.

soak [səuk] vt (drench) empapar; (put in water) remojar // vi remojarse, estar a remojo; to ~ in vi penetrar; to ~ up vt absorber.

soap [səup] n jabón m; ~flakes npl escamas fpl de jabón; ~ powder n jabón en polvo; ~y a jabonoso.

soar [sɔ:*] vi (on wings) remontarse; (building etc) elevarse.

sob [sɔb] n sollozo // vi sollozar.

sober ['səubə*] a (serious) serio; (sensible) sensato; (moderate) moderado; ~ (not drunk) sobrio; (colour, style) discreto; to ~ up vi pasársele a uno la borrachera.

Soc. abbr of **society**.

so-called ['səu'kɔ:ld] a llamado.

soccer ['sɔkə*] n fútbol m.

sociable ['səuʃəbl] a sociable.

social ['səuʃl] a (gen) social; (sociable) sociable // n velada, fiesta; ~ climber n arribista m/f; ~ club n club m; ~ism n socialismo; ~ist a, n socialista m/f; ~ly ad socialmente; ~ science n ciencias fpl sociales; ~ security n seguridad f social; ~ work n asistencia social; ~ worker n asistente/a m/f social.

society [sə'saɪətɪ] n sociedad f; (club) asociación f; (also: high ~) buena sociedad.

sociologist [səusɪ'ɔlədʒɪst] n sociólogo; **sociology** [-dʒɪ] n sociología.

sock [sɔk] n calcetín m.

socket ['sɔkɪt] n (ELEC) enchufe m.

sod [sɔd] n (of earth) césped m; (col!) cabrón/ona m/f.

soda ['səudə] n soda; (also: ~ water) sifón m.

sodden ['sɔdn] a empapado.

sodium ['səudiəm] n sodio.

sofa ['səufə] n sofá m.

soft [sɔft] a (gen) blando; (gentle, not loud) suave; (kind) tierno, compasivo; (weak) débil; (stupid) tonto; ~ **drink** n bebida no alcohólica; ~**en** ['sɔfn] vt ablandar; suavizar; debilitar // vi ablandarse; suavizarse; debilitarse; ~**hearted** a compasivo, bondadoso; ~**ly** ad suavemente; (gently) delicadamente, con delicadeza; ~**ness** n blandura; suavidad f, (sweetness) dulzura; (tenderness) ternura.

soggy ['sɔgi] a empapado.

soil [sɔil] n (earth) tierra, suelo // vt ensuciar; ~**ed** a sucio.

solace ['sɔlis] n consuelo.

solar ['səulə*] a solar.

sold [səuld] pt, pp of sell; ~ **out** (COMM) agotado.

solder ['səuldə*] vt soldar // n soldadura.

soldier ['səuldʒə*] n (gen) soldado; (army man) militar m.

sole [səul] n (of foot) planta; (of shoe) suela; (fish, pl inv) lenguado // a único; ~**ly** ad únicamente, sólo, solamente.

solemn ['sɔləm] a solemne.

solicitor [sə'lisitə*] n (for wills etc) notario; (in court) abogado.

solid ['sɔlid] a (not hollow) sólido; (gold etc) macizo; (person) serio // n sólido.

solidarity [sɔli'dæriti] n solidaridad f.

solidify [sə'lidifai] vi solidificarse.

solitaire [sɔli'tɛə*] n (game, gem) solitario.

solitary ['sɔlitəri] a solitario, solo; (isolated) apartado, aislado; (only) único; ~ **confinement** n incomunicación f.

solitude ['sɔlitju:d] n soledad f.

solo ['səuləu] n solo; ~**ist** n solista m/f.

soluble ['sɔljubl] a soluble.

solution [sə'lu:ʃən] n solución f.

solve [sɔlv] vt resolver, solucionar.

solvent ['sɔlvənt] a (COMM) solvente // n (CHEM) solvente m.

sombre, somber (US) ['sɔmbə*] a sombrío.

some [sʌm] det (a few) algunos(as); (certain) algún/una; (a certain number or amount) see phrases below; (unspecified) algo de // pron algunos/as; (a bit) algo // ad: ~ **10 people** unas 10 personas; ~ **children came** vinieron algunos niños; **have ~ tea** tome té; **there's ~ milk in the fridge** hay leche en la refrigeradora; ~ **was left** quedaba algo; **I've got ~** (books etc) tengo algunos; (milk, money etc) tengo algo; ~**body** pron alguien; ~ **day** ad algún día; ~**how** ad de alguna manera; (for some reason) por una u otra razón; ~**one** pron = ~**body**.

somersault ['sʌməsɔ:lt] n (deliberate) salto mortal; (accidental) vuelco // vi dar un salto mortal; dar vuelcos.

something ['sʌmθiŋ] pron algo.

sometime ['sʌmtaim] ad (in future) algún día, en algún momento; (in past): ~ **last month** durante el mes pasado.

sometimes ['sʌmtaimz] ad a veces.

somewhat ['sʌmwɔt] ad algo.

somewhere ['sʌmwɛə*] ad (be) en alguna parte; (go) a alguna parte; ~ **else** (be) en otra parte; (go) a otra parte.

son [sʌn] n hijo.

song [sɔŋ] n canción f; ~**writer** n compositor/a m/f de canciones.

sonic ['sɔnik] a (boom) sónico.

son-in-law ['sʌninlɔ:] n yerno.

sonnet ['sɔnit] n soneto.

soon [su:n] ad pronto, dentro de poco; (early) temprano; ~

afterwards poco después; *see also* as; **~er** *ad* (*time*) antes, más temprano; (*preference*): **I would ~er do that** preferiría hacer eso; **~er or later** tarde o temprano.

soot [sut] *n* hollín *m*.

soothe [su:ð] *vt* tranquilizar; (*pain*) aliviar.

sophisticated [sə'fıstıkeıtıd] *a* sofisticado.

soporific [sɔpə'rıfık] *a* soporífero.

sopping ['sɔpıŋ] *a:* **~ wet** totalmente empapado.

soppy ['sɔpı] *a* (*pej*) bobo, tonto.

soprano [sə'prɑːnəu] *n* soprano *f*.

sorcerer ['sɔːsərə*] *n* hechicero.

sordid ['sɔːdıd] *a* (*dirty*) sucio, asqueroso; (*wretched*) miserable.

sore [sɔː*] *a* (*painful*) doloroso, que duele; (*offended*) resentido // *n* llaga; **~ly** *ad:* **I am ~ly tempted** casi estoy por.

sorrow ['sɔrəu] *n* pena, dolor *m*; **~ful** *a* afligido, triste.

sorry ['sɔrı] *a* (*regretful*) arrepentido; (*condition, excuse*) lastimoso; **~!** ¡lo siento!, ¡perdón!, ¡perdone!; **to feel ~ for sb** sentir lástima por uno; **I feel ~ for him** me da lástima.

sort [sɔːt] *n* clase *f*, género, tipo // *vt* (*also:* **~ out:** *papers*) clasificar; (: *problems*) arreglar, solucionar; **~ing office** *n* oficina de distribución de correos.

SOS *n abbr of* **save our souls.**

so-so ['səusəu] *ad* regular, así-así.

soufflé ['suːfleı] *n* suflé *m*.

sought [sɔːt] *pt, pp of* **seek.**

soul [səul] *n* alma *m*; **~-destroying** *a* embrutecedor(a); **~ful** *a* lleno de sentimiento; **~less** *a* desalmado.

sound [saund] *a* (*healthy*) sano; (*safe, not damaged*) firme, sólido; (*secure*) seguro; (*reliable, not superficial*) formal, digno de confianza; (*sensible*) sensato, razonable // *ad:* **~ asleep** profundamente dormido // *n* (*noise*) sonido, ruido; (*GEO*) estrecho // *vt* (*alarm*) sonar; (*also:* **~ out:** *opinions*) consultar, sondear // *vi* sonar, resonar; (*fig: seem*) parecer; **to ~ like** sonar a; **~ barrier** *n* barrera del sonido; **~ effects** *npl* efectos *mpl* sonoros; **~ing** *n* (NAUT *etc*) sondeo; **~ly** *ad* (*sleep*) profundamente; (*beat*) completamente; **~proof** *a* a prueba de sonidos; **~track** *n* (*of film*) banda sonora.

soup [suːp] *n* (*thick*) sopa; (*thin*) caldo; **in the ~** (*fig*) en apuros; **~spoon** *n* cuchara sopera.

sour ['sauə*] *a* agrio; (*milk*) cortado; (*fig*) desabrido, acre.

source [sɔːs] *n* fuente *f*.

south [sauθ] *n* sur *m* // *a* del sur // *ad* al sur, hacia el sur; **S~ Africa** *n* África del Sur; **S~ African** *a, n* sudafricano/a; **S~ America** *n* América (del Sur); **S~ American** *a, n* sudamericano/a; **~-east** *n* sudeste *m*; **~erly** ['sʌðəlı] *a* sur; (*from the ~*) del sur; **~ern** ['sʌðən] *a* del sur, meridional; **S~ Pole** *n* Polo Sur; **~ward(s)** *ad* hacia el sur; **~-west** *n* suroeste *m*.

souvenir [suːvə'nıə*] *n* recuerdo.

sovereign ['sɔvrın] *a, n* soberano; **~ty** *n* soberanía.

soviet ['səuvıət] *a* soviético; **the S~ Union** la Unión Soviética.

sow [sau] *n* cerda, puerca // *vt* [səu], *pt* **sowed**, *pp* **sown** [səun] (*gen*) sembrar; (*spread*) esparcir.

soy [sɔı] *n:* **~ sauce** salsa de soja.

soya bean ['sɔıəbiːn] *n* semilla de soja.

spa [spɑː] *n* (*spring*) baños *mpl* térmicos; (*town*) balneario.

space [speıs] *n* (*gen*) espacio; (*room*) sitio // *vt* (*also:* **~ out**) espaciar; **~craft** *n* nave *f* espacial; **~man/woman** *n* astronauta *m/f*, cosmonauta *m/f*; **spacing** *n* espaciamiento.

spacious ['speıʃəs] *a* amplio.

spade [speıd] *n* (*tool*) pala, laya;

~s npl (CARDS: British) picos mpl; (: Spanish) espadas fpl.

spaghetti [spə'geti] n espaguetis mpl, fideos mpl.

Spain [spein] n España.

span [spæn] n (of bird, plane) envergadura; (of hand) palmo; (of arch) luz f; (in time) lapso // vt extenderse sobre, cruzar; (fig) abarcar.

Spaniard ['spænjəd] n español/a m/f.

spaniel ['spænjəl] n perro de aguas.

Spanish ['spæniʃ] a español(a) // n (LING) español m, castellano.

spank [spæŋk] vt zurrar.

spanner ['spænə*] n llave f (inglesa).

spar [spɑ:*] n palo, verga // vi (BOXING) entrenarse.

spare [spɛə*] a (free) desocupado; (surplus) sobrante, de más; (available) disponible // n (part) pieza de repuesto // vt (do without) pasarse sin; (afford to give) tener de sobra; (refrain from hurting) perdonar; (be grudging with) escatimar; ~ **part** n pieza de repuesto; ~ **time** n ratos mpl de ocio, tiempo libre.

sparing ['spɛəriŋ] a: **to be ~ with** ser parco en; ~**ly** ad escasamente.

spark [spɑ:k] n chispa; (fig) chispazo; ~(**ing**) **plug** n bujín.

sparkle ['spɑ:kl] n centelleo, destello // vi centellear; (shine) relucir, brillar; **sparkling** a centelleante; (wine) espumoso.

sparrow ['spærəu] n gorrión m.

sparse [spɑ:s] a esparcido, escaso.

spasm ['spæzəm] n (MED) espasmo; (fig) arranque m, acceso; ~**odic** ['mɔdik] a espasmódico.

spastic ['spæstik] n espástico/a.

spat [spæt] pt, pp of **spit**.

spate [speit] n (fig): ~ **of** torrente m de; **in** ~ (river) crecido.

spatter ['spætə*] vt salpicar, rociar.

spatula ['spætjulə] n espátula.

spawn [spɔ:n] vi desovar, frezar // n huevas fpl.

speak [spi:k], pt **spoke**, pp **spoken** vt (language) hablar; (truth) decir // vi hablar; (make a speech) intervenir; **to ~ to sb/of or about sth** hablar con uno/de o sobre algo; ~ **up!** ¡habla fuerte!, ~**er** n (in public) orador/a m/f; (also: **loud~er**) altavoz m, parlante m; (POL): **the S~ or** el Presidente del Congreso.

spear [spiə*] n lanza; (for fishing) arpón m // vt alancear; arponear; ~**head** n punta de lanza.

special ['speʃl] a especial; (edition etc) extraordinario; (delivery) urgente; **take ~ care** ponga un cuidado especial; ~**ist** n especialista m/f; ~**ity** [speʃi'æliti] n especialidad f; ~**ize vi: to ~ ize (in)** especializarse en; ~**ly** ad sobre todo, en particular.

species ['spi:ʃi:z] n especie f.

specific [spə'sifik] a específico; ~**ally** ad específicamente.

specification [spesifi'keiʃən] n especificación f; ~s npl presupuesto; **specify** ['spesifai] vt, vi especificar, precisar.

specimen ['spesimən] n ejemplar m, espécimen m.

speck [spek] n grano, mota.

speckled ['spekld] a moteado.

specs [speks] mpl (col) gafas fpl.

spectacle ['spektəkl] n espectáculo; ~s npl gafas fpl, anteojos mpl; **spectacular** [-'tækjulə*] a espectacular; (success) impresionante.

spectator [spek'teitə*] n espectador/a m/f.

spectre, specter (US) ['spektə*] n espectro, fantasma m.

spectrum ['spektrəm], pl -**tra** [-trə] n espectro.

speculate ['spekjuleit] vi especular; (try to guess): **to ~ about** especular sobre; **speculation** [-'leiʃən] n especulación f.

speech [spi:tʃ] n (faculty) habla,
palabra; (formal talk) discurso;
(talk) palabras fpl; (language)
idioma m, lenguaje m; ~**less** a
mudo, estupefacto.

speed [spi:d] n velocidad f, rapidez
f; (haste) prisa; (promptness)
prontitud f; **at full** or **top** ~ a
máxima velocidad; **to** ~ **up** vi
acelerarse // vt acelerar; ~**boat** n
lancha motora; ~**ily** ad rápido,
rápidamente; ~**ing** n (AUT) exceso
de velocidad; ~ **limit** n límite m de
velocidad, velocidad f máxima;
~**ometer** [spi'dɔmitə*] n
velocímetro; ~**way** n (SPORT)
carreras fpl de moto; ~**y** a (fast)
veloz, rápido; (prompt) pronto.

spell [spel] n (also: **magic** ~)
encanto, hechizo; (period of time)
rato, período; (turn) turno // vt, pt,
pp **spelt** or **spelled** (also: ~ **out**)
deletrear; (fig) anunciar, presagiar;
to cast a ~ **on sb** hechizar a uno; **he
can't** ~ no sabe escribir bien, sabe
poco de ortografía; ~**bound** a
embelesado, hechizado; ~**ing** n
ortografía.

spend [spend], pt, pp **spent** [spent]
vt (money) gastar; (time) pasar;
(life) dedicar; ~**thrift** n derro-
chador/a m/f, pródigo/a.

sperm [spə:m] n esperma; ~ **whale**
n cachalote m.

spew [spju:] vt vomitar, arrojar.

sphere [sfiə*] n esfera; **spherical**
['sferikl] a esférico.

sphinx [sfiŋks] n esfinge f.

spice [spais] n especia // vt
especiar; **spicy** a especiado, (fig)
picante.

spider ['spaidə*] n araña.

spike [spaik] n (point) punta; (ZOOL)
pincho, púa; (BOT) espiga.

spill [spil], pt, pp **spilt** or **spilled**
vt derramar, verter // vi
derramarse; **to** ~ **over** desbordarse.

spin [spin] n (revolution of wheel)
vuelta, revolución f; (AVIAT)

barrena; (trip in car) paseo (en
coche) // (vb: pt, pp **spun**) vt (wool
etc) hilar; (wheel) girar // vi girar,
dar vueltas; **to** ~ **out** vt alargar,
prolongar.

spinach ['spinitʃ] n espinaca; (as
food) espinacas fpl.

spinal ['spainl] a espinal; ~ **cord** n
columna vertebral.

spindly ['spindli] a zanquivano.

spin-drier [spin'draiə*] n secador
m centrífugo.

spine [spain] n espinazo, columna
vertebral; (thorn) espina; ~**less** a
(fig) débil, flojo.

spinning ['spinin] n (of thread)
hilado; (art) hilandería; ~ **top** n
peonza; ~ **wheel** n rueca, torno de
hilar.

spinster ['spinstə*] n soltera; (pej)
solterona.

spiral ['spaiərl] n espiral m // a en
espiral; ~ **staircase** n escalera de
caracol.

spire ['spaiə*] n aguja, chapitel m.

spirit ['spirit] n (gen) espíritu m;
(soul) alma m; (ghost) fantasma m;
(humour) humor m; (courage) valor
m, ánimo; ~**s** npl (drink) alcohol m,
bebidas fpl alcohólicas; **in good** ~**s**
alegre, de buen ánimo; ~**ed** a
enérgico, vigoroso; ~ **level** n nivel
m de aire.

spiritual ['spiritjuəl] a espiritual //
n (also: **Negro** ~) canción f
religiosa, espiritual m; ~**ism** n
espiritualismo.

spit [spit] n (for roasting) asador m,
espetón m // vi, pt, pp **spat** escupir;
(sound) chisporrotear.

spite [spait] n rencor m, ojeriza //
vt causar pena a, mortificar; **in
spite of** a pesar de, pese a; ~**ful** a
rencoroso, malévolo.

spittle ['spitl] n saliva, baba.

splash [splæʃ] n (sound) chapoteo;
(of colour) mancha // vt salpicar de
// vi (also: ~ **about**) chapotear.

spleen [spli:n] n (ANAT) bazo.

splendid ['splendid] a espléndido.

splendour, splendor (US) [-də*] n esplendor m; (of achievement) brillo, gloria.

splint [splɪnt] n tablilla.

splinter ['splɪntə*] n (of wood) astilla; (in finger) espigón m // vi astillarse, hacer astillas.

split [splɪt] n hendedura, raja; (fig) división f; (POL) escisión f // (vb: pt, pp split) vt partir, rajar; (party) dividir; (work, profits) repartir // (divide) dividirse, escindirse; to ~ up vi (couple) separarse; (meeting) acabarse.

splutter ['splʌtə*] vi chisporrotear; (person) balbucear.

spoil [spɔɪl], pt, pp **spoilt** or **spoiled** vt (damage) dañar; (mar) estropear, echar a perder; (child) mimar, consentir; ~s npl despojo sg, botín m; ~sport n aguafiestas m inv.

spoke [spəuk] pt of **speak** // n rayo, radio.

spoken ['spəukn] pp of **speak**.

spokesman ['spəuksmən] n vocero, portavoz m.

sponge [spʌndʒ] n esponja; (cake) pastel m // vt (wash) lavar con esponja // vi: to ~ on sb vivir a costa de uno // ~ bag n esponjera; ~ cake n bizcocho, pastel m; **spongy** a esponjoso.

sponsor ['spɔnsə*] n (RADIO, TV) patrocinador/a m/f; (for membership) padrino; (COMM) fiador/a m/f // vt patrocinar; apadrinar; (idea etc) presentar, promover; ~**ship** n patrocinio.

spontaneous [spɔn'teɪnɪəs] a espontáneo.

spool [spuːl] n carrete m; (of sewing machine) canilla.

spoon [spuːn] n cuchara; ~**feed** vt dar de comer con cuchara; (fig) tratar como un niño; ~**ful** n cucharada.

sporadic [spə'rædɪk] a esporádico.

sport [spɔːt] n deporte m; (person) buen perdedor m; ~**ing** a deportivo;

~s car n coche m sport; ~s jacket n chaqueta sport; **sportsman** n deportista m; **sportsmanship** n deportividad f; **sportswear** n trajes mpl de deporte o sport; **sportswoman** n deportista f; ~y a deportivo.

spot [spɔt] n sitio, lugar m; (dot: on pattern) punto, mancha; (pimple) grano; (freckle) peca; (small amount): a ~ of un poquito de // (notice) notar, observar; on the ~ en el acto, acto seguido; (in difficulty) en un aprieto; ~ check n reconocimiento rápido; ~less a limpio, perfectamente nítido, limpio; ~light n foco, reflector m; ~ted a (pattern) de puntos; ~ty a (face) con granos.

spouse [spauz] n cónyuge m/f.

spout [spaut] n (of jug) pico; (pipe) caño // vi chorrear.

sprain [spreɪn] n torcedura // vt: to ~ one's ankle torcerse el tobillo.

sprang [spræŋ] pt of **spring**.

sprawl [sprɔːl] vi tumbarse.

spray [spreɪ] n rociada; (of sea) espuma; (container) atomizador m; (of paint) pistola rociadora; (of flowers) ramita // vt rociar; (crops) regar.

spread [spred] n extensión f; (distribution) diseminación f, propagación f; (col: food) comilona f // (vb: pt, pp spread) vt extender, diseminar; (butter) untar; (wings, sails) desplegar; (scatter) esparcir // vi extenderse; diseminarse; untarse; desplegarse; esparcirse.

spree [spriː] n: to go on a ~ ir de juerga.

sprightly ['spraɪtlɪ] a vivo, enérgico.

spring [sprɪŋ] n (leap) salto, brinco; (coiled metal) resorte m; (season) primavera; (of water) fuente f, manantial f // vi, pt **sprang**, pp **sprung** (arise) brotar, nacer; (leap) saltar, brincar; to ~ up vi nacer de repente, aparecer repentinamente;

~board n trampolín m; **~-clean** n (also: **~-cleaning**) limpieza general; **~time** n primavera; **~y** a elástico; (grass) muelle.

sprinkle ['sprɪŋkl] vt (pour) rociar; **to ~ water on, ~ with water** rociar o salpicar de agua; **~d with** (fig) sembrado o salpicado de.

sprint [sprɪnt] n sprint m // vi (gen) correr a toda velocidad; (SPORT) sprintar; **~er** n sprinter m/f, corredor/a m/f.

sprite [spraɪt] n duende m.

sprout [spraut] vi brotar, retoñar; (Brussels) **~s** npl coleccillos mpl de Bruselas.

spruce [spru:s] n (BOT) pícea // a aseado, pulcro.

sprung [sprʌŋ] pp of **spring.**

spry [spraɪ] a ágil, activo.

spun [spʌn] pt, pp of **spin.**

spur [spə:*] n espuela; (fig) estímulo, aguijón m // vt (also: **~ on**) estimular, incitar; **on the ~ of the moment** de improviso.

spurn [spə:n] vt desdeñar, rechazar.

spurt [spə:t] n esfuerzo supremo; (of energy) arrebato // vi hacer un esfuerzo supremo.

spy [spaɪ] n espía m/f // vi: **to ~ on** espiar a // vt (see) divisar, lograr ver; **~ing** n espionaje m.

sq. abbr of **square.**

squabble ['skwɔbl] n riña, pelea // vi reñir, pelear.

squad [skwɔd] n (MIL, POLICE) pelotón m, escuadra.

squadron ['skwɔdrn] n (MIL) escuadrón m; (AVIAT, NAUT) escuadra.

squalid ['skwɔlɪd] a vil, miserable, escuálido.

squall [skwɔ:l] n (storm) chubasco; (wind) ráfaga.

squalor ['skwɔlə*] n miseria.

squander ['skwɔndə*] vt (money) derrochar, despilfarrar; (chances) desperdiciar.

square [skwɛə*] n cuadro; (in town) plaza // a cuadrado; (col: ideas,

tastes) pasota // vt (arrange) arreglar; (MATH) cuadrar; **all ~** igual(es); **a ~ meal** una comida abundante; **2 metres ~** 2 metros en cuadro; **1 ~ metre** un metro cuadrado; **~ly** ad en cuadro; (fully) de lleno.

squash [skwɔʃ] n (drink): **lemon/orange ~** zumo de limón/naranja; (SPORT) squash m, frontenis m // vt aplastar; **to ~ together** apiñar.

squat [skwɔt] a achaparrado // vi agacharse, sentarse en cuclillas; **~ter** n persona que ocupa ilegalmente una casa.

squawk [skwɔ:k] vi graznar.

squeak [skwi:k] n chirrido, rechinamiento; (of shoe) crujido; (of mouse) chillido // vi chirriar, rechinar; crujir; chillar.

squeal [skwi:l] vi chillar, dar gritos agudos.

squeamish ['skwi:mɪʃ] a delicado, remilgado.

squeeze [skwi:z] n (gen) estrujón m; (of hand) apretón m; (in bus etc) apiñamiento // vt estrujar, apretar; (hand, arm) apretar; **to ~ out** vt exprimir; (fig) excluir; **to ~ through** abrirse paso con esfuerzos.

squelch [skwɛltʃ] vi aplastar, despachurrar.

squid [skwɪd] n calamar m.

squint [skwɪnt] vi bizquear, ser bizco // n (MED) estrabismo; **to ~ at** sth mirar algo de soslayo.

squirm [skwə:m] vi retorcerse, revolverse.

squirrel ['skwɪrəl] n ardilla.

squirt [skwə:t] vi salir a chorros.

Sr abbr of **senior.**

St abbr of **saint; street.**

stab [stæb] n (with knife etc) puñalada; (of pain) pinchazo; (col: try): **to have a ~ at (doing)** sth intentar (hacer) algo // vt apuñalar.

stability [stə'bɪlɪtɪ] n estabilidad f; **stabilize** ['steɪbəlaɪz] vt estabilizar // vi estabilizarse; **stable** ['steɪbl] a cotable // n cuadra, caballeriza.

stack [stæk] n montón m, pila // vt amontonar, apilar.

stadium ['steidiəm] n estadio.

staff [staːf] n (work force) personal m, plantilla; (stick) bastón m // vt proveer de personal.

stag [stæg] n ciervo, venado.

stage [steidʒ] n escena; (profession): the ~ el escenario, el teatro; (point) etapa; (platform) plataforma // vt (play) poner en escena, representar; (demonstration) montar, organizar; (fig: perform: recovery etc) llevar a cabo; ~coach n diligencia; ~ door n entrada de artistas; ~ manager n director/a m/f de escena.

stagger ['stægə*] vi tambalear // vt (amaze) asombrar; (hours, holidays) escalonar; ~ing a (amazing) asombroso, pasmoso.

stagnant ['stægnənt] a estancado.

stagnate [-'neit] vi estancarse.

stag party n fiesta de solteros.

staid [steid] a serio, formal.

stain [stein] n mancha; (colouring) tintura // vt manchar; (wood) teñir; ~ed glass window n vidriera de colores; ~less a (steel) inoxidable.

stair [steə*] n (step) peldaño, escalón m; ~s npl escaleras fpl; ~case, ~way n escalera.

stake [steik] n estaca, poste m; (BETTING) apuesta // vt apostar; to be at ~ estar en juego.

stalactite ['stæləktait] n estalactita.

stalagmite ['stæləgmait] n estalagmita.

stale [steil] a (bread) duro; (food) no fresco, pasado.

stalemate ['steilmeit] n tablas fpl (por ahogado); (fig) estancamiento.

stalk [stɔːk] n tallo, caña // vt acechar, cazar al acecho; to ~ off irse con paso airado.

stall [stɔːl] n (in market) puesto; (in stable) casilla (de establo) // vt (AUT) parar // vi (AUT) pararse;

(fig) buscar evasivas; ~s npl (in cinema, theatre) butacas fpl.

stallion ['stæliən] n caballo padre, semental m.

stalwart ['stɔːlwət] n (in build) fornido; (in spirit) valiente.

stamina ['stæminə] n resistencia.

stammer ['stæmə*] n tartamudeo, balbuceo // vi tartamudear, balbucir.

stamp [stæmp] n sello, estampilla; (mark, also fig) marca, huella; (on document) timbre m // vt patear; (mark) marcar con el pie; (in dance) zapatear; (letter) poner sellos en; (with rubber) marcar con estampilla; ~ album n álbum m para sellos; ~ collecting n filatelia.

stampede [stæm'piːd] n estampida.

stance [stæns] n postura.

stand [stænd] n (position) posición f, postura; (for taxis) parada; (hall ~) perchero; (music ~) atril m; (SPORT) tribuna; (news ~) quiosco // (vb: pt, pp stood) vi (be) estar, encontrarse; (be on foot) estar de pie; (rise) levantarse; (remain) quedar en pie // vt (place) poner, colocar; (tolerate, withstand) aguantar, soportar; (cost) pagar; (invite) invitar; to make a ~ resistir; (fig) aferrarse a un principio; to ~ for parliament presentarse como candidato al parlamento; to ~ by vi (be ready) estar listo // vt fus (opinion) aferrarse a; to ~ for vt fus (defend) apoyar; (signify) significar; (tolerate) aguantar, permitir; to ~ in for vt fus suplir a; to ~ out vi (be prominent) destacarse; to ~ up vi (rise) levantarse, ponerse de pie; to ~ up for vt fus defender; to ~ up to vt fus hacer frente a.

standard ['stændəd] n patrón m, norma; (flag) estandarte m; (degree) grado // a (size etc) normal, corriente, estándar; ~s npl (morals) valores mpl morales; ~ize *vt* estandarizar; ~ **lamp** *n* lámpara de pie; ~ **of living** *n* nivel *m* de vida.

stand-by ['stændbaɪ] *n* (alert) alerta, aviso; **to be on** ~ estar sobre aviso; ~ **ticket** *n* (AVIAT) billete *m* standby.

stand-in ['stændɪn] *n* suplente *m/f*; (CINEMA) doble *m/f*.

standing ['stændɪŋ] *a* (upright) derecho; (on foot) de pie, en pie // *n* reputación *f*; **of many years'** ~ que lleva muchos años; ~ **order** *n* (at bank) giro bancario; ~ **orders** *npl* (MIL) reglamento *sg* general; ~ **room** *n* sitio para estar de pie.

stand-: ~**offish** *a* reservado, poco afable; ~**point** *n* punto de vista; ~**still** *n*: **at a** ~**still** paralizado, en paro; **to come to a** ~**still** pararse, quedar paralizado.

stank [stæŋk] *pt of* **stink**.

staple ['steɪpl] *n* (for papers) grapa // *a* (food etc) corriente // *vt* unir con grapa, engrapar; **stapler** *n* grapadora.

star [stɑː*] *n* estrella; (celebrity) estrella, astro // *vi*: **to** ~ **in** ser la estrella *o* el astro de.

starboard ['stɑːbəd] *n* estribor *m*.

starch [stɑːtʃ] *n* almidón *m*; ~**ed** *a* (collar) almidonado; ~**y** *a* feculento.

stardom ['stɑːdəm] *n* estrellato, calidad *f* de estrella.

stare [stɛə*] *n* mirada fija // *vt*: **to** ~ **at** mirar fijo.

starfish ['stɑːfɪʃ] *n* estrella de mar.

stark [stɑːk] *a* (bleak) severo, escueto // *ad*: ~ **naked** en cueros, en pelota.

starlight ['stɑːlaɪt] *n*: **by** ~ a la luz de las estrellas.

starling ['stɑːlɪŋ] *n* estornino.

starry ['stɑːrɪ] *a* estrellado; ~**-eyed** *a* (innocent) inocentón(ona), ingenuo.

start [stɑːt] *n* (beginning) principio, comienzo; (departure) salida; (sudden movement) salto, sobre-

salto; (advantage) ventaja // *vt* empezar, comenzar; (cause) causar; (found) fundar; (engine) poner en marcha // *vi* (begin) comenzar, empezar; (with fright) asustarse, sobresaltarse; (train etc) salir; **to** ~ **off** *vi* empezar, comenzar; (leave) salir, ponerse en camino; **to** ~ **up** *vi* comenzar; (car) ponerse en marcha // *vt* comenzar; (car) poner en marcha; ~**er** *n* (AUT) botón *m* de arranque; (SPORT: official) juez *m/f* de salida; (: runner) corredor/a *m/f*; (CULIN) entrada; ~**ing point** *n* punto de partida.

startle ['stɑːtl] *vt* asustar, sobrecoger; **startling** *a* alarmante.

starvation [stɑː'veɪʃən] *n* hambre *f*; (MED) inanición *f*; **starve** *vi* pasar hambre; (to death) morir de hambre // *vt* hacer pasar hambre; (fig) privar; **I'm starving** estoy muerto de hambre.

state [steɪt] *n* estado // *vt* (say, declare) afirmar; (a case) presentar, exponer; **the S~s** los Estados Unidos; **to be in a** ~ estar agitado; ~**ly** *a* majestuoso, imponente; ~**ment** *n* afirmación *f*; (LAW) declaración *f*; **statesman** *n* estadista *m*.

static ['stætɪk] *n* (RADIO) parásitos *mpl* // *a* estático; ~ **electricity** *n* estática.

station ['steɪʃən] *n* (gen) estación *f*; (place) puesto, sitio; (RADIO) emisora; (rank) posición *f* social // *vt* colocar, situar; (MIL) apostar.

stationary ['steɪʃnərɪ] *a* estacionario, fijo.

stationer's (shop) ['steɪʃənəz] *n* papelería; **stationery** [-nərɪ] *n* papel *m* de escribir.

station master *n* (RAIL) jefe *m* de estación.

station wagon *n* (US) break *m*.

statistic [stə'tɪstɪk] *n* estadística; ~**s** *npl* (science) estadística *sg*; ~**al** *a* estadístico.

statue ['stætjuː] *n* estatua.

stature ['stætʃə*] n estatura; (fig) talla.

status ['steitəs] n condición f, estado; (reputation) reputación f, status m; **the ~ quo** el status quo; **~ symbol** n símbolo de prestigio.

statute ['stætjuːt] n estatuto, ley f; **statutory** a estatutario.

staunch [stɔːntʃ] a firme, incondicional.

stave [steiv] vt: **to ~ off** (attack) rechazar; (threat) evitar.

stay [stei] n (period of time) estancia // vi (remain) quedar, quedarse; (as guest) hospedarse; (spend some time) pasar (un) tiempo; **to ~ put** seguir en el mismo sitio; **to ~ the night** pasar la noche; **to ~ behind** vi quedar atrás; **to ~ in** vi (at home) quedarse en casa; **to ~ on** vi quedarse; **to ~ out** vi (of house) no volver a casa; **to ~ up** vi (at night) velar, no acostarse; **~ing power** n resistencia.

steadfast ['stedfəst] a firme, resuelto.

steadily ['stedili] ad (firmly) firmemente; (unceasingly) sin parar; (fixedly) fijamente; (walk) normalmente; (drive) a velocidad constante.

steady ['stedi] a (constant) constante, fijo; (unswerving) firme; (regular) regular; (person, character) sensato, juicioso; (diligent) trabajador; (calm) sereno // vt (hold) mantener firme; (stabilize) estabilizar; (nerves) calmar; **to o.s. on or against** sth afirmarse en algo.

steak [steik] n (gen) filete m; (beef) bistec m.

steal [stiːl], pt **stole**, pp **stolen** vt vi robar.

stealth [stelθ] n: **by ~** a escondidas, sigilosamente; **~y** a cauteloso, sigiloso.

steam [stiːm] n vapor m; (mist) vaho, humo // vt empañar; (CULIN) cocer al vapor // vi echar vapor;

(ship): **to ~ along** avanzar, avanzando; **~ engine** n máquina de vapor; **~er** n vapor m; **~roller** n apisonadora; **~y** a vaporoso; (room) lleno de vapor; (window) empañado.

steel [stiːl] n acero // a de acero; **~works** n (fábrica) siderúrgica.

steep [stiːp] a escarpado, abrupto; (stair) empinado; (price) exorbitante, excesivo // vt empapar, remojar.

steeple ['stiːpl] n aguja, campanario; **~chase** n carrera de obstáculos; **~jack** n reparador m de chimeneas.

steer [stiə*] vt conducir, dirigir // vi conducir; **~ing** n (AUT) dirección f; **~ing wheel** n volante m.

stellar ['stelə*] a estelar.

stem [stem] n (of plant) tallo; (of glass) pie m; (of pipe) cañón m // vt detener; (blood) restañar; **to ~ from** vt fus proceder de.

stench [stentʃ] n hedor m.

stencil ['stensl] n (typed) cliché m, clisé m; (lettering) plantilla // vt hacer un cliché de.

step [step] n paso; (sound) paso, pisada; (stair) peldaño, escalón m // vi: **to ~ forward** dar un paso adelante; **~s** npl = **~ladder**; **to ~ down** vi (fig) retirarse; **to ~ off** vt fus bajar de; **to ~ on** vt fus pisar; **to ~ over** vt fus pasar por encima de; **to ~ up** vt (increase) aumentar; **~brother** n hermanastro; **~daughter** n hijastra; **~father** n padrastro; **~ladder** n escalera de tijera o doble; **~mother** n madrastra; **~ping stone** n pasadera; **~sister** n hermanastra; **~son** n hijastro.

stereo ['steriəu] n estéreo // a (also: **~phonic**) estereofónico.

stereotype ['stiəriətaip] n estereotipo // vt estereotipar.

sterile ['sterail] a estéril; **sterility** [-'riliti] n esterilidad f; **sterilization** [-'zeiʃən] n esterilización f; **sterilize** ['sterilaiz] vt esterilizar.

sterling ['stɜːlɪŋ] a esterlina; (silver) de ley; (fig) auténtico.

stern [stɜːn] a severo, austero // n (NAUT) popa.

stethoscope ['steθəskəup] n estetoscopio.

stew [stjuː] n cocido, estofado; (fig: mess) apuro // vt, vi estofar, guisar; (fruit) cocer.

steward [stjuːəd] n (gen) camarero; ~ess n azafata.

stick [stɪk] n palo; (as weapon) porra; (walking ~) bastón m // (vb: pt, pp **stuck**) vt (glue) pegar; (thrust): **to ~ sth into** clavar o hincar algo en; (col: put) meter; (col: tolerate) aguantar, soportar // vi pegar, pegarse; (come to a stop) quedarse parado; (in mind etc) atascarse; (pin etc) clavarse; **to ~ out, ~ up** vi sobresalir; **to ~ up for** vt fus defender; ~**er** n etiqueta engomada.

stickler ['stɪklə*] n: **to be a ~ for** dar mucha importancia a.

stick-up ['stɪkʌp] n asalto, atraco.

sticky ['stɪkɪ] a pegajoso; (label) engomado; (fig) difícil.

stiff [stɪf] a rígido, tieso; (hard) duro; (difficult) difícil; (person) inflexible; (price) exorbitante; ~**en** vt hacer más rígido; (limb) entumecer o vi endurecerse; (grow stronger) fortalecerse; ~**ness** n rigidez f, tiesura; dificultad f; (character) frialdad f.

stifle ['staɪfl] vt ahogar, sofocar; **stifling** a (heat) sofocante, bochornoso.

stigma ['stɪɡmə], pl (BOT, MED, REL) ~**ta** [-tə], (fig) ~**s** n estigma m.

stile [staɪl] n escalera para pasar una cerca.

stiletto [stɪ'letəu] n (also: ~ **heel**) tacón m de aguja.

still [stɪl] a inmóvil, quieto // ad (up to this time) todavía; (even) aún; (nonetheless) sin embargo, aun así; ~**born** a nacido muerto; ~ **life** n naturaleza muerta.

stilt [stɪlt] n zanco; (pile) pilar m, soporte m.

stilted ['stɪltɪd] a afectado.

stimulant ['stɪmjulənt] n estimulante m.

stimulate ['stɪmjuleɪt] vt estimular; **stimulating** a estimulante; **stimulation** [-'leɪʃən] n estímulo.

stimulus ['stɪmjuləs], pl **-li** [-laɪ] n estímulo, incentivo.

sting [stɪŋ] n (wound) picadura; (pain) escozor m, picazón m; (organ) aguijón m // (vb: pt, pp **stung**) vt picar // vi picar, escocer.

stingy ['stɪndʒɪ] a tacaño.

stink [stɪŋk] n hedor m, tufo // vi, pt **stank**, pp **stunk** heder, apestar; ~**ing** a hediondo, fétido.

stint [stɪnt] n tarea, destajo; **to do one's ~** hacer su parte // vi: **to ~ on** escatimar.

stipend ['staɪpend] n (of vicar etc) estipendio, sueldo.

stipulate ['stɪpjuleɪt] vt estipular, poner como condición; **stipulation** [-'leɪʃən] n estipulación f, condición f.

stir [stɜː*] n (fig: agitation) conmoción f // vt (tea etc) remover; (fire) atizar; (move) mover; (fig: emotions) conmover // vi moverse, menearse; **to ~ up** vt excitar; (trouble) fomentar; ~**ring** a conmovedor(a).

stirrup ['stɪrəp] n estribo.

stitch [stɪtʃ] n (SEWING) puntada; (KNITTING) punto; (MED) punto de sutura; (pain) punzada // vt coser; (MED) suturar.

stoat [stəut] n armiño.

stock [stɒk] n (COMM. reserves) existencias fpl, stock m; (: selection) surtido; (AGR) ganado, ganadería; (CULIN) caldo; (fig: lineage) estirpe f; (FINANCE) capital m; (: shares) acciones fpl // a (fig: reply etc) clásico, acostumbrado // vt (have in ~) tener o en existencia o almacén); (supply) proveer, abastecer; **to take ~ of** (fig) asesorar, examinar; **to ~ up with** vt abastecerse de; ~**s** npl cepo sg; ~**s and shares** acciones y valores.

stockade [stɔ'keid] n estacada.

stockbroker ['stɔkbrəukə*] n agente m/f o corredor/a m/f de bolsa.

stock exchange n bolsa.

stocking ['stɔkiŋ] n media.

stock market n bolsa (de valores).

stockpile ['stɔkpail] n reserva // vt acumular, almacenar.

stocktaking ['stɔkteikiŋ] n (COMM) inventario, balance m.

stocky ['stɔki] a (strong) robusto, (short) achaparrado.

stodgy ['stɔdʒi] a indigesto, pesado

stoical ['stəuikəl] a estoico.

stoke [stəuk] vt cargar, cebar.

stole [stəul] pt of **steal** // n estola.

stolen ['stəuln] pp of **steal**.

stomach ['stʌmək] n (ANAT) estómago; (belly) vientre m; (appetite) apetito // vt tragar, aguantar; ~**ache** n dolor m de estómago.

stone [stəun] n piedra; (in fruit) hueso, (weight) medida de peso (6.348kg) // a de piedra // vt apedrear; ~**cold** a helado; ~**deaf** a totalmente sordo; ~**work** n (art) cantería; (stones) piedras fpl; **stony** a pedregoso; (glance) glacial.

stood [stud] pt, pp of **stand**.

stool [stu:l] n taburete m.

stoop [stu:p] vi (also: have a ~) ser cargado de espaldas; (bend) inclinarse, encorvarse.

stop [stɔp] n parada, alto; (in punctuation) punto // vt parar, detener; (break off) suspender; (block) tapar, cerrar; (also: put a ~ to) terminar, poner término a // vi pararse, detenerse; (end) acabarse; **to ~ doing sth** dejar de hacer algo; **to ~ dead** vi pararse en seco; **to ~ off** vi interrumpir el viaje; **to ~ up** vt (hole) tapar; ~**gap** n recurso (temporal); ~**lights** npl (AUT) luces

fpl de detención; ~**over** n parada intermedia.

stoppage ['stɔpidʒ] n (strike) paro; (temporary stop) interrupción f; (of pay) suspensión f; (blockage) obstrucción f.

stopper ['stɔpə*] n tapón m.

stopwatch ['stɔpwɔtʃ] n cronómetro.

storage ['stɔ:ridʒ] n almacenaje m.

store [stɔ:*] n (stock) provisión f; (depot, large shop) almacén m; (reserve) reserva, repuesto; ~**s** npl víveres mpl // vt almacenar; (keep) guardar; **to ~ up** vt acumular; ~**room** n despensa.

storey, story (US) ['stɔ:ri] n piso.

stork [stɔ:k] n cigüeña.

storm [stɔ:m] n tormenta, (wind) vendaval m, (fig) tempestad f // vi (fig) rabiar // vt tomar por asalto, asaltar; ~ **cloud** n nubarrón m; ~**y** a tempestuoso.

story ['stɔ:ri] n historia, relato; (joke) cuento, chiste m; (plot) argumento; (lie) cuento, embuste m; (US) = **storey**; ~**book** n libro de cuentos; ~**teller** n cuentista m/f.

stout [staut] a (strong) sólido, macizo; (fat) gordo, corpulento // n cerveza negra.

stove [stəuv] n (for cooking) cocina; (for heating) estufa.

stow [stəu] vt meter, poner (NAUT) estibar; ~**away** n polizón/ona m/f.

straddle ['strædl] vt montar a horcajadas.

straggle ['strægl] vi (wander) vagar en desorden; (lag behind) rezagarse; **straggler** n rezagado/a, **straggling, straggly** a (hair) desordenado.

straight [streit] a recto, derecho; (honest) honrado, (frank) franco, directo; (simple) sencillo; (in order) en orden // ad derecho, directamente; (drink) sin mezcla; **to put o get sth ~** = dejar algo en claro; ~ **away, ~ off** (at once) en seguida; ~**en** vt (also: ~**en out**) enderezar, poner derecho; ~-**faced** a solemne, sin expresión; ~**forward** a (simple) sencillo; (honest) honrado, franco.

strain [streɪn] n (gen) tensión f; (TECH) esfuerzo; (MED) torcedura; (breed) raza // vt (back etc) torcerse; (tire) cansar; (stretch) estirar; (filter) filtrar // vi esforzarse; ~s npl (MUS) son m; ~**ed** a (muscle) torcido; (laugh) forzado; (relations) tenso; ~**er** n colador m.

strait [streɪt] n (GEO) estrecho; ~-**jacket** n camisa de fuerza; ~-**laced** a mojigato, gazmoño.

strand [strænd] n (of thread) hebra; (of hair) trenza; (of rope) ramal m; ~**ed** a abandonado (sin recursos), desamparado.

strange [streɪndʒ] a (not known) desconocido; (odd) extraño, raro; **stranger** n desconocido/a; (from another area) forastero/a.

strangle [ˈstræŋgl] vt estrangular; (sobs etc) ahogar; ~**hold** n (fig) dominio completo; **strangulation** [-ˈleɪʃən] n estrangulación f.

strap [stræp] n correa; (of slip, dress) tirante m // vt atar con correa; (punish) azotar.

strapping [ˈstræpɪŋ] a robusto, fornido.

strata [ˈstrɑːtə] pl of **stratum**.

stratagem [ˈstrætɪdʒəm] n estrategema.

strategic [strəˈtiːdʒɪk] a estratégico.

strategy [ˈstrætɪdʒɪ] n estrategia.

stratum [ˈstrɑːtəm], pl -ta n estrato.

straw [strɔː] n paja; (drinking ~) caña, pajita.

strawberry [ˈstrɔːbərɪ] n fresa.

stray [streɪ] a (animal) extraviado; (bullet) perdido; (scattered) disperso // vi extraviarse, perderse.

streak [striːk] n raya; (fig: of madness etc) vena // vt rayar // vi:

to ~ **past** pasar como un rayo; ~**y** a rayado.

stream [striːm] n riachuelo, arroyo; (jet) chorro; (current) corriente f; (of people) oleada // vt (SCOL) dividir en grupos por habilidad // vi correr, fluir; to ~ **in/out** (people) entrar/salir en tropel.

streamer [ˈstriːmə*] n serpentina.

streamlined [ˈstriːmlaɪnd] a aerodinámico.

street [striːt] n calle f // a callejero; ~**car** n (US) tranvía; ~ **lamp** n farol m.

strength [streŋθ] n fuerza; (of girder, knot etc) resistencia; ~**en** vt fortalecer, reforzar.

strenuous [ˈstrenjuəs] a (tough) arduo; (energetic) enérgico; (determined) tenaz.

stress [stres] n (force, pressure) presión f; (mental strain) tensión f; (accent) énfasis m, acento; (TECH) tensión f, carga // vt subrayar, recalcar.

stretch [stretʃ] n (of sand etc) trecho, tramo // vi estirarse; (extend): to ~ **to** or **as far as** extenderse hasta // vt extender, estirar; (make demands of) exigir el máximo esfuerzo a; to ~ **out** vi tenderse // vt (arm etc) extender; (spread) estirar.

stretcher [ˈstretʃə*] n camilla.

strewn [struːn] a: ~ **with** cubierto o sembrado de.

stricken [ˈstrɪkən] a (wounded) herido; (ill) enfermo.

strict [strɪkt] a (person) severo, riguroso; (precise) estricto, exacto; ~**ly** ad (exactly) estrictamente; (totally) terminantemente; (severely) rigurosamente; ~**ness** n exactitud f; rigor m, severidad f.

stride [straɪd] n zancada, tranco // vi, pt **strode**, pp **stridden** [ˈstrɪdn] dar zancadas, andar a trancos.

strident [ˈstraɪdnt] a estridente; (colour) chillón(ona).

strife [straɪf] n lucha.

strike [straɪk] n huelga; (of oil etc) descubrimiento; (attack) ataque m; (SPORT) golpe m // (vb: pt, pp **struck**) vt descubrir; (obstacle) topar con // vi declarar la huelga; (attack) atacar; (clock) dar la hora; **to ~ a match** encender un fósforo; **to ~ down** vt derribar; **to ~ out** vt borrar, tachar; **to ~ up** vt (MUS) empezar a tocar; (conversation) entablar; (friendship) trabar; **~-breaker** n rompehuelgas m/t inv; **striker** n huelgista m/t; (SPORT) delantero; **striking** a impresionante; (nasty) chocante; (colour) llamativo.

string [strɪŋ] n (gen) cuerda; (row) hilera // vt, pp **strung**: **to ~ together** ensartar // vi: **to ~ out** extenderse; **the ~s** npl (MUS) los instrumentos de cuerda; **to pull ~s** (fig) mover palancas; **~ bean** n judía verde, habichuela; **~(ed) instrument** n (MUS) instrumento de cuerda.

stringent ['strɪndʒənt] a riguroso, severo.

strip [strɪp] n tira; (of land) franja; (of metal) cinta, lámina // vt desnudar; (also: **~ down**: machine) desmontar // vi desnudarse; **~ cartoon** n tira cómica.

stripe [straɪp] n raya; (MIL) galón m; **~d** a a rayas, rayado.

stripper ['strɪpə*] n artista de striptease.

striptease ['strɪptiːz] n striptease m.

strive [straɪv], pt **strove**, pp **striven** ['strɪvn] vi: **to ~ to do sth** esforzarse o luchar por hacer algo.

strode [strəud] pt of **stride**.

stroke [strəuk] n (blow) golpe m; (MED) ataque m fulminante; (caress) caricia; (of pen) trazo // vt acariciar, frotar suavemente; **at a ~ de golpe**.

stroll [strəul] n paseo, vuelta // vi dar un paseo o una vuelta.

strong [strɔŋ] a fuerte; **they are 50**

~ son 50; **~box** n caja fuerte; **~hold** n fortaleza; (fig) baluarte m; **~ly** ad fuertemente, con fuerza; (believe) firmemente; **~room** n cámara acorazada.

strove [strəuv] pt of **strive**.

struck [strʌk] pt, pp of **strike**.

structural ['strʌktʃərəl] a estructural; **structure** n estructura; (building) construcción f.

struggle ['strʌgl] n lucha // vi luchar.

strum [strʌm] vt (guitar) rasguear.

strung [strʌŋ] pt, pp of **string**.

strut [strʌt] n puntal m // vi pavonearse.

stub [stʌb] n (of ticket etc) talón m; (of cigarette) colilla; **to ~ out** vt apagar; **to ~ one's toe** dar con el dedo contra algo.

stubble ['stʌbl] n rastrojo; (on chin) barba (de pocos días).

stubborn ['stʌbən] a terco, testarudo.

stuck [stʌk] pt, pp of **stick** // a (jammed) atascado; **~-up** a engreído, presumido.

stud [stʌd] n (shirt ~) botón m; (of boot) taco; (of horses) caballeriza; (also: **~ horse**) caballo padre o semental // vt (fig): **~ded with** sembrado de.

student ['stjuːdənt] n estudiante m/t // a estudiantil.

studio ['stjuːdɪəu] n estudio; (sculptor's) taller m.

studious ['stjuːdɪəs] a aplicado; (studied) calculado; **~ly** ad (carefully) con esmero.

study ['stʌdɪ] n (gen) estudio // vt estudiar; (examine) examinar, escudriñar // vi estudiar.

stuff [stʌf] n materia; (cloth) tela; (substance) material m, sustancia // vt llenar; (CULIN) rellenar; (animals) disecar; **~ing** n relleno; **~y** a (room) mal ventilado; (person) de miras estrechas.

stumble ['stʌmbl] vi tropezar, dar un traspié; **to ~ across** (fig) tropezar con; **stumbling block** n tropiezo, obstáculo.

stump [stʌmp] n (of tree) tocón m; (of limb) muñón m // vi: **to be ~ed** quedar perplejo.

stun [stʌn] vt dejar sin sentido.

stung [stʌŋ] pt, pp of **sting**.

stunk [stʌŋk] pp of **stink**.

stunning [stʌnɪŋ] a (fig) pasmoso.

stunt [stʌnt] n proeza excepcional; (AVIAT) vuelo acrobático; (publicity ~) truco publicitario; **~ed** a enano, achaparrado; **~man** n doble m.

stupefy ['stju:pɪfaɪ] vt dejar estupefacto.

stupendous [stju:'pɛndəs] a estupendo, asombroso.

stupid ['stju:pɪd] a estúpido, tonto; **~ity** [-'pɪdɪtɪ] n estupidez f; **~ly** ad estúpidamente.

stupor ['stju:pə*] n estupor m.

sturdy ['stɜ:dɪ] a robusto, fuerte.

stutter ['stʌtə*] n tartamudeo // vi tartamudear.

sty [staɪ] n (for pigs) pocilga.

stye [staɪ] n (MED) orzuelo.

style [staɪl] n estilo; **stylish** a elegante, a la moda.

stylus ['staɪləs] n (of record player) aguja.

suave [swɑːv] a cortés, fino.

sub... [sʌb] pref sub...; **~conscious** a subconsciente // n subconsciente m; **~divide** vt subdividir; **~division** n subdivisión f.

subdue [səb'dju:] vt sojuzgar; (passions) dominar; **~d** a (light) tenue; (person) sumiso, manso.

subject ['sʌbdʒɪkt] n súbdito; (SCOL) tema m, materia // vt [səb'dʒɛkt]: **to ~ sb to sth** someter a uno a algo; **to be ~ to** (law) estar sujeto a; **~ion** [-'dʒɛkʃən] n sometimiento, sujeción f; **~ive** a subjetivo; **~ matter** n materia; (content) contenido.

subjugate ['sʌbdʒugeɪt] vt subyugar.

sublet [sʌb'lɛt] vt subarrendar.

sublime [sə'blaɪm] a sublime.

submachine gun [sʌbmə'ʃiːn-] n metralleta.

submarine [sʌbmə'riːn] n submarino.

submerge [səb'mɜːdʒ] vt sumergir; (flood) inundar // vi sumergirse.

submission [səb'mɪʃən] n sumisión f; **submissive** [-'mɪsɪv] a sumiso.

submit [səb'mɪt] vt someter // vi someterse.

subnormal [sʌb'nɔːməl] a anormal; (backward) retrasado.

subordinate [sə'bɔːdɪnət] a, n subordinado.

subpoena [səb'piːnə] (LAW) n comparendo, citación f // vt mandar comparecer.

subscribe [səb'skraɪb] vi suscribir; **to ~ to** (opinion, fund) suscribir, aprobar; (newspaper) suscribirse a; **subscriber** n (to periodical, telephone) abonado/a.

subscription [səb'skrɪpʃən] n abono, suscripción f.

subsequent ['sʌbsɪkwənt] a subsiguiente, posterior; **~ly** ad después, más tarde.

subside [səb'saɪd] vi hundirse; (flood) bajar; (wind) amainar; **subsidence** [-'saɪdns] n hundimiento; (in road) socavón m.

subsidiary [səb'sɪdɪərɪ] n sucursal f, filial f.

subsidize ['sʌbsɪdaɪz] vt subvencionar; **subsidy** [-dɪ] n subvención f.

subsistence [səb'sɪstəns] n subsistencia; (allowance) dietas fpl.

substance ['sʌbstəns] n sustancia; (fig) esencia.

substandard [sʌb'stændəd] a inferior.

substantial [səb'stænʃl] a sustancial, sustancioso; (fig) importante; **~ly** ad sustancialmente.

substantiate [səb'stænʃɪeɪt] vt comprobar.

substitute ['sʌbstɪtjuːt] n (person) suplente m/f; (thing) sustituto // vt: **to ~ A for B** sustituir B por A, reemplazar A por B; **substitution**

[-'tju:ʃən] n sustitución f, reemplazo.

subterfuge ['sʌbtəfju:dʒ] n subterfugio.

subterranean [sʌbtə'reɪnɪən] a subterráneo.

subtitle ['sʌbtaɪtl] n subtítulo.

subtle ['sʌtl] a sutil; ~ty n sutileza.

subtract [sʌb'trækt] vt sustraer, restar; ~ion [-'trækʃən] n sustracción f, resta.

suburb ['sʌbɜ:b] n arrabal m, suburbio; ~an [sə'bɜ:bən] a suburbano; (train etc) de cercanías.

subversive [sʌb'vɜ:sɪv] a subversivo.

subway ['sʌbweɪ] n (Brit) paso subterráneo o inferior; (US) metro.

succeed [sək'si:d] vi (person) tener éxito; (plan) salir bien // vt suceder a; to ~ in doing lograr hacer; ~ing a (following) sucesivo, seguido.

success [sək'ses] n éxito; (gain) triunfo; ~ful a (venture) de éxito; to be ~ful (in doing) lograr (hacer); ~fully ad con éxito.

succession [sək'seʃən] n (series) sucesión f, serie f; (descendants) descendencia; **successive** [-'sesɪv] a sucesivo, consecutivo; **successor** [-'sesə] n sucesor/a m/f.

succinct [sək'sɪŋkt] a sucinto.

succulent ['sʌkjulənt] a suculento.

succumb [sə'kʌm] vi sucumbir.

such [sʌtʃ] a, det tal, semejante; (of that kind): ~ a book un libro parecido; ~ books tales libros; (so much): ~ courage tanto valor; ~ a long trip un viaje tan largo; ~ a lot of tanto; ~ as (like) tal como; a noise ~ as to un ruido tal que; as ~ ad como tal // pron los/los que; ~-and-~ det tal o cual; until ~ time as hasta que.

suck [sʌk] vt chupar; (bottle) sorber; (breast) mamar; ~er n (BOT) serpollo; (ZOOL) ventosa; (col) bobo, primo.

suckle ['sʌkl] vt amamantar.

suction ['sʌkʃən] n succión f.

sudden ['sʌdn] a (rapid) repentino;

súbito; (unexpected) imprevisto; **all of a** ~, **~-ly** ad de repente; (unexpectedly) inesperadamente.

suds [sʌdz] npl jabonaduras fpl.

sue [su:] vt demandar.

suede [sweɪd] n ante m.

suet ['suɪt] n sebo.

suffer ['sʌfə] vt sufrir, padecer; (bear) aguantar; (allow) permitir, tolerar // vi sufrir, padecer; ~er n víctima m/f; (MED) enfermo; ~ing n sufrimiento, padecimiento; (pain) dolor m.

suffice [sə'faɪs] vi bastar, ser suficiente.

sufficient [sə'fɪʃənt] a suficiente, bastante.

suffix ['sʌfɪks] n sufijo.

suffocate ['sʌfəkeɪt] vi ahogarse, asfixiarse; **suffocation** [-'keɪʃən] n sofocación f, asfixia.

suffrage ['sʌfrɪdʒ] n sufragio; (vote) derecho de votar.

sugar ['ʃugə] n azúcar m // vt echar azúcar a; ~ **beet** n remolacha; ~ **cane** n caña de azúcar; ~y a azucarado.

suggest [sə'dʒest] vt sugerir; (advise) aconsejar; ~**ion** [-'dʒestʃən] n sugerencia; (hypnotic) sugestión f; ~**ive** a sugestivo; (pej) indecente.

suicidal [suɪ'saɪdl] a suicida; **suicide** ['suɪsaɪd] n suicidio; (person) suicida m/f.

suit [su:t] n (man's) traje m; (woman's) conjunto; (LAW) litigio, pleito; (CARDS) palo // vt (gen) convenir; (clothes) sentar a, ir bien a; (adapt): **to** ~ **sth to** adaptar o ajustar algo a; ~**able** a conveniente; (apt) indicado; ~**ably** ad convenientemente, en forma debida.

suitcase ['su:tkeɪs] n maleta.

suite [swi:t] n (of rooms) grupo de habitaciones; (MUS) suite f; (furniture): **bedroom/dining room** ~ (juego de) dormitorio/comedor m.

suitor ['su:tə] n pretendiente m.

sulk [sʌlk] vi tener mohino; ~**y** a con mohino.

sullen ['sʌlən] a hosco, malhumorado.

sulphur, sulfur (US) ['sʌlfə*] n azufre m.

sultan ['sʌltən] n sultán m.

sultana [sʌl'tɑːnə] n (fruit) pasa de Esmirna.

sultry ['sʌltrɪ] a (weather) bochornoso; (seductive) seductor(a).

sum [sʌm] n (gen) suma; (total) total m; **to ~ up** vt recapitular // vi hacer un resumen.

summarize ['sʌmərɑɪz] vt resumir.

summary ['sʌmərɪ] n resumen m // a (justice) sumario.

summer ['sʌmə*] n verano // a de verano; ~**house** n (in garden) cenador m, glorieta; ~**time** n (season) verano; ~ **time** n (by clock) hora de verano.

summit ['sʌmɪt] n cima, cumbre f; ~ (**conference**) n conferencia cumbre.

summon ['sʌmən] vt (person) llamar; (meeting) convocar; (LAW) citar; **to ~ up** vt cobrar; ~**s** n llamamiento, llamada // vt citar, emplazar.

sump [sʌmp] n (AUT) cárter m.

sumptuous ['sʌmptjuəs] a suntuoso.

sun [sʌn] n sol m; ~**bathe** vi tomar el sol; ~ **burn** n (painful) quemadura; (tan) bronceado; ~**burnt** a (tanned) bronceado; (painfully) quemado por el sol.

Sunday ['sʌndɪ] n domingo.

sundial ['sʌndaɪəl] n reloj m de sol.

sundry ['sʌndrɪ] a varios, diversos; **all and ~** todos y cada uno; **sundries** npl géneros mpl diversos.

sunflower ['sʌnflauə*] n girasol m.

sung [sʌŋ] pp of sing.

sunglasses ['sʌnˌglɑːsɪz] npl gafas ↑ de sol.

[san]k] pp of sink.

~**light** n luz f del sol; ~**lit** a ↑o por el sol; ~**ny** a soleado;

(day) de sol; (fig) alegre; ~**rise** n salida del sol; ~**set** n puesta del sol; ~**shade** n (over table) sombrilla; ~**shine** n sol m; ~**spot** n mancha solar; ~**stroke** n insolación f; ~ **tan** n bronceado; ~ **tan oil** n bronceador m, crema bronceadora.

super ['suːpə*] a (col) bárbaro.

superannuation [suːpərænjuˈeɪʃən] n jubilación f.

superb [suːˈpəːb] a magnífico, espléndido.

supercilious [suːpəˈsɪlɪəs] a (disdainful) desdeñoso; (haughty) altanero.

superficial [suːpəˈfɪʃəl] a superficial.

superfluous [suˈpəːfluəs] a superfluo, de sobra.

superhuman [suːpəˈhjuːmən] a sobrehumano.

superimpose ['suːpərɪmˈpəuz] vt sobreponer.

superintendent [suːpərɪnˈtendənt] n superintendente m/f; (POLICE) subjefe m.

superior [suˈpɪərɪə*] a superior; (smug) desdeñoso // n superior m; ~**ity** [-ˈɔrɪtɪ] n superioridad f, desdén f m.

superlative [suˈpəːlətɪv] a, n superlativo.

superman ['suːpəmæn] n superhombre m.

supermarket ['suːpəmɑːkɪt] n supermercado m.

supernatural [suːpəˈnætʃərəl] a sobrenatural.

superpower ['suːpəpauə*] n (POL) superpotencia.

supersede [suːpəˈsiːd] vt suplantar.

supersonic ['suːpəˈsɔnɪk] a supersónico.

superstition [suːpəˈstɪʃən] n superstición f; **superstitious** [-ʃəs] a supersticioso.

supertanker ['suːpətæŋkə*] n superpetrolero.

supervise ['suːpəvaɪz] vt supervisar; **supervision** [-ˈvɪʒən] n supervisión f; **supervisor** n supervisor/a m/f.

supper ['sʌpə*] n cena; **to have ~** cenar.

supple ['sʌpl] a flexible.

supplement ['sʌplimənt] // vt suplemento // vt ['sʌpli'mɛnt] suplir; **~ary** [-'mɛntəri] a suplementario.

supplier [sə'plaiə*] n suministrador/a m/f; (COMM) distribuidor/a m/f.

supply [sə'plai] vt (provide) suministrar, facilitar; (equip): **to ~ (with)** abastecer (de) // n suministro, provisión f; (supplying) abastecimiento // a (teacher etc) suplente; **supplies** npl (food) víveres mpl; (MIL) pertrechos mpl; **~ and demand** la oferta y la demanda.

support [sə'pɔ:t] n (moral, financial etc) apoyo; (TECH) soporte m // vt apoyar; (financially) mantener; (uphold) sostener; **~er** n (POL etc) partidario/a; (SPORT) aficionado/a.

suppose [sə'pəuz] vt, vi (gen) suponer; (imagine) imaginarse; **to be ~d to do sth** deber hacer algo; **~dly** [sə'pəuzidli] ad uno se supone, según cabe suponer; **supposing** conj en caso de que; **supposition** [sʌpə'ziʃən] n suposición f.

suppository [sə'pɔzitəri] n supositorio.

suppress [sə'pres] vt suprimir; (yawn) ahogar; **~ion** [sə'preʃən] n represión f.

supremacy [su'preməsi] n supremacía; **supreme** [-'pri:m] a supremo.

surcharge ['sə:tʃɑ:dʒ] n sobrecarga; (extra tax) recargo.

sure [ʃuə*] a (gen) seguro; (definite, convinced) cierto; (aim) certero; **~!** (of course) ¡claro!, por supuesto!; **~-footed** a de pie firme; **~ly** ad (certainly) seguramente.

surety ['ʃuərəti] n garantía, fianza; (person) fiador/a m/f.

surf [sə:f] n olas fpl.

surface ['sə:fis] n superficie f // vt (road) revestir // vi salir a la superficie.

surfboard ['sə:fbɔ:d] n plancha (de surfing), acuaplano.

surfeit ['sə:fit] n: **a ~ of** exceso de.

surfing ['sə:fiŋ] n surfing m.

surge [sə:dʒ] n oleada, oleaje m // vi avanzar a tropel.

surgeon ['sə:dʒən] n cirujano; **dental ~** odontólogo.

surgery ['sə:dʒəri] n cirugía; (room) consultorio; **to undergo ~** operarse; **~ hours** npl horas fpl de consulta.

surgical ['sə:dʒikl] a quirúrgico; **~ spirit** n alcohol m.

surly ['sə:li] a hosco, malhumorado.

surmount [sə:'maunt] vt superar, sobreponerse a

surname ['sə:neim] n apellido.

surpass [sə:'pɑ:s] vt superar, exceder.

surplus ['sə:pləs] n (gen) excedente m; (COMM) superávit m // a excedente, sobrante.

surprise [sə'praiz] n (gen) sorpresa; (astonishment) asombro // vt sorprender; asombrar; **surprising** a sorprendente; asombroso.

surrealist [sə'riəlist] a surrealista.

surrender [sə'rendə*] n rendición f, entrega // vi rendirse, entregarse.

surreptitious [sʌrəp'tiʃəs] a subrepticio.

surround [sə'raund] vt rodear, circundar; (MIL etc) cercar; **~ing** a circundante; **~ings** npl alrededores mpl, cercanías fpl.

surveillance [sə:'veiləns] n vigilancia.

survey ['sə:vei] n inspección f, examen m; (inquiry) encuesta // vt [sə:'vei] (gen) examinar, inspeccionar; (look at) mirar, contemplar; (make inquiries about) hacer una encuesta sobre; **~or** n agrimensor m.

survival [sə'vaivl] n supervivencia; **survive** vi sobrevivir; (custom etc)

perdurar // vt sobrevivir a;
survivor n superviviente m/f.

susceptible [səˈseptəbl] a: ~ **(to)**
susceptible o sensible (a).

suspect n [ˈsʌspekt] a, n sospechoso
// vt [səsˈpekt] sospechar.

suspend [səsˈpend] vt suspender;
~er belt n portaligas m inv; **~ers**
npl ligas fpl; (US) tirantes mpl.

suspense [səsˈpens] n incertidumbre f, duda; (in film etc) suspense m.

suspension [səsˈpenʃən] n (gen,
AUT) suspensión f; (of driving
licence) privación f; ~ **bridge** n
puente m colgante.

suspicion [səsˈpɪʃən] n (gen)
sospecha; (distrust) recelo; (trace)
traza; **suspicious** [-ʃəs] a
(suspecting) receloso; (causing ~)
sospechoso.

sustain [səsˈteɪn] vt sostener,
apoyar; (suffer) sufrir, padecer;
~ed a (effort) sostenido.

sustenance [ˈsʌstɪnəns] n sustento.

swab [swɔb] n (MED) algodón m,
torunda.

swagger [ˈswægə*] vi pavonearse.

swallow [ˈswɔləu] n (bird)
golondrina; (of food etc) trago // vt
tragar; **to ~ up** (savings etc)
consumir.

swam [swæm] pt of **swim**.

swamp [swɔmp] n pantano,
ciénaga // vt abrumar, agobiar; **~y**
a pantanoso.

swan [swɔn] n cisne m.

swap [swɔp] n canje m, intercambio
// vt: **to ~ (for)** canjear (por).

swarm [swɔːm] n (of bees)
enjambre m; (gen) multitud f // vi
hormiguear, pulular.

swarthy [ˈswɔːðɪ] a moreno.

swastika [ˈswɔstɪkə] n suástika,
cruz f gamada.

swat [swɔt] vt aplastar.

sway [sweɪ] vi mecerse, balancearse // vt (influence) mover,
influir en.

swear [swɛə*], pt swore, pp

sworn vi jurar; **to ~ to sth**
declarar algo bajo juramento;
~word n taco, palabrota.

sweat [swet] n sudor m // vi sudar.

sweater [ˈswetə*] n suéter m.

sweaty [ˈswetɪ] a sudoroso.

swede [swiːd] n nabo.

Swede [swiːd] n sueco/a; **Sweden**
n Suecia; **Swedish** a, n (LING) sueco.

sweep [swiːp] n (act) barredura; (of
arm) golpe m; (range) extensión f,
alcance m; (also: **chimney ~**)
deshollinador m // (vb: pt, pp
swept) vt barrer; (mines) rastrear
// vi barrer; **to ~ away** vt barrer;
(rub out) borrar; **to ~ past** vi pasar
rápidamente; (brush by) rozar; **to ~
up** vi recoger la basura; **~ing** a
(gesture) dramático; (generalized)
generalizado.

sweet [swiːt] n (candy) dulce m,
caramelo; (pudding) postre m // a
dulce; (sugary) azucarado; (fresh)
fresco, nuevo; (fig) dulce, amable;
~corn n maíz m; **~en** vt endulzar;
(add sugar to) poner azúcar a;
~heart n novio/a; (in speech)
amor; **~ly** ad dulcemente; (gently)
suavemente; **~ness** n (gen)
dulzura; (amount of sugar) lo dulce,
lo azucarado; **~ pea** n guisante m
de olor.

swell [swel] n (of sea) marejada,
oleaje m // a (col: excellent)
estupendo, excelente // (vb: pt
swelled, pp **swollen** or **swelled**) vt
hinchar, inflar // vi hincharse,
inflarse; **~ing** n (MED) hinchazón
m.

sweltering [ˈsweltərɪŋ] a sofocante, de mucho calor.

swept [swept] pt, pp of **sweep**.

swerve [swɜːv] vi desviarse
bruscamente.

swift [swɪft] n (bird) vencejo // a
rápido, veloz; **~ness** n rapidez f,
velocidad f.

swig [swɪg] n (col: drink) trago.

swill [swɪl] n bazofia // vt (also: ~

out, ~ **down**) lavar, limpiar con agua.

swim [swɪm] n: to go for a ~ ir a nadar // (vb: pt **swam**, pp **swum**) vi nadar; (head, room) dar vueltas // vt pasar a nado; ~**mer** n nadador/a m/f; ~**ming** n natación f; ~**ming baths** npl piscina sg; ~**ming cap** n gorro de baño; ~**ming costume** n bañador m, traje m de baño; ~**ming pool** n piscina; ~**suit** n bañador m, traje m de baño.

swindle ['swɪndl] n estafa // vt estafar, **swindler** n estafador/a m/f.

swine [swaɪn] n, pl inv cerdos mpl, puercos mpl; (col!) canalla sg.

swing [swɪŋ] n (in playground) columpio; (movement) balanceo, vaivén m; (change of direction) viraje m; (rhythm) ritmo // (vb: pt, pp **swung**) vt balancear; (on a ~) columpiar; (also: ~ **round**) voltear bruscamente // vi balancearse, columpiarse; (also: ~ **round**) volver bruscamente; to be in full ~ estar en plena marcha; ~ **bridge** n puente m giratorio; ~ **door** n puerta giratoria.

swipe [swaɪp] n golpe m fuerte // vt (hit) golpear fuerte; (col: steal) guindar.

swirl [swɜːl] vi arremolinarse.

Swiss [swɪs] a, n, pl inv suizo/a.

switch [swɪtʃ] n (for light, radio etc) interruptor m; (change) cambio; (of hair) trenza postiza // vt (change) cambiar de; to ~ **off** vt apagar; (engine) parar; to ~ **on** vt encender, prender; (engine, machine) arrancar; ~**board** n (TEL) central f de teléfonos.

Switzerland ['switsələnd] n Suiza.

swivel ['swɪvl] vi (also: ~ **round**) girar.

swollen ['swəʊlən] pp of swell.

swoon [swuːn] vi desmayarse, desvanecerse.

swoop [swuːp] n (by police etc) redada // vi (also: ~ **down**) calarse, precipitarse.

swop [swɒp] = swap.

sword [sɔːd] n espada; ~**fish** n pez m espada.

swore [swɔː*] pt of swear.

sworn [swɔːn] pp of swear.

swot [swɒt] vt, vi empollar.

swum [swʌm] pp of swim.

swung [swʌŋ] pt, pp of swing.

sycamore ['sɪkəmɔː*] n sicómoro.

syllable ['sɪləbl] n sílaba.

syllabus ['sɪləbəs] n programa m de estudios.

symbol ['sɪmbl] n símbolo, ~**ic(al)** [-'bɒlɪk(l)] a simbólico; ~**ism** n simbolismo; ~**ize** vt simbolizar.

symmetrical [sɪ'metrɪkl] a simétrico; **symmetry** ['sɪmɪtrɪ] n simetría.

sympathetic [sɪmpə'θetɪk] a compasivo; (pleasant) simpático; ~**ally** ad con compasión.

sympathize ['sɪmpəθaɪz] vi: to ~ **with sb** compadecerse de uno; **sympathizer** n (POL) simpatizante m/f.

sympathy ['sɪmpəθɪ] n (pity) compasión f; (liking) simpatía; **with our deepest** ~ nuestro más sentido pésame; ~ **strike** n huelga por solidaridad.

symphony ['sɪmfənɪ] n sinfonía; ~ **orchestra** n orquesta sinfónica.

symposium [sɪm'pəʊzɪəm] n simposio.

symptom ['sɪmptəm] n síntoma m, indicio; ~**atic** [-'mætɪk] a sintomático.

synagogue ['sɪnəgɒg] n sinagoga.

synchronize ['sɪŋkrənaɪz] vt sincronizar // vi: to ~ **with** sincronizarse con.

syndicate ['sɪndɪkɪt] n (gen) sindicato; (of newspapers) cadena.

syndrome ['sɪndrəʊm] n síndrome m.

synonym ['sɪnənɪm] n sinónimo; ~**ous** [sɪ'nɒnɪməs] a. ~**ous (with)** sinónimo (con).

synopsis [sɪ'nɒpsɪs], pl -**ses** [-siːz] n sinopsis f inv.

syntax ['sɪntæks] n sintáxis f.
synthesis ['sɪnθəsɪs], pl -ses [-si:z] n síntesis f inv.
synthetic [sɪn'θetɪk] a sintético.
syphilis ['sɪfɪlɪs] n sífilis f.
syphon ['saɪfən] = **siphon**.
Syria ['sɪrɪə] n Siria; ~n a, n sirio/a.
syringe [sɪ'rɪndʒ] n jeringa.
syrup ['sɪrəp] n jarabe m, almíbar m.
system ['sɪstəm] n (gen) sistema; (method) método; (ANAT) organismo; ~atic [-'mætɪk] a sistemático; metódico; ~s analyst n analista m/f de sistemas.

T

ta [tɑ:] excl (Brit: col) gracias.
tab [tæb] n (gen) lengüeta; (label) etiqueta; **to keep ~s on** (fig) vigilar.
tabby ['tæbɪ] n (also: ~ cat) gato atigrado.
table ['teɪbl] n mesa; (of statistics etc) cuadro, tabla // vt (motion etc) presentar; **to lay** or **set the ~** poner la mesa; **~cloth** n mantel m; **~ d'hôte** [tɑ:bl'dəʊt] n menú m; **~mat** n mantel m individual; **~spoon** n cuchara grande; (also: **~spoonful**: as measurement) cucharada.
tablet ['tæblɪt] n (MED) tableta, pastilla; (for writing) bloc m; (of stone) lápida.
table: ~ **tennis** n ping-pong m, tenis m de mesa; ~ **wine** n vino de mesa.
taboo [tə'bu:] n tabú m // a tabú.
tacit ['tæsɪt] a tácito.
taciturn ['tæsɪtə:n] a taciturno.
tack [tæk] n (nail) tachuela, chincheta; (stitch) hilván m; (NAUT) bordada // vt (nail) clavar con chinchetas; (stitch) hilvanar // vi virar.
tackle ['tækl] n (gear) equipo; (also: **fishing ~**) aparejo; (for lifting)

polea; (RUGBY) atajo // vt (difficulty) enfrentar; (grapple with) agarrar; (RUGBY) atajar.
tacky ['tækɪ] a pegajoso.
tact [tækt] n tacto, discreción f; ~**ful** a discreto, diplomático; ~**fully** ad discretamente.
tactical ['tæktɪkl] a táctico; **tactics** [-tɪks], n, npl táctica sg.
tactless ['tæktlɪs] a indiscreto, falto de tacto; ~**ly** ad indiscretamente.
tadpole ['tædpəʊl] n renacuajo.
tag [tæg] n (label) etiqueta; (loose end) cabo; **to ~ along with sb** acompañar a uno.
tail [teɪl] n (gen) cola; (ZOOL) rabo; (of shirt, coat) faldón m // vt (follow) seguir los talones a; **to ~ away, ~ off** vi (in size, quality etc) ir disminuyendo; ~**coat** n frac m; ~ **end** n cola, parte f final; ~**gate** n puerta trasera.
tailor ['teɪlə*] n sastre m; ~**ing** n (cut) corte m; (craft) sastrería; ~**made** a hecho a la medida; (fig) especial.
tailwind ['teɪlwɪnd] n viento de cola.
tainted ['teɪntɪd] a (food) pasado; (water, air) contaminado; (fig) manchado.
take [teɪk], pt **took**, pp **taken** n (gen) tomar; (grab) coger; (gain: prize) ganar; (require: effort, courage) exigir, hacer falta; (tolerate) aguantar; (hold: passengers etc) tener cabida para; (accompany, bring, carry) llevar; (exam) presentarse a; **to ~ sth from** (drawer etc) sacar algo de; (person) coger algo a; **I ~ it that...** supongo que...; **to ~ after** vt fus parecerse a; **to ~ apart** vt desmontar; **to ~ away** vt (remove) quitar; (carry off) llevar; **to ~ back** vt (return) devolver; (one's words) retractar; **to ~ down** vt (building) demoler; (letter etc) poner por escrito; **to ~ in** vt (deceive) engañar; (understand) entender;

(include) abarcar; (lodger) acoger, recibir; to ~ off vi (AVIAT) despegar // vt (remove) quitar; (imitate) imitar; to ~ on vt (work) emprender; (employee) contratar; (opponent) desafiar; to ~ out vt sacar; (remove) quitar; to ~ over vt (business) tomar posesión de // vi: to ~ over from sb relevar a uno; to ~ to vt fus (person) coger simpatía a; (activity) aficionarse a; to ~ up vt (a dress) acortar; (occupy: time, space) ocupar; (engage in: hobby etc) dedicarse a; ~away a (food) para llevar; ~home pay n salario neto; ~off n (AVIAT) despegue m; ~over n (COMM) absorción f; ~over bid n oferta de compra.

takings ['teɪkɪŋz] npl (COMM) ingresos mpl.

talc [tælk] n (also: ~um powder) talco.

tale [teɪl] n (story) cuento; (account) relación f; to tell ~s (fig: lie) chismear.

talent ['tælnt] n talento; ~ed a talentoso, de talento.

talk [tɔ:k] n (gen) charla, (gossip) habladurías fpl, chismes mpl; (conversation) conversación f // vi (speak) hablar; (chatter) charlar; to ~ about hablar de, to ~ sb into doing sth convencer a uno de que debe hacer algo; to ~ sb out of doing sth disuadir a uno de algo; to ~ shop hablar de asuntos profesionales; to ~ over vt hablar de; ~ative a hablador(a).

tall [tɔ:l] a (gen) alto; (tree) grande; to be 6 feet ~ medir 6 pies, tener 6 pies de alto; ~boy n cómoda alta; ~ness n altura; ~ story n historia inverosímil.

tally ['tælɪ] n cuenta // vi: to ~ (with) corresponder (con).

talon ['tælən] n garra.

tambourine [tæmbə'ri:n] n pandereta.

tame [teɪm] a (mild) manso;

(tamed) domesticado; (fig: story, style) soso.

tamper ['tæmpə*] vi: to ~ with entrometerse en.

tampon ['tæmpən] n tampón m.

tan [tæn] n (also: sun~) bronceado // vi broncear // vi ponerse moreno // a (colour) marrón.

tandem ['tændəm] n tándem m.

tang [tæŋ] n sabor m fuerte.

tangerine [tændʒə'ri:n] n mandarina.

tangible ['tændʒəbl] n tangible.

tangle ['tæŋgl] n enredo; to get in(to) a ~ enredarse.

tango ['tæŋgəu] n tango.

tank [tæŋk] n (water ~) depósito, tanque m; (for fish) acuario; (MIL) tanque m.

tanker ['tæŋkə*] n (ship) petrolero; (truck) camión m cisterna o tanque.

tanned [tænd] a (skin) moreno, bronceado.

tantalizing ['tæntəlaɪzɪŋ] a tentador(a).

tantamount ['tæntəmaunt] a: to equivalente a.

tantrum ['tæntrəm] n rabieta.

tap [tæp] n (on sink etc) grifo; (gentle blow) golpecito; (gas ~) llave f // vt dar golpecitos; (resources) utilizar, explotar; ~dancing n zapateado.

tape [teɪp] n cinta; (also: magnetic ~) cinta magnética; (sticky ~) cinta adhesiva // vt (record) grabar (en cinta); ~ measure n cinta métrica; metro

taper ['teɪpə*] n cirio // vi afilarse.

tape recorder [teɪp rɪ'kɔ:də*] n grabadora.

tapered ['teɪpəd], **tapering** ['teɪpərɪŋ] a afilado.

tapestry ['tæpɪstrɪ] n (object) tapiz m; (art) tapicería.

tapioca [tæpɪ'əukə] n tapioca.

tar [tɑ:] n alquitrán m, brea.

tarantula [tə'ræntjulə] n tarántula.

target ['tɑ:gɪt] n (gen) blanco; ~ practice tiro al blanco.

tariff ['tærɪf] n tarifa.

tarmac ['tɑːmæk] n (on road) alquitranado; (AVIAT) pista de aterrizaje.

tarnish ['tɑːnɪʃ] vt quitar el brillo a.

tarpaulin [tɑː'pɔːlɪn] n alquitranado.

tarragon ['tærəgən] n estragón m.

tart [tɑːt] n (CULIN) tarta; (col: pej: woman) fulana // a (flavour) agrio, ácido.

tartan ['tɑːtn] n tartán m, escocés m // a de tartán.

tartar ['tɑːtə*] n (on teeth) sarro; ~(e) sauce n salsa tártara.

task [tɑːsk] n tarea; **to take to** ~ reprender; ~ **force** n (MIL, POLICE) destacamento especial.

tassel ['tæsl] n borla.

taste [teɪst] n sabor m, gusto; (also: after~) dejo; (sip) sorbo; (fig: glimpse, idea) muestra, idea // vt probar // vi: **to** ~ **of or like** (fish etc) saber a; **you can** ~ **the garlic (in it)** se nota el sabor a ajo; **can I have a** ~ **of this wine?** ¿puedo probar el vino?; **to have a** ~ **for** ser aficionado a algo; **in good/bad** ~ de buen/mal gusto; ~**ful** a de buen gusto; ~**less** a (food) insípido; (remark) de mal gusto; **tasty** a sabroso, rico.

tattered ['tætəd] a see **tatters**.

tatters ['tætəz] npl: **in** ~ (also: **tattered**) hecho jirones.

tattoo [tə'tuː] n tatuaje m; (spectacle) espectáculo militar // vt tatuar.

tatty ['tætɪ] a (col) raído.

taught [tɔːt] pt, pp of **teach**.

taunt [tɔːnt] n burla // vt burlarse de.

Taurus ['tɔːrəs] n Tauro.

taut [tɔːt] a tenso, tirante.

tawdry ['tɔːdrɪ] a cursi, de mal gusto.

tawny ['tɔːnɪ] a leonado.

tax [tæks] n impuesto // vt gravar (con un impuesto); (fig: test)

abrumar; (: patience) agotar; **direct** ~ contribución directa; ~**ation** [-'seɪʃən] n impuestos mpl; ~ **collector** n recaudador/a m/f; ~**free** a libre de impuestos.

taxi ['tæksɪ] n taxi m // vi (AVIAT) rodar de suelo.

taxidermist ['tæksɪdəːmɪst] n taxidermista m/f.

taxi: ~ **driver** n taxista m/f; ~ **rank,** ~ **stand** n parada de taxis.

tax: ~ **payer** n contribuyente m/f; ~ **return** n declaración f de ingresos.

TB abbr of **tuberculosis.**

tea [tiː] n té m; (snack) merienda; **high** ~ merienda-cena; ~ **bag** n bolsa de té; ~ **break** n descanso para el té; ~**cake** n bollo.

teach [tiːtʃ], pt, pp **taught** vt: **to** ~ **sb sth,** ~ **sth to sb** enseñar algo a uno // vi enseñar; (be a teacher) ser profesor/a; ~**er** n (in secondary school) profesor/a m/f; (in primary school) maestro/a; ~**ing** n enseñanza.

tea: ~ **cosy** n cubretetera; ~**cup** n taza para té.

teak [tiːk] n (madera de) teca.

tea leaves npl hojas fpl de té.

team [tiːm] n equipo; (of animals) pareja; ~**work** n trabajo de equipo.

teapot ['tiːpɔt] n tetera.

tear [tɛə*] n rasgón m, desgarrón m // n [tɪə*] lágrima // (vb: pt **tore,** pp **torn**) vt romper, rasgar // vi rasgarse; ~ **s** llorando; **to burst into** ~**s** deshacerse en lágrimas; **to** ~ **along** vi (rush) precipitarse; ~**ful** a lloroso; ~ **gas** n gas m lacrimógeno.

tearoom ['tiːruːm] n salón m de té, cafetería.

tease [tiːz] n bromista m/f // vt bromear, tomar el pelo a.

tea: ~ **set** n juego de té; ~**spoon** n cucharilla; (also: ~**spoonful:** as measurement) cucharadita.

teat [tiːt] n (of bottle) tetina.

ea: ~**time** n hora del té; ~ **towel** n rapo de cocina.

chnical ['teknɪkl] a técnico; ~**ity** [-'kælɪtɪ] n detalle m técnico; ~**ly** ad écnicamente.

chnician [tek'nɪʃn] n técnico.

chnique [tek'niːk] n técnica.

chnological [teknə'lɔdʒɪkl] a ecnológico; **technology** [-'nɔlədʒɪ] n ecnología.

eddy (**bear**) ['tedɪ] n osito de elpa.

dious ['tiːdɪəs] a pesado, aburrido.

e [tiː] n (GOLF) tee m.

em [tiːm] vi abundar, pulular; to ~ **with** rebosar de; **it is ~ing** (**with ain**) llueve a mares.

enage ['tiːneɪdʒ] a (fashions etc) ~o para los jóvenes; **teenager** n oven m/f (de 13 a 19 años).

ens [tiːnz] npl: **to be in one's ~** er un adolescente, no haber umplido los 20.

e-shirt ['tiːʃət] n = T-shirt.

eeter ['tiːtə*] vi balancearse.

eeth [tiːθ] pl of tooth.

eethe [tiːð] vi echar los dientes.

eething ['tiːðɪŋ]: ~ **ring** n nordedor m; ~ **troubles** npl (fig) iificultades fpl iniciales.

eetotal ['tiː'təutl] a (person) bstemio.

elecommunications [tel komjuːnɪ'keɪʃənz] n telecomunicaiones fpl.

elegram ['telɪɡræm] n telegrama m.

elegraph ['telɪɡrɑːf] n telégrafo; **ic** [-'ɡræfɪk] a telegráfico; ~ **pole** n poste m de telégrafos.

elepathic [telɪ'pæθɪk] a telepático; **telepathy** [tə'lepəθɪ] n telepatía.

elephone ['telɪfəun] n teléfono // t (person) llamar por teléfono; (message) telefonear; ~ **booth**, ~ **box** n cabina telefónica; ~ **call** n lamada (telefónica); ~ **directory** n ruía f telefónica; ~ **exchange** n entral f telefónica; ~ **number** n número de teléfono; **telephonist**

[tə'lefənɪst] n telefonista m/f.

telephoto ['telɪ'fəutəu] a: ~ **lens** teleobjetivo.

teleprinter ['telɪprɪntə*] n teletipo.

telescope ['telɪskəup] n telescopio; **telescopic** [-'skɔpɪk] a telescópico.

televise ['telɪvaɪz] vt televisar.

television ['telɪvɪʒən] n televisión f; ~ **set** n televisor m.

telex ['teleks] n telex m.

tell pt, pp **told** vt decir; (relate: story) contar; (distinguish): **to** ~ **sth from** distinguir algo de // vi (have effect) tener efecto; **to** ~ **sb to do sth** mandar a uno que haga algo; **to** ~ **sb off** reñir o regañar a uno; ~**er** n (in bank) cajero; ~**ing** a (remark, detail) revelador(a); ~**tale** a (sign) indicador(a).

telly ['telɪ] n (col) abbr of television.

temerity [tə'merɪtɪ] n temeridad f.

temper ['tempə*] n (nature) carácter m; (mood) humor m; (bad ~) genio, mal genio; (fit of anger) cólera; (of child) rabieta // vt (moderate) moderar; **to be in a** ~ estar de mal humor; **to lose one's** ~ perder la paciencia.

temperament ['tempərəmənt] n (nature) temperamento; ~**al** [-'mentl] a temperamental.

temperance ['tempərəns] n moderación f; (in drinking) sobriedad f.

temperate ['tempərət] a moderado; (climate) templado.

temperature ['temprətʃə*] n temperatura; **to have** o **run a** ~ tener fiebre.

tempered ['tempəd] a (steel) templado.

tempest ['tempɪst] n tempestad f.

temple ['templ] n (building) templo; (ANAT) sien f.

tempo ['tempəu] pl ~**s** or **tempi** [-piː] n tiempo; (fig: of life etc) ritmo.

temporal ['tempərəl] a temporal.

temporarily ['tempərərɪlɪ] ad temporalmente.

temporary ['tempərərɪ] a

provisional, temporal; (*passing*) transitorio; (*worker*) temporero.

tempt [tempt] *vt* tentar; **to ~ sb into doing sth** tentar o inducir a uno a hacer algo; **~ation** [-'teɪʃən] *n* tentación *f*; **~ing** a tentador(a).

ten [ten] *num* diez.

tenable ['tenəbl] a sostenible.

tenacious [tə'neɪʃəs] a tenaz; **tenacity** [-'næsɪtɪ] *n* tenacidad *f*.

tenancy ['tenənsɪ] *n* alquiler *m*; (*of house*) inquilinato; **tenant** *n* (*rent-payer*) inquilino; (*occupant*) habitante *m/f*.

tend [tend] *vt* cuidar // *vi*: **to ~ to do sth** tener tendencia a hacer algo.

tendency ['tendənsɪ] *n* tendencia.

tender ['tendə*] a tierno, blando; (*delicate*) delicado; (*sore*) sensible, dolorido; (*affectionate*) tierno, cariñoso // *n* (*COMM. offer*) oferta; (*money*): **legal ~** moneda de curso legal // *vt* ofrecer; **~ize** *vt* (*CULIN*) ablandar; **~ness** *n* ternura; (*of meat*) blandura.

tendon ['tendən] *n* tendón *m*.

tenement ['tenəmənt] *n* casa de pisos.

tennis ['tenɪs] *n* tenis *m*; **~ ball** *n* pelota de tenis; **~ court** *n* pista de tenis; **~ racket** *n* raqueta de tenis.

tenor ['tenə*] *n* (*MUS*) tenor *m*.

tenpin bowling ['tenpɪn-] *n* los bolos *mpl*.

tense [tens] a tenso; (*stretched*) tirante; (*stiff*) rígido, tieso // *n* (*LING*) tiempo; **~ness** *n* tensión *f*.

tension ['tenʃən] *n* tensión *f*.

tent [tent] *n* tienda (de campaña).

tentacle ['tentəkl] *n* tentáculo.

tentative ['tentətɪv] a experimental; (*conclusion*) provisional.

tenterhooks ['tentəhuks] *npl*: **on ~** sobre ascuas.

tenth [tenθ] a décimo.

tent: **~ peg** *n* clavija, estaquilla; **~ pole** *n* mástil *m*.

tenuous ['tenjuəs] a tenue.

tenure ['tenjuə*] *n* posesión *f*, tenencia.

tepid ['tepɪd] a tibio.

term [tə:m] *n* (*limit*) límite *m*; (*COMM*) plazo; (*word*) término; (*period*) período; (*SCOL*) trimestre *m* // *vt* llamar; **~s** *npl* (*conditions*) condiciones *fpl*; (*COMM*) precio, tarifa; **in the short/long ~** a corto/largo plazo; **to be on good ~ with sb** llevarse bien con uno; **to come to ~s with** (*person*) llegar a un acuerdo con; (*problem*) adaptarse a.

terminal ['tə:mɪnl] a terminal; (*disease*) mortal // *n* (*ELEC*) born *m*; (*also*: **air ~**) terminal *f*; (*also*: **coach ~**) estación *f* terminal.

terminate ['tə:mɪneɪt] *vt* terminar // *vi*: **to ~ in** acabar por; **termination** [-'neɪʃən] *n* terminación *f*, (*of contract*) conclusión *f*.

terminology [tə:mɪ'nɔlədʒɪ] *n* terminología.

terminus ['tə:mɪnəs], *pl* **-mini** [-mɪnaɪ] *n* término, estación terminal.

termite ['tə:maɪt] *n* termita.

terrace ['terəs] *n* terraza; (*row of houses*) hilera de casas adosadas; **the ~s** (*SPORT*) gradas *fpl*; **~ed** a (*garden*) escalonado; (*house*) adosado.

terrain [te'reɪn] *n* terreno.

terrible ['terɪbl] a terrible, horrible; (*fam*) malísimo; **terribly** *ad* terriblemente; (*very badly*) malísimamente.

terrier ['terɪə*] *n* terrier *m*.

terrific [tə'rɪfɪk] a fantástico, fenomenal; (*wonderful*) maravilloso.

terrify ['terɪfaɪ] *vt* aterrar.

territorial [terɪ'tɔ:rɪəl] a territorial.

territory ['terɪtərɪ] *n* territorio.

terror ['terə*] *n* terror *m*; **~ism** *n* terrorismo; **~ist** *n* terrorista *m/f*; **~ize** *vt* aterrorizar.

terse [tə:s] a (*style*) conciso; (*reply*) brusco.

test [test] *n* (*trial, check*) prueba, ensayo; (: *of goods in factory*)

control m; (of courage etc, CHEM)
prueba; (MED) examen m; (exam)
examen m, test m; (also: driving ~)
examen m de conducir // vt probar,
poner a prueba.

estament ['testamant] n testamento; **the Old/New T~** el
Antiguo/Nuevo Testamento.

esticle ['testikl] n testículo.

estify ['testifai] vi (LAW) prestar
declaración; **to ~ to sth** atestiguar
algo.

estimonial [testi'maunial] a
(reference) recomendación f; (gift)
obsequio.

estimony ['testimani] n (LAW)
testimonio, declaración f.

est   match n (CRICKET, RUGBY)
partido internacional; **~ pilot** n
piloto de pruebas; **~ tube** n probeta.

esty ['testi] a irritable.

etanus ['tetanas] n tétano.

ether ['teðə*] n atar (con una
cuerda) // n. **at the end of one's ~**
a punto de perder la paciencia.

ext [tekst] n texto, **~book** n libro de
texto.

extiles ['tekstailz] npl textiles mpl,
tejidos mpl.

exture ['tekstʃə*] n textura.

Thai [tai] a, n tailandés/esa m/f;
~land n Tailandia

Thames [temz] n: **the ~** el (río)
Támesis.

than [ðæn, ðən] conj que; (with
numerals): **more ~ 10**/once más de
10/una vez; **I have more/less ~ you**
tengo más/menos que tú.

thank [θæŋk] vt dar las gracias a,
agradecer; **~ you (very much)**
muchas gracias; **~s** npl gracias fpl,
~s to prep gracias a; **~ful** a (~ful
for agradecido por; **~less** a ingrato;
Thanksgiving (Day) n día m de
acción de gracias.

that [ðæt, ðət] conj que // det
ese/esa; (more remote) aquel/
aquella // pron ése/ésa; aquél/
aquélla. (neuter) eso; aquello
(relative: subject) que; (: object)

que, el cual/la cual etc; (with time):
on the day ~ he came el día que
vino // ad: **~ high** tan alto, así de
alto; **it's about ~ high** es más o
menos así de alto; **~ one** ése/ésa;
aquél/aquélla; **what's ~?** ¿qué es
eso?; **who's ~?** ¿quién es?; **is ~**
you? ¿eres tú?; (formal) ¿es usted?;
~'s what he said eso es lo que dijo;
all ~ todo eso; **I can't work ~**
much no puedo trabajar tanto.

thatched [θætʃt] a (roof) de paja;
~ cottage casa con tejado de paja.

thaw [θɔ:] n deshielo // vi (ice)
derretirse; (food) descongelarse //
vt (food) descongelar.

the [ði:, ðə] def art el/la; (pl) los/las;
(neuter) lo; **~ sooner ~ better**
cuanto antes mejor.

theatre, theater (US) ['θiətə*] n
teatro; **~-goer** n aficionado al
teatro.

theatrical [θi'ætrikl] a teatral.

theft [θeft] n robo.

their [ðeə*] a su; **~s** pron (el)
suyo/(la) suya etc; **a friend of ~s**
un amigo suyo.

them [ðem, ðəm] pron (direct)
los/las; (indirect) les; (stressed, after
prep) ellos/ellas; **I see ~** los veo;
give ~ the book dales el libro.

theme [θi:m] n tema m; **~ song**
tema (musical).

themselves [ðəm'selvz] pl pron
(subject) ellos mismos/ellas mismas; (complement) se; (after prep)
sí (mismos/as).

then [ðen] ad (at that time)
entonces; (next) pues; (later) luego,
después; (and also) además // conj
(therefore) en ese caso, entonces //
a: **the ~ president** el entonces
presidente; **from ~ on** desde
entonces.

theological [θiə'lɒdʒikl] a teoló-
gico; **theology** n [θi'ɒlədʒi] n teología.

theorem ['θiərəm] n teorema m.

theoretical [θiə'retikl] a teórico;
theorize ['θiəraiz] vi elaborar una
teoría; **theory** ['θiəri] n teoría.

therapeutic(al) [θerə'pju:tɪk(l)] a terapéutico.

therapist ['θerəpɪst] n terapeuta m/f; **therapy** n terapia.

there [ðeə*] ad allí, allá, ahí; ~, ~! ¡cálmate!; **it's** ~ está ahí; ~ **is**, ~ **are** hay; ~ **he is** ahí está; **on/in** ~ allí encima/dentro; ~**abouts** ad por ahí; ~**after** ad después; ~**fore** ad por lo tanto; ~'**s** = ~ **is**; ~ **has**.

thermal [θə:ml] a termal.

thermometer [θə'mɔmɪtə*] n termómetro.

Thermos [θə:məs] n termo.

thermostat [θə:məustæt] n termostato.

thesaurus [θɪ'sɔ:rəs] n tesoro.

these [ði:z] pl det estos/as // pl pron éstos/as.

thesis ['θi:sɪs], pl **-ses** [-si:z] n tesis f.

they [ðeɪ] pl pron ellos/ellas; (stressed) ellos (mismos)/ellas (mismas); ~ **say that**... (it is said that) se dice que...; ~'**d** = they had; they would; ~'**ll** = they shall, they will; ~'**re** = they are; ~'**ve** = they have.

thick [θɪk] a espeso; (fat) gordo; (dense) denso, espeso; (stupid) torpe // n: **in the** ~ **of the battle** en plena batalla; **it's 20 cm** ~ tiene 20 cm de espesor; ~**en** vi espesarse // vt espesar; ~**ness** n espesor m, grueso; ~**set** a rechoncho; ~**skinned** a (fig) insensible.

thief [θi:f], pl **thieves** [θi:vz] n ladrón/ona m/f.

thieving [θi:vɪŋ] n robo.

thigh [θaɪ] n muslo.

thimble [θɪmbl] n dedal m.

thin [θɪn] a (gen) delgado; (watery) aguado; (light) tenue; (hair, crowd) escaso; (fog) poco denso // vt: **to** ~ (**down**) (sauce, paint) diluir.

thing [θɪŋ] n (gen) cosa; (object) objeto, artículo; (matter) asunto; (mania) manía; ~**s** npl (belongings) efectos mpl (personales); **the best**

think [θɪŋk], pt, pp **thought** vt pensar // vt pensar, creer; (imagine) imaginar; **what did you** ~ **of them?** ¿qué te parecieron?; to ~ **about sth/sb** pensar en algo/alguien; **I'll** ~ **about it** lo pensaré; to ~ **of doing sth** pensar en hacer algo; **I** ~ **so/not** creo que sí/no; to ~ **well of sb** tener buen concepto de alguien; to ~ **over** v reflexionar sobre, meditar; **to** ~ **up** vt imaginar; ~**ing** a pensante.

thinly [θɪnlɪ] ad (cut) en lonchas finas; (spread) con una capa fina.

thinness [θɪnnɪs] n delgadez f.

third [θə:d] a tercer(a) // n tercero; (fraction) tercio; (SCOL: degree) de tercera clase; ~**ly** ad en tercer lugar; ~ **party insurance** n seguro contra terceras personas; ~**rate** a (de calidad) mediocre; **the T~ World** n el Tercer Mundo.

thirst [θə:st] n sed f; ~**y** a (person) sediento; to **be** ~**y** tener sed.

thirteen [θə:'ti:n] num trece.

thirty [θə:tɪ] num treinta.

this [ðɪs] det este/esta // pron éste/ésta; (neuter) esto; ~ **is wha** he said esto es lo que dijo; ~ **hig** así de alto.

thistle [θɪsl] n cardo.

thong [θɔŋ] n correa.

thorn [θɔ:n] n espina; ~**y** espinoso.

thorough [θʌrə] a (search minucioso; (knowledge, research profundo; ~**bred** a (horse) de pur sangre; ~**fare** n calle f; '**no** ~**fare** "prohibido el paso"; ~**ly** ad minuciosamente; profundamente, a fondo.

those [ðəuz] pl pron esos/esas; (more remote) aquellos/as // pl de esos/ésas; aquéllos/as.

though [ðəu] conj aunque // ad sin embargo.

thought [θɔ:t] pt, pp de **think** // pensamiento; (opinion) opinión f (*intention*) intención *f*; ~**ful** a pensativo; (*considerate*) considerado; ~**less** a desconsiderado.

thousand ['θauzənd] *num* mil; **two ~** dos mil; ~**s of** miles de; ~**th** a milésimo.

thrash [θræʃ] *vt* apalear; (*defeat*) derrotar; **to ~ about** *vi* revolcarse; **to ~ out** *vt* discutir largamente.

thread [θrɛd] *n* hilo; (*of screw*) rosca // *vt* (*needle*) enhebrar; ~**bare** a raído.

threat [θrɛt] *n* amenaza; ~**en** *vi* amenazar // *vt*: **to ~en sb with sth/to do** amenazar a uno con algo/ con hacer.

three [θriː] *num* tres; ~**-dimensional** a tridimensional; ~**fold** ad: **to increase** ~**fold** triplicar; ~**-piece suit** *n* traje *m* de tres piezas; ~**-piece suite** *n* tresillo; ~**-ply** a (*wool*) triple; ~**-wheeler** *n* (*car*) coche *m* de tres ruedas.

thresh [θrɛʃ] *vt* (*AGR*) trillar.

threshold ['θrɛʃhəuld] *n* umbral *m*.

threw [θruː] *pt* of **throw**.

thrift [θrɪft] *n* economía; ~**y** a económico.

thrill [θrɪl] *n* (*excitement*) emoción *f*, (*shudder*) estremecimiento // *vt* emocionar; estremecer; **to be** ~**ed** (*with gift etc*) estar encantado; ~**er** *n* película/novela de suspense.

thrive [θraɪv], *pt* **thrived** or **throve** [θrəuv], *pp* **thrived** or **thriven** ['θrɪvn] *vi* (*grow*) crecer; (*do well*) prosperar; **thriving** a próspero.

throat [θrəut] *n* garganta; **to have a sore** ~ tener dolor de garganta.

throb [θrɔb] *n* (*of heart*) latido; (*of engine*) vibración *f* // *vi* latir; vibrar; (*pain*) dar punzadas.

throes [θrəuz] *npl*: **in the** ~ **of** en medio de.

thrombosis [θrɔm'bəusɪs] *n* trombosis *f*.

throne [θrəun] *n* trono.

throttle ['θrɔtl] *n* (*AUT*) acelerador *m* // *vt* ahogar.

through [θruː] *prep* por, a través de; (*time*) durante; (*by means of*) por medio de, mediante; (*owing to*) gracias a // a (*ticket, train*) directo // ad completamente, de parte a parte; **to put sb ~ to sb** (*TEL*) poner a alguien (en comunicación) con alguien; **to be ~** (*TEL*) tener comunicación; (*have finished*) haber terminado; **"no ~ way"** "calle sin salida"; ~**out** *prep* (*place*) por todas partes de, por todo; (*time*) durante todo, en todo // ad por todas partes.

throw [θrəu] *n* tirada, tiro; (*SPORT*) lanzamiento // *vt*, *pt* **threw**, *pp* **thrown** tirar, echar; (*SPORT*) lanzar; (*rider*) derribar; (*fig*) desconcertar; **to ~ a party** dar una fiesta; **to ~ away** *vt* tirar; **to ~ off** *vt* deshacerse de; **to ~ out** *vt* tirar; **to ~ up** *vi* vomitar; ~**away** a para tirar, desechable; ~**in** *n* (*SPORT*) saque *m*.

thru [θruː] (*US*) = **through**.

thrush [θrʌʃ] *n* zorzal *m*, tordo.

thrust [θrʌst] *n* (*TECH*) empuje *m* // *vt*, *pt*, *pp* **thrust** empujar; (*push in*) introducir.

thud [θʌd] *n* golpe *m* sordo.

thug [θʌg] *n* (*criminal*) criminal *m/f*, (*pej*) bruto.

thumb [θʌm] *n* (*anat*) pulgar *m*, dedo gordo (*col*) // *vt* (*book*) hojear; **to ~ a lift** hacer dedo o autostop; ~**tack** *n* (*US*) chinche *m*.

thump [θʌmp] *n* golpe *m*; (*sound*) porrazo // *vt*, *vi* golpear.

thunder ['θʌndə*] *n* (*gen*) trueno; (*sudden noise*) ruido; (*of applause etc*) estruendo // *vi* tronar; (*train etc*): **to ~ past** pasar como un trueno; ~**bolt** *n* rayo; ~**clap** *n* trueno; ~**storm** *n* tormenta; ~**struck** a pasmado; ~**y** a tormentoso.

Thursday ['θəːzdɪ] *n* jueves *m*.

thus [ðʌs] ad así, de este modo.

thwart [θwɔːt] *vt* frustrar.

thyme [taɪm] *n* tomillo.

thyroid [ˈθaɪrɔɪd] n tiroides m.

tiara [tɪˈɑːrə] n tiara, diadema.

tic [tɪk] n tic m.

tick [tɪk] n (sound: of clock) tictac m; (mark) palomita; (ZOOL) garrapata; (col): **in a** ~ en un instante // vi hacer tictac // vt marcar; **to** ~ **off** vt marcar; (person) poner como un trapo.

ticket [ˈtɪkɪt] n billete m, tíquet m; (for cinema) entrada; (in shop: on goods) etiqueta; (for library) tarjeta; ~ **collector** n revisor m; ~ **office** n taquilla.

tickle [ˈtɪkl] n cosquillas fpl // vt hacer cosquillas a; **ticklish** a que tiene cosquillas.

tidal [ˈtaɪdl] a de marea; ~ **wave** n maremoto.

tiddlywinks [ˈtɪdlɪwɪŋks] n juego de la pulga.

tide [taɪd] n marea; (fig: of events) curso, marcha.

tidiness [ˈtaɪdɪnɪs] n (good order) buen orden m; (neatness) limpieza, aseo.

tidy [ˈtaɪdɪ] a (room) ordenado; (dress, work) limpio; (person) bien arreglado // vt (also: ~ **up**) poner en orden.

tie [taɪ] n (string etc) atadura; (also: neck~) corbata; (fig: link) vínculo, lazo; (SPORT: draw) empate m // vt (gen) atar // vi (SPORT) empatar; **to** ~ **in a bow** hacer un lazo; **to** ~ **a knot in sth** hacer un nudo a algo; **to** ~ **down** vt atar; (fig): **to** ~ **sb down** to obligar a uno a; **to** ~ **up** vt (parcel) envolver; (dog) atar; (boat) amarrar; (arrangements) concluir, despachar; **to be** ~**d up** (busy) estar ocupado.

tier [tɪəˈ] n grada; (of cake) piso.

tiger [ˈtaɪgəˈ] n tigre m/f.

tight [taɪt] a (rope) tirante; (money) escaso; (clothes) ajustado; (budget, programme) apretado; (col: drunk) borracho // ad (squeeze) muy fuerte; (shut) herméticamente; ~ **s** npl pantimedias fpl; (for gym) malla sg; ~**en** vt (rope) estirar; (screw) apretar // vi apretarse, estirarse; ~**fisted** a tacaño; ~**ly** ad (grasp) muy fuerte; ~**rope** n cuerda floja.

tile [taɪl] n (on roof) teja; (on floor) baldosa; (on wall) azulejo, baldosín m; ~**d** a embaldosado.

till [tɪl] n caja (registradora) // vt (land) cultivar // prep, conj = **until**.

tiller [ˈtɪləˈ] n (NAUT) caña del timón.

tilt [tɪlt] vt inclinar // vi inclinarse.

timber [ˈtɪmbəˈ] n (material) madera; (trees) árboles mpl.

time [taɪm] n tiempo; (epoch: often pl) época; (by clock) hora; (moment) momento; (occasion) vez f; (MUS) compás m // vt (gen) calcular o medir el tiempo de; (race) cronometrar; (remark etc) elegir el momento para; **a long** ~ mucho tiempo; **for the** ~ **being** de momento, por ahora; **from** ~ **to** ~ de vez en cuando; **in** ~ (soon enough) a tiempo; (after some time) con el tiempo; (MUS) al compás; **in a week's** ~ dentro de una semana; **on** ~ a la hora; **5** ~**s 5** 5 por 5; **what** ~ **is it?** ¿qué hora es?; **to have a good** ~ pasarlo bien, divertirse; ~ **bomb** n bomba de efecto retardado; ~**keeper** n (SPORT) cronómetro; ~**less** a eterno; ~ **limit** n limitación f de tiempo; (COMM) plazo; ~**ly** a oportuno; ~ **off** n tiempo libre; **timer** n (in kitchen) reloj m programador; ~ **switch** n interruptor m; ~**table** n horario; ~ **zone** n huso horario.

timid [ˈtɪmɪd] a tímido.

timing [ˈtaɪmɪŋ] n (SPORT) cronometraje m; (gen) elección f de momento; **the** ~ **of his resignation** el momento que eligió para dimitir.

timpani [ˈtɪmpənɪ] npl tímpanos mpl.

tin [tɪn] n estaño; (also: ~ **plate**) hojalata; (can) lata; ~ **foil** n papel m de estaño.

tinge [tɪndʒ] n matiz m // vt: ~d with teñido de.

tingle [tɪŋgl] n picotazo // vi sentir picazón.

tinker [tɪŋkə*] n calderero; (gipsy) gitano; **to ~ with** vt manosear.

tinkle [tɪŋkl] vi tintinear // n (col): **to give sb a ~** dar un telefonazo a alguien.

tinned [tɪnd] a (food) en lata, en conserva.

tin opener [tɪnəupnə*] n abrelatas m inv.

tinsel [tɪnsl] n oropel m.

tint [tɪnt] n matiz m; (for hair) tinte m.

tiny [taɪnɪ] a minúsculo, pequeñito.

tip [tɪp] n (end) punta; (gratuity) propina; (for rubbish) basurero; (advice) aviso // vt (waiter) dar una propina a; (tilt) inclinar; (overturn: also: ~ over) volcar; (empty: also: ~ out) vaciar, echar; ~-off n (hint) aviso, advertencia; ~ped a (cigarette) con filtro.

tipsy [tɪpsɪ] a algo borracho, mareado.

tiptoe [tɪptəu] n: **on ~** de puntillas.

tiptop [tɪptɒp] a: **in ~ condition** en perfectas condiciones.

tire [taɪə*] n (US) = **tyre** // vt cansar // vi (gen) cansarse; (become bored) aburrirse; ~d a cansado; **to be ~d of sth** estar cansado o harto de algo; **tiredness** n cansancio; ~less a incansable; ~some a aburrido; **tiring** a cansado.

tissue [tɪʃu:] n tejido; (paper handkerchief) pañuelo de papel, kleenex m; ~ **paper** n papel m de seda.

tit [tɪt] n (bird) herrerillo común; **to give ~ for tat** dar ojo por ojo.

titbit [tɪtbɪt] n (food) golosina; (news) suceso.

titillate [tɪtɪleɪt] vt estimular, excitar.

titivate [tɪtɪveɪt] vt emperejilar.

title [taɪtl] n título; ~ **deed** n (LAW) título de propiedad; ~ **role** n papel m principal.

titter [tɪtə*] vi reírse entre dientes.

titular [tɪtjulə*] a (in name only) nominal.

to [tu:, tə] prep a; (towards) hacia; (of time) a, hasta; (of) de; **give it ~ me** dámelo; **the key ~ the front door** la llave de la puerta; **the main thing is ~...** lo importante es...; **to go ~ France/school** ir a Francia/al colegio; **a quarter ~ 5** las 5 menos cuarto; **pull/push the door ~** tirar/empujar la puerta; **to go ~ and fro** ir y venir.

toad [təud] n sapo; ~**stool** n hongo venenoso.

toast [təust] n (CULIN: also: piece of ~) tostada; (drink, speech) brindis m // vt (CULIN) tostar; (drink to) brindar; ~**er** n tostador m.

tobacco [təbækəu] n tabaco; ~**nist** n estanquero; ~**nist's (shop)** n estanco.

toboggan [təbɒgən] n tobogán m.

today [tədeɪ] ad, n (also fig) hoy m.

toddler [tɒdlə*] n niño que empieza a andar.

toddy [tɒdɪ] n ponche m.

toe [təu] n dedo (del pie); (of shoe) punta; **to ~ the line** (fig) conformarse; ~**nail** n uña del pie.

toffee [tɒfɪ] n caramelo; ~ **apple** n pirulí m.

toga [təugə] n toga.

together [təgeðə*] ad juntos; (at same time) al mismo tiempo, a la vez; ~ **with** prep junto con; ~**ness** n compañerismo.

toil [tɔɪl] n trabajo duro, labor f // vi esforzarse.

toilet [tɔɪlət] n (lavatory) servicios mpl, wáter m // cpd (bag, soap etc) de aseo; ~ **bowl** n palangana; ~ **paper** n papel m higiénico; ~**ries** npl artículos mpl de aseo; (make-up etc) artículos mpl de tocador; ~ **roll** n rollo de papel higiénico; ~ **water** n agua de tocador.

token ['təukən] n (sign) señal f, muestra; (souvenir) recuerdo; (voucher) cupón m; **book/record ~** vale m para comprar libros/discos.

told [təuld] pt, pp of **tell**.

tolerable ['tɔlərəbl] a (bearable) soportable; (fairly good) pasable.

tolerance ['tɔlərns] n (also: TECH) tolerancia; **tolerant** a: **tolerant of** tolerante con.

tolerate ['tɔləreit] vt tolerar; **toleration** [-'reiʃən] n tolerancia.

toll [təul] n (of casualties) número de víctimas; (tax, charge) peaje m // vi (bell) doblar; **~bridge** n puente m de peaje.

tomato [tə'mɑ:təu], pl **~es** n tomate m.

tomb [tu:m] n tumba.

tombola [tɔm'bəulə] n tómbola.

tomboy ['tɔmbɔi] n marimacho.

tombstone ['tu:mstəun] n lápida.

tomcat ['tɔmkæt] n gato.

tomorrow [tə'mɔrəu] ad, n (also fig) mañana; **the day after ~** pasado mañana; **~ morning** mañana por la mañana.

ton [tʌn] n tonelada; **~s of** (col) montones mpl de.

tone [təun] n tono // vi armonizar; **to ~ down** vt (colour, criticism) suavizar; (sound) bajar; (MUS) entonar; **to ~ up** vt (muscles) tonificar; **~-deaf** a que no tiene oído.

tongs [tɔŋz] npl (for coal) tenazas fpl; (for hair) tenacillas fpl.

tongue [tʌŋ] n lengua; **~ in cheek** ad irónicamente; **~-tied** a (fig) mudo; **~-twister** n trabalenguas m inv.

tonic ['tɔnik] n (MED) tónico; (MUS) tónica; (also: **~ water**) agua tónica.

tonight [tə'nait] ad, n esta noche.

tonnage ['tʌnidʒ] n (NAUT) tonelaje m.

tonsil ['tɔnsl] n amígdala, anginas fpl (col); **~litis** [-'laitis] n

amigdalitis f, (inflamación f de las) anginas.

too [tu:] ad (excessively) demasiado; (very) muy; (also) también; **~ much** ad demasiado; **~ many** de demasiados/as.

took [tuk] pt of **take**.

tool [tu:l] n herramienta; **~ box** n caja de herramientas.

toot [tu:t] n (of horn) bocinazo; (of whistle) silbido // vi (with car-horn) tocar la bocina.

tooth [tu:θ], pl **teeth** n (ANAT, TECH) diente m; (molar) muela; **~ache** n dolor m de muelas; **~brush** n cepillo de dientes; **~paste** n pasta de dientes; **~pick** n palillo.

top [tɔp] n (of mountain) cumbre f, cima; (of head) coronilla; (of ladder) lo alto; (of cupboard, table) superficie f; (lid: of box, jar) tapa, tapadera; (: of bottle) tapón m; (of list etc) cabeza; (toy) peonza // a más alto; (in rank) principal, primero; (best) mejor // vt (exceed) exceder; (be first in) ir a la cabeza de; **on ~ of** sobre, encima de; **from ~ to toe** de pies a cabeza; **to ~ up** vt llenar; **~coat** n sobretodo; **~ hat** n sombrero de copa; **~-heavy** a (object) desequilibrado.

topic ['tɔpik] n tema m, tópico; **~al** a actual.

top: ~less a (bather etc) con el pecho al descubierto, topless; **~-level** a (talks) al más alto nivel; **~most** a más alto.

topple ['tɔpl] vt volcar, derribar // vi caerse.

topsy-turvy ['tɔpsi'tə:vi] a, ad patas arriba.

torch [tɔ:tʃ] n antorcha; (electric) linterna.

tore [tɔ:*] pt of **tear**.

torment ['tɔ:ment] n tormento // vt [tɔ:'ment] atormentar; (fig: annoy) fastidiar.

torn [tɔ:n] pp of **tear**.

ornado ['tɔːneɪdəu], pl ~es n tornado.

orpedo [tɔːˈpiːdəu], pl ~es n torpedo.

orrent ['tɒrnt] n torrente m; ~ial [tɒˈrenʃl] a torrencial.

orso ['tɔːsəu] n torso.

ortoise ['tɔːtəs] n tortuga; ~shell ['tɔːtəʃel] a de carey.

ortuous ['tɔːtjuəs] a tortuoso.

orture ['tɔːtʃə*] n tortura // vt torturar; (fig) atormentar.

ory ['tɔːrɪ] a, n conservador a m/f.

oss [tɒs] vt tirar, echar; (head) sacudir (la cabeza); to ~ a coin echar a cara o cruz; to ~ up for sth jugar a cara o cruz algo; to ~ and turn in bed dar vueltas en la cama.

ot [tɒt] n (drink) copita; (child) nene/a m/f.

otal ['təutl] a total, entero // n total m, suma // vt (add up) sumar; (amount to) ascender a.

otalitarian [təutælɪˈteərɪən] a totalitario.

otem pole ['təutəm-] n poste m totémico.

otter ['tɒtə*] vi tambalearse.

ouch [tʌtʃ] n (gen) tacto; (contact) contacto; (FOOTBALL) fuera de juego // vt (gen) tocar; (emotionally) conmover; there's no ~ of (fig) una pizca o un poquito de; to get in ~ with sb ponerse en contacto con uno; to lose ~ (friends) perder contacto; to ~ on vt fus (topic) aludir (brevemente) a; to ~ up vt (paint) retocar; ~-and-go a arriesgado; ~down n aterrizaje m; (on sea) amaraje m; ~ed a conmovido; (col) chiflado; ~ing a conmovedor(a); ~line n (SPORT) línea de banda; ~y a (person) susceptible.

ough [tʌf] a (gen) duro; (difficult) difícil; (resistant) resistente; (person) fuerte; (: pej) bruto // n (gangster etc) gorila m; ~en vt endurecer; ~ness n dureza; dificultad f; resistencia; fuerza.

toupee ['tuːpeɪ] n peluca.

tour ['tuə*] n viaje m, vuelta; (also: package ~) viaje m organizado; (of town, museum) visita // vt viajar por; ~ing n viajes mpl turísticos, turismo.

tourism ['tuərɪzm] n turismo.

tourist ['tuərɪst] n turista m/f // cpd turístico; ~ office n oficina de turismo.

tournament ['tuənəmənt] n torneo.

tousled ['tauzld] a (hair) despeinado.

tout [taut] vi: to ~ for solicitar clientes para // n: ticket ~ revendedor/a m/f.

tow [təu] vt remolcar, 'on ~' (AUT) "a remolque".

toward(s) [təˈwɔːd(z)] prep hacia; (of attitude) respecto a, con; (of purpose) para.

towel ['tauəl] n toalla; ~ling n (fabric) felpa; ~ rail n toallero.

tower ['tauə*] n torre f; ~ block n rascacielos m inv, ~ing a muy alto, imponente.

town [taun] n ciudad f; to go to ~ ir a la ciudad; (fig) hacer con entusiasmo; ~ clerk n secretario del Ayuntamiento; ~ council n consejo municipal; ~ hall n Ayuntamiento; ~ planning n urbanismo.

towrope ['təurəup] n cable m de remolque.

toxic ['tɒksɪk] a tóxico.

toy [tɔɪ] n juguete m; to ~ with vt fus jugar con; (idea) acariciar; ~shop n juguetería.

trace [treɪs] n rastro // vt (draw) trazar, delinear; (follow) seguir la pista de; (locate) encontrar.

track [træk] n (mark) huella, pista; (path: gen) camino, senda; (: of bullet etc) trayectoria; (: of suspect, animal) pista, rastro; (RAIL) vía; (on tape, SPORT) pista // vt seguir la pista de; to keep ~ of mantenerse al tanto de, seguir; to ~ down vt (*prey*) averiguar el paradero de; (*sth lost*) buscar y encontrar; ~ **suit** *n* chandal *m*.

tract [trækt] *n* (GEO) región *f*; (*pamphlet*) folleto.

tractor ['træktə*] *n* tractor *m*.

trade [treɪd] *n* comercio, negocio; (*skill, job*) oficio, empleo // *vi* negociar, comerciar; **to ~ in** *vt* (*old car etc*) ofrecer como parte del pago; ~**-in price** *n* valor *m* de un objeto usado que se descuenta del precio de otro nuevo; ~**mark** *n* marca de fábrica; ~ **name** *n* marca registrada; **trader** *n* comerciante *m/f*; **tradesman** *n* (*shopkeeper*) tendero; ~ **union** *n* sindicato; ~ **unionism** *n* sindicalismo; **trading** *n* comercio; **trading estate** *n* zona comercial.

tradition [trə'dɪʃən] *n* tradición *f*; ~**al** *a* tradicional.

traffic ['træfɪk] *n* (*gen, AUT*) tráfico, circulación *f*; (*air ~ etc*) tránsito // *vi*: **to ~ in** (*pej: liquor, drugs*) traficar en; ~ **circle** *n* (*US*) cruce *m* giratorio; ~ **jam** *n* embotellamiento; ~ **lights** *npl* semáforo *sg*; ~ **warden** *n* guardia *m/f* de tráfico.

tragedy ['trædʒədɪ] *n* tragedia.

tragic ['trædʒɪk] *a* trágico.

trail [treɪl] *n* (*tracks*) rastro, pista; (*path*) camino, sendero; (*wake*) estela // *vt* (*drag*) arrastrar; (*follow*) seguir la pista de; (*follow closely*) vigilar // *vi* arrastrarse; **to ~ behind** *vi* quedar a la zaga; ~**er** *n* (AUT) remolque *m*; (*US*) caravana; (CINEMA) trailer *m*, ávance *m*.

train [treɪn] *n* tren *m*; (*of dress*) cola; (*series*) serie *f*; (*followers*) séquito // *vt* (*educate*) formar; (*teach skills to*) adiestrar; (*sportsman*) entrenar; (*dog*) amaestrar; (*point: gun etc*): **to ~ on** apuntar a // *vi* (SPORT) entrenarse; (*be educated*) recibir una formación; ~**ed** *a* (*worker*) cualificado, adiestrado; (*teacher*)

diplomado; (*animal*) amaestrado; ~**ee** [treɪ'niː] *n* persona que está aprendiendo; (*in trade*) aprendiz/a *m/f*, ~**er** *n* (SPORT) entrenador/a *m/f*; (*of animals*) domador/a *m/f*; ~**ing** *n* formación *f*, adiestramiento; entrenamiento; **in ~ing** (SPORT) en forma; ~**ing college** *n* (*for teachers*) escuela normal; (*gen*) colegio de formación profesional.

traipse [treɪps] *vi* andar con desgana.

trait [treɪt] *n* rasgo.

traitor ['treɪtə*] *n* traidor/a *m/f*.

tram [træm] *n* (*also*: ~**car**) tranvía *m*.

tramp [træmp] *n* (*person*) vagabundo // *vi* andar con pasos pesados.

trample ['træmpl] *vt*: **to ~ (underfoot)** pisotear.

trampoline ['træmpəliːn] *n* trampolín *m*.

trance [trɑːns] *n* trance *m*; (MED) catalepsia.

tranquil ['træŋkwɪl] *a* tranquilo; ~**lity** *n* tranquilidad *f*; ~**lizer** *n* (MED) tranquilizante *m*.

transact [træn'zækt] *vt* (*business*) tramitar; ~**ion** [-'zækʃən] *n* transacción *f*, negocio.

transatlantic ['trænzət'læntɪk] *a* transatlántico.

transcend [træn'send] *vt* trascender.

transcript ['trænskrɪpt] *n* copia; ~**ion** [-'skrɪpʃən] *n* transcripción *f*.

transept ['trænsept] *n* crucero.

transfer ['trænsfə*] *n* (*gen*) transferencia; (SPORT) traspaso; (*picture, design*) calcomanía // [træns'fəː*] trasladar, pasar; **to ~ the charges** (TEL) llamar a cobro revertido; ~**able** [-'fɑːrəbl] *a* transferible; **'not ~able'** 'intransferible'.

transform [træns'fɔːm] *vt* transformar; ~**ation** [-'meɪʃən] *n* transformación *f*; ~**er** *n* (ELEC) transformador *m*.

ransfusion [træns'fju:ʒən] n transfusión f.

ransient ['trænzɪənt] a transitorio.

ransistor [træn'zɪstə*] n (ELEC) transistor m; ~ **radio** n radio f a transistores.

ransit ['trænzɪt] n: **in ~** de tránsito, de paso.

ransition [træn'zɪʃən] n transición f; **~al** a transitorio.

ransitive ['trænzɪtɪv] a (LING) transitivo.

ransitory ['trænzɪtərɪ] a transitorio.

ranslate [trænz'leɪt] vt traducir; **translation** [-'leɪʃən] n traducción f; **translator** n traductor/a m/f.

ransmission [trænz'mɪʃən] n transmisión f.

ransmit [trænz'mɪt] vt transmitir; **~ter** n transmisor m; **(station)** emisora f.

ransparency [træns'pɛərnsɪ] n (PHOT) diapositiva f.

ransparent [træns'pærnt] a transparente.

ransplant [træns'plɑ:nt] vt transplantar // n ['trænsplɑ:nt] (MED) transplante m.

ransport [træns'pɔ:t] n (gen) transporte m; (also: **road/rail ~**) transporte por carretera/ferrocarril // vt transportar; (carry) acarrear; **~ation** [-'teɪʃən] n transporte m; **~ café** n cafetería de carretera.

ransverse ['trænzvɜ:s] a transversal.

ransvestite [trænz'vestaɪt] n travesti m/f.

rap [træp] n (snare, trick) trampa; (carriage) cabriolé m // vt coger en una trampa; (immobilize) bloquear; (jam) atascar; **~ door** n escotilla.

rapeze [trə'pi:z] n trapecio.

rappings ['træpɪŋz] npl adornos mpl.

rash [træʃ] n (pej: goods) pacotilla; (: nonsense) basura; **~ can** n (US) cubo de la basura.

trauma ['trɔ:mə] n trauma m; **~tic** [-'mætɪk] a traumático.

travel ['trævl] n viaje m // vi viajar // vt (distance) recorrer; **~ agency** n agencia de viajes; **~ler**, **~er** (US) n viajero/a; **~ler's cheque** n cheque m de viajero; **~ling**, **~ing** (US) n los viajes mpl, el viajar; **~ sickness** n mareo.

traverse ['trævəs] vt atravesar, cruzar.

travesty ['trævəstɪ] n parodia.

trawler ['trɔ:lə*] n barco rastreador o de rastra.

tray [treɪ] n (for carrying) bandeja; (on desk) cajón m.

treacherous ['tretʃərəs] a traidor(a); **treachery** n traición f.

treacle ['tri:kl] n melaza.

tread [tred] n (step) paso, pisada; (sound) ruido de pasos; (of tyre) banda de rodadura // vi, pt **trod**, pp **trodden** pisar; **to ~ on** vt fus pisar sobre.

treason ['tri:zn] n traición f.

treasure ['treʒə*] n tesoro // vt (value) apreciar, valorar; **~ hunt** n caza del tesoro.

treasurer ['treʒərə*] n tesorero/a.

treasury ['treʒərɪ] n: **the T~** (POL) el Ministerio de Hacienda.

treat [tri:t] n (present) regalo; (pleasure) placer m // vt tratar; **to ~ sb to sth** invitar a uno a algo.

treatise ['tri:tɪz] n tratado.

treatment ['tri:tmənt] n tratamiento.

treaty ['tri:tɪ] n tratado.

treble ['trebl] a triple // n (MUS) tiple m // vt, vi triplicar // vi triplicarse.

tree [tri:] n árbol m; **~ trunk** n tronco de árbol.

trek [trek] n (long journey) viaje m largo y peligroso; (tiring walk) caminata; (as holiday) excursión f.

trellis ['trelɪs] n enrejado.

tremble ['trembl] vi temblar; **trembling** n temblor m // a tembloroso.

tremendous [trɪ'mendəs] *a*
tremendo; (*enormous*) enorme;
(*excellent*) estupendo.

tremor ['tremə*] *n* temblor *m*;
(*also*: **earth ~**) temblor *m* de tierra.

trench [trentʃ] *n* trinchera.

trend [trend] *n* (*tendency*)
tendencia; (*of events*) curso;
(*fashion*) moda; **~y** *a* (*idea*) según
las tendencias actuales; (*clothes*) a
la última moda.

trepidation [trepɪ'deɪʃən] *n* agitación *f*; (*fear*) ansia.

trespass ['trespəs] *vi*: **to ~ on**
entrar sin permiso en; **"no ~ing"**
"prohibido el paso".

tress [tres] *n* trenza.

trestle ['tresl] *n* caballete *m*; **~
table** *n* mesa de caballete.

trial ['traɪəl] *n* (*LAW*) juicio, proceso;
(*test: of machine etc*) prueba;
(*hardship*) desgracia; **by ~ and
error** por tanteo.

triangle ['traɪæŋgl] *n* (*MATH*, *MUS*)
triángulo; **triangular** [-'æŋgjulə*] *a*
triangular.

tribal ['traɪbəl] *a* tribal.

tribe [traɪb] *n* tribu *f*; **tribesman** *n*
miembro de una tribu.

tribulation [trɪbju'leɪʃən] *n* tribu-
lación *f*, sufrimiento.

tribunal [traɪ'bjuːnl] *n* tribunal *m*.

tributary ['trɪbjutəri] *n* (*river*)
afluente *m*.

tribute ['trɪbjuːt] *n* homenaje *m*;
(*payment*) tributo; **to pay ~ to**
rendir homenaje a.

trice [traɪs] *n*: **in a ~** en un
santiamén.

trick [trɪk] *n* trampa; (*deceit*) truco;
(*joke*) broma; (*CARDS*) baza // *vt*
engañar; **to play a ~ on sb** gastar
una broma a uno; **~ery** *n* astucia.

trickle ['trɪkl] *n* (*of water etc*)
hilillo // *vi* gotear.

tricky ['trɪkɪ] *a* difícil, delicado.

tricycle ['traɪsɪkl] *n* triciclo.

trifle ['traɪfl] *n* bagatela; (*CULIN*)
dulce *m* de bizcocho, fruta y natillas
// *ad*: **a ~ long** un poquito largo;

trifling *a* insignificante.

trigger ['trɪgə*] *n* (*of gun*) gatillo;
to ~ off *vt* desencadenar.

trigonometry [trɪgə'nɒmətrɪ] *n*
trigonometría.

trill [trɪl] *n* (*of bird*) trino.

trim [trɪm] *a* (*elegant*) aseado;
(*house, garden*) en buen estado;
(*figure*) con buen tipo // *n* (*haircut
etc*) recorte *m*; (*on car*) tapicería //
vt arreglar; (*cut*) recortar
(*decorate*) adornar; (*NAUT*: *a sail*)
orientar; **~mings** *npl* decoraciones
fpl; (*cuttings*) recortes *mpl*.

Trinity ['trɪnɪtɪ] *n*: **the ~** la
Trinidad.

trinket ['trɪŋkɪt] *n* chuchería; (*piece
of jewellery*) baratija.

trio ['triːəu] *n* trío.

trip [trɪp] *n* viaje *m*; (*excursion*)
excursión *f*; (*stumble*) traspié *m* //
vi (*also*: **~ up**) tropezar; (*go lightly*)
andar a paso ligero // *vt* poner la
zancadilla a.

tripe [traɪp] *n* (*CULIN*) callos *mpl*;
(*pej*: *rubbish*) bobadas *fpl*.

triple ['trɪpl] *a* triple.

triplets ['trɪplɪts] *npl* trillizos/as
m/fpl.

triplicate ['trɪplɪkət] *n*: **in ~** por
triplicado.

tripod ['traɪpɒd] *n* trípode *m*.

trite [traɪt] *a* gastado, trillado.

triumph ['traɪʌmf] *n* triunfo // *vi*:
to ~ (over) vencer; **~ant** [-'ʌmfənt]
a triunfante.

trivia ['trɪvɪə] *npl* trivialidades *fpl*.

trivial ['trɪvɪəl] *a* insignificante,
(*commonplace*) trivial; **~ity** [-'ælɪtɪ]
n trivialidad *f*.

trod [trɒd], **trodden** ['trɒdn] *pt*, *pp*
of **tread**.

trolley ['trɒlɪ] *n* carrito; **~ bus** *n*
trolebús *m*.

trombone [trɒm'bəun] *n* trombón
m.

troop [truːp] *n* grupo, banda; **~s**
(*MIL*) tropas *fpl*; **to ~ in/out** *vi*
entrar/salir en grupo; **~er** *n* (*MIL*)
soldado de caballería.

trophy ['trəufɪ] n trofeo.

tropic ['trɒpɪk] n trópico; ~al a tropical.

trot [trɒt] n trote m // vi trotar; **on the ~** (fig: col) de corrido.

trouble ['trʌbl] n problema m, dificultad f, (worry) preocupación f, (bother, effort) molestia, esfuerzo; (unrest) inquietud f; (MED): **stomach ~** problemas mpl gástricos // vt molestar; (worry) preocupar, inquietar // vi: **to ~** **to do sth** molestarse en hacer algo; ~s npl (POL etc) conflictos mpl; **to be in ~** estar en un apuro; **to go to the ~ of doing sth** tomarse la molestia de hacer algo; **what's the ~?** ¿qué pasa?; **~d** a (person) preocupado; (epoch, life) agitado; **~maker** n elemento perturbador; (child) niño alborotado; **~shooter** n (in conflict) conciliador m; **~some** a molesto, inoportuno.

trough [trɒf] n (also: drinking ~) abrevadero; (also: feeding ~) comedero; (channel) canal m.

troupe [truːp] n grupo.

trousers ['trauzəz] npl pantalones mpl.

trousseau ['truːsəu] pl **~x** or **~s** [-z] n ajuar m.

trout [traut] n, pl inv trucha.

trowel ['trauəl] n paleta.

truant ['truənt] n: **to play ~** hacer novillos.

truce [truːs] n tregua.

truck [trʌk] n camión m; (RAIL) vagón m; **~ driver** n camionero; **~ farm** n (US) huerto de hortalizas.

truculent ['trʌkjulənt] a agresivo.

trudge [trʌdʒ] vi andar con dificultad o pesadamente.

true [truː] a verdadero; (accurate) exacto; (genuine) auténtico; (faithful) fiel.

truffle ['trʌfl] n trufa.

truly ['truːlɪ] ad auténticamente; (truthfully) verdaderamente; (faithfully) fielmente; **yours ~** (in letter) (le saluda) atentamente.

trump [trʌmp] n triunfo; **~ed-up** a inventado.

trumpet ['trʌmpɪt] n trompeta.

truncheon ['trʌntʃən] n porra.

trundle ['trʌndl] vt, vi: **to ~ along** rodar haciendo ruido.

trunk [trʌŋk] n (of tree, person) tronco; (of elephant) trompa; (case) baúl m; **~s** npl (also: swimming **~s**) bañador m; **~ call** n (TEL) llamada interurbana.

truss [trʌs] n (MED) braguero; **to ~ (up)** vt atar.

trust [trʌst] n confianza; (COMM) trust m, cartel m; (obligation) responsabilidad f; (LAW) fideicomiso // vt (rely on) tener confianza en; (entrust): **to ~ sth to sb** confiar algo a uno; (trust): **to ~ed** a de confianza; **~ee** [trʌs'tiː] n (LAW) depositario, fideicomisario; (of school etc) administrador/a m/f; **~ful, ~ing** a confiado; **~worthy** a digno de confianza; **~y** a fiel.

truth [truːθ], pl **~s** [truːðz] n verdad f; **~ful** a (person) que dice la verdad; **~fully** ad sinceramente; **~fulness** n veracidad f.

try [traɪ] n tentativa, intento; (RUGBY) ensayo // vt (LAW) juzgar, procesar; (test: sth new) probar, someter a prueba; (attempt) intentar; (strain) hacer sufrir // vi probar; **to ~ to do sth** intentar hacer algo; **to ~ on** vt (clothes) probarse; **to ~ out** vt probar, poner a prueba; **~ing** a penoso, cansado.

tsar [zɑː] n zar m.

T shirt ['tiːʃəːt] n camiseta.

tub [tʌb] n cubo; (bath) tina, bañera.

tuba ['tjuːbə] n tuba.

tubby ['tʌbɪ] a regordete.

tube [tjuːb] n tubo; (underground) metro; (for tyre) cámara de aire; **~less** a sin cámara.

tuberculosis [tjubəːkju'ləusɪs] n tuberculosis f.

tube station n estación f de metro.

tubing ['tju:bɪŋ] n tubería; **a piece of** ~ un trozo de tubo.

tubular ['tju:bjulə*] a tubular; (furniture) de tubo.

TUC n abbr of **Trades Union Congress.**

tuck [tʌk] n (SEWING) pliegue m // vt (put) poner; **to** ~ **away** vt esconder; **to** ~ **in** vt meter; (child) arropar // vi (eat) comer con mucho apetito; **to** ~ **up** vt (child) arropar; ~ **shop** n tienda de golosinas.

Tuesday ['tju:zdɪ] n martes m.

tuft [tʌft] n mechón m; (of grass etc) manojo.

tug [tʌg] n (ship) remolcador m // vt remolcar; ~-**of-war** n lucha de la cuerda.

tuition [tju:'ɪʃən] n enseñanza; (private ~) clases fpl particulares.

tulip ['tju:lɪp] n tulipán m.

tumble ['tʌmbl] n (fall) caída // vi caerse, tropezar // vt tirar; ~**s down** a destartalado; ~ **dryer** n secador m de ropa automático.

tumbler ['tʌmblə*] n vaso.

tummy ['tʌmɪ] n (col: belly) barriga; (: stomach) vientre m.

tumour ['tju:mə*] n tumor m.

tumult ['tju:mʌlt] n tumulto; ~**uous** [-'mʌltjuəs] a tumultuoso.

tuna ['tju:nə] n, pl inv (also: ~ **fish**) atún m.

tune [tju:n] n (melody) melodía // vt (MUS) afinar; (RADIO, TV, AUT) sintonizar; **to be in/out of** ~ (instrument) estar afinado/ desafinado; (singer) cantar bien/ mal; **to be in/out of** ~ **with** (fig) armonizar/desentonar con; **to** ~ **up** vi (musician) afinar (su instrumento); ~**ful** a melodioso; **tuner** n (radio set) sintonizador m; **piano tuner** afinador m de pianos.

tunic ['tju:nɪk] n túnica.

tuning ['tju:nɪŋ] n sintonización f; (MUS) afinación f; ~ **fork** n diapasón m.

Tunisia [tju:'nɪzɪə] n Tunez m.

tunnel ['tʌnl] n túnel m; (in mine) galería // vi construir un túnel/una galería.

tunny ['tʌnɪ] n atún m.

turban ['tə:bən] n turbante m.

turbine ['tə:baɪn] n turbina.

turbulence ['tə:bjuləns] n (AVIAT) turbulencia; **turbulent** a turbulento.

tureen [tə'ri:n] n sopera.

turf [tə:f] n turba; (clod) césped m // vt poner césped; **to** ~ **out** vt (col) echar a la calle.

turgid ['tə:dʒɪd] a (speech) pesado.

Turk [tə:k] n turco/a.

turkey ['tə:kɪ] n pavo.

Turkey ['tə:kɪ] n Turquía; **Turkish** a, n turco; **Turkish bath** n baño turco.

turmoil ['tə:mɔɪl] n desorden m, alboroto.

turn [tə:n] n turno; (in road) curva; (tendency: of mind, events) disposición f, propensión f; (THEATRE) número; (MED) desmayo // vt girar, volver; (collar, steak) dar la vuelta a; (change): **to** ~ **sth into** convertir algo en // vi volver; (person: look back) volverse; (reverse direction) dar la vuelta; (milk) cortarse; (change) cambiar; (become) convertirse en; **a good** ~ un favor; **it gave me quite a** ~ me dio un susto (bastante grande); **'no left** ~' (AUT) 'prohibido girar a la izquierda'; **it's your** ~ te toca a ti; **in** ~ por turnos; **to take** ~**s** turnarse; **to** ~ **about** vi dar una vuelta completa; **to** ~ **away** vi volver la cabeza; **to** ~ **back** vi volverse atrás; **to** ~ **down** vt (refuse) rechazar; (reduce) bajar; (fold) doblar (hacia abajo); **to** ~ **in** vi (col: go to bed) acostarse // vt (fold) doblar hacia dentro; **to** ~ **off** vi (from road) desviarse // vt (light, radio etc) apagar; (engine) parar; **to** ~ **on** vt (light, radio etc) encender; (engine) poner en marcha; **to** ~ **out** vt (light, gas) apagar // vi: **to** ~ **out to be...** resultar ser...; **to** ~ **up**

(person) llegar, presentarse; (lost object) aparecer // vt (gen) subir; ~ing n (in road) vuelta; ~ing point n (fig) momento decisivo.

turnip ['tə:nɪp] n nabo.

turnout ['tə:naut] n asistencia, número de asistentes.

turnover ['tə:nəuvə*] n (comm: amount of money) cifra de negocios; (: of goods) movimiento.

turnpike ['tə:npaɪk] n (US) autopista de peaje.

turnstile ['tə:nstaɪl] n torniquete m.

turntable ['tə:nteɪbl] n (on record player) plato.

turn-up ['tə:nʌp] n (on trousers) vuelta.

turpentine ['tə:pəntaɪn] n (also: turps) trementina.

turquoise ['tə:kwɔɪz] n (stone) turquesa // a color turquesa.

turret ['tʌrɪt] n torrecilla.

turtle ['tə:tl] n tortuga marina.

tusk [tʌsk] n colmillo.

tussle ['tʌsl] n (fight) lucha; (scuffle) pelea.

tutor ['tju:tə*] n (gen) profesor/a m/f; ~ial [-'tɔ:rɪəl] n (scol) seminario.

T.V. [ti:'vi:] n abbr of television.

twaddle ['twɔdl] n tonterías fpl, bobadas fpl.

twang [twæŋ] n (of instrument) punteado; (of voice) timbre m nasal // vi vibrar // vt (guitar) puntear.

tweed [twi:d] n tweed m.

tweezers ['twi:zəz] npl pinzas fpl de depilar.

twelfth [twelfθ] a duodécimo; T~ Night n Día de Reyes.

twelve [twelv] num doce.

twentieth ['twentɪəθ] a vigésimo.

twenty ['twentɪ] num veinte.

twerp [twə:p] n (col) imbécil m/f.

twice [twaɪs] ad dos veces; ~ as much dos veces más.

twig [twɪg] n ramita // vi (col) caer en la cuenta.

twilight ['twaɪlaɪt] n crepúsculo, ocaso.

twin [twɪn] a, n gemelo/a // vt tener como gemelo.

twine [twaɪn] n bramante m // vi (plant) enroscarse.

twinge [twɪndʒ] n (of pain) punzada; (of conscience) remordimiento.

twinkle ['twɪŋkl] n centelleo // vi centellear; (eyes) parpadear.

twirl [twə:l] n giro // vt dar vueltas a // vi girar rápidamente.

twist [twɪst] n (action) torsión f; (in road, coil) vuelta; (in wire, flex) enroscadura; (in story) cambio imprevisto // vt torcer, retorcer; (weave) entrelazar; (roll around) enrollar; (fig) deformar // vi serpentear.

twit [twɪt] n (col) tonto.

twitch [twɪtʃ] n sacudida; (nervous) tic m nervioso // vi moverse nerviosamente.

two [tu:] num dos; to put ~ and ~ together (fig) atar cabos; ~-door a (AUT) de dos puertas; ~-faced a (pej: person) falso; ~-fold ad: to increase ~fold duplicar; ~-piece (suit) n traje m de dos piezas; ~-piece (swimsuit) n dos piezas m inv, bikini m; ~-seater n (plane) avión m biplaza; (car) coche m de dos plazas; ~some n (people) pareja; ~-way a: ~-way traffic circulación f en ambas direcciones.

tycoon [taɪ'ku:n] n: (business) ~ magnate m.

type [taɪp] n (category) tipo, género; (model) modelo; (TYP) tipo, letra // vt (letter etc) escribir a máquina; ~-cast a (actor) encasillado; ~-script n texto mecanografiado; ~-writer n máquina de escribir; ~-written n mecanografiado.

typhoid ['taɪfɔɪd] n tifoidea.

typhoon [taɪ'fu:n] n tifón m.

typhus ['taɪfəs] n tifus m.

typical ['tɪpɪkl] a típico; **typify** [-faɪ] vt ser típico de.

typing ['taɪpɪŋ] n mecanografía;
typist n mecanógrafa.
tyranny ['tɪrənɪ] n tiranía.
tyrant ['taɪərnt] n tirano/a.
tyre, tire (US) ['taɪə*] n neumático,
llanta.
tzar [zɑ:*] n = **tsar**.

U

U-bend ['ju:bend] n (in pipe)
recodo.
ubiquitous [ju:'bɪkwɪtəs] a ubicuo,
omnipresente.
udder ['ʌdə*] n ubre f.
UFO ['ju:fəu] n abbr of **unidentified
flying object** O.V.N.I. m (objeto
volante no identificado).
ugliness ['ʌglɪnɪs] n fealdad f; **ugly**
a feo; (dangerous) peligroso.
U.K. n abbr of **United
Kingdom.**
ulcer ['ʌlsə*] n úlcera.
Ulster ['ʌlstə*] n Ulster m, Irlanda
del Norte.
ulterior [ʌl'tɪərɪə*] a ulterior; ~
motive motivo oculto.
ultimate ['ʌltɪmət] a último, final;
(authority) supremo; ~**ly** ad (in the
end) por último, al final;
(fundamentally) en el fondo.
ultimatum [ʌltɪ'meɪtəm] n ulti-
mátum m.
ultraviolet [ʌltrə'vaɪəlɪt] a ultra-
violeta.
umbilical cord [ʌmbɪ'laɪkl-] n
cordón m umbilical.
umbrella [ʌm'brelə] n paraguas m
inv.
umpire ['ʌmpaɪə*] n árbitro // vt
arbitrar.
umpteen [ʌmp'ti:n] a tantísimos;
for the ~th time por enésima vez.
UN, UNO abbr of **United
Nations (Organization).**
unable [ʌn'eɪbl] a: **to be ~ to do sth**
ser incapaz o no poder hacer algo.

unabridged [ʌnə'brɪdʒd] a íntegro.
unaccompanied [ʌnə'kʌmpənɪd]
a no acompañado.
unaccountably [ʌnə'kauntəblɪ] ad
inexplicablemente.
unaccustomed [ʌnə'kʌstəmd] a:
to be ~ to no tener costumbre de.
unaided [ʌn'eɪdɪd] a sin ayuda, por
sí solo.
unanimous [ju:'nænɪməs] a
unánime; ~**ly** ad unánimemente.
unarmed [ʌn'ɑ:md] a (without a
weapon) desarmado; (defenceless)
inerme.
unassuming [ʌnə'sju:mɪŋ] a
modesto, sin pretensiones.
unattached [ʌnə'tætʃt] a (person)
libre; (part etc) suelto, separable.
unattended [ʌnə'tendɪd] a (car,
luggage) sin vigilancia.
unattractive [ʌnə'træktɪv] a poco
atractivo.
unauthorized [ʌn'ɔ:θəraɪzd] a desautorizado.
unavoidable [ʌnə'vɔɪdəbl] a inevitable.
unaware [ʌnə'weə*] a: **to be ~ of**
ignorar, no darse cuenta de; ~**s** ad
de improviso.
unbalanced [ʌn'bælənst] a desequilibrado; (mentally) trastornado.
unbearable [ʌn'beərəbl] a insoportable.
unbeatable [ʌn'bi:təbl] a (team)
imbatible; (price) inmejorable.
unbeaten [ʌn'bi:tn] a imbatido.
unbeknown(st) [ʌnbɪ'nəun(st)]
ad: ~ **to me** sin saberlo (yo).
unbelievable [ʌnbɪ'li:vəbl] a
increíble.
unbend [ʌn'bend] (irg: like bend) vi
suavizarse // vt (wire) enderezar.
unblock [ʌn'blɔk] vt (pipe)
desatascar.
unborn [ʌn'bɔ:n] a sin nacer.
unbounded [ʌn'baundɪd] a ilimitado, sin límite.
unbreakable [ʌn'breɪkəbl] a
irrompible.

unbridled [ʌn'braɪdld] a (fig) desenfrenado.

unbroken [ʌn'brəukən] a (seal) intacto; (series) continuo; (record) imbatido; (spirit) indómito.

unburden [ʌn'bɜːdn] vr: **to ~ o.s.** desahogarse.

unbutton [ʌn'bʌtn] vt desabrochar.

uncalled-for [ʌn'kɔːldfɔː*] a gratuito, inmerecido.

uncanny [ʌn'kænɪ] a extraño, extraordinario.

unceasing [ʌn'siːsɪŋ] a incesante.

uncertain [ʌn'sɜːtn] a incierto; (character) indeciso; **~ty** n incertidumbre f.

unchanged [ʌn'tʃeɪndʒd] a sin cambiar o alterar.

uncharitable [ʌn'tʃærɪtəbl] a poco caritativo.

uncharted [ʌn'tʃɑːtɪd] a inexplorado.

unchecked [ʌn'tʃekt] a desenfrenado.

uncivil [ʌn'sɪvɪl] a grosero.

uncle ['ʌŋkl] n tío.

uncomfortable [ʌn'kʌmfətəbl] a incómodo; (uneasy) molesto.

uncommon [ʌn'kɔmən] a poco común, raro.

unconcerned [ʌnkən'sɜːnd] a indiferente, despreocupado.

unconditional [ʌnkən'dɪʃənl] a incondicional.

unconscious [ʌn'kɔnʃəs] a sin sentido; (unaware) inconsciente // n: **the ~** el inconsciente; **~ly** ad inconscientemente.

uncontrollable [ʌnkən'trəuləbl] a (temper) ingobernable; (laughter) incontenible.

uncouth [ʌn'kuːθ] a grosero, inculto.

uncover [ʌn'kʌvə*] vt (gen) descubrir; (take lid off) destapar.

undecided [ʌndɪ'saɪdɪd] a (character) indeciso; (question) no resuelto, pendiente.

undeniable [ʌndɪ'naɪəbl] a innegable.

under ['ʌndə*] prep debajo de; (less than) menos de; (according to) según, de acuerdo con // ad debajo, abajo; **~ there** allí abajo; **~ repair** en reparación.

under... [ʌndə*] pref sub; **~age** a menor de edad; **~carriage** n tren m de aterrizaje; **~clothes** npl ropa sg interior; **~coat** n (paint) primera mano; **~cover** a clandestino; **~current** n corriente f submarina; (fig) tendencia oculta; **~cut** vt irg rebajar los precios para competir con; **~developed** a subdesarrollado; **~dog** n desvalido; **~done** a (CULIN) poco hecho; **~estimate** vt subestimar; **~exposed** a (PHOT) subexpuesto; **~fed** a subalimentado; **~foot** ad bajo los pies; **~go** vt irg sufrir; (treatment) recibir; **~graduate** n estudiante m/f; **~ground** n (railway) metro, (POL) movimiento clandestino // a subterráneo; **~growth** n maleza; **~hand(ed)** a (fig) turbio; **~lie** vt irg estar debajo de; (fig) ser la razón fundamental de; **~line** vt subrayar; **~ling** ['ʌndəlɪŋ] n (pej) subalterno; **~mine** vt socavar, minar; **~neath** [ʌndə'niːθ] ad debajo // prep debajo de, bajo; **~paid** a mal pagado; **~pants** npl (Brit) calzoncillos mpl; **~pass** n paso subterráneo; **~price** vt vender demasiado barato; **~privileged** a desamparado; **~rate** vt menospreciar, subestimar; **~side** n parte f inferior, revés m; **~skirt** n enaguas fpl.

understand [ʌndə'stænd] (irg: like stand) vt, vi entender, comprender; (assume) sobreentender; **~able** a comprensible; **~ing** a comprensivo // n comprensión f, entendimiento f; (agreement) acuerdo.

understatement [ʌndə'steɪtmənt] n descripción f insuficiente; (quality) modestia (excesiva).

understood [ʌndə'stud] pt, pp of

understand // a entendido; (*implied*) sobreentendido.

understudy ['ʌndəstʌdɪ] n suplente m/f.

undertake [ʌndə'teɪk] (*irg: like take*) vt acometer; to ~ to do sth comprometerse a hacer algo.

undertaker ['ʌndəteɪkə*] n director m de pompas fúnebres, sepulturero.

undertaking [ʌndə'teɪkɪŋ] n empresa; (*promise*) promesa.

underwater [ʌndə'wɔ:tə*] ad bajo el agua // a submarino.

underwear ['ʌndəwɛə*] n ropa interior.

underweight [ʌndə'weɪt] a de peso insuficiente; (*person*) demasiado delgado.

underworld ['ʌndəwə:ld] n (*of crime*) hampa, inframundo.

underwriter ['ʌndəraɪtə*] n (*INSURANCE*) (re)asegurador/a m/f.

undesirable [ʌndɪ'zaɪərəbl] a indeseable.

undies ['ʌndɪz] npl (col) paños mpl menores.

undignified [ʌn'dɪgnɪfaɪd] a indecoroso.

undisputed [ʌndɪ'spju:tɪd] a incontestable.

undo [ʌn'du:] (*irg: like do*) vt deshacer; ~ing n ruina, perdición f.

undoubted [ʌn'dautɪd] a indudable; ~ly ad indudablemente, sin duda.

undress [ʌn'dres] vi desnudarse.

undue [ʌn'dju:] a indebido, excesivo.

undulating ['ʌndjuleɪtɪŋ] a ondulante.

unduly [ʌn'dju:lɪ] ad excesivamente, demasiado.

unearth [ʌn'ə:θ] vt desenterrar.

unearthly [ʌn'ə:θlɪ] a (*hour*) inverosímil.

uneasy [ʌn'i:zɪ] a intranquilo; (*worried*) preocupado.

uneconomic(al) ['ʌni:kə'nɔmɪk(l)] a antieconómico.

uneducated [ʌn'edjukeɪtɪd] a sin educación, inculto.

unemployed [ʌnɪm'plɔɪd] a parado, sin trabajo // n: the ~ los parados; **unemployment** [-'plɔɪmənt] n paro, desempleo.

unending [ʌn'endɪŋ] a interminable.

unenthusiastic [ʌnɪnθu:zɪ'æstɪk] a poco entusiasta.

unerring [ʌn'ə:rɪŋ] a infalible.

uneven [ʌn'i:vn] a desigual; (*road etc*) quebrado, accidentado.

unexpected [ʌnɪk'spektɪd] a inesperado.

unfair [ʌn'fɛə*] a: ~ (to) injusto (con); ~ly ad injustamente.

unfaithful [ʌn'feɪθful] a infiel.

unfamiliar [ʌnfə'mɪlɪə*] a nuevo, desconocido.

unfashionable [ʌn'fæʃnəbl] a pasado o fuera de moda.

unfasten [ʌn'fɑ:sn] vt desatar.

unfavourable, unfavorable (*US*) [ʌn'feɪvərəbl] a desfavorable.

unfeeling [ʌn'fi:lɪŋ] a insensible.

unfinished [ʌn'fɪnɪʃt] a incompleto, sin terminar.

unfit [ʌn'fɪt] a con mala salud, enfermo; (*incompetent*) incompetente, incapaz; ~ for work no apto para trabajar.

unflagging [ʌn'flægɪŋ] a incansable.

unfold [ʌn'fəuld] vt desdoblar; (*fig*) revelar // vi abrirse; revelarse.

unforeseen ['ʌnfɔ:'si:n] a imprevisto.

unforgettable [ʌnfə'getəbl] a inolvidable.

unforgivable [ʌnfə'gɪvəbl] a imperdonable.

unfortunate [ʌn'fɔ:tʃnət] a desgraciado; (*event, remark*) inoportuno; ~ly ad desgraciadamente.

unfounded [ʌn'faundɪd] a infundado.

unfriendly [ʌn'frendlɪ] a antipático.

unfurnished [ʌn'fə:nɪʃt] a desamueblado.

ungainly [ʌn'geɪnlɪ] a desgarbado.

unhappiness [ʌnˈhæpɪnɪs] n tristeza; **unhappy** a (sad) triste; (unfortunate) desgraciado; (childhood) infeliz; **unhappy with** (arrangements etc) poco contento con, descontento de.

unharmed [ʌnˈhɑːmd] a ileso; (col) sano y salvo.

unhealthy [ʌnˈhelθɪ] a (gen) malsano; (person) enfermizo, con poca salud.

unheard-of [ʌnˈhəːdɔv] a inaudito, sin precedente.

unhook [ʌnˈhuk] vt desenganchar; (from wall) descolgar; (dress) desabrochar.

unhurt [ʌnˈhəːt] a ileso.

unidentified [ʌnaɪˈdentɪfaɪd] a no identificado.

uniform [ˈjuːnɪfɔːm] n uniforme m // a uniforme; **~ity** [-ˈfɔːmɪtɪ] n uniformidad f.

unify [ˈjuːnɪfaɪ] vt unificar, unir.

unilateral [juːnɪˈlætərəl] a unilateral.

unintentional [ʌnɪnˈtenʃənəl] a involuntario.

union [ˈjuːnjən] n unión f; (also: trade ~) sindicato // a sindical; **U~ Jack** n bandera del Reino Unido.

unique [juːˈniːk] a único.

unison [ˈjuːnɪsn] n: **in ~** en armonía.

unit [ˈjuːnɪt] n unidad f; (team, squad) grupo; **kitchen ~** mueble m de cocina.

unite [juːˈnaɪt] vt unir // vi unirse; **~d** a unido; **U~d Kingdom (U.K.)** n Reino Unido; **U~d Nations (Organization) (UN, UNO)** n (Las) Naciones Unidas fpl (O.N.U.); **U~d States (of America) (US, USA)** n (Los) Estados Unidos mpl (EE.UU.).

unity [ˈjuːnɪtɪ] n unidad f.

universal [juːnɪˈvəːsl] a universal.

universe [ˈjuːnɪvəːs] n universo.

university [juːnɪˈvəːsɪtɪ] n universidad f.

unjust [ʌnˈdʒʌst] a injusto.

unkempt [ʌnˈkempt] a descuidado; (hair) despeinado.

unkind [ʌnˈkaɪnd] a poco amable; (comment etc) cruel.

unknown [ʌnˈnəun] a desconocido.

unladen [ʌnˈleɪdn] a (ship, weight) vacío.

unleash [ʌnˈliːʃ] vt soltar; (fig) desencadenar.

unless [ʌnˈles] conj a menos que, a no ser que; **~ he comes** a menos que venga; **~ otherwise stated** salvo indicación contraria.

unlike [ʌnˈlaɪk] a distinto // prep a diferencia de.

unlikely [ʌnˈlaɪklɪ] a improbable.

unlimited [ʌnˈlɪmɪtɪd] a ilimitado.

unload [ʌnˈləud] vt descargar.

unlock [ʌnˈlɔk] vt abrir con (llave).

unlucky [ʌnˈlʌkɪ] a desgraciado, (object, number) que da mala suerte; **to be ~** tener mala suerte.

unmarried [ʌnˈmærɪd] a soltero.

unmask [ʌnˈmɑːsk] vt desenmascarar.

unmistakable [ʌnmɪsˈteɪkəbl] a inconfundible.

unmitigated [ʌnˈmɪtɪgeɪtɪd] a no mitigado, absoluto.

unnatural [ʌnˈnætʃrəl] a (gen) antinatural; (manner) afectado, (habit) perverso.

unnecessary [ʌnˈnesəsərɪ] a innecesario, inútil.

unnoticed [ʌnˈnəutɪst] a: **to go ~** pasar desapercibido.

unobtainable [ʌnəbˈteɪnəbl] a inconseguible.

unoccupied [ʌnˈɔkjupaɪd] a (seat etc) libre.

unofficial [ʌnəˈfɪʃl] a no oficial; (strike) espontáneo, sin la aprobación de la central.

unorthodox [ʌnˈɔːθədɔks] a poco ortodoxo.

unpack [ʌnˈpæk] vi deshacer las maletas.

unpalatable [ʌnˈpælətəbl] a (truth) desagradable.

unparalleled [ʌnˈpærəleld] a

(*unequalled*) sin par; (*unique*) sin precedentes.

unpleasant [ʌn'plɛznt] *a* (*disagreeable*) desagradable; (*person, manner*) antipático.

unplug [ʌn'plʌg] *vt* desenchufar, desconectar.

unpopular [ʌn'pɒpjulə*] *a* poco popular.

unprecedented [ʌn'prɛsidɛntid] *a* sin precedentes.

unpredictable [ʌnpri'diktəbl] *a* imprevisible.

unproductive [ʌnprə'dʌktiv] *a* improductivo.

unqualified [ʌn'kwɒlifaid] *a* (*teacher*) sin título, no cualificado; (*success*) total, incondicional.

unravel [ʌn'rævl] *vt* desenmarañar.

unreal [ʌn'riəl] *a* irreal.

unrealistic [ʌnriə'listik] *a* poco realista.

unreasonable [ʌn'riːznəbl] *a* poco razonable; (*demand*) excesivo.

unrelated [ʌnri'leitid] *a* sin relación; (*family*) sin parentesco.

unrelenting [ʌnri'lentiŋ] *a* implacable.

unreliable [ʌnri'laiəbl] *a* (*person*) informal; (*machine*) de poca confianza.

unrelieved [ʌnri'liːvd] *a* (*monotony*) monótono.

unrepeatable [ʌnri'piːtəbl] *a* (*offer*) irrepetible.

unrepresentative [ʌnrɛpri'zɛntətiv] *a* poco representativo o característico.

unrest [ʌn'rɛst] *n* inquietud f, malestar *m*; (POL) disturbios *mpl*.

unroll [ʌn'rəul] *vt* desenrollar.

unruly [ʌn'ruːli] *a* indisciplinado.

unsafe [ʌn'seif] *a* (*journey*) peligroso; (*car etc*) inseguro.

unsaid [ʌn'sɛd] *a*: to leave sth ~ dejar algo sin decir.

unsatisfactory [ʌnsætis'fæktəri] *a* insatisfactorio.

unsavoury, unsavory (US) [ʌn'seivəri] *a* (*fig*) repugnante.

unscathed [ʌn'skeiðd] *a* ileso.

unscrew [ʌn'skruː] *vt* destornillar.

unscrupulous [ʌn'skruːpjuləs] *a* sin escrúpulos.

unsettled [ʌn'sɛtld] *a* inquieto, inestable; (*weather*) variable.

unshaven [ʌn'feivn] *a* sin afeitar.

unsightly [ʌn'saitli] *a* feo.

unskilled [ʌn'skild] *a*: ~ worker obrero no cualificado.

unspeakable [ʌn'spiːkəbl] *a* indecible; (*bad*) horrible.

unsteady [ʌn'stɛdi] *a* inestable.

unstuck [ʌn'stʌk] *a*: to come ~ despegarse; (*fig*) fracasar.

unsuccessful [ʌnsək'sɛsful] *a* (*attempt*) infructuoso; (*proposal*) sin éxito; to be ~ (*in attempting sth*) no tener éxito, fracasar; ~ly *ad* en vano, sin éxito.

unsuitable [ʌn'suːtəbl] *a* inconveniente, inapropiado.

unsure [ʌn'juə*] *a* inseguro, poco seguro.

unsuspecting [ʌnsə'spɛktiŋ] *a* confiado.

unswerving [ʌn'swɜːviŋ] *a* inquebrantable.

untangle [ʌn'tæŋgl] *vt* desenredar.

untapped [ʌn'tæpt] *a* (*resources*) sin explotar.

unthinkable [ʌn'θiŋkəbl] *a* inconcebible, impensable.

untidy [ʌn'taidi] *a* (*room*) desordenado, en desorden; (*appearance*) descuidado.

untie [ʌn'tai] *vt* desatar.

until [ən'til] *prep* hasta // *conj* hasta que; ~ he comes hasta que venga; ~ then hasta entonces.

untimely [ʌn'taimli] *a* inoportuno; (*death*) prematuro.

untold [ʌn'təuld] *a* (*story*) inédito; (*suffering*) indecible; (*wealth*) incalculable.

untoward [ʌntə'wɔːd] *a* desfavorable.

unused [ʌn'juːzd] *a* sin usar, nuevo.

unusual [ʌn'juːʒuəl] *a* insólito, poco común.

unveil [ʌn'veil] vt *(statue)* descubrir.

unwavering [ʌn'weivəriŋ] a inquebrantable.

unwelcome [ʌn'welkəm] a *(at a bad time)* inoportuno; *(unpleasant)* desagradable.

unwell [ʌn'wel] a: **to feel** ~ estar indispuesto; **to be** ~ estar enfermo.

unwieldy [ʌn'wi:ldi] a difícil de manejar.

unwilling [ʌn'wiliŋ] a: **to be** ~ **to do sth** estar poco dispuesto a hacer algo; ~**ly** ad de mala gana.

unwind [ʌn'waind] *(irg: like wind)* vt desenvolver // vi *(relax)* relajarse.

unwitting [ʌn'witiŋ] a inconsciente.

unworthy [ʌn'wə:ði] a indigno.

unwrap [ʌn'ræp] vt desenvolver.

up [ʌp] prep: **to go/be** ~ **sth** subir/estar encima de algo // ad hacia arriba, arriba; ~ **there** allí arriba; ~ **above** encima, allí arriba; **to be** ~ *(out of bed)* estar levantado; **it is** ~ **to you** Ud. decide/tú decides; **what is he** ~ **to?** ¿qué es lo que quiere?, ¿qué está tramando?; **he is not** ~ **to it** no es capaz de hacerlo; ~**and-coming** a prometedor(a); ~**s and downs** npl *(fig)* altibajos mpl.

upbringing ['ʌpbriŋiŋ] n educación f.

update [ʌp'deit] vt poner al día, modernizar; *(contract etc)* actualizar.

upgrade [ʌp'greid] vt ascender; *(job)* revalorizar.

upheaval [ʌp'hi:vl] n trastorno, conmoción f.

uphill [ʌp'hil] a cuesta arriba; *(fig: task)* penoso, difícil // ad: **to go** ~ ir cuesta arriba.

uphold [ʌp'həuld] *(irg: like hold)* vt sostener.

upholstery [ʌp'həulstəri] n tapicería.

upkeep ['ʌpki:p] n mantenimiento.

upon [ə'pɔn] prep sobre.

upper ['ʌpə*] a superior, de arriba // n *(of shoe)* pala; ~**-class** a de clase alta; ~**most** a el más alto; **what was** ~**most in my mind** lo que me preocupaba más.

upright ['ʌprait] a vertical; *(fig)* honrado.

uprising ['ʌpraiziŋ] n sublevación f.

uproar ['ʌprɔ:*] n tumulto, escándalo.

uproot [ʌp'ru:t] vt desarraigar.

upset ['ʌpset] n *(to plan etc)* revés m, contratiempo; *(MED)* trastorno // vt [ʌp'set] *(irg: like set)* *(glass etc)* volcar; *(spill)* derramar; *(plan)* alterar; *(person)* molestar, perturbar // a [ʌp'set] preocupado, perturbado; *(stomach)* trastornado.

upshot ['ʌpʃɔt] n resultado.

upside-down ['ʌpsaiddaun] ad al revés.

upstairs [ʌp'steəz] ad arriba // a *(room)* de arriba // n el piso superior.

upstart ['ʌpsta:t] n advenedizo.

upstream [ʌp'stri:m] ad río arriba.

uptake ['ʌpteik] n: **he is quick/slow on the** ~ es muy listo/ algo torpe.

up-to-date ['ʌptə'deit] a moderno, actual.

upturn ['ʌptə:n] n *(in luck)* mejora.

upward ['ʌpwəd] a ascendente; ~**(s)** ad hacia arriba.

uranium [juə'reiniəm] n uranio.

urban ['ə:bən] a urbano.

urbane [ə:'bein] a cortés.

urchin ['ə:tʃin] n pilluelo, golfillo.

urge [ə:dʒ] n *(force)* impulso; *(desire)* deseo // vt: **to** ~ **sb to do sth** incitar a uno a hacer algo.

urgency ['ə:dʒənsi] n urgencia; *(of tone)* insistencia, urgent a urgente.

urinal ['juərinl] n urinario.

urinate ['juərineit] vi orinar; **urine** n orina, orines mpl.

urn [ə:n] n urna; *(also: tea* ~*)* tetera.

us [ʌs] pron nos; *(after prep)* nosotros/as.

US, USA n abbr of **United States (of America).**

usage ['juːzɪdʒ] n uso, costumbre f.

use [juːs] n uso, empleo; (usefulness) utilidad f // vt [juːz] usar, emplear; she ~d to do it (ella) solía hacerlo; in ~ en uso; out of ~ anticuado, que ya no se usa; to be of ~ servir; it's no ~ (pointless) es inútil; (not useful) no sirve; to be ~d to estar acostumbrado a; to ~ up vt agotar, consumir; ~d a (car) usado; ~ful a útil; to be ~ful servir; ~less a inútil; **user** n usuario/a.

usher ['ʌʃə*] n ujier m, portero; ~ette [-'rɛt] n (in cinema) acomodadora.

USSR n: the ~ la U.R.S.S.

usual ['juːʒuəl] a normal, corriente; ~ly ad normalmente.

usurp [juː'zɜːp] vt usurpar.

utensil [juː'tɛnsl] n utensilio; **kitchen** ~s batería sg de cocina.

uterus ['juːtərəs] n útero.

utilitarian [juːtɪlɪ'tɛərɪən] a utilitario.

utility [juː'tɪlɪtɪ] n utilidad f; ~ **room** n trascocina.

utilize ['juːtɪlaɪz] vt utilizar.

utmost ['ʌtməust] a mayor // n: to do one's ~ hacer todo lo posible.

utter ['ʌtə*] a total, completo // vt pronunciar, proferir; ~ance n palabras fpl, declaración f; ~ly ad completamente, totalmente.

U-turn ['juː'tɜːn] n viraje m en U.

V

v. abbr of **verse; versus; volt;** vide véase.

vacancy ['veɪkənsɪ] n (job) vacante f; (room) cuarto libro; **vacant** a desocupado, libre; (expression) distraído; **vacate** [və'keɪt] vt (house) desocupar; (job) salir de; (throne) renunciar a.

vacation [və'keɪʃən] n vacaciones fpl.

vaccinate ['væksɪneɪt] vt vacunar; **vaccination** [-'neɪʃən] n vacunación f.

vaccine ['væksiːn] n vacuna.

vacuum ['vækjum] n vacío; ~ **cleaner** n aspiradora; ~ **flask** n termo.

vagabond ['vægəbɔnd] n vagabundo.

vagina [və'dʒaɪnə] n vagina.

vagrant ['veɪgrnt] n vagabundo.

vague [veɪg] a vago; (blurred: memory) borroso; (uncertain) incierto, impreciso; (person) distraído; ~ly ad vagamente.

vain [veɪn] a (conceited) vanidoso; (useless) vano, inútil; in ~ en vano.

vale [veɪl] n valle m.

valentine ['væləntaɪn] n: V~'s Day n Día m de los Enamorados.

valid ['vælɪd] a válido; (ticket) valedero; (law) vigente; ~ity [-'lɪdɪtɪ] n validez f; vigencia.

valley ['vælɪ] n valle m.

valour, valor (US) ['vælə*] n valor m, valentía.

valuable ['væljuəbl] a (jewel) de valor; (time) valioso; ~s npl objetos mpl de valor.

valuation [vælju'eɪʃən] n tasación f, valuación f.

value ['væljuː] n valor m; (importance) importancia // vt (fix price of) tasar, valorar; (esteem) apreciar; (cherish) tener en mucho; ~ **added tax** (VAT) n tasa al valor añadido o agregado; ~d a (appreciated) apreciado.

valve [vælv] n (gen) válvula; (MED) valva.

vampire ['væmpaɪə*] n vampiro/vampiresa.

van [væn] n (AUT) furgoneta; (RAIL) furgón m de equipajes.

vandal ['vændl] n vándalo; ~**ism** n vandalismo; ~**ize** vt dañar, destruir.

vanilla [və'nɪlə] n vainilla.

vanish ['vænɪʃ] vi desvanecerse, esfumarse.

vanity ['vænɪtɪ] n vanidad f; ~ **case** n neceser m.

vantage point ['vɑ:ntɪdʒ-] n posición f ventajosa.

vapour, vapor (US) ['veɪpə*] n vapor m; (steam) vaho.

variable ['vɛərɪəbl] a variable.

variance ['vɛərɪəns] n: to be at ~ (with) desentonar (con), estar en desacuerdo (con).

variation [vɛərɪ'eɪʃən] n variedad f; (in opinion) variación f.

varicose ['værɪkəus] a: ~ **veins** varices fpl.

varied ['vɛərɪd] a variado(a).

variety [və'raɪətɪ] n variedad f, diversidad f; (quantity) surtido; ~ **show** n variedades fpl.

various ['vɛərɪəs] a varios(as), diversos(as).

varnish ['vɑ:nɪʃ] n (gen) barniz m; (nail ~) esmalte m // vt (gen) barnizar; (nails) pintar (con esmalte).

vary ['vɛərɪ] vt variar; (change) cambiar // vi variar; (disagree) discrepar; (deviate) desviarse; ~ing a diversos(as).

vase [vɑːz] n florero.

vaseline ['væsɪliːn] ® n vaselina f.

vast [vɑːst] a enorme; (success) abrumador(a); ~**ness** n inmensidad f.

vat [væt] n tina, tinaja.

VAT [væt] n abbr of **Value Added Tax**.

Vatican ['vætɪkən] n: the ~ el Vaticano.

vault [vɔːlt] n (of roof) bóveda; (tomb) tumba; (in bank) sótano // vt (also: ~ over) saltar (por encima de).

veal [viːl] n ternera.

veer [vɪə*] vi virar.

vegetable ['vɛdʒtəbl] n (BOT) vegetal m; (edible plant) legumbre f, hortaliza; ~**s** npl (cooked)

verduras fpl // a vegetal; ~ **garden** n huerto.

vegetarian [vɛdʒɪ'tɛərɪən] a, n vegetariano/a.

vegetate ['vɛdʒɪteɪt] vi vegetar.

vegetation [vɛdʒɪ'teɪʃən] n vegetación f.

vehement ['viːɪmənt] a vehemente; (impassioned) apasionado.

vehicle ['viːɪkl] n vehículo.

veil [veɪl] n velo // vt velar.

vein [veɪn] n vena; (of ore etc) veta.

velocity [vɪ'lɒsɪtɪ] n velocidad f.

velvet ['vɛlvɪt] n terciopelo // a aterciopelado.

vendetta [vɛn'dɛtə] n vendetta.

vending machine ['vɛndɪŋ-] n distribuidor m automático.

vendor ['vɛndə*] n vendedor/a m/f.

veneer [və'nɪə*] n chapa, enchapado; (fig) barniz m, apariencia.

venereal [vɪ'nɪərɪəl] a: ~ **disease** (VD) enfermedad f venérea.

Venetian blind [vɪ'niːʃən-] n persiana.

Venezuela [vɛnɛ'zweɪlə] n Venezuela; ~**n** a, n venezolano/a.

vengeance ['vɛndʒəns] n venganza; **with a** ~ (fig) con creces.

venison ['vɛnɪsn] n carne f de venado.

venom ['vɛnəm] n veneno; ~**ous** a venenoso.

vent [vɛnt] n (opening) abertura; (air-hole) respiradero; (in wall) rejilla (de ventilación) // vt (fig: feelings) desahogar.

ventilate ['vɛntɪleɪt] vt ventilar; **ventilation** [-'leɪʃən] n ventilación f; **ventilator** n ventilador m.

ventriloquist [vɛn'trɪləkwɪst] n ventrílocuo.

venture ['vɛntʃə*] n empresa // vt aventurar; (opinion) ofrecer // vi arriesgarse, lanzarse.

venue ['vɛnjuː] n lugar m; (meeting place) lugar m de reunión.

veranda(h) [vəˈrændə] n terraza; (*with glass*) galería.

verb [vəːb] n verbo; ~**al** a verbal.

verbatim [vəːˈbeɪtɪm] a, ad palabra por palabra.

verbose [vəːˈbəus] a prolijo.

verdict [ˈvəːdɪkt] n veredicto, fallo; (*fig*) opinión f, juicio.

verge [vəːdʒ] n borde m, margen m; **to be on the ~ of doing sth** estar a punto de hacer algo; **to ~ on** vt fus rayar en.

verify [ˈverɪfaɪ] vt comprobar, verificar.

vermin [ˈvəːmɪn] npl (*animals*) bichos mpl; (*insects, fig*) sabandijas fpl.

vermouth [ˈvəːməθ] n vermut m.

vernacular [vəˈnækjulə*] n vernáculo.

versatile [ˈvəːsətaɪl] a (*person*) de talentos variados; (*machine, tool etc*) que tiene muchos usos; (*mind*) ágil, flexible.

verse [vəːs] n versos mpl, poesía; (*stanza*) estrofa; (*in bible*) versículo.

versed [vəːst] a: (**well-**)~ **in** versado en, conocedor de.

version [ˈvəːʃən] n versión f.

versus [ˈvəːsəs] prep contra.

vertebra [ˈvəːtɪbrə], pl ~**e** [-briː] n vértebra; **vertebrate** [-brɪt] n vertebrado.

vertical [ˈvəːtɪkl] a vertical.

vertigo [ˈvəːtɪgəu] n vértigo.

very [ˈverɪ] ad muy // a: **the ~ book which** el mismo libro que; **the ~ last** el último (de todos); **at the ~ least** al menos; ~ **much** muchísimo.

vespers [ˈvespəz] npl vísperas fpl.

vessel [ˈvesl] n (*ANAT, NAUT*) vaso; (*container*) vasija.

vest [vest] n camiseta; (*US: waistcoat*) chaleco; ~**ed interests** npl (*COMM*) intereses mpl creados.

vestibule [ˈvestɪbjuːl] n vestíbulo.

vestige [ˈvestɪdʒ] n vestigio, rastro.

vestry [ˈvestrɪ] n sacristía.

vet [vet] n abbr of **veterinary**

surgeon // vt repasar, revisar.

veteran [ˈvetərn] n veterano; ~ **car** n coche m antiguo.

veterinary [ˈvetrɪnərɪ] a veterinario; ~ **surgeon** n veterinario.

veto [ˈviːtəu], pl ~**es** n veto // vt vetar, vedar.

vex [veks] vt (*irritate*) fastidiar; (*make impatient*) impacientar; ~**ed** a (*question*) batallón(ona), controvertido.

via [ˈvaɪə] prep por, por vía de.

viable [ˈvaɪəbl] a viable.

viaduct [ˈvaɪədʌkt] n viaducto.

vibrate [vaɪˈbreɪt] vi vibrar; **vibration** [-ˈbreɪʃən] n vibración f.

vicar [ˈvɪkə*] n párroco; ~**age** n parroquia.

vice [vaɪs] n (*evil*) vicio; (*TECH*) torno de banco.

vice- [vaɪs] pref vice; ~**chairman** n vicepresidente m.

vice versa [ˈvaɪsɪˈvəːsə] ad viceversa.

vicinity [vɪˈsɪnɪtɪ] n (*area*) vecindad f; (*nearness*) proximidad f.

vicious [ˈvɪʃəs] a (*violent*) violento; (*depraved*) depravado; (*cruel*) cruel; (*bitter*) rencoroso; ~**ness** n violencia; depravación f; crueldad f; rencor m.

victim [ˈvɪktɪm] n víctima m/f; ~**ization** [-zeɪʃən] n (*gen*) persecución f; (*in strike*) represalias fpl; ~**ize** vt (*strikers etc*) tomar represalias contra.

victor [ˈvɪktə*] n vencedor/a m/f.

Victorian [vɪkˈtɔːrɪən] a victoriano.

victorious [vɪkˈtɔːrɪəs] a vencedor(a).

victory [ˈvɪktərɪ] n victoria.

video [ˈvɪdɪəu] cpd video; ~**(-tape) recorder** n video-grabadora.

vie [vaɪ] vi: **to ~ with** competir con.

Vienna [vɪˈenə] n Viena.

view [vjuː] n vista, perspectiva; (*landscape*) paisaje m; (*opinion*) opinión f, criterio // vt (*look at*) mirar; (*examine*) examinar; **on ~** (*in museum etc*) expuesto; **in full ~**

(of) en plena vista (de); **in ~ of the fact that** en vista del hecho de que; **~er** n (small projector) visionadora; (TV) televidente m/f; **~finder** n visor m de imagen; **~point** n punto de vista.

vigil ['vɪdʒɪl] n vigilia; **to keep ~** velar; **~ance** n vigilancia; **~ant** a vigilante.

vigorous ['vɪgərəs] a enérgico, vigoroso; **vigour, vigor** (US) n energía, vigor m.

vile [vaɪl] a (action) vil, infame; (smell) asqueroso.

vilify ['vɪlɪfaɪ] vt vilipendiar.

villa ['vɪlə] n (country house) casa de campo; (suburban house) chalet m.

village ['vɪlɪdʒ] n aldea; **villager** n aldeano/a.

villain ['vɪlən] n (scoundrel) malvado; (criminal) maleante m/f.

vindicate ['vɪndɪkeɪt] vt vindicar, justificar.

vindictive [vɪn'dɪktɪv] a vengativo.

vine [vaɪn] n vid f.

vinegar ['vɪnɪgə*] n vinagre m.

vineyard ['vɪnjɑːd] n viña, viñedo.

vintage ['vɪntɪdʒ] n (year) vendimia, cosecha; **~ wine** n vino añejo.

vinyl ['vaɪnl] n vinilo.

violate ['vaɪəleɪt] vt violar; **violation** [-'leɪʃən] n violación f.

violence ['vaɪələns] n violencia; **violent** a (gen) violento; (intense) intenso.

violet ['vaɪələt] a violado, violeta f; n (plant) violeta.

violin [vaɪə'lɪn] n violín m; **~ist** n violinista m/f.

VIP n abbr of **very important person**.

viper ['vaɪpə*] n víbora.

virgin ['vɜːdʒɪn] n virgen m/f // a virgen; **the Blessed V~** la Santísima Virgen; **~ity** [-'dʒɪnɪtɪ] n virginidad f.

Virgo ['vɜːgəu] n Virgo.

virile ['vɪraɪl] a viril; **virility**

virility [vɪ'rɪlɪtɪ] n virilidad f; (fig) machismo.

virtually ['vɜːtjuəlɪ] ad (almost) virtualmente.

virtue ['vɜːtjuː] n virtud f; **by ~ of** en virtud de.

virtuoso [vɜːtju'əuzəu] n virtuoso.

virtuous ['vɜːtjuəs] a virtuoso.

virulent ['vɪrulənt] a virulento.

virus ['vaɪərəs] n virus m.

visa ['viːzə] n visado, visa (AM).

vis-à-vis [viːzə'viː] prep respecto de.

visibility [vɪzɪ'bɪlɪtɪ] n visibilidad f.

visible ['vɪzəbl] a visible; **visibly** ad visiblemente.

vision ['vɪʒən] n (sight) vista; (foresight, in dream) visión f; **~ary** n visionario.

visit ['vɪzɪt] n visita // vt (person) visitar, hacer una visita a; (place) ir a, (ir a) conocer; **~or** n (gen) visitante m/f; (to one's house) visita; (tourist) turista m/f; (tripper) excursionista m/f; **~ors' book** n libro de visitas.

visor ['vaɪzə*] n visera.

vista ['vɪstə] n vista, panorama.

visual ['vɪzjuəl] a visual; **~ize** vt imaginarse; (foresee) prever.

vital ['vaɪtl] a (essential) esencial, imprescindible; (important) (crucial) de suma importancia; (person) enérgico, vivo; (of life) vital; **~ity** [-'tælɪtɪ] n energía, vitalidad f; **~ly** ad: **~ly important** de primera importancia.

vitamin ['vɪtəmɪn] n vitamina.

vivacious [vɪ'veɪʃəs] a vivaz, alegre.

vivid ['vɪvɪd] a (account) gráfico; (light) intenso; (imagination) vivo.

vivisection [vɪvɪ'sekʃən] n vivisección f.

V-neck ['viːnek] n cuello de pico.

vocabulary [vəu'kæbjulərɪ] n vocabulario.

vocal ['vəukl] a vocal; (noisy) ruidoso; **~ chords** npl cuerdas fpl vocales; **~ist** n cantante m/f.

vocation [vəu'keɪʃən] n vocación f; ~al a vocacional.

vociferous [və'sɪfərəs] a vociferglero.

vodka ['vɔdkə] n vodka.

vogue [vəug] n boga, moda.

voice [vɔɪs] n voz f // vt (opinion) expresar.

void [vɔɪd] n vacío; (hole) hueco // a (gen) vacío; (vacant) vacante; (null) nulo, inválido.

volatile ['vɔlətaɪl] a volátil.

volcanic [vɔl'kænɪk] a volcánico; **volcano** [-'keɪnəu], pl -es n volcán m.

volley ['vɔlɪ] n (of gunfire) descarga; (of stones etc) lluvia; (TENNIS etc) volea; ~ball n balonvolea, vol(e)ibol m (AM).

volt [vəult] n voltio; ~age n voltaje m.

voluble ['vɔljubl] a locuaz, hablador(a).

volume ['vɔlju:m] n (gen) volumen m; (book) tomo.

voluntarily ['vɔləntrɪlɪ] ad libremente, de su propia voluntad.

voluntary ['vɔləntərɪ] a voluntario, espontáneo; (unpaid) (a título) gratuito.

volunteer [vɔlən'tɪə*] n voluntario // vi ofrecerse de voluntario).

voluptuous [və'lʌptjuəs] a voluptuoso.

vomit ['vɔmɪt] n vómito // vt, vi vomitar.

vote [vəut] n voto; (votes cast) votación f; (right to ~) derecho de votar; (franchise) sufragio // vt (chairman) elegir // vi votar, ir a votar; **voter** n votante m/f; **voting** n votación f.

vouch [vautʃ]: to ~ for vt garantizar, responder de.

voucher ['vautʃə*] n (for meal, petrol) vale m.

vow [vau] n voto // vi hacer voto.

vowel ['vauəl] n vocal f.

voyage ['vɔɪdʒ] n (journey) viaje m; (crossing) travesía.

vulgar ['vʌlgə*] a (rude) ordinario,

grosero; (in bad taste) de mal gusto; ~ity [-'gærɪtɪ] n grosería; mal gusto.

vulnerable ['vʌlnərəbl] a vulnerable.

vulture ['vʌltʃə*] n buitre m.

W

wad [wɔd] n (of cotton wool, paper) bolita; (of banknotes etc) fajo.

waddle ['wɔdl] vi anadear.

wade [weɪd] vi: to ~ through caminar por el agua; (fig: a book) leer con dificultad.

wafer ['weɪfə*] n (biscuit) galleta, barquillo; (REL) oblea.

waffle ['wɔfl] n (CULIN) buñuelo, panqueque m // vi meter paja.

waft [wɔft] vt hacer flotar // vi flotar.

wag [wæg] vt menear, agitar // vi moverse, menearse.

wage [weɪdʒ] n (also: ~s) sueldo, salario // vt: to ~ war hacer la guerra; ~ **claim** n demanda de aumento de sueldo; ~ **earner** n asalariado/a; ~ **freeze** n congelación f de salarios.

wager ['weɪdʒə*] n apuesta // vt apostar.

waggle ['wægl] vt menear, mover.

wag(g)on ['wægən] n (horse-drawn) carro; (truck) camión m; (RAIL) vagón m.

wail [weɪl] n gemido // vi gemir.

waist [weɪst] n cintura, talle m; ~**coat** n chaleco; ~**line** n talle m.

wait [weɪt] n espera; (interval) pausa // vi esperar; to lie in ~ for acechar a; I can't ~ to (fig) estoy deseando; to ~ for esperar (a); to ~ on vt fus servir a; 'no ~ing' (AUT) 'prohibido aparcar'; ~**er** n camarero; ~**ing list** n lista de espera; ~**ing room** n sala de espera; ~**ress** n camarera.

waive [weɪv] vt renunciar a.

wake [weɪk], *pt* **woke** *or* **waked**, *pp* **woken** *or* **waked** *vt* (also: ~ **up**) despertar // *vi* (also: ~ **up**) despertarse // *n* (for dead person) vela, velatorio; (NAUT) estela; **waken** *vt*, *vi* = **wake**.

Wales [weɪlz] *n* País *m* de Gales.

walk [wɔːk] *n* paseo; (hike) excursión *f* a pie, caminata; (gait) paso, andar *m*; (in park etc) paseo, alameda // *vi* andar; (for pleasure, exercise) pasearse // *vt* (distance) recorrer a pie, andar; (dog) sacar de paseo, pasear; **10 minutes' ~ from here** desde aquí hay 10 minutos a pie; **people from all ~s of life** gente de todas las esferas; **~er** *n* (person) paseante *m/f*, caminante *m/f*; **~ie-talkie** [wɔːkɪˈtɔːkɪ] *n* walkie-talkie *m*, transmisor-receptor *m* (portátil); **~ing** *n* el andar; **~ing shoes** *npl* zapatos *mpl* para andar; **~ing stick** *n* bastón *m*; **~out** *n* (of workers) huelga sorpresa; **~over** *n* (col) triunfo fácil; **~way** *n* paseo.

wall [wɔːl] *n* pared *f*; (exterior) muro; (city ~ etc) muralla; **~ed** *a* (city) amurallado; (garden) con tapia.

wallet ['wɔlɪt] *n* cartera.

wallflower ['wɔːlflauə*] *n* alhelí *m*; **to be a ~** (fig) comer pavo.

wallop ['wɔləp] *vt* (col) zurrar.

wallow ['wɔləu] *vi* revolcarse.

wallpaper ['wɔːlpeɪpə*] *n* papel *m* pintado.

walnut ['wɔːlnʌt] *n* nuez *f*; (tree) nogal *m*.

walrus ['wɔːlrəs], *pl* ~ *or* ~**es** *n* morsa.

waltz [wɔːlts] *n* vals *m* // *vi* bailar el vals.

wand [wɔnd] *n* (also: **magic ~**) varita (mágica).

wander ['wɔndə*] *vi* (person) vagar, deambular; (thoughts) divagar; (get lost) extraviarse // *vt* recorrer, vagar por; **~er** *n*

vagabundo; **~ing** *a* errante; (thoughts) distraído.

wane [weɪn] *vi* menguar.

wangle ['wæŋgl] *vt* (col): **to ~ sth** agenciarse algo.

want [wɔnt] *vt* (wish for) querer, desear; (demand) exigir; (need) necesitar; (lack) carecer de // *n*: **for ~ of** por falta de; **~s** *npl* (needs) necesidades *fpl*; **to ~ to do** querer hacer; **to ~ sb to do sth** querer que uno haga algo; **~ing** *a* falto, deficiente; **to be found ~ing** no estar a la altura de las circunstancias.

wanton ['wɔntn] *a* (playful) juguetón(ona); (licentious) lascivo.

war [wɔː*] *n* guerra; **to make ~** hacer la guerra.

ward [wɔːd] *n* (in hospital) sala; (POL) distrito electoral; (LAW: child) pupilo; **to ~ off** *vt* desviar, parar; (attack) rechazar.

warden ['wɔːdn] *n* (of institution) director *m*; (of park, game reserve) guardián *m*; (also: **traffic ~**) guardia *m/f*.

warder ['wɔːdə*] *n* guardián *m*, carcelero.

wardrobe ['wɔːdrəub] *n* (cupboard) armario; (clothes) guardarropa.

warehouse ['weəhaus] *n* almacén *m*, depósito.

wares [weəz] *npl* mercancías *fpl*.

warfare *n* guerra; **~head** *n* cabeza armada.

warily ['weərɪlɪ] *ad* con cautela, cautelosamente.

warlike ['wɔːlaɪk] *a* guerrero.

warm [wɔːm] *a* caliente; (thanks) efusivo; (clothes etc) cálido; (welcome, day) caluroso; **it's ~** hace calor; **I'm ~** tengo calor; **to ~ up** *vi* (person, room) calentarse; (athlete) hacer ejercicios de calentamiento; (discussion) acalorarse // *vt* calentar; **~-hearted** *a* afectuoso; **~ly** *ad* afectuosamente; **~th** *n* calor *m*.

warn [wɔːn] *vt* avisar, prevenir;

~ing n aviso, advertencia; **~ing light** n luz f de advertencia.

warp [wɔːp] vi diformarse.

warrant ['wɔrnt] n (guarantee) garantía; (LAW) mandato judicial.

warranty ['wɔrəntɪ] n garantía.

warren ['wɔrən] n (of rabbits) madriguera; (house) conejera.

warrior ['wɔrɪə*] n guerrero.

warship ['wɔːʃɪp] n buque m o barco de guerra.

wart [wɔːt] n verruga.

wartime ['wɔːtaɪm] n: **in** ~ en tiempos de guerra, en la guerra.

wary ['wɛərɪ] a cauteloso, cauto.

was [wɔz] pt of be.

wash [wɔʃ] vt lavar // vi lavarse // n (clothes etc) lavado; (bath) baño; (of ship) estela; **to have a** ~ lavarse; **to** ~ **away** vt (stain) quitar lavando; (subj: river etc) llevarse; (fig) regar; **to** ~ **off** vt quitar lavando; **to** ~ **up** vi fregar los platos; **~able** a lavable; **~basin** n lavabo; **~er** n (TECH) arandela; **~ing** n (dirty) ropa sucia; (clean) colada; **~ing machine** n lavadora; **~ing powder** n jabón m en polvo; **~ing-up** n fregado, platos mpl (para fregar); **~out** n (col) fracaso; **~room** n servicios mpl.

wasn't ['wɔznt] = **was not.**

wasp [wɔsp] n avispa.

wastage ['weɪstɪdʒ] n desgaste m; (loss) pérdida; **natural** ~ desgaste natural.

waste [weɪst] n derroche m, despilfarro; (wastage) desgaste m; (of time) pérdida; (food) sobras fpl; (rubbish) basura, desperdicios mpl // a (material) de desecho; (left over) sobrante; (land) baldío // vt (squander) malgastar, derrochar; (time) perder; (opportunity) desperdiciar; (use up) consumir; **to** ~ **away** vi consumirse; **~bin** n cubo de la basura; **~ disposal unit** n triturador m de basura; **~ful** a derrochador(a); (process) antieconómico; ~ **ground** n terreno baldío;

~ **paper basket** n papelera; ~ **pipe** n tubo de desagüe.

watch [wɔtʃ] n reloj m; (act of watching) vigilia; (vigilance) vigilancia; (guard: MIL) centinela m; (NAUT: spell of duty) guardia // vt (look at) mirar, observar; (: match, programme) ver; (spy on, guard) vigilar; (be careful of) cuidarse de, tener cuidado de // vi ver, mirar; (keep guard) montar guardia; **to** ~ **out** vi cuidarse, tener cuidado; **~dog** n perro guardián; **~ful** a vigilante, observador(a); **~maker** n relojero; **~man** n guardián m; (also: **night ~man**) sereno; (in factory) vigilante m nocturno; **~strap** n pulsera (de reloj); **~word** n lema m.

water ['wɔːtə*] n agua // vt (plant) regar; **to** ~ **down** vt (milk) aguar; ~ **closet** n wáter m; ~ **colour** n acuarela; **~cress** n berro; ~ **fall** n cascada, salto de agua; ~ **hole** n charco; **~ing can** n regadera; ~ **level** n nivel m del agua; ~ **lily** n nenúfar m; **~line** n (NAUT) línea de flotación; **~logged** a empapado; ~ **main** n cañería del agua; **~mark** n (on paper) filigrana; **~melon** n sandía; ~ **polo** n polo acuático; **~proof** a impermeable; **~shed** n (GEO) cuenca; (fig) momento crítico; **~skiing** n esquí m acuático; ~ **tank** n depósito de agua; **~tight** a hermético; **~works** npl central f depuradora; **~y** a (colour) desvaído; (coffee) aguado; (eyes) lloroso.

watt [wɔt] n vatio.

wave [weɪv] n ola; (of hand) ademán m, señal f; (RADIO) onda; (in hair) ondulación f; (fig) oleada // vi agitar la mano; (flag) ondear // vt (handkerchief) agitar; (weapon) blandir; (hair) ondular; **~length** n longitud f de onda.

waver ['weɪvə*] vi oscilar; (person) vacilar.

wavy ['weɪvɪ] a ondulado.

wax [wæks] n cera // vt encerar // vi (moon) crecer; ~works npl museo sg de cera.

way [weɪ] n (gen) camino; (distance) trayecto, recorrido; (direction) dirección f, sentido; (manner) modo, manera, (habit) costumbre f; (condition) estado, which ~? ¿por dónde?, ¿en qué dirección?; to be on one's ~ estar en camino; to be in the ~ bloquear el camino; to go out of one's ~ to do sth desvivirse por hacer algo; to lose one's ~ extraviarse; in a ~ en cierto modo o sentido; by the ~ a propósito; '~ out' 'salida'; the ~ back el camino de vuelta; 'give ~' (AUT) 'ceda el paso'.

waylay [weɪˈleɪ] (irg: like lay) vt acechar.

wayward [ˈweɪwəd] a (wilful) voluntarioso; (capricious) caprichoso; (naughty) travieso.

W.C. [ˈdʌbljuːˈsiː] n wáter m.

we [wiː] pl pron nosotros/as.

weak [wiːk] a (gen) débil, flojo; (tea) claro; ~en vi debilitarse; (give way) ceder // vt debilitar; (lessen) disminuir; ~ling n persona débil o delicada; ~ness n debilidad f; (fault) punto débil.

wealth [welθ] n (money, resources) riqueza; (of details) abundancia; ~y a rico.

wean [wiːn] vt destetar.

weapon [ˈwepən] n arma.

wear [wɛə*] n (use) uso; (deterioration through use) desgaste m, (clothing): sports/baby ~ ropa de deportes/para niños // (vb: pt wore, pp worn) vt (clothes) llevar; (shoes) calzar; (put on) ponerse; (damage: through use) gastar, usar // vi (last) durar; (rub through etc) desgastarse; ~ and tear n desgaste m; to ~ away vt gastar // vi desgastarse; to ~ down vt gastar; (strength) agotar; to ~ off vi (pain etc) pasar, desaparecer; to ~ out vt desgastar; (person, strength) agotar.

weariness [ˈwɪərɪnɪs] n cansancio; (boredom) aburrimiento, hastío.

weary [ˈwɪərɪ] a (tired) cansado; (dispirited) abatido // vt cansar // vi: to ~ of cansarse de, aburrirse de.

weasel [ˈwiːzl] n (zool) comadreja.

weather [ˈwɛðə*] n tiempo // vt (storm, crisis) hacer frente a; ~beaten a curtido; ~ cock n veleta; ~ forecast n boletín m meteorológico; ~ vane n = ~cock.

weave [wiːv] pt wove, pp woven vt (cloth) tejer; (fig) entretejer; weaver n tejedor/a m/f; weaving n tejeduría.

web [web] n (of spider) telaraña; (on foot) membrana; (network) red f; ~bed a (foot) palmeado; ~bing n (on chair) cinchas fpl.

wed [wed], pt, pp wedded vt casar // vi casarse // n: the newly-~s los recién casados.

we'd [wiːd] = we had; we would.

wedded [ˈwedɪd] pt, pp of wed.

wedding [ˈwedɪŋ] n boda, casamiento; silver/golden ~ bodas fpl de plata/de oro; ~ day n día de la boda; ~ dress n traje m de novia; ~ present n regalo de boda; ~ ring n anillo de boda.

wedge [wedʒ] n (of wood etc) cuña; (of cake) porción f // vt (pack tightly) apretar.

wedlock [ˈwedlɒk] n matrimonio.

Wednesday [ˈwednzdɪ] n miércoles m.

wee [wiː] a (Scottish) pequeñito.

weed [wiːd] n mala hierba, maleza // vt escardar, deshierbar; ~killer n herbicida m.

week [wiːk] n semana; ~day n día m laborable; ~end n fin m de semana; ~ly ad semanalmente, cada semana // a semanal // n semanario.

weep [wiːp], pt, pp wept vi, vt

llorar; ~**ing willow** n sauce m
llorón.

weigh [wei] vt, vi pesar; **to ~ down**
vt sobrecargar; (fig: with worry)
agobiar; **to ~ up** vt pesar; ~**bridge**
n báscula-puente f.

weight [weit] n peso; (on scale)
pesa; **to lose/put on ~**
adelgazarse/engordarse; ~**less-**
ness n ingravidez f; **~ lifter** n
levantador m de pesos; **~y** a
pesado.

weir [wiə*] n presa.

weird [wiəd] a raro, extraño.

welcome ['welkəm] a bienvenido
// n bienvenida // vt dar la
bienvenida a; (be glad of) alegrarse
de; **welcoming** a acogedor(a);
(speech) de bienvenida.

weld [weld] n soldadura // vt soldar;
~**er** n (person) soldador m; ~**ing** n
soldadura.

welfare ['welfeə*] n bienestar m;
(social aid) asistencia social; ~
state n estado de bienestar.

well [wel] n fuente f, pozo // ad bien
// a: **to be ~** estar bien (de salud)
// excl ¡vaya!, ¡bueno!; **as ~**
también; **as ~ as** igual que; ~
done! ¡bien hecho!; **get ~ soon!** ¡que
te mejores pronto!; **to do ~** ir o salir
bien; **to ~ up** vi brotar.

we'll [wi:l] = **we will, we shall.**

well-: ~**behaved** a bien educado,
formal; ~**being** n bienestar m;
~**built** a (person) fornido; ~**de-**
served a merecido; ~**developed** a
bien desarrollado; ~**dressed** a bien
vestido; ~**heeled** a (col: wealthy)
rico; ~**informed** a enterado.

wellingtons ['weliŋtənz] n (also:
wellington boots) botas fpl de
goma.

well-: ~**known** a (person)
conocido; ~**mannered** a educado;
~**meaning** a bienintencionado;
~**off** a pudiente, con dinero;
~**read** a culto; ~**to-do** a
acomodado; ~**wisher** n admi-
rador/a m/f, amigo.

Welsh [welʃ] a galés(esa) //
(LING) galés m; ~**man/woman** n
galés/esa m/f.

went [went] pt of **go.**

wept [wept] pt, pp of **weep.**

were [wə:*] pt of **be.**

we're [wiə*] = **we are.**

weren't [wə:nt] = **were not.**

west [west] n oeste m // a
occidental, del oeste // ad hacia el o
al oeste; **the W~** n el Oeste, el
Occidente; **the W~ Country** n el
suroeste de Inglaterra; ~**erly** a
(situation) oeste; (wind) del oeste;
~**ern** a occidental // n (CINEMA)
película del oeste; **W~ Germany** n
Alemania Occidental; **W~ Indies**
npl Antillas fpl; ~**ward(s)** ad hacia
el oeste.

wet [wet] a (damp) húmedo; (~
through) mojado; (rainy) lluvioso; **to**
get ~ mojarse; '~ **paint**' 'recién
pintado'; **to be a ~ blanket** (fig) ser
un/una aguafiestas; ~ n
humedad f; **~ suit** n traje m de
buzo.

we've [wi:v] = **we have.**

whack [wæk] vt dar un buen golpe
a; ~**ed** a (col: tired) reventado.

whale [weil] n (ZOOL) ballena.

wharf [wɔ:f], pl **wharves** [wɔ:vz] n
muelle m.

what [wɔt] excl ¡qué!, ¡cómo! // det
que // pron (interrogative) ¿qué?,
¿cómo?; (relative, indirect: object)
lo que; (: subject) el/la que; ~ **are**
you doing? ¿qué haces?; **I saw ~**
you did he visto lo que hiciste; ~ **a**
mess! ¡que lío!; ~ **is it called?**
¿cómo se llama?; ~ **about me?** ¿y
yo?; ~**ever** det: ~**ever book you**
choose cualquier libro que elijas //
pron: **do** ~**ever is necessary** haga
lo que sea necesario; **no reason**
~**ever** or ~**soever** ninguna razón
sea la que sea; **nothing** ~**ever** nada
en absoluto.

wheat [wi:t] n trigo.

wheel [wi:l] n rueda; (AUT: also:
steering ~) volante m; (NAUT)

timón m // vt (pram etc) empujar // vi (also: ~ round) dar la vuelta, girar; ~barrow n carretilla, ~chair n silla de ruedas; ~house n timonera.

wheeze [wi:z] n respiración f ruidosa // vi resollar.

when [wen] ad cuándo // conj cuando; (whereas) mientras; on the day ~ I met him el día que le conocí; las veces que; (every time that) siempre que.

~ever conj cuando, todas

where [weə*] ad dónde // conj donde; this is ~ aquí es donde; ~abouts ad ¿dónde? // n: nobody knows his ~abouts nadie conoce su paradero; ~as conj visto que, mientras; wherever [-'evə*] ad dondequiera que; (interrogative) ¿dónde?; ~withal n recursos mpl.

whet [wet] vt estimular.

whether ['weðə*] conj si; I don't know ~ to accept or not no sé si aceptar o no; ~ you go or not vayas o no vayas.

which [wɪtʃ] det (interrogative) ¿qué?, ¿cuál?; ~ one of you? ¿cuál de vosotros?; ~ picture do you want? ¿qué cuadro quieres? // pron (interrogative) ¿cuál?; (relative: subject) que, lo que; (: object) el que etc, el cual etc, lo cual, lo que; I don't mind ~ no me importa cuál; the apple is on the table la manzana que está sobre la mesa; the chair on ~ you are sitting la silla sobre la que estás sentado; he said he knew, ~ is true él dijo que sabía, lo cual es cierto; in ~ case en cuyo caso, ~ever det take ~ever book you prefer coja el libro que prefiera; you take ~ever book you take cualquier libro que coja.

whiff [wif] n bocanada.

while [waɪl] n rato, momento // conj durante; (as long as) mientras; (although) aunque; for a ~ durante algún tiempo.

whim [wɪm] n capricho.

whimper ['wɪmpə*] n (weeping)

lloriqueo; (moan) quejido // vi lloriquear; quejarse.

whimsical ['wɪmzɪkl] a (person) caprichoso; (look) extraño.

whine [waɪn] n (of pain) gemido; (of engine) zumbido // vi gemir; zumbar.

whip [wɪp] n látigo; (for riding) fusta; (Brit: POL) oficial disciplinario del partido // vt azotar; (snatch) arrebatar; ~ped cream n crema batida; ~round n colecta.

whirl [wə:l] n remolino // vt hacer girar, dar vueltas a // vi girar, dar vueltas; (leaves, water etc) arremolinarse; ~pool n remolino; ~wind n torbellino.

whirr [wə:*] vi rechinar, zumbar.

whisk [wɪsk] n (CULIN) batidor m // vt batir; to ~ sth away from sb arrebatarle algo a uno; to ~ sb away or off llevar rápidamente a uno.

whisker ['wɪskə*] n: ~s (of animal) bigotes mpl; (of man) patillas fpl.

whisk(e)y ['wɪskɪ] n whisky m.

whisper ['wɪspə*] n cuchicheo; (rumour) rumor m; (fig) susurro, murmullo // vi cuchichear, hablar bajo; (fig) susurrar.

whist [wɪst] n whist m.

whistle ['wɪsl] n (sound) silbido; (object) silbato // vi silbar.

white [waɪt] a blanco; (pale) pálido // n blanco; (of egg) clara; ~collar worker n oficinista m/f; ~ elephant n (fig) maula; ~ lie n mentira piadosa; ~ness n blancura; ~ paper n (POL) libro rojo; ~wash n (paint) jalbegue m cal f // vt enjalbegar; (fig) encubrir.

whiting ['waɪtɪŋ] n, pl inv (fish) pescadilla.

Whitsun ['wɪtsn] n pentecostés m.

whittle ['wɪtl] vt: to ~ away, ~ down reducir poco a poco.

whizz [wɪz] vi: to ~ past or by pasar a toda velocidad; ~ kid n (col) prodigio, portento.

who [hu:] pron (relative) que, el que

etc, quien; (*interrogative*) ¿quién?; (*pl*) ¿quiénes?; ~**ever** *pron*: ~**ever finds it** cualquiera o quienquiera que lo encuentre; **ask** ~**ever you like** pregunta a quien quieras; ~**ever he marries** no importa con quién se case.

whole [həul] *a* (*complete*) todo, entero; (*not broken*) intacto // *n* (*total*) total *m*; (*sum*) conjunto; **the** ~ **of the town** toda la ciudad, la ciudad entera; **on the** ~, **as a** ~ en general; ~**hearted** *a* sincero, cordial; ~**sale** *n* venta al por mayor // *a* al por mayor; (*destruction*) sistemático; ~**saler** *n* mayorista *m/f*; ~**some** *a* sano; **wholly** *ad* totalmente, enteramente.

whom [hu:m] *pron* que, a quien; (*interrogative*) ¿a quién?

whooping cough ['hu:piŋkɔf] *n* tos *f* ferina.

whopper ['wɔpə*] *n* cosa muy grande; (*lie*) bola; **whopping** *a* (*col: big*) enorme.

whore [hɔ:*] *n* (*col: pej*) puta.

whose [hu:z] *det*: ~ **book is this?** ¿de quién es este libro?; **the man** ~ **son you rescued** el hombre cuyo hijo salvaste; **the girl** ~ **sister you were speaking to** la chica con cuya hermana estabas hablando // *pron*: ~ **is this?** ¿de quién es esto?; **I know** ~ **it is** yo sé de quién es.

why [wai] *ad* por qué; (*interrogative*) ¿por qué?, ¿para qué? // *excl* ¡toma!, ¡cómo!; **tell me** ~ **dime** por qué, dime la razón; ~**ever** *ad* por qué.

wick [wik] *n* mecha.

wicked ['wikid] *a* malvado, cruel.

wicker ['wikə*] *n* (*also*: ~**work**) artículos *mpl* de mimbre.

wicket ['wikit] *n* (CRICKET) palos *mpl*.

wide [waid] *a* ancho; (*region, knowledge*) vasto, grande; (*choice*) grande // *ad*: **to open** ~ abrir de par en par; **to shoot** ~ errar el tiro; ~**-awake** *a* bien despierto; (*fig*)

despabilado; ~**ly** *ad* (*different*) muy; **it is** ~ **believed that...** hay una convicción general de que...; **widen** *vt* ensanchar; ~**ness** *n* anchura; ~ **open** *a* abierto de par en par; ~**spread** *a* (*belief etc*) extendido, general.

widow ['widəu] *n* viuda; ~**ed** *a* viudo; ~**er** *n* viudo.

width [widθ] *n* anchura; (*of cloth*) ancho.

wield [wi:ld] *vt* (*sword*) manejar; (*power*) ejercer.

wife [waif], *pl* **wives** [waivz] *n* mujer *f*, esposa.

wig [wig] *n* peluca.

wiggle ['wigl] *vt* menear (rápidamente) // *vi* menearse.

wild [waild] *a* (*animal*) salvaje; (*plant*) silvestre; (*rough*) furioso, violento; (*idea*) disparatado, descabellado; (*person*) loco; ~**s** *npl* regiones *fpl* salvajes, tierras *fpl* vírgenes; ~**erness** ['wildənis] *n* desierto; ~**life** *n* fauna; ~**ly** *ad* (*roughly*) violentamente, (*foolishly*) locamente, (*rashly*) descabelladamente.

wilful ['wilful] *a* (*person*) voluntarioso; (*action*) deliberado; (*obstinate*) testarudo; (*child*) travieso.

will [wil] *auxiliary vb*: **he** ~ **come** vendrá // *vt, pt, pp* **willed**: **to** ~ **sb to do sth** desear que alguien haga algo; **he** ~**ed himself to go on** con gran fuerza de voluntad, continuó // *n* voluntad *f*; (*testament*) testamento; ~**ing** *a* (*with goodwill*) de buena voluntad; (*submissive*) complaciente; ~**ingly** *ad* con mucho gusto; ~**ingness** *n* buena voluntad.

willow ['wiləu] *n* sauce *m*.

will power *n* fuerza de voluntad.

wilt [wilt] *vi* marchitarse.

wily ['waili] *a* astuto.

win [win] *n* (*in sports etc*) victoria, triunfo // (*vb*: *pt, pp* **won**) *vt* ganar; (*obtain*) conseguir, lograr // *vi* ganar, tener éxito; **to** ~ **over**, ~ **round** *vt* atraerse.

wince [wɪns] vi estremecerse.

winch [wɪntʃ] n torno.

wind [wɪnd] n viento; (MED) flatulencia; (breath) aliento // (vb: [waɪnd], pt, pp wound) vt enrollar; (wrap) envolver; (clock, toy) dar cuerda a // vi (road, river) serpentear // [wɪnd] (take breath away from) dejar sin aliento a; to ~ up vt (clock) dar cuerda a; (debate) concluir, terminar; ~break n abrigada; ~fall n golpe m de suerte; ~ing a (road) tortuoso; ~ instrument n (MUS) instrumento de viento; ~mill n molino de viento.

window [wɪndəu] n ventana; (in car, train) ventanilla; (in shop etc) escaparate m; ~ box n jardinera (de ventana); ~ cleaner n (person) limpiacristales m inv; ~ ledge n alféizar m; ~ pane n cristal m; ~sill n alféizar m.

windpipe [wɪndpaɪp] n tráquea.

windscreen [wɪndskriːn], windshield [wɪndʃiːld] (US) n parabrisas m inv; ~ washer n lavaparabrisas m inv; ~ wiper n limpiaparabrisas m inv.

windswept [wɪndswɛpt] a azotado por el viento.

windy [wɪndɪ] a de mucho viento; it's ~ hace viento.

wine [waɪn] n vino; ~ cellar n bodega; ~ glass n copa (para vino); ~ list n lista de vinos; ~ merchant n vinatero; ~ tasting n degustación f de vinos.

wing [wɪŋ] n (gen) ala; (AUT) aleta, guardabarros m inv; (THEATRE) bastidores mpl; ~er n (SPORT) extremo.

wink [wɪŋk] n guiño, pestañeo // vi guiñar, pestañear; (light etc) parpadear.

winner [wɪnə*] n ganador/a m/f.

winning [wɪnɪŋ] a (team) ganador(a); (goal) decisivo; ~s npl ganancias fpl; ~ post n meta.

winter [wɪntə*] n invierno // vi invernar; ~ sports npl deportes mpl de invierno.

wintry [wɪntrɪ] a invernal.

wipe [waɪp] n: to give sth a ~ pasar un trapo sobre algo; to ~ limpiar; to ~ off vt limpiar con un trapo; to ~ out vt (debt) liquidar; (memory) borrar; (destroy) destruir.

wire [waɪə*] n alambre m; (ELEC) cable m (eléctrico); (TEL) telegrama m // vt (house) instalar el alambrado de; (also: ~ up) conectar // vi poner un telegrama.

wireless [waɪəlɪs] n radio f.

wiring [waɪərɪŋ] n instalación f eléctrica, alambrado.

wiry [waɪərɪ] a nervioso, nervudo.

wisdom [wɪzdəm] n sabiduría, saber m; (good sense) cordura; (care) prudencia; ~ tooth n muela del juicio.

wise [waɪz] a sabio; (sensible) cuerdo; (careful) prudente.

...wise [waɪz] suff: time~ en cuanto a o respecto al tiempo.

wisecrack [waɪzkræk] n broma.

wish [wɪʃ] n (desire) deseo // vt desear; (want) querer; best ~es (on birthday etc) felicidades fpl; with best ~es (in letter) saludos mpl, recuerdos mpl; to ~ sb goodbye despedirse de uno; he ~ed me well me deseó mucha suerte; to ~ to do/sb to do sth querer hacer/que alguien haga algo; to ~ for desear; it's ~ful thinking es un espejismo.

wisp [wɪsp] n mechón m: (of smoke) voluta.

wistful [wɪstful] a pensativo.

wit [wɪt] n (wittiness) ingenio, gracia; (intelligence) entendimiento; (person) chistoso/a.

witch [wɪtʃ] n bruja; ~craft n brujería.

with [wɪð, wɪθ] prep con; red ~ anger rojo de cólera; the man ~ the grey hair el hombre del sombrero gris; to be ~ it (fig) estar al tanto o a la moda; I am ~ you (I

understand) te entiendo.
withdraw [wɪð'drɔ:] (*irg: like draw*) *vt* retirar, sacar // *vi* retirarse; (*go back on promise*) retractarse; **to ~ money (from the bank)** retirar fondos (del banco); **~al** *n* retirada; **~n** *a (person)* reservado, introvertido.

wither ['wɪðə*] *vi* marchitarse; **~ed** *a* marchito.

withhold [wɪð'həuld] (*irg: like hold*) *vt (money)* retener; *(decision)* aplazar; *(permission)* negar; *(information)* ocultar.

within [wɪð'ɪn] *prep* dentro de // *ad* dentro; **~ reach** al alcance de la mano; **~ sight of** a la vista de; **~ the week** antes de acabar la semana.

without [wɪð'aut] *prep* sin.

withstand [wɪð'stænd] (*irg: like stand*) *vt* resistir a.

witness ['wɪtnɪs] *n (person)* testigo; *(evidence)* testimonio // *vt (event)* presenciar; *(document)* atestiguar la veracidad de; **~ box, ~ stand** *(US)* *n* tribuna de los testigos.

witticism ['wɪtɪsɪzm] *n* dicho ingenioso.

witty ['wɪtɪ] *a* ingenioso, salado.

wives [waɪvz] *pl of* **wife**.

wizard ['wɪzəd] *n* hechicero.

wk *abbr of* **week**.

wobble ['wɔbl] *vi* tambalearse; *(chair)* ser poco firme.

woe [wəu] *n* desgracia.

woke [wəuk], **woken** ['wəukən] *pt, pp of* **wake**.

wolf [wulf], *pl* **wolves** [wulvz] *n* lobo.

woman ['wumən], *pl* **women** ['wɪmɪn] *n* mujer *f*; **~ly** *a* femenino.

womb [wu:m] *n (ANAT)* matriz *f*, útero.

women ['wɪmɪn] *pl of* **woman**.

won [wʌn] *pt, pp of* **win**.

wonder ['wʌndə*] *n* maravilla, prodigio; *(feeling)* asombro // *vi*: **to ~ whether** preguntarse si; **to ~ at** asombrarse de; **to ~ about** pensar

sobre *o* en; **it's no ~ that** no es de extrañarse que; **~ful** *a* maravilloso; **~fully** *ad* maravillosamente, estupendamente.

won't [wəunt] = **will not**.

woo [wu:] *vt (woman)* cortejar.

wood [wud] *n (timber)* madera; *(forest)* bosque *m*; **~ carving** *n* escultura de madera; **~ed** *a* arbolado; **~en** *a* de madera; *(fig)* inexpresivo; **~pecker** *n* pájaro carpintero; **~wind** *n (MUS)* instrumentos *mpl* de viento de madera; **~work** *n* carpintería; **~worm** *n* carcoma.

wool [wul] *n* lana; **to pull the ~ over sb's eyes** *(fig)* dar a uno gato por liebre; **~len, ~en** *(US)* *a* de lana; **~lens** *npl* géneros *mpl* de lana; **~ly, ~y** *(US)* *a* lanudo, de lana; *(fig: ideas)* confuso.

word [wə:d] *n* palabra; *(news)* noticia; *(message)* aviso // *vt* redactar; **in other ~s** en otras palabras; **to break/keep one's ~** faltar a la palabra/cumplir la promesa; **~ing** *n* redacción *f*.

wore [wɔ:*] *pt of* **wear**.

work [wə:k] *n (gen)* trabajo; *(job)* empleo, trabajo; *(ART, LITERATURE)* obra // *vi* trabajar; *(mechanism)* funcionar, marchar; *(medicine)* ser eficaz, surtir efecto // *vt (clay, wood etc)* tallar; *(mine etc)* explotar; *(machine)* manejar, hacer funcionar; *(cause)* producir; **to be out of ~** estar parado, no tener trabajo; **~s** *n (factory)* fábrica // *npl (of clock, machine)* mecanismo *sg*; **to ~ loose** *vi (part)* desprenderse; *(knot)* aflojarse; **to ~ on** *vt fus* trabajar en, dedicarse a; *(principle)* basarse en; **to ~ out** *vi (plans etc)* salir bien, funcionar // *vt (problem)* resolver; *(plan)* elaborar; **does it ~ out?** ¿da resultado?; **it ~s out at £100** suma 100 libras; **to get ~ed up** exaltarse; **~able** *a (solution)* práctico, factible; **~er** *n* trabajador/a,

obrero; ~ing class n clase f obrera;
~ing-class a de clase obrera; in
~ing order en funcionamiento; ~
-man n obrero; ~manship n (art)
hechura, arte m; (skill) habilidad f,
trabajo; ~shop n taller m; ~-to-
rule n huelga de celo.

world [wɜːld] n mundo // cpd
(champion) del mundo; (power,
war) mundial; to think the ~ of sb
(fig) tener un concepto muy alto de
uno; ~ly a mundano; ~-wide a
mundial, universal.

worm [wɜːm] n gusano; (earth~)
lombriz f.

worn [wɔːn] pp of wear // a usado;
~-out a (object) gastado; (person)
rendido, agotado.

worried ['wʌrɪd] a preocupado.

worry ['wʌrɪ] n preocupación f // vt
preocupar, inquietar // vi preocuparse; ~ing a inquietante.

worse [wɜːs] a, ad peor, inferior // n
el peor (lo peor); a change for the ~
un empeoramiento; worsen vt, vi
empeorar; ~ off a (fig): you'll be ~
off this way de esta forma estarás
peor que nunca.

worship ['wɜːʃɪp] n culto; (act)
adoración f // vt adorar; Your W~
(to mayor) señor alcalde; (to judge)
señor juez, ~per n devoto/a.

worst [wɜːst] a (ol/la) peor // ad
peor // n lo peor; at ~ en lo peor de
los casos.

worth [wɜːθ] n valor m // a: to be ~
valer, it's ~ it vale o merece la
pena; ~less a sin valor; (useless)
inútil; ~while a (activity) que
merece la pena; (cause) loable.

worthy [ˈwɜːðɪ] a (person) respetable; (motive) honesto; ~ of digno
de.

would [wʊd] auxiliary vb: she ~
come ella vendría; he ~ have come
él hubiera venido; ~ you like a
biscuit? ¿quieres una galleta?; he
~ go on Mondays solía ir los lunes;
~-be a (pej) presunto, aspirante.

wound [waʊnd] pt, pp of wind // n

[wuːnd] herida // vt [wuːnd] herir.

wove [wəuv], woven [ˈwəuvən] pt,
pp of weave.

wrangle [ˈræŋgl] n riña // vi reñir.

wrap [ræp] n (stole) chal m; (cape)
capa // vt (also: ~ up) envolver;
~per n (of book) cubierta, tapa;
~ping paper n papel m de
envolver.

wrath [rɔːθ] n cólera.

wreath [riːθ], pl ~s [riːðz] n
(funeral) corona; (of flowers)
guirnalda.

wreathe [riːð] vt ceñir.

wreck [rɛk] n naufragio; (ship)
restos mpl del barco; (pej: person)
ruina f // vt destrozar, hundir; (fig)
arruinar; ~age n restos mpl; (of
building) escombros mpl.

wren [rɛn] n (ZOOL) reyezuelo.

wrench [rɛntʃ] n (TECH) llave f
inglesa; (tug) tirón m // vt
arrancar; to ~ sth from sb
arrebatar algo violentamente a uno.

wrestle [ˈrɛsl] vi: to ~ (with sb)
luchar (con o contra uno); wrestler
n luchador m (de lucha libre);
wrestling n lucha libre; wrestling
match n partido de lucha libre.

wretched [ˈrɛtʃɪd] a miserable.

wriggle [ˈrɪgl] n (gen) culebreo //
vi (gen) serpentear.

wring [rɪŋ], pt, pp wrung vt
torcer, retorcer; (wet clothes)
escurrir; (fig): to ~ sth out of sb
sacar algo por la fuerza a uno.

wrinkle [ˈrɪŋkl] n arruga // vt
arrugar // vi arrugarse.

wrist [rɪst] n muñeca; ~ watch n
reloj m de pulsera.

writ [rɪt] n mandato judicial; to
issue a ~ against sb demandar a
uno (en juicio).

write [raɪt], pt wrote, pp
written vt, vi escribir; to ~ down
vt escribir; (note) apuntar; to ~ off
vt (debt) borrar (como incobrable);
(depreciate) depreciar; to ~ out
vt escribir; to ~ up vt redactar; ~-off
n pérdida total; the car is a ~-off el

coche es pura chatarra; **writer** n
escritor/a m/f.
writhe [raið] vi retorcerse.
writing ['raitiŋ] n escritura;
(hand–~) letra; (of author) obra; in
~ por escrito; ~ **paper** n papel m
de escribir.
written ['ritn] pp of **write**.
wrong [rɔŋ] a (bad) malo; (unfair)
injusto; (incorrect) equivocado,
incorrecto; (not suitable) inoportuno, inconveniente // ad mal;
equivocadamente // n mal m; (pl)
~ (injustice) injusticia // vt ser injusto
con; (hurt) agraviar; **you are** ~ **to
do it** estás equivocado en hacerlo,
cometes un error al hacerlo; **you
are** ~ **about that, you've got it** ~
en eso, estás equivocado en eso; **to be
in the** ~ no tener razón, tener la
culpa; **what's** ~? ¿qué pasa?; **to go**
~ (person) equivocarse; (plan) salir
mal; (machine) tener una avería;
~**ful** a injusto; ~**ly** ad injustamente.
wrote [rəut] pt of **write**.
wrought [rɔːt] a: ~ **iron** hierro m
forjado.
wrung [rʌŋ] pt, pp of **wring**.
wry [rai] a irónico.
wt. abbr of **weight**.

X

Xmas ['eksməs] n abbr of
Christmas.
X-ray [eks'rei] n radiografía; ~**s**
npl rayos mpl X // vt hacer una
radiografía a.
xylophone ['zailəfəun] n xilófono.

Y

yacht [jɔt] n yate m; ~**ing** n (sport)
balandrismo; **yachtsman** n
balandrista m.
Yank [jæŋk] n (pej) yanqui m/f.
yap [jæp] vi (dog) aullar.
yard [jɑːd] n patio; (measure) yarda;
~ **stick** n (fig) criterio, norma.
yarn [jɑːn] n hilo; (tale) cuento,
historia.
yawn [jɔːn] n bostezo // vi bostezar.
yd. abbr of **yard(s)**.
year [jiə*] n año; **to be 8** ~**s old**
tener 8 años; ~**ly** a anual // ad
anualmente, cada año.
yearn [jɔːn] vi: **to** ~ **for sth** añorar
o suspirar por algo; ~**ing** n ansia,
añoranza.
yeast [jiːst] n levadura.
yell [jel] n grito, alarido // vi gritar.
yellow ['jeləu] a, n amarillo.
yelp [jelp] n aullido // vi aullar.
yeoman ['jəumən] n: **Y**~ **of the
Guard** alabardero de la Casa Real.
yes [jes] ad, n sí m.
yesterday ['jestədi] ad, n ayer m.
yet [jet] ad todavía // conj sin
embargo, a pesar de todo; **it is not
finished** ~ todavía no está
acabado; **the best** ~ el mejor hasta
ahora; **as** ~ hasta ahora, todavía.
yew [juː] n tejo.
Yiddish ['jidiʃ] n judío.
yield [jiːld] n producción f; (AGR)
cosecha; (COMM) rendimiento // vt
(gen) producir; (profit) rendir // vi
rendirse, ceder.
yoga [jəuɡə] n yoga.
yog(h)ourt, yog(h)urt ['jəuɡət]
n yogur m.
yoke [jəuk] n (of oxen) yunta; (on
shoulders) balancín m; (fig) yugo //
vt acoplar.
yolk [jəuk] n yema (de huevo).
yonder ['jɔndə*] ad allá (a lo lejos).
you [juː] pron tú; (pl) vosotros;
(polite form) usted; (: pl) ustedes;
(complement) te; (: pl) os; (after

prep) tí; (: pl) vosotros; (: formal) le/la; (: pl) les; (after prep) usted; (: pl) ustedes; (one): ~ never know uno nunca sabe; (impersonal): ~ can't do that eso no se hace.

you'd [ju:d] = you had; you would.

you'll [ju:l] = you will, you shall.

young [jʌŋ] a joven // npl (of animal) la cría sg; (people): the ~ los jóvenes, la juventud sg; ~er a (brother etc) menor; ~ish a bastante joven; ~ster n joven m/f.

your [jɔ:*] a tu; (pl) vuestro; (formal) su.

you're [juə*] = you are.

yours [jɔz] pron tuyo; (: pl) vuestro; (formal) suyo, su; ~ is ~ (en tuya etc?; ~ sincerely or faithfully le saluda atentamente.

yourself [jɔ:'self] pron (reflexive) tú mismo; (complement) te; (after prep) tí (mismo); (formal) usted mismo; (: complement) se; (after prep) sí (mismo); **yourselves** pl pron vosotros mismos; (after prep) vosotros (mismos); (formal) ustedes (mismos); (: complement) se; (: after prep) sí mismos.

youth [ju:θ] n juventud f; (young man: pl ~s [ju:ðz]) joven m; ~ful a juvenil; ~ hostel n albergue m de juventud.

you've [ju:v] = you have.

Yugoslav ['ju:gəu'slɑ:v] a, n

yugoeslavo/a; ~ia n Yugoslavia.
Yuletide ['ju:ltaɪd] n Navidad f.

Z

zany ['zeɪnɪ] a tonto.
zeal [zi:l] n celo, entusiasmo; ~ous ['zeləs] a celoso, entusiasta.
zebra ['zi:brə] n cebra; ~ crossing n paso de peatones.
zenith ['zenɪθ] n cénit m.
zero ['zɪərəu] n cero.
zest [zest] n ánimo, vivacidad f.
zigzag ['zɪgzæg] n zigzag m // vi zigzaguear.
zinc [zɪŋk] n cinc m, zinc m.
Zionism ['zaɪənɪzm] n sionismo; **Zionist** n sionista m/f.
zip [zɪp] n (also: ~ fastener, ~per) cremallera // vt (also: ~ up) cerrar la cremallera.
zodiac ['zəudɪæk] n zodiaco.
zombie ['zɒmbɪ] n (fig): like a ~ como un sonámbulo.
zone [zəun] n zona.
zoo [zu:] n (parque m) zoológico.
zoological [zuə'lɒdʒɪkl] a zoológico.
zoologist [zu'ɒlədʒɪst] n zoólogo.
zoology [zu'ɒlədʒɪ] n zoología.
zoom [zu:m] vi: to ~ past pasar zumbando; ~ lens n zoom m.

SPANISH VERB TABLES

1 Gerund. *2* Imperative. *3* Present. *4* Preterite. *5* Future. *6* Present subjunctive. *7* Imperfect subjunctive. *8* Past participle. *9* Imperfect.

Etc indicates that the irregular root is used for all persons of the tense, e.g. **oír**: *6* oiga, oigas, oigamos, oigáis, oigan.

acertar *2* acierta *3* acierto, aciertas, acierta, aciertan *6* acierte, aciertes, acierte, acierten

acordar *2* acuerda *3* acuerdo, acuerdas, acuerda, acuerdan *6* acuerde, acuerdes, acuerde, acuerden

advertir *1* advirtiendo *2* advierte *3* advierto, adviertes, advierte, advierten *4* advirtió, advirtieron *6* advierta, adviertas, advierta, adviertan, advirtáis, adviertan *7* advirtiera *etc*

agradecer *3* agradezco *6* agradezca *etc*

aparecer *3* aparezco *6* aparezca *etc*

aprobar *2* aprueba *3* apruebo, apruebas, aprueba, aprueban *6* apruebe, apruebes, apruebe, aprueben

atravesar *2* atraviesa *3* atravieso, atraviesas, atraviesa, atraviesan *6* atraviese, atravieses, atraviese, atraviesen

caber *3* quepo *4* cupe, cupiste, cupo, cupimos, cupisteis, cupieron *5* cabré *6* quepa *etc* *7* cupiera *etc*

caer *1* cayendo *3* caigo *4* cayó, cayeron *6* caiga *etc* *7* cayera *etc*

calentar *2* calienta *3* caliento, calientas, calienta, calientan *6* caliente, calientes, caliente, calienten

cerrar *2* cierra *3* cierro, cierras, cierra, cierran *6* cierre, cierres, cierre, cierren

COMER *1* comiendo *2* come, comed *3* como, comes, come, comemos, coméis, comen *4* comí, comiste,

comió, comimos, comisteis, comieron *5* comeré, comerás, comerá, comeremos, comeréis, comerán *6* coma, comas, coma, comamos, comáis, coman *7* comiera, comieras, comiera, comiéramos, comierais, comieran *8* comido *9* comía, comías, comía, comíamos, comíais, comían

conocer *3* conozco *6* conozca *etc*

contar *2* cuenta *3* cuento, cuentas, cuenta, cuentan *6* cuente, cuentes, cuente, cuenten

costar *3* cuesta *6* cueste

dar *3* doy *4* di, diste, dio, dimos, disteis, dieron *7* diera *etc*

decir *1* diciendo *2* di *3* digo, dices, dice, dicen *4* dije, dijiste, dijo, dijimos, dijisteis, dijeron *5* diré *etc* *6* diga *etc* *7* dijera *etc* *8* dicho

despertar *2* despierta *3* despierto, despiertas, despierta, despiertan *6* despierte, despiertes, despierte, despierten

divertir *1* divirtiendo *2* divierte *3* divierto, diviertes, divierte, divierten *4* divirtió, divirtieron *6* divierta, diviertas, divierta, divirtamos, divirtáis, diviertan *7* divirtiera *etc*

dormir *1* durmiendo *2* duerme *3* duermo, duermes, duerme, duermen *4* durmió, durmieron *6* duerma, duermas, duerma, durmamos, durmáis, duerman 7 durmiera etc | iba, ibas, iba, íbamos, ibais, iban

empezar 2 empieza 3 empiezo, empiezas, empieza, empiezan 4 empecé 6 empiece, empieces, empiece, empecemos, empecéis, empiecen

encontrar 2 encuentra 3 encuentro, encuentras, encuentra, encuentran 6 encuentre, encuentres, encuentre, encuentren

entender 2 entiende 3 entiendo, entiendes, entiende, entienden 6 entienda, entiendas, entienda, entiendan

ESTAR 2 está 3 estoy, estás, está, están 4 estuve, estuviste, estuvo, estuvimos, estuvisteis, estuvieron 6 esté, estés, esté, estén 7 estuviera etc

HABER 3 he, has, ha, hemos, han 4 hube, hubiste, hubo, hubimos, hubisteis, hubieron 5 habré etc 6 haya etc 7 hubiera etc

HABLAR 1 hablando 2 habla, hablad 3 hablo, hablas, habla, hablamos, habláis, hablan 4 hablé etc. hablaste, habló, hablamos, hablasteis, hablaron 5 hablaré, hablarás, hablará, hablaremos, hablaréis, hablarán 6 hable, hables, hable, hablemos, habléis, hablen 7 hablara, hablaras, hablara, habláramos, hablarais, hablaran 8 hablado 9 hablaba, hablabas, hablaba, hablábamos, hablabais, hablaban

hacer 2 haz 3 hago 4 hice, hiciste, hizo, hicimos, hicisteis, hicieron 5 haré 6 haga etc 7 hiciera etc 8 hecho

instruir 1 instruyendo 2 instruye 3 instruyo, instruyes, instruye, instruyen 4 instruyó, instruiste 6 instruya etc 7 instruyera etc

ir 1 yendo 2 ve 3 voy, vas, va, vamos, vais, van 6 vaya, vayas, vaya, vayamos, vayáis, vayan 7 fuera etc

jugar 2 juega 3 juego, juegas, juega, juegan 4 jugué 6 juegue etc

leer 1 leyendo 4 leyó, leyeron 7 leyera etc

morir 1 muriendo 2 muere 3 muero, mueres, muere, mueren 4 murió, murieron 6 muera, mueras, muera, muramos, muráis, mueran 7 muriera etc 8 muerto

mostrar 2 muestra 3 muestro, muestras, muestra, muestran 6 muestre, muestres, muestre, muestren

mover 2 mueve 3 muevo, mueves, mueve, mueven 6 mueva, muevas, mueva, muevan

negar 2 niega 3 niego, niegas, niega, niegan 4 negué 6 niegue, niegues, niegue, neguemos, neguéis, nieguen

ofrecer 3 ofrezco 6 ofrezca etc

oír 1 oyendo 2 oye 3 oigo, oyes, oye, oyen 4 oyó, oyeron 6 oiga etc 7 oyera etc

oler 2 huele 3 huelo, hueles, huele, huelen 6 huela, huelas, huela, huelan

parecer 3 parezco 6 parezca etc

pedir 1 pidiendo 2 pide 3 pido, pides, pide, piden 4 pidió, pidieron 6 pida etc 7 pidiera etc

pensar 2 piensa 3 pienso, piensas, piensa, piensan 6 piense, pienses, piense, piensen

perder 2 pierde 3 pierdo, pierdes, pierde, pierden 6 pierda, pierdas, pierda, pierdan

poder 1 pudiendo 2 puede 3 puedo, puedes, puede, pueden 4 pude, pudiste, pudo, pudimos, pudisteis, pudieron 5 podré etc 6 pueda, puedas, pueda, puedan 7 pudiera etc

poner 2 pon 3 pongo 4 puse, pusiste, puso, pusimos, pusisteis, pusieron 5 pondré etc 6 ponga etc 7 pusiera etc 8 puesto

preferir 1 prefiriendo 2 prefiere 3

prefiero, prefieres, prefiere, prefieren *4* prefirió, prefirieron *6* prefiera, prefieras, prefiera, prefiramos, prefiráis, prefieran *7* prefiriera *etc*

querer *2* quiere *3* quiero, quieres, quiere, quieren, quieren *4* quise, quisimos, quisisteis, quisieron *5* querré *etc 6* quiera, quieras, quiera, quieran *7* quisiera *etc*

reír *2* ríe *3* río, ríes, ríe, ríen *4* rió, rieron *6* ría, rías, ría, riamos, riáis, rían *7* riera *etc*

repetir *1* repitiendo *2* repite *3* repito, repites, repite, repiten *4* repitió, repitieron *6* repita *etc 7* repitiera *etc*

rogar *2* ruega *3* ruego, ruegas, ruega, ruegan *4* rogué *6* ruegue, ruegues, ruegue, roguemos, roguéis, rueguen

saber *3* sé *4* supe, supiste, supo, supimos, supisteis, supieron *5* sabré *etc 6* sepa *etc 7* supiera *etc*

salir *2* sal *3* salgo *5* saldré *etc 6* salga *etc*

seguir *1* siguiendo *2* sigue *3* sigo, sigues, sigue, siguen *4* siguió, siguieron *6* siga *etc 7* siguiera *etc*

sentar *2* sienta *3* siento, sientas, sienta, sientan *4* siente, sientes, siente, sienten

sentir *1* sintiendo *2* siente *3* siento, sientes, siente, sienten *4* sintió, sintieron *6* sienta, sientas, sienta, sintamos, sintáis, sintáis, sintieran *etc*

SER *2* sé *3* soy, eres, es, somos, sois, son *4* fui, fuiste, fue, fuimos, fuisteis, fueron *6* sea *etc 7* fuera *etc 9* era, eras, era, éramos, erais, eran

servir *1* sirviendo *2* sirve *3* sirvo, sirves, sirve, sirven *4* sirvió, sirvieron *6* sirva *etc 7* sirviera *etc*

soñar *2* sueña *3* sueño, sueñas, sueña, sueñan *6* sueñe, sueñes, sueñe, sueñen

tener *2* ten *3* tengo, tienes, tiene, tienen *4* tuve, tuviste, tuvo, tuvimos, tuvisteis, tuvieron *5* tendré *etc 6* tenga *etc 7* tuviera *etc*

traer *1* trayendo *3* traigo *4* traje, trajiste, trajo, trajimos, trajisteis, trajeron *6* traiga *etc 7* trajera *etc*

valer *2* val *3* valgo *5* valdré *etc 6* valga *etc*

venir *2* ven *3* vengo, vienes, viene, vienen *4* vine, viniste, vino, vinimos, vinisteis, vinieron *5* vendré *etc 6* venga *etc 7* viniera *etc*

ver *3* veo *6* vea *etc 8* visto *9* veía *etc*

vestir *1* vistiendo *2* viste *3* visto, vistes, viste, visten *4* vistió, vistieron *6* vista *etc 7* vistiera *etc*

VIVIR *1* viviendo *2* vive, vivid *3* vivo, vives, vive, vivimos, vivís, viven *4* viví, viviste, vivió, vivimos, vivisteis, vivieron *5* viviré, vivirás, vivirá, viviremos, viviréis, vivirán *6* viva, vivas, viva, vivamos, viváis, vivan *7* viviera, vivieras, viviera, viviéramos, vivierais, vivieran *8* vivido *9* vivía, vivías, vivía, vivíamos, vivíais, vivían

volver *2* vuelve *3* vuelvo, vuelves, vuelve, vuelven *6* vuelva, vuelvas, vuelva, vuelvan *8* vuelto.

VERBOS IRREGULARES EN INGLÉS

present	pt	pp	present	pt	pp
arise	arose	arisen	deal	dealt	dealt
awake	awoke	awaked	dig	dug	dug
be (am, is, are; being)	was, were	been	do (3rd person; he/she/it/does)	did	done
bear	bore	born(e)	draw	drew	drawn
beat	beat	beaten	dream	dreamed, dreamt	dreamed, dreamt
become	became	become			
befall	befell	befallen			
begin	began	begun	drink	drank	drunk
behold	beheld	beheld	drive	drove	driven
bend	bent	bent	dwell	dwelt	dwelt
beseech	besought	besought	eat	ate	eaten
beset	beset	beset	fall	fell	fallen
bet	bet, betted	bet, betted	feed	fed	fed
			feel	felt	felt
bid	bid	bid	fight	fought	fought
bind	bound	bound	find	found	found
bite	bit	bitten	flee	fled	fled
bleed	bled	bled	fling	flung	flung
blow	blew	blown	fly	flew	flown
break	broke	broken	forbid	forbade	forbidden
breed	bred	bred	forego	forewent	foregone
bring	brought	brought	foresee	foresaw	foreseen
build	built	built	foretell	foretold	foretold
burn	burnt, burned	burnt, burned	forget	forgot	forgotten
			forgive	forgave	forgiven
burst	burst	burst	forsake	forsook	forsaken
buy	bought	bought	freeze	froze	frozen
can	could	(been able)	get	got	got, (US) gotten
cast	cast	cast			
catch	caught	caught	give	gave	given
choose	chose	chosen	go (goes)	went	gone
cling	clung	clung			
come	came	come	grind	ground	ground
cost	cost	cost	grow	grew	grown
creep	crept	crept	hang	hung, hanged	hung, hanged
cut	cut	cut			

622

present	pt	pp	present	pt	pp
have	had	had	ride	rode	ridden
hear	heard	heard	ring	rang	rung
hide	hid	hidden	rise	rose	risen
hit	hit	hit	run	ran	run
hold	held	held	saw	sawed	sawn
hurt	hurt	hurt	say	said	said
keep	kept	kept	see	saw	seen
kneel	knelt,	knelt,	seek	sought	sought
	kneeled	kneeled	sell	sold	sold
know	knew	known	send	sent	sent
lay	laid	laid	set	set	set
lead	led	led	shake	shook	shaken
lean	leant,	leant,	shall	should	—
	leaned	leaned	shear	sheared	shorn,
leap	leapt,	leapt,			sheared
	leaped	leaped	shed	shed	shed
learn	learnt,	learnt,	shine	shone	shone
	learned	learned	shoot	shot	shot
leave	left	left	show	showed	shown
lend	lent	lent	shrink	shrank	shrunk
let	let	let	shut	shut	shut
lie	lay	lain	sing	sang	sung
(lying)			sink	sank	sunk
light	lit,	lit,	sit	sat	sat
	lighted	lighted	slay	slew	slain
lose	lost	lost	sleep	slept	slept
make	made	made	slide	slid	slid
may	might	—	sling	slung	slung
mean	meant	meant	slit	slit	slit
meet	met	met	smell	smelt,	smelt,
mistake	mistook	mistaken		smelled	smelled
mow	mowed	mown,	sow	sowed	sown,
		mowed			sowed
must	(had to)	(had to)	speak	spoke	spoken
pay	paid	paid	speed	sped,	sped,
put	put	put		speeded	speeded
quit	quit,	quit,	spell	spelt,	spelt,
	quitted	quitted		spelled	spelled
read	read	read	spend	spent	spent
rent	rent	rent	spill	spilt,	spilt,
rid	rid	rid		spilled	spilled

623

present	pt	pp	present	pt	pp
spin	spun	spun	take	took	taken
spit	spat	spat	teach	taught	taught
split	split	split	tear	tore	torn
spoil	spoiled, spoilt	spoiled, spoilt	tell	told	told
			think	thought	thought
spread	spread	spread	throw	threw	thrown
spring	sprang	sprung	thrust	thrust	thrust
stand	stood	stood	tread	trod	trodden
steal	stole	stolen	wake	woke, waked	woken, waked
stick	stuck	stuck			
sting	stung	stung	waylay	waylaid	waylaid
stink	stank	stunk	wear	wore	worn
stride	strode	strode	weave	wove, weaved	woven, weaved
strike	struck	struck, stricken	wed	wedded, wed	wedded, wed
strive	strove	striven			
swear	swore	sworn	weep	wept	wept
sweep	swept	swept	win	won	won
swell	swelled	swollen, swelled	wind	wound	wound
			wring	wrung	wrung
swim	swam	swum	write	wrote	written
swing	swung	swung			

LOS NÚMEROS

NUMBERS

un, uno(a)/primer, primero(a)	1	one/first
dos/segundo(a)	2	two/second
tres/tercer, tercero(a)	3	three/third
cuatro/cuarto(a)	4	four/fourth
cinco/quinto(a)	5	five/fifth
seis/sexto(a)	6	six/sixth
siete/séptimo(a)	7	seven/seventh
ocho/octavo(a)	8	eight/eighth
nueve/noveno(a)	9	nine/ninth
diez/décimo(a)	10	ten/tenth
once/undécimo(a)	11	eleven/eleventh
doce/duodécimo(a)	12	twelve/twelfth
trece/decimotercio(a)	13	thirteen/thirteenth
catorce/decimocuarto(a)	14	fourteen/fourteenth
quince/decimoquinto(a)	15	fifteen/fifteenth
dieciséis/decimosexto(a)	16	sixteen/sixteenth
diecisiete/decimoséptimo(a)	17	seventeen/seventeenth
dieciocho/decimooctavo(a)	18	eighteen/eighteenth
diecinueve/decimonoveno(a)	19	nineteen/nineteenth
veinte/vigésimo(a)	20	twenty/twentieth
veintiuno	21	twenty-one
veintidós	22	twenty-two
treinta	30	thirty
treinta y uno(a)	31	thirty-one
treinta y dos	32	thirty-two
cuarenta	40	forty
cuarenta y uno(a)	41	forty-one
cincuenta	50	fifty
cincuenta y uno(a)	51	fifty-one
sesenta	60	sixty
sesenta y uno(a)	61	sixty-one
setenta	70	seventy
setenta y uno(a)	71	seventy-one
setenta y dos	72	seventy-two
ochenta	80	eighty
ochenta y uno(a)	81	eighty-one
noventa	90	ninety
noventa y uno(a)	91	ninety-one
cien, ciento/centésimo(a)	100	a hundred, one hundred/hundredth

ciento uno(a)	101	a hundred and one
doscientos(as)	200	two hundred
doscientos(as) uno(a)	201	two hundred and one
trescientos(as)	300	three hundred
trescientos(as) uno(a)	301	three hundred and one
quatrocientos(as)	400	four hundred
quinientos(as)	500	five hundred
seiscientos(as)	600	six hundred
setecientos(as)	700	seven hundred
ochocientos(as)	800	eight hundred
novecientos(as)	900	nine hundred
mil/milésimo(a)	1000	a thousand, one thousand/ thousandth
mil dos	1002	a thousand and two
cinco mil	5000	five thousand
un millón	1,000,000	a million, one million

Ejemplos	Examples
va a llegar el 7 (de mayo)	he's arriving on the 7th (of May)
vive en el número 7	he lives at number 7
el capítulo/la página 7	chapter/page 7
llegó séptimo	he came in 7th
1º (1ª), 2º (2ª), 3º (3ª), 4º (4ª), 5º (5ª)	1st, 2nd, 3rd, 4th, 5th

N.B. In Spanish the ordinal numbers from 1 to 10 are commonly used; from 11 to 20 rather less; above 21 they are rarely written and almost never heard in speech. The custom is to replace the forms for 21 and above by the cardinal number.

LA HORA	THE TIME
¿qué hora es?	*what time is it?*
es/son	*it's o it is*
¿a qué hora?	*(at) what time?*
a	*at*

medianoche, las doce (de la noche)	midnight
la una (de la madrugada)	one (o'clock) (a.m. o in the morning), 1 a.m.
la una y diez	ten past one
la una y cuarto *or* quince	a quarter past one, one fifteen
la una y media *or* treinta	half past one, one thirty
las dos menos cuarto, la una cuarenta y cinco	a quarter to two, one forty-five
la dos menos diez, la una cincuenta	ten to two, one fifty
mediodía, las doce (de la tarde)	twelve (o'clock), midday, noon
la una (de la tarde), las trece (horas)	one (o'clock) (p.m. o in the afternoon)
las siete (de la tarde), las diecinueve (horas)	seven (o'clock) (p.m. o at night)
las nueve y media (de la noche), las veintiuna (horas) y media	nine thirty (p.m. o at night)